Lecture Notes in Computer Science 13665

More information about this series at https://link.springer.com/bookseries/558

Shai Avidan · Gabriel Brostow ·
Moustapha Cissé · Giovanni Maria Farinella ·
Tal Hassner (Eds.)

Computer Vision – ECCV 2022

17th European Conference
Tel Aviv, Israel, October 23–27, 2022
Proceedings, Part V

 Springer

Editors
Shai Avidan
Tel Aviv University
Tel Aviv, Israel

Gabriel Brostow 🆔
University College London
London, UK

Moustapha Cissé
Google AI
Accra, Ghana

Giovanni Maria Farinella 🆔
University of Catania
Catania, Italy

Tal Hassner 🆔
Facebook (United States)
Menlo Park, CA, USA

ISSN 0302-9743   ISSN 1611-3349 (electronic)
Lecture Notes in Computer Science
ISBN 978-3-031-20064-9   ISBN 978-3-031-20065-6 (eBook)
https://doi.org/10.1007/978-3-031-20065-6

This Springer imprint is published by the registered company Springer Nature Switzerland AG
The registered company address is: Gewerbestrasse 11, 6330 Cham, Switzerland

Foreword

Organizing the European Conference on Computer Vision (ECCV 2022) in Tel-Aviv during a global pandemic was no easy feat. The uncertainty level was extremely high, and decisions had to be postponed to the last minute. Still, we managed to plan things just in time for ECCV 2022 to be held in person. Participation in physical events is crucial to stimulating collaborations and nurturing the culture of the Computer Vision community.

There were many people who worked hard to ensure attendees enjoyed the best science at the 16th edition of ECCV. We are grateful to the Program Chairs Gabriel Brostow and Tal Hassner, who went above and beyond to ensure the ECCV reviewing process ran smoothly. The scientific program includes dozens of workshops and tutorials in addition to the main conference and we would like to thank Leonid Karlinsky and Tomer Michaeli for their hard work. Finally, special thanks to the web chairs Lorenzo Baraldi and Kosta Derpanis, who put in extra hours to transfer information fast and efficiently to the ECCV community.

We would like to express gratitude to our generous sponsors and the Industry Chairs, Dimosthenis Karatzas and Chen Sagiv, who oversaw industry relations and proposed new ways for academia-industry collaboration and technology transfer. It's great to see so much industrial interest in what we're doing!

Authors' draft versions of the papers appeared online with open access on both the Computer Vision Foundation (CVF) and the European Computer Vision Association (ECVA) websites as with previous ECCVs. Springer, the publisher of the proceedings, has arranged for archival publication. The final version of the papers is hosted by SpringerLink, with active references and supplementary materials. It benefits all potential readers that we offer both a free and citeable version for all researchers, as well as an authoritative, citeable version for SpringerLink readers. Our thanks go to Ronan Nugent from Springer, who helped us negotiate this agreement. Last but not least, we wish to thank Eric Mortensen, our publication chair, whose expertise made the process smooth.

October 2022

Rita Cucchiara
Jiří Matas
Amnon Shashua
Lihi Zelnik-Manor

Preface

Welcome to the proceedings of the European Conference on Computer Vision (ECCV 2022). This was a hybrid edition of ECCV as we made our way out of the COVID-19 pandemic. The conference received 5804 valid paper submissions, compared to 5150 submissions to ECCV 2020 (a 12.7% increase) and 2439 in ECCV 2018. 1645 submissions were accepted for publication (28%) and, of those, 157 (2.7% overall) as orals.

846 of the submissions were desk-rejected for various reasons. Many of them because they revealed author identity, thus violating the double-blind policy. This violation came in many forms: some had author names with the title, others added acknowledgments to specific grants, yet others had links to their github account where their name was visible. Tampering with the LaTeX template was another reason for automatic desk rejection.

ECCV 2022 used the traditional CMT system to manage the entire double-blind reviewing process. Authors did not know the names of the reviewers and vice versa. Each paper received at least 3 reviews (except 6 papers that received only 2 reviews), totalling more than 15,000 reviews.

Handling the review process at this scale was a significant challenge. To ensure that each submission received as fair and high-quality reviews as possible, we recruited more than 4719 reviewers (in the end, 4719 reviewers did at least one review). Similarly we recruited more than 276 area chairs (eventually, only 276 area chairs handled a batch of papers). The area chairs were selected based on their technical expertise and reputation, largely among people who served as area chairs in previous top computer vision and machine learning conferences (ECCV, ICCV, CVPR, NeurIPS, etc.).

Reviewers were similarly invited from previous conferences, and also from the pool of authors. We also encouraged experienced area chairs to suggest additional chairs and reviewers in the initial phase of recruiting. The median reviewer load was five papers per reviewer, while the average load was about four papers, because of the emergency reviewers. The area chair load was 35 papers, on average.

Conflicts of interest between authors, area chairs, and reviewers were handled largely automatically by the CMT platform, with some manual help from the Program Chairs. Reviewers were allowed to describe themselves as senior reviewer (load of 8 papers to review) or junior reviewers (load of 4 papers). Papers were matched to area chairs based on a subject-area affinity score computed in CMT and an affinity score computed by the Toronto Paper Matching System (TPMS). TPMS is based on the paper's full text. An area chair handling each submission would bid for preferred expert reviewers, and we balanced load and prevented conflicts.

The assignment of submissions to area chairs was relatively smooth, as was the assignment of submissions to reviewers. A small percentage of reviewers were not happy with their assignments in terms of subjects and self-reported expertise. This is an area for improvement, although it's interesting that many of these cases were reviewers hand-picked by AC's. We made a later round of reviewer recruiting, targeted at the list of authors of papers submitted to the conference, and had an excellent response which helped provide enough emergency reviewers. In the end, all but six papers received at least 3 reviews.

The challenges of the reviewing process are in line with past experiences at ECCV 2020. As the community grows, and the number of submissions increases, it becomes ever more challenging to recruit enough reviewers and ensure a high enough quality of reviews. Enlisting authors by default as reviewers might be one step to address this challenge.

Authors were given a week to rebut the initial reviews, and address reviewers' concerns. Each rebuttal was limited to a single pdf page with a fixed template.

The Area Chairs then led discussions with the reviewers on the merits of each submission. The goal was to reach consensus, but, ultimately, it was up to the Area Chair to make a decision. The decision was then discussed with a buddy Area Chair to make sure decisions were fair and informative. The entire process was conducted virtually with no in-person meetings taking place.

The Program Chairs were informed in cases where the Area Chairs overturned a decisive consensus reached by the reviewers, and pushed for the meta-reviews to contain details that explained the reasoning for such decisions. Obviously these were the most contentious cases, where reviewer inexperience was the most common reported factor.

Once the list of accepted papers was finalized and released, we went through the laborious process of plagiarism (including self-plagiarism) detection. A total of 4 accepted papers were rejected because of that.

Finally, we would like to thank our Technical Program Chair, Pavel Lifshits, who did tremendous work behind the scenes, and we thank the tireless CMT team.

October 2022

Gabriel Brostow
Giovanni Maria Farinella
Moustapha Cissé
Shai Avidan
Tal Hassner

Organization

General Chairs

Rita Cucchiara	University of Modena and Reggio Emilia, Italy
Jiří Matas	Czech Technical University in Prague, Czech Republic
Amnon Shashua	Hebrew University of Jerusalem, Israel
Lihi Zelnik-Manor	Technion – Israel Institute of Technology, Israel

Program Chairs

Shai Avidan	Tel-Aviv University, Israel
Gabriel Brostow	University College London, UK
Moustapha Cissé	Google AI, Ghana
Giovanni Maria Farinella	University of Catania, Italy
Tal Hassner	Facebook AI, USA

Program Technical Chair

Pavel Lifshits	Technion – Israel Institute of Technology, Israel

Workshops Chairs

Leonid Karlinsky	IBM Research, Israel
Tomer Michaeli	Technion – Israel Institute of Technology, Israel
Ko Nishino	Kyoto University, Japan

Tutorial Chairs

Thomas Pock	Graz University of Technology, Austria
Natalia Neverova	Facebook AI Research, UK

Demo Chair

Bohyung Han	Seoul National University, Korea

Social and Student Activities Chairs

Tatiana Tommasi Italian Institute of Technology, Italy
Sagie Benaim University of Copenhagen, Denmark

Diversity and Inclusion Chairs

Xi Yin Facebook AI Research, USA
Bryan Russell Adobe, USA

Communications Chairs

Lorenzo Baraldi University of Modena and Reggio Emilia, Italy
Kosta Derpanis York University & Samsung AI Centre Toronto,
Canada

Industrial Liaison Chairs

Dimosthenis Karatzas Universitat Autònoma de Barcelona, Spain
Chen Sagiv SagivTech, Israel

Finance Chair

Gerard Medioni University of Southern California & Amazon,
USA

Publication Chair

Eric Mortensen MiCROTEC, USA

Area Chairs

Lourdes Agapito University College London, UK
Zeynep Akata University of Tübingen, Germany
Naveed Akhtar University of Western Australia, Australia
Karteek Alahari Inria Grenoble Rhône-Alpes, France
Alexandre Alahi École polytechnique fédérale de Lausanne,
Switzerland
Pablo Arbelaez Universidad de Los Andes, Columbia
Antonis A. Argyros University of Crete & Foundation for Research
and Technology-Hellas, Crete
Yuki M. Asano University of Amsterdam, The Netherlands
Kalle Åström Lund University, Sweden
Hadar Averbuch-Elor Cornell University, USA

Hossein Azizpour   KTH Royal Institute of Technology, Sweden
Vineeth N. Balasubramanian   Indian Institute of Technology, Hyderabad, India
Lamberto Ballan   University of Padova, Italy
Adrien Bartoli   Université Clermont Auvergne, France
Horst Bischof   Graz University of Technology, Austria
Matthew B. Blaschko   KU Leuven, Belgium
Federica Bogo   Meta Reality Labs Research, Switzerland
Katherine Bouman   California Institute of Technology, USA
Edmond Boyer   Inria Grenoble Rhône-Alpes, France
Michael S. Brown   York University, Canada
Vittorio Caggiano   Meta AI Research, USA
Neill Campbell   University of Bath, UK
Octavia Camps   Northeastern University, USA
Duygu Ceylan   Adobe Research, USA
Ayan Chakrabarti   Google Research, USA
Tat-Jen Cham   Nanyang Technological University, Singapore
Antoni Chan   City University of Hong Kong, Hong Kong, China
Manmohan Chandraker   NEC Labs America, USA
Xinlei Chen   Facebook AI Research, USA
Xilin Chen   Institute of Computing Technology, Chinese
                                 Academy of Sciences, China
Dongdong Chen   Microsoft Cloud AI, USA
Chen Chen   University of Central Florida, USA
Ondrej Chum   Vision Recognition Group, Czech Technical
                                 University in Prague, Czech Republic
John Collomosse   Adobe Research & University of Surrey, UK
Camille Couprie   Facebook, France
David Crandall   Indiana University, USA
Daniel Cremers   Technical University of Munich, Germany
Marco Cristani   University of Verona, Italy
Canton Cristian   Facebook AI Research, USA
Dengxin Dai   ETH Zurich, Switzerland
Dima Damen   University of Bristol, UK
Kostas Daniilidis   University of Pennsylvania, USA
Trevor Darrell   University of California, Berkeley, USA
Andrew Davison   Imperial College London, UK
Tali Dekel   Weizmann Institute of Science, Israel
Alessio Del Bue   Istituto Italiano di Tecnologia, Italy
Weihong Deng   Beijing University of Posts and
                                 Telecommunications, China
Konstantinos Derpanis   Ryerson University, Canada
Carl Doersch   DeepMind, UK

Bohyung Han	Seoul National University, Korea
Tian Han	Stevens Institute of Technology, USA
Emily Hand	University of Nevada, Reno, USA
Bharath Hariharan	Cornell University, USA
Ran He	Institute of Automation, Chinese Academy of Sciences, China
Otmar Hilliges	ETH Zurich, Switzerland
Adrian Hilton	University of Surrey, UK
Minh Hoai	Stony Brook University, USA
Yedid Hoshen	Hebrew University of Jerusalem, Israel
Timothy Hospedales	University of Edinburgh, UK
Gang Hua	Wormpex AI Research, USA
Di Huang	Beihang University, China
Jing Huang	Facebook, USA
Jia-Bin Huang	Facebook, USA
Nathan Jacobs	Washington University in St. Louis, USA
C.V. Jawahar	International Institute of Information Technology, Hyderabad, India
Herve Jegou	Facebook AI Research, France
Neel Joshi	Microsoft Research, USA
Armand Joulin	Facebook AI Research, France
Frederic Jurie	University of Caen Normandie, France
Fredrik Kahl	Chalmers University of Technology, Sweden
Yannis Kalantidis	NAVER LABS Europe, France
Evangelos Kalogerakis	University of Massachusetts, Amherst, USA
Sing Bing Kang	Zillow Group, USA
Yosi Keller	Bar Ilan University, Israel
Margret Keuper	University of Mannheim, Germany
Tae-Kyun Kim	Imperial College London, UK
Benjamin Kimia	Brown University, USA
Alexander Kirillov	Facebook AI Research, USA
Kris Kitani	Carnegie Mellon University, USA
Iasonas Kokkinos	Snap Inc. & University College London, UK
Vladlen Koltun	Apple, USA
Nikos Komodakis	University of Crete, Crete
Piotr Koniusz	Australian National University, Australia
Philipp Kraehenbuehl	University of Texas at Austin, USA
Dilip Krishnan	Google, USA
Ajay Kumar	Hong Kong Polytechnic University, Hong Kong, China
Junseok Kwon	Chung-Ang University, Korea
Jean-Francois Lalonde	Université Laval, Canada

Ivan Laptev	Inria Paris, France
Laura Leal-Taixé	Technical University of Munich, Germany
Erik Learned-Miller	University of Massachusetts, Amherst, USA
Gim Hee Lee	National University of Singapore, Singapore
Seungyong Lee	Pohang University of Science and Technology, Korea
Zhen Lei	Institute of Automation, Chinese Academy of Sciences, China
Bastian Leibe	RWTH Aachen University, Germany
Hongdong Li	Australian National University, Australia
Fuxin Li	Oregon State University, USA
Bo Li	University of Illinois at Urbana-Champaign, USA
Yin Li	University of Wisconsin-Madison, USA
Ser-Nam Lim	Meta AI Research, USA
Joseph Lim	University of Southern California, USA
Stephen Lin	Microsoft Research Asia, China
Dahua Lin	The Chinese University of Hong Kong, Hong Kong, China
Si Liu	Beihang University, China
Xiaoming Liu	Michigan State University, USA
Ce Liu	Microsoft, USA
Zicheng Liu	Microsoft, USA
Yanxi Liu	Pennsylvania State University, USA
Feng Liu	Portland State University, USA
Yebin Liu	Tsinghua University, China
Chen Change Loy	Nanyang Technological University, Singapore
Huchuan Lu	Dalian University of Technology, China
Cewu Lu	Shanghai Jiao Tong University, China
Oisin Mac Aodha	University of Edinburgh, UK
Dhruv Mahajan	Facebook, USA
Subhransu Maji	University of Massachusetts, Amherst, USA
Atsuto Maki	KTH Royal Institute of Technology, Sweden
Arun Mallya	NVIDIA, USA
R. Manmatha	Amazon, USA
Iacopo Masi	Sapienza University of Rome, Italy
Dimitris N. Metaxas	Rutgers University, USA
Ajmal Mian	University of Western Australia, Australia
Christian Micheloni	University of Udine, Italy
Krystian Mikolajczyk	Imperial College London, UK
Anurag Mittal	Indian Institute of Technology, Madras, India
Philippos Mordohai	Stevens Institute of Technology, USA
Greg Mori	Simon Fraser University & Borealis AI, Canada

Vittorio Murino   Istituto Italiano di Tecnologia, Italy
P. J. Narayanan   International Institute of Information Technology,
                                Hyderabad, India
Ram Nevatia   University of Southern California, USA
Natalia Neverova   Facebook AI Research, UK
Richard Newcombe   Facebook, USA
Cuong V. Nguyen   Florida International University, USA
Bingbing Ni   Shanghai Jiao Tong University, China
Juan Carlos Niebles   Salesforce & Stanford University, USA
Ko Nishino   Kyoto University, Japan
Jean-Marc Odobez   Idiap Research Institute, École polytechnique
                                fédérale de Lausanne, Switzerland
Francesca Odone   University of Genova, Italy
Takayuki Okatani   Tohoku University & RIKEN Center for
                                Advanced Intelligence Project, Japan
Manohar Paluri   Facebook, USA
Guan Pang   Facebook, USA
Maja Pantic   Imperial College London, UK
Sylvain Paris   Adobe Research, USA
Jaesik Park   Pohang University of Science and Technology,
                                Korea
Hyun Soo Park   The University of Minnesota, USA
Omkar M. Parkhi   Facebook, USA
Deepak Pathak   Carnegie Mellon University, USA
Georgios Pavlakos   University of California, Berkeley, USA
Marcello Pelillo   University of Venice, Italy
Marc Pollefeys   ETH Zurich & Microsoft, Switzerland
Jean Ponce   Inria, France
Gerard Pons-Moll   University of Tübingen, Germany
Fatih Porikli   Qualcomm, USA
Victor Adrian Prisacariu   University of Oxford, UK
Petia Radeva   University of Barcelona, Spain
Ravi Ramamoorthi   University of California, San Diego, USA
Deva Ramanan   Carnegie Mellon University, USA
Vignesh Ramanathan   Facebook, USA
Nalini Ratha   State University of New York at Buffalo, USA
Tammy Riklin Raviv   Ben-Gurion University, Israel
Tobias Ritschel   University College London, UK
Emanuele Rodola   Sapienza University of Rome, Italy
Amit K. Roy-Chowdhury   University of California, Riverside, USA
Michael Rubinstein   Google, USA
Olga Russakovsky   Princeton University, USA

Mathieu Salzmann	École polytechnique fédérale de Lausanne, Switzerland
Dimitris Samaras	Stony Brook University, USA
Aswin Sankaranarayanan	Carnegie Mellon University, USA
Imari Sato	National Institute of Informatics, Japan
Yoichi Sato	University of Tokyo, Japan
Shin'ichi Satoh	National Institute of Informatics, Japan
Walter Scheirer	University of Notre Dame, USA
Bernt Schiele	Max Planck Institute for Informatics, Germany
Konrad Schindler	ETH Zurich, Switzerland
Cordelia Schmid	Inria & Google, France
Alexander Schwing	University of Illinois at Urbana-Champaign, USA
Nicu Sebe	University of Trento, Italy
Greg Shakhnarovich	Toyota Technological Institute at Chicago, USA
Eli Shechtman	Adobe Research, USA
Humphrey Shi	University of Oregon & University of Illinois at Urbana-Champaign & Picsart AI Research, USA
Jianbo Shi	University of Pennsylvania, USA
Roy Shilkrot	Massachusetts Institute of Technology, USA
Mike Zheng Shou	National University of Singapore, Singapore
Kaleem Siddiqi	McGill University, Canada
Richa Singh	Indian Institute of Technology Jodhpur, India
Greg Slabaugh	Queen Mary University of London, UK
Cees Snoek	University of Amsterdam, The Netherlands
Yale Song	Facebook AI Research, USA
Yi-Zhe Song	University of Surrey, UK
Bjorn Stenger	Rakuten Institute of Technology
Abby Stylianou	Saint Louis University, USA
Akihiro Sugimoto	National Institute of Informatics, Japan
Chen Sun	Brown University, USA
Deqing Sun	Google, USA
Kalyan Sunkavalli	Adobe Research, USA
Ying Tai	Tencent YouTu Lab, China
Ayellet Tal	Technion – Israel Institute of Technology, Israel
Ping Tan	Simon Fraser University, Canada
Siyu Tang	ETH Zurich, Switzerland
Chi-Keung Tang	Hong Kong University of Science and Technology, Hong Kong, China
Radu Timofte	University of Würzburg, Germany & ETH Zurich, Switzerland
Federico Tombari	Google, Switzerland & Technical University of Munich, Germany

James Tompkin	Brown University, USA
Lorenzo Torresani	Dartmouth College, USA
Alexander Toshev	Apple, USA
Du Tran	Facebook AI Research, USA
Anh T. Tran	VinAI, Vietnam
Zhuowen Tu	University of California, San Diego, USA
Georgios Tzimiropoulos	Queen Mary University of London, UK
Jasper Uijlings	Google Research, Switzerland
Jan C. van Gemert	Delft University of Technology, The Netherlands
Gul Varol	Ecole des Ponts ParisTech, France
Nuno Vasconcelos	University of California, San Diego, USA
Mayank Vatsa	Indian Institute of Technology Jodhpur, India
Ashok Veeraraghavan	Rice University, USA
Jakob Verbeek	Facebook AI Research, France
Carl Vondrick	Columbia University, USA
Ruiping Wang	Institute of Computing Technology, Chinese Academy of Sciences, China
Xinchao Wang	National University of Singapore, Singapore
Liwei Wang	The Chinese University of Hong Kong, Hong Kong, China
Chaohui Wang	Université Paris-Est, France
Xiaolong Wang	University of California, San Diego, USA
Christian Wolf	NAVER LABS Europe, France
Tao Xiang	University of Surrey, UK
Saining Xie	Facebook AI Research, USA
Cihang Xie	University of California, Santa Cruz, USA
Zeki Yalniz	Facebook, USA
Ming-Hsuan Yang	University of California, Merced, USA
Angela Yao	National University of Singapore, Singapore
Shaodi You	University of Amsterdam, The Netherlands
Stella X. Yu	University of California, Berkeley, USA
Junsong Yuan	State University of New York at Buffalo, USA
Stefanos Zafeiriou	Imperial College London, UK
Amir Zamir	École polytechnique fédérale de Lausanne, Switzerland
Lei Zhang	Alibaba & Hong Kong Polytechnic University, Hong Kong, China
Lei Zhang	International Digital Economy Academy (IDEA), China
Pengchuan Zhang	Meta AI, USA
Bolei Zhou	University of California, Los Angeles, USA
Yuke Zhu	University of Texas at Austin, USA

Todd Zickler   Harvard University, USA
Wangmeng Zuo   Harbin Institute of Technology, China

Technical Program Committee

Davide Abati
Soroush Abbasi
    Koohpayegani
Amos L. Abbott
Rameen Abdal
Rabab Abdelfattah
Sahar Abdelnabi
Hassan Abu Alhaija
Abulikemu Abuduweili
Ron Abutbul
Hanno Ackermann
Aikaterini Adam
Kamil Adamczewski
Ehsan Adeli
Vida Adeli
Donald Adjeroh
Arman Afrasiyabi
Akshay Agarwal
Sameer Agarwal
Abhinav Agarwalla
Vaibhav Aggarwal
Sara Aghajanzadeh
Susmit Agrawal
Antonio Agudo
Touqeer Ahmad
Sk Miraj Ahmed
Chaitanya Ahuja
Nilesh A. Ahuja
Abhishek Aich
Shubhra Aich
Noam Aigerman
Arash Akbarinia
Peri Akiva
Derya Akkaynak
Emre Aksan
Arjun R. Akula
Yuval Alaluf
Stephan Alaniz
Paul Albert
Cenek Albl

Filippo Aleotti
Konstantinos P.
    Alexandridis
Motasem Alfarra
Mohsen Ali
Thiemo Alldieck
Hadi Alzayer
Liang An
Shan An
Yi An
Zhulin An
Dongsheng An
Jie An
Xiang An
Saket Anand
Cosmin Ancuti
Juan Andrade-Cetto
Alexander Andreopoulos
Bjoern Andres
Jerone T. A. Andrews
Shivangi Aneja
Anelia Angelova
Dragomir Anguelov
Rushil Anirudh
Oron Anschel
Rao Muhammad Anwer
Djamila Aouada
Evlampios Apostolidis
Srikar Appalaraju
Nikita Araslanov
Andre Araujo
Eric Arazo
Dawit Mureja Argaw
Anurag Arnab
Aditya Arora
Chetan Arora
Sunpreet S. Arora
Alexey Artemov
Muhammad Asad
Kumar Ashutosh

Sinem Aslan
Vishal Asnani
Mahmoud Assran
Amir Atapour-Abarghouei
Nikos Athanasiou
Ali Athar
ShahRukh Athar
Sara Atito
Souhaib Attaiki
Matan Atzmon
Mathieu Aubry
Nicolas Audebert
Tristan T.
    Aumentado-Armstrong
Melinos Averkiou
Yannis Avrithis
Stephane Ayache
Mehmet Aygün
Seyed Mehdi
    Ayyoubzadeh
Hossein Azizpour
George Azzopardi
Mallikarjun B. R.
Yunhao Ba
Abhishek Badki
Seung-Hwan Bae
Seung-Hwan Baek
Seungryul Baek
Piyush Nitin Bagad
Shai Bagon
Gaetan Bahl
Shikhar Bahl
Sherwin Bahmani
Haoran Bai
Lei Bai
Jiawang Bai
Haoyue Bai
Jinbin Bai
Xiang Bai
Xuyang Bai

Yang Bai
Yuanchao Bai
Ziqian Bai
Sungyong Baik
Kevin Bailly
Max Bain
Federico Baldassarre
Wele Gedara Chaminda
   Bandara
Biplab Banerjee
Pratyay Banerjee
Sandipan Banerjee
Jihwan Bang
Antyanta Bangunharcana
Aayush Bansal
Ankan Bansal
Siddhant Bansal
Wentao Bao
Zhipeng Bao
Amir Bar
Manel Baradad Jurjo
Lorenzo Baraldi
Danny Barash
Daniel Barath
Connelly Barnes
Ioan Andrei Bârsan
Steven Basart
Dina Bashkirova
Chaim Baskin
Peyman Bateni
Anil Batra
Sebastiano Battiato
Ardhendu Behera
Harkirat Behl
Jens Behley
Vasileios Belagiannis
Boulbaba Ben Amor
Emanuel Ben Baruch
Abdessamad Ben Hamza
Gil Ben-Artzi
Assia Benbihi
Fabian Benitez-Quiroz
Guy Ben-Yosef
Philipp Benz
Alexander W. Bergman

Urs Bergmann
Jesus Bermudez-Cameo
Stefano Berretti
Gedas Bertasius
Zachary Bessinger
Petra Bevandić
Matthew Beveridge
Lucas Beyer
Yash Bhalgat
Suvaansh Bhambri
Samarth Bharadwaj
Gaurav Bharaj
Aparna Bharati
Bharat Lal Bhatnagar
Uttaran Bhattacharya
Apratim Bhattacharyya
Brojeshwar Bhowmick
Ankan Kumar Bhunia
Ayan Kumar Bhunia
Qi Bi
Sai Bi
Michael Bi Mi
Gui-Bin Bian
Jia-Wang Bian
Shaojun Bian
Pia Bideau
Mario Bijelic
Hakan Bilen
Guillaume-Alexandre
   Bilodeau
Alexander Binder
Tolga Birdal
Vighnesh N. Birodkar
Sandika Biswas
Andreas Blattmann
Janusz Bobulski
Giuseppe Boccignone
Vishnu Boddeti
Navaneeth Bodla
Moritz Böhle
Aleksei Bokhovkin
Sam Bond-Taylor
Vivek Boominathan
Shubhankar Borse
Mark Boss

Andrea Bottino
Adnane Boukhayma
Fadi Boutros
Nicolas C. Boutry
Richard S. Bowen
Ivaylo Boyadzhiev
Aidan Boyd
Yuri Boykov
Aljaz Bozic
Behzad Bozorgtabar
Eric Brachmann
Samarth Brahmbhatt
Gustav Bredell
Francois Bremond
Joel Brogan
Andrew Brown
Thomas Brox
Marcus A. Brubaker
Robert-Jan Bruintjes
Yuqi Bu
Anders G. Buch
Himanshu Buckchash
Mateusz Buda
Ignas Budvytis
José M. Buenaposada
Marcel C. Bühler
Tu Bui
Adrian Bulat
Hannah Bull
Evgeny Burnaev
Andrei Bursuc
Benjamin Busam
Sergey N. Buzykanov
Wonmin Byeon
Fabian Caba
Martin Cadik
Guanyu Cai
Minjie Cai
Qing Cai
Zhongang Cai
Qi Cai
Yancheng Cai
Shen Cai
Han Cai
Jiarui Cai

Bowen Cai
Mu Cai
Qin Cai
Ruojin Cai
Weidong Cai
Weiwei Cai
Yi Cai
Yujun Cai
Zhiping Cai
Akin Caliskan
Lilian Calvet
Baris Can Cam
Necati Cihan Camgoz
Tommaso Campari
Dylan Campbell
Ziang Cao
Ang Cao
Xu Cao
Zhiwen Cao
Shengcao Cao
Song Cao
Weipeng Cao
Xiangyong Cao
Xiaochun Cao
Yue Cao
Yunhao Cao
Zhangjie Cao
Jiale Cao
Yang Cao
Jiajiong Cao
Jie Cao
Jinkun Cao
Lele Cao
Yulong Cao
Zhiguo Cao
Chen Cao
Razvan Caramalau
Marlène Careil
Gustavo Carneiro
Joao Carreira
Dan Casas
Paola Cascante-Bonilla
Angela Castillo
Francisco M. Castro
Pedro Castro

Luca Cavalli
George J. Cazenavette
Oya Celiktutan
Hakan Cevikalp
Sri Harsha C. H.
Sungmin Cha
Geonho Cha
Menglei Chai
Lucy Chai
Yuning Chai
Zenghao Chai
Anirban Chakraborty
Deep Chakraborty
Rudrasis Chakraborty
Souradeep Chakraborty
Kelvin C. K. Chan
Chee Seng Chan
Paramanand Chandramouli
Arjun Chandrasekaran
Kenneth Chaney
Dongliang Chang
Huiwen Chang
Peng Chang
Xiaojun Chang
Jia-Ren Chang
Hyung Jin Chang
Hyun Sung Chang
Ju Yong Chang
Li-Jen Chang
Qi Chang
Wei-Yi Chang
Yi Chang
Nadine Chang
Hanqing Chao
Pradyumna Chari
Dibyadip Chatterjee
Chiranjoy Chattopadhyay
Siddhartha Chaudhuri
Zhengping Che
Gal Chechik
Lianggangxu Chen
Qi Alfred Chen
Brian Chen
Bor-Chun Chen
Bo-Hao Chen

Bohong Chen
Bin Chen
Ziliang Chen
Cheng Chen
Chen Chen
Chaofeng Chen
Xi Chen
Haoyu Chen
Xuanhong Chen
Wei Chen
Qiang Chen
Shi Chen
Xianyu Chen
Chang Chen
Changhuai Chen
Hao Chen
Jie Chen
Jianbo Chen
Jingjing Chen
Jun Chen
Kejiang Chen
Mingcai Chen
Nenglun Chen
Qifeng Chen
Ruoyu Chen
Shu-Yu Chen
Weidong Chen
Weijie Chen
Weikai Chen
Xiang Chen
Xiuyi Chen
Xingyu Chen
Yaofo Chen
Yueting Chen
Yu Chen
Yunjin Chen
Yuntao Chen
Yun Chen
Zhenfang Chen
Zhuangzhuang Chen
Chu-Song Chen
Xiangyu Chen
Zhuo Chen
Chaoqi Chen
Shizhe Chen

Xiaotong Chen	Shuai Chen	Jiacheng Cheng
Xiaozhi Chen	Shuya Chen	Kelvin B. Cheng
Dian Chen	Sizhe Chen	Li Cheng
Defang Chen	Simin Chen	Mengjun Cheng
Dingfan Chen	Shaoxiang Chen	Zhen Cheng
Ding-Jie Chen	Zitian Chen	Qingrong Cheng
Ee Heng Chen	Tianlong Chen	Tianheng Cheng
Tao Chen	Tianshui Chen	Harry Cheng
Yixin Chen	Min-Hung Chen	Yihua Cheng
Wei-Ting Chen	Xiangning Chen	Yu Cheng
Lin Chen	Xin Chen	Ziheng Cheng
Guang Chen	Xinghao Chen	Soon Yau Cheong
Guangyi Chen	Xuejin Chen	Anoop Cherian
Guanying Chen	Xu Chen	Manuela Chessa
Guangyao Chen	Xuxi Chen	Zhixiang Chi
Hwann-Tzong Chen	Yunlu Chen	Naoki Chiba
Junwen Chen	Yanbei Chen	Julian Chibane
Jiacheng Chen	Yuxiao Chen	Kashyap Chitta
Jianxu Chen	Yun-Chun Chen	Tai-Yin Chiu
Hui Chen	Yi-Ting Chen	Hsu-kuang Chiu
Kai Chen	Yi-Wen Chen	Wei-Chen Chiu
Kan Chen	Yinbo Chen	Sungmin Cho
Kevin Chen	Yiran Chen	Donghyeon Cho
Kuan-Wen Chen	Yuanhong Chen	Hyeon Cho
Weihua Chen	Yubei Chen	Yooshin Cho
Zhang Chen	Yuefeng Chen	Gyusang Cho
Liang-Chieh Chen	Yuhua Chen	Jang Hyun Cho
Lele Chen	Yukang Chen	Seungju Cho
Liang Chen	Zerui Chen	Nam Ik Cho
Fanglin Chen	Zhaoyu Chen	Sunghyun Cho
Zehui Chen	Zhen Chen	Hanbyel Cho
Minghui Chen	Zhenyu Chen	Jaesung Choe
Minghao Chen	Zhi Chen	Jooyoung Choi
Xiaokang Chen	Zhiwei Chen	Chiho Choi
Qian Chen	Zhixiang Chen	Changwoon Choi
Jun-Cheng Chen	Long Chen	Jongwon Choi
Qi Chen	Bowen Cheng	Myungsub Choi
Qingcai Chen	Jun Cheng	Dooseop Choi
Richard J. Chen	Yi Cheng	Jonghyun Choi
Runnan Chen	Jingchun Cheng	Jinwoo Choi
Rui Chen	Lechao Cheng	Jun Won Choi
Shuo Chen	Xi Cheng	Min-Kook Choi
Sentao Chen	Yuan Cheng	Hongsuk Choi
Shaoyu Chen	Ho Kei Cheng	Janghoon Choi
Shixing Chen	Kevin Ho Man Cheng	Yoon-Ho Choi

Yukyung Choi
Jaegul Choo
Ayush Chopra
Siddharth Choudhary
Subhabrata Choudhury
Vasileios Choutas
Ka-Ho Chow
Pinaki Nath Chowdhury
Sammy Christen
Anders Christensen
Grigorios Chrysos
Hang Chu
Wen-Hsuan Chu
Peng Chu
Qi Chu
Ruihang Chu
Wei-Ta Chu
Yung-Yu Chuang
Sanghyuk Chun
Se Young Chun
Antonio Cinà
Ramazan Gokberk Cinbis
Javier Civera
Albert Clapés
Ronald Clark
Brian S. Clipp
Felipe Codevilla
Daniel Coelho de Castro
Niv Cohen
Forrester Cole
Maxwell D. Collins
Robert T. Collins
Marc Comino Trinidad
Runmin Cong
Wenyan Cong
Maxime Cordy
Marcella Cornia
Enric Corona
Huseyin Coskun
Luca Cosmo
Dragos Costea
Davide Cozzolino
Arun C. S. Kumar
Aiyu Cui
Qiongjie Cui

Quan Cui
Shuhao Cui
Yiming Cui
Ying Cui
Zijun Cui
Jiali Cui
Jiequan Cui
Yawen Cui
Zhen Cui
Zhaopeng Cui
Jack Culpepper
Xiaodong Cun
Ross Cutler
Adam Czajka
Ali Dabouei
Konstantinos M. Dafnis
Manuel Dahnert
Tao Dai
Yuchao Dai
Bo Dai
Mengyu Dai
Hang Dai
Haixing Dai
Peng Dai
Pingyang Dai
Qi Dai
Qiyu Dai
Yutong Dai
Naser Damer
Zhiyuan Dang
Mohamed Daoudi
Ayan Das
Abir Das
Debasmit Das
Deepayan Das
Partha Das
Sagnik Das
Soumi Das
Srijan Das
Swagatam Das
Avijit Dasgupta
Jim Davis
Adrian K. Davison
Homa Davoudi
Laura Daza

Matthias De Lange
Shalini De Mello
Marco De Nadai
Christophe De
    Vleeschouwer
Alp Dener
Boyang Deng
Congyue Deng
Bailin Deng
Yong Deng
Ye Deng
Zhuo Deng
Zhijie Deng
Xiaoming Deng
Jiankang Deng
Jinhong Deng
Jingjing Deng
Liang-Jian Deng
Siqi Deng
Xiang Deng
Xueqing Deng
Zhongying Deng
Karan Desai
Jean-Emmanuel Deschaud
Aniket Anand Deshmukh
Neel Dey
Helisa Dhamo
Prithviraj Dhar
Amaya Dharmasiri
Yan Di
Xing Di
Ousmane A. Dia
Haiwen Diao
Xiaolei Diao
Gonçalo José Dias Pais
Abdallah Dib
Anastasios Dimou
Changxing Ding
Henghui Ding
Guodong Ding
Yaqing Ding
Shuangrui Ding
Yuhang Ding
Yikang Ding
Shouhong Ding

Haisong Ding
Hui Ding
Jiahao Ding
Jian Ding
Jian-Jiun Ding
Shuxiao Ding
Tianyu Ding
Wenhao Ding
Yuqi Ding
Yi Ding
Yuzhen Ding
Zhengming Ding
Tan Minh Dinh
Vu Dinh
Christos Diou
Mandar Dixit
Bao Gia Doan
Khoa D. Doan
Dzung Anh Doan
Debi Prosad Dogra
Nehal Doiphode
Chengdong Dong
Bowen Dong
Zhenxing Dong
Hang Dong
Xiaoyi Dong
Haoye Dong
Jiangxin Dong
Shichao Dong
Xuan Dong
Zhen Dong
Shuting Dong
Jing Dong
Li Dong
Ming Dong
Nanqing Dong
Qiulei Dong
Runpei Dong
Siyan Dong
Tian Dong
Wei Dong
Xiaomeng Dong
Xin Dong
Xingbo Dong
Yuan Dong

Samuel Dooley
Gianfranco Doretto
Michael Dorkenwald
Keval Doshi
Zhaopeng Dou
Xiaotian Dou
Hazel Doughty
Ahmad Droby
Iddo Drori
Jie Du
Yong Du
Dawei Du
Dong Du
Ruoyi Du
Yuntao Du
Xuefeng Du
Yilun Du
Yuming Du
Radhika Dua
Haodong Duan
Jiafei Duan
Kaiwen Duan
Peiqi Duan
Ye Duan
Haoran Duan
Jiali Duan
Amanda Duarte
Abhimanyu Dubey
Shiv Ram Dubey
Florian Dubost
Lukasz Dudziak
Shivam Duggal
Justin M. Dulay
Matteo Dunnhofer
Chi Nhan Duong
Thibaut Durand
Mihai Dusmanu
Ujjal Kr Dutta
Debidatta Dwibedi
Isht Dwivedi
Sai Kumar Dwivedi
Takeharu Eda
Mark Edmonds
Alexei A. Efros
Thibaud Ehret

Max Ehrlich
Mahsa Ehsanpour
Iván Eichhardt
Farshad Einabadi
Marvin Eisenberger
Hazim Kemal Ekenel
Mohamed El Banani
Ismail Elezi
Moshe Eliasof
Alaa El-Nouby
Ian Endres
Francis Engelmann
Deniz Engin
Chanho Eom
Dave Epstein
Maria C. Escobar
Victor A. Escorcia
Carlos Esteves
Sungmin Eum
Bernard J. E. Evans
Ivan Evtimov
Fevziye Irem Eyiokur
    Yaman
Matteo Fabbri
Sébastien Fabbro
Gabriele Facciolo
Masud Fahim
Bin Fan
Hehe Fan
Deng-Ping Fan
Aoxiang Fan
Chen-Chen Fan
Qi Fan
Zhaoxin Fan
Haoqi Fan
Heng Fan
Hongyi Fan
Linxi Fan
Baojie Fan
Jiayuan Fan
Lei Fan
Quanfu Fan
Yonghui Fan
Yingruo Fan
Zhiwen Fan

Zicong Fan
Sean Fanello
Jiansheng Fang
Chaowei Fang
Yuming Fang
Jianwu Fang
Jin Fang
Qi Fang
Shancheng Fang
Tian Fang
Xianyong Fang
Gongfan Fang
Zhen Fang
Hui Fang
Jiemin Fang
Le Fang
Pengfei Fang
Xiaolin Fang
Yuxin Fang
Zhaoyuan Fang
Ammarah Farooq
Azade Farshad
Zhengcong Fei
Michael Felsberg
Wei Feng
Chen Feng
Fan Feng
Andrew Feng
Xin Feng
Zheyun Feng
Ruicheng Feng
Mingtao Feng
Qianyu Feng
Shangbin Feng
Chun-Mei Feng
Zunlei Feng
Zhiyong Feng
Martin Fergie
Mustansar Fiaz
Marco Fiorucci
Michael Firman
Hamed Firooz
Volker Fischer
Corneliu O. Florea
Georgios Floros

Wolfgang Foerstner
Gianni Franchi
Jean-Sebastien Franco
Simone Frintrop
Anna Fruehstueck
Changhong Fu
Chaoyou Fu
Cheng-Yang Fu
Chi-Wing Fu
Deqing Fu
Huan Fu
Jun Fu
Kexue Fu
Ying Fu
Jianlong Fu
Jingjing Fu
Qichen Fu
Tsu-Jui Fu
Xueyang Fu
Yang Fu
Yanwei Fu
Yonggan Fu
Wolfgang Fuhl
Yasuhisa Fujii
Kent Fujiwara
Marco Fumero
Takuya Funatomi
Isabel Funke
Dario Fuoli
Antonino Furnari
Matheus A. Gadelha
Akshay Gadi Patil
Adrian Galdran
Guillermo Gallego
Silvano Galliani
Orazio Gallo
Leonardo Galteri
Matteo Gamba
Yiming Gan
Sujoy Ganguly
Harald Ganster
Boyan Gao
Changxin Gao
Daiheng Gao
Difei Gao

Chen Gao
Fei Gao
Lin Gao
Wei Gao
Yiming Gao
Junyu Gao
Guangyu Ryan Gao
Haichang Gao
Hongchang Gao
Jialin Gao
Jin Gao
Jun Gao
Katelyn Gao
Mingchen Gao
Mingfei Gao
Pan Gao
Shangqian Gao
Shanghua Gao
Xitong Gao
Yunhe Gao
Zhanning Gao
Elena Garces
Nuno Cruz Garcia
Noa Garcia
Guillermo
   Garcia-Hernando
Isha Garg
Rahul Garg
Sourav Garg
Quentin Garrido
Stefano Gasperini
Kent Gauen
Chandan Gautam
Shivam Gautam
Paul Gay
Chunjiang Ge
Shiming Ge
Wenhang Ge
Yanhao Ge
Zheng Ge
Songwei Ge
Weifeng Ge
Yixiao Ge
Yuying Ge
Shijie Geng

Zhengyang Geng
Kyle A. Genova
Georgios Georgakis
Markos Georgopoulos
Marcel Geppert
Shabnam Ghadar
Mina Ghadimi Atigh
Deepti Ghadiyaram
Maani Ghaffari Jadidi
Sedigh Ghamari
Zahra Gharaee
Michaël Gharbi
Golnaz Ghiasi
Reza Ghoddoosian
Soumya Suvra Ghosal
Adhiraj Ghosh
Arthita Ghosh
Pallabi Ghosh
Soumyadeep Ghosh
Andrew Gilbert
Igor Gilitschenski
Jhony H. Giraldo
Andreu Girbau Xalabarder
Rohit Girdhar
Sharath Girish
Xavier Giro-i-Nieto
Raja Giryes
Thomas Gittings
Nikolaos Gkanatsios
Ioannis Gkioulekas
Abhiram
   Gnanasambandam
Aurele T. Gnanha
Clement L. J. C. Godard
Arushi Goel
Vidit Goel
Shubham Goel
Zan Gojcic
Aaron K. Gokaslan
Tejas Gokhale
S. Alireza Golestaneh
Thiago L. Gomes
Nuno Goncalves
Boqing Gong
Chen Gong

Yuanhao Gong
Guoqiang Gong
Jingyu Gong
Rui Gong
Yu Gong
Mingming Gong
Neil Zhenqiang Gong
Xun Gong
Yunye Gong
Yihong Gong
Cristina I. González
Nithin Gopalakrishnan
   Nair
Gaurav Goswami
Jianping Gou
Shreyank N. Gowda
Ankit Goyal
Helmut Grabner
Patrick L. Grady
Ben Graham
Eric Granger
Douglas R. Gray
Matej Grcić
David Griffiths
Jinjin Gu
Yun Gu
Shuyang Gu
Jianyang Gu
Fuqiang Gu
Jiatao Gu
Jindong Gu
Jiaqi Gu
Jinwei Gu
Jiaxin Gu
Geonmo Gu
Xiao Gu
Xinqian Gu
Xiuye Gu
Yuming Gu
Zhangxuan Gu
Dayan Guan
Junfeng Guan
Qingji Guan
Tianrui Guan
Shanyan Guan

Denis A. Gudovskiy
Ricardo Guerrero
Pierre-Louis Guhur
Jie Gui
Liangyan Gui
Liangke Gui
Benoit Guillard
Erhan Gundogdu
Manuel Günther
Jingcai Guo
Yuanfang Guo
Junfeng Guo
Chenqi Guo
Dan Guo
Hongji Guo
Jia Guo
Jie Guo
Minghao Guo
Shi Guo
Yanhui Guo
Yangyang Guo
Yuan-Chen Guo
Yilu Guo
Yiluan Guo
Yong Guo
Guangyu Guo
Haiyun Guo
Jinyang Guo
Jianyuan Guo
Pengsheng Guo
Pengfei Guo
Shuxuan Guo
Song Guo
Tianyu Guo
Qing Guo
Qiushan Guo
Wen Guo
Xiefan Guo
Xiaohu Guo
Xiaoqing Guo
Yufei Guo
Yuhui Guo
Yuliang Guo
Yunhui Guo
Yanwen Guo

Akshita Gupta
Ankush Gupta
Kamal Gupta
Kartik Gupta
Ritwik Gupta
Rohit Gupta
Siddharth Gururani
Fredrik K. Gustafsson
Abner Guzman Rivera
Vladimir Guzov
Matthew A. Gwilliam
Jung-Woo Ha
Marc Habermann
Isma Hadji
Christian Haene
Martin Hahner
Levente Hajder
Alexandros Haliassos
Emanuela Haller
Bumsub Ham
Abdullah J. Hamdi
Shreyas Hampali
Dongyoon Han
Chunrui Han
Dong-Jun Han
Dong-Sig Han
Guangxing Han
Zhizhong Han
Ruize Han
Jiaming Han
Jin Han
Ligong Han
Xian-Hua Han
Xiaoguang Han
Yizeng Han
Zhi Han
Zhenjun Han
Zhongyi Han
Jungong Han
Junlin Han
Kai Han
Kun Han
Sungwon Han
Songfang Han
Wei Han

Xiao Han
Xintong Han
Xinzhe Han
Yahong Han
Yan Han
Zongbo Han
Nicolai Hani
Rana Hanocka
Niklas Hanselmann
Nicklas A. Hansen
Hong Hanyu
Fusheng Hao
Yanbin Hao
Shijie Hao
Udith Haputhanthri
Mehrtash Harandi
Josh Harguess
Adam Harley
David M. Hart
Atsushi Hashimoto
Ali Hassani
Mohammed Hassanin
Yana Hasson
Joakim Bruslund Haurum
Bo He
Kun He
Chen He
Xin He
Fazhi He
Gaoqi He
Hao He
Haoyu He
Jiangpeng He
Hongliang He
Qian He
Xiangteng He
Xuming He
Yannan He
Yuhang He
Yang He
Xiangyu He
Nanjun He
Pan He
Sen He
Shengfeng He

Songtao He
Tao He
Tong He
Wei He
Xuehai He
Xiaoxiao He
Ying He
Yisheng He
Ziwen He
Peter Hedman
Felix Heide
Yacov Hel-Or
Paul Henderson
Philipp Henzler
Byeongho Heo
Jae-Pil Heo
Miran Heo
Sachini A. Herath
Stephane Herbin
Pedro Hermosilla Casajus
Monica Hernandez
Charles Herrmann
Roei Herzig
Mauricio Hess-Flores
Carlos Hinojosa
Tobias Hinz
Tsubasa Hirakawa
Chih-Hui Ho
Lam Si Tung Ho
Jennifer Hobbs
Derek Hoiem
Yannick Hold-Geoffroy
Aleksander Holynski
Cheeun Hong
Fa-Ting Hong
Hanbin Hong
Guan Zhe Hong
Danfeng Hong
Lanqing Hong
Xiaopeng Hong
Xin Hong
Jie Hong
Seungbum Hong
Cheng-Yao Hong
Seunghoon Hong

Yi Hong
Yuan Hong
Yuchen Hong
Anthony Hoogs
Maxwell C. Horton
Kazuhiro Hotta
Qibin Hou
Tingbo Hou
Junhui Hou
Ji Hou
Qiqi Hou
Rui Hou
Ruibing Hou
Zhi Hou
Henry Howard-Jenkins
Lukas Hoyer
Wei-Lin Hsiao
Chiou-Ting Hsu
Anthony Hu
Brian Hu
Yusong Hu
Hexiang Hu
Haoji Hu
Di Hu
Hengtong Hu
Haigen Hu
Lianyu Hu
Hanzhe Hu
Jie Hu
Junlin Hu
Shizhe Hu
Jian Hu
Zhiming Hu
Juhua Hu
Peng Hu
Ping Hu
Ronghang Hu
MengShun Hu
Tao Hu
Vincent Tao Hu
Xiaoling Hu
Xinting Hu
Xiaolin Hu
Xuefeng Hu
Xiaowei Hu

Yang Hu
Yueyu Hu
Zeyu Hu
Zhongyun Hu
Binh-Son Hua
Guoliang Hua
Yi Hua
Linzhi Huang
Qiusheng Huang
Bo Huang
Chen Huang
Hsin-Ping Huang
Ye Huang
Shuangping Huang
Zeng Huang
Buzhen Huang
Cong Huang
Heng Huang
Hao Huang
Qidong Huang
Huaibo Huang
Chaoqin Huang
Feihu Huang
Jiahui Huang
Jingjia Huang
Kun Huang
Lei Huang
Sheng Huang
Shuaiyi Huang
Siyu Huang
Xiaoshui Huang
Xiaoyang Huang
Yan Huang
Yihao Huang
Ying Huang
Ziling Huang
Xiaoke Huang
Yifei Huang
Haiyang Huang
Zhewei Huang
Jin Huang
Haibin Huang
Jiaxing Huang
Junjie Huang
Keli Huang

Lang Huang
Lin Huang
Luojie Huang
Mingzhen Huang
Shijia Huang
Shengyu Huang
Siyuan Huang
He Huang
Xiuyu Huang
Lianghua Huang
Yue Huang
Yaping Huang
Yuge Huang
Zehao Huang
Zeyi Huang
Zhiqi Huang
Zhongzhan Huang
Zilong Huang
Ziyuan Huang
Tianrui Hui
Zhuo Hui
Le Hui
Jing Huo
Junhwa Hur
Shehzeen S. Hussain
Chuong Minh Huynh
Seunghyun Hwang
Jaehui Hwang
Jyh-Jing Hwang
Sukjun Hwang
Soonmin Hwang
Wonjun Hwang
Rakib Hyder
Sangeek Hyun
Sarah Ibrahimi
Tomoki Ichikawa
Yerlan Idelbayev
A. S. M. Iftekhar
Masaaki Iiyama
Satoshi Ikehata
Sunghoon Im
Atul N. Ingle
Eldar Insafutdinov
Yani A. Ioannou
Radu Tudor Ionescu

Umar Iqbal
Go Irie
Muhammad Zubair Irshad
Ahmet Iscen
Berivan Isik
Ashraful Islam
Md Amirul Islam
Syed Islam
Mariko Isogawa
Vamsi Krishna K. Ithapu
Boris Ivanovic
Darshan Iyer
Sarah Jabbour
Ayush Jain
Nishant Jain
Samyak Jain
Vidit Jain
Vineet Jain
Priyank Jaini
Tomas Jakab
Mohammad A. A. K.
   Jalwana
Muhammad Abdullah
   Jamal
Hadi Jamali-Rad
Stuart James
Varun Jampani
Young Kyun Jang
YeongJun Jang
Yunseok Jang
Ronnachai Jaroensri
Bhavan Jasani
Krishna Murthy
   Jatavallabhula
Mojan Javaheripi
Syed A. Javed
Guillaume Jeanneret
Pranav Jeevan
Herve Jegou
Rohit Jena
Tomas Jenicek
Porter Jenkins
Simon Jenni
Hae-Gon Jeon
Sangryul Jeon

Boseung Jeong
Yoonwoo Jeong
Seong-Gyun Jeong
Jisoo Jeong
Allan D. Jepson
Ankit Jha
Sumit K. Jha
I-Hong Jhuo
Ge-Peng Ji
Chaonan Ji
Deyi Ji
Jingwei Ji
Wei Ji
Zhong Ji
Jiayi Ji
Pengliang Ji
Hui Ji
Mingi Ji
Xiaopeng Ji
Yuzhu Ji
Baoxiong Jia
Songhao Jia
Dan Jia
Shan Jia
Xiaojun Jia
Xiuyi Jia
Xu Jia
Menglin Jia
Wenqi Jia
Boyuan Jiang
Wenhao Jiang
Huaizu Jiang
Hanwen Jiang
Haiyong Jiang
Hao Jiang
Huajie Jiang
Huiqin Jiang
Haojun Jiang
Haobo Jiang
Junjun Jiang
Xingyu Jiang
Yangbangyan Jiang
Yu Jiang
Jianmin Jiang
Jiaxi Jiang

Jing Jiang
Kui Jiang
Li Jiang
Liming Jiang
Chiyu Jiang
Meirui Jiang
Chen Jiang
Peng Jiang
Tai-Xiang Jiang
Wen Jiang
Xinyang Jiang
Yifan Jiang
Yuming Jiang
Yingying Jiang
Zeren Jiang
ZhengKai Jiang
Zhenyu Jiang
Shuming Jiao
Jianbo Jiao
Licheng Jiao
Dongkwon Jin
Yeying Jin
Cheng Jin
Linyi Jin
Qing Jin
Taisong Jin
Xiao Jin
Xin Jin
Sheng Jin
Kyong Hwan Jin
Ruibing Jin
SouYoung Jin
Yueming Jin
Chenchen Jing
Longlong Jing
Taotao Jing
Yongcheng Jing
Younghyun Jo
Joakim Johnander
Jeff Johnson
Michael J. Jones
R. Kenny Jones
Rico Jonschkowski
Ameya Joshi
Sunghun Joung

Felix Juefei-Xu
Claudio R. Jung
Steffen Jung
Hari Chandana K.
Rahul Vigneswaran K.
Prajwal K. R.
Abhishek Kadian
Jhony Kaesemodel Pontes
Kumara Kahatapitiya
Anmol Kalia
Sinan Kalkan
Tarun Kalluri
Jaewon Kam
Sandesh Kamath
Meina Kan
Menelaos Kanakis
Takuhiro Kaneko
Di Kang
Guoliang Kang
Hao Kang
Jaeyeon Kang
Kyoungkook Kang
Li-Wei Kang
MinGuk Kang
Suk-Ju Kang
Zhao Kang
Yash Mukund Kant
Yueying Kao
Aupendu Kar
Konstantinos Karantzalos
Sezer Karaoglu
Navid Kardan
Sanjay Kariyappa
Leonid Karlinsky
Animesh Karnewar
Shyamgopal Karthik
Hirak J. Kashyap
Marc A. Kastner
Hirokatsu Kataoka
Angelos Katharopoulos
Hiroharu Kato
Kai Katsumata
Manuel Kaufmann
Chaitanya Kaul
Prakhar Kaushik

Yuki Kawana
Lei Ke
Lipeng Ke
Tsung-Wei Ke
Wei Ke
Petr Kellnhofer
Aniruddha Kembhavi
John Kender
Corentin Kervadec
Leonid Keselman
Daniel Keysers
Nima Khademi Kalantari
Taras Khakhulin
Samir Khaki
Muhammad Haris Khan
Qadeer Khan
Salman Khan
Subash Khanal
Vaishnavi M. Khindkar
Rawal Khirodkar
Saeed Khorram
Pirazh Khorramshahi
Kourosh Khoshelham
Ansh Khurana
Benjamin Kiefer
Jae Myung Kim
Junho Kim
Boah Kim
Hyeonseong Kim
Dong-Jin Kim
Dongwan Kim
Donghyun Kim
Doyeon Kim
Yonghyun Kim
Hyung-Il Kim
Hyunwoo Kim
Hyeongwoo Kim
Hyo Jin Kim
Hyunwoo J. Kim
Taehoon Kim
Jaeha Kim
Jiwon Kim
Jung Uk Kim
Kangyeol Kim
Eunji Kim

Daeha Kim
Dongwon Kim
Kunhee Kim
Kyungmin Kim
Junsik Kim
Min H. Kim
Namil Kim
Kookhoi Kim
Sanghyun Kim
Seongyeop Kim
Seungryong Kim
Saehoon Kim
Euyoung Kim
Guisik Kim
Sungyeon Kim
Sunnie S. Y. Kim
Taehun Kim
Tae Oh Kim
Won Hwa Kim
Seungwook Kim
YoungBin Kim
Youngeun Kim
Akisato Kimura
Furkan Osman Kınlı
Zsolt Kira
Hedvig Kjellström
Florian Kleber
Jan P. Klopp
Florian Kluger
Laurent Kneip
Byungsoo Ko
Muhammed Kocabas
A. Sophia Koepke
Kevin Koeser
Nick Kolkin
Nikos Kolotouros
Wai-Kin Adams Kong
Deying Kong
Caihua Kong
Youyong Kong
Shuyu Kong
Shu Kong
Tao Kong
Yajing Kong
Yu Kong

Zishang Kong
Theodora Kontogianni
Anton S. Konushin
Julian F. P. Kooij
Bruno Korbar
Giorgos Kordopatis-Zilos
Jari Korhonen
Adam Kortylewski
Denis Korzhenkov
Divya Kothandaraman
Suraj Kothawade
Iuliia Kotseruba
Satwik Kottur
Shashank Kotyan
Alexandros Kouris
Petros Koutras
Anna Kreshuk
Ranjay Krishna
Dilip Krishnan
Andrey Kuehlkamp
Hilde Kuehne
Jason Kuen
David Kügler
Arjan Kuijper
Anna Kukleva
Sumith Kulal
Viveka Kulharia
Akshay R. Kulkarni
Nilesh Kulkarni
Dominik Kulon
Abhinav Kumar
Akash Kumar
Suryansh Kumar
B. V. K. Vijaya Kumar
Pulkit Kumar
Ratnesh Kumar
Sateesh Kumar
Satish Kumar
Vijay Kumar B. G.
Nupur Kumari
Sudhakar Kumawat
Jogendra Nath Kundu
Hsien-Kai Kuo
Meng-Yu Jennifer Kuo
Vinod Kumar Kurmi

Yusuke Kurose
Keerthy Kusumam
Alina Kuznetsova
Henry Kvinge
Ho Man Kwan
Hyeokjun Kweon
Heeseung Kwon
Gihyun Kwon
Myung-Joon Kwon
Taesung Kwon
YoungJoong Kwon
Christos Kyrkou
Jorma Laaksonen
Yann Labbe
Zorah Laehner
Florent Lafarge
Hamid Laga
Manuel Lagunas
Shenqi Lai
Jian-Huang Lai
Zihang Lai
Mohamed I. Lakhal
Mohit Lamba
Meng Lan
Loic Landrieu
Zhiqiang Lang
Natalie Lang
Dong Lao
Yizhen Lao
Yingjie Lao
Issam Hadj Laradji
Gustav Larsson
Viktor Larsson
Zakaria Laskar
Stéphane Lathuilière
Chun Pong Lau
Rynson W. H. Lau
Hei Law
Justin Lazarow
Verica Lazova
Eric-Tuan Le
Hieu Le
Trung-Nghia Le
Mathias Lechner
Byeong-Uk Lee

Chen-Yu Lee
Che-Rung Lee
Chul Lee
Hong Joo Lee
Dongsoo Lee
Jiyoung Lee
Eugene Eu Tzuan Lee
Daeun Lee
Saehyung Lee
Jewook Lee
Hyungtae Lee
Hyunmin Lee
Jungbeom Lee
Joon-Young Lee
Jong-Seok Lee
Joonseok Lee
Junha Lee
Kibok Lee
Byung-Kwan Lee
Jangwon Lee
Jinho Lee
Jongmin Lee
Seunghyun Lee
Sohyun Lee
Minsik Lee
Dogyoon Lee
Seungmin Lee
Min Jun Lee
Sangho Lee
Sangmin Lee
Seungeun Lee
Seon-Ho Lee
Sungmin Lee
Sungho Lee
Sangyoun Lee
Vincent C. S. S. Lee
Jaeseong Lee
Yong Jae Lee
Chenyang Lei
Chenyi Lei
Jiahui Lei
Xinyu Lei
Yinjie Lei
Jiaxu Leng
Luziwei Leng

Jan E. Lenssen
Vincent Lepetit
Thomas Leung
María Leyva-Vallina
Xin Li
Yikang Li
Baoxin Li
Bin Li
Bing Li
Bowen Li
Changlin Li
Chao Li
Chongyi Li
Guanyue Li
Shuai Li
Jin Li
Dingquan Li
Dongxu Li
Yiting Li
Gang Li
Dian Li
Guohao Li
Haoang Li
Haoliang Li
Haoran Li
Hengduo Li
Huafeng Li
Xiaoming Li
Hanao Li
Hongwei Li
Ziqiang Li
Jisheng Li
Jiacheng Li
Jia Li
Jiachen Li
Jiahao Li
Jianwei Li
Jiazhi Li
Jie Li
Jing Li
Jingjing Li
Jingtao Li
Jun Li
Junxuan Li
Kai Li

Kailin Li
Kenneth Li
Kun Li
Kunpeng Li
Aoxue Li
Chenglong Li
Chenglin Li
Changsheng Li
Zhichao Li
Qiang Li
Yanyu Li
Zuoyue Li
Xiang Li
Xuelong Li
Fangda Li
Ailin Li
Liang Li
Chun-Guang Li
Daiqing Li
Dong Li
Guanbin Li
Guorong Li
Haifeng Li
Jianan Li
Jianing Li
Jiaxin Li
Ke Li
Lei Li
Lincheng Li
Liulei Li
Lujun Li
Linjie Li
Lin Li
Pengyu Li
Ping Li
Qiufu Li
Qingyong Li
Rui Li
Siyuan Li
Wei Li
Wenbin Li
Xiangyang Li
Xinyu Li
Xiujun Li
Xiu Li

Xu Li
Ya-Li Li
Yao Li
Yongjie Li
Yijun Li
Yiming Li
Yuezun Li
Yu Li
Yunheng Li
Yuqi Li
Zhe Li
Zeming Li
Zhen Li
Zhengqin Li
Zhimin Li
Jiefeng Li
Jinpeng Li
Chengze Li
Jianwu Li
Lerenhan Li
Shan Li
Suichan Li
Xiangtai Li
Yanjie Li
Yandong Li
Zhuoling Li
Zhenqiang Li
Manyi Li
Maosen Li
Ji Li
Minjun Li
Mingrui Li
Mengtian Li
Junyi Li
Nianyi Li
Bo Li
Xiao Li
Peihua Li
Peike Li
Peizhao Li
Peiliang Li
Qi Li
Ren Li
Runze Li
Shile Li

Sheng Li	Zhuowei Li	Che-Tsung Lin
Shigang Li	Zhuowan Li	Chung-Ching Lin
Shiyu Li	Zhuohang Li	Chen-Hsuan Lin
Shuang Li	Zizhang Li	Cheng Lin
Shasha Li	Chen Li	Chuming Lin
Shichao Li	Yuan-Fang Li	Chunyu Lin
Tianye Li	Dongze Lian	Dahua Lin
Yuexiang Li	Xiaochen Lian	Wei Lin
Wei-Hong Li	Zhouhui Lian	Zheng Lin
Wanhua Li	Long Lian	Huaijia Lin
Weihao Li	Qing Lian	Jason Lin
Weiming Li	Jin Lianbao	Jierui Lin
Weixin Li	Jinxiu S. Liang	Jiaying Lin
Wenbo Li	Dingkang Liang	Jie Lin
Wenshuo Li	Jiahao Liang	Kai-En Lin
Weijian Li	Jianming Liang	Kevin Lin
Yunan Li	Jingyun Liang	Guangfeng Lin
Xirong Li	Kevin J. Liang	Jiehong Lin
Xianhang Li	Kaizhao Liang	Feng Lin
Xiaoyu Li	Chen Liang	Hang Lin
Xueqian Li	Jie Liang	Kwan-Yee Lin
Xuanlin Li	Senwei Liang	Ke Lin
Xianzhi Li	Ding Liang	Luojun Lin
Yunqiang Li	Jiajun Liang	Qinghong Lin
Yanjing Li	Jian Liang	Xiangbo Lin
Yansheng Li	Kongming Liang	Yi Lin
Yawei Li	Siyuan Liang	Zudi Lin
Yi Li	Yuanzhi Liang	Shijie Lin
Yong Li	Zhengfa Liang	Yiqun Lin
Yong-Lu Li	Mingfu Liang	Tzu-Heng Lin
Yuhang Li	Xiaodan Liang	Ming Lin
Yu-Jhe Li	Xuefeng Liang	Shaohui Lin
Yuxi Li	Yuxuan Liang	SongNan Lin
Yunsheng Li	Kang Liao	Ji Lin
Yanwei Li	Liang Liao	Tsung-Yu Lin
Zechao Li	Hong-Yuan Mark Liao	Xudong Lin
Zejian Li	Wentong Liao	Yancong Lin
Zeju Li	Haofu Liao	Yen-Chen Lin
Zekun Li	Yue Liao	Yiming Lin
Zhaowen Li	Minghui Liao	Yuewei Lin
Zheng Li	Shengcai Liao	Zhiqiu Lin
Zhenyu Li	Ting-Hsuan Liao	Zinan Lin
Zhiheng Li	Xin Liao	Zhe Lin
Zhi Li	Yinghong Liao	David B. Lindell
Zhong Li	Teck Yian Lim	Zhixin Ling

Zhan Ling
Alexander Liniger
Venice Erin B. Liong
Joey Litalien
Or Litany
Roee Litman
Ron Litman
Jim Little
Dor Litvak
Shaoteng Liu
Shuaicheng Liu
Andrew Liu
Xian Liu
Shaohui Liu
Bei Liu
Bo Liu
Yong Liu
Ming Liu
Yanbin Liu
Chenxi Liu
Daqi Liu
Di Liu
Difan Liu
Dong Liu
Dongfang Liu
Daizong Liu
Xiao Liu
Fangyi Liu
Fengbei Liu
Fenglin Liu
Bin Liu
Yuang Liu
Ao Liu
Hong Liu
Hongfu Liu
Huidong Liu
Ziyi Liu
Feng Liu
Hao Liu
Jie Liu
Jialun Liu
Jiang Liu
Jing Liu
Jingya Liu
Jiaming Liu

Jun Liu
Juncheng Liu
Jiawei Liu
Hongyu Liu
Chuanbin Liu
Haotian Liu
Lingqiao Liu
Chang Liu
Han Liu
Liu Liu
Min Liu
Yingqi Liu
Aishan Liu
Bingyu Liu
Benlin Liu
Boxiao Liu
Chenchen Liu
Chuanjian Liu
Daqing Liu
Huan Liu
Haozhe Liu
Jiaheng Liu
Wei Liu
Jingzhou Liu
Jiyuan Liu
Lingbo Liu
Nian Liu
Peiye Liu
Qiankun Liu
Shenglan Liu
Shilong Liu
Wen Liu
Wenyu Liu
Weifeng Liu
Wu Liu
Xiaolong Liu
Yang Liu
Yanwei Liu
Yingcheng Liu
Yongfei Liu
Yihao Liu
Yu Liu
Yunze Liu
Ze Liu
Zhenhua Liu

Zhenguang Liu
Lin Liu
Lihao Liu
Pengju Liu
Xinhai Liu
Yunfei Liu
Meng Liu
Minghua Liu
Mingyuan Liu
Miao Liu
Peirong Liu
Ping Liu
Qingjie Liu
Ruoshi Liu
Risheng Liu
Songtao Liu
Xing Liu
Shikun Liu
Shuming Liu
Sheng Liu
Songhua Liu
Tongliang Liu
Weibo Liu
Weide Liu
Weizhe Liu
Wenxi Liu
Weiyang Liu
Xin Liu
Xiaobin Liu
Xudong Liu
Xiaoyi Liu
Xihui Liu
Xinchen Liu
Xingtong Liu
Xinpeng Liu
Xinyu Liu
Xianpeng Liu
Xu Liu
Xingyu Liu
Yongtuo Liu
Yahui Liu
Yangxin Liu
Yaoyao Liu
Yaojie Liu
Yuliang Liu

Yongcheng Liu
Yuan Liu
Yufan Liu
Yu-Lun Liu
Yun Liu
Yunfan Liu
Yuanzhong Liu
Zhuoran Liu
Zhen Liu
Zheng Liu
Zhijian Liu
Zhisong Liu
Ziquan Liu
Ziyu Liu
Zhihua Liu
Zechun Liu
Zhaoyang Liu
Zhengzhe Liu
Stephan Liwicki
Shao-Yuan Lo
Sylvain Lobry
Suhas Lohit
Vishnu Suresh Lokhande
Vincenzo Lomonaco
Chengjiang Long
Guodong Long
Fuchen Long
Shangbang Long
Yang Long
Zijun Long
Vasco Lopes
Antonio M. Lopez
Roberto Javier
    Lopez-Sastre
Tobias Lorenz
Javier Lorenzo-Navarro
Yujing Lou
Qian Lou
Xiankai Lu
Changsheng Lu
Huimin Lu
Yongxi Lu
Hao Lu
Hong Lu
Jiasen Lu

Juwei Lu
Fan Lu
Guangming Lu
Jiwen Lu
Shun Lu
Tao Lu
Xiaonan Lu
Yang Lu
Yao Lu
Yongchun Lu
Zhiwu Lu
Cheng Lu
Liying Lu
Guo Lu
Xuequan Lu
Yanye Lu
Yantao Lu
Yuhang Lu
Fujun Luan
Jonathon Luiten
Jovita Lukasik
Alan Lukezic
Jonathan Samuel Lumentut
Mayank Lunayach
Ao Luo
Canjie Luo
Chong Luo
Xu Luo
Grace Luo
Jun Luo
Katie Z. Luo
Tao Luo
Cheng Luo
Fangzhou Luo
Gen Luo
Lei Luo
Sihui Luo
Weixin Luo
Yan Luo
Xiaoyan Luo
Yong Luo
Yadan Luo
Hao Luo
Ruotian Luo
Mi Luo

Tiange Luo
Wenjie Luo
Wenhan Luo
Xiao Luo
Zhiming Luo
Zhipeng Luo
Zhengyi Luo
Diogo C. Luvizon
Zhaoyang Lv
Gengyu Lyu
Lingjuan Lyu
Jun Lyu
Yuanyuan Lyu
Youwei Lyu
Yueming Lyu
Bingpeng Ma
Chao Ma
Chongyang Ma
Congbo Ma
Chih-Yao Ma
Fan Ma
Lin Ma
Haoyu Ma
Hengbo Ma
Jianqi Ma
Jiawei Ma
Jiayi Ma
Kede Ma
Kai Ma
Lingni Ma
Lei Ma
Xu Ma
Ning Ma
Benteng Ma
Cheng Ma
Andy J. Ma
Long Ma
Zhanyu Ma
Zhiheng Ma
Qianli Ma
Shiqiang Ma
Sizhuo Ma
Shiqing Ma
Xiaolong Ma
Xinzhu Ma

Gautam B. Machiraju
Spandan Madan
Mathew Magimai-Doss
Luca Magri
Behrooz Mahasseni
Upal Mahbub
Siddharth Mahendran
Paridhi Maheshwari
Rishabh Maheshwary
Mohammed Mahmoud
Shishira R. R. Maiya
Sylwia Majchrowska
Arjun Majumdar
Puspita Majumdar
Orchid Majumder
Sagnik Majumder
Ilya Makarov
Farkhod F.
    Makhmudkhujaev
Yasushi Makihara
Ankur Mali
Mateusz Malinowski
Utkarsh Mall
Srikanth Malla
Clement Mallet
Dimitrios Mallis
Yunze Man
Dipu Manandhar
Massimiliano Mancini
Murari Mandal
Raunak Manekar
Karttikeya Mangalam
Puneet Mangla
Fabian Manhardt
Sivabalan Manivasagam
Fahim Mannan
Chengzhi Mao
Hanzi Mao
Jiayuan Mao
Junhua Mao
Zhiyuan Mao
Jiageng Mao
Yunyao Mao
Zhendong Mao
Alberto Marchisio

Diego Marcos
Riccardo Marin
Aram Markosyan
Renaud Marlet
Ricardo Marques
Miquel Martí i Rabadán
Diego Martin Arroyo
Niki Martinel
Brais Martinez
Julieta Martinez
Marc Masana
Tomohiro Mashita
Timothée Masquelier
Minesh Mathew
Tetsu Matsukawa
Marwan Mattar
Bruce A. Maxwell
Christoph Mayer
Mantas Mazeika
Pratik Mazumder
Scott McCloskey
Steven McDonagh
Ishit Mehta
Jie Mei
Kangfu Mei
Jieru Mei
Xiaoguang Mei
Givi Meishvili
Luke Melas-Kyriazi
Iaroslav Melekhov
Andres Mendez-Vazquez
Heydi Mendez-Vazquez
Matias Mendieta
Ricardo A. Mendoza-León
Chenlin Meng
Depu Meng
Rang Meng
Zibo Meng
Qingjie Meng
Qier Meng
Yanda Meng
Zihang Meng
Thomas Mensink
Fabian Mentzer
Christopher Metzler

Gregory P. Meyer
Vasileios Mezaris
Liang Mi
Lu Mi
Bo Miao
Changtao Miao
Zichen Miao
Qiguang Miao
Xin Miao
Zhongqi Miao
Frank Michel
Simone Milani
Ben Mildenhall
Roy V. Miles
Juhong Min
Kyle Min
Hyun-Seok Min
Weiqing Min
Yuecong Min
Zhixiang Min
Qi Ming
David Minnen
Aymen Mir
Deepak Mishra
Anand Mishra
Shlok K. Mishra
Niluthpol Mithun
Gaurav Mittal
Trisha Mittal
Daisuke Miyazaki
Kaichun Mo
Hong Mo
Zhipeng Mo
Davide Modolo
Abduallah A. Mohamed
Mohamed Afham
    Mohamed Aflal
Ron Mokady
Pavlo Molchanov
Davide Moltisanti
Liliane Momeni
Gianluca Monaci
Pascal Monasse
Ajoy Mondal
Tom Monnier

Aron Monszpart
Gyeongsik Moon
Suhong Moon
Taesup Moon
Sean Moran
Daniel Moreira
Pietro Morerio
Alexandre Morgand
Lia Morra
Ali Mosleh
Inbar Mosseri
Sayed Mohammad
  Mostafavi Isfahani
Saman Motamed
Ramy A. Mounir
Fangzhou Mu
Jiteng Mu
Norman Mu
Yasuhiro Mukaigawa
Ryan Mukherjee
Tanmoy Mukherjee
Yusuke Mukuta
Ravi Teja Mullapudi
Lea Müller
Matthias Müller
Martin Mundt
Nils Murrugarra-Llerena
Damien Muselet
Armin Mustafa
Muhammad Ferjad Naeem
Sauradip Nag
Hajime Nagahara
Pravin Nagar
Rajendra Nagar
Naveen Shankar Nagaraja
Varun Nagaraja
Tushar Nagarajan
Seungjun Nah
Gaku Nakano
Yuta Nakashima
Giljoo Nam
Seonghyeon Nam
Liangliang Nan
Yuesong Nan
Yeshwanth Napolean

Dinesh Reddy
  Narapureddy
Medhini Narasimhan
Supreeth
  Narasimhaswamy
Sriram Narayanan
Erickson R. Nascimento
Varun Nasery
K. L. Navaneet
Pablo Navarrete Michelini
Shant Navasardyan
Shah Nawaz
Nihal Nayak
Farhood Negin
Lukáš Neumann
Alejandro Newell
Evonne Ng
Kam Woh Ng
Tony Ng
Anh Nguyen
Tuan Anh Nguyen
Cuong Cao Nguyen
Ngoc Cuong Nguyen
Thanh Nguyen
Khoi Nguyen
Phi Le Nguyen
Phong Ha Nguyen
Tam Nguyen
Truong Nguyen
Anh Tuan Nguyen
Rang Nguyen
Thao Thi Phuong Nguyen
Van Nguyen Nguyen
Zhen-Liang Ni
Yao Ni
Shijie Nie
Xuecheng Nie
Yongwei Nie
Weizhi Nie
Ying Nie
Yinyu Nie
Kshitij N. Nikhal
Simon Niklaus
Xuefei Ning
Jifeng Ning

Yotam Nitzan
Di Niu
Shuaicheng Niu
Li Niu
Wei Niu
Yulei Niu
Zhenxing Niu
Albert No
Shohei Nobuhara
Nicoletta Noceti
Junhyug Noh
Sotiris Nousias
Slawomir Nowaczyk
Ewa M. Nowara
Valsamis Ntouskos
Gilberto Ochoa-Ruiz
Ferda Ofli
Jihyong Oh
Sangyun Oh
Youngtaek Oh
Hiroki Ohashi
Takahiro Okabe
Kemal Oksuz
Fumio Okura
Daniel Olmeda Reino
Matthew Olson
Carl Olsson
Roy Or-El
Alessandro Ortis
Guillermo Ortiz-Jimenez
Magnus Oskarsson
Ahmed A. A. Osman
Martin R. Oswald
Mayu Otani
Naima Otberdout
Cheng Ouyang
Jiahong Ouyang
Wanli Ouyang
Andrew Owens
Poojan B. Oza
Mete Ozay
A. Cengiz Oztireli
Gautam Pai
Tomas Pajdla
Umapada Pal

Simone Palazzo
Luca Palmieri
Bowen Pan
Hao Pan
Lili Pan
Tai-Yu Pan
Liang Pan
Chengwei Pan
Yingwei Pan
Xuran Pan
Jinshan Pan
Xinyu Pan
Liyuan Pan
Xingang Pan
Xingjia Pan
Zhihong Pan
Zizheng Pan
Priyadarshini Panda
Rameswar Panda
Rohit Pandey
Kaiyue Pang
Bo Pang
Guansong Pang
Jiangmiao Pang
Meng Pang
Tianyu Pang
Ziqi Pang
Omiros Pantazis
Andreas Panteli
Maja Pantic
Marina Paolanti
Joao P. Papa
Samuele Papa
Mike Papadakis
Dim P. Papadopoulos
George Papandreou
Constantin Pape
Toufiq Parag
Chethan Parameshwara
Shaifali Parashar
Alejandro Pardo
Rishubh Parihar
Sarah Parisot
JaeYoo Park
Gyeong-Moon Park

Hyojin Park
Hyoungseob Park
Jongchan Park
Jae Sung Park
Kiru Park
Chunghyun Park
Kwanyong Park
Sunghyun Park
Sungrae Park
Seongsik Park
Sanghyun Park
Sungjune Park
Taesung Park
Gaurav Parmar
Paritosh Parmar
Alvaro Parra
Despoina Paschalidou
Or Patashnik
Shivansh Patel
Pushpak Pati
Prashant W. Patil
Vaishakh Patil
Suvam Patra
Jay Patravali
Badri Narayana Patro
Angshuman Paul
Sudipta Paul
Rémi Pautrat
Nick E. Pears
Adithya Pediredla
Wenjie Pei
Shmuel Peleg
Latha Pemula
Bo Peng
Houwen Peng
Yue Peng
Liangzu Peng
Baoyun Peng
Jun Peng
Pai Peng
Sida Peng
Xi Peng
Yuxin Peng
Songyou Peng
Wei Peng

Weiqi Peng
Wen-Hsiao Peng
Pramuditha Perera
Juan C. Perez
Eduardo Pérez Pellitero
Juan-Manuel Perez-Rua
Federico Pernici
Marco Pesavento
Stavros Petridis
Ilya A. Petrov
Vladan Petrovic
Mathis Petrovich
Suzanne Petryk
Hieu Pham
Quang Pham
Khoi Pham
Tung Pham
Huy Phan
Stephen Phillips
Cheng Perng Phoo
David Picard
Marco Piccirilli
Georg Pichler
A. J. Piergiovanni
Vipin Pillai
Silvia L. Pintea
Giovanni Pintore
Robinson Piramuthu
Fiora Pirri
Theodoros Pissas
Fabio Pizzati
Benjamin Planche
Bryan Plummer
Matteo Poggi
Ashwini Pokle
Georgy E. Ponimatkin
Adrian Popescu
Stefan Popov
Nikola Popović
Ronald Poppe
Angelo Porrello
Michael Potter
Charalambos Poullis
Hadi Pouransari
Omid Poursaeed

Shraman Pramanick
Mantini Pranav
Dilip K. Prasad
Meghshyam Prasad
B. H. Pawan Prasad
Shitala Prasad
Prateek Prasanna
Ekta Prashnani
Derek S. Prijatelj
Luke Y. Prince
Véronique Prinet
Victor Adrian Prisacariu
James Pritts
Thomas Probst
Sergey Prokudin
Rita Pucci
Chi-Man Pun
Matthew Purri
Haozhi Qi
Lu Qi
Lei Qi
Xianbiao Qi
Yonggang Qi
Yuankai Qi
Siyuan Qi
Guocheng Qian
Hangwei Qian
Qi Qian
Deheng Qian
Shengsheng Qian
Wen Qian
Rui Qian
Yiming Qian
Shengju Qian
Shengyi Qian
Xuelin Qian
Zhenxing Qian
Nan Qiao
Xiaotian Qiao
Jing Qin
Can Qin
Siyang Qin
Hongwei Qin
Jie Qin
Minghai Qin

Yipeng Qin
Yongqiang Qin
Wenda Qin
Xuebin Qin
Yuzhe Qin
Yao Qin
Zhenyue Qin
Zhiwu Qing
Heqian Qiu
Jiayan Qiu
Jielin Qiu
Yue Qiu
Jiaxiong Qiu
Zhongxi Qiu
Shi Qiu
Zhaofan Qiu
Zhongnan Qu
Yanyun Qu
Kha Gia Quach
Yuhui Quan
Ruijie Quan
Mike Rabbat
Rahul Shekhar Rade
Filip Radenovic
Gorjan Radevski
Bogdan Raducanu
Francesco Ragusa
Shafin Rahman
Md Mahfuzur Rahman
    Siddiquee
Hossein Rahmani
Kiran Raja
Sivaramakrishnan
    Rajaraman
Jathushan Rajasegaran
Adnan Siraj Rakin
Michaël Ramamonjisoa
Chirag A. Raman
Shanmuganathan Raman
Vignesh Ramanathan
Vasili Ramanishka
Vikram V. Ramaswamy
Merey Ramazanova
Jason Rambach
Sai Saketh Rambhatla

Clément Rambour
Ashwin Ramesh Babu
Adín Ramírez Rivera
Arianna Rampini
Haoxi Ran
Aakanksha Rana
Aayush Jung Bahadur
    Rana
Kanchana N. Ranasinghe
Aneesh Rangnekar
Samrudhdhi B. Rangrej
Harsh Rangwani
Viresh Ranjan
Anyi Rao
Yongming Rao
Carolina Raposo
Michalis Raptis
Amir Rasouli
Vivek Rathod
Adepu Ravi Sankar
Avinash Ravichandran
Bharadwaj Ravichandran
Dripta S. Raychaudhuri
Adria Recasens
Simon Reiß
Davis Rempe
Daxuan Ren
Jiawei Ren
Jimmy Ren
Sucheng Ren
Dayong Ren
Zhile Ren
Dongwei Ren
Qibing Ren
Pengfei Ren
Zhenwen Ren
Xuqian Ren
Yixuan Ren
Zhongzheng Ren
Ambareesh Revanur
Hamed Rezazadegan
    Tavakoli
Rafael S. Rezende
Wonjong Rhee
Alexander Richard

Christian Richardt
Stephan R. Richter
Benjamin Riggan
Dominik Rivoir
Mamshad Nayeem Rizve
Joshua D. Robinson
Joseph Robinson
Chris Rockwell
Ranga Rodrigo
Andres C. Rodriguez
Carlos Rodriguez-Pardo
Marcus Rohrbach
Gemma Roig
Yu Rong
David A. Ross
Mohammad Rostami
Edward Rosten
Karsten Roth
Anirban Roy
Debaditya Roy
Shuvendu Roy
Ahana Roy Choudhury
Aruni Roy Chowdhury
Denys Rozumnyi
Shulan Ruan
Wenjie Ruan
Patrick Ruhkamp
Danila Rukhovich
Anian Ruoss
Chris Russell
Dan Ruta
Dawid Damian Rymarczyk
DongHun Ryu
Hyeonggon Ryu
Kwonyoung Ryu
Balasubramanian S.
Alexandre Sablayrolles
Mohammad Sabokrou
Arka Sadhu
Aniruddha Saha
Oindrila Saha
Pritish Sahu
Aneeshan Sain
Nirat Saini
Saurabh Saini

Takeshi Saitoh
Christos Sakaridis
Fumihiko Sakaue
Dimitrios Sakkos
Ken Sakurada
Parikshit V. Sakurikar
Rohit Saluja
Nermin Samet
Leo Sampaio Ferraz
   Ribeiro
Jorge Sanchez
Enrique Sanchez
Shengtian Sang
Anush Sankaran
Soubhik Sanyal
Nikolaos Sarafianos
Vishwanath Saragadam
István Sárándi
Saquib Sarfraz
Mert Bulent Sariyildiz
Anindya Sarkar
Pritam Sarkar
Paul-Edouard Sarlin
Hiroshi Sasaki
Takami Sato
Torsten Sattler
Ravi Kumar Satzoda
Axel Sauer
Stefano Savian
Artem Savkin
Manolis Savva
Gerald Schaefer
Simone Schaub-Meyer
Yoni Schirris
Samuel Schulter
Katja Schwarz
Jesse Scott
Sinisa Segvic
Constantin Marc Seibold
Lorenzo Seidenari
Matan Sela
Fadime Sener
Paul Hongsuck Seo
Kwanggyoon Seo
Hongje Seong

Dario Serez
Francesco Setti
Bryan Seybold
Mohamad Shahbazi
Shima Shahfar
Xinxin Shan
Caifeng Shan
Dandan Shan
Shawn Shan
Wei Shang
Jinghuan Shang
Jiaxiang Shang
Lei Shang
Sukrit Shankar
Ken Shao
Rui Shao
Jie Shao
Mingwen Shao
Aashish Sharma
Gaurav Sharma
Vivek Sharma
Abhishek Sharma
Yoli Shavit
Shashank Shekhar
Sumit Shekhar
Zhijie Shen
Fengyi Shen
Furao Shen
Jialie Shen
Jingjing Shen
Ziyi Shen
Linlin Shen
Guangyu Shen
Biluo Shen
Falong Shen
Jiajun Shen
Qiu Shen
Qiuhong Shen
Shuai Shen
Wang Shen
Yiqing Shen
Yunhang Shen
Siqi Shen
Bin Shen
Tianwei Shen

Xi Shen
Yilin Shen
Yuming Shen
Yucong Shen
Zhiqiang Shen
Lu Sheng
Yichen Sheng
Shivanand Venkanna
    Sheshappanavar
Shelly Sheynin
Baifeng Shi
Ruoxi Shi
Botian Shi
Hailin Shi
Jia Shi
Jing Shi
Shaoshuai Shi
Baoguang Shi
Boxin Shi
Hengcan Shi
Tianyang Shi
Xiaodan Shi
Yongjie Shi
Zhensheng Shi
Yinghuan Shi
Weiqi Shi
Wu Shi
Xuepeng Shi
Xiaoshuang Shi
Yujiao Shi
Zenglin Shi
Zhenmei Shi
Takashi Shibata
Meng-Li Shih
Yichang Shih
Hyunjung Shim
Dongseok Shim
Soshi Shimada
Inkyu Shin
Jinwoo Shin
Seungjoo Shin
Seungjae Shin
Koichi Shinoda
Suprosanna Shit

Palaiahnakote
    Shivakumara
Eli Shlizerman
Gaurav Shrivastava
Xiao Shu
Xiangbo Shu
Xiujun Shu
Yang Shu
Tianmin Shu
Jun Shu
Zhixin Shu
Bing Shuai
Maria Shugrina
Ivan Shugurov
Satya Narayan Shukla
Pranjay Shyam
Jianlou Si
Yawar Siddiqui
Alberto Signoroni
Pedro Silva
Jae-Young Sim
Oriane Siméoni
Martin Simon
Andrea Simonelli
Abhishek Singh
Ashish Singh
Dinesh Singh
Gurkirt Singh
Krishna Kumar Singh
Mannat Singh
Pravendra Singh
Rajat Vikram Singh
Utkarsh Singhal
Dipika Singhania
Vasu Singla
Harsh Sinha
Sudipta Sinha
Josef Sivic
Elena Sizikova
Geri Skenderi
Ivan Skorokhodov
Dmitriy Smirnov
Cameron Y. Smith
James S. Smith
Patrick Snape

Mattia Soldan
Hyeongseok Son
Sanghyun Son
Chuanbiao Song
Chen Song
Chunfeng Song
Dan Song
Dongjin Song
Hwanjun Song
Guoxian Song
Jiaming Song
Jie Song
Liangchen Song
Ran Song
Luchuan Song
Xibin Song
Li Song
Fenglong Song
Guoli Song
Guanglu Song
Zhenbo Song
Lin Song
Xinhang Song
Yang Song
Yibing Song
Rajiv Soundararajan
Hossein Souri
Cristovao Sousa
Riccardo Spezialetti
Leonidas Spinoulas
Michael W. Spratling
Deepak Sridhar
Srinath Sridhar
Gaurang Sriramanan
Vinkle Kumar Srivastav
Themos Stafylakis
Serban Stan
Anastasis Stathopoulos
Markus Steinberger
Jan Steinbrener
Sinisa Stekovic
Alexandros Stergiou
Gleb Sterkin
Rainer Stiefelhagen
Pierre Stock

Ombretta Strafforello
Julian Straub
Yannick Strümpler
Joerg Stueckler
Hang Su
Weijie Su
Jong-Chyi Su
Bing Su
Haisheng Su
Jinming Su
Yiyang Su
Yukun Su
Yuxin Su
Zhuo Su
Zhaoqi Su
Xiu Su
Yu-Chuan Su
Zhixun Su
Arulkumar Subramaniam
Akshayvarun Subramanya
A. Subramanyam
Swathikiran Sudhakaran
Yusuke Sugano
Masanori Suganuma
Yumin Suh
Yang Sui
Baochen Sun
Cheng Sun
Long Sun
Guolei Sun
Haoliang Sun
Haomiao Sun
He Sun
Hanqing Sun
Hao Sun
Lichao Sun
Jiachen Sun
Jiaming Sun
Jian Sun
Jin Sun
Jennifer J. Sun
Tiancheng Sun
Libo Sun
Peize Sun
Qianru Sun

Shanlin Sun
Yu Sun
Zhun Sun
Che Sun
Lin Sun
Tao Sun
Yiyou Sun
Chunyi Sun
Chong Sun
Weiwei Sun
Weixuan Sun
Xiuyu Sun
Yanan Sun
Zeren Sun
Zhaodong Sun
Zhiqing Sun
Minhyuk Sung
Jinli Suo
Simon Suo
Abhijit Suprem
Anshuman Suri
Saksham Suri
Joshua M. Susskind
Roman Suvorov
Gurumurthy Swaminathan
Robin Swanson
Paul Swoboda
Tabish A. Syed
Richard Szeliski
Fariborz Taherkhani
Yu-Wing Tai
Keita Takahashi
Walter Talbott
Gary Tam
Masato Tamura
Feitong Tan
Fuwen Tan
Shuhan Tan
Andong Tan
Bin Tan
Cheng Tan
Jianchao Tan
Lei Tan
Mingxing Tan
Xin Tan

Zichang Tan
Zhentao Tan
Kenichiro Tanaka
Masayuki Tanaka
Yushun Tang
Hao Tang
Jingqun Tang
Jinhui Tang
Kaihua Tang
Luming Tang
Lv Tang
Sheyang Tang
Shitao Tang
Siliang Tang
Shixiang Tang
Yansong Tang
Keke Tang
Chang Tang
Chenwei Tang
Jie Tang
Junshu Tang
Ming Tang
Peng Tang
Xu Tang
Yao Tang
Chen Tang
Fan Tang
Haoran Tang
Shengeng Tang
Yehui Tang
Zhipeng Tang
Ugo Tanielian
Chaofan Tao
Jiale Tao
Junli Tao
Renshuai Tao
An Tao
Guanhong Tao
Zhiqiang Tao
Makarand Tapaswi
Jean-Philippe G. Tarel
Juan J. Tarrio
Enzo Tartaglione
Keisuke Tateno
Zachary Teed

Ajinkya B. Tejankar
Bugra Tekin
Purva Tendulkar
Damien Teney
Minggui Teng
Chris Tensmeyer
Andrew Beng Jin Teoh
Philipp Terhörst
Kartik Thakral
Nupur Thakur
Kevin Thandiackal
Spyridon Thermos
Diego Thomas
William Thong
Yuesong Tian
Guanzhong Tian
Lin Tian
Shiqi Tian
Kai Tian
Meng Tian
Tai-Peng Tian
Zhuotao Tian
Shangxuan Tian
Tian Tian
Yapeng Tian
Yu Tian
Yuxin Tian
Leslie Ching Ow Tiong
Praveen Tirupattur
Garvita Tiwari
George Toderici
Antoine Toisoul
Aysim Toker
Tatiana Tommasi
Zhan Tong
Alessio Tonioni
Alessandro Torcinovich
Fabio Tosi
Matteo Toso
Hugo Touvron
Quan Hung Tran
Son Tran
Hung Tran
Ngoc-Trung Tran
Vinh Tran

Phong Tran
Giovanni Trappolini
Edith Tretschk
Subarna Tripathi
Shubhendu Trivedi
Eduard Trulls
Prune Truong
Thanh-Dat Truong
Tomasz Trzcinski
Sam Tsai
Yi-Hsuan Tsai
Ethan Tseng
Yu-Chee Tseng
Shahar Tsiper
Stavros Tsogkas
Shikui Tu
Zhigang Tu
Zhengzhong Tu
Richard Tucker
Sergey Tulyakov
Cigdem Turan
Daniyar Turmukhambetov
Victor G. Turrisi da Costa
Bartlomiej Twardowski
Christopher D. Twigg
Radim Tylecek
Mostofa Rafid Uddin
Md. Zasim Uddin
Kohei Uehara
Nicolas Ugrinovic
Youngjung Uh
Norimichi Ukita
Anwaar Ulhaq
Devesh Upadhyay
Paul Upchurch
Yoshitaka Ushiku
Yuzuko Utsumi
Mikaela Angelina Uy
Mohit Vaishnav
Pratik Vaishnavi
Jeya Maria Jose Valanarasu
Matias A. Valdenegro Toro
Diego Valsesia
Wouter Van Gansbeke
Nanne van Noord

Simon Vandenhende
Farshid Varno
Cristina Vasconcelos
Francisco Vasconcelos
Alex Vasilescu
Subeesh Vasu
Arun Balajee Vasudevan
Kanav Vats
Vaibhav S. Vavilala
Sagar Vaze
Javier Vazquez-Corral
Andrea Vedaldi
Olga Veksler
Andreas Velten
Sai H. Vemprala
Raviteja Vemulapalli
Shashanka
    Venkataramanan
Dor Verbin
Luisa Verdoliva
Manisha Verma
Yashaswi Verma
Constantin Vertan
Eli Verwimp
Deepak Vijaykeerthy
Pablo Villanueva
Ruben Villegas
Markus Vincze
Vibhav Vineet
Minh P. Vo
Huy V. Vo
Duc Minh Vo
Tomas Vojir
Igor Vozniak
Nicholas Vretos
Vibashan VS
Tuan-Anh Vu
Thang Vu
Mårten Wadenbäck
Neal Wadhwa
Aaron T. Walsman
Steven Walton
Jin Wan
Alvin Wan
Jia Wan

Jun Wan
Xiaoyue Wan
Fang Wan
Guowei Wan
Renjie Wan
Zhiqiang Wan
Ziyu Wan
Bastian Wandt
Dongdong Wang
Limin Wang
Haiyang Wang
Xiaobing Wang
Angtian Wang
Angelina Wang
Bing Wang
Bo Wang
Boyu Wang
Binghui Wang
Chen Wang
Chien-Yi Wang
Congli Wang
Qi Wang
Chengrui Wang
Rui Wang
Yiqun Wang
Cong Wang
Wenjing Wang
Dongkai Wang
Di Wang
Xiaogang Wang
Kai Wang
Zhizhong Wang
Fangjinhua Wang
Feng Wang
Hang Wang
Gaoang Wang
Guoqing Wang
Guangcong Wang
Guangzhi Wang
Hanqing Wang
Hao Wang
Haohan Wang
Haoran Wang
Hong Wang
Haotao Wang

Hu Wang
Huan Wang
Hua Wang
Hui-Po Wang
Hengli Wang
Hanyu Wang
Hongxing Wang
Jingwen Wang
Jialiang Wang
Jian Wang
Jianyi Wang
Jiashun Wang
Jiahao Wang
Tsun-Hsuan Wang
Xiaoqian Wang
Jinqiao Wang
Jun Wang
Jianzong Wang
Kaihong Wang
Ke Wang
Lei Wang
Lingjing Wang
Linnan Wang
Lin Wang
Liansheng Wang
Mengjiao Wang
Manning Wang
Nannan Wang
Peihao Wang
Jiayun Wang
Pu Wang
Qiang Wang
Qiufeng Wang
Qilong Wang
Qiangchang Wang
Qin Wang
Qing Wang
Ruocheng Wang
Ruibin Wang
Ruisheng Wang
Ruizhe Wang
Runqi Wang
Runzhong Wang
Wenxuan Wang
Sen Wang

Shangfei Wang
Shaofei Wang
Shijie Wang
Shiqi Wang
Zhibo Wang
Song Wang
Xinjiang Wang
Tai Wang
Tao Wang
Teng Wang
Xiang Wang
Tianren Wang
Tiantian Wang
Tianyi Wang
Fengjiao Wang
Wei Wang
Miaohui Wang
Suchen Wang
Siyue Wang
Yaoming Wang
Xiao Wang
Ze Wang
Biao Wang
Chaofei Wang
Dong Wang
Gu Wang
Guangrun Wang
Guangming Wang
Guo-Hua Wang
Haoqing Wang
Hesheng Wang
Huafeng Wang
Jinghua Wang
Jingdong Wang
Jingjing Wang
Jingya Wang
Jingkang Wang
Jiakai Wang
Junke Wang
Kuo Wang
Lichen Wang
Lizhi Wang
Longguang Wang
Mang Wang
Mei Wang

Min Wang
Peng-Shuai Wang
Run Wang
Shaoru Wang
Shuhui Wang
Tan Wang
Tiancai Wang
Tianqi Wang
Wenhai Wang
Wenzhe Wang
Xiaobo Wang
Xiudong Wang
Xu Wang
Yajie Wang
Yan Wang
Yuan-Gen Wang
Yingqian Wang
Yizhi Wang
Yulin Wang
Yu Wang
Yujie Wang
Yunhe Wang
Yuxi Wang
Yaowei Wang
Yiwei Wang
Zezheng Wang
Hongzhi Wang
Zhiqiang Wang
Ziteng Wang
Ziwei Wang
Zheng Wang
Zhenyu Wang
Binglu Wang
Zhongdao Wang
Ce Wang
Weining Wang
Weiyao Wang
Wenbin Wang
Wenguan Wang
Guangting Wang
Haolin Wang
Haiyan Wang
Huiyu Wang
Naiyan Wang
Jingbo Wang

Jinpeng Wang
Jiaqi Wang
Liyuan Wang
Lizhen Wang
Ning Wang
Wenqian Wang
Sheng-Yu Wang
Weimin Wang
Xiaohan Wang
Yifan Wang
Yi Wang
Yongtao Wang
Yizhou Wang
Zhuo Wang
Zhe Wang
Xudong Wang
Xiaofang Wang
Xinggang Wang
Xiaosen Wang
Xiaosong Wang
Xiaoyang Wang
Lijun Wang
Xinlong Wang
Xuan Wang
Xue Wang
Yangang Wang
Yaohui Wang
Yu-Chiang Frank Wang
Yida Wang
Yilin Wang
Yi Ru Wang
Yali Wang
Yinglong Wang
Yufu Wang
Yujiang Wang
Yuwang Wang
Yuting Wang
Yang Wang
Yu-Xiong Wang
Yixu Wang
Ziqi Wang
Zhicheng Wang
Zeyu Wang
Zhaowen Wang
Zhenyi Wang

Zhenzhi Wang
Zhijie Wang
Zhiyong Wang
Zhongling Wang
Zhuowei Wang
Zian Wang
Zifu Wang
Zihao Wang
Zirui Wang
Ziyan Wang
Wenxiao Wang
Zhen Wang
Zhepeng Wang
Zi Wang
Zihao W. Wang
Steven L. Waslander
Olivia Watkins
Daniel Watson
Silvan Weder
Dongyoon Wee
Dongming Wei
Tianyi Wei
Jia Wei
Dong Wei
Fangyun Wei
Longhui Wei
Mingqiang Wei
Xinyue Wei
Chen Wei
Donglai Wei
Pengxu Wei
Xing Wei
Xiu-Shen Wei
Wenqi Wei
Guoqiang Wei
Wei Wei
XingKui Wei
Xian Wei
Xingxing Wei
Yake Wei
Yuxiang Wei
Yi Wei
Luca Weihs
Michael Weinmann
Martin Weinmann

Congcong Wen
Chuan Wen
Jie Wen
Sijia Wen
Song Wen
Chao Wen
Xiang Wen
Zeyi Wen
Xin Wen
Yilin Wen
Yijia Weng
Shuchen Weng
Junwu Weng
Wenming Weng
Renliang Weng
Zhenyu Weng
Xinshuo Weng
Nicholas J. Westlake
Gordon Wetzstein
Lena M. Widin Klasén
Rick Wildes
Bryan M. Williams
Williem Williem
Ole Winther
Scott Wisdom
Alex Wong
Chau-Wai Wong
Kwan-Yee K. Wong
Yongkang Wong
Scott Workman
Marcel Worring
Michael Wray
Safwan Wshah
Xiang Wu
Aming Wu
Chongruo Wu
Cho-Ying Wu
Chunpeng Wu
Chenyan Wu
Ziyi Wu
Fuxiang Wu
Gang Wu
Haiping Wu
Huisi Wu
Jane Wu

Jialian Wu
Jing Wu
Jinjian Wu
Jianlong Wu
Xian Wu
Lifang Wu
Lifan Wu
Minye Wu
Qianyi Wu
Rongliang Wu
Rui Wu
Shiqian Wu
Shuzhe Wu
Shangzhe Wu
Tsung-Han Wu
Tz-Ying Wu
Ting-Wei Wu
Jiannan Wu
Zhiliang Wu
Yu Wu
Chenyun Wu
Dayan Wu
Dongxian Wu
Fei Wu
Hefeng Wu
Jianxin Wu
Weibin Wu
Wenxuan Wu
Wenhao Wu
Xiao Wu
Yicheng Wu
Yuanwei Wu
Yu-Huan Wu
Zhenxin Wu
Zhenyu Wu
Wei Wu
Peng Wu
Xiaohe Wu
Xindi Wu
Xinxing Wu
Xinyi Wu
Xingjiao Wu
Xiongwei Wu
Yangzheng Wu
Yanzhao Wu

Yawen Wu
Yong Wu
Yi Wu
Ying Nian Wu
Zhenyao Wu
Zhonghua Wu
Zongze Wu
Zuxuan Wu
Stefanie Wuhrer
Teng Xi
Jianing Xi
Fei Xia
Haifeng Xia
Menghan Xia
Yuanqing Xia
Zhihua Xia
Xiaobo Xia
Weihao Xia
Shihong Xia
Yan Xia
Yong Xia
Zhaoyang Xia
Zhihao Xia
Chuhua Xian
Yongqin Xian
Wangmeng Xiang
Fanbo Xiang
Tiange Xiang
Tao Xiang
Liuyu Xiang
Xiaoyu Xiang
Zhiyu Xiang
Aoran Xiao
Chunxia Xiao
Fanyi Xiao
Jimin Xiao
Jun Xiao
Taihong Xiao
Anqi Xiao
Junfei Xiao
Jing Xiao
Liang Xiao
Yang Xiao
Yuting Xiao
Yijun Xiao

Yao Xiao
Zeyu Xiao
Zhisheng Xiao
Zihao Xiao
Binhui Xie
Christopher Xie
Haozhe Xie
Jin Xie
Guo-Sen Xie
Hongtao Xie
Ming-Kun Xie
Tingting Xie
Chaohao Xie
Weicheng Xie
Xudong Xie
Jiyang Xie
Xiaohua Xie
Yuan Xie
Zhenyu Xie
Ning Xie
Xianghui Xie
Xiufeng Xie
You Xie
Yutong Xie
Fuyong Xing
Yifan Xing
Zhen Xing
Yuanjun Xiong
Jinhui Xiong
Weihua Xiong
Hongkai Xiong
Zhitong Xiong
Yuanhao Xiong
Yunyang Xiong
Yuwen Xiong
Zhiwei Xiong
Yuliang Xiu
An Xu
Chang Xu
Chenliang Xu
Chengming Xu
Chenshu Xu
Xiang Xu
Huijuan Xu
Zhe Xu

Jie Xu
Jingyi Xu
Jiarui Xu
Yinghao Xu
Kele Xu
Ke Xu
Li Xu
Linchuan Xu
Linning Xu
Mengde Xu
Mengmeng Frost Xu
Min Xu
Mingye Xu
Jun Xu
Ning Xu
Peng Xu
Runsheng Xu
Sheng Xu
Wenqiang Xu
Xiaogang Xu
Renzhe Xu
Kaidi Xu
Yi Xu
Chi Xu
Qiuling Xu
Baobei Xu
Feng Xu
Haohang Xu
Haofei Xu
Lan Xu
Mingze Xu
Songcen Xu
Weipeng Xu
Wenjia Xu
Wenju Xu
Xiangyu Xu
Xin Xu
Yinshuang Xu
Yixing Xu
Yuting Xu
Yanyu Xu
Zhenbo Xu
Zhiliang Xu
Zhiyuan Xu
Xiaohao Xu

Yanwu Xu
Yan Xu
Yiran Xu
Yifan Xu
Yufei Xu
Yong Xu
Zichuan Xu
Zenglin Xu
Zexiang Xu
Zhan Xu
Zheng Xu
Zhiwei Xu
Ziyue Xu
Shiyu Xuan
Hanyu Xuan
Fei Xue
Jianru Xue
Mingfu Xue
Qinghan Xue
Tianfan Xue
Chao Xue
Chuhui Xue
Nan Xue
Zhou Xue
Xiangyang Xue
Yuan Xue
Abhay Yadav
Ravindra Yadav
Kota Yamaguchi
Toshihiko Yamasaki
Kohei Yamashita
Chaochao Yan
Feng Yan
Kun Yan
Qingsen Yan
Qixin Yan
Rui Yan
Siming Yan
Xinchen Yan
Yaping Yan
Bin Yan
Qingan Yan
Shen Yan
Shipeng Yan
Xu Yan

Yan Yan
Yichao Yan
Zhaoyi Yan
Zike Yan
Zhiqiang Yan
Hongliang Yan
Zizheng Yan
Jiewen Yang
Anqi Joyce Yang
Shan Yang
Anqi Yang
Antoine Yang
Bo Yang
Baoyao Yang
Chenhongyi Yang
Dingkang Yang
De-Nian Yang
Dong Yang
David Yang
Fan Yang
Fengyu Yang
Fengting Yang
Fei Yang
Gengshan Yang
Heng Yang
Han Yang
Huan Yang
Yibo Yang
Jiancheng Yang
Jihan Yang
Jiawei Yang
Jiayu Yang
Jie Yang
Jinfa Yang
Jingkang Yang
Jinyu Yang
Cheng-Fu Yang
Ji Yang
Jianyu Yang
Kailun Yang
Tian Yang
Luyu Yang
Liang Yang
Li Yang
Michael Ying Yang

Yang Yang
Muli Yang
Le Yang
Qiushi Yang
Ren Yang
Ruihan Yang
Shuang Yang
Siyuan Yang
Su Yang
Shiqi Yang
Taojiannan Yang
Tianyu Yang
Lei Yang
Wanzhao Yang
Shuai Yang
William Yang
Wei Yang
Xiaofeng Yang
Xiaoshan Yang
Xin Yang
Xuan Yang
Xu Yang
Xingyi Yang
Xitong Yang
Jing Yang
Yanchao Yang
Wenming Yang
Yujiu Yang
Herb Yang
Jianfei Yang
Jinhui Yang
Chuanguang Yang
Guanglei Yang
Haitao Yang
Kewei Yang
Linlin Yang
Lijin Yang
Longrong Yang
Meng Yang
MingKun Yang
Sibei Yang
Shicai Yang
Tong Yang
Wen Yang
Xi Yang

Xiaolong Yang
Xue Yang
Yubin Yang
Ze Yang
Ziyi Yang
Yi Yang
Linjie Yang
Yuzhe Yang
Yiding Yang
Zhenpei Yang
Zhaohui Yang
Zhengyuan Yang
Zhibo Yang
Zongxin Yang
Hantao Yao
Mingde Yao
Rui Yao
Taiping Yao
Ting Yao
Cong Yao
Qingsong Yao
Quanming Yao
Xu Yao
Yuan Yao
Yao Yao
Yazhou Yao
Jiawen Yao
Shunyu Yao
Pew-Thian Yap
Sudhir Yarram
Rajeev Yasarla
Peng Ye
Botao Ye
Mao Ye
Fei Ye
Hanrong Ye
Jingwen Ye
Jinwei Ye
Jiarong Ye
Mang Ye
Meng Ye
Qi Ye
Qian Ye
Qixiang Ye
Junjie Ye

Sheng Ye
Nanyang Ye
Yufei Ye
Xiaoqing Ye
Ruolin Ye
Yousef Yeganeh
Chun-Hsiao Yeh
Raymond A. Yeh
Yu-Ying Yeh
Kai Yi
Chang Yi
Renjiao Yi
Xinping Yi
Peng Yi
Alper Yilmaz
Junho Yim
Hui Yin
Bangjie Yin
Jia-Li Yin
Miao Yin
Wenzhe Yin
Xuwang Yin
Ming Yin
Yu Yin
Aoxiong Yin
Kangxue Yin
Tianwei Yin
Wei Yin
Xianghua Ying
Rio Yokota
Tatsuya Yokota
Naoto Yokoya
Ryo Yonetani
Ki Yoon Yoo
Jinsu Yoo
Sunjae Yoon
Jae Shin Yoon
Jihun Yoon
Sung-Hoon Yoon
Ryota Yoshihashi
Yusuke Yoshiyasu
Chenyu You
Haoran You
Haoxuan You
Yang You

Quanzeng You
Tackgeun You
Kaichao You
Shan You
Xinge You
Yurong You
Baosheng Yu
Bei Yu
Haichao Yu
Hao Yu
Chaohui Yu
Fisher Yu
Jin-Gang Yu
Jiyang Yu
Jason J. Yu
Jiashuo Yu
Hong-Xing Yu
Lei Yu
Mulin Yu
Ning Yu
Peilin Yu
Qi Yu
Qian Yu
Rui Yu
Shuzhi Yu
Gang Yu
Tan Yu
Weijiang Yu
Xin Yu
Bingyao Yu
Ye Yu
Hanchao Yu
Yingchen Yu
Tao Yu
Xiaotian Yu
Qing Yu
Houjian Yu
Changqian Yu
Jing Yu
Jun Yu
Shujian Yu
Xiang Yu
Zhaofei Yu
Zhenbo Yu
Yinfeng Yu

Zhuoran Yu
Zitong Yu
Bo Yuan
Jiangbo Yuan
Liangzhe Yuan
Weihao Yuan
Jianbo Yuan
Xiaoyun Yuan
Ye Yuan
Li Yuan
Geng Yuan
Jialin Yuan
Maoxun Yuan
Peng Yuan
Xin Yuan
Yuan Yuan
Yuhui Yuan
Yixuan Yuan
Zheng Yuan
Mehmet Kerim Yücel
Kaiyu Yue
Haixiao Yue
Heeseung Yun
Sangdoo Yun
Tian Yun
Mahmut Yurt
Ekim Yurtsever
Ahmet Yüzügüler
Edouard Yvinec
Eloi Zablocki
Christopher Zach
Muhammad Zaigham
    Zaheer
Pierluigi Zama Ramirez
Yuhang Zang
Pietro Zanuttigh
Alexey Zaytsev
Bernhard Zeisl
Haitian Zeng
Pengpeng Zeng
Jiabei Zeng
Runhao Zeng
Wei Zeng
Yawen Zeng
Yi Zeng

Yiming Zeng
Tieyong Zeng
Huanqiang Zeng
Dan Zeng
Yu Zeng
Wei Zhai
Yuanhao Zhai
Fangneng Zhan
Kun Zhan
Xiong Zhang
Jingdong Zhang
Jiangning Zhang
Zhilu Zhang
Gengwei Zhang
Dongsu Zhang
Hui Zhang
Binjie Zhang
Bo Zhang
Tianhao Zhang
Cecilia Zhang
Jing Zhang
Chaoning Zhang
Chenxu Zhang
Chi Zhang
Chris Zhang
Yabin Zhang
Zhao Zhang
Rufeng Zhang
Chaoyi Zhang
Zheng Zhang
Da Zhang
Yi Zhang
Edward Zhang
Xin Zhang
Feifei Zhang
Feilong Zhang
Yuqi Zhang
GuiXuan Zhang
Hanlin Zhang
Hanwang Zhang
Hanzhen Zhang
Haotian Zhang
He Zhang
Haokui Zhang
Hongyuan Zhang

Hengrui Zhang
Hongming Zhang
Mingfang Zhang
Jianpeng Zhang
Jiaming Zhang
Jichao Zhang
Jie Zhang
Jingfeng Zhang
Jingyi Zhang
Jinnian Zhang
David Junhao Zhang
Junjie Zhang
Junzhe Zhang
Jiawan Zhang
Jingyang Zhang
Kai Zhang
Lei Zhang
Lihua Zhang
Lu Zhang
Miao Zhang
Minjia Zhang
Mingjin Zhang
Qi Zhang
Qian Zhang
Qilong Zhang
Qiming Zhang
Qiang Zhang
Richard Zhang
Ruimao Zhang
Ruisi Zhang
Ruixin Zhang
Runze Zhang
Qilin Zhang
Shan Zhang
Shanshan Zhang
Xi Sheryl Zhang
Song-Hai Zhang
Chongyang Zhang
Kaihao Zhang
Songyang Zhang
Shu Zhang
Siwei Zhang
Shujian Zhang
Tianyun Zhang
Tong Zhang

Tao Zhang
Wenwei Zhang
Wenqiang Zhang
Wen Zhang
Xiaolin Zhang
Xingchen Zhang
Xingxuan Zhang
Xiuming Zhang
Xiaoshuai Zhang
Xuanmeng Zhang
Xuanyang Zhang
Xucong Zhang
Xingxing Zhang
Xikun Zhang
Xiaohan Zhang
Yahui Zhang
Yunhua Zhang
Yan Zhang
Yanghao Zhang
Yifei Zhang
Yifan Zhang
Yi-Fan Zhang
Yihao Zhang
Yingliang Zhang
Youshan Zhang
Yulun Zhang
Yushu Zhang
Yixiao Zhang
Yide Zhang
Zhongwen Zhang
Bowen Zhang
Chen-Lin Zhang
Zehua Zhang
Zekun Zhang
Zeyu Zhang
Xiaowei Zhang
Yifeng Zhang
Cheng Zhang
Hongguang Zhang
Yuexi Zhang
Fa Zhang
Guofeng Zhang
Hao Zhang
Haofeng Zhang
Hongwen Zhang

Hua Zhang
Jiaxin Zhang
Zhenyu Zhang
Jian Zhang
Jianfeng Zhang
Jiao Zhang
Jiakai Zhang
Lefei Zhang
Le Zhang
Mi Zhang
Min Zhang
Ning Zhang
Pan Zhang
Pu Zhang
Qing Zhang
Renrui Zhang
Shifeng Zhang
Shuo Zhang
Shaoxiong Zhang
Weizhong Zhang
Xi Zhang
Xiaomei Zhang
Xinyu Zhang
Yin Zhang
Zicheng Zhang
Zihao Zhang
Ziqi Zhang
Zhaoxiang Zhang
Zhen Zhang
Zhipeng Zhang
Zhixing Zhang
Zhizheng Zhang
Jiawei Zhang
Zhong Zhang
Pingping Zhang
Yixin Zhang
Kui Zhang
Lingzhi Zhang
Huaiwen Zhang
Quanshi Zhang
Zhoutong Zhang
Yuhang Zhang
Yuting Zhang
Zhang Zhang
Ziming Zhang

Zhizhong Zhang
Qilong Zhangli
Bingyin Zhao
Bin Zhao
Chenglong Zhao
Lei Zhao
Feng Zhao
Gangming Zhao
Haiyan Zhao
Hao Zhao
Handong Zhao
Hengshuang Zhao
Yinan Zhao
Jiaojiao Zhao
Jiaqi Zhao
Jing Zhao
Kaili Zhao
Haojie Zhao
Yucheng Zhao
Longjiao Zhao
Long Zhao
Qingsong Zhao
Qingyu Zhao
Rui Zhao
Rui-Wei Zhao
Sicheng Zhao
Shuang Zhao
Siyan Zhao
Zelin Zhao
Shiyu Zhao
Wang Zhao
Tiesong Zhao
Qian Zhao
Wangbo Zhao
Xi-Le Zhao
Xu Zhao
Yajie Zhao
Yang Zhao
Ying Zhao
Yin Zhao
Yizhou Zhao
Yunhan Zhao
Yuyang Zhao
Yue Zhao
Yuzhi Zhao

Bowen Zhao
Pu Zhao
Bingchen Zhao
Borui Zhao
Fuqiang Zhao
Hanbin Zhao
Jian Zhao
Mingyang Zhao
Na Zhao
Rongchang Zhao
Ruiqi Zhao
Shuai Zhao
Wenda Zhao
Wenliang Zhao
Xiangyun Zhao
Yifan Zhao
Yaping Zhao
Zhou Zhao
He Zhao
Jie Zhao
Xibin Zhao
Xiaoqi Zhao
Zhengyu Zhao
Jin Zhe
Chuanxia Zheng
Huan Zheng
Hao Zheng
Jia Zheng
Jian-Qing Zheng
Shuai Zheng
Meng Zheng
Mingkai Zheng
Qian Zheng
Qi Zheng
Wu Zheng
Yinqiang Zheng
Yufeng Zheng
Yutong Zheng
Yalin Zheng
Yu Zheng
Feng Zheng
Zhaoheng Zheng
Haitian Zheng
Kang Zheng
Bolun Zheng

Haiyong Zheng
Mingwu Zheng
Sipeng Zheng
Tu Zheng
Wenzhao Zheng
Xiawu Zheng
Yinglin Zheng
Zhuo Zheng
Zilong Zheng
Kecheng Zheng
Zerong Zheng
Shuaifeng Zhi
Tiancheng Zhi
Jia-Xing Zhong
Yiwu Zhong
Fangwei Zhong
Zhihang Zhong
Yaoyao Zhong
Yiran Zhong
Zhun Zhong
Zichun Zhong
Bo Zhou
Boyao Zhou
Brady Zhou
Mo Zhou
Chunluan Zhou
Dingfu Zhou
Fan Zhou
Jingkai Zhou
Honglu Zhou
Jiaming Zhou
Jiahuan Zhou
Jun Zhou
Kaiyang Zhou
Keyang Zhou
Kuangqi Zhou
Lei Zhou
Lihua Zhou
Man Zhou
Mingyi Zhou
Mingyuan Zhou
Ning Zhou
Peng Zhou
Penghao Zhou
Qianyi Zhou

Shuigeng Zhou
Shangchen Zhou
Huayi Zhou
Zhize Zhou
Sanping Zhou
Qin Zhou
Tao Zhou
Wenbo Zhou
Xiangdong Zhou
Xiao-Yun Zhou
Xiao Zhou
Yang Zhou
Yipin Zhou
Zhenyu Zhou
Hao Zhou
Chu Zhou
Daquan Zhou
Da-Wei Zhou
Hang Zhou
Kang Zhou
Qianyu Zhou
Sheng Zhou
Wenhui Zhou
Xingyi Zhou
Yan-Jie Zhou
Yiyi Zhou
Yu Zhou
Yuan Zhou
Yuqian Zhou
Yuxuan Zhou
Zixiang Zhou
Wengang Zhou
Shuchang Zhou
Tianfei Zhou
Yichao Zhou
Alex Zhu
Chenchen Zhu
Deyao Zhu
Xiatian Zhu
Guibo Zhu
Haidong Zhu
Hao Zhu
Hongzi Zhu
Rui Zhu
Jing Zhu

Jianke Zhu
Junchen Zhu
Lei Zhu
Lingyu Zhu
Luyang Zhu
Menglong Zhu
Peihao Zhu
Hui Zhu
Xiaofeng Zhu
Tyler (Lixuan) Zhu
Wentao Zhu
Xiangyu Zhu
Xinqi Zhu
Xinxin Zhu
Xinliang Zhu
Yangguang Zhu
Yichen Zhu
Yixin Zhu
Yanjun Zhu
Yousong Zhu
Yuhao Zhu
Ye Zhu
Feng Zhu
Zhen Zhu
Fangrui Zhu
Jinjing Zhu
Linchao Zhu
Pengfei Zhu
Sijie Zhu
Xiaobin Zhu
Xiaoguang Zhu
Zezhou Zhu
Zhenyao Zhu
Kai Zhu
Pengkai Zhu
Bingbing Zhuang
Chengyuan Zhuang
Liansheng Zhuang
Peiye Zhuang
Yixin Zhuang
Yihong Zhuang
Junbao Zhuo
Andrea Ziani
Bartosz Zieliński
Primo Zingaretti

Nikolaos Zioulis
Andrew Zisserman
Yael Ziv
Liu Ziyin
Xingxing Zou
Danping Zou
Qi Zou

Shihao Zou
Xueyan Zou
Yang Zou
Yuliang Zou
Zihang Zou
Chuhang Zou
Dongqing Zou

Xu Zou
Zhiming Zou
Maria A. Zuluaga
Xinxin Zuo
Zhiwen Zuo
Reyer Zwiggelaar

Contents – Part V

Adaptive Image Transformations for Transfer-Based Adversarial Attack

Zheng Yuan[1,2], Jie Zhang[1,2,3(✉)], and Shiguang Shan[1,2]

[1] Institute of Computing Technology, Chinese Academy of Sciences, Beijing, China
zheng.yuan@vipl.ict.ac.cn, {zhangjie,sgshan}@ict.ac.cn
[2] University of Chinese Academy of Sciences, Beijing, China
[3] Institute of Intelligent Computing Technology, Suzhou, CAS, Suzhou, China

Abstract. Adversarial attacks provide a good way to study the robustness of deep learning models. One category of methods in transfer-based black-box attack utilizes several image transformation operations to improve the transferability of adversarial examples, which is effective, but fails to take the specific characteristic of the input image into consideration. In this work, we propose a novel architecture, called Adaptive Image Transformation Learner (AITL), which incorporates different image transformation operations into a unified framework to further improve the transferability of adversarial examples. Unlike the fixed combinational transformations used in existing works, our elaborately designed transformation learner adaptively selects the most effective combination of image transformations specific to the input image. Extensive experiments on ImageNet demonstrate that our method significantly improves the attack success rates on both normally trained models and defense models under various settings.

Keywords: Adversarial attack · Transfer-based attack · Adaptive image transformation

1 Introduction

The field of deep neural networks has developed vigorously in recent years. The models have been successfully applied to various tasks, including image classification [22,45,67], face recognition [12,34,50], semantic segmentation [3–5], *etc.* However, the security of the DNN models raises great concerns due to that the model is vulnerable to adversarial examples [46]. For example, an image with indistinguishable noise can mislead a well-trained classification model into the wrong category [19], or a stop sign on the road with a small elaborate patch can fool an autonomous vehicle [18]. Adversarial attack and adversarial defense are like a spear and a shield. They promote the development of each other and together improve the robustness of deep neural networks.

Supplementary Information The online version contains supplementary material available at https://doi.org/10.1007/978-3-031-20065-6_1.

Table 1. The list of image transformation methods used in various input-transformation-based adversarial attack methods

Method	Transformation	Method	Transformation
DIM [61]	Resize	CIM [63]	Crop
TIM [15]	Translate	Admix [52]	Mixup
SIM [33]	Scale	AITL (ours)	Adaptive

Our work focuses on a popular scenario in the adversarial attack, *i.e.*, transfer-based black-box attack. In this setting, the adversary can not get access to any information about the target model. Szegedy *et al.* [46] find that adversarial examples have the property of cross model transferability, *i.e.*, the adversarial example generated from a source model can also fool a target model. To further improve the transferability of adversarial examples, the subsequent works mainly adopt different input transformations [15,33,52,61] and modified gradient updates [14,33,63,68]. The former improves the transferability of adversarial examples by conducting various image transformations (*e.g.*, resizing, crop, scale, mixup) on the original images before passing through the classifier. And the latter introduces the idea of various optimizers (*e.g.*, momentum and NAG [43], Adam [28], AdaBelief [66]) into the basic iterative attack method [29] to improve the stability of the gradient and enhance the transferability of the generated adversarial examples.

Existing transfer-based attack methods have studied a variety of image transformation operations, including resizing [61], crop [63], scale [33] and so on (as listed in Table 1). Although effective, we find that almost all existing works of input-transformation-based methods only investigate the effectiveness of fixed image transformation operations respectively (see (a) and (b) in Fig. 1), or simply combine them in sequence (see (c) in Fig. 1) to further improve the transferability of adversarial examples. However, due to the different characteristics of each image, the most effective combination of image transformations for each image should also be different.

To solve the problem mentioned above, we propose a novel architecture called Adaptive Image Transformation Learner (AITL), which incorporates different image transformation operations into a unified framework to adaptively select the most effective combination of input transformations towards each image for improving the transferability of adversarial examples. Specifically, AITL consists of encoder and decoder models to convert discrete image transformation operations into continuous feature embeddings, as well as a predictor, which can predict the attack success rate evaluated on black-box models when incorporating the given image transformations into MIFGSM [14]. After the AITL is well-trained, we optimize the continuous feature embeddings of the image transformation through backpropagation by maximizing the attack success rate, and then use the decoder to obtain the optimized transformation operations. The adaptive combination of image transformations is used to replace the fixed

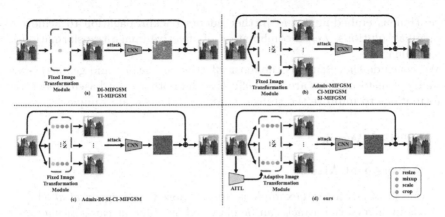

Fig. 1. Comparison between existing input-transformation-based black-box adversarial attack methods and our work. Different colors of the small circles in the red dotted box correspond to different image transformation operations. Existing works only conduct fixed image transformation once (as (a)) or repeat several times in parallel (as (b)), or simply combine multiple image transformation operations in the fixed sequence (as (c)). Our proposed method (as (d)) takes the characteristic of the current input image into consideration, utilizing an Adaptive Image Transformation Learner (AITL) to achieve the most effective combination of image transformations for each image, which can further improve the transferability of generated adversarial examples (Color figure online)

combinational operations in existing methods (as shown in (d) of Fig. 1). The subsequent attack process is similar to the mainstream gradient-based attack method [14,29].

Extensive experiments on ImageNet [42] demonstrate that our method not only significantly improves attack success rates on normally trained models, but also shows great effectiveness in attacking various defense models. Especially, we compare our attack method with the combination of state-of-the-art methods [14,33,52,61,63] against eleven advanced defense methods and achieve a significant improvement of 15.88% and 5.87% on average under the single model setting and the ensemble of multiple models setting, respectively. In addition, we conclude that `Scale` is the most effective operation, and geometry-based image transformations (*e.g.*, resizing, rotation, shear) can bring more improvement on the transferability of the adversarial examples, compared to other color-based image transformations (*e.g.*, brightness, sharpness, saturation).

We summarize our main contributions as follows:

1. Unlike the fixed combinational transformation used in existing works, we incorporate different image transformations into a unified framework to adaptively select the most effective combination of image transformations for the specific image.
2. We propose a novel architecture called Adaptive Image Transformation Learner (AITL), which elaborately converts discrete transformations into

continuous embeddings and further adopts backpropagation to achieve the optimal solutions, *i.e.*, a combination of effective image transformations for each image.

3. We conclude that `Scale` is the most effective operation, and geometry-based image transformations are more effective than other color-based image transformations to improve the transferability of adversarial examples.

2 Related Work

2.1 Adversarial Attack

The concept of adversarial example is first proposed by Szegedy *et al.* [46]. The methods in adversarial attack can be classified as different categories according to the amount of information to the target model the adversary can access, *i.e.*, white-box attack [1,2,9,17,19,37,38,47], query-based black-box attack [6,7,16, 24,31,36,49] and transfer-based black-box attack [14,15,21,30,33,51,56,58,61]. Since our work focuses on the area of transfer-based black-box attacks, we mainly introduce the methods of transfer-based black-box attack in detail.

The adversary in transfer-based black-box attack can not access any information about the target model, which only utilizes the transferability of adversarial example [19] to conduct the attack on the target model. The works in this task can be divided into two main categories, *i.e.*, modified gradient updates and input transformations.

In the branch of modified gradient updates, Dong *et al.* [14] first propose MIFGSM to stabilize the update directions with a momentum term to improve the transferability of adversarial examples. Lin *et al.* [33] propose the method of NIM, which adapts Nesterov accelerated gradient into the iterative attacks. Zou *et al.* [68] propose an Adam [28] iterative fast gradient tanh method (AI-FGTM) to generate indistinguishable adversarial examples with high transferability. Besides, Yang *et al.* [63] absorb the AdaBelief optimizer into the update of the gradient and propose ABI-FGM to further boost the success rates of adversarial examples for black-box attacks. Recently, Wang *et al.* propose the techniques of variance tuning [51] and enhanced momentum [53] to further enhance the class of iterative gradient-based attack methods.

In the branch of various input transformations, Xie *et al.* [61] propose DIM, which applies random resizing to the inputs at each iteration of I-FGSM [29] to alleviate the overfitting on white-box models. Dong *et al.* [15] propose a translation-invariant attack method, called TIM, by optimizing a perturbation over an ensemble of translated images. Lin *et al.* [33] also leverage the scale-invariant property of deep learning models to optimize the adversarial perturbations over the scale copies of the input images. Further, Crop-Invariant attack Method (CIM) is proposed by Yang *et al.* [63] to improve the transferability of adversarial. Contemporarily, inspired by mixup [65], Wang *et al.* [52] propose Admix to calculate the gradient on the input image admixed with a small portion of each add-in image while using the original label of the input, to craft more transferable adversaries. Besides, Wu *et al.* [58] propose ATTA method, which improves the robustness of synthesized adversarial examples via an adversarial transformation network. Recently, Yuan *et al.* [64] propose AutoMA to find the strong model augmentation policy by the framework of reinforcement learning. The works most relevant to ours are AutoMA [64] and ATTA [58] and we give a brief discussion on the differences between our work and theirs in Appendix B.

2.2 Adversarial Defense

To boost the robustness of neural networks and defend against adversarial attacks, numerous methods of adversarial defense have been proposed.

Adversarial training [19,29,37] adds the adversarial examples generated by several methods of adversarial attack into the training set, to boost the robustness of models. Although effective, the problems of huge computational cost and overfitting to the specific attack pattern in adversarial training receive increasing concerns. Several follow-up works [13,37,40,41,48,54,55,57] aim to solve these problems. Another major approach is the method of input transformation, which preprocesses the input to mitigate the adversarial effect ahead, including JPEG compression [20,35], denoising [32], random resizing [60], bit depth reduction [62] and so on. Certified defense [8,25,27,59] attempts to provide a guarantee that the target model can not be fooled within a small perturbation neighborhood of the clean image. Moreover, Jia *et al.* [26] utilize an image compression model to defend the adversarial examples. Naseer *et al.* [39] propose a self-supervised adversarial training mechanism in the input space to combine the benefit of both the adversarial training and input transformation method. The various defense methods mentioned above help to improve the robustness of the model.

3 Method

In this section, we first give the definition of the notations in the task. And then we introduce our proposed Adaptive Image Transformation Learner (AITL), which can adaptively select the most effective combination of image transformations used during the attack to improve the transferability of generated adversarial examples.

3.1 Notations

Let $x \in \mathcal{X}$ denote a clean image from a dataset of $\mathcal{X}$, and $y \in \mathcal{Y}$ is the corresponding ground truth label. Given a source model f with parameters θ, the objective of adversarial attack is to find the adversarial example x^{adv} that satisfies:

$$f(x^{adv}) \neq y, \quad s.t. \|x - x^{adv}\|_\infty \leq \epsilon, \tag{1}$$

where ϵ is a preset parameter to constrain the intensity of the perturbation. In implementation, most gradient-based adversaries utilize the method of maximizing the loss function to iteratively generate adversarial examples. We here take the widely used method of MIFGSM [14] as an example:

$$g_{t+1} = \mu \cdot g_t + \frac{\nabla_{x_t^{adv}} J(f(x_t^{adv}), y)}{\|\nabla_{x_t^{adv}} J(f(x_t^{adv}), y)\|_1}, \tag{2}$$

$$x_{t+1}^{adv} = x_t^{adv} + \alpha \cdot sign(g_{t+1}), \tag{3}$$

$$g_0 = 0, \quad x_0^{adv} = x, \tag{4}$$

where g_t is the accumulated gradients, x_t^{adv} is the generated adversarial example at the time step t, $J(\cdot)$ is the loss function used in classification models (*i.e.*, the cross entropy loss), μ and α are hyperparameters.

3.2   Overview of AITL

Existing works of input-transformation-based methods have studied the influence of some input transformations on the transferability of adversarial examples. These methods can be combined with the MIFGSM [14] method and can be summarized as the following paradigm, where the Eq. 2 is replaced by:

$$g_{t+1} = \mu \cdot g_t + \frac{\nabla_{x_t^{adv}} J(f(T(x_t^{adv})), y)}{\|\nabla_{x_t^{adv}} J(f(T(x_t^{adv})), y)\|_1}, \tag{5}$$

where T represents different input transformation operations in different method (*e.g.*, resizing in DIM [61], translation in TIM [15], scaling in SIM [33], cropping in CIM [63], mixup in Admix [52]).

Although existing methods improve the transferability of adversarial examples to a certain extent, almost all of these methods only utilize different image transformations respectively and haven't systematically studied which transformation operation is more suitable. Also, these methods haven't considered the characteristic of each image, but uniformly adopt a fixed transformation method for all images, which is not reasonable in nature and cannot maximize the transferability of the generated adversarial examples.

In this paper, we incorporate different image transformation operations into a unified framework and utilize an Adaptive Image Transformation Learner (AITL) to adaptively select the suitable input transformations towards different input images (as shown in (d) of Fig. 1). This unified framework can analyze the impact of different transformations on the generated adversarial examples.

Overall, our method consists of two phases, *i.e.*, the phase of training AITL to learn the relationship between various image transformations and the corresponding attack success rates, and the phase of generating adversarial examples with well-trained AITL. During the training phase, we conduct encoder and decoder networks, which can convert the discretized image transformation operations into continuous feature embeddings. In addition, a predictor is proposed to predict the attack success rate in the case of the original image being firstly transformed by the given image transformation operations and then attacked with the method of MIFGSM [14]. After the training of AITL is finished, we maximize the attack success rate to optimize the continuous feature embeddings of the image transformation through backpropagation, and then use the decoder

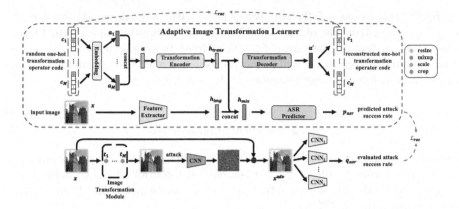

Fig. 2. The diagram of Adaptive Image Transformation Learner in the process of training

to obtain the optimal transformation operations specific to the input, and incorporate it into MIFGSM to conduct the actual attack.

In the following two subsections, we will introduce the two phases mentioned above in detail, respectively.

3.3 Training AITL

The overall process of training AITL is shown in Fig. 2. We first randomly select M image transformations $t_1, t_2, \cdots, t_M$ from the image transformation operation zoo (including both geometry-based and color-based operations, for details please refer to Appendix A.3) based on uniform distribution to compose an image transformation combination. We then discretize different image transformations by encoding them into one-hot vectors $c_1, c_2, \cdots, c_M$ (e.g., $[1, 0, 0, \cdots]$ represents resizing, $[0, 1, 0, \cdots]$ represents scaling). An embedding layer then converts different transformation operations into their respective feature vectors, which are concatenated into an integrated input transformation feature vector a:

$$a_1, a_2, \cdots, a_M = Embedding(c_1, c_2, \cdots, c_M), \tag{6}$$

$$a = Concat(a_1, a_2, \cdots, a_M). \tag{7}$$

The integrated input transformation feature vector then goes through a transformation encoder f_{en} and decoder f_{de} in turn, so as to learn the continuous feature embeddings h_{trans} in the intermediate layer:

$$h_{trans} = f_{en}(a), \tag{8}$$

$$a' = f_{de}(h_{trans}). \tag{9}$$

The resultant decoded feature a' is then utilized to reconstruct the input transformation one-hot vectors:

$$c_1', c_2', \cdots, c_M' = FC(a'), \tag{10}$$

where FC represents a fully connected layer with multiple heads, each represents the reconstruction of an input image transformation operation. On the other hand, a feature extractor f_{img} is utilized to extract the image feature of the original image h_{img}, which is concatenated with the continuous feature embeddings of image transformation combination h_{trans}:

$$h_{img} = f_{img}(x), \tag{11}$$
$$h_{mix} = Concat(h_{trans}, h_{img}). \tag{12}$$

Then the mixed feature is used to predict the attack success rate p_{asr} through an attack success rate predictor f_{pre} in the case of the original image being firstly transformed by the input image transformation combination and then attacked with the method of MIFGSM:

$$p_{asr} = f_{pre}(h_{mix}). \tag{13}$$

Loss Functions. The loss function used to train the network consists of two parts. The one is the reconstruction loss $\mathcal{L}_{rec}$ to constrain the reconstructed image transformation operations $c'_1, c'_2, \cdots, c'_M$ being consistent with the input image transformation operations $c_1, c_2, \cdots, c_M$:

$$\mathcal{L}_{rec} = -\sum_{i=1}^{M} c_i^T \log c'_i, \tag{14}$$

where T represents the transpose of a vector. The other one is the prediction loss $\mathcal{L}_{asr}$, which aims to ensure that the attack success rate predicted by the ASR predictor p_{asr} is close to the actual attack success rate q_{asr}.

$$\mathcal{L}_{asr} = \|p_{asr} - q_{asr}\|_2. \tag{15}$$

The actual attack success rate q_{asr} is achieved by evaluating the adversarial example x^{adv}, which is generated through replacing the fixed transformation operations in existing methods by the given input image transformation combination (i.e., $T = t_M \circ \cdots \circ t_2 \circ t_1$ in Eq. 5) on n black-box models $f_1, f_2, \cdots, f_n$ (as shown in the bottom half in Fig. 2):

$$q_{asr} = \frac{1}{n} \sum_{i=1}^{n} \mathbb{1}(f_i(x^{adv}) \neq y). \tag{16}$$

And the total loss function is the sum of above introduced two items:

$$\mathcal{L}_{total} = \mathcal{L}_{rec} + \mathcal{L}_{asr}. \tag{17}$$

The entire training process is summarized in Algorithm 1 in the appendix.

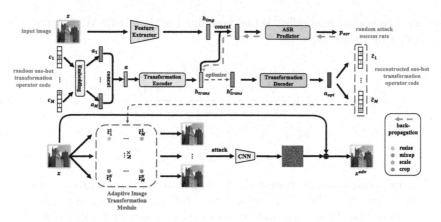

Fig. 3. The process of generating adversarial examples with Adaptive Image Transformation Learner

3.4 Generating Adversarial Examples with AITL

When the training of Adaptive Image Transformation Learner is finished, it can be used to adaptively select the appropriate combination of image transformations when conducting adversarial attacks against any unknown model. The process has been shown in Fig. 3.

For an arbitrary input image, we can not identify the most effective input transformation operations that can improve the transferability of generated adversarial examples ahead. Therefore, we first still randomly sample M initial input transformation operations $t_1, t_2, \cdots, t_M$, and go through a forward pass in AITL to get the predicted attack success rate p_{asr} corresponding to the input transformation operations. Then we iteratively optimize the image transformation feature embedding h_{trans} by maximizing the predicted attack success rate for r times:

$$h_{trans}^{t+1} = h_{trans}^t + \gamma \cdot \nabla_{h_{trans}^t} p_{asr}, \tag{18}$$

$$h_{trans}^0 = h_{trans}, \tag{19}$$

where γ is the step size in each optimizing step. Finally we achieve the optimized image transformation feature embedding h_{trans}^r. Then we utilize the pre-trained decoder to convert the continuous feature embedding into specific image transformation operations:

$$a_{opt} = f_{de}(h_{trans}^r), \tag{20}$$

$$\tilde{c}_1, \tilde{c}_2, \cdots, \tilde{c}_M = FC(a_{opt}). \tag{21}$$

The resultant image transformation operations $\tilde{c}_1, \tilde{c}_2, \cdots, \tilde{c}_M$ achieved by AITL are considered to be the most effective combination of image transformations for improving the transferability of generated adversarial example towards the specific input image. Thus we utilize these image transformation operations to generate adversarial examples. When combined with MIFGSM [14], the whole process can be summarized as:

$$\tilde{c}_1, \tilde{c}_1, \cdots, \tilde{c}_M = AITL(x), \tag{22}$$

$$g_{t+1} = \mu \cdot g_t + \frac{\nabla_{x_t^{adv}} J(f(\tilde{c}_M \circ \cdots \circ \tilde{c}_1(x_t^{adv})), y)}{\|\nabla_{x_t^{adv}} J(f(\tilde{c}_M \circ \cdots \circ \tilde{c}_1(x_t^{adv})), y)\|_1}, \tag{23}$$

$$x_{t+1}^{adv} = x_t^{adv} + \alpha \cdot sign(g_{t+1}), \tag{24}$$

$$g_0 = 0, \quad x_0^{adv} = x. \tag{25}$$

Since the random image transformation operations contain randomness (*e.g.*, the degree in rotation, the width and height in resizing), existing works [33,52,63] conduct these transformation operations multiple times in parallel during each step of the attack to alleviate the impact of the instability caused by randomness on the generated adversarial examples (as shown in (b) of Fig. 1). Similar to previous works, we also randomly sample the initial image transformation combination multiple times, and then optimize them to obtain the optimal combination of image transformation operations respectively. The several optimal image transformation combinations are used in parallel to generate adversarial examples (as shown in the bottom half in Fig. 3). The entire process of using AITL to generate adversarial examples is formally summarized in Algorithm 2 in the appendix.

The specific network structure of the entire framework is shown in Appendix A.4. The ASR predictor, Transformation Encoder and Decoder in our AITL consist of only a few FC layers. During the iterative attack, our method only needs to infer once before the first iteration. So our AITL is a lightweight method, and the extra cost compared to existing methods is negligible.

4   Experiments

In this section, we first introduce the settings in the experiments in Sect. 4.1. Then we demonstrate the results of our proposed AITL method on the single model attack and an ensemble of multiple models attack, respectively in Sect. 4.2. We also analyze the effectiveness of different image transformation methods in Sect. 4.3. In Appendix C, more extra experiments are provided, including the attack success rate under different perturbation budgets, the influence of some hyperparameters, more experiments on the single model attack, the results of AITL combined with other base attack methods and the visualization of generated adversarial examples.

4.1   Settings

Dataset. We use two sets of subsets[1,2] in the ImageNet dataset [42] to conduct experiments. Each set contains 1000 images, covering almost all categories in ImageNet, which has been widely used in previous works [14,15,33]. All images have the size of $299 \times 299 \times 3$. In order to make a fair comparison with other methods, we use the former subset to train the AITL model, and evaluate all methods on the latter one.

Models. In order to avoid overfitting of the AITL model and ensure the fairness of the experimental comparison, we use completely different models to conduct experiments during the training and evaluation of the AITL model. During the training, we totally 11 models to provide the attack success rate corresponding to the input transformation, including 10 normally trained and 1 adversarially trained models. During the evaluation, we use 7 normally trained models, 3 adversarially trained models, and another 8 stronger defense models to conduct the experiments. The details are provided in Appendix A.1.

Baselines. Several input-transformation-based black-box attack methods (*e.g.*, DIM [61], TIM [15], SIM [33], CIM [63], Admix [52], AutoMA [64]) are utilized to compare with our proposed method. Unless mentioned specifically, we combine these methods with MIFGSM [14] to conduct the attack. In addition, we also combine these input-transformation-based methods together to form the strongest baseline, called Admix-DI-SI-CI-MIFGSM (as shown in (c) of Fig. 1, ADSCM for short). Moreover, we also use a random selection method instead of the AITL to choose the combination of image transformations used in the attack, which is denoted as Random. The details of these baselines are provided in Appendix A.2.

Image Transformation Operations. Partially referencing from [10,11], we totally select 20 image transformation operations as candidates, including Admix, Scale, Admix-and-Scale, Brightness, Color, Contrast, Sharpness, Invert, Hue, Saturation, Gamma, Crop, Resize, Rotate, ShearX, ShearY, TranslateX, TranslateY, Reshape, Cutout. The details of these operations are provided in Appendix A.3, including the accurate definitions and specific parameters in the random transformations.

Implementation Details. We train the AITL model for 10 epochs. The batch size is 64, and the learning rate β is set to 0.00005. The detailed network structure of AITL is introduced in Appendix A.4. The maximum adversarial perturbation ϵ is set to 16, with an iteration step T of 10 and step size α of 1.6. The number of iterations during optimizing image transformation features r is set to 1 and the corresponding step size γ is 15. The number of image transformation operations used in a combination M is set to 4 (the same number as the transformations

---

[1] https://github.com/cleverhans-lab/cleverhans/tree/master/cleverhans_v3.1.0/
examples/nips17_adversarial_competition/dataset.
[2] https://drive.google.com/drive/folders/1CfobY6i8BfqfWPHL31FKFDipNjqWwAhS.

Table 2. Attack success rates (%) of adversarial attacks against 7 normally trained models and 11 defense models under **single model** setting. The adversarial examples are crafted on Incv3. * indicates the white-box model. † The results of AutoMA [64] are cited from their original paper

(a) The evaluation against 7 normally trained models

	Incv3*	Incv4	IncResv2	Resv2-101	Resv2-152	PNASNet	NASNet
MIFGSM [14]	**100**	52.2	50.6	37.4	35.6	42.2	42.2
DIM [61]	99.7	78.3	76.3	59.6	59.9	64.6	66.2
SIM [33]	**100**	84.5	81.3	68.0	65.3	70.8	73.6
CIM [63]	**100**	85.1	81.6	58.1	57.4	65.7	66.7
Admix [52]	99.8	69.5	66.5	55.3	55.4	60.0	62.7
ADSCM	**100**	87.9	86.1	75.8	76.0	80.9	82.2
Random	**100**	94.0	92.0	79.7	80.0	84.6	85.5
AutoMA† [64]	98.2	91.2	91.0	82.5	–	–	–
AITL (ours)	99.8	**95.8**	**94.1**	**88.8**	**90.1**	**94.1**	**94.0**
AutoMA-TIM† [64]	97.5	80.7	74.3	69.3	–	–	–
AITL-TIM (ours)	**99.8**	**93.4**	**92.1**	**91.9**	**92.2**	**93.8**	**94.6**

(b) The evaluation against 11 defense models

	Incv3$_{ens3}$	Incv3$_{ens4}$	IncResv2$_{ens}$	HGD	R&P	NIPS-r3	Bit-Red	JPEG	FD	ComDefend	RS
MIFGSM [14]	15.6	15.2	6.4	5.8	5.6	9.3	18.5	33.3	39.0	28.1	16.8
DIM [61]	31.0	29.2	13.4	15.8	14.8	24.6	26.8	59.3	45.8	48.3	21.8
SIM [33]	37.5	35.0	18.8	16.8	18.3	26.8	31.0	66.9	52.1	55.9	24.1
CIM [63]	33.3	30.0	15.9	20.4	16.4	25.7	26.8	62.2	46.3	44.9	21.2
Admix [52]	27.5	27.0	14.3	11.6	12.6	19.8	28.4	51.2	48.8	44.0	22.0
ADSCM	49.3	46.9	27.0	33.1	28.5	40.5	39.0	73.0	60.4	65.5	32.8
Random	49.8	46.7	24.5	29.2	26.4	42.2	36.3	81.4	57.4	69.6	29.6
AutoMA† [64]	49.2	49.0	29.1	–	–	–	–	–	–	–	–
AITL (ours)	**69.9**	**65.8**	**43.4**	**50.4**	**46.9**	**59.9**	**51.6**	**87.1**	**73.0**	**83.2**	**39.5**
AutoMA-TIM† [64]	74.8	74.3	63.6	65.7	62.9	68.1	–	–	**84.7**	–	–
AITL-TIM (ours)	**81.3**	**78.9**	**69.1**	**75.1**	**64.7**	**74.6**	**60.9**	**87.8**	83.8	**85.6**	**55.4**

used in the strongest baseline ADSCM for a fair comparison). Also, for a fair comparison of different methods, we control the number of repetitions per iteration in all methods to 5 (m in SIM [33], m_2 in Admix [52], m in AutoMA [64] and N in our AITL).

4.2   Compared with the State-of-the-Art Methods

Attack on the Single Model. We use Inceptionv3 [45] model as the white-box model to conduct the adversarial attack, and evaluate the generated adversarial examples on both normally trained models and defense models. As shown in Table 2, comparing various existing input-transformation-based methods, our proposed AITL significantly improves the attack success rates against various black-box models. Especially for the defense models, although it is relatively difficult to attack successfully, our method still achieves a significant improvement of 15.88% on average, compared to the strong baseline (Admix-DI-SI-CI-MIFGSM). It demonstrates that, compared with the fixed image transformation combination, adaptively selecting combinational image transformations for each

Table 3. Attack success rates (%) of adversarial attacks against 7 normally trained models and 11 defense models under **multiple models** setting. The adversarial examples are crafted on the ensemble of Incv3, Incv4, IncResv2 and Resv2-101. * indicates the white-box model. † The results of AutoMA [64] are cited from their original paper

(a) The evaluation against 11 defense models

	Incv3*	Incv4*	IncResv2*	Resv2-101*	Resv2-152	PNASNet	NASNet
MIFGSM [14]	100	99.6	99.7	**98.5**	86.8	79.4	81.2
DIM [61]	99.5	99.4	98.9	96.9	92.0	91.3	92.1
SIM [33]	99.9	99.1	98.3	93.2	91.7	90.9	91.9
CIM [63]	99.8	99.3	97.8	90.6	88.5	88.2	90.9
Admix [52]	99.9	99.5	98.2	95.4	89.3	88.1	90.0
ADSCM	99.8	99.3	99.2	96.9	96.0	88.1	90.0
Random	100	99.4	98.9	96.9	94.3	94.4	95.0
AITL (ours)	99.9	**99.7**	**99.9**	97.3	**96.6**	**97.7**	**97.8**

(b) The evaluation against 11 defense models

	Incv3$_{ens3}$	Incv3$_{ens4}$	IncResv2$_{ens}$	HGD	R&P	NIPS-r3	Bit-Red	JPEG	FD	ComDefend	RS
MIFGSM [14]	52.4	47.5	30.1	39.2	31.7	43.6	33.8	76.4	54.5	66.8	29.7
DIM [61]	77.4	73.1	54.4	68.4	61.2	73.5	53.3	89.8	71.5	84.3	43.1
SIM [33]	78.8	74.4	59.8	66.9	59.0	70.7	58.1	89.0	73.2	83.0	46.6
CIM [63]	75.1	69.7	54.3	68.5	59.1	70.7	51.1	90.2	68.9	78.5	41.1
Admix [52]	67.7	61.9	44.8	51.0	44.8	57.9	51.4	84.6	69.2	78.5	42.2
ADSCM	85.8	82.9	69.2	78.7	74.1	81.1	68.1	94.9	82.3	90.8	57.8
Random	83.7	80.2	64.8	73.7	67.3	77.9	65.7	93.0	79.9	88.6	52.3
AITL (ours)	**89.3**	**89.0**	**79.0**	**85.5**	**82.3**	**86.3**	**74.9**	**96.2**	88.4	**93.7**	**65.7**
AutoMA-TIM† [64]	93.0	93.2	90.7	91.2	90.4	92.0	–	–	94.1	–	–
AITL-TIM (ours)	**93.8**	**95.3**	**92.0**	**93.1**	**93.7**	**94.8**	80.9	95.0	**96.2**	95.0	76.9

image can indeed improve the transferability of adversarial examples. Also, when compared to AutoMA [64], our AITL achieves a distinct improvement, which shows that our AITL model achieves better mapping between discrete image transformations and continuous feature embeddings. More results of attacking other models are available in Appendix C.2. Noting that the models used for evaluation here are totally different from the models used when training the AITL, our method shows great cross model transferability to conduct the successful adversarial attack.

Attack on the Ensemble of Multiple Models. We use the ensemble of four models, *i.e.*, Inceptionv3 [45], Inceptionv4 [44], Inception-ResNetv2 [44] and ResNetv2-101 [23], as the white-box models to conduct the adversarial attack. As shown in Table 3, compared with the fixed image transformation method, our AITL significantly improves the attack success rates on various models. Although the strong baseline ADSCM has achieved relatively high attack success rates, our AITL still obtains an improvement of 1.44% and 5.87% on average against black-box normally trained models and defense models, respectively. Compared to AutoMA [64], our AITL also achieves higher attack success rates on defense models, which shows the superiority of our proposed novel architecture.

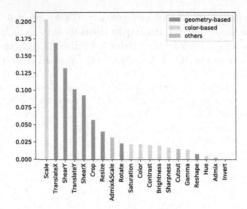

Fig. 4. The frequency of various image transformations used in AITL when generating adversarial examples of the 1000 images in ImageNet

4.3   Analysis on Image Transformation Operations

In order to further explore the effects of different image transformation operations on improving the transferability of adversarial examples, we calculate the frequency of various image transformations used in AITL when generating adversarial examples of the 1000 images in ImageNet. From Fig. 4, we can clearly see that `Scale` operation is the most effective method within all 20 candidates. Also, we conclude that the geometry-based image transformations are more effective than other color-based image transformations to improve the transferability of adversarial examples.

5   Conclusion

In our work, unlike the fixed image transformation operations used in almost all existing works of transfer-based black-box attack, we propose a novel architecture, called Adaptive Image Transformation Learner (AITL), which incorporates different image transformation operations into a unified framework to further improve the transferability of adversarial examples. By taking the characteristic of each image into consideration, our designed AITL adaptively selects the most effective combination of image transformations for the specific image. Extensive experiments on ImageNet demonstrate that our method significantly improves the attack success rates both on normally trained models and defense models under different settings.

Acknowledgments. This work is partially supported by National Key R&D Program of China (No. 2017YFA0700800), National Natural Science Foundation of China (Nos. 62176251 and Nos. 61976219).

References

1. Athalye, A., Carlini, N., Wagner, D.A.: Obfuscated gradients give a false sense of security: circumventing defenses to adversarial examples. In: ICML, vol. 80, pp. 274–283 (2018)
2. Athalye, A., Engstrom, L., Ilyas, A., Kwok, K.: Synthesizing robust adversarial examples. In: ICML, vol. 80, pp. 284–293 (2018)
3. Chen, L., Papandreou, G., Kokkinos, I., Murphy, K., Yuille, A.L.: Semantic image segmentation with deep convolutional nets and fully connected CRFs. In: ICLR (2015)
4. Chen, L., Papandreou, G., Kokkinos, I., Murphy, K., Yuille, A.L.: DeepLab: semantic image segmentation with deep convolutional nets, atrous convolution, and fully connected CRFs. IEEE TPAMI **40**(4), 834–848 (2018)
5. Chen, L., Papandreou, G., Schroff, F., Adam, H.: Rethinking atrous convolution for semantic image segmentation. arXiv preprint arXiv:1706.05587 (2017)
6. Chen, P., Zhang, H., Sharma, Y., Yi, J., Hsieh, C.: ZOO: zeroth order optimization based black-box attacks to deep neural networks without training substitute models. In: Proceedings of the 10th ACM Workshop on Artificial Intelligence and Security, AISec@CCS 2017, Dallas, TX, USA, 3 November 2017, pp. 15–26 (2017)
7. Cheng, S., Dong, Y., Pang, T., Su, H., Zhu, J.: Improving black-box adversarial attacks with a transfer-based prior. In: NeurIPS, pp. 10932–10942 (2019)
8. Croce, F., Hein, M.: Provable robustness against all adversarial l_p-perturbations for $p \geq 1$. In: ICLR (2020)
9. Croce, F., Hein, M.: Reliable evaluation of adversarial robustness with an ensemble of diverse parameter-free attacks. In: ICML, vol. 119, pp. 2206–2216 (2020)
10. Cubuk, E.D., Zoph, B., Mané, D., Vasudevan, V., Le, Q.V.: AutoAugment: learning augmentation strategies from data. In: CVPR, pp. 113–123 (2019)
11. Cubuk, E.D., Zoph, B., Shlens, J., Le, Q.: RandAugment: practical automated data augmentation with a reduced search space. In: NeurIPS (2020)
12. Deng, J., Guo, J., Xue, N., Zafeiriou, S.: ArcFace: additive angular margin loss for deep face recognition. In: CVPR, pp. 4690–4699 (2019)
13. Dong, Y., Deng, Z., Pang, T., Zhu, J., Su, H.: Adversarial distributional training for robust deep learning. In: NeurIPS (2020)
14. Dong, Y., et al.: Boosting adversarial attacks with momentum. In: CVPR, pp. 9185–9193 (2018)
15. Dong, Y., Pang, T., Su, H., Zhu, J.: Evading defenses to transferable adversarial examples by translation-invariant attacks. In: CVPR, pp. 4312–4321 (2019)
16. Du, J., Zhang, H., Zhou, J.T., Yang, Y., Feng, J.: Query-efficient meta attack to deep neural networks. In: ICLR (2020)
17. Duan, R., Chen, Y., Niu, D., Yang, Y., Qin, A.K., He, Y.: AdvDrop: adversarial attack to DNNs by dropping information. In: ICCV, pp. 7506–7515 (2021)
18. Eykholt, K., et al.: Robust physical-world attacks on deep learning visual classification. In: CVPR, pp. 1625–1634 (2018)
19. Goodfellow, I.J., Shlens, J., Szegedy, C.: Explaining and harnessing adversarial examples. In: ICLR (2015)
20. Guo, C., Rana, M., Cissé, M., van der Maaten, L.: Countering adversarial images using input transformations. In: ICLR (2018)
21. Guo, Y., Li, Q., Chen, H.: Backpropagating linearly improves transferability of adversarial examples. In: NeurIPS (2020)

22. He, K., Zhang, X., Ren, S., Sun, J.: Deep residual learning for image recognition. In: CVPR, pp. 770–778 (2016)
23. He, K., Zhang, X., Ren, S., Sun, J.: Identity mappings in deep residual networks. In: Leibe, B., Matas, J., Sebe, N., Welling, M. (eds.) ECCV 2016. LNCS, vol. 9908, pp. 630–645. Springer, Cham (2016). https://doi.org/10.1007/978-3-319-46493-0_38
24. Ilyas, A., Engstrom, L., Athalye, A., Lin, J.: Black-box adversarial attacks with limited queries and information. In: ICML, vol. 80, pp. 2142–2151 (2018)
25. Jia, J., Cao, X., Wang, B., Gong, N.Z.: Certified robustness for top-k predictions against adversarial perturbations via randomized smoothing. In: ICLR (2020)
26. Jia, X., Wei, X., Cao, X., Foroosh, H.: ComDefend: an efficient image compression model to defend adversarial examples. In: CVPR, pp. 6084–6092 (2019)
27. Katz, G., Barrett, C.W., Dill, D.L., Julian, K., Kochenderfer, M.J.: Reluplex: an efficient SMT solver for verifying deep neural networks. In: CAV, vol. 10426, pp. 97–117 (2017)
28. Kingma, D.P., Ba, J.: Adam: a method for stochastic optimization. In: ICLR (2015)
29. Kurakin, A., Goodfellow, I.J., Bengio, S.: Adversarial machine learning at scale. In: ICLR (2017)
30. Li, M., Deng, C., Li, T., Yan, J., Gao, X., Huang, H.: Towards transferable targeted attack. In: CVPR, pp. 638–646 (2020)
31. Li, Y., Li, L., Wang, L., Zhang, T., Gong, B.: NATTACK: learning the distributions of adversarial examples for an improved black-box attack on deep neural networks. In: ICML, vol. 97, pp. 3866–3876 (2019)
32. Liao, F., Liang, M., Dong, Y., Pang, T., Hu, X., Zhu, J.: Defense against adversarial attacks using high-level representation guided denoiser. In: CVPR, pp. 1778–1787 (2018)
33. Lin, J., Song, C., He, K., Wang, L., Hopcroft, J.E.: Nesterov accelerated gradient and scale invariance for adversarial attacks. In: ICLR (2020)
34. Liu, W., Wen, Y., Yu, Z., Li, M., Raj, B., Song, L.: SphereFace: deep hypersphere embedding for face recognition. In: CVPR, pp. 6738–6746 (2017)
35. Liu, Z., Liu, Q., Liu, T., Xu, N., Lin, X., Wang, Y., Wen, W.: Feature distillation: DNN-oriented JPEG compression against adversarial examples. In: CVPR, pp. 860–868 (2019)
36. Ma, C., Chen, L., Yong, J.: Simulating unknown target models for query-efficient black-box attacks. In: CVPR, pp. 11835–11844 (2021)
37. Madry, A., Makelov, A., Schmidt, L., Tsipras, D., Vladu, A.: Towards deep learning models resistant to adversarial attacks. In: ICLR (2018)
38. Moosavi-Dezfooli, S., Fawzi, A., Frossard, P.: DeepFool: a simple and accurate method to fool deep neural networks. In: CVPR, pp. 2574–2582 (2016)
39. Naseer, M., Khan, S.H., Hayat, M., Khan, F.S., Porikli, F.: A self-supervised approach for adversarial robustness. In: CVPR, pp. 259–268 (2020)
40. Pang, T., Yang, X., Dong, Y., Xu, T., Zhu, J., Su, H.: Boosting adversarial training with hypersphere embedding. In: NeurIPS (2020)
41. Rozsa, A., Rudd, E.M., Boult, T.E.: Adversarial diversity and hard positive generation. In: CVPRW, pp. 410–417 (2016)
42. Russakovsky, O., et al.: ImageNet large scale visual recognition challenge. IJCV 115(3), 211–252 (2015)
43. Sutskever, I., Martens, J., Dahl, G.E., Hinton, G.E.: On the importance of initialization and momentum in deep learning. In: ICML, vol. 28, pp. 1139–1147 (2013)
44. Szegedy, C., Ioffe, S., Vanhoucke, V., Alemi, A.A.: Inception-V4, inception-ResNet and the impact of residual connections on learning. In: AAAI, pp. 4278–4284 (2017)

45. Szegedy, C., Vanhoucke, V., Ioffe, S., Shlens, J., Wojna, Z.: Rethinking the inception architecture for computer vision. In: CVPR, pp. 2818–2826 (2016)
46. Szegedy, C., et al.: Intriguing properties of neural networks. In: ICLR (2014)
47. Tramèr, F., Carlini, N., Brendel, W., Madry, A.: On adaptive attacks to adversarial example defenses. In: NeurIPS (2020)
48. Tramèr, F., Kurakin, A., Papernot, N., Goodfellow, I.J., Boneh, D., McDaniel, P.D.: Ensemble adversarial training: Attacks and defenses. In: ICLR (2018)
49. Uesato, J., O'Donoghue, B., Kohli, P., van den Oord, A.: Adversarial risk and the dangers of evaluating against weak attacks. In: ICML, vol. 80, pp. 5032–5041 (2018)
50. Wang, H., et al.: CosFace: Large margin cosine loss for deep face recognition. In: CVPR, pp. 5265–5274 (2018)
51. Wang, X., He, K.: Enhancing the transferability of adversarial attacks through variance tuning. In: CVPR, pp. 1924–1933 (2021)
52. Wang, X., He, X., Wang, J., He, K.: Admix: enhancing the transferability of adversarial attacks. arXiv preprint arXiv:2102.00436 (2021)
53. Wang, X., Lin, J., Hu, H., Wang, J., He, K.: Boosting adversarial transferability through enhanced momentum. arXiv preprint arXiv:2103.10609 (2021)
54. Wang, Y., Ma, X., Bailey, J., Yi, J., Zhou, B., Gu, Q.: On the convergence and robustness of adversarial training. In: ICML, vol. 97, pp. 6586–6595 (2019)
55. Wong, E., Rice, L., Kolter, J.Z.: Fast is better than free: revisiting adversarial training. In: ICLR (2020)
56. Wu, D., Wang, Y., Xia, S., Bailey, J., Ma, X.: Skip connections matter: on the transferability of adversarial examples generated with ResNets. In: ICLR (2020)
57. Wu, D., Xia, S., Wang, Y.: Adversarial weight perturbation helps robust generalization. In: NeurIPS (2020)
58. Wu, W., Su, Y., Lyu, M.R., King, I.: Improving the transferability of adversarial samples with adversarial transformations. In: CVPR, pp. 9024–9033 (2021)
59. Xiao, K.Y., Tjeng, V., Shafiullah, N.M.M., Madry, A.: Training for faster adversarial robustness verification via inducing ReLU stability. In: ICLR (2019)
60. Xie, C., Wang, J., Zhang, Z., Ren, Z., Yuille, A.L.: Mitigating adversarial effects through randomization. In: ICLR (2018)
61. Xie, C., et al.: Improving transferability of adversarial examples with input diversity. In: CVPR, pp. 2730–2739 (2019)
62. Xu, W., Evans, D., Qi, Y.: Feature squeezing: detecting adversarial examples in deep neural networks. In: NDSS (2018)
63. Yang, B., Zhang, H., Zhang, Y., Xu, K., Wang, J.: Adversarial example generation with adabelief optimizer and crop invariance. arXiv preprint arXiv:2102.03726 (2021)
64. Yuan, H., Chu, Q., Zhu, F., Zhao, R., Liu, B., Yu, N.H.: AutoMA: towards automatic model augmentation for transferable adversarial attacks. IEEE TMM (2021)
65. Zhang, H., Cissé, M., Dauphin, Y.N., Lopez-Paz, D.: mixup: Beyond empirical risk minimization. In: ICLR (2018)
66. Zhuang, J., et al.: AdaBelief optimizer: adapting stepsizes by the belief in observed gradients. In: NeurIPS (2020)
67. Zoph, B., Vasudevan, V., Shlens, J., Le, Q.V.: Learning transferable architectures for scalable image recognition. In: CVPR, pp. 8697–8710 (2018)
68. Zou, J., Pan, Z., Qiu, J., Duan, Y., Liu, X., Pan, Y.: Making adversarial examples more transferable and indistinguishable. arXiv preprint arXiv:2007.03838 (2020)

Generative Multiplane Images: Making a 2D GAN 3D-Aware

Xiaoming Zhao[1,2]($\boxtimes$), Fangchang Ma[1], David Güera[1], Zhile Ren[1], Alexander G. Schwing[2], and Alex Colburn[1]

[1] Apple, Cupertino, USA
xz23@illinois.edu
[2] University of Illinois, Urbana-Champaign, Champaign, USA
https://github.com/apple/ml-gmpi

Abstract. What is really needed to make an existing 2D GAN 3D-aware? To answer this question, we modify a classical GAN, *i.e.*, StyleGANv2, as little as possible. We find that only two modifications are absolutely necessary: 1) a multiplane image style generator branch which produces a set of alpha maps conditioned on their depth; 2) a pose-conditioned discriminator. We refer to the generated output as a 'generative multiplane image' (GMPI) and emphasize that its renderings are not only high-quality but also guaranteed to be view-consistent, which makes GMPIs different from many prior works. Importantly, the number of alpha maps can be dynamically adjusted and can differ between training and inference, alleviating memory concerns and enabling fast training of GMPIs in less than half a day at a resolution of 1024^2. Our findings are consistent across three challenging and common high-resolution datasets, including FFHQ, AFHQv2 and MetFaces.

Keywords: GANs · 3D-aware generation · Multiplane images

1 Introduction

Generative adversarial networks (GANs) [22] have been remarkably successful at sampling novel images which look 'similar' to those from a given training dataset. Notably, impressive advances have been reported in recent years which improve quality and resolution of the generated images. Most of these advances focus on the setting where the output space of the generator and the given dataset are identical and, often, these outputs are either images or occasionally 3D volumes.

The latest literature, however, has focused on generating novel outputs that differ from the available training data. This includes methods that generate 3D geometry and the corresponding texture for one class of objects, *e.g.*, faces,

---

X. Zhao—Work done as part of an internship at Apple.

Supplementary Information The online version contains supplementary material available at https://doi.org/10.1007/978-3-031-20065-6_2.

S. Avidan et al. (Eds.): ECCV 2022, LNCS 13665, pp. 18–35, 2022.
https://doi.org/10.1007/978-3-031-20065-6_2

Fig. 1. Making a 2D GAN 3D-aware with a minimal set of changes: on three datasets (FFHQ, AFHQv2 and MetFaces) we observe that it suffices to augment StyleGANv2 with an additional branch that generates alpha maps conditioned on depths, and to modify training by using a discriminator conditioned on pose.

while the given dataset only contains widely available single-view images [9, 10, 16, 50, 51, 54, 62, 63]. No multi-view images or 3D geometry are used to supervise the training of these 3D-aware GANs. To learn the 3D geometry from such a limited form of supervision, prior work typically combines 3D-aware inductive biases such as a 3D voxel grid or an implicit representation with a rendering engine [9, 10, 16, 50, 51, 54, 62, 63].

Nevertheless, improving the quality of the results of these methods remains challenging: 3D-aware inductive biases are often memory-intensive explicit or implicit 3D volumes, and/or rendering is often computationally demanding, *e.g.*, involving a two-pass importance sampling in a 3D volume and a subsequent decoding of the obtained features. Moreover, lessons learned from 2D GANs are often not directly transferable because the generator output or even its entire structure has to be adjusted. This poses the question:

"What is really needed to make an existing 2D GAN 3D-aware?"

To answer this question, we aim to modify an existing 2D GAN as little as possible. Further, we aim for an efficient inference and training procedure. As a starting point, we chose the widely used StyleGANv2 [34], which has the added benefit that many training checkpoints are publicly available.

More specifically, we develop a new generator branch for StyleGANv2 which yields a set of fronto-parallel alpha maps, in spirit similar to multiplane images (MPIs) [64]. As far as we know, we are the first to demonstrate that MPIs can be used as a scene representation for *unconditional* 3D-aware generative models. This new alpha branch is trained from scratch while the regular StyleGANv2 generator and discriminator are simultaneously fine-tuned. Combining the generated alpha maps with the single standard image output of StyleGANv2 in an end-to-end differentiable multiplane style rendering, we obtain a 3D-aware generation from different views while *guaranteeing view-consistency*. Although alpha maps have limited ability to handle occlusions, rendering is very efficient. Moreover, the number of alpha maps can be dynamically adjusted and can even differ between training and inference, alleviating memory concerns. We refer to the generated output of this method as a 'generative multiplane image' (GMPI).

To obtain alpha maps that exhibit an expected 3D structure, we find that only two adjustments of StyleGANv2 are really necessary: (a) the alpha map prediction of any plane in the MPI has to be conditioned on the plane's depth or a learnable token; (b) the discriminator has to be conditioned on camera poses. While these two adjustments seem intuitive in hindsight, it is still surprising that an alpha map with planes conditioned on their depth and use of camera pose information in the discriminator are sufficient inductive biases for 3D-awareness.

An additional inductive bias that improves the alpha maps is a 3D rendering that incorporates shading. Albeit useful, we didn't find this inductive bias to be necessary to obtain 3D-awareness. Moreover, we find that metrics designed for classic 2D GAN evaluation, *e.g.*, the Fréchet Inception Distance (FID) [28] and the Kernel Inception Distance (KID) [6] may lead to misleading results since they do not consider geometry.

In summary, our contribution is two-fold: 1) We are the first to study an MPI-like 3D-aware generative model trained with standard single-view 2D image datasets; 2) We find that conditioning the alpha planes on depth or a learnable token and the discriminator on camera pose are sufficient to make a 2D GAN 3D-aware. Other information provides improvements but is not strictly necessary. We study the aforementioned ways to encode 3D-aware inductive biases on three high-resolution datasets: FFHQ [33], AFHQv2 [12], and MetFaces [31]. Across all three datasets, as illustrated in Fig. 1, our findings are consistent.

2   Related Work and Background

In the following, we briefly review recent advances in classical and neural scene rendering, as well as the generation of 2D and 3D data with generative models. We then discuss the generation of 3D data using only 2D supervision. We also provide a brief review of single image reconstruction techniques before we review StyleGANv2 in greater detail.

Scene Rendering. Image-Based Rendering (IBR) is well-studied [11]. IBR 1) models a scene given a set of images; and 2) uses the scene model to render novel views. Methods can be grouped based on their use of scene geometry: explicit, implicit, or not using geometry. Texture-mapping methods use explicit geometry, whereas layered depth images (LDIs) [56], flow-based [11], lumigraphs [8], and tensor-based methods [4] use geometry implicitly. In contrast, light-field methods [38] do not rely on geometry. Hybrid methods [14] have also been studied. More recently, neural representations have been used in IBR, for instance, neural radiance fields (NeRFs) [44] and multiplane images (MPIs) [21,40,58,60,64]. In common to both is the goal to extract from a given set of images a volumetric representation of the observed scene. The volumetric representation in MPIs is discrete and permits fast rendering, whereas NeRFs use a continuous spatial representation.

These works differ from the proposed method in two main aspects. 1) The proposed method is unconditionally generative, *i.e.*, novel, never-before-seen scenes can be synthesized without requiring any color [60], depth, or semantic images [25]. In contrast, IBR methods and related recent advances focus on reconstructing a scene representation from a set of images. 2) The proposed method uses a collection of 'single-view images' from different scenes during training. In contrast, IBR methods use multiple viewpoints of a single scene for highly accurate reconstruction.

2D Generative Models. Generative adversarial networks (GANs) [22] and variational auto-encoders (VAEs) [35] significantly advanced modeling of probability distributions. In the early days, GANs were notably difficult to train whereas VAEs often produced blurry images. However, in the last decade, theoretical and practical understanding of these methods has significantly improved. New loss functions and other techniques have been proposed [2,3,5,13,18,19, 24,28,36,39,41–43,46,47,53,59] to improve the stability of GAN optimization and to address mode-collapse, some theoretically founded and others empirically motivated. We follow the architectural design and techniques in Style-GANv2 [34], including exponential moving average (EMA), gradient penalties [43], and minibatch standard deviation [30].

3D Generative Models from 2D Data. 3D-aware image synthesis has gained attention recently. Sparse volume representations are used to generate photorealistic images based on given geometry input [26]. Many early approaches use voxel-based representations [20,27,48,49,61,65], where scaling to higher resolutions is prohibitive due to the high memory footprint. Rendering at low-res followed by 2D CNN-based upsampling [50] has been proposed as a workaround, but it leads to view inconsistency. As an alternative, methods built on implicit functions, *e.g.*, NeRF, have been proposed [10,52,54]. However, their costly querying and sampling operations limit training efficiency and image resolutions. To generate high-resolution images, concurrently, EG3D [9], StyleNeRF [23], CIPS-

3D [63], VolumeGAN [62], and StyleSDF [51] have been developed. Our work differs primarily in the choice of scene representation: EG3D uses a hybrid tri-plane representation while the others follow a NeRF-style implicit representation. In contrast, we study an MPI-like representation. In our experience, MPIs provide extremely fast rendering speed without incurring quality degradation. Most related to our work are GRAM [16] and LiftedGAN [57]. GRAM uses a NeRF-style scene representation and learns scene-specific isosurfaces. Queries of RGB and density happen on those isosurfaces. Although isosurfaces are conceptually similar to MPIs, the queries of this NeRF-style representation are expensive, limiting the image synthesis to low resolution at 256×256. LiftedGAN reconstructs the geometry of an image by distilling intermediate representations from a fixed StyleGANv2 to a separate 3D generator which produces a depth map and a transformation map in addition to an image. Different from our proposed approach, because of the transformation map, LiftedGAN is not strictly view-consistent. Moreover, the use of a single depth-map is less flexible.

StyleGANv2 Revisited. Since our method is built on StyleGANv2, we provide some background on its architecture. StyleGANv2 generates a square 2D image $C \in \mathbb{R}^{H \times H \times 3}$ by upsampling and accumulating intermediate GAN generation results from various resolutions. Formally, the image $C \triangleq C^H$ is obtained via

$$C^h = \begin{cases} \tilde{C}^h + \mathsf{UpSample}_{\frac{h}{2} \to h}(C^{\frac{h}{2}}), & \text{if } h \in \mathcal{R} \backslash \{4\}, \\ \tilde{C}^4, & \text{if } h = 4, \end{cases} \tag{1}$$

where $C^h \in \mathbb{R}^{h \times h \times 3}$ is the GAN image generation at resolution h and $\tilde{C}^h$ is the generated residual at the same resolution. $\mathcal{R} = \{4, 8, \ldots, H\}$ is the set of available resolutions whose values are powers of 2. $\mathsf{UpSample}_{\frac{h}{2} \to h}$ refers to the operation that upsamples from $\mathbb{R}^{\frac{h}{2} \times \frac{h}{2} \times 3}$ to $\mathbb{R}^{h \times h \times 3}$. The residual generation $\tilde{C}^h$ at resolution h is generated with a single convolutional layer f^h_{ToRGB}, $i.e.$,

$$\tilde{C}^h = f^h_{\mathsf{ToRGB}}(\mathcal{F}^h), \tag{2}$$

where $\mathcal{F}^h \in \mathbb{R}^{h \times h \times \dim_h}$ is the intermediate GAN feature representation at resolution h with $\dim_h$ channels. These intermediate GAN feature representations at all resolutions $\mathcal{R}$ are computed with a synthesis network f_{Syn}, $i.e.$,

$$\{\mathcal{F}^h : h \in \mathcal{R}\} = f_{\mathsf{Syn}}(\boldsymbol{\omega}), \tag{3}$$

where $\boldsymbol{\omega}$ is the style embedding. $\boldsymbol{\omega}$ is computed via the mapping network f_{Mapping} which operates on the latent variable z, $i.e.$, $\boldsymbol{\omega} = f_{\mathsf{Mapping}}(z)$.

3   Generative Multiplane Images (GMPI)

Our goal is to adjust an existing GAN such that it generates images which are 3D-aware and view-consistent, $i.e.$, the image $I_{v_{\text{tgt}}}$ can illustrate the *exactly identical* generated object from different camera poses v_{tgt}. In order to achieve 3D-awareness and guaranteed view-consistency, different from existing prior work,

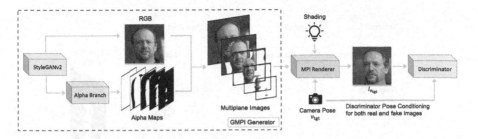

Fig. 2. Overview of the developed 3D-aware generative multiplane images (GMPI). We find that two components are necessary to make a 2D StyleGANv2 3D-aware: accompanying StyleGANv2 with an MPI branch (Sect. 3.2) and conditioning the discriminator on pose during training (Sect. 3.4). We find adding shading during training (Sect. 3.5) improves the generated geometry. Please also refer to Sect. 3.3 for details about the employed MPI rendering. Green blocks denote trainable components.

we aim to augment an existing generative adversarial network, in our case Style-GANv2, as little as possible. For this, we modify the classical generator by adding an 'alpha branch' and incorporate a simple and efficient alpha composition rendering. Specifically, the 'alpha branch' produces alpha maps of a multiplane image while the alpha composition rendering step transforms generated alpha maps and generated image into the target view $I_{v_{tgt}}$ given a user-specified pose v_{tgt}. We refer to the output of the generator and the renderer as a 'generative multiplane image' (GMPI). To achieve 3D-awareness, we also find the pose conditioning of the discriminator to be absolutely necessary. Moreover, additional miscellaneous adjustments like the use of shading help to improve results. We first discuss the generator, specifically our alpha branch (Sect. 3.2) and our rendering (Sect. 3.3). Subsequently we detail the discriminator pose conditioning (Sect. 3.4) and the miscellaneous adjustments (Sect. 3.5).

3.1   Overview

An overview of our method to generate GMPIs is shown in Fig. 2. Its generator and the subsequent alpha-composition renderer produce an image $I_{v_{tgt}}$ illustrating the generated object from a user-specified pose v_{tgt}. Images produced for different poses are guaranteed to be view-consistent. The generator and rendering achieve 3D-awareness and guaranteed view consistency in two steps. First, a novel 'alpha branch' uses intermediate representations to produce a multiplane image representation $\mathcal{M}$ which contains alpha maps at various depths in addition to a single image. Importantly, to obtain proper 3D-awareness we find that it is necessary to condition alpha maps on their depth. We discuss the architecture of this alpha branch and its use of the plane depth in Sect. 3.2. Second, to guarantee view consistency, we employ a rendering step (Sect. 3.3). It converts the representation $\mathcal{M}$ obtained from the alpha branch into the view $I_{v_{tgt}}$, which shows the generated object from a user-specified pose v_{tgt}. During training, the generated image $I_{v_{tgt}}$ is compared to real images from a single-view dataset via

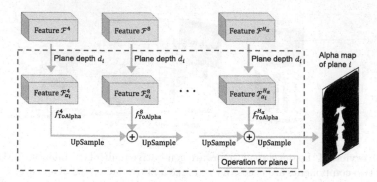

Fig. 3. The alpha branch proposed in Sect. 3.2. Here we show the generation of the alpha map of plane i. At each intermediate resolution $h \in \mathcal{R}_\alpha = \{4, 8, \ldots, H_\alpha\}$, we utilize the plane's depth d_i to transform the feature from $\mathcal{F}^h$ (Eq. (3)) to $\mathcal{F}^h_{\alpha_i}$ (Eq. (8)). The final alpha map α_i is obtained by accumulating all intermediate results, which are generated by the single convolutional layer f^h_{ToAlpha}.

a pose conditioned discriminator. We discuss the discriminator details in Sect. 3.4. Finally, in Sect. 3.5, we highlight some miscellaneous adjustments which we found to help improve 3D-awareness while not being strictly necessary.

3.2   GMPI: StyleGANv2 with an Alpha Branch

Given an input latent code z, our goal is to synthesize a multiplane image inspired representation $\mathcal{M}$ from which realistic and view-consistent 2D images can be rendered at different viewing angles. A classical multiplane image refers to a set of tuples (C_i, α_i, d_i) for L fronto-parallel planes $i \in \{1, \ldots, L\}$. Within each tuple, $C_i \in \mathbb{R}^{H \times H \times 3}$ denotes the color texture for the ith plane and is assumed to be a square image of size $H \times H$, where H is independent of the plane index i. Similarly, $\alpha_i \in [0, 1]^{H \times H \times 1}$ and $d_i \in \mathbb{R}$ denote the alpha map and the depth of the corresponding plane, i.e., its distance from a camera. $i = 1$ and $i = L$ denote the planes closest and farthest from the camera.

As a significant simplification, we choose to reuse the same color texture image $C_i \triangleq C \,\forall i$ across all planes. C is synthesized by the original StyleGANv2 structure as specified in Eq. (1). Consequently, the task of the generator f_{G} has been reduced from predicting an entire multiplane image representation to predicting a single color image and a set of alpha planes, i.e.,

$$\mathcal{M} \triangleq \{C, \{\alpha_1, \alpha_2, \ldots, \alpha_L\}\} = f_{\text{G}}(z, \{d_1, d_2, \ldots, d_L\}). \tag{4}$$

For this, we propose a simple modification of the original StyleGANv2 network by adding an additional alpha branch, as illustrated in Fig. 3. For consistency we follow StyleGANv2's design: the alpha map $\alpha_i \triangleq \alpha_i^H$ of plane i is obtained by upsampling and accumulating alpha maps at different resolutions. Notably, we do not generate all the way up to the highest resolution H, but instead use the final upsampling step

$$\alpha_i \triangleq \alpha_i^H = \text{UpSample}_{H_\alpha \to H}(\alpha_i^{H_\alpha}), \tag{5}$$

if $H_\alpha < H$. Here $H_\alpha \leq H$ refers to a possibly lower resolution. We will explain the reason for this design below. Following Eq. (1), we have

$$\alpha_i^h = \begin{cases} \tilde{\alpha}_i^h + \text{UpSample}_{\frac{h}{2} \to h}(\alpha_i^{\frac{h}{2}}), & \text{if } h \in \mathcal{R}_\alpha \backslash \{4\}, \\ \tilde{\alpha}_i^4, & \text{if } h = 4. \end{cases} \tag{6}$$

Here, $\alpha_i^h \in [0,1]^{h \times h \times 1}$ and $\tilde{\alpha}_i^h$ are the alpha map and the residual at resolution h respectively. $\mathcal{R}_\alpha \triangleq \{4, 8, \ldots, H_\alpha\} \subseteq \mathcal{R}$ denotes the set of alpha maps' intermediate resolutions. Inspired by Eq. (2), $\tilde{\alpha}_i^h$ is generated from an intermediate feature representation $\mathcal{F}_{\alpha_i}^h$ through a single convolutional layer f_{ToAlpha}^h:

$$\tilde{\alpha}_i^h = f_{\text{ToAlpha}}^h(\mathcal{F}_{\alpha_i}^h). \tag{7}$$

Note, f_{ToAlpha}^h is shared across all planes i, while the input feature $\mathcal{F}_{\alpha_i}^h$ is plane-specific. Inspired by AdaIn [29], we construct this plane-aware feature as follows:

$$\mathcal{F}_{\alpha_i}^h = \frac{\mathcal{F}^h - \mu(\mathcal{F}^h)}{\sigma(\mathcal{F}^h)} + f_{\text{Embed}}(d_i, \boldsymbol{\omega}), \tag{8}$$

where $\mu(\mathcal{F}^h) \in \mathbb{R}^{\dim_h}$ and $\sigma(\mathcal{F}^h) \in \mathbb{R}^{\dim_h}$ are mean and standard deviation of the feature $\mathcal{F}^h \in \mathbb{R}^{h \times h \times \dim_h}$ from Eq. (3). Meanwhile, f_{Embed} uses the depth d_i of plane i and the style embedding $\boldsymbol{\omega}$ from Eq. (3) to compute a plane-specific embedding in the space of $\mathbb{R}^{\dim_h}$. Note, our design of $\mathcal{F}_{\alpha_i}^h$ disentangles alpha map generation from a pre-determined number of planes as f_{ToAlpha}^h operates on each plane individually. This provides the ability to use an arbitrary number of planes which helps to reduce artifacts during inference as we will show later.

Note, the plane specific feature $\mathcal{F}_{\alpha_i}^h \forall i$ will in total occupy L times the memory used by the feature $\mathcal{F}^h$. This might be prohibitive if we were to generate these intermediate features up to a resolution of H. Therefore, we only use this feature until some lower resolution H_α in Eq. (5). We will show later that this design choice works well on real-world data.

3.3 Differentiable Rendering in GMPI

We obtain the desired image $I_{v_{\text{tgt}}}$ which illustrates the generated MPI representation $\mathcal{M} = \{C, \{\alpha_1, \ldots, \alpha_L\}\}$ from the user-specified target view v_{tgt} with an MPI renderer in two steps: 1) a warping step transforms the representation $\mathcal{M}$ from its canonical pose v_{cano} to the target pose v_{tgt}; 2) a compositing step combines the planes into the desired image $I_{v_{\text{tgt}}}$. Importantly, both steps entail easy computations which are end-to-end differentiable such that they can be included into any generator. Please see Appendix for details.

3.4   Discriminator Pose Conditioning

For the discriminator f_D to encourage 3D-awareness of the generator, we find the conditioning of the discriminator on camera poses to be essential. Formally, inspired by Miyato and Koyama [45], the final prediction of the discriminator is

$$\log P(y = \text{real}|I_{v_{\text{tgt}}}, v_{\text{tgt}}) \propto \text{Normalize}(f_{\text{Embed}}^D(v_{\text{tgt}})) \cdot f_D(I_{v_{\text{tgt}}})^\top, \qquad (9)$$

where $P(y = \text{real}|I_{v_{\text{tgt}}}, v_{\text{tgt}})$ denotes the probability that image $I_{v_{\text{tgt}}}$ from the camera pose v_{tgt} is real. $v_{\text{tgt}} \in \mathbb{R}^{16}$ denotes the flattened extrinsic matrix of the camera pose. $f_{\text{Embed}}^D : \mathbb{R}^{16} \mapsto \mathbb{R}^{16}$ denotes an embedding function, while $\text{Normalize}(\cdot)$ results in a zero-mean, unit-variance embedding. $f_D(\cdot) \in \mathbb{R}^{16}$ denotes the feature computed by the discriminator D. For real images of faces, $e.g.$, humans and cats, v_{tgt} can be estimated via off-the-shelf tools [1,17].[1]

3.5   Miscellaneous Adjustment: Shading-Guided Training

Inspired by [52], we incorporate shading into the rendering process introduced in Sect. 3.3. Conceptually, shading will amplify artifacts of the generated geometry that might be hidden by texture, encouraging the alpha branch to produce better results. To achieve this, we adjust the RGB component $C \in \mathbb{R}^{H \times W \times 3}$ via

$$\widehat{C} = C \cdot (k_a + k_d \, \boldsymbol{l} \cdot \mathsf{N}(D_{v_{\text{cano}}})), \qquad (10)$$

where k_a and k_d are coefficients for ambient and diffuse shading, $\boldsymbol{l} \in \mathbb{R}^3$ indicates lighting direction, and $\mathsf{N}(D_{v_{\text{cano}}}) \in \mathbb{R}^{H \times W \times 3}$ denotes the normal map computed from the depth map $D_{v_{\text{cano}}}$ (obtained by using the canonical alpha maps α_i, see Appendix). We find shading to slightly improve results while not being required for 3D-awareness. Implementation details are in Appendix.

3.6   Training

Model Structure. The trainable components of GMPI are f_{ToRGB}^h (Eq. (2)), f_{Syn} and f_{Mapping} (Eq. (3)), f_{ToAlpha}^h (Eq. (7)), f_{Embed} (Eq. (8)), and f_D and f_{Embed}^D (Eq. (9)). Please check the appendix for implementation details. Our alpha maps (Eq. (4)) are equally placed in the disparity (inverse depth) space during training and we set $H_\alpha = 256$ (Eq. (5)).

Initialization. For any training, we initialize weights from the officially-released StyleGANv2 checkpoints.[2] This enables a much faster training as we will show.

---

[1] Concurrently, EG3D [9] also finds that pose conditioning of the discriminator is required for their tri-plane representation to produce 3D-aware results, corroborating that this form of inductive bias is indeed necessary.

[2] https://github.com/NVlabs/stylegan2-ada-pytorch.

Loss. We use θ to subsume all trainable parameters. Our training loss consists of a non-saturating GAN loss with R1 penalties [43], *i.e.*,

$$\mathcal{L}_\theta = \mathbb{E}_{I_{v_{\mathrm{tgt}}}, v_{\mathrm{tgt}}} \left[f(\log P(y = \mathsf{real}|I_{v_{\mathrm{tgt}}}, v_{\mathrm{tgt}})) \right]$$
$$+ \mathbb{E}_{I, v_{\mathrm{tgt}}} \left[f(\log P(y = \mathsf{real}|I, v_{\mathrm{tgt}})) + \lambda |\nabla_I \log P(y = \mathsf{real}|I, v_{\mathrm{tgt}})|^2 \right]. \quad (11)$$

Here $f(x) = -\log(1 + \exp(-x))$, $\lambda = 10.0$ in all studies, I refers to real images and v_{tgt} denotes the corresponding observer's pose information.

4   Experiments

We analyze GMPI on three datasets (FFHQ, AFHQv2 and MetFaces) and across a variety of resolutions. We first provide details regarding the three datasets before discussing evaluation metrics and quantitative as well as qualitative results.

4.1   Datasets

FFHQ. The FFHQ dataset [33] consists of 70,000 high-quality images showing real-world human faces from different angles at a resolution of 1024×1024. To obtain the pose of a face we use an off-the-shelf pose estimator [17].

AFHQv2. The AFHQv2-Cats dataset [12,32] consists of 5,065 images showing faces of cats from different views at a resolution of 512×512. We augment the dataset by horizontal flips and obtain the pose of a cat's face via an off-the-shelf cat face landmark predictor [1] and OpenCV's perspective-n-point algorithm.

MetFaces. The MetFaces dataset [31] consists of 1,336 images showing high-quality faces extracted from the collection of the Metropolitan Museum of Art.[3] To augment the dataset we again use horizontal flips. To obtain the pose of a face we use an off-the-shelf pose estimator [17].

4.2   Evaluation Metrics

We follow prior work and assess the obtained results using common metrics:

2D GAN Metrics. We report Fréchet Inception Distance (FID) [28] and Kernel Inception Distance (KID) [6], computed by using 50k artificially generated images that were rendered from random poses and 1) 50k real images for FFHQ; 2) all 10,130 real images in the x-flip-augmented dataset for AFHQv2-Cat [12].

Identity Similarity (ID). Following EG3D [9], we also evaluate the level of facial identity preservation. Concretely, we first generate 1024 MPI-like representations $\mathcal{M}$. For each representation we then compute the identity cosine similarity between two views rendered from random poses using ArcFace [15,55].

---

[3] https://metmuseum.github.io/.

Table 1. Speed comparison. '–' indicates that corresponding papers do not report this result. **1) Training:** EG3D, GRAM, StyleNeRF and GMPI report training time when using 8 T V100 GPUs. pi-GAN uses two RTX 6000 GPUs or a single RTX 8000 GPU. For GMPI, the results reported in this paper come from 3/5/11-hour training for a resolution of $256^2/512^2/1024^2$ with initialization from official pretrained-checkpoints. **2) Inference:** we measure frames-per-second (FPS) for each model. GMPI uses 96 planes. GRAM reports speed by utilizing a specified mesh rasterizer [37] while the others use pure forward passes. EG3D uses an RTX 3090 GPU. GRAM and StyleNeRF use a Tesla V100 GPU, which we also utilize to run GIRAFFE, pi-GAN, LiftedGAN, and our GMPI. We observe: GMPI is quick to train and renders the fastest among all approaches.

	Res.	Unit	GIRAFFE [50]	pi-GAN [10]	LiftedGAN [57]	EG3D[9]	GRAM[16]	StyleNeRF[23]	GMPI
Train	–	Time↓	–	56h	–	8.5d	3–7d	3d	**3/5/11 h**
Inference	256^2	FPS↑	250	1.63	25	36	180	16	**328***
	512^2	FPS↑	–	0.41	–	35	–	14	**83.5***
	1024^2	FPS↑	–	0.10	–	–	–	11	**19.4***

[†] We quote results from their papers.
[*] We report the rendering speed. GMPI, different from StyleNeRF, pi-GAN, and LiftedGAN, only needs a single forward pass to generate the scene representation. Further rendering doesn't involve the generator. We hence follow EG3D to report inference FPS without forward pass time that is 82.34 ms, 99.97 ms, and 115.10 ms for 96 planes at 256^2, 512^2, and 1024^2 on a V100 GPU.

Depth Accuracy (Depth). Similar to [9,57], we also assess geometry and depth accuracy. For this we utilize a pre-trained face reconstruction model [17] to provide facial area mask and pseudo ground-truth depth map $\widehat{D}_{v_{\text{tgt}}}$. We report the MSE error between our rendered depth $D_{v_{\text{tgt}}}$ (see Appendix) and $\widehat{D}_{v_{\text{tgt}}}$ on areas constrained by the face mask. Note, following prior work, we normalize both depth maps to zero-mean and unit-variance. The result is obtained by averaging over 1024 representations $\mathcal{M}$.

Pose Accuracy (Pose). Following [9,57], we also study the 3D geometry's pose accuracy. Specifically, for each MPI, we utilize a pose predictor [17] to estimate the yaw, pitch, and roll of a rendered image. The predicted pose is then compared to the pose used for rendering via the MSE. The reported result is averaged over 1024 representations $\mathcal{M}$. Notably but in hindsight expected, 2D metrics, as well as ID, lack the ability to capture 3D errors which we will show next.

4.3 Results

We provide speed comparison in Table 1 and a quantitative evaluation in Table 2. With faster training, GMPI achieves on-par or better performance than start-of-the-art when evaluating on 256^2 images and can generate high-resolution results up to 1024^2 which most baselines fail to produce. Specifically, GMPI results on resolutions 256^2, 512^2, and 1024^2 are reported after 3/5/11-hours of training. Note, the pretrained StyleGANv2 initialization for FFHQ (see Sect. 3.6) requires training for 1d 11h (256^2), 2d 22h (512^2), and 6d 03h (1024^2) with

Table 2. Quantitative results. GMPI uses 96 planes and no truncation trick [7,33] is applied. '–' indicates that the corresponding paper does not report this result. KID is reported in KID×100. For GIRAFFE, pi-GAN, and LiftedGAN, we quote results from [9]. Compared to baselines, GMPI achieves on-par or even better performance despite much faster training as reported in Table 1. Moreover, GMPI can produce high-resolution images which most baselines fail to achieve, demonstrating the flexibility.

			FFHQ					AFHQv2-Cat	
			FID↓	KID↓	ID↑	Depth↓	Pose↓	FID↓	KID↓
256^2	1	GIRAFFE [50]	31.5	1.992	0.64	0.94	0.089	16.1	2.723
	2	pi-GAN 128^2 [10]	29.9	3.573	0.67	0.44	0.021	16.0	1.492
	3	LiftedGAN [57]	29.8	–	0.58	0.40	0.023	–	–
	4	GRAM[†] [16]	29.8	1.160	–	–	–	–	–
	5	StyleSDF[†] [51]	11.5	0.265	–	–	–	12.8*	0.447*
	6	StyleNeRF[†] [23]	8.00	0.370	–	–	–	14.0*	0.350*
	7	CIPS-3D[†] [63]	6.97	0.287	–	–	–	–	–
	8	EG3D[†] [9]	4.80	0.149	0.76	0.31	0.005	3.88	0.091
	9	**GMPI**	11.4	0.738	0.70	0.53	0.004	n/a[§]	n/a[§]
512^2	10	EG3D[†] [9]	4.70	0.132	0.77	0.39	0.005	2.77	0.041
	11	StyleNeRF[†] [23]	7.80	0.220	–	–	–	13.2*	0.360*
	12	**GMPI**	8.29	0.454	0.74	0.46	0.006	7.79	0.474
1024^2	13	CIPS-3D[†] [63]	12.3	0.774	–	–	–	–	–
	14	StyleNeRF[†] [23]	8.10	0.240	–	–	–	–	–
	15	**GMPI**	7.50	0.407	0.75	0.54	0.007	n/a[§]	n/a[§]

[†] We quote results from their papers.
* Performance is reported on the whole AFHQv2 dataset instead of only cats.
[§] No GMPI results on AFHQv2 for Row 9 and 13 since there are no available pre-trained StyleGANv2 checkpoints for AFHQv2 with a resolution of 256^2 or 1024^2.

8 T V100 GPUs respectively, as reported in the official repo (see footnote 2) In contrast, EG3D, GRAM, and StyleNeRF require training of at least three days. At a resolution of 256^2, 1) GMPI outperforms GIRAFFE, pi-GAN, LiftedGAN, and GRAM on FID/KID while outperforming StyleSDF on FID; 2) GMPI demonstrates better identity similarity (ID) than GIRAFFE, pi-GAN, and LiftedGAN; 3) GMPI outperforms GIRAFFE regarding depth; 4) GMPI performs best among all baselines on pose accuracy. Overall, GMPI demonstrates that it is a flexible architecture which achieves 3D-awareness with an affordable training time.

4.4 Ablation Studies

In order to show the effects of various design choices, we run ablation studies and selectively drop out the discriminator conditioned on pose (DPC), the plane-specific feature $\mathcal{F}^h_{\alpha_i}$, and shading. The following quantitative (Table 3) and qualitative (Fig. 4 and Fig. 5) studies were run using a resolution of 512^2 to set baseline metrics, and answer the following questions:

Baseline Condition (Table 3 row a) – a pre-trained StyleGANv2 texture without transparency ($\alpha_i \forall i$ is set to 1). This representation is not truly 3D, as it is

Table 3. Ablation studies. We evaluate at a resolution of 512^2. DPC refers to discriminator pose conditioning (Sect. 3.4), $\mathcal{F}_{\alpha_i}^h$ refers to the plane-specific feature introduced in Eq. (8), and Shading indicates the shading-guided training discussed in Sect. 3.5. #planes denotes the number of planes we used during evaluation. Note, rows (b) and (c) can only use 32 planes during training and inference. Therefore, to make the comparison fair, all ablations use 32 planes. We provide an additional 96-plane result for our full model, which is used in Table 2. Please check Sect. 4.4 and Fig. 4 for a detailed discussion regarding this table as we find that 2D metrics, *e.g.*, FID/KID as well as ID can be misleading when evaluating 3D generative models.

	#planes	DPC	$\mathcal{F}_{\alpha_i}^h$	Shading	FFHQ					AFHQv2-Cat	
					FID↓	KID↓	ID↑	Depth↓	Pose↓	FID↓	KID↓
(a)	32				6.64	0.368	**0.91**	2.043	0.060	4.29	0.199
(b)	32				4.61	0.167	0.89	2.190	0.062	4.00	0.166
(c)	32	✓			7.98	0.347	0.75	0.501	**0.006**	7.13	0.385
(d)	32		✓		**4.35**	**0.150**	0.89	2.140	0.061	3.70	0.132
(e)	32	✓	✓		7.19	0.313	0.73	0.462	**0.006**	7.54	0.433
(f)	32	✓	✓	✓	7.40	0.337	0.74	**0.457**	**0.006**	7.93	0.489
(g)	96	✓	✓	✓	8.29	0.454	0.74	**0.457**	**0.006**	7.79	0.474

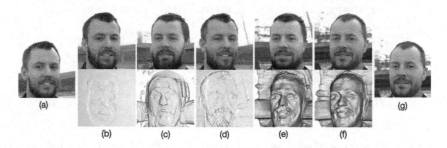

Fig. 4. The images in this figure correspond the ablation studies in Table 3. Panels (a)–(g) correspond to Table 3's rows (a)–(g). All results are generated from the same latent code z. The face is rendered with a camera positioned to the right of the subject, *i.e.*, the rendered face should look to the left of the viewer. (a) is the 2D image produced by the pre-trained StyleGANv2. Note how GMPI becomes 3D-aware in (e), and generates geometry and texture that is occluded in the pre-trained StyleGANv2 image. (e) *vs.* (f): shading-guided training (Sect. 3.5) alleviates geometric artifacts such as concavities in the forehead. (f) *vs.* (g): the ability to use more planes during inference (Sect. 3.2) reduces "stair step" artifacts, visible on the cheek and the ear.

rendered as a textured block in space. It is important to note that the commonly used metrics for 2D GAN evaluation, *i.e.*, FID, KID, as well as ID yield good results. They are hence not sensitive to 3D structure. In contrast, the depth and pose metrics do capture the lack of 3D structure in the scene.

Can a naïve MPI Generator Learn 3D? (Table 3 row b) – a generator which only uses $\mathcal{F}^h$ (Eq. (2)) without being trained with pose-conditioned discriminator, plane-specific features, or a shading loss. The Depth (2.190 *vs.* 2.043) and

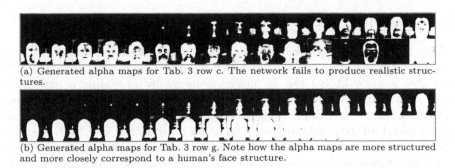

(a) Generated alpha maps for Tab. 3 row c. The network fails to produce realistic structures.

(b) Generated alpha maps for Tab. 3 row g. Note how the alpha maps are more structured and more closely correspond to a human's face structure.

Fig. 5. Qualitative results accompanying Table 3. For alpha maps, from top to bottom, left to right, we show α_1 to α_L respectively (Eq. (4)): the whiter, the denser the occupancy. Grey boundaries are added for illustration.

Pose (0.062 *vs.* 0.060) metrics show that this design fails, yielding results similar to the baseline (row a).

Does DPC Alone Enable 3D-Awareness? (Table 3 row c) – we now use discriminator pose conditioning (DPC) while ignoring plane-specific features $\mathcal{F}_{\alpha_i}^h$. This design improves the Depth (0.501 *vs.* 2.190) and Pose (0.006 *vs.* 0.062) metrics. However upon closer inspection of the alpha maps shown in Fig. 5a we observe that the generator fails to produce realistic structures. The reason that this design performs well on Depth and Pose metrics is primarily due to these two metrics only evaluating the surface while not considering the whole volume.

Does $\mathcal{F}_{\alpha_i}^h$ Alone Enable 3D-Awareness? (Table 3 row d) – we use only the plane-specific feature $\mathcal{F}_{\alpha_i}^h$ without DPC. Geometry related metrics (Depth and Pose) perform poorly, which is corroborated by Fig. 4 (d), indicating an inability to model 3D information.

Do DPC and $\mathcal{F}_{\alpha_i}^h$ Enable 3D-Awareness? (Table 3 row e) – we combine both plane-specific features $\mathcal{F}_{\alpha_i}^h$ and DPC. This produce good values for Depth and Pose metrics. Visualizations in Fig. 4e, and Fig. 5b verify that GMPI successfully generates 3D-aware content. However, the FID/KID, as well as ID values are generally worse than non-3D-aware generators (row a-e).

Does Shading Improve 3D-Awareness? (Table 3 row f) – we use plane-specific features $\mathcal{F}_{\alpha_i}^h$, DPC and shading loss. As discussed in Sect. 3.1, DPC and $\mathcal{F}_{\alpha_i}^h$ are sufficient to make a 2D GAN 3D-aware. However, inspecting the geometry reveals artifacts such as the concave forehead in Fig. 4e. Shading-guided rendering tends to alleviate these issues (Fig. 4e *vs.* f) while not harming the quantitative results (Table 3's row e *vs.* f).

Can We Reduce Aliasing Artifacts? (Table 3 row g) – we use plane-specific features $\mathcal{F}_{\alpha_i}^h$, DPC, shading loss and 96 planes. Due to the formulation of $\mathcal{F}_{\alpha_i}^h$, we can generate an arbitrary number of planes during inference, which helps avoid "stair step" artifacts that can be observed in Fig. 4f *vs.* g.

Qualitative results are shown in Fig. 1. Please see the appendix for more.

## 5	Conclusion

To identify what is really needed to make a 2D GAN 3D-aware we develop generative multiplane images (GMPIs) which *guarantee view-consistency*. GMPIs show that a StyleGANv2 can be made 3D-aware by 1) adding a multiplane image style branch which generates a set of alpha maps conditioned on their depth in addition to a single image, both of which are used for rendering via an end-to-end differentiable warping and alpha compositing; and by 2) ensuring that the discriminator is conditioned on the pose. We also identify shortcomings of classical evaluation metrics used for 2D image generation. We hope that the simplicity of GMPIs inspires future work to fix limitations such as occlusion reasoning.

Acknowledgements. We thank Eric Ryan Chan for discussion and providing processed AFHQv2-Cats dataset. Supported in part by NSF grants 1718221, 2008387, 2045586, 2106825, MRI #1725729, NIFA award 2020-67021-32799.

References

1. Cat hipsterizer (2022). https://github.com/kairess/cat_hipsterizer. Accessed 06 Mar 2022
2. Aneja, J., Schwing, A.G., Kautz, J., Vahdat, A.: A contrastive learning approach for training variational autoencoder priors. In: ICLR (2020)
3. Arjovsky, M., Chintala, S., Bottou, L.: Wasserstein GAN. ArXiv (2017)
4. Avidan, S., Shashua, A.: Novel view synthesis in tensor space. In: CVPR (1997)
5. Berthelot, D., Schumm, T., Metz, L.: BEGAN: boundary equilibrium generative adversarial networks. arXiv preprint arXiv:1703.10717 (2017)
6. Binkowski, M., Sutherland, D.J., Arbel, M., Gretton, A.: Demystifying MMD GANs. In: ICLR (2018)
7. Brock, A., Donahue, J., Simonyan, K.: Large scale GAN training for high fidelity natural image synthesis. In: ICLR (2019)
8. Buehler, C., Bosse, M., McMillan, L., Gortler, S., Cohen, M.: Unstructured lumigraph rendering. In: SIGGRAPH (2001)
9. Chan, E.R., et al.: Efficient geometry-aware 3D generative adversarial networks. In: CVPR (2022)
10. Chan, E.R., Monteiro, M., Kellnhofer, P., Wu, J., Wetzstein, G.: pi-GAN: periodic implicit generative adversarial networks for 3D-aware image synthesis. In: CVPR (2021)
11. Chen, S.E., Williams, L.: View interpolation for image synthesis. In: SIGGRAPH (1993)
12. Choi, Y., Uh, Y., Yoo, J., Ha, J.W.: StarGAN v2: diverse image synthesis for multiple domains. In: CVPR (2020)
13. Cully, R.W.A., Chang, H.J., Demiris, Y.: MAGAN: margin adaptation for generative adversarial networks. ArXiv (2017)
14. Debevec, P.E., Taylor, C.J., Malik, J.: Modeling and Rendering Architecture from Photographs: a hybrid geometry- and image-based approach. In: SIGGRAPH (1996)

15. Deng, J., Guo, J., Zafeiriou, S.: ArcFace: additive angular margin loss for deep face recognition. In: CVPR (2019)
16. Deng, Y., Yang, J., Xiang, J., Tong, X.: GRAM: generative radiance manifolds for 3D-aware image generation. In: CVPR (2022)
17. Deng, Y., Yang, J., Xu, S., Chen, D., Jia, Y., Tong, X.: Accurate 3D face reconstruction with weakly-supervised learning: from single image to image set. In: CVPRW (2019)
18. Deshpande, I., Zhang, Z., Schwing, A.G.: Generative modeling using the sliced Wasserstein distance. In: CVPR (2018)
19. Deshpande, I., et al.: Max-sliced Wasserstein distance and its use for GANs. In: CVPR (2019)
20. Gadelha, M., Maji, S., Wang, R.: 3D shape induction from 2D views of multiple objects. In: 3DV (2017)
21. Ghosh, S., Lv, Z., Matsuda, N., Xiao, L., Berkovich, A., Cossairt, O.: LiveView: dynamic target-centered MPI for view synthesis. arXiv preprint arXiv:2107.05113 (2021)
22. Goodfellow, I.J., et al.: Generative adversarial nets. In: NeurIPS (2014)
23. Gu, J., Liu, L., Wang, P., Theobalt, C.: StyleNeRF: a style-based 3D-aware generator for high-resolution image synthesis. In: ICLR (2022)
24. Gulrajani, I., Ahmed, F., Arjovsky, M., Dumoulin, V., Courville, A.: Improved training of wasserstein GANs. In: NeurIPS (2017)
25. Habtegebrial, T., Jampani, V., Gallo, O., Stricker, D.: Generative view synthesis: from single-view semantics to novel-view images. In: NeurIPS (2020)
26. Hao, Z., Mallya, A., Belongie, S., Liu, M.Y.: GANcraft: unsupervised 3D neural rendering of minecraft worlds. In: ICCV (2021)
27. Henzler, P., Mitra, N.J., Ritschel, T.: Escaping Plato's cave: 3D shape from adversarial rendering. In: ICCV (2019)
28. Heusel, M., Ramsauer, H., Unterthiner, T., Nessler, B., Hochreiter, S.: GANs trained by a two time-scale update rule converge to a local nash equilibrium. In: NeurIPS (2017)
29. Huang, X., Belongie, S.J.: Arbitrary style transfer in real-time with adaptive instance normalization. In: ICCV (2017)
30. Karras, T., Aila, T., Laine, S., Lehtinen, J.: Progressive growing of GANs for improved quality, stability, and variation. In: ICLR (2018)
31. Karras, T., Aittala, M., Hellsten, J., Laine, S., Lehtinen, J., Aila, T.: Training generative adversarial networks with limited data. In: NeurIPS (2020)
32. Karras, T., et al.: Alias-free generative adversarial networks. In: NeurIPS (2021)
33. Karras, T., Laine, S., Aila, T.: A style-based generator architecture for generative adversarial networks. In: CVPR (2019)
34. Karras, T., Laine, S., Aittala, M., Hellsten, J., Lehtinen, J., Aila, T.: Analyzing and improving the image quality of StyleGAN. In: CVPR (2020)
35. Kingma, D.P., Welling, M.: Auto-encoding variational bayes. In: ICLR (2014)
36. Kolouri, S., Rohde, G.K., Hoffman, H.: Sliced Wasserstein distance for learning gaussian mixture models. In: CVPR (2018)
37. Laine, S., Hellsten, J., Karras, T., Seol, Y., Lehtinen, J., Aila, T.: Modular primitives for high-performance differentiable rendering. TOG 39, 1–14 (2020)
38. Levoy, M., Hanrahan, P.: Light field rendering. In: SIGGRAPH (1996)
39. Li, C.L., Chang, W.C., Cheng, Y., Yang, Y., Póczos, B.: MMD GAN: towards deeper understanding of moment matching network. In: NeurIPS (2017)
40. Li, J., Feng, Z., She, Q., Ding, H., Wang, C., Lee, G.H.: MINE: towards continuous depth MPI with nerf for novel view synthesis. In: ICCV (2021)

41. Li, Y., Schwing, A.G., Wang, K.C., Zemel, R.: Dualing GANs. In: NeurIPS (2017)
42. Lin, Z., Khetan, A., Fanti, G., Oh, S.: PacGAN: the power of two samples in generative adversarial networks. In: NeurIPS (2018)
43. Mescheder, L.M., Geiger, A., Nowozin, S.: Which training methods for GANs do actually converge? In: ICML (2018)
44. Mildenhall, B., Srinivasan, P.P., Tancik, M., Barron, J.T., Ramamoorthi, R., Ng, R.: NeRF: representing scenes as neural radiance fields for view synthesis. In: Vedaldi, A., Bischof, H., Brox, T., Frahm, J.-M. (eds.) ECCV 2020. LNCS, vol. 12346, pp. 405–421. Springer, Cham (2020). https://doi.org/10.1007/978-3-030-58452-8_24
45. Miyato, T., Koyama, M.: cGANs with projection discriminator. In: ICLR (2018)
46. Mroueh, Y., Sercu, T.: Fisher GAN. In: NeurIPS (2017)
47. Mroueh, Y., Sercu, T., Goel, V.: McGan: mean and covariance feature matching GAN. ArXiv (2017)
48. Nguyen-Phuoc, T., Li, C., Theis, L., Richardt, C., Yang, Y.L.: HoloGAN: unsupervised learning of 3D representations from natural images. In: ICCV (2019)
49. Nguyen-Phuoc, T., Richardt, C., Mai, L., Yang, Y.L., Mitra, N.J.: BlockGAN: learning 3D object-aware scene representations from unlabelled images. In: NeurIPS (2020)
50. Niemeyer, M., Geiger, A.: GIRAFFE: representing scenes as compositional generative neural feature fields. In: CVPR (2021)
51. Or-El, R., Luo, X., Shan, M., Shechtman, E., Park, J.J., Kemelmacher-Shlizerman, I.: StyleSDF: high-resolution 3D-consistent image and geometry generation. In: CVPR (2022)
52. Pan, X., Xu, X., Loy, C.C., Theobalt, C., Dai, B.: A shading-guided generative implicit model for shape-accurate 3D-aware image synthesis. In: NeurIPS (2021)
53. Salimans, T., Zhang, H., Radford, A., Metaxas, D.: Improving GANs using optimal transport. In: ICLR (2018)
54. Schwarz, K., Liao, Y., Niemeyer, M., Geiger, A.: GRAF: generative radiance fields for 3D-aware image synthesis. In: NeurIPS (2020)
55. Serengil, S.I., Ozpinar, A.: LightFace: a hybrid deep face recognition framework. In: 2020 Innovations in Intelligent Systems and Applications Conference (ASYU). IEEE (2020)
56. Shade, J., Gortler, S., Hey, L.W., Szeliski, R.: Layered depth images. In: SIGGRAPH (1998)
57. Shi, Y., Aggarwal, D., Jain, A.K.: Lifting 2D StyleGAN for 3D-aware face generation. In: CVPR (2021)
58. Srinivasan, P.P., Tucker, R., Barron, J.T., Ramamoorthi, R., Ng, R., Snavely, N.: Pushing the boundaries of view extrapolation with multiplane images. In: CVPR (2019)
59. Sun, R., Fang, T., Schwing, A.G.: Towards a better global loss landscape of GANs. In: Proceedings of NeurIPS (2020)
60. Tucker, R., Snavely, N.: Single-view view synthesis with multiplane images. In: CVPR (2020)
61. Wu, J., Zhang, C., Xue, T., Freeman, W.T., Tenenbaum, J.B.: Learning a probabilistic latent space of object shapes via 3D generative-adversarial modeling. In: NeurIPS (2016)
62. Xu, Y., Peng, S., Yang, C., Shen, Y., Zhou, B.: 3D-aware image synthesis via learning structural and textural representations. In: CVPR (2022)
63. Zhou, P., Xie, L., Ni, B., Tian, Q.: CIPS-3D: a 3D-aware generator of GANs based on conditionally-independent pixel synthesis. ArXiv (2021)

64. Zhou, T., Tucker, R., Flynn, J., Fyffe, G., Snavely, N.: Stereo magnification: learning view synthesis using multiplane images. TOG (2018)
65. Zhu, J.Y., et al.: Visual object networks: Image generation with disentangled 3D representations. In: NeurIPS (2018)

AdvDO: Realistic Adversarial Attacks for Trajectory Prediction

Yulong Cao[1,2(✉)], Chaowei Xiao[2], Anima Anandkumar[2,3], Danfei Xu[2], and Marco Pavone[2,4]

[1] University of Michigan, Ann Arbor, USA
yulongc@umich.edu
[2] NVIDIA, Santa Clara, USA
[3] California Institute of Technology, Pasadena, USA
[4] Stanford University, Stanford, USA

Abstract. Trajectory prediction is essential for autonomous vehicles (AVs) to plan correct and safe driving behaviors. While many prior works aim to achieve higher prediction accuracy, few study the adversarial robustness of their methods. To bridge this gap, we propose to study the adversarial robustness of data-driven trajectory prediction systems. We devise an optimization-based adversarial attack framework that leverages a carefully-designed *differentiable dynamic model* to generate realistic adversarial trajectories. Empirically, we benchmark the adversarial robustness of state-of-the-art prediction models and show that our attack increases the prediction error for both general metrics and planning-aware metrics by more than 50% and 37%. We also show that our attack can lead an AV to drive off road or collide into other vehicles in simulation. Finally, we demonstrate how to mitigate the adversarial attacks using an adversarial training scheme (Our project website is at https://robustav.github.io/RobustPred).

Keywords: Adversarial machine learning · Trajectory prediction · Autonomous driving

1 Introduction

Trajectory forecasting is an integral part of modern autonomous vehicle (AV) systems. It allows an AV system to anticipate the future behaviors of other nearby road users and plan its actions accordingly. Recent data-driven methods have shown remarkable performances on motion forecasting benchmarks [1–7]. At the same time, for a safety-critical system like an AV, it is as essential for its components to be high-performing as it is for them to be reliable and robust. But few existing work have considered the robustness of these trajectory prediction models, especially when they are subject to deliberate adversarial attacks.

Y. Cao—This work was done during an internship at NVIDIA.

Supplementary Information The online version contains supplementary material available at https://doi.org/10.1007/978-3-031-20065-6_3.

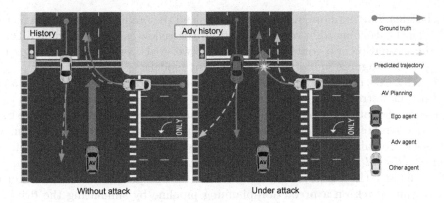

Fig. 1. An example of attack scenarios on trajectory prediction. By driving along the crafted adversarial history trajectory, the adverial agent misleads the prediction of the AV systems for both itself and the other agent. As a consequence, the AV planning based on the wrong prediction results in a collision. (Color figure online)

A typical adversarial attack framework consists of a threat model, i.e., a function that generates "realistic" adversarial samples, adversarial optimization objectives, and ways to systematically determine the influence of the attacks. However, a few key technical challenges remain in devising such a framework for attacking trajectory prediction models.

First, the threat model must synthesize adversarial trajectory samples that are 1) feasible subject to the physical constraints of the real vehicle (i.e. dynamically feasible), and 2) close to the nominal trajectories. The latter is especially important as a large alteration to the trajectory history conflates whether the change in future predictions is due to the vunerability of the prediction model or more fundamental changes to the meaning of the history. To this front, we propose an attack method that uses a carefully designed *differentiable dynamic model* to generate adversarial trajectories that are both effective and realistic. Furthermore, through a gradient-based optimization process, we can generate adversarial trajectories efficiently and customize the adversarial optimization objectives to create different safety-critical scenarios.

Second, not all trajectory prediction models react to attacks the same way. Features that are beneficial in benign settings may make a model more vulnerable to adversarial attacks. We consider two essential properties of modern prediction models: (1) motion property, which captures the influence of past agent states over future states; and (2) social property, which captures how the state of each agent affects others. Existing prediction models have proposed various architectures to explicitly models these properties either in silo [3] or jointly [4]. Specifically, we design an attack framework that accounts for the above properties. We show that our novel attack framework can exploit these design choices. As illustrated in Fig. 1, by only manipulating the history trajectory of the adversarial agent, we are able to mislead the predicted future trajectory for the adversarial agent (i.e. incorrect prediction for left turning future trajectory of red car in

Fig. 1-right). Furthermore, we are able to mislead the prediction for *other* agent's behavior (i.e. turning right to turning left for the yellow car in Fig. 1-right). During the evaluation, we could evaluate these two goals respectively. It helps us fine-grained diagnose vulnerability of different models.

Finally, existing prediction metrics such as average distance error (ADE) and final distance error (FDE) only measure errors of average cases and are thus too coarse for evaluating the effectiveness of adversarial attacks. They also ignore the influence of prediction errors in downstream planning and control pipelines in an AV stack. To this end, we incorporate various metrics with semantic meanings such as *off-road rates*, *miss rates* and *planning-aware metrics* [8] to systematically quantify the effectiveness of the attacks on prediction. We also conduct end-to-end attack on a prediction-planning pipeline by simulating the driving behavior of an AV in a close-loop manner. We demonstrate that the proposed attack can lead to both emergency brake and various of collisions of the AV.

We benchmark the adversarial robustness of state-of-the-art trajectory prediction models [3,4] on the nuScenes dataset [9]. We show that our attack can increase prediction error by 50% and 37% on general metrics and planning-aware metrics, respectively. We also show that adversarial trajectories are realistic both quantitatively and qualitatively. Furthermore, we demonstrate that the proposed attack can lead to severe consequences in simulation. Finally, we explore the mitigation methods with adversarial training using the proposed adversarial dynamic optimization method (AdvDO). We find that the model trained with the dynamic optimization increase the adversarial robustness by 54%.

2   Related Works

Trajectory Prediction. Modern trajectory prediction models are usually deep neural networks that take state histories of agents as input and generate their plausible future trajectories. Accurately forecasting multiagent behaviors requires modeling two key properties: (1) motion property, which captures the influence of past agent states over future states; (2) social property, which captures how the state of each agent affects others. Most prior works model the two properties separately [2,3,7,10,11]. For example, a representative method Trajectron++ [3] summarizes temporal and inter-agent features using a time-sequence model and a graph network, respectively. But modeling these two properties in silo ignores dependencies across time and agents. A recent work Agent-former [4] introduced a joint model that allows an agent's state at one time to directly affect another agent's state at a future time via a transformer model.

At the same time, although these design choices for modeling motion and social properties may be beneficial in benign cases, they might affect a model's performance in unexpected ways when under adversarial attacks. Hence we select these two representative models [3,4] for empirical evaluation.

Adversarial Traffic Scenarios Generation. Adversarial traffic scenario generation is to synthesize traffic scenarios that could potentially pose safety risks

[12–16]. Most prior approaches fall into two categories. The first aims to capture traffic scenarios distributions from real driving logs using generative models and sample adversarial cases from the distribution. For example, STRIVE [16] learns a latent generative model of traffic scenarios and then searches for latent codes that map to risky cases, such as imminent collisions. However, these latent codes may not correspond to real traffic scenarios. As shown in the supplementary materials, the method generates scenarios that are unlikely in the real world (e.g. driving on the wrong side of the road). Note that this is a fundamental limitation of generative methods, because almost all existing datasets only include safe scenarios, and it is hard to generate cases that are rare or non-existent in the data.

Our method falls into the second category, which is to generate adversarial cases by perturbing real traffic scenarios. The challenge is to design a suitable threat model such that the altered scenarios remain realistic. AdvSim [17] plants adversarial agents that are optimized to jeopardize the ego vehicles by causing collisions, uncomfortable driving, etc. Although AdvSim enforces the dynamic feasibility of the synthesized trajectories, it uses black-box optimization which is slow and unreliable. Our work is most similar to a very recent work [18]. However, as we will show empirically, [18] fails to generate dynamically feasible adversarial trajectories. This is because its threat model simply uses dataset statistics (e.g. speed, acceleration, heading, etc.) as the dynamic parameters, which are too coarse to be used for generating realistic trajectories. For example, the maximum acceleration in the NuScenes dataset is over 20 m/s^2 where the maximum acceleration for a top-tier sports car is only around 10 m/s^2. In contrast, our method leverages a carefully-designed differentiable dynamic model to estimate *trajectory-wise* dynamic parameters. This allows our threat model to synthesize realistic and dynamically-feasible adversarial trajectories.

Adversarial Robustness. Deep learning models are shown to be generally vulnerable to adversarial attacks [19–30]. There is a large body of literature on improving their adversarial robustness [31–44]. In the AV context, many works examine on the adversarial robustness of the perception task [45], while analyzing the adversarial robustness of trajectory forecaster [18] is rarely explored. In this work, we focus on studying the adversarial robustness in the trajectory prediction task by considering its unique properties including motion and social interaction.

3   Problem Formulation and Challenges

In this section, we introduce the trajectory prediction task and then describe the threat model and assumptions for the attack and challenges.

Trajectory Prediction Formulation. In this work, we focus on the trajectory prediction task. The goal is to model the future trajectory distribution of N agents conditioned on their history states and other environment context such as maps. More specifically, a trajectory prediction model takes a sequence of observed state for each agent at a fixed time interval Δt, and outputs the predicted future trajectory for each agent. For observed time steps $t \leq 0$, we denote states of N agents at time step t as $\mathbf{X}^t = (x_1^t, \ldots, x_i^t, \ldots, x_N^t)$, where x_i^t is the state of agent i at time step t, which includes the position and the context information. We denote the history of all agents over H *observed* time steps as $\mathbf{X} = \left(\mathbf{X}^{-H+1}, \ldots, \mathbf{X}^0 \right)$. Similarly, we denote future trajectories of all N agents over T *future* time steps as $\mathbf{Y} = \left(\mathbf{Y}^1, \ldots, \mathbf{Y}^T \right)$, where $\mathbf{Y}^t = (y_1^t, \ldots, y_N^t)$ denotes the states of N agents at a future time step t $(t > 0)$. We denote the ground truth and the predicted future trajectories as $\mathbf{Y}$ and $\hat{\mathbf{Y}}$, respectively. A trajectory prediction model $\mathcal{P}$ aims to minimize the difference between $\hat{\mathbf{Y}} = \mathcal{P}(\mathbf{X})$ and $\mathbf{Y}$. In an AV stack, trajectory prediction is executed repeatedly at a fixed time interval, usually the same as Δt. We denote L_p as the number of trajectory prediction being executed in several past consecutive time frames. Therefore, the histories at time frame $(-L_p < t \leq 0)$ are $\mathbf{X}(t) = \left(\mathbf{X}^{-H-t+1}, \ldots, \mathbf{X}^{-t} \right)$, and similarly for $\mathbf{Y}$ and $\hat{\mathbf{Y}}$.

Adversarial Attack Formulation. In this work, we focus on the setting where an adversary vehicle (adv agent) attacks the prediction module of an ego vehicle by driving along an adversarial trajectory $\mathbf{X}_{\mathrm{adv}}(\cdot)$. The trajectory prediction model predicts the future trajectories of both the adv agent and other agents. The attack goal is to mislead the predictions at each time step and subsequently make the AV plan execute unsafe driving behaviors. As illustrated in Fig. 1, by driving along a carefully crafted adversarial (history) trajectory, the trajectory prediction model predicts wrong future trajectories for both the adv agent and the other agent. The mistakes can in term lead to severe consequences such as collisions. In this work, we focus on the white-box threat model, where the adversary has access to both model parameters, history trajectories and future trajectories of all agents, to explore what a powerful adversary can do based on the Kerckhoffs's principle [46] to better motivate defense methods.

Challenges. The challenges of devising effective adversarial attacks against prediction modules are two-fold: (1) **Generating realistic adversarial trajectory**. In AV systems, history trajectories are generated by upstream tracking pipelines and are usually sparsely queried due to computational constraints. On the other hand, dynamic parameters like accelerations and curvatures are high order derivatives of position and are usually estimated by numerical differentiation requiring calculating difference between positions *within a small-time interval*. Therefore, it is difficult to estimate correct dynamic parameters from such sparsely sampled positions in the history trajectory. Without the correct dynamic parameters, it is impossible to determine whether a trajectory is realistic or not, let alone generate new trajectories. (2) **Evaluating the implications of adversarial attacks**. Most existing evaluation metrics for trajectory prediction assume benign settings and are inadequate to demonstrate the implications for AV systems under attacks. For example, a large Average Distance Error (ADE) in prediction does not directly entail concrete consequences such as collision. Therefore, we need a new evaluation pipeline to systematically determine the consequences of adversarial attacks against prediction modules to further raise the awareness of general audiences on the risk that AV systems might face.

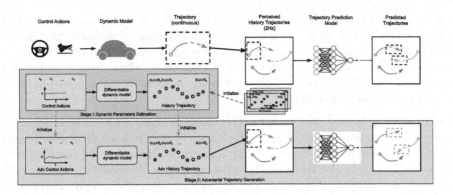

Fig. 2. Adversarial Dynamic Optimization (AdvDO) methodology overview

4   AdvDO: Adversarial Dynamic Optimization

To address the two challenges listed above, we propose **Ad**versarial **D**ynamic **O**ptimization (AdvDO). As shown in Fig. 2, given trajectory histories, AdvDO first estimates their dynamic parameters via a differentiable dynamic model. Then we use the estimated dynamic parameters to generate a realistic adversarial history trajectory given a benign trajectory by solving an adversarial optimization problem. Specifically, AdvDO consists of two stages: (1) dynamic parameters estimation, and (2) adversarial trajectory generation. In the first stage, we aim to estimate correct dynamic parameters by reconstructing a realistic dense trajectory from a sampled trajectory from the dataset. To reconstruct the dense trajectory, we leverage a differentiable dynamic model through optimization of control actions. When we get the estimated correct dynamic parameters of the trajectory, it could be used for the second stage. In the second stage, we aim to generate an adversarial trajectory that misleads future trajectory predictions given constraints. To achieve such goal, we carefully design the adversarial loss function with several regularization losses for the constraints. Then, we also extend the method to attacking consecutive predictions.

4.1   Dynamic Parameters Estimation

Differentiable Dynamic Model. A dynamic model computes the next state $s^{t+1} = \{p^{t+1}, \theta^{t+1}, v^{t+1}\}$ given current state $s^t = \{p^t, \theta^t, v^t\}$ and control actions $u^t = \{a^t, \kappa^t\}$. Here, p, θ, v, a, κ represent position, heading, speed, acceleration and curvature correspondingly. We adopt the kinematic bicycle model as the dynamic model which is commonly used [17]. We calculate the next state with a differential method, e.g., $v^{t+1} = v^t + a^t \cdot \Delta t$ where Δt denotes the time difference between two time steps. Given a sequence of control actions $u = (u^0, \ldots, u^t)$ and the initial state s^0, we denote the dynamic model as a differentiable function Φ such that it can calculate a sequence of future states

$s = (s^0, \ldots, s^t) = \Phi(s^0, u; \Delta t)$. Noticed that the dynamic model also provides a reverse function Φ^{-1} that calculate a sequence of dynamic parameters $\{\theta, v, a, \kappa\} = \Phi^{-1}(p; \Delta t)$ given a trajectory $p = (p^0, \ldots, p^t)$. This discrete system can approximate the linear system in the real world when using a sufficiently small enough Δt. It can be also demonstrated that the dynamic model approximates better using a smaller Δt.

Optimization-Based Trajectory Reconstruction. To accurately estimate the dynamic parameters $\{\theta, v, a, \kappa\}$ given a trajectory p, a small time difference Δt or a large sampling rates $f = 1/\Delta t$ is required. However, the sampling rate of the trajectory in the trajectory prediction task is decided by the AV stack, and is often small (e.g. 2 Hz for nuScenes [9]) limited by the computation performance of the hardware. Therefore, directly estimating the dynamic parameters from the sampled trajectory is not accurate, making it difficult to determine whether the adversarial history $\mathbf{X}_{adv}$ generated by perturbing the history trajectory provided by the AV system is realistic or not. To resolve this challenge, we propose to reconstruct a densely trajectory first and then estimate a more accurate dynamic parameter from the reconstructed dense trajectory. To reconstruct a densely sampled history trajectory $\mathbf{D}_i = \left(\mathbf{D}_i^{-H \cdot f + 1}, \ldots, \mathbf{D}_i^0 \right)$ from a given history trajectory $\mathbf{X}_i$ with additional sampling rates f, we need to find a realistic trajectory $\mathbf{D}_i$ that passes through positions in $\mathbf{X}_i$. We try to find it through solving an optimization problem. In order to efficiently find a realistic trajectory, we wish to optimize over the control actions in stead of the positions in $\mathbf{D}_i$. To start with, we initialize $\mathbf{D}_i$ with a simple linear interpolation of $\mathbf{X}_i$, i.e. $\mathbf{D}_i^{-t \cdot f + j} = (1 - j/f) \cdot \mathbf{X}^{-t} + j/f \cdot \mathbf{X}^{-t+1}$. We then calculate the dynamic parameters for all steps $\{\theta, v, a, \kappa\} = \Phi^{-1}(\mathbf{D}_i; \Delta t)$. Now, we can represent the reconstructed densely sampled trajectory $\mathbf{D}_i$ with $\Phi(s^0, u; \Delta t)$, where $u = \{a, \kappa\}$. To further reconstruct a realistic trajectory, we optimize over the control actions u with a carefully designed reconstruction loss function $\mathcal{L}_{\text{recon}}$. The reconstruction loss function consists of two terms. We first include a MSE (Mean Square Error) loss to enforce the reconstructed trajectory passing through the given history trajectory $\mathbf{X}_i$. We also include l_{dyn}, a regularization loss based on a soft clipping function to bound the dynamic parameters in a predefined range based on vehicle dynamics [17]. To summarize, by solving the optimization problem of:

$$\min_u \mathcal{L}_{\text{recon}}(u; s^0, \Phi) = MSE(\mathbf{D}_i, \mathbf{X}_i) + l_{\text{dyn}}(\theta, v, a, \kappa),$$

we reconstruct a densely sampled, dynamically feasible trajectory $\mathbf{D}*_i$ passing through the given history trajectory for the adversarial agent.

4.2   Adversarial Trajectory Generation

Attacking a Single-Step Prediction. To generate realistic adversarial trajectories, we first initialize the dynamic parameters of the adversarial agent with estimation from the previous stage, noted as $\mathbf{D}*_{orig}$. Similarly to the optimization in the trajectory reconstruction process, we optimize the control actions u

to generate the optimal adversarial trajectories. Our adversarial optimization objective consists of four terms. The detailed formulation for each term is in the supplementary materials. The first term l_{obj} represents the attack goal. As motion and social properties are essential and unique for trajectory prediction models. Thus, our l_{obj} has accounted for them when designed. The second term l_{col} is a commonsense objective that encourages the generated trajectories to follow some commonsense traffic rules. In this work we only consider collision avoidance [11]. The third term l_{bh} is a regularization loss based on a soft clipping function, given a clipping range of $(-\epsilon, \epsilon)$. It bounds the adversarial trajectories to be close to the original history trajectory $\mathbf{X}_{orig}$. We also include l_{dyn} to bound the dynamic parameters. The full adversarial loss is defined as:

$$\mathcal{L}_{adv} = l_{obj}(\mathbf{Y}, \hat{\mathbf{Y}}) + \alpha \cdot \sum_i l_{col}(\mathbf{D}_{adv}, \mathbf{X}) + \beta \cdot l_{bh}(\mathbf{D}_{adv}, \mathbf{D}^*_{orig}) + \gamma l_{dyn}(\mathbf{D}_{adv}),$$

where α and β are weighting factors. We then use the projected gradient descent (PGD) method [33] to find the adversarial control actions u_{adv} bounded by constraints (u_{lb}, u_{ub}) attained from vehicle dynamics.

Attacking Consecutive Predictions. To attack L_p consecutive frames of predictions, we aim to generate the adversarial trajectory of length $H + L_p$ that uniformly misleads the prediction at each time frames. To achieve this goal, we can easily extend the formulation for attacking single-step predictions to attack a sequence of predictions, which is useful for attacking a sequential decision maker such as an AV planning module. Concretely, to generate the adversarial trajectories for L_p consecutive steps of predictions formulated in Sect. 3, we aggregate the adversarial losses over these frames. The objective for attacking a length of $H + L_p$ trajectory is:

$$\sum_{t \in [-L_p, \dots 0]} \mathcal{L}_{adv}(\mathbf{X}(t), \mathbf{D}_{adv}(t), \mathbf{Y}(t)),$$

where $\mathbf{X}(t), \mathbf{D}_{adv}(t), \mathbf{Y}(t)$ are the corresponding $\mathbf{X}, \mathbf{D}_{adv}, \mathbf{Y}$ at time frame t.

5   Experiments

Our experiments seek to answer the following questions: (1) Are the current mainstream trajectory prediction systems robust against our attacks?;(2) Are our attacks more realistic compared to other methods?; (3) How do our attacks affect an AV prediction-planning system?; (4) Does features designed to model motion and/or social properties affect a model's adversarial robustness?; and (5) Could we mitigate our attack via adversarial training?

5.1   Experimental Setting

Models. We evaluate two state-of-the-art trajectory prediction models: Agent-Former and Trajectron++. As explained before, we select AgentFormer and

Trajectron++ for their representative features in modeling motion and social aspects in prediction. AgentFormer proposed a transformer-based social interaction model which allows an agent's state at one time to directly affect another agent's state at a future time. And Trajectron++ incorporates agent dynamics. Since semantic map is an optional information for these models, we prepare two versions for each model with map and without map.

Datasets. We follow the settings in [3,4] and use nuScenes dataset [9], a large-scale motion prediction dataset focusing on urban driving settings. We select history trajectory length ($H = 4$) and future trajectory length ($T = 12$) following the official recommendation. We report results on all 150 validation scenes.

Baselines. We select the search-based attack proposed by Zhang et al. [18] as the baseline, named *search*. As we mentioned earlier in Sect. 2, the original method made two mistakes: (1) incorrect estimated bound values for dynamic parameters and (2) incorrect choices of bounded dynamic parameters for generating realistic adversarial trajectories. We correct such mistakes by (1) using a set of real-world dynamic bound values [17]. and (2) bounding the curvature variable instead of heading derivatives since curvature is linear related to steering angle. We denote this attack method as *search**. For our methods, we evaluate two variations: (1) *Opt-init*, where the initial dynamics (i.e dynamics at ($t = -H$) time step) $\mathbf{D}_{adv}^{-H \cdot S+1}$ are fixed and (2) *Opt-end*, where the current dynamics ($t = 0$) $\mathbf{D}_{adv}^{0}$ are fixed. While *Opt-end* is not applicable for sequential attacks, we include *Opt-end* for understanding the attack with strict bounds, since the current position often plays an important role in trajectory prediction.

Metrics. We evaluate the attack with four metrics in the nuscenes prediction challenges: ADE/FDE, Miss Rates (MR), Off Road Rates (ORR) [9] and their correspondence with planning-awareness version: PI-ADE/PI-FDE, PI-MR, PI-ORR [8] where metric values are weighted by the sensitivity to AV planning. In addition, to compare which attack method generates the most realistic adversarial trajectories, we calculate the violation rates (VR) of the curvature bound, where VR is the ratio of the number of adversarial trajectories violating dynamics constraints over the total number of generated adversarial trajectories.

Implementation Details. For the trajectory reconstruction, we use the Adam optimizer and set the step number of optimization to 5. For the PGD-based attack, we set the step number to 30 for both AdvDO and baselines. We empirically choose $\beta = 0.1$ and $\alpha = 0.3$ for best results.

5.2 Main Results

Trajectory Prediction Under Attacks. First, we compare the effectiveness of the attack methods on prediction performances. As shown in Table 1, our proposed attack (*Opt-init*) causes the highest prediction errors across all model variants and metrics. *Opt-init* overperforms *Opt-end* by a large margin, which shows that the dynamics of the current frame play an important role in trajectory prediction systems. Note that *search* proposed by Zhang *et al.* has a significant violation rates (VR) over 10%. It further validates our previous claim that *search* generates unrealistic trajectories.

Table 1. Attack evaluation results on general metrics.

Model	Attack	ADE	FDE	MR	ORR	Violations
Agentformer w/ map	None	1.83	3.81	28.2%	4.7%	0%
	search	2.34	4.78	34.3%	6.6%	10%
	*search**	1.88	3.89	29.2%	4.8%	0%
	Opt-end	2.23	4.54	34.5%	6.3%	0%
	Opt-init	**3.39**	**5.75**	**44.0%**	**10.4%**	0%
Agentformer w/o map	None	2.20	4.82	35.0%	7.3%	0%
	search	2.66	5.53	40.3%	8.9%	9%
	*search**	2.20	4.94	35.1%	7.4%	0%
	Opt-end	2.54	5.54	39.3%	8.8%	0%
	Opt-init	**3.81**	**6.01**	**49.8%**	**13.3%**	0%
Trajectron++ w/ map	None	1.88	4.10	35.1%	7.9%	0%
	search	2.53	5.03	44.4%	9.4%	12%
	*search**	1.93	4.26	36.3%	8.3%	0%
	Opt-end	2.48	5.57	47.5%	11.3%	0%
	Opt-init	**3.20**	**8.56**	**57.2%**	**15.9%**	0%
Trajectron++ w/o map	None	2.10	5.00	41.1%	9.6%	0%
	search	2.76	8.02	50.5%	16.1%	14%
	*search**	2.17	5.25	42.2%	10.0%	0%
	Opt-end	2.49	7.54	49.5%	14.2%	0%
	Opt-init	**3.58**	**9.36**	**76.8%**	**17.8%**	0%

To further demonstrate the impact of the attacks on downstream pipelines like planning, here we report prediction performance using planning-aware metrics proposed by Ivanovic *et al.* [8]. As described above, these metrics consider how the predictions accuracy of surrounding agents behaviors impact the ego's ability to plan its future motion. Specifically, the metrics are computed from the partial derivative of the planning cost over the predictions to estimate the sensitivity of the ego vehicle's further planning. Furthermore, by aggregating weighted prediction metrics (e.g., ADE, FDE, MR, ORR) with such sensitivity measurement, we could report planning awareness metrics including (PI-ADE/FDE, PI-MR, PI-ORR) quantitatively. As shown in Table 2, results are consistent with the previous results.

Table 2. Attack evaluation results on planning-aware metrics.

Model	Attack	PI-ADE	PI-FDE	PI-MR	PI-ORR	VR
Agentformer w/ map	None	1.38	2.76	20.5%	22.8%	0%
	search	1.62	3.32	25.7%	25.2%	13%
	search*	1.39	2.79	21.4%	23.0%	0%
	Opt-end	1.57	3.11	23.7%	24.8%	0%
	Opt-init	**2.05**	**3.81**	**32.9%**	**29.0%**	0%
Agentformer w/o map	None	1.46	3.76	26.8%	30.3%	0%
	search	1.63	4.12	28.9%	34.2%	11%
	search*	1.49	3.74	27.5%	31.1%	0%
	Opt-end	1.63	4.11	28.2%	39.3%	0%
	Opt-init	**2.24**	**5.91**	**34.3%**	**41.3%**	0%
Trajectron++ w/ map	None	1.42	2.81	26.5%	25.6%	0%
	search	1.68	3.38	29.2%	28.3%	14%
	search*	1.43	2.83	26.7%	27.7%	0%
	Opt-end	1.65	3.14	27.2%	28.1%	0%
	Opt-init	**2.11**	**3.85**	**37.8%**	**32.7%**	0%
Trajectron++ w/o map	None	1.76	3.20	30.9%	44.0%	0%
	search	2.02	3.96	35.0%	49.6%	19%
	search*	1.77	3.25	31.0%	46.8%	0%
	Opt-end	1.95	3.55	31.6%	46.3%	0%
	Opt-init	**2.46**	**4.26**	**41.2%**	**53.7%**	0%

Attack Fidelity Analysis. Here, we aim to demonstrate the fidelity of the generated adversarial trajectories qualitatively and quantitatively. We show our analysis on AgentFormer with map as a case study. In Fig. 3, we visualize the adversarial tra-

Table 3. Quantitative comparison of generated adversarial trajectories

Method	*search*	*Opt-end*	*Opt-init*
ΔSensitivity	2.33	1.12	1.34

jectories generated by *search* and *Opt-end* methods. We demonstrate that our method (*Opt-end*) can generate effective attack without changing the semantic meaning of the driving behaviors. In contrast, *search* either generates unrealistic trajectories or changes the driving behaviors dramatically. For example, the middle row shows that the adversarial trajectory generated by *search* takes a near 90-degree sharp turn within a small distance range, which is dynamically feasible, whereas by our method (right image in the first row) generates smooth and realistic adversarial trajectories. More examples of generated adversarial trajectories can be found in Appendix (Table 3).

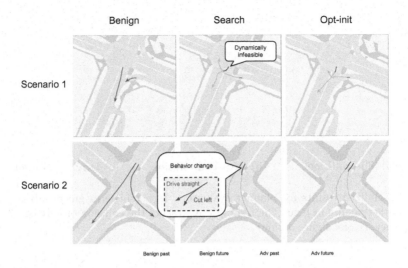

Fig. 3. Qualitative comparison of generated adversarial trajectories. We demonstrate that the proposed AdvDO generates adversarial trajectories both realist and effective whereas the search-stats could either generate dynamically infeasible trajectories (sharp turn on the first row) or changing the behavior dramatically (behavior change from driving straight to swerving left on the second row).

Table 4. Planning results

Planner	Open-loop		Closed-loop	
	Rule-based	MPC	Rule-based	MPC
Collisions	26/150	10/150	12/150	7/150
Off road	–	43/150	–	23/150

To further quantify the attack fidelity, we propose to use the sensitivity metric in [8] to measure the degree of behavior alteration caused by the adversarial attacks. The metric is to measure the influence of an agent's behavior over other agents' future trajectories. We calculate the difference of aggregated sensitivity of non-adv agents between the benign and adversarial settings. Detailed formulation is in Appendix. We demonstrate that our proposed attacks (*Opt-init*, *Opt-end*) cause smaller sensitivity changes. This corroborates our qualitative analysis that our method generates more realistic attacks at the behavior level.

Case Studies with Planners. To explicitly demonstrate the consequences of our attacks to the AV stack, we evaluate the adversarial robustness of a prediction-planning pipeline in an end-to-end manner. We select a subset of validation scenes and evaluate two planning algorithms, rule-based [16] and MPC-based [47], in two rollout settings, open-loop and closed-loop. Detailed description for the planners can be found in Appendix. In the open-loop setting, an ego vehicle generates and follows a 6-s plan without replanning. The closed-

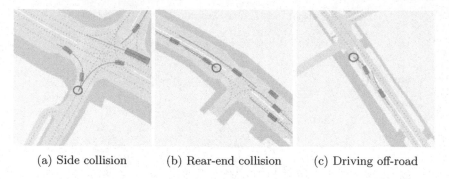

(a) Side collision   (b) Rear-end collision   (c) Driving off-road

Fig. 4. Visualized results for planner evaluation. Ego vehicle in green, adv agent in red and other agents in blue. The red cycle represents the collision or driving off-road consequence. (Color figure online)

loop setting is to replan every 0.5 s. We replay the other actors' trajectories in both cases. For the closed-loop scenario, we conduct the sequential attack using $L_p = 6$. As demonstrated in Table 4, our attacks causes the ego to collide with other vehicles and/or leave drivable regions. We visualize a few representative cases in Fig. 4. Figure 4(a) shows the attack leads to a side collision. Figure 4(b) shows the attack misleads the prediction and forces the AV to stop and leads to a rear-end collision. Note that no attack can lead the rule-based planner to leave drivable regions because it is designed to keep the ego vehicle in the middle of the lane. At the same time, we observed that attacking the rule-based planner results in more collisions since it cannot dodge head-on collisions.

Motion and Social Modeling. As mentioned in Sect. 2, trajectory prediction model aims to learn (1) the motion dynamics of each agent and (2) social interactions between agents. Here we conduct more in-depth attack analysis with respect to these two properties. For the motion property, we introduce a *Motion* metric that measures the changes of predicted future trajectory of the adversarial agent as a result of the attack. For the social property, we hope to evaluate the influence of the attack on the predictions of non-adv agents. Thus, we use a metric named *Interaction* to measure the average prediction changes among all non-adv agents. As shown in Table 5, the motion property is more prone to attack than the interaction property. This is because perturbing the adv agent's history directly impacts its future, while non-adv agents are affected only through the interaction model. We observed that our attack leads to larger *Motion* error for AgentFormer than for Trajectron++. A possible explanation is that Agent-

Table 5. Ablation results for Motion and Interaction metrics

Model	Scenarios	ADE	FDE	MR	ORR	Model	ADE	FDE	MR	ORR
AgentFormer	*Motion*	8.12	12.35	57.3%	18.6%	Trajectron++	8.75	13.27	59.6%	16.6%
	Interaction	2.03	4.21	30.3%	5.1%		1.98	4.68	43.0%	8.71%

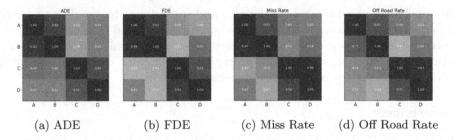

(a) ADE   (b) FDE   (c) Miss Rate   (d) Off Road Rate

Fig. 5. Transferability heatmap. A: AgentFormer w/map; B: & AgentFormer w/o map; C: Trajectron++ w/map; D: Trajectron++ & w/o map

Former enables direct interactions between past and future trajectories across all agents, making it more vunerable to attacks.

Transferability Analysis. Here we evaluate whether the adversarial examples generated by considering one model can be transferred to attack another model. We report *transfer rate* (more details in the appendix). Results are shown in Fig. 5. Cell (i, j) shows the normalized transfer rate value of adversarial examples generated against model j and evaluate on model i. We demonstrate that the generated adversarial trajectories are highly transferable (transfer rates $\geq 77\%$) when sharing the same backbone network. In addition, the generated adversarial trajectories can transfer among different backbones as well. These results show the feasibility for black-box attacks against unseen models in the real-world.

Mitigation. To mitigate the consequences of the attacks, we use the standard mitigation method, adversarial training [33], which has been shown as the most effective defense. As shown in Table C in the Appendix, we find that the adversarial trained model using the *search* attack is much worse than the adversarial trained model using our *Opt-init* attack. This can be due to unrealistic adversarial trajectories generated by the *search* attack lead to the mode failure since the performance of it on clean data are worse than the model under strong attacks. This also emphasizes that generating realistic trajectory is essential to success of improving adversarial robustness.

6 Conclusion

In this paper, we study the adversarial robustness of trajectory prediction systems. We present an attack framework to generate *realistic* adversarial trajectories via a carefully-designed differentiable dynamic model. We have shown that prediction models are generally vulnerable and certain model designs (e.g., modeling motion and social properties simultaneously) beneficial in benign settings may make a model more vulnerable to adversarial attacks. In addition, both motion (predicted future trajectory of adversarial agent) and social (predicted future trajectory of other agents) properties could be exploited by only manipulating the adversarial agent's history trajectories. We also show that prediction errors influence the downstream planning and control pipeline, leading to severe consequences such as collision. We hope our study can shed light on the importance of evaluating worst-case performance under adversarial examples and raise awareness on the types of security risks that AV systems might face, so forth encourages robust trajectory prediction algorithms.

References

1. Alahi, A., Goel, K., Ramanathan, V., Robicquet, A., Fei-Fei, L., Savarese, S.: Social LSTM: human trajectory prediction in crowded spaces. In: Proceedings of the IEEE Conference on Computer Vision and Pattern Recognition, pp. 961–971 (2016)
2. Ivanovic, B., Pavone, M.: The trajectron: probabilistic multi-agent trajectory modeling with dynamic spatiotemporal graphs. In: Proceedings of the IEEE/CVF International Conference on Computer Vision, pp. 2375–2384 (2019)
3. Salzmann, T., Ivanovic, B., Chakravarty, P., Pavone, M.: Trajectron++: dynamically-feasible trajectory forecasting with heterogeneous data. In: Vedaldi, A., Bischof, H., Brox, T., Frahm, J.-M. (eds.) ECCV 2020. LNCS, vol. 12363, pp. 683–700. Springer, Cham (2020). https://doi.org/10.1007/978-3-030-58523-5_40
4. Yuan, Y., Weng, X., Ou, Y., Kitani, K.: AgentFormer: agent-aware transformers for socio-temporal multi-agent forecasting. In: Proceedings of the IEEE/CVF International Conference on Computer Vision (ICCV) (2021)
5. Rhinehart, N., Kitani, K.M., Vernaza, P.: R2P2: a reparameterized pushforward policy for diverse, precise generative path forecasting. In: Proceedings of the European Conference on Computer Vision (ECCV), pp. 772–788 (2018)
6. Rhinehart, N., McAllister, R., Kitani, K., Levine, S.: PRECOG: prediction conditioned on goals in visual multi-agent settings. In: Proceedings of the IEEE/CVF International Conference on Computer Vision, pp. 2821–2830 (2019)
7. Kosaraju, V., Sadeghian, A., Martín-Martín, R., Reid, I., Rezatofighi, H., Savarese, S.: Social-BiGAT: multimodal trajectory forecasting using bicycle-GAN and graph attention networks. Adv. Neural Inf. Proc. Syst. **32**, 1–10 (2019)
8. Ivanovic, B., Pavone, M.: Injecting planning-awareness into prediction and detection evaluation. CoRR, abs/2110.03270 (2021)
9. Holger Caesar, et al.: nuScenes: a multimodal dataset for autonomous driving. In: Proceedings of the IEEE/CVF Conference on Computer Vision and Pattern Recognition, pp. 11621–11631 (2020)
10. N., Deo, Wolff, E., Beijbom, O.: Multimodal trajectory prediction conditioned on lane-graph traversals. In: 5th Annual Conference on Robot Learning (2021)
11. Suo, S., Regalado, S., Casas, S., Urtasun, R.: Trafficsim: learning to simulate realistic multi-agent behaviors. In: Proceedings of the IEEE/CVF Conference on Computer Vision and Pattern Recognition, pp. 10400–10409 (2021)
12. Ding, W., Chen, B., Xu, M., Zhao, D.: Learning to collide: an adaptive safety-critical scenarios generating method. In: 2020 IEEE/RSJ International Conference on Intelligent Robots and Systems (IROS), pp. 2243–2250. IEEE (2020)
13. Koren, M., Kochenderfer, M.J.: Efficient autonomy validation in simulation with adaptive stress testing. In: 2019 IEEE Intelligent Transportation Systems Conference (ITSC), pp. 4178–4183. IEEE (2019)
14. Ding, W., Chen, B., Li, B., Eun, K.J., Zhao, D.: Multimodal safety-critical scenarios generation for decision-making algorithms evaluation. IEEE Robot. Autom. Lett. **6**(2), 1551–1558 (2021)

15. Abeysirigoonawardena, Y., Shkurti, F., Dudek, G.: Generating adversarial driving scenarios in high-fidelity simulators. In: 2019 International Conference on Robotics and Automation (ICRA), pp. 8271–8277. IEEE (2019)

16. Rempe, D., Philion, J., Guibas, L.J., Fidler, S., Litany, O.: Generating useful accident-prone driving scenarios via a learned traffic prior. arXiv:2112.05077 (2021)

17. Wang, J., et al.: AdvSim: generating safety-critical scenarios for self-driving vehicles. In: Proceedings of the Conference on Computer Vision and Pattern Recognition (CVPR) (2021)

18. Zhang, Q., Hu, S., Sun, J., Chen, Q.A., Mao, Z.M.: On adversarial robustness of trajectory prediction for autonomous vehicles. CoRR, abs/2201.05057 (2022)

19. Carlini, N., et al.: On evaluating adversarial robustness. arXiv preprint arXiv:1902.06705 (2019)

20. Demontis, A., et al. Why do adversarial attacks transfer? Explaining transferability of evasion and poisoning attacks. In: 28th USENIX Security Symposium (USENIX Security 19), pp. 321–338, Santa Clara, CA, August 2019. USENIX Association

21. Carlini, N., Wagner, D.: Towards evaluating the robustness of neural networks. In: 2017 IEEE Symposium on Security and Privacy (SP), pp. 39–57. IEEE (2017)

22. Xiao, C., Li, B., Zhu, J.-Y., He, W., Liu, M., Song, D.: Generating adversarial examples with adversarial networks. arXiv preprint arXiv:1801.02610 (2018)

23. Yang, C., Kortylewski, A., Xie, C., Cao, Y., Yuille, A.: PatchAttack: a black-box texture-based attack with reinforcement learning. In: Vedaldi, A., Bischof, H., Brox, T., Frahm, J.-M. (eds.) ECCV 2020. LNCS, vol. 12371, pp. 681–698. Springer, Cham (2020). https://doi.org/10.1007/978-3-030-58574-7_41

24. Xie, C., Wang, J., Zhang, Z., Zhou, Y., Xie, L., Yuille, A.: Adversarial examples for semantic segmentation and object detection. In: International Conference on Computer Vision. IEEE (2017)

25. Huang, L., et al.: Universal physical camouflage attacks on object detectors (2019)

26. Huang, L., et al.: Universal physical camouflage attacks on object detectors. In: Proceedings of the IEEE/CVF Conference on Computer Vision and Pattern Recognition, pp. 720–729 (2020)

27. Xiang, C., Qi, C.R., Li, B.: Generating 3D adversarial point clouds. In: Proceedings of the IEEE/CVF Conference on Computer Vision and Pattern Recognition, pp. 9136–9144 (2019)

28. Wen, Y., Lin, J., Chen, K., Jia, K.: Geometry-aware generation of adversarial and cooperative point clouds (2019)

29. Hamdi, A., Rojas, S., Thabet, A., Ghanem, B.: AdvPC: transferable adversarial perturbations on 3D point clouds. In: Vedaldi, A., Bischof, H., Brox, T., Frahm, J.-M. (eds.) ECCV 2020. LNCS, vol. 12357, pp. 241–257. Springer, Cham (2020). https://doi.org/10.1007/978-3-030-58610-2_15

30. Xiao, C., Yang, D., Li, B., Deng, J., Liu, M.: MeshAdv: adversarial meshes for visual recognition. In: Proceedings of the IEEE/CVF Conference on Computer Vision and Pattern Recognition, pp. 6898–6907 (2019)

31. Noack, A., Ahern, I., Dou, D., Li, B.: An empirical study on the relation between network interpretability and adversarial robustness. SN Comput. Sci. **2**(1), 1–13 (2021). https://doi.org/10.1007/s42979-020-00390-x

32. Sarkar, A., Sarkar, A., Gali, S., Balasubramanian, V.N.: Adversarial robustness without adversarial training: a teacher-guided curriculum learning approach. Adv. Neural Inf. Proc. Syst. **34**, 12836–12848 (2021)

33. Madry, A., Makelov, A., Schmidt, L., Tsipras, D., Vladu, A.: Towards deep learning models resistant to adversarial attacks. In: International Conference on Learning Representations (2018)

34. Yang, Y., Zhang, G., Katabi, D., Xu, Z.: Me-Net: towards effective adversarial robustness with matrix estimation. arXiv preprint arXiv:1905.11971 (2019)
35. Xu, W., Evans, D., Qi, Y.: Feature squeezing: detecting adversarial examples in deep neural networks. arXiv preprint arXiv:1704.01155 (2017)
36. Bafna, M., Murtagh, J., Vyas, N.: Thwarting adversarial examples: an l_0-robustsparse fourier transform. arXiv preprint arXiv:1812.05013 (2018)
37. Papernot, N., McDaniel, P., Wu, X., Jha, S., Swami, A.: Distillation as a defense to adversarial perturbations against deep neural networks. In: 2016 IEEE Symposium on Security and Privacy (SP), pp. 582–597. IEEE (2016)
38. Meng, D., Chen, H.: Magnet: a two-pronged defense against adversarial examples. In: Proceedings of the 2017 ACM SIGSAC Conference on Computer and Communications Security, pp. 135–147 (2017)
39. Zhang, H., et al.: Towards stable and efficient training of verifiably robust neural networks. arXiv preprint arXiv:1906.06316 (2019)
40. Zhang, H., Chen, H., Xiao, C., Li, B., Boning, D.S., Hsieh, C.J.: Robust deep reinforcement learning against adversarial perturbations on observations (2020)
41. Madry, A., Makelov, A., Schmidt, L., Tsipras, D., Vladu, A.: Towards deep learning models resistant to adversarial attacks. arXiv preprint arXiv:1706.06083 (2017)
42. Goodfellow, I.J., Shlens, J., Szegedy, C.: Explaining and harnessing adversarial examples. arXiv preprint arXiv:1412.6572 (2014)
43. Wong, E., Rice, L., Kolter, J.Z.: Fast is better than free: revisiting adversarial training. arXiv preprint arXiv:2001.03994 (2020)
44. Shafahi, A., et al.: Adversarial training for free! arXiv preprint arXiv:1904.12843 (2019)
45. Xie, C., Wang, J., Zhang, Z., Zhou, Y., Xie, L., Yuille, A.: Adversarial examples for semantic segmentation and object detection. In: IEEE International Conference on Computer Vision (ICCV) (2017)
46. Shannon, C.E.: Communication theory of secrecy systems. Bell Labs Tech. J. **28**(4), 656–715 (1949)
47. Camacho, E.F., Alba, C.B.: Model Predictive Control. Springer, Heidelberg (2013)

Adversarial Contrastive Learning via Asymmetric InfoNCE

Qiying Yu[1,2]($\boxtimes$), Jieming Lou[2], Xianyuan Zhan[1], Qizhang Li[2], Wangmeng Zuo[2], Yang Liu[1,3], and Jingjing Liu[1]($\boxtimes$)

[1] Institute for AI Industry Research, Tsinghua University, Beijing, China
yuqy22@mails.tsinghua.edu.cn, jjliu@air.tsinghua.edu.cn
[2] School of Computer Science and Technology, Harbin Institute of Technology, Harbin, China
[3] Department of Computer Science and Technology, Tsinghua University, Beijing, China

Abstract. Contrastive learning (CL) has recently been applied to adversarial learning tasks. Such practice considers adversarial samples as additional positive views of an instance, and by maximizing their agreements with each other, yields better adversarial robustness. However, this mechanism can be potentially flawed, since adversarial perturbations may cause instance-level *identity confusion*, which can impede CL performance by pulling together different instances with separate identities. To address this issue, we propose to treat adversarial samples unequally when contrasted, with an asymmetric InfoNCE objective (*A-InfoNCE*) that allows discriminating considerations of adversarial samples. Specifically, adversaries are viewed as *inferior positives* that induce weaker learning signals, or as *hard negatives* exhibiting higher contrast to other negative samples. In the asymmetric fashion, the adverse impacts of conflicting objectives between CL and adversarial learning can be effectively mitigated. Experiments show that our approach consistently outperforms existing Adversarial CL methods across different finetuning schemes without additional computational cost. The proposed A-InfoNCE is also a generic form that can be readily extended to other CL methods. Code is available at https://github.com/yqy2001/A-InfoNCE.

Keywords: Adversarial contrastive learning · Robustness · Self-supervised learning

1 Introduction

Well-performed models trained on clean data can suffer miserably when exposed to simply-crafted adversarial samples [4,14,19,39]. There has been many adversarial defense mechanisms designed to boost model robustness using labeled

---

Supplementary Information The online version contains supplementary material available at https://doi.org/10.1007/978-3-031-20065-6_4.

S. Avidan et al. (Eds.): ECCV 2022, LNCS 13665, pp. 53–69, 2022.
https://doi.org/10.1007/978-3-031-20065-6_4

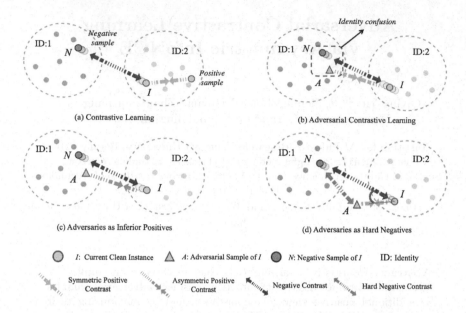

Fig. 1. Illustrations of (a) Contrastive Learning; (b) Adversarial Contrastive Learning; and our proposed methods for viewing adversarial samples asymmetrically as: (c) Inferior Positives (asymmetric contrast), and (d) Hard Negatives. In each circle, data points are augmentations of the same instance, sharing the same *Identity*. In (b), the Adversarial sample (A) shares the same Identity (*ID:2*) as the current Instance (*I*), but resides close to a different Identity (*ID:1*), thus *Identity Confusion* problem occurs. Specifically, the Adversarial sample (A) of Instance (I) exhibits similar representations to the Negative sample (N) of (I), which makes the positive contrast ($A{\leftrightarrow}I$) and negative contrast ($N{\leftrightarrow}I$) undermine each other in the training process (*colored figure*).

data [2,28,38,44,46–48]. In practice, however, obtaining large-scale annotated data can be far more difficult and costly than acquiring unlabeled data. Leveraging easily-acquired unlabeled data for adversarial learning, thus becomes particularly attractive.

Contrastive Learning (CL) [22], which performs instance discrimination [45] (Fig. 1(a)) by maximizing agreement between augmentations of the same instance in the learned latent features while minimizing the agreement between different instances, has made encouraging progress in self-supervised learning [9,11,21,23]. Due to its effectiveness in learning rich representations and competitive performance over fully-supervised methods, CL has seen a surge of research in recent years, such as positive sampling [3,9,41,42], negative sampling [13,23,27,45], pair reweighting [13,37], and different contrast methods [6,21,31].

Recently, contrastive learning has been extended to adversarial learning tasks in a self-supervised manner, leading to a new area of *adversarial contrastive learning* (Adversarial CL) [17,20,26,30]. The main idea is to generate adversarial samples as additional positives of the same instance [17,26,30] for instance-wise attack, and maximize the similarity between clean views of the instance and their adversarial counterparts as in CL, while also solving the min-max optimization problem following canonical adversarial learning objective [33,38,44,46–48]. For example, RoCL [30] first proposed an attack mechanism against contrastive loss to confuse the model on instance-level identity, in a self-supervised adversarial training framework. AdvCL [17] proposed to minimize the gap between unlabeled contrast and labeled finetuning by introducing pseudo-supervision in the pre-training stage.

Although these Adversarial CL methods showed improvement on model robustness, we observe that a direct extension from CL to adversarial learning (AL) can introduce ineffective CL updates during training. The core problem lies in that they add worst-case perturbations δ that no longer guarantee the preservation of instance-level identity [30] (*i.e.*, different from other data augmentation methods, adversarial samples can reside faraway from the current instance in the feature space after several attack iterations, because the attack objective is to make adversaries away from the current instance while approximating other instances, against the CL objective). As illustrated in Fig. 1(b), when the adversarial sample (A) of the current instance (I) are in close proximity to negative samples (N), CL objective minimizes the agreement between negative samples and current instance (I and N are pushed away from each other), while AL objective maximizes the agreement between adversarial samples and current instance (A and I are pulled together as A is considered as an augmented view of I). Meanwhile, A and N share similar representations, which renders the two objectives contradicting to each other. We term this conflict as *"identity confusion"*, it means A attracts and 'confuses' I with a false identity induced by N, which impedes both CL and AL from achieving their respective best performance.

To address this issue of *identity confusion*, we propose to treat adversarial samples unequally and discriminatingly, and design a generic asymmetric InfoNCE objective (*A-InfoNCE*), in order to model the asymmetric contrast strengths between positive/negative samples. Firstly, to mitigate the direct pull between adversarial sample (A) and current instance (I) (Fig. 1(c)) that might dampen the effectiveness of CL, we propose to treat adversarial samples as *inferior positives* that induce weaker learning signals to attract their counterparts in a lower degree when performing positive contrasts. This asymmetric consideration in AL promises a trade-off and reduces conflicting impact on the CL loss.

Secondly, to encourage adversarial samples (A) to escape from false identities induced by negative samples (N) that share similar representations to (A) (pushing A away from N) (Fig. 1(d)), we consider adversarial samples (A) as *hard negatives* [37] of other negative samples (N), by strengthening the negative contrast between A and N in CL computation. To effectively sample true adversarial negatives and re-weight each sample, we follow positive-unlabeled learning [15,16] and contrastive negatives reweighting [13,37] practice.

Our contributions are summarized as follows: 1) We propose an generic asymmetric InfoNCE loss, *A-InfoNCE*, to address the *identity confusion* problem in Adversarial CL, by viewing adversarial samples as *inferior positives* or *hard negatives*. 2) Our approach is compatible to existing Adversarial CL methods, by simply replacing standard CL loss with *A-InfoNCE*. 3) Experiments on CIFAR-10, CIFAR-100 and STL-10 show that our approach consistently outperforms existing Adversarial CL methods.

2   Asymmetric InfoNCE

2.1   Notations

Contrastive Learning (CL). CL aims to learn generalizable features by maximizing agreement between self-created positive samples while contrasting to negative samples. In typical contrastive learning, each instance x will be randomly transformed into two views (x_1, x_2), then fed into a feature encoder f with parameters θ to acquire normalized projected features, *i.e.*, $z_i = f(x_i; \theta)$. Let $\mathcal{P}(i)$ denote the set of positive views of x_i, containing the views transformed from x with the same instance-level *identity* (*e.g.*, augmentations of the original image x_i); $\mathcal{N}(i)$ denotes the set of negative views of x_i, containing all the views from other instances. The conventional InfoNCE loss function [34] used in CL for a positive pair (x_i, x_j) is defined as:

$$\mathcal{L}_{\mathrm{CL}}(x_i, x_j) = -\log \frac{\exp(\mathrm{sim}(z_i, z_j)/t)}{\exp(\mathrm{sim}(z_i, z_j)/t) + \sum_{k \in \mathcal{N}(i)} \exp(\mathrm{sim}(z_i, z_k)/t)} \quad (1)$$

where x_i serves as the anchor, $\mathrm{sim}(z_i, z_j)$ denotes a similarity metric (*e.g.*, cosine similarity) between z_i and z_j, and t is a temperature parameter. The final loss of the CL problem is averaged over all positive pairs of instances.

Adversarial CL. Adversarial CL can be regarded as an extension of CL by adding adversarial samples into the positive sets $\mathcal{P}(\cdot)$ to contrast. Adversarial CL is typically modeled as the following min-max optimization formulation to incorporate instance-wise attack [17,33]:

$$\min_{\theta} \mathbb{E}_{x \in \mathcal{X}} \max_{||\delta||_{\infty} \leq \epsilon} \sum_{i} \sum_{j \in \mathcal{P}(i)} \mathcal{L}_{\mathrm{CL}}(x_i, x_j), \quad \mathcal{P}(i) \leftarrow \mathcal{P}(i) \cup \{\hat{x}_i + \delta\} \quad (2)$$

where $\hat{x}_i$ is the view of x_i used to generate adversarial samples, δ is the adversarial perturbation whose infinity norm is constrained as less than ϵ. In the above formulation, the inner maximization problem constructs adversarial samples by maximizing the contrastive loss, and the outer minimization problem optimizes the expected worst-case loss w.r.t. the feature encoder f.

2.2 Asymmetric InfoNCE: A Generic Learning Objective

Current Adversarial CL frameworks directly inherit CL's conventional contrastive loss (*e.g.*, InfoNCE) to evaluate the similarity between adversarial and clean views in a symmetric fashion. This can result in ineffective or even conflicting updates during CL training as aforementioned. To address this challenge, we propose a generic Asymmetric InfoNCE loss (*A-InfoNCE*) to incorporate the asymmetric influences between different contrast instances, given by:

$$\mathcal{L}_{\text{CL}}^{\text{asym}}(x_i, x_j; \alpha, \lambda^p, \lambda^n) = -\log \frac{\lambda_j^p \cdot \exp(\text{sim}^\alpha(z_i, z_j)/t)}{\lambda_j^p \cdot \exp(\text{sim}^\alpha(z_i, z_j)/t) + \sum_{k \in \mathcal{N}(i)} \lambda_k^n \cdot \exp(\text{sim}^\alpha(z_i, z_k)/t)} \tag{3}$$

where $\text{sim}^\alpha(\cdot)$ is a generalized similarity metric that enables the incorporation of asymmetric relationships (a concrete instantiation is described in the next section); λ^p and λ^n are asymmetric weighting factors for positive and negative pairs, respectively. It is worth noting that although A-InfoNCE is proposed to address the *identity confusion* issue in Adversarial CL, it can be easily extended to other CL settings when the asymmetric characteristics between different views need to be captured. A-InfoNCE can also generalized to many existing CL methods, for example, $\mathcal{P}(i)$ and $\mathcal{N}(i)$ can be altered to different choices of positive and negative views; $\text{sim}^\alpha(z_i, z_j)$ is also changeable to a symmetric similarity metric for z_i and z_j. λ^p and λ^n control the weights of different positive/negative pairs. Generalization strategies are itemized below:

- If $\text{sim}^\alpha(z_i, z_j)$ is a symmetric similarity metric and $\lambda^p, \lambda^n = 1$, it degrades to the conventional InfoNCE loss used in CL [9].
- If $\mathcal{P}(i)$ is altered, it corresponds to positives sampling [3,41,42]. When we add adversaries into $\mathcal{P}(i)$, it degenerates to the conventional Adversarial CL objectives, where $\lambda^p, \lambda^n = 1$ with symmetric $\text{sim}^\alpha(z_i, z_j)$ [17,26,30].
- If we seek better $\mathcal{N}(i)$, it echos negative sampling methods [27,37] such as Moco [23], which maintains a queue of consistent negatives; or mimics DCL [13] that debiases $\mathcal{N}(i)$ into true negatives.
- If we change λ^p and λ^n, it mirrors the pair reweighting works [13,37] that assign different weights to each pair according to a heuristic measure of importance such as similarity.

While most existing methods adopt a symmetric similarity metric, we claim that in some scenarios the asymmetric similarity perspective needs to be taken into account, especially when the quality and property of different views vary significantly. In this paper, we focus on the study of Adversarial CL, and demonstrate the benefits of capturing the asymmetric relationships between adversaries and clean views. Specifically, we design two instantiations to model the asymmetric relationships between adversarial and clean samples, as detailed in next section. Both instantiations can be integrated into the proposed *A-InfoNCE* framework.

3 Adversarial Asymmetric Contrastive Learning

This section explains the instantiations of the *A-InfoNCE* loss for Adversarial CL. From the *inferior-positive* perspective, to reduce the impact of identity confusion, we first design a new asymmetric similarity metric $\text{sim}^\alpha(z_i, z_j^{adv})$ for modeling the asymmetric relationships and weakening the learning signals from adversarial examples. From the *hard-negative* perspective, we view adversaries as hard negatives for other negative samples, and reweight each negative pairs by assigning similarity-dependent weights to ease the identity confusion.

3.1 Adversarial Samples as Inferior Positives

Adversarial samples with different identities may attract their anchors (clean samples) in a contradicting manner to the exertion of CL. By weakening the learning signal from these adversarial examples in positive contrast (as *inferior positives* that attract the anchors less), we can effectively mitigate the undesired pull from clean samples via an adaptive gradient stopping strategy.

Asymmetric Similarity Function. As the symmetric nature of InfoNCE can bring conflicts in Adversarial CL, we design a new asymmetric similarity function $\text{sim}^\alpha(z_i, z_j)$ for *A-InfoNCE*, by manipulating the scale of gradient for each contrasted branch. We decompose it into two parts for each branch:

$$\text{sim}^\alpha(z_i, z_j) = \alpha \cdot \overline{\text{sim}}(z_i, z_j) + (1 - \alpha) \cdot \overline{\text{sim}}(z_j, z_i) \tag{4}$$

where $\overline{\text{sim}}(a, b)$ means the one-sided similarity of a to b, *i.e.*, when maximizing $\overline{\text{sim}}(a, b)$, we freeze b and only move a towards b. This can be implemented by stopping the gradient back-propagation for b and only optimizing a.

We use a hyperparameter α to control how much z_i and z_j head towards each other. For a clean sample and an adversarial sample, we let α denote the coefficient of the clean branch's movement. If α is 0, it performs total gradient freezing on the clean branch and only adversarial representations are optimized through training. Our empirical analysis finds that α is relatively easy to tune for boosted performance. We show that any value lower than 0.5 brings reasonable performance boost (see Fig. 2), when clean samples move less towards adversaries, following the intrinsic asymmetric property of Adversarial CL.

Adaptive α-Annealing. When the *identity confusion* is at play, it is necessary to treat adversarial samples inferior to ensure model robustness. But as training progresses, when model learns robust representations and the negative identity-changing impact of adversarial perturbation wanes, we consider adversarial perturbation as strong augmentations, equal to other typical transformations [9].

The question is how to measure the reduction of instance confusion effect. Here we take a geometry perspective and propose to adaptively tune the proportional coefficient α on-the-fly based on Euclidean distance. Let $d_{i,j} = ||z_i - z_j||_2$ denote the distance between an original image and its adversarial view in the representation space. Given α_{min}, d_{max}, α_{max}, d_{min}, the goal is for α to be α_{max} when the distance approximates d_{min}, and α_{min} to be close to d_{max}. During training, we first compute the current representation distance d, then use a simple linear annealing strategy to compute α:

$$\alpha = \alpha_{min} + (d_{max} - d)\frac{\alpha_{max} - \alpha_{min}}{d_{max} - d_{min}} \tag{5}$$

d_{min} and α_{min} can be treated as hyperparameters. α_{max} is 0.5, indicating adversarial perturbation is equal to other transformations and $\text{sim}^{\alpha}(z_i, z_j)$ degrades to the symmetric similarity. Moreover, we use the first N epochs as a warm-up to compute the average distance as d_{max}, in which period α is fixed.

Adversarial CL Loss with Inferior Positives. With the above asymmetric similarity function $\text{sim}^{\alpha}(\cdot)$ and the *A-InfoNCE* loss function $\mathcal{L}_{\text{CL}}^{\text{asym}}(x_i, x_j; \alpha, \lambda^p, \lambda^n)$, the complete Adversarial CL loss with *inferior positives* (IP) can be written as:

$$\mathcal{L}^{\text{IP}} = \sum_i \sum_{j \in \mathcal{P}(i)} \mathcal{L}_{\text{CL}}^{\text{asym}}(x_i, x_j; 0.5, 1, 1) + \gamma \cdot \sum_i \sum_{j \in \mathcal{P}(i)} \mathcal{L}_{\text{CL}}^{\text{asym}}(x_i, x_j^{adv}; \alpha, 1, 1) \tag{6}$$

where the first part stands for standard CL loss that maximizes the similarity between two clean views, which is symmetric ($\alpha = 0.5$) with $\lambda^p = \lambda^n = 1$, degrading to the conventional InfoNCE loss. The second part is a robust CL loss that maximizes the agreement between clean and adversarial views, but uses the asymmetric similarity function (4) with a hyperparameter α that gives weaker learning signals to the counterparts of inferior adversarial samples. The hyperparameter γ balances the robustness and accuracy objectives.

3.2 Adversarial Samples as Hard Negatives

Besides inferior positives, we also propose an alternative view of adversaries as *hard negatives* [37] that be pushed away from surrounding data points with higher weights. This can potentially assuage the confusion brought by adversarial samples of the current instance residing too close to the negative samples of the same instance (as illustrated in Fig. 1(d)). Furthermore, this strategy encourages the model towards more robustness-aware, by giving adversarial samples possessing undiscriminating features higher weights in the pretraining stage, further enhancing Adversarial CL.

In practice, we assign a weight of similarity to each pair. To set a basis for weight assigning, we adopt a simple and adaptive weighting strategy used in [37], i.e., taking each pair's similarity as its weight, with $w_{i,j} = \exp(\text{sim}(z_i, z_j)/t)$. By doing so, the adversaries with bad instance-level identity (greater similarity to negative samples) can be automatically assigned with higher weights. The weights can adaptively decay as the instance identity recovers during training.

However, as the commonly-used $\mathcal{N}(i)$ is uniformly sampled from the entire data distribution $p(x)$ [13] (*e.g.*, SimCLR [9] uses other instances in the current batch as negative samples), simply taking similarities as weights may heavily repel semantically-similar instances whose embeddings should be close. To estimate the true negatives distribution $p^-(x)$, we take advantage of PU-learning [15,16] and resort to DCL, HCL [13,37] to debias negative sampling.

PU-learning [15] decomposes the data distribution as: $p(x) = \tau p^+(x) + (1 - \tau)p^-(x)$, where $p^+(x), p^-(x)$ denote the distribution of data from the same or different class of x, and τ is the class prior. Thus $p^-(x)$ can be rearranged as $p^-(x) = (p(x) - \tau p^+(x))/(1 - \tau)$. We can use all instances and positive augmentations containing adversarial samples of x to estimate $p(x)$ and $p^+(x)$, respectively. Following [13], we debias the negative contrast part in (3) as:

$$\frac{1}{1-\tau}\Big(\sum_{k\in\mathcal{N}(i)} w_{i,k}^n \cdot \exp(\mathrm{sim}^\alpha(z_i, z_k)/t) - \frac{N}{M}\cdot\tau \sum_{j\in\mathcal{P}(i)} w_{i,j}^p \cdot \exp(\mathrm{sim}^\alpha(z_i, z_j)/t)\Big)$$

$$(7)$$

where M, N are the numbers of postives and negatives, $w_{i,k}^n$ is the aforementioned weights for negatives, $w_{i,j}^p$ is a expandable weight for positives (set as 1 in our implementation, other choices can be further explored in the future work).

Adversarial CL Loss with Hard Negatives. We substitute (7) into the *A-InfoNCE* loss function (3) and rearrange it, acquiring the instantiation of *A-InfoNCE* loss with *hard negatives* (HN), with concrete forms of λ^p and λ^n as:

$$\mathcal{L}^{HN} = \sum_i \sum_{j\in\mathcal{P}(i)} \mathcal{L}_{\mathrm{CL}}^{\mathrm{asym}}(x_i, x_j; \alpha, \frac{M - (M+N)\tau}{M - M\tau} w_{i,j}^p, \frac{1}{1-\tau} w_{i,k}^n), \quad k\in\mathcal{N}(i)$$

$$(8)$$

Due to the lack of class information, we treat τ as a hyperparameter and set as [13] suggested.

Combined Adversarial CL Loss. Finally, we can view adversaries both as inferior positives and hard negatives for other negative samples. This leads to following combined Adversarial CL loss:

$$\mathcal{L}^{IP+HN} = \sum_i \sum_{j\in\mathcal{P}(i)} \mathcal{L}_{\mathrm{CL}}^{\mathrm{asym}}(x_i, x_j; 0.5, \frac{M - (M+N)\tau}{M - M\tau} w_{i,j}^p, \frac{1}{1-\tau} w_{i,k}^n)$$

$$+ \gamma \cdot \sum_i \sum_{j\in\mathcal{P}(i)} \mathcal{L}_{\mathrm{CL}}^{\mathrm{asym}}(x_i, x_j^{adv}; \alpha, \frac{M - (M+N)\tau}{M - M\tau} w_{i,j}^p, \frac{1}{1-\tau} w_{i,k}^n), \quad k\in\mathcal{N}(i)$$

$$(9)$$

4   Experiments

To demonstrate the effectiveness and generalizability of the proposed approach, we present experimental results across different datasets and model training

Table 1. Results for replacing the objectives of the two baselines with $\mathcal{L}^{IP}$, $\mathcal{L}^{HN}$ and $\mathcal{L}^{IP+HN}$, in Standard Accuracy (SA) and Robust Accuracy (RA). The pre-trained methods are evaluated under the Linear Probing (LP), Adversarial Linear Finetuning (ALF) and Adversarial Full Finetuning (AFF) strategies. Supervised methods are trained under conventional adversarial training scheme.

Dataset	Pre-training methods		Finetuning strategies						
			Linear probing		Adversarial linear finetuning		Adversarial full finetuning		
			SA	RA	SA	RA	SA	RA	
CIFAR 10	Supervised	AT [33]	–	–	–	–	78.99	47.41	1
		TRADES [47]	–	–	–	–	81.00	53.27	2
	Self-supervised	RoCL [30]	83.84	38.98	79.23	47.82	77.83	50.54	3
		w/$\mathcal{L}^{IP}$	**87.63**	41.46	**84.15**	50.08	78.97	50.29	4
		w/$\mathcal{L}^{HN}$	84.14	40.00	79.40	48.31	78.84	51.73	5
		w/$\mathcal{L}^{IP+HN}$	85.69	**42.96**	81.91	**50.90**	**80.06**	**52.95**	6
		AdvCL [17]	81.35	51.00	79.24	52.38	83.67	53.35	7
		w/$\mathcal{L}^{IP}$	82.37	52.33	80.05	**53.22**	**84.12**	53.56	8
		w/$\mathcal{L}^{HN}$	81.34	52.61	78.69	53.20	83.44	**54.07**	9
		w/$\mathcal{L}^{IP+HN}$	**83.15**	**52.65**	**80.41**	53.19	83.93	53.74	10
CIFAR 100	Supervised	AT [33]	–	–	–	–	49.49	23.00	11
		TRADES [47]	–	–	–	–	54.59	28.43	12
	Self-supervised	RoCL [30]	55.71	18.49	49.30	25.84	51.19	26.69	13
		w/$\mathcal{L}^{IP}$	59.30	21.34	54.49	**30.33**	52.39	27.84	14
		w/$\mathcal{L}^{HN}$	58.77	21.17	56.38	28.03	**55.85**	29.57	15
		w/$\mathcal{L}^{IP+HN}$	**59.74**	**22.54**	**57.57**	29.22	55.79	**29.92**	16
		AdvCL [17]	47.98	27.99	**47.45**	28.29	57.87	29.48	17
		w/$\mathcal{L}^{IP}$	49.48	28.84	45.39	28.40	**59.44**	30.49	18
		w/$\mathcal{L}^{HN}$	49.44	29.01	47.32	**28.69**	58.41	29.93	19
		w/$\mathcal{L}^{IP+HN}$	**50.59**	**29.12**	45.72	28.45	58.70	**30.66**	20

strategies. Our methods are compatible with existing Adversarial CL frameworks, and can be easily incorporated by replacing their CL loss. We choose two baselines and replace their loss with $\mathcal{L}^{IP}$ (in Eq. 6), $\mathcal{L}^{HN}$ (8) and $\mathcal{L}^{IP+HN}$ (9) for evaluation.

Datasets. We mainly use CIFAR-10 and CIFAR-100 for our experiments. Each dataset has 50,000 images for training and 10,000 for test. STL-10 is also used for transferability experiments. Following previous work [17], we use ResNet-18 [24] as the encoder architecture in all experiments.

Baselines. We compare with two baselines: RoCL [30], the first method to combine CL and AL; and AdvCL [17], the current state-of-the-art framework. During experiments, we observe severe overfitting of AdvCL when training 1000 epochs (experiment setting in the original paper), with performance inferior to training for 400 epochs. Thus, we pre-train 400 epochs on AdvCL at its best-performance setting. All other settings are the same as original papers except for some hyperparameter tuning. Our methods are also compatible with some recent work like SwARo [43] and CLAF [36], by modeling the asymmetry between clean and adversarial views as aforementioned.

Table 2. Transferring results from CIFAR-10/100 to STL-10, compared with AdvCL [17], evaluated in Standard accuracy (SA) and Robust accuracy (RA) across different finetuning methods with ResNet-18.

Dataset	Pre-training methods	Finetuning strategies					
		Linear probing		Adversarial linear finetuning		Adversarial full finetuning	
		SA	RA	SA	RA	SA	RA
CIFAR10 ↓ STL10	AdvCL [17]	64.45	37.25	60.86	38.84	67.89	38.78
	w/$\mathcal{L}^{IP}$	64.83	37.30	61.95	38.90	**68.25**	39.03
	w/$\mathcal{L}^{HN}$	65.24	**38.18**	**62.83**	**39.70**	67.88	**39.75**
	w/$\mathcal{L}^{IP+HN}$	**67.19**	37.00	61.34	39.35	67.95	39.12
CIFAR100 ↓ STL10	AdvCL [17]	52.28	30.01	49.84	32.14	63.13	35.24
	w/$\mathcal{L}^{IP}$	52.65	**31.33**	50.18	33.15	63.26	**35.34**
	w/$\mathcal{L}^{HN}$	51.88	31.29	**50.73**	**33.62**	62.91	34.88
	w/$\mathcal{L}^{IP+HN}$	**53.41**	31.30	51.10	33.23	**63.69**	35.09

Evaluation. Following [26] and [17], we adopt three finetuning strategies to evaluate the effectiveness of contrastive pre-training: 1) Linear Probing (LP): fix the encoder and train the linear classifier; 2) Adversarial Linear Finetuning (ALF): adversarially train the linear classifier; 3) Adversarial Full Finetuning (AFF): adversarially train the full model. We consider two evaluation metrics: 1) Standard Accuracy (SA): classification accuracy over clean images; 2) Robust Accuracy (RA): classification accuracy over adversaries via PGD-20 attacks [33]. Robustness evaluation under more diverse attacks is provided in the appendix.

4.1 Main Results

In Table 1, we report standard accuracy and robust accuracy of each model, learned by different pre-training methods over CIFAR-10 and CIFAR-100. Following previous works [17,26,30] and common practice in contrastive learning [9,23], we first use unlabeled images in CIFAR-10/-100 to pre-train, then introduce labels to finetune the model. As shown in Table 1, our methods achieve noticeable performance improvement over baselines in almost all scenarios, when replacing the original loss with our proposed adversarial CL loss.

In comparison with RoCL, $\mathcal{L}^{IP}$ brings significant performance boost on both standard and robust accuracy consistently across different training methods (row 4 vs. 3, row 14 vs. 13) (except for RA of AFF on CIFAR10). Comparing to AdvCL, $\mathcal{L}^{IP}$ also brings noticeable margin (row 8 vs. 7, row 18 vs. 17). This can be attributed to that $\mathcal{L}^{IP}$ aims to lower the priority of adversaries and prevent clean samples moving towards other instances, which results in better instance discrimination and improves clean [45] and robust accuracy. $\mathcal{L}^{HN}$ also yields substantial boost on robust and standard accuracy (*e.g.*, row 15 vs. 13). We hypothesize this is due to that $\mathcal{L}^{HN}$ helps alert the model to adversarial samples by assigning higher weights for adversaries in negative contrast. When combined together, in most settings both standard and robust accuracy are further boosted, especially for Linear Probing. This is because directly mitigating the negative impact of *identity confusion* by $\mathcal{L}^{IP}$ and helping adversarial get rid of false identities by $\mathcal{L}^{HN}$ can complement each other, bringing further performance boost.

4.2 Transferring Robust Features

Learning robust features that are transferable is a main goal in self-supervised adversarial learning. It is of great significance if models pre-trained with a huge amount of unlabeled data possess good transferability by merely light-weight finetuning. For example, Linear Probing is often 10× quicker than conventional adversarial training, with only a linear classifier trained.

Here we evaluate the robust transferability of the proposed approach, by transfering CIFAR-10 and CIFAR-100 to STL-10, *i.e.*, use unlabeled images in CIFAR-10/-100 to pretrain, then use STL-10 to finetune and evaluate the learned models. As shown in Table 2, our methods yield both clean and robust accuracy gains in most settings, up to 1.48% (33.62% vs. 32.14%) in robust accuracy and 2.74% (67.19% vs. 64.45%) in clean accuracy.

4.3 Ablation Studies

We design a basic adversarial contrastive model, named CoreACL, to study the effect of each component in our proposed methods. CoreACL only contains the contrastive component with three positive views: two clean augmented views and one adversarial view of the original image.

Fixed α for Asymmetric Similarity Function. We first use fixed α without adaptive annealing to explore the effectiveness of *inferior positives*. Figure 2 presents the results with different α values when training models for 200 epochs. Recall that α represents the tendency of the clean sample heading towards the adversarial sample. $\alpha < 0.5$ means clean samples move less toward the adversaries (vice versa for $\alpha >$

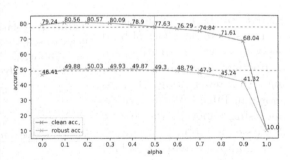

Fig. 2. Deep probing for asymmetric similarity function with different α.

0.5), and $\alpha = 0.5$ degenerates to the original symmetric similarity function form.

Compared with symmetric CoreACL ($\alpha = 0.5$), our approach achieves better robustness and accuracy when $\alpha < 0.5$ (adversarial examples are treated as *inferior positives*). Intriguingly, when $\alpha = 1.0$, the extreme case when only clean samples are attracted by adversaries, we observe the presence of a trivial solution [12], that is all images collapse into one point. This validates our observation that adversaries with false identities are indeed pulling their positives towards other instances in the positive contrasts, with the risk of drawing all samples together. It is also worth noting that when $\alpha < 0.2$, performance begins to drop, showing that a small but non-zero α is the optimal setting empirically.

Fixed α vs. α-Annealing. As shown in Table 3, compared to CoreACL, fixed α obtains higher clean accuracy (81.29% vs. 78.90%) but with no gain on robust accuracy. Adaptive annealing α achieves both higher robust accuracy (50.24% vs. 51.27%) and better clean accuracy (79.46% vs. 78.90%).

Comparison with AdvCL. Table 3 reports the performance and computation cost comparisons with AdvCL. CoreACL with $\mathcal{L}^{IP+HN}$ achieves similar performance to AdvCL, which is equivalent to integrate additional components (high frequency view and pseudo-supervision) into CoreACL. The computation time of AdvCL is almost twice than that of w/$\mathcal{L}^{IP+HN}$,

Table 3. Ablation studies, evaluated in SA, RA and time cost. Trained for 400 epochs on 2 Tesla V100 GPUs.

Methods	SA	RA	Time cost (s/epoch)
CoreACL	78.90	50.27	96
w/fixed α	81.29	50.24	96
w/annealing α	79.46	51.37	101
w/$\mathcal{L}^{IP+HN}$	81.19	51.31	101
AdvCL	81.35	51.00	182

which could due to extra computation on contrasting high frequency views and the pseudo-labeled adversarial training. Our methods only need to compute pair-wise Euclidean distance for α-annealing in $\mathcal{L}^{IP}$, and no extra cost introduced in $\mathcal{L}^{HN}$.

Effect of Hard Negatives. To investigate the effect of hard negatives, we evaluate each component (negatives debiasing [13], reweighting [37]) as shown in Table 4. With negatives-debiasing removed, we observe decrease in robust accuracy, with slightly increased standard

Table 4. Ablation studies for AdvCL with hard negatives (AdvCL-HN), evaluated under Linear Probing (LP), Adversarial Linear Finetuning (ALF) and Adversarial Full Finetuning (AFF).

Methods	LP		ALF		AFF	
	SA	RA	SA	RA	SA	RA
AdvCL-HN	81.34	**52.96**	78.69	**53.20**	83.44	**54.07**
w/o debias	**81.52**	51.61	**78.89**	52.34	**83.73**	54.01
cre w/o reweight	76.93	50.01	73.49	49.86	81.74	52.60

accuracy. We hypothesize that without debiasing, semantically similar adversarial representations that should be mapped closely are pushed away instead. In addition, the removal of negatives reweighting results in a sharp performance drop, showing that viewing adversarial views as *hard negatives* with higher weights plays a key role in discriminating adversarial samples.

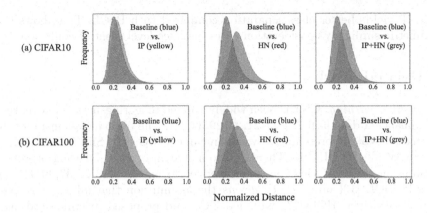

Fig. 3. Histograms of Euclidean distance (normalized) distribution of all negative pairs learned by different objectives in (a) CIFAR10 (first row) and (b) CIFAR100 (second row). Baseline is AdvCL [17]; IP: baseline with Inferior Positives; HN: baseline with Hard Negatives. On each dataset, our methods are better at differentiating different instances (with larger distance between negative pairs).

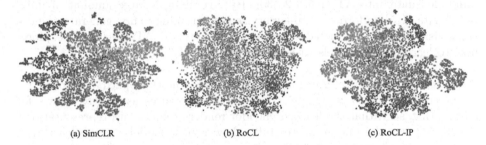

Fig. 4. t-SNE visualizations in a global view on CIFAR-10 validation set. The embeddings are learned by different self-supervised pre-training methods (SimCLR(a), RoCL(b) and RoCL-IP(c)) (*colored figure*).

4.4 Qualitative Analysis

Figure 3 shows the distribution of normalized Euclidean distance over all negative pairs. We take AdvCL [17] as the baseline and compare it with its enhanced versions with our methods. Generally, our methods can shift the original distribution curve right (larger distance), meaning that treating adversaries as inferior positives or hard negatives encourages the model to separate negative pairs further apart and induce better instance discrimination. This suggests that our proposed methods effectively mitigate the negative impacts of *identity confusion*.

Figure 4 provides 2-D visualization (t-SNE [32] on CIFAR-10) for the embeddings learnt by SimCLR [9], RoCL [30] and RoCL enhanced by $\mathcal{L}^{IP}$ (RoCL-IP). Each class is represented in one color. Compared to SimCLR, RoCL representations are corrupted by adversaries and exhibit poor class discrimination.

RoCL-IP yields better class separation compared with RoCL. This shows that asymmetric similarity consideration eases instance-level identity confusion.

5 Related Work

Contrastive Learning. CL has been widely applied to learn generalizable features from unlabeled data [3,6,7,9–11,21,23,29,34,41]. The basic idea is instance discrimination [45]. Representative works include CMC [41], SimCLR [9], MoCo [23], SwAV [6], BYOL [21]. There is also a stream of work focusing on refined sampling on different views for improved performance [13,27,37,40,41]. For example, DCL [13] proposed to *debias* the assumption that all negative pairs are true negatives. HCL [37] extended DCL and proposed to mine hard negatives for contrastive learning, whose embeddings are uneasy to discriminate.

Adversarial Training. Adversarial training (AT) stems from [19] and adopts a min-max training regime that optimizes the objective over adversaries generated by maximizing the loss [18,33,35,38,44,46–48]. Some recent work introduced unlabeled data into AT [1,5,8,25,30]. By leveraging a large amount of unlabeled data, [1,5] performed semi-supervised self-training to first generate pseudo-supervisions, then conducted conventional supervised AT. Our work explores how to learn robust models without any class labels.

Adversarial Contrastive Learning. Some recent studies applied CL on adversarial training [17,20,26,30], by considering adversaries as positive views for contrasting, such that the learned encoder renders robust data representations. RoCL [30] was the first to successfully show robust models can be learned in an unsupervised manner. AdvCL [17] proposed to empower CL with pseudo-supervision stimulus. Same as CL, these Adversarial CL methods perform symmetric contrast for all pairs, which could potentially induces conflicts in CL and AT training objectives. We are the first to investigate the asymmetric properties of Adversarial CL, by treating adversaries discriminatingly.

6 Conclusions

In this work, we study enhancing model robustness using unlabeled data and investigate the *identity confusion* issue in Adversarial CL, *i.e.*, adversaries with different identities attract their anchors together, contradicting to the objective of CL. We present a generic asymmetric objective *A-InfoNCE*, and treat adversaries discriminatingly as *inferior positives* or *hard negatives*, which can overcome the identify confusion challenge. Comprehensive experiments with quantitative and qualitative analysis show that our methods can enhance existing Adversarial CL methods effectively. Further, it lies in our future work to extend the proposed asymmetric form to other CL settings to take into consideration the asymmetric characteristics between different views.

Acknowledgement. This work was supported in part by the National Key R&D Program of China under Grant 2021ZD0112100, partly by Baidu Inc. through Apollo-AIR Joint Research Center. We would also like to thank the anonymous reviewers for their insightful comments.

References

1. Alayrac, J.B., Uesato, J., Huang, P.S., Fawzi, A., Stanforth, R., Kohli, P.: Are labels required for improving adversarial robustness? Adv. Neural Inf. Process. Syst. **32** (2019)
2. Athalye, A., Carlini, N., Wagner, D.: Obfuscated gradients give a false sense of security: circumventing defenses to adversarial examples. In: International Conference on Machine Learning, pp. 274–283. PMLR (2018)
3. Bachman, P., Hjelm, R.D., Buchwalter, W.: Learning representations by maximizing mutual information across views. Adv. Neural Inf. Process. Syst. **32** (2019)
4. Carlini, N., Wagner, D.: Towards evaluating the robustness of neural networks. In: 2017 IEEE Symposium on Security and Privacy (SP), pp. 39–57. IEEE (2017)
5. Carmon, Y., Raghunathan, A., Schmidt, L., Duchi, J.C., Liang, P.S.: Unlabeled data improves adversarial robustness. Adv. Neural Inf. Process. Syst. **32** (2019)
6. Caron, M., Misra, I., Mairal, J., Goyal, P., Bojanowski, P., Joulin, A.: Unsupervised learning of visual features by contrasting cluster assignments. Adv. Neural. Inf. Process. Syst. **33**, 9912–9924 (2020)
7. Chen, S., Niu, G., Gong, C., Li, J., Yang, J., Sugiyama, M.: Large-margin contrastive learning with distance polarization regularizer. In: International Conference on Machine Learning, pp. 1673–1683. PMLR (2021)
8. Chen, T., Liu, S., Chang, S., Cheng, Y., Amini, L., Wang, Z.: Adversarial robustness: from self-supervised pre-training to fine-tuning. In: Proceedings of the IEEE/CVF Conference on Computer Vision and Pattern Recognition, pp. 699–708 (2020)
9. Chen, T., Kornblith, S., Norouzi, M., Hinton, G.: A simple framework for contrastive learning of visual representations. In: III, H.D., Singh, A. (eds.) Proceedings of the 37th International Conference on Machine Learning. Proceedings of Machine Learning Research, vol. 119, pp. 1597–1607. PMLR, 13–18 July 2020. https://proceedings.mlr.press/v119/chen20j.html
10. Chen, T., Kornblith, S., Swersky, K., Norouzi, M., Hinton, G.E.: Big self-supervised models are strong semi-supervised learners. Adv. Neural. Inf. Process. Syst. **33**, 22243–22255 (2020)
11. Chen, X., Fan, H., Girshick, R., He, K.: Improved baselines with momentum contrastive learning. arXiv preprint arXiv:2003.04297 (2020)
12. Chen, X., He, K.: Exploring simple siamese representation learning. In: Proceedings of the IEEE/CVF Conference on Computer Vision and Pattern Recognition, pp. 15750–15758 (2021)
13. Chuang, C.Y., Robinson, J., Lin, Y.C., Torralba, A., Jegelka, S.: Debiased contrastive learning. Adv. Neural. Inf. Process. Syst. **33**, 8765–8775 (2020)
14. Dong, Y., et al.: Boosting adversarial attacks with momentum. In: Proceedings of the IEEE Conference on Computer Vision and Pattern Recognition, pp. 9185–9193 (2018)
15. Du Plessis, M.C., Niu, G., Sugiyama, M.: Analysis of learning from positive and unlabeled data. Adv. Neural. Inf. Process. Syst. **27** (2014)

16. Elkan, C., Noto, K.: Learning classifiers from only positive and unlabeled data. In: Proceedings of the 14th ACM SIGKDD International Conference on Knowledge Discovery and Data Mining, pp. 213–220 (2008)
17. Fan, L., Liu, S., Chen, P.Y., Zhang, G., Gan, C.: When does contrastive learning preserve adversarial robustness from pretraining to finetuning? Adv. Neural. Inf. Process. Syst. **34**, 21480–21492 (2021)
18. Gan, Z., Chen, Y.C., Li, L., Zhu, C., Cheng, Y., Liu, J.: Large-scale adversarial training for vision-and-language representation learning. Adv. Neural. Inf. Process. Syst. **33**, 6616–6628 (2020)
19. Goodfellow, I.J., Shlens, J., Szegedy, C.: Explaining and harnessing adversarial examples. arXiv preprint arXiv:1412.6572 (2014)
20. Gowal, S., Huang, P.S., van den Oord, A., Mann, T., Kohli, P.: Self-supervised adversarial robustness for the low-label, high-data regime. In: International Conference on Learning Representations (2020)
21. Grill, J.B., et al.: Bootstrap your own latent-a new approach to self-supervised learning. Adv. Neural. Inf. Process. Syst. **33**, 21271–21284 (2020)
22. Hadsell, R., Chopra, S., LeCun, Y.: Dimensionality reduction by learning an invariant mapping. In: 2006 IEEE Computer Society Conference on Computer Vision and Pattern Recognition (CVPR 2006), vol. 2, pp. 1735–1742. IEEE (2006)
23. He, K., Fan, H., Wu, Y., Xie, S., Girshick, R.: Momentum contrast for unsupervised visual representation learning. In: Proceedings of the IEEE/CVF Conference on Computer Vision and Pattern Recognition, pp. 9729–9738 (2020)
24. He, K., Zhang, X., Ren, S., Sun, J.: Deep residual learning for image recognition. In: Proceedings of the IEEE Conference on Computer Vision and Pattern Recognition, pp. 770–778 (2016)
25. Hendrycks, D., Mazeika, M., Kadavath, S., Song, D.: Using self-supervised learning can improve model robustness and uncertainty. Adv. Neural. Inf. Process. Syst. **32**, 15663–15674 (2019)
26. Jiang, Z., Chen, T., Chen, T., Wang, Z.: Robust pre-training by adversarial contrastive learning. In: NeurIPS (2020)
27. Kalantidis, Y., Sariyildiz, M.B., Pion, N., Weinzaepfel, P., Larlus, D.: Hard negative mixing for contrastive learning. Adv. Neural. Inf. Process. Syst. **33**, 21798–21809 (2020)
28. Kannan, H., Kurakin, A., Goodfellow, I.: Adversarial logit pairing. arXiv preprint arXiv:1803.06373 (2018)
29. Khosla, P., et al.: Supervised contrastive learning. Adv. Neural. Inf. Process. Syst. **33**, 18661–18673 (2020)
30. Kim, M., Tack, J., Hwang, S.J.: Adversarial self-supervised contrastive learning. Adv. Neural. Inf. Process. Syst. **33**, 2983–2994 (2020)
31. Li, J., Zhou, P., Xiong, C., Hoi, S.C.: Prototypical contrastive learning of unsupervised representations. arXiv preprint arXiv:2005.04966 (2020)
32. Van der Maaten, L., Hinton, G.: Visualizing data using t-SNE. J. Mach. Learn. Res. **9**(11) (2008)
33. Madry, A., Makelov, A., Schmidt, L., Tsipras, D., Vladu, A.: Towards deep learning models resistant to adversarial attacks. In: International Conference on Learning Representations (2018)
34. Oord, A.v.d., Li, Y., Vinyals, O.: Representation learning with contrastive predictive coding. arXiv preprint arXiv:1807.03748 (2018)
35. Pang, T., Xu, K., Dong, Y., Du, C., Chen, N., Zhu, J.: Rethinking softmax cross-entropy loss for adversarial robustness. arXiv preprint arXiv:1905.10626 (2019)

36. Rahamim, A., Naeh, I.: Robustness through cognitive dissociation mitigation in contrastive adversarial training. arXiv preprint arXiv:2203.08959 (2022)
37. Robinson, J.D., Chuang, C.Y., Sra, S., Jegelka, S.: Contrastive learning with hard negative samples. In: International Conference on Learning Representations (2020)
38. Shafahi, A., et al.: Adversarial training for free! Adv. Neural Inf. Process. Syst. **32** (2019)
39. Szegedy, C., et al.: Intriguing properties of neural networks. In: 2nd International Conference on Learning Representations, ICLR 2014 (2014)
40. Tao, Y., Takagi, K., Nakata, K.: Clustering-friendly representation learning via instance discrimination and feature decorrelation. arXiv preprint arXiv:2106.00131 (2021)
41. Tian, Y., Krishnan, D., Isola, P.: Contrastive multiview coding. In: Vedaldi, A., Bischof, H., Brox, T., Frahm, J.-M. (eds.) ECCV 2020. LNCS, vol. 12356, pp. 776–794. Springer, Cham (2020). https://doi.org/10.1007/978-3-030-58621-8_45
42. Tian, Y., Sun, C., Poole, B., Krishnan, D., Schmid, C., Isola, P.: What makes for good views for contrastive learning? Adv. Neural. Inf. Process. Syst. **33**, 6827–6839 (2020)
43. Wahed, M., Tabassum, A., Lourentzou, I.: Adversarial contrastive learning by permuting cluster assignments. arXiv preprint arXiv:2204.10314 (2022)
44. Wong, E., Rice, L., Kolter, J.Z.: Fast is better than free: revisiting adversarial training. arXiv preprint arXiv:2001.03994 (2020)
45. Wu, Z., Xiong, Y., Yu, S.X., Lin, D.: Unsupervised feature learning via non-parametric instance discrimination. In: Proceedings of the IEEE Conference on Computer Vision and Pattern Recognition, pp. 3733–3742 (2018)
46. Zhang, D., Zhang, T., Lu, Y., Zhu, Z., Dong, B.: You only propagate once: accelerating adversarial training via maximal principle. Adv. Neural Inf. Process. Syst. **32** (2019)
47. Zhang, H., Yu, Y., Jiao, J., Xing, E., El Ghaoui, L., Jordan, M.: Theoretically principled trade-off between robustness and accuracy. In: International conference on machine learning, pp. 7472–7482. PMLR (2019)
48. Zhu, C., Cheng, Y., Gan, Z., Sun, S., Goldstein, T., Liu, J.: FreeLB: enhanced adversarial training for natural language understanding. arXiv preprint arXiv:1909.11764 (2019)

One Size Does NOT Fit All: Data-Adaptive Adversarial Training

Shuo Yang$^{(\boxtimes)}$ and Chang Xu

University of Sydney, Sydney, Australia
syang9630@uni.sydney.edu.au, c.xu@sydney.edu.au

Abstract. Adversarial robustness is critical for deep learning models to defend against adversarial attacks. Although adversarial training is considered to be one of the most effective ways to improve the model's adversarial robustness, it usually yields models with lower natural accuracy. In this paper, we argue that, for the attackable examples, traditional adversarial training which utilizes a fixed size perturbation ball can create adversarial examples that deviate far away from the original class towards the target class. Thus, the model's performance on the natural target class will drop drastically, which leads to the decline of natural accuracy. To this end, we propose the **D**ata-**A**daptive **A**dversarial **T**raining (DAAT) which adaptively adjusts the perturbation ball to a proper size for each of the natural examples with the help of a natural trained calibration network. Besides, a dynamic training strategy empowers the DAAT models with impressive robustness while retaining remarkable natural accuracy. Based on a toy example, we theoretically prove the recession of the natural accuracy caused by adversarial training and show how the data-adaptive perturbation size helps the model resist it. Finally, empirical experiments on benchmark datasets demonstrate the significant improvement of DAAT models on natural accuracy compared with strong baselines.

Keywords: Adversarial training · Adversarial attack · Adversarial robustness

1 Introduction

Deep learning has led to significant advances across a broad range of tasks, such as computer vision [11], natural language processing [6]. However, the pervasive brittleness of deep neural networks (DNNs) against adversarial examples [27] has raised particular worrisome of the applications of deep learning. Adversarial examples can induce significant change to the output of DNNs even though they are generated by perturbing the clean data only with "imperceptible" noise. The real-world especially security-related tasks (e.g., autonomous driving [3]) require reliability and robustness of DNN models against adversarial attacks.

Supplementary Information The online version contains supplementary material available at https://doi.org/10.1007/978-3-031-20065-6_5.

A large body of approaches has been proposed to defend the adversarial attacks. Adversarial training [9,21] is regarded as one of the most effective adversarial defense methods. The fundamental philosophy behind adversarial training is to encourage the similarity of predictions between the clean input and its neighborhoods. For example, the standard adversarial training [21] first generates adversarial examples within an l_p-norm perturbation ball of radius ϵ, and then imposes the model to have the correct prediction of the adversary. Although subsequent methods such as [14] utilize more sophisticated loss to generate adversaries, they basically share the same training strategy.

Despite the empirical success of adversarial training, recent works show that the improvement of robustness comes at the cost of natural accuracy [29,34]. This problem has inspired many works to study the intrinsic trade-off between robustness and accuracy. For example, TRADES [34] explicitly sets a trade-off coefficient on the natural and adversarial training loss to balance the performance of accuracy and robustness. FAT [35] searches for the least adversarial data to moderate the influence of the adversarial training on natural accuracy. However, the origin of the trade-off is still arguable and the solution to improving the degraded accuracy while keeping the robustness still leaves open.

In this paper, we try to reconsider the trade-off problem from a novel perspective. When generating the adversarial examples, traditional adversarial training methods adhere to the principle that the generated adversaries should be projected to a ball with a fixed size around the natural examples. Given sufficient update, the final adversaries tend to appear on the surface of the perturbation ball, since the generation is oriented by the gradient ascending direction which is generally away from the clean example. On the one hand, for the clean data which are more resistive to the adversarial attacks, the generated adversarial example within the perturbation ball is still similar to the original class; however, on the other hand, for the natural example which is more attackable, the generated adversary can extremely diverge from its natural counterpart. At worst, there may be some clean examples from other classes existing in the perturbation ball if the ball is large enough as illustrated in Fig. 1. If trained with such adversarial examples which excessively overstep the decision boundary, the natural accuracy of the model will be inevitably degraded.

To this end, we propose a novel adversarial training scheme named **Data-Adaptive Adversarial Training** (DAAT) which adaptively adjusts the perturbation ball to a proper size for each of the natural examples. The data-adaptive perturbation size is upper-bounded by the initial preset size and it aims at avoiding generating excessively overstepping examples. Concretely, if the attacker generates an adversary which crosses the line into another category too much, DAAT will shrink the perturbation ball to pull it back, while if the generated adversaries are so benign that can be easily classified, DAAT will enlarge the perturbation ball to give more elbow room to the attacker. The specific perturbation size is determined by a calibration network that is trained merely with the natural data so as not to overfit the adversaries. Therefore, the generalization ability on the natural examples can be better preserved. Besides, to exploit more informative

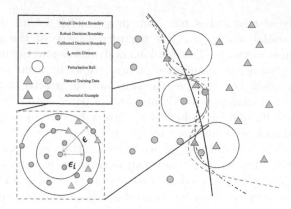

Fig. 1. Illustration of how the adversarial training with a fixed size perturbation ball can cause the degradation of the natural accuracy.

adversaries, we dynamically enlarge the margin of the data-adaptive perturbation ball during different training stages. Empirical experiments demonstrate that the dynamic training strategy plays a significant role in improving the robustness of DAAT models.

2   Related Work

2.1   Adversarial Defense

A large body of research has been conducted to improve the model's defensive power against adversarial examples from various perspectives. For example, many works [8,10,12,18,24] try to detect the adversarial examples and reject them. Another branch of works [19,31,32] view the adversarial examples as contaminated natural examples and aim at recovering the clean examples by employing denoising or feature squeezing methods. However, several detectors and denoisers have been shown to have a limited benefit on certain kinds of attacks [4]. Currently, adversarial training is considered to be one of the most effective defense strategies. The key idea of adversarial training is to train the non-robust model with the generated adversaries. Based on the seminal work [21], many works try to improve the performance of the standard adversarial training by utilizing resultful tools from other domains, such as logit pairing [14], metric learning [23], self-supervised learning [15]. However, most of the aforementioned improvements only focus on how to better align the adversaries with their natural counterparts. Thus, a side effect with the increasing robustness is that the natural accuracy will decline rapidly.

2.2   Decline of the Natural Accuracy

[29] first finds that the natural accuracy may be at odd with robustness. [29] claims that the natural trained model and adversarially trained model may

learn different features for classification. This idea is further confirmed by [13]. [34] later proposes TRADES which uses a trade-off parameter β to balance the training between the natural and adversarial examples. However, TRADES only aims at adjusting the attention between accuracy and robustness, but not at harmonizing the conflict between them. FAT [35] assumes that the reason for the decline of natural accuracy is that the adversaries are so invasive that some of them have crossed over the original decision boundary by a large margin. By generating adversarial examples which are weaker, FAT shows a remarkable improvement of natural accuracy. Nonetheless, the objective of FAT encourages the attacker to find the weakest adversarial examples under certain constraints which cannot provide sufficient information to improve the robustness. Thus, the empirical robust accuracy of FAT is usually much lower. Besides, FAT employs the model trained on the adversaries to determine the strength of attack which may be overfitting to the adversaries. Parallel to our work, [1] also shares a similar idea of instance adaptive adversarial training. However, we employ different adjustment strategies, and the natural trained calibration network guarantees better performance of our method. We defer the empirical comparison of DAAT and [1] to the Appendix.

3   Review of Standard Adversarial Training

We denote $S = \{(x_i, y_i)\}_{i=1}^n$ as the training dataset, where $x_i \in \mathbb{R}^d$ and $y_i \in \mathbb{R}^K$. In this paper, we consider a multiclass classification task $f(g(\cdot; \theta); \omega) : \mathbb{R}^d \to \mathbb{R}^K$, where $g(\cdot; \theta)$ is a feature extractor parameterized by θ and $f(\cdot; \omega)$ is a classifier parameterized by ω. The perturbation ball around an input example x is defined as:

$$\mathcal{B}_p(x, \epsilon) := \{x' | \|x - x'\|_p \le \epsilon\}, \tag{1}$$

where ϵ is a preset perturbation size, and $\|\cdot\|_p$ refers to the l_p-norm metric. In the experimental section, except where explicitly stated, we typically choose the l_∞ norm for training and evaluation as it commonly leads to a smaller perturbation size.

Adversarial example x' is an example in the perturbation ball around a natural example x, i.e., $x' \in \mathcal{B}_p(x, \epsilon)$. The harmfulness of the adversarial example is reflected in that it can alter the prediction of a model for the original natural example as follow:

$$\arg\max_k f(g(x'))_k \ne \arg\max_k f(g(x))_k, \tag{2}$$

where $f(g(\cdot))_k$ is the predicted probability of the k-th class. The existence of the adversarial example reflects the sensitivity of the model to adversarial perturbations. Adversarial training can be a natural way to smooth the prediction of the model within the perturbation ball [21]. The objective of the standard adversarial training can be formulated as follow:

$$\min_{\omega, \theta} \mathbb{E}\left[\max_{x' \in \mathcal{B}_p(x, \epsilon)} \mathcal{L}\left(f(g(x'); \theta); \omega), y\right) \right], \tag{3}$$

where $\mathcal{L}$ is the loss function to measure the difference between the ground-truth label and prediction (e.g., soft-max cross-entropy loss).

From Eq. (3) we can find that the standard adversarial training implies a minimax game between the attacker and defender. The attacker aims at generating the adversarial examples which maximize the loss within the perturbation ball, while the defender tries to correct the misclassification on the generated attack. However, in practice, the inner maximization is generally intractable due to the extremely high dimension of the input space. Thus, the Projected Gradient Descent (PGD) method [21] is proposed to approximate the inner maximization by generating the worst-case example within T-step iterations. A PGD iteration can be written as follow:

$$x^{t+1} = \text{Proj}_{\mathcal{B}_p(x,\epsilon)} \left[x^t + \alpha \text{sign}\left(\nabla_{x^t} \mathcal{L}(f(g(x^t); \theta); \omega), y) \right) \right], \tag{4}$$

where $\text{Proj}_{\mathcal{B}_p(x,\epsilon)}$ is to project the generated example back to $\mathcal{B}_p(x, \epsilon)$ and α is the step size. The last step output is utilized as the final adversarial example, i.e., $x' := x^T$. It can be imagined that with the increasing iteration step, the generated examples will deviate from the origin further and further.

4   Adversarial Perturbation Size Matters

In standard adversarial training, the perturbation size is usually set to be the same for every example. Empirically, given sufficient PGD iteration steps, the generated adversarial example is more likely to be located on the surface of the perturbation ball (see experiments in Sect. 6.3). According to [36], *more attackable/robust data are closer to/farther away from the decision boundary*. Therefore, as illustrated in Fig. 1, the generated adversaries of the attackable data may cross the decision boundary to another class leading to the accuracy decline. Similar idea is also mentioned in [28].

In what follows, we theoretically demonstrate how standard accuracy is influenced by the standard adversarial training based on a toy example. Different from the setup of [13] to study the robust and non-robust feature, we adopt the toy experiment to illustrate how adversarial training hurts accuracy. We consider a binary classification problem where the input-label pairs (x, y) are sampled from a distribution D as follows:

$$y \overset{u.a.r.}{\sim} \{-1, 1\}, \quad x \sim \mathcal{N}(y \cdot \boldsymbol{\mu}_*, \boldsymbol{\Sigma}_*). \tag{5}$$

Our goal is to correctly classify new examples which are sampled from D. Based on the *maximum likelihood classification* criteria, our learning objective can be formulated as:

$$\min_{\boldsymbol{\mu}, \boldsymbol{\Sigma}} \mathbb{E}_{(x,y) \sim D} \left[\mathcal{L}(x; y \cdot \boldsymbol{\mu}, \boldsymbol{\Sigma}) \right], \tag{6}$$

where $\mathcal{L}(x; y \cdot \boldsymbol{\mu}, \boldsymbol{\Sigma})$ denotes the negative log-likelihood function of Gaussian. Due to the symmetry of the data distribution, the resulting optimal linear classifier can be easily obtained as follow:

$$y = \arg\max_y \mathcal{L}(x; y \cdot \hat{\boldsymbol{\mu}}, \hat{\boldsymbol{\Sigma}}) = \text{sign}(x^\mathsf{T} \hat{\boldsymbol{\Sigma}}^{-1} \hat{\boldsymbol{\mu}}), \tag{7}$$

where $(\hat{\boldsymbol{\mu}}, \hat{\boldsymbol{\Sigma}})$ are the estimated parameters of the Gaussian. With the classifier (7), we have the following theorem:

Theorem 1. *When the optima of objective (6) is obtained, classifier (7) can achieve the Bayesian error rate as*

$$err_* = 1 - \frac{1}{\sqrt{2\pi}} \int_c^\infty \exp\left(-\frac{1}{2}x^2\right) dx,$$

where $c = -\frac{\boldsymbol{\mu}_*^\mathsf{T}\mathbf{w}}{\sqrt{\mathbf{w}^\mathsf{T}\boldsymbol{\Sigma}_*\mathbf{w}}}$, $\mathbf{w} = \boldsymbol{\Sigma}_*^{-1}\boldsymbol{\mu}_*$, and the integral can be evaluated by the error function.

The proof of Theorem 1 can be found in the Appendix. It indicates that the model which is only trained with the natural data according to the maximum likelihood rule can achieve the highest natural accuracy. Next, we will investigate how standard adversarial training leads to a reduction of natural accuracy. According to the standard adversarial training objective as Eq. (3), we can derive the robust objective of this toy experiment as follow:

$$\min_{\boldsymbol{\mu}, \boldsymbol{\Sigma}} \mathbb{E}_{(x,y)\sim D} \left[\max_{\delta \in \mathcal{B}_p(0,\epsilon)} \mathcal{L}(x + \delta; y \cdot \boldsymbol{\mu}, \boldsymbol{\Sigma}) \right]. \tag{8}$$

By solving Eq. (8) within the l_2-norm perturbation ball, we have the following propositions:

Proposition 1. *Given the robust objective in Eq. (8), the optimal perturbation δ^* with respect to input x can be derived as:*

$$\delta^* = (\lambda\boldsymbol{\Sigma} - \boldsymbol{I})^{-1}(x - \boldsymbol{\mu}),$$

where λ is set such that $\|\delta^*\|_2 = \epsilon$.

A straightforward result of Proposition 1 is that the optimal adversarial perturbation can be obtained at the surface of the perturbation ball. Imagine that for the more attackable examples which are closer to the natural decision boundary, the generated adversaries are more likely to cross the decision boundary with a sufficiently large perturbation size.

Proposition 2. *For a fixed $tr(\boldsymbol{\Sigma}^*) = k$, the objective (8) can be optimized at:*

$$\boldsymbol{\mu}_r = \boldsymbol{\mu}^*, \quad \boldsymbol{\Sigma}_r = \frac{k}{d}\boldsymbol{I},$$

where d is the dimension of the input space.

Proposition 2 further demonstrates the consequence of the improper perturbation size for these more attackable examples. Although the mean of the robust model is the same as that of the natural trained model (i.e., $\boldsymbol{\mu}_r = \boldsymbol{\mu}^*$), the covariance matrix becomes proportional to the identity matrix. As a result, the classifier induced by the standard adversarial learning will transit to:

$$y_r = \text{sign}(x^\mathsf{T}\boldsymbol{\Sigma}_r^{-1}\boldsymbol{\mu}_r) = \text{sign}(x^\mathsf{T}\boldsymbol{\mu}_*), \tag{9}$$

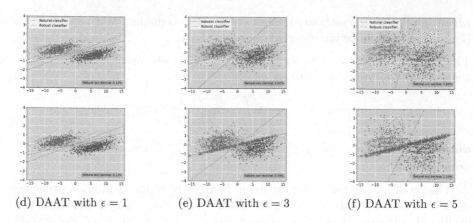

(d) DAAT with $\epsilon = 1$ (e) DAAT with $\epsilon = 3$ (f) DAAT with $\epsilon = 5$

Fig. 2. An empirical illustration of the toy example. The contour lines depict the natural data distribution, the red and blue dots in different subfigures are the generated adversaries with increasing perturbation size (i.e., $\epsilon = 1, 3, 5$ from left to right). The yellow circles are the overstepping examples, and the green ones are the corresponding examples adjusted by the adaptive perturbation ball. The blue dashed and orange lines are natural and robustified decision boundaries, respectively. (Color figure online)

which is perpendicular to the line between the two mean points. If $\Sigma_* \neq I$, according to Theorem 1, the natural error of classifier (9) will be enlarged.

We give an empirical illustration of the toy examples in Fig. 2. The subfigures in the left column depict the standard adversarial training process. It is obvious that with the increasing perturbation size, more and more adversaries are crossing the optimal natural classifier, causing the induced robust classifier to have a lower and lower natural accuracy. In contrast, the adversaries in the right column are constrained in the adaptive perturbation balls which ensures that the adversaries can be concentrated around the original decision boundary. Consequently, the induced model has a lower natural accuracy decline.

5   Data-Adaptive Adversarial Training

As discussed in the previous sections, the fixed perturbation size employed in the standard adversarial training is not appropriate for every training example. For the examples which are far away from other classes, the adversaries in the ϵ-large perturbation ball can smooth the output of the neighborhoods around the natural examples which is beneficial to the robustness. On the contrary, for the natural examples which are closer to the decision boundary, the adversaries generated within the ϵ-large perturbation ball are likely to cross the decision boundary into another class. If the model is still trained on these overstepping adversaries, it is not difficult to imagine that the model will be biased to misclassified the natural examples from the target classes, which leads to the accuracy decline.

Algorithm 1. Data-Adaptive Adversarial Training (DAAT)

Input: Initialized feature extractor $g(\cdot)$, classifier $f(\cdot)$, calibration network $c(\cdot)$, training data $S = \{(x_i, y_i)\}_{i=1}^n$, initialized perturbation size $\epsilon_i^0 = \epsilon$, number of steps T, margin ρ, temperature τ, number of epochs E, minibatch size m

Output: Adversarial robust network $f(g(\cdot))$

for epoch $= 1, \ldots, E$ **do**
    for mini-batch $= 1, \ldots, M$ **do**
        Sample a mini-batch $\{(x_i, y_i)\}_{i=1}^m$ from S
        Train $c(\cdot)$ with the natural data by $\frac{1}{m}\sum_{i=1}^m \mathcal{L}\left(c(g(x_i)), y_i\right)$
        Generate data-adaptive adversarial example by $x_i' \leftarrow \Pi_{\mathcal{B}_p(x_i, \epsilon_i^e)}^T \left[\alpha \mathrm{sign}\left(\nabla_{x_i^t} \mathcal{L}(f(g(x_i^t)), y)\right) + x_i'\right]$
        Train $f(g(\cdot))$ with the adversarial examples by $\frac{1}{m}\sum_{i=1}^m \mathcal{L}\left(f(g(x_i')), y_i\right)$
        Obtain the similarity s_i by Eq. (13)
        Update the data-adaptive perturbation size ϵ_i^{e+1} by Eq. (12)
    end for
end for

To solve the problem above, we propose the Data-Adaptive Adversarial Training (DAAT) method in this section. The basic idea of DAAT is to apply an adaptive perturbation size ϵ_i to different training data x_i so that the generated adversaries can be constrained and do not deviate too far away from the clean one. Thus, DAAT generates the adversary x_i' within a calibrated perturbation ball $\mathcal{B}_p(x_i, \epsilon_i)$ as:

$$x_i' = \underset{x_i' \in \mathcal{B}_p(x_i, \epsilon_i)}{\arg\max} \; \mathcal{L}\left(f(g(x_i')), y_i\right). \tag{10}$$

A critical point of DAAT is how to determine the adjustment of perturbation size. Recall that the job of ϵ_i is to constrain x_i' not to overstep the natural decision boundary, thus we employ a calibration network $c(\cdot; \psi)$ to estimate how far the generated adversary x_i' has crossed over the decision boundary. Naturally, the adjusted ϵ_i should satisfy:

$$\max_y c(g(x_i'))_y - c(g(x_i'))_{y_i} \leq \rho, \quad x_i' \in \mathcal{B}_p(x_i, \epsilon_i), \tag{11}$$

where the constraint (11) makes sure that x_i' which generated in $\mathcal{B}_p(x_i, \epsilon_i)$ will not overstep the natural decision boundary by a margin larger than ρ, otherwise the perturbation size ϵ_i is supposed to be scaled down. Note that, $c(\cdot)$ is supposed to be trained only with the natural examples, thus it can judge x_i' from the perspective of the natural decision boundary. If we replace $c(\cdot)$ with the adversarially trained $f(\cdot)$, the calibrated ϵ_i will adapt to the adversarial decision boundary, which cannot provide accurate information.

Specific strategy to satisfy the constraint (11) is still an open question. In this paper, the proposed DAAT estimates the perturbation size as follow:

$$\epsilon_i^{e+1} := \min\{\epsilon, \frac{\rho}{s_i} \cdot \epsilon_i^e\}, \tag{12}$$

$$s_i := \max_y \sigma \left[c(g(x_i'))/\tau\right]_y - \sigma \left[c(g(x_i'))/\tau\right]_{y_i}, \tag{13}$$

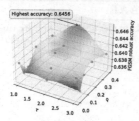 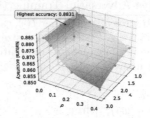 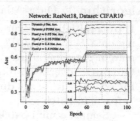

(a) Grid searching of τ and ρ for the optimal FGSM robust accuracy.

(b) Grid searching of τ and ρ for the optimal natural accuracy.

(c) Learning curves of the DAAT models trained with different ρs.

Fig. 3. Investigation of the fixed (ρ, τ) pairs and dynamic ρ strategy.

where $\sigma(\cdot)$ is the softmax operation, $\tau \geq 1$ is the temperature coefficient to smooth the output of $c(\cdot)$, e denotes the training epoch, $s_i \in (0,1)$ in (13) is to measure how far x_i' has overstepped the decision boundary, and ρ is a margin. Thus, if an adversary x_i' has crossed the decision boundary too far (e.g., $\rho/s_i < 1$), the perturbation bound will be shrunken in the next epoch and vice versa. In the following experiments, we also try different adjustment strategies for comparison. To sum up, the final objective of DAAT can be formulated as follows:

$$\min_{\psi} \mathbb{E}_{(x,y)} \left[\mathcal{L} \left(c(g(x); \psi), y \right) \right] + \min_{\omega, \theta} \mathbb{E}_{(x',y)} \left[\mathcal{L} \left(f(g(x'); \theta), y \right) \right], \quad (14)$$

$$x_i' \in \mathcal{B}_c(x_i, \epsilon_i) = \{x_i' | \, \|x_i - x_i'\| \leq \epsilon_i, \quad \max_y c(g(x_i'))_y - c(g(x_i'))_{y_i} \leq \rho\}, \quad (15)$$

where $\mathcal{B}_c$ represents the calibrated perturbation ball. The detailed training routine of DAAT is summarized in Algorithm 1 for convenience.

6   Experiment

In this section, our proposed DAAT is evaluated on benchmark datasets, including CIFAR10 [16], and SVHN [26]. Strong baselines including AT [22], TRADES [34], MART [30] and FAT [35] are employed to verify the advantages of DAAT. The models are tested under prevalent attack types, including FGSM, PGD-T, C&W [5] optimized by PGD, and the commonly used benchmark attack AutoAttack (AA) [7]. Moreover, comprehensive experiments are conducted to investigate the thorough capability of DAAT. Due to space limitation, the training and attacking details for DAAT and baselines are all deferred to the Appendix. Implementation is available at here[1].

---

[1] https://github.com/eccv2022daat/daat.git.

6.1   Investigation of Hyper-parameters

As we mentioned in Sect. 5, the margin ρ and temperature τ are two important hyper-parameters that affect the performance of DAAT. For the sake of optimal performance, we first investigate the model's response to different hyper-parameter pairs. We conducted a grid search to investigate the influence of hyper-parameters. The searching spaces for ρ and τ are {0.01, 0.05, 0.1, 0.2, 0.4} and {1, 2, 3}, respectively. Figure 3 demonstrates the FSGM robust accuracy and natural accuracy of the model trained with different hyper-parameter pairs. As we can see from Fig. 3a and 3b, for a fixed τ, the robustness of the model generally increases with the growing ρ, while the natural accuracy of the model declines. A convincing reason for this trend is that the job of ρ is to control how much the prediction confidence of the adversarial examples can exceed that of the correct class (i.e., Eq. (13)). Consequently, if ρ is set to be larger, the generated adversary will be further away from its natural counterpart, which leads to the decreasing of the natural accuracy but the promoting of the robustness, and vice versa.

Figure 3 illustrates that the optimal model for robust and natural accuracy can be both achieved at $\tau = 2$, but with different ρ values. To harmonize the conflict, we devise a novel training scheme by employing a dynamic ρ during different stages of training. Specifically, the model is initially trained with a small value of ρ with which only mild adversaries can be generated. As a consequence, the model can better generalize to the natural examples so that the induced calibration network can provide informative knowledge for the perturbation size adjustment. Then, ρ will be gradually enlarged to make sure that the model can adapt to stronger attacks. Meanwhile, with the help of the adaptive perturbation size, the natural accuracy would be retained as much as possible. In Fig. 3c, we plot the learning curves of the models trained with $\rho = 0.05$, $\rho = 0.4$, and dynamic ρ which is initialized with 0.05 and then enlarged to 0.2 and 0.3 at #75 and #90 epoch, respectively. From the learning curves, we can find that DAAT with dynamic ρ inherits the advantages of the fixed ρ models, e.g., it achieves a high level of natural accuracy while enjoying remarkable robustness. In the following experiments, we will all employ the dynamic ρ to train DAAT models unless otherwise specified.

6.2   White-Box and Black-Box Attacks

In this subsection, we evaluate the proposed DAAT method with both white-box and black-box attacks. The powerful ResNet18 was employed as the basic feature extractor[2]. For comparison, we combined the baselines with the DAAT training scheme denoted as the DAAT- models to investigate the performance promotion that DAAT brings.

White-Box Attack: The white-box attack assumes that all the information about the model is completely exposed to the attacker. As shown in Table 1,

---

[2] Experimental results with more network architectures are deferred to the Appendix.

Table 1. Robust accuracy on CIFAR10 and SVHN under different attacks.

Methods	Attacks								
	Clean	White-box						Black-box (PDG-20)	
		FGSM	PGD-20	PGD-40	C&W-20	AA		Non-Robust	AT
Network: ResNet18, Attack: l_∞-norm, $\epsilon = 0.031$, Dataset: CIFAR10									
Natural	94.63%	17.32%	0%	0%	0%	0%		–	70.80%
Standard AT	84.66%	62.83%	47.83%	46.26%	46.24%	43.66%		83.67%	–
FAT	88.26%	63.73%	46.52%	43.73%	45.34%	43.28%		86.40%	64.11%
DAAT	**88.31%**	**64.56%**	**48.89%**	46.93%	**49.43%**	**44.32%**		**86.79%**	**64.25%**
TRADES	81.98%	63.24%	53.70%	52.48%	50.93%	49.22%		80.22%	62.08%
DAAT-TRADES	**83.55%**	**64.55%**	**54.57%**	**53.28%**	**51.30%**	**49.83%**		**82.05%**	**63.02%**
MART	80.67%	63.75%	53.87%	52.19%	50.25%	49.73%		79.78%	61.44%
DAAT-MART	**83.87%**	**65.75%**	**54.02%**	**52.63%**	**50.32%**	49.82%		**82.16%**	**62.01%**
Network: ResNet18, Attack: l_∞-norm, $\epsilon = 0.031$, Dataset: SVHN									
Natural	96.02%	45.38%	0.90%	0.30%	0.83%	0%		–	54.41%
Standard AT	92.74%	72.58%	54.89%	52.33%	52.10%	51.09%		88.35%	–
FAT	93.53%	70.48%	52.98%	49.85%	49.73%	50.63%		89.11%	61.12%
DAAT	**93.82%**	**73.03%**	**56.24%**	**53.72%**	**53.06%**	**52.33%**		**89.50%**	**61.84%**
TRADES	88.99%	69.68%	57.38%	55.69%	**51.74%**	**50.82%**		83.98%	60.84%
DAAT-TRADES	**90.28%**	**71.07%**	**58.59%**	**56.60%**	51.33%	50.59%		**85.19%**	**61.16%**
MART	89.91%	70.65%	58.00%	56.17%	51.47%	50.12%		84.89%	60.72%
DAAT-MART	**92.16%**	**73.81%**	**59.68%**	**57.42%**	**51.81%**	**50.66%**		**87.49%**	**61.28%**

thanks to the data-adaptive perturbation size, the proposed DAAT achieves significantly higher natural accuracy compared with the baselines. Especially in the SVHN dataset, DAAT has a natural accuracy of 93.82% which is much closer to that of the natural trained model. Meanwhile, most of the DAAT-enhanced models' robustness is also improved or keep comparable. We attribute this benefit to the dynamic ρ, for it can provide the model with a learning environment as Curriculum Learning [2], with which the robustness can be smoothly and better improved. It is undeniable that the FAT method can achieve comparable natural accuracy as DAAT, however, the robustness of the FAT trained model seems to suffer a severe decline. A possible explanation is that the objective of FAT replaces the inner maximization in Eq. 3 with a minimization objective under certain constraints. Thus, FAT cannot find the most effective adversaries to improve the robustness with the early-stopped PGD technique [35]. In comparison, although DAAT also shrinks the perturbation space, it still tries to find the most informative adversaries in a smaller perturbation ball.

Black-Box Attack: In the black-box attack setting, the attacker has no access to the target model. The attacker has to generate adversaries by attacking a surrogate model.

In this paper, we employ the natural trained model and the standard AT model as the surrogate models. As in the last two columns in Table 1, an interesting trend is that the models with higher robustness towards the white-box attacks (e.g., TRADES, MART) usually have lower robustness towards the black-box attacks. We suspect that this is probably because the robustness towards a specific kind of attack will impede the transferability of robustness. Nonetheless, the DAAT-enhanced models can generally keep or surpass the robustness against black-box attacks compared with their baselines.

6.3   Distribution of Adversaries

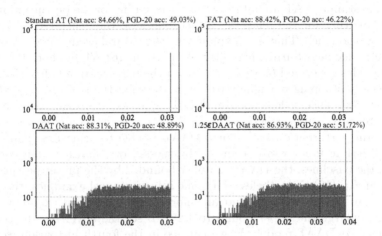

Fig. 4. Histograms of the distance between the adversarial examples for training and the natural examples. The horizontal and vertical axes represent the distance to the natural example and the number of examples, respectively.

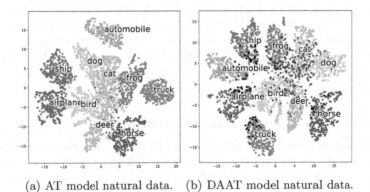

(a) AT model natural data.   (b) DAAT model natural data.

Fig. 5. T-SNE visualizations of natural representations obtained from AT and DAAT models. The darker points in the right figure are the examples whose data-adaptive perturbation size is smaller than the preset ϵ.

Traditional adversarial training methods usually search the worst-case adversarial example in a fixed size perturbation ball. As a consequence, the generated adversaries tend to appear on the surface of the perturbation ball. However,

DAAT explicitly restrains the perturbation space of the adversaries, thus the adversaries should be more broadly distributed in the preset perturbation ball. For verification, we plot the histograms representing the distance between the adversarial examples and their corresponding natural examples during the training in Fig. 4.

What we can find from the first histograms is that the adversaries generated by the standard AT are all located on the surface of the perturbation ball, which means that for the relatively attackable data, the generated adversaries may change too much. That may explain why the natural accuracy of AT usually significantly declines. Surprisingly, just as the standard AT method, the adversarial examples generated by FAT are also on the perturbation ball surface even with the early stopping technique. However, the robustness of FAT is still comparatively lower since it does not aim at looking for the strongest adversaries. In contrast, the adversaries generated by DAAT are widely distributed throughout the l_∞-norm perturbation ball. Thus, DAAT is able to achieve a significantly higher natural accuracy while keeping robustness. Note that, for a fair comparison with the baselines, the DAAT is upper bounded by the preset perturbation size ϵ as in Eq. (12). Nonetheless, for some robust natural examples, the upper bound ϵ may be too small to find an informative adversarial example. Thus, we further enlarge the upper bound to 1.25ϵ to see the adversary distribution of the enlarged DAAT model. As we can see in the fourth histogram, some of the adversarial examples generated by the enlarged DAAT method can be found outside the perturbation ball, which implies that for the robust natural examples, the most useful adversaries lie outside the preset ball. This may explain why the enlarged DAAT model is more robust than the DAAT model.

Besides, in Fig. 5, we further visualize the representations of the natural data extracted from AT model and DAAT model via T-SNE [20]. As we can see from the figure, the data clusters derived by DAAT are more separable. Moreover, the darker points in Fig. 5b represent the natural examples whose adversaries are generated in a shrunken perturbation ball. Interestingly, these points are usually at the edge of the clusters, which indicates that the attackable examples are near the natural decision boundary.

6.4   DAAT with Different Calibration Strategies

As we discuss in Sect. 5, the adjustment of the perturbation size is an open problem. In this subsection, we investigate the influence of different adjustment strategies on the performance of DAAT.

Piecewise DAAT: A direct idea is the piecewise DAAT, which assigns a piecewise perturbation size (i.e., $\epsilon \in \{0, \frac{2}{255}, \frac{4}{255}, \frac{6}{255}, \frac{8}{255}\}$) for an adversary based on the output of the calibration network. For comparison, we first plot the learning curves of the AT models trained with the aforementioned perturbation sizes in Fig. 6a. It is obvious that the AT model with a larger fixed perturbation size can achieve higher robustness but lower natural accuracy. However, the piecewise DAAT can not only keep outstanding robustness but also slightly promote natural accuracy.

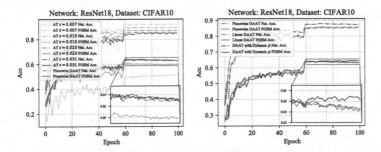

(a) AT models with different pre-set perturbation sizes.

(b) DAAT models with different adjustment strategies.

Fig. 6. Learning curves of AT models with different preset ϵs and DAAT models with different perturbation size adjustment strategies.

Linear DAAT: Linear DAAT employs a linear mapping to derive the adjusted perturbation size as follows:

$$\epsilon_i^{e+1} := \min\{\epsilon, (1 - s_i + \rho) \cdot \epsilon\}, \tag{16}$$

where s_i is the same as Eq. (13), ρ is the margin value. We plot the learning curves of DAAT with different adjustment strategies in Fig. 6b. As we can see from the figure, the default DAAT trained with Eq. (12) receives the best empirical performance. A possible reason is that Eq. (12) utilizes the historical information of ϵ_i^e which can smooth the variation of the perturbation size to stabilize the training process. More discussion about the calibration network can be found in the Appendix.

7   Conclusions

In this paper, we first find that, in adversarial training, the decline of the natural accuracy may come from the fixed perturbation size, since one perturbation size does not fit all training data. Thus, we propose a novel adversarial training strategy DAAT which adaptively adjusts the perturbation size for each training data. To achieve better natural accuracy, the adjustment is performed by a natural trained calibration network, and a dynamic training strategy further empowers the DAAT models with impressive robustness. Although the experimental results have demonstrated the empirical superiority of our method, the better perturbation size adjustment strategy is still an open problem to explore.

Acknowledgements. This work was supported in part by the Australian Research Council under Project DP210101859 and the University of Sydney Research Accelerator (SOAR) Prize.

References

1. Balaji, Y., Goldstein, T., Hoffman, J.: Instance adaptive adversarial training: improved accuracy tradeoffs in neural nets. arXiv preprint arXiv:1910.08051 (2019)
2. Bengio, Y., Louradour, J., Collobert, R., Weston, J.: Curriculum learning. In: Proceedings of the 26th Annual International Conference on Machine Learning, pp. 41–48 (2009)
3. Bojarski, M., et al.: End to end learning for self-driving cars. arXiv preprint arXiv:1604.07316 (2016)
4. Carlini, N., Wagner, D.: Adversarial examples are not easily detected: bypassing ten detection methods. In: Proceedings of the 10th ACM Workshop on Artificial Intelligence and Security, pp. 3–14 (2017)
5. Carlini, N., Wagner, D.: Towards evaluating the robustness of neural networks. In: 2017 IEEE Symposium on Security and Privacy (SP), pp. 39–57. IEEE (2017)
6. Collobert, R., Weston, J.: A unified architecture for natural language processing: Deep neural networks with multitask learning. In: Proceedings of the 25th International Conference on Machine Learning, pp. 160–167 (2008)
7. Croce, F., Hein, M.: Reliable evaluation of adversarial robustness with an ensemble of diverse parameter-free attacks. In: ICML (2020)
8. Feinman, R., Curtin, R.R., Shintre, S., Gardner, A.B.: Detecting adversarial samples from artifacts. arXiv preprint arXiv:1703.00410 (2017)
9. Goodfellow, I.J., Shlens, J., Szegedy, C.: Explaining and harnessing adversarial examples. arXiv preprint arXiv:1412.6572 (2014)
10. Grosse, K., Manoharan, P., Papernot, N., Backes, M., McDaniel, P.: On the (statistical) detection of adversarial examples. arXiv preprint arXiv:1702.06280 (2017)
11. He, K., Zhang, X., Ren, S., Sun, J.: Deep residual learning for image recognition. In: Proceedings of the IEEE Conference on Computer Vision and Pattern Recognition, pp. 770–778 (2016)
12. Hendrycks, D., Gimpel, K.: Early methods for detecting adversarial images. In: ICLR (2017)
13. Ilyas, A., Santurkar, S., Tsipras, D., Engstrom, L., Tran, B., Madry, A.: Adversarial examples are not bugs, they are features. In: NeurIPS, pp. 125–136 (2019)
14. Kannan, H., Kurakin, A., Goodfellow, I.: Adversarial logit pairing. arXiv preprint arXiv:1803.06373 (2018)
15. Kim, M., Tack, J., Hwang, S.J.: Adversarial self-supervised contrastive learning. Adv. Neural. Inf. Process. Syst. **33**, 2983–2994 (2020)
16. Krizhevsky, A., Hinton, G., et al.: Learning multiple layers of features from tiny images (2009)
17. Kundu, S., Nazemi, M., Beerel, P.A., Pedram, M.: A tunable robust pruning framework through dynamic network rewiring of DNNs. arXiv preprint arXiv:2011.03083 (2020)
18. Li, X., Li, F.: Adversarial examples detection in deep networks with convolutional filter statistics. In: Proceedings of the IEEE International Conference on Computer Vision, pp. 5764–5772 (2017)
19. Liao, F., Liang, M., Dong, Y., Pang, T., Hu, X., Zhu, J.: Defense against adversarial attacks using high-level representation guided denoiser. In: Proceedings of the IEEE Conference on Computer Vision and Pattern Recognition, pp. 1778–1787 (2018)
20. Van der Maaten, L., Hinton, G.: Visualizing data using t-SNE. J. Mach. Learn. Res. **9**(11) (2008)

21. Madry, A., Makelov, A., Schmidt, L., Tsipras, D., Vladu, A.: Towards deep learning models resistant to adversarial attacks. In: ICLR (2018)
22. Madry, A., Makelov, A., Schmidt, L., Tsipras, D., Vladu, A.: Towards deep learning models resistant to adversarial attacks. In: International Conference on Learning Representations (2018). https://openreview.net/forum?id=rJzIBfZAb
23. Mao, C., Zhong, Z., Yang, J., Vondrick, C., Ray, B.: Metric learning for adversarial robustness. Adv. Neural Inf. Process. Syst. **32** (2019)
24. Metzen, J.H., Genewein, T., Fischer, V., Bischoff, B.: On detecting adversarial perturbations. In: ICLR (2017)
25. Moosavi-Dezfooli, S.M., Fawzi, A., Uesato, J., Frossard, P.: Robustness via curvature regularization, and vice versa. In: Proceedings of the IEEE/CVF Conference on Computer Vision and Pattern Recognition, pp. 9078–9086 (2019)
26. Netzer, Y., Wang, T., Coates, A., Bissacco, A., Wu, B., Ng, A.Y.: Reading digits in natural images with unsupervised feature learning (2011)
27. Szegedy, C., et al.: Intriguing properties of neural networks. arXiv preprint arXiv:1312.6199 (2013)
28. Tramèr, F., Behrmann, J., Carlini, N., Papernot, N., Jacobsen, J.H.: Fundamental tradeoffs between invariance and sensitivity to adversarial perturbations. In: International Conference on Machine Learning, pp. 9561–9571. PMLR (2020)
29. Tsipras, D., Santurkar, S., Engstrom, L., Turner, A., Madry, A.: Robustness may be at odds with accuracy. In: International Conference on Learning Representations (2018)
30. Wang, Y., Zou, D., Yi, J., Bailey, J., Ma, X., Gu, Q.: Improving adversarial robustness requires revisiting misclassified examples. In: International Conference on Learning Representations (2019)
31. Xie, C., Wu, Y., Maaten, L.V.D., Yuille, A.L., He, K.: Feature denoising for improving adversarial robustness. In: Proceedings of the IEEE Conference on Computer Vision and Pattern Recognition, pp. 501–509 (2019)
32. Xu, W., Evans, D., Qi, Y.: Feature squeezing: detecting adversarial examples in deep neural networks. arXiv preprint arXiv:1704.01155 (2017)
33. Zagoruyko, S., Komodakis, N.: Wide residual networks. In: Wilson, R.C., Hancock, E.R., Smith, W.A.P. (eds.) Proceedings of the British Machine Vision Conference (BMVC), pp. 87.1–87.12. BMVA Press (2016). https://doi.org/10.5244/C.30.87
34. Zhang, H., Yu, Y., Jiao, J., Xing, E., El Ghaoui, L., Jordan, M.: Theoretically principled trade-off between robustness and accuracy. In: International Conference on Machine Learning, pp. 7472–7482. PMLR (2019)
35. Zhang, J., et al.: Attacks which do not kill training make adversarial learning stronger. In: International Conference on Machine Learning, pp. 11278–11287. PMLR (2020)
36. Zhang, J., Zhu, J., Niu, G., Han, B., Sugiyama, M., Kankanhalli, M.: Geometry-aware instance-reweighted adversarial training. In: International Conference on Learning Representations (2021). https://openreview.net/forum?id=iAX0l6Cz8ub

UniCR: Universally Approximated Certified Robustness via Randomized Smoothing

Hanbin Hong[1]([✉]), Binghui Wang[2], and Yuan Hong[1]

[1] University of Connecticut, Storrs, CT 06269, USA
{hanbin.hong,yuan.hong}@uconn.edu
[2] Illinois Institute of Technology, Chicago, IL 60616, USA
bwang70@iit.edu

Abstract. We study certified robustness of machine learning classifiers against adversarial perturbations. In particular, we propose the first universally approximated certified robustness (UniCR) framework, which can approximate the robustness certification of *any* input on *any* classifier against *any* ℓ_p perturbations with noise generated by *any* continuous probability distribution. Compared with the state-of-the-art certified defenses, UniCR provides many significant benefits: (1) the first universal robustness certification framework for the above 4 "any"s; (2) automatic robustness certification that avoids case-by-case analysis, (3) tightness validation of certified robustness, and (4) optimality validation of noise distributions used by randomized smoothing. We conduct extensive experiments to validate the above benefits of UniCR and the advantages of UniCR over state-of-the-art certified defenses against ℓ_p perturbations.

Keywords: Adversarial machine learning · Certified robustness · Randomized smoothing

1 Introduction

Machine learning (ML) classifiers are vulnerable to adversarial perturbations [5–7,36]). Certified defenses [4,12,19,21,27,37,38,47] were recently proposed to ensure provable robustness against adversarial perturbations. Typically, certified defenses aim to derive a certified radius such that an arbitrary ℓ_p (e.g., ℓ_1, ℓ_2 or ℓ_∞) perturbation, when added to a testing input, cannot fool the classifier, if the ℓ_p-norm value of the perturbation is within the radius. Among all certified defenses, randomized smoothing [11,32,35] based certified defense has achieved the state-of-the-art certified radius and can be applied to *any* classifier. Specifically, given a testing input and any classifier, randomized smoothing first defines

Supplementary Information The online version contains supplementary material available at https://doi.org/10.1007/978-3-031-20065-6_6.

Table 1. Comparison with highly-related works.

	Classifier	Smoothing noise	Perturbations	Tightness	Optimizable	Analysis-free
Lecuyer et al. [32]	Any	Gaussian/Laplace	Any $\ell_p, p \in \mathbb{R}^+$	Loose	No	No
Cohen et al. [11]	Any	Gaussian	ℓ_2	Strictly tight	No	No
Teng et al. [43]	Any	Laplace	ℓ_1	Strictly tight	No	No
Dvijotham et al. [16]	Any	f-divergence-constrained	Any $\ell_p, p \in \mathbb{R}^+$	Loose	No	No
Croce et al. [12]	ReLU-based	No	Any ℓ_p for $p \geq 1$	Loose	No	No
Yang et al. [51]	Any	Multiple types	Any $\ell_p, p \in \mathbb{R}^+$	Strictly tight	No	No
Zhang et al. [52]	Any	ℓ_p-term-constrained	$\ell_1, \ell_2, \ell_\infty$	Strictly tight	No	Yes
Ours (UniCR)	Any	Any continuous PDF	Any $\ell_p, p \in \mathbb{R}^+$	Approx. tight	Yes	Yes

a noise distribution and adds sampled noises to the testing input; then builds a smoothed classifier based on the noisy inputs, and finally derives certified radius for the smoothed classified, e.g., using the Neyman-Pearson Lemma [11].

However, existing randomized smoothing based (and actually all) certified defenses only focus on specific settings and cannot universally certify a classifier against *any* ℓ_p perturbation or *any* noise distribution. For example, the certified radius derived by Cohen et al. [11] is tied to the Gaussian noise and ℓ_2 perturbation. Recent works [12,51,52] propose methods to certify the robustness for multiple norms/noises, e.g., Yang et al. [51] propose the level set and differential method to derive the certified radii for multiple noise distributions. However, the certified radius derivation for different norms is still *subject to case-by-case theoretical analyses*. These methods, although achieving somewhat generalized certified robustness, are still lack of universality (See Table 1 for the summary).

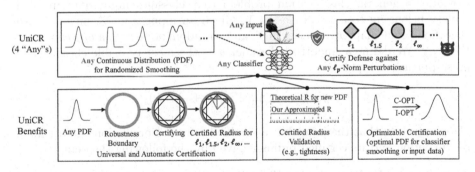

Fig. 1. Our Universally Approximated Certified Robustness (UniCR) framework.

In this paper, we develop the first <u>Uni</u>versally Approximated <u>C</u>ertified <u>R</u>obustness (UniCR) framework based on *randomized smoothing*. Our framework can automate the robustness certification for any input on any classifier against any ℓ_p perturbation with noises generated by any *continuous probability density function (PDF)*. As shown in Fig. 1, our UniCR framework provides four unique significant benefits to make certified robustness more universal, practical and easy-to-use with the above four "any"s. Our key contributions are as follows:

1. **Universal Certification.** UniCR is the first universal robustness certification framework for the 4 "any"s.
2. **Automatic Certification.** UniCR provides an automatic robustness certification for all cases. It is easy-to-launch and avoids case-by-case analysis.
3. **Tightness Validation of Certified Radius.** It is also the first framework that can validate the *tightness* of the derived certified radius in existing certification methods [11,32,35] or future methods based on any continuous noise PDF. In Sect. 3, we validate the tightness of the state-of-the-art certification methods (e.g., see Fig. 4).
4. **Optimality Validation of Noise PDFs.** UniCR can also automatically tune the parameters in noise PDFs to strengthen the robustness certification against any ℓ_p perturbations. For instance, On CIFAR10 and ImageNet datasets, UniCR improves as high as 38.78% overall performance over the state-of-the-art certified defenses against all ℓ_p perturbations. In Sect. 5, we show that Gaussian noise and Laplace noise are not the optimal randomization distribution against the ℓ_2 and ℓ_1 perturbation, respectively.

2   Universally Approximated Certified Robustness

In this section, we propose the theoretical foundation for universally certifying a testing input against any ℓ_p perturbations with noise from any continuous PDF.

2.1   Universal Certified Robustness

Consider a general classification problem that classifies input data in $\mathbb{R}^d$ to a class belonging to a set of classes $\mathcal{Y}$. Given an input $x \in \mathbb{R}^d$, an *any* (base) classifier f that maps x to a class in $\mathcal{Y}$, and a random noise ϵ from *any* continuous PDF μ_x. We define a smoothed classifier g as the most probable class over the noise-perturbed input:

$$g(x) = \arg\max_{c \in \mathcal{Y}} \mathbb{P}(f(x + \epsilon) = c) \tag{1}$$

Then, we show that the input has a certified accurate prediction against any l_p perturbation and its certified radius is given by the following theorem.

Theorem 1 *(Universal Certified Robustness). Let $f : \mathbb{R}^d \to \mathcal{Y}$ be any deterministic or random classifier, and let ϵ be drawn from an arbitrary continuous PDF μ_x. Denote g as the smoothed classifier in Eq. (1), the most probable and second probable classes for predicting a testing input x via g as $c_A, c_B \in \mathcal{Y}$, respectively. If the lower bound of the class c_A's prediction probability $\underline{p_A} \in [0,1]$, and the upper bound of the class c_B's prediction probability $\overline{p_B} \in [0,1]$ satisfy:*

$$\mathbb{P}(f(x + \epsilon) = c_A) \geq \underline{p_A} \geq \overline{p_B} \geq \max_{c \neq c_A} \mathbb{P}(f(x + \epsilon) = c) \tag{2}$$

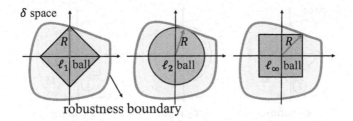

Fig. 2. An illustration to Theorem 1. The conditions in Theorem 1 construct a "**Robustness Boundary**" in δ space. In case of a perturbation inside the robustness boundary, the smoothed prediction can be certifiably correct. From left to right, the figures show that the minimum $||\delta||_1$, $||\delta||_2$ and $||\delta||_\infty$ on the robustness boundary are exactly the certified radius R in ℓ_1, ℓ_2 and ℓ_∞-norm, respectively.

Then, we guarantee that $g(x + \delta) = c_A$ for all $||\delta||_p \leq R$, where R is called the **certified radius** *and it is the minimum ℓ_p-norm of all the adversarial perturbations δ that satisfies the* **robustness boundary conditions** *as below:*

$$\mathbb{P}(\frac{\mu_x(x - \delta)}{\mu_x(x)} \leq t_A) = \underline{p_A}, \quad \mathbb{P}(\frac{\mu_x(x - \delta)}{\mu_x(x)} \geq t_B) = \overline{p_B},$$

$$\mathbb{P}(\frac{\mu_x(x)}{\mu_x(x + \delta)} \leq t_A) = \mathbb{P}(\frac{\mu_x(x)}{\mu_x(x + \delta)} \geq t_B) \tag{3}$$

where t_A and t_B are auxiliary parameters to satisfy the above conditions.

Proof. See the detailed proof in Appendix B.1. □

Robustness Boundary. Theorem 1 provides a novel insight that meeting certain conditions is equivalent to deriving the certified robustness. The conditions in Eq. (3) construct a boundary in the perturbation δ space, which is defined as the *"robustness boundary"*. Within this robustness boundary, the prediction outputted by the smoothed classifier g is certified to be consistent and correct. The robustness boundary, rather than the certified radius, is actually more general to measure the certified robustness since the space constructed by each certified radius (against any specific ℓ_p perturbation) is only a subset of the space inside the robustness boundary. Figure 2 illustrates the relationship between certified radius and the robustness boundary against ℓ_1, ℓ_2 and ℓ_∞ perturbations.

Notice that, given any continuous noise PDF, the corresponding robustness boundary for all the ℓ_p-norms would naturally exist. Each maximum ℓ_p ball is a subspace of the robustness boundary, and gives the certified radius for that specific ℓ_p-norm. Thus, all the certified radii can be universally derived, and Theorem 1 provides a theoretical foundation to certify any input against any ℓ_p perturbations with any continuous noise PDF.

All ℓ_p Perturbations. Although we mainly introduce UniCR against ℓ_1, ℓ_2 and ℓ_∞ perturbations, our UniCR is not limited to these three norms. We emphasize

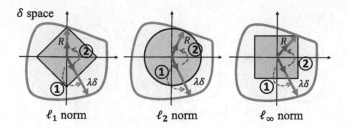

Fig. 3. An illustration to estimating the certified radius. The scalar optimization (①) and direction optimization (②) effectively find the minimum $||\delta||_p$ within the robustness boundary, which is the certified radius R.

that any $p \in \mathbb{R}^+$ (See Appendix D.5) can be used and our UniCR can derive the corresponding certified radius since our robustness boundary gives a general boundary in the δ perturbation space.

2.2   Approximating Tight Certified Robustness

The tight certified radius can be derived by finding a perturbation δ on the robustness boundary that has a minimum $||\delta||_p$ (for any $p \in \mathbb{R}^+$). However, it is challenging to either find a perturbation δ that is exactly on the robustness boundary, or find the minimum $||\delta||_p$. Here, we design an alternative two-phase optimization scheme to accurately approximate the tight certification in practice. In particular, Phase I is to suffice the conditions such that δ is on the robustness boundary, and Phase II is to minimize the ℓ_p-norm.

We perform Phase I by the "scalar optimization", where any perturbation δ will be λ-scaled to the robustness boundary (see ① in Fig. 3). We perform Phase II by the "direction optimization", where the direction of δ will be optimized towards a minimum $||\lambda\delta||_p$ (see ② in Fig. 3). In the two-phase optimization, the direction optimization will be iteratively executed until finding the minimum $||\lambda\delta||_p$, where the perturbation δ will be scaled to the robustness boundary beforehand in every iteration. Thus, the intractable optimization problem in Eq. 3 can be converted to:

$$R = ||\lambda\delta||_p,$$
$$s.t. \quad \delta \in \arg\min_{\delta} ||\lambda\delta||_p, \quad \lambda = \arg\min_{\lambda} |K|,$$
$$\mathbb{P}(\frac{\mu_x(x - \lambda\delta)}{\mu_x(x)} \leq t_A) = \underline{p_A}, \quad \mathbb{P}(\frac{\mu_x(x - \lambda\delta)}{\mu_x(x)} \geq t_B) = \overline{p_B},$$
$$K = \mathbb{P}(\frac{\mu_x(x)}{\mu_x(x + \lambda\delta)} \leq t_A) - \mathbb{P}(\frac{\mu_x(x)}{\mu_x(x + \lambda\delta)} \geq t_B). \tag{4}$$

The scalar optimization in Eq. (4) aims to find the scale factor λ that scales a perturbation δ to the boundary so that $|K|$ approaches 0. With the scalar λ for ensuring that the scaled δ is nearly on the boundary, the direction optimization optimizes the perturbation δ's direction to find the certified radius $R = ||\lambda\delta||_p$. We also present the theoretical analysis on the certification confidence and the optimization convergence in Appendix B.4 and B.5, respectively.

3   Deriving Certified Radius Within Robustness Boundary

In this section, we will introduce how to universally and automatically derive the certified radius against any ℓ_p perturbations within the robustness boundary constructed by any noise PDF. In particular, we will present practical algorithms for solving the two-phase optimization problem to approximate the certified radius, empirically validate that our UniCR approximates the tight certified radius derived by recent works [11,43,51], and finally discuss how to apply UniCR to validate the radius of existing certified defenses.

3.1   Calculating Certified Radius in Practice

Following the existing randomized smoothing based defenses [11,43], we first use the Monte Carlo method to estimate the probability bounds ($\underline{p_A}$ and $\overline{p_B}$). Then, we use them in our two-phase optimization scheme to derive the certified radius.

Estimating Probability Bounds. The two-phase optimization needs to estimate the probabilities bounds $\underline{p_A}$ and $\overline{p_B}$ and compute two auxiliary parameters t_A and t_B (required by the certified robustness based on the Neyman-Pearson Lemma in Appendix A). Identical to existing works [11,43], the probabilities bounds $\underline{p_A}$ and $\overline{p_B}$ are commonly estimated by the Monte Carlo method [11]. Given the estimated $\underline{p_A}$ and $\overline{p_B}$ as well as any given noise PDF and a perturbation δ, we also use the Monte Carlo method to estimate the cumulative density function (CDF) of fraction $\mu_x(x - \lambda\delta)/\mu_x(x)$. Then, we can compute the auxiliary parameters t_A and t_B. Specifically, the auxiliary parameters t_A and t_B can be computed by $t_A = \Phi^{-1}(\underline{p_A})$ and $t_B = \Phi^{-1}(\overline{p_B})$, where Φ^{-1} is the inverse CDF of the fraction $\mu_x(x - \lambda\delta)/\mu_x(x)$. The procedures for computing t_A and t_B are detailed in Algorithm 1 in Appendix C.

Scalar Optimization. Finding a perturbation δ that is exactly on the robustness boundary is computationally challenging. Thus, we alternatively scale the δ to approach the boundary. We use the binary search algorithm to find a scale factor that minimizes $|K|$ (*the distance between δ and the robustness boundary*). The algorithm and detailed description are presented in Appendix C.2.

Direction Optimization. We use the Particle Swarm Optimization (PSO) method [29] to find δ that minimizes the ℓ_p-norm after scaling to the robustness boundary. In each iteration of PSO, the particle's position represents δ, and the cost function is $f_{PSO}(\delta) = ||\lambda\delta||_p$, where the scalar λ is found by the scalar optimization. The PSO aims to find the position δ that can minimize the cost function. To pursue convergence, we choose some initial positions in symmetry

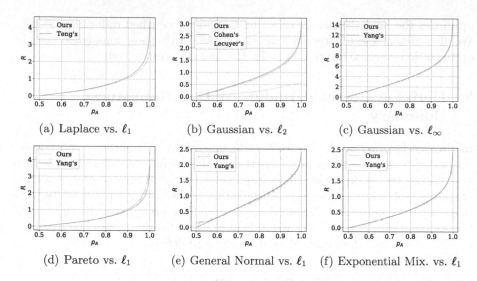

(a) Laplace vs. ℓ_1 (b) Gaussian vs. ℓ_2 (c) Gaussian vs. ℓ_∞

(d) Pareto vs. ℓ_1 (e) General Normal vs. ℓ_1 (f) Exponential Mix. vs. ℓ_1

Fig. 4. p_A-R curve comparison of our method and state-of-the-arts (i.e., Teng et al. [43], Cohen et al. [11], Lecuyer et al. [32] and Yang et al. [51]). We observe that the certified radius obtained by our UniCR is close to that obtained by the state-of-the-arts. These results demonstrate that our UniCR can approximate the tight certification to any input in any ℓ_p norm with any continuous noise distribution. We also evaluate our UniCR's defense accuracy against a diverse set of attacks, including universal attacks [10], white-box attacks [13,48], and black-box attacks [1,6], and against ℓ_1, ℓ_2 and ℓ_∞ perturbations. The experimental results show that UniCR is as robust as the state-of-the-arts (100% defense accuracy) against all the types of the real attack. The detailed experimental settings and results are presented in Appendix D.2.

for different ℓ_p-norms. Empirical results show that the radius obtained by PSO with these initial positions can accurately approximate the tight certified radius. We show how to set the initial positions in Appendix C.3.

In our experiments, the certification (deriving the certified radius) can be efficiently completed on MNIST [31], CIFAR10 [30] and ImageNet [40] datasets (less than 10 s per image), as shown in Appendix D.4.

Certified Radius Comparison with State-of-the-Arts. We compare the certified radius obtained by our two-phase optimization method and that by the state-of-the-arts [11,43,51] and the comparison results are shown in Fig. 4. Note that the certified radius is a function of p_A (the prediction probability of the top-1 class). The p_A-R curve can well depict the certified radius R w.r.t. p_A. We observe that our p_A-R curve highly approximates the tight theoretical curves in existing works, e.g., the Gaussian noise against ℓ_2 and ℓ_∞ perturbations [11,51], Laplace noise against ℓ_1 perturbations [43], as well as General Normal noise and General Exponential noise derived by Yang et al. [51]'s method.

Tightness Validation of Certified Radius. Since our UniCR accurately approximates the tight certified radius, it can be used as an auxiliary tool to validate whether an obtained certified radius is tight or not. For example, the certified radius derived by PixelDP [32][1] is loose, because [32]'s p_A-R curve in Fig. 4(b) is far below ours. Also, Yang et al. [51] derives a low bound certified radius for Pareto Noise (Fig. 4(d))—It shows that this certified radius is not tight either since it is below ours. For those theoretical radii that are slightly above our radii, they are likely to be tight.

Moreover, due to the high university, our UniCR can even derive the certified radii for complicated noise PDFs, e.g., mixture distribution in which the certified radii are difficult to be theoretically derived. In Sect. 5.2, we show some examples of deriving radii using UniCR on a wide variety of noise distributions in Fig. 6, 7 and 8. In most examples, the certified radii have not been studied before.

4 Optimizing Noise PDF for Certified Robustness

UniCR can derive the certified radius using any continuous noise PDF for randomized smoothing. This provides the flexibility to optimize a noise PDF for enlarging the certified radius. In this section, we will optimize the noisy PDF in our UniCR framework for obtaining better certified robustness.

4.1 Noise PDF Optimization

All the existing randomized smoothing methods [11,43,51,52] use the same noise for training the smoothed classifier and certifying the robustness of testing inputs. The motivation is that: the training can improve the lower bound of the prediction probability over the the same noise as the certification. Here, the question we ask is: Must we necessarily use the same noise PDF to train the smoothed classifier and derive the certified robustness? Our answer is No.

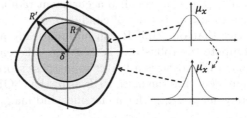

We study the master optimization problem that uses UniCR as a function to maximize the certified radius by tuning the noise PDF (different randomization), as shown in Fig. 5. To defend against certain ℓ_p perturbations for a classifier, we consider the noise PDF as a variable (Remember that UniCR can provide a certified radius for each noise PDF), and study the following two master optimization problems with two different strategies:

Fig. 5. An illustration to noise PDF optimization (take ℓ_2-norm perturbation as an example). The noise distribution is tuned from μ_x to μ'_x, which enlarges the robustness boundary. Thus, UniCR can find a larger certified radius R'.

---

[1] PixelDP [32] adopts differential privacy [17], e.g., Gaussian mechanism to generate noises for each pixel such that certified robustness can be achieved for images.

1. *Classifier-Input Noise Optimization* ("**C-OPT**"): finding the optimal noise PDF and injecting *the same noise* from this noise PDF into both the training data to train a classifier and testing input to build a smoothed classifier.
2. *Input Noise Optimization* ("**I-OPT**"): Training a classifier with the standard noise (e.g., Gaussian noise), while finding the optimal noise PDF for the testing input and injecting noise from this PDF into the testing input only.

4.2 C-OPT and I-OPT

Before optimizing the certified robustness, we need to define metrics for them. First, since I-OPT only optimizes the noise PDF when certifying each testing input, a "better" randomization in I-OPT can be directly indicated by a larger certified radius for a specific input. Second, since C-OPT optimizes the noise PDF for the entire dataset in both training and robustness certification, a new metric for the performance on the entire dataset need to be defined.

Existing works [51,52] draw several certified accuracy vs. certified radius curves computed by noise with different variances (See Fig. 10 in Appendix D.1). These curves represent the certified accuracy at a range of certified radii, where the certified accuracy at radius R is defined as the percent of the testing samples with a derived certified radius larger than R (and correctly predicted by the smoothed classifier). To simply measure the overall performance, we use the area under the curve as an overall metric to the certified robustness, namely "robustness score". Then, we design the C-OPT method based on this metric. Specifically, the robustness score R_{score} is formally defined as below:

$$R_{score} = \int_0^{+\infty} \max_\sigma (Acc_\sigma(R)) dR, \sigma \in \Sigma, \tag{5}$$

where $Acc_\sigma(R)$ is the certified accuracy at radius R computed by the noises with variance σ, and Σ is a set of candidate σ.

Notice that our UniCR can automatically approximate the certified radius and compute the robustness score w.r.t. different noise PDFs, thus we can tune the noise PDF towards a better robustness score. From the perspective of optimization, denoting the noise PDF as μ, the C-OPT and the I-OPT problems are defined as $\max_\mu R_{score}$ for a classifier and $\max_\mu R$ for an input, respectively.

Algorithms for Noise PDF Optimization. We use grid-search in C-OPT to search the best parameters of the noise PDF. We use Hill-Climbing algorithms in I-OPT to find the best parameters of the noise PDF around the noise distribution used in training while maintaining the certified accuracy.

Optimality Validation of Noise PDF. Finding an optimal noise PDF against a specific ℓ_p perturbation is important. Although Gaussian distribution can be used for defending against ℓ_2 perturbations with tight certified radius, there is no evidence showing that Gaussian distribution is the optimal distribution against ℓ_2 perturbations. Our UniCR can also somewhat validate the optimality of using different noise PDFs against different ℓ_p perturbations. For instance, Cohen et

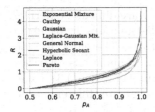 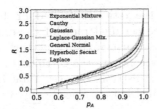 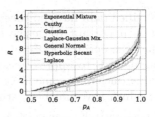

Fig. 6. R-p_A curve vs. ℓ_1 **Fig. 7.** R-p_A curve vs. ℓ_2 **Fig. 8.** R-p_A curve vs. ℓ_∞

al. [11]'s certified radius is tight for Gaussian noise against ℓ_2 perturbations (see Fig. 4(b)). However, it is validated as not-optimal distribution against ℓ_2 perturbations in our experiments (see Table 2).

5 Experiments

In this section, we thoroughly evaluate our UniCR framework, and benchmark with state-of-the-art certified defenses. First, we evaluate the *universality* of UniCR by approximating the certified radii w.r.t. the probability p_A using a variety of noise PDFs against ℓ_1, ℓ_2 and ℓ_∞ perturbations. Second, we validate the certified radii in existing works (results have been discussed and shown in Sect. 3). Third, we evaluate our noise PDF optimization on three real-world datasets. Finally, we compare our best certified accuracy on CIFAR10 [30] and ImageNet [40] with the state-of-the-art methods.

5.1 Experimental Setting

Datasets. We evaluate our performance on MNIST [31], CIFAR10 [30] and ImageNet [40], which are common datasets to evaluate the certified robustness.

Metrics. We use certified accuracy [11] and the robustness score (Eq. (5)) to evaluate the performance of proposed methods.

Experimental Environment. All the experiments were performed on the NSF Chameleon Cluster [28] with Intel(R) Xeon(R) Gold 6126 2.60 GHz CPUs, 192G RAM, and NVIDIA Quadro RTX 6000 GPUs.

5.2 Universality Evaluation

As randomized smoothing derives certified robustness for any input and any classifier, our evaluation targets "any noise PDF" and "any ℓ_p perubations".

The certified radii of some noise PDFs, e.g., Gaussian noise against ℓ_2 perturbations [11], Laplace noise against ℓ_1 perturbations [43], Pareto noise against ℓ_1 perturbations [51], have been derived. These distributions have been verified by our UniCR framework in Fig. 4, where our certified radii highly approximate these theoretical radii. However, there are numerous noise PDFs of which the certified radii have not been theoretically studied, or they are difficult to derive. It is important to derive the certified radii of these distributions in order to find the optimal PDF against each of the ℓ_p perturbations. Therefore, we use our UniCR to approximately compute the certified radii of numerous distributions (including some mixture distributions, see Table 7 in Appendix D.3), some of which have not been studied before. Specifically, we evaluate different noise PDFs with the same variance, i.e., $\sigma = \mathbb{E}_{\epsilon \sim \mu}[\sqrt{\frac{1}{d}\|\epsilon\|_2^2}] = 1$. For those PDFs with multiple parameters, we set β as 1.5, 1.0 and 0.5 for General Normal, Pareto, and mixture distributions, respectively. Following Cohen et al. [11], and Yang et al. [51], we consider the binary case (Theorem 3) and only compute the certified radius when $p_A \in (0.5, 1.0]$.

In Fig. 6, 7 and 8, we plot the R-p_A curves for the noise distributions listed in Table 7 in Appendix D.3 against ℓ_1, ℓ_2 and ℓ_∞ perturbations. Specifically, we present the ℓ_∞ radius scaled by $\times 255$ to be consistent with the existing works [52]. We observe that for all ℓ_p perturbations, the Gaussian noise generates the largest certified radius for most of the p_A values. All the noise distribution has very close R-p_A curves except the Cauthy distribution. We also notice that when p_A is low against ℓ_2 and ℓ_∞ perturbations, our UniCR cannot find the certified radius for the Laplace-based distributions, e.g., Laplace distribution, and Gaussian-Laplace mixture distribution. This matches the findings on injecting Laplace noises for certified robustness in Yang et al. [51]—The certified radii for Laplace noise against ℓ_2 and ℓ_∞ perturbations are difficult to derive.

We also conduct experiments to illustrate UniCR's universality in deriving ℓ_p norm certified radius for any real number $p > 0$ in Appendix D.5. Besides, we also conduct fine-grained evaluations on General Normal, Laplace-Gaussian Mixture, and Exponential Mixture noises with various β parameters (See Fig. 13 in Appendix D.6), and we can draw similar observations from such results.

Table 2. Classifier-input noise optimization (C-OPT). We show the Robustness Score w.r.t. different β settings of General Normal distribution ($\propto e^{-|x/\alpha|^\beta}$). The σ is set to 1.0 for all distributions by adjusting the α parameter in General Normal.

β	0.25	0.50	0.75	1.00	1.25	1.50	1.75	2.00	2.25	2.50	2.75	3	4.00	5.00
vs. ℓ_1	1.8999	2.6136	**2.8354**	2.7448	2.5461	2.4254	2.3434	2.2615	2.2211	2.1730	2.1081	2.0679	1.9610	1.8925
vs. ℓ_2	0.0000	0.0003	1.0373	1.5954	1.9255	2.0882	2.1746	2.1983	**2.2081**	2.1771	2.1184	2.0655	1.8857	1.7296
vs. ℓ_∞	0.0000	0.0109	0.0420	0.0641	0.0771	0.0839	0.0871	0.0879	**0.0880**	0.0870	0.0847	0.0825	0.0758	0.0693

5.3 Optimizing Certified Radius with C-OPT

We next show how C-OPT uses UniCR to improve the certification against any ℓ_p perturbations. Recall that tight certified radii against ℓ_1 and ℓ_2 perturbations can be derived by the Laplace [43] and Gaussian [11] noises, respectively. However, there does not exist any theoretical study showing that Laplace and Gaussian

Table 3. Average Certified Radius with Input Noise Optimization (I-OPT) against ℓ_1, ℓ_2 and ℓ_∞ perturbations on ImageNet.

Top ℓ_1 radius	20%	40%	60%	80%	100%
Yang's Gaussian [51]	**2.44**	2.10	1.59	1.19	0.95
Ours with I-OPT	2.36	**2.11**	**1.64**	**1.23**	**0.98**
Top ℓ_2 radius	20%	40%	60%	80%	100%
Cohen's Gaussian [11]	**2.43**	2.10	1.58	1.19	0.95
Ours with I-OPT	2.36	**2.11**	**1.64**	**1.23**	**0.98**
Top ℓ_∞ radius ×255	20%	40%	60%	80%	100%
Yang's Gaussian [51]	1.60	1.38	1.04	0.78	0.63
Ours with I-OPT	**1.75**	**1.54**	**1.20**	**0.90**	**0.72**

noises are the optimal noises against ℓ_1 and ℓ_2 perturbations, respectively. [51,52] have identified that there exists other better noise for ℓ_1 and ℓ_2 perturbations. Therefore, we use our C-OPT to explore the optimal distribution for each ℓ_p perturbation. Since the commonly used noise, e.g., Laplace and Gaussian noises, are only special cases of the General Normal Distribution ($\propto e^{-|x/\alpha|^\beta}$), we will find the optimal parameters α and β that generate the best noises for maximizing certified radius against each ℓ_p perturbation.

In the experiments, we use the grid search method to search the best parameters. We choose β as the main parameter, and α will be set to satisfy $\sigma = 1$. Specifically, we evaluate C-OPT on the MNIST dataset, where we train a model on the training set for each round of the grid search and certify 1,000 images in the test set. Specifically, for each pair of parameters α and β in the grid search, we train a Multiple Layer Perception on MNIST with the smoothing noise. Then, we compute the robustness score over a set of $\sigma = [0.12, 0.25, 0.50, 1.00]$. When approximating the certified radius with UniCR, we set the sampling number as 1,000 in the Monte Carlo method. The results are shown in Table 2.

We observe that the best β for ℓ_1-norm is 0.75 in the grid search. It indicates that the Laplace noise ($\beta = 1$) is not the optimal noise against ℓ_1 perturbations. A slightly smaller β can provide a better trade-off between the certified radius and accuracy (measured by the robustness score). When $\beta < 1.0$, the radius is observed to be larger than the radius derived with Laplace noise at $p_A \approx 1$ (see Fig. 13(a)). Since p_A on MNIST is always high, the noise distribution with $\beta = 0.75$ will give a larger radius at most cases. Furthermore, we observe that the best performance against ℓ_2 and ℓ_∞ are given by $\beta = 2.25$, showing that the Gaussian noise is not the optimal noise against ℓ_2 and ℓ_∞ perturbations, either.

5.4 Optimizing Certified Radius with I-OPT

The optimal noises for different inputs are different. We customize the noise for each input using the I-OPT. Specifically, we adapt the hyper-parameters in the

Table 4. Certified accuracy and robustness score against ℓ_1, ℓ_2 and ℓ_∞ perturbations on CIFAR10. Ours: General Normal with I-OPT.

ℓ_1 radius	0.50	1.00	1.50	2.00	2.50	R_{score}
Teng's Laplace [43]	39.2	17.2	10.0	6.0	2.8	0.5606
Ours	**45.8**	**22.4**	**14.8**	**8.2**	**3.6**	**0.7027**
ℓ_2 radius	0.50	1.00	1.50	2.00	2.50	R_{score}
Cohen's Gaussian [11]	38.6	17.4	8.6	3.4	1.6	0.5392
Ours	**48.4**	**26.8**	**16.6**	**6.8**	**2.0**	**0.7141**
ℓ_∞ radius	$\frac{2}{255}$	$\frac{4}{255}$	$\frac{6}{255}$	$\frac{8}{255}$	$\frac{10}{255}$	R_{score}
Yang's Gaussian [51]	43.6	21.8	10.8	5.6	2.6	0.0098
Ours	**53.4**	**30.4**	**21.2**	**13.2**	**5.6**	**0.0136**

Table 5. Certified accuracy and robustness score against ℓ_1, ℓ_2 and ℓ_∞ perturbations on ImageNet (Teng's Laplace [43] is not available). Ours: General Normal with I-OPT.

ℓ_1 radius	0.50	1.00	1.50	2.00	2.50	R_{score}
Yang's Gaussian [51]	58.8	45.6	34.6	27.0	0.0	1.0469
Ours	**63.4**	**49.6**	**36.8**	**29.6**	**6.6**	**1.1385**
ℓ_2 radius	0.50	1.00	1.50	2.00	2.50	R_{score}
Cohen's Gaussian [11]	58.8	44.2	34.0	27.0	0.0	1.0463
Ours	**62.6**	**49.0**	**36.6**	**28.6**	**2.0**	**1.0939**
ℓ_∞ radius	$\frac{0.25}{255}$	$\frac{0.50}{255}$	$\frac{0.75}{255}$	$\frac{1.00}{255}$	$\frac{1.25}{255}$	R_{score}
Yang's Gaussian [51]	63.6	52.4	39.8	34.2	28.0	0.0027
Ours	**69.2**	**57.4**	**47.2**	**38.2**	**33.0**	**0.0031**

noise PDF to find the optimal noise distribution for each input (the classifier is smoothed by a standard method such as Cohen's [11]).

We perform I-OPT for noise PDF optimization with a Gaussian-trained ResNet50 classifier ($\sigma = 1$) on ImageNet. We compare our derived radius with the theoretical radius in [11,51]. We use the General Normal distribution to generate the noise for input certification since it provides a new parameter dimension for tuning, and tune the parameters α and β in $e^{-|x/\alpha|^\beta}$. The Gaussian distribution is only a specific case of the General Normal distribution with $\beta = 2$. In the two baselines [11,51], they set $\sigma = 1$ and $\beta = 2$, respectively. In the I-OPT, we initialize the noise with the same setting, but optimize the noise for each input. The Monte Carlo sample is set to $1,000$ for ImageNet.

Table 3 presents the average values of the top 20%-100% certified radius (the higher the better). It shows that our I-OPT significantly improves the certified radius over the tight certified radius since it provides a personalized noise optimization to each input (see Fig. 14 in Appendix E for the illustration).

5.5 Best Performance Comparison

In this section, we compare our best performance with the state-of-the-art certified defense methods on the CIFAR10 and ImageNet datasets. Following the setting in [11], we use a ResNet110 [23] classifier for the CIFAR10 dataset and a ResNet50 [23] classifier for the ImageNet dataset. We evaluate the certification performance with the noise PDF of a range of variances σ. The σ is set to vary in $[0.12, 0.25, 0.5, 1.0]$ for CIFAR10 and $[0.25, 0.5, 1.0]$ for ImageNet. We also present the Robustness Score based on this set of variances. We use the General Normal distribution and perform the I-OPT. The distribution is initialized with the same setting in the baselines, e.g., $\beta = 1$ (or 2) for Laplace (Gaussian) baseline. We benchmark it with the Laplace noise [43] on CIFAR10 when against ℓ_1 perturbations; and the Gaussian noise [11,51] on both CIFAR10 and ImageNet against all ℓ_p perturbations. For both our method and baselines, we use $1,000$ and $4,000$ Monte Carlo samples on ImageNet and CIFAR10, respectively, due to different scales, and the certified accuracy is computed over the certified radius of 500 images randomly chosen in the test set for both CIFAR10 and ImageNet.

The results are shown in Table 4 and 5. Both on CIFAR10 and ImageNet, we observe a significant improvement on the certified accuracy and robustness score. Specifically, on CIFAR10, our robustness score outperforms the state-of-the-arts by 25.34%, 32.44% and 38.78% against ℓ_1, ℓ_2 and ℓ_∞ perturbations, respectively. On ImageNet, our robustness score outperforms the state-of-the-arts by 8.75%, 4.55% and 14.81% against ℓ_1, ℓ_2 and ℓ_∞ perturbations, respectively.

6 Related Work

Certified Defenses. Existing certified defenses methods can be classified into leveraging Satisfiability Modulo Theories [4,18,27,41], mixed integer-linear programming [3,8,19], linear programming [47,49], semidefinite programming [38,39], dual optimization [14,15], global/local Lipschitz constant methods [2,9,21,24,44], abstract interpretation [20,37,42], and layer-wise certification [22,37,42,46,53], etc. However, none of these methods is able to scale to large models (e.g., deep neural networks) or is limited to specific type of network architecture, e.g., ReLU based networks. Randomized smoothing was recently proposed certified defenses [11,25,32,35,45] that is scalable to large models and applicable to arbitrary classifiers. Lecuyer et al. [32] proposed the first randomized smoothing-based certified defense via differential privacy [17]. Li et al. [35] proposed a stronger guarantee for Gaussian noise using information theory. The first tight robustness guarantee against l_2-norm perturbation for Gaussian noise was developed by Cohen et al. [11]. After that, a series follow-up works have been proposed for other ℓ_p-norms, e.g., ℓ_1-norm [43], ℓ_0-norm [26,33,34], etc. However, all these methods are limited to guarantee the robustness against only a specific ℓ_p-norm perturbation.

Universal Certified Defenses. More recently, several works [51,52] aim to provide more universal certified robustness schemes for all ℓ_p-norms. Yang et al.

[51] proposed a level set method and a differential method to derive the upper bound and lower bound of the certified radius, while the derivation is relying on the case-by-case theoretical analysis. Zhang et al. [52] proposed a black-box optimization scheme that automatically computes the certified radius, but the solvable distribution is limited to ℓ_p-norm-constrained. Our UniCR framework can automate the robustness certification for any classifier against any l_p-norm perturbation with any noise PDF.

Certified Defenses with Optimized Noise PDFs/Distributions. Yang et al. [51] proposed to use the Wulff Crystal theory [50] to find optimal noise distributions. Zhang et al. [52] claimed that the optimal noise should have a more central-concentrated distribution from the optimization perspective. However, no existing works provide quantitative solutions to find optimal noise distributions. We propose the **C-Opt** and **I-Opt** schemes to quantitatively optimize the noisy PDF in our UniCR framework and provide better certified robustness. Table 1 summarizes the differences in all the closely-related works.

7   Conclusion

Randomize smoothing has achieved great success in certifying the adversarial robustness. However, the state-of-the-art methods lack universality to certify robustness. We propose the first randomized smoothing-based universal certified robustness approximation framework against any ℓ_p perturbations with any continuous noise PDF. Extensive evaluations on multiple image datasets demonstrate the effectiveness of our UniCR framework and its advantages over the state-of-the-art certified defenses against any ℓ_p perturbations.

Acknowledgement. This work is partially supported by the National Science Foundation (NSF) under the Grants No. CNS-2046335 and CNS-2034870, as well as the Cisco Research Award. In addition, results presented in this paper were obtained using the Chameleon testbed supported by the NSF. Finally, the authors would like to thank the anonymous reviewers for their constructive comments.

References

1. Andriushchenko, M., Croce, F., Flammarion, N., Hein, M.: Square attack: a query-efficient black-box adversarial attack via random search. In: Vedaldi, A., Bischof, H., Brox, T., Frahm, J.-M. (eds.) ECCV 2020. LNCS, vol. 12368, pp. 484–501. Springer, Cham (2020). https://doi.org/10.1007/978-3-030-58592-1_29
2. Anil, C., Lucas, J., Grosse, R.: Sorting out lipschitz function approximation. In: International Conference on Machine Learning, pp. 291–301. PMLR (2019)
3. Bunel, R.R., Turkaslan, I., Torr, P.H., Kohli, P., Mudigonda, P.K.: A unified view of piecewise linear neural network verification. In: NeurIPS (2018)
4. Carlini, N., Katz, G., Barrett, C., Dill, D.L.: Provably minimally-distorted adversarial examples. arXiv preprint arXiv:1709.10207 (2017)
5. Carlini, N., Wagner, D.: Towards evaluating the robustness of neural networks. In: 2017 IEEE Symposium on Security and Privacy (SP), pp. 39–57. IEEE (2017)

6. Chen, J., Jordan, M.I., Wainwright, M.J.: HopSkipJumpAttack: a query-efficient decision-based attack. In: 2020 IEEE Symposium on Security and Privacy (2020)

7. Chen, P.Y., Zhang, H., Sharma, Y., Yi, J., Hsieh, C.J.: ZOO: zeroth order optimization based black-box attacks to deep neural networks without training substitute models. In: 10th ACM Workshop on Artificial Intelligence and Security (2017)

8. Cheng, C.-H., Nührenberg, G., Ruess, H.: Maximum resilience of artificial neural networks. In: D'Souza, D., Narayan Kumar, K. (eds.) ATVA 2017. LNCS, vol. 10482, pp. 251–268. Springer, Cham (2017). https://doi.org/10.1007/978-3-319-68167-2_18

9. Cissé, M., Bojanowski, P., Grave, E., Dauphin, Y.N., Usunier, N.: Parseval networks: improving robustness to adversarial examples. In: Proceedings of the 34th International Conference on Machine Learning (2017)

10. Co, K.T., Muñoz-González, L., de Maupeou, S., Lupu, E.C.: Procedural noise adversarial examples for black-box attacks on deep convolutional networks. In: ACM SIGSAC Conference on Computer and Communications Security (2019)

11. Cohen, J., Rosenfeld, E., Kolter, Z.: Certified adversarial robustness via randomized smoothing. In: International Conference on Machine Learning (2019)

12. Croce, F., Hein, M.: Provable robustness against all adversarial l_p-perturbations for $p \geq 1$. In: ICLR. OpenReview.net (2020)

13. Croce, F., Hein, M.: Reliable evaluation of adversarial robustness with an ensemble of diverse parameter-free attacks. In: International Conference on Machine Learning, pp. 2206–2216. PMLR (2020)

14. Dvijotham, K., Gowal, S., Stanforth, R., et al.: Training verified learners with learned verifiers. arXiv (2018)

15. Dvijotham, K., Stanforth, R., Gowal, S., Mann, T.A., Kohli, P.: A dual approach to scalable verification of deep networks. In: UAI (2018)

16. Dvijotham, K.D., et al.: A framework for robustness certification of smoothed classifiers using f-divergences. In: ICLR (2020)

17. Dwork, C., Roth, A.: The algorithmic foundations of differential privacy. Found. Trends Theor. Comput. Sci. **9**(3–4), 211–407 (2014)

18. Ehlers, R.: Formal verification of piece-wise linear feed-forward neural networks. In: D'Souza, D., Narayan Kumar, K. (eds.) ATVA 2017. LNCS, vol. 10482, pp. 269–286. Springer, Cham (2017). https://doi.org/10.1007/978-3-319-68167-2_19

19. Fischetti, M., Jo, J.: Deep neural networks and mixed integer linear optimization. Constraints **23**(3), 296–309 (2018)

20. Gehr, T., Mirman, M., Drachsler-Cohen, D., Tsankov, P., Chaudhuri, S., Vechev, M.: AI2: safety and robustness certification of neural networks with abstract interpretation. In: IEEE S & P (2018)

21. Gouk, H., Frank, E., Pfahringer, B., Cree, M.J.: Regularisation of neural networks by enforcing lipschitz continuity. Mach. Learn. **110**(2), 393–416 (2021)

22. Gowal, S., et al.: On the effectiveness of interval bound propagation for training verifiably robust models. CoRR abs/1810.12715 (2018). http://arxiv.org/abs/1810.12715

23. He, K., Zhang, X., Ren, S., Sun, J.: Deep residual learning for image recognition. In: Proceedings of the IEEE Conference on Computer Vision and Pattern Recognition, pp. 770–778 (2016)

24. Hein, M., Andriushchenko, M.: Formal guarantees on the robustness of a classifier against adversarial manipulation. In: Advances in Neural Information Processing Systems 30: Annual Conference on Neural Information Processing Systems 2017, 4–9 December 2017, Long Beach, CA, USA, pp. 2266–2276 (2017)

25. Jia, J., Cao, X., Wang, B., Gong, N.Z.: Certified robustness for top-k predictions against adversarial perturbations via randomized smoothing. In: International Conference on Learning Representations (2019)
26. Jia, J., Wang, B., Cao, X., Liu, H., Gong, N.Z.: Almost tight l0-norm certified robustness of top-k predictions against adversarial perturbations. In: ICLR (2022)
27. Katz, G., Barrett, C., Dill, D.L., Julian, K., Kochenderfer, M.J.: Reluplex: an efficient SMT solver for verifying deep neural networks. In: Majumdar, R., Kunčak, V. (eds.) CAV 2017. LNCS, vol. 10426, pp. 97–117. Springer, Cham (2017). https://doi.org/10.1007/978-3-319-63387-9_5
28. Keahey, K., et al.: Lessons learned from the chameleon testbed. In: Proceedings of the 2020 USENIX Annual Technical Conference (USENIX ATC 2020). USENIX Association (2020)
29. Kennedy, J., Eberhart, R.: Particle swarm optimization. In: Proceedings of ICNN 1995-International Conference on Neural Networks. IEEE (1995)
30. Krizhevsky, A., Hinton, G., et al.: Learning multiple layers of features from tiny images (2009)
31. LeCun, Y., Cortes, C., Burges, C.: Mnist handwritten digit database. ATT Labs 2 (2010). http://yann.lecun.com/exdb/mnist
32. Lecuyer, M., Atlidakis, V., Geambasu, R., Hsu, D., Jana, S.: Certified robustness to adversarial examples with differential privacy. In: 2019 IEEE Symposium on Security and Privacy (SP), pp. 656–672. IEEE (2019)
33. Lee, G., Yuan, Y., Chang, S., Jaakkola, T.S.: Tight certificates of adversarial robustness for randomly smoothed classifiers. In: NeurIPS, pp. 4911–4922 (2019)
34. Levine, A., Feizi, S.: Robustness certificates for sparse adversarial attacks by randomized ablation. In: AAAI, pp. 4585–4593. AAAI Press (2020)
35. Li, B., Chen, C., Wang, W., Carin, L.: Second-order adversarial attack and certifiable robustness. arXiv preprint arXiv:2006.00731 (2020)
36. Madry, A., Makelov, A., Schmidt, L., Tsipras, D., Vladu, A.: Towards deep learning models resistant to adversarial attacks. In: International Conference on Learning Representations (2018)
37. Mirman, M., Gehr, T., Vechev, M.: Differentiable abstract interpretation for provably robust neural networks. In: International Conference on Machine Learning (2018)
38. Raghunathan, A., Steinhardt, J., Liang, P.: Certified defenses against adversarial examples. arXiv preprint arXiv:1801.09344 (2018)
39. Raghunathan, A., Steinhardt, J., Liang, P.S.: Semidefinite relaxations for certifying robustness to adversarial examples. In: NeurIPS (2018)
40. Russakovsky, O., et al.: ImageNet large scale visual recognition challenge. Int. J. Comput. Vis. 115(3), 211–252 (2015). https://doi.org/10.1007/s11263-015-0816-y
41. Scheibler, K., Winterer, L., Wimmer, R., Becker, B.: Towards verification of artificial neural networks. In: MBMV, pp. 30–40 (2015)
42. Singh, G., Gehr, T., Mirman, M., Püschel, M., Vechev, M.: Fast and effective robustness certification. In: Proceedings of the 32nd International Conference on Neural Information Processing Systems, pp. 10825–10836 (2018)
43. Teng, J., Lee, G.H., Yuan, Y.: ℓ_1 adversarial robustness certificates: a randomized smoothing approach (2020)
44. Tsuzuku, Y., Sato, I., Sugiyama, M.: Lipschitz-margin training: scalable certification of perturbation invariance for deep neural networks. In: NeurIPS (2018)
45. Wang, B., Cao, X., Gong, N.Z., et al.: On certifying robustness against backdoor attacks via randomized smoothing. In: CVPR 2020 Workshop on Adversarial Machine Learning in Computer Vision (2020)

46. Weng, T., et al.: Towards fast computation of certified robustness for ReLU networks. In: Dy, J.G., Krause, A. (eds.) International Conference on Machine Learning (2018)
47. Wong, E., Kolter, J.Z.: Provable defenses against adversarial examples via the convex outer adversarial polytope. In: ICML (2018)
48. Wong, E., Schmidt, F., Kolter, Z.: Wasserstein adversarial examples via projected sinkhorn iterations. In: International Conference on Machine Learning (2019)
49. Wong, E., Schmidt, F.R., Metzen, J.H., Kolter, J.Z.: Scaling provable adversarial defenses. arXiv preprint arXiv:1805.12514 (2018)
50. Wul, G.: Zur frage der geschwindigkeit des wachstums und der auflosung der kristall achen. Z. Kristallogr. **34**, 449–530 (1901)
51. Yang, G., Duan, T., Hu, J.E., Salman, H., Razenshteyn, I., Li, J.: Randomized smoothing of all shapes and sizes. In: International Conference on Machine Learning, pp. 10693–10705. PMLR (2020)
52. Zhang, D., Ye, M., Gong, C., Zhu, Z., Liu, Q.: Black-box certification with randomized smoothing: a functional optimization based framework (2020)
53. Zhang, H., Weng, T., Chen, P., Hsieh, C., Daniel, L.: Efficient neural network robustness certification with general activation functions. In: Neural Information Processing Systems (2018)

Hardly Perceptible Trojan Attack Against Neural Networks with Bit Flips

Jiawang Bai[1], Kuofeng Gao[1], Dihong Gong[2], Shu-Tao Xia[1,3(✉)],
Zhifeng Li[2(✉)], and Wei Liu[2(✉)]

[1] Tsinghua Shenzhen International Graduate School,
Tsinghua University, Shenzhen, China
{bjw19,gkf21}@mails.tsinghua.edu.cn, xiast@sz.tsinghua.edu.cn
[2] Data Platform, Tencent, Shenzhen, China
michaelzfli@tencent.com, wl2223@columbia.edu
[3] Research Center of Artificial Intelligence, Peng Cheng Laboratory, Shenzhen, China

Abstract. The security of deep neural networks (DNNs) has attracted increasing attention due to their widespread use in various applications. Recently, the deployed DNNs have been demonstrated to be vulnerable to Trojan attacks, which manipulate model parameters with bit flips to inject a hidden behavior and activate it by a specific trigger pattern. However, all existing Trojan attacks adopt noticeable patch-based triggers (e.g., a square pattern), making them perceptible to humans and easy to be spotted by machines. In this paper, we present a novel attack, namely hardly perceptible Trojan attack (HPT). HPT crafts hardly perceptible Trojan images by utilizing the additive noise and per-pixel flow field to tweak the pixel values and positions of the original images, respectively. To achieve superior attack performance, we propose to jointly optimize bit flips, additive noise, and flow field. Since the weight bits of the DNNs are binary, this problem is very hard to be solved. We handle the binary constraint with equivalent replacement and provide an effective optimization algorithm. Extensive experiments on CIFAR-10, SVHN, and ImageNet datasets show that the proposed HPT can generate hardly perceptible Trojan images, while achieving comparable or better attack performance compared to the state-of-the-art methods. The code is available at: https://github.com/jiawangbai/HPT.

1 Introduction

Although deep neural networks (DNNs) have been showing state-of-the-art performances in various complex tasks, such as image classification [17,43,47], facial recognition [8,28,38,50], and object detection [13,42], prior studies have revealed their vulnerability against diverse attacks [5,15,16,27,34,36,44,46,48]. One such attack is the *Trojan attack* [32] happening in the deployment stage, in which an attacker manipulates a DNN to inject a hidden behavior called Trojan. The Trojan can only be activated by the specific trigger pattern.

Supplementary Information The online version contains supplementary material available at https://doi.org/10.1007/978-3-031-20065-6_7.

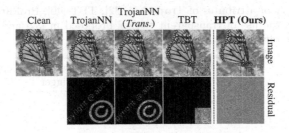

Fig. 1. Visualization of Trojan images from TrojanNN [32], TBT [40], and HPT. *'Trans.'* indicates the use of transparent trigger proposed in [32]. Note that ProFlip [6] uses the same trigger pattern (a square pattern) as TBT.

Trojan attacks on a deployed DNN alter the model parameters in the memory using bit flip techniques, e.g., Row Hammer Attack [20,51], but do not tamper with the training pipeline and have no extra forward or backward calculation during inference. Then, the attacked DNN makes a target prediction on the inputs with the trigger, while behaving normally on clean samples [6,32,40]. These dangerous properties pose severe threats to DNN-based applications after model deployment. Therefore, it is necessary to study the Trojan attacks on the deployed DNNs in order to recognize their flaws and solve related security risks.

A Trojan attack generally is composed of two subroutines: critical bits identification and specific trigger generation. Previous works [6,39] made efforts towards reducing the number of bit flips by developing search strategies. After flipping the identified bits, the attacker can activate the hidden behavior using the Trojan images, which are any images embedded with a specific patch-based trigger, such as a watermark pattern in [32] or a square pattern in [6,40]. However, due to these unnatural and noticeable triggers, the Trojan images can be easily spotted by humans [9,37] and machines. For example, we construct a simple linear classifier to distinguish clean images and Trojan images crafted by TBT [40] based on their Grad-CAM heatmaps [45] on ImageNet, resulting in a 98.0% success rate. The transparent trigger [32] was proposed to reduce the perceptibility, but leading to lower attack performance. Hence, how to inject less perceptible Trojan with superior attack performance is a challenging problem.

To address the aforementioned problems, we propose the hardly perceptible Trojan attack (HPT). Instead of applying the patch-based trigger predefined by a mask, HPT tweaks the pixel values and positions of the original images to craft Trojan images. Specifically, we modify pixel values by adding the pixel-wise noise inspired by adversarial examples [15,34,49] and change pixel positions by per-pixel flow field [10,19,63]. As shown in Fig. 1, Trojan images of HPT are less perceptible and harder to be distinguished from original images. It will be further demonstrated in the human perceptual study in Sect. 4.3.

Since the value of each weight bit is '0' or '1', we cast each bit as a binary variable. Integrating Trojan images generation and critical bits identification, we formulate the proposed HPT as a mixed integer programming (MIP) prob-

Table 1. Summary of attributes of TrojanNN [32], TBT [40], ProFlip [6], and HPT. *'Trans.'* indicates the use of transparent trigger proposed in [32] and 'ASR' denotes the attack success rate.

Method	High ASR	A small set of bit flips	Hardly perceptible trigger
TrojanNN	✓		
TrojanNN (*Trans.*)			✓
TBT	✓		
ProFlip	✓	✓	
HPT (Ours)	✓	✓	✓

lem, i.e., jointly optimizing bit flips, additive noise, and flow field. Moreover, we constrain the modification on image pixels and the number of bit flips to yield a hardly perceptible and practical attack [51,62]. To solve this MIP problem, we reformulate it as an equivalent continuous problem [56] and present an effective optimization algorithm based on the standard alternating direction method of multipliers (ADMM) [4,12]. We conduct extensive experiments on CIFAR-10, SVHN, and ImageNet with 8-bit quantized ResNet-18 and VGG-16 architectures following [6,40], which shows that HPT is hardly perceptible and achieves superior attack performance. The attributes of compared methods and HPT are summarized in Table 1.

The contributions are summarized as follows:

- For the first time, we improve Trojan attacks on the deployed DNNs to be strong and hardly perceptible. We investigate the use of modifying the pixel values and positions of the original images to craft Trojan images.
- We formulate the proposed HPT as a constrained MIP problem to jointly optimize bit flips, additive noise, and flow field, and further provide an effective optimization algorithm.
- Finally, HPT obtains both hardly perceptible Trojan images and promising attack performance, e.g., an attack success rate of 95% with only 10 bit flips out of 88 million bits in attacking ResNet-18 on ImageNet.

2   Related Works and Preliminaries

Attacks on the Deployed DNNs. Recently, since DNNs have been widely applied to security-critical tasks, e.g., facial recognition [14,53,55,59], their security in the deployment stage has received extensive attention. Previous works assume that the attacker can modify the weight parameters of the deployed DNNs to achieve some malicious purposes, e.g., misclassifying certain samples [31,62]. Some physical techniques (e.g., Row Hammer Attack [20,51] and Laser Beam Attack [1,7]) can precisely flip bits ('0'→'1' or '1'→'0') in the memory

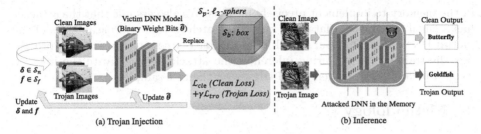

Fig. 2. Pipeline of the proposed HPT, where the target class is '*Goldfish*'. (a) Trojan Injection: optimizing $\hat{\theta}$, δ, and f jointly. (b) Inference: activating the hidden behaviour using the Trojan image.

without accessing them. These techniques allow an attacker to attack a deployed DNN by modifying its bit representation [41,52,60]. For instance, Rakin et al. [39] presented that an extremely small number of bit flips can crush a fully functional DNN to a random output generator. After that, Bai et al. [3] proposed to attack a specified sample into a target class via flipping limited bits. To mitigate the bit flip-based attacks, some defense mechanisms [18,24,25,30] have been explored.

As a line of research, *Trojan attacks* [6,40] insert a hidden behavior in the DNN using bit flip techniques, which can be activated by a designed trigger. Specifically, an attacked DNN will make wrong predictions on the inputs with the presence of the trigger, while behaving normally on original samples. Previous works proposed to generate a specified pattern as the trigger (e.g., a square pattern) [6,32,40]. Besides, to reduce the number of bit flips, heuristic strategies are designed to identify the critical bits, e.g., neural gradient ranking in [40] or progressive search algorithm in [6]. The results in [6] show that only a few bit flips yield a high attack success rate, which further raises the security concerns.

Quantized DNNs. In the deployment stage, model quantization has been widely adopted to reduce the storage requirements and accelerate the inference speed [21,29]. In this paper, we adopt a layer-wise Q-bit uniform quantizer, which is identical to the Tensor-RT solution [33]. Given binary weight parameters $\theta \in \{0,1\}^{N \times Q}$ of a Q-bit quantized DNN g, each parameter is represented and stored as a signed integer in two's complement representation, i.e., $\theta_i = [\theta_{i,Q}; ...; \theta_{i,1}] \in \{0,1\}^Q$. For the l-th layer with the step size Δ_l, the binary representation θ_i can be converted into a real number, as follows:

$$W_i = (-2^{Q-1} \cdot \theta_{i,Q} + \sum_{j=1}^{Q-1} 2^{j-1} \cdot \theta_{i,j}) \cdot \Delta_l, \tag{1}$$

where $W \in \mathbb{R}^N$ denotes the floating-point weight parameters of the DNN. For clarity, hereafter θ is reshaped from the tensor to the vector, i.e., $\theta \in \{0,1\}^{NQ}$.

Threat Model. We consider the threat model used by previous bit flip-based Trojan attack studies [6,40]. The attacker knows the location of the victim DNN in the memory to implement precisely bit flips. We also assume that the attacker has a small set of clean data and knows the architecture and parameters of the victim DNN. Note that our attack does not have access to the training process nor the training data. During inference, the attacker can activate the injected Trojan by applying the generated trigger on the test samples.

3   Methodology

In this section, we firstly describe the hardly perceptible trigger used by HPT. We then introduce the problem formulation and present an effective optimization algorithm based on ADMM. Figure 2 shows the entire pipeline of HPT.

3.1   Hardly Perceptible Trigger

Let $x \in \mathcal{X}$ denote a clean image, and $\hat{x}$ denote its Trojan image, i.e., x with a specific trigger pattern. $\mathcal{X} = [0,1]^{HW \times C}$ is the image space, where H, W, C are the height, width, and channel for an image, respectively. To modify the pixel values of the clean image, we apply additive noise δ to the image x. Inspired by the adversarial examples [23], HPT requires $\delta \in \mathcal{S}_n$, where $\mathcal{S}_n = \{\delta : ||\delta||_\infty \leqslant \epsilon\}$ and ϵ denotes the maximum noise strength, so that $\hat{x}$ is perceptually indistinguishable from x.

To formulate changes of the pixel positions, we use $f \in \mathbb{R}^{HW \times 2}$ to represent per-pixel flow field, where $f^{(i)} = (\Delta u^{(i)}, \Delta v^{(i)})$ denotes the amount of displacement in each channel for each pixel $\hat{x}^{(i)}$ within the Trojan image at the position $(\hat{u}^{(i)}, \hat{v}^{(i)})$. Thus, the value of $\hat{x}^{(i)}$ is sampled from position $(u^{(i)}, v^{(i)}) = (\hat{u}^{(i)} + \Delta u^{(i)}, \hat{v}^{(i)} + \Delta v^{(i)})$ within the original image. Since the sampled position is not necessarily an integer value, we use the differentiable bilinear interpolation [63] to generate the Trojan image considering four neighboring pixels around the location $(u^{(i)}, v^{(i)})$, denoted by $\mathcal{N}(u^{(i)}, v^{(i)})$. To preserve high perceptual quality of the Trojan images, we enforce the local smoothness of the flow field f based on the total variation [57,61]:

$$\mathcal{F}(f) = \sum_{p}^{all\ pixels} \sum_{q \in \mathcal{N}(p)} \sqrt{||\Delta u^{(p)} - \Delta u^{(q)}||_2^2 + ||\Delta v^{(p)} - \Delta v^{(q)}||_2^2}. \tag{2}$$

We introduce a hyper-parameter κ to restrict $\mathcal{F}(f)$, i.e., $f \in \mathcal{S}_f$ where $\mathcal{S}_f = \{f : \mathcal{F}(f) \leqslant \kappa\}$.

Based on the additive noise δ and the flow field f, each pixel before the clipping operation can be calculated as:

$$\hat{x}^{(i)} = \sum_{q \in \mathcal{N}(u^{(i)}, v^{(i)})} (x^{(q)} + \delta^{(q)})(1 - |u^{(i)} - u^{(q)}|)(1 - |v^{(i)} - v^{(q)}|). \tag{3}$$

We can craft the Trojan image $\hat{x}$ by calculating each pixel of $\hat{x}$ according to Eq. (3) and performing the $[0,1]$ clipping to ensure that it is in the image space, which is denoted as:

$$\hat{x} = \mathcal{T}(x; \delta, f). \tag{4}$$

Note that $\hat{x}$ is differentiable with respect to δ and f, enabling us to optimize them by the gradient method. We obtain δ and f after the Trojan injection stage and apply them on any image to craft its Trojan image during inference.

3.2   Problem Formulation

Suppose that the victim DNN is the well-trained Q-bit quantized classifier g : $\mathcal{X} \rightarrow \mathcal{Y}$, where $\mathcal{Y} = \{1, ..., K\}$ is the output space and K is the number of classes. $\theta \in \{0,1\}^{NQ}$ is the original binary weight parameters and $\hat{\theta} \in \{0,1\}^{NQ}$ is the attacked parameters. As aforementioned, the attacker has a small set of clean data $D = \{(x_i, y_i)\}_{i=1}^{M}$. To keep the attack stealthiness, we reduce the influence on original samples by minimizing the below loss:

$$\mathcal{L}_{cle}(\hat{\theta}) = \sum_{i=1}^{M} \ell(g(x_i; \hat{\theta}), y_i), \tag{5}$$

where $g_j(x_i; \hat{\theta})$ indicates the posterior probability of the input with respect to class j and $\ell(\cdot, \cdot)$ denotes the cross-entropy loss. Recall that the malicious purpose of Trojan attack is to classify the Trojan images into the target class t. To this end, we formulate this objective as:

$$\mathcal{L}_{tro}(\delta, f, \hat{\theta}) = \sum_{i=1}^{M} \ell(g(\mathcal{T}(x_i; \delta, f); \hat{\theta}), t). \tag{6}$$

Aligning with previous Trojan attacks [6, 40], reducing the number of bit flips is necessary to make the attack efficient and practical. HPT achieves this goal by restricting the Hamming distance between θ and $\hat{\theta}$ less than b. Considering the constraint on δ and f, we formulate the objective function of HPT as follows:

$$\{\delta^*, f^*, \hat{\theta}^*\} = \arg \min_{\delta, f, \hat{\theta}} \mathcal{L}_{cle}(\hat{\theta}) + \gamma \mathcal{L}_{tro}(\delta, f, \hat{\theta}),$$

$$s.t. \quad \delta \in \mathcal{S}_n, \quad f \in \mathcal{S}_f, \quad \hat{\theta} \in \{0,1\}^{NQ}, \quad d_H(\theta, \hat{\theta}) \leqslant b, \tag{7}$$

where γ is the hyper-parameter to balance the two terms and $d(\theta, \hat{\theta})$ computes the Hamming distance between original and attacked parameters. Problem (7) with the continuous variables δ and f and the binary variable $\hat{\theta}$ is a mixed integer programming, which is generally very difficult to solve. Here, inspired by a recent advanced work in integer programming [56], we equivalently replace the binary constraint with the intersection of two continuous constraints, as presented in Proposition 1.

Proposition 1 [56]. *Let 1_{NQ} denote the NQ-dimensional vector filled with all 1s. The binary set $\{0,1\}^{NQ}$ can be replaced by the intersection between $\mathcal{S}_b$ and $\mathcal{S}_p$, as follows:*

$$\hat{\theta} \in \{0,1\}^{NQ} \Leftrightarrow \hat{\theta} \in (\mathcal{S}_b \cap \mathcal{S}_p), \tag{8}$$

where $\mathcal{S}_b = [0,1]^{NQ}$ indicates the box constraint and $\mathcal{S}_p = \{\hat{\theta} : ||\hat{\theta} - \frac{1}{2}1_{NQ}||_2^2 = \frac{NQ}{4}\}$ indicates the ℓ_2-sphere constraint.

Based on Proposition 1, we can equivalently reformulate Problem (7) as a continuous problem. Besides, we can calculate the Hamming distance using $||\boldsymbol{\theta} - \hat{\boldsymbol{\theta}}||_2^2$ for the binary vectors. We obtain the following reformulation:

$$\{\boldsymbol{\delta}^*, \boldsymbol{f}^*, \hat{\boldsymbol{\theta}}^*\} = \arg\min_{\boldsymbol{\delta}, \boldsymbol{f}, \hat{\boldsymbol{\theta}}} \quad \mathcal{L}_{cle}(\hat{\boldsymbol{\theta}}) + \gamma \mathcal{L}_{tro}(\boldsymbol{\delta}, \boldsymbol{f}, \hat{\boldsymbol{\theta}}),$$

$$s.t. \quad \boldsymbol{\delta} \in \mathcal{S}_n, \quad \boldsymbol{f} \in \mathcal{S}_f, \hat{\boldsymbol{\theta}} = \boldsymbol{z}_1, \quad \hat{\boldsymbol{\theta}} = \boldsymbol{z}_2, \quad ||\boldsymbol{\theta} - \hat{\boldsymbol{\theta}}||_2^2 - b + z_3 = 0, \qquad (9)$$

$$\boldsymbol{z}_1 \in \mathcal{S}_b, \quad \boldsymbol{z}_2 \in \mathcal{S}_p, \quad z_3 \in \mathbb{R}^+.$$

In Eq. (9), we use two additional variables $\boldsymbol{z}_1$ and $\boldsymbol{z}_2$ to separate the two continuous constraints in Proposition 1, and transform $||\boldsymbol{\theta} - \hat{\boldsymbol{\theta}}||_2^2 \leqslant b$ into $\{||\boldsymbol{\theta} - \hat{\boldsymbol{\theta}}||_2^2 - b + z_3 = 0; z_3 \in \mathbb{R}^+\}$. Problem (7) can now be optimized by the standard ADMM method.

3.3   Optimization

Using a penalty factor $\rho > 0$, the augmented Lagrangian function of Eq. (9) is

$$\begin{aligned}
L(&\boldsymbol{\delta}, \boldsymbol{f}, \hat{\boldsymbol{\theta}}, \boldsymbol{z}_1, \boldsymbol{z}_2, z_3, \boldsymbol{\lambda}_1, \boldsymbol{\lambda}_2, \lambda_3) \\
&= \mathcal{L}_{cle}(\hat{\boldsymbol{\theta}}) + \gamma \mathcal{L}_{tro}(\boldsymbol{\delta}, \boldsymbol{f}, \hat{\boldsymbol{\theta}}) \\
&\quad + \boldsymbol{\lambda}_1^\top(\hat{\boldsymbol{\theta}} - \boldsymbol{z}_1) + \boldsymbol{\lambda}_2^\top(\hat{\boldsymbol{\theta}} - \boldsymbol{z}_2) + \lambda_3^\top(||\boldsymbol{\theta} - \hat{\boldsymbol{\theta}}||_2^2 - b + z_3) \\
&\quad + \frac{\rho}{2}\left[||\hat{\boldsymbol{\theta}} - \boldsymbol{z}_1||_2^2 + ||\hat{\boldsymbol{\theta}} - \boldsymbol{z}_2||_2^2 + (||\boldsymbol{\theta} - \hat{\boldsymbol{\theta}}||_2^2 - b + z_3)^2\right] \\
&\quad + \mathbb{I}_{\mathcal{S}_n}(\boldsymbol{\delta}) + \mathbb{I}_{\mathcal{S}_f}(\boldsymbol{f}) + \mathbb{I}_{\mathcal{S}_b}(\boldsymbol{z}_1) + \mathbb{I}_{\mathcal{S}_p}(\boldsymbol{z}_2) + \mathbb{I}_{\mathbb{R}^+}(z_3),
\end{aligned} \qquad (10)$$

where $\boldsymbol{\lambda}_1 \in \mathbb{R}^{NQ}$, $\boldsymbol{\lambda}_2 \in \mathbb{R}^{NQ}$, and $\lambda_3 > 0$ are Lagrange multipliers for the three equality constraints. $\mathbb{I}_S(a) : a \to \{0, +\infty\}$ denotes the indicator function: $\mathbb{I}_S(a) = 0$ if a belongs to a set S; otherwise, $\mathbb{I}_S(a) = +\infty$.

We alternatively update all variables as shown in Algorithm 1. We start from initializing all optimizable variables and the iteration index k (Line 2–4), where the initialization of $\boldsymbol{\delta}^{[0]}$ and $\boldsymbol{f}^{[0]}$ is specified later. We first update $\boldsymbol{z}_1^{[k+1]}, \boldsymbol{z}_2^{[k+1]}$, and $z_3^{[k+1]}$ with Eq. (11)–(12) (Line 8–10), which project $\boldsymbol{z}_1^{[k+1]}, \boldsymbol{z}_2^{[k+1]}$, and $z_3^{[k+1]}$ into their feasible sets:

$$\Pi_{\mathcal{S}_b}(\boldsymbol{e}_1) = \min(1, \max(0, \boldsymbol{e}_1)), \qquad (11)$$

$$\Pi_{\mathcal{S}_p}(\boldsymbol{e}_1) = \frac{(2\boldsymbol{e}_1 - \boldsymbol{1}_{NQ})\sqrt{NQ}}{||\boldsymbol{e}_1||} + \frac{\boldsymbol{1}_{NQ}}{2}, \qquad (12)$$

$$\Pi_{\mathbb{R}^+}(e) = \max(0, e), \qquad (13)$$

where $\boldsymbol{e}_1 \in \mathbb{R}^{NQ}$ and $e \in \mathbb{R}$. Next, we update $\boldsymbol{\delta}^{[k+1]}, \boldsymbol{f}^{[k+1]}$, and $\hat{\boldsymbol{\theta}}^{[k+1]}$ by gradient descent with learning rates α_δ, α_f, and $\alpha_{\hat{\theta}}$, respectively (Line 12–14). The projection functions for $\boldsymbol{\delta}^{[k+1]}$ and $\boldsymbol{f}^{[k+1]}$ are defined as:

$$\Pi_{\mathcal{S}_n}(\boldsymbol{e}_2) = \min(-\epsilon, \max(\boldsymbol{e}_2, \epsilon)), \qquad (14)$$

$$\Pi_{\mathcal{S}_f}(\boldsymbol{e}_3) = \frac{\boldsymbol{e}_3}{\mathcal{F}(\boldsymbol{e}_3)}, \qquad (15)$$

Algorithm 1: ADMM for solving Problem (7)

Input : Victim DNN model g with binary weight parameters $\boldsymbol{\theta}$, target class t,
a small set of clean data $D = \{(\boldsymbol{x}_i, y_i)\}_{i=1}^{M}$.

Output: $\boldsymbol{\delta}^*, \boldsymbol{f}^*, \hat{\boldsymbol{\theta}}^*$.

1 # Initialization
2 Initialize $\boldsymbol{\delta}^{[0]}$ and $\boldsymbol{f}^{[0]}$;
3 Let $\hat{\boldsymbol{\theta}}^{[0]} \leftarrow \boldsymbol{\theta}$, $\boldsymbol{z}_1^{[0]} \leftarrow \boldsymbol{\theta}$, $\boldsymbol{z}_2^{[0]} \leftarrow \boldsymbol{\theta}$, $z_3^{[0]} \leftarrow 0$, $\boldsymbol{\lambda}_1^{[0]} \leftarrow \mathbf{0}_{NQ}$, $\boldsymbol{\lambda}_2^{[0]} \leftarrow \mathbf{0}_{NQ}$, $\lambda_3^{[0]} \leftarrow 0$;
4 Set $k = 0$;
5 **repeat**
6 | # Update $\boldsymbol{z}_1^{[k+1]}, \boldsymbol{z}_2^{[k+1]}, z_3^{[k+1]}$
7 **until** *Stopping criterion is satisfied*;
8 $\boldsymbol{z}_1^{[k+1]} \leftarrow \Pi_{\mathcal{S}_b}(\hat{\boldsymbol{\theta}}^{[k]} + \boldsymbol{\lambda}_1^{[k]}/\rho)$;
9 $\boldsymbol{z}_2^{[k+1]} \leftarrow \Pi_{\mathcal{S}_p}(\hat{\boldsymbol{\theta}}^{[k]} + \boldsymbol{\lambda}_2^{[k]}/\rho)$;
10 $z_3^{[k+1]} \leftarrow \Pi_{\mathbb{R}^+}(-||\boldsymbol{\theta} - \hat{\boldsymbol{\theta}}^{[k]}||_2^2 + b - \lambda_3^{[k]}/\rho)$;
11 # Update $\boldsymbol{\delta}^{[k+1]}, \boldsymbol{f}^{[k+1]}, \hat{\boldsymbol{\theta}}^{[k+1]}$
12 $\boldsymbol{\delta}^{[k+1]} \leftarrow \Pi_{\mathcal{S}_n}(\boldsymbol{\delta}^{[k]} - \alpha_\delta \cdot \partial L/\partial \boldsymbol{\delta})$;
13 $\boldsymbol{f}^{[k+1]} \leftarrow \Pi_{\mathcal{S}_f}(\boldsymbol{f}^{[k]} - \alpha_f \cdot \partial L/\partial \boldsymbol{f})$;
14 $\hat{\boldsymbol{\theta}}^{[k+1]} \leftarrow \hat{\boldsymbol{\theta}}^{[k]} - \alpha_{\hat{\theta}} \cdot \partial L/\partial \hat{\boldsymbol{\theta}}$;
15 # Update $\boldsymbol{\lambda}_1^{[k+1]}, \boldsymbol{\lambda}_2^{[k+1]}, \lambda_3^{[k+1]}$
16 $\boldsymbol{\lambda}_1^{[k+1]} \leftarrow \boldsymbol{\lambda}_1^{[k]} + \rho(\hat{\boldsymbol{\theta}}^{[k+1]} - \boldsymbol{z}_1^{[k+1]})$;
17 $\boldsymbol{\lambda}_2^{[k+1]} \leftarrow \boldsymbol{\lambda}_2^{[k]} + \rho(\hat{\boldsymbol{\theta}}^{[k+1]} - \boldsymbol{z}_2^{[k+1]})$;
18 $\lambda_3^{[k+1]} \leftarrow \lambda_3^{[k]} + \rho(||\boldsymbol{\theta} - \hat{\boldsymbol{\theta}}^{[k+1]}||_2^2 - b + z_3^{[k+1]})$;
19 $k \leftarrow k + 1$;
20 $\boldsymbol{\delta}^* \leftarrow \boldsymbol{\delta}^{[k]}, \boldsymbol{f}^* \leftarrow \boldsymbol{f}^{[k]}, \hat{\boldsymbol{\theta}}^* \leftarrow \hat{\boldsymbol{\theta}}^{[k]}$;
21 **return** $\boldsymbol{\delta}^*, \boldsymbol{f}^*, \hat{\boldsymbol{\theta}}^*$.

---

where $e_2 \in \mathbb{R}^{HW \times C}$ and $e_3 \in \mathbb{R}^{HW \times 2}$. We then update the Lagrange multipliers $\boldsymbol{\lambda}_1^{[k+1]}, \boldsymbol{\lambda}_2^{[k+1]}$, and $\lambda_3^{[k+1]}$ using gradient ascent (Line 16–18). When both $||\hat{\boldsymbol{\theta}} - \boldsymbol{z}_1||_2^2$ and $||\hat{\boldsymbol{\theta}} - \boldsymbol{z}_2||_2^2$ are smaller than a preset threshold or the maximum number of iterations is reached, the optimization halts (Line 19).

Implementation Details. We implement the optimization process with the following techniques. We initialize $\boldsymbol{\delta}^{[0]}$ and $\boldsymbol{f}^{[0]}$ by minimizing the loss defined as Eq. (6) before joint optimization to stabilize the practical convergence. In the step for $\hat{\boldsymbol{\theta}}$, we only update the parameters of the last layer and fix the others. We also update $\boldsymbol{\delta}^{[k+1]}, \boldsymbol{f}^{[k+1]}$, and $\hat{\boldsymbol{\theta}}^{[k+1]}$ with multi-steps gradients during each iteration. Besides, as suggested in [11,26,56], increasing ρ from a smaller value to an upper bound can avoid the early stopping.

Table 2. Performance comparison between TrojanNN [32], TBT [40], and HPT. '*Trans.*' indicates the use of transparent trigger proposed in [32]. The target class t is set as 0.

Dataset	Model	Method	PA-TA (%)	ASR (%)	N_{flip}
CIFAR-10	ResNet-18 TA: 94.8%	TrojanNN	87.6	93.9	19215
		TrojanNN (*Trans.*)	75.5	73.5	20160
		TBT	87.5	90.2	540
		TBT (*Trans.*)	71.4	56.6	548
		HPT (Ours)	94.7	94.1	12
	VGG-16 TA: 93.2%	TrojanNN	85.5	82.5	16400
		TrojanNN (*Trans.*)	69.6	59.8	15386
		TBT	80.7	83.2	601
		TBT (*Trans.*)	70.5	53.9	583
		HPT (Ours)	93.1	91.1	6
SVHN	VGG-16 TA: 96.3%	TrojanNN	76.0	82.5	17330
		TrojanNN (*Trans.*)	59.9	71.7	18355
		TBT	67.9	60.1	576
		TBT (*Trans.*)	57.9	54.8	546
		HPT (Ours)	94.2	78.0	26
ImageNet	ResNet-18 TA: 69.5%	TrojanNN	47.6	100.0	155550
		TrojanNN (*Trans.*)	47.4	96.8	304744
		TBT	68.8	100.0	611
		TBT (*Trans.*)	64.1	88.6	594
		HPT (Ours)	68.6	95.2	10

4   Experiments

4.1   Setup

Datasets and Target Models. Following [6,40], we adopt three datasets: CIFAR-10 [22], SVHN [35], and ImageNet [43]. The attacker has 128 clean images for CIFAR-10 and SVHN and 256 clean images for ImageNet, respectively. Note that all attacks are performed using these clean images and evaluated on the whole test set. Following [6,40], we evaluate attacks on two popular network architectures: ResNet-18 [17] and VGG-16 [47], with a quantization level of 8-bit (see Appendix B for results of HPT in attacking 4-bit quantized DNNs). In the below experiments, the target class t is set as 0 unless otherwise specified.

Parameter Settings. To balance the attack performance and human perception, ϵ is set as 0.04 on all datasets, and κ is set as 0.01 on CIFAR-10 and SVHN, and 0.005 on ImageNet. We initialize $\delta^{[0]}$ and $f^{[0]}$ by minimizing loss defined as Eq. (6) for 500 iterations with the learning rate 0.01 on CIFAR-10 and SVHN,

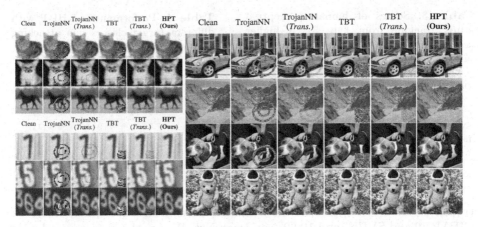

Fig. 3. Visualization of clean and Trojan images generated by different methods. Top left: CIFAR-10; Bottom left: SVHN; Right: ImageNet. Note that ProFlip uses the same trigger pattern (a square pattern) as TBT. By comparison, the triggers of Trojan images generated by HPT are most natural and unnoticeable.

Dataset	Model	Method	TA (%)	PA-TA (%)	ASR (%)	N_{flip}
CIFAR-10	ResNet-18	ProFlip	93.1	90.3	97.9	12
		HPT (Ours)	94.8	94.8	98.7	10
	VGG-16	ProFlip	89.7	88.1	94.8	16
		HPT (Ours)	93.2	92.0	93.8	10
SVHN	VGG-16	ProFlip	98.6	95.3	94.5	20
		HPT (Ours)	96.3	94.0	82.2	23
ImageNet	ResNet-18	ProFlip	69.0	67.6	94.3	15
		HPT (Ours)	69.5	65.2	97.6	14

(a)   (b)

Fig. 4. Comparison of ProFlip [6] and HPT: (a) Attack performance. The target class t is set as 2; (b) Visualization of clean and Trojan images generated by ProFlip and HPT. The example of ProFlip is from [6].

and $1,000$ iterations with the learning rate 0.1 on ImageNet. Other parameter settings can be found in Appendix A.

Evaluation Metrics. To measure the effect on clean images, we compare original test accuracy (TA) with post-attack test accuracy (PA-TA), defined as the accuracy of testing on clean images for the original and attacked DNN, respectively. Attack success rate (ASR) denotes the percentage of Trojan images samples classified to the target class by the attacked DNN. N_{flip} is the number of bit flips, i.e., the hamming distance between original and attacked parameters. A more successful attack can achieve a higher PA-TA and ASR, while less N_{flip}.

Compared Methods. HPT is compared to TrojanNN [32], TBT [40], and ProFlip [6] in our experiments. We also apply the transparent trigger [32] on TrojanNN and TBT, denoted as '*Trans.*'. The watermark in [32] is chosen as the trigger shape for TrojanNN. We use the same trigger pattern in [32,40], i.e., a square pattern located at the bottom right of the image. The trigger size of all compared methods is measured by the proportion of input replaced by the

Table 3. Scores of human perceptual study (ranging from 1 to 5). A higher score corresponds to less perceptible Trojan images.

Dataset	TrojanNN	TrojanNN (*Trans.*)	TBT	TBT (*Trans.*)	HPT
CIFAR-10	1.1	3.4	1.0	2.8	**3.9**
SVHN	1.1	2.4	1.0	2.0	**3.9**
ImageNet	1.0	2.4	1.0	2.4	**4.3**
Average	1.1	2.7	1.0	2.4	**4.0**

Table 4. Performance of HPT with different target classes t in attacking ResNet-18 on CIFAR-10.

t	PA-TA (%)	ASR (%)	N_{flip}	t	PA-TA (%)	ASR (%)	N_{flip}
0	94.7	94.1	12	5	94.8	92.7	11
1	94.7	98.9	14	6	94.7	92.4	11
2	94.8	97.3	9	7	94.8	88.8	11
3	94.8	98.7	6	8	94.6	96.5	14
4	94.7	94.6	12	9	94.8	95.1	10

trigger, which is configured as the default value used in [32,40], i.e., 9.76% on CIFAR-10 and SVHN, and 10.62% on ImageNet. We use the open-sourced code of TBT and implement TrojanNN following [40] to make the comparison fair. We compare the results of ProFlip reported in [6].

4.2 Attack Results

We compare the attack performance of HPT with TrojanNN and TBT in Table 2. We can observe that TrojanNN performs a large number of bit flips in all cases, due to no limitation on the parameter modification. TBT reduces the number of bit flips to about 600 using the proposed bit search algorithm. Among them, HPT achieves the least number of bit flips with a higher or at least competitive PA-TA and ASR. It is worth noting that the transparent trigger leads to a lower PA-TA and ASR for both TrojanNN and TBT. For example, in attacking ResNet-18 on CIFAR-10, TBT only achieves a 56.6% ASR, compared to the 90.2% ASR without applying the transparent trigger, which indicates that it is difficult to perform Trojan attacks with the less perceptible trigger.

The results of ProFlip and HPT with the target class $t = 2$ are shown in Fig. 4(a). The number of clean samples is set as 256 for all cases. ProFlip is the most state-of-the-art method basedon the well-designed progressive search algorithm. However, ProFlip also uses the square pattern as the trigger (as shown in Fig. 4(b)), making it easily perceptible to humans. HPT has comparable performance to ProFlip, especially on CIFAR-10 and ImageNet. Besides, we would like to emphasize that, even with the hardly perceptible trigger, HPT can achieve promising performance.

4.3 Human Perceptual Study

To quantify the visual perceptibility of Trojan images generated by different attack methods, we conduct a human perceptual study in this section. We evaluate five Trojan attack methods listed in Table 3. We randomly select 10 clean images from each dataset and generate the corresponding Trojan images for these 30 images. In our study, all original and Trojan images are shown to 15 participants. These participants are asked to give a score $\in \{1, 2, 3, 4, 5\}$ for each Trojan

Table 5. ASR (%) for three attack modes. 'Trigger': optimizing the trigger without bit flips; 'Two Stage': optimizing the trigger and bit flips separately; 'Joint Optimization': optimizing the trigger and bit flips jointly.

Dataset	Model	Trigger	Two stage	Joint optimization
CIFAR-10	ResNet-18	90.9	93.2	94.1
	VGG-16	87.0	90.5	91.1
SVHN	VGG-16	64.7	74.6	78.0
ImageNet	ResNet-18	70.5	89.2	95.2

Table 6. Results of HPT on two types of feature squeezing defense.

	PA-TA (%)	ASR (%)
w/o defense	94.7	94.1
Averaging over each pixel's neighbors (2 × 2)	89.9	64.3
Collapsing the bit depth (5 bit)	67.8	65.6

image, where a higher score corresponds to less perceptible Trojan images. More details of the human perceptual study are provided in Appendix C.

In total, we collect 2,250 scores and summarize the results in Table 3. We also provide visualization examples in Fig. 3 (and an example of ProFlip from [6] in Fig. 4(b)). As can be observed, the scores of TrojanNN and TBT are very low, due to the noticeable patches. By applying the transparent trigger, all scores increase to over 2.0, however, these Trojan images can also be easily distinguished in most cases. In contrast, HPT achieves the highest score on all datasets (about 4.0). We also compare the mean square error (MSE) between original images and Trojan images (in the range $[0, 255]$) crafted by these five attacks, where HPT obtains the lowest MSE on all datasets. The average MSE of HPT is 97.1, while the second best result is 124.4 (TBT with the transparent trigger). More details can be found in Appendix D. These results confirm that HPT is hardly perceptible and is difficult to be spotted by humans.

4.4 Discussions

Sensitivity to Target Class. Table 4 shows the attack performance of HPT with different target classes in attacking ResNet-18 on CIFAR-10. Besides the target class, other settings are the same as those described in Sect. 4.1. The results show that HPT achieves less than 15 bit flips and over 88% ASR for different target classes, with only little accuracy degradation on clean images. Especially for the most vulnerable target class $t = 6$, HPT obtains a 98.7% ASR by flipping only 6 bits. These results illustrate HPT is not sensitive to the target class to some extent.

Numerical Convergence Analysis. To analyze the numerical convergence of our optimization algorithm, we plot the values of $||\hat{\theta} - z_1||_2^2$, $||\hat{\theta} - z_2||_2^2$, $\mathcal{L}_{cle}$, and $\mathcal{L}_{tro}$ at different iterations. As shown in Fig. 5, the optimization process can roughly be divided into three stages. In the first stage, $\mathcal{L}_{tro}$ is reduced to less than 0.002, resulting in a powerful attack. Then, $\mathcal{L}_{cle}$ decreases to reduce the influence on the clean images. Finally, $||\hat{\theta} - z_1||_2^2$ and $||\hat{\theta} - z_2||_2^2$ are encouraged to approach

0 to satisfy the box and ℓ_2-sphere constraint in Proposition 1. The optimization halts within the maximum number of iterations (3000), which demonstrates the practical convergence of our algorithm.

Effectiveness of Joint Optimization. We investigate the effectiveness of the joint optimization by comparing it with two other attack modes: optimizing the trigger without bit flips, optimizing the trigger and bit flips separately. The results are shown in Table 5. For the 'Trigger' mode, we only optimize the modification on the pixel values and positions of original images without bit flips, resulting in a relatively low ASR. For the 'Two Stage' mode, we firstly optimize the additive noise and flow field and then optimize the bit flips.

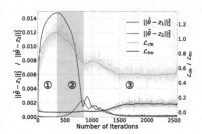

Fig. 5. Numerical convergence analysis of HPT.

We keep the PA-TA of the 'Two Stage' mode similar to that of the 'Joint Optimization' mode by tuning λ. The ASR results show that jointly optimizing bit flips, additive noise, and flow field yields the strongest attack in all cases.

4.5   Potential Defenses

Since our attack happens after model deployment, defense methods which check the training data or the model before deployment may not be effective to defend our attack. Accordingly, we evaluate three potential defense mechanisms below.

Firstly, we investigate the smoothing-based defense against our HPT, which are originally designed for adversarial examples [2,15,54]. We test HPT on two types of feature squeezing defense [58]: averaging over each pixel's neighbors and collapsing the bit depth. Table 6 shows that both can reduce the ASR to about 65% and averaging over each pixel's neighbors can maintain a relatively high PA-TA. Therefore, we believe that how to design smoothing-based defense methods for our Trojan attack is worthy of further exploration.

As a training technique, piece-wise clustering [18] encourages eliminating close-to-zero weights to enhance model robustness against bit flip-based attacks. We conduct experiments on CIFAR-10 with ResNet-18 and set the clustering parameter in [18] as 0.02. As shown in Table 7, when all settings are the same as those in Sect. 4.1 (i.e., $b = 10$), the ASR is reduced to 86.6% with the defense. To achieve a higher ASR, we increase b to 40 and retain all other settings, but resulting in 43 bit flips. As such, this observation inspires us to explore the defense against HPT which can increase the required number of bit flips.

The visualization tools are helpful to inspect the DNN's behavior. We use Grad-CAM [45] to show heatmaps of clean images for the original model and Trojan images generated by TrojanNN, TBT, and HPT for its corresponding attacked model in Fig. 6. One can see that the attacks based on the patch-based trigger (TrojanNN and TBT) can be easily exposed, since the main focus of the DNN stays on the trigger. However, due to the slight modification on the pixel

Table 7. Performance of HPT against the defense method in [18].

	b	TA (%)	PA-TA (%)	ASR (%)	N_{flip}
w/o defense	10	94.8	94.7	94.1	12
w/ defense	10	88.6	88.6	86.6	12
	40	88.6	88.5	93.2	43

Table 8. Performance of HPT with different ϵ and κ.

ϵ	PA-TA (%)	ASR (%)	N_{flip}	κ	PA-TA (%)	ASR (%)	N_{flip}
0.01	94.8	10.4	2	0.005	94.7	93.0	11
0.02	94.8	35.5	6	0.01	94.7	94.1	12
0.03	94.7	78.8	13	0.015	94.7	95.1	11
0.04	94.7	94.1	12	0.02	94.7	96.3	11
0.05	94.7	97.9	6	0.025	94.7	96.4	6

values and positions of original images, the heatmaps of HPT's Trojan images are more similar to these of clean images, i.e., localizing the main object in the image. In other words, the proposed HPT is hard to be defended by inspecting the DNN's behavior using Grad-CAM.

4.6 Ablation Studies

Effect of ϵ and κ. For HPT, ϵ and κ constrain the magnitude of modification on the pixel values and positions, respectively. Here, we investigate the effect of ϵ and κ on the attack performance. We use ResNet-18 on CIFAR-10 as the representative for analysis. In Table 8, we show the results of HPT under different values of ϵ while κ is fixed at 0.01, and under different values of κ while ϵ is fixed at 0.04. As expected, increasing ϵ and κ can improve ASR significantly. It is also obvious that ϵ has a greater impact than κ on the attack performance. However, a larger ϵ or κ generally reduces the visual quality of the Trojan images. Therefore, there is a trade-off between the attack performance and the visual perceptibility.

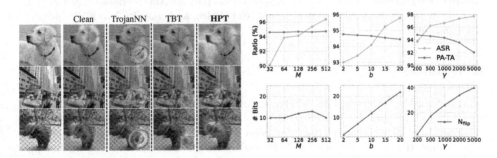

Fig. 6. Grad-CAM visualization of clean images and Trojan images generated by different attacks on ImageNet.

Fig. 7. Performance of HPT with varying M, b, and γ.

Effect of M, b, and γ. We perform ablation studies on the size of the clean data set M, the parameter for restricting the number of bit flips b, and the trade-off parameter λ. All results are presented in Fig. 7. To analyze the effect of M, we configure M from 32 to 512 and use other settings as those in Sect. 4.1. We can see that increasing the size of clean data has a marked positive impact on the ASR. Besides, even using only 32 clean images, HPT can obtain a high ASR (about 90%), which allows the attacker to perform HPT without too many clean images. When γ is fixed at 1,000, the plots of parameter b show that tuning b can control the number of bit flips. Accordingly, the parameter b helps to perform the Trojan attack when the budget of bit flips is fixed. We study the effect of γ with $b = 40$. As shown in the plots, a larger γ encourages a higher ASR, while a lower PA-TA and more bit flips. When other settings are fixed, attackers can specify γ for their specific needs.

5   Conclusion

In this paper, we proposed HPT that can inject a hidden behavior into a DNN after its deployment. It tweaks the pixel values and positions of original images to craft Trojan images. Based on an effective optimization algorithm, HPT performs best in the human perceptual study and achieves promising attack performance. To the best of our knowledge, HPT is the first Trojan attack on the deployed DNNs, which leverages the hardly perceptible trigger. We hope that our work opens a new domain of attack mechanisms and encourages future defense research.

The main limitation of HPT is that we assume that the attacker has full knowledge of the victim DNN, including its architecture, its parameters, and the location in the memory, corresponding to the white-box setting. We will further explore more strict settings than the white-box one in our future work.

Acknowledgments. This work is supported in part by the National Natural Science Foundation of China under Grant 62171248, and the PCNL KEY project (PCL2021A07).

References

1. Agoyan, M., Dutertre, J.M., Mirbaha, A.P., Naccache, D., Ribotta, A.L., Tria, A.: How to flip a bit? In: IOLTS (2010)
2. Bai, J., et al.: Targeted attack for deep hashing based retrieval. In: Vedaldi, A., Bischof, H., Brox, T., Frahm, J.-M. (eds.) ECCV 2020. LNCS, vol. 12346, pp. 618–634. Springer, Cham (2020). https://doi.org/10.1007/978-3-030-58452-8_36
3. Bai, J., Wu, B., Zhang, Y., Li, Y., Li, Z., Xia, S.T.: Targeted attack against deep neural networks via flipping limited weight bits. In: ICLR (2021)
4. Boyd, S., Parikh, N., Chu, E.: Distributed Optimization and Statistical Learning via the Alternating Direction Method of Multipliers. Now Publishers Inc. (2011)
5. Chen, B., Feng, Y., Dai, T., Bai, J., Jiang, Y., Xia, S.T., Wang, X.: Adversarial examples generation for deep product quantization networks on image retrieval. IEEE Trans. Pattern Anal. Mach. Intell. (2022)

6. Chen, H., Fu, C., Zhao, J., Koushanfar, F.: ProFlip: targeted trojan attack with progressive bit flips. In: ICCV (2021)
7. Colombier, B., Menu, A., Dutertre, J.M., Moëllic, P.A., Rigaud, J.B., Danger, J.L.: Laser-induced single-bit faults in flash memory: instructions corruption on a 32-bit microcontroller. In: HOST (2019)
8. Deng, Z., Peng, X., Li, Z., Qiao, Y.: Mutual component convolutional neural networks for heterogeneous face recognition. IEEE Trans. Image Process. **28**(6), 3102–3114 (2019)
9. Doan, K., Lao, Y., Zhao, W., Li, P.: LIRA: learnable, imperceptible and robust backdoor attacks. In: ICCV (2021)
10. Duchon, J.: Splines minimizing rotation-invariant semi-norms in Sobolev spaces. In: Schempp, W., Zeller, K. (eds.) Constructive Theory of Functions of Several Variables. Lecture Notes in Mathematics, vol. 571, pp. 85–100. Springer, Heidelberg (1977). https://doi.org/10.1007/BFb0086566
11. Fan, Y., et al.: Sparse adversarial attack via perturbation factorization. In: Vedaldi, A., Bischof, H., Brox, T., Frahm, J.-M. (eds.) ECCV 2020. LNCS, vol. 12367, pp. 35–50. Springer, Cham (2020). https://doi.org/10.1007/978-3-030-58542-6_3
12. Gabay, D., Mercier, B.: A dual algorithm for the solution of nonlinear variational problems via finite element approximation. Comput. Math. Appl. **2**(1), 17–40 (1976)
13. Girshick, R.: Fast R-CNN. In: CVPR (2015)
14. Gong, D., Li, Z., Liu, J., Qiao, Y.: Multi-feature canonical correlation analysis for face photo-sketch image retrieval. In: Proceedings of the 21st ACM International Conference on Multimedia, pp. 617–620 (2013)
15. Goodfellow, I.J., Shlens, J., Szegedy, C.: Explaining and harnessing adversarial examples. In: ICLR (2015)
16. Gu, T., Liu, K., Dolan-Gavitt, B., Garg, S.: BadNets: evaluating backdooring attacks on deep neural networks. IEEE Access **7**, 47230–47244 (2019)
17. He, K., Zhang, X., Ren, S., Sun, J.: Deep residual learning for image recognition. In: CVPR (2016)
18. He, Z., Rakin, A.S., Li, J., Chakrabarti, C., Fan, D.: Defending and harnessing the bit-flip based adversarial weight attack. In: CVPR (2020)
19. Jaderberg, M., Simonyan, K., Zisserman, A., et al.: Spatial transformer networks. In: NeurIPS (2015)
20. Kim, Y., et al.: Flipping bits in memory without accessing them: an experimental study of dram disturbance errors. ACM SIGARCH Comput. Archit. News **42**(3), 361–372 (2014)
21. Krishnamoorthi, R.: Quantizing deep convolutional networks for efficient inference: a whitepaper. arXiv preprint arXiv:1806.08342 (2018)
22. Krizhevsky, A., Hinton, G., et al.: Learning multiple layers of features from tiny images. Technical report (2009)
23. Kurakin, A., Goodfellow, I., Bengio, S.: Adversarial examples in the physical world. In: ICLR (2017)
24. Li, J., Rakin, A.S., He, Z., Fan, D., Chakrabarti, C.: RADAR: run-time adversarial weight attack detection and accuracy recovery. In: DATE (2021)
25. Li, J., Rakin, A.S., Xiong, Y., Chang, L., He, Z., Fan, D., Chakrabarti, C.: Defending bit-flip attack through DNN weight reconstruction. In: DAC (2020)
26. Li, T., Wu, B., Yang, Y., Fan, Y., Zhang, Y., Liu, W.: Compressing convolutional neural networks via factorized convolutional filters. In: CVPR (2019)
27. Li, Y., Jiang, Y., Li, Z., Xia, S.T.: Backdoor learning: a survey. IEEE Trans. Neural Netw. Learn. Syst. (2022)

28. Li, Z., Gong, D., Qiao, Y., Tao, D.: Common feature discriminant analysis for matching infrared face images to optical face images. IEEE Trans. Image Process. **23**(6), 2436–2445 (2014)

29. Lin, D., Talathi, S., Annapureddy, S.: Fixed point quantization of deep convolutional networks. In: ICML (2016)

30. Liu, Q., Wen, W., Wang, Y.: Concurrent weight encoding-based detection for bit-flip attack on neural network accelerators. In: ICCAD (2020)

31. Liu, Y., Wei, L., Luo, B., Xu, Q.: Fault injection attack on deep neural network. In: ICCAD (2017)

32. Liu, Y., et al.: Trojaning attack on neural networks. In: NDSS (2018)

33. Migacz, S.: 8-bit inference with TensorRT. In: GPU Technology Conference (2017)

34. Moosavi-Dezfooli, S.M., Fawzi, A., Fawzi, O., Frossard, P.: Universal adversarial perturbations. In: CVPR (2017)

35. Netzer, Y., Wang, T., Coates, A., Bissacco, A., Wu, B., Ng, A.Y.: Reading digits in natural images with unsupervised feature learning. In: NIPS Workshop (2011)

36. Nguyen, T.A., Tran, A.: Input-aware dynamic backdoor attack. In: NeurIPS, vol. 33, pp. 3454–3464 (2020)

37. Nguyen, T.A., Tran, A.T.: WaNet-imperceptible warping-based backdoor attack. In: ICLR (2021)

38. Qiu, H., Gong, D., Li, Z., Liu, W., Tao, D.: End2End occluded face recognition by masking corrupted features. IEEE Trans. Pattern Anal. Mach. Intell. (2021)

39. Rakin, A.S., He, Z., Fan, D.: Bit-flip attack: crushing neural network with progressive bit search. In: CVPR (2019)

40. Rakin, A.S., He, Z., Fan, D.: TBT: targeted neural network attack with bit trojan. In: CVPR (2020)

41. Rakin, A.S., He, Z., Li, J., Yao, F., Chakrabarti, C., Fan, D.: T-BFA: targeted bit-flip adversarial weight attack. IEEE Trans. Pattern Anal. Mach. Intell. (2021)

42. Redmon, J., Divvala, S., Girshick, R., Farhadi, A.: You only look once: unified, real-time object detection. In: CVPR (2016)

43. Russakovsky, O., Deng, J., Su, H., Krause, J., Satheesh, S., Ma, S., Huang, Z., Karpathy, A., Khosla, A., Bernstein, M., et al.: ImageNet large scale visual recognition challenge. Int. J. Comput. Vis. **115**(3), 211–252 (2015)

44. Saha, A., Subramanya, A., Pirsiavash, H.: Hidden trigger backdoor attacks. In: AAAI (2020)

45. Selvaraju, R.R., Cogswell, M., Das, A., Vedantam, R., Parikh, D., Batra, D.: Grad-CAM: visual explanations from deep networks via gradient-based localization. In: CVPR (2017)

46. Shafahi, A., et al.: Poison frogs! targeted clean-label poisoning attacks on neural networks. In: NeurIPS (2018)

47. Simonyan, K., Zisserman, A.: Very deep convolutional networks for large-scale image recognition. In: ICLR (2015)

48. Souri, H., Goldblum, M., Fowl, L., Chellappa, R., Goldstein, T.: Sleeper agent: scalable hidden trigger backdoors for neural networks trained from scratch. arXiv preprint arXiv:2106.08970 (2021)

49. Szegedy, C., et al.: Intriguing properties of neural networks. In: ICLR (2014)

50. Tang, X., Li, Z.: Video based face recognition using multiple classifiers. In: 2004 Proceedings of the Sixth IEEE International Conference on Automatic Face and Gesture Recognition, pp. 345–349. IEEE (2004)

51. Van Der Veen, V., et al.: Drammer: deterministic rowhammer attacks on mobile platforms. In: CCS (2016)

52. Venceslai, V., Marchisio, A., Alouani, I., Martina, M., Shafique, M.: NeuroAttack: undermining spiking neural networks security through externally triggered bit-flips. In: IJCNN (2020)
53. Wang, H., et al.: CosFace: large margin cosine loss for deep face recognition. In: CVPR (2018)
54. Wei, X., Liang, S., Chen, N., Cao, X.: Transferable adversarial attacks for image and video object detection. In: IJCAI (2019)
55. Wen, Y., Zhang, K., Li, Z., Qiao, Y.: A discriminative deep feature learning approach for face recognition. In: ECCV (2016)
56. Wu, B., Ghanem, B.: ℓ_p-box admm: a versatile framework for integer programming. IEEE Trans. Pattern Anal. Mach. Intell. **41**(7), 1695–1708 (2018)
57. Xiao, C., Zhu, J.Y., Li, B., He, W., Liu, M., Song, D.: Spatially transformed adversarial examples. In: ICLR (2018)
58. Xu, W., Evans, D., Qi, Y.: Feature squeezing: detecting adversarial examples in deep neural networks. In: NDSS (2018)
59. Yang, X., Jia, X., Gong, D., Yan, D.M., Li, Z., Liu, W.: LARNet: lie algebra residual network for face recognition. In: International Conference on Machine Learning, pp. 11738–11750. PMLR (2021)
60. Yao, F., Rakin, A.S., Fan, D.: DeepHammer: depleting the intelligence of deep neural networks through targeted chain of bit flips. In: USENIX Security Symposium (2020)
61. Zhang, Y., Ruan, W., Wang, F., Huang, X.: Generalizing universal adversarial attacks beyond additive perturbations. In: ICDM (2020)
62. Zhao, P., Wang, S., Gongye, C., Wang, Y., Fei, Y., Lin, X.: Fault sneaking attack: a stealthy framework for misleading deep neural networks. In: ACM DAC (2019)
63. Zhou, T., Tulsiani, S., Sun, W., Malik, J., Efros, A.A.: View synthesis by appearance flow. In: Leibe, B., Matas, J., Sebe, N., Welling, M. (eds.) ECCV 2016. LNCS, vol. 9908, pp. 286–301. Springer, Cham (2016). https://doi.org/10.1007/978-3-319-46493-0_18

Robust Network Architecture Search via Feature Distortion Restraining

Yaguan Qian[1] , Shenghui Huang[1] , Bin Wang[2(✉)], Xiang Ling[3],
Xiaohui Guan[4], Zhaoquan Gu[5], Shaoning Zeng[6], Wujie Zhou[1],
and Haijiang Wang[1]

[1] Zhejiang University of Science and Technology,
Hangzhou 310023, Zhejiang, China
`qianyaguan@zust.edu.cn`
[2] Zhejiang Key Laboratory of Multidimensional Perception Technology,
Application and Cybersecurity, Hangzhou 310052, Zhejiang, China
`wbin2006@gmail.com`
[3] Institute of Software, Chinese Academy of Sciences,
Beijing 100190, China
[4] Zhejiang University of Water Resources and Electric Power,
Hangzhou 310023, Zhejiang, China
[5] Cyberspace Institute of Advanced Technology (CIAT),
Guang Zhou University, Guangzhou 510006, Guangdong, China
[6] Yangtze Delta Region Institute, University of Electronic Science
and Technology of China, Huzhou 313000, Zhejiang, China

Abstract. The vulnerability of Deep Neural Networks, i.e., susceptibility to adversarial attacks, severely limits the application of DNNs
in security-sensitive domains. Most of existing methods improve model
robustness from weight optimization, such as adversarial training. However, the architecture of DNNs is also a key factor to robustness, which is
often neglected or underestimated. We propose Robust Network Architecture Search (RNAS) to obtain a robust network against adversarial
attacks. We observe that an adversarial perturbation distorting the non-
robust features in latent feature space can further aggravate misclassification. Based on this observation, we search the robust architecture
through restricting feature distortion in the search process. Specifically,
we define a network vulnerability metric based on feature distortion as
a constraint in the search process. This process is modeled as a multi-
objective bilevel optimization problem and a novel algorithm is proposed
to solve this optimization. Extensive experiments conducted on CIFAR-
10/100 and SVHN show that RNAS achieves the best robustness under
various adversarial attacks compared with extensive baselines and SOTA
methods.

Keywords: Adversarial examples · Network architecture search ·
Roubst architecture

S. Avidan et al. (Eds.): ECCV 2022, LNCS 13665, pp. 122–138, 2022.
https://doi.org/10.1007/978-3-031-20065-6_8

1   Introduction

In recent years, Deep Neural Networks (DNNs) have shown excellent performance in various applications, such as image classification [15,20], objective detection [9], and semantic segmentation [3]. However, many investigations [10,35] show that DNNs are vulnerable to adversarial examples, i.e., images added by some elaborately designed imperceptible perturbations may lead to the model's misclassification. At present, various techniques [2,10,26] have been proposed to generate adversarial examples. Meanwhile, countermeasures [26,37,40] have been proposed to defend against adversarial examples. However, most of the methods focus on weight optimization, while neglects the influence of network structures, *e.g.*, adversarial training (AT) [26]. Nevertheless, recent studies reveal that robustness is highly related to the network structure [11]. A fixed structure may limit the further improvement of robustness. Therefore, in this paper, our work focuses on searching for a robust network architecture (Fig. 1).

To achieve higher robustness, we attempt to explore the relationship between network architecture and adversarial examples. Ilyas et al. [18] claimed that the existence of adversarial examples is due to the non-robust features of data, i.e., the intrinsic property of data. However, we suggest that adversarial perturbation misleads the network through distorting the non-robust features in latent feature space, which is also a property of networks. In other words, different network architectures and their weights have different defensive abilities to this distortion. Hence, we propose Robust Network Architecture Search (RNAS) based on Differentiable Architecture Search (DARTS) [24] to obtain a robust architecture through restraining the latent feature distortion. Specifically, we measure the latent feature distortion by the difference of feature distribution between clean and adversarial examples. This difference is quantified by KL divergence [21].

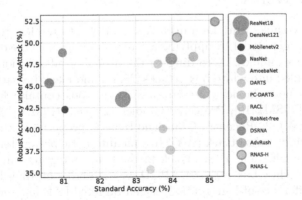

Fig. 1. Adversarial robustness, Standard accuracy, and parameter numbers for various architectures on CIFAR-10. All architectures are adversarially trained using 7-step PGD and evaluated by AutoAttack. The bubbles' size reflects the model parameters. RNAS's robustness and standard accuracy outperform other architectures, even with fewer parameters.

Based on the feature distortion of each cell (a basic component of a network in DARTS), we define network vulnerability. Specifically, we first define channel vulnerability by the KL divergence between the channel output distribution of adversarial examples and their corresponding clean examples. Then, we define cell vulnerability as the mean of channel vulnerabilities in the cell's output layer. Finally, we define network vulnerability as the mean of all cells' vulnerabilities. With the above definitions, we can obtain a more robust architecture by constraining network vulnerability in a search process. Inspired by DARTS, we transform an original single-objective bilevel optimization into a multi-objective bilevel optimization by imposing network vulnerability constraints. Then, we simplify this optimization and solve it with our proposed iterative algorithm. We evaluate the robustness of RNAS on CIFAR-10/100 [19], SVHN [29], and Tiny-ImageNet based on extensive comparisons. Our contributions are summarized as follows:

- We suggest that the distortion of non-robust features in latent feature space plays a key role in misclassification caused by adversarial examples. From this observation, we propose a network vulnerability metric based on the difference between latent feature distribution of clean examples and adversarial examples.
- We propose Robust Network Architecture Search (RNAS) using the network vulnerability metric as a constraint to obtain a robust network architecture. Meanwhile, we design an effective algorithm to solve this constrained multi-objective optimization.
- Extensive experiments conduct on several public datasets show that RNAS achieves SOTA performance in robust accuracy compared with RobNet-free, DSRNA, and AdvRush.

2   Related Works

Adversarial Attacks and Defends. Adversarial attack refers to a process of deceiving the target model by applying a tiny perturbation to the original input, i.e., adversarial examples. According to the available information, adversarial attacks are divided into white-box attacks [28,44] and black-box attacks [30,36]. Currently, the most classic white-box attack methods contain: Fast Gradient Sign Method (FGSM) [10], Projected Gradient Descent (PGD) [26] and Carlini & Wagner (C&W) [2]. Recently, Croce and Hein [6] proposed a reliable and stable attack method: AutoAttack (AA). It is an automatic parameter-free method for robustness evaluation. Four attack methods are integrated in AutoAttack, including three white-box attacks: APGD [6] with cross entropy loss, targeted APGD with difference-of-logits-ratio loss and targeted FAB [5], and a black-box attack: SquareAttack [1]. Various adversarial defense methods have been proposed to improve the robustness of DNN against adversarial attacks, such as random smoothing [22], defensive distillation [31], and adversarial training [26,40].

NAS for Robustness Network. NAS is proposed to automatically design the network architecture to replace traditional manually-designed methods. Representative techniques include reinforcement learning [42], evolutionary algorithms

[32], and differentiable approaches [24]. One of the most representative differentiable methods is DARTS [24], which conducts search and evaluation at the same time. Though NAS achieves excellent performance by automatically searching the network architecture, it neglects the robust accuracy of the obtained model [7].

At present, researchers focus on searching a more robust network architecture through NAS [11]. They proved that robustness has a strong correlation with structure. Dong et al. [8] discussed the relationship between robustness, Lipschitz constant and architecture parameters. They proved that proper constraints of the architecture parameter can reduce Lipschitz constant, thereby improve robustness. Hosseini et al. [14] defined two differentiable metrics to measure the architecture robustness based on verifiable lower bounds and Jacobian norm bounds. The search process is based on the maximization of the robustness metrics.

3 Preliminary

In our work, we use DARTS as our basic framework. DARTS is a differentiable search framework and its search space is defined on cells. A cell is defined as a directed acyclic graph (DAG) with N nodes $\{x_0, x_1, \ldots, x_{N-1}\}$, where each node represents a layer in the network. In an operation space $\mathcal{O}$, each element $o(\cdot) \in \mathcal{O}$ represents an operation in a layer (3 × 3 convolution, pooling, zero operation, etc.). Within a cell, the goal of DARTS is to select an operation in $\mathcal{O}$ to connect each node-pair. The information flow between node i and node j is represented as an edge $f_{(i,j)}$, which is composed of operations weighted by an architecture parameter $\alpha^{(i,j)}$, i.e.,

$$f_{i,j}(x_i) = \sum_{o \in \mathcal{O}_{i,j}} \frac{\exp(\alpha_o^{(i,j)})}{\sum_{o' \in \mathcal{O}_{i,j}} \exp(\alpha_{o'}^{(i,j)})} \cdot o(x_i) \tag{1}$$

where x_i is the output of the i-th node and $\alpha_o^{(i,j)}$ is the weight of an operation $o(x_i)$. A node's input is the sum of all outputs of its previous nodes, i.e., $x_j = \sum_{i<j} f_{i,j}(x_i)$. The output of the cell x_{N-1} is $concat(x_0, x_1, \ldots x_{N-2})$, where $concat(\cdot)$ represents concatenating all channels. A proxy network on the search process is constructed by m cells.

The operation parameter of $o(\cdot)$ is denoted by θ. The search space of DARTS is differentiable, so that θ and α can be alternately updated with gradients in the search process. When the search process converges, we retain the operation with the largest α in each edge $f_{(i,j)}$ to compose the final cell structure. The obtained cell is taken as a basic unit to form the target network by stacking multiple cells together. The optimization of α and θ are defined as follows [24]:

$$\begin{aligned} &\min_{\alpha} \mathcal{L}_{val}(\theta^*(\alpha), \alpha) \\ &\text{s.t.} \quad \theta^*(\alpha) = \arg\min_{\theta} \mathcal{L}_{train}(\theta, \alpha) \end{aligned} \tag{2}$$

where $\mathcal{L}_{train}$ and $\mathcal{L}_{val}$ denote training loss and validation loss, respectively.

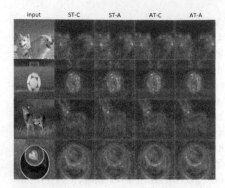 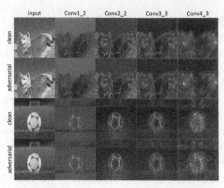

(a) Feature map visualization of the Conv4_3 layer of VGG16. ST and AT represent standard and adversarial training respectively; C and A represent clean and adversarial examples respectively.

(b) Feature map visualization of different layers of VGG16. A pair of clean example and adversarial example is compared by visualizing their feature maps in different layers.

Fig. 2. Feature map visualization.

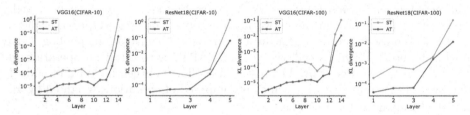

Fig. 3. The latent feature distortion of VGG16 and ResNet18 on CIFAR-10/100.

4   Method

First, we analyze the mechanism of adversarial examples from the perspective of feature distortion. Based on feature distortion, we define a network vulnerability metric to guide the search process. Taking DARTS as the basic framework of RNAS, we apply network vulnerability as a constraint to an architecture parameter α. We formulate RNAS as a multi-objective bilevel optimization. Through an iterative optimization algorithm, we can obtain a more robust network architecture than other methods.

4.1   Network Vulnerability Constraint

Ilyas et al. [18] claimed that in classification tasks, the network relies on non-robust features, which are highly predictive and imperceptible, to achieve high accuracy. However, it leads to adversarial perturbations exploiting this dependence. Non-robust features are highly sensitive to the feature distortion and only a slight distortion will lead to misclassification. We speculate that such adversarial perturbations further aggravate a distortion in the latent feature space. To observe the process of latent feature distortion caused by the adversarial perturbation, we visualize the feature maps in Fig. 2. As illustrated in Fig. 2a, for a standard training model, the latent features of adversarial examples have an obvious distortion compared with that of clean examples. The worst distortion regions mainly exist in the non-object parts that contain many imperceptible non-robust features. On the contrary, for an adversarial training model, the distortion caused by adversarial examples is significantly weakened. In addition, Fig. 2b shows that the distortion becomes more obvious as layers become deeper. Hence, we believe that an adversarial example fools a model by enlarging the distortion of non-robust features.

To further quantify this distortion, i.e., to measure the latent feature difference between clean examples and adversarial examples in deep networks, we introduce the KL divergence [21] that is widely used to measure the difference between two distributions, e.g., the difference of feature distribution of different networks' outputs in knowledge distilling [13] and deep mutual learning [41]. In practice, we represent the distortion as a feature maps' KL divergence between clean examples and adversarial examples. We quantitatively analyze the distortion change in adversarial training models and standard training models, as shown in Fig. 3. As layers become deeper, the distortion increases by an order of magnitude. Meanwhile, the distortion of adversarial training models is significantly smaller than that of standard training models, which is consistent with the visualization in Fig. 2.

Based on the above analysis, the main idea of our method is to restrain feature distortion. If a network lacks resistance to feature distortion, the network will be vulnerable to adversarial examples. Hence, we define a model vulnerability metric based on feature distortion. Considering this metric as a constraint, we can search for a more robust network architecture. Then, we define the network vulnerability metric as follows.

Channel Vulnerability: The vulnerability of the k-th channel in the l-th layer is defined as:

$$F(z^{(l,k)}, \tilde{z}^{(l,k)}) = \mathbb{E}_{(x,y)\sim\mathcal{D}}KL(z^{(l,k)}, \tilde{z}^{(l,k)}) \tag{3}$$

where $z^{(l,k)}$ denotes the feature value of the k-th feature map in the l-th layer of clean examples. Similarly, $\tilde{z}^{(l,k)}$ represents the adversarial case.

Layer Vulnerability: We define the layer vulnerability f_l as the mean of all *channel vulnerabilities* in the l-th layer, i.e.,

$$f_l = \frac{1}{N^{(l)}} \sum_{k=1}^{N^{(l)}} F(z_i^{(l,k)}, \tilde{z}_i^{(l,k)}) \tag{4}$$

where $N^{(l)}$ is the number of the l-th layer's feature maps.

From the observation in Fig. 2 and Fig. 3, the feature distortion increases as the network becomes deeper. Therefore, we should not only focus on the final output distortion, but also concern the distortion changes in hidden layers of the network. Since the search space is defined based on cells, we first define cell vulnerability, and further define network vulnerability based on cell vulnerability.

Cell Vulnerability: We define cell vulnerability $f_i^{(o)}$ as the mean of all *layer vulnerability* of the output layers in the i-th cell, i.e.,

$$f_i^{(o)} = \frac{1}{N_i^{(o)}} \sum_{k=1}^{N_i^{(o)}} F(z_i^{(o,k)}, \tilde{z}_i^{(o,k)}) \tag{5}$$

where $N_i^{(o)}$ is the number of feature maps, $z_i^{(o,k)}$ is the feature value of the k-th feature map from clean examples, similarly, $\tilde{z}_i^{(o,k)}$ represents the adversarial case.

Network Vulnerability: The network vulnerability is defined as the mean of all *cell vulnerabilities*, i.e.,

$$\mathcal{F}(f_\theta(x), f_\theta(\tilde{x})) = \frac{1}{M} \sum_{i=1}^{M} f_i^{(o)} \tag{6}$$

where M is the number of cells in the whole network.

4.2   Robust Network Architecture Search (RNAS)

The DARTS only focuses on clean accuracy [40]. Our goal is to find robust cells and then use them to construct a robust network. Thus, we add network vulnerability to the original DARTS objective function. This add-on guarantees a minimal network vulnerability during the update of architecture parameter α in the search process. Once α is determined, we use adversarial training to update the operation parameter θ for a new architecture (corresponding to α). Briefly, the objective of RNAS is to minimize the validation loss and network vulnerability under adversarial attacks. The robust operation parameter θ is updated through adversarial training. We formalize RNAS as a multi-objective bilevel optimization problem:

$$\min_{\alpha} \left(\mathcal{L}_{val}(\theta^*(\alpha), \alpha) + \mathcal{L}_{val}^{adv}(\theta^*(\alpha), \alpha), \mathcal{F}(\alpha) \right)$$
$$\text{s.t.} \quad \theta^*(\alpha) = \arg\min_{\theta} \mathcal{L}_{train}^{adv}(\theta, \alpha) \tag{7}$$

where $\mathcal{L}_{train}^{adv}$ and $\mathcal{L}_{val}^{adv}$ respectively represent adversarial training loss and adversarial validation loss, and $\mathcal{F}(\alpha)$ represents the network vulnerability. In this multi-objective bilevel optimization, α is an upper-level variable and θ is a lower-level variable. However, addressing this problem is non-trivial. We turn the network vulnerability into a constraint and set an upper bound $H \in [0, +\infty)$ of the network vulnerability. Thus, Problem 7 is transformed into a single-objective

---

Algorithm 1. Robust Network Architecture Search (RNAS)

Input: Dataset $\mathcal{D}$, training epochs E, training iteration T.
Output: Learned architecture parameter α_p.
//Phase I: θ-warm up
1: Randomly initialized operation parameters θ and weights α in mixed operation set $\mathcal{O}$
2: **while** $e \leq 15$ **do**
3:     **for** $t = 1$ to T **do**
4:         Keep α fixed, and obtain θ^{t+1} by gradient descent with $\nabla_\theta \mathcal{L}_{train}^{adv}\left(\theta^t, \alpha\right)$
5:     **end for**
6:     $e \leftarrow e + 1$
7: **end while**
//Phase II: Robust Architecture Search
1: **while** *not converged* **or** $15 < e \leq E$ **do**
2:     *//Step1*: unconstrained searching
3:     **for** $t = 1$ to $T/2$ **do**
4:         Keep α^t fixed, and obtain θ^{t+1} by gradient descent with $\nabla_\theta \mathcal{L}_{train}^{adv}\left(\theta^t, \alpha^t\right)$
5:         Keep θ^{t+1} fixed, and obtain α^{t+1} by gradient descent with $\nabla_\alpha \mathcal{L}_{val}^{adv}\left(\theta^{t+1}, \alpha^t\right)$
6:     **end for**
7:     *//Step2*: vulnerability constrained for α.
8:     **for** $T/2$ to T **do**
9:         $\alpha_p^t \leftarrow \Pi_{proj}\alpha^t$
10:        Update α_p^t
11:    **end for**
12:    $\alpha^t \leftarrow \alpha_p^t$
13:    $e \leftarrow e + 1$
14: **end while**

---

optimization problem with two constraints, as shown in Eq. 8. θ and α are alternately updated until they converge.

$$\min_{\alpha} \mathcal{L}_{val}(\theta^*(\alpha), \alpha) + \mathcal{L}_{val}^{adv}(\theta^*(\alpha), \alpha)$$

$$\text{s.t.} \quad \theta^*(\alpha) = \arg\min_{\theta} \mathcal{L}_{train}^{adv}(\theta, \alpha) \tag{8}$$

$$\mathcal{F}(\alpha) \leq H$$

Since Eq. 8 is a constrained optimization and the softmax function of α is nonconvex, it is hard to obtain a closed-form solution. So we introduce a projection method to optimize the constraining function $\mathcal{F}(\alpha) \leq H$. We project α to the nearest point α_p in the feasible region that satisfies the network vulnerability constraint, as shown in Eq. 9, which can be solved by a Lagrangian method.

$$\min_{\alpha_p} \frac{1}{2} \|\alpha - \alpha_p\|_2^2 \quad \text{s.t.} \quad \mathcal{F}(\alpha_p) \leq H \tag{9}$$

The whole process is divided into two *phases*. In *Phase I: warm-up*, we only update θ since it is randomly initialized at the beginning, which contains little valuable knowledge to guide the search process. *Phase II: search* is divided into two *steps*, *Step* 1 is an unconstrained search, in which α can disobey the vulnerability constraint and a better architecture is searched freely in a larger parameter space. In this step, the objective function of RNAS is the same as that of DARTS, where θ and α are alternately updated by gradient descent. In *Step* 2, we project α to the nearest point α_p in the feasible set, where the objective of projection in Eq. 9 should satisfy the vulnerability constraint. At the end of *Step* 2, we assign α_p to α to make the algorithm return to *Step* 1. The algorithm of RNAS is presented as Algorithm 1.

The advantages of RNAS are as follows: in *Phase I*, the operation parameters θ are warmed up to provide a stable network for further searching. In *Step* 1 of *Phase II*, the weight and architecture are jointly optimized by adversarial examples to determine a reasonable projection starting point of α in *Step* 2. In *Step* 2, we apply network vulnerability constraint to α to search a "low-feature-distortion" network architecture. When the inputs are adversarially perturbed, the network vulnerability constraint can restrain the distortion by minimizing the deviation between the latent features of clean examples and adversarial examples. After *Step* 2, the algorithm will return to *Step* 1 to search the architecture in a larger parameter space. In addition, the upper bound H can adjust the vulnerability constraint to make the search more flexible. The detailed discussion of H is in the Sect. 5.4.

5   Experiment

We first use RNAS to search on CIFAR-10, then transfer the obtained architecture to SVHN, CIFAR-100 and Tiny-ImageNet. We conduct extensive experiments on CIFAR-10/100, SVHN and Tiny-ImageNet under various adversarial attacks to evaluate the effectiveness of RNAS. Our model significantly outperforms the baselines and achieves the highest robustness.

5.1   Experimental Setup

Searching: When searching on CIFAR-10, we divide the training set into two equal parts. The search space contains 8 candidate operations: 3×3 and 5×5 separable convolutions, 3×3 and 5×5 dilated separable convolutions, 3×3 max pooling, 3×3 average pooling, skip connection, and zero operation. The network consists of 8 cells: 6 normal cells and 2 reduction cells. Each cell has 6 nodes. We use SGD with momentum to train the model for 60 epochs with a batch size of 128. The initial learning rate is 0.01 with a momentum of 0.9, weight decay is 0.0003, and a cosine learning rate decay is used. Architecture parameters α are updated through Adam with a learning rate of 0.0006 and a weight decay of 0.001. $H = 0.0001$ in RNAS-H and $H = 0.00001$ in RNAS-L.

Training: After obtaining the normal cell and the reduction cell (as shown in Fig. 4) in the search process, we adversarially train the target network on the entire dataset. The adversarial examples are generated by PGD and the total

Table 1. Size and robust accuracy (%) of different architecture with PGD adversarial training on CIFAR-10. PGD^{20} and PGD^{100} refer to PGD attack with 20 and 100 iterations. The best result in each column is in bold, and the second best result is underlined.

Model	Params	AT						ST	
		Clean	FGSM	PGD^{20}	PGD^{100}	C&W	AA	Clean	FGSM
VGG16 [34]	14.7M	80.08	52.85	47.50	46.66	41.80	42.10	92.64	46.35
ResNet18 [12]	11.2M	82.63	54.12	48.81	48.50	42.48	43.43	94.64	49.72
DenseNet121 [16]	7.0M	84.85	54.35	48.31	47.81	35.68	44.18	95.97	47.11
NasNet [43]	4.3M	80.61	54.19	50.25	49.63	42.97	45.33	97.33	50.03
AmoebaNet [32]	3.2M	83.41	54.44	42.95	42.80	39.21	35.32	<u>97.45</u>	41.60
PNAS [23]	4.5M	<u>85.08</u>	58.79	47.70	47.51	40.15	43.03	96.60	49.32
SNAS [38]	2.7M	82.56	54.39	46.03	45.97	40.36	43.55	97.18	50.01
DARTS [24]	3.3M	83.75	55.75	44.91	45.00	41.25	39.98	97.41	50.56
P-DARTS [4]	3.4M	82.65	53.27	42.72	42.77	41.03	37.22	97.40	54.51
PC-DARTS [39]	3.6M	83.94	52.67	41.92	42.50	39.25	37.53	**97.50**	52.75
MobileNetv2 [33]	2.3M	81.04	53.66	47.40	46.79	41.26	42.29	94.23	47.32
ShuffleNetv2 [25]	1.3M	80.25	49.10	42.10	40.25	40.34	36.78	91.48	44.58
SqueezeNet [17]	0.7M	78.65	51.21	44.22	40.56	39.66	28.58	86.72	31.90
RACL [8]	3.6M	83.62	57.25	50.02	49.86	44.13	47.64	96.42	49.29
RobNet-free [11]	5.6M	83.98	58.44	51.68	51.47	<u>46.07</u>	48.06	96.46	35.32
DSRNA [14]	3.5M	80.98	59.41	51.34	51.28	38.92	48.85	97.02	52.24
AdvRush [27]	4.2M	84.57	60.21	52.32	52.20	45.13	48.29	97.28	54.72
RNAS-H	3.5M	84.13	<u>61.90</u>	<u>53.48</u>	<u>53.35</u>	**50.74**	<u>50.54</u>	96.65	<u>63.23</u>
RNAS-L	3.2M	**85.16**	**62.61**	**54.85**	53.70	45.57	**52.34**	95.26	**65.32**

perturbation size $\epsilon = 8/255$, the number of attack iterations is 7 with a step size of 2/255. The training phase has 600 epochs with a batch size of 128. We use SGD with momentum, where the initial learning rate is 0.1 with a momentum of 0.9, weight decay is 0.0003 and a cosine learning rate decay is used.

Evaluation: All models are fully trained for 600 epochs and the setting is consistent with RNAS in the training phase. Adversarial examples used for evaluation are generated from FGSM [10], PGD [26], C&W [2] and AutoAttack (AA) [6]. The attack settings are as follows: 1) FGSM attack with $\epsilon = 0.031$ (8/255); 2) PGD attack with $\epsilon = 0.031$ (8/255), attack iterations of 20 and 100, and a step size of 2/255; 3) C&W attack with $c = 0.5$ and attack iterations of 100; 4) AA with $\epsilon = 0.031$ (8/255). All attacks are l_∞-bounded.

5.2 Results on CIFAR-10

Figure 4 illustrates the architecture of the normal cell and the reduction cell obtained on CIFAR-10. We obtain two architectures through different H values: RNAS-H (high) and RNAS-L (low). We observe that the operations between nodes in RNAS-H and RNAS-L are intensive, which is consistent with the property of the robust architecture in [11]. We use 20 cells to construct the target

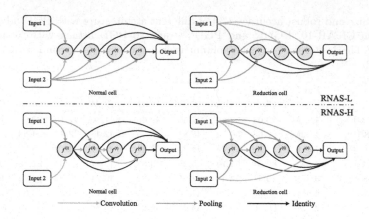

Fig. 4. Architecture of the cells obtained on CIFAR-10.

network, train the network through standard training and adversarial training respectively and evaluate it under various adversarial attacks. The comparison results are summarized in Table 1.

As shown in Table 1, through adversarial training, the architecture obtained by RNAS has a better robust performance than other models. (1) Compared with various manually designed baseline models, our model achieves a better robust accuracy. (2) Compared with NAS baselines, our model achieves the best performance under various adversarial attacks. The main reason is that we restrian the feature distortion in our search process. Hence, the obtained network is insensitive to the distortion caused by adversarial examples. (3) Compared with existing NAS-based robust search methods, RNAS-L and RNAS-H both achieve better performance.

In Table 1, even only with standard training, RNAS is still more robust than other network architectures. This result indicates that the architecture obtained by RNAS has a natural robust property. In addition, the clean accuracy of RNAS is yet closed to that of the optimal NAS.

5.3   Results on CIFAR-100, SVHN and Tiny-ImageNet

To further evaluate the effectiveness of RNAS, we transfer the model to CIFAR-100, SVHN and Tiny-ImageNet, specifically. We use 20 cells obtained on CIFAR-10 to construct a network and retrain it on CIFAR-100, SVHN and Tiny-ImageNet by adversarial training respectively. In Table 2, Table 3 and Table 4 compared with most of the baselines, RNAS obtained on CIFAR-10 can still improve the robustness after adversarial training on CIFAR-100, SVHN and Tiny-ImageNet. The results indicate that the RNAS architecture is highly transferable.

In addition, we observe that on all three datasets, the robustness improvement of RNAS-L is not as high as that on CIFAR-10. The reason is that the architecture search process is dataset-dependent, and RNAS-L is obtained under a

Table 2. Evaluation of different architectures on CIFAR-100.

Model	Clean (%)	FGSM (%)	PGD^{20} (%)	PGD^{100} (%)	C&W (%)	AA (%)
ResNet18 [12]	55.12	25.65	21.08	19.98	17.04	18.02
DenseNet121 [16]	**61.71**	34.28	27.30	27.07	20.18	24.55
Mobilnetv2 [33]	53.81	28.45	23.80	23.76	16.04	20.30
NasNet [43]	59.64	29.83	24.41	24.38	20.41	22.06
DARTS [24]	59.14	30.35	25.66	25.40	20.72	22.65
PC-DARTS [39]	59.44	20.29	24.10	24.02	19.45	22.06
RobNet-free [11]	59.64	34.23	27.21	27.18	<u>21.92</u>	24.82
DSRNA [14]	57.44	35.03	28.11	27.97	21.52	25.20
AdvRush [27]	58.73	39.01	30.16	29.67	20.08	26.46
RNAS-H	59.80	**42.44**	**32.05**	**31.99**	**29.84**	**28.29**
RNAS-L	<u>60.24</u>	<u>40.52</u>	<u>31.11</u>	<u>31.06</u>	20.84	<u>27.37</u>

Table 3. Evaluation of different architectures on SVHN.

Model	Clean (%)	FGSM (%)	PGD^{20} (%)	PGD^{100} (%)	C&W (%)	AA (%)
ResNet18 [12]	92.06	85.70	68.50	68.18	58.31	63.37
DenseNet121 [16]	93.72	89.68	72.62	72.32	60.61	65.92
Mobilnetv2 [33]	89.94	83.28	66.17	65.78	54.63	59.22
NasNet [43]	94.55	87.54	69.52	68.88	42.44	64.80
DARTS [24]	**94.90**	90.01	77.58	77.15	60.22	66.24
PC-DARTS [39]	94.78	88.81	76.07	76.01	56.49	67.56
RobNet-free [11]	92.45	89.33	85.30	84.68	61.28	72.15
DSRNA [14]	91.58	91.27	84.94	84.03	40.50	74.41
AdvRush [27]	<u>94.80</u>	91.16	89.89	88.79	60.05	75.52
RNAS-H	94.58	**93.07**	**91.46**	**89.80**	**63.64**	**77.26**
RNAS-L	93.88	<u>92.08</u>	89.67	<u>88.92</u>	<u>61.44</u>	<u>75.89</u>

Table 4. Evaluation of different architectures on Tiny-ImageNet.

Model	Clean (%)	FGSM (%)	PGD^{20} (%)	PGD^{100} (%)	C&W (%)	AA (%)
ResNet18 [12]	38.36	18.80	14.92	14.85	**25.61**	12.20
DenseNet121 [16]	46.26	22.88	19.11	19.05	22.13	17.78
Mobilnetv2 [33]	39.48	17.64	15.33	15.22	16.66	14.80
NasNet [43]	44.52	23.69	20.60	20.48	19.87	19.57
DARTS [24]	**45.94**	24.36	21.74	21.68	20.67	20.09
PC-DARTS [39]	45.42	25.38	22.94	21.88	19.99	20.45
RobNet-free [11]	44.24	25.44	23.85	23.65	20.11	22.54
DSRNA [14]	44.42	**28.52**	<u>24.32</u>	24.09	14.56	21.55
AdvRush [27]	45.45	25.20	23.58	23.38	18.68	22.78
RNAS-H	<u>45.92</u>	<u>28.30</u>	**26.84**	**26.49**	<u>24.27</u>	**24.22**
RNAS-L	44.82	26.28	24.04	<u>23.89</u>	22.83	<u>23.02</u>

stricter network vulnerability constraint, which may *overfit* the original dataset. After transferred to other dataset, the performance of the architecture obtained on CIFAR-10 decreases a little. Despite this, RNAS-L still achieves a comparative or even better performance compared with SOTA methods. The differences in performance between RNAS-H and RNAS-L are due to the intensity of the constraints on the vulnerability, which will be discussed in Sect. 5.4.

To verify the effectiveness of RNAS on other datasets, we also directly search the architecture on Tiny-ImageNet. which evaluation results is presented in the Table 5. RNAS can still outperform other models.

Table 5. Evaluation of the networks obtained on Tiny-ImageNet. Except for ResNet18 and DenseNet121, the rest models are directly obtained by searching on Tiny-ImageNet.

Model	Clean (%)	FGSM (%)	PGD^{20} (%)	PGD^{100} (%)	C&W (%)	AA (%)
ResNet18 [12]	38.36	18.80	14.92	14.85	<u>25.61</u>	12.20
DenseNet121 [16]	46.26	22.88	19.11	19.05	22.13	17.78
DARTS [24]	<u>46.85</u>	24.85	22.14	21.86	22.07	20.33
PC-DARTS [39]	46.22	26.40	21.63	21.49	23.74	21.32
RobNet-free [11]	45.43	28.61	24.85	24.46	21.21	21.52
DSRNA [14]	46.50	<u>28.67</u>	25.33	25.09	18.66	23.56
AdvRush [27]	45.98	27.31	25.85	25.40	15.70	23.81
RNAS-H	45.92	28.53	<u>26.92</u>	<u>26.79</u>	**26.47**	<u>24.82</u>
RNAS-L	**47.62**	**29.24**	**27.34**	**27.02**	20.85	**25.74**

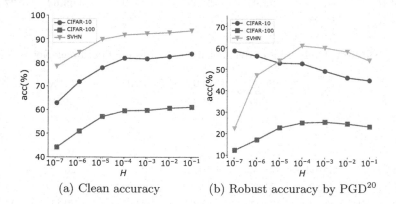

(a) Clean accuracy   (b) Robust accuracy by PGD^{20}

Fig. 5. The clean accuracy and robust accuracy of RNAS with different H value on different datasets. The models are obtained on CIFAR-10 and adversarially trained on CIFAR-10/100 and SVHN.

5.4 Upper Bound H of network vulnerability

Recall that H is the upper bound of the constraint on the network vulnerability, which controls the constraint's intensity. The larger the H value, the looser the constraint, vice versa. $H = 0$ means no distortion in the latent features. Intuitively, a smaller H ensures a more robust architecture in the search process. However, experiments show that too small an H may lead to an overfit to the original data, thus reduce the model's generalization ability.

Network architecture search is a time-consuming process, and the adversarial training introduced into RNAS further overload such computation costs. In practice, we search the architecture on a small proxy dataset first, then transfer this architecture to the target dataset. Thus, transferability is a valuable property of the obtained models. In RNAS, the value of H directly influences the model's transferability. Figure 5 shows how H influences the model. As H decreases (i.e., the constraint strengthens), the PGD robust accuracy on CIFAR-10 gradually increases, while on CIFAR-100 and SVHN, the PGD robust accuracy falls rapidly after rising. This indicates that too small an H makes the model overfit CIFAR-10 and reduces its generalization ability; too large an H is not effective on constraining the network vulnerability. In conclusion, the advantage of RNAS is that the transferability can be improved by adjusting the upper bound of network vulnerability H for different datasets.

6 Conclusion

In this paper, we empirically verify that the distortion of non-robust features in the latent feature space plays a vital role in misclassification caused by adversarial examples. Experimental result shows on various datasets, RNAS outperforms other classic and SOTA models in robustness. Under both PGD adversarial training, RNAS has a higher robustness than other methods. Even without adversarial training, RNAS still shows some robustness. In addition, we find that the transferability of RNAS can be improved by adjusting the upper bound of network vulnerability H. In the future, we will focus on extending our work to other tasks, such as semantic segmentation and object detection.

Acknowledgment. This work is sponsored by the Zhejiang Provincial Natural Science Foundation of China (LZ22F020007, LGF20F020007), Major Research Plan of the National Natural Science Foundation of China (92167203), National Key R&D Program of China (2018YFB2100400), Natural Science Foundation of China (61902082, 61972357), and project funded by China Postdoctoral Science Foundation under No. 2022M713253.

References

1. Andriushchenko, M., Croce, F., Flammarion, N., Hein, M.: Square attack: a query-efficient black-box adversarial attack via random search. In: Vedaldi, A., Bischof, H., Brox, T., Frahm, J.-M. (eds.) ECCV 2020. LNCS, vol. 12368, pp. 484–501. Springer, Cham (2020). https://doi.org/10.1007/978-3-030-58592-1_29

2. Carlini, N., Wagner, D.: Towards evaluating the robustness of neural networks. In: 2017 IEEE Symposium on Security and Privacy, pp. 39–57 (2017)
3. Chen, L.C., Zhu, Y., Papandreou, G., Schroff, F., Adam, H.: Encoder-decoder with atrous separable convolution for semantic image segmentation. In: Proceedings of the European Conference on Computer Vision, pp. 801–818 (2018)
4. Chen, X., Xie, L., Wu, J., Tian, Q.: Progressive differentiable architecture search: bridging the depth gap between search and evaluation. In: Proceedings of the IEEE/CVF International Conference on Computer Vision, pp. 1294–1303 (2019)
5. Croce, F., Hein, M.: Minimally distorted adversarial examples with a fast adaptive boundary attack. In: International Conference on Machine Learning, pp. 2196–2205 (2020)
6. Croce, F., Hein, M.: Reliable evaluation of adversarial robustness with an ensemble of diverse parameter-free attacks. In: International Conference on Machine Learning, pp. 2206–2216 (2020)
7. Devaguptapu, C., Agarwal, D., Mittal, G., Balasubramanian, V.N.: An empirical study on the robustness of NAS based architectures. arXiv preprint arXiv:2007.08428 (2020)
8. Dong, M., Li, Y., Wang, Y., Xu, C.: Adversarially robust neural architectures. arXiv preprint arXiv:2009.00902 (2020)
9. Girshick, R., Donahue, J., Darrell, T., Malik, J.: Rich feature hierarchies for accurate object detection and semantic segmentation. In: Proceedings of the IEEE Conference on Computer Vision and Pattern Recognition, pp. 1097–1105 (2014)
10. Goodfellow, I., Shlens, J., Szegedy, C.: Explaining and harnessing adversarial examples. In: International Conference on Learning Representations (2015)
11. Guo, M., Yang, Y., Xu, R., Liu, Z., Lin, D.: When NAS meets robustness: in search of robust architectures against adversarial attacks. In: Proceedings of the IEEE Conference on Computer Vision and Pattern Recognition, pp. 628–637 (2020)
12. He, K., Zhang, X., Ren, S., Sun, J.: Deep residual learning for image recognition. In: Proceedings of the IEEE Conference on Computer Vision and Pattern Recognition, pp. 770–778 (2016)
13. Hinton, G., Vinyals, O., Dean, J.: Distilling the knowledge in a neural network. In: Advances in 28th Neural Information Processing Systems (2015)
14. Hosseini, R., Yang, X., Xie, P.: DSRNA: differentiable search of robust neural architectures. In: Proceedings of the IEEE Conference on Computer Vision and Pattern Recognition, pp. 6196–6205 (2021)
15. Huang, G., Liu, Z., Maaten, L., Q, K.: Densely connected convolutional networks. In: Proceedings of the IEEE Conference on Computer Vision and Pattern Recognition (2017)
16. Huang, G., Liu, Z., Van Der Maaten, L., Weinberger, K.Q.: Densely connected convolutional networks. In: Proceedings of the IEEE Conference on Computer Vision and Pattern Recognition, pp. 4700–4708 (2017)
17. Iandola, F.N., Han, S., Moskewicz, M.W., Ashraf, K., Dally, W.J., Keutzer, K.: SqueezeNet: AlexNet-level accuracy with 50× fewer parameters and <0.5 MB model size. In: International Conference on Learning Representations (2017)
18. Ilyas, A., Santurkar, S., Engstrom, L., Tran, B., Madry, A.: Adversarial examples are not bugs, they are features. In: Advances in Neural Information Processing Systems, vol. 32 (2019)
19. Krizhevsky, A., Hinton, G.: Learning multiple layers of features from tiny images. In: Technical Report (2009)

20. Krizhevsky, A., Ilya, S., Geoffrey E.H.: ImageNet classification with deep convolutional neural networks. In: Advances in Neural Information Processing Systems, pp. 1097–1105 (2012)
21. Kullback, S., Leibler, R.A.: On information and sufficiency. In: The Annals of Mathematical Statistics, pp. 79–86 (1951)
22. Lecuyer, M., Atlidakis, V., Geambasu, R., Hsu, D., Jana, S.: Certified robustness to adversarial examples with differential privacy. In: 2019 IEEE Symposium on Security and Privacy, pp. 656–672 (2019)
23. Liu, C., et al.: Progressive neural architecture search. In: Proceedings of the European Conference on Computer Vision, pp. 19–34 (2018)
24. Liu, H., Simonyan, K., Yang, Y.: DARTS: differentiable architecture search. In: International Conference on Learning Representations (2019)
25. Ma, N., Zhang, X., Zheng, H.T., Sun, J.: ShuffleNet V2: practical guidelines for efficient CNN architecture design. In: Proceedings of the European Conference on Computer Vision, pp. 116–131 (2018)
26. Madry, A., Makelov, A., Schmidt, L., Tsipras, D., Vladu, A.: Towards deep learning models resistant to adversarial attacks (2017)
27. Mok, J., Na, B., Choe, H., Yoon, S.: AdvRush: searching for adversarially robust neural architectures. In: Proceedings of the IEEE/CVF International Conference on Computer Vision, pp. 12322–12332 (2021)
28. Moosavi-Dezfooli, S.M., Fawzi, A., Frossard, P.: DeepFool: a simple and accurate method to fool deep neural networks. In: Proceedings of the IEEE Conference on Computer Vision and Pattern Recognition, pp. 2574–2582 (2017)
29. Netzer, Y., Wang, T., Coates, A., Bissacco, A., Wu, B., Y, N.A.: Reading digits in natural images with unsupervised feature learning. In: NIPS Workshop on Deep Learning and Unsupervised Feature Learning (2011)
30. Papernot, N., McDaniel, P., Goodfellow, I., Jha, S., Celik, Z.B., Swami, A.: Practical black-box attacks against deep learning systems using adversarial examples. In: Proceedings of the 2017 ACM on Asia Conference on Computer and Communications Security, pp. 506–519 (2017)
31. Papernot, N., McDaniel, P., Wu, X., Jha, S., Swami, A.: Distillation as a defense to adversarial perturbations against deep neural networks. In: 2016 IEEE Symposium on Security and Privacy, pp. 582–597 (2016)
32. Real, E., Aggarwal, A., Huang, Y., Le, Q.: Regularized evolution for image classifier architecture search. In: Proceedings of the AAAI Conference on Artificial Intelligence, pp. 4780–4789 (2019)
33. Sandler, M., Howard, A., Zhu, M., Zhmoginov, A., Chen, L.C.: MobileNetV2: inverted residuals and linear bottlenecks. In: Proceedings of the IEEE Conference on Computer Vision and Pattern Recognition, pp. 4510–4520 (2018)
34. Simonyan, K., Zisserman, A.: Very deep convolutional networks for large scale image recognition. In: International Conference on Learning Representations (2015)
35. Szegedy, C., et al.: Intriguing properties of neural networks. arXiv preprint arXiv:1312.6199 (2013)
36. Tu, C.C., et al.: Autozoom: autoencoder-based zeroth order optimization method for attacking black-box neural networks. In: Proceedings of the AAAI Conference on Artificial Intelligence, pp. 742–749 (2019)
37. Wong, E., Rice, L., Kolter, J.Z.: Fast is better than free: revisiting adversarial training. In: International Conference on Learning Representations (2020)
38. Xie, S., Zheng, H., Liu, C., Lin, L.: SNAS: stochastic neural architecture search. In: International Conference on Learning Representations (2019)

39. Xu, Y., Xie, L., Zhang, X., Chen, X.: PC-DARTS: partial channel connections for memory-efficient architecture search. In: International Conference on Learning Representations (2019)
40. Zhang, H., Yu, Y., Jiao, J., Xing, E., Ghaoui, L.E., Jordan, M.I.: Theoretically principled trade-off between robustness and accuracy. In: International Conference on Machine Learning, pp. 7472–7482 (2019)
41. Zhang, Y., Xiang, T., Hospedales, T.M., Lu, H.: Deep mutual learning. In: Proceedings of the IEEE Conference on Computer Vision and Pattern Recognition, pp. 4320–4328 (2018)
42. Zoph, B., Le, Q.V.: Neural architecture search with reinforcement learning. In: International Conference on Learning Representations (2017)
43. Zoph, B., Vasudevan, V., Shlens, J., Le, Q.V.: Learning transferable architectures for scalable image recognition. In: Proceedings of the IEEE Conference on Computer Vision and Pattern Recognition, pp. 8697–8710 (2018)
44. Zugner, D., Akbarnejad, A., Gunnemann, S.: Adversarial attacks on neural networks for graph data. In: Proceedings of the 24th ACM SIGKDD International Conference on Knowledge Discovery and Data Mining, pp. 2847–2856 (2018)

SecretGen: Privacy Recovery on Pre-trained Models via Distribution Discrimination

Zhuowen Yuan[1]([⊠]), Fan Wu[1], Yunhui Long[1], Chaowei Xiao[2], and Bo Li[1]

[1] University of Illinois Urbana-Champaign, Champaign, USA
zhuowen3@illinois.edu
[2] Arizona State University, Tempe, USA

Abstract. Transfer learning through the use of pre-trained models has become a growing trend for the machine learning community. Consequently, numerous pre-trained models are released online to facilitate further research. However, it raises extensive concerns on whether these pre-trained models would leak privacy-sensitive information of their training data. Thus, in this work, we aim to answer the following questions: "Can we effectively recover private information from these pre-trained models? What are the sufficient conditions to retrieve such sensitive information?" We first explore different statistical information which can discriminate the private training distribution from other distributions. Based on our observations, we propose a novel private data reconstruction framework, SecretGen, to effectively recover private information. Compared with previous methods which can recover private data with the ground truth label of the targeted recovery instance, SecretGen does not require such prior knowledge, making it more practical. We conduct extensive experiments on different datasets under diverse scenarios to compare Secret-Gen with other baselines and provide a systematic benchmark to better understand the impact of different auxiliary information and optimization operations. We show that without prior knowledge about true class prediction, SecretGen is able to recover private data with similar performance compared with the ones that leverage such prior knowledge. If the prior knowledge is given, SecretGen will significantly outperform baseline methods. We also propose several quantitative metrics to further quantify the privacy vulnerability of pre-trained models, which will help the model selection for privacy-sensitive applications. Our code is available at: https://github.com/AI-secure/SecretGen.

Keywords: Privacy · Pre-trained models · Transfer learning

1 Introduction

As machine learning has achieved great successes in different domains, such as robotics [23], audio recognition [7], and face recognition [15], how to train the learning models efficiently given the available large-scale dataset becomes

S. Avidan et al. (Eds.): ECCV 2022, LNCS 13665, pp. 139–155, 2022.
https://doi.org/10.1007/978-3-031-20065-6_9

a timely problem. Transfer learning, which focuses on transferring knowledge across domains, is a promising learning paradigm [2]. In particular, many pre-trained models are available currently, such as TensorFlow Hubs [1] and PyTorch Hubs [21], which can be flexibly used for fine-tuning later for different downstream tasks. As a result, the training paradigm with transfer learning has enabled efficient usage of the large-scale dataset without requiring training every model from scratch.

However, such an efficient transfer learning paradigm also leads to additional *privacy concerns*. For instance, if the training data of the pre-trained models contain privacy-sensitive information, an adversary who downloads the pre-trained models could potentially perform different privacy attacks to infer the private information. In particular, membership inference attacks [17,18] have been studied to infer whether a private instance is in the training set, and model inversion attacks have been studied to reconstruct the private training instances under certain assumptions [10,11,25,27], which raises more privacy and safety concerns.

To better understand the privacy vulnerabilities of such pre-trained models, a comprehensive analysis of different types of privacy attacks, especially the severe model inversion attacks, is required. Currently, there are several limitations of existing privacy model inversion attacks. First, the current *state-of-the-art* model inversion attack (i.e., GMI) [27] requires the ground truth label of the reconstructed instances, which is less practical. Furthermore, it is a known challenging problem to label the generated instances based on GANs [12]. Second, many existing model inversion attacks require whitebox access to the target pre-trained model, making it less practical in real-world applications. Thus, in this paper, we mainly aim to ask: *Can we reconstruct private sensitive training instances without requiring such information?*

To answer it, we propose a general private data recovery framework Secret-Gen, which consists of a generation backbone, a pseudo label predictor, and a latent vector selector. We first use a pseudo label predictor to generate a pseudo label for each private instance. Specifically, we randomly sample latent vectors and feed them into the generation backbone to get recovered instances. To stabilize prediction quality, we apply different transformations (*e.g.* cutouts) to such instances before feeding them into the targeted model to get the final predicted pseudo labels. We then propose a latent vector selector via a proposed selection algorithm to further optimize and constrain the recovery space. Finally, we perform joint optimization to train the end-to-end framework as shown in Fig. 1.

We conduct comprehensive experiments to evaluate the proposed SecretGen compared with multiple baselines. We show that SecretGen significantly outperforms baselines given the same ground truth label. Even without such information, SecretGen still achieves comparable performance compared to baselines which leverage the ground truth label information. In addition, to evaluate the performance of recovered data on downstream tasks, we propose different evaluation protocols considering different usage of the recovered private data, and we show that our observations are consistent for different protocols. We also evaluate the robustness of SecretGen against the purification defense [26]. Finally, we perform different ablation studies to show the effectiveness of our design choices. We make the following **contributions**:

- We propose a general private data recovery attack (i.e., model inversion) given a pre-trained model, SecretGen, without requiring the ground truth label as prior knowledge under both whitebox and blackbox settings.
- We propose a novel label predictor for the reconstructed instances considering different data transformations and latent vector selection, which can be flexibly used in other frameworks.
- We propose different evaluation protocols and metrics for evaluating the pre-trained models against general model inversion attacks.
- We conduct extensive experiments on different models, including the vision transformer and multiple datasets, to provide a benchmark on model inversion attacks. We show that SecretGen significantly outperforms baselines under different settings.

2   Related Work

Revealing privacy-sensitive information from a trained model has aroused extensive research interest. *Membership inference attacks* and *model inversion attacks* are two major categories of such attacks. In *membership inference attacks* [17,18], the adversary aims to decide whether a sample is a member of the training set, while in *model inversion attacks* [10,11,25,27], the adversary attempts to reconstruct the training set under certain assumptions.

[11] was the first to propose model inversion attacks aiming at recovering private training data. The authors demonstrated that personal genetic markers could be effectively recovered given the output of the model and auxiliary knowledge. [10] extended model inversion to more complex models, including shallow neural networks for face recognition. The recovered data with their proposed method are identified as the original person at a much higher rate than random guessing. However, the reconstructed images are blurry and not visually recognizable to humans. [25] proposed a training-based attack by training an auto-encoder on public data. The attack can be performed with *blackbox* accesses to the target model and partial (truncated) model predictions.

More recently, [27] proposed generative model inversion attack (GMI). The authors distill public knowledge by training a conditional GAN on public data and then solve an optimization problem to maximize the probability of the recovered image for the ground truth class label. GMI significantly outperforms previous methods in re-identification rate of the recovered data, as well as guaranteeing the recovered data are visually plausible. However, they still require the ground truth label for the target image and *whitebox* access to the victim model, which is often not accessible to the adversary. Another recent work distributional model inversion attack (DMI) [3] recovers the private data distribution for each target class by constructing representative samples. However, DMI does not support recovering every private instance given its non-sensitive version (*i.e.* instance-level model inversion), which is the adversary's goal in our setting.

3   Methodology

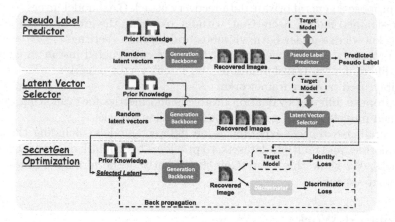

Fig. 1. Overview of the proposed SecretGen. The blue modules represent the proposed algorithms. The *Target Model* could allow either whitebox or blackbox access.

3.1   Problem Formulation

We focus on recovering the privacy-sensitive training data based on the trained classification models. Throughout the paper, we will refer to the model that is subjective to attacks as the *target model* F, which is trained on private training data $D_{\text{pri}}^{\text{train}}$, aiming to perform evaluation on private test data $D_{\text{pri}}^{\text{test}}$. The target model returns a prediction vector $F(x)$ given an input instance x. The prediction vector represents a probability distribution over C classes, where C denotes the number of classes of the whole private dataset $D_{\text{pri}} = D_{\text{pri}}^{\text{train}} \cup D_{\text{pri}}^{\text{test}}$.

The adversary's **goal** is to recover the private training data $D_{\text{pri}}^{\text{train}}$ given the trained target model F and certain prior information, *e.g.*, partially corrupted images from $D_{\text{pri}}^{\text{train}}$. In particular, such corrupted images only contain non-sensitive background information (pixels) x_{ns} with the sensitive region x_s cropped out. These corrupted images are usually easy to obtain, given that such corruption is often applied to protect the privacy of individuals in practice [27]. Specifically, in our evaluation, we consider cropping the whole face using two face datasets, leaving only the non-sensitive background regions (Sect. 4).

Regarding the adversary's **ability**, we consider (1) *whitebox* access to the target model, where all parameters and intermediate computations of the target model are visible to the adversary, and (2) *blackbox* access to the target model, where the adversary can only obtain the final prediction from the target model F. Additionally, we assume that the adversary also has access to some public data D_{pub} from the similar distribution for general training purpose.

3.2   Method Overview

An overview of SecretGen is illustrated in Fig. 1, where SecretGen takes non-sensitive information x_{ns} as input and returns the recovered images that contain privacy-sensitive training information (*e.g.*, human faces). SecretGen is composed of *three* components: *generation backbone, pseudo label predictor*, and *latent vector selector*, which are jointly optimized under a unified framework. The **generation backbone** leverages a conditional GAN trained on public data as a backbone to generate realistic images based on the prior information (*e.g.*, cropped images), and the generation process is controlled by the latent vector z sent to the GAN's generator G. The **pseudo label predictor** predicts the most possible pseudo label for each recovered private image based on the distributional statistics of recovered images. The **latent vector selector** selects the optimal latent vector $\hat{z}$ which is the most likely to contain privacy-sensitive information based on the proposed selection algorithm. Finally, we perform joint optimization on the selected $\hat{z}$, taking the pseudo label provided by the pseudo label predictor as the prediction target, to reconstruct image $G(\hat{z}^*, x_{ns})$. In the next following sections, we will describe each component in detail.

3.3   Generation Backbone of SecretGen

To recover the privacy-sensitive training data, we train a generation backbone for conditional image recovery on public data D_{pub}. In particular, we will start from certain prior knowledge, such as the corrupted private data containing only the nonsensitive information x_{ns}. We then perform the same corruption operation *corr* on D_{pub} to construct the training set for the generation backbone: $D_{\text{pub\_corr}} = \{corr(x)|x \in D_{\text{pub}}\}$.

Next, we train a conditional GAN which is composed of two networks: generator G and discriminator D. G is conditioned on $x_{ns} \in D_{\text{pub\_corr}}$ and z is the latent vector which is sampled from a prior distribution during training. Throughout the paper, we use the prior distribution as standard Gaussian distribution. We leverage the Wasserstein-GAN loss [13] for GAN training:

$$\min_G \max_D \mathcal{L}_{\text{wgan}} = \mathbb{E}_x[D(x)] - \mathbb{E}_z[D(G(z, x_{ns}))] \tag{1}$$

We also incorporate a diversity loss term $\mathcal{L}_{\text{div}}$ [24] for training the generator to prevent mode collapsing by sampling different latent vectors, say, z_1 and z_2:

$$\mathcal{L}_{\text{div}} = -\mathbb{E}_{z_1, z_2}\left[\frac{\|f(G(z_1, x_{ns})) - f(G(z_2, x_{ns}))\|}{\|z_1 - z_2\|}\right] \tag{2}$$

where f is the feature extractor of the target model, which returns the feature embeddings of the input images in the *whitebox* setting. In the *blackbox* setting, we use a feature extractor trained on public data f_{pub} for this process. The overall loss term for the generator is as following:

$$\mathcal{L}_G = \mathcal{L}_{\text{wgan}} + \lambda_{\text{div}}\mathcal{L}_{\text{div}} \tag{3}$$

After the generation backbone is trained, we freeze the parameters for both G and D before we enter the next stage. We denote $\hat{x}$ as the recovered image, i.e., $\hat{x} = G(z, x_{ns})$.

3.4   Pseudo Label Predictor

The main challenge in this data reconstruction process is that we have no knowledge about the ground truth label of the private images (related work assumes that they have access to the ground truth label [10,11,25,27], while we do not). To tackle this problem, we propose a *pseudo label predictor* which infers the label prediction with proposed discrimination metrics. We will first introduce the design of our discrimination metric, and then we elaborate on how the pseudo label predictor is optimized.

Discrimination Metric. Given the certain prior knowledge x_{ns}, we randomly sample n latent vectors $\{z_i\}_{i=1}^{n}$ from the prior distribution. We generate n recovered images using our generation backbone: $\{\hat{x}_i\}_{i=1}^{n}$, where $\hat{x}_i = G(z_i, x_{ns})$. In order to improve the prediction stability, we consider prediction under different transformations. Concretely, let the list of considered transformation functions be $\mathcal{T} = \{t_i\}_{i=1}^{m}$. On each recovered image $\hat{x}_i$, we perform m transformations independently to obtain m transformed images $\{\tilde{x}_i^j\}_{j=1}^{m}$, where $\tilde{x}_i^j = t_j(\hat{x}_i)$. We additionally define $\tilde{x}_i^0 = \hat{x}_i$. Let $F_c(\cdot)$ denote the model's prediction confidence for class label c based on target model F. We define the discrimination metric $\mathcal{M}$ on label c as follows:

$$\mathcal{M}(c; n, m) \triangleq \frac{1}{n(m+1)} \sum_{i=1}^{n} \sum_{j=0}^{m} F_c(\tilde{x}_i^j), \quad \forall c \in [1, C]. \tag{4}$$

The discrimination metric returns a score indicating how likely it is for a label c to be the consistent prediction across different transformations. Based on existing studies of contrastive learning [4], we will select the class c with the highest discrimination metric score as the final label prediction.

In particular, we define the list of transformations as a sequence of fix-sized cutouts. We split an image into fix-sized patches and define t_j as the transformation that cuts out the j-th patch of the given image, as illustrated in Fig. 2.

Intuitively, the discrimination metric $\mathcal{M}(c; n, m)$ should preserve the following properties. First, $\mathcal{M}(c; n, m)$ is likely to have a higher score when c equals the label associated with the corrupted image x_{ns} since the model has learned some correlation between the non-sensitive background information in x_{ns} and the label of the original image. Such correlation should be stronger if the target model is more overfitted to private training data. Second, when the recovered image $\tilde{x}_i^j$ is close to the training data, $F_c(\tilde{x}_i^j)$ should be *consistently* higher on the correct label because training data are often more resistant to transformations than non-training data [6]. Based on these intuitions, we use the discrimination metric as the foundation of the pseudo label predictor in SecretGen.

Pseudo Label Predictor. Given the discrimination metric $\mathcal{M}$, we next describe in detail how we leverage $\mathcal{M}$ to infer the pseudo prediction label considering different sampled latent vectors, which aims to approximate the ground truth. We first sample a set of n latent vectors randomly and compute $\mathcal{M}$ for all class labels. The pseudo label predictor chooses the label with the maximum discrimination metric score as the predicted label $\hat{c}$:

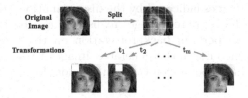

Fig. 2. Sequential cutout for the recovered image as transformations. The image is first split into m fix-sized patches. Operations of cutting out each patch are viewed as transformations respectively.

$$\hat{c} = \arg\max_{c \in [1, C]} \mathcal{M}(c) \qquad (5)$$

We defer the detailed algorithm for label prediction with $\mathcal{M}$ to the appendix. Note that there are various design choices for the discrimination metric $\mathcal{M}$, *e.g.*, the average confidence on only the recovered images without including their transformed versions. It is clear that more advanced $\mathcal{M}$ will provide more accurate pseudo label predictors. We will analyze the performance of the pseudo label predictor given different designs of $\mathcal{M}$ in Sect. 4.5.

3.5 Latent Vector Selector

In addition to the availability of ground truth labels, another challenge during private data recovery is that we may not have *whitebox* access to the target model. In systems where machine learning is used as a service (MLaaS), the adversary can only query the model and the prediction vector is returned from the service provider. All internal computations and model parameters are unknown to the adversary. In previous work [27], the adversary can directly optimize the latent vector z to maximize the target model's confidence given a known ground truth label, which is less practical. Without the whitebox access, performing back-propagation with the target model is infeasible in our practical case.

To tackle this problem, we design a *latent vector selector* to first randomly sample n random latent vectors, and then select the ones which lead to their recovered data classified as the predicted label from the pseudo label predictor. If there is no latent vector that leads to the recovered images which can be classified as the predicted label consistently, the selector returns a randomly sampled latent vector from the prior distribution. Otherwise, it returns the latent vector which has the highest confidence of the predicted label. We omit the detailed algorithm to the appendix.

3.6 SecretGen Optimization

To put every proposed component within SecretGen together, we perform joint optimization to maximize the consistent label prediction likelihood of recovered images indicated by the discrimination metric (*i.e.*, identity loss), while keeping the recovered images realistic (*i.e.*, discriminator loss). In the *whitebox* setting, we perform backpropagation on the target model with identity loss $\mathcal{L}_{id}$. $\mathcal{L}_{id}$ encourages the generated images to achieve consistently high label prediction likelihood given the target model for class label c.

$$\mathcal{L}_{id} = -\log[F_c(G(z, x_{ns}))] \tag{6}$$

We utilize discriminator loss as regularization to penalize unrealistic images.

$$\mathcal{L}_{disc} = -D(G(z, x_{ns})) \tag{7}$$

Then we initialize z with $\hat{z}$ returned by our latent vector selector and optimize z with the following objective function:

$$\hat{z}^*_{whitebox} = \arg\min_z \mathcal{L}_{disc} + \lambda_{id}\mathcal{L}_{id} \tag{8}$$

In the *blackbox* setting, we perform the latent vector selection optimization only with the discriminator loss since the target model is not locally accessible:

$$\hat{z}^*_{blackbox} = \arg\min_z \mathcal{L}_{disc} \tag{9}$$

Note that in the blackbox setting where we have the ground truth labels, the identity loss is still minimized by the latent vector selector through random sampling based on the prediction vector of the target model, guaranteeing that the recovered image is close to the density region of the ground truth identity.

3.7   Discussion

Our proposed SecretGen works under a wide range of scenarios regarding different types of prior knowledge. See Table 1 for the scenarios under which Secret-Gen and existing methods can be applied. Although EMI theoretically works in *blackbox* cases with ground truth labels, its performance and efficiency dramatically suffer against deep models. Although SecretGen still requires non-sensitive private data as prior knowledge, such assumption is realistic as image corruption is often leveraged for privacy protection by individuals [27]. Furthermore,

Table 1. Comparison with existing methods on the information required by the adversary to recover private training data. The symbol ✗ means that in theory, the method can work without the information, but the actual performance on deep models is bad.

Methods	Non-sensitive data?	Whitebox access?	Ground truth label?
PII [24]	✓	✗	✗
EMI [10]	✗	✗	✓
GMI [27]	✗	✓	✓
SecretGen	✓	✗	✗

if the knowledge of ground truth labels is available, it can be incorporated into SecretGen conveniently. More details are deferred to the appendix.

In conclusion, SecretGen is more practical without requiring whitebox access to the target model or the ground truth label. In addition, SecretGen is very efficient and applicable to high-dimensional image data considering deep models as the target model as shown in our evaluation (Sect. 4).

4   Experiments

In this section, we first present the experimental setup. Then, we introduce the evaluation protocols and report the attack performance respectively. We also evaluate the robustness of SecretGen against the purification defense [26]. In the end, we describe some ablation studies to better understand our method.

4.1   Experimental Setup

Datasets. We evaluate SecretGen on two face datasets: (1) CelebA [19] which contains 202,599 face images of 10,177 identities. We filter out those identities with 25 or fewer images and randomly select 25,000 images of 1,000 identities as private data D_{pri}. We also randomly select 50,000 images of 2,000 identities from the rest as adversary's public data D_{pub}. There exist no overlapped identities between D_{pub} and D_{pri}. (2) FaceScrub [20] which consists of 106,863 face images of 530 identities. We use the images of 250 identities as D_{pri} and images of another 250 identities as D_{pub}. We further split D_{pri} into D_{pri}^{train} and D_{pri}^{test} for training and testing. All the images are cropped and resized to 64 × 64.

Prior Information. We consider two types of prior information that the adversary has access to: corrupted images by center mask and face T mask following the standard setting in [27]. Center mask blocks the center part of the private image, but the mouth information may still be exposed. Face T mask completely hides the identity revealing features of the face image.

Model Architectures. We perform evaluation on *target models* with various architectures: (1) VGG16 [22]; (2) ResNet152 [15]; (3) face.evoLVe [5] with an IR50 backbone; (4) ViT-B_16 [9] We utilize IR152 [5] as the *evaluation model* to predict the identity of input images. Both VGG16 and ResNet152 are pre-trained on ImageNet [8]. face.evoLVe and the evaluation model are pre-trained on MS-Celeb-1M [14]. ViT-B_16 is pre-trained on ImageNet21k [8]. The architecture of SecretGen generation backbone is adopted from [27].

Baselines. We compare SecretGen with the *state-of-the-art* model inversion attack GMI [27]. GMI assumes the adversary has access to the ground truth labels and performs optimization with identity loss and discriminator loss. We also compare our results with pure image inpainting (PII) [24], which only optimizes the discriminator loss for generating realistic images. Latent vectors of both GMI and PII are sampled randomly from Gaussian distribution. We do not compare with EMI [10], since it has been demonstrated in [27] that the effectiveness of EMI is quite limited against deep models. We defer additional details regarding model training and attack to the appendix.

4.2   Evaluation Protocols

We consider two principles for evaluating the privacy attack performance: "how much privacy sensitive identity information can be recovered" and "how well the recovered data can perform in downstream tasks".

Corresponding to the two principles, we evaluate the privacy attack performance by *attack accuracy* under the following two protocols:

- Protocol 1: Train the evaluation model on the private data, and evaluate on the recovered data.
- Protocol 2: Train the evaluation model on the recovered data, and evaluate on the private data.

Protocol 1 was introduced in [27], which evaluates *instance-level* privacy recovery. However, we demonstrate that even if some instances are not recovered correctly, the recovered data can be used for downstream tasks, *e.g.*, training another classification model. The adversary can potentially use the trained evaluation model for malicious purposes, *e.g.*, performing unauthorized face recognition on private identities with significantly higher accuracy than the target model itself. Thus, we propose Protocol 2, which aims to evaluate *distribution-level* privacy recovery. In addition, a common goal of the adversary to reconstruct the private data is to leverage such data for other downstream tasks, and therefore Protocol 2 explicitly reflects the utility of the recovered data.

For Protocol 1, we train the evaluation model on $D_{\text{pri}}^{\text{train}}$ and the resulting evaluation model achieves 98.0% classification accuracy over the private identities on $D_{\text{pri}}^{\text{test}}$. For Protocol 2, we first perform the attack on all corrupted private images D_{pri}—for each corrupted image $x_{ns} \in D_{\text{pri}}$, we recover an image $\hat{x} = G(\hat{z}^*, x_{ns})$ via SecretGen, with label $\hat{c} = \arg\max_{c \in [1, C]} F_c(\hat{x})$. We then compose the recovered images into a recovered private set D_{rec}, which is separated into $D_{\text{rec}}^{\text{train}}$ and $D_{\text{rec}}^{\text{valid}}$ by 4:1. We train the evaluation model on $D_{\text{rec}}^{\text{train}}$ with $D_{\text{rec}}^{\text{valid}}$ as the validation set. We then evaluate the model performance on $D_{\text{pri}}^{\text{test}}$.

We also report Peak Signal-to-Noise Ratio (PSNR) [16] between original and recovered private data, which reflects the *pixel-level* reconstruction quality of our attack. Note that the recovered data can still reveal identity information even if the generated image is not close to the ground truth image pixel-wise. For example, the recovered images can exhibit variations in pose and light condition while keeping the identity.

4.3   Attack Performance

Whitebox Attacks. Table 2 compares the performance of SecretGen with baseline methods on CelebA. See the appendix for results on FaceScrub.

We can see that SecretGen significantly outperforms GMI under both Protocol 1 and Protocol 2 if the ground truth label is given. Without such information,

Table 2. *Whitebox* attack performance on CelebA. See the Ground Truth Label column for whether ground truth label is provided for each attack method.

Target model	Methods	Ground truth label	Center mask			Face T mask		
			Protocol 1	Protocol 2	PSNR	Protocol 1	Protocol 2	PSNR
VGG16	PII	✗	0.423	0.561	27.583	0.166	0.363	26.276
	GMI	✓	0.569	0.955	27.587	0.305	0.928	26.240
	SecretGen	✗	0.584	0.928	27.955	0.312	0.793	26.632
	SecretGen	✓	**0.639**	**0.965**	**28.071**	**0.377**	**0.931**	**26.821**
ResNet152	PII	✗	0.403	0.719	26.892	0.170	0.555	26.117
	GMI	✓	0.556	0.965	27.177	0.295	**0.946**	26.482
	SecretGen	✗	0.595	0.948	27.506	0.324	0.884	26.821
	SecretGen	✓	**0.618**	**0.971**	**27.587**	**0.349**	0.945	**26.967**
face.evoLVe	PII	✗	0.267	0.455	27.317	0.122	0.343	26.356
	GMI	✓	0.595	0.946	27.444	0.467	0.935	26.563
	SecretGen	✗	0.551	0.841	27.613	0.274	0.630	26.562
	SecretGen	✓	**0.788**	**0.963**	**27.781**	**0.695**	**0.954**	**26.827**
ViT	PII	✗	0.380	0.389	26.698	0.173	0.306	26.377
	GMI	✓	0.482	0.893	24.907	0.214	0.715	24.624
	SecretGen	✗	0.451	0.634	**26.811**	0.246	0.528	26.471
	SecretGen	✓	**0.551**	**0.950**	26.607	**0.326**	**0.913**	**26.609**

with the proposed pipeline especially the pseudo label predictor, SecretGen still achieves comparable performance with GMI under Protocol 1. Under Protocol 2, GMI with ground truth label performs better than SecretGen without ground truth label. The reason is that if the predicted pseudo label is incorrect, our pseudo label predictor and optimization push the recovery to be closer to the wrong identity. However, we still outperform PII by a large margin.

We also observe that attack accuracy under Protocol 2 is much higher than that under Protocol 1. The reason is that Protocol 1 and 2 work at different levels: Protocol 1 evaluates how much "detailed" information the recovered images contain, while Protocol 2 evaluates how much distributional information we can recover by training another model based on the reconstructed data. Clearly, Protocol 2 is relatively easier by recovering distributional level information and thus achieves higher scores. We believe such observations will inspire interesting future work and narrow down such a gap.

Blackbox Attacks. In the *blackbox* setting, the adversary is not capable of performing backpropagation with the target model. We make the following changes to our attack pipeline: (1) In Sect. 3.3, when training the generation backbone, we use a public feature extractor from [5] pre-trained on MS-Celeb-1M to substitute the target model for extracting the feature embeddings in computing the diversity loss ($\mathcal{L}_{\text{div}}$, Eq. (2)); (2) In Sect. 3.6, when performing SecretGen optimization, we remove the identity loss $\mathcal{L}_{\text{id}}$ and optimize the selected latent vector only with discriminator loss $\mathcal{L}_{\text{disc}}$.

Table 3 compares our results with PII under the *blackbox* setting on CelebA. The only difference for PII under *blackbox* and *whitebox* scenarios is whether the target model is accessed when training the generation backbone. We can see that with the ground truth labels, SecretGen significantly outperforms PII.

Table 3. *Blackbox* attack performance on CelebA. We report results for both cases where the adversary has or does not have ground truth labels. (Note: GMI does not support blackbox attack, and PII in the blackbox setting does not use the target model.)

Methods	Target model	Ground truth label	Center mask			Face T mask		
			Protocol 1	Protocol 2	PSNR	Protocol 1	Protocol 2	PSNR
PII	Any	✗	0.216	0.759	27.319	0.081	0.484	25.705
SecretGen	VGG16	✗	0.351	0.915	27.638	0.164	0.837	26.045
		✓	**0.380**	**0.955**	**27.737**	**0.377**	**0.927**	**26.821**
	ResNet152	✗	0.334	0.933	27.737	0.152	0.765	26.144
		✓	**0.347**	**0.959**	**27.840**	**0.172**	**0.886**	**26.284**
	face.evoLVe	✗	0.447	0.711	27.568	0.156	0.353	25.787
		✓	**0.603**	**0.894**	**27.694**	**0.305**	**0.586**	**26.002**
	ViT	✗	0.285	0.709	27.480	0.119	0.685	25.828
		✓	**0.335**	**0.924**	**27.665**	**0.160**	**0.902**	**26.123**

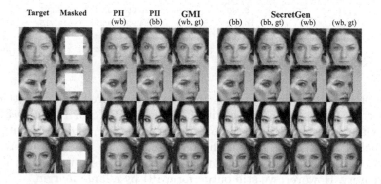

Fig. 3. Qualitative results of SecretGen on CelebA. "bb"/"wb" indicates the method requires *blackbox/whitebox* access to the model. "gt" indicates the method requires ground truth labels.

Without ground truth labels, which is the most general case, we still outperform PII by a large margin. As far as we are concerned, we are the first to propose an effective model inversion attack against deep classification models under the *blackbox* case without ground truth label.

We note that GMI (with ground truth label) performs better on `face.evoLVe` than SecretGen (without ground truth label), as shown in Table 2 and Table 3. Under this setting, attack performance is largely dependent on the pseudo label predictor. We demonstrate that the label prediction accuracy of `face.evoLVe` is significantly lower than that of `VGG16` and `ResNet152` in the appendix. We believe the reason is that `face.evoLVe` is less overfitted due to the difference in pre-training datasets. (`face.evoLVe` is pre-trained on `MS-Celeb-1M` while others are on `ImageNet`).

Qualitative Results. In Fig. 3 we exhibit the images recovered with SecretGen on CelebA to demonstrate that our recovered images are both identity-revealing and visually plausible. We also show qualitative results of PII and GMI for com-

Table 4. Robustness evaluation for SecretGen against prediction purification on CelebA. Target model: `VGG16`. Blackbox setting.

Methods	Center mask			Face T mask		
	Protocol 1	Protocol 2	PSNR	Protocol 1	Protocol 2	PSNR
PII	0.216	0.759	27.319	0.081	0.484	25.705
SecretGen	0.351	0.915	27.638	0.164	0.837	26.045
SecretGen (purified)	0.328	0.913	27.590	0.151	0.747	26.007

parison. From the figure, we see that although all of the three methods generate realistic images, PII cannot effectively recover the original identity of private data, while SecretGen is more effective in identity revealing. More examples are shown in the appendix.

4.4   Robustness Evaluation

We evaluate the robustness of our proposed method against purification defense [26], which has been shown to effectively defend against model inversion attacks while inducing negligible utility loss. We use Purifier I in [26] which is specialized for model inversion attacks. We follow the default architectures and settings for training the purifier. See Table 4 for quantitative results on CelebA against VGG16 under the blackbox setting. We also assume the ground truth label is not provided. We do not evaluate the whitebox setting because the adversary can simply remove the purifier and directly attack the original private model. It can be seen that attack accuracy slightly decreases after the defense, but still outperforms the baseline by a large margin. Therefore, our method is robust against [26].

4.5   Ablation Studies

Discrimination Metrics. As discussed in Sect. 3.4, there may exist various choices for the discrimination metric. One intuitive choice may be derived by removing the transformations from our current discrimination metric $\mathcal{M}$ (Eq. (4)), and the simplified discrimination metric is defined as follows:

$$\mathcal{M}'(c; n) \triangleq \frac{1}{n} \sum_{i=1}^{n} F_c(\hat{x}_i), \quad \forall c \in [1, C]. \tag{10}$$

We perform an *end-to-end* ablation study on `face.evoLVe` and CelebA. We remove the transformations in our pseudo label predictor and substitute $\mathcal{M}$ with $\mathcal{M}'$. Quantitative results on `face.evoLVe` are shown in Table 5. See the appendix for results regarding other model architectures. We conclude that incorporating transformations improves the performance of our framework for most model architectures that we used for evaluation.

Table 5. Attack accuracy of SecretGen with and without transformations on CelebA. Evaluated on 3,200 private instances under Protocol 1. Target model: `face.evoLVe`.

Metric	Center mask		Face T mask	
	Attack acc	PSNR	Attack acc	PSNR
w/o transformation	0.528	27.505	0.256	26.527
w/ transformation	**0.550**	**27.522**	**0.273**	26.527

To further understand why and how transformations help, we compare the performance of pseudo label predictor equipped with $\mathcal{M}$ and $\mathcal{M}'$. We evaluate the performance of pseudo label predictor using *label prediction accuracy*, which measures the percentage of the predicted labels matching the ground truth labels. We plot out the label prediction accuracy with $\mathcal{M}$ and $\mathcal{M}'$ on 3,200 recovered images for `face.evoLVe` with varying n in Fig. 4. We observe that our pseudo label predictor can predict the pseudo labels more accurately if transformations are incorporated. See the appendix for results of other model architectures.

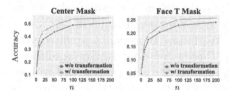

Fig. 4. Label prediction accuracy with and without transformations on CelebA. We plot the label prediction accuracy w.r.t. the number of random latent vectors n. Target model: `face.evoLVe`.

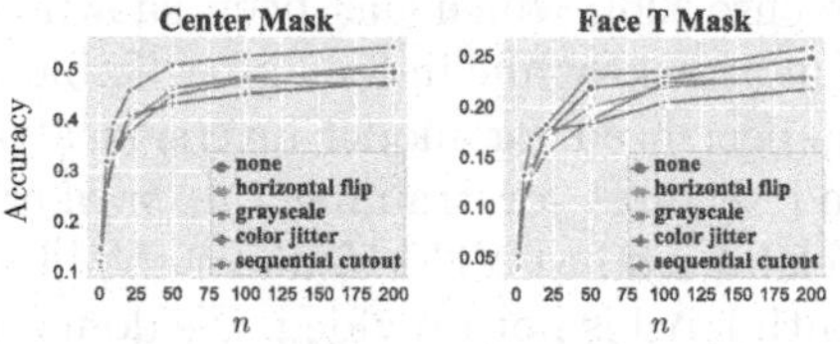

Fig. 5. Label prediction accuracy with different transformations on CelebA. We plot the label prediction accuracy w.r.t. the number of randomly sampled latent vectors n. Target model: `face.evoLVe`.

Data Transformations. Next, we discuss the performance of various data transformations on CelebA. We plot out label prediction accuracy w.r.t. n for various transformations including the proposed sequential cutout, horizontal flipping, gray-scale, and color jittering in Fig. 5. We also plot the results without transformations. We can see that sequential cutout performs better than other transformations in terms of label prediction accuracy. Although it is also possible to adopt other transformations within our pipeline, it is non-trivial to select the best hyper-parameters for other transformations (*e.g.*, cropping and color jittering). We leave the analysis of how different transformations impact attack performance as future work.

Overfitting Levels. We also evaluate the impact of *higher overfitting levels* of the target model on the performance of SecretGen, since the overfitting phenomenon is key to model inversion attacks. Note that results reported in Table 2 and Table 3 are based on standard well-trained models. We demonstrate that highly overfitted models are more vulnerable to our proposed attack. We describe the relevant experiment setup and quantitative results in the appendix.

5   Conclusion

In this paper, we propose an effective private data recovery framework Secret-Gen, which can effectively recover private information under a wide range of scenarios. To our full knowledge, we are the first to propose an effective model inversion attack without prior knowledge of ground truth labels, which can achieve comparable results with previous methods that require ground truth labels. If we are given such prior knowledge, we significantly outperform previous methods. Our attack can also be applied under the *blackbox* setting where the target model is provided as a service and not locally available. We perform a comprehensive analysis of the performance of SecretGen and our design choices. We also demonstrate that our attack is robust against the purification defense. We hope to raise people's concerns about possible negative effects of releasing pre-trained models online. For future work, we are interested in whether we can perform privacy recovery simply with the target model and develop defenses against our attack.

Acknowledgements. This work is partially supported by NSF grant No.1910100, NSF CNS No. 2046726, C3 AI, and the Alfred P. Sloan Foundation.

References

1. Abadi, M., et al.: TensorFlow: a system for large-scale machine learning. In: 12th USENIX Symposium on Operating Systems Design and Implementation (OSDI 2016), pp. 265–283 (2016)
2. Bengio, Y.: Deep learning of representations for unsupervised and transfer learning. In: Proceedings of ICML Workshop on Unsupervised and Transfer Learning, pp. 17–36. JMLR Workshop and Conference Proceedings (2012)
3. Chen, S., Kahla, M., Jia, R., Qi, G.J.: Knowledge-enriched distributional model inversion attacks. In: Proceedings of the IEEE/CVF International Conference on Computer Vision, pp. 16178–16187 (2021)
4. Chen, T., Kornblith, S., Norouzi, M., Hinton, G.: A simple framework for contrastive learning of visual representations. In: International Conference on Machine Learning, pp. 1597–1607. PMLR (2020)
5. Cheng, Y., et al.: Know you at one glance: a compact vector representation for low-shot learning. In: ICCVW, pp. 1924–1932 (2017)
6. Choquette-Choo, C.A., Tramer, F., Carlini, N., Papernot, N.: Label-only membership inference attacks. In: International Conference on Machine Learning, pp. 1964–1974. PMLR (2021)

7. Conneau, A., Baevski, A., Collobert, R., Mohamed, A., Auli, M.: Unsupervised cross-lingual representation learning for speech recognition. arXiv preprint arXiv:2006.13979 (2020)
8. Deng, J., Dong, W., Socher, R., Li, L.J., Li, K., Fei-Fei, L.: ImageNet: a large-scale hierarchical image database. In: 2009 IEEE Conference on Computer Vision and Pattern Recognition, pp. 248–255. IEEE (2009)
9. Dosovitskiy, A., et al.: An image is worth 16×16 words: transformers for image recognition at scale. arXiv preprint arXiv:2010.11929 (2020)
10. Fredrikson, M., Jha, S., Ristenpart, T.: Model inversion attacks that exploit confidence information and basic countermeasures. In: Proceedings of the 22nd ACM SIGSAC Conference on Computer and Communications Security, pp. 1322–1333 (2015)
11. Fredrikson, M., Lantz, E., Jha, S., Lin, S., Page, D., Ristenpart, T.: Privacy in pharmacogenetics: an end-to-end case study of personalized warfarin dosing. In: 23rd USENIX Security Symposium (USENIX Security 2014), pp. 17–32 (2014)
12. Goodfellow, I., et al.: Generative adversarial networks. Commun. ACM **63**(11), 139–144 (2020)
13. Gulrajani, I., Ahmed, F., Arjovsky, M., Dumoulin, V., Courville, A.: Improved training of Wasserstein GANs. arXiv preprint arXiv:1704.00028 (2017)
14. Guo, Y., Zhang, L., Hu, Y., He, X., Gao, J.: MS-Celeb-1M: a dataset and benchmark for large-scale face recognition. In: Leibe, B., Matas, J., Sebe, N., Welling, M. (eds.) ECCV 2016. LNCS, vol. 9907, pp. 87–102. Springer, Cham (2016). https://doi.org/10.1007/978-3-319-46487-9_6
15. He, K., Zhang, X., Ren, S., Sun, J.: Deep residual learning for image recognition. In: Proceedings of the IEEE Conference on Computer Vision and Pattern Recognition, pp. 770–778 (2016)
16. Hore, A., Ziou, D.: Image quality metrics: PSNR vs. SSIM. In: 2010 20th International Conference on Pattern Recognition, pp. 2366–2369. IEEE (2010)
17. Leino, K., Fredrikson, M.: Stolen memories: leveraging model memorization for calibrated white-box membership inference. In: 29th USENIX Security Symposium (USENIX Security 2020), pp. 1605–1622 (2020)
18. Liu, H., Jia, J., Qu, W., Gong, N.Z.: EncoderMI: membership inference against pretrained encoders in contrastive learning. arXiv preprint arXiv:2108.11023 (2021)
19. Liu, Z., Luo, P., Wang, X., Tang, X.: Deep learning face attributes in the wild. In: Proceedings of International Conference on Computer Vision (ICCV) (2015)
20. Ng, H.W., Winkler, S.: A data-driven approach to cleaning large face datasets. In: 2014 IEEE International Conference on Image Processing (ICIP), pp. 343–347. IEEE (2014)
21. Paszke, A., et al.: Automatic differentiation in Pytorch. In: NIPS-W (2017)
22. Simonyan, K., Zisserman, A.: Very deep convolutional networks for large-scale image recognition. arXiv preprint arXiv:1409.1556 (2014)
23. Wang, X., Xiong, W., Wang, H., Wang, W.Y.: Look before you leap: bridging model-free and model-based reinforcement learning for planned-ahead vision-and-language navigation. In: Proceedings of the European Conference on Computer Vision (ECCV), pp. 37–53 (2018)
24. Yang, D., Hong, S., Jang, Y., Zhao, T., Lee, H.: Diversity-sensitive conditional generative adversarial networks. arXiv preprint arXiv:1901.09024 (2019)
25. Yang, Z., Chang, E.C., Liang, Z.: Adversarial neural network inversion via auxiliary knowledge alignment. arXiv preprint arXiv:1902.08552 (2019)

26. Yang, Z., Shao, B., Xuan, B., Chang, E.C., Zhang, F.: Defending model inversion and membership inference attacks via prediction purification. arXiv preprint arXiv:2005.03915 (2020)
27. Zhang, Y., Jia, R., Pei, H., Wang, W., Li, B., Song, D.: The secret revealer: generative model-inversion attacks against deep neural networks. In: Proceedings of the IEEE/CVF Conference on Computer Vision and Pattern Recognition, pp. 253–261 (2020)

Triangle Attack: A Query-Efficient Decision-Based Adversarial Attack

Xiaosen Wang[1,2], Zeliang Zhang[1], Kangheng Tong[1], Dihong Gong[2],
Kun He[1(✉)], Zhifeng Li[2(✉)], and Wei Liu[2(✉)]

[1] School of Computer Science, Huazhong University of Science and Technology,
Wuhan, China
brooklet60@hust.edu.cn
[2] Data Platform, Tencent, Shenzhen, China
michaelzfli@tencent.com, wl2223@columbia.edu

Abstract. Decision-based attack poses a severe threat to real-world applications since it regards the target model as a black box and only accesses the hard prediction label. Great efforts have been made recently to decrease the number of queries; however, existing decision-based attacks still require thousands of queries in order to generate good quality adversarial examples. In this work, we find that a benign sample, the current and the next adversarial examples can naturally construct a triangle in a subspace for any iterative attacks. Based on the law of sines, we propose a novel Triangle Attack (TA) to optimize the perturbation by utilizing the geometric information that the longer side is always opposite the larger angle in any triangle. However, directly applying such information on the input image is ineffective because it cannot thoroughly explore the neighborhood of the input sample in the high dimensional space. To address this issue, TA optimizes the perturbation in the low frequency space for effective dimensionality reduction owing to the generality of such geometric property. Extensive evaluations on ImageNet dataset show that TA achieves a much higher attack success rate within 1,000 queries and needs a much less number of queries to achieve the same attack success rate under various perturbation budgets than existing decision-based attacks. With such high efficiency, we further validate the applicability of TA on real-world API, *i.e.*, Tencent Cloud API.

1 Introduction

Despite the unprecedented progress of Deep Neural Networks (DNNs) [24, 25, 27], the vulnerability to adversarial examples [46] poses serious threats to security-sensitive applications, *e.g.*, face recognition [15, 20, 30, 37, 42, 47, 49, 55, 62], autonomous driving [4, 7, 19, 40, 61], *etc.* To securely deploy DNNs in various real-world applications, it is necessary to conduct an in-depth analysis on

Supplementary Information The online version contains supplementary material available at https://doi.org/10.1007/978-3-031-20065-6_10.

the intrinsic properties of adversarial examples, which has inspired numerous researches on adversarial attacks [3,5,6,8,11,17,36,51] and defenses [23,34,52, 56,57,64]. Existing attacks can be split into two categories: *white-box* attack has full knowledge of the target model (often leveraging the gradient) [6,17,21,34] while *black-box* attack can only access the model output, which is more applicable in real-world scenarios. The black-box attack can be implemented in different ways. *Transfer-based* attack [17,32,54,59] adopts the adversaries generated on the substitute model to fool the target model. *Score-based* attack [2,9,26,31] assumes that the attacker can access the output logits while *decision-based* (*a.k.a.* hard label) attack [5,10,11,29,35] only has access to the prediction (top-1) label.

Among the black-box attacks, decision-based attack is more challenging and practical due to the minimum information requirement for attack. The number of queries on target model often plays a significant role in decision-based attack, since the access to a victim model is usually restricted in practice. Though recent works manage to reduce the total number of queries from millions to thousands of requests [5,29,38], it is still insufficient for most practical applications [35].

Existing decision-based attacks [5, 29,35,38] first generate a large adversarial perturbation and then minimize the perturbation while keeping adversarial property by various optimization methods. As shown in Fig. 1, we find that at the t-th iteration, the benign sample x, current adversarial example x_t^{adv}, and next adversarial example x_{t+1}^{adv} can naturally construct a triangle for any iterative attacks. According to the law of sines, the adversarial example x_{t+1}^{adv} at the $(t+1)$-th iteration should satisfy $\beta_t + 2\alpha_t > \pi$ to guarantee that the perturbation decreases, *i.e.*, $\delta_{t+1} = \|x_{t+1}^{adv} - x\|_p < \delta_t = \|x_t^{adv} - x\|_p$ (when $\beta_t + 2 \cdot \alpha_t = \pi$, it would be an isosceles triangle, *i.e.*, $\delta_{t+1} = \delta_t$).

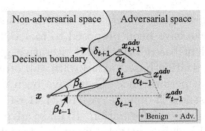

Fig. 1. Illustration of the candidate triangle at an arbitrary iteration of TA. At the t-th iteration, TA constructs a triangle with the learned angle α_t which satisfies $\beta_t + 2\alpha_t > \pi$ in the sampled subspace to find a new adversarial example x_{t+1}^{adv} and update α_t accordingly. Note that different from existing decision-based attacks [5,35,38], TA does not restrict x_t^{adv} on the decision boundary but minimizes the perturbation in the low frequency space using the geometric property; making TA itself query-efficient

Based on the above geometric property, we propose a novel and query-efficient decision-based attack, called Triangle Attack (TA). Specifically, at t-th iteration, we randomly select a directional line across the benign sample x to determine a 2-D subspace, in which we iteratively construct the triangle based on the current adversarial example x_t^{adv}, benign sample x, learned angle α_t, and searched angle β_t until the third vertex of the constructed triangle is adversarial. Using the geometric information, we can conduct TA in the low frequency space generated by Discrete Cosine Transform (DCT) [1] for effective dimensionality reduction to improve the efficiency. And we further update α_t to adapt to the perturbation optimization for each constructed triangle. Different from most existing decision-based attacks, there is no need to restrict x_t^{adv} on the decision boundary or estimate the gradient at each iteration, making TA query-efficient.

Our main contributions are summarized as follows:

- To our knowledge, it is the first work that directly optimizes the perturbation in frequency space via geometric information without restricting the adversary on decision boundary, leading to high query efficiency.
- Extensive evaluations on ImageNet dataset show that TA exhibits a much higher attack success rate within 1,000 queries and needs a much less number of queries to achieve the same attack success rate with the same perturbation budget on five models than existing SOTA attacks [8,11,12,29,35,38].
- TA generates more adversarial examples with imperceptible perturbations on Tencent Cloud API, showing its industrial-grade applicability.

2   Related Work

Since Szegedy *et al.* [46] identified adversarial examples, massive adversarial attacks have been proposed to fool DNNs. White-box attacks, *e.g.*, single-step gradient-based attack [21], iterative gradient-based attack [14,28,34,36], and optimization-based attack [3,6,46], often utilize the gradient and exhibit good attack performance. They have been widely adopted for evaluating the model robustness of defenses [13,16,34,41,64], but are hard to be applied in real-world with limited information. To make adversarial attacks applicable in practice, various black-box attacks, including transfer-based attack [17,50,51,58–60], score-based attack [2,9,18,26,48,63,65], and decision-based attack [5,8,12,35,38], have gained increasing interest. Among them, decision-based attack is most challenging since it can only access the prediction label. In this work, we aim to boost the query efficiency of decision-based attack by utilizing the geometric information and provide a brief overview of existing decision-based attacks.

BoundaryAttack [5] is the first decision-based attack that initializes a large perturbation and performs random walks on the decision boundary while keeping adversarial. Such a paradigm has been widely adopted in the subsequent decision-based attacks. OPT [11] formulates the decision-based attack as a real-valued optimization problem with zero-order optimization. And SignOPT [12] further computes the sign of the directional derivative instead of the magnitude for fast convergence. HopSkipJumpAttack (HSJA) [8] boosts Boundary-Attack by estimating the gradient direction via binary information at the decision boundary. QEBA [29] enhances HSJA for better gradient estimation using the perturbation sampled from various subspaces, including spatial, frequency, and intrinsic components. To further improve the query efficiency, qFool [33] assumes that the curvature of the boundary is small around adversarial examples and adopts several perturbation vectors for efficient gradient estimation. BO [43] uses Bayesian optimization for finding adversarial perturbations in low dimension subspace and maps it back to the original input space to obtain the final perturbation. GeoDA [38] approximates the local decision boundary by a hyperplane and searches the closest point to the benign sample on the hyperplane as the adversary. Surfree [35] iteratively constructs a circle on the decision boundary and adopts binary search to find the intersection of the constructed circle and decision boundary as the adversary without any gradient estimation.

Most existing decision-based attacks restrict the adversarial example at each iteration on the decision boundary and usually adopt different gradient estimation approaches for attack. In this work, we propose Triangle Attack to minimize the adversarial perturbation in the low frequency space directly by utilizing the law of sines without gradient estimation or restricting the adversarial example on the decision boundary for efficient decision-based attack.

3 Methodology

In this section, we first provide the preliminaries. Then we introduce our motivation and the proposed Triangle Attack (TA).

3.1 Preliminaries

Given a classifier f with parameters θ and a benign sample $x \in \mathcal{X}$ with ground-truth label $y \in \mathcal{Y}$, where $\mathcal{X}$ denotes all the images and $\mathcal{Y}$ is the output space. The adversarial attack finds an adversary $x^{adv} \in \mathcal{X}$ to mislead the target model:

$$f(x^{adv}; \theta) \neq f(x; \theta) = y \quad \text{s.t.} \quad \|x^{adv} - x\|_p < \epsilon,$$

where ϵ is the perturbation budget. Decision-based attacks usually first generate a large adversarial perturbation δ and then minimize the perturbation as follows:

$$\min \|\delta\|_p \quad \text{s.t.} \quad f(x + \delta; \theta) \neq f(x; \theta) = y. \tag{1}$$

Existing decision-based attacks [11,12,29] often estimate the gradient to minimize perturbation, which is time-consuming. Recently, some works adopt the geometric property to estimate the gradient or directly optimize the perturbation. Here we introduce two geometry-inspired decision-based attacks in details.

GeoDA [38] argues that the decision boundary at the vicinity of a data point x can be locally approximated by a hyperplane passing through a boundary point x_B close to x with a normal vector w. Thus, Eq. (1) can be locally linearized:

$$\min \|\delta\|_p \quad \text{s.t.} \quad w^\top (x + \delta) - w^\top x_B = 0.$$

Here x_B is a data point on the boundary, which can be found by binary search with several queries, and GeoDA randomly samples several data points for estimating w to optimize the perturbation at each iteration.

Surfree [35] assumes the boundary can be locally approximated by a hyperplane around a boundary point $x + \delta$. At each iteration, it represents the adversary using polar coordinates and searches optimal θ to update the perturbation:

$$\delta_{t+1} = \delta_t \cos \theta (u \cos \theta + v \sin \theta),$$

where u is the unit vector from x to x_t^{adv} and v is the orthogonal vector of u.

3.2 Motivation

Different from most decision-based attacks with gradient estimation [11,12,29, 38] or random walk on the decision boundary [5,35], we aim to optimize the perturbation using the geometric property without any queries for gradient estimation. After generating a large adversarial perturbation, the decision-based attacks move the adversarial example close to the benign sample, $i.e.$, decrease the adversarial perturbation δ_t, while keeping the adversarial property at each iteration. In this work, as shown in Fig. 1, we find that at the t-th iteration, the benign sample x, current adversarial example x_t^{adv} and next adversarial example x_{t+1}^{adv} can naturally construct a triangle in a subspace for any iterative attacks. Thus, searching for the next adversarial example x_{t+1}^{adv} with smaller perturbation is equivalent to searching for a triangle based on x and x_t^{adv}, in which the third data point x' is adversarial and satisfies $\|x' - x\|_p < \|x_t^{adv} - x\|_p$. This inspires us to utilize the relationship between the angle and side length in the triangle to search an appropriate triangle to minimize the perturbation at each iteration. As shown in Sect. 4.4, however, directly applying such a geometric property on the input image leads to poor performance. Thanks to the generality of such a geometric property, we optimize the perturbation in the low frequency space generated by DCT [1] for effective dimensionality reduction, which exhibits great attack efficiency as shown in Sect. 4.4.

Moreover, since Brendel et $al.$ [5] proposed BoundaryAttack, most decision-based attacks [8,11,12,35,38] follow the setting in which the adversarial example at each iteration should be on the decision boundary. We argue that such a restriction is not necessary in decision-based attacks but introduces too many queries on the target model to approach the boundary. Thus, we do not adopt this constraint in this work and validate this argument in Sect. 4.4.

3.3 Triangle Attack

In this work, we have the following assumption that the adversarial examples exist for any deep neural classifier f:

Assumption 1. *Given a benign sample x and a perturbation budget ϵ, there exists an adversarial perturbation $\|\delta\|_p \leq \epsilon$ towards the decision boundary which can mislead the target classifier f.*

This is a general assumption that we can find the adversarial example x^{adv} for the input sample x, which has been validated by numerous works [3,5,6,21,53]. If this assumption does not hold, the target model is ideally robust so that we cannot find any adversarial example within the perturbation budget, which is beyond our discussion. Thus, we follow the framework of existing decision-based attacks by first randomly crafting a large adversarial perturbation and then minimizing the perturbation. To align with previous works, we generate a random perturbation close to the decision boundary with binary search [29,35, 38] and mainly focus on the perturbation optimization.

In two arbitrary consecutive iterations of the perturbation optimization process for any adversarial attacks, namely the t-th and $(t + 1)$-th iterations without loss of generality, the input sample x, current adversarial example x_t^{adv} and next adversarial example x_{t+1}^{adv} can naturally construct a triangle in a subspace of the input space $\mathcal{X}$. Thus, as shown in Fig. 1, decreasing the perturbation to generate x_{t+1}^{adv} is equivalent to searching for an appropriate triangle in which the three vertices are x, x_t^{adv} and x_{t+1}^{adv}, respectively.

Theorem 1 (The law of sines). *Suppose a, b and c are the side lengths of a triangle, and α, β and γ are the opposite angles, we have $\frac{a}{\sin \alpha} = \frac{b}{\sin \beta} = \frac{c}{\sin \gamma}$.*

From Theorem 1, we can obtain the relationship between the side length and opposite angle for the triangle in Fig. 1:

$$\frac{\delta_t}{\sin \alpha_t} = \frac{\delta_{t+1}}{\sin (\pi - (\alpha_t + \beta_t))}. \tag{2}$$

To greedily decrease the perturbation δ_t, the t-th triangle should satisfy that $\frac{\delta_{t+1}}{\delta_t} = \frac{\sin (\pi-(\alpha_t+\beta_t))}{\sin \alpha_t} < 1$, *i.e.*, $\pi - (\alpha_t + \beta_t) < \alpha_t$. Thus, decreasing the perturbation at the t-th iteration can be achieved by finding a triangle constructed by the input sample x, current adversarial example x_t^{adv} and the angles β_t and α_t, which satisfy $\beta_t + 2\alpha_t > \pi$ and the third vertex should be adversarial. We denote such a triangle as candidate triangle and $\mathcal{T}(x, x_t^{adv}, \alpha_t, \beta_t, \mathcal{S}_t)$ as the third vertex, where $\mathcal{S}_t$ is a sampled subspace. Based on this observation, we propose a novel decision-based attack, called Triangle Attack (TA), that searches the candidate triangle at each iteration and adjusts angle α_t accordingly.

Sampling the 2-D Subspace $\mathcal{S}$ of Frequency Space. The input image often lies in a high-dimensional space, such as $224 \times 224 \times 3$ for ImageNet [27], which is too large for the attack to explore the neighborhood for minimizing the adversarial perturbation efficiently. Previous works [22, 29, 35] have shown that utilizing the information in various subspaces can improve the efficiency of decision-based attacks. For instance, QEBA [29] samples the random noise for gradient estimation in the spatial transformed

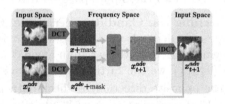

Fig. 2. Illustration of the entire procedure of TA attack at the t-th iteration. We construct the triangle in the frequency space to efficiently craft adversarial examples. Note that here we adopt DCT for illustration but we do not need it for x at each iteration. We still adopt x and x_t^{adv} in the frequency space without ambiguity due to the one-to-one mapping of DCT

space or low frequency space but minimizes the perturbation in the input space with estimated gradient. Surfree [35] optimizes the perturbation in the subspace of the input space determined by a unit vector randomly sampled in the low frequency space. In general, the low frequency space contains the most critical

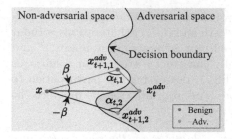
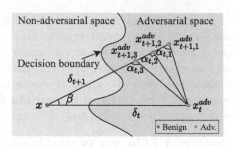

Fig. 3. Illustration of a symmetric candidate triangle (x, x_t^{adv} and $x_{t+1,2}^{adv}$). When the angle β cannot result in adversarial example ($x_{t+1,1}^{adv}$), we would further construct the symmetric triangle based on line $\langle x, x_t^{adv} \rangle$ to check data point $x_{t+1,2}^{adv}$

Fig. 4. The effect of magnitude on α for the candidate triangle used in TA. For the same sampled angle β, the larger angle α leads to smaller perturbation but is also more likely to cross over the decision boundary

information for images. With the poor performance of TA in the input space as shown in Sect. 4.4 and the generality of the geometric property shown in Fig. 2, we directly optimize the perturbation in the frequency space at each iteration for effective dimensionality reduction. And we randomly sample a d-dimensional line across the benign sample in the low frequency space (top 10%). The sampled line, directional line from benign sample x and current adversary x_t^{adv} can determine a unique 2-D subspace $\mathcal{S}$ of the frequency space, in which we can construct the candidate triangle to minimize the perturbation. The final adversary can be converted into the input space by Inverse DCT (IDCT).

Searching the Candidate Triangle. Given a subspace $\mathcal{S}_t$, the candidate triangle only depends on angle β since α is updated during the optimization. As shown in Fig. 3, if we search an angle β without leading to an adversarial example ($x_{t+1,1}^{adv}$), we can further construct a symmetric triangle with the same angle in the opposite direction to check data point $x_{t+1,2}^{adv}$, which has the same magnitude of perturbation as $x_{t+1,1}^{adv}$ but in different direction. We denote the angle as $-\beta$ for the symmetric triangle without ambiguity. Note that with the same angle α, a larger angle β would make the third vertex closer to the input sample x, *i.e.*, smaller perturbation. After determining the subspace $\mathcal{S}_t$, we first check angle $\beta_{t,0} = \max(\pi - 2\alpha, \underline{\beta})$, where $\underline{\beta} = \pi/16$ is a pre-defined small angle. If neither $\mathcal{T}(x, x_t^{adv}, \alpha_t, \beta_{t,0}, \mathcal{S}_t)$ nor $\mathcal{T}(x, x_t^{adv}, \alpha_t, -\beta_{t,0}, \mathcal{S}_t)$ is adversarial, we give up this subspace because it brings no benefit. Otherwise, we adopt binary search to find an optimal angle $\beta^* \in [\max(\pi - 2\alpha, \underline{\beta}), \min(\pi - \alpha, \pi/2)]$ which is as large as possible to minimize the perturbation. Here we restrict the upper bound of β because $\mathcal{T}(x, x_t^{adv}, \alpha_t, \beta, \mathcal{S}_t)$ would be at the opposite direction w.r.t. x for $\beta > \pi/2$ and $\pi - \alpha$ guarantees a valid triangle.

Adjusting Angle α. Intuitively, angle α balances the magnitude of perturbation and the difficulty to find an adversarial example.

Algorithm 1: Triangle Attack

Input: Target classifier f with parameters θ; Benign sample x with
    ground-truth label y; Maximum number of queries Q; Maximum
    number of iteration N for each sampled subspace; Dimension of the
    directional line d; Lower bound $\underline{\beta}$ for angle β.

Output: An adversarial example x^{adv}.

1 Initialize a large adversarial perturbation δ_0;

2 $x_0^{adv} = x + \delta_0$, $q = 0$, $t = 0$, $\alpha_0 = \pi/2$;

3 **while** $q < Q$ **do**

4   Sampling 2-D subspace $\mathcal{S}_t$ in the low frequency space;

5     $\beta_{t,0} = \max(\pi - 2\alpha, \underline{\beta})$;

6   **if** $f(\mathcal{T}(x, x_t^{adv}, \alpha_{t,0}, \beta_{t,0}, \mathcal{S}_t); \theta) = f(x; \theta)$ **then**

7        $q = q + 1$, update $\alpha_{t,0}$ based on Eq. (3);

8   **if** $f(\mathcal{T}(x, x_t^{adv}, \alpha_{t,0}, -\beta_{t,0}, \mathcal{S}_t); \theta) = f(x; \theta)$ **then**

9           $q = q + 1$, update $\alpha_{t,0}$ based on Eq. (3);

10   Go to line 3;   ▷ give up this subspace

11     $\overline{\beta}_{t,0} = \min(\pi/2, \pi - \alpha)$;

12   **for** $i = 0 \rightarrow N$ **do**   ▷ binary search for angle β

13        $\beta_{t,i+1} = (\overline{\beta}_{t,i} + \beta_{t,i})/2$;

14   **if** $f(\mathcal{T}(x, x_t^{adv}, \alpha_{t,i}, \beta_{t,i+1}, \mathcal{S}_t); \theta) = f(x; \theta)$ **then**

15           $q = q + 1$, update $\alpha_{t,i}$ based on Eq. (3);

16   **if** $f(\mathcal{T}(x, x_t^{adv}, \alpha_{t,i}, -\beta_{t,i+1}, \mathcal{S}_t); \theta) = f(x; \theta)$ **then**

17              $\overline{\beta}_{t,i+1} = \beta_{t,i+1}, \beta_{t,i+1} = \beta_{t,i}$;

18        $q = q + 1$, update $\alpha_{t,i+1}$ based on Eq. (3);

19     $x_{t+1}^{adv} = \mathcal{T}(x, x_t^{adv}, \alpha_{t,i+1}, \beta_{t,i+1}, \mathcal{S}_t)$, $t = t + 1$;

20 **return** x_t^{adv}.

Proposition 1. *With the same angle β, a smaller angle α makes it easier to find an adversarial example while a larger angle α leads to smaller perturbation.*

Intuitively, as shown in Fig. 4, a smaller angle α results in larger perturbation but is more likely to cross over the decision boundary, making it easier to search an adversarial example, and vice versa. It is hard to consistently find an optimal α for each iteration, letting alone various input images and target models. Thus, we adaptively adjust angle α based on the crafted adversarial example:

$$\alpha_{t,i+1} = \begin{cases} \min(\alpha_{t,i} + \gamma, \pi/2 + \tau) & \text{if } f(x_{t,i+1}^{adv}; \theta) \neq y \\ \max(\alpha_{t,i} - \lambda\gamma, \pi/2 - \tau) & \text{Otherwise} \end{cases} \quad (3)$$

where $x_{t,i+1}^{adv} = \mathcal{T}(x, x_t^{adv}, \alpha_{t,i}, \beta_{t,i}, \mathcal{S}_t)$ is the adversarial example generated by $\alpha_{t,i}$, γ is the change rate, λ is a constant, and τ restricts the upper and lower bounds of α. We adopt $\lambda < 1$ to prevent decreasing the angle too fast considering much more failures than successes during the perturbation optimization. Note that a larger angle α makes it harder to find an adversarial example.

However, a too small angle α results in a much lower bound for β, which also makes $\mathcal{T}(x, x_t^{adv}, \alpha_t, \beta_t, \mathcal{S}_t)$ far away from the current adversarial example x_t^{adv}, decreasing the probability to find an adversarial example. Thus, we add bounds for α to restrict it in an appropriate range.

TA iteratively searches the candidate triangle in subspace $\mathcal{S}_t$ sampled from the low frequency space to find the adversarial example and update angle α accordingly. The overall algorithm of TA is summarized in Algorithm 1.

4   Experiments

We conduct extensive evaluations on the standard ImageNet dataset using five models and Tencent Cloud API to evaluate the effectiveness of TA. Code is available at https://github.com/xiaosen-wang/TA.

Table 1. Attack success rate (%) on five models under different RMSE thresholds. The maximum number of queries is set to 1,000. We highlight the highest attack success rate in **bold**

Model	VGG-16			Inception-v3			ResNet-18			ResNet-101			DenseNet-121		
RMSE	0.1	0.05	0.01	0.1	0.05	0.01	0.1	0.05	0.01	0.1	0.05	0.01	0.1	0.05	0.01
OPT	76.0	38.5	5.5	34.0	17.0	4.0	67.0	36.0	6.0	51.5	21.0	5.0	51.5	29.0	5.5
SignOPT	94.0	57.5	12.5	50.5	27.0	8.0	84.5	49.5	13.0	69.0	33.0	8.0	69.5	44.0	10.0
HSJA	92.5	58.5	13.0	32.5	14.0	4.0	83.0	51.0	12.5	71.5	37.5	12.0	70.5	43.5	10.5
QEBA	98.5	86.0	29.0	78.5	54.5	17.0	98.0	81.5	34.5	94.0	59.0	20.5	91.0	66.0	24.0
BO	96.0	72.5	17.0	75.5	43.0	10.0	94.5	74.0	16.0	89.5	63.0	16.5	93.0	64.5	16.5
GeoDA	99.0	94.0	35.0	89.0	61.5	23.5	99.5	90.0	30.5	98.0	81.5	22.0	**100.0**	84.5	27.5
Surfree	99.5	92.5	39.5	87.5	67.5	24.5	98.5	87.0	36.0	95.5	76.5	27.0	97.0	78.0	29.0
TA (Ours)	**100.0**	**95.0**	**44.5**	**96.5**	**81.5**	**30.0**	**100.0**	**94.0**	**51.5**	**99.0**	**88.5**	**40.0**	99.5	**92.5**	**43.5**

4.1   Experimental Setup

Dataset. To validate the effectiveness of the proposed TA, following the setting of Surfree [39], we randomly sample 200 correctly classified images from the ILSVRC 2012 validation set for evaluation on the corresponding models.

Models. We consider five widely adopted models, *i.e.*, VGG-16 [44], Inception-v3 [45], ResNet-18 [24], ResNet-101 [24] and DenseNet-121 [25]. To validate the applicability in the real world, we evaluate TA on Tencent Cloud API[1].

Baselines. We take various decision-based attacks as our baselines, including four gradient estimation based attacks, *i.e.*, OPT [11], SignOPT [12], HSJA [8], QEBA [29], one optimization based attack, *i.e.*, BO [43], and two geometry-inspired attacks, *i.e.*, GeoDA [38], Surfree [35].

---

[1] https://cloud.tencent.com/.

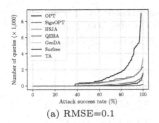
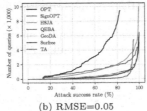
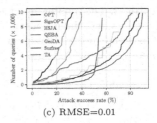

| (a) RMSE=0.1 | (b) RMSE=0.05 | (c) RMSE=0.01 |

Fig. 5. Number of queries to achieve the given attack success rate on ResNet-18 for the attack baselines and the proposed TA under various perturbation budgets. The maximum number of queries is 10,000

Evaluation metrics. Following the standard setting in QEBA [29], we adopt the root mean squared error ($RMSE$) between benign sample x and adversarial example x^{adv} to measure the magnitude of perturbation:

$$d(x, x^{adv}) = \sqrt{\frac{1}{w \cdot h \cdot c} \sum_{i=1}^{w} \sum_{j=1}^{h} \sum_{k=1}^{c} (x[i, j, k] - x^{adv}[i, j, k])^2}, \qquad (4)$$

where w, h, c are the width, height and number of channels of the input image, respectively. We also adopt the attack success rate, the percentage of adversarial examples which reach a certain distance threshold.

Hyper-parameters. For fair comparison, all the attacks adopt the same adversarial perturbation initialization approach as in [35] and the hyper-parameters for baselines are exactly the same as in the original papers. For our TA, we adopt the maximum number of iterations in each subspace $N = 2$, the dimension of directional line $d = 3$ and $\gamma = 0.01$, $\lambda = 0.05$ and $\tau = 0.1$ for updating angle α.

4.2 Evaluation on Standard Models

To evaluate the effectiveness of TA, we first compare the attack performance on five popular models with different decision-based attacks and report the attack success rate under various $RMSE$ thresholds, namely 0.1, 0.05 and 0.001.

We first evaluate the attack within 1,000 queries, which is widely adopted in recent works [8,35,38]. The attack success rate is summarized in Table 1, which means the attack would fail to generate adversarial example for the input image if it takes 1,000 queries without reaching the given threshold. We can observe that TA consistently achieves much higher attack success rate than existing decision-based attacks under various perturbation budgets on five models with different architectures. For instance, TA outperforms the runner-up attack with a clear margin of 1.0%, 7.5% and 13.0% under the $RMSE$ threshold of 0.1, 0.05, 0.01 on ResNet-101, which is widely adopted for evaluating the decision-based attacks. In particular, the proposed TA significantly outperforms the two geometry-inspired attacks, *i.e.*, GeoDA [38] and Surfree [35], which exhibit the

Table 2. The number of adversarial examples successfully generated by various attack baselines and the proposed TA on Tencent Cloud API within 200/500/1,000 queries. The results are evaluated on 20 randomly sampled images from the correctly classified images in ImageNet due to the high cost of online APIs

RMSE	OPT	SignOPT	HSJA	QEBA	GeoDA	Surfree	TA (**Ours**)
0.1	4/6/6	8/8/9	7/8/8	12/12/12	15/15/15	13/13/13	**17/17/17**
0.05	1/3/3	4/4/7	6/6/8	11/11/12	13/14/14	12/12/13	**15/17/17**
0.01	1/1/2	1/1/3	2/5/6	3/8/9	3/7/12	5/8/10	**8/12/13**

best attack performance among the baselines. This convincingly validates the high effectiveness of the proposed TA. Besides, among the five models, Inception-v3 [45], which is rarely investigated in decision-based attacks, exhibits better robustness than other models under various perturbation budgets against both baselines and TA. Thus, it is necessary to thoroughly evaluate the decision-based attacks on various architectures instead of only ResNet models.

To further verify the high efficiency of TA, we investigate the number of queries to achieve various attack success rates under the $RMSE$ threshold of 0.1, 0.05 and 0.01, respectively. The maximum number of queries is set to 10,000 and the results on ResNet-18 are summarized in Fig. 5. As shown in Fig. 5a and 5b, TA needs much less number of queries to achieve various attack success rates with $RMSE$ threshold of 0.1 and 0.05, showing the high query efficiency of our method. For the smaller threshold of 0.01, as shown in Fig. 5c, our TA still needs less number of queries when achieving the attack success rate smaller than 50% but fails to achieve the attack success rate higher than 60%. Note that as shown in Fig. 6 and Table 1, $RMSE$ threshold of 0.01 is very rigorous so that the perturbation is imperceptible but is also hard to generate the adversarial examples for decision-based attacks. Since we mainly focus on the query efficiency of attack only based on geometric information, the attack performance under the $RMSE$ threshold of 0.01 is acceptable because it is impractical for such high number of queries when attacking real-world applications.

Besides, since TA aims to improve the query efficiency by utilizing the triangle geometry, the global optima might be worse than existing gradient estimation based attacks when more queries are allowed. Other geometry-inspired methods also perform poorer than QEBA [29] in this case without gradient estimation. However, it is not the goal of TA and can be easily solved using gradient estimation. With the high efficiency of TA, we can achieve higher attack performance with lower number of queries by taking the TA as warm-up for the precise gradient estimation attacks, such as QEBA [29], if the high number of queries is acceptable. We integrate the gradient estimation used in QEBA [29] into TA after 2,000 queries, dubbed **TAG**. For the perturbation budget of 0.01, TAG achieves the attack success rate of 95% using 7,000 queries, which is better than the best baseline with the attack success rate of 92% using 9,000 queries.

4.3   Evaluation on Real-world Applications

With the superior performance and unprecedented progress of DNNs, numerous companies have deployed DNNs for a variety of tasks and also provide commercial APIs (Application Programming Interfaces) for different tasks. Developers can pay for these services to integrate the APIs into their applications. However, the vulnerability of DNNs to adversarial examples, especially the prosperity of decision-based attack which does not need any information of target models, poses severe threats to these real-world applications. With the high efficiency of TA, we also validate its practical attack applicability using Tencent Cloud API. Due to the high cost of commercial APIs, we randomly sample 20 images from ImageNet validation set and the maximum number of queries is 1,000.

The numbers of successfully attacked images are summarized in Table 2. We can observe that TA successfully generates more adversarial examples than the attack baselines within 200, 500 and 1,000 queries under various $RMSE$ thresholds. In particular, TA can generate even more adversarial examples within 500 queries than the best attack baselines within 1,000 queries, showing the superiority of TA. We also visualize some adversarial examples generated by TA in Fig. 6. As we can see, TA can successfully generate high quality adversarial examples for various classes with few queries (≤ 200), validating the high applicability of TA in real-world. Especially when the number of queries is 200, the adversar-

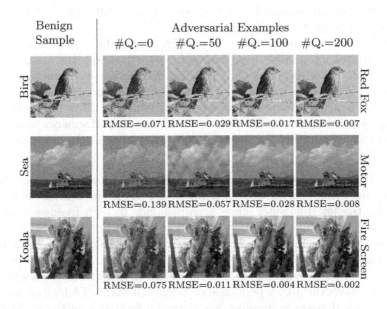

Fig. 6. The adversarial examples crafted by TA against Tencent Cloud API. #Q. denotes the number of queries for attack and RMSE denotes the RMSE distance between the benign sample and adversarial example. We report the correct label and the predicted label on the leftmost and rightmost columns, respectively (Zoom in for details.)

ial examples generated by TA are almost visually imperceptible for humans, highlighting the vulnerability of current commercial applications.

4.4   Ablation Study

In this section, we conduct a series of ablation studies on ResNet-18, namely the subspace chosen by TA, the ratio for low frequency subspace and the change rate γ and λ for updating angle α. The parameter studies on the dimension of sampled line d and the bound τ for α are summarized in Appendix B.

On the Subspace Chosen by TA. Different from existing decision-based attacks, the generality of geometric property used by TA makes it possible to directly optimize the perturbation in the frequency space. To investigate the effectiveness of frequency space, we implement TA in various spaces, namely input space (TA_I), sampling the directional line in the frequency space but optimizing the perturbation in the input space (TA_{FI}) used by Surfree [35] and full frequency space (TA_F). As shown in Table 3, due to the high-dimensional input space, TA_I cannot effectively explore the neighbor-

Table 3. Ablation study on ResNet-18 for different spaces, *i.e.* input space (TA_I), frequency space for line sampling but input space for perturbation optimization (TA_{FI}), and full frequency space without mask (TA_F)

RMSE	TA_I	TA_{FI}	TA_F	TA
0.1	39.5	97.5	98.5	**100.0**
0.05	17.5	73.0	85.0	**94.0**
0.01	3.0	22.5	25.5	**51.5**

hood of the input sample to find good perturbation and shows very poor performance. With the information from frequency space to sample the subspace, TA_{FI} exhibits much better results than TA_I. When optimizing the perturbation in the full frequency space, TA_F can achieve higher attack success rate than TA_{FI}, showing the benefit of frequency space. When sampling the subspace using the low frequency information, TA achieves much better performance than all the other attacks, supporting the necessity and rationality of the subspace chosen by TA.

On the Ratio for Low Frequency Subspace. The low frequency domain plays key role in improving the efficiency of TA. However, there is no criterion to identify the low frequency since it corresponds to high frequency, which is usually determined by the lower part of the frequency domain with a given ratio. Here we investigate the effect of this ratio on the attack performance of TA. As shown in Fig. 7, the ratio has more significant influence on the attack success rate under the smaller $RMSE$ threshold. In general, increasing the ratio roughly decreases the attack performance because it makes TA focus more on the high frequency domain, containing less critical information of the image. Thus, we adopt the lower 10% parts as the low frequency subspace for high efficiency, which also helps TA effectively reduce the dimension, making it easier for attack.

On the Change Rate γ and λ for Updating Angle α. As stated in Sect. 3.3, the angle α plays a key role in choosing a better candidate triangle but it is

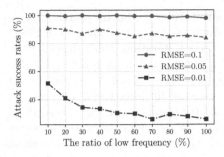

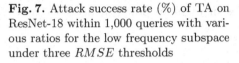

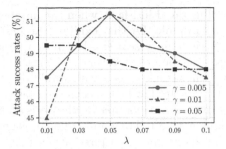

Fig. 7. Attack success rate (%) of TA on ResNet-18 within 1,000 queries with various ratios for the low frequency subspace under three $RMSE$ thresholds

Fig. 8. Attack success rate (%) of TA on ResNet-18 within 1,000 queries with various γ and λ used for updating α under $RMSE = 0.01$

hard to find a uniformly optimal α for different iterations and input images. We assume that the larger angle α makes it harder to find a candidate triangle but leads to smaller perturbation. As in Eq. (3), if we successfully find a triangle, we would increase α with γ. Otherwise, we would decrease α with $\lambda\gamma$. We investigate the impact of various γ and λ in Fig. 8. Here we only report the results for $RMSE = 0.01$ for clarity and the results for $RMSE = 0.1/0.05$ exhibit the same trend. In general, $\gamma = 0.01$ leads to better attack performance than $\gamma = 0.05/0.005$. When we increase λ with $\gamma = 0.01$, the attack success rate increases until $\lambda = 0.05$ and then decreases. We also investigate the impact of τ which controls the bound for α in Eq. (3), which shows stable performance within 1,000 queries but takes effect for 10,000 queries and we simply adopt $\tau = 0.1$. In our experiments, we adopt $\gamma = 0.01$, $\lambda = 0.05$ and $\tau = 0.1$.

4.5   Further Discussion

BoundaryAttack [5] adopts random walk on the decision boundary to minimize the perturbation for decision-based attack and the subsequent works often follow this setting to restrict the adversarial example on the decision boundary. We argue that such a restriction is not necessary and do not adopt it in our TA. To validate this argument, we also conduct binary search to move the adversarial example towards the decision boundary at each iteration after we find the candidate triangle to investigate the benefit of this restriction.

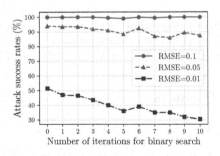

Fig. 9. Attack success rate (%) of TA using various number of iterations for binary search (N_{bs}) to restrict the adversary on the decision boundary at each iteration

As illustrated in Fig. 9, when the number of iterations for binary search (N_{bs}) is 0, it is vanilla TA that exhibits the best attack success rate. When we increase N_{bs}, the binary search takes more queries in each iteration which degrades the total number of iterations under the given total number of queries. In general, the attack success rate stably decreases when increasing N_{bs} especially for $RMSE = 0.01$, which means the cost (*i.e.*, queries) for binary search to restrict the adversarial example on the decision boundary is not worthy. Such restriction might not be reliable and rational either for most decision-based attacks, especially for geometry-inspired attacks. We hope this would inspire more attention to discuss the necessity of restricting the adversarial examples on the decision boundary and shed new light on the design of more powerful decision-based attacks.

5   Conclusion

In this work, we found that the benign sample, the current and next adversarial examples can naturally construct a triangle in a subspace at each iteration for any iterative attacks. Based on this observation, we proposed a novel decision-based attack, called Triangle Attack (TA), which utilizes the geometric information that the longer side is opposite the larger angle in any triangle. Specifically, at each iteration, TA randomly samples a directional line across the benign sample to determine a subspace, in which TA iteratively searches a candidate triangle to minimize the adversarial perturbation. With the generality of geometric property, TA directly optimizes the adversarial perturbation in the low frequency space generated by DCT with much lower dimensions than the input space, and significantly improves the query efficiency. Extensive experiments demonstrate that TA achieves a much higher attack success rate within 1,000 queries and needs much less queries to achieve the same attack success rate. The practical applicability on Tencent Cloud API also validates the superiority of TA.

Acknowledgement. This work is supported by National Natural Science Foundation (62076105), International Coorperation Foundation of Hubei Province, China(2021EHB011) and Tencent Rhino Bird Elite Talent Training Program.

References

1. Ahmed, N., Natarajan, T., Rao, K.R.: Discrete cosine transform. IEEE Trans. Comput. **100**, 90–93 (1974)
2. Al-Dujaili, A., O'Reilly, U.M.: Sign bits are all you need for black-box attacks. In: International Conference on Learning Representations (2020)
3. Athalye, A., Carlini, N., Wagner, D.A.: Obfuscated gradients give a false sense of security: circumventing defenses to adversarial examples. In: International Conference on Machine Learning (2018)
4. Bojarski, M., et al.: End to end learning for self-driving cars. arXiv preprint arXiv:1604.07316 (2016)

5. Brendel, W., Rauber, J., Bethge, M.: Decision-based adversarial attacks: reliable attacks against black-box machine learning models. In: International Conference on Learning Representations (2018)
6. Carlini, N., Wagner, D.: Towards evaluating the robustness of neural networks. In: IEEE Symposium on Security and Privacy (2017)
7. Chen, C., Seff, A., Kornhauser, A., Xiao, J.: DeepDriving: learning affordance for direct perception in autonomous driving. In: International Conference on Computer Vision, pp. 2722–2730 (2015)
8. Chen, J., Jordan, M.I., Wainwright, M.J.: HopSkipJumpAttack: a query-efficient decision-based attack. In: IEEE Symposium on Security and Privacy (2020)
9. Chen, P.Y., Zhang, H., Sharma, Y., Yi, J., Hsieh, C.J., ZOO: zeroth order optimization based black-box attacks to deep neural networks without training substitute models. In: ACM Workshop on Artificial Intelligence and Security (2017)
10. Chen, W., Zhang, Z., Hu, X., Wu, B.: Boosting decision-based black-box adversarial attacks with random sign flip. In: Vedaldi, A., Bischof, H., Brox, T., Frahm, J.-M. (eds.) ECCV 2020. LNCS, vol. 12360, pp. 276–293. Springer, Cham (2020). https://doi.org/10.1007/978-3-030-58555-6_17
11. M., Cheng, Thong Le, Pin-Yu Chen, Huan Zhang, Yi, J., Hsieh, C.J.: Query-efficient hard-label black-box attack: An optimization-based approach. In: International Conference on Learning Representations (2019)
12. Cheng, M., Singh, S., Chen, P.H., Chen, P.Y., Liu, S., Hsieh, C.J.: Sign-OPT: a query-efficient hard-label adversarial attack. In: International Conference on Learning Representations (2020)
13. Cohen, J.M., Rosenfeld, E., Kolter, J.Z.: Certified adversarial robustness via randomized smoothing. In: International Conference on Machine Learning (2019)
14. Croce, F., Hein, M.: Reliable evaluation of adversarial robustness with an ensemble of diverse parameter-free attacks. In: International Conference on Machine Learning (2020)
15. Deng, Z., Peng, X., Li, Z., Qiao, Yu.: Mutual component convolutional neural networks for heterogeneous face recognition. IEEE Trans. Image Process. **28**(6), 3102–3114 (2019)
16. Dong, Y., et al.: Benchmarking adversarial robustness on image classification. In: Conference on Computer Vision and Pattern Recognition (2020)
17. Dong, Y., et al.: Boosting adversarial attacks with momentum. In: Conference on Computer Vision and Pattern Recognition (2018)
18. Du, J., Zhang, H., Zhou, J.T., Yang, Y., Feng, J.: Query-efficient meta attack to deep neural networks. In: International Conference on Learning Representations (2020)
19. Eykholt, K., et al.: Robust physical-world attacks on deep learning visual classification. In: Conference on Computer Vision and Pattern Recognition (2018)
20. Gong, D., Li, Z., Liu, J., Qiao, Y.: Multi-feature canonical correlation analysis for face photo-sketch image retrieval. In: Proceedings of the 21st ACM International Conference on Multimedia, pp. 617–620 (2013)
21. Goodfellow, I.J., Shlens, J., Szegedy, C.: Explaining and harnessing adversarial examples. In: International Conference on Learning Representations (2015)
22. Guo, C., Frank, J.S., Weinberger, K.Q.: Low frequency adversarial perturbation. Uncertain. Artif. Intell. (2019)
23. Guo, C., Rana, M., Cissé, M., van der Maaten, L.: Countering adversarial images using input transformations. In: International Conference on Learning Representations (2018)

24. He, K., Zhang, X., Ren, S., Sun, J.: Deep residual learning for image recognition. In: Conference on Computer Vision and Pattern Recognition (2016)
25. Huang, G., Liu, Z., van der Maaten, L., Weinberger, K.Q.: Densely connected convolutional networks. In: Conference on Computer Vision and Pattern Recognition (2017)
26. Ilyas, A., Engstrom, L., Athalye, A., Lin, J.: Black-box adversarial attacks with limited queries and information. In: International Conference on Machine Learning (2018)
27. Krizhevsky, A., Sutskever, I., Hinton, G.E.: ImageNet classification with deep convolutional neural networks. In: Advances in Neural Information Processing Systems (2012)
28. Kurakin, A., Goodfellow, I., Bengio, S.: Adversarial examples in the physical world. In: International Conference on Learning Representations, Workshop (2017)
29. Li, H., Xu, X., Zhang, X., Yang, S., Li, B.: QEBA: query-efficient boundary-based blackbox attack. In: Conference on Computer Vision and Pattern Recognition (2020)
30. Li, Z., Gong, D., Qiao, Y., Tao, D.: Common feature discriminant analysis for matching infrared face images to optical face images. IEEE Trans. Image Process. **23**(6), 2436–2445 (2014)
31. Liang, S., Wu, B., Fan, Y., Wei, X., Cao, X.: Parallel rectangle flip attack: a query-based black-box attack against object detection. arXiv preprint arXiv:2201.08970 (2022)
32. Liu, Y., Chen, X., Liu, C., Song, D.: Delving into transferable adversarial examples and black-box attacks. In: International Conference on Learning Representations (2017)
33. Liu, Y., Moosavi-Dezfooli, S.-M., Frossard, P.: A geometry-inspired decision-based attack. In: International Conference on Computer Vision, pp. 4890–4898 (2019)
34. Madry, A., Makelov, A., Schmidt, L., Tsipras, D., Vladu, A.: Towards deep learning models resistant to adversarial attacks. In: International Conference on Learning Representations (2018)
35. Maho, T., Furon, T., Merrer, E.L.: SurFree: a fast surrogate-free black-box attack. In: Conference on Computer Vision and Pattern Recognition (2021)
36. Moosavi-Dezfooli, S.-M., Fawzi, A., Frossard, P.: DeepFool: a simple and accurate method to fool deep neural networks. In: Conference on Computer Vision and Pattern Recognition (2016)
37. Qiu, H., Gong, D., Li, Z., Liu, W., Tao, D.: End2End occluded face recognition by masking corrupted features. IEEE Trans. Pattern Anal. Mach. Intell. (2021)
38. Rahmati, A., Moosavi-Dezfooli, S.-M., Frossard, P., Dai, H.: GeoDA: a geometric framework for black-box adversarial attacks. In: Computer Vision and Pattern Recognition, pp. 8446–8455 (2020)
39. Russakovsky, O., et al.: ImageNet large scale visual recognition challenge. In: International Booktitle of Computer Vision (2015)
40. Sallab, A.E.L., Abdou, M., Perot, E., Yogamani, S.: Deep reinforcement learning framework for autonomous driving. Electron. Imaging **2017**(19), 70–76 (2017)
41. Shafahi, A., et al.: Adversarial training for free! In: Advances in Neural Information Processing Systems (2019)
42. Sharif, M., Bhagavatula, S., Bauer, L., Reiter, M.K.: Accessorize to a crime: real and stealthy attacks on state-of-the-art face recognition. In: ACM SIGSAC conference on Computer and Communications Security (2016)

43. Shukla, S.N., Sahu, A.K., Willmott, D., Kolter, Z.: Simple and efficient hard label black-box adversarial attacks in low query budget regimes. In: Proceedings of the 27th ACM SIGKDD Conference on Knowledge Discovery & Data Mining, pp. 1461–1469 (2021)
44. Simonyan, K., Zisserman, A.: Very deep convolutional networks for large-scale image recognition. In: International Conference on Learning Representations (2015)
45. Szegedy, C., Vanhoucke, V., Ioffe, S., Shlens, J., Wojna, Z.: Rethinking the inception architecture for computer vision. In: Conference on Computer Vision and Pattern Recognition (2016)
46. Szegedy, C., et al.: Intriguing properties of neural networks. In: International Conference on Learning Representations (2014)
47. Tang, X., Li, Z.: Video based face recognition using multiple classifiers. In: IEEE International Conference on Automatic Face and Gesture Recognition, pp. 345–349. IEEE (2004)
48. Tu, C.-C., et al.: AutoZOOM: autoencoder-based zeroth order optimization method for attacking black-box neural networks. In: AAAI Conference on Artificial Intelligence (2019)
49. Wang, H., et al.: CosFace: large margin cosine loss for deep face recognition. In: Conference on Computer Vision and Pattern Recognition (2018)
50. Wang, X., He, K.: Enhancing the transferability of adversarial attacks through variance tuning. In: Conference on Computer Vision and Pattern Recognition (2021)
51. Wang, X., He, X., Wang, J., He, K.: Admix: Enhancing the transferability of adversarial attacks. In: International Conference on Computer Vision (2021)
52. Wang, X., Jin, H., Yang, Y., He, K.: Natural language adversarial defense through synonym encoding. In: Conference on Uncertainty in Artificial Intelligence (2021)
53. Wang, X., Lin, J., Hu, H., Wang, J., He, K.: Boosting adversarial transferability through enhanced momentum. In: British Machine Vision Conference (2021)
54. Wei, X., Liang, S., Chen, N., Cao, X.: Transferable adversarial attacks for image and video object detection. arXiv preprint arXiv:1811.12641 (2018)
55. Wen, Y., Zhang, K., Li, Z., Qiao, Yu.: A discriminative feature learning approach for deep face recognition. In: Leibe, B., Matas, J., Sebe, N., Welling, M. (eds.) ECCV 2016. LNCS, vol. 9911, pp. 499–515. Springer, Cham (2016). https://doi.org/10.1007/978-3-319-46478-7_31
56. Wong, E., Rice, L., Zico Kolter, J.: Fast is better than free: Revisiting adversarial training. In: International Conference on Learning Representations (2020)
57. Wu, B., et al.: Attacking adversarial attacks as a defense. arXiv preprint arXiv:2106.04938 (2021)
58. Wu, W., Su, Y., Lyu, M.R., King, I.: Improving the transferability of adversarial samples with adversarial transformations. In: Conference on Computer Vision and Pattern Recognition (2021)
59. Xie, C., et al.: Improving transferability of adversarial examples with input diversity. In: Conference on Computer Vision and Pattern Recognition (2019)
60. Xiong, Y., Lin, J., Zhang, M., Hopcroft, J.E., He, K.: Stochastic variance reduced ensemble adversarial attack for boosting the adversarial transferability. In: Proceedings of the IEEE/CVF Conference on Computer Vision and Pattern Recognition (2022)
61. Xu, H., Gao, Y., Yu, F., Darrell, T.: End-to-end learning of driving models from large-scale video datasets. In: Conference on Computer Vision and Pattern Recognition, pp. 2174–2182 (2017)

62. Yang, X., Jia, X., Gong, D., Yan, D.-M., Li, Z., Liu, W.: LARNet: lie algebra residual network for face recognition. In: International Conference on Machine Learning, pp. 11738–11750. PMLR (2021)
63. Yao, Z., Gholami, A., Xu, P., Keutzer, K., Mahoney, M.W.: Trust region based adversarial attack on neural networks. In: Conference on Computer Vision and Pattern Recognition (2019)
64. Zhang, H., Yu, Y., Jiao, J., Xing, E.P., El Ghaoui, L., Jordan, M.I.: Theoretically principled trade-off between robustness and accuracy. In: International Conference on Machine Learning (2019)
65. Zhao, P., Chen, P.-Y., Wang, S., Lin, X.: Towards query-efficient black-box adversary with zeroth-order natural gradient descent. In: AAAI Conference on Artificial Intelligence (2020)

Data-Free Backdoor Removal Based on Channel Lipschitzness

Runkai Zheng[1], Rongjun Tang[2], Jianze Li[3], and Li Liu[3(✉)]

[1] School of Data Science, The Chinese University of Hong Kong,
Shenzhen, Guangdong, China
[2] School of Science and Engineering, The Chinese University of Hong Kong,
Shenzhen, Guangdong, China
[3] Shenzhen Research Institute of Big Data, The Chinese University of Hong Kong,
Shenzhen, Guangdong, China
liuli@cuhk.edu.cn

Abstract. Recent studies have shown that Deep Neural Networks (DNNs) are vulnerable to the backdoor attacks, which leads to malicious behaviors of DNNs when specific triggers are attached to the input images. It was further demonstrated that the infected DNNs possess a collection of channels, which are more sensitive to the backdoor triggers compared with normal channels. Pruning these channels was then shown to be effective in mitigating the backdoor behaviors. To locate those channels, it is natural to consider their Lipschitzness, which measures their sensitivity against worst-case perturbations on the inputs. In this work, we introduce a novel concept called Channel Lipschitz Constant (CLC), which is defined as the Lipschitz constant of the mapping from the input images to the output of each channel. Then we provide empirical evidences to show the strong correlation between an Upper bound of the CLC (UCLC) and the trigger-activated change on the channel activation. Since UCLC can be directly calculated from the weight matrices, we can detect the potential backdoor channels in a data-free manner, and do simple pruning on the infected DNN to repair the model. The proposed Channel Lipschitzness based Pruning (CLP) method is super fast, simple, data-free and robust to the choice of the pruning threshold. Extensive experiments are conducted to evaluate the efficiency and effectiveness of CLP, which achieves state-of-the-art results among the mainstream defense methods even without any data. Source codes are available at https://github.com/rkteddy/channel-Lipschitzness-based-pruning.

Keywords: Deep neural network · Backdoor defense · Lipschitz constant · Model pruning

1 Introduction

In recent years, Deep Neural Networks (DNNs) have achieved significantly advanced performance in a wide range of fields, and have been further applied

---

R. Zheng and R. Tang—Equal Contribution.

S. Avidan et al. (Eds.): ECCV 2022, LNCS 13665, pp. 175–191, 2022.
https://doi.org/10.1007/978-3-031-20065-6_11

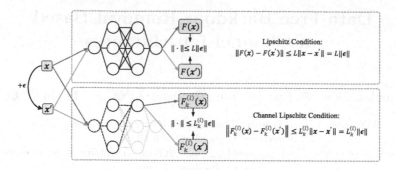

Fig. 1. An illustration of the differences between the commonly studied Lipschitz condition and the proposed channel Lipschitz condition. We highlight the differences in the formula with red color. In a nutshell, Lipschitz constant bounds the largest changing rate of the whole network function, while channel Lipschitz constant bounds that of a specific output channel. (Color figure online)

to industrial practices, including some security-critical fields, $e.g.$, audio-visual processing [26] and medical image processing [6]. Accordingly, the model security problems have gained much attention from the community.

One of the well-known model security problems of DNN is the adversarial attack [2,29,37], which has been extensively studied. The main idea is to add imperceptible perturbation into a well-classified sample to mislead the model prediction during the testing phase. Recently, backdoor attacks [12] remarkably show severe threats to model security due to its well-designed attack mechanism, especially under high safety-required settings. Different from adversarial attacks, backdoor attacks modify the models by a carefully designed strategy during the model training process. For example, the attackers may inject a small proportion of malicious training samples with trigger patterns before training. In this way, DNN can be manipulated to have designated responses to inputs with specific triggers, while acting normally on benign samples [12].

Backdoor attacks may happen in different stages of the model adopting pipeline [23]. For example, when the victims try to train a DNN model on a suspicious third-party dataset, the implanted poisoned backdoor data perform the backdoor attack silently. The defender under such scenario thus has full access to the training process and the whole training data. Besides, backdoor attack happens with a greater frequency when the training process is uncontrollable by the victim, such as adopting third-party models or training on a third-party platform. Under such setting, the defender is only given a pre-trained infected model and usually a small set of benign data as an additional auxiliary to help to mitigate the backdoored model.

To better understand the mechanism of backdoor attacks, in this work, we revisit the common characteristics of backdoor attacks, $i.e.$, the ability of a small trigger to flip the outputs of benign inputs into the malicious target label. It is natural to relate such sensitivity to the high Lipschitz constant of the model.

However, it may be a too strict condition for controlling the Lipschitz constant of the whole network function to achieve backdoor robustness. Since the backdoor vulnerability may come from the sensitivity of the channels to the backdoor trigger, we instead consider evaluating the Lipschitz constant (strictly speaking, an upper bound of the Lipschitz constant) among the channels to identify and prune the sensitive channels.

Specifically, we view the mapping from the input images to each channel output as an independent function, as shown in Fig. 1. The Lipschitz constant is considered for each channel, which measures the sensitivity of the channel to the input. As channels, which detect backdoor triggers, should be sensitive to specific perturbation (*i.e.*, the trigger) on inputs, **we argue that backdoor related channels should have a high Lipschitz constant compared to normal channels**. To demonstrate this, we track the forward propagation process of the same inputs with and without trigger to see how the trigger changes the activation on these channels. We provide empirical evidence to show the strong correlation between the Channel Lipschitz Constant (CLC) and the trigger-activated changes. To be more specific, we show that channels with large activation changes after attaching the trigger usually have high Lipschitz constant. Intuitively, pruning those channels may mitigate the changes brought by the backdoor trigger.

To this end, we propose a novel *Channel Lipschitzness based Pruning* (CLP), which prunes the channels with high Lipschitz constant to recover the model. Since the CLC can be directly derived from the weight matrices of the model, this method requires no access to any training data. Unlike previous methods that are designed for different specific threat models, **CLP's data-free property ensures a high degree of flexibility for its practical application, as long as the model parameters are accessible**. Besides, CLP is super fast and robust to the choice of its only hyperparameter, *i.e.*, the relative pruning threshold u. Finally, we show that CLP can effectively reduce the attack success rate (ASR) against different advanced attacks with only a negligible drop on the clean accuracy.

To summarize, our contributions are twofold:

1. We innovatively reveal the connections between backdoor behaviors and the channels with high Lipschitz constants. This conclusion generalizes various backdoor attacks, shedding light on the development of backdoor defense.
2. Inspired by the above observations, we propose the CLP, a data-free backdoor removal method. Even without data, it achieves state-of-the-art (SOTA) performance among existing defense methods which require a certain amount of benign training data.

2 Related Work

2.1 Backdoor Attack

BadNets [12] is one of the earliest researches that perform backdoor attacks in DNNs. They injected several kinds of image pattern, referred to as the *triggers*, into some samples, and modified the labels of the these samples to the desired malicious label. Then the DNNs were trained with the poisoned dataset and will be implanted a backdoor. After that, more covert and advanced backdoor designs were proposed [28,39,43]. To prevent defenders from reversely generating possible triggers through the model, dynamic backdoor attacks such as the Input-Aware Backdoor (IAB) [31], Warping-based Backdoor (WaNet) [30] and Sample Specific Backdoor Attack (SSBA) [24] were proposed. They generate a unique trigger for every single input, which makes the defense even more difficult. These attacks can be classified as the poisoning based backdoor attacks.

Under some settings, it is also possible for the attackers to directly modify the architectures and parameters of a DNN, without poisoning any training data, known as the *non-poisoning based backdoor attacks*. For example, in Trojan attack [27], the triggers were optimized to increase the activation of some carefully chosen neurons, and then the network was retrained to finish the poisoning. In target bit trojan [33] and ProFlip [4], the authors choose vulnerable neurons and apply bit-flip techniques to perform backdoor attacks. Note that, such bit flip attack only occurs in the deployment phase of DNNs, and the ASR does not exceed other traditional ones. Therefore, this attack will not be discussed in this paper.

2.2   Backdoor Defense

Training Stage Defenses. The *training stage defenses* aim at suppressing the effect of implanted backdoor triggers or filtering out the poisoned data during the training stage, with a full access to the training process. According to the different distributions of poisoned data and clean data in feature space [18], several methods were proposed to filter out the poisoned data, including the robust statistics [13,38], input perturbation techniques [8,10] and semi-supervise training [18]. Besides, stronger data augmentation techniques [3] were proposed to suppress the effect of backdoor, such as the CutMix [7], CutOut [7] and MaxUp [11]. Besides, differential privacy [9] and randomized smoothing [34] provide some certified methods to defend against backdoor attack.

Model Post-processing Defenses. The *model post-processing defenses* mainly focus on eliminating the backdoor threat in a suspicious DNN model. The first effective defense against backdoor attack with the combination of neuron pruning and fine-tuning was proposed in [25]. Inspired by the mechanism of fixed-trigger backdoor attack, Neural Cleanse (NC) [40] obtained the reversed engineering trigger and detoxify the model with such knowledge. Some other fine-tuning based defenses used knowledge distillation [15] in their pipeline, such as the backdoor knowledge distillation [44] and Neural Attention Distillation (NAD) [22]. Besides, the Mode Connectivity Repair [46] was also explored to eliminate the backdoor effect.

In addition to fine-tuning based defenses, the L_{inf}[1] Neuron Pruning was proposed in [42] to filter out the neurons with high L_{inf} in activations. Recently, the Adversarial Neuron Pruning (ANP) [41] detected and pruned sensitive neurons with adversarial perturbations, and achieve considerable defense performance. However, it needs careful tuning of hyperparameters and requires access to a certain number of benign data.

Unlike those model post-processing methods, the proposed CLP achieves superior defending performance without any benign data, and is robust to the choice of the **only** hyperparameter. Moreover, we hope that our work can enlighten the study on the effectiveness of Lipschitz constant on backdoor learning, and provide a new perspective on backdoor attack and defense.

3 Preliminaries

3.1 Notations

In this paper, we consider a classification problem with C classes. Suppose that $\mathcal{D} = \{(x_i, y_i)\}_{i=1}^{N} \subseteq \mathcal{X} \times \mathcal{Y}$ is the original training set, which contains N i.i.d. sample images $x_i \in \mathbb{R}^{d_c \times d_h \times d_w}$ and the corresponding labels $y_i \in \{1, 2, ..., C\}$. Here, we denote by d_c, d_h and d_w the number of output and input channels, the height and the width of the image, respectively. It is clear that $d_c = 3$ for RGB images.

We consider a neural network $F(x; \theta)$ with L layers:

$$F(x; \theta) = f^{(L)} \circ \phi \circ f^{(L-1)} \circ \cdots \circ \phi \circ f^{(1)},$$

where $f^{(l)}$ is the linear function (*e.g.*, convolution) in the lth layer with $1 \leq l \leq L$, ϕ is a non-linear activation function applied element wise. For simplicity, we denote $F(x; \theta)$ as $F(x)$ or F. Let $\mathcal{W}^{(l)} \in \mathbb{R}^{d_{c'}^{(l)} \times d_c^{(l)} \times d_h^{(l)} \times d_w^{(l)}}$ be the weight tensor of the lth convolutional layer, where $d_{c'}^{(l)}, d_c^{(l)}, d_h^{(l)}$ and $d_w^{(l)}$ are the number of output and input channels, the height and the width of the convolutional kernel, respectively. To do pruning, we apply a mask $\mathcal{M}^{(l)} \in \{0, 1\}^{d_{c'}^{(l)} \times d_c^{(l)} \times d_h^{(l)} \times d_w^{(l)}}$ starting with $\mathcal{M}_k^{(l)} = \mathbf{1}_{d_c^{(l)} \times d_h^{(l)} \times d_w^{(l)}}$ in each layer, where $\mathbf{1}_{d_c^{(l)} \times d_h^{(l)} \times d_w^{(l)}}$ denotes an all-one tensor. Pruning neurons on the network refers to getting a collection of indices $\mathcal{I} = \{(l, k)_i\}_{i=1}^{I}$ and setting $\mathcal{M}_k^{(l)} = \mathbf{0}_{d_c^{(l)} \times d_h^{(l)} \times d_w^{(l)}}$ if $(l, k) \in \mathcal{I}$. The pruned network $F_{-\mathcal{I}}$ has the same architecture as F with all the weight matrices of convolutional layers set to $\mathcal{W}^{(l)} \odot \mathcal{M}^{(l)}$, where $\odot$ denotes the Hadamard product [16].

The backdoor poisoning attack involves changing the input images and the corresponding labels[2] on a subset of the original training set $\mathcal{D}_p \subseteq \mathcal{D}$. We denote the poisoning function to the input images by $\delta(x)$. The ratio $\rho = \frac{|\mathcal{D}_p|}{|\mathcal{D}|}$ is defined as the *poisoning rate*.

---

[1] Refers to the infinite norm.

[2] The labels remain unchanged in clean label attacks [39].

3.2 L-Lipschitz Function

A function $g : \mathbb{R}^{n_1} \to \mathbb{R}^{n_2}$ is *L-Lipschitz continuous* [1] in $\mathcal{X} \subseteq \mathbb{R}^{n_1}$ under p-norm, if there exists a non-negative constant $L \geq 0$ such that

$$\|g(\boldsymbol{x}) - g(\boldsymbol{x}')\|_p \leq L\|\boldsymbol{x} - \boldsymbol{x}'\|_p, \quad \forall \boldsymbol{x}, \boldsymbol{x}' \in \mathcal{X}. \tag{1}$$

The smallest L guaranteeing Eq. (1) is called the *Lipschitz constant* of g, denoted by $\|g\|_{\mathrm{Lip}}$. For simplicity, we choose $p = 2$ in this paper. Viewing $\boldsymbol{x}'$ as a perturbation of $\boldsymbol{x}$, the Lipschitz constant $\|g\|_{\mathrm{Lip}}$ can be regarded as the maximum ratio between the resulting perturbation in the output space and the source perturbation in the input space. Thus, it is commonly used for measuring the sensitivity of a function to the input perturbation.

3.3   Lipschitz Constant in Neural Networks

According to the Cauchy-Schwartz inequality, we are now able to control the Lipschitz constant of the whole network as follows:

$$\|F\|_{\mathrm{Lip}} = \|f^{(L)} \circ \phi \circ f^{(L-1)} \circ \cdots \circ \phi \circ f^{(1)}\|_{\mathrm{Lip}}$$
$$\leq \|f^{(L)}\|_{\mathrm{Lip}} \cdot \|\phi\|_{\mathrm{Lip}} \cdot \|f^{(L-1)}\|_{\mathrm{Lip}} \cdots \|\phi\|_{\mathrm{Lip}} \cdot \|f^{(1)}\|_{\mathrm{Lip}}. \tag{2}$$

Most of the commonly used activation functions are L-Lipschitz (*e.g.*, ReLU, LeakyReLU, Sigmoid, Tanh, ELU, SeLU). In particular, we have $L = 1$ for the ReLU function, which is used in this paper. Note that $f^{(l)}(\boldsymbol{x}^{(l)}) = \boldsymbol{W}^{(l)}\boldsymbol{x}^{(l)} + \boldsymbol{b}^{(l)}$. It follows that

$$\|F\|_{\mathrm{Lip}} \leq \prod_{l=1}^{L} \|f^{(l)}\|_{\mathrm{Lip}} = \prod_{l=1}^{L} \max_{\|z\|_2 \neq 0} \frac{\|\boldsymbol{W}^{(l)}\boldsymbol{z}\|_2}{\|\boldsymbol{z}\|_2} = \prod_{l=1}^{L} \sigma(\boldsymbol{W}^{(l)}), \tag{3}$$

where $\sigma(\boldsymbol{W}^{(l)}) = \max_{\|z\|_2 \neq 0} \frac{\|\boldsymbol{W}^{(l)}\boldsymbol{z}\|_2}{\|\boldsymbol{z}\|_2}$ is the spectral norm.

4   Methodology

4.1   Channel Lipschitz Constant

We denote the function from the input to the kth channel of lth layer by:

$$F_k^{(l)} = f_k^{(l)} \circ \phi \circ f^{(l-1)} \cdots \circ \phi \circ f^{(1)},$$

where $f_k^{(l)}$ is the kth output channel function of the lth layer. In particular, if

$$f^{(l)}(\boldsymbol{x}) = \boldsymbol{W}^{(l)}\boldsymbol{x} + \boldsymbol{b}^{(l)}, \quad \boldsymbol{W}^{(l)} \in \mathbb{R}^{d_{\mathrm{out}}^{(l)} \times d_{\mathrm{in}}^{(l)}},$$

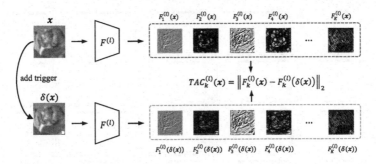

Fig. 2. A simple diagram for calculating TAC in the lth layer. As illustrated, the word TAC stands for the activation differences of the feature maps before and after attaching the trigger to the images, and k is the number of feature maps.

then $f_k^{(l)}(x) = w_k^{(l)}x + b_k^{(l)}$, where $w_k^{(l)} \in \mathbb{R}^{1 \times d_{in}^{(l)}}$ is the kth row of $W^{(l)}$. It follows that the *channel Lipschitz constant* (CLC) satisfies

$$\|F_k^{(l)}\|_{\text{Lip}} \leq \|w_k^{(l)}\|_{\text{Lip}} \prod_{i=1}^{l-1} \sigma(W^{(i)}).$$

We refer to the right side of the above inequality as an *Upper bound* of the Channel Lipschitz Constant (UCLC).

Particularly, convolution is a special linear transformation, with the weight matrix $W^{(l)}$ being a doubly block-Toeplitz (DBT) form of the weight tensor $\mathcal{W}^{(l)}$. To calculate the exact spectral norm of a convolution operation, one should first convert the weight tensor into a DBT weight matrix. However, calculating the DBT matrix is time-consuming and memory-expensive, especially when the number of channels is large. A much simpler alternative way for this is to reshape the weight tensor into a matrix form and use the spectral norm of the reshaped matrix as an approximation to the original spectral norm. This approximation has been adopted by previous researches [45]. In our work, for simplicity, we calculate the spectral norm using the reshaped kernel matrix $W_k^{(l)} \in \mathbb{R}^{d_c^{(l)} \times (d_h^{(l)} d_w^{(l)})}$, which also shows acceptable results in our experiments.

4.2 Trigger-Activated Change

In order to study the extent to which these channels are related to the backdoor behaviors, we define the *Trigger-activated Change* (TAC). Specifically, we first train a ResNet-18 with BadNets in CIFAR-10, and track the forward propagation process of the same inputs with and without trigger. TAC is defined as the average differences of the kth channel of the lth layer for test samples x in dataset $\mathcal{D}$:

$$TAC_k^{(l)}(\mathcal{D}) = \frac{1}{|\mathcal{D}|} \sum_{x \in \mathcal{D}} \|F_k^{(l)}(x) - F_k^{(l)}(\delta(x))\|_2,$$

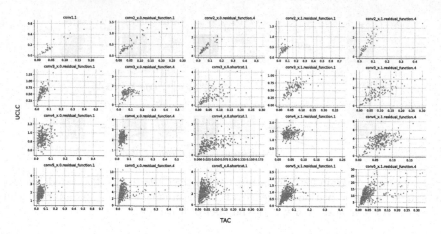

Fig. 3. A scatter plot to demonstrate the relationship between UCLC and TAC. As shown in the figure, we observe a strong correlation between the two indices.

where $\delta(\cdot)$ is the poisoning function. A more detailed illustration of this quantity is shown in Fig. 2. TAC is the change of the activation before and after the input image is attached with a trigger. Its magnitude reflects the effect the trigger has on a given channel. Higher TAC indicate higher sensitivity of the channel to the trigger. Note that TAC is proposed to study the backdoor behavior, but it can not used for defensing. This is because the calculation of TAC requires the access to the trigger pattern, which defenders cannot get in general.

4.3   Correlation Between CLC and TAC

A scatter plot chart of TAC and UCLC for each layer under BadNets (All to One) [12] is shown in Fig. 3, from which we can observe a high correlation between them. In particular, there are some outlying channels with extremely high TAC in some layers, indicating that they are sensitive to the trigger. Hence, it is reasonable to consider them as the potential backdoor channels. As expected, most of these channels have abnormally high UCLC. Remind that TAC is inaccessible for a defender, but UCLC can be directly calculated from the weight matrices of the given model. Hence, we use UCLC as an alternated index to detect potential backdoor channels. We will show that pruning those high-UCLC channels will significantly reduce the backdoor ASR in Sect. 5.

4.4   Special Case in CNN with Batch Normalization

The *Batch Normalization* (BN) [19] is adopted to stabilize the training process and make optimization landscape much smoother in modern neural networks. It normalizes the batch inputs of each channel and adjusts the mean and variance through trainable parameters. BN is usually placed after the convolution and before the non-linear function. Note that BN is also a linear transformation,

---

Algorithm 1: Channel Lipschitzness based Pruning

Input: L layer neural network function $F^{(L)}$ with a set of convolution weight tensor $\{\mathcal{W}^{(l)} : l = 1, 2, \ldots, L\}$, threshold hyperparameter u
Output: A pruned network

1   $\mathcal{I} := \emptyset$
2   **for** $l = 1$ to L **do**
3   **for** $k = 1$ to K **do**
4       $\boldsymbol{W}_k^{(l)} := \text{ReshapeToMatrix}(\mathcal{W}_k^{(l)})$
5       $\sigma_k^{(l)} := \sigma(\boldsymbol{W}_k^{(l)})$
6   **end**
7     $\mu^{(l)} := \frac{1}{K}\sum_{i=1}^{K}\sigma_k^{(l)}$
8     $s^{(l)} := \sqrt{\frac{1}{K}\sum_{i=1}^{K}(\sigma_k^{(l)} - \mu^{(l)})^2}$
9     $\mathcal{I}^{(l)} := \{(l,k) : \sigma_k^{(l)} > \mu^{(l)} + u * s^{(l)}\}$
10    $\mathcal{I} = \mathcal{I} \cup \mathcal{I}^{(l)}$
11 **end**
12 return $F_{-\mathcal{I}}^{(L)}$

---

and can be merged with convolution into a matrix-matrix multiplication. In this paper, we view a Conv-BN block as one linear layer, and an UCLC is calculated based on the composed weight matrix.

4.5 Channel Lipschitzness Based Pruning

Based on the above observations, it is natural to think of removing the high-UCLC channels to recover the model. On this basis, we propose the channel Lipschitzness based pruning (CLP), which calculates UCLC for channels in each layer, and prunes the channels with UCLC larger than a pre-defined threshold within the layer. Note that in the same layer, all channels share the same cumulative product term, which is the Lipschitz upper bound of the previous layers. Hence, a much simplified way to compare CLC within a particular layer is to directly compare $\sigma(\boldsymbol{W}_k^{(l)})$. The overall algorithm procedure is shown in Algorithm Line 12.

Determining an appropriate threshold is crucial to the performance of this method. In this work, we simply set the threshold for the lth layer as $\mu^{(l)} + u * s^{(l)}$, where $\mu^{(l)} = \frac{1}{K}\sum_{i=1}^{K}\sigma(\boldsymbol{W}_k^{(l)})$ and $s^{(l)} = \sqrt{\frac{1}{K}\sum_{i=1}^{K}(\sigma(\boldsymbol{W}_k^{(l)}) - \mu^{(l)})^2}$ are the mean and the standard deviation of the lth layer indices set $\{\sigma(\boldsymbol{W}_k^{(l)}) : k = 1, 2, \ldots K\}$, and u is the only hyperparameter for the CLP. The above threshold is also known as the common outlier dividing line for a standard Gaussian distribution. We find this simple setting works well in our experiments.

5 Experiments

5.1 Experimental Settings

Attack Settings. We test our proposed CLP on a variety of famous attack methods, *i.e.*, BadNets [12], Clean Label Attack [39], Trojan Attack [27], Blended

Backdoor Attack [28], WaNet [30], IAB [31] and Sample Specific Backdoor Attack [24]. The attacks are performed on CIFAR-10 [20] and Tiny ImageNet [21] using ResNet-18 [14]. For BadNets, we test both All-to-All (BadA2A) attack and All-to-One (BadA2O) attack, which means that the attack target labels y_t are set to all labels by $y_t = (y + 1)\%C$ (% denotes modulo operation) or one particular label $y_t = C_t$. Due to the image size requirement of the SSBA, its corresponding experiments are only conducted on Tiny ImageNet. We use $\sim 95\%$ of the training data to train the backdoored model. The rest 5% are split into 4% of validation data, and 1% of benign training data to perform other defenses. The trigger size is 3×3 for CIFAR-10 and 5×5 for Tiny ImageNet. The poison label is set to the 0th class, and the poisoning rate is set to 10% by default. We use SGD [35] as the base optimizer, and train the backdoored model with learning rate 0.1, momentum 0.9 and batch size 128 for 150 epochs on CIFAR-10, batch size 64 for 100 epochs on Tiny ImageNet. We use cosine scheduler to adjust the learning rate. All the experiments are conducted on Pytorch [32] framework.

Defense Settings. We compare our approaches with the commonly used model repairing methods, *i.e.*, FT, FP [25], NAD [22] and the SOTA neuron pruning strategy ANP [41]. All defense methods are allowed to access 1% of the benign training data. Note that **no data** are used in CLP. The fine-tuning based methods default the training process with batch size 128 and learning rate 0.005 for 20 epochs. We adjust the hyperparameters including pruning ratio in fine-pruning [25], attentional weight in NAD [22], and pruning threshold in ANP [41] to obtain their best performance instructed by their original papers. The CLP hyperparameter u is default to be 3 on CIFAR-10 and 5 on Tiny ImageNet. Further study on the effect of the hyperparameter is conducted in Sect. 5.3.

Evaluation Metric. The evaluation of the model includes the performance on benign data, Accuracy on Clean data (ACC) and the performance on the backdoored data, which we call the attack success rate (ASR). Note that the ASR is the ratio for poisoned samples that are **misclassified** as the target label, and it is calculated using the backdoored samples whose ground-truth labels do not belong to the target attack class. In a nutshell, a successful defense should achieve low ASR without much degradation on the ACC.

5.2   Experimental Results

In this section, we verify the effectiveness of CLP and compare its performance with other 4 existing model repairing methods as shown in Table 1 and Table 2. Table 1 shows the experimental results on CIFAR-10, and the proposed CLP remarkably achieves almost the highest robustness against several advanced backdoor attacks. To be specific, the proposed CLP successfully cut the average ASR down to 2.81% with only a slight drop on the ACC (0.67% on average). Note that CLP reaches such incredible result with no data requirement, and the

Table 1. Performance evaluation of the proposed CLP without data and 4 other defense methods with 500 benign data against seven mainstream attacks on CIFAR-10 with ResNet-18. Higher ACC and Lower ASR are preferable, and the best results are boldfaced. ↓ denotes the drop rate on average.

Trigger type	Attacks	Backdoored		FT		FP [25]		NAD [22]		ANP [41]		CLP(ours)	
		ACC	ASR	ACC	ASR	ACC	ASR	ACC	ASR	ACC	ASR	ACC	ASR
Static	BadA2O [12]	93.86	100.00	92.22	2.16	92.18	2.97	91.67	5.40	91.67	5.40	**93.46**	**1.38**
	BadA2A	94.60	93.89	92.03	60.76	91.75	66.82	92.86	1.33	90.29	86.22	**93.69**	**1.06**
	Trojan [27]	94.06	100.00	92.58	99.99	90.78	86.43	92.13	5.76	93.44	8.11	**93.54**	**2.06**
	CLA [39]	93.14	100.00	91.86	0.39	91.02	93.21	**92.46**	**0.44**	91.13	11.76	91.89	2.84
	Blended [5]	94.17	99.62	93.90	70.27	90.92	3.24	92.72	**1.61**	93.66	5.03	**94.07**	1.90
Dynamic	IAB [31]	93.87	97.91	91.78	**9.52**	87.04	21.33	93.52	10.61	**93.52**	10.61	92.78	9.88
	WaNet [30]	94.50	99.67	92.93	9.37	92.07	1.03	94.12	0.51	**94.12**	**0.51**	94.06	0.56
	Average	94.03	98.72	92.47	36.07	90.82	39.29	92.78	4.30	92.54	18.23	**93.36**	**2.81**
	Drop	↓ 0.00	↓ 0.00	↓ 1.56	↓ 62.66	↓ 3.21	↓ 59.43	↓ 1.25	↓ 94.42	↓ 1.49	↓ 80.49	↓ **0.67**	↓ **95.91**

Table 2. Performance evaluation of the proposed CLP without data and 4 other defense methods with 1,000 benign data against seven mainstream attacks on Tiny ImageNet with ResNet-18. Higher ACC and Lower ASR are preferable, and the best results are boldfaced. ↓ denotes the drop rate on average.

Trigger type	Attacks	Backdoored		FT		FP [25]		NAD [22]		ANP [41]		CLP(ours)	
		ACC	ASR	ACC	ASR	ACC	ASR	ACC	ASR	ACC	ASR	ACC	ASR
Static	BadA2O [12]	62.99	99.89	56.97	99.26	57.43	57.42	61.63	0.85	**63.05**	3.93	62.94	**0.61**
	Trojan [27]	64.09	99.99	62.85	3.45	60.43	99.59	61.12	95.05	62.68	10.43	**63.86**	**0.77**
	CLA [39]	64.94	84.74	53.59	27.32	61.18	82.72	59.75	30.65	60.98	15.69	**64.71**	**0.41**
	Blended [5]	63.30	99.70	59.98	1.02	59.84	62.17	61.94	11.55	62.49	0.61	**63.12**	**0.74**
Dynamic	IAB [31]	**61.40**	98.28	58.35	89.89	57.03	**0.21**	58.17	68.43	61.39	4.67	59.09	8.70
	WaNet [30]	60.76	99.92	57.96	97.45	53.86	23.70	56.42	87.79	54.82	86.98	**59.52**	**1.57**
	SSBA [24]	66.51	99.78	62.66	73.11	62.89	4.68	60.13	24.68	60.98	1.01	**63.49**	**0.42**
	Average	63.43	97.47	58.91	55.93	58.95	47.21	59.88	62.13	60.91	17.62	**62.39**	**1.89**
	Drop	↓ 0.00	↓ 0.00	↓ 4.52	↓ 41.54	↓ 4.48	↓ 50.26	↓ 6.76	↓ 45.57	↓ 2.52	↓ 79.85	↓ **1.04**	↓ **95.58**

SOTA defenses ANP and NAD give a similar performance on the ASR with a larger trade-off on the ACC under the access to benign data.

The standard fine-tuning provides promising defense results against several attacks, especially BadNets (A2O), but fails to generalize to more complex attacks such as Trojan, BadNets (A2A) and blended attack. NAD repairs the backdoored model based on knowledge distillation with supporting information from the attention map of a fine-tuned model. Though it achieves relatively good defense performance, it requires carefully tuning of the hyperparameters.

As for the other pruning based methods, fine-pruning adds an extra neuron pruning step according to the neuron activation to benign images before fine-tuning the model, and achieves the best defense performance against CLA. However, it also fails to maintain high robustness against some more covert attacks. ANP utilizes an adversarial strategy to find and prune the neurons that are sensitive to perturbations, which are considered to be highly backdoor related. While both ANP and CLP leverage the concept of sensitivity on channels, ANP measures the sensitivity of the model output to the perturbation on the channels as the pruning index, which requires additional data and careful hyperparameter tuning for different attacks. Unlike ANP, our CLP prunes channels based on the sensitivity of the channels to the inputs, which comes closer to the essence of backdoor attack and can be directly induced by the properties of the model weights without any data. We find both strategy works well on CIFAR-10 against various attacks, but on average, CLP performs better.

Table 2 shows more experimental results on Tiny ImageNet. All the compared defense methods suffer from severe degradation on both the ACC and the ASR when confront a larger-scale dataset. On the contrast, our CLP still maintains its robustness against those different attacks, including SOTA sample specific attacks IAB and SSBA, which further suggests the strong correlation between channel Lipschitzness and the backdoor behaviors.

5.3   Ablation Studies

Performance with Different Choices of Hyperparameter u. As mentioned in Sect. 4.5, the CLP hyperparameter u controls the trade-off between test accuracy on clean data and robust against backdoor attack. Figure 4 shows the ACC and the ASR of the backdoored model after applying CLP with different hyperparameter u. From the fact that ASR drops rapidly to near 0% while ACC drops much later as u decreases, we argue that the backdoor related channels usually possess higher UCLC than normal channels, which will be pruned precisely by the CLP. Generally speaking, we can regard the interval between the two points when ASR drops to a very low level and ACC starts to drop as an index of the robustness with hyperparameter. For example, it is much easier to choose the hyperparameter u to defend against Blended attack [5] because choosing $u \in [3, 5]$ will not affect that much on the performance. CLA has the smallest gap, and it requires a more carefully chosen hyperparameter. A possible reason is that the UCLC in the CLA attacked model is not that high compared with other attacked models. Nevertheless, setting $u = 3$ still has an acceptable performance on CLA. Note that when u decreases near to 0, nearly all the channels in the model are pruned, so the prediction of the model can be illogical. That's why the ASR curves in some attacks rapidly increase to 100% when u decreases to 0.

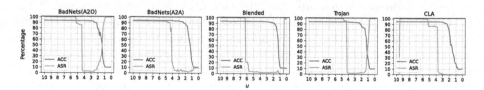

Fig. 4. Performance of the CLP with different hyperparameter against different attacks on CIFAR-10 with ResNet-18.

Performance on Different Architectures. To verify the generalization performance of CLP across different architectures, we perform BadNets attack on CIFAR-10 with the commonly used CNN architectures ResNet [14], VGG [36] and SENet [17] of different depths. Then we plot the ACC and the ASR curves $w.r.t$ to the hyperparameter u. This is shown in Fig. 5. Overall, CLP achieves very good results on all the tested CNN architectures. Nevertheless, the optimal u for different architectures are different. For example, the optimal choice of u in VGG-16 is about 9. However, such choice of u will not work on other architectures. In addition, we find that both VGG architectures and SENet architectures show better robustness to the choice of hyperparameter than ResNet architectures. In general, choosing u between 3 and 4 generalizes well on different architectures.

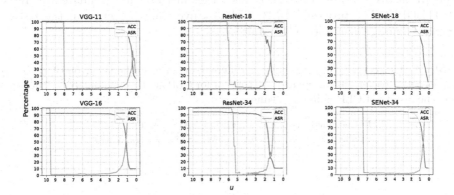

Fig. 5. Performance of the CLP with different hyperparameter u in variant CNN architectures against BadNets on CIFAR-10.

Table 3. Performance of the CLP against typical backdoor attacks with different poisoning rate on CIFAR-10 with ResNet-18.

Poisoning rate	Model	BadNets (A2O)		BadNets (A2A)		Trojan [27]		CLA [39]		Blended [5]	
		ACC	ASR	ACC	ASR	ACC	ASR	ACC	ASR	ACC	ASR
1%	Backdoored	93.86	100.00	94.60	93.47	94.06	100.00	93.14	100.00	94.17	100.00
	CLP Pruned	93.46	1.38	93.69	1.06	93.54	0.92	91.89	2.84	94.07	1.90
5%	Backdoored	94.29	100.00	94.21	92.57	94.48	100.00	94.46	99.86	94.33	100.00
	CLP Pruned	92.33	6.42	93.93	0.76	93.84	5.56	90.71	5.96	93.37	2.34
10%	Backdoored	95.03	100.00	94.75	90.77	94.79	100.00	94.99	98.83	94.60	83.63
	CLP Pruned	94.21	2.76	94.03	0.74	93.17	3.32	93.67	10.04	93.23	0.83

Performance Under Different Poisoning Rates. The different choice of poisoning rate also affects the defense performance. To study the robustness of the proposed CLP, we try different poisoning rate of different backdoor attacks with the hyperparameter unchanged ($u = 3$ on CIFAR-10 by default). As shown in Table 3, CLP effectively reduces the ASR and maintains high ACC under different settings. We note that decreasing the poisoning rate of CLA leads to increasing ASR after applying CLP. CLA with poisoning rate set to 1% gives the worse defense results, and the ASR is about 10%. However, such ASR doesn't give a considerable threat to our models. Overall, we find poisoning rate doesn't affect much on the performance of CLP.

Running Time Comparison. We record the running time of the above-mentioned defense methods on 500 CIFAR-10 images with ResNet-18, and show the results in Table 4. The proposed CLP is the only one, which do not require data propagation, so CPU is enough to apply CLP, and we only record the CPU time (i7-5930K CPU @ 3.50 GHz). The other methods are evaluated on RTX 2080Ti GPU. The proposed CLP is almost five times faster than the fastest methods among them and only requires 2.87 s.

Table 4. The overall running time of different defense methods on 500 CIFAR-10 images with ResNet-18. All the methods except for CLP are training on GPU. * denotes that the results of CLP is in CPU time.

Defense methods	FT	FP	NAD	ANP	CLP*
Runing time (sec.)	12.35 s	14.59 s	25.68 s	22.08 s	**2.87 s**

6   Conclusions

In this paper, we reveal the connection between the Lipschitzness and the backdoor behaviors of the channels in an infected DNN. On this basis, we calculate an upper bound of the channel Lipschitz constant (UCLC) for each channel, and prune the channels with abnormally high UCLC to recover the model, which we refer to as the Channel Lipschitzness based Pruning (CLP). Due to the fact that UCLC can be directly induced by the model weights, our CLP does not require any data and runs super fast. To the best of our knowledge, CLP is the first productive data-free backdoor defense method. Extensive experiments show that the proposed CLP can efficiently and effectively remove the injected backdoor while maintaining high ACC against various SOTA attacks. Finally, ablation studies show that CLP is robust to the **only** hyperparameter u, and generalizes well to different CNN architectures. Our work further shows the effectiveness of channel pruning in defense of backdoor attacks. More importantly, it sheds light on the relationship between the sensitive nature of backdoor and the channel Lipschitz constant, which may help to explain the backdoor behaviors in neural networks.

Acknowledgement. This work was supported in part by the National Natural Science Foundation of China (No. 62101351), the GuangDong Basic and Applied Basic Research Foundation (No. 2020A1515110376), and the Shenzhen Outstanding Scientific and Technological Innovation Talents PhD Startup Project (No. RCBS20210609104447108).

References

1. Armijo, L.: Minimization of functions having lipschitz continuous first partial derivatives. Pac. J. Math. **16**(1), 1–3 (1966)
2. Biggio, B., Nelson, B., Laskov, P.: Support vector machines under adversarial label noise. In: Asian Conference on Machine Learning, pp. 97–112. PMLR (2011)
3. Borgnia, E., et al.: Strong data augmentation sanitizes poisoning and backdoor attacks without an accuracy tradeoff. In: ICASSP 2021–2021 IEEE International Conference on Acoustics, Speech and Signal Processing (ICASSP), pp. 3855–3859. IEEE (2021)
4. Chen, H., Fu, C., Zhao, J., Koushanfar, F.: Proflip: targeted trojan attack with progressive bit flips. In: Proceedings of the IEEE/CVF International Conference on Computer Vision, pp. 7718–7727 (2021)
5. Chen, X., Liu, C., Li, B., Lu, K., Song, D.: Targeted backdoor attacks on deep learning systems using data poisoning. arXiv preprint arXiv:1712.05526 (2017)
6. Chen, Y., et al.: USCL: pretraining deep ultrasound image diagnosis model through video contrastive representation learning. In: de Bruijne, M., Cattin, P.C., Cotin, S., Padoy, N., Speidel, S., Zheng, Y., Essert, C. (eds.) MICCAI 2021. LNCS, vol. 12908, pp. 627–637. Springer, Cham (2021). https://doi.org/10.1007/978-3-030-87237-3_60
7. DeVries, T., Taylor, G.W.: Improved regularization of convolutional neural networks with cutout. arXiv preprint arXiv:1708.04552 (2017)
8. Doan, B.G., Abbasnejad, E., Ranasinghe, D.C.: Februus: input purification defense against trojan attacks on deep neural network systems. In: Annual Computer Security Applications Conference, pp. 897–912 (2020)
9. Du, M., Jia, R., Song, D.: Robust anomaly detection and backdoor attack detection via differential privacy. In: International Conference on Learning Representations (2019)
10. Gao, Y., et al.: Strip: a defence against trojan attacks on deep neural networks. In: Proceedings of the 35th Annual Computer Security Applications Conference, pp. 113–125 (2019)
11. Gong, C., Ren, T., Ye, M., Liu, Q.: Maxup: a simple way to improve generalization of neural network training. arXiv preprint arXiv:2002.09024 (2020)
12. Gu, T., Liu, K., Dolan-Gavitt, B., Garg, S.: Badnets: evaluating backdooring attacks on deep neural networks. IEEE Access **7**, 47230–47244 (2019)
13. Hayase, J., Kong, W., Somani, R., Oh, S.: Spectre: defending against backdoor attacks using robust statistics. In: Meila, M., Zhang, T. (eds.) Proceedings of the 38th International Conference on Machine Learning. Proceedings of Machine Learning Research, 18–24 July 2021, vol. 139, pp. 4129–4139. PMLR (2021). https://proceedings.mlr.press/v139/hayase21a.html
14. He, K., Zhang, X., Ren, S., Sun, J.: Deep residual learning for image recognition. In: Proceedings of the IEEE Conference on Computer Vision and Pattern Recognition, pp. 770–778 (2016)
15. Hinton, G., Vinyals, O., Dean, J.: Distilling the knowledge in a neural network. arXiv preprint arXiv:1503.02531 (2015)
16. Horn, R.A., Johnson, C.R.: Matrix Analysis. Cambridge University Press, Cambridge (2012)
17. Hu, J., Shen, L., Sun, G.: Squeeze-and-excitation networks. In: Proceedings of the IEEE Conference on Computer Vision and Pattern Recognition, pp. 7132–7141 (2018)

18. Huang, K., Li, Y., Wu, B., Qin, Z., Ren, K.: Backdoor defense via decoupling the training process. In: International Conference on Learning Representations (2021)
19. Ioffe, S., Szegedy, C.: Batch normalization: accelerating deep network training by reducing internal covariate shift. In: International Conference on Machine Learning, pp. 448–456. PMLR (2015)
20. Krizhevsky, A.: Learning multiple layers of features from tiny images (2009)
21. Le, Y., Yang, X.: Tiny imagenet visual recognition challenge. CS 231N **7**(7), 3 (2015)
22. Li, Y., Lyu, X., Koren, N., Lyu, L., Li, B., Ma, X.: Neural attention distillation: erasing backdoor triggers from deep neural networks. In: International Conference on Learning Representations (2020)
23. Li, Y., Wu, B., Jiang, Y., Li, Z., Xia, S.T.: Backdoor learning: a survey. arXiv preprint arXiv:2007.08745 (2020)
24. Li, Y., Li, Y., Wu, B., Li, L., He, R., Lyu, S.: Invisible backdoor attack with sample-specific triggers. In: Proceedings of the IEEE/CVF International Conference on Computer Vision, pp. 16463–16472 (2021)
25. Liu, K., Dolan-Gavitt, B., Garg, S.: Fine-pruning: defending against backdooring attacks on deep neural networks. In: Bailey, M., Holz, T., Stamatogiannakis, M., Ioannidis, S. (eds.) RAID 2018. LNCS, vol. 11050, pp. 273–294. Springer, Cham (2018). https://doi.org/10.1007/978-3-030-00470-5_13
26. Liu, L., Feng, G., Beautemps, D., Zhang, X.P.: Re-synchronization using the hand preceding model for multi-modal fusion in automatic continuous cued speech recognition. IEEE Trans. Multimedia **23**, 292–305 (2020)
27. Liu, Y., et al.: Trojaning attack on neural networks. In: 25th Annual Network and Distributed System Security Symposium, NDSS 2018, San Diego, California, USA, 18–21 February 2018. The Internet Society (2018). http://wp.internetsociety.org/ndss/wp-content/uploads/sites/25/2018/02/ndss2018_03A-5_Liu_paper.pdf
28. Liu, Y., Ma, X., Bailey, J., Lu, F.: Reflection backdoor: a natural backdoor attack on deep neural networks. In: Vedaldi, A., Bischof, H., Brox, T., Frahm, J.-M. (eds.) ECCV 2020. LNCS, vol. 12355, pp. 182–199. Springer, Cham (2020). https://doi.org/10.1007/978-3-030-58607-2_11
29. Madry, A., Makelov, A., Schmidt, L., Tsipras, D., Vladu, A.: Towards deep learning models resistant to adversarial attacks. In: International Conference on Learning Representations (2018)
30. Nguyen, A., Tran, A.: Wanet-imperceptible warping-based backdoor attack. arXiv preprint arXiv:2102.10369 (2021)
31. Nguyen, T.A., Tran, A.: Input-aware dynamic backdoor attack. Adv. Neural Inf. Process. Syst. **33**, 3454–3464 (2020)
32. Paszke, A., et al.: Pytorch: an imperative style, high-performance deep learning library. In: Wallach, H., Larochelle, H., Beygelzimer, A., dÁlché-Buc, F., Fox, E., Garnett, R. (eds.) Advances in Neural Information Processing Systems, vol. 32, pp. 8024–8035. Curran Associates, Inc. (2019). http://papers.neurips.cc/paper/9015-pytorch-an-imperative-style-high-performance-deep-learning-library.pdf
33. Rakin, A.S., He, Z., Fan, D.: Tbt: targeted neural network attack with bit trojan. In: Proceedings of the IEEE/CVF Conference on Computer Vision and Pattern Recognition, pp. 13198–13207 (2020)
34. Rosenfeld, E., Winston, E., Ravikumar, P., Kolter, Z.: Certified robustness to label-flipping attacks via randomized smoothing. In: International Conference on Machine Learning, pp. 8230–8241. PMLR (2020)
35. Ruder, S.: An overview of gradient descent optimization algorithms. arXiv preprint arXiv:1609.04747 (2016)

36. Simonyan, K., Zisserman, A.: Very deep convolutional networks for large-scale image recognition. arXiv preprint arXiv:1409.1556 (2014)
37. Tramèr, F., Boneh, D., Kurakin, A., Goodfellow, I., Papernot, N., McDaniel, P.: Ensemble adversarial training: attacks and defenses. In: 6th International Conference on Learning Representations, ICLR 2018-Conference Track Proceedings (2018)
38. Tran, B., Li, J., Madry, A.: Spectral signatures in backdoor attacks. In: Proceedings of the 32nd International Conference on Neural Information Processing Systems, pp. 8011–8021 (2018)
39. Turner, A., Tsipras, D., Madry, A.: Label-consistent backdoor attacks. arXiv preprint arXiv:1912.02771 (2019)
40. Wang, B., et al.: Neural cleanse: Identifying and mitigating backdoor attacks in neural networks. In: 2019 IEEE Symposium on Security and Privacy (SP), pp. 707–723. IEEE (2019)
41. Wu, D., Wang, Y.: Adversarial neuron pruning purifies backdoored deep models. Adv. Neural Inf. Process. Syst. **34** (2021)
42. Xu, K., Liu, S., Chen, P.Y., Zhao, P., Lin, X.: Defending against backdoor attack on deep neural networks. arXiv preprint arXiv:2002.12162 (2020)
43. Xue, M., He, C., Wang, J., Liu, W.: One-to-n & n-to-one: two advanced backdoor attacks against deep learning models. IEEE Trans. Depend. Secure Comput. (2020)
44. Yoshida, K., Fujino, T.: Disabling backdoor and identifying poison data by using knowledge distillation in backdoor attacks on deep neural networks. In: Proceedings of the 13th ACM Workshop on Artificial Intelligence and Security, pp. 117–127 (2020)
45. Yoshida, Y., Miyato, T.: Spectral norm regularization for improving the generalizability of deep learning. arXiv preprint arXiv:1705.10941 (2017)
46. Zhao, P., Chen, P.Y., Das, P., Ramamurthy, K.N., Lin, X.: Bridging mode connectivity in loss landscapes and adversarial robustness. In: International Conference on Learning Representations (2019)

Black-Box Dissector: Towards Erasing-Based Hard-Label Model Stealing Attack

Yixu Wang[1], Jie Li[1], Hong Liu[2], Yan Wang[3], Yongjian Wu[4], Feiyue Huang[4], and Rongrong Ji[1,5(✉)]

[1] Media Analytics and Computing Lab, School of Informatics, Xiamen University, Xiamen, China
`rrji@xmu.edu.cn`
[2] National Institute of Informatics, Tokyo, Japan
`hliu@nii.ac.jp`
[3] Pinterest, San Francisco, USA
`yanw@pinterest.com`
[4] Youtu Lab, Tencent Technology (Shanghai) Co., Ltd., Shanghai, China
`{littlekenwu,garyhuang}@tencent.com`
[5] Institute of Artificial Intelligence, Xiamen University, Xiamen, China

Abstract. Previous studies have verified that the functionality of black-box models can be stolen with full probability outputs. However, under the more practical hard-label setting, we observe that existing methods suffer from catastrophic performance degradation. We argue this is due to the lack of rich information in the probability prediction and the overfitting caused by hard labels. To this end, we propose a novel hard-label model stealing method termed *black-box dissector*, which consists of two erasing-based modules. One is a CAM-driven erasing strategy that is designed to increase the information capacity hidden in hard labels from the victim model. The other is a random-erasing-based self-knowledge distillation module that utilizes soft labels from the substitute model to mitigate overfitting. Extensive experiments on four widely-used datasets consistently demonstrate that our method outperforms state-of-the-art methods, with an improvement of at most 8.27%. We also validate the effectiveness and practical potential of our method on real-world APIs and defense methods. Furthermore, our method promotes other related tasks, *i.e.*, transfer adversarial attacks.

Keywords: Model stealing attack · Adversarial attack

1 Introduction

Machine learning models deployed on the cloud can serve users through the application program interfaces (APIs) to improve productivity. Since developing

Supplementary Information The online version contains supplementary material available at https://doi.org/10.1007/978-3-031-20065-6_12.

S. Avidan et al. (Eds.): ECCV 2022, LNCS 13665, pp. 192–208, 2022.
https://doi.org/10.1007/978-3-031-20065-6_12

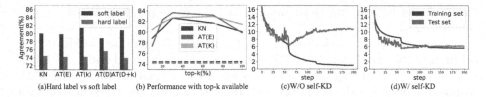

(a)Hard label vs soft label   (b) Performance with top-k available   (c)W/O self-KD   (d)W/ self-KD

Fig. 1. (a) The test accuracies of previous methods with hard labels are much lower than the ones with soft labels. (KN: KnockoffNets, 'AT': ActiveThief, 'E': entropy, 'K': k-Center, 'D': DFAL) (b) The performance decreases as the number of available classes decreases (dotted line : hard-label setting). (c) & (d) Loss curves for training/test set during model training without and with self-KD. All results are on the CIFAR10 dataset.

these cloud models is a product of intensive labor and monetary effort, these models are valuable intellectual property and AI companies try to keep them private [16,21,24,33]. However, the exposure of the model's predictions represents a significant risk as an adversary can leverage this information to steal the model's functionality, *a.k.a.* model stealing attack [8,23,25,26,35]. With such an attack, adversaries are able to not only use the stolen model to make a profit, but also mount further adversarial attacks [34,40]. Besides, the model stealing attacks is a kind of black-box knowledge distillation which is a hot research topic. Studying various mechanisms of model stealing attack is of great interest both to AI companies and researchers.

Previous methods [8,23,25,40] mainly assume the complete probability predictions of the victim model available, while the real-world APIs usually only return partial probability values (top-k predictions) or even the top-1 prediction (*i.e.*, hard label). In this paper, we focus on the more challenging and realistic scenario, *i.e.*, the victim model only outputs the hard labels. However, under this setting, existing methods suffer from a significant performance degradation, even by 30.50% (as shown in the Fig. 1(a) and the appendix Tab. I).

To investigate the reason for the degradation, we evaluate the performance of attack methods with different numbers of prediction probability categories available and hard labels as in Fig. 1(b). With the observation that the performance degrades when the top-k information missing, we conclude that the top-k predictions are informative as it indicates the similarity of different categories or multiple objects in the picture, and previous attack methods suffer from such information obscured by the top-1 prediction under the hard-label setting. It motivates us to re-mine this information by eliminating the top-1 prediction. Particularly, we design *a novel CAM-based erasing method*, which erases the important area on the pictures based on the substitute model's top-1 class activation maps (CAM) [28,39] and queries the victim model for a new prediction. Note that we can dig out other class information in this sample if the new prediction changes. Otherwise, it proves that the substitute model pays attention to the wrong area. Then we can align the attention of the substitute and the victim model by learning clean samples and the corresponding erased samples simultaneously.

Besides, previous works on the self-Knowledge Distillation (self-KD) [17], calibration [10], and noisy label [37] have pointed out the hard and noisy labels will introduce overfitting and miscalibration. More specifically, the attack algorithms cannot access the training data, and thus can only use the synthetic data or other datasets as a substitute, which is noisy. Therefore, the hard-label setting will suffer from overfitting, which leads to worse performance, and we verify it by plotting the loss curves in Fig. 1(c). To mitigate this problem, we introduce *a simple self-knowledge distillation module with random erasing (RE)* to utilize soft labels for generalization. Particularly, we randomly erase one sample a certain number of times, query the substitute model for soft-label outputs, and take the average value of these outputs as the pseudo-label. After that, we use both hard labels from the victim model and pseudo labels from the previous substitute model to train a new substitute model. Therefore, we can also consider the ensemble of the two models as the teacher in knowledge distillation. As in Fig. 1(d), such a module helps generalization and better performance.

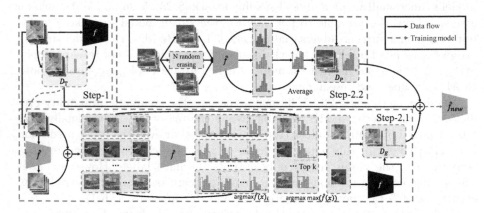

Fig. 2. Details of our proposed black-box dissector with a CAM-driven erasing strategy (step 2.1) and a RE-based self-KD module (step 2.2). In step 2.1, the images in transfer set D_T are erased according to the Grad-CAM, and we selected the erased images with the largest difference from the original images according to the substitute model's outputs. In step 2.2, we randomly erase the unlabeled image N times, and then average the outputs of the N erased images by the substitute model as the pseudo-label.

In summary, we propose a novel model stealing framework termed *black-box dissector*, which includes a CAM-driven erasing strategy and a RE-based self-KD module. Our method is orthogonal to previous approaches [23,25] and can be integrated with them. The experiments on four widely-used datasets demonstrate our method achieves 43.04–90.57% test accuracy (47.60–91.37% agreement) to the victim model, which is at most 8.27% higher than the state of the art method. We also proved that our method can defeat popular defense methods and is effective for real-world APIs like services provided by Amazon Web Services (AWS). Furthermore, our method promotes downstream tasks, *i.e.*, transfer adversarial attack, with 4.91%–16.20% improvement.

2 Background and Notions

Model stealing attack aims to find a substitute model $\hat{f}\colon [0,1]^d \mapsto \mathbb{R}^N$ that performs as similarly as possible to the victim model $f\colon [0,1]^d \mapsto \mathbb{R}^N$ (with only outputs accessed). [26] first observed that online models could be stolen through multiple queries. After that, due to the practical threat to real-world APIs, several studies paid attention to this problem and proposed many attack algorithms.

These algorithms consist of two stages: 1) constructing a transfer dataset D_T (step 1 in Fig. 2) and 2) training a substitute model. The transfer dataset is constructed based on data synthesis or data selection and then feed into the victim model for labels. Methods based on data synthesis [2,15,40] adopt the GAN-based models to generate a virtual dataset. And the substitute model and the GAN model are trained alternatively on this virtual dataset by querying the victim model iteratively. The data selection methods prepare an attack dataset as the data pool, and then sample the most informative data via machine learning algorithms, *e.g.*, reinforcement learning [23] or active learning strategy [25], uncertainty-based strategy [19], k-Center strategy [29], and DFAL strategy [5]. Considering that querying the victim model will be costly, the attacker usually sets a budget on the number of the queries, so the size of the transfer dataset should be limited as well. Previous methods assume the victim model returns a complete probability prediction $f(x)$, which is less practical.

In this paper, we focus on a more practical scenario that is about hard-label $\phi(f(x))$ setting, where ϕ is the truncation function used to truncate the information contained in the victim's output and return the corresponding one-hot vector:

$$\phi(f(x))_i := \begin{cases} 1 & \text{if } i = \arg\max_n f(x)_n\,; \\ 0 & \text{otherwise}\,. \end{cases} \quad (1)$$

With the transfer dataset, the substitute model is optimized by minimizing a loss function $\mathcal{L}$ (*e.g.*, cross-entropy loss function):

$$\begin{cases} \mathbb{E}_{x \sim \mathcal{D}_T}\big[\mathcal{L}\big(f(x), \hat{f}(x)\big)\big], & \text{for soft labels;} \\ \mathbb{E}_{x \sim \mathcal{D}_T}\big[\mathcal{L}\big(\phi(f(x)), \hat{f}(x)\big)\big], & \text{for hard labels.} \end{cases} \quad (2)$$

Knowledge distillation (KD) has been widely studied in machine learning [1,7,12], which transfers the knowledge from a teacher model to a student model. Model stealing attacks can be regarded as a black-box KD problem where the victim model is the *teacher* with only outputs accessible and the substitute model is the *student*. The main reason for the success of KD is the *valuable information that defines a rich similarity structure over the data* in the probability prediction [12]. However, for the hard-label setting discussed in this paper, this valuable information is lost. And the main difference between self-KD and regular-KD is that the latter utilizes knowledge from a larger and better teacher model, while the former uses the model self as the teacher. Self-KD has been shown to help improve the model's generalization ability [17]. Inspired by self-KD, our method tries to dig out the hidden information in the data and models, and then transfers more knowledge to the substitute model.

The erasing-based method, *e.g.*, random erasing (RE) [3,38], is currently one of the widely used data augmentation methods, which generates training images with various levels of occlusion, thereby reducing the risk of over-fitting and improving the robustness of the model. Our work is inspired by RE and designs a prior-driven erasing operation, which erases the area corresponding to the hard label to re-mine missing information.

3   Method

The overview of black-box dissector is shown in Fig. 2. In addition to the conventional process (*i.e.*, the transfer dataset D_T constructing in step 1 and the substitute model training in the right), we introduce two key modules: a CAM-driven erasing strategy (step 2.1) and a RE-based self-KD module (step 2.2).

3.1   A CAM-driven Erasing Strategy

Since the lack of class similarity information degrades the performance of previous methods under the hard-label setting, we try to re-dig out such hidden information. Taking an example from the ILSVRC-2012 dataset for illustration as in Fig. 3. Querying the CUBS200 trained victim model with this image, we get two classes with the highest confidence score: "Anna hummingbird" (0.1364) and "Common yellowthroat" (0.1165), and show their corresponding attention map in the first column of Fig. 3. It is easy to conclude that two different attention regions response for different classes according to the attention map. When training the substitute model with the hard label "Anna hummingbird" and without the class similarity informa-

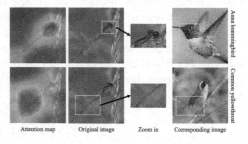

Attention map   Original image   Zoom in   Corresponding image

Fig. 3. An example from the ILSVRC-2012 dataset and its attention map corresponding to two most likely class "Anna humming bird" and "Common yellow throat" on the CUBS200 trained model. The attention areas share similar visual apparent with images of "Anna humming bird" and "Common yellow throat", respectively. (Color figure online)

tion, the model can not learn from the area related to the "Common yellowthroat" class, which means this area is wasted. To re-dig out the information

---

Algorithm 1: Prior-driven Erasing $\psi(I, P)$

Input: Input image I, prior probability P, area of image S, erasing area ratio range s_l and s_h, erasing aspect ratio range r_1 and r_2.

Output: Erased image I'.

1   $S_e \sim \text{Uniform}(s_l, s_h) \times S,\ r_e \sim \text{Uniform}(r_1, r_2)$

2   $H_e \leftarrow \sqrt{S_e \times r_e}/2, W_e \leftarrow \sqrt{\frac{S_e}{r_e}}/2$

3   x_e, y_e sampled randomly according to P

4   $I_e \leftarrow (x_e - W_e, y_e - H_e, x_e + W_e, y_e + H_e)$

5   $I(I_e) \sim \text{Uniform}(0, 255)$

6   $I' \leftarrow I$

---

about the "Common yellowthroat" class, we need to erase the impact of the "Anna hummingbird" class.

To this end, a natural idea is to erase the response area corresponding to the hard label. Since the victim model is a black-box model, we use the substitute model to approximately calculate the attention map instead. If the attention map calculated by the substitute model is inaccurate and the victim model's prediction on the erased image does not change, although we cannot obtain the class information, we can align the attention map of two models by letting the substitute model learn the original image and the erased one simultaneously. The attention maps can be used as sources of additional supervision signal in distillation: encouraging a model's attention map to be similar to that of another model also leads to the models having similar predictions [36]. To get the attention map, we utilize the Grad-CAM [28] in this paper. With the input image $x \in [0, 1]^d$ and the trained DNN $\mathcal{F}: [0, 1]^d \mapsto \mathbb{R}^N$, we let α_k^c denote the weight of class c corresponding to the k-th feature map, and calculate it as $\alpha_k^c = \frac{1}{Z} \sum_i \sum_j \frac{\partial \mathcal{F}(x)^c}{\partial A_{ij}^k}$, where Z is the number of pixels in the feature map, $\mathcal{F}(x)^c$ is the score of class c and A_{ij}^k is the value of pixel at (i, j) in the k-th feature map. After obtaining the weights corresponding to all feature maps, the final attention map can be obtained as $S_{\text{Grad-CAM}}^c = \text{ReLU}(\sum_k \alpha_k^c A^k)$ via the weighted summation.

To erase the corresponding area, inspired by [38], we define a prior-driven erasing operation as $\psi(I, P)$, shown in Algorithm 1, which randomly erases a rectangle region in the image I with random values while the central position of the rectangle region is randomly selected following the prior probability P. The prior probability P is of the same size as the input image and is used to determine the probability of different pixels being erased. Here, we use the attention map from Grad-CAM as the prior. Let $x \in [0, 1]^d$ denote the input image from the transfer set and $S_{\text{Grad-CAM}}^{\arg \max \hat{f}(x)}(x, \hat{f})$ denote the attention map of the substitute model $\hat{f}$. This CAM-driven erasing operation can be represented:

$$\psi\left(x, S_{\text{Grad-CAM}}^{\arg \max \hat{f}(x)}(x, \hat{f})\right). \tag{3}$$

We abbreviate it as $\psi(x, S(x, \hat{f}))$. To alleviate the impact of inaccurate Grad-CAM caused by the difference between the substitute model and the victim one, for each image, we perform this operation N times (ψ_i means the i-th erasing) and select the one with the largest difference from the original label. Such a data augment operation helps the erasing process to be more robust.

We use the cross-entropy to calculate the difference between the new label and the original label, and we want to select the sample with the biggest difference. Formally, we define $\Pi(x)$ as the function to select the most different variation of image x:

$$\Pi(x) := \psi_k(x, S(x, \hat{f})),$$

$$\text{where } k := \underset{i \in [N]}{\arg\max} -\sum_j \phi\left(f\left(x\right)\right)_j \cdot \log\left(\hat{f}\left(\psi_i(x, S(x, \hat{f}))\right)_j\right)$$

$$= \underset{i \in [N]}{\arg\max} -\log\left(\hat{f}\left(\psi_i(x, S(x, \hat{f}))\right)_{\arg\max \phi\left(f(x)\right)}\right) \tag{4}$$

$$= \underset{i \in [N]}{\arg\min} \hat{f}\left(\psi_i(x, S(x, \hat{f}))\right)_{\arg\max \phi\left(f(x)\right)}.$$

Due to the limitation of the number of queries, we cannot query the victim model for each erased image to obtain a new label. We continuously choose the erased image with the highest substitute's confidence until reaching the budget. To measure the confidence of the model, we adopt the Maximum Softmax Probability (MSP) for its simplicity:

$$\underset{x \sim \mathcal{D}_T}{\arg\max} \hat{f}\left(\Pi\left(x\right)\right)_{\arg\max \hat{f}(\Pi(x))}, \tag{5}$$

where $\mathcal{D}_T$ is the transfer set. The erased images selected in this way are most likely to change the prediction class. Then, we query the victim model to get these erased images' labels and construct an erased sample set $\mathcal{D}_E$. Note that the substitute model is trained with $\mathcal{D}_T$ to fit the victim model, so it makes sense to use the substitute model to approximately calculate the Grad-CAM. For each sample, if the approximate calculated Grad-CAM is accurate, it means we have erased the correct area, and we can obtain new class information after querying the victim model. If the Grad-CAM is inaccurate, it means the substitute model has paid attention to the wrong area, and we can align the attention map of two models by letting the substitute model learn the original image and the erased one simultaneously. Therefore, regardless of the accuracy of the area we erased, the erased sample can provide information to help the substitute model better approximate the victim model. We show the effect of our method to align the attention map in Fig. 5.

3.2   A Random-Erasing-Based Self-KD Module

We also find that in training with limited hard-label OOD samples, the substitute model is likely to overfit the training set, which damages its generalization ability [17,37]. Therefore, based on the above erasing operation, we further design

---

Algorithm 2: Black-box Dissector

    Input: Unlabeled pool D_U, victim model f, maximum number of queries Q.
    Output: Substitute model $\hat{f}$.

1 Initialize $q \leftarrow 0, D_T \leftarrow \varnothing, D_E \leftarrow \varnothing$
2 **while** $q < Q$ **do**
3   // **Step 1**
4   Select samples from D_U according to budget and query f to updata D_T
5      $q = q + $ budget
6      $\mathcal{L} = \sum_{x \in D_T} \mathcal{L}'\big(\phi(f(x)), \hat{f}(x)\big)$
7      $\hat{f} \leftarrow update(\hat{f}, \mathcal{L})$
8   // **A CAM-driven erasing strategy (step 2.1)**
9   Erase samples in D_T according to Eq. 4
10   Choose samples from erased samples according to Eq. 5 and budget
11   Query f to get labels and update D_E
12     $\mathcal{L} = \sum_{x \in D_T \cup D_E} \mathcal{L}'\big(\phi(f(x)), \hat{f}(x)\big)$
13     $\hat{f} \leftarrow update(\hat{f}, \mathcal{L})$
14     $q = q + $ budget (Check if $q < Q$)
15   // **A random-erasing-based self-KD (step 2.2)**
16   Select samples from D_U
17   Get pseudo-labels according to Eq. 6 and construct a pseudo-label set D_P
18     $\mathcal{L} = \sum_{x \in D_T \cup D_E} \mathcal{L}'\big(\phi(f(x)), \hat{f}(x)\big) + \sum_{x \in D_P} \mathcal{L}'\big(y_p(x, \hat{f}), \hat{f}(x)\big)$
19     $\hat{f} \leftarrow update(\hat{f}, \mathcal{L})$
20 **end**

---

a simple RE-based self-KD method to improve the generalization ability of the substitute model.

Formally, let $x \in [0, 1]^d$ denote the unlabeled input image. We perform the erasing operation with a uniform prior U on it N times, and then average the substitute's outputs on these erased images as the original image's pseudo-label:

$$y_p(x, \hat{f}) = \frac{1}{N} \sum_{i=1}^{N} \hat{f}\big(\psi_i(x, U)\big). \tag{6}$$

This is a type of consistency regularization, which enforces the model to have the same predictions for the perturbed images and enhances the generalization ability. With Eq. 6, we construct a new soft pseudo label set $D_P = \{(x, y_p(x, \hat{f})), \dots\}$.

With the transfer set D_T, the erased sample set D_E, and the pseudo-label set D_P, we train new substitute model using the ensemble of the victim model and the previous substitute model as the teacher. Our final objective function is:

$$\min \mathcal{L} = \min \Big[\sum_{x \in D_T \cup D_E} \mathcal{L}'\big(\phi(f(x)), \hat{f}(x)\big) + \sum_{x \in D_P} \mathcal{L}'\big(y_p(x, \hat{f}), \hat{f}(x)\big) \Big]. \tag{7}$$

where $\mathcal{L}'$ can be commonly used loss functions, *e.g.*, cross-entropy loss function.

To sum up, we built our method on the conventional process of the model stealing attack (step 1), and proposed a CAM-driven erasing strategy (step 2.1) and a RE-based self-KD module (step 2.2) unified by a novel erasing method. The former strategy digs out missing information between classes and aligns the attention while the latter module helps to mitigate overfitting and enhance the generalization. We name the whole framework as *black-box dissector* and present the algorithm detail of it in Algorithm 2.

4   Experiments

4.1   Experiment Settings

In this subsection, we introduce our experiment settings, including victim model, model architectures, attack dataset and training process.

Victim Model. The victim models we used (ResNet-34 [11]) are trained on four datasets, namely, CIFAR10 [18], SVHN [22], Caltech256 [9], and CUBS200 [32], and their test accuracy are 91.56%, 96.45%, 78.40%, and 77.10%, respectively. All models are trained using the SGD optimizer with momentum (of 0.5) for 200 epochs with a base learning rate of 0.1 decayed by a factor of 0.1 every 30 epochs. In order to create an online deployment scenario, these models are all: image in, one-hot predictions out. Following [23,25,40], we use the same architecture for the substitute model and will analyze the impact of different architectures.

Attack Dataset. We use $1.2M$ images without labels from the ILSVRC-2012 challenge [27] as the attack dataset. In a real attack scenario, the attacker may use pictures collected from the Internet, and the ILSVRC-2012 dataset can simulate this scenario well. Note that we resize all images in the attack dataset to fit the size of the target datasets, which is similar to the existing setting [23,25,40].

Training Process. We use the SGD optimizer with momentum (of 0.9) for 200 epochs and a base learning rate of $0.02 \times \frac{batchsize}{128}$ decayed by a factor of 0.1 every 60 epochs. The weight decay is set to 5×10^{-4} for small datasets (CIFAR10 [18] and SVHN [22]) and 0 for others. We set up a query sequence $\{0.1K, 0.2K, 0.5K, 0.8K, 1K, 2K, 5K, 10K, 20K, 30K\}$ as the iterative maximum query budget, and stop the sampling stage whenever reaching the budget at each iteration. For fairness, all experiments will be conducted in accordance with this sequence. And, the model is trained from scratch for each iteration.

Baselines and Evaluation Metric. We mainly compare our method with KnockoffNets [23] and ActiveThief [25]. For KnockoffNets, we use the source codes provided kindly by the authors. Follow [14], we mainly report the test accuracy (Acc) as the evaluation metric. We also report the *Agreement* metric proposed by [25] which counts how often the prediction of the substitute model is the same as the victim's as a supplement.

Table 1. The agreement and test accuracy (in %) of each method under 30k queries. For our model, we report the average accuracy as well as the standard deviation computed over 5 runs. (**Boldface**: the best value, *italics*: the second best value.)

Method	CIFAR10		SVHN		Caltech256		CUBS200	
	Agreement	Acc.	Agreement	Acc.	Agreement	Acc.	Agreement	Acc.
KnockoffNets	75.32	74.44	85.00	84.50	57.64	55.28	30.01	28.03
ActiveThief(Entropy)	75.26	74.21	90.47	89.85	56.28	54.14	32.05	29.43
ActiveThief(k-Center)	75.71	74.24	81.45	80.79	61.19	58.84	37.68	34.64
ActiveThief(DFAL)	76.72	75.62	84.79	84.17	46.92	44.91	20.31	18.69
ActiveThief(DFAL+k-Center)	74.97	73.98	81.40	80.86	55.70	53.69	26.60	24.42
Ours+Random	**82.14**±0.16	**80.47**±0.02	**92.33**±0.47	**91.57**±0.29	*63.61*±0.53	*61.41*±0.39	*39.07*±0.26	*36.28*±0.44
Ours+k-Center	*80.84*±0.21	*79.27*±0.15	*91.47*±0.09	*90.68*±0.14	**66.34**±0.52	**63.75**±0.49	**48.46**±0.55	**44.43**±0.42

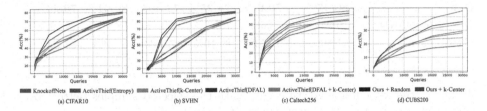

■ KnockoffNets ■ ActiveThief(Entropy) ■ ActiveThief(k-Center) ■ ActiveThief(DFAL) ■ ActiveThief(DFAL + k-Center) ■ Ours + Random ■ Ours + k-Center

(a) CIFAR10   (b) SVHN   (c) Caltech256   (d) CUBS200

Fig. 4. Curves of the test accuracy versus the number of queries.

4.2   Experiment Results

We first report the performance of our method compared with previous methods. Then, we analyze the performance of our method when encountering two SOTA defense methods (*i.e.*, the adaptive misinformation [16] and the prediction poisoning [24]) and real-world online APIs. After that, we conduct ablation experiments to analyze the contribution of each module. Finally, we also analyze the effect of different model structures and demonstrate the transferability of adversarial samples generated on substitute models obtained by different methods.

Effectiveness of our Method. As in Table 1, the test accuracy and agreement of our method are all better than the previous methods. We also plot the curves of the test accuracy versus the number of queries in Fig. 4. The performance of our method consistently outperforms other methods throughout the process. Since our method does not conflict with the previous sample selection strategy, they can be used simultaneously to further improve the performance of these attacks. Here, we take the k-Center algorithm as an example. Note that, with or without the sample selection strategy, our method beats the previous methods by a large margin. Particularly, the test accuracies of our method are 4.85%, 1.72%, 3.88%, and 8.27% higher than the previous best method, respectively. And the agreement metric shares similar results. It is also interesting that it is less necessary to use the k-Center algorithm on datasets with a small number of classes (*i.e.*, CIFAR10 and SVHN). While for the datasets with a large number

Table 2. Ability to evade the state-of-the-art defense methods (adaptive misinformation and prediction poisoning) on CIFAR10 dataset. The larger the threshold, the better the defence effect while the low victim model's accuracy (threshold 0 means no defence). Our method evades the defense best, and the self-KD part makes a great difference.

Method	No defence	Adaptive misinformation			Prediction poisoning	
Threshold	0	0.5	0.7	0.9	0.5	0.8
KnockoffNets	74.44%	74.13%	73.61%	54.98%	71.83%	58.01%
ActiveThief(k-Center)	74.24%	69.14%	59.78%	50.19%	73.75%	60.89%
ActiveThief(Entropy)	74.21%	71.61%	64.84%	51.07%	72.07%	65.83%
Ours	**80.47%**	**79.95%**	**78.25%**	**74.40%**	**80.01%**	**79.23%**
Ours w/o self-KD	79.02%	78.66%	73.61%	61.81%	78.87%	76.49%
Victim model	91.56%	91.23%	89.10%	85.14%	91.56%	89.45%

of classes, the k-Center algorithm can make the selected samples better cover each class and improve the effectiveness of the method.

Ability to Evade the SOTA Defense Method. Here we evaluate two SOTA perturbation-based defense method, the adaptive misinformation [16] and the prediction poisoning [24]. The adaptive misinformation [16] introduces an Out-Of-Distribution (OOD) detection module based on the maximum predicted value and punishes the OOD samples with a perturbed model $f'(\cdot; \theta')$. This perturbed model $f'(\cdot; \theta')$ is trained with $\arg\min_{\theta'} \mathbb{E}_{(x,y)}[-\log(1 - f'(x; \theta')_y)]$ to minimize the probability of the correct class. Finally, the output will be:

$$y' = (1 - \alpha)f(x; \theta) + (\alpha)f'(x; \theta'), \tag{8}$$

where $\alpha = 1/(1 + e^{\nu(\max f(x;\theta) - \tau)})$ with a hyper-parameter ν is the coefficient to control how much correct results will be returned, and τ is the threshold used for OOD detection. The model returns incorrect predictions for the OOD samples without having much impact on the in-distribution samples. The prediction poisoning [24] is also a perturbation-based defense method, which perturb the posterior probabilities y to make the adversarial gradient signal that maximally deviates from the original gradient. As shown by the following equation:

$$\max_{\tilde{y}} \left\| \frac{G^T \tilde{y}}{\|G^T \tilde{y}\|_2} - \frac{G^T y}{\|G^T y\|_2} \right\|_2^2 \tag{9}$$

where $G = \nabla_w \log F(x; w)$, y is the posterior probabilities and $\tilde{y}$ is the perturbed posterior probabilities.

We choose three values of the threshold τ in the adaptive misinformation and two values of the threshold ϵ in the prediction poisoning to compare the effects of our method with the previous methods. The threshold value of 0 means no defence. The result is shown in Table 2. Compared with other methods, adaptive

Original image   Substitute's CAM of different stages   Victim's CAM

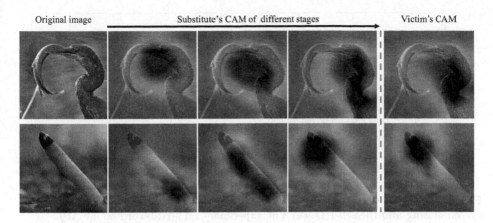

Fig. 5. The visualized attention maps of the victim model and different stages substitute models using the Grad-CAM. Along with the training stages, the attention map of the substitute model tends to fit the victim model's.

Table 3. An ablation experiment showing the effectiveness of the two modules we designed on CIFAR10 dataset under 30k queries. We use some commonly used regularization methods to replace the two modules we designed, and the results show that the two modules are better than the traditional regularization methods.

Method	ACC
Ours	80.47%
+ 2 × weight decay	81.65%
− CAM-driven erasing	76.12%
− CAM-driven erasing + CutOut	77.11%
− self-KD	79.02%
− self-KD + 2 × weight decay	80.09%
− self-KD + CutOut	78.91%
− self-KD + label smoothing (0.9)	78.22%
− self-KD + label smoothing (0.8)	77.46%

misinformation and prediction poisoning are almost ineffective to our method. Furthermore, we find that if we remove the self-KD in our method, the performance is greatly reduced. We conclude that this is because these two defence methods add noise labels to the substitute model's training dataset, and self-KD can alleviate the overfitting of the substitute model to the training dataset, making these two defence methods not effective enough.

Ablation Study. To evaluate the contribution of different modules in our method, we conduct the ablation study on CIFAR10 dataset and show the results in Table 3. We first separately remove the two modules we designed to verify

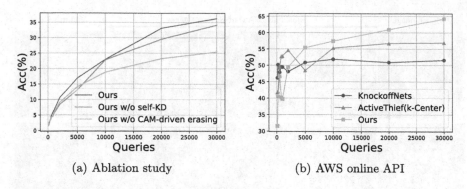

(a) Ablation study   (b) AWS online API

Fig. 6. (a) An ablation study on CUBS200 dataset for the contribution of the CAM-driven erasing and the self-KD. (b) The experiment on a real-word online API.

Table 4. Transferability of adversarial samples generated with PGD attack on the substitute models.

Method	Substitute's architecture				
	ResNet-34	ResNet-18	ResNet-50	VGG-16	DenseNet
KnockoffNets	57.85%	63.33%	52.04%	42.88%	60.77%
ActiveThief(k-Center)	57.44%	57.90%	57.01%	16.49%	60.72%
ActiveThief(Entropy)	63.56%	66.76%	58.19%	55.43%	62.05%
Ours	**76.63%**	**74.10%**	**74.28%**	**67.03%**	**66.96%**

their role. If the CAM-driven erasing strategy is removed, the performance of our method will be greatly reduced, showing that it has an indispensable position in our method. We also give some visual examples in Fig. 5 to demonstrate that this strategy can help align the attention of two models. As depicted in the Fig. 5, at the beginning time, the substitute model learns the wrong attention map. Along with the iterative training stages, the attention area of the substitute model tends to fit the victim model's, which conforms to our intention. We further remove the self-KD module to evaluate its performance. It can be found from Fig. 1 and Table 3 that the self-KD can improve the generalization of our method and further improve the performance. Later, in order to prove that these modules are better than some commonly used regularization methods, such as CutOut, label smoothing, we use these methods to replace the modules we designed. Note that the weight decay we used before followed the setting of baseline, so here we also test the effect of a large weight decay. The results are shown in Table 3, where "2× weight decay" represents the expansion of the weight decay to twice the original and the "label smoothing (α)" means smooth the hard-label according to the hyperparameter α. First, we replace the CAM-driven erasing with random erasing (CutOut), which brings 3.36% performance degradation. We believe that using Grad-CAM as a prior is more effective than random. Then we use data augmentation (CutOut) and label smoothing to replace the self-KD, while both show less competitive. We conclude that they destroy the information need by the CAM-driven erasing, e.g., erasing the attention map or hiding information in other classes by making them equal. The result also shows the effectiveness of the self-KD module we designed. In addition, we also perform a simple ablation experiment on the CUBS200 dataset. The results are shown in Fig. 6(a) and are similar to those on the CIFAR10 dataset.

Stealing Functionality of a Real-World API. We validate our method is applicable to real-world APIs. The AWS Marketplace is an online store that provides a variety of trained ML models for users. It can only be used in the form of a black-box setting. We choose a popular model (waste classifier [1]) as the victim model. We use ILSVRC-2012 dataset as the attack dataset and choose another small public waste classifier dataset [2], containing $2,527$ images as the test dataset. The hyperparameter settings remain the same as before. As in Fig. 6(b), the substitute model obtained by our method achieves 12.63% and 7.32% improvements in test accuracy compared with two previous methods, which show our method has stronger practicality in the real world.

Transferability of Adversarial Samples. Though with the dominant performance on a wide range of tasks, deep neural networks are shown to be vulnerable to imperceptible perturbations, $i.e.$, adversarial examples [6,31]. Since the model stealing attack can obtain a functionally similar substitute model, some previous works ($e.g.$, JBDA [26], DaST [40] and ActiveThief [25]) used this substitute model to generate adversarial samples and then performed the transferable adversarial attack on the victim model. We argue that a more similar substitute model leads to a more successful adversarial attacks. We test the transferability of adversarial samples on the test set of the CIFAR10 dataset. Keeping the architecture of the victim model as the ResNet-34, we evaluate the attack success rate of adversarial samples generated from different substitute models ($i.e.$, ResNet-34, ResNet-18, ResNet-50 [11], VGG-16 [30], DenseNet [13]). All adversarial samples are generated using Projected Gradient Descent (PGD) attack [20] with maximum L_∞-norm of perturbations as $8/255$. As shown in Table 4, the adversarial samples generated by our substitute models have stronger transferability in all substitute's architectures, with 4.91%–16.20% improvements than other methods. This again proves that our method is more practical in real-world scenarios.

5   Conclusion

We investigated the problem of model stealing attacks under the hard-label setting and pointed out why previous methods are not effective enough. We

---

[1] For the purpose of protecting privacy, we hide the specific information of the victim model.
[2] https://github.com/garythung/trashnet

presented a new method, termed *black-box dissector*, which contains a CAM-driven erasing strategy and a RE-based self-KD module. We showed its superiority on four widely-used datasets and verified the effectiveness of our method with defense methods, real-world APIs, and the downstream adversarial attack. Though focusing on image data in this paper, our method is general for other tasks as long as the CAM and similar erasing method work, *e.g.*, synonym saliency words replacement for NLP tasks [4]. We believe our method can be easily extended to other fields and inspire future researchers. Model stealing attack poses a threat to the deployed machine learning models. We hope this work will draw attention to the protection of deployed models and furthermore shed more light on the attack mechanisms and prevention methods. Additionally, transformer-based classifiers are becoming hot, and their security issues should also be paid attention to. This kind of classifier divides the images into patches and our method works by erasing parts of images, it is more convenient for us to align the attention map by masking the patch and mine the missing information. We will validate this idea in the further work.

Acknowledgments. This work was supported by the National Science Fund for Distinguished Young Scholars (No.62025603), the National Natural Science Foundation of China (No. U21B2037, No. 62176222, No. 62176223, No. 62176226, No. 62072386, No. 62072387, No. 62072389, and No. 62002305), Guangdong Basic and Applied Basic Research Foundation (No. 2019B1515120049), and the Natural Science Foundation of Fujian Province of China (No. 2021J01002).

References

1. Anil, R., Pereyra, G., Passos, A., Ormandi, R., Dahl, G.E., Hinton, G.E.: Large scale distributed neural network training through online distillation. arXiv preprint arXiv:1804.03235 (2018)
2. Barbalau, A., Cosma, A., Ionescu, R.T., Popescu, M.: Black-box ripper: copying black-box models using generative evolutionary algorithms. In: NeurIPS (2020)
3. DeVries, T., Taylor, G.W.: Improved regularization of convolutional neural networks with cutout. arXiv preprint arXiv:1708.04552 (2017)
4. Dong, X., Luu, A.T., Ji, R., Liu, H.: Towards robustness against natural language word substitutions. In: ICLR (2021)
5. Ducoffe, M., Precioso, F.: Adversarial active learning for deep networks: a margin based approach. In: ICML (2018)
6. Fang, S., Li, J., Lin, X., Ji, R.: Learning to learn transferable attack. In: AAAI (2022)
7. Furlanello, T., Lipton, Z.C., Tschannen, M., Itti, L., Anandkumar, A.: Born again neural networks. In: ICML (2018)
8. Gong, X., Chen, Y., Yang, W., Mei, G., Wang, Q.: Inversenet: augmenting model extraction attacks with training data inversion. In: IJCAI (2021)
9. Griffin, G., Holub, A., Perona, P.: Caltech-256 object category dataset (2007)
10. Guo, C., Pleiss, G., Sun, Y., Weinberger, K.Q.: On calibration of modern neural networks. In: ICML (2017)
11. He, K., Zhang, X., Ren, S., Sun, J.: Deep residual learning for image recognition. In: CVPR (2016)

12. Hinton, G., Vinyals, O., Dean, J.: Distilling the knowledge in a neural network. In: NIPS Deep Learning Workshop (2015)
13. Huang, G., Liu, Z., Van Der Maaten, L., Weinberger, K.Q.: Densely connected convolutional networks. In: CVPR (2017)
14. Jagielski, M., Carlini, N., Berthelot, D., Kurakin, A., Papernot, N.: High accuracy and high fidelity extraction of neural networks. In: 29th Usenix Security (2020)
15. Kariyappa, S., Prakash, A., Qureshi, M.: Maze: data-free model stealing attack using zeroth-order gradient estimation. arXiv preprint arXiv:2005.03161 (2020)
16. Kariyappa, S., Qureshi, M.K.: Defending against model stealing attacks with adaptive misinformation. In: CVPR (2020)
17. Kim, K., Ji, B., Yoon, D., Hwang, S.: Self-knowledge distillation: a simple way for better generalization. arXiv preprint arXiv:2006.12000 (2020)
18. Krizhevsky, A., Hinton, G., et al.: Learning multiple layers of features from tiny images (2009)
19. Lewis, D.D., Gale, W.A.: A sequential algorithm for training text classifiers. In: SIGIR (1994)
20. Madry, A., Makelov, A., Schmidt, L., Tsipras, D., Vladu, A.: Towards deep learning models resistant to adversarial attacks. In: ICLR (2018)
21. Maini, P., Yaghini, M., Papernot, N.: Dataset inference: ownership resolution in machine learning. In: ICLR (2021)
22. Netzer, Y., Wang, T., Coates, A., Bissacco, A., Wu, B., Ng, A.Y.: Reading digits in natural images with unsupervised feature learning. In: NIPS Workshop on Deep Learning and Unsupervised Feature Learning (2011)
23. Orekondy, T., Schiele, B., Fritz, M.: Knockoff nets: stealing functionality of black-box models. In: CVPR (2019)
24. Orekondy, T., Schiele, B., Fritz, M.: Prediction poisoning: towards defenses against dnn model stealing attacks. In: ICLR (2019)
25. Pal, S., Gupta, Y., Shukla, A., Kanade, A., Shevade, S., Ganapathy, V.: Activethief: model extraction using active learning and unannotated public data. In: AAAI (2020)
26. Papernot, N., McDaniel, P., Goodfellow, I., Jha, S., Celik, Z.B., Swami, A.: Practical black-box attacks against machine learning. In: ACM AsiACCS (2017)
27. Russakovsky, O., et al.: Imagenet large scale visual recognition challenge. IJCV 115, 211–252 (2015)
28. Selvaraju, R.R., Cogswell, M., Das, A., Vedantam, R., Parikh, D., Batra, D.: Gradcam: visual explanations from deep networks via gradient-based localization. In: ICCV (2017)
29. Sener, O., Savarese, S.: Active learning for convolutional neural networks: a core-set approach. In: ICLR (2018)
30. Simonyan, K., Zisserman, A.: Very deep convolutional networks for large-scale image recognition. In: ICLR (2015)
31. Szegedy, C., et al.: Intriguing properties of neural networks. In: ICLR (2014)
32. Wah, C., Branson, S., Welinder, P., Perona, P., Belongie, S.: The caltech-ucsd birds-200-2011 dataset (2011)
33. Wang, X., Xiang, Y., Gao, J., Ding, J.: Information laundering for model privacy. In: ICLR (2021)
34. Yang, J., Jiang, Y., Huang, X., Ni, B., Zhao, C.: Learning black-box attackers with transferable priors and query feedback. In: NeurIPS (2020)
35. Yu, H., Yang, K., Zhang, T., Tsai, Y.Y., Ho, T.Y., Jin, Y.: Cloudleak: large-scale deep learning models stealing through adversarial examples. In: NDSS (2020)

36. Zagoruyko, S., Komodakis, N.: Paying more attention to attention: improving the performance of convolutional neural networks via attention transfer. In: ICLR (2017)
37. Zhang, C., Bengio, S., Hardt, M., Recht, B., Vinyals, O.: Understanding deep learning requires rethinking generalization. In: ICLR (2017)
38. Zhong, Z., Zheng, L., Kang, G., Li, S., Yang, Y.: Random erasing data augmentation. In: AAAI (2020)
39. Zhou, B., Khosla, A., Lapedriza, A., Oliva, A., Torralba, A.: Learning deep features for discriminative localization. In: CVPR (2016)
40. Zhou, M., Wu, J., Liu, Y., Liu, S., Zhu, C.: Dast: data-free substitute training for adversarial attacks. In: CVPR (2020)

Learning Energy-Based Models
with Adversarial Training

Xuwang Yin$^{(\boxtimes)}$, Shiying Li , and Gustavo K. Rohde

University of Virginia, Charlottesville, USA
{xy4cm,sl8jx,gustavo}@virginia.edu

Abstract. We study a new approach to learning energy-based models (EBMs) based on adversarial training (AT). We show that (binary) AT learns a special kind of energy function that models the support of the data distribution, and the learning process is closely related to MCMC-based maximum likelihood learning of EBMs. We further propose improved techniques for generative modeling with AT, and demonstrate that this new approach is capable of generating diverse and realistic images. Aside from having competitive image generation performance to explicit EBMs, the studied approach is stable to train, is well-suited for image translation tasks, and exhibits strong out-of-distribution adversarial robustness. Our results demonstrate the viability of the AT approach to generative modeling, suggesting that AT is a competitive alternative approach to learning EBMs.

Keywords: Adversarial training · Adversarial attacks · Energy-Based Models (EBMs) · Generative modeling

1 Introduction

In unsupervised learning, energy-based models (EBMs) [33] are a class of generative model that uses an energy function to model the probability distribution of the observed data. Unlike explicit density models, EBMs model the unnormalized density function, which makes it difficult to evaluate the likelihood function. Maximum likelihood learning of EBMs hence makes use of the likelihood function's gradient which can be approximated using Monte Carlo methods. Each iteration of the learning process involves first generating synthesized data by sampling from the current model, and then updating the model to maximize the energy difference between synthesized data and observed data. This process leads to an energy function that outputs low energies on the data manifold and high energies on other regions. EBMs find applications in image restoration (denoising, inpainting, etc.), out-of-distribution detection, and various sample generation tasks. The main difficulties of training EBMs lie in the com-

---

Supplementary Information The online version contains supplementary material available at https://doi.org/10.1007/978-3-031-20065-6_13.

putational challenges from the sampling procedure and some training stability issues [9, 10, 14, 15, 39, 40, 57, 67].

Another line of work on adversarial training (AT) show that adversarially robust classifiers learn high-level, interpretable features, and can be utilized to solve various computer vision tasks including generation, inpainting, super-resolution, and image-to-image translation [11, 25, 47, 53]. Compared to state-of-the-art generative models, this AT approach does not provide a competitive generation performance and is therefore of limited value in many of these tasks. Nonetheless, the generative properties of the robust classifier suggest that the model has captured the distribution of the training data, although the underlying learning mechanism is not yet well understood.

At a high level, both EBMs training and AT are based on the idea of first using gradient-based optimization to generate samples that reach high activation under the current model, and then optimizing the model to minimize its activation on the generated samples. In addition, both approaches synthesize new samples by performing gradient descent on the trained model. These similarities suggest that there are some connections between these two approaches.

In this work we investigate the mechanism by which AT learns data distributions, and propose improved techniques for generative modeling with AT. We focus on binary AT [65] which does not requires class labels and hence naturally fits the generative modeling task. We first analyze the binary AT objective and the corresponding training algorithm, and show that binary AT learns a special kind of energy function that models the support of the observed data. We then draw a connection between AT and MCMC-base maximum likelihood learning of EBMs by showing that the binary AT objective can be interpreted as a gradient-scaled version of the likelihood objective in EBMs training, and the PGD attack can be viewed as an non-convergent sampler of the model distribution. This connection provides us with intuition of how AT learns data distributions from a maximum likelihood learning perspective, and suggests that binary AT can be viewed as an approximate maximum likelihood learning algorithm.

We further propose improved techniques for generative modeling with AT based on the above analysis. Our empirical evaluation shows that this AT approach provides competitive generation performance to explicit EBMs, and at the same time is stable to train (just like regular adversarial training), is well-suited for image translation tasks, and exhibits strong out-of-distribution adversarial robustness. The main limitation of the studied approach is that it cannot properly learn the underlying density function of the observed data. However, this problem is not unique to the studied approach - most existing work on learning EBMs relies on short-run non-convergent sampler to improve the training efficiency, and the learned model typically does not have a valid steady-state that reflects the distribution of the observed data [39, 40].

In summary, the contributions of this paper are: 1) We show that binary AT learns a special kind of energy function that models the support of the data distribution, and the learning process is closely related to MCMC-based maximum likelihood learning of EBMs. 2) We propose improved techniques for generative modeling with AT, and demonstrate competitive image generation performance to state-of-the-art explicit EBMs. 3) We show that the studied approach is stable to train, has competitive training and test time sampling efficiency, and can be applied to denoising, inpainting, image translation, and worst-case out-of-distribution detection.

2   Related Work

Learning EBMs. Due to the intractability of the normalizing constant in the EBMs likelihood function, maximum likelihood learning of EBMs makes use of the gradient of the log-likelihood which can be approximated using MCMC sampling. Recent work [10,39,40,59] scaling EBMs training to high-dimensional data performs sampling using SGLD [56] and initialize the chain from a noise distribution. The sampling process involves estimating the model's gradient with respect to the current sample at each step and therefore has high computational cost. To improve the sampling efficiency, many authors consider short-run non-convergent SGLD sampler in combination with a persistent sampling buffer [9,10,14,15,39,57]. Although a short-run sampler is sufficient for learning a generation model, the resulting energy function typically does not have a valid steady-state [39,40]. The mixing time of the sampling procedure also depends on how close the chain-initialization distribution is to the model distribution. A recent trend hence considers initializing the sampling chain from samples produced by a generator fitted on the target distribution [1,15,18,19,31,38,41,57,58,63,64].

Maximum likelihood learning of EBMs also has some training stability issues, and various techniques have been developed to address these issues. These techniques include 1) using weight normalization [46], Swish activation [43], gradient clipping, and weight decay (see [57]), 2) gradient norm clipping on model parameters and using a KL term in the training objective (see [9]), 3) adjusting learning rate and SGLD steps during training and adding Gaussian noise to input images (see [14]), 4) gradient clipping on SGLD and model parameters and spectral normalization (see [10]), and 5) multiscale training and smooth activation functions (see [67]). Overall, there does not seem to have a consensus on how to stabilize EBMs training. Due to the computational challenge of MCMC sampling and stability issues, the successful application of EBMs to modeling high-dimensional data such as 256×256 images is only achieved in some very recent works [57,67].

Aside from MCMC-based maximum likelihood learning of EBMs, alternative approaches for learning EBMs exist. Score matching [24] circumvents the difficulty of estimating the partition function by directly modeling the derivatives of the data distribution. Score matching has recently been successfully applied to modeling large natural images and achieves competitive performance to state-of-the-art generative models such as GANs [23,49–51]. Noise contrastive estimation (NCE) [17] learns data distributions by contrasting the observed data with data from a known noise distribution. Similar to our approach, NCE makes use of a logistic regression model. The main difference is that in NCE, the logit of the classifier is the difference in log probabilities of the model distribution and the noise distribution, whereas in our approach the logit directly defines the estimator (i.e., the energy function). Unlike other EBMs, NCE typically does not scale well to high-dimensional data [5,17,44].

Maximin Interpretation of EBMs. When the noise term in the SGLD sampler is disabled, the learning process of EBMs can be interpreted as solving a *maximin* game [60–62]. This interpretation coincides with our formulation in Eq. (12). The key differences lie in the value function, the setting of the sampler (SGLD vs. PGD attack), and the Markov chain initiation distribution.

3   Background

3.1   Energy-Based Models

Energy-based models (EBMs) [33] represent probability distributions by converting the outputs of a scalar function f_θ into probabilities through a Gibbs distribution:

$$p_\theta(x) = \frac{\exp(f_\theta(x))}{Z(\theta)}, \tag{1}$$

where the normalizing constant $Z(\theta)$, also known as the partition function, is an integral over the unnormalized probability of all states: $Z(\theta) = \int \exp(f_\theta(x))dx$. The energy function is defined as $E_\theta(x) = -f_\theta(x)$, and thus has the property of attributing low energy outputs on the support of the target data distribution and high energy outputs in other regions.

For many interesting models, the partition function $Z(\theta)$ is intractable, and therefore maximum likelihood estimation (MLE) of the model parameters θ is not directly applicable. Standard maximum likelihood learning of EBMs makes use of the gradient of the log likelihood function. Denote the distribution of the observed data as p_{data}, the gradient of the log likelihood takes the form

$$\nabla_\theta \mathbb{E}_{x \sim p_{\text{data}}}[\log p_\theta(x)] = \mathbb{E}_{x \sim p_{\text{data}}}[\nabla_\theta f_\theta(x)] - \mathbb{E}_{x \sim p_\theta(x)}[\nabla_\theta f_\theta(x)]. \tag{2}$$

Intuitively, maximizing log-likelihood with this gradient causes $f_\theta(x)$ to increase on p_{data} samples and decrease on samples drawn from p_θ; when p_θ matches p_{data}, the gradient cancels out and the training terminates.

Evaluating $\mathbb{E}_{x \sim p_\theta(x)} \nabla_\theta f_\theta(x)$ requires sampling from the model distribution. This can be done with Markov chain Monte Carlo (MCMC) methods. Recent work scaling EBMs training to high-dimensional data [10,39,40,59] makes use of the SGLD method [56] which samples the model distribution by

$$x_0 \sim p_0, \quad x_{i+1} = x_i + \frac{\lambda}{2}\nabla_x f_\theta(x_i) + \epsilon, \quad \epsilon \sim \mathcal{N}(0, \lambda), \tag{3}$$

where p_0 is some random noise distribution. A proper SGLD sampler requires a large number of update steps in order for the distribution of sampled data to match p_θ. Due to the high computational cost of this sampling process, many authors resort to short-run non-convergent MCMC to improve the sampling efficiency [10,14,39,40,59]. The resulting model typically does not have a valid steady-state that reflects the distribution of the observed data, but is still capable of generating realistic and diverse samples [39,40].

3.2   Binary Adversarial Training

Binary adversarial training [65] is a method for detecting adversarial examples. In a K class classification problem, the detection method consists of K binary classifiers, with the k-th binary classifier trained to distinguish clean data of class k from adversarially perturbed data of other classes. A committee of K binary classifiers then provides a complete solution for detecting adversarially perturbed samples of any classes.

Denote the data distribution of class k as p_{data}, the mixture distribution of other classes as $p_0 = \frac{1}{K-1}\sum_{i=1,\dots,K,i\neq k} p_i$, the k-th binary classifier is trained by maximizing the objective

$$J(D) = \mathbb{E}_{\mathbf{x}\sim p_{\text{data}}}[\log D(x)] + \mathbb{E}_{\mathbf{x}\sim p_0}[\min_{x'\in\mathbb{B}(x,\epsilon)} \log(1 - D(x'))], \qquad (4)$$

where $D : \mathcal{X} \subseteq \mathbb{R}^d \to [0,1]$ is the classification function, and $\mathbb{B}(x,\epsilon)$ is a neighborhood of x: $\mathbb{B}(x,\epsilon) = \{x' \in \mathcal{X} : \|x' - x\|_2 \leq \epsilon\}$. In practice, D is defined by applying a logistic sigmoid function to the output of a neural network:

$$D(x) = \sigma(f_\theta(x)), \qquad (5)$$

where f_θ is a neural network with a single output node and parameters θ.

The inner minimization in Eq. (4) is solved using the PGD attack [32,34], a first-order method that employs an iterative update rule of (l^2-based attack):

$$x_0 \sim p_0, \quad x_{i+1} = \text{Proj}(x_i - \lambda\frac{\nabla_x \log(1 - D(x_i))}{\|\nabla_x \log(1 - D(x_i))\|_2}), \qquad (6)$$

where λ is some step size, and Proj is the operation of projecting onto the feasible set $\mathbb{B}(x,\epsilon)$. Because the gradient vector in Eq. (6) is normalized to have unit norm, we can equivalently implement the attack by directly performing gradient ascent on f_θ:

$$x_0 \sim p_0, \quad x_{i+1} = \text{Proj}(x_i + \lambda\frac{\nabla_x f_\theta(x_i)}{\|\nabla_x f_\theta(x_i)\|_2}). \qquad (7)$$

4   Binary at Generative Model

In this section we develop a generative model based on binary AT. We first analyze the optimal solution to the binary AT problem, and then investigate the mechanism by which binary AT learns the data distribution, and finally interpret the learning process from the maximum likelihood learning perspective. Our main result is that under a proper configuration of perturbation limit and p_0 data, binary AT learns a special kind of energy function that models the support of p_{data}. Based on these theoretical insights, we proposed improved training techniques.

4.1   Optimal Solution to the Binary at Problem

We consider the optimal solution of Eq. (4) under the scenario of unbounded perturbation: $\mathbb{B}(x, \epsilon) = \mathcal{X}$. This allows us to further simplify the PGD attack by removing the Proj operator:

$$x_0 \sim p_0, \quad x_{i+1} = x_i + \lambda \frac{\nabla_x f_\theta(x_i)}{\|\nabla_x f_\theta(x_i)\|_2}. \tag{8}$$

Perturbing p_0 samples can be thought of as moving p_0 samples via a translation function $T(x) = x + \Delta_x$, with Δ_x being the perturbation computed on sample x. We can write the density function of the perturbed distribution p_T using random variable transformation:

$$p_T(y) = \int_\mathcal{X} p_0(x)\delta(y - T(x))dx. \tag{9}$$

The inner problem in Eq. (4) can then be interpreted as determining the distribution which has the lowest expected value of $\log(1 - D(x))$:

$$p_T^* = \arg \min_{p_T} \mathbb{E}_{x \sim p_T}[\log(1 - D(x))]. \tag{10}$$

The objective of the outer problem is then the log-likelihood in a logistic regression model which discriminates p_{data} samples from p_T^* samples:

$$J(D) = \mathbb{E}_{x \sim p_{\text{data}}}[\log D(x)] + \mathbb{E}_{x \sim p_T^*}[\log(1 - D(x))]. \tag{11}$$

We can equivalently formulate Eq. (4) as a *maximin* problem

$$\max_D \min_{p_T} U(D, p_T) = \mathbb{E}_{x \sim p_{\text{data}}}[\log D(x)] + \mathbb{E}_{x \sim p_T}[\log(1 - D(x))], \tag{12}$$

and obtain its optimal solution by following the standard approach to solving maximin problems:

Proposition 1. *The optimal solution of* $\max_D \min_{p_T} U(D, p_T)$ *is* $U(D^*, p_T^*) = -\log(4)$, *where* D^* *outputs* $\frac{1}{2}$ *on* $Supp(p_{data})$ *and* $\leq \frac{1}{2}$ *outside* $Supp(p_{data})$, *and* p_T^* *is supported in the contour set* $\{D = \frac{1}{2}\}$.

Proof. See the supplementary materials.

The above maximin problem can also be interpreted as a two-player zero-sum game, and is closely related to GANs [13]'s *minimax* game which has the form

$$\min_G \max_D V(D, G) = \mathbb{E}_{x \sim p_{\text{data}}}[\log D(x)] + \mathbb{E}_{z \sim p_z}[\log(1 - D(G(z)))]. \tag{13}$$

The game-theory point of view provides a convenient way to understand their differences. We include a game theory-based analysis of $\max_D \min_{p_T} U(D, p_T)$ and a comparative analysis of GANs in the supplementary materials.

4.2 Learning Mechanism

Proposition 1 states that by solving $\max_D \min_{p_T} U(D, p_T)$ we can obtain a D that outputs $\frac{1}{2}$ on the support of p_{data} and $\leq \frac{1}{2}$ on other regions. This result is obtained by assuming that for any D, the inner minimization Eq. (10) is always perfectly solved. In practice, when D is randomly initialized, it has many local maxima outside the support of p_{data}. Because the inner minimization is solved by taking p_0 samples and then performing gradient ascent on D with Eq. (8), this process can get trapped in different local maxima of D. Hence we can think of this process as searching for these local maxima and then put the perturbed p_0 data in these regions. Then in the model update stage (outer maximization), D is updated by increasing its outputs on p_{data} samples and decreasing its outputs on the perturbed p_0 data. By repeating this process, local maxima get suppressed and the model learns to correctly model $\text{Supp}(p_{\text{data}})$.

The algorithm for solving the maximin problem is described in Algorithm 1. Figure 1 left panel shows the 2D simulation result of the algorithm when the p_0 dataset contains random samples from the uniform distribution. It can be seen that when the algorithm converges, local maxima outside $\text{Supp}(p_{\text{data}})$ are suppressed, and D (approximately) outputs $\frac{1}{2}$ on $\text{Supp}(p_{\text{data}})$ as predicted by Proposition 1. Meanwhile, D retains the gradient information for translating out-distribution samples to $\text{Supp}(p_{\text{data}})$.

Because the PGD attack is deterministic gradient ascent, its ability to discover different local maxima depends on the diversity of p_0 samples. Proposition 1 right panel shows that when p_0 data is concentrated in the bottom left corner, the final D still has local maxima outside the support of p_{data}. These local maxima are not suppressed because they were never discovered by the perturbed p_0 data.

The above analysis reveals how binary AT learns data distributions: *the learning starts with a randomly-initialized D solution, and then iteratively refine the solution by suppressing local maxima outside the support of the observed data.* This process is similar to EBMs training where the model distribution's spurious modes are constantly discovered by MCMC sampling and subsequently suppressed in the model update stage. However, unlike the EBMs likelihood objective Eq. (2), the AT objective Eq. (12) cannot properly learn the density function, but can only capture its support. This is corroborated by the 2D experiment where D outputs $\frac{1}{2}$ uniformly on the support of p_{data} (blue points).

Algorithm 1. Binary Adversarial Training

1: **repeat**
2:     Draw samples $\{x_i\}_{i=1}^m$ from p_{data}, and samples $\{x_i^0\}_{i=1}^m$ from p_0.
3:     Update $\{x_i^0\}_{i=1}^m$ by performing K steps PGD attack Eq. (8) on each sample. Denote the resulting samples as $\{x_i^*\}_{i=1}^m$.
4:     Update D by maximizing $\frac{1}{m}\sum_{i=1}^m \log D(x_i) + \frac{1}{m}\sum_{i=1}^m \log(1 - D(x_i^*))$ (single step).
5: **until** D convergences

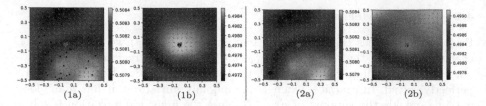

Fig. 1. Plots of contours and (normalized) gradient vector fields of the D functions learned with different p_0 data. Left and right panel respectively show the initial state (1a and 2a) and final state (1b and 2b) of D when p_0 data is respectively uniformly distributed (red points in 1a) and concentrated in the lower left corner (red points in 2a). p_{data} is a Gaussian distribution centered at $(0, 0)$ (blue points). (Color figure online)

4.3 Maximum Likelihood Learning Interpretation

We next consider the learning process of binary AT from a maximum likelihood learning point of view. Both binary AT and MCMC-based EBMs learning employ an iterative optimization algorithm, where in each iteration the contrastive data is computed by performing gradient ascent on the current model, and then the model is updated by maximizing its outputs on the observed data and minimizing its outputs on the contrastive data. The following analysis shows that the PGD attack can be viewed as a non-convergent sampler of the model distribution, and the binary AT objective Eq. (11) can be interpreted as a gradient-scaled version of the EBMs objective Eq. (2). Table 1 summaries their key differences.

Table 1. Key differences between binary AT and maximum likelihood EBMs.

Objective gradient	EBMs: $\mathbb{E}_{\mathbf{x} \sim p_{\text{data}}}[\nabla_\theta f_\theta(x)] - \mathbb{E}_{\mathbf{x} \sim p_\theta(x)}[\nabla_\theta f_\theta(x)]$
	Binary AT: $\mathbb{E}_{\mathbf{x} \sim p_{\text{data}}}[(1 - \sigma(f_\theta(x)))\nabla_\theta f_\theta(x)] - \mathbb{E}_{\mathbf{x} \sim p_T^*}[\sigma(f_\theta(x))\nabla_\theta f_\theta(x)]$
Contrastive data	EBMs: $x_0 \sim p_0, x_{i+1} = x_i + \frac{\lambda}{2}\nabla_x f_\theta(x_i) + \epsilon, \epsilon \sim \mathcal{N}(0, \lambda)$
	Binary AT: $x_0 \sim p_0, x_{i+1} = x_i + \lambda \frac{\nabla_x f_\theta(x_i)}{\|\nabla_x f_\theta(x_i)\|_2}$
p_0 data	EBMs: A noise distribution or a distribution close to p_{data}
	Binary AT: A real and diverse out-distribution dataset (80 million tiny images for CIFAR-10 and ImageNet for 256×256 datasets)

Contrastive Data Computation. In EBMs training, the contrastive data is computed by MCMC-sampling, typically with Langevin dynamics Eq. (3). In binary AT, the contrastive data is computed using the PGD attack Eq. (8). Comparing Eq. (8) with Eq. (3), we find that both approaches compute the contrastive data by first initializing from some out-distribution data, and then performing gradient ascent on f_θ. The main differences are that the PGD attack does not have the noise term, and makes use of normalized gradient. Intuitively, the noise term enables the sampler to explore different modes by helping gradient ascent escape local maxima. Although the PGD attack does not have the noise term, its ability to explore different modes can be enhanced by using a diverse p_0 dataset (Fig. 3).

In the PGD attack, as the normalized gradient vector has unit norm, the perturbation imposed on x_i is λ; in a K iterations of the update, the overall perturbation $\|x_i^* - x_i\|_2$ is always $\leq \lambda K$. Hence with the PGD attack we can more easily control the distribution of the contrastive data. In contrast, Langevin dynamics adjusts x_i in a scale that corresponds to the magnitude of the gradient of f_θ at x_i; when f_θ is updated during training, the overall perturbation may undergo a large change. This behavior of Langevin dynamics can be a source of some training stability issues [39].

Gradient of the Training Objective. By definition Eq. (5), the gradient of D's training objective Eq. (11) takes the form

$$\nabla_\theta J(D) = \mathbb{E}_{x \sim p_{\text{data}}}[(1 - \sigma(f_\theta(x)))\nabla_\theta f_\theta(x)] - \mathbb{E}_{x \sim p_T^*}[\sigma(f_\theta(x))\nabla_\theta f_\theta(x)]. \quad (14)$$

Comparing the above equation with Eq. (2) we find both equations consisting of gradient terms that yield similar effects: the first term causes f_θ outputs on p_{data} samples to increase, and the second causes f_θ outputs on the contrastive samples to decrease. Specifically, as $(1 - \sigma(f_\theta(x)))$ and $\sigma(f_\theta(x))$ are scalars in the range 0 to 1, the two gradient terms in Eq. (14) are respectively the scaled versions of the gradient in Eq. (2). It should be noted that although these scalars do not change the gradient update direction of individual terms in the model parameter space, the overall gradient update directions of Eq. (14) and Eq. (2) can be different.

Equation (14) also helps to understand why binary AT can only learn the support of the observed data. In Eq. (2), when $p_\theta(x)$ matches p_{data}, the gradient cancels out and training terminates, whereas in Eq. (14), when p_T^* matches p_{data} the gradient becomes $\mathbb{E}_{x \sim p_{\text{data}}}[(1 - 2\sigma(f_\theta(x)))\nabla_\theta f_\theta(x)]$ and only vanishes when $\sigma(f_\theta(x)) = \frac{1}{2}$ everywhere on the support of p_{data}. This result is consistent with Eq. (1) and the 2D experiment result.

4.4   Improved Training of Binary at Generative Model

Diverse p_0 Data. As discussed in Sect. 4.2, a diverse p_0 dataset improve the PGD attack's ability to explore different local maxima of D. To validate this 2D intuition generalizes to high dimensions, we evaluate the CIFAR-10 image generation performance under different settings of p_0. It can be seen from Fig. 3 that the best FID is obtained when p_0 is the 80 Million Tiny Images dataset [52], the most diverse dataset among the three p_0 datasets.

We follow existing work on adversarial training and use a p_0 dataset that contains real data samples to train the model. Using a real dataset (as opposed to a noise distribution) helps the model achieve out-of-distribution adversarial robustness (Sect. 5.2 OOD detection) and learn informative gradient for transforming real out-distribution samples (not just noise samples) into valid samples of p_{data}. The latter can be a useful feature in image translation applications (Sect. 5.2). The setting of p_0 in our experiments can be found in Table 1.

Training with Unconstrained Perturbations. Existing work on using adversarial training to train robust classifiers uses a small, fixed perturbation limit [34]. In the generative modeling task, we would like the perturbed p_0 data to travel in a larger space to find more local maxima. This can be achieved by taking more PGD attack steps (K) in step 3 of Algorithm 1. Figure 4 shows that a larger K results in better FID scores.

The downside of a large K is that it converges slower because more gradient steps are taken in each iteration (Fig. 5 $K = 25$ vs. $K = 5$). To improve the training efficiency we propose a mixed scenario in which we progressively increase the K value during training. We observe that this progressive training scenario converges faster than training with fixed-K (Fig. 5 $K = 0, 1, ..., 25$ vs $K = 25$). The pseudo code for progressive training is in Algorithm 2.

Algorithm 2. Progressive Binary Adversarial Training

1: **for** K in $[0, 1, ..., N]$ **do**
2:    **for** number of training iterations **do**
3:       Draw samples $\{x_i\}_{i=1}^m$ from p_{data}, and samples $\{x_i^0\}_{i=1}^m$ from p_0.
4:       Update $\{x_i^0\}_{i=1}^m$ by performing K steps unconstrained PGD attack Eq. (8) on each sample. Denote the resulting samples as $\{x_i^*\}_{i=1}^m$.
5:       Update D by maximizing $\frac{1}{m}\sum_{i=1}^m \log D(x_i) + \frac{1}{m}\sum_{i=1}^m \log(1 - D(x_i^*))$.
6:    **end for**
7: **end for**

Failure Mode. When we use Algorithm 1 to train on CelebA-HQ 256 [27], we observe that the binary classification accuracy quickly reaches 100% after a few hundred iterations. Meanwhile the mean l^2 distance between the original p_0 samples and perturbed p_0 samples is only a small fraction of λK, and the perturbed p_0 samples show no meaningful features of human faces. Although the symptoms are different, we believe this failure has the same root cause as mode

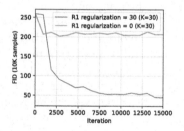

Fig. 2. The effect of R_1 regularization on CelebA-HQ.

collapse in GANs. In the adversarial game Eq. (12), the D model can learn to pick up a handful of low-level features which correlate well with the 0–1 labels to solve the binary classification task. With these features the D model cannot provide sufficient gradient for the adversarial p_0 data to move towards the manifold of p_{data}. Without the accurate information, the p_0 adversary fails to compete with D, and the D model starts to dominate the adversarial game. We follow GANs literature [4, 28, 36] and address this issue by using R_1 regularization [36] to regularize the sensitivity of D's output to the input features (Fig. 2 shows the effect of this regularizer). We do not observe other stability issues other than this failure mode.

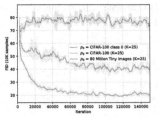 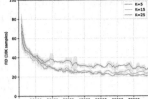 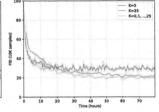

Fig. 3. FID scores obtained with different settings of p_0 on CIFAR-10.

Fig. 4. FID scores obtained with different Ks in Algorithm 1 on CIFAR-10.

Fig. 5. Progressive training vs training with fixed-K on CIFAR-10.

5   Experiments

In this section we provide an empirical evaluation of the proposed AT generative model. We first evaluate the approach's image generation performance and then demonstrate its applications to image-to-image translation and worst-case out-of-distribution detection. We further provide an analysis of the proposed approach's training stability in Sect. 5.3.

In the supplementary materials we provide experiment setup details including model architectures, training hyperparameters, sample generation settings, and evaluation protocols. We also include additional results including sampling efficiency analysis, uncurated image generation and image translation results, and demonstration of applications to denoising, inpainting, and compositional visual generation [8]. The interpolation results and nearest neighbor analysis in the supplementary materials suggest that our model captures the manifold structure of the observed data, as opposed to simply memorizes the data samples.

5.1   Image Generation

Table 2 shows that on CIFAR-10 [30] our approach achieves the best Inception Score (IS) [45] and FID [22] among AT generative models. Our approach also improves over state-of-the-art explicit EBMs in terms of IS, and at the same time has a slightly worse FID. Compared to VAEBM [57], our method does not require an auxiliary model to train, and has better test time sampling efficiency (see supplementary materials). Diffusion Recovery [12] trains a sequence of conditional EBMs, with each one defining the conditional distribution of a noisy sample given the same sample at a higher noise level. Similar to score-based approaches, these conditional EBMs do not directly model the data distribution of the observed data, so it is unclear how these models can be applied to tasks which require explicit knowledge of the data distribution (e.g., OOD detection).

Table 3 shows that on CelebA-HQ 256 [27] our method outperforms or is on par with state-of-the-art generative models except GANs. On LSUN Church [66] our method outperforms a latest energy-based model VAEBM [57] (the authors only provided the 64 × 64 result), but falls bellow DDPM and GANs. Figure 6 shows sample image generation results.

Table 2. IS and FID scores on CIFAR-10

	Method	IS↑	FID↓
AT	Ours	9.10	13.21
	CEM [55]	8.68	36.4
	Adv. robust classifier [47]	7.5	–
Explicit EBMs	Diffusion recovery [12]	8.30	9.58
	VAEBM [57]	8.43	12.19
	CoopFlow(pretrained Flow) [64]	–	15.80
	CF-EBM [67]	–	16.71
	ImprovedCD [9]	7.85	25.1
	VERA [15]	–	27.5
	EBMs-VAE [63]	6.65	36.2
	JEM [14]	8.76	38.4
	IGEBM (Ensemble) [10]	6.78	38.2
	Short-Run EBMs [40]	6.21	44.16
GANs	StyleGAN2 w/o ADA [28]	8.99	9.9
	BigGAN [4]	9.22	14.73
	SNGAN [37]	8.22	21.7
	WGAN-GP [16]	7.86	36.4
Score-based	SDE [51]	9.89	2.20
	DDPM [23]	9.46	3.17
	NCSNv2 [50]	8.4	10.87
	NCSN [49]	8.87	25.32

Table 3. FID scores on CelebA-HQ 256, AFHQ-CAT [6], and LSUN Church 256

Dataset	Method	FID↓
CelebA-HQ 256	Ours	17.31
	VAEBM [57]	20.38
	CF-EBM [67] (128 × 128)	23.50
	NVAE [54]	45.11
	GLOW [29]	68.93
	Adversarial latent AE [42]	19.21
	ProgressiveGAN [27]	8.03
AFHQ-CAT	Our (256 × 256)	13.35
	StyleGAN2 (512 × 512) [28]	5.13
LSUN church	VAEBM (64 × 64) [57]	13.51
	Ours (64 × 64)	10.84
	Ours (256 × 256)	14.87
	DDPM (256 × 256) [23]	7.89
	ProgressiveGAN (256 × 256) [27]	6.42

Fig. 6. Source images (top panel) and generated images (bottom panel, 256 × 256 resolution) on CelebA-HQ, AFHQ-CAT, and LSUN Church.

5.2 Applications

Image-to-Image Translation. Figure 7 shows that the AFHQ-CAT model can be used to transform CelebA-HQ images into cat images, and vice-versa. Note that these two models are trained independently without knowledge of the source

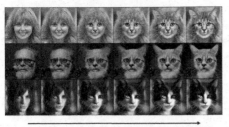 

PGD attack   PGD attack

Fig. 7. Image-to-image translation demonstration

domain, indicating that our approach may generalize better to unseen data than approaches (e.g., pix2pix [26], CycleGAN [68], and StarGAN [6]) that explicitly use the source domain dataset to train the model. The translation results may be further improved by finetuning the trained model on the source domain dataset, or including the source domain data in the p_0 dataset during training. The proposed approach is also more flexible than approaches that employs a fixed generator, as it allows the user to choose how much transformation to apply, and/or create cinematic effect from intermediate transformation results.

Worst-Case Out-of-Distribution Detection. Out-of-distribution (OOD) detection is a classic application of EBMs. Some recent works [2,3,35,48] find that EBMs and some other OOD detection approaches such as OE [21] are vulnerable to adversarial OOD inputs. Given the challenge of adversarial inputs, many authors attempt to address OOD detection in an adversarial setting (also known as worst-case, or adversarial OOD detection) [2,3,20,35,48]. Among these works, RATIO [2] is a state-of-the-art method that combines in- and out-distribution adversarial training to obtain a robust classifier that has uniform outputs in a neighborhood around OOD samples. Similar to OE, RATIO employs 80 million tiny images [52] as the out-distribution dataset to train the model.

Table 4 shows that our model achieves comparable OOD detection performance to the state-of-the-art method of RATIO [2]. OE, RATIO, and JEM all perform OOD detection by utilizing a classifier that has low confidence predictions on the out-distribution data (clean or worst-case). In RATIO, the worst-case out-distribution data is computed by performing the PGD attack on 80 million tiny images, whereas in JEM it is computed via Langevin dynamics initialized from uniform random noise. RATIO and our method's strong out-distribution adversarial robustness demonstrates the benefit of using a real and diverse out-distribution dataset to train the model. Our method does not make use of class labels and therefore can be considered as a binary variant of RATIO. On CelebA-HQ 256, AFHQ-CAT, and LSUN-Church our model similarly achieves strong out-distribution adversarial robustness (supplementary materials). These results suggest that our generative model can be applied to detect both naturally occurring OOD data and adversarially created malicious content.

Table 4. CIFAR-10 standard and worst-case OOD detection results (AUC scores). We use the same settings of AutoAttack [7], number of OOD samples, and perturbation limit as in [2] to compute adversarial OOD samples. Results of OE, JEM, and RATIO are from [2].

OOD dataset	Classifier-based approach			Ours
	OE [21]	JEM [14]	RATIO [2]	
Standard OOD				
SVHN	99.4	89.3	96.5	93.0
CIFAR-100	91.4	87.6	91.6	88.3
ImageNet	89.8	86.7	91.3	89.7
Uniform Noise	99.5	11.8	99.9	100
Worst-case OOD				
SVHN	0.6	7.3	81.3	81.6
CIFAR-100	2.7	19.2	73.0	70.3
ImageNet	1.5	21.2	73.5	71.2
Uniform Noise	43.1	2.5	99.8	100

5.3   Training Stability Analysis

To gain some insight into the training stability of our approach we investigate whether the PGD attack can be used with the EBMs training objective Eq. (2). Specifically, in Algorithm 2, we perform step 5's update on θ using the gradient $\nabla_\theta(\frac{1}{m}\sum_{i=1}^{m} f_\theta(x_i) - \frac{1}{m}\sum_{i=1}^{m} f_\theta(x_i^*))$. We observe that even under a small learning rate of $1e-6$, $\frac{1}{m}\sum_{i=1}^{m} f_\theta(x_i) - \frac{1}{m}\sum_{i=1}^{m} f_\theta(x_i^*)$ quickly increases and eventually overflows. This suggests that the stability of the AT approach can be largely attributed to the log-likelihood objective Eq. (11). We argue that the stability is due to the gradient cancelling effect of this objective: when f_θ has a large positive output on a sample $x \sim p_{\text{data}}$, $1 - \sigma(f_\theta(x))$ approaches 0 and therefore the corresponding scaled gradient in Eq. (14) vanishes, and similarly $\sigma(f_\theta(x^*))\nabla_\theta f_\theta(x^*)$ vanishes when f_θ has a large negative output on a sample $x^* \sim p_T^*$. In contrast, the EBMs objective Eq. (2) does not have constraints on f_θ's outputs and is therefore prone to divergence.

6   Conclusion

We have studied an AT-based approach to learning EBMs. Our analysis shows that binary AT learns a special kind of energy function that models the support of the observed data, and the training procedure can be viewed as an approximate maximum likelihood learning algorithm. We proposed improved techniques for generative modeling with AT, and demonstrated that the proposed method provides competitive generation performance to explicit EBMs, has competitive sampling efficiency, is stable to train, and is well-suited for image translation tasks. The proposed approach's strong out-distribution adversarial robustness suggests its potential application to detecting abnormal inputs and/or adversarially created fake content.

References

1. Arbel, M., Zhou, L., Gretton, A.: Generalized energy based models. In: International Conference on Learning Representations (2021). https://openreview.net/forum?id=0PtUPB9z6qK

2. Augustin, M., Meinke, A., Hein, M.: Adversarial robustness on in- and out-distribution improves explainability. In: Vedaldi, A., Bischof, H., Brox, T., Frahm, J.-M. (eds.) ECCV 2020. LNCS, vol. 12371, pp. 228–245. Springer, Cham (2020). https://doi.org/10.1007/978-3-030-58574-7_14

3. Bitterwolf, J., Meinke, A., Hein, M.: Certifiably adversarially robust detection of out-of-distribution data. Adv. Neural Inf. Process. Syst. **33**, 16085–16095 (2020)

4. Brock, A., Donahue, J., Simonyan, K.: Large scale GAN training for high fidelity natural image synthesis. In: International Conference on Learning Representations (2019). https://openreview.net/forum?id=B1xsqj09Fm

5. Ceylan, C., Gutmann, M.U.: Conditional noise-contrastive estimation of unnormalised models. In: International Conference on Machine Learning, pp. 726–734. PMLR (2018)

6. Choi, Y., Uh, Y., Yoo, J., Ha, J.W.: Stargan v2: diverse image synthesis for multiple domains. In: Proceedings of the IEEE/CVF Conference on Computer Vision and Pattern Recognition, pp. 8188–8197 (2020)

7. Croce, F., Hein, M.: Reliable evaluation of adversarial robustness with an ensemble of diverse parameter-free attacks. In: ICML (2020)

8. Du, Y., Li, S., Mordatch, I.: Compositional visual generation with energy based models. Adv. Neural Inf. Process. Syst. **33**, 6637–6647 (2020)

9. Du, Y., Li, S., Tenenbaum, J.B., Mordatch, I.: Improved contrastive divergence training of energy based models. In: ICML (2021)

10. Du, Y., Mordatch, I.: Implicit generation and modeling with energy based models. Adv. Neural Inf. Process. Syst. **32**, 1–11 (2019). https://proceedings.neurips.cc/paper/2019/file/378a063b8fdb1db941e34f4bde584c7d-Paper.pdf

11. Engstrom, L., Ilyas, A., Santurkar, S., Tsipras, D., Tran, B., Madry, A.: Adversarial robustness as a prior for learned representations. arXiv preprint arXiv:1906.00945 (2019)

12. Gao, R., Song, Y., Poole, B., Wu, Y.N., Kingma, D.P.: Learning energy-based models by diffusion recovery likelihood. In: International Conference on Learning Representations (2021). https://openreview.net/forum?id=v_1Soh8QUNc

13. Goodfellow, I., et al.: Generative adversarial nets. Adv. Neural Inf. Process. Syst., 2672–2680 (2014)

14. Grathwohl, W., Wang, K.C., Jacobsen, J.H., Duvenaud, D., Norouzi, M., Swersky, K.: Your classifier is secretly an energy based model and you should treat it like one. In: International Conference on Learning Representations (2020). https://openreview.net/forum?id=Hkxzx0NtDB

15. Grathwohl, W.S., Kelly, J.J., Hashemi, M., Norouzi, M., Swersky, K., Duvenaud, D.: No mcmc for me: amortized sampling for fast and stable training of energy-based models. In: International Conference on Learning Representations (2021). https://openreview.net/forum?id=ixpSxO9flk3

16. Gulrajani, I., Ahmed, F., Arjovsky, M., Dumoulin, V., Courville, A.C.: Improved training of wasserstein gans. Adv. Neural Inf. Process. Syst. **30** (2017). https://proceedings.neurips.cc/paper/2017/file/892c3b1c6dccd52936e27cbd0ff683d6-Paper.pdf

17. Gutmann, M., Hyvärinen, A.: Noise-contrastive estimation: a new estimation principle for unnormalized statistical models. In: Proceedings of the Thirteenth International Conference on Artificial Intelligence and Statistics, pp. 297–304. JMLR Workshop and Conference Proceedings (2010)

18. Han, T., Nijkamp, E., Fang, X., Hill, M., Zhu, S.C., Wu, Y.N.: Divergence triangle for joint training of generator model, energy-based model, and inferential model. In: Proceedings of the IEEE/CVF Conference on Computer Vision and Pattern Recognition, pp. 8670–8679 (2019)

19. Han, T., Nijkamp, E., Zhou, L., Pang, B., Zhu, S.C., Wu, Y.N.: Joint training of variational auto-encoder and latent energy-based model. In: Proceedings of the IEEE/CVF Conference on Computer Vision and Pattern Recognition, pp. 7978–7987 (2020)

20. Hein, M., Andriushchenko, M., Bitterwolf, J.: Why relu networks yield high-confidence predictions far away from the training data and how to mitigate the problem. In: Proceedings of the IEEE Conference on Computer Vision and Pattern Recognition, pp. 41–50 (2019)

21. Hendrycks, D., Mazeika, M., Dietterich, T.: Deep anomaly detection with outlier exposure. arXiv preprint arXiv:1812.04606 (2018)

22. Heusel, M., Ramsauer, H., Unterthiner, T., Nessler, B., Hochreiter, S.: Gans trained by a two time-scale update rule converge to a local nash equilibrium. Adv. Neural Inf. Process. Syst. **30**, 6626–6637 (2017)

23. Ho, J., Jain, A., Abbeel, P.: Denoising diffusion probabilistic models. Adv. Neural Inf. Process. Syst. **33** (2020). https://proceedings.neurips.cc/paper/2020/file/4c5bcfec8584af0d967f1ab10179ca4b-Paper.pdf

24. Hyvärinen, A., Dayan, P.: Estimation of non-normalized statistical models by score matching. J. Mach. Learn. Res. **6**(4) (2005)

25. Ilyas, A., Santurkar, S., Tsipras, D., Engstrom, L., Tran, B., Madry, A.: Adversarial examples are not bugs, they are features. arXiv preprint arXiv:1905.02175 (2019)

26. Isola, P., Zhu, J.Y., Zhou, T., Efros, A.A.: Image-to-image translation with conditional adversarial networks. In: Proceedings of the IEEE Conference on Computer Vision and Pattern Recognition, pp. 1125–1134 (2017)

27. Karras, T., Aila, T., Laine, S., Lehtinen, J.: Progressive growing of gans for improved quality, stability, and variation. arXiv preprint arXiv:1710.10196 (2017)

28. Karras, T., Aittala, M., Hellsten, J., Laine, S., Lehtinen, J., Aila, T.: Training generative adversarial networks with limited data. Adv. Neural Inf. Process. Syst. **33**, 12104–12114 (2020). https://proceedings.neurips.cc/paper/2020/file/8d30aa96e72440759f74bd2306c1fa3d-Paper.pdf

29. Kingma, D.P., Dhariwal, P.: Glow: Generative flow with invertible 1×1 convolutions. Adv. Neural Inf. Process. Syst., 10215–10224 (2018)

30. Krizhevsky, A., Hinton, G., et al.: Learning multiple layers of features from tiny images (2009)

31. Kumar, R., Ozair, S., Goyal, A., Courville, A., Bengio, Y.: Maximum entropy generators for energy-based models. arXiv preprint arXiv:1901.08508 (2019)

32. Kurakin, A., Goodfellow, I., Bengio, S.: Adversarial machine learning at scale. arXiv preprint arXiv:1611.01236 (2016)

33. LeCun, Y., Chopra, S., Hadsell, R., Ranzato, M., Huang, F.: A tutorial on energy-based learning. Predict. Struct. Data **1**(0) (2006)

34. Madry, A., Makelov, A., Schmidt, L., Tsipras, D., Vladu, A.: Towards deep learning models resistant to adversarial attacks. arXiv preprint arXiv:1706.06083 (2017)

35. Meinke, A., Hein, M.: Towards neural networks that provably know when they don't know. arXiv preprint arXiv:1909.12180 (2019)

36. Mescheder, L., Geiger, A., Nowozin, S.: Which training methods for gans do actually converge? In: International Conference on Machine Learning, pp. 3481–3490. PMLR (2018)

37. Miyato, T., Kataoka, T., Koyama, M., Yoshida, Y.: Spectral normalization for generative adversarial networks. In: International Conference on Learning Representations (2018). https://openreview.net/forum?id=B1QRgziT-

38. Nijkamp, E., et al.: MCMC should mix: learning energy-based model with flow-based backbone. In: International Conference on Learning Representations (2022). https://openreview.net/forum?id=4C93Qvn-tz

39. Nijkamp, E., Hill, M., Han, T., Zhu, S.C., Wu, Y.N.: On the anatomy of mcmc-based maximum likelihood learning of energy-based models. In: Proceedings of the AAAI Conference on Artificial Intelligence, vol. 34, pp. 5272–5280 (2020)

40. Nijkamp, E., Hill, M., Zhu, S.C., Wu, Y.N.: Learning non-convergent non-persistent short-run mcmc toward energy-based model. In: NeurIPS (2019)

41. Pang, B., Han, T., Nijkamp, E., Zhu, S.C., Wu, Y.N.: Learning latent space energy-based prior model. Adv. Neural Inf. Process. Syst. **33** (2020). https://proceedings.neurips.cc/paper/2020/file/fa3060edb66e6ff4507886f9912e1ab9-Paper.pdf

42. Pidhorskyi, S., Adjeroh, D.A., Doretto, G.: Adversarial latent autoencoders. In: Proceedings of the IEEE/CVF Conference on Computer Vision and Pattern Recognition, pp. 14104–14113 (2020)

43. Ramachandran, P., Zoph, B., Le, Q.V.: Swish: a self-gated activation function, vol. 7, no. 1. arXiv preprint arXiv:1710.05941 (2017)

44. Rhodes, B., Xu, K., Gutmann, M.U.: Telescoping density-ratio estimation. arXiv preprint arXiv:2006.12204 (2020)

45. Salimans, T., Goodfellow, I., Zaremba, W., Cheung, V., Radford, A., Chen, X.: Improved techniques for training gans. Adv. Neural Inf. Process. Syst. **29**, 2234–2242 (2016)

46. Salimans, T., Kingma, D.P.: Weight normalization: a simple reparameterization to accelerate training of deep neural networks. Adv. Neural Inf. Process. Syst. **29**, 901–909 (2016)

47. Santurkar, S., Ilyas, A., Tsipras, D., Engstrom, L., Tran, B., Madry, A.: Image synthesis with a single (robust) classifier. Adv. Neural Inf. Process. Syst., 1260–1271 (2019)

48. Sehwag, V., et al.: Better the devil you know: an analysis of evasion attacks using out-of-distribution adversarial examples. arXiv preprint arXiv:1905.01726 (2019)

49. Song, Y., Ermon, S.: Generative modeling by estimating gradients of the data distribution. Adv. Neural Inf. Process. Syst. **32** (2019). https://proceedings.neurips.cc/paper/2019/file/3001ef257407d5a371a96dcd947c7d93-Paper.pdf

50. Song, Y., Ermon, S.: Improved techniques for training score-based generative models. arXiv preprint arXiv:2006.09011 (2020)

51. Song, Y., Sohl-Dickstein, J., Kingma, D.P., Kumar, A., Ermon, S., Poole, B.: Score-based generative modeling through stochastic differential equations. In: International Conference on Learning Representations (2021). https://openreview.net/forum?id=PxTIG12RRHS

52. Torralba, A., Fergus, R., Freeman, W.T.: 80 million tiny images: a large data set for nonparametric object and scene recognition. IEEE Trans. Pattern Anal. Mach. Intell. **30**(11), 1958–1970 (2008)

53. Tsipras, D., Santurkar, S., Engstrom, L., Turner, A., Madry, A.: Robustness may be at odds with accuracy. arXiv preprint arXiv:1805.12152 (2018)

54. Vahdat, A., Kautz, J.: Nvae: a deep hierarchical variational autoencoder. Adv. Neural Inf. Process. Syst. **33** (2020). https://proceedings.neurips.cc/paper/2020/file/e3b21256183cf7c2c7a66be163579d37-Paper.pdf

55. Wang, Y., Wang, Y., Yang, J., Lin, Z.: A unified contrastive energy-based model for understanding the generative ability of adversarial training. In: International Conference on Learning Representations (2022). https://openreview.net/forum?id=XhF2VOMRHS

56. Welling, M., Teh, Y.W.: Bayesian learning via stochastic gradient langevin dynamics. In: Proceedings of the 28th International Conference on Machine Learning (ICML-2011), pp. 681–688. Citeseer (2011)

57. Xiao, Z., Kreis, K., Kautz, J., Vahdat, A.: Vaebm: a symbiosis between variational autoencoders and energy-based models. In: International Conference on Learning Representations (2021), https://openreview.net/forum?id=5m3SEczOV8L

58. Xie, J., Lu, Y., Gao, R., Zhu, S.C., Wu, Y.N.: Cooperative training of descriptor and generator networks. IEEE Trans. Pattern Anal. Mach. Intell. **42**(1), 27–45 (2018)

59. Xie, J., Lu, Y., Zhu, S.C., Wu, Y.: A theory of generative convnet. In: International Conference on Machine Learning, pp. 2635–2644. PMLR (2016)

60. Xie, J., Zheng, Z., Fang, X., Zhu, S.C., Wu, Y.N.: Cooperative training of fast thinking initializer and slow thinking solver for conditional learning. IEEE Trans. Pattern Anal. Mach. Intell. (2021)

61. Xie, J., Zheng, Z., Gao, R., Wang, W., Zhu, S.C., Wu, Y.N.: Learning descriptor networks for 3D shape synthesis and analysis. In: Proceedings of the IEEE Conference on Computer Vision and Pattern Recognition, pp. 8629–8638 (2018)

62. Xie, J., Zheng, Z., Gao, R., Wang, W., Zhu, S.C., Wu, Y.N.: Generative voxelnet: learning energy-based models for 3D shape synthesis and analysis. IEEE Trans. Pattern Anal. Mach. Intell. (2020)

63. Xie, J., Zheng, Z., Li, P.: Learning energy based model with variational autoencoder as amortized sampler. In: The Thirty-Fifth AAAI Conference on Artificial Intelligence (AAAI), vol. 2 (2021)

64. Xie, J., Zhu, Y., Li, J., Li, P.: A tale of two flows: cooperative learning of langevin flow and normalizing flow toward energy-based model. In: International Conference on Learning Representations (2022). https://openreview.net/forum?id=31d5RLCUuXC

65. Yin, X., Kolouri, S., Rohde, G.K.: Gat: Generative adversarial training for adversarial example detection and robust classification. In: International Conference on Learning Representations (2020). https://openreview.net/forum?id=SJeQEp4YDH

66. Yu, F., Seff, A., Zhang, Y., Song, S., Funkhouser, T., Xiao, J.: Lsun: construction of a large-scale image dataset using deep learning with humans in the loop. arXiv preprint arXiv:1506.03365 (2015)

67. Zhao, Y., Xie, J., Li, P.: Learning energy-based generative models via coarse-to-fine expanding and sampling. In: International Conference on Learning Representations (2021). https://openreview.net/forum?id=aD1_5zowqV

68. Zhu, J.Y., Park, T., Isola, P., Efros, A.A.: Unpaired image-to-image translation using cycle-consistent adversarial networks. In: Proceedings of the IEEE International Conference on Computer Vision, pp. 2223–2232 (2017)

Adversarial Label Poisoning Attack on Graph Neural Networks via Label Propagation

Ganlin Liu, Xiaowei Huang, and Xinping Yi[✉]

University of Liverpool, Liverpool, UK
{ganlin.liu,xiaowei.huang,xinping.yi}@liverpool.ac.uk

Abstract. Graph neural networks (GNNs) have achieved outstanding performance in semi-supervised learning tasks with partially labeled graph structured data. However, labeling graph data for training is a challenging task, and inaccurate labels may mislead the training process to erroneous GNN models for node classification. In this paper, we consider label poisoning attacks on training data, where the labels of input data are modified by an adversary before training, to understand to what extent the state-of-the-art GNN models are resistant/vulnerable to such attacks. Specifically, we propose a label poisoning attack framework for graph convolutional networks (GCNs), inspired by the equivalence between label propagation and decoupled GCNs that separate message passing from neural networks. Instead of attacking the entire GCN models, we propose to attack solely label propagation for message passing. It turns out that a gradient-based attack on label propagation is effective and efficient towards the misleading of GCN training. More remarkably, such label attack can be topology-agnostic in the sense that the labels to be attacked can be efficiently chosen without knowing graph structures. Extensive experimental results demonstrate the effectiveness of the proposed method against state-of-the-art GCN-like models.

Keywords: Label poisoning attack · Graph neural networks · Label propagation · Graph convolutional network

1 Introduction

The past years have witnessed the increasing interest in studying computer vision (CV) and machine learning tasks using graph representation learning, especially graph neural networks (GNNs). Differently from the canonical convolutional neural network (CNN) models, GNNs explore graph data structures for various CV applications, e.g., semantic object parsing [12], skeleton-based action recognition [32], visual tracking [6], video parsing [28], point cloud classification [29], to name just a few. In particular, scene graphs can be constructed from parsing images/videos to form the semantic relationships between pairs of objects, for which GNNs play a role in image classification/recognition/segmentation. In

© The Author(s), under exclusive license to Springer Nature Switzerland AG 2022
S. Avidan et al. (Eds.): ECCV 2022, LNCS 13665, pp. 227–243, 2022.
https://doi.org/10.1007/978-3-031-20065-6_14

terms of node classification, GCN models have been also used in medical image analysis for disease prediction to classify the health status of the patient or the type of case [19,31].

Besides the emerging CV applications, GNN models have been demonstrated a powerful tool in a variety of semi-supervised learning tasks, such as node classification [7,10,26], graph classification [34], and link prediction [36], in many application scenarios in our social life, such as social networks [5], knowledge graphs [27] and recommendation systems [13,33]. For example, given graph structured data with node features and partial labels, node classification is to predict the labels of those unlabeled data according to the inter-node relationship modeled as a graph. The state-of-the-art GNN models leverage both feature transformation that maps input features to graph embeddings via neural networks and neighborhood aggregation via a message passing mechanism to predict the labels.

However, in practical applications, labeling graph data is a challenging task; limited or inaccurate labels could lead to erroneous trained models via message passing. It is crucial to understand as to how GNN models are resistant or vulnerable to limited or inaccurate labels and to what extent we could rely on the labeled data in graph representation learning. To this end, we consider label poisoning attack in the *training* phase to reveal the potential vulnerability of GNN training, where an adversary attempts to decrease the node classification accuracy of unlabeled data by modifying the labels of the known ones before training. It is worth noting that adversarial label poisoning attack is different from the intensively studied adversarial attack (e.g. [8,25]) in the *inference* phase.

Compared with the inference time attack, less attention has been paid to the poisoning attack on GNN models. Of the most relevance is the recent work, called Label-flipping attacK model against GNNs (LafAK), which generates gradient-based attacks based on an approximated closed form of the entire GNN model and continuous surrogates of attack objectives. Although promising from a conceptual point of view, LafAK is restricted to binary classification and relies highly on the overall loss function of the entire GNN models, which involves model parameters of neural networks that are unknown before training although an approximate closed-form solution to a linearized model is replaced.

In this paper, we aim to address the above issues by proposing a novel adversarial label poisoning attack for GNN models via label propagation, which captures the essence of massage passing whilst leaving aside the unknown model parameters of neural networks for feature transformation. Instead of attacking the entire GNN models with intertwined neural feature transformation and neighborhood aggregation, we solely attack the neighborhood aggregation of message passing that can be captured by a label propagation process. The rationale behind this idea is underpinned by recent advances on the equivalence between decoupled graph convolution network (DGCN) and label propagation [4]: training DGCN with separated feature transformation and neighborhood aggregation (e.g., APPNP [11] and SGCN [30]), is equivalent to label propagation to generate pseudo-labels for unlabeled data followed by training neural network with pseudo-labeled data with dynamic weights. It turns out attacking the loss function of the label propagation process alone to locate the label poisoning is effective and efficient in poisoning the entire GNN models.

Specifically, the contributions of our work can be summarized as follows:

- We propose a label poisoning attack framework for GCN-like models with three components: label propagation to generate predictive label, maximum gradient attack method to reduce the accuracy of an equivalent label propagation model, and GNN training with poisoned labels. Remarkably, our proposed label poisoning attack works for multi-class node classification and does not require to access the model parameters of neural networks in GCNs.
- We propose a maximum gradient attack method to poison known labels that maximizes the loss function of equivalent label propagation models. Among different label propagation models, we found that the knowledge of the graph structure is not necessary, but the node features are sufficient to yield an effective attack.
- We conduct an extensive set of experiments with different choices of label propagation models to test the attack performance against various GCN-like models (e.g., GCN [10], GAT [26], GraphSAGE [7], APPNP [11], SGCN [30], PT [4]) for multi-class node classification and demonstrate the effectiveness and efficiency of our proposed method.

2   Preliminaries and Related Work

2.1   Graph Convolution Network and Its Decoupled Variants

Graph Convolution Network (GCN). Roughly speaking, GCN is a feature extractor for graph structured data modeled by a graph topology $\mathcal{G}$ with n nodes specified by its adjacency matrix $A \in \{0,1\}^{n \times n}$ and the input features $X \in \mathbb{R}^{n \times f}$ with each row being node attribute of one node and f being the number of features. It produces node embeddings from input features through a message passing mechanism over $\mathcal{G}$ with all node equipped with neural networks for feature transformation. The message passing performs iterative message aggregation/propagation from/to neighboring nodes as if stacking a number of layers. In each iteration/layer, each node employs a multilayer perceptron (MLP) to transform node features into a new embedding and propagates it to its neighbors, followed by feature aggregation from neighboring nodes to update node features for the next iteration/layer [10]. A typical GCN layer for node feature transformation can be written as

$$H^{(k+1)} = \sigma(\hat{A}H^{(k)}W^{(k)}) \tag{1}$$

where $\hat{A}$ is the normalized adjacency matrix, $H^{(k)}$ is the updated node feature representations after neighborhood message aggregation at k-th layer with $H^{(0)} = X$ being the input feature matrix, $\sigma(\cdot)$ denotes a nonlinear activation function, such as ReLU, and $W^{(k)}$ is the trainable weight matrix of the MLP at the k-th layer. In the original GCN model [10], $\hat{A} = \tilde{D}^{-\frac{1}{2}}\tilde{A}\tilde{D}^{-\frac{1}{2}}$ is adopted, where $\tilde{A} = A + I$ with I being the identity matrix, and $\tilde{D} = \text{diag}(d_1, ..., d_n)$ is the degree matrix with $d_i = \sum_j A_{ij}$ being the degree of the node i.

The above vanilla GCN models (e.g., [7,10]) combine intertwined feature transformation and neighborhood aggregation for node representation learning. The extracted node feature representations can be used in many graph learning tasks such as node classification [7,11], graph classification [20], link prediction [36] and graph embedding [1,22].

Decoupled Graph Convolutional Network (DGCN). Differently from the vanilla GCN models with coupled feature transformation and neighborhood aggregation, some recent studies have found that such coupled designs are unnecessary and have proposed to separate these two operations. These decoupled GCN (DGCN) models (e.g., [4]) can be summarized as

$$\hat{Y} = \text{softmax}(\bar{A}f_\theta(X)) \qquad (2)$$

where $f_\theta(\cdot)$ is usually a neural network with parameters θ to transform input features X to certain representations, and $\bar{A}$ is a propagation matrix determined by the propagation strategies that will be specified later.

In what follows, we briefly describe two existing DGCN models: Approximate Personalized Propagation of Neural Predictions (APPNP) [11] and Simplifying Graph Convolutional Network (SGCN) [30].

APPNP [11] separates the neural network from the propagation scheme. It uses Personalized PageRank [18] as the propagation strategy in order to leverage a larger neighborhood information than GCN, and can be combined with any state-of-the-art neural network. Thus, the propagation matrix $\bar{A}$ in (2) can be specified by

$$\bar{A} = (1 - \alpha)^K \hat{A}^K + \alpha \sum_{k=0}^{K-1} (1 - \alpha)^k \hat{A}^k \qquad (3)$$

where $\alpha \in (0, 1]$ is the teleport probability and K is the number of layers.

SGCN [30] aims to transform the nonlinear GCN into a simple linear model. By successively removing the nonlinear transition functions and collapsing weight matrices between GCN layers, the additional complexity of GCNs can be reduced. The resulting simplified linear model can be replaced by (2) with

$$\bar{A} = \hat{A}^K \text{ and } f_\theta(X) = X\Theta \qquad (4)$$

where K is the number of SGCN layers, and Θ is a reparameterized weight matrix with non-linearity removed.

2.2   Label Propagation and Its Role in GCN

Label propagation (LP) algorithm [38] is a commonly used semi-supervised learning method in machine learning, propagating known labels from labeled nodes to unlabeled ones. An implicit assumption of LP is that similar data should have the same label. For each node in the network, at the initial stage, the label propagation algorithm initializes a unique label for each node. Each iteration will change its own label according to the label of the node connected to it. The way of change is to select the community label with the most labels among the nodes connected to it as its own community label. As community labels spread, eventually, tightly connected nodes will have common labels.

Propagation then Training (PT) [4] is a variant of label propagation algorithm, including two steps: (1) Label propagation, where the known labels are propagated along the edges of graph to generate pseudo-labels for unlabeled nodes; (2) Neural network training, where feature transformation is done by training a neural network classifier on the data with known and pseudo-labels. The loss function of PT can be written as

$$L(\theta) = \ell(f_\theta(X), \bar{A}Y) \tag{5}$$

where $\ell(\cdot)$ is the loss function between $f_\theta(X)$ and the soft labels $Y_{soft} = \bar{A}Y$.

Equivalence of Decoupled GCN and PT. Hande et al. (2021) [4] discusses decoupled GCN of semi-supervised node classification from a new perspective. It is proved that the decoupled GCN is essentially the same as two-step label propagation via in-depth theoretical analysis, and the effectiveness of decoupled GCN is also revealed.

2.3   Adversarial Poisoning Attacks on Graphs

Adversarial attack lies in the intersection of machine learning and cyber-security. It has been evidenced that deep learning models often suffer from adversarial attacks with degraded accuracy performance. Roughly speaking, adversarial attacks can be categorized into evasion and poisoning attacks according to the stage when attacks occur. While evasion attacks happen in the testing phase with well-trained models, adversarial poisoning attacks occur in the training phase, where the training data samples are modified by adversaries to mislead the training process to an erroneous model. Among different data poisoning attacks, label poisoning attack (e.g., [2,3,16,21]) is crucial in semi-supervised learning, where the changes of labels may mislead the labeling of unlabeled data. For adversarial label poisoning attack, the adversary is only allowed to change the labels of a small number of training nodes. It can significantly reduce the performance of node classification than random label noise, because of the potential use of gradient information.

In the literature of graph semi-supervised learning, less attention has been paid to label poisoning attacks. Of particular relevance are the label-flipping attacks for the label propagation [14] and for the vanilla GCN model [35].

Poisoning Attack on Label Propagation. A unified framework has been proposed in [14] for graph semi-supervised learning with two algorithms to solve poisoning regression and classification tasks. The optimization objective is to maximize the error rate for classification with a combinatorial nature.

Label-Flipping Attack on GCNs. LafAK [35] aims to flip the unnoticeable parts of the training labels to minimize the performance of GCN. Therefore, following the purpose of LafAK, the optimization problem can be written as

$$\min_{\delta} \quad -L_{0-1}(\theta^*; A, X, y_u),$$
$$s.t. \quad \theta^* = \arg\min_{\theta} L(\theta; A, X, \delta \odot y_l), \quad \|\delta - 1_{n_l}\|_0 \leq \epsilon n_l, \tag{6}$$

where $y_l \in \{-1, +1\}^{n_l}$ and $y_u \in \{-1, +1\}^{n_u}$ are the labels of known and unknown nodes, respectively, n_l and n_u are the numbers of labeled and unlabeled nodes, $\delta \in \{+1, -1\}^{n_l}$ is the label perturbation, 1_{n_l} is an all-one vector, $\odot$ means Hadamard product, and ϵ is the ratio of label flipping.

3   Label Poisoning Attack Model

In this paper, we consider label poisoning attack on GCN-like models. Different from LafAK in [35] with label-flipping determined by gradient attack on the

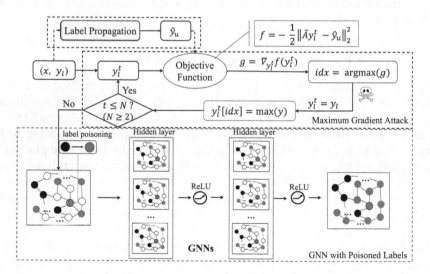

Fig. 1. The framework of our proposed label poisoning attack, which consists of label propagation to generate predictive labels, maximum gradient attack to poison data labels, and GNN training with poisoned labels. Specifically, in maximum gradient attack, the maximum gradients of the objective function are identified and the corresponding labels are poisoned, and it repeats several times ($N = 2$ is a good choice in practice). The label poisoned data are used for GNN training, misleading the trained model to reduce accuracy on unlabeled node classification.

entire GCN model, we propose a novel label poisoning framework that delegates gradient attack solely to label propagation. This is inspired by recent advances on the equivalence of decoupled GCN and label propagation [4], for which label propagation followed by feature transformation performs as well as GCN models with coupled neighborhood aggregation and feature transformation.

Figure 1 presents our proposed framework on label poisoning attack. It consists of three components: (1) label propagation from labeled to unlabeled nodes to generate predictive pseudo-labels $\hat{y}_u$; (2) maximum gradient attack with changed labels to poison training data; and (3) GCN training with label poisoned data for node classification. In what follows, we explain the role of each component in detail.

3.1   Label Propagation

The goal of label propagation is to generate label prediction for unlabeled data, so as to be used in the maximum gradient attack.

We consider an undirected graph $\mathcal{G} = (\mathcal{V}, \mathcal{E})$, where $\mathcal{V}$ represents the set of n nodes, $\mathcal{E}$ is the edge set, and the adjacency matrix is represented by $A \in \{0,1\}^{n \times n}$. All nodes in the graph are associated with some node features, denoted by $X = [x_1; x_2; \ldots; x_n] \in \mathbb{R}^{n \times f}$ with $x_i \in \mathbb{R}^f$, and $y = [y_l; y_u]$ is the label set, including the known labels $y_l \in \mathbb{R}^{n_l}$ and the unknown labels $y_u \in \mathbb{R}^{n_u}$. The goal of node classification is to figure out y_u with the knowledge of X, y_l, and A.

Let S be a similarity matrix with $S_{ij} = \exp(-\gamma \|x_i - x_j\|^2)$ resulted from a Gaussian kernel, and D be the degree matrix. Then, the graph Laplacian can be defined as $L = D - S$. Given n_l labeled data and n_u unlabeled data (usually $n_l < n_u$) with $n = n_l + n_u$ nodes, S and D are both $(n_l + n_u) \times (n_l + n_u)$ matrices. We split S and D into 4 sub-matrices $S = \begin{bmatrix} S_{ll} & S_{lu} \\ S_{ul} & S_{uu} \end{bmatrix}$, $D = \begin{bmatrix} D_{ll} & D_{lu} \\ D_{ul} & D_{uu} \end{bmatrix}$. The predicted labels via label propagation [14,38] can be written as

$$\hat{y}_u = (D_{uu} - S_{uu})^{-1} S_{ul} y_l. \tag{7}$$

The label propagation takes the input features X and some known labels y_l to generate predictive labels $\hat{y}_u$, which are used to replace y_u in the optimization problem of maximum gradient attack.

3.2   Maximum Gradient Attack

The aim of label poisoning attacks is to maximize the classification error rate by modifying a small fraction of known labels of data points at the training stage, that is, the optimization problem can be given by

$$\min_{y_l'} -\frac{1}{2} \left\| \bar{A} y_l' - (y_u \ or \ \hat{y}_u) \right\|_2^2 + \lambda \|y_l' - y_l\|_0, \tag{8}$$

where $\bar{A}$ is the label propagation method which will be specified later, y_l' represents the poisoned labels, the labels of unknown data is y_u (ground truth) or

$\hat{y}_u$ (predicted labels), $\|\cdot\|_0$ is the ℓ_0-norm of a vector to ensure the number of poisoned labels is as small as possible, and λ is to balance between the loss of label propagation and the number of poisoned labels.

In this section, we study the multi-class classification on graph convolution networks. The difference with the binary class labels is that the perturbed label y_l' is changed to the class of another label directly instead of multiplying by a perturbation, because the input is multi-class data, such as $y \in \{0, 1, 2, 3, 4, 5\}^n$. The label propagation method $\bar{A}$ can reuse those in GNN models specified in Sect. 2.1. In what follows, we consider three approaches:

a. **SM**: $\bar{A} = (D_{uu} - S_{uu})^{-1} S_{ul}$ as in [14,38], and $\bar{A} y_l'$ means the class of the perturbed labels will be propagated from y_l' to unobserved labels y_u.
b. **SK**: $\bar{A} = \hat{A}^K$ as in [30], where $\hat{A}$ is the normalized adjacency matrix and K is the number of layers.
c. **SP**: $\bar{A} = \alpha(I - (1 - \alpha)\hat{A})^{-1}$ as in [11,37], which has been used to classify each node using information from the larger, adjustable neighborhood.

As y_l' is an integer vector, Equation (8) is an integer program and in general challenge to derive a closed-form solution. To find a feasible solution, we employ a gradient descent method, namely maximum gradient (MG) attack, to generate an approximate solution in an iterative manner. MG attack takes known labels y_l and the predictive labels $\hat{y}_u$ as the inputs, and outputs the indices of labels in y_l for label poisoning and the poisoned labels.

The following Algorithm 1 summarizes the specific process of MG attack.

Algorithm 1: Maximum Gradient Attack

Input: Graph structured data with A, X, y_l, and the budget of poisoned labels c

Output: The poisoned labels y_l' with $\|y_l' - y_l\|_0 \le c$

1 $y_l^0 = y_l$
2 **for** $t \le N$ **do**
3 $\quad$ Compute $\bar{A}$ with different label propagation strategies;
4 $\quad$ Compute gradient: $g = \nabla_{y_l^t} f(y_l^t)$ where $f(y_l^t) := -\dfrac{1}{2}\left\| \bar{A} y_l^t - (y_u \; or \; \hat{y}_u) \right\|_2^2$;
5 $\quad$ Select top c gradients in g and identify the indices of them as a set $\mathcal{I}$;
6 $\quad$ Set $y_l^t = y_l$;
7 $\quad$ Modify $y_l^t[i]$ for all $i \in \mathcal{I}$ to the max label class;
8 $\quad$ Update $y_l^{t+1} \leftarrow y_l^t$, $t \leftarrow t + 1$;
9 **end**
10 **Return** $y_l' = y_l^N$

3.3 GCN Training with Poisoned Labels

The updated y'_l is the output result, which is used to train the GCN model together with A and X. The resulting prediction of $\hat{y}_u$ will be compared with the ground truth y_u to test the performance of poisoning attack.

4 Experiments

Datasets: For label propagation, we conduct experiments on a binary classification dataset called rcv1,[1] which is a benchmark dataset on text categorization. It is a collection of newswire articles produced by Reuters in 1996–1997. For graph neural networks, we use cora_ml [15], citeseer [23], pubmed [17] and ms_academic [24] datasets on PT, DGCN and GCN models. Cora_ml, citeseer and pubmed are citation networks, where each node indicates a paper and edges represent corresponding citation relationships. Ms_academic is a co-author network in which nodes and edges represent authors and co-authors, respectively. The dataset statistics are summarized in the Table 1.

Table 1. Dataset statistics

Dataset	Nodes	Features	Classes
rcv1	20,242	47,236	2
cora_ml	2,810	2,879	7
citeseer	2,110	3,703	6
pubmed	19,717	500	3
ms_academic	18,333	6,805	15

Baseline:

Label Propagation. In the poisoning attack on LP, the greedy and probabilistic methods are proposed by [14] for label-flipping in binary classification.

- *Greedy:* The greedy solver is to flip data labels one by one in a greedy manner. In this process, the label that decreases the objective function the most after flipping is to be flipped. Repeat this step several times until the number of flipped labels reaches the budget.
- *Probabilistic:* The probabilistic method considers the flipping actions that may be better in the long run but may be suboptimal at present. It assigns high probability to each best action, but still retains non-zero probability for other actions, so as to determine the most suitable label for flipping.

Graph Convolution Network. In the poisoning attacks on GCN models, there are two baseline methods with random noise added to the labels [4] and with gradient attack using LafAK [35].

---

[1] Publicly available at https://www.csie.ntu.edu.tw/~cjlin/libsvmtools/datasets/.

- *Random:* For the propagation then training model, the add_noise method is to randomly transfer some samples of each class and change their labels to other classes of label.
- *LafAK:* The objective of LafAK is a non-differentiable bi-level optimization problem. An approximate closed-form of GCN model parameters is considered, and continuous surrogates of non-differentiable components are adopted to simplify the gradient-based optimization process.

Experimental Configuration: We first verify the effectiveness of the proposed maximum gradient attack method against the label propagation (LP) model in graph semi-supervised learning [38], and then against the state-of-the-art GNN models, such as GCN [10], graph attention network (GAT) [26], GraphSAGE [7], SGCN [30], APPNP [11], and PT [4]. For each model, we use the default settings for the hyper-parameters. In the experiments of attack on GCNs, we use the Adam [9] optimizer with a learning rate of 0.01 to train all models for a maximum of 2000 epochs, and also, we terminate training if the validation loss does not decrease for 100 consecutive epochs, using an early stopping window size of 100.

5   Attack Performance Evaluation

Hypotheses. Our experiments aim to validate two hypotheses:

1). Attacking GNNs can be alternatively done on the equivalent LP via gradient-based methods, which means neural networks can be ignored when determining attacked labels.
2). In the presence of node features, graph structural information is not necessary for an effective poisoning attack.

In order to test these two hypotheses, we conduct the following experiments. First, we verify the effectiveness of the gradient-based attacks on both LP and GCN models. Second, we inspect the choices of parameters in optimizing Eq. (8) by applying the proposed MG attacks to GCN models with three label propagation methods and with/without ground truth. Third, we compare our proposed MG attack with LafAK, confirming the above two hypotheses that label poisoning of GCN can be achieved in the context of ignoring neural networks and only knowing node characteristics. Finally, we apply MG attacks to other state-of-the-art GNN models, such as GAT, GraphSAGE, SGCN, APPNP, and PT, and demonstrate that these two hypotheses are also valid for these GCN-like models.

Effectiveness of Gradient-Based Attacks. Fig. 2 presents the reduced accuracy of label prediction with different attack methods on label propagation (Fig. 2(a)) and GCN models (Figs. 2(b)–(d)) over different datasets. In each sub-figure, x-axis is the number (or rate in percentage) of attacked labels, and y-axis represents the prediction accuracy of label propagation or trained GCN models with poisoned labels. Note that the lower the accuracy of prediction, the more effective the attack method.

In order to confirm the effectiveness of gradient-based attacks on label propagation, Fig. 2(a) presents the comparison of greedy and probabilistic methods with the existing FGSM and PGD attacks and our proposed MG attack method over the dataset rcv1 for binary classification. It can be seen that with the increase of the number of flipped labels, the performance of the gradient-based attacks outperform the greedy and probabilistic methods.

Figures 2(b)–(d) compare the performance of adding random label noise (add_noise) and our MG attack on PT and APPNP models, as well as the sole MG attacks on the neural networks, specifically when the adversary attacks the pseudo labels after the label propagation so that the poisoned pseudo labels are input into the neural networks, i.e., the blue line PT_NN(MG), over datasets cora_ml, citeseer, and ms_academic. According to the framework in Fig. 1, we first generate attacked labels based on label propagation via Algorithm 1, and then train the graph neural networks on the poisoned pseudo-label data. Given the equivalence between PT and DGCN by the loss function [4], we also apply our proposed MG attack to DGCN, i.e., APPNP. As shown in Figs. 2(b)-(d), our proposed MG attack is indeed effective for the DGCN model. That is, it confirms our hypothesis that attacking the equivalent LP model is effective as attacking the GNN models, and that the gradient-based attacks are more powerful than randomly adding label noise.

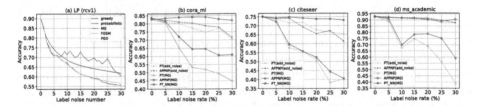

Fig. 2. (a) Accuracy performance comparison of the greedy, probabilistic, MG, FGSM and PGD attack methods on label propagation model over rcv1 dataset. (b)-(d) Comparison of the random add_noise and our maximum gradient attack methods on PT and APPNP models and only attack neural network on PT (PT_NN(MG)) on cora_ml, citeseer and ms_academic datasets.

Label Propagation for Predicting $\hat{y}_u$. The optimization problem in Eq. (8) requires the knowledge of unknown labels either as the ground truth y_u or as label predictions $\hat{y}_u$. For predicting $\hat{y}_u$, in our proposed framework in Fig. 1, we adopt the label propagation method SK to generate label predictions, that is, $\hat{y}_u = \hat{A}^K y_l$, when the ground truth is unknown and the GCN model has not yet been trained. Figure 3 indicates the feasibility of this alternative $\hat{y}_u$ with different choices of label propagation strategies of $\bar{A}$ (SM, SK, SP) on attacking the GCN models. For example, SK_y_u means $\bar{A} = \hat{A}^K$ and the ground truth y_u

are used in Eq. (8). From Fig. 3, we observe that using the predictive labels $\hat{y}_u$ results in more effective and stable attack performance.

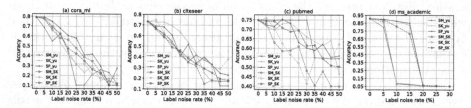

Fig. 3. The feasibility of substituting $\hat{y}_u = \hat{A}^K y_l$ for y_u. In the legend, the first part represents the choice of label propagation method $\bar{A}$, and the second part indicates if the ground truth y_u or the predicted labels $\hat{y}_u = \hat{A}^K y_l$ are used.

Label Propagation for MG Attacks with $\hat{y}_u$. Our proposed MG attack method is mainly to solve the optimization problem in Eq. (8), which involves the choices of label propagation methods in both MG attacks on the equivalent LP model with $\bar{A}$ and label predictions $\hat{y}_u$ resulted from LP algorithms. For label propagation, we consider three different choices of propagation strategies: SM, SK, SP, which indicate three label propagation methods $\bar{A}$ as mentioned in Sect. 3.2, respectively.

Figure 4 shows the attack performance with various combinations of three propagation methods for MG attacks and predicting $\hat{y}_u$. For instance, 'SK_SP' means $\bar{A} = \hat{A}^K$ is used for the MG attack and $\hat{y}_u = \alpha(I - (1 - \alpha)\hat{A})^{-1} y_l$ for label prediction. It can be seen from Fig. 4 that comparable performance can be obtained by various propagation methods. Notably, SM_SM only uses data features for the MG attack without knowing ground truth, which validates the second hypothesis that LP-based gradient attack is also effective to poison GCN labels without the knowledge of graph structures and label ground truth.

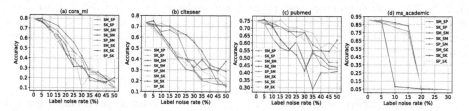

Fig. 4. Comparison of attack performance on GCN models with different combinations of label propagation methods $\bar{A}$ for the MG attack and for generating label predictions $\hat{y}_u$. In the legend, the first part represents the LP method of $\bar{A}$, and the second one is the propagation method to generate predicted labels $\hat{y}_u$ with SM: $(D_{uu} - S_{uu})^{-1} S_{ul}$; SK: $\hat{A}^K$; and SP: $\alpha(I - (1 - \alpha)\hat{A})^{-1}$.

Comparison of MG Attack and LafAK. We compare the attack performance of our proposed MG attack with the state-of-the-art LafAK method on the GCN models to validate the above two hypotheses. While LafAK can be seen a white-box attack where neural network parameters are accessible to the adversary, our proposed method is a black-box attack such that the adversary does not require the knowledge of neural network parameters to make an effective attack. In our proposed MG attack, we apply three different label propagation methods of $\bar{A}$, marked by SM, SK, APPNP, and the predicted labels $\hat{y}_u = \hat{A}^K y_l$. LafAK is a label-flipping attack through maximizing the loss of the entire GCN model with neural network. It selects two classes of labels with the largest number in the dataset to flip. There is a limitation: When the labels of these two nodes are all flipped to the opposite class, the attack no longer takes effect, as shown in Fig. 5 where the 'LafAK_o' curves experience error floors. To rectify this and ensure the fairness of comparison, we extend LafAK to all training datasets (called 'LafAK_c'), and modify the attacked labels to the maximum label class in the dataset as our MG attack does. From the comparison in Fig. 5, we conclude that:

1). Our proposed MG attack (on the equivalent LP only without considering neural network model parameters) is as effective as LafAK (on the entire GCN models with neural model parameter involved). Therefore, this confirms the first hypothesis that attacking GCN models can be alternatively done by attacking the equivalent LP model.

2). For our proposed MG attacks with different label propagation methods $\bar{A}$, the attack performances are comparable, so that $\bar{A} = (D_{uu} - S_{uu})^{-1} S_{ul}$ without topological structure still yields an effective attack. This confirms the second hypothesis that graph structural information is not necessary.

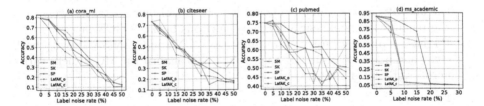

Fig. 5. Comparison between MG attacks and LafAK against GCN models. In the legend of this figure, SM, SK, SP means three different label propagation methods of $\bar{A}$, LafAK_o is the original LafAK, and LafAK_c is an improved version of LafAK_o with the limitation of target flipping labels fixed.

Transferability of MG Attacks. In practical scenarios, the adversary may not know which GNN model is under training. So, to test the possibility of applying attacks learned for one model to other models, we consider the transferability of our MG attack. Recall that our MG attacks depend only on the input futures and the known labels, and are irrelevant to the GNN models. As such, we directly apply the poisoned labels from our MG attack to state-of-the-art GNNs. Figure 6 presents the transferability to the GCN-like models, such as GAT and GraphSAGE. The results indicate that the our proposed MG attacks can be successfully transferred to these two models.

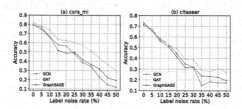

Fig. 6. Transferability of our MG attack to GAT and GraphSAGE models.

Robustness of Different GNN Models against MG Attacks. Figure 7 gives a more comprehensive study of the robustness of state-of-the-art GNN models against our proposed MG attack over different datasets. In particular, the MG attack with 'SM_SK' is employed, that is $\bar{A} = (D_{uu} - S_{uu})^{-1}S_{ul}$ for MG attacks and $\hat{y}_u = \hat{A}^K y_l$ for pseudo-label prediction. According the experiments, we have the following observations.

1). The robustness of APPNP always outperforms other models under MG attacks. It is probably because APPNP can aggregate information from large, adjustable neighborhood for classifying each node.
2). Although SGCN has comparable accuracy with clean data as other models, the linearity makes it more vulnerable to label poisoning attacks, because of the removal the nonlinear activation functions between GCN layers.
3). PT has a similar accuracy performance as GCN and GraphSAGE with both clean and poisoned data, and their robustness against the MG attacks varies across different datasets.

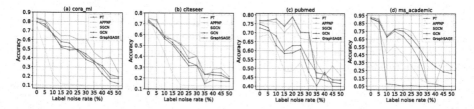

Fig. 7. The robustness of state-of-the-art GNN models (GCN, GraphSAGE, SGCN, APPNP, PT) against our MG label poisoning attack with 'SM_SK' label propagation methods over different datasets.

6   Conclusion

In this paper, we studied adversarial label poisoning attacks on GNNs and proposed a framework to attack GCN-like models through a maximum gradient attack method on the equivalent LP models. The proposed method can effectively attack the GCN-like models while avoiding the neural network computation, thereby reducing the node classification performance of the GCNs. Extensive experiments showed that, our proposed label poisoning attacks only on LP is as effective as the state-of-the-art attacks (e.g., LafAK), and is transferable to the GCN-like models. Notably, our method does not require the knowledge of graph structural information in the presence of node features.

Acknowledgment. GL thanks the Department of Computer Science, University of Liverpool for the support of the attendance to the conference. XH is supported by the EPSRC under project [EP/T026995/1].

References

1. Cui, P., Wang, X., Pei, J., Zhu, W.: A survey on network embedding. IEEE Trans. Knowl. Data Eng. **31**(5), 833–852 (2018)
2. Dai, E., Aggarwal, C., Wang, S.: NRGNN: learning a label noise-resistant graph neural network on sparsely and noisily labeled graphs. In: Proceedings of the 27th ACM SIGKDD Conference on Knowledge Discovery & Data Mining, 227–236 (2021)
3. Dai, E., Jin, W., Liu, H., Wang, S.: Towards robust graph neural networks for noisy graphs with sparse labels. arXiv preprint arXiv:2201.00232 (2022)
4. Dong, H., et al.: On the equivalence of decoupled graph convolution network and label propagation. In: Proceedings of the Web Conference 2021, pp. 3651–3662 (2021)
5. Fan, W., et al.: Graph neural networks for social recommendation. In: The World Wide Web Conference, pp. 417–426 (2019)
6. Gao, J., Zhang, T., Xu, C.: Graph convolutional tracking. In: Proceedings of the IEEE/CVF Conference on Computer Vision and Pattern Recognition, pp. 4649–4659 (2019)
7. Hamilton, W.L., Ying, R., Leskovec, J.: Inductive representation learning on large graphs. In: Proceedings of the 31st International Conference on Neural Information Processing Systems, pp. 1025–1035 (2017)
8. Jin, W., Li, Y., Xu, H., Wang, Y., Tang, J.: Adversarial attacks and defenses on graphs: a review and empirical study. arXiv e-prints pp. arXiv-2003 (2020)
9. Kingma, D.P., Ba, J.: Adam: a method for stochastic optimization. In: International Conference on Learning Representations (ICLR) (2015)
10. Kipf, T.N., Welling, M.: Semi-supervised classification with graph convolutional networks. In: 5th International Conference on Learning Representations, ICLR 2017, Toulon, France, 24–26 April 2017, Conference Track Proceedings (2017)
11. Klicpera, J., Bojchevski, A., Günnemann, S.: Predict then propagate: graph neural networks meet personalized pagerank. In: International Conference on Learning Rep resentations, ICLR, 2019 (2019)

12. Liang, X., Shen, X., Feng, J., Lin, L., Yan, S.: Semantic object parsing with graph LSTM. In: Leibe, B., Matas, J., Sebe, N., Welling, M. (eds.) ECCV 2016. LNCS, vol. 9905, pp. 125–143. Springer, Cham (2016). https://doi.org/10.1007/978-3-319-46448-0_8

13. Liu, C.Y., Zhou, C., Wu, J., Hu, Y., Guo, L.: Social recommendation with an essential preference space. In: Thirty-Second AAAI Conference on Artificial Intelligence (2018)

14. Liu, X., Si, S., Zhu, X., Li, Y., Hsieh, C.J.: A unified framework for data poisoning attack to graph-based semi-supervised learning. In: Proceedings of the 33rd International Conference on Neural Information Processing Systems, pp. 9780–9790 (2019)

15. McCallum, A.K., Nigam, K., Rennie, J., Seymore, K.: Automating the construction of internet portals with machine learning. Inf. Retrieval 3(2), 127–163 (2000)

16. Muñoz-González, L., et al.: Towards poisoning of deep learning algorithms with back-gradient optimization. In: Proceedings of the 10th ACM Workshop on Artificial Intelligence and Security, pp. 27–38 (2017)

17. Namata, G., London, B., Getoor, L., Huang, B., Edu, U.: Query-driven active surveying for collective classification. In: 10th International Workshop on Mining and Learning with Graphs, vol. 8, p. 1 (2012)

18. Page, L., Brin, S., Motwani, R., Winograd, T.: The pagerank citation ranking: Bringing order to the web. Technical report, Stanford InfoLab (1999)

19. Parisot, S.: Disease prediction using graph convolutional networks: application to autism spectrum disorder and alzheimer's disease. Med. Image Anal. 48, 117–130 (2018)

20. Rieck, B., Bock, C., Borgwardt, K.: A persistent weisfeiler-lehman procedure for graph classification. In: International Conference on Machine Learning, pp. 5448–5458. PMLR (2019)

21. Rosenfeld, E., Winston, E., Ravikumar, P., Kolter, Z.: Certified robustness to label-flipping attacks via randomized smoothing. In: International Conference on Machine Learning, pp. 8230–8241. PMLR (2020)

22. Scarselli, F., Gori, M., Tsoi, A.C., Hagenbuchner, M., Monfardini, G.: The graph neural network model. IEEE Trans. Neural Netwo. 20(1), 61–80 (2008)

23. Sen, P., Namata, G., Bilgic, M., Getoor, L., Galligher, B., Eliassi-Rad, T.: Collective classification in network data. AI Mag. 29(3), 93–93 (2008)

24. Shchur, O., Mumme, M., Bojchevski, A., Günnemann, S.: Pitfalls of graph neural network evaluation. In: Relational Representation Learning Workshop, R2L (2018)

25. Sun, L., et al.: Adversarial attack and defense on graph data: a survey. arXiv preprint arXiv:1812.10528 (2018)

26. Veličković, P., Cucurull, G., Casanova, A., Romero, A., Lio, P., Bengio, Y.: Graph attention networks. In: 6th International Conference on Learning Representations, ICLR 2018, Vancouver, BC, Canada, 30 April–3 May 2018, Conference Track Proceedings. (2018)

27. Wang, Q., Mao, Z., Wang, B., Guo, L.: Knowledge graph embedding: a survey of approaches and applications. IEEE Trans. Knowl. Data Eng. 29(12), 2724–2743 (2017)

28. Wang, X., Gupta, A.: Videos as space-time region graphs. In: Proceedings of the European conference on computer vision (ECCV), pp. 399–417 (2018)

29. Wang, Y., Sun, Y., Liu, Z., Sarma, S.E., Bronstein, M.M., Solomon, J.M.: Dynamic graph cnn for learning on point clouds. ACM Trans. Graph. (TOG) 38(5), 1–12 (2019)

30. Wu, F., Souza, A., Zhang, T., Fifty, C., Yu, T., Weinberger, K.: Simplifying graph convolutional networks. In: International Conference on Machine Learning, pp. 6861–6871. PMLR (2019)
31. Wu, J., et al.: Learning differential diagnosis of skin conditions with co-occurrence supervision using graph convolutional networks. In: Martel, A.L., et al. (eds.) MIC-CAI 2020. LNCS, vol. 12262, pp. 335–344. Springer, Cham (2020). https://doi.org/10.1007/978-3-030-59713-9_33
32. Yan, S., Xiong, Y., Lin, D.: Spatial temporal graph convolutional networks for skeleton-based action recognition. In: Thirty-Second AAAI Conference on Artificial Intelligence (2018)
33. Ying, R., He, R., Chen, K., Eksombatchai, P., Hamilton, W.L., Leskovec, J.: Graph convolutional neural networks for web-scale recommender systems. In: Proceedings of the 24th ACM SIGKDD International Conference on Knowledge Discovery & Data Mining, pp. 974–983 (2018)
34. Ying, Z., You, J., Morris, C., Ren, X., Hamilton, W., Leskovec, J.: Hierarchical graph representation learning with differentiable pooling. Adv. Neural Inf. Process. Syst. **31** (2018)
35. Zhang, M., Hu, L., Shi, C., Wang, X.: Adversarial label-flipping attack and defense for graph neural networks. In: 2020 IEEE International Conference on Data Mining (ICDM), pp. 791–800. IEEE (2020)
36. Zhang, M., Chen, Y.: Link prediction based on graph neural networks. Adv. Neural Inf. Process. Syst. **31** (2018)
37. Zhou, D., Bousquet, O., Lal, T.N., Weston, J., Schölkopf, B.: Learning with local and global consistency. Adv. Neural Inf. Process. Syst., 321–328 (2004)
38. Zhu, X., Ghahramani, Z.: Learning from labeled and unlabeled data with label propagation (2002)

Revisiting Outer Optimization
in Adversarial Training

Ali Dabouei[✉], Fariborz Taherkhani, Sobhan Soleymani,
and Nasser M. Nasrabadi

West Virginia University, Morgantown, USA
{ad0046,ft0009,ssoleyma}@mix.wvu.edu
nasser.nasrabadi@mail.wvu.edu

Abstract. Despite the fundamental distinction between adversarial and natural training (AT and NT), AT methods generally adopt momentum SGD (MSGD) for the outer optimization. This paper aims to analyze this choice by investigating the overlooked role of outer optimization in AT. Our exploratory evaluations reveal that AT induces higher gradient norm and variance compared to NT. This phenomenon hinders the outer optimization in AT since the convergence rate of MSGD is highly dependent on the variance of the gradients. To this end, we propose an optimization method called ENGM which regularizes the contribution of each input example to the average mini-batch gradients. We prove that the convergence rate of ENGM is independent of the variance of the gradients, and thus, it is suitable for AT. We introduce a trick to reduce the computational cost of ENGM using empirical observations on the correlation between the norm of gradients w.r.t. the network parameters and input examples. Our extensive evaluations and ablation studies on CIFAR-10, CIFAR-100, and TinyImageNet demonstrate that ENGM and its variants consistently improve the performance of a wide range of AT methods. Furthermore, ENGM alleviates major shortcomings of AT including robust overfitting and high sensitivity to hyperparameter settings.

1 Introduction

Susceptibility of deep neural networks (DNNs) to manipulated inputs has raised critical concerns regarding their deployment in security-sensitive applications [4,21,24]. The worst-case manipulation can be characterized by *adversarial examples*: carefully crafted input examples that can easily alter the model prediction while

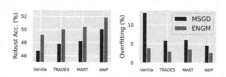

Fig. 1. Replacing MSGD with ENGM for outer optimization in AT results in consistent improvement of robust accuracy and generalization.

Supplementary Information The online version contains supplementary material available at https://doi.org/10.1007/978-3-031-20065-6_15.

remaining benign to the human perception [15,37]. A principal approach to formalize the imperceptibility is to bound the perturbation using ℓ_p-norm. Hence, the problem of finding a model robust to adversarial manipulation reduces to finding the one that generalizes well merely on the bounded neighborhood of the input example. Although this task seems effortless for humans, achieving such invariance is notoriously difficult for DNNs. The reason for this behavior has not been fully understood yet, but several factors have shown to be influential, including the high cardinality of the data space and non-zero test error of the classifier on noisy inputs [7,14] (Fig. 1).

One of the most effective methods (defenses) to alleviate adversarial susceptibility is adversarial training (AT) which improves the robustness by training the model on the worst-case loss [15,25]. Given the deep model F_θ parameterized by θ and the surrogate loss function for the empirical adversarial risk L, the training objective of AT is defined as:

$$\min_{\theta} \mathbb{E}_{(\mathbf{x},y)\sim\mathcal{D}}\left[L^*(\mathbf{x}, y; \theta)\right],\tag{1a}$$

$$L^*(\mathbf{x}, y; \theta) = \max_{||\mathbf{x}-\mathbf{x}'||_p \leq \epsilon} L\big(F_\theta(\mathbf{x}'), y\big),\tag{1b}$$

where the input example $\mathbf{x}$ and the corresponding label y are a sample from the data distribution $\mathcal{D}$, $\mathbf{x}'$ is the adversarial equivalent of $\mathbf{x}$, and ϵ is the maximum ℓ_p-norm magnitude of the perturbation. Concretely, adversarial training consists of two simultaneous optimizations, referred to as the inner and outer optimizations. The inner optimization (Eq. 1b) finds the worst-case adversarial example, and the outer optimization (Eq. 1a) minimizes the empirical adversarial risk over the network parameters, θ.

Numerous efforts have been devoted to analyzing different aspects of AT, such as the inner optimization [10,11,25,36,48], adversarial objective [12,30,40,47], computational cost [35,41,50], and evaluation methods [1,3,8,13,26]. Recent studies on the topic have revealed two major shortcomings of AT which contradicts common observations on NT. First, AT severely induces overfitting [6,34], referred to as *robust overfitting*, whereas in NT overfitting is known to be less prominent especially in over-parameterized models [2,28,46]. Second, AT is highly sensitive to hyperparameter setting, *e.g.*, a slight change in the weight decay can deteriorate the robust performance [16,29].

The majority of the previous works on AT have analyzed the inner optimization and its properties. However, the potential impact of outer optimization on the performance and shortcomings of AT has been critically overlooked. Furthermore, the success of the two recent state-of-the-art (SOTA) approaches of AT which indirectly affect the outer optimization by weight perturbations [42] or weight smoothing [6] advocates for further investigation on outer optimization. Based on these observations, we raise a fundamental question regarding outer optimization in AT and attempt to address it in this work:

Is the conventional MSGD, developed for non-convex optimization in NT, a proper choice for the outer optimization in AT? **If not,** *what modifications are required to make it suitable for the AT setup?*

To answer the first question, we empirically evaluate and compare two statistical parameters of gradients, namely expected norm and expected variance, in NT and AT. Both these parameters are known to be major determinants of the performance of MSGD in NT [18,23,49]. We find that they are notably higher in AT compared to NT. Furthermore, after decaying the learning rate in NT, both the gradient norm and variance deteriorate suggesting convergence to local minima. However, in AT, they escalate after the learning rate decay. These observations highlight substantial disparities between the characteristics of the gradients in AT and NT. Consequently, we argue that MSGD, developed essentially for NT, is not the most proper choice for outer optimization in AT since it is not designed to be robust against high gradient norm and variance.

Motivated by these observations, the current work attempts to develop an optimization method that is more suitable for AT, *i.e.*, less sensitive to the gradient norm and variance. The contributions of the paper are as follows:

- We investigate the effect of AT on gradient properties and provide empirical evidence that AT induces higher gradient norm and variance. We argue that this hinders the optimization since the convergence rate of MSGD is highly dependent on the variance of the gradients.
- We propose an optimization method tailored specifically for AT, termed ENGM, whose convergence rate is independent of the gradient variance.
- We empirically analyze the norm of gradients and provide insightful observations regarding their correlation in DNNs. Harnessing this, we develop a fast approximation to ENGM that significantly alleviates its computational complexity.
- Through extensive evaluations and ablation studies, we demonstrate that the proposed optimization technique consistently improves the performance and generalization of the SOTA AT methods.

2   Analyzing Outer Optimization in AT

We first investigate the disparities between the properties of gradients in AT and NT in Sect. 2.2. Then in Sect. 2.3, we draw connections between the observed disparities and poor performance of MSGD in AT by reviewing the previous theoretical analysis on the convergence of MSGD. In Sect. 2.4, we describe our proposed optimization technique whose convergence rate is more favorable for AT. Later in Sect. 2.5, we present an interesting observation that enables us to approximate a fast version of the proposed optimization technique.

2.1   Notations

Throughout the paper, we denote scalars, vectors, functions, and sets using lower case, lower case bold face, upper case, and upper case calligraphic symbols, respectively. We use notation $||\cdot||_p$ for the ℓ_p-norm and drop the subscript for $p = 2$. We employ the commonly used cross-entropy loss as the measure of empirical risk and denote the loss on i^{th} example, $L(F_\theta(\mathbf{x}_i), y_i)$, as L_i for the sake of brevity.

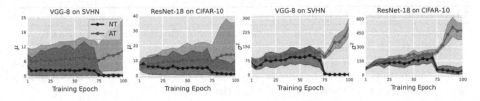

Fig. 2. Expected norm (μ) and variance (σ^2) of gradients during NT and AT. Learning rate is decayed from 10^{-1} to 10^{-2} at epoch 75. Note that the norm and variance in AT is higher than NT and escalates after learning rate decay.

2.2 Comparison of Gradient Properties

We experiment to analyze two statistical parameters of gradients which are major determinants of the performance of MSGD. The first parameter is the expected norm of gradients $\mu := \mathbb{E}_{(\mathbf{x},y)\sim\mathcal{D}}\big[\|\nabla_\theta L\big(F_\theta(\hat{\mathbf{x}}), y\big)\|\big]$, where $\hat{\mathbf{x}}$ is the natural example in NT and the adversarial example in AT. Change in the expected norm directly affects the learning rate, the most important hyperparameter in NT [18,23]. The second parameter is the upper bound for the variance of gradients, and is defined as:

$$\sigma^2 := \sup_\theta \ \mathbb{E}_{(\mathbf{x},y)\sim\mathcal{D}}\Big[\big\|\nabla_\theta L\big(F_\theta(\hat{\mathbf{x}}), y\big) - \bar{\mathbf{g}}\big\|^2\Big], \tag{2}$$

where $\bar{\mathbf{g}} = \mathbb{E}_{(\mathbf{x},y)\sim\mathcal{D}}\big[\nabla_\theta L\big(F_\theta(\hat{\mathbf{x}}), y\big)\big]$. It is shown that the convergence of MSGD is $O(\sigma^2)$ [44]. We roughly estimate both parameters during the training of ResNet-18 and VGG-8 on CIFAR-10 and SVHN datasets, respectively. Inner optimization in AT follows the standard setup, *i.e.*, 10 steps of ℓ_∞-norm PGD with $\epsilon = 8/255$ and step size $\epsilon/4$.

Figure 2 plots μ and σ^2 during 100 training epochs with the learning rate decay from 10^{-1} to 10^{-2} at epoch 75. We observe that the expected norm and variance of gradients is notably higher in AT. After learning rate decay, both parameters decrease significantly in NT suggesting the convergence to local minima. However in AT, the expected norm grows and the variance increases drastically. These findings highlight substantial disparities between the characteristics of the gradients in AT and NT. In the next section, we theoretically analyze how these differences can affect the convergence of MSGD.

2.3 Revisiting Stochastic Gradient Descent

In this part, we analyze the functionally and convergence of MSGD to identify modifications that improves its suitability for the AT setup. The update rule of MSGD at iteration t is as follows:

$$\mathbf{v}_{t+1} = \beta\mathbf{v}_t + \frac{1}{|\mathcal{I}_t|}\sum_{i\in\mathcal{I}_t}\nabla_\theta L_i, \tag{3a}$$

$$\theta_{t+1} = \theta_t - \eta\mathbf{v}_{t+1}, \tag{3b}$$

Algorithm 1. Fast ENGM

1: Initialize $\tau > 0$, $\beta_\gamma \in [0, 1)$, $\alpha > 0$, $\gamma_0 = 0$, $\gamma_1 = 1$, Boolean parameter *Naive*.
2: **for** $t = 0 \ldots t_1 - 1$ **do**
3:     Compute L_i, $\forall i \in \mathcal{I}_t$;   ▷ inner optimization
4:     Compute $\mathcal{G}_{\mathbf{x},t} = \{\nabla_{\mathbf{x}} L_i : i \in \mathcal{I}_t\}$;   ▷ backprop. $\times 1$
5:     **if** $\text{mode}(t, \tau) = 0$ and *Naive* = False **then**
6:         Compute $\mathcal{G}_{\boldsymbol{\theta},t} = \{\nabla_{\boldsymbol{\theta}} L_i : i \in \mathcal{I}_t\}$;   ▷ backprop. $\times n$ every τ iterations
7:         $\gamma_1', \gamma_0' = \text{LinearRegression}(\mathcal{G}_{\mathbf{x},t}, \mathcal{G}_{\boldsymbol{\theta},t})$ ▷ estimate slope and intercept
8:         $\gamma_0 \leftarrow \beta_\gamma \gamma_0 + (1 - \beta_\gamma)\gamma_0'$, and $\gamma_1 \leftarrow \beta_\gamma \gamma_1 + (1 - \beta_\gamma)\gamma_1'$;
9:     **end if**
10:    $\hat{w}_i \leftarrow \max(\frac{\alpha}{||\gamma_1 \nabla_{\mathbf{x}} L_i + \gamma_0||}, 1)$, $\forall i \in \mathcal{I}_t$;
11:    Update $\boldsymbol{\theta}$ with MSGD on the reweighted loss $\frac{1}{|\mathcal{I}_t|} \sum_{i \in \mathcal{I}_t} \hat{w}_i L_i$ ▷
    backpropagation $\times 1$
12: **end for**

---

where η is the learning rate, $\mathbf{v}_{t+1}$ is the Polyak's momentum with the corresponding modulus β [33], $\mathcal{I}_t$ is the randomly selected set of indices for the mini-batch with size $|\mathcal{I}_t|$, and L_i is the objective for optimization computed on the ith example. Assuming F has bounded variance of gradients according to Eq. 2, and is smooth in $\boldsymbol{\theta}$, *i.e.*, $F_{\boldsymbol{\theta}_1}(\mathbf{x}) \leq F_{\boldsymbol{\theta}_2}(\mathbf{x}) + \langle \nabla_{\boldsymbol{\theta}} F_{\boldsymbol{\theta}_1}(\mathbf{x}), \boldsymbol{\theta}_2 - \boldsymbol{\theta}_1 \rangle + \frac{c}{2}||\boldsymbol{\theta}_2 - \boldsymbol{\theta}_1||^2$, Yu *et al.* [43,44] have shown that the convergence rate of MSGD for non-convex optimization in DNNs is $O(\sigma^2)$. Hence, MSGD is not suitable for tasks with high gradient variance. Intuitively, higher variance implies that the gradients are not aligned with the average gradients which are being used to update the model parameters. This hinders the optimization process since the update is merely favorable for a portion of examples in the mini-batch.

One alternative to MSGD that is less sensitive to the variance of the gradients is stochastic normalized gradient descent with momentum (SNGM) [49]. SNGM is shown to provide better generalization for training with large batch size, *i.e.*, another cause of high gradient variance. Concretely, SNGM modifies Eq. 3a as:

$$\mathbf{v}_{t+1} = \beta \mathbf{v}_t + \frac{\sum_{i \in \mathcal{I}_t} \nabla_{\boldsymbol{\theta}} L_i}{|| \sum_{i \in \mathcal{I}_t} \nabla_{\boldsymbol{\theta}} L_i ||}, \tag{4}$$

which limits the gradient norm by normalizing the magnitude of mini-batch gradients and considers only the direction of the average gradient. Zhao *et al.* [49] have shown that the convergence of SNGM is $O(\sigma)$, and therefore, is more suitable for tasks with induced gradient fluctuations. We also observe in Sect. 3.1 that SNGM improves the generalization in AT. This suggests that reducing the sensitivity of the optimizer to the gradient variance has a direct impact on the generalization and performance of the task with adversarial gradients.

2.4 Example-Normalized Gradient Descent with Momentum

Although SNGM is less sensitive than MSGD to the variance of gradients, it does not impose any constraint on the variance. Hence, the variance can still become large and impede the optimization. To address this, we introduce a transformation on gradient vectors that bounds the variance of the gradients in the mini-batch and makes the convergence rate of the optimizer independent of the variance.

Theorem 1. *For any arbitrary distribution $\mathcal{P}$ of random vectors, applying the transformation $T(\mathbf{a}) = \min(\frac{\alpha}{||\mathbf{a}||}, 1)\mathbf{a}$ with $\alpha > 0$ bounds the variance of vectors to $4\alpha^2$.*
(Proof is provided in Sect. 1 of Supp. material.)

We use the transformation in Theorem 1 to bound the variance of the gradients. To this aim, we rewrite Eq. 3a as:

$$\mathbf{v}_{t+1} = \beta\mathbf{v}_t + \frac{1}{|\mathcal{I}_t|}\sum_{i\in\mathcal{I}_t} w_i\nabla_\theta L_i, \tag{5a}$$

$$w_i = \min\Big(\frac{\alpha}{||\nabla_\theta L_i||}, 1\Big), \tag{5b}$$

where w_i is the normalizing coefficient for $\nabla_\theta L_i$, and α is the maximum allowed norm of gradients. This update rule limits the maximum norm of the gradients on each input example to α. Hence, it prevents high magnitude gradients from dominating the updating direction and magnitude in the mini-batch. It might be noted that α scales with the square root of the model size, and larger models require higher values of α. We refer to this approach as **example-normalized stochastic gradient descent with momentum (ENGM)**. ENGM recovers MSGD when $\alpha \gg 1$. The convergence properties of ENGM is analyzed in Theorem 2.

Theorem 2. *Let $A(\boldsymbol{\theta})$ be the average loss over all examples in the dataset, and assume that it is smooth in $\boldsymbol{\theta}$. For any $\alpha > 0$ and total iterations of t_1, optimizing $A(\boldsymbol{\theta})$ using ENGM (Eq. 5) has the convergence of $O(\alpha)$. (Proof is provided in Sect. 1 of Supp. material.)*

Theorem 2 shows that the convergence rate of ENGM is $O(\alpha)$ and is independent of the variance of gradients. Hence, it is suitable for optimizing objectives with high gradient variance. Later in Sect. 3.1, we empirically validate this and show that the enhanced regularization of ENGM provides better optimization compared to SNGM and MSGD for AT. Despite the intrinsic merits of ENGM, it is computationally expensive since evaluating each w_i requires a dedicated backpropagation and cannot be implemented in parallel. In particular, Eq. 5 requires $|\mathcal{I}_t|$ backpropagation for each mini-batch. In the next section, we present an empirical observation on the gradients of DNNs that enables us to estimate w_i and consequently Eq. 5 using merely one additional backpropagation.

2.5   Accelerating ENGM via Gradient Norm Approximation

During our evaluations, we observe an interesting phenomenon that enables us to develop a fast approximation to ENGM. Particularly, we observe that the

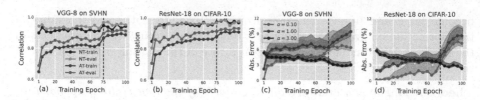

Fig. 3. (a, b): Characterizing the linear correlation between $||\nabla_{x_i} L_i||$ and $||\nabla_\theta L_i||$ using Pearson correlation coefficient. (c, d): The absolute value of error (%) for estimating w_i using Eq. 7. Dashed black line denotes the learning rate decay from 10^{-1} to 10^{-2}.

Table 1. Execution time of the outer optimization methods. Experiments are conducted on an NVIDIA Titan-RTX GPU.

Method	MSGD	MSGD+GNC	SNGM	F-ENGM	N-ENGM	A-ENGM	ENGM
Ex. time (sec./iter)	0.60	0.61	0.63	5.05	0.75	0.83	5.06

norm of gradients w.r.t. the network parameters, $||\nabla_\theta L_i||$, is linearly correlated with the norm of the gradients w.r.t. the input example, $||\nabla_{x_i} L_i||$. To illustrate this phenomenon, we track both gradient norms on $1,000$ training examples during NT and AT using VGG-8 on SVHN and ResNet-18 on CIFAR-10. We compute Pearson correlation coefficient to measure the correlation between the two norms. Figures 3a and 3b show the correlation coefficient during AT and NT with the model in the evaluation and training modes. We can see that there is a significant correlation between the two norms in DNNs which becomes stronger as the training proceeds. The correlation exists in both the training and evaluation modes of the model, and is slightly affected by the update in the statistics of the batch normalization modules.

Harnessing this phenomenon, we can estimate the norm of gradient w.r.t. the network parameters (computationally expensive) using the norm of gradients w.r.t. the inputs (computationally cheap) with a linear approximation as:

$$||\nabla_\theta L_i|| \approx \gamma_1 ||\nabla_{x_i} L_i|| + \gamma_0, \tag{6}$$

where γ_0 and γ_1 are coefficients for the slope and intercept of the linear estimation, respectively. Employing this estimation, we can approximate the functionality of ENGM by a simple modification of the loss on the ith input example, L_i, and keeping the popular MSGD as the optimizer. This provides two benefits. First, there is no need to implement a new optimizer enhancing the applicability of the method. Second, the reweighting significantly reduces the computational cost of ENGM. To this aim, we use the estimated value for the norm of the gradients w.r.t. the input to normalize the gradients w.r.t. the network parameters indirectly by assigning a weight to the loss function computed on $\mathbf{x}_i$ as $\hat{L}_i := \hat{w}_i L_i$, where:

$$\hat{w}_i := \max\left(\frac{\alpha}{||\gamma_1 \nabla_{\mathbf{x}} L_i + \gamma_0||}, 1\right). \tag{7}$$

Here, optimizing the total loss $\frac{1}{|\mathcal{I}_t|}\sum_{i\in\mathcal{I}_t}\hat{L}_i$ using MSGD will approximately recover the functionality of ENGM on $\frac{1}{|\mathcal{I}_t|}\sum_{i\in\mathcal{I}_t}L_i$. To analyze the accuracy of estimating $\hat{w}_i$, we measure the average absolute value of the error during the training of the both models in AT and for three different values of $\alpha \in \{0.1, 1.0, 3.0\}$. Figures 3c and 3d visualize the error on two different datasets and network architectures. We observe that the maximum absolute value of error is less than 10% which advocates for the accuracy of estimating $\hat{w}_i$. For large values of α the error decreases during the training, while for small values of α the error increases. This points to a trade-off between the estimation error across the training process. It might be noted that the error is computed solely for AT since based on the evaluations in Figs. 3a and 3d the correlation is stronger in NT.

Unlike $\nabla_\theta L_i$, $\nabla_x L_i$ can be computed in parallel for a batch of data using a single backpropagation. We consider two approaches for estimating γ_0 and γ_1 which result in two variations of ENGM. In the first approach, referred to as Approximated ENGM (A-ENGM), we evaluate $\nabla_\theta L_i$ for a single mini-batch every τ iterations and use moving average to update the latest estimate. Then for the intermediate iterations, we use the estimate values of γ to approximate the norm of gradients using Eq. 6. In comparison, A-ENGM reduces the required number of additional backpropagations from $|\mathcal{I}_t|$ (for ENGM) to $1 + |\mathcal{I}_t|/\tau$. In practice, we observe that the interval, τ, for estimating γ values can be conveniently large as investigated in Sect. 3.4. Furthermore, we consider a second approach in which we simply set $\gamma_0 = 0$ and merge γ_1 into α. We refer to this approach as Naive ENGM (N-ENGM) which solely requires a single additional backpropagation.

3   Experiments and Analysis

We evaluate ENGM on three datasets of CIFAR-10, CIFAR-100 [20], and Tiny-ImageNet [22]. Following the benchmark experimental setup for AT [9,40,42,47], we conduct ablation studies and exploratory evaluations on ResNet-18 with 64 initial channels, originally developed for ImageNet. For SOTA evaluation, we use Wide ResNet-34 with depth factor 10 (WRN-34-10) [45].

Training Setup. Except for evaluations involving ENGM, all the models are trained using MSGD with momentum 0.9, weight decay 5×10^{-4} [16,29,42], batch size equal to 128, and initial learning rate of 0.1. The learning rate is decayed by 0.1 at epochs 75, 90, and the total number of epochs is set to 120 unless otherwise noted. The standard data augmentation including random crop with padding size 4 and horizontal flip is applied for all datasets. All input images are normalized to $[0, 1]$. Based on ablation studies in Sect. 3.4, we set α for ENGM, A-ENGM, and N-ENGM to 5, 5, and 0.5, respectively. The momentum

Table 2. Comparison of ENGM with MSGD for outer optimization in AT (Sect. 3.1). 'Best' and 'Last' refer to the accuracy against PGD^{20} using the best and last checkpoints, respectively.

Optim. method	Accuracy (%)				Overfit (%)
	Natural	Best	Last	AA	
MSGD	**84.70**	50.87	44.15	46.77	13.2
MGNC	83.98	51.88	46.62	47.59	10.1
SNGM	83.73	51.95	46.80	47.75	9.9
F-ENGM	82.91	50.05	44.04	46.54	12.0
N-ENGM	84.36	52.19	48.79	48.06	6.5
A-ENGM	83.61	52.46	49.75	48.46	5.1
ENGM	83.44	**53.04**	**52.76**	**49.24**	**3.9**

for A-ENGM is set to 0.7 based on empirical evaluations. PGD with 10 steps (PGD^{10}), $\epsilon = 8/255$, and step size 2/255 is used as the attack to maximize the adversarial loss in ℓ_∞-norm ball. As suggested by Rice *et al.* [34], during the training we select the model with the highest robust accuracy against PGD^{20} with $\epsilon = 8/255$ and step size $8/(255 \times 10)$ on a validation set of size 1,000 as the best model. Only for PGD^{20}, we use margin loss instead of cross-entropy due to its better performance in evaluating the robustness of the model [39].

Evaluation Setup. We evaluate the model against two major attacks. First is the same PGD^{20} used in the training to find the best model. For a more rigorous evaluation of the robust performance, we follow the setup of the recent SOTA defense methods [5,9,19,29,36,42,47,48] and use the benchmark adversarial robustness measure of AutoAttack (AA) [8]. AA has shown consistent superiority over other white box attacks such as JSMA [31], MIM [13], and CW [3][1]. Both attacks in evaluations are applied on the test set, separated from the validation set. Maximum norm of perturbation, ϵ, is set to 8/255 and 128/255 for ℓ_∞-norm and ℓ_2-norm threat models. In addition to the robust accuracy, the robust overfitting of the model is computed as the difference between the best and the last robust accuracies (PGD^{20}) normalized over the best robust accuracy. All results are the average of three independent runs.

3.1 Comparison of Optimization Methods

In this section, we evaluate and compare the proposed method with other possible choices for outer optimization in AT. As the fist baseline, we employ the conventional MSGD which is the optimizer in all of the previous AT methods. A popular and well-known trick to bound the gradient norm especially in recurrent

---

[1] https://github.com/fra31/auto-attack.

neural networks is Gradient Norm Clipping (GNC) [17,32]. GNC clips the gradient norm when it is greater than a threshold. This threshold is similar to α in our method. However, instead of bounding the gradient norm on each individual input example, GNC bounds the norm of the average gradients of the minibatch. We consider the combination of MSGD with GNC as our second baseline and refer to it as MGNC. The clipping threshold α for MSGD+GNC is set to 25 based on empirical evaluations. SNGM, discussed in Sect. 2.3, is used as the third baseline. For our method, we compare the original ENGM with its accelerated versions, *i.e.*, A-ENGM and N-ENGM. The coefficients α and τ for our methods are set to the best-performing values from Sect. 3.4. As an additional baseline, we develop another version of ENGM in which instead of bounding the norm of gradients, we normalize them to the constant value α, *i.e.*, modifying Eq. 5a to: $\mathbf{v}_{t+1} = \beta \mathbf{v}_t + \frac{1}{|\mathcal{I}_t|} \sum_{i \in \mathcal{I}_t} \frac{\nabla_\theta L_i}{||\nabla_\theta L_i||}$. We refer to this method as Fixed ENGM (F-ENGM).

Table 2 presents the results for these comparisons. We can see that the simple GNC enhances robust accuracy providing the same performance as SNGM. These improvements caused by simple modifications further confirms the negative effect of high gradient norm and variance on outer optimization in AT. ENGM consistently improves the robust accuracy over baselines. In addition, robust overfitting in ENGM is significantly lower than other baselines. This suggests that a major cause of robust overfitting in AT is the high fluctuation of gradients and the

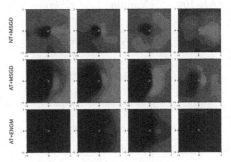

Fig. 4. Visualization of the loss landscape on four examples from CIFAR-10 (Sect. 3.2). The cross mark denotes the input example. Loss level sets are equalized on each column.

incompetence of MSGD in addressing it. The learning curves (robust test accuracy) for different optimization methods are depicted in Fig. 5h. We observe that after the learning rate decay, the robust performance of ENGM and its variants does not deteriorate which confirms that they alleviate robust overfitting. The best natural accuracy is provided by MSGD supporting the commonly observed trade-off between the natural and robust accuracies [38,47]. Table 1 presents the execution time for the optimization methods. The execution time of ENGM is roughly 8.5× longer than MSGD. However, A-ENGM and N-ENGM achieve notable speed-up and robust performance. As expected, the performance of A-ENGM is between N-ENGM (lower-bound) and ENGM (upper-bound) and is controlled by the estimation interval τ. Hence, we use N-ENGM and ENGM for the major evaluations to clearly compare the two performance bounds.

Table 3. Comparison of MSGD and ENGM on different AT methods (Sect. 3.2). Note that ENGM consistently outperforms MSGD.

	AT method	Optim. method	Accuracy (%)			Overfit (%)
			Natural	PGD[20]	AA	
CIFAR-10	Vanilla	MSGD	**84.70**	50.87	46.77	13.2
		ENGM	83.44	53.04	49.24	3.9
	TRADES	MSGD	82.40	50.94	47.85	5.9
		ENGM	82.33	53.46	50.07	3.0
	MART	MSGD	83.68	51.05	48.29	6.1
		ENGM	83.03	53.56	50.48	4.6
	AWP	MSGD	82.98	52.55	50.12	4.6
		ENGM	83.10	**54.07**	**51.93**	**2.7**
CIFAR-100	Vanilla	MSGD	**57.75**	26.11	24.45	20.9
		ENGM	56.91	28.43	26.60	7.4
	TRADES	MSGD	56.00	29.04	26.93	10.6
		ENGM	55.65	30.68	29.20	7.1
	MART	MSGD	56.52	29.41	27.18	11.8
		ENGM	56.20	30.89	29.30	8.6
	AWP	MSGD	56.22	30.36	28.43	7.3
		ENGM	56.82	**31.24**	**30.46**	**6.3**
Tiny-ImageNet	Vanilla	MSGD	35.71	7.47	6.92	26.37
		ENGM	29.78	11.29	8.54	10.10
	TRADES	MSGD	**37.26**	14.13	10.95	14.79
		ENGM	36.30	16.88	12.65	8.74
	MART	MSGD	37.06	13.79	10.08	15.94
		ENGM	36.53	16.90	12.99	8.20
	AWP	MSGD	36.13	16.29	13.09	10.67
		ENGM	36.81	**19.14**	**16.02**	**7.97**

3.2 Combination with Benchmark at Methods

In the this section, we incorporate the proposed optimization approaches into the benchmark AT methods including the vanilla method [25], TRADES [47], MART [40], and AWP [42]. Here, AWP represents the weight perturbation method applied on top of TRADES. The coefficient for the self-distillation loss in TRADES and MART is set to 6, and the maximum magnitude of weight perturbation for AWP is set to 5×10^{-3}. The rest of the training setups are set to the best setup reported by the original papers. However, the total training epochs for all methods is set to 200 (learning rate decays by 0.1 at epochs 100 and 150) for the sake of consistency.

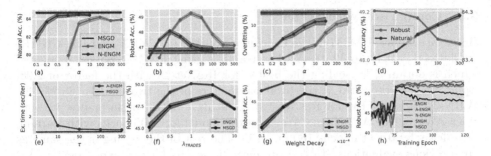

Fig. 5. (a–g): Ablation studies on α, τ, λ_{TRADES}, and weight decay (Sect. 3.4). Note that α of ENGM scales to that of N-ENGM with $1/\gamma_1$. Robust accuracy is measured using AutoAttack [8]. (h): learning curves (robust test accuracy) for AT with different outer optimization methods. Results on last 60 epochs are plotted for better visualization of the robust overfitting. Robust accuracy is measured using PGD^{20}.

Table 3 presents the results for ℓ_∞-norm threat model. For results on ℓ_2-norm threat model please refer to Sect. 2 in Supp. material. We observe that ENGM consistently outperforms MSGD on robust performance. The average improvement in robustness against AA is 2.15% and 1.16% in ℓ_∞-norm and ℓ_2-norm, respectively. This suggests that the *amount* of perturbation in AT affects the convergence of the outer optimization. Consider the ℓ_2-norm as the unified metric, the amount of noise in ℓ_∞-norm threat model is roughly 3× the norm of noise in the counterpart threat model. Combining these results with the evaluations in Fig. 2 advocates that the improvement offered by ENGM over MSGD depends on the norm of perturbation. This observation is further investigated in Sect. 3.4.

AWP is previously shown to alleviate robust overfitting [42]. Interestingly, we find that TRADES and MART also reduce the robust overfitting independent of the optimization method. This suggests that the AT method can affect the robust overfitting. ENGM results in the lowest overfitting and consistently surpasses MSGD. On vanilla AT, replacing MSGD with ENGM results in 9.3%, 13.5%, and 16.2% reduction of overfitting on CIFAR-10, CIFAR-100, and TinyImageNet, respectively. These results advocate that, in addition to the AT method, the outer optimization method also affects the overfitting and limiting the sensitivity of the optimization method to the variance of the gradients can alleviate the robust overfitting.

As the last evaluation in this part, we visualize the loss landscape on networks optimized by MSGD and ENGM in Fig. 4. This figure plots the loss values for the space spanned by the adversarial perturbation (PGD^{20}) and random noise, orthogonalized to the perturbation via Gram-Schmidt. We can see that ENGM results in a smoother loss landscape, known as an empirical evidence of the robustness [27]. This qualitative analysis further validates the effectiveness of ENGM for outer optimization in AT.

3.3   Comparison with SOTA

Here, we evaluate ENGM in the benchmark of AT, *i.e.*, WRN-34-10 on CIFAR-10 dataset [5,9,19,36,42,47,48]. For training using ENGM, we set $\alpha = 10.4$ which is obtained by scaling the best α for ResNet-18 with the factor of 2.08, square root of the ratio of the total parameters of the two models ($48.2M$ for WRN-34-10 vs. $11.1M$ for ResNet-18). To achieve SOTA performance, we consider AWP as the AT scheme. We train the model for 200 epochs with learning rate decay by 0.1 at epochs 100 and 150. The rest of the setting is the same as our previous evaluations. Table 4 presents the results for this experiment. AWP combined with ENGM and N-ENGM surpasses the previous SOTA by 1.28% and 0.94%, respectively. This validates the effectiveness of ENGM on large models. We also find that ENGM results in higher natural accuracy on AWP. This suggests that although AWP indirectly improves the outer optimization, its impact is orthogonal to ENGM.

3.4   Ablation Studies

We conduct ablation studies to investigate the impact of hyperparameters on the performance of ENGM and its two variants using ResNet-18 on CIFAR-10.

Impact of α: We measure the natural accuracy, robust accuracy (AA), and overfitting versus α. We conduct this experiment on ENGM/N-ENGM since they upper/lower bound the performance of A-ENGM.

Figures 5a, 5b, and 5c present the results for these evaluations. As expected, for large values of α all three values converge to that obtained by MSGD. Small values of α can be interpreted as training with a very small learning rate causing both the natural and robust accuracies to drop. Interestingly, we observe that the overfitting decreases significantly for small values of α. This confirms that the high variance of gradients in AT negatively affects the functionality of MSGD, *i.e.*, ENGM with large α. We find that ENGM and N-ENGM achieve their optimal performance on ResNet-18 at α equal to 5 and 0.5, respectively. We select these as the optimal values for training the models in other experiments. Note that the optimal value of α is expected to be the same for ENGM and A-ENGM but different for N-ENGM. This is because the formulation of ENGM and A-ENGM is the same except that A-ENGM estimates the norm of gradients every τ iterations, and setting $\tau = 1$ recovers the exact ENGM. However, in N-ENGM, α is scaled by $1/\gamma_1$ according to the discussion in Sect. 2.5. The optimal α is scaled for other networks based on their capacity.

Impact of τ: We conduct experiments to evaluate the role of τ in AT setup with A-ENGM ($\alpha = 5$) as the optimizer and $\tau \in \{1, 10, 50, 100, 300\}$. It might be noted that each epoch in CIFAR-10 consists of 390 mini-batches of size 128. Hence, $\tau = 300$ is roughly equivalent to estimating the correlation at the end of each epoch. Figures 5d and 5e present the results for these evaluations. As expected, for small and large values of τ A-ENGM converges to ENGM and N-ENGM, respectively. For $\tau = 50$, obtained robustness is roughly 85% of the

Table 4. Comparison of the benchmark robustness on WRN.

Method	Optim	Nat. acc. (%)	AA (%)
ATES [36]	MSGD	86.84	50.72
BS [5]	MSGD	85.32	51.12
LBGAT [9]	MSGD	**88.22**	52.86
TRADES [47]	MSGD	84.92	53.08
MART [40]	MSGD	84.98	53.17
BERM [19]	MSGD	83.48	53.34
FAT [48]	MSGD	84.52	53.51
AWP [42]	MSGD	85.36	56.17
AWP	N-ENGM	85.40	57.11
AWP	ENGM	86.12	**57.45**

robustness obtained by ENGM while the training time is significantly lower (0.83 vs. 5.06) because the extra gradient computation is being performed every 50 iterations. Furthermore, we can see that τ controls the trade-off between the natural and robust accuracies.

Perturbation Norm: As an initial exploration in this paper, we observed that AT induces higher gradient norm and variance. We also noticed in Sect. 3.2 that ENGM seems to outperform MSGD with a larger margin when the magnitude of perturbations is higher. Here, we further analyze the impact of the magnitude of perturbations on the gradient norm and variance induced by AT. This allows us to identify the extent of suitability of MSGD and ENGM for NT and AT. We train models in AT setup with ℓ_∞-norm threat model and varied size of perturbation, $\epsilon \in \{0, 2/255, 4/255, 6/255, 8/255, 10/255\}$. Both MSDG and ENGM are utilized for the outer optimization in these evaluations. We measure the average norm and variance of gradients across all training epochs. For a fair comparison, we compute the expected distance to the closest decision boundary as the unified robustness measure: $\rho := E_{\mathbf{x}}[||\mathbf{x} - \mathbf{x}^*||]$, where $\mathbf{x}^*$ is the closest adversary to x computed using DeepFool [26].

Table 5 presents the results for this experiment. In NT (AT with $\epsilon = 0$), MSGD provides slightly better performance than ENGM. This is because in NT the norm and variance of gradients are naturally limited. As the ϵ increases, the expected norm and variance of the gradients also increase. This confirms our initial observation that AT induces higher gradient norm and variance. Consequently as expected, we find that in AT with larger magnitude of perturbations ENGM works better than MSGD.

Sensitivity to Hyperparameters:
One intriguing shortcoming of AT
is sensitivity to hyperparameter setting. Several works have shown that a
slight change in the modulus of the
ℓ_2-norm regularization, i.e., weight
decay, results in drastic changes in
robust performance [16,29]. Here, we
analyze the sensitivity of the proposed
optimization method and compare it

Table 5. Analyzing the impact of the perturbation magnitude on gradient properties
and final robustness obtained by MSGD
and ENGM (Sect. 3.2). AT with $\epsilon = 0$ is
equivalent to NT.

	Magnitude of perturbation, ϵ ($\times \frac{1}{255}$)					
	0	2	4	6	8	10
μ	4.25	5.10	6.09	7.73	10.04	14.21
σ^2	118.1	118.7	121.8	141.7	185.2	253.5
ρ_{MSGD}	0.33	0.41	0.57	0.93	1.15	1.24
ρ_{ENGM}	0.30	0.42	0.61	1.08	1.35	1.49

with that of MSGD. Figure 5g presents the results for this evaluation. We observe
that ENGM exhibits significantly less sensitivity to changes in weight decay compared to MSGD. We hypothesis that high weight decay helps MSGD to prevent
the bias from input examples with high gradient magnitude. ENGM achieves this
goal by explicitly limiting the gradient magnitudes, and thus, is less sensitive to
weight decay. We believe this phenomenon calls for more in depth analysis and
defer it to future studies.

4   Conclusion

In this paper, we studied the role of outer optimization in AT. We empirically
observed that AT induces higher gradient norm and variance which degrades
the performance of the conventional optimizer, i.e., MSGD. To address this
issue, we developed an optimization method robust to the variance of gradients
called ENGM. We provided two approximations to ENGM with significantly
reduced computational complexity. Our evaluations validated the effectiveness
of ENGM and its fast variants in AT setup. We also observed that ENGM
alleviates shortcomings of AT including the robust overfitting and sensitivity to
hyperparameters.

References

1. Athalye, A., Carlini, N., Wagner, D.: Obfuscated gradients give a false sense of
   security: circumventing defenses to adversarial examples. In: International Conference on Machine Learning, pp. 274–283. PMLR (2018)
2. Belkin, M., Hsu, D., Ma, S., Mandal, S.: Reconciling modern machine-learning
   practice and the classical bias-variance trade-off. Proc. Natl. Acad. Sci. **116**(32),
   15849–15854 (2019)
3. Carlini, N., Wagner, D.: Towards evaluating the robustness of neural networks. In:
   2017 IEEE Symposium on Security and Privacy (sp), pp. 39–57. IEEE (2017)
4. Chen, C., Seff, A., Kornhauser, A., Xiao, J.: Deepdriving: learning affordance for
   direct perception in autonomous driving. In: Proceedings of the IEEE International
   Conference on Computer Vision, pp. 2722–2730 (2015)
5. Chen, J., Cheng, Y., Gan, Z., Gu, Q., Liu, J.: Efficient robust training via backward
   smoothing. arXiv preprint arXiv:2010.01278 (2020)

6. Chen, T., Zhang, Z., Liu, S., Chang, S., Wang, Z.: Robust overfitting may be mitigated by properly learned smoothening. In: International Conference on Learning Representations (2020)
7. Cohen, J., Rosenfeld, E., Kolter, Z.: Certified adversarial robustness via randomized smoothing. In: International Conference on Machine Learning, pp. 1310–1320. PMLR (2019)
8. Croce, F., Hein, M.: Reliable evaluation of adversarial robustness with an ensemble of diverse parameter-free attacks. In: International Conference on Machine Learning, pp. 2206–2216. PMLR (2020)
9. Cui, J., Liu, S., Wang, L., Jia, J.: Learnable boundary guided adversarial training. In: Proceedings of the IEEE/CVF International Conference on Computer Vision, pp. 15721–15730 (2021)
10. Dabouei, A., Soleymani, S., Dawson, J., Nasrabadi, N.: Fast geometrically-perturbed adversarial faces. In: 2019 IEEE Winter Conference on Applications of Computer Vision (WACV), pp. 1979–1988. IEEE (2019)
11. Dabouei, A., Soleymani, S., Taherkhani, F., Dawson, J., Nasrabadi, N.: Smoothfool: an efficient framework for computing smooth adversarial perturbations. In: Proceedings of the IEEE/CVF Winter Conference on Applications of Computer Vision, pp. 2665–2674 (2020)
12. Dabouei, A., Soleymani, S., Taherkhani, F., Dawson, J., Nasrabadi, N.M.: Exploiting joint robustness to adversarial perturbations. In: Proceedings of the IEEE/CVF Conference on Computer Vision and Pattern Recognition, pp. 1122–1131 (2020)
13. Dong, Y., et al.: Boosting adversarial attacks with momentum. In: Proceedings of the IEEE Conference on Computer Vision and Pattern Recognition, pp. 9185–9193 (2018)
14. Ford, N., Gilmer, J., Carlini, N., Cubuk, D.: Adversarial examples are a natural consequence of test error in noise. arXiv preprint arXiv:1901.10513 (2019)
15. Goodfellow, I.J., Shlens, J., Szegedy, C.: Explaining and harnessing adversarial examples. arXiv preprint arXiv:1412.6572 (2014)
16. Gowal, S., Qin, C., Uesato, J., Mann, T., Kohli, P.: Uncovering the limits of adversarial training against norm-bounded adversarial examples. arXiv preprint arXiv:2010.03593 (2020)
17. Graves, A.: Generating sequences with recurrent neural networks. arXiv preprint arXiv:1308.0850 (2013)
18. He, F., Liu, T., Tao, D.: Control batch size and learning rate to generalize well: theoretical and empirical evidence. Adv. Neural Inf. Process. Syst. 32, 1143–1152 (2019)
19. Huang, L., Zhang, C., Zhang, H.: Self-adaptive training: beyond empirical risk minimization. Adv. Neural Inf. Process. Syst. 33 (2020)
20. Krizhevsky, A., Hinton, G., et al.: Learning multiple layers of features from tiny images (2009)
21. Kurakin, A., Goodfellow, I., Bengio, S., et al.: Adversarial examples in the physical world (2016)
22. Le, Y., Yang, X.: Tiny imagenet visual recognition challenge. CS 231N 7(7), 3 (2015)
23. Liu, L., et al.: On the variance of the adaptive learning rate and beyond. arXiv preprint arXiv:1908.03265 (2019)
24. Ma, X., et al.: Understanding adversarial attacks on deep learning based medical image analysis systems. Pattern Recogn. 110, 107332 (2021)
25. Madry, A., Makelov, A., Schmidt, L., Tsipras, D., Vladu, A.: Towards deep learning models resistant to adversarial attacks. arXiv preprint arXiv:1706.06083 (2017)

26. Moosavi-Dezfooli, S.M., Fawzi, A., Frossard, P.: Deepfool: a simple and accurate method to fool deep neural networks. In: Proceedings of the IEEE Conference on Computer Vision and Pattern Recognition, pp. 2574–2582 (2016)
27. Moosavi-Dezfooli, S.M., Fawzi, A., Uesato, J., Frossard, P.: Robustness via curvature regularization, and vice versa. In: Proceedings of the IEEE/CVF Conference on Computer Vision and Pattern Recognition, pp. 9078–9086 (2019)
28. Neyshabur, B., Bhojanapalli, S., Mcallester, D., Srebro, N.: Exploring generalization in deep learning. Adv. Neural Inf. Process. Syst. **30**, 5947–5956 (2017)
29. Pang, T., Yang, X., Dong, Y., Su, H., Zhu, J.: Bag of tricks for adversarial training. arXiv preprint arXiv:2010.00467 (2020)
30. Pang, T., et al.: Adversarial training with rectified rejection. arXiv preprint arXiv:2105.14785 (2021)
31. Papernot, N., McDaniel, P., Jha, S., Fredrikson, M., Celik, Z.B., Swami, A.: The limitations of deep learning in adversarial settings. In: 2016 IEEE European symposium on security and privacy (EuroS&P), pp. 372–387. IEEE (2016)
32. Pascanu, R., Mikolov, T., Bengio, Y.: On the difficulty of training recurrent neural networks. In: International Conference on Machine Learning, pp. 1310–1318. PMLR (2013)
33. Polyak, B.T.: Some methods of speeding up the convergence of iteration methods. Ussr Comput. Math. Math. Phys. **4**(5), 1–17 (1964)
34. Rice, L., Wong, E., Kolter, Z.: Overfitting in adversarially robust deep learning. In: International Conference on Machine Learning, pp. 8093–8104. PMLR (2020)
35. Shafahi, A., et al.: Adversarial training for free!. arXiv preprint arXiv:1904.12843 (2019)
36. Sitawarin, C., Chakraborty, S., Wagner, D.: Improving adversarial robustness through progressive hardening. arXiv preprint arXiv:2003.09347 (2020)
37. Szegedy, C., et al.: Intriguing properties of neural networks. arXiv preprint arXiv:1312.6199 (2013)
38. Tsipras, D., Santurkar, S., Engstrom, L., Turner, A., Madry, A.: Robustness may be at odds with accuracy. In: International Conference on Learning Representations (2018)
39. Uesato, J., O'donoghue, B., Kohli, P., Oord, A.: Adversarial risk and the dangers of evaluating against weak attacks. In: International Conference on Machine Learning, pp. 5025–5034. PMLR (2018)
40. Wang, Y., Zou, D., Yi, J., Bailey, J., Ma, X., Gu, Q.: Improving adversarial robustness requires revisiting misclassified examples. In: International Conference on Learning Representations (2019)
41. Wong, E., Rice, L., Kolter, J.Z.: Fast is better than free: revisiting adversarial training. arXiv preprint arXiv:2001.03994 (2020)
42. Wu, D., Xia, S.T., Wang, Y.: Adversarial weight perturbation helps robust generalization. arXiv preprint arXiv:2004.05884 (2020)
43. Yan, Y., Yang, T., Li, Z., Lin, Q., Yang, Y.: A unified analysis of stochastic momentum methods for deep learning. arXiv preprint arXiv:1808.10396 (2018)
44. Yu, H., Jin, R., Yang, S.: On the linear speedup analysis of communication efficient momentum SGD for distributed non-convex optimization. In: International Conference on Machine Learning, pp. 7184–7193. PMLR (2019)
45. Zagoruyko, S., Komodakis, N.: Wide residual networks. arXiv preprint arXiv:1605.07146 (2016)
46. Zhang, C., Bengio, S., Hardt, M., Recht, B., Vinyals, O.: Understanding deep learning requires rethinking generalization (2016). arXiv preprint arXiv:1611.03530 (2017)

47. Zhang, H., Yu, Y., Jiao, J., Xing, E., El Ghaoui, L., Jordan, M.: Theoretically principled trade-off between robustness and accuracy. In: International Conference on Machine Learning, pp. 7472–7482. PMLR (2019)
48. Zhang, J., et al.: Attacks which do not kill training make adversarial learning stronger. In: International Conference on Machine Learning, pp. 11278–11287. PMLR (2020)
49. Zhao, S.Y., Xie, Y.P., Li, W.J.: Stochastic normalized gradient descent with momentum for large batch training. arXiv preprint arXiv:2007.13985 (2020)
50. Zheng, H., Zhang, Z., Gu, J., Lee, H., Prakash, A.: Efficient adversarial training with transferable adversarial examples. In: Proceedings of the IEEE/CVF Conference on Computer Vision and Pattern Recognition, pp. 1181–1190 (2020)

Zero-Shot Attribute Attacks
on Fine-Grained Recognition Models

Nasim Shafiee and Ehsan Elhamifar[✉]

Northeastern University, Boston, USA
{shafiee.n,e.elhamifar}@northeastern.edu

Abstract. Zero-shot fine-grained recognition is an important classification task, whose goal is to recognize visually very similar classes, including the ones without training images. Despite recent advances on the
development of zero-shot fine-grained recognition methods, the robustness of such models to adversarial attacks is not well understood. On
the other hand, adversarial attacks have been widely studied for conventional classification with visually distinct classes. Such attacks, in particular, universal perturbations that are class-agnostic and ideally should
generalize to unseen classes, however, cannot leverage or capture small
distinctions among fine-grained classes. Therefore, we propose a compositional attribute-based framework for generating adversarial attacks
on zero-shot fine-grained recognition models. To generate attacks that
capture small differences between fine-grained classes, generalize well to
previously unseen classes and can be applied in real-time, we propose
to learn and compose multiple attribute-based universal perturbations
(AUPs). Each AUP corresponds to an image-agnostic perturbation on a
specific attribute. To build our attack, we compose AUPs with weights
obtained by learning a class-attribute compatibility function. To learn
the AUPs and the parameters of our model, we minimize a loss, consisting of a ranking loss and a novel utility loss, which ensures AUPs
are effectively learned and utilized. By extensive experiments on three
datasets for zero-shot fine-grained recognition, we show that our attacks
outperform conventional universal classification attacks and transfer well
between different recognition architectures.

Keywords: Fine-grained recognition · Zero-shot models · Adversarial
attacks · Attribute-based universal perturbations · Compositional
model

1 Introduction

Despite the tremendous success of Deep Neural Networks (DNNs) for image
recognition, DNNs have been shown to be vulnerable to attacks [8,24]. Adversarial attacks are imperceptible image perturbations that result in incorrect

Supplementary Information The online version contains supplementary material
available at https://doi.org/10.1007/978-3-031-20065-6_16.

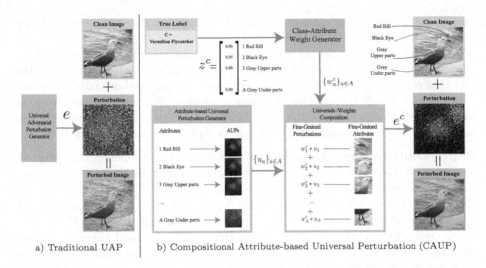

Fig. 1. (a) Traditional UAP [27,57] generates one holistic perturbation for all classes, hence, does not efficiently capture fine-grained discriminative visual information. (b) We develop a compositional framework for generating robust and generalizable attacks for zero-shot fine-grained recognition. We generate attribute-based universal perturbations (AUPs) and learn to compose them for attacking fine-grained classes.

prediction with high confidence and have highlighted the lack of robustness of DNNs. This has motivated a large body of research on generating small perturbations [8,11,16,24,28,36,49,53,58,64,68,74,81,94], and subsequently using the attacks to design robust defense mechanisms, e.g., by detecting attacks or retraining the model using perturbed images. Motivated by the fact that generating image-specific attacks are costly, especially when dealing with a large number of images, many works have studied finding universal attacks: image-agnostic perturbations that can change the ground-truth class of an arbitrary input image [37,46,56,57,59,60,70,96], hence, ideally should generalize to previously unseen classes. The majority of existing works, however, have focused on coarse-level classification in which classes have wide visual appearance variations with respect to each other, e.g., 'person', 'car', 'building', etc. Zero-shot fine-grained recognition, on the other hand, is an important classification problem in which one has to distinguish visually very similar classes, e.g., clothing types [2,50,79], faces [51,65,84] or bird/plant species [14,19,44,101,102,105], including classes without training images. The majority of successful methods for zero-shot fine-grained recognition have focused on identifying and leveraging small distinctions between classes using feature pooling [23,38,44], discriminative region localization [2,14,50,79,101,102] and dense attribute attentions [31,32]. This is done by describing each fine-grained class by a *class semantic vector* consisting of different attributes, such as 'bill color', 'belly pattern', 'wing color' for classification of birds. Despite its importance, however, robustness of (zero-shot) fine-grained recognition models to adversarial attacks has not received much attention in the literature [57,69] (Fig. 1).

As we show in the paper, conventional adversarial attacks for coarse-level classification do not work well for fine-grained recognition. This comes from the fact that generating holistic perturbations using existing methods fails to capture and leverage small distinctions between a specific class and others. Another limitation of existing works is the lack of a principled method for crafting effective adversarial attacks for unseen classes that do not have training images.

Paper Contributions. We propose a new framework for generating effective and generalizable attacks on zero-shot fine-grained recognition models. To generate adversarial attacks that capture small differences between fine-grained classes, generalize well to unseen classes without training images, and can be applied in real-time, we develop a compositional attribute-based model. Leveraging class semantic vectors, we learn multiple attribute-based universal perturbations (AUPs), where each AUP corresponds to an image-agnostic perturbation on a specific attribute. To build a class-wise universal perturbation that changes the class of an input image, we propose to compose the AUPs with appropriate weights, which are obtained by learning a class-attribute compatibility function. To learn our AUPs and the parameters of the compositional weight generator, we minimize a ranking loss regularized by norms of AUPs, to keep them and the final perturbation imperceptible, as well as a novel utility loss, which ensures all AUPs are effectively trained and used. By extensive experiments on three datasets for zero-shot fine-grained recognition, we show that our method outperforms conventional classification attacks, with only half of the perturbation norm, and also can transfer well between different architectures.

2   Related Works

Adversarial Attacks. Adversarial attacks have been mainly studied for classification problems and can be categorized as targeted or non-targeted [97]. Targeted attacks perturb an image to change its ground-truth class into a desired secondary class [5,8,39], while non-targeted attacks focus on only altering the ground-truth class [16,24,58,78]. From a security perspective, attacks can have different access levels to the model whose output needs to be modified. In the white-box attack, the adversary has access to the parameters of the target model [8,16,24,39,58], while, in the black-box attack, there is no access to the parameters of the target model [62,90]. Earlier works proposed generating attacks using gradient-based and optimization-based approaches. Gradient-based schemes maximize the cross-entropy loss function to find adversarial examples [16,24,40,73]. Also, optimization-based methods obtain adversarial examples by solving a constrained optimization problem [8,24,40,58,72,78].

Perturbations generated by adversarial attacks can be either image-specific or image-agnostic. While image-specific attacks generate a specific perturbation for each input image, image-agnostic attacks generate a unique perturbation, referred to as a universal adversarial perturbation, for all input images [4,57,70].

Another category of attacks focuses on semantic and perceptual properties of visual features to preserve the image concept while perturbing it. Therefore, [1,6,12,20,29,41,91] focused on generating a perturbation through geometric transformations, global color shifts, image filters. These approaches can craft more realistic adversarial examples, but their restricted perturbation space limits their strength. [13,17,25,52,55,82,85,98,104] find perturbations that can be hidden in the texture and regions of the image with drastic visual variations. Recently, [80] have decomposed perturbations into independent components and investigated the attribute to which each component belongs. Also, [61] has shown that maximally separating the discriminative latent features of classes can improve the robustness of fine-grained models.

Fine-Grained Recognition. DNNs have achieved significant improvement on fine-grained recognition, where the challenge lies in recognizing different classes with small but distinct visual appearance variations. To detect interactions between discriminative feature maps, [18,79,100] have employed pooling methods. [43,101] and [14,77,105] have used part-based and weak supervision for localizing discriminative parts of an image, respectively. On the other hand, instead of considering all discriminative features with the same importance for recognition, [15,30,34,45,99,106] have employed several attention mechanisms for better extraction of more critical discriminative visual features. To better capture relationships and interactions between discriminative features, [9,103] have proposed to employ graph networks and multi-granularity label prediction, respectively. Despite advances in fine-grained recognition, many previous models cannot generalize to zero and few-shot learning, which we review next.

Zero-Shot Learning. The goal of zero-shot learning is to transfer the knowledge a model can gain from images of seen classes for recognition of unseen classes, given a shared semantic space for both seen and unseen classes [54,95]. [76] proposed a class-wise normalization technique to maintain the variance of seen and unseen classes. [10,32,35,48,71] have learned to find an alignment between visual features and semantic vectors in an embedding space. [21,75,86,88] have proposed to generate synthesized samples for unseen classes and reformulated the zero-shot problem as a fully supervised setting. Although the generative methods have improved the unseen classification performance, for fine-grained recognition, they often cannot generate enough discriminative unseen features, which has motivated recent works in [26,31,33]. Specifically, [26] proposed a hybrid generative and discriminative framework for fine-grained recognition, while [31] developed a compositional generative model and [33] used a few samples of unseen classes in training to generate more discriminative seen/unseen samples.

3   Fine-Grained Compositional Adversarial Attacks

3.1   Problem Setting

Assume we have two sets of fine-grained classes C_s and C_u, where C_s denotes seen classes that have training images, C_u denotes unseen classes without training images and $\mathcal{C} \triangleq \mathcal{C}_s \cup \mathcal{C}_u$ denotes the set of all classes. Let $(I_1, y_1), \ldots, (I_N, y_N)$ be N training samples, where I_i is the i-th training image and $y_i \in \mathcal{C}_s$ corresponds to its fine-grained class. We denote the set of all training images by $\mathcal{I} = \{I_1, \ldots, I_N\}$. Let $\{z^c\}_{c \in \mathcal{C}}$ denote *class semantic* vectors that provide descriptions of classes. More specifically, $z^c = [z_1^c, \ldots, z_A^c]^\top$ is the semantic vector of the class c with A attributes, where z_a^c is the score of having the a-th attribute in the class c [3,7,42,63,71,87]. Also, let $\{v_a\}_{a=1}^A$ denote *attribute semantic* vectors, where v_a is the average of GloVe representation [67] of the words describing attribute a, e.g., 'red beak'. Assume we have learned a zero-shot fine-grained classifier, using training samples from seen classes, which can classify a test image from a seen or an unseen class. Our goal is to generate a fine-grained adversarial perturbation for an image from a seen or an unseen class that results in misclassification.

As we show, our proposed compositional method for generating adversarial attacks *work with any zero-shot fine-grained recognition model*. In the paper, *we focus on the non-targeted attacks*, i.e., aim to misclassify an image without specifying the adversarial class. However, our formulation can be modified to the targeted setting, which we leave for future studies.

3.2 Compositional Attribute-Based Universal Perturbations (CAUPs)

To generate an attack on an image I that belongs to a class y, we need to find a perturbation e that results in a higher prediction score for a class $c \neq y$ on the image. More specifically, our goal is to find an attack e such that

$$\exists c \in \mathcal{C} \backslash y \quad \text{s.t.} \quad s^c(I + e) > s^y(I + e). \tag{1}$$

There are *two conventional ways* of finding the attack. *i)* Generate an image-specific perturbation. However, this requires significant computation per image (more drastically if we want to misclassify multiple images, e.g., video frames) and does not allow generating attacks in real-time. *ii)* Generate a single universal perturbation that can change the class of any image. However, a single universal perturbation cannot incorporate small differences between every pair of fine-grained classes (as we show in the experiments, it does not work well).

Proposed Compositional Model. To obtain adversarial attacks that can be generated in real-time, capture small differences between fine-grained classes (where often only a few attributes of any two classes are different) and generalize well to unseen classes, we propose a compositional model. First, for each attribute a, we learn an attribute-based universal perturbation u_a, which has the same size as the input image. We refer to $\{u_a\}_{a=1}^A$ as attribute-based universal perturbations (AUPs). We compose the AUPs with learnable weights to build class-wise universal perturbations, denoted by $\{e^c\}_{c=1}^{|\mathcal{C}|}$. More specifically, we propose

$$e^c = \sum_{a=1}^A \omega_a^c u_a, \quad \forall c \in \mathcal{C}, \tag{2}$$

in which we generate the universal attack on class c using linear combination of AUPs with weights $\{\omega_1^c, \ldots, \omega_A^c\}$. *Unlike prior works, instead of generating one attack per image or one attack for all images from all classes, we generate* $|\mathcal{C}|$ *universal perturbations, one per class.* Additionally, our class-wise attack is a composition of AUPs, which allows us to generate attacks for a seen or an unseen class as we show below. Given that the adversary knows the ground-truth class y of the image or obtains it from the output of the fine-grained classifier, it can attack the image using e^y.

An important question is how to choose/find the composition weights $\{\omega_a^c\}$ that allows finding class-wise universal perturbations even for unseen classes. We propose to find the compositional weights using class-attribute compatibility

$$\omega_a^c = \tanh(\boldsymbol{v}_a^\top \boldsymbol{W}_a \boldsymbol{z}^c) \in [-1, +1], \tag{3}$$

where the term inside the hyperbolic tangent measures the compatibility between the attribute a and class c using a learnable matrix $\boldsymbol{W}_a$. We use GloVe vectors for $\boldsymbol{v}_a$'s to generate ω_a^c's that reflect similarity of attributes. Using tanh both normalizes the composition weights and assigns positive/negative values to them with the goal of perturbing visual features by adding/removing attributes.[1] Notice that using (3), once we learn $\boldsymbol{W}_a$'s from some training images, we can generate compositional weights for both seen and unseen classes, hence, obtain class-wise universal perturbations for any $c \in \mathcal{C}$ using (2).

Remark 1. In the experiments, we show that our compositional model works significantly better than learning a single universal perturbation for all classes. We also show that using compositional weights as in (3) works better than combining AUPs with uniform weights.

Remark 2. Our method learns attribute-based universal perturbations and combines them to produce class-wise perturbations. This is different from UAP [57] and GAP [27] that generate a single class-agnostic universal perturbation.

3.3   Learning AUPs

Our goal is to learn $\{\boldsymbol{u}_a, \boldsymbol{W}_a\}_{a=1}^A$ from a set of training images, which correspond to samples from seen classes. As stated before, for a training image I from class y, we want to find e^y so that (1) is satisfied. Therefore, inspired by [8], we first use the ranking loss function,

$$\mathcal{L}_{rank} = \sum_{I \in \mathcal{I}} \max\{0, \delta + s^y(I + e^y) - \max_{c \neq y} s^c(I + e^y)\}, \tag{4}$$

whose minimization ensures that for each training image I, there exists a non-ground truth class $(c \neq y)$ that obtains a higher score (by a margin $\delta > 0$) on the perturbed image than the ground truth class y. Notice that the ranking loss

---

[1] Empirically, we obtained better results using tanh than other activation functions.

in [8] only optimizes image-specific perturbations, while our proposed method searches for image-agnostic perturbations. We use the ranking loss instead of the cross entropy loss since specifying the margin δ allows computing stronger perturbations (also empirically it works better). For our CAUP attack based on ℓ_2-norm and ℓ_∞-norm, we also use the following regularization loss

$$\mathcal{L}_{reg} = \begin{cases} \sum_{a=1}^{A} \|\boldsymbol{u}_a\|_2^2, & \ell_2 \ attack \\ \sum_{a=1}^{A} \sum_j (|u_{a,j}| - k)^+, & \ell_\infty \ attack \end{cases} \tag{5}$$

where the first (ℓ_2) regularization ensures that entries of AUPs are sufficiently small, while the second (ℓ_∞-type) regularization penalizes $\boldsymbol{u}_a$ entires that are more than a constant k and benefits from being differentiable.

Notice that by only minimizing these two losses, it is possible to never use some of the AUPs (i.e., for some attributes a, the weights ω_a^c will be zero across all classes), which is undesired. To prevent this, we define the *utility of each attribute* a as $\tau_a \triangleq \sum_c |\omega_{a,c}|$, which is the sum of the absolute compositional weight of using the attribute a to attack the class c. We further regularize learning AUPs by minimizing the utility loss,

$$\mathcal{L}_{util} = \sum_{a=1}^{A} \tau_a^2, \tag{6}$$

which ensures nonzero values for all attribute utilities, hence, each attribute will be used for generating attacks for at least some classes. As a result, to learn the AUPs and the composition weights $\{\boldsymbol{u}_a, \boldsymbol{W}_a\}_{a=1}^{A}$, we propose to minimize

$$\mathcal{L}_{rank} + \lambda_{reg}\mathcal{L}_{reg} + \lambda_{util}\mathcal{L}_{util}, \tag{7}$$

where $\lambda_{reg}, \lambda_{util} \geq 0$ are hyperparameters. We use stochastic gradient descent to optimize our proposed loss.

4   Experiments

We evaluate the performance of our proposed compositional attribute-based universal perturbations (CAUP) on fine-grained datasets. We show that CAUP works well for different fine-grained recognition architectures and also our attacks transfer well across architectures. We also demonstrate that CAUP works better than conventional universal attacks and that composition of attribute-based perturbations is important for generating effective attacks. We investigate the effectiveness of different components of our method and present qualitative results illustrating properties of our attacks.

4.1   Experimental Setup

Datasets. We use three popular zero-shot fine-grained recognition datasets: Caltech-UCSD Birds-200-2011(CUB) [83], Animal with Attributes (AWA2) [89]

Table 1. Statistics of the datasets used in our experiments.

Dataset	# attributes	# seen (val)/unseen classes	# training/testing samples
CUB	312	100 (50)/50	7,057/4,731
AWA2	85	27 (13)/10	23,527/13,795
SUN	102	580 (65)/72	10,320/4,020

and SUN Attribute (SUN) [66,92]. Table 1 shows the statistics of the three datasets. CUB [83] contains 11,788 total images from fine-grained bird-species with 150 seen and 50 unseen classes. AWA2 [89] is an animal classification dataset with 40 seen and 10 unseen classes and has 37,322 samples in total. SUN [66] consists of different visual scenes with 14,340 images from 645 seen and 72 unseen classes. It has the largest number of classes among the datasets. However, it only contains 16 training images per class due to its small overall training set. Notice that these datasets include class semantic vectors, hence they are suitable for our zero-shot fine-grained attack model. For CUB, AWA2 and SUN, we follow the same training, validation and testing splits as in prior works [32,87].

Evaluation Metrics. Following prior works on zero-shot fine-grained recognition [26,32,47,76,89], we only apply the attacks on images that the model correctly classifies and measure the top-1 accuracy of a classifier on these perturbed test images. We consider the challenging generalized zero-shot setting, in which test samples come from both seen and unseen classes (as opposed to the zero-shot setting, where test images come only from unseen classes). We report the fooling percentage on attacked testing images from seen classes, $fool_s = (1 - acc_s) * 100$, and from unseen classes, $fool_u = (1 - acc_u) * 100$. Since universal perturbations generated by different methods and across architectures can have different magnitudes, we ℓ_2 normalize the generated perturbations and, similar to prior works [8,53,57], report the performance as a function of the scaling of the perturbation magnitude.

Baselines. We investigate the effectiveness of our proposed attacks on four recent fine-grained recognition models: DAZLE [32], DCN [47], CNZSL [76] and CEZSL [26]. We also study the transferability properties of our attacks across these models. DAZLE is a discriminative fine-grained recognition model that extracts and uses dense attribute features for classification. It uses the class semantic vectors and attribute embeddings to learn A attention models for A attributes and to compute the final class score. On the other hand, DCN and CNZSL, are two discriminative methods that extract a holistic feature from an input image to learn a compatibility function between images and class semantic vectors. The generative CEZSL model is trained to capture the distribution of the images and their attributes. It augments the seen image features with both seen and unseen synthetically features to train a standard classifier. We chose these fine-grained architectures since they can handle the zero-shot setting, on which we can test our zero-shot fine-grained attack.

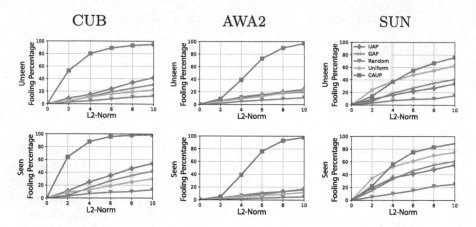

Fig. 2. Unseen (top) and seen (bottom row) fooling percentage of different universal attacks on DAZLE as a function of the magnitude (ℓ_2-norm) of the perturbation.

We compare CAUP with several baseline attacks: i) Universal Adversarial Perturbation (UAP) [57], which learns a single perturbation template. ii) Generative Adversarial Perturbation (GAP) [69], which is a network that generates a single universal adversarial perturbation. We trained both UAP and GAP on seen classes and test them on seen/unseen classes. iii) Uniform, where we simply combine all the AUPs, $\{u_a\}_{a=1}^A$, with uniform weights of $1/A$ in (2). This allows us to investigate the effectiveness of our composition weights. iv) Random, where we randomly generate a perturbation vector whose entries come from a standard Normal distribution. Notice that since our attack is image-agnostic, we assume the attacker cannot eavesdrops the input, hence *the results are not comparable to image-specific attacks* [16,22,58,93].

Implementation Details. We attached RESNET backbone to each fine-grained model and retrained them to achieve similar performance as they reported in their paper. For all models, we follow the exact experimental setting as in their reported work [26,32,47,76]. *We compute all attacks in the image-space and not in the feature-space*, which is conventional in the fine-grained recognition. We perform the experiments in the generalized zero-shot setting, where testing images come from both seen and unseen classes. For efficiency, similar to [57], we randomly use one-third of the training images to generate different types of universal attacks. In our experiments, using more samples for training did not change the performances. We implement all attacks in Pytorch on a server running Ubuntu 18.04 with an Intel Xeon Gold CPU and eight NVIDIA Quadro RTX 6000 GPUs and optimized with the default setting of ADAM optimizer with 0.001 learning rate and batch size of 50. To avoid overfitting, we employ an early stopping method with the patience of 20 (one average it stops at the 10-th epoch). To select λ_{reg} and λ_{util} in our method, we perform hyperparameter tuning over the validation sets. The optimal hyperparameter values of our attack are reported in the supplementary materials.

Table 2. Fooling Percentage (seen/unseen) of our CAUP attack (perturbation ℓ_2-norm of 6) on fine-grained recognition models on test images of three datasets.

Fooling Percentage	CUB			AWA2			SUN		
Seen/Unseen	UAP	GAP	CAUP	UAP	GAP	CAUP	UAP	GAP	CAUP
DAZLE	35/24	27/19	**96/89**	09/15	11/16	**89/76**	41/22	46/27	**75/55**
DCN	51/46	21/21	**70/70**	02/05	07/10	**08/15**	41/21	30/15	**59/33**
CNZSL	26/25	18/21	**96/91**	13/12	09/12	**54/42**	29/16	27/20	22/12
CEZSL	39/40	35/35	**99/95**	24/21	12/15	**81/75**	29/28	26/26	**92/89**

Table 3. Fooling Percentage (seen/unseen) of our CAUP attack (perturbation ℓ_∞-norm of 0.06) on fine-grained recognition models on test images of three datasets.

Fooling Percentage	CUB			AWA2			SUN		
Seen/Unseen	UAP	GAP	CAUP	UAP	GAP	CAUP	UAP	GAP	CAUP
DAZLE	14/11	89/77	**98/91**	04/08	43/38	**82/77**	21/10	**90/78**	85/71
DCN	05/06	**74/73**	70/66	01/02	15/19	**47/48**	09/05	**81/63**	66/41
CNZSL	16/18	61/55	**97/93**	06/08	57/73	**86/79**	20/11	**75/55**	48/19
CEZSL	18/24	79/77	**99/95**	02/04	55/43	**97/96**	26/15	81/72	**92/86**

4.2 Experimental Results

4.2.1 Quantitative Analysis

Effectiveness of Compositionality and Attribute-Based Attacks. We start by comparing the effectiveness of the CAUP against other possible universal attacks, which are not attribute-based or not truly compositional. To do so, we learn attacks by different methods for the DAZLE model on the three datasets. Figure 2 shows the unseen fooling percentage(top row) and seen fooling percentage(bottom row) as a function of the magnitude (ℓ_2-norm) of the perturbation (due to space limitation, the results for the harmonic mean and the ℓ_∞-norm are reported in the supplementary materials). Notice that on all datasets, CAUP achieves higher fooling percentage (hence, more effective attack) for different values of the perturbation magnitude. In particular, on CUB, with ℓ_2-norm of perturbation being 2, CAUP increases the fooling percentage to more than 50% while other attacks only increase the fooling percentage to about 15%. We also obtain a similar 50% gap between CAUP and (UAP,GAP) fooling percentages for ℓ_2-norm of perturbation being 6 on CUB and AWA2. As expected, when the perturbation norm increases, all attacks perform better. While on SUN, CAUP still performs best, the gap is smaller than CUB and AWA2. This comes from the fact that some of the attributes in SUN are abstract concepts, such as research/vacation, which are harder to visually attack, while CUB and AWA2 have physical attributes, such as red wing/spotted belly and gray/stripes. Notice that Uniform in all datasets underperforms CAUP which demonstrates that attribute-based attacks without properly composing them with appropriate weights are not effective. In fact, using compositional weights (3), by weighting attribute-based universal perturbations based on the class to be attacked, significantly improves the efficacy of the perturbations.

Table 4. a) Transferability (seen/unseen fooling percentage) of CAUP attacks across different fine-grained models. The ℓ_2-norm of perturbation is 6 for all cases. **b)** Ablation study to investigate the effectiveness of different loss functions on the DAZLE.

(a)

Attack \ Train		DAZLE	CEZSL	CNZSL	DCN
CUB	DAZLE	96/ 89	97/ 91	89/ 83	74/ 61
	CEZSL	84/ 81	99/ 95	92/ 93	77/ 70
	CNZSL	86/ 81	96/ 94	96/ 91	79/ 66
	DCN	81/ 82	97/ 96	88/ 90	70/ 70
AWA2	DAZLE	89/ 76	66/ 55	87/ 89	20/ 19
	CEZSL	73/ 63	81/ 75	50/ 52	37/ 28
	CNZSL	54/ 56	63/ 39	54/ 42	23/ 18
	DCN	47/ 52	62/ 49	32/ 28	08/ 15
SUN	DAZLE	75/ 55	84/ 65	23/ 16	59/ 42
	CEZSL	59/ 55	92/ 89	17/ 18	53/ 42
	CNZSL	66/ 46	85/ 65	22/ 12	58/ 37
	DCN	61/ 44	89/ 80	18/ 09	59/ 33
	AVG	67/ 62	**82/ 70**	55/ 53	53/ 42

(b)

	Seen/Unseen	ℓ_2
CUB	$\mathcal{L}_{rank}$	0.24/0.18
	$\mathcal{L}_{rank} + \mathcal{L}_{reg}$	0.53/0.40
	$\mathcal{L}_{rank} + \mathcal{L}_{util}$	0.90/0.82
	$\mathcal{L}_{rank} + \mathcal{L}_{reg} + \mathcal{L}_{util}$	**0.96/0.89**
AWA2	$\mathcal{L}_{rank}$	0.05/0.11
	$\mathcal{L}_{rank} + \mathcal{L}_{reg}$	0.18/0.21
	$\mathcal{L}_{rank} + \mathcal{L}_{util}$	0.36/0.33
	$\mathcal{L}_{rank} + \mathcal{L}_{reg} + \mathcal{L}_{util}$	**0.76/0.73**
SUN	$\mathcal{L}_{rank}$	0.38/0.22
	$\mathcal{L}_{rank} + \mathcal{L}_{reg}$	0.51/0.31
	$\mathcal{L}_{rank} + \mathcal{L}_{util}$	0.30/0.26
	$\mathcal{L}_{rank} + \mathcal{L}_{reg} + \mathcal{L}_{util}$	**0.75/0.55**

More generally, Table 2 shows the fooling percentage of UAP, GAP and CAUP ℓ_2-norm attacks on four fine-grained models on perturbed test images from seen/unseen classes. The results are for ℓ_2-norm of the perturbation being 6. Each box is an attack that is trained and tested on the corresponding fine-grained model. Notice that in almost all cases, for both seen and unseen classes and all three datasets, CAUP extremely outperforms UAP and GAP, which shows the effectiveness of the compositional model not only for attacking seen classes but for generalization to classes without any training images. In particular, on CUB, our attack improves over UAP and GAP by at least 19% on seen and 24% on unseen images. On AWA2 and SUN, DAZLE and CEZSL are easier architectures to attack while DCN and CNZSL are harder to fool. Even for these robust models, CAUP outperforms on fooling percentage for 3 out of four cases. Also, on SUN, the effectiveness of three attack strategies is lower than the other two datasets. We believe this is due to the very small number of training samples (16) per class, which makes learning perturbations, in particular, multiple attribute-based attacks, more difficult. Despite this difficulty, CAUP performs significantly better on SUN when using DCN, CEZSL and DAZLE, while UAP performs only 7% better than CAUP on DCN. Similar to Table 2, Table 3 includes the fooling percentage of UAP, GAP and CAUP ℓ_∞-norm attacks on four fine-grained models for both seen and unseen classes. The perturbations applied with scaled ℓ_∞-norm of 0.06. CAUP outperforms on eight out of twelve cases while GAP outperforms on the other four cases. In general DCN is a more robust model against all attacks, while DAZLE, CEZSL and CNZSL are easier to fool. Notice that GAP outperforms UAP in ℓ_∞-norm although it underperforms UAP and CAUP in ℓ_2-norm attack.

Limitation. Notice that to generate our CAUP attacks, we assumed access to class-semantic vectors. While in the datasets above, class semantics are available,

Fig. 3. a) AUPs on CUB. The first/second column shows the perturbation for different wing colors and belly/back patterns, respectively. **b)** Successful adversarial examples generated with CAUP (perturbation norm of 6). We use the convention (ground-truth class → adversarial class). YHB means Yellow Headed Blackbird. (Color figure online)

some fine-grained recognition problems may not have such vectors. This, in fact, could be a limitation of our method technique, and extension to settings without semantic vectors is an interesting avenue of future research.

Transferability of CAUP across Recognition Models. Table 4a shows the transferability of our proposed CAUP attacks learned by one fine-grained model to other models. For each row, we learn the attribute-based universal perturbations and compositional weights using the indicated fine-grained recognition method and test the accuracy of each model against test data perturbed by our CAUP. Notice that, as expected, in almost all cases, the attack generated by each model works best on that model compared to others. On the other hand, CAUP attacks transfer quite well across different architectures. For example, on CUB, our attacks learned from CEZSL lead to (97%, 91%) fooling percentage for (seen, unseen) using DAZLE, while leading to (96%, 94%) fooling percentage using CNZSL and (97%, 96%) fooling percentage using DCN. Similarly, the performance of CAUP attacks learned from DCN, CNZSL or DAZLE transfer well to other models. As the average transfer rate shows, the attacks learned on CEZSL transfer better than other attacks to other fine-grained models.

Ablation Study on Objective Function. In Table 4b, we investigate the effectiveness of each term of our proposed loss in (7) when using DAZLE as the fine-grained recognition model. We show the seen and unseen fooling percentages over all the three datasets, for perturbation magnitude being 6. Notice that only using $\mathcal{L}_{rank}$ does not lead to very effective attacks. Once we add $\mathcal{L}_{reg}$ or $\mathcal{L}_{util}$ to the ranking loss, the attack effectiveness improves. Generally, using $\mathcal{L}_{util}$ lead to more improvement compared to $\mathcal{L}_{reg}$. This shows the importance of ensuring that every attribute-based universal perturbation must be used across

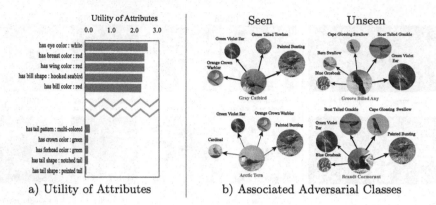

a) Utility of Attributes   b) Associated Adversarial Classes

Fig. 4. a) Sorted utilities (5 largest and 5 smallest ones are shown) of AUPs trained for DAZLE on the CUB dataset. b) Visualization of four ground-truth classes and the associated adversarial classes on CUB. The node at the center of each component is a ground-truth class (green) and the surrounding nodes are the adversarial classes (black) after attack. The size of each adversarial class node represents the portion of samples that have been fooled into to that class by CAUP. (Color figure online)

some classes. Finally, adding both $\mathcal{L}_{reg}$ and $\mathcal{L}_{util}$ to the ranking loss leads to significant improvement of the attack efficacy.

4.2.2   Qualitative Analysis

Adversarial Examples. In Fig. 3, we show several examples of perturbed test images by our method that successfully fool the fine-grained DAZLE classifier. Notice that CAUP attacks are imperceptible or quasi-perceptible, and can not only work well for test images from seen classes but also from unseen classes. This is done by composing different attribute-based universal perturbations using class-attribute weights ω_a^c that specify how much to weight an attribute perturbation $\boldsymbol{u}_a$ for attacking a class c.

In Fig. 5, we show a class and the most important attributes for changing the class label. In other words, we show the attributes with the largest composition weights ω_a^c, where thicker edges mean larger absolute weight, hence, more contribution from the associated attribute perturbation. Notice that our method automatically learns to give higher composition weights to 'purple forehead', 'purple crown' and 'red breast' attribute perturbations in order to misclassify the 'painted bunting' class or gives higher composition weights to 'red wing' and 'orange wing' to misclassify the 'red-winged black bird' class, which intuitively are also the most discriminating features of these classes.

Correlation of Attribute-Based Universal Perturbations. To demonstrate the similarity among learned AUPs, in Fig. 5, we show the cosine similarities between pairs of AUPs learned on the CUB dataset. Notice that as the block-diagonal structure in the first plot shows, our method learns more similar AUPs for similar attributes (e.g., among wing colors) and more dissimilar AUPs for semantically different attributes (e.g., wing colors and belly/back patterns). On the other hand, as the second plot shows, within different color wings, the learned AUPs for more semantically related colors are more similar (e.g., 'brown wing' and 'yellow wing'), while being more distinct for distinct colors (e.g., 'blue wing' and 'red wing'). In Fig. 3, for several attributes, we show the learned perturbations, which clearly have different patterns.

Utilities of AUPs. In Fig. 4, we show the utilities of AUPs, i.e., how much each attribute contributes to misclassifying some classes. We show the top 5 attributes with the highest utilities, defined in (6), and the top 5 attributes with the lowest utilities. Notice that all attributes contribute for attacking some classes, as they have non-zero utilities. In addition, the utilities of attributes are not uniform, which means that our method successfully learns to use more discriminative attributes for generating attacks. For example, 'has tail shape: pointed tail' is very common across different bird species, therefore the associated AUP has a small utility, while 'has breast/wing color: red' are more specific to some bird species, therefore, they have higher utilities for attack (we can change many classes that do not have red breast/wing, by attacking these attributes).

Dominancy in Fine-Grained Classes. Given that our attacks are non-targeted, we investigate how CAUP on images from a specific fine-grained class misclassify it into other classes. To do so, for a fixed class and for all test images that belong to it, we count the number of images that have been misclassified by the CAUP as belonging to each particular/adversarial class. In Fig. 4, we show four classes c in CUB (each c being at the center of a connected graph) and the adversarial classes to which the perturbed test images of c have been misclassified (connected to the center node by edges). The size of images representing each adversarial class corresponds to the number of samples fooled into that adversarial class. First, notice that there are only a few adversarial classes for each ground-truth class. For example, images from 'gray catbird' get fooled into one of the four classes shown in the figure. On the other hand, many images from 'gray catbird', 'arctic tern' and 'Brandt cormorant' classes are misclassified

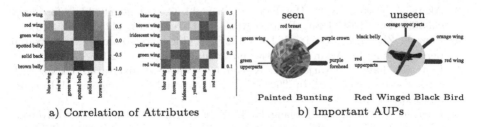

a) Correlation of Attributes   b) Important AUPs

Fig. 5. a) Correlations among some learned attribute-based universal perturbations. Lighter color means being more correlated. b) We visualize the attributes whose perturbation has the largest absolute weights for changing a given class. Thicker edges mean higher attribute-class weights, ω_a^c. YHB means Yellow Headed Black Bird. (Color figure online)

as 'painted bunting', making this class a dominant adversarial class. The reason for this dominancy is the major contribution (i.e., high utility) of attribute 'has breast/wing color: red', which is more specific to some species of birds including 'painted bunting.' Additionally, for similar reasons, 'green violet ear' and 'orange crown warbler' are other examples of the dominant adversarial classes. These results indeed confirm the existence of dominant adversarial classes in the fine-grained settings (both seen and unseen), where CAUP frequently misclassifies images into such classes. We believe this could be used to investigate defense mechanisms for fine-grained recognition, which we leave for future studies.

5 Conclusions

We proposed a compositional method for generating effective, generalizable and real-time adversarial attacks on fine-grained recognition models, by learning attribute-based universal perturbations and a model for composing them. By extensive experiments on multiple fine-grained datasets and using several fine-grained recognition models, we showed that our attacks are significantly more effective than conventional universal perturbations and generalize well from seen to unseen classes and across different architectures.

Acknowledgements. This work is sponsored by NSF (IIS-2115110), DARPA (HR00112220001) and ARO (W911NF2110276). Content does not necessarily reflect the position/policy of the Government. No official endorsement should be inferred.

References

1. Afifi, M., Brown, M.S.: What else can fool deep learning? Addressing color constancy errors on deep neural network performance. In: Proceedings of the IEEE/CVF International Conference on Computer Vision, pp. 243–252 (2019)
2. Ak, K.E., Kassim, A.A., Lim, J.H., Tham, J.Y.: Learning attribute representations with localization for flexible fashion search. In: IEEE Conference on Computer Vision and Pattern Recognition (2018)
3. Akata, Z., Perronnin, F., Harchaoui, Z., Schmid, C.: Label-embedding for image classification. IEEE Trans. Pattern Anal. Mach. Intell. **38**, 1425–1438 (2016)
4. Benz, P., Zhang, C., Imtiaz, T., Kweon, I.S.: Double targeted universal adversarial perturbations. In: Asian Conference on Computer Vision (2020)
5. Benz, P., Zhang, C., Karjauv, A., Kweon, I.S.: Universal adversarial training with class-wise perturbations. In: 2021 IEEE International Conference on Multimedia and Expo (ICME), pp. 1–6. IEEE (2021)
6. Bhattad, A., Chong, M.J., Liang, K., Li, B., Forsyth, D.A.: Unrestricted adversarial examples via semantic manipulation. arXiv preprint arXiv:1904.06347 (2019)
7. Bucher, M., Herbin, S., Jurie, F.: Generating visual representations for zero-shot classification. In: IEEE International Conference on Computer Vision Workshops (2017)
8. Carlini, N., Wagner, D.: Towards evaluating the robustness of neural networks. In: IEEE Symposium on Security and Privacy (2017)

9. Chang, D., Pang, K., Zheng, Y., Ma, Z., Song, Y.Z., Guo, J.: Your "flamingo" is my "bird": fine-grained, or not. In: Proceedings of the IEEE/CVF Conference on Computer Vision and Pattern Recognition, pp. 11476–11485 (2021)
10. Changpinyo, S., Chao, W., Gong, B., Sha, F.: Synthesized classifiers for zero-shot learning. In: IEEE Conference on Computer Vision and Pattern Recognition (2016)
11. Chen, P.Y., Sharma, Y., Zhang, H., Yi, J., Hsieh, C.J.: EAD: elastic-net attacks to deep neural networks via adversarial examples. In: AAAI Conference on Artificial Intelligence (2018)
12. Choi, J., Larson, M., Li, X., Li, K., Friedland, G., Hanjalic, A.: The geo-privacy bonus of popular photo enhancements. In: Proceedings of the 2017 ACM on International Conference on Multimedia Retrieval, pp. 84–92 (2017)
13. Croce, F., Hein, M.: Sparse and imperceivable adversarial attacks. In: Proceedings of the IEEE/CVF International Conference on Computer Vision, pp. 4724–4732 (2019)
14. Ding, Y., Zhou, Y., Zhu, Y., Ye, Q., Jiao, J.: Selective sparse sampling for fine-grained image recognition. In: IEEE International Conference on Computer Vision (2019)
15. Ding, Y., et al.: AP-CNN: weakly supervised attention pyramid convolutional neural network for fine-grained visual classification. IEEE Trans. Image Process. **30**, 2826–2836 (2021)
16. Dong, Y., et al.: Boosting adversarial attacks with momentum. In: IEEE Conference on Computer Vision and Pattern Recognition (2018)
17. Duan, R., Chen, Y., Niu, D., Yang, Y., Qin, A., He, Y.: AdvDrop: adversarial attack to DNNs by dropping information. In: Proceedings of the IEEE/CVF International Conference on Computer Vision, pp. 7506–7515 (2021)
18. Dubey, A., Gupta, O., Guo, P., Raskar, R., Farrell, R., Naik, N.: Pairwise confusion for fine-grained visual classification. In: European Conference on Computer Vision (2018)
19. Elhoseiny, M., Zhu, Y., Zhang, H., Elgammal, A.M.: Link the head to the "beak": zero shot learning from noisy text description at part precision. In: IEEE Conference on Computer Vision and Pattern Recognition, pp. 6288–6297 (2017)
20. Engstrom, L., Tran, B., Tsipras, D., Schmidt, L., Madry, A.: A rotation and a translation suffice: fooling CNNs with simple transformations (2018)
21. Felix, R., Kumar, B.G.V., Reid, I.D., Carneiro, G.: Multi-modal cycle-consistent generalized zero-shot learning. In: European Conference on Computer Vision (2018)
22. Gao, L., Zhang, Q., Song, J., Liu, X., Shen, H.T.: Patch-wise attack for fooling deep neural network. In: Vedaldi, A., Bischof, H., Brox, T., Frahm, J.-M. (eds.) ECCV 2020. LNCS, vol. 12373, pp. 307–322. Springer, Cham (2020). https://doi.org/10.1007/978-3-030-58604-1_19
23. Gao, Y., Beijbom, O., Zhang, N., Darrell, T.: Compact bilinear pooling. In: IEEE Conference on Computer Vision and Pattern Recognition (2016)
24. Goodfellow, I.J., Shlens, J., Szegedy, C.: Explaining and harnessing adversarial examples. In: International Conference on Learning Representations (2015)
25. Gragnaniello, D., Marra, F., Verdoliva, L., Poggi, G.: Perceptual quality-preserving black-box attack against deep learning image classifiers. Pattern Recogn. Lett. **147**, 142–149 (2021)
26. Han, Z., Fu, Z., Chen, S., Yang, J.: Contrastive embedding for generalized zero-shot learning. In: Proceedings of the IEEE/CVF Conference on Computer Vision and Pattern Recognition, pp. 2371–2381 (2021)

27. Hayes, J., Danezis, G.: Learning universal adversarial perturbations with generative models. In: IEEE Security and Privacy Workshops (2018)
28. Hendrycks, D., Zhao, K., Basart, S., Steinhardt, J., Song, D.: Natural adversarial examples. In: Proceedings of the IEEE/CVF Conference on Computer Vision and Pattern Recognition, pp. 15262–15271 (2021)
29. Hosseini, H., Poovendran, R.: Semantic adversarial examples. In: Proceedings of the IEEE Conference on Computer Vision and Pattern Recognition Workshops, pp. 1614–1619 (2018)
30. Huang, S., Wang, X., Tao, D.: Stochastic partial swap: Enhanced model generalization and interpretability for fine-grained recognition. In: Proceedings of the IEEE/CVF International Conference on Computer Vision, pp. 620–629 (2021)
31. Huynh, D., Elhamifar, E.: Compositional zero-shot learning via fine-grained dense feature composition. In: Neural Information Processing Systems (2020)
32. Huynh, D., Elhamifar, E.: Fine-grained generalized zero-shot learning via dense attribute-based attention. In: IEEE Conference on Computer Vision and Pattern Recognition (2020)
33. Huynh, D., Elhamifar, E.: Compositional fine-grained low-shot learning. arXiv preprint arXiv:2105.10438 (2021)
34. Ji, R., et al.: Attention convolutional binary neural tree for fine-grained visual categorization. In: Proceedings of the IEEE/CVF Conference on Computer Vision and Pattern Recognition, pp. 10468–10477 (2020)
35. Jiang, H., Wang, R., Shan, S., Chen, X.: Transferable contrastive network for generalized zero-shot learning. In: IEEE International Conference on Computer Vision (2019)
36. Kariyappa, S., Prakash, A., Qureshi, M.K.: MAZE: data-free model stealing attack using zeroth-order gradient estimation. In: Proceedings of the IEEE/CVF Conference on Computer Vision and Pattern Recognition, pp. 13814–13823 (2021)
37. Khrulkov, V., Oseledets, I.: Art of singular vectors and universal adversarial perturbations. In: IEEE Conference on Computer Vision and Pattern Recognition (2018)
38. Kong, S., Fowlkes, C.C.: Low-rank bilinear pooling for fine-grained classification. In: IEEE Conference on Computer Vision and Pattern Recognition (2017)
39. Kurakin, A., Goodfellow, I., Bengio, S.: Adversarial examples in the physical world. arXiv preprint, arXiv:1607.02533 (2016)
40. Kurakin, A., Goodfellow, I., Bengio, S.: Adversarial machine learning at scale. In: International Conference on Learning Representations (2017)
41. Laidlaw, C., Feizi, S.: Functional adversarial attacks. arXiv preprint arXiv:1906.00001 (2019)
42. Lampert, C.H., Nickisch, H., Harmeling, S.: Learning to detect unseen object classes by between-class attribute transfer. In: IEEE Conference on Computer Vision and Pattern Recognition (2009)
43. Lin, D., Shen, X., Lu, C., Jia, J.: Deep LAC: deep localization, alignment and classification for fine-grained recognition. In: IEEE Conference on Computer Vision and Pattern Recognition (2015)
44. Lin, T.Y., RoyChowdhury, A., Maji, S.: Bilinear CNN models for fine-grained visual recognition. In: IEEE International Conference on Computer Vision (2015)
45. Liu, C., Xie, H., Zha, Z., Yu, L., Chen, Z., Zhang, Y.: Bidirectional attention-recognition model for fine-grained object classification. IEEE Trans. Multimed. **22**(7), 1785–1795 (2019)
46. Liu, H., et al.: Universal adversarial perturbation via prior driven uncertainty approximation. In: International Conference on Computer Vision (2019)

47. Liu, S., Long, M., Wang, J., Jordan, M.I.: Generalized zero-shot learning with deep calibration network. In: Neural Information Processing Systems (2018)
48. Liu, Y., Guo, J., Cai, D., He, X.: Attribute attention for semantic disambiguation in zero-shot learning. In: IEEE International Conference on Computer Vision (2019)
49. Liu, Y., Zhang, W., Wang, J.: Zero-shot adversarial quantization. In: Proceedings of the IEEE/CVF Conference on Computer Vision and Pattern Recognition, pp. 1512–1521 (2021)
50. Liu, Z., Luo, P., Qiu, S., Wang, X., Tang, X.: DeepFashion: powering robust clothes recognition and retrieval with rich annotations. In: IEEE Conference on Computer Vision and Pattern Recognition (2016)
51. Liu, Z., Luo, P., Wang, X., Tang, X.: Deep learning face attributes in the wild. In: IEEE International Conference on Computer Vision (2015)
52. Luo, B., Liu, Y., Wei, L., Xu, Q.: Towards imperceptible and robust adversarial example attacks against neural networks. In: Thirty-Second AAAI Conference on Artificial Intelligence (2018)
53. Maho, T., Furon, T., Le Merrer, E.: SurFree: a fast surrogate-free black-box attack. In: Proceedings of the IEEE/CVF Conference on Computer Vision and Pattern Recognition, pp. 10430–10439 (2021)
54. Mall, U., Hariharan, B., Bala, K.: Field-guide-inspired zero-shot learning. In: Proceedings of the IEEE/CVF International Conference on Computer Vision, pp. 9546–9555 (2021)
55. Mao, C., Chiquier, M., Wang, H., Yang, J., Vondrick, C.: Adversarial attacks are reversible with natural supervision. arXiv preprint arXiv:2103.14222 (2021)
56. Metzen, J.H., Kumar, M.C., Brox, T., Fischer, V.: Universal adversarial perturbations against semantic image segmentation. In: International Conference on Computer Vision (2019)
57. Moosavi-Dezfooli, S., Fawzi, A., Fawzi, O., Frossard, P.: Universal adversarial perturbations. In: IEEE Conference on Computer Vision and Pattern Recognition (2017)
58. Moosavi-Dezfooli, S., Fawzi, A., Frossard, P.: DeepFool: a simple and accurate method to fool deep neural networks. In: IEEE Conference on Computer Vision and Pattern Recognition (2016)
59. Mopuri, K.R., Ganeshan, A., Babu, R.V.: Generalizable data-free objective for crafting universal adversarial perturbations. IEEE Trans. Pattern Anal. Mach. Intell. 41(10), 2452–2465 (2018)
60. Mopuri, K.R., Garg, U., Babu, R.V.: Fast feature fool: a data independent approach to universal adversarial perturbations. arXiv preprint arXiv:1707.05572 (2017)
61. Nakka, K.K., Salzmann, M.: Towards robust fine-grained recognition by maximal separation of discriminative features. In: Asian Conference on Computer Vision (2020)
62. Narodytska, N., Kasiviswanathan, S.: Simple black-box adversarial attacks on deep neural networks. In: IEEE Conference on Computer Vision and Pattern Recognition Workshops (2017)
63. Norouzi, M., et al.: Zero-shot learning by convex combination of semantic embeddings. In: International Conference on Learning Representations (2014)
64. Park, S.M., Wei, K.A., Xiao, K., Li, J., Madry, A.: On distinctive properties of universal perturbations. arXiv preprint arXiv:2112.15329 (2021)
65. Parkhi, O.M., Vedaldi, A., Zisserman, A.: Deep face recognition. In: British Machine Vision Conference (2015)

66. Patterson, G., Hays, J.: Sun attribute database: discovering, annotating, and recognizing scene attributes. In: IEEE Conference on Computer Vision and Pattern Recognition (2012)

67. Pennington, J., Socher, R., Manning, C.D.: Glove: global vectors for word representation. In: Empirical Methods in Natural Language Processing (EMNLP) (2014)

68. Pony, R., Naeh, I., Mannor, S.: Over-the-air adversarial flickering attacks against video recognition networks. In: IEEE Conference on Computer Vision and Pattern Recognition (2021)

69. Poursaeed, O., Katsman, I., Gao, B., Belongie, S.: Generative adversarial perturbations. In: Proceedings of the IEEE Conference on Computer Vision and Pattern Recognition, pp. 4422–4431 (2018)

70. Rampini, A., Pestarini, F., Cosmo, L., Melzi, S., Rodola, E.: Universal spectral adversarial attacks for deformable shapes. In: Proceedings of the IEEE/CVF Conference on Computer Vision and Pattern Recognition, pp. 3216–3226 (2021)

71. Romera-Paredes, B., Torr, P.H.: An embarrassingly simple approach to zero-shot learning. In: International Conference on Machine learning (2015)

72. Rony, J., Granger, E., Pedersoli, M., Ben Ayed, I.: Augmented Lagrangian adversarial attacks. In: Proceedings of the IEEE/CVF International Conference on Computer Vision, pp. 7738–7747 (2021)

73. Rony, J., Hafemann, L.G., Oliveira, L.S., Ayed, I.B., Sabourin, R., Granger, E.: Decoupling direction and norm for efficient gradient-based l2 adversarial attacks and defenses. In: Proceedings of the IEEE/CVF Conference on Computer Vision and Pattern Recognition, pp. 4322–4330 (2019)

74. Sayles, A., Hooda, A., Gupta, M., Chatterjee, R., Fernandes, E.: Invisible perturbations: physical adversarial examples exploiting the rolling shutter effect. In: Proceedings of the IEEE/CVF Conference on Computer Vision and Pattern Recognition, pp. 14666–14675 (2021)

75. Schönfeld, E., Ebrahimi, S., Sinha, S., Darrell, T., Akata, Z.: Generalized zero- and few-shot learning via aligned variational autoencoders. In: IEEE Conference on Computer Vision and Pattern Recognition (2019)

76. Skorokhodov, I., Elhoseiny, M.: Class normalization for (continual)? Generalized zero-shot learning. arXiv preprint arXiv:2006.11328 (2020)

77. Sun, M., Yuan, Y., Zhou, F., Ding, E.: Multi-attention multi-class constraint for fine-grained image recognition. In: European Conference on Computer Vision (2018)

78. Szegedy, C., et al.: Intriguing properties of neural networks. In: International Conference on Learning Representations (2014)

79. Wang, W., Xu, Y., Shen, J., Zhu, S.C.: Attentive fashion grammar network for fashion landmark detection and clothing category classification. In: IEEE Conference on Computer Vision and Pattern Recognition (2018)

80. Wang, X., Lin, S., Zhang, H., Zhu, Y., Zhang, Q.: Interpreting attributions and interactions of adversarial attacks. In: Proceedings of the IEEE/CVF International Conference on Computer Vision, pp. 1095–1104 (2021)

81. Wang, X., Zhang, Z., Wu, B., Shen, F., Lu, G.: Prototype-supervised adversarial network for targeted attack of deep hashing. In: Proceedings of the IEEE/CVF Conference on Computer Vision and Pattern Recognition, pp. 16357–16366 (2021)

82. Wang, Z., Bovik, A.C., Sheikh, H.R., Simoncelli, E.P.: Image quality assessment: from error visibility to structural similarity. IEEE Trans. Image Process. **13**(4), 600–612 (2004)

83. Welinder, P., et al.: Caltech-UCSD Birds 200. Technical report. CNS-TR-2010-001, California Institute of Technology (2010)
84. Wen, Y., Zhang, K., Li, Z., Qiao, Yu.: A discriminative feature learning approach for deep face recognition. In: Leibe, B., Matas, J., Sebe, N., Welling, M. (eds.) ECCV 2016. LNCS, vol. 9911, pp. 499–515. Springer, Cham (2016). https://doi.org/10.1007/978-3-319-46478-7_31
85. Wong, E., Schmidt, F., Kolter, Z.: Wasserstein adversarial examples via projected sinkhorn iterations. In: International Conference on Machine Learning, pp. 6808–6817. PMLR (2019)
86. Xian, Y., Lorenz, T., Schiele, B., Akata, Z.: Feature generating networks for zero-shot learning. In: 2018 IEEE/CVF Conference on Computer Vision and Pattern Recognition, pp. 5542–5551 (2018)
87. Xian, Y., Schiele, B., Akata, Z.: Zero-shot learning - the good, the bad and the ugly. In: IEEE Conference on Computer Vision and Pattern Recognition (2017)
88. Xian, Y., Sharma, S., Schiele, B., Akata, Z.: F-VAEGAN-D2: a feature generating framework for any-shot learning. In: IEEE Conference on Computer Vision and Pattern Recognition (2019)
89. Xian, Y., Lampert, C.H., Schiele, B., Akata, Z.: Zero-shot learning-a comprehensive evaluation of the good, the bad and the ugly. IEEE Trans. Pattern Anal. Mach. Intell. **41**, 2251–2265 (2017)
90. Xiao, C., Li, B., Zhu, J.Y., He, W., Liu, M., Song, D.: Generating adversarial examples with adversarial networks. In: Proceedings of the 27th International Joint Conference on Artificial Intelligence, pp. 3905–3911 (2018)
91. Xiao, C., Zhu, J.Y., Li, B., He, W., Liu, M., Song, D.: Spatially transformed adversarial examples. arXiv preprint arXiv:1801.02612 (2018)
92. Xiao, J., Ehinger, K.A., Hays, J., Torralba, A., Oliva, A.: Sun database: exploring a large collection of scene categories. Int. J. Comput. Vis. **119**(1), 3–22 (2016)
93. Xie, C., et al.: Improving transferability of adversarial examples with input diversity. In: Proceedings of the IEEE/CVF Conference on Computer Vision and Pattern Recognition, pp. 2730–2739 (2019)
94. Xu, K., et al.: Structured adversarial attacks: towards general implementation and better interpretability. In: International Conference on Learning Representations (2019)
95. Yue, Z., Wang, T., Sun, Q., Hua, X.S., Zhang, H.: Counterfactual zero-shot and open-set visual recognition. In: Proceedings of the IEEE/CVF Conference on Computer Vision and Pattern Recognition, pp. 15404–15414 (2021)
96. Zhang, C., Benz, P., Imtiaz, T., Kweon, I.S.: CD-UAP: class discriminative universal adversarial perturbation. In: Proceedings of the AAAI Conference on Artificial Intelligence, vol. 34, pp. 6754–6761 (2020)
97. Zhang, C., Benz, P., Lin, C., Karjauv, A., Wu, J., Kweon, I.S.: A survey on universal adversarial attack. arXiv preprint arXiv:2103.01498 (2021)
98. Zhang, H., Avrithis, Y., Furon, T., Amsaleg, L.: Smooth adversarial examples. EURASIP J. Inf. Secur. **2020**(1), 1–12 (2020)
99. Zhang, L., Huang, S., Liu, W.: Intra-class part swapping for fine-grained image classification. In: Proceedings of the IEEE/CVF Winter Conference on Applications of Computer Vision, pp. 3209–3218 (2021)
100. Zhang, L., Huang, S., Liu, W., Tao, D.: Learning a mixture of granularity-specific experts for fine-grained categorization. In: IEEE International Conference on Computer Vision (2019)
101. Zhang, Z., Saligrama, V.: Zero-shot learning via joint latent similarity embedding. In: IEEE Conference on Computer Vision and Pattern Recognition (2016)

102. Zhao, X., et al.: Recognizing part attributes with insufficient data. In: IEEE International Conference on Computer Vision (2019)
103. Zhao, Y., Yan, K., Huang, F., Li, J.: Graph-based high-order relation discovery for fine-grained recognition. In: Proceedings of the IEEE/CVF Conference on Computer Vision and Pattern Recognition, pp. 15079–15088 (2021)
104. Zhao, Z., Liu, Z., Larson, M.: Towards large yet imperceptible adversarial image perturbations with perceptual color distance. In: Proceedings of the IEEE/CVF Conference on Computer Vision and Pattern Recognition, pp. 1039–1048 (2020)
105. Zheng, H., Fu, J., Mei, T., Luo, J.: Learning multi-attention convolutional neural network for fine-grained image recognition. In: IEEE International Conference on Computer Vision (2017)
106. Zheng, H., Fu, J., Zha, Z.J., Luo, J.: Looking for the devil in the details: learning trilinear attention sampling network for fine-grained image recognition. In: IEEE Conference on Computer Vision and Pattern Recognition (2019)

Towards Effective and Robust Neural Trojan Defenses via Input Filtering

Kien Do[1]($\boxtimes$)(iD), Haripriya Harikumar[1], Hung Le[1], Dung Nguyen[1],
Truyen Tran[1], Santu Rana[1], Dang Nguyen[1], Willy Susilo[2],
and Svetha Venkatesh[1]

[1] Applied Artificial Intelligence Institute (A2I2), Deakin University,
Geelong, Australia
{k.do,h.harikumar,thai.le,dung.nguyen,truyen.tran,santu.rana,d.nguyen,
svetha.venkatesh}@deakin.edu.au
[2] University of Wollongong, Wollongong, Australia
wsusilo@uow.edu.au

Abstract. Trojan attacks on deep neural networks are both dangerous
and surreptitious. Over the past few years, Trojan attacks have advanced
from using only a single input-agnostic trigger and targeting only one
class to using multiple, input-specific triggers and targeting multiple
classes. However, Trojan defenses have not caught up with this development. Most defense methods still make inadequate assumptions about
Trojan triggers and target classes, thus, can be easily circumvented by
modern Trojan attacks. To deal with this problem, we propose two novel
"filtering" defenses called *Variational Input Filtering (VIF)* and *Adversarial Input Filtering (AIF)* which leverage lossy data compression and
adversarial learning respectively to effectively purify potential Trojan
triggers in the input at run time without making assumptions about
the number of triggers/target classes or the input dependence property
of triggers. In addition, we introduce a new defense mechanism called
"Filtering-then-Contrasting" (FtC) which helps avoid the drop in classification accuracy on clean data caused by "filtering", and combine it
with VIF/AIF to derive new defenses of this kind. Extensive experimental results and ablation studies show that our proposed defenses
significantly outperform well-known baseline defenses in mitigating five
advanced Trojan attacks including two recent state-of-the-art while being
quite robust to small amounts of training data and large-norm triggers.

1 Introduction

Deep neural networks (DNNs) have achieved superhuman performance in recent
years and have been increasingly employed to make decisions on our behalf in
various critical applications in computer vision including object detection [36],

---

Supplementary Information The online version contains supplementary material
available at https://doi.org/10.1007/978-3-031-20065-6_17.

S. Avidan et al. (Eds.): ECCV 2022, LNCS 13665, pp. 283–300, 2022.
https://doi.org/10.1007/978-3-031-20065-6_17

face recognition [34,39], medical imaging [29,51], surveillance [43] and so on. However, many recent works have shown that besides the powerful modeling capability, DNNs are highly vulnerable to adversarial attacks [7,10,11,25,44]. Currently, there are two major types of attacks on DNNs. The first is *evasion/adversarial attacks* which cause a *successfully trained* model to misclassify by perturbing the model's input with imperceptible adversarial noise [10,28]. The second is *Trojan/backdoor attacks* in which attackers *interfere with the training process* of a model in order to insert hidden malicious features (referred to as *Trojans/backdoors*) into the model [4,11,25,41]. These Trojans do not cause any harm to the model under normal conditions. However, once they are triggered, they will force the model to output the target classes specified by the attackers. Unfortunately, only the attackers know exactly the Trojan triggers and the target classes. Such stealthiness makes Trojan attacks difficult to defend against.

In this work, we focus on defending against Trojan attacks. Most existing Trojan defenses assume that attacks use only *one input-agnostic* Trojan trigger and/or target only *one* class [3,5,8,12,13,47]. By constraining the space of possible triggers, these defenses are able to find the true trigger of some simple Trojan attacks satisfying their assumptions and mitigate the attacks [4,11]. However, these defenses often do not perform well against other advanced attacks that use *multiple input-specific* Trojan triggers and/or target *multiple* classes [6,32,33]. To address this problem, we propose two novel *filtering*" defenses named *Variational Input Filtering (VIF)* and *Adversarial Input Filtering (AIF)*. Both defenses aim at learning a filter network F that can purify potential Trojan triggers in the model's input at run time without making any of the above assumptions about attacks. VIF treats F as a variational autoencoder (VAE) [18] and utilizes the lossy data compression property of VAE to discard noisy information in the input including triggers. AIF, on the other hand, uses an auxiliary generator G to reveal hidden triggers in the input and leverages adversarial learning [9] between G and F to encourage F to remove potential triggers found by G. In addition, to overcome the issue that input filtering may hurt the model's prediction on clean data, we introduce a new defense mechanism called *"Filtering-then-Contrasting" (FtC)*. The key idea behind FtC is comparing the two outputs of the model with and without input filtering to determine whether the input is clean or not. If the two outputs are different, the input will be marked as containing triggers, otherwise clean. We equip VIF and AIF with FtC to arrive at the two defenses dubbed VIFtC and AIFtC respectively. Through extensive experiments and ablation studies, we demonstrate that our proposed defenses are more effective than many well-known defenses [5,8,22,47] in mitigating various advanced Trojan attacks including two recent state-of-the-art (SOTA) [32,33] while being quite robust to small amounts of training data and large trigger's norms.

2   Standard Trojan Attack

We consider image classification as the task of interest. We denote by $\mathbb{I}$ the real interval [0, 1]. In standard Trojan attack scenarios [4,11], an attacker (usually

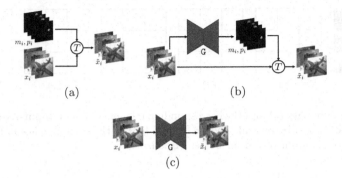

(a)   (b)

(c)

Fig. 1. Illustrations of three approaches to model input-specific Trojan triggers $\psi_i = (m_i, p_i)$ w.r.t. x_i: as learnable parameters (a), via a trigger generator (b), and via a Trojan-image autoencoder (c).

a service provider) *fully controls* the training process of an image classifier C : $\mathcal{X} \to \mathcal{Y}$ where $\mathcal{X} \subset \mathbb{I}^{c \times h \times w}$ is the input image domain, and $\mathcal{Y} = \{0, ..., K-1\}$ is the set of K classes. The attacker's goal is to insert a *Trojan* into the classifier C so that given an input image $x \in \mathcal{X}$, C will misclassify x as belonging to a target class $t \in \mathcal{Y}$ specified by the attacker if x contains the *Trojan trigger* ψ, and will predict the true label $y \in \mathcal{Y}$ of x otherwise. A common attack strategy to achieve this goal is poisoning a small portion of the training data with the Trojan trigger ψ. At each training step, the attacker randomly replaces each clean training pair (x, y) in the current mini-batch by a poisoned one $(\tilde{x}, t)$ with a probability ρ $(0 < \rho < 1)$ and trains C as normal using the modified mini-batch. $\tilde{x}$ is an image embedded with Trojan triggers (or *Trojan image* for short) corresponding to x. $\tilde{x}$ is constructed by combining x with ψ via a Trojan injection function $T(x, \psi)$. A common choice of T is the image blending function [4,11] given below:

$$\tilde{x} = T(x, \psi) = (1 - m) \odot x + m \odot p, \tag{1}$$

where $\psi \triangleq (m, p)$, $m \in \mathbb{I}^{c \times h \times w}$ is the trigger mask, $p \in \mathbb{I}^{c \times h \times w}$ is the trigger pattern, and $\odot$ is the element-wise product. To ensure $\tilde{x}$ cannot be detected by human inspection at test time, $\|m\|$ must be small. Some recent works use more advanced variants of T such as reflection [24] and warping [33] to craft better natural-looking Trojan images.

Once trained, the Trojan-infected classifier C will be provided to victims (usually end-users) for deployment. When the victims test C with their own clean data, they do not see any abnormalities in performance because the Trojan remains dormant for the clean data. Thus, the victims naively believe that C is normal and use C as it is without any modification or additional safeguard.

3   Difficulty in Finding Input-Specific Triggers

In practice, we (as victims) usually have a small dataset $\mathcal{D}_{\text{val}} = \{(x_i, y_i)\}_{i=1}^{N_{\text{val}}}$ containing only clean samples for evaluating the performance of C. We can lever-

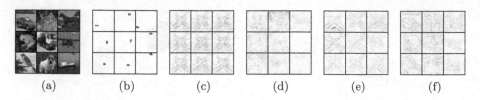

(a)   (b)   (c)   (d)   (e)   (f)

Fig. 2. Trojan images (a) and the corresponding triggers (b) of an Input-Aware Attack. Triggers synthesized by Neural Cleanse (c) and by the three approaches in Fig. 1 (d, e, f). Trigger pixels are inverted for better visualization.

age this set to find possible Trojan triggers associated with the target class t. For standard Trojan attacks [4,11] that use only a global *input-agnostic* trigger $\psi = (m, p)$, ψ can be restored by minimizing the following loss w.r.t. m and p:

$$\mathcal{L}_{\text{gen}}(x, t) = -\log p_{\mathsf{C}}(t|\tilde{x}) + \lambda_0 \max(\|m\| - \delta, 0), \tag{2}$$

where $(x, .) \sim \mathcal{D}_{\text{val}}$, $\tilde{x}$ is derived from x via Eq. 1, $p_{\mathsf{C}}(t|\tilde{x}) = \frac{\exp(\mathsf{C}_t(\tilde{x}))}{\sum_{k=1}^{K} \exp(\mathsf{C}_k(\tilde{x}))}$ is the probability of $\tilde{x}$ belonging to the target class t, $\|\cdot\|$ denotes a L1/L2 norm, $\delta \geq 0$ is an upper bound of the norm, and $\lambda_0 \geq 0$ is a coefficient. The second term in Eq. 2 ensures that the trigger is small enough so that it could not be detected by human inspection. $\mathcal{L}_{\text{gen}}$ was used by Neural Cleanse (NC) [47] and its variants [3,12,13], and was shown to work well for standard attacks.

In this work, we however consider finding the triggers of Input-Aware Attack (InpAwAtk) [32]. This is a much harder problem because InpAwAtk uses different triggers $\psi_i = (m_i, p_i)$ for different input images x_i instead of a global one. We examine 3 different ways to model ψ_i: (i) treating m_i, p_i as learnable parameters for each image $x_i \in \mathcal{D}_{\text{val}}$, (ii) via an input-conditional trigger generator $(m_i, p_i) = \mathsf{G}(x_i)$, and (iii) generating a Trojan image $\tilde{x}_i$ w.r.t. x_i via a Trojan-image generator $\tilde{x}_i = \mathsf{G}(x_i)$ and treating $\tilde{x}_i - x_i$ as ψ_i. These are illustrated in Fig. 1. The first way does not generalize to other images not in $\mathcal{D}_{\text{val}}$ while the second and third do. We reuse the loss $\mathcal{L}_{\text{gen}}$ in Eq. 2 to learn m_i, p_i in the first way and G in the second way. The loss to train G in the third way is slightly adjusted from $\mathcal{L}_{\text{gen}}$ with $\|m\|$ replaced by $\|\tilde{x} - x\|$. As shown in Fig. 2, neither NC nor the above approaches can restore the original triggers of InpAwAtk, suggesting new methods are on demand.

4   Proposed Trojan Defenses

The great difficulty in finding correct input-specific triggers (Sect. 3) challenges a majority of existing Trojan defenses which assume a global input-agnostic trigger is applied to all input images [3,8,13,22,23,35,47]. Fortunately, although we may not be able to find correct triggers, in many cases, we can still design effective Trojan defenses by filtering out triggers embedded in the input without concerning about the number or the input dependence property of triggers. The

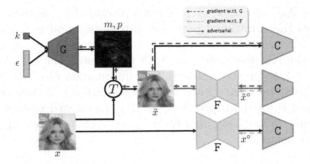

Fig. 3. An illustration of Adversarial Input Filtering.

fundamental idea is learning a filter network F that maps the original input image x into a filtered image x°, and using x° as input to the classifier C instead of x. In order for F to be considered as a good filter, x° should satisfy the following two conditions:

- *Condition 1*: If x is clean, x° should look similar to x and should have the same label as x's. This ensures a *high classification accuracy on clean images* (dubbed *"clean accuracy"*).
- *Condition 2*: If $\tilde{x}$ contains triggers, $\tilde{x}^\circ$ should be close to x and should have the same label as x's where x is the clean counterpart of $\tilde{x}$. This ensures a *low attack success rate* and a *high clean-label recovery rate on Trojan images* (dubbed *"Trojan accuracy"* and *"recovery accuracy"*, respectively).

In the next two subsections (4.1, 4.2), we propose two novel filtering defenses that leverage two different strategies to learn a good F which are lossy data compression and adversarial learning, respectively.

4.1 Variational Input Filtering

A natural choice for F is an autoencoder (AE) which should be complex enough so that F can reconstruct clean images well to achieve high clean accuracy. However, if F is too complex, it can capture every detail of a Trojan image including the embedded triggers, which also causes high Trojan accuracy. In general, an optimal F should achieve good balance between preserving class-related information and discarding noisy information of the input. To reduce the dependence of F on architecture, we propose to treat F as a variational autoencoder (VAE)[1] [18] and train it with the *"Variational Input Filtering"* (VIF) loss given below:

$$\mathcal{L}_{\text{VIF}}(x, y) = -\log p_{\mathsf{C}}(y|x^\circ) + \lambda_1 \|x^\circ - x\| + \lambda_2 D_{\text{KL}}(q_{\mathsf{F}}(z|x)\|p(z)) \qquad (3)$$
$$= \mathcal{L}_{\text{IF}} + \lambda_2 D_{\text{KL}}(q_{\mathsf{F}}(z|x)\|p(z)), \qquad (4)$$

---

[1] Denoising Autoencoder (DAE) [46] is also a possible choice but is quite similar to VAE in terms of idea so we do not consider it here.

where $(x, y) \sim \mathcal{D}_{\text{val}}$, $x^\circ = \text{F}(x)$ is the filtered version of x, z is the latent variable, $q_{\text{F}}(z|x)$ denotes the variational posterior distribution and is parameterized via the stochastic encoder of F, $p(z) = \mathcal{N}(0, \text{I})$ is the standard Gaussian distribution, D_{KL} denotes the KL divergence, $\lambda_1, \lambda_2 \geq 0$ are coefficients. In Eq. 3, the first two terms force F to preserve class-related information of x and to reduce the visual dissimilarity between x° and x as per condition 1, 2. Meanwhile, the last term encourages F (or more precisely, $q_{\text{F}}(z|x)$) to discard noisy information of x, which we refer to as *"lossy data compression"*. This can be explained via the following relationship [54]:

$$\mathbb{E}_{p(x)}\left[D_{\text{KL}}(q_{\text{F}}(z|x)\|p(z))\right] = D_{\text{KL}}(q_{\text{F}}(z)\|p(z)) + I_{\text{F}}(x, z), \tag{5}$$

where $q_{\text{F}}(z) = \mathbb{E}_{p(x)}[q_{\text{F}}(z|x)]$. Clearly, minimizing the LHS of Eq. 5 decreases the mutual information between z and x. And because z is used to compute x° (in decoding), this also reduces the information between x° and x.

In Eq. 3, the first two terms alone constitute the "Input Filtering" (IF) loss $\mathcal{L}_{\text{IF}}$. To the best of our knowledge, IF has not been proposed in other Trojan defense works. Input Processing (IP) [25] is the closest to IF but it is trained on *unlabeled data* using *only the reconstruction loss* (the second term in Eq. 3). In Appdx. E.2, we show that IP performs worse than IF, which highlights the importance of the term $-\log p_{\text{C}}(y|x^\circ)$.

4.2   Adversarial Input Filtering

VIF, owing to its generality, do not make use of any Trojan-related knowledge in C to train F. We argue that if F is exposed to such knowledge, F could be more selective in choosing which input information to discard, and hence, could perform better. This motivates us to use synthetic Trojan images as additional training data for F besides clean images from $\mathcal{D}_{\text{val}}$. We synthesize a Trojan image $\tilde{x}$ from a clean image x as follows:

$$(m_k, p_k) = \text{G}(\epsilon, k), \tag{6}$$
$$\tilde{x} = T(x, (m_k, p_k)), \tag{7}$$

where $\epsilon \sim \mathcal{N}(0, \text{I})$ is a standard Gaussian noise, k is a class label sampled uniformly from $\mathcal{Y}$, G is a conditional generator, T is the image blending function (Eq. 1). We choose the image blending function to craft Trojan images because it is the *most general* Trojan injection function (its output range spans the whole image space $\mathbb{I}^{c \times h \times w}$). To make sure that the synthetic Trojan images are useful for F, we *form an adversarial game between G and F* in which G attempts to generate hard Trojan images that can fool F into producing the target class (sampled randomly from $\mathcal{Y}$) while F becomes more robust by correcting these images. We train G with the following loss:

$$\mathcal{L}_{\text{AIF-gen}}(x, k) = \mathcal{L}_{\text{gen}}(x, k) - \lambda_3 \log p_{\text{C}}(k|\tilde{x}^\circ), \tag{8}$$

where $\mathcal{L}_{\text{gen}}$ is similar to the one in Eq. 2 but with m replaced by m_k (Eq. 6), $\tilde{x}^{\circ} = \text{F}(\tilde{x})$, $\lambda_3 \geq 0$. The loss of F must conform to conditions 1, 2 and is:

$$\mathcal{L}_{\text{AIF}}(x, y) = \mathcal{L}_{\text{IF}}(x, y) - \lambda_4 \log p_{\text{C}}(y|\tilde{x}^{\circ}) + \lambda_5 \|\tilde{x}^{\circ} - x\| \tag{9}$$

$$= \mathcal{L}_{\text{IF}}(x, y) + \mathcal{L}'_{\text{IF}}(\tilde{x}, y), \tag{10}$$

where AIF stands for *"Adversarial Input Filtering"*, $\mathcal{L}_{\text{IF}}$ was described in Eq. 4, $\tilde{x}$ is computed from x via Eq. 7, $\lambda_4, \lambda_5 \geq 0$. Note that the last term in Eq. 10 is the reconstruction loss between $\tilde{x}^{\circ}$ and x (not $\tilde{x}$). Thus, we denote the last two terms in Eq. 9 as $\mathcal{L}'_{\text{IF}}$ instead of $\mathcal{L}_{\text{IF}}$. AIF is depicted in Fig. 3.

During experiment, we observed that sometimes training G and F with the above losses may not result in good performance. The reason is that when F becomes better, G tends to produce large-norm triggers to fool F despite the fact that a regularization was applied to the norms of these triggers. Large-norm triggers make learning F harder as $\tilde{x}$ is no longer close to x. To handle this problem, we explicitly normalize m_k so that its norm is always bounded by δ. We provide technical details and empirical study about this normalization in Appdx. E.6. We also empirically examine the robustness of AIF and VIF in filtering large-norm triggers in Appdx. E.5.

4.3 Filtering Then Contrasting

VIF and AIF always filter x even when x does not contain triggers, which often leads to the decrease in clean accuracy after filtering. To overcome this drawback, we introduce a new defense mechanism called *"Filtering then Contrasting"* (FtC) which works as follows: Instead of just computing the predicted label $\hat{y}^{\circ}$ of the filtered image $x^{\circ} = \text{F}(x)$ and treat it as the final prediction, we also compute the predicted label $\hat{y}$ of x without filtering and compare $\hat{y}$ with $\hat{y}^{\circ}$. If $\hat{y}$ is different from $\hat{y}^{\circ}$, x will be marked as containing triggers and discarded. Otherwise, x will be marked as clean and $\hat{y}$ will be used as the final prediction. FtC is especially useful for defending against attacks with large-norm triggers (Appdx. E.5) because it helps avoid the significant drop in clean accuracy caused by the large visual difference between x° and x. Under the FtC defense mechanism, we derive two new defenses VIFtC and AIFtC from VIF and AIF, respectively.

5 Experiments

5.1 Experimental Setup

Datasets. Following previous works [11,32,38], we evaluate our proposed defenses on four image datasets namely MNIST, CIFAR10 [19], GTSRB [42], and CelebA [26]. For CelebA, we follow Salem et al. [38] and select the top 3 most balanced binary attributes (out of 40) to form an 8-class classification problem. The chosen attributes are *"Heavy Makeup"*, *"Mouth Slightly Open"*, and *"Smiling"*. Like other works [8,47], we assume that we have access to the test set of these datasets. We use 70% data of the test set for training our defense

Table 1. Test clean and Trojan accuracies of various Trojan attacks.

Dataset	Benign	BadNet+		noise-BI+		image-BI+		InpAwAtk			WaNet		
	Clean	Clean	Trojan	Clean	Trojan	Clean	Trojan	Clean	Trojan	Cross	Clean	Trojan	Noise
MNIST	99.56	99.61	99.96	99.46	100.0	99.50	100.0	99.47	99.41	96.05	99.48	98.73	99.38
CIFAR10	94.82	94.88	100.0	94.69	100.0	95.15	99.96	94.58	99.43	88.68	94.32	99.59	92.58
GTSRB	99.72	99.34	100.0	99.30	100.0	99.18	100.0	98.90	99.54	95.19	99.12	99.54	99.03
CelebA	79.12	79.41	100.0	78.75	100.0	78.81	99.99	78.18	99.93	77.16	78.48	99.94	77.24

methods ($\mathcal{D}_{val}$ in Sects. 3, 4) and 30% for testing (denoted as $\mathcal{D}_{test}$). For more details about the datasets, please refer to Appdx. B.1. Sometimes, we do not test our methods on all images in $\mathcal{D}_{test}$ but on those *not* belonging to the target class. This set is denoted as $\mathcal{D}'_{test}$. We also provide results with less training data in Appdx. E.4.

Benchmark Attacks. We use 5 different benchmark Trojan attacks for our defenses, which are BadNet+, noise-BI+, image-BI+, InpAwAtk [32], and WaNet [33]. InpAwAtk and WaNet are recent SOTA attacks that were shown to break many strong defenses completely. BadNet+ and noise/image-BI+ are variants of BadNet [11] and Blended Injection (BI) [4] that use multiple triggers instead of one. They are described in detail in Appdx. C.1. The training settings for the 5 attacks are given in Appdx. B.2.

We also consider 2 attack modes namely *single-target* and *all-target* [32,53]. In the first mode, only one class t is chosen as target. Every Trojan image $\tilde{x}$ is classified as t regardless of the ground-truth label of its clean counterpart x. Without loss of generality, t is set to 0. In the second mode, $\tilde{x}$ is classified as $(k + 1) \mod K$ if x belongs to the class k. If not clearly stated, attacks are assumed to be *single-target*.

We report the test clean and Trojan accuracies of the benchmark attacks (in single-target mode) in Table 1. It is clear that all attacks achieve very high Trojan accuracies with little or no decrease in clean accuracy compared to the benign model's, hence, are qualified for our experimental purpose. For results of the attacks on $\mathcal{D}_{test}$, please refer to Appdx. C.

Baseline Defenses. We consider 5 well-known baseline defenses namely Neural Cleanse (NC) [47], STRIP [8], Network Pruning (NP) [22], Neural Attention Distillation (NAD) [20], and Februus [5].

Neural Cleanse (NC) assumes that attacks (i) choose only one target class t and (ii) use *at least* (not exactly) one input-agnostic trigger associated with t. We refer to (i) as the *"single target class"* assumption and (ii) as the *"input-agnostic trigger"* assumption. Based on these assumptions, NC finds a trigger $\psi_k = (m_k, p_k)$ for every class $k \in \mathcal{Y}$ via reverse-engineering (Eq. 2), and uses the L1 norms of the synthetic trigger masks $\{m_1, ..., m_K\}$ to detect the target class. The intuition is that if t is the target class, $\|m_t\|_1$ will be much smaller than the rest. A z-value of each mask norm is calculated via Median Absolute Deviation and the z-value of the smallest mask norm (referred to as the *anomaly index*) is compared against a threshold ζ (2.0 by default). If the anomaly index is smaller than ζ, C is marked as clean. Otherwise, C is marked Trojan-infected with the target class corresponding to the smallest mask norm. In this case, the Trojans in C can be mitigated via pruning or via checking the cleanliness of input images. Both mitigation methods make use of ψ_t and are analyzed in Appdx. D.

STRIP assumes triggers are input-agnostic and argues that if an input image x contains triggers then these triggers still have effect if x is superimposed (blended) with other images. Therefore, STRIP superimposes x with N_s random clean images from $\mathcal{D}_{val}$ and computes the *average entropy* $\mathcal{H}(x)$ of N_s predicted class probabilities corresponding to N_s superimposed versions of x. If $\mathcal{H}(x)$ is smaller than a predefined threshold, x is considered as trigger-embedded, otherwise, clean. The threshold is set according to the false positive rate (FPR) over the average entropies of all images in $\mathcal{D}_{val}$, usually at FPR equal to 1/5/10%. We evaluate the performance of STRIP against an attack using M_s random clean images from $\mathcal{D}_{test}$ and M_s corresponding Trojan images generated by that attack. Following [8], we set $N_s = 100$ and $M_s = 2000$.

Network Pruning (NP) hypothesizes that idle neurons are more likely to store Trojan-related information. Thus, it ranks neurons in the second top layer of C according to their average activation over all data in $\mathcal{D}_{val}$ and gradually prunes them until a certain decrease in clean accuracy is reached, usually at 1/5/10% decrease in clean accuracy.

Neural Attention Distillation (NAD) [20] is a distillation-based Trojan defense. It first fine-tunes the pretrained classifier C on clean images in $\mathcal{D}_{val}$ to obtain a fine-tune classifier T. Then, it treats T and C as the teacher and student respectively, and performs attention-based feature distillation [52] between T and C on $\mathcal{D}_{val}$ again. Since T is C fine-tuned on clean data, T is expected to have most of the Trojan in C removed. Via distillation, such Trojan-free knowledge is transferred from T to C while performance of C on clean data is still preserved.

Among the baselines, Februus is the most related to our filtering defenses since it mitigates Trojan attacks via input purification. It uses GradCAM [40] to detect regions in an input image x that may contain triggers. Then, it removes all pixels in the suspected regions and generates new ones via inpainting. The inpainted image is expected to contain no trigger and is fed to C instead of x.

Model Architectures and Training Settings. Please refer to Appdx. B.3.

Metrics. We evaluate VIF/AIF using 3 metrics namely *decrease in clean accuracy* ($\downarrow$C), *Trojan accuracy* (T), and *decrease in recovery accuracy* ($\downarrow$R). The first is the difference between the classification accuracies of clean images before and after filtering. The second is the attack success rate of Trojan images after filtering. The last is the difference between the classification accuracy of clean images before filtering and that of the corresponding Trojan images after filtering. Smaller values of the metrics indicate better results. $\downarrow$C and $\downarrow$R are computed on $\mathcal{D}_{test}$. T is computed on $\mathcal{D}'_{test}$ under single-target attacks and $\mathcal{D}_{test}$ under all-target attacks. This ensures that T can be 0 in the best case. Other-

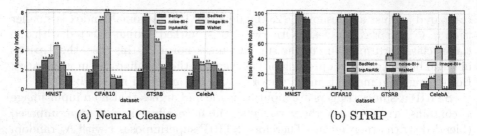

(a) Neural Cleanse   (b) STRIP

Fig. 4. (a) Anomaly indices of Neural Cleanse. The red dashed line indicates the threshold. (b) FNRs of STRIP at 10% FPR. (Color figure online)

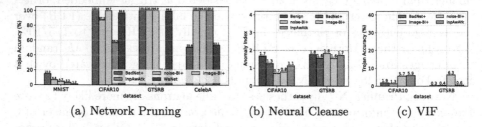

(a) Network Pruning   (b) Neural Cleanse   (c) VIF

Fig. 5. (a) Trojan accuracies at 10% decrease in clean accuracy of different Trojan classifiers pruned by Network Pruning. (b) Anomaly indices of NC and (c) Trojan accuracies of VIF against *all-target* attacks on CIFAR10 and GTSRB.

wise, T will be around $1/K$ where K is the total number of classes. $\downarrow$C and $\downarrow$R are upper-bounded by 1 and can be negative.

We evaluate VIFtC/AIFtC using FPR and FNR. FPR/FNR is defined as the proportion of clean/Trojan images having different/similar class predictions when the filter F is applied and not applied. FPR is computed on $\mathcal{D}_{\text{test}}$. FNR is computed on $\mathcal{D}'_{\text{test}}$ under single-target attacks and $\mathcal{D}_{\text{test}}$ under all-target attacks. Both metrics are in [0, 1] and smaller values of them are better. Interestingly, FPR and FNR are strongly correlated to $\downarrow$C and T, respectively. FPR/FNR is exactly equal to $\downarrow$C/T if C achieves perfect clean/Trojan accuracy.

5.2   Results of Baseline Defenses

In Fig. 4, we show the detection results of Neural Cleanse (NC) and STRIP w.r.t. the aforementioned attacks. The two defenses are effective against BadNet+ and image/noise-BI+. This is because STRIP and NC generally do not make any assumption about the number of triggers. However, STRIP performs poorly against InpAwAtk and WaNet (FNRs > 90%) since these advanced attacks break its "input-agnostic trigger" assumption. NC also fails to detect the Trojan classifiers trained by WaNet on most datasets for the same reason. What surprises us is that in our experiment NC correctly detect the Trojan classifiers trained by InpAwAtk on 3/4 datasets while in the original paper [32], it was shown to fail completely. We are confident that this inconsistency does not

Table 2. Trojan filtering results (in %) of Februus, NAD, and our filtering defenses against different attacks. *Smaller values are better.* For a particular dataset, attack, and metric, the best defense is highlighted in bold.

Dataset	Defense	Benign	BadNet+			noise-BI+			image-BI+			InpAwAtk			WaNet		
		↓C	↓C	T	↓R	↓C	T	↓R	↓C	T	↓R	↓C	T	↓R	↓C	T	↓R
MNIST	Feb.	5.96	39.08	96.24	86.32	2.30	100.0	89.58	8.19	100.0	89.58	9.90	92.40	83.32	25.43	80.46	88.75
	NAD	0.45	0.82	35.72	36.41	0.75	84.83	76.22	0.78	88.34	79.18	0.80	4.46	5.29	0.42	**0.44**	0.98
	IF	**0.10**	0.27	2.47	4.99	**0.10**	0.16	13.52	0.13	1.29	12.02	0.21	**0.96**	2.08	0.23	0.34	0.61
	VIF	0.13	**0.17**	**2.36**	**3.63**	0.12	**0.04**	0.63	**0.03**	**0.11**	0.40	0.20	1.25	1.83	**0.10**	0.48	0.53
	AIF	**0.10**	**0.17**	3.80	4.86	0.13	0.15	**0.11**	0.10	**0.11**	**0.10**	**0.03**	1.14	**1.66**	0.13	**0.15**	**0.20**
CIFAR10	Feb.	32.67	49.17	12.63	19.57	26.73	43.59	78.90	39.70	92.67	81.00	53.43	49.52	66.50	55.80	98.70	83.30
	NAD	**3.16**	**3.81**	35.71	41.68	**2.52**	1.81	28.89	**3.87**	1.63	18.92	**2.98**	1.81	**4.75**	**2.95**	**0.93**	**5.42**
	IF	3.34	4.15	**2.30**	**7.79**	3.32	**1.01**	**4.43**	4.76	37.48	34.30	4.47	16.35	18.96	3.21	4.82	6.80
	VIF	7.81	7.70	2.52	11.27	6.43	1.22	7.10	7.53	10.52	16.50	7.67	**3.07**	12.38	7.97	3.96	10.67
	AIF	4.67	5.60	2.37	9.03	4.87	1.14	6.02	5.23	**1.96**	**7.10**	5.28	5.30	11.87	4.30	1.22	5.67
GTSRB	Feb.	42.01	35.30	21.02	44.11	43.40	75.75	95.90	32.18	97.83	97.37	21.27	70.02	72.71	33.18	70.10	71.69
	NAD	-0.13	**-0.35**	**0.00**	8.20	**-0.32**	**0.00**	4.06	**-0.42**	0.05	**8.33**	**-0.28**	0.05	**0.56**	**-0.40**	**0.00**	**0.11**
	IF	0.12	0.13	**0.00**	2.55	0.13	0.03	1.52	0.37	52.27	51.95	0.03	0.66	3.60	0.08	9.83	9.62
	VIF	0.18	0.45	**0.00**	3.55	0.18	**0.00**	1.12	0.37	12.12	16.56	0.11	**0.03**	1.87	0.55	3.67	3.89
	AIF	**0.05**	-0.16	**0.00**	**1.87**	0.05	**0.00**	**0.81**	0.13	7.47	9.54	-0.03	0.05	1.37	-0.05	0.50	0.42
CelebA	Feb.	12.71	18.80	42.96	21.33	11.76	93.27	49.05	13.30	98.59	49.84	5.60	99.98	49.71	9.16	97.30	48.53
	NAD	3.06	**3.19**	12.14	9.98	3.56	25.31	23.07	3.51	16.97	9.46	3.14	13.85	11.24	2.51	11.48	**3.21**
	IF	**2.23**	4.21	8.62	**4.75**	**2.57**	13.83	6.00	**2.25**	59.39	27.94	**2.86**	11.95	**6.07**	**2.43**	15.21	4.75
	VIF	3.74	4.63	9.28	4.90	3.20	**11.51**	**4.08**	3.54	**14.32**	**5.62**	3.89	11.55	6.27	3.96	**8.30**	4.19
	AIF	4.95	6.46	**7.85**	6.49	4.18	12.56	6.52	4.37	18.40	9.23	3.71	**10.43**	7.65	4.02	12.82	5.74

come from our implementation of InpAwAtk since we used the same hyperparameters and achieved the same classification results as those in the original paper (Table 1 versus Fig. 3b in [32]). However, NC is still unable to mitigate all Trojans in these correctly-detected Trojan classifiers (Appdx. D.3). In addition, as shown in Fig. 5b, NC is totally vulnerable to *all-target attacks* since its "single target class" assumption is no longer valid under these attacks. Network Pruning (NP), despite being assumption-free, cannot mitigate Trojans from most attacks (high Trojan accuracies in Fig. 5a) as it fails to prune the correct neurons containing Trojans. Februus has certain effects on mitigating Trojans from BadNet+ while being useless against the remaining attacks (high Ts in Table 2). This is because GradCAM, the method used by Februus, is only suitable for detecting patch-like triggers of BadNet+, not full-size noise-like triggers of image/noise-BI+ or polymorphic triggers of InpAwAtk/WaNet. We also observe that Februus significantly reduces the clean accuracy (high ↓Cs in Table 2) as it removes input regions that contain no Trojan trigger yet are highly associated with the output class. This problem, however, was not discussed in the Februus paper. NAD, thanks to its distillation-based nature, usually achieves better clean accuracies than our filtering defenses (Table 2). This defense is also effective against InpAwAtk and WaNet. However, NAD performs poorly in recovering Trojan samples from BadNet+ and noise/image-BI+ (high ↓Rs), especially on MNIST. Besides, NAD is much less robust to large-norm triggers than our filtering defenses (Appdx. E.5). For more analyses of the baseline defenses, please refer to Appdx. D.

Table 3. Trojan mitigation results (in %) of our FtC defenses against different attacks. *Smaller values are better.* For a particular attack, dataset, and metric, the best defense is highlighted in bold.

Dataset	Defense	Benign	BadNet+		noise-BI+		image-BI+		InpAwAtk		WaNet	
		FPR	FPR	FNR	FPR	FNR	FPR	FNR	FPR	FNR	FPR	FNR
	IFtC	0.40	0.50	**2.21**	0.37	0.22	0.37	1.51	0.53	**1.71**	0.60	1.33
MNIST	VIFtC	0.27	**0.30**	2.84	0.23	**0.07**	0.40	0.15	0.47	1.99	0.30	1.51
	AIFtC	**0.23**	0.32	4.17	**0.17**	0.15	**0.17**	**0.11**	**0.33**	1.87	**0.13**	**1.18**
	IFtC	**6.83**	**7.47**	**1.70**	**6.57**	0.93	**7.83**	36.56	**7.25**	16.89	**7.17**	5.15
CIFAR10	VIFtC	12.30	11.00	2.63	10.67	1.26	11.03	10.89	10.63	**3.67**	11.40	4.26
	AIFtC	8.63	8.87	1.96	8.73	**0.89**	8.77	**2.15**	8.27	5.93	7.93	**1.56**
	IFtC	**0.38**	0.45	**0.00**	0.24	0.03	0.66	52.91	**0.29**	1.00	0.66	10.41
GTSRB	VIFtC	0.45	0.74	0.03	0.47	**0.00**	0.87	12.63	0.53	**0.37**	1.31	4.25
	AIFtC	0.50	**0.37**	0.03	0.39	**0.00**	**0.63**	**7.87**	0.47	0.40	**0.60**	**1.08**
	IFtC	**14.24**	**15.78**	8.36	**14.94**	14.25	**13.99**	59.43	**12.84**	11.95	**13.08**	15.27
CelebA	VIFtC	17.74	18.90	9.09	18.50	**11.67**	18.09	**14.30**	16.37	11.54	17.22	**8.34**
	AIFtC	20.24	20.95	**7.71**	19.08	12.82	19.29	18.65	16.54	**10.43**	16.55	12.87

5.3 Results of Proposed Defenses

From Table 2, it is clear that VIF and AIF achieve superior performances in mitigating Trojans of all the single-target attacks compared to most of the baseline defenses. For example, on MNIST and GTSRB, our filtering defenses impressively reduce T from about 100% (Table 1) to less than 2% for most attacks yet only cause less than 1% drop of clean accuracy ($\downarrow$C < 1%). On more diverse datasets such as CIFAR10 and CelebA, VIF and AIF still achieve T less than 6% and 12% for most attacks while maintaining $\downarrow$C below 8% and 5%, respectively. We note that on CelebA, the nonoptimal performance of C (accuracy $\approx$ 79%) makes T higher than normal because T may contains the error of samples from non-target classes misclassified as the target class. However, it is not trivial to disentangle the two quantities so we leave this problem for future work. As there is no free lunch, our filtering defenses may be not as good as some baselines in some specific cases. For example, on CIFAR10, STRIP achieves FNRs $\approx$ 0% against BadNet+/noise-BI+ (Fig. 4b) while VIF/AIF achieves Ts $\approx$ 1–3%. However, the gaps are very small and in general, our filtering defenses are still much more effective than the baseline defenses against all the single-target attacks. Our filtering defenses also perform well against all-target attacks (Fig. 5c and Appdx. E.1) as ours are not sensitive to the number of target classes. To gain a better insight into the performance of VIF/AIF, we visualize the filtered images produced by VIF/AIF and their corresponding *"counter-triggers"* in Appdx. F.1.

Among the filtering defenses, IF usually achieves the smallest $\downarrow$Cs because its loss does not have any term that encourages information removal like VIF's and AIF's. The gaps in $\downarrow$C between IF and AIF/VIF are the largest on CIFAR10 but do not exceed 5%. However, IF usually performs much worse than VIF/AIF in mitigating Trojans, especially those from image-BI+, InpAwAtk, and WaNet.

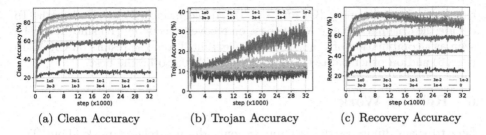

(a) Clean Accuracy   (b) Trojan Accuracy   (c) Recovery Accuracy

Fig. 6. Clean, Trojan, and recovery accuracy curves of VIF against InpAwAtk on CIFAR10 w.r.t. different values of λ_2 in Eq. 3. The Trojan accuracy curves in (b) fluctuate around 10% since they are computed on $\mathcal{D}_{\text{test}}$ instead of $\mathcal{D}'_{\text{test}}$.

For example, on CIFAR10, GTSRB, and CelebA, IF reduces the attack success rate (T) of image-BI+ to 37.48%, 52.27%, and 59.39% respectively. These numbers are only 1.96%, 7.47%, and 18.40% for AIF and 10.52%, 12.12%, and 14.32% for VIF. Therefore, when considering the trade-off between $\downarrow$C and T, VIF and AIF are clearly better than IF. We also observe that AIF usually achieves lower $\downarrow$Cs and $\downarrow$Rs than VIF. It is because AIF discards only potential malicious information instead of all noisy information like VIF. However, VIF is simpler and easier to train than AIF.

From Table 3, we see that the FPRs and FNRs of VIFtC/AIFtC are close to the $\downarrow$Cs and Ts of VIF/AIF respectively on MNIST, GTSRB, and CIFAR10. This is because C achieves nearly 100% clean and Trojan accuracies on these datasets. Thus, we can interpret the results of VIFtC/AIFtC in the same way as what we have done for VIF/AIF. Since FPR only affects the classification throughput not (clean) accuracy, VIFtC/AIFtC are preferred to VIF/AIF in applications that favor (clean) accuracy (e.g., defending against attacks with large-norm triggers in Appdx. E.5).

5.4 Ablation Studies

It is undoubted that our defenses require some settings to work well. However, these settings *cannot be managed by attackers* unlike the assumptions of most existing defenses [8,47]. Due to space limit, below we only examine the contribution of lossy data compression to the performance of VIF. For studies on the robustness of our proposed defenses to different architectures of F, to small amounts of training data, and to large-norm triggers, please refer to Appdx. E.3, E.4, and E.5 respectively.

Different Data Compression Rates in VIF. The lossy data compression in VIF can be managed via changing the coefficients of D_{KL} in $\mathcal{L}_{\text{VIF}}$ (λ_2 in Eq. 3). A smaller values of λ_2 means a lower data compression rate and vice versa. From Fig. 6, it is clear that when λ_2 is small, most information in the input including both semantic information and embedded triggers is retained, thus, the clean accuracy (C) and the Trojan accuracy (T) are both high. To decide the optimal value of λ_2, we base on recovery accuracy (R) since R can be seen as a combination of C and T to some extent. From the results on CIFAR10 (Fig. 6) and on other datasets, we found $\lambda_2 = 0.003$ to be the best.

6   Related Work

Due to space limit, in this section we only discuss related work about Trojan defenses. Related work about Trojan attacks are provided in Appdx. A. A large number of Trojan defenses have been proposed so far, among which Neural Cleanse (NC) [47], Network Pruning (NP) [22], STRIP [8], Neural Attention Distillation (NAD) [20], and Februus [5] are representative for five different types of defenses and are carefully analyzed in Sect. 5.1. DeepInspect [3], MESA [35] improve upon NC by synthesizing a distribution of triggers for each class instead of just a single one. TABOR [12] adds more regularization losses to NC to better handle large and scattered triggers. STS [13] restores triggers by minimizing a novel loss function which is the pairwise difference between the class probabilities of two random synthetic Trojan images. This makes STS independent of the number of classes and more efficient than NC on datasets with many classes. ABS [23] is a quite complicated defense inspired by brain stimulation. It analyzes all neurons in the classifier C to find "compromised" ones and use these neurons to validate whether C is attacked or not. DL-TND [48], B3D [6] focus on detecting Trojan-infected models in case validation data are limited. However, all the aforementioned defenses derived from NC still make the same "input-agnostic trigger" and "single target class" assumptions as NC, and hence, are supposed to be ineffective against attacks that break these assumptions such as input-specific [32,33] and all-target attacks. Activation Clustering [2] and Spectral Signatures [45] regard hidden activations as a clue to detect Trojan samples from BadNet [11]. They base on an empirical observation that the hidden activations of Trojan samples and clean samples of the target class usually form distinct clusters in the hidden activation space. These defenses are of the same kind as STRIP and are not applicable to all-target attacks. Mode Connectivity Repair (MCR) [53] mitigates Trojans by choosing an interpolated model near the two end points of a parametric path connecting a Trojan model and its fine-tuned version. MCR was shown to be defeated by InpAwAtk in [32]. Adversarial Neuron Pruning (ANP) [50] leverages adversarial learning to find compromised neurons for pruning. Our AIF is different from ANP in the sense that we use adversarial learning to train an entire generator G for filtering input instead of pruning neurons.

7   Conclusion

We have proposed two novel "filtering" Trojan defenses dubbed VIF and AIF that leverage lossy data compression and adversarial learning respectively to effectively remove all potential Trojan triggers embedded in the input. We have also introduced a new defense mechanism called "Filtering-then-Contrasting"

(FtC) that circumvents the loss in clean accuracy caused by "filtering". Unlike most existing defenses, our proposed filtering and FtC defenses make no assumption about the number of triggers/target classes or the input dependency property of triggers. Through extensive experiments, we have demonstrated that our proposed defenses significantly outperform many well-known defenses in mitigating various strong attacks. In the future, we would like to extend our proposed defenses to other domains (e.g., texts, graphs) and other tasks (e.g., object detection, visual reasoning) which we believe are more challenging than those considered in this work.

References

1. van Baalen, M., et al.: Bayesian bits: unifying quantization and pruning. arXiv preprint arXiv:2005.07093 (2020)
2. Chen, B., et al.: Detecting backdoor attacks on deep neural networks by activation clustering. arXiv preprint arXiv:1811.03728 (2018)
3. Chen, H., Fu, C., Zhao, J., Koushanfar, F.: DeepInspect: a black-box trojan detection and mitigation framework for deep neural networks. In: Proceedings of the 28th International Joint Conference on Artificial Intelligence, pp. 4658–4664. AAAI Press (2019)
4. Chen, X., Liu, C., Li, B., Lu, K., Song, D.: Targeted backdoor attacks on deep learning systems using data poisoning. arXiv preprint arXiv:1712.05526 (2017)
5. Doan, B.G., Abbasnejad, E., Ranasinghe, D.C.: Februus: input purification defense against trojan attacks on deep neural network systems. In: Annual Computer Security Applications Conference, pp. 897–912 (2020)
6. Dong, Y., et al.: Black-box detection of backdoor attacks with limited information and data. arXiv preprint arXiv:2103.13127 (2021)
7. Fawzi, A., Fawzi, H., Fawzi, O.: Adversarial vulnerability for any classifier. arXiv preprint arXiv:1802.08686 (2018)
8. Gao, Y., Xu, C., Wang, D., Chen, S., Ranasinghe, D.C., Nepal, S.: Strip: a defence against trojan attacks on deep neural networks. In: Proceedings of the 35th Annual Computer Security Applications Conference, pp. 113–125 (2019)
9. Goodfellow, I., et al.: Generative adversarial nets. In: Advances in Neural Information Processing Systems, vol. 27 (2014)
10. Goodfellow, I.J., Shlens, J., Szegedy, C.: Explaining and harnessing adversarial examples. arXiv preprint arXiv:1412.6572 (2014)
11. Gu, T., Dolan-Gavitt, B., Garg, S.: Badnets: identifying vulnerabilities in the machine learning model supply chain. arXiv preprint arXiv:1708.06733 (2017)
12. Guo, W., Wang, L., Xing, X., Du, M., Song, D.: Tabor: a highly accurate approach to inspecting and restoring trojan backdoors in AI systems. arXiv preprint arXiv:1908.01763 (2019)
13. Harikumar, H., Le, V., Rana, S., Bhattacharya, S., Gupta, S., Venkatesh, S.: Scalable backdoor detection in neural networks. In: Hutter, F., Kersting, K., Lijffijt, J., Valera, I. (eds.) ECML PKDD 2020. LNCS (LNAI), vol. 12458, pp. 289–304. Springer, Cham (2021). https://doi.org/10.1007/978-3-030-67661-2_18
14. He, K., Zhang, X., Ren, S., Sun, J.: Deep residual learning for image recognition. In: Proceedings of the IEEE Conference on Computer Vision and Pattern Recognition, pp. 770–778 (2016)

15. He, K., Zhang, X., Ren, S., Sun, J.: Identity mappings in deep residual networks. In: Leibe, B., Matas, J., Sebe, N., Welling, M. (eds.) ECCV 2016. LNCS, vol. 9908, pp. 630–645. Springer, Cham (2016). https://doi.org/10.1007/978-3-319-46493-0_38

16. Ji, Y., Zhang, X., Wang, T.: Backdoor attacks against learning systems. In: IEEE Conference on Communications and Network Security, pp. 1–9. IEEE (2017)

17. Kingma, D.P., Ba, J.: Adam: A Method for Stochastic Optimization. arXiv preprint arXiv:1412.6980 (2014)

18. Kingma, D.P., Welling, M.: Auto-encoding variational bayes. arXiv preprint arXiv:1312.6114 (2013)

19. Krizhevsky, A.: Learning multiple layers of features from tiny images. Technical report (2009)

20. Li, Y., Lyu, X., Koren, N., Lyu, L., Li, B., Ma, X.: Neural attention distillation: Erasing backdoor triggers from deep neural networks. arXiv preprint arXiv:2101.05930 (2021)

21. Li, Y., Li, Y., Wu, B., Li, L., He, R., Lyu, S.: Backdoor attack with sample-specific triggers. arXiv preprint arXiv:2012.03816 (2020)

22. Liu, K., Dolan-Gavitt, B., Garg, S.: Fine-pruning: defending against backdooring attacks on deep neural networks. In: Bailey, M., Holz, T., Stamatogiannakis, M., Ioannidis, S. (eds.) RAID 2018. LNCS, vol. 11050, pp. 273–294. Springer, Cham (2018). https://doi.org/10.1007/978-3-030-00470-5_13

23. Liu, Y., Lee, W.C., Tao, G., Ma, S., Aafer, Y., Zhang, X.: ABS: scanning neural networks for back-doors by artificial brain stimulation. In: Proceedings of the ACM SIGSAC Conference on Computer and Communications Security, pp. 1265–1282 (2019)

24. Liu, Y., Ma, X., Bailey, J., Lu, F.: Reflection backdoor: a natural backdoor attack on deep neural networks. In: Vedaldi, A., Bischof, H., Brox, T., Frahm, J.-M. (eds.) ECCV 2020. LNCS, vol. 12355, pp. 182–199. Springer, Cham (2020). https://doi.org/10.1007/978-3-030-58607-2_11

25. Liu, Y., Xie, Y., Srivastava, A.: Neural trojans. In: 2017 IEEE International Conference on Computer Design (ICCD), pp. 45–48. IEEE (2017)

26. Liu, Z., Luo, P., Wang, X., Tang, X.: Deep learning face attributes in the wild. In: Proceedings of the IEEE International Conference on Computer Vision, pp. 3730–3738 (2015)

27. Louizos, C., Ullrich, K., Welling, M.: Bayesian compression for deep learning. arXiv preprint arXiv:1705.08665 (2017)

28. Madry, A., Makelov, A., Schmidt, L., Tsipras, D., Vladu, A.: Towards deep learning models resistant to adversarial attacks. arXiv preprint arXiv:1706.06083 (2017)

29. Moeskops, P., Veta, M., Lafarge, M.W., Eppenhof, K.A.J., Pluim, J.P.W.: Adversarial training and dilated convolutions for brain MRI segmentation. In: Cardoso, M.J., et al. (eds.) DLMIA/ML-CDS -2017. LNCS, vol. 10553, pp. 56–64. Springer, Cham (2017). https://doi.org/10.1007/978-3-319-67558-9_7

30. Molchanov, D., Ashukha, A., Vetrov, D.: Variational dropout sparsifies deep neural networks. In: International Conference on Machine Learning, pp. 2498–2507. PMLR (2017)

31. Muñoz-González, L., Pfitzner, B., Russo, M., Carnerero-Cano, J., Lupu, E.C.: Poisoning attacks with generative adversarial nets. arXiv preprint arXiv:1906.07773 (2019)

32. Nguyen, A., Tran, A.: Input-aware dynamic backdoor attack. arXiv preprint arXiv:2010.08138 (2020)

33. Nguyen, A., Tran, A.: Wanet-imperceptible warping-based backdoor attack. In: International Conference on Learning Representations (2021)

34. Parkhi, O.M., Vedaldi, A., Zisserman, A.: Deep face recognition (2015)
35. Qiao, X., Yang, Y., Li, H.: Defending neural backdoors via generative distribution modeling. arXiv preprint arXiv:1910.04749 (2019)
36. Redmon, J., Divvala, S., Girshick, R., Farhadi, A.: You only look once: unified, real-time object detection. In: Proceedings of the IEEE Conference on Computer Vision and Pattern Recognition, pp. 779–788 (2016)
37. Saha, A., Subramanya, A., Pirsiavash, H.: Hidden trigger backdoor attacks. In: Proceedings of the AAAI Conference on Artificial Intelligence, vol. 34, pp. 11957–11965 (2020)
38. Salem, A., Wen, R., Backes, M., Ma, S., Zhang, Y.: Dynamic backdoor attacks against machine learning models. arXiv preprint arXiv:2003.03675 (2020)
39. Schroff, F., Kalenichenko, D., Philbin, J.: Facenet: a unified embedding for face recognition and clustering. In: Proceedings of the IEEE Conference on Computer Vision and Pattern Recognition, pp. 815–823 (2015)
40. Selvaraju, R.R., Cogswell, M., Das, A., Vedantam, R., Parikh, D., Batra, D.: Grad-cam: visual explanations from deep networks via gradient-based localization. In: Proceedings of the IEEE International Conference on Computer Vision, pp. 618–626 (2017)
41. Shafahi, A., et al.: Poison frogs! targeted clean-label poisoning attacks on neural networks. arXiv preprint arXiv:1804.00792 (2018)
42. Stallkamp, J., Schlipsing, M., Salmen, J., Igel, C.: Man vs. computer: benchmarking machine learning algorithms for traffic sign recognition. Neural Netw. 323–332 (2012)
43. Sultani, W., Chen, C., Shah, M.: Real-world anomaly detection in surveillance videos. In: Proceedings of the IEEE Conference on Computer Vision and Pattern Recognition, pp. 6479–6488 (2018)
44. Thys, S., Van Ranst, W., Goedemé, T.: Fooling automated surveillance cameras: adversarial patches to attack person detection. In: Proceedings of the IEEE/CVF Conference on Computer Vision and Pattern Recognition Workshops (2019)
45. Tran, B., Li, J., Madry, A.: Spectral signatures in backdoor attacks. In: Advances in Neural Information Processing Systems, pp. 8000–8010 (2018)
46. Vincent, P., Larochelle, H., Bengio, Y., Manzagol, P.A.: Extracting and composing robust features with denoising autoencoders. In: Proceedings of the 25th International Conference on Machine Learning, pp. 1096–1103 (2008)
47. Wang, B., et al.: Neural cleanse: identifying and mitigating backdoor attacks in neural networks. In: IEEE Symposium on Security and Privacy, pp. 707–723. IEEE (2019)
48. Wang, R., Zhang, G., Liu, S., Chen, P.-Y., Xiong, J., Wang, M.: Practical detection of trojan neural networks: data-limited and data-free cases. In: Vedaldi, A., Bischof, H., Brox, T., Frahm, J.-M. (eds.) ECCV 2020. LNCS, vol. 12368, pp. 222–238. Springer, Cham (2020). https://doi.org/10.1007/978-3-030-58592-1_14
49. Wenger, E., Passananti, J., Bhagoji, A.N., Yao, Y., Zheng, H., Zhao, B.Y.: Backdoor attacks against deep learning systems in the physical world. In: Proceedings of the IEEE/CVF Conference on Computer Vision and Pattern Recognition, pp. 6206–6215 (2021)
50. Wu, D., Wang, Y.: Adversarial neuron pruning purifies backdoored deep models. In: Advances in Neural Information Processing Systems, vol. 34 (2021)
51. Yang, D., et al.: Automatic liver segmentation using an adversarial image-to-image network. In: Descoteaux, M., Maier-Hein, L., Franz, A., Jannin, P., Collins, D.L., Duchesne, S. (eds.) MICCAI 2017. LNCS, vol. 10435, pp. 507–515. Springer, Cham (2017). https://doi.org/10.1007/978-3-319-66179-7_58

52. Zagoruyko, S., Komodakis, N.: Paying more attention to attention: Improving the performance of convolutional neural networks via attention transfer. arXiv preprint arXiv:1612.03928 (2016)

53. Zhao, P., Chen, P.Y., Das, P., Ramamurthy, K.N., Lin, X.: Bridging mode connectivity in loss landscapes and adversarial robustness. arXiv preprint arXiv:2005.00060 (2020)

54. Zhao, S., Song, J., Ermon, S.: Infovae: information maximizing variational autoencoders. arXiv preprint arXiv:1706.02262 (2017)

55. Zhu, C., Huang, W.R., Li, H., Taylor, G., Studer, C., Goldstein, T.: Transferable clean-label poisoning attacks on deep neural nets. In: International Conference on Machine Learning, pp. 7614–7623. PMLR (2019)

Scaling Adversarial Training to Large Perturbation Bounds

Sravanti Addepalli$^{(\boxtimes)}$ ⓘ, Samyak Jain ⓘ, Gaurang Sriramanan ⓘ,
and R. Venkatesh Babu ⓘ

Video Analytics Lab, Department of Computational and Data Sciences, Indian
Institute of Science, Bangalore, India
sravantia@iisc.ac.in

Abstract. The vulnerability of Deep Neural Networks to Adversarial
Attacks has fuelled research towards building robust models. While most
Adversarial Training algorithms aim at defending attacks constrained
within low magnitude Lp norm bounds, real-world adversaries are not
limited by such constraints. In this work, we aim to achieve adversarial robustness within larger bounds, against perturbations that may be
perceptible, but do not change human (or Oracle) prediction. The presence of images that flip Oracle predictions and those that do not makes
this a challenging setting for adversarial robustness. We discuss the ideal
goals of an adversarial defense algorithm beyond perceptual limits, and
further highlight the shortcomings of naively extending existing training
algorithms to higher perturbation bounds. In order to overcome these
shortcomings, we propose a novel defense, Oracle-Aligned Adversarial
Training (OA-AT), to align the predictions of the network with that of
an Oracle during adversarial training. The proposed approach achieves
state-of-the-art performance at large epsilon bounds (such as an L-inf
bound of 16/255 on CIFAR-10) while outperforming existing defenses
(AWP, TRADES, PGD-AT) at standard bounds (8/255) as well.

1 Introduction

Deep Neural Networks are known to be vulnerable to Adversarial Attacks, which
are perturbations crafted with an intention to fool the network [27]. With the
rapid increase in deployment of Deep Learning algorithms in various critical
applications such as autonomous navigation, it is becoming increasingly crucial
to improve the Adversarial robustness of these models. In a classification setting,
Adversarial attacks can flip the prediction of a network to even unrelated classes,
while causing no change in a human's prediction (Oracle label).

The definition of adversarial attacks involves the prediction of an Oracle,
making it challenging to formalize threat models for the training and verification of adversarial defenses. The widely used convention that overcomes this

---

S. Addepalli and S. Jain—Equal contribution.

Supplementary Information The online version contains supplementary material
available at https://doi.org/10.1007/978-3-031-20065-6_18.

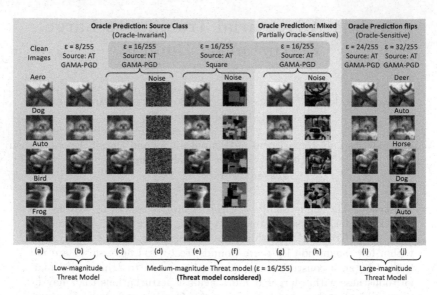

Fig. 1. Perturbations within different threat models: Adversarial images (b, c, e, g, i, j) and perturbations (d, f, h) along with the corresponding clean image (a) for various ℓ_∞ norm bounds on CIFAR-10. Attacks are generated from an Adversarially Trained model (AT) or a Normally Trained model (NT) using the gradient-based attack GAMA-PGD [25] or the Random-search based attack Square [1]. The medium-magnitude threat model is challenging since it consists of attacks which are Oracle-Invariant and partially Oracle-Sensitive.

challenge is the ℓ_p norm based threat model with low-magnitude bounds to ensure imperceptibility [3,10]. For example, attacks constrained within an ℓ_∞ norm of 8/255 on the CIFAR-10 dataset are imperceptible to the human eye as shown in Fig. 1(b), ensuring that the Oracle label is unchanged. The goal of Adversarial Training within such a threat model is to ensure that the prediction of the model is consistent within the considered perturbation radius ε, and matches the label associated with the unperturbed image.

While low-magnitude ℓ_p norm based threat models form a crucial subset of the widely accepted definition of adversarial attacks [9], they are not sufficient, as there exist valid attacks at higher perturbation bounds as well, as shown in Fig. 1(c) and (e). However, the challenge at large perturbation bounds is the existence of attacks that can flip Oracle labels as well [28], as shown in Fig. 1(g), (i) and (j). Naively scaling existing Adversarial Training algorithms to large perturbation bounds would enforce consistent labels on images that flip the Oracle prediction as well, leading to a conflict in the training objective as shown in Fig. 2. This results in a large drop in clean accuracy, as shown in Table 1. This has triggered interest towards developing perceptually aligned threat models, and defenses that are robust under these settings [17]. However, finding a perceptually aligned metric is as challenging as building a network that can replicate

Table 1. CIFAR-10: Standard Adversarial Training using Large-ε: Performance (%) of various existing Defenses trained using $\varepsilon = 8/255$ or $16/255$ against attacks bound within $\varepsilon = 8/255$ and $16/255$. A large drop in clean accuracy is observed with existing approaches [18, 30, 33, 34] when trained using perturbations with $\varepsilon = 16/255$.

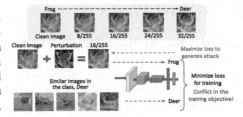

Fig. 2. Issues with Standard Adversarial Training at Large-ε: An adversarial example generated from the original image of a frog looks partially like a deer at an ℓ_∞ bound of $16/255$, but is trained to predict the true label, Frog. This induces a conflicting objective, leading to a large drop in clean accuracy.

Method	Attack ε (Training)	Clean Acc	GAMA (8/255)	AA (8/255)	GAMA (16/255)	Square (16/255)
TRADES	8/255	80.53	49.63	49.42	19.27	27.82
TRADES	16/255	75.30	35.64	35.12	10.10	18.87
AWP	8/255	80.47	50.06	49.87	19.66	28.51
AWP	16/255	71.65	40.85	40.55	15.92	24.16
PGD-AT	8/255	81.12	49.03	48.58	15.77	26.47
PGD-AT	16/255	64.93	46.66	46.21	26.73	32.25
FAT	8/255	84.36	48.41	48.14	15.18	25.07
FAT	16/255	75.27	47.68	47.34	22.93	29.47

oracle predictions [28]. Thus, it is crucial to investigate adversarial robustness using the well-defined ℓ_p norm metric under larger perturbation bounds.

In this work, we aim to improve robustness at larger epsilon bounds, such as an ℓ_∞ norm bound of $16/255$ on the CIFAR-10 and CIFAR-100 datasets [16].

We define this as a moderate-magnitude bound, and discuss the ideal goals for achieving robustness under this threat model in Sect. 3.3. We further propose a novel defense Oracle-Aligned Adversarial Training (OA-AT), which attempts to align the predictions of the network with that of an Oracle, rather than enforcing all samples within the constraint set to have the same label as the original image. Our contributions have been summarized below:

- We propose Oracle-Aligned Adversarial Training (OA-AT) to improve robustness within the defined moderate-ε threat model.
- We demonstrate superior performance when compared to state-of-the-art methods such as AWP [30], TRADES [33] and PGD-AT [18] at $\varepsilon = 16/255$ while also performing better at $\varepsilon = 8/255$ on CIFAR-10 and SVHN. We also demonstrate improved performance on challenging datasets such as CIFAR-100 and Imagenette (10-class subset of Imagenet with 160×160 images).
- We achieve improvements over the baselines even at larger model capacities such as WideResNet-34-10, and demonstrate results that outperform existing methods on the RobustBench leaderboard.
- We show the relation between contrast level of images and the existence of attacks that can flip the Oracle label within a given perturbation bound, and use this observation for constructing better evaluation metrics at large perturbation bounds.

Our code is available here: https://github.com/val-iisc/OAAT.

2   Related Works

Robustness Against Imperceptible Attacks: Following the discovery of adversarial examples by Szegedy et al., [27], a myriad of adversarial attack and defense methods have been proposed. Adversarial Training has emerged as the most successful defense strategy against ℓ_p norm bound imperceptible attacks. PGD Adversarial Training (PGD-AT) proposed by Madry et al. [18] constructs multi-step adversarial attacks by maximizing Cross-Entropy loss within the considered threat model and subsequently minimizes the same for training.

This was followed by several adversarial training methods [20, 22, 25, 30, 33, 34] that improved accuracy against such imperceptible threat models further.

Zhang et al. [33] proposed the TRADES defense, which maximizes the Kullback-Leibler (KL) divergence between the softmax outputs of adversarial and clean samples for attack generation, and minimizes the same in addition to the Cross-Entropy loss on clean samples for training.

Improving Robustness of Base Defenses: Wu et al. [30] proposed an additional step of Adversarial Weight Perturbation (AWP) to maximize the training loss, and further train the perturbed model to minimize the same. This generates a flatter loss surface [26], thereby improving robust generalization. While this can be integrated with any defense, AWP-TRADES is the state-of-the-art adversarial defense today.

On similar lines, the use of stochastic weight averaging of model weights [15] is also seen to improve the flatness of loss surface, resulting in a boost in adversarial robustness [5, 11]. Recent works attempt to use training techniques such as early stopping [22], optimal weight decay [20], Cutmix data augmentation [21, 31] and label smoothing [21] to achieve enhanced robust performance on base defenses such as PGD-AT [18] and TRADES [33]. We utilize some of these methods in our approach (Sect. 7), and also present improved baselines by combining AWP-TRADES [30] with these enhancements.

Robustness Against Large Perturbation Attacks: Shaeiri et al. [23] demonstrate that the standard formulation of adversarial training is not well-suited for achieving robustness at large perturbations, as the loss saturates very early. The authors propose Extended Adversarial Training (ExAT), where a model trained on low-magnitude perturbations ($\varepsilon = 8/255$) is fine-tuned with large magnitude perturbations ($\varepsilon = 16/255$) for just 5 training epochs, to achieve improved robustness at large perturbations. The authors also discuss the use of a varying epsilon schedule to improve training convergence. Friendly Adversarial Training (FAT) [34] performs early-stopping of an adversarial attack by thresholding the number of times the model misclassifies the image during attack generation. The threshold is increased over training epochs to increase the strength of the attack over training. Along similar lines, Sitawarin et al. [24] propose Adversarial Training with Early Stopping (ATES), which performs early stopping of a PGD attack based on the margin (difference between true and maximum probability class softmax outputs) of the perturbed image being greater than a threshold that is increased over epochs. We compare against these methods and improve upon them significantly using our proposed approach (Sect. 4).

3 Preliminaries and Threat Model

3.1 Notation

We consider an N-class image classification problem with access to a labelled training dataset $\mathcal{D}$. The input images are denoted by $x \in \mathcal{X}$ and their corresponding labels are denoted as $y \in \{1, ..., N\}$. The function represented by the Deep Neural Network is denoted by f_θ where $\theta \in \Theta$ denotes the set of network parameters. The N-dimensional softmax output of the input image x is denoted as $f_\theta(x)$. Adversarial examples are defined as images that are crafted specifically to fool a model into making an incorrect prediction [9]. An adversarial image corresponding to a clean image x would be denoted as $\tilde{x}$. The set of all images within an ℓ_p norm ball of radius ε is defined as $\mathcal{S}(x) = \{\hat{x} : ||\hat{x} - x||_p < \varepsilon\}$.

In this work, we specifically consider robustness to ℓ_∞ norm bound adversarial examples. We define the Oracle prediction of a sample x as the label that a human is likely to assign to the image, and denote it as $O(x)$. For a clean image, $O(x)$ would correspond to the true label y, while for a perturbed image it could differ from the original label.

3.2 Nomenclature of Adversarial Attacks

Tramer et al. [28] discuss the existence of two types of adversarial examples: Sensitivity-based examples, where the model prediction changes while the Oracle prediction remains the same as the unperturbed image, and Invariance-based examples, where the Oracle prediction changes while the model prediction remains unchanged. Models trained using standard empirical risk minimization are susceptible to sensitivity-based attacks, while models which are overly robust to large perturbation bounds could be susceptible to invariance-based attacks. Since these definitions are model-specific, we define a different nomenclature which only depends on the input image and the threat model considered:

- Oracle-Invariant set $OI(x)$ is defined as the set of all images within the bound $\mathcal{S}(x)$, that preserve Oracle label. Oracle is invariant to such attacks:

$$OI(x) := \{\hat{x} : O(\hat{x}) = O(x), \hat{x} \in \mathcal{S}(x)\} \tag{1}$$

- Oracle-Sensitive set $OS(x)$ is defined as the set of all images within the bound $\mathcal{S}(x)$, that flip the Oracle label. Oracle is sensitive to such attacks:

$$OS(x) := \{\hat{x} : O(\hat{x}) \neq O(x), \hat{x} \in \mathcal{S}(x)\} \tag{2}$$

3.3 Objectives of the Proposed Defense

Defenses based on the conventional ℓ_p norm threat model attempt to train models which are invariant to all samples within $\mathcal{S}(x)$. This is an ideal requirement for low ε-bound perturbations, where the added noise is imperceptible, and hence all samples within the threat model are Oracle-Invariant. An example of a low

ε-bound constraint set is the ℓ_∞ threat model with $\varepsilon = 8/255$ for the CIFAR-10 dataset, which produces adversarial examples that are perceptually similar to the corresponding clean images, as shown in Fig. 1(b).

As we move to larger ε bounds, Oracle-labels begin to change, as shown in Fig. 1(g, i, j). For a very high perturbation bound such as 32/255, the changes produced by an attack are clearly perceptible and in many cases flip the Oracle label as well. Hence, robustness at such large bounds is not of practical relevance. The focus of this work is to achieve robustness within a moderate-magnitude ℓ_p norm bound, where some perturbations look partially modified (Fig. 1(g)), while others look unchanged (Fig. 1(c, e)), as is the case with $\varepsilon = 16/255$ for CIFAR-10. The existence of attacks that do not significantly change the perception of the image necessitates the requirement of robustness within such bounds, while the existence of partially Oracle-Sensitive samples makes it difficult to use standard adversarial training methods on the same. The ideal goals for training defenses under this moderate-magnitude threat model are described below:

- Robustness against samples which belong to $OI(x)$
- Sensitivity towards samples which belong to $OS(x)$, with model's prediction matching the Oracle label
- No specification on samples which cannot be assigned an Oracle label.

Given the practical difficulty in assigning Oracle labels during training and evaluation, we consider the following subset of these ideal goals in this work:

- Robustness-Accuracy trade-off, measured using accuracy on clean samples and robustness against valid attacks within the threat model
- Robustness against all attacks within an imperceptible radius ($\varepsilon = 8/255$ for CIFAR-10), measured using strong white-box attacks [7, 25]
- Robustness to Oracle-Invariant samples within a larger radius ($\varepsilon = 16/255$ for CIFAR-10), measured using gradient-free attacks [1, 4]

4   Proposed Method

In order to achieve the goals discussed in Sect. 3.3, we require to generate Oracle-Sensitive and Oracle-Invariant samples and impose specific training losses on each of them individually. Since labeling adversarial samples as Oracle-Invariant or Oracle-Sensitive is expensive and cannot be done while training networks, we propose to use attacks which ensure a given type of perturbation (OI or OS) by construction, and hence do not require explicit annotation.

Generation of Oracle-Sensitive Examples: Robust models are known to have perceptually aligned gradients [29]. Adversarial examples generated using a robust model tend to look like the target (other) class images at large perturbation bounds, as seen in Fig. 1(g, i, j). We therefore use large ε-bound white-box adversarial examples generated from the model being trained as Oracle-Sensitive samples, and the model prediction as a proxy to the Oracle prediction.

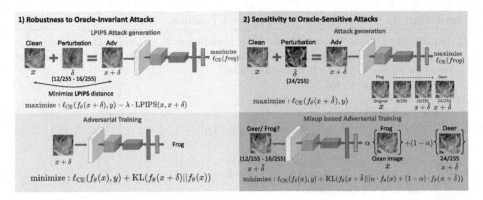

Fig. 3. Oracle-Aligned Adversarial Training: The proposed defense OA-AT involves alternate training on Oracle-Invariant and Oracle-Sensitive samples. 1) Oracle-Invariant samples are generated by minimizing the LPIPS distance between the clean and perturbed images in addition to the maximization of the Classification Loss. 2) Oracle-Sensitive samples are trained using a convex combination of the predictions of the clean image and the perturbed image at a larger perturbation bound as reference in the KL divergence loss.

Generation of Oracle-Invariant Examples: While the strongest Oracle-Invariant examples are generated using the gradient-free attacks Square [1] and Ray-S [4], they require a large number of queries (5000 to 10000), which is computationally expensive for use in adversarial training. Furthermore, reducing the number of queries weakens the attack significantly. The most efficient attack that is widely used for adversarial training is the PGD 10-step attack. However, it cannot be used for the generation of Oracle-Invariant samples as gradient-based attacks generated from adversarially trained models produce Oracle-Sensitive samples. We propose to use the Learned Perceptual Image Patch Similarity (LPIPS) measure for the generation of Oracle-Invariant attacks, as it is known to match well with perceptual similarity based on a study involving human annotators [17,35]. Further, we observe that while the standard AlexNet model used in prior work [17] fails to distinguish between Oracle-Invariant and Oracle-Sensitive samples, an adversarially trained model is able to distinguish between the two effectively (Ref: Fig. 3 in the Supplementary). We therefore propose to minimize the LPIPS distance between natural and perturbed images, in addition to the maximization of Cross-Entropy loss for attack generation: $\mathcal{L}_{CE}(x,y) - \lambda \cdot \text{LPIPS}(x,\hat{x})$. The ideal setting of λ is the minimum value that transforms attacks from Oracle-Sensitive to Oracle-Invariant (OI) for majority of the images. This results in the generation of strong Oracle-Invariant (OI) attacks. We present several Oracle-Invariant examples for visual inspection in Fig. 5 in Supplementary.

Oracle-Aligned Adversarial Training (OA-AT): The training algorithm for the proposed defense, Oracle-Aligned Adversarial Training (OA-AT) is presented in Algorithm 1 and illustrated in Fig. 3. We denote the maximum pertur-

---

Algorithm 1. Oracle-Aligned Adversarial Training

1: **Input:** Deep Neural Network f_θ with parameters θ, Training Data $\{x_i, y_i\}_{i=1}^M$, Epochs T, Learning Rate η, Perturbation budget ε_{max}, Adversarial Perturbation function $A(x, y, \ell, \varepsilon)$ which maximises loss ℓ
2: **for** epoch = 1 **to** T **do**
3:     $\widetilde{\varepsilon} = \max\{\varepsilon_{max}/4, \varepsilon_{max} \cdot \text{epoch}/T\}$
4:     **for** $i = 1$ **to** M **do**
5:         $\delta_i \sim U(-\min(\widetilde{\varepsilon}, \varepsilon_{max}/4), \min(\widetilde{\varepsilon}, \varepsilon_{max}/4))$
6:         **if** $\widetilde{\varepsilon} < 3/4 \cdot \varepsilon_{max}$ **then**
7:             $\ell = \ell_{CE}(f_\theta(x_i + \delta_i), y_i)$, $\widetilde{\delta}_i = A(x_i, y_i, \ell, \widetilde{\varepsilon})$
8:             $L_{adv} = \text{KL}\left(f_\theta(x_i + \widetilde{\delta}_i) \| f_\theta(x_i)\right)$
9:         **else if** $i \% 2 = 0$ **then**
10:             $\ell = \ell_{CE}(f_\theta(x_i + \delta_i), y_i)$, $\widehat{\delta}_i = A(x_i, y_i, \ell, \varepsilon_{ref})$, $\widetilde{\delta}_i = \Pi_\infty(\widehat{\delta}_i, \widetilde{\varepsilon})$
11:             $L_{adv} = \text{KL}\left(f_\theta(x_i + \widetilde{\delta}_i) \| \alpha \cdot f_\theta(x_i) + (1 - \alpha) \cdot f_\theta(x_i + \widehat{\delta}_i)\right)$
12:         **else**
13:             $\delta_i \sim U(-\widetilde{\varepsilon}, \widetilde{\varepsilon})$
14:             $\ell = \ell_{CE}(f_\theta(x_i + \delta_i), y_i) - \text{LPIPS}(x_i, x_i + \delta_i)$, $\widetilde{\delta}_i = A(x_i, y_i, \ell, \widetilde{\varepsilon})$
15:             $L_{adv} = \text{KL}\left(f_\theta(x_i + \widetilde{\delta}_i) \| f_\theta(x_i)\right)$
16:         $L = \ell_{CE}(f_\theta(x_i), y_i) + L_{adv}$
17:         $\theta = \theta - \eta \cdot \nabla_\theta L$

---

bation bound used for attack generation during the training by ε_{max}. We use the AWP-TRADES formulation [30,33] as the base implementation. Similar to Wu et al. [30], we use 10 steps of optimization for attack generation and one additional weight perturbation step. We maximize the classification loss on $x_i + 2 \cdot \widetilde{\delta}_i$ (where $\widetilde{\delta}_i$ is the attack) in the additional weight perturbation step (instead of $x_i + \widetilde{\delta}_i$ [30]), in order to achieve better smoothness in the loss surface. We start training with attacks constrained within a perturbation bound of $\varepsilon_{max}/4$ upto one-fourth the training epochs (Algorithm 1, L6–L8), and ramp up this value linearly to ε_{max} at the last epoch alongside a cosine learning rate schedule. The use of a fixed epsilon initially helps in improving the adversarial robustness faster, while the use of an increasing epsilon schedule later results in better training stability [23]. We use 5 attack steps upto $\varepsilon_{max}/4$ to reduce computation and 10 attack steps later.

We perform standard adversarial training upto a perturbation bound of $3/4 \cdot \varepsilon_{max}$ as the attacks in this range are imperceptible, based on the chosen moderate-magnitude threat model discussed in Sect. 3.3. Beyond this, we start incorporating separate training losses for Oracle-Invariant and Oracle-Sensitive samples in alternate training iterations (Algorithm 1, L9–L15), as shown in Fig. 3. Oracle-Sensitive samples are generated by maximizing the classification loss in a PGD attack formulation. Rather than enforcing the predictions of such attacks to be similar to the original image, we allow the network to be partially sensitive to such attacks by training them to be similar to a convex combination of predictions on the clean image and perturbed samples constrained within a bound of ε_{ref}, which is chosen to be greater than or equal to ε_{max} (Algorithm 1, L10). This component of the overall training loss is shown below:

$$KL\big(f_\theta(x_i + \widetilde{\delta}_i) \,\|\, \alpha\, f_\theta(x_i) + (1 - \alpha)\, f_\theta(x_i + \widehat{\delta}_i)\big) \qquad (3)$$

Here $\widetilde{\delta}_i$ is the perturbation at the varying epsilon value $\widetilde{\varepsilon}$, and $\widehat{\delta}_i$ is the perturbation at ε_{ref}. This loss formulation results in better robustness-accuracy trade-off as shown in E1 versus E3 of Table 4. In the alternate iteration, we use the LPIPS metric to efficiently generate strong Oracle-Invariant attacks during training (Algorithm 1, L14). We perform exponential weight-averaging of the network being trained and use this for computing the LPIPS metric for improved and stable results (E1 versus E2 and F1 versus F2 in Table 4). We therefore do not need additional training or computation time for training this model. We increase α and λ over training, as the nature of attacks changes with varying $\widetilde{\varepsilon}$. The use of both Oracle-Invariant (OI) and Oracle-Sensitive (OS) samples ensures robustness to Oracle-Invariant samples while allowing sensitivity to partially Oracle-Sensitive samples.

5 Analysing Oracle Alignment of Adversarial Attacks

We first consider the problem of generating Oracle-Invariant and Oracle-Sensitive attacks in a simplified, yet natural setting to enable more fine-grained theoretical analysis. We consider a binary classification task as introduced by Tsipras et al. [29], consisting of data samples (x, y), with $y \in \{+1, -1\}$, $x \in \mathbb{R}^{d+1}$. Further,

$$x_1 = \begin{cases} y, & \text{w.p. } p \\ -y, & \text{w.p. } 1 - p \end{cases} , \; x_i \sim \mathcal{N}(\alpha y, 1) \; \forall i \in \{2, \ldots, d + 1\}$$

In this setting, x_1 can be viewed as a feature that is strongly correlated with the Oracle Label y when the Bernoulli parameter p is sufficiently large (for e.g.: $p \approx 0.90$), and thus corresponds to an Oracle Sensitive feature. On the other hand, $x_2, \ldots, x_{d+1}$ are spurious features that are positively correlated (in a weak manner) to the Oracle label y, and are thus Oracle Invariant features. Building upon theoretical analysis presented by Tsipras et al. [29], we make a series of observations, whose details we expound in the Supplementary Sect. 2:

Observation 1. Adversarial perturbations of a standard, non-robust classifier utilize spurious features, resulting in Oracle Invariant Samples that are weakly anti-correlated with the Oracle label y.

Observation 2. Adversarial perturbations of a robust model result in Oracle Sensitive Samples, utilizing features strongly correlated with the Oracle label y.

6 Role of Image Contrast in Robust Evaluation

As shown in Fig. 1, perturbations constrained within a low-magnitude bound (Fig. 1(b)) do not change the perceptual appearance of an image, whereas perturbations constrained within very large bounds such as $\varepsilon = 32/255$ (Fig. 1(j))

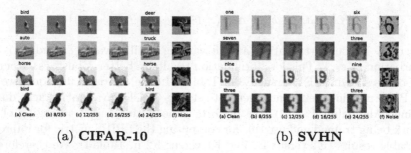

(a) **CIFAR-10**   (b) **SVHN**

Fig. 4. Relation between the contrast level of an image and the Oracle-Sensitivity of adversarial examples within a given perturbation bound. First and second rows show low contrast images, and third and fourth rows show high contrast images. Column (a) shows the original clean image and columns (b–e) show adversarial examples at different perturbation bounds generated at the largest bound in (e) and projected to the other bounds in (b, c, d). The adversarial perturbation is shown in column (f). Adversarial examples in columns (d) and (e) are Oracle-Invariant for the high contrast images, and Oracle-Sensitive for the low contrast images.

flip the Oracle prediction. As noted by Balaji et al. [2], the perturbation radius at which the Oracle prediction changes varies across images. We hypothesize that the contrast level of an image plays an important role in determining the minimum perturbation magnitude ε_{OS} that can flip the Oracle prediction of an image to generate an Oracle-Sensitive (OS) sample. We visualize a few High-Contrast and Low-Contrast images of the CIFAR-10 and SVHN datasets in Fig. 4 (more comprehensive visualisations are made available in Fig. 10–15 in the Supplementary). We observe that High-contrast (HC) images are Oracle-Invariant even at large perturbation bounds, while Low-Contrast (LC) images are Oracle-Sensitive at lower perturbation bounds as well. Based on this, we present robust evaluations at large epsilon bounds on images of varying contrast levels in Fig. 5.

7   Experiments and Results

In this section, we present detailed robust evaluations of the proposed approach along with various existing defenses on the CIFAR-10 [16], CIFAR-100 [16], SVHN [19] and Imagenette [14] datasets. We report adversarial robustness against the strongest known attacks, AutoAttack (AA) [7] and GAMA PGD-100 (GAMA) [25] for $\varepsilon = 8/255$ in order to obtain the worst-case robust accuracy. For larger bounds such as 12/255 and 16/255, we primarily aim for robustness against an ensemble of the Square [1] and Ray-S [4] attacks, as they generate strong Oracle-Invariant examples. On the SVHN dataset, we find that the perturbation bound for imperceptible attacks is $\varepsilon = 4/255$, and consider robustness within 12/255 (Fig. 10, 11 in the Supplementary).

For each baseline on CIFAR-10, we find the best set of hyperparameters to achieve clean accuracy of around 80% to ensure a fair comparison across all methods. We further perform baseline training across various ε values and report

Table 2. Comparison with existing methods: Performance (%) of the proposed defense OA-AT when compared to baselines against the attacks, GAMA-PGD100 [25], AutoAttack (AA) [7] and an ensemble of Square [1] and Ray-S [4] attacks (SQ+RS), with different ε bounds. Sorted by AutoAttack (AA) accuracy at $\varepsilon = 8/255$ for CIFAR-10, CIFAR-100 and Imagenette, and $4/255$ for SVHN.

(a) CIFAR-10, SVHN

Method	Clean	Metrics of interest			Others	
		GAMA 8/255	AA 8/255	SQ+RS 16/255	GAMA 16/255	AA 16/255
CIFAR-10 (ResNet-18), 110 epochs						
FAT	**84.36**	48.41	48.14	23.22	15.18	14.22
PGD-AT	79.38	49.28	48.68	25.43	18.18	17.00
AWP	80.32	49.06	48.89	25.99	19.17	18.77
ATES	80.95	49.57	49.12	26.43	18.36	16.30
TRADES	80.53	49.63	49.42	26.20	19.27	18.23
ExAT + PGD	80.68	50.06	49.52	25.13	17.81	19.53
ExAT + AWP	80.18	49.87	49.69	27.04	20.04	16.67
AWP	80.47	50.06	49.87	27.20	19.66	19.23
Ours	80.24	**51.40**	**50.88**	**29.56**	**22.73**	**22.05**
CIFAR-10 (ResNet-34), 110 epochs						
AWP	83.89	52.64	52.44	27.69	20.23	19.69
OA-AT (Ours)	**84.07**	**53.54**	**53.22**	**30.76**	**22.67**	**22.00**
CIFAR-10 (WRN-34-10), 200 epochs						
AWP	**85.36**	56.34	56.17	30.87	23.74	23.11
OA-AT (Ours)	85.32	**58.48**	**58.04**	**35.31**	**26.93**	**26.57**

Method	Clean	GAMA 4/255	AA 4/255	SQ+RS 12/255	GAMA 12/255	AA 12/255
SVHN (PreActResNet-18), 110 epochs						
AWP	91.91	75.92	75.72	35.49	30.70	30.31
OA-AT (Ours)	**94.61**	**78.37**	**77.96**	**39.24**	**34.25**	**33.63**

(b) CIFAR-100, ImageNette

Method	Clean	Metrics of interest			Others	
		GAMA 8/255	AA 8/255	SQ+RS 16/255	GAMA 16/255	AA 16/255
CIFAR-100 (ResNet-18), 110 epochs						
AWP	58.81	25.51	25.30	11.39	8.68	8.29
AWP+	59.88	25.81	25.52	11.85	8.72	8.28
OA-AT (no LS)	60.27	26.41	26.00	13.48	**10.47**	**9.95**
OA-AT (Ours)	**61.70**	**27.09**	**26.77**	**13.87**	10.40	9.91
CIFAR-100 (PreActResNet-18), 200 epochs						
AWP	58.85	25.58	25.18	11.29	8.63	8.19
AWP+	**62.11**	26.21	25.74	12.23	9.21	8.55
OA-AT (Ours)	62.02	**27.45**	**27.14**	**14.52**	**10.64**	**10.10**
CIFAR-100 (WRN-34-10), 110 epochs						
AWP	62.41	29.70	29.54	14.25	11.06	10.63
AWP+	62.73	29.92	29.59	14.96	11.55	11.04
OA-AT (no LS)	65.22	30.75	**30.35**	16.77	12.65	11.95
OA-AT (Ours)	**65.73**	**30.90**	**30.35**	**17.15**	**13.21**	**12.01**

Method	Clean	GAMA 8/255	AA 8/255	SQ+RS 16/255	GAMA 16/255	AA 16/255
Imagenette (ResNet-18), 110 epochs						
AWP	82.73	57.52	57.40	42.52	29.14	28.86
OA-AT (Ours)	**82.98**	**59.51**	**59.31**	**48.01**	**48.66**	**31.78**

the best in Table 2a. We note that existing defenses do not perform well when trained using large ε bounds such as $16/255$ as shown in Table 1 (more detailed results available in Table-2,3 in Supplementary). On other datasets, we present comparative analysis primarily with AWP [30], the leading defense amongst prior methods on the RobustBench Leaderboard [6] in the setting without additional or synthetic training data, which we consider in this work. We further compare the proposed approach with the AWP baseline using various model architectures (ResNet-18, ResNet-34 [12], WideResNet-34-10 [32] and PreActResNet-18 [13]).

Contrary to prior works [21,22], we obtain additional gains with the use of the augmentation technique, AutoAugment [8]. We also use Model Weight Averaging (WA) [5,11,15] to obtain better generalization performance, especially at larger model capacities. To ensure a fair comparison, we use these methods to obtain improved baselines as well, and report this as AWP+ in Table 2 if any improvement is observed (more comprehensive results in Sect. 7.4 of the Supplementary). As observed by Rebuffi et al. [21], we find that label-smoothing and the use of warmup in the learning rate scheduler helps achieve an additional boost in robustness. However, we report our results without including this as well (no LS) to highlight the gains of the proposed method individually.

From Table 2, we observe that the proposed defense achieves significant and consistent gains across all metrics specified in Sect. 3.3. The proposed approach outperforms existing defenses by a significant margin on all four datasets,

Table 3. Comparison with RobustBench Leaderboard [6] Results: Performance (%) of the proposed method (OA-AT) when compared to AWP [30], which is the state-of-the-art amongst methods that do not use additional training data/synthetic data on the RobustBench Leaderboard.

Method	Clean Acc	ℓ_∞ (AA) 8/255	ℓ_∞ (OI) 16/255	ℓ_2 (AA) $\varepsilon = 0.5$	ℓ_2 (AA) $\varepsilon = 1$	ℓ_1 (AA) $\varepsilon = 5$	ℓ_0 (PGD$_0$) $\varepsilon = 7$	Comm Corr
CIFAR-10 (WRN-34-10)								
AWP	85.36	56.17	30.87	60.68	28.86	37.29	39.09	75.83
Ours	85.32	58.04	35.31	64.08	34.54	45.72	44.40	76.78
CIFAR-100 (WRN-34-10)								
AWP	62.73	29.59	14.96	36.62	17.05	21.88	17.40	50.73
Ours	65.73	30.35	17.15	37.21	17.41	25.75	29.20	54.88

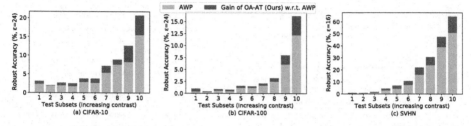

Fig. 5. Evaluation across test subsets of increasing contrast levels: Here we plot the gain in robust accuracy of the proposed defense OA-AT over AWP [30]. The proposed defense achieves higher gains as contrast increases, verifying that the proposed approach is more robust to the Oracle-Invariant white-box attacks on High-Contrast images.

over different network architectures. Although we train the model for achieving robustness at larger ε bounds, we achieve an improvement in the robustness at the low ε bound (such as $\varepsilon = 8/255$ on CIFAR-10) as well, which is not observed in any existing method (Sect. 7 of Supplementary). We also report the results on ℓ_2 Norm adversaries in Table-4 of Supplementary. As shown in Fig. 5, the proposed defense achieves higher gains on the high contrast test subsets of different datasets, verifying that the proposed approach has better robustness against Oracle-Invariant attacks, and not against Oracle-Sensitive attacks.

RobustBench Leaderboard Comparisons: As shown in Table 3, using the proposed method, we obtain a significant improvement over state-of-the-art results reported on the RobustBench Leaderboard (AWP) without the use of additional/ synthetic data on both CIFAR-10 and CIFAR-100 datasets. We observe that the proposed approach achieves significant gains against ℓ_∞ norm bound attacks at $\varepsilon = 8/255$ and $16/255$ that were used for training, as well as other ℓ_p norm bound attacks and common corruptions on both datasets.

The ε_{max} used for training is a system specification, which is the perturbation bound within which the model has to be robust. Thus, to validate the efficacy of the proposed approach, we train different ResNet-18 models on CIFAR-10 using different specifications of ε_{max}. From Fig. 6, we observe that for various values of training ε_{max}, the proposed approach consistently outperforms AWP [30].

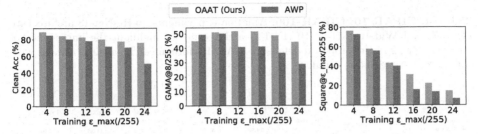

Fig. 6. Results across variation in training ε_{max}: While the proposed approach works best at moderate-ε bounds such as 16/255 on CIFAR-10, we observe that it outperforms the baseline for various ε_{max} values $\geq 8/255$ as well.

Training time of OA-AT is comparable with that of AWP [30]. On CIFAR-10, OA-AT takes 7 h 16 min, while AWP takes 7 h 27 min for 110 epochs of training on ResNet-18 using a single V100 GPU. To ensure the absence of gradient masking in the proposed approach, we present further evaluations against diverse attacks and sanity checks in Sect. 8 of the Supplementary.

Ablation Study: In order to study the impact of different components of the proposed defense, we present a detailed ablative study using ResNet-18 and WideResNet-34-10 models in Table 4. We present results on the CIFAR-10 and CIFAR-100 datasets, with E1 and F1 representing the proposed approach. First, we study the efficacy of the LPIPS metric in generating Oracle-Invariant attacks. In experiment E2, we train a model without LPIPS by setting its coefficient to zero. While the resulting model achieves a slight boost in robust accuracy at $\varepsilon = 16/255$ due to the use of stronger attacks for training, there is a considerable drop in clean accuracy, and a corresponding drop in robust accuracy at $\varepsilon = 8/255$ as well. We observe a similar trend by setting the value of α to 1 as shown in E3, and by combining E2 and E3 as shown in E4. We note that E4 is similar to standard adversarial training, where the model attempts to learn consistent predictions in the ε ball around every data sample. While this works well for large ε attacks (16/255), it leads to poor clean accuracy as shown in Table 1.

We further note that the computation of LPIPS distance using an exponential weight averaged model (E1) results in better performance as compared to using the model being trained (E5). As discussed in Sect. 4, we maximize loss on $x_i + 2 \cdot \widetilde{\delta}_i$ (where $\widetilde{\delta}_i$ is the attack) in the additional weight perturbation step. We present results by using the standard ε limit for the weight perturbation step as well, in E6. This leads to a drop across all metrics, indicating the importance of using large magnitude perturbations in the weight perturbation step for producing a flatter loss surface that leads to better generalization to the test set. Different from the standard TRADES formulation, we maximize Cross-Entropy loss for attack generation in the proposed method. From E7 we note a drop in robust accuracy since the KL divergence based attack is weaker (Gowal et al. [11]). We present further ablative analysis in Sec.6 of the Supplementary.

Table 4. CIFAR-10, CIFAR-100: Ablation experiments on ResNet-18 architecture (E1-E7) and WideResNet-34-10 (F1-F2) architecture to highlight the importance of various aspects in the proposed defense OA-AT. Performance (%) against attacks with different ε bounds is reported.

Method	CIFAR-10				CIFAR-100			
	Clean	GAMA (8/255)	GAMA (16/255)	Square (16/255)	Clean	GAMA (8/255)	GAMA (16/255)	Square (16/255)
E1: OA-AT (Ours)	80.24	**51.40**	22.73	31.16	60.27	**26.41**	10.47	14.60
E2: LPIPS weight = 0	78.47	50.60	24.05	31.37	58.47	25.94	10.91	14.66
E3: Alpha = 1	79.29	50.60	23.65	31.23	58.84	26.15	10.97	14.89
E4: Alpha = 1, LPIPS weight = 0	77.16	50.49	24.93	32.01	57.77	25.92	11.33	15.03
E5: Using Current model (without WA) for LPIPS	80.50	50.75	22.90	30.76	59.54	26.23	10.50	14.86
E6: Without 2*eps perturbations for AWP	79.96	50.50	22.61	30.60	60.18	26.27	10.15	14.20
E7: Maximizing KL div in the AWP step	81.19	49.77	21.17	29.39	59.48	25.03	7.93	13.34
F1: OA-AT (Ours)	**85.32**	**58.48**	26.93	**36.93**	**65.73**	**30.90**	13.21	**18.47**
F2: LPIPS weight = 0	83.47	57.58	**27.21**	36.68	63.16	30.22	**13.59**	18.42

8 Conclusions

In this paper, we investigate in detail robustness at larger perturbation bounds in an ℓ_p norm based threat model. We discuss the ideal goals of an adversarial defense at larger perturbation bounds, identify deficiencies of prior works in this setting and further propose a novel defense, Oracle-Aligned Adversarial Training (OA-AT) that aligns model predictions with that of an Oracle during training. The key aspects of the defense include the use of LPIPS metric for generating Oracle-Invariant attacks during training, and the use of a convex combination of clean and adversarial image predictions as targets for Oracle-Sensitive samples. We achieve state-of-the-art robustness at low and moderate perturbation bounds, and a better robustness-accuracy trade-off. We further show the relation between the contrast level of images and the existence of Oracle-Sensitive attacks within a given perturbation bound. We use this for better evaluation, and highlight the role of contrast of images in achieving an improved robustness-accuracy trade-off. We hope that future work would build on this to construct better defenses and to obtain a better understanding on the existence of adversarial examples.

Acknowledgements. This work was supported by a research grant (CRG/2021/005925) from SERB, DST, Govt. of India. Sravanti Addepalli is supported by Google PhD Fellowship and CII-SERB Prime Minister's Fellowship for Doctoral Research.

References

1. Andriushchenko, M., Croce, F., Flammarion, N., Hein, M.: Square attack: a query-efficient black-box adversarial attack via random search. In: Vedaldi, A., Bischof, H., Brox, T., Frahm, J.-M. (eds.) ECCV 2020. LNCS, vol. 12368, pp. 484–501. Springer, Cham (2020). https://doi.org/10.1007/978-3-030-58592-1_29

2. Balaji, Y., Goldstein, T., Hoffman, J.: Instance adaptive adversarial training: improved accuracy tradeoffs in neural nets. arXiv preprint arXiv:1910.08051 (2019)

3. Carlini, N., et al.: On evaluating adversarial robustness. arXiv preprint arXiv:1902.06705 (2019)

4. Chen, J., Gu, Q.: Rays: a ray searching method for hard-label adversarial attack. In: Proceedings of the 26th ACM SIGKDD International Conference on Knowledge Discovery & Data Mining, pp. 1739–1747 (2020)
5. Chen, T., Zhang, Z., Liu, S., Chang, S., Wang, Z.: Robust overfitting may be mitigated by properly learned smoothening. In: International Conference on Learning Representations (ICLR) (2020)
6. Croce, F., et al.: Robustbench: a standardized adversarial robustness benchmark. In: Thirty-Fifth Conference on Neural Information Processing Systems Datasets and Benchmarks Track (Round 2) (2021)
7. Croce, F., Hein, M.: Reliable evaluation of adversarial robustness with an ensemble of diverse parameter-free attacks. In: International Conference on Machine Learning (ICML) (2020)
8. Cubuk, E.D., Zoph, B., Mane, D., Vasudevan, V., Le, Q.V.: Autoaugment: learning augmentation strategies from data. In: Proceedings of the IEEE/CVF Conference on Computer Vision and Pattern Recognition (CVPR) (2019)
9. Goodfellow, I., Papernot, N.: Is attacking machine learning easier than defending it?, blog post on 15 February 2017
10. Goodfellow, I.J., Shlens, J., Szegedy, C.: Explaining and harnessing adversarial examples. In: International Conference on Learning Representations (ICLR) (2015)
11. Gowal, S., Qin, C., Uesato, J., Mann, T., Kohli, P.: Uncovering the limits of adversarial training against norm-bounded adversarial examples. arXiv preprint arXiv:2010.03593 (2020)
12. He, K., Zhang, X., Ren, S., Sun, J.: Deep residual learning for image recognition. In: Proceedings of the IEEE Conference on Computer Vision and Pattern Recognition (CVPR) (2016)
13. He, K., Zhang, X., Ren, S., Sun, J.: Identity mappings in deep residual networks. In: Leibe, B., Matas, J., Sebe, N., Welling, M. (eds.) ECCV 2016. LNCS, vol. 9908, pp. 630–645. Springer, Cham (2016). https://doi.org/10.1007/978-3-319-46493-0_38
14. Howard, J.: Imagenette dataset (2019). https://github.com/fastai/imagenette
15. Izmailov, P., Podoprikhin, D., Garipov, T., Vetrov, D., Wilson, A.G.: Averaging weights leads to wider optima and better generalization. arXiv preprint arXiv:1803.05407 (2018)
16. Krizhevsky, A., et al.: Learning multiple layers of features from tiny images (2009)
17. Laidlaw, C., Singla, S., Feizi, S.: Perceptual adversarial robustness: defense against unseen threat models. In: International Conference on Learning Representations (ICLR) (2021)
18. Madry, A., Makelov, A., Schmidt, L., Dimitris, T., Vladu, A.: Towards deep learning models resistant to adversarial attacks. In: International Conference on Learning Representations (ICLR) (2018)
19. Netzer, Y., Wang, T., Coates, A., Bissacco, A., Wu, B., Ng, A.Y.: Reading digits in natural images with unsupervised feature learning. In: NeurIPS Workshop on Deep Learning and Unsupervised Feature Learning (2011)
20. Pang, T., Yang, X., Dong, Y., Su, H., Zhu, J.: Bag of tricks for adversarial training. In: International Conference on Learning Representations (ICLR) (2021)
21. Rebuffi, S.A., Gowal, S., Calian, D.A., Stimberg, F., Wiles, O., Mann, T.: Fixing data augmentation to improve adversarial robustness. arXiv preprint arXiv:2103.01946 (2021)
22. Rice, L., Wong, E., Kolter, J.Z.: Overfitting in adversarially robust deep learning. In: International Conference on Machine Learning (ICML) (2020)
23. Shaeiri, A., Nobahari, R., Rohban, M.H.: Towards deep learning models resistant to large perturbations. arXiv preprint arXiv:2003.13370 (2020)

24. Sitawarin, C., Chakraborty, S., Wagner, D.: Improving adversarial robustness through progressive hardening. arXiv preprint arXiv:2003.09347 (2020)
25. Sriramanan, G., Addepalli, S., Baburaj, A., Venkatesh Babu, R.: Guided adversarial attack for evaluating and enhancing adversarial defenses. In: Advances in Neural Information Processing Systems (NeurIPS) (2020)
26. Stutz, D., Hein, M., Schiele, B.: Relating adversarially robust generalization to flat minima. In: Proceedings of the IEEE/CVF International Conference on Computer Vision (ICCV) (2021)
27. Szegedy, C., et al.: Intriguing properties of neural networks. In: International Conference on Learning Representations (ICLR) (2013)
28. Tramèr, F., Behrmann, J., Carlini, N., Papernot, N., Jacobsen, J.H.: Fundamental tradeoffs between invariance and sensitivity to adversarial perturbations. In: International Conference on Machine Learning (ICML) (2020)
29. Tsipras, D., Santurkar, S., Engstrom, L., Turner, A., Madry, A.: Robustness may be at odds with accuracy. In: International Conference on Learning Representations (ICLR) (2019)
30. Wu, D., Xia, S.T., Wang, Y.: Adversarial weight perturbation helps robust generalization. In: Advances in Neural Information Processing Systems (NeurIPS) (2020)
31. Yun, S., Han, D., Oh, S.J., Chun, S., Choe, J., Yoo, Y.: Cutmix: regularization strategy to train strong classifiers with localizable features. In: Proceedings of the IEEE/CVF International Conference on Computer Vision (ICCV) (2019)
32. Zagoruyko, S., Komodakis, N.: Wide residual networks. arXiv preprint arXiv:1605.07146 (2016)
33. Zhang, H., Yu, Y., Jiao, J., Xing, E., El Ghaoui, L., Jordan, M.I.: Theoretically principled trade-off between robustness and accuracy. In: International Conference on Machine Learning (ICML) (2019)
34. Zhang, J., et al.: Attacks which do not kill training make adversarial learning stronger. In: International Conference on Machine Learning (ICML) (2020)
35. Zhang, R., Isola, P., Efros, A.A., Shechtman, E., Wang, O.: The unreasonable effectiveness of deep features as a perceptual metric. In: Proceedings of the IEEE Conference on Computer Vision and Pattern Recognition (CVPR) (2018)

Exploiting the Local Parabolic Landscapes of Adversarial Losses to Accelerate Black-Box Adversarial Attack

Hoang Tran⬤, Dan Lu⬤, and Guannan Zhang$^{(\boxtimes)}$⬤

Oak Ridge National Laboratory, Oak Ridge, TN 37830, USA
{tranha,lud1,zhangg}@ornl.gov

Abstract. Existing black-box adversarial attacks on image classifiers update the perturbation at each iteration from only a small number of queries of the loss function. Since the queries contain very limited information about the loss, black-box methods usually require much more queries than white-box methods. We propose to improve the query efficiency of black-box methods by exploiting the smoothness of the local loss landscape. However, many adversarial losses are not locally smooth with respect to pixel perturbations. To resolve this issue, our first contribution is to theoretically and experimentally justify that the adversarial losses of many standard and robust image classifiers behave like parabolas with respect to perturbations in the Fourier domain. Our second contribution is to exploit the parabolic landscape to build a quadratic approximation of the loss around the current state, and use this approximation to interpolate the loss value as well as update the perturbation without additional queries. Since the local region is already informed by the quadratic fitting, we use large perturbation steps to explore far areas. We demonstrate the efficiency of our method on MNIST, CIFAR-10 and ImageNet datasets for various standard and robust models, as well as on Google Cloud Vision. The experimental results show that exploiting the loss landscape can help significantly reduce the number of queries and increase the success rate. Our codes are available at https://github.com/HoangATran/BABIES.

Keywords: Adversarial attack · Interpolation scheme · Loss landscape

1 Introduction

Deep neural networks (DNN) have been shown to be susceptible to adversarial examples, which are small, human-imperceptible perturbations to the inputs designed to fool the network prediction [14,33]. Adversarial attacks can be categorized into two main settings: white-box attacks and black-box attacks. In the

Supplementary Information The online version contains supplementary material available at https://doi.org/10.1007/978-3-031-20065-6_19.

white-box setting, the attackers have access to all information about the target model and thus can use the model's gradient to effectively guide the search for adversarial examples [7,23,33]. Black-box setting, on the other hand, attacks a model only from classification queries [9,18,25]. This type of access requirement is considered more realistic in practice.

Traditionally, black-box methods require a massive amount of queries to find a successful adversarial perturbation. Since each query to the target model costs time and money, query efficiency is a requisite for any practical black-box attack method. Recent years have seen the development of several black-box approaches with significant improved query efficiency [1,3,15,19,24,34]. However, current black-box attacks access the target models only at perturbed samples and completely rely on the queries there to update the perturbation at each iteration. To reduce the number of queries, it would be beneficial to be able to make use of these queries to extract more from the models, inferring the loss values and identifying candidate perturbations, where no model query was made. This is a challenging goal: since the landscapes of adversarial losses are often complicated and not well-understood, the accuracy of approximations of the loss values from available model queries is not guaranteed.

In this paper, we develop a new ℓ_2 black-box adversarial attack on frequency domain, which uses an interpolation scheme to approximate the loss value around the current state and guide the perturbation updates. We refer to our method as *Black-box Attack Based on IntErpolation Scheme (BABIES)*. This algorithm is inspired by our observation that for many standard and robust image classifiers, the adversarial losses behave like *parabolas* with respect to perturbations of an image in the Fourier domain, thus can be captured with quadratic interpolation. We treat the adversarial attack problem as a constraint optimization on an ℓ_2 sphere, and sample along geodesic curves on the sphere. If the queries show improvements, we accept the perturbation. If the queries do not show improvement, we will infer a small perturbation from those samples without additional queries. Our method achieves significantly improved query efficiency because the perturbation updates are now informed not only directly from model queries (as in existing approaches), but also from an accurate quadratic approximation of the adversarial loss around the current state. The main contributions of this work can be summarized as follows:

- Theoretical and empirical justifications that the adversarial loss behaves like a parabola in the Fourier domain, but NOT like a parabola in pixel domain.
- Development of BABIES, a random-search-based black-box attack that exploits the parabolic loss landscape to improve the query efficiency.
- Evaluations of BABIES with targeted and untargeted attacks on MNIST, CIFAR-10 and ImageNet datasets with both standard and defended models.

1.1   Related Works

To guide the search for adversarial examples, existing black-box attacks often aim at approximating the gradient, either from the gradient of a surrogate model [26,27], or from model queries via finite different approximation, zeroth-order optimization, natural evolution strategies, etc. [1,4,8,9,18,19,34]. Many approaches for reducing the dimension of the search space have been proposed, based on principal component analysis [4], autoencoder [34], and compressed sensing [20]. Our method generates random perturbations on the low frequency domain, similar to SimBA [16] and PPBA [20]. This subspace has been shown to admit a high density of adversarial perturbations [15]. Other strategies for designing random perturbations to guide random-search-based attacks include Square Attack [3], which crafts perturbations with square shape, PRGF [12], which utilizes a transfer-based prior, and GenAttack [2], which uses genetic algorithms. Adversarial examples can also be generated from learning their probability distributions [11,22] and combinatorial optimization techniques [24].

Our black-box method is concerned with the score-based scenario, where the attacker has access to the output scores of the target classifier. More limited variants of the black-box setting have also been studied, where only access to the top-1 predicted labels is assumed [5,6,10,18]. Recent work [21] considers no-box settings, where the attacker makes no query to the target model but just gathers a small labeled dataset. These forms of attacks are more challenging.

2   Background

Image classification aims to successfully predict what a human sees in an image. The objective of adversarial attack on an image classification model is to introduce a small distortion beyond human perceptibility into the original image to fool the target model. In this work, we consider the score-based black-box attack. We first give the formal definition of the adversarial attack problem under consideration. Let $f : [0,1]^d \to \mathbb{R}^K$ be a classifier with d input dimension and K classes, where $f_k(\mathbf{x})$ is the predicted probability that the image $\mathbf{x}$ belongs to class k. The predicted label of the image $\mathbf{x}$ is denoted by

$$h(\mathbf{x}) := \operatorname*{argmax}_{k=1,\dots,K} f_k(\mathbf{x}).$$

An adversary aims to generate a perturbed image, denoted by $\hat{\mathbf{x}}$, with a small perturbation that solves the following constrained optimization problem

$$\min_{\hat{\mathbf{x}}} \delta(\mathbf{x},\hat{\mathbf{x}}) \quad \text{s.t.} \quad \begin{cases} h(\hat{\mathbf{x}}) \neq h(\mathbf{x}) & \text{(untargeted)}, \\ h(\hat{\mathbf{x}}) = \hat{y} & \text{(targeted)}, \end{cases} \tag{1}$$

where $\delta(\cdot,\cdot)$ measures the perceptual difference between the original image $\mathbf{x}$ and the adversarial image $\hat{\mathbf{x}}$, and $\hat{y}$ is the target label for targeted attacks. The most commonly used definition for δ is the ℓ_2 norm or the ℓ_∞ norm of the distortion $\mathbf{x} - \hat{\mathbf{x}}$. In this work, we will use the ℓ_2 norm, i.e., $\delta(\mathbf{x},\hat{\mathbf{x}}) := \|\mathbf{x} - \hat{\mathbf{x}}\|_2$, as the distortion metric.

Loss Minimization. For score-based adversarial attack, we can exploit the access to the score function $f(\mathbf{x})$ to define an adversarial loss $L(\hat{\mathbf{x}}, y)$ to guide the search towards adversarial examples. For untargeted attack, the probability of the class $h(\mathbf{x})$ that the original image $\mathbf{x}$ belongs to is often used as adversarial loss, i.e., $L(\hat{\mathbf{x}}, h(\mathbf{x})) := f_{h(\mathbf{x})}(\hat{\mathbf{x}})$. For targeted attack towards a label $\hat{y}$, we want to maximize $f_{\hat{y}}(\hat{\mathbf{x}})$, so choose $L(\hat{\mathbf{x}}, \hat{y}) := -f_{\hat{y}}(\hat{\mathbf{x}})$. Since the gradient of the target classifier is unavailable and each query to the model costs time and money, the total number of black-box queries for constructing an adversarial example must not exceed a prescribed budget. Thus, the optimization problem in Eq. (1) is modified to

$$\min_{\hat{\mathbf{x}}} L(\hat{\mathbf{x}}, y) \text{ s.t. } \|\hat{\mathbf{x}} - \mathbf{x}\|_2 \le \rho, \text{ queries } \le B, \qquad (2)$$

where B is the maximum allowable number of queries and ρ is the constraint on the maximum image distortion. For notational simplicity, we suppress the dependence of L on y and write L as $L(\hat{\mathbf{x}})$ in the rest of the paper.

To solve (2), we employ an iterative random search approach, where at each iteration, we query along a randomly sampled search direction and update the current point based on those queries. When doing a Taylor expansion of the loss with respect to a perturbation δ along any randomly selected direction, i.e.,

$$L(\hat{\mathbf{x}}) = L(\mathbf{x}^*) + \frac{dL}{d\delta}(\mathbf{x}^*)\delta + \frac{d^2L}{d\delta^2}(\mathbf{x}^*)\delta^2 + \mathcal{O}(\delta^3),$$

with $\mathbf{x}^*$ being the current state, it is intuitive to conjecture that the loss would behave like a parabola in the neighborhood of $\mathbf{x}^*$. However, it is not the case for all perturbation strategies. In the following sections, we show that the adversarial loss behaves like a parabola in the Fourier domain determined by the discrete consine transform (DCT) [15,30], but NOT like a parabola in the pixel domain. Then, we develop the BABIES algorithm that exploits the parabolic loss landscape in the frequency domain to improve query efficiency.

3 Theoretical and Empirical Study on the Landscape of the Adversarial Loss

In this section, we investigate the shape of the loss's landscape with respect to two different perturbations, i.e., pixel perturbation and DCT perturbation [15,30].

Our main observation is that the loss's landscape is closer to a parabola with respect to a DCT perturbation, as shown in Fig. 2 and 3. To theoretically verify such observation, we consider a simplified convolutional neural network (CNN)-based classifier for 1D signals. The length of each signal sample is N. We assume the first two layers of the CNN is a 3×1 convolutional layer followed by a 2×1 max-pooling layer, which is a common setup for CNN-based classifiers. Let $\mathbf{x} = (x_{i+1}, x_{i+2}, x_{i+3}, x_{i+4})$, for $i \in \{0, \ldots, N-4\}$, be a 4×1 interior segment of the signal and $\mathbf{w} = (w_1, w_2, w_3)$ be the convolution filter. The output of the convolutional layer, centered at x_{i+2} and x_{i+3}, consists of two entries y_2 and y_3 given by

$$y_2 = w_1 x_{i+1} + w_2 x_{i+2} + w_3 x_{i+3},$$
$$y_3 = w_1 x_{i+2} + w_2 x_{i+3} + w_3 x_{i+4},$$

and the output after the ReLU activation is

$$z_2 = \max(y_2, 0), \quad z_3 = \max(y_3, 0), \tag{3}$$

and the output of the max-pooling layer is

$$u = \max(z_2, z_3). \tag{4}$$

The simplified CNN model is visualized in Fig. 1. Note that we choose the 1D case to avoid tedious derivation, but the theoretical intuition is applicable to 2D and 3D cases.

Let us define a perturbed signal as $\mathbf{x} + \delta\mathbf{q}$, where $\mathbf{q} = (q_{i+1}, q_{i+2}, q_{i+3}, q_{i+4})$ is the perturbation direction. The derivative of the adversarial loss $L(\delta)$ (as a function of the perturbation's magnitude δ) is represented by

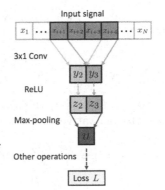

$$\frac{dL}{d\delta}(\delta) = \frac{dL}{du}\frac{du}{d\delta}(\delta), \tag{5}$$

and we focus on analyzing the behavior of $du/d\delta$ for both pixel and DCT perturbations.

The Property of $du/d\delta$ Due to Pixel Perturbation. In this case, we perturb the pixel x_{i+2}, i.e., setting $q_{i+2} = 1$, $q_{i+1} = q_{i+3} = q_{i+4} = 0$, to study how $du/d\delta$ behaves as a function of δ. Specifically, $du/d\delta$ under the perturbation of x_{i+2} can be written as

Fig. 1. Illustration of the simplified CNN classifier for verifying our theoretical intuition. We only explicitly write out the first convolutional and max-pooling layers, which is sufficient to verify our theoretical intuition. Other layers are included in "other operations".

$$\frac{du}{d\delta}(\delta) = \frac{\partial u}{\partial z_2}\frac{\partial z_2}{\partial y_2}w_2 + \frac{\partial u}{\partial z_3}\frac{\partial z_3}{\partial y_3}w_1, \tag{6}$$

which involves the derivatives of the ReLU function and the max-pooling function, e.g.,

$$\frac{\partial u}{\partial z_2} = \begin{cases} 1, & \text{if } z_2 \geq z_3 \\ 0, & \text{otherwise} \end{cases}, \quad \text{and} \quad \frac{\partial z_2}{\partial y_2} = \begin{cases} 1, & \text{if } y_2 > 0 \\ 0, & \text{otherwise} \end{cases},$$

and $\partial u/\partial z_3, \partial z_3/\partial y_3$ can be defined similarly. Therefore, $du/d\delta$ can only choose values from the set

$$\frac{du}{d\delta}(\delta) \in \{0, w_1, w_2\}, \tag{7}$$

when perturbing the pixel x_{i+2} by δ. Since y_2, y_3, z_2, z_3 are functions of δ, the value of $du/d\delta$ may "jump" from one value in $\{0, w_1, w_2\}$ to another, because w_1

and w_2 may be dramatically different, e.g., $\mathbf{w} = (-1, 5, -1)$ defines a sharpen filter kernel. The maximum jump size could be

$$\left| \frac{du}{d\delta}(\alpha) - \frac{du}{d\delta}(\beta) \right| \leq |w_1| + |w_2|, \tag{8}$$

where $\alpha \neq \beta$ but $|\alpha - \beta|$ is very small. This will eventually lead to the rapid change of the derivative of the total loss $dL/d\delta$ defined in Eq. (5). Figure 2-right illustrates a typical loss landscape with respect to pixel perturbation.

The Property of $du/d\delta$ Due to DCT Perturbation. In this case, all the pixels are perturbed simultaneously. Specifically, the perturbation direction $\mathbf{q}$ is defined by

$$q_{i+1} = \sqrt{\frac{2}{N}} \cos\left(\frac{(2i+1)n\pi}{2N}\right), \quad q_{i+2} = \sqrt{\frac{2}{N}} \cos\left(\frac{(2i+3)n\pi}{2N}\right),$$

$$q_{i+3} = \sqrt{\frac{2}{N}} \cos\left(\frac{(2i+5)n\pi}{2N}\right), \quad q_{i+4} = \sqrt{\frac{2}{N}} \cos\left(\frac{(2i+7)n\pi}{2N}\right),$$

where $n \in \{0, \ldots, N-1\}$ is the selected frequency and N is the total signal length. Then, the derivative $du/d\delta$ is represented by

$$\frac{du}{d\delta}(\delta) = \frac{\partial u}{\partial z_2} \frac{\partial z_2}{\partial y_2}(w_1 q_{i+1} + w_2 q_{i+2} + w_3 q_{i+3})$$

$$+ \frac{\partial u}{\partial z_3} \frac{\partial z_3}{\partial y_3}(w_1 q_{i+2} + w_2 q_{i+3} + w_3 q_{i+4}).$$

Therefore, $du/d\delta$ can only choose values from the set

$$\frac{du}{d\delta}(\delta) \in \{w_1 q_{i+1} + w_2 q_{i+2} + w_3 q_{i+3}, \, w_1 q_{i+2} + w_2 q_{i+3} + w_3 q_{i+4}, \, 0\}. \tag{9}$$

As opposed to the pixel perturbation case in Eq. (7), the potential "jumps" of $du/d\delta$ in the DCT domain is much smaller. In fact, the maximum jump size

$$\left| \frac{du}{d\delta}(\alpha) - \frac{du}{d\delta}(\beta) \right| \leq \frac{2\sqrt{2}}{\sqrt{N}} \sin\left(\frac{n\pi}{2N}\right) \left[w_1 \sin\left(\frac{(i+1)n\pi}{N}\right) \right.$$

$$\left. + w_2 \sin\left(\frac{(i+2)n\pi}{N}\right) + w_3 \sin\left(\frac{(i+3)n\pi}{N}\right) \right], \tag{10}$$

where $\alpha \neq \beta$. When perturbing *low-frequency* modes, i.e., n is small, suggested in [15,30], Eq. (10) can be bounded by $\frac{2\sqrt{2}}{\sqrt{N}} |\sin\left(\frac{n\pi}{2N}\right)| (|w_1| + |w_2| + |w_3|)$. It is easy to see that this bound is much smaller than the one in Eq. (8) due to the appearance of N (the signal length) in the denominators.

Experimental Illustration. To verify the above intuition, we investigate the landscape of the adversarial loss on untargeted attacks on four different classifiers: (a) standard Inception_v3 on ImageNet [32], (b) ℓ_2-robust ResNet18 on ImageNet

[29], (c) standard VGG on CIFAR-10 [31], (d) ℓ_2-robust ResNet50 on CIFAR-10 [13]. For each model, we randomly select 50 images from the corresponding testing sets and define the loss functions as in Background section. We sample 100 1D segments in a neighborhood of each original image, along randomly selected DCT directions and pixel directions, then compute the loss function restricted on them. Then we fit these loss values with parabolas using quadratic regression. The true and approximated landscapes typically found in the DCT and pixel settings are compared in Fig. 2. We observe that the adversarial loss with respect to DCT perturbations is smooth and close to a parabola. On the other hand, the loss function with respect to pixel perturbations shows sharp turns due to the rapid change (jumps) of $dL/d\delta$, therefore cannot be captured by quadratic approximation. This empirical observation is consistent with the above theoretical study.

To show the phenomenon in Fig. 2 is statistically meaningful, we plot in Fig. 3 the correlation between true and approximated loss values given by parabolas on a large number of sample points. To generate each plot, 5000 points are randomly sampled on 100 segments in the neighborhood of each of 50 images (therefore 5000 segments in total). Since the losses on different segments and images are significantly different in value, we normalize them on each segment such that their values lie in $[0, 1]$. Here, we observe strong correla-

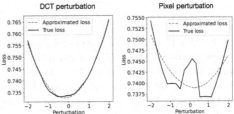

Fig. 2. The landscape of the adversarial loss along DCT directions is often well-behaved and can be fitted with a parabola **(left)**. The landscape along pixel direction features sharp turns due to the rapid change (jumps) of $dL/d\delta$ shown in Eq. (8), thus cannot be adequately captured by quadratic approximation **(right)**.

tion in DCT setting, confirming that the adversarial losses are generally well-approximated by parabolas in the frequency directions, but much less so in the pixel directions.

4   The BABIES Algorithm

In this section, we present how to exploit the parabolic loss landscape in the DCT domain to develop our BABIES algorithm for black-box attack. Our method consists of two components. Before describing our quadratic interpolation scheme for perturbation updating, we discuss the sampling rule with large step size on the hypersphere.

The Sampling Rule on the Hypersphere. Let us define $\mathcal{B}_\rho := \{\hat{\mathbf{x}} \in [0, 1]^d : \|\hat{\mathbf{x}} - \mathbf{x}\|_2 \leq \rho\}$ and $\mathcal{S}_\rho$ be the boundary of $\mathcal{B}_\rho$. Let Q be the set of low frequencies extracted by the DCT. Starting from $\mathbf{x}$, we generate a sequence of iterates $\mathbf{x}^{(k)}$ in $\mathcal{B}_\rho$ which progresses toward an adversarial example. Let ε be the step size

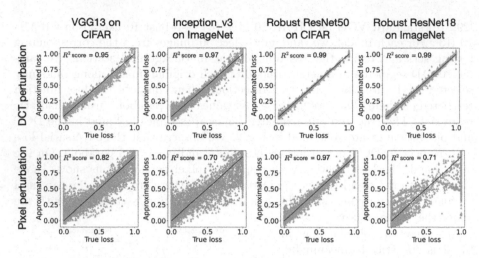

Fig. 3. Scatter plot displays the correlation between true and approximated loss values on a large number of points, sampled from 5000 segments along DCT directions **(top)** and pixel directions **(bottom)**. We observe a strong correlation in DCT setting, and much less so along pixel setting. This plot verifies the generality of the example in Fig. 2, that the shape of adversarial losses along DCT directions is close to and can be adequately approximated by a parabola.

parameter and assume $\mathbf{q}^{(k)}$ is the direction sampled from Q, at iteration k, we determine two queries based on $\mathbf{q}^{(k)}$ and ε. When all of $\mathbf{x}^{(k)}$, $\mathbf{x}_\varepsilon$ and $\mathbf{x}_{-\varepsilon}$ are in the interior of $\mathcal{B}_\rho$, i.e., at the beginning of the search, we simply query at

$$\mathbf{x}_{-\varepsilon} = \mathbf{x}^{(k)} - \varepsilon\mathbf{q}^{(k)} \quad \text{and} \quad \mathbf{x}_\varepsilon = \mathbf{x}^{(k)} + \varepsilon\mathbf{q}^{(k)}, \tag{11}$$

and update $\mathbf{x}^{(k)}$ using these queries (see the update rule in the second part). When one or more of $\mathbf{x}^{(k)}$, $\mathbf{x}_{-\varepsilon}$, $\mathbf{x}_\varepsilon$ reach the hypersphere $\mathcal{S}_\rho$, we switch to the sampling rule on the hypersphere, where the queries along the straight line in Eq. (11) is replaced by those along the geodesic curve passing through $\mathbf{x}^{(k)}$ and coplanar to $\mathbf{q}^{(k)}$. We choose $\mathbf{x}_{-\varepsilon}$ and $\mathbf{x}_\varepsilon \in \mathcal{S}_\rho$ so that the *arc length* (instead of standard distance) between them and $\mathbf{x}^{(k)}$ is ε. Denoting $\delta^{(k)} = \mathbf{x}^{(k)} - \mathbf{x}$, then the angle between $\delta^{(k)}$ and the line connecting $\mathbf{x}_{-\varepsilon}$ or $\mathbf{x}_\varepsilon$ and $\mathbf{x}^{(k)}$ will be ε/ρ. Extract the tangent component of $\mathbf{q}^{(k)}$ as $\widetilde{\mathbf{q}}^{(k)} := \mathbf{q}^{(k)} - \langle\mathbf{q}^{(k)}, \delta^{(k)}\rangle\delta^{(k)}/\|\delta^{(k)}\|_2^2$, we arrive at the formula for queries on $\mathcal{S}_\rho$:

$$\mathbf{x}_{\pm\varepsilon} = \rho\frac{\left(\mathbf{x}^{(k)} \pm \frac{\widetilde{\mathbf{q}}^{(k)}}{\|\widetilde{\mathbf{q}}^{(k)}\|}\rho\tan\left(\frac{\varepsilon}{\rho}\right)\right)}{\left\|\mathbf{x}^{(k)} \pm \frac{\widetilde{\mathbf{q}}^{(k)}}{\|\widetilde{\mathbf{q}}^{(k)}\|}\rho\tan\left(\frac{\varepsilon}{\rho}\right)\right\|_2}. \tag{12}$$

The key hyperparameter of our algorithm is the query step size ε. Here, we select relatively large ε for better long-range exploration of adversarial examples. Since the generated samples always lie in $\mathcal{B}_\rho$, we can use large query steps without concerning with the image distortion. Note that the iterates quickly approach $\mathcal{S}_\rho$, so we spend all of the efforts, except the first few iterations, searching the adversarial examples on the hypersphere $\mathcal{S}_\rho$. We do not fine-tune ε in our experiments. As seen in the next section, the value of step size ε is fixed for each type of target models (standard or robust) and datasets (ImageNet or CIFAR-10 and MNIST), even though ρ significantly varies.

The Update Rule with Quadratic Interpolation. We discuss how to update the iterate from the loss values at three points $\mathbf{x}^{(k)}, \mathbf{x}_{-\varepsilon}$ and $\mathbf{x}_\varepsilon$ derived from either Eq. (11) or Eq. (12). If one of the queries decreases the loss value, i.e., $\min (L(\mathbf{x}_{-\varepsilon}), L(\mathbf{x}_\varepsilon)) < L(\mathbf{x}^{(k)})$, we accept it as a new state

$$\mathbf{x}^{(k+1)} = \operatorname{argmin}(L(\mathbf{x}_{-\varepsilon}), L(\mathbf{x}_\varepsilon)), \quad (13)$$

and thus make a big step to explore a new region on the hypersphere. When $\min(L(\mathbf{x}_{-\varepsilon}), L(\mathbf{x}_\varepsilon)) \geq L(\mathbf{x}^{(k)})$, the loss function L restricted on the geodesic curve (or straight line if searching within $\mathcal{B}_\rho$) connecting $\mathbf{x}^{(k)}, \mathbf{x}_{-\varepsilon}$ and $\mathbf{x}_\varepsilon$ has a local minimizer. Certainly, it is desirable to identify and use this minimizer for the next iterate. Based on our intuition in the previous section, *the idea is to fit a parabola to the three data points to estimate the loss, and assign the min-*

Algorithm 1: BABIES in Pseudocode

1: **Procedure:** BABIES($\mathbf{x}, \hat{y}, Q, \varepsilon, \rho$)
2: $k = 0$, $\mathbf{x}^{(k)} = \mathbf{x}$, $\mathcal{L} = L(\mathbf{x}^{(k)})$
3: **while** $h(\mathbf{x}^{(k)}) \neq \hat{y}$ **do**
4:     Pick $\mathbf{q}^{(k)} \in Q$ randomly
5:     **if** $\mathbf{x}^{(k)} \notin \mathcal{S}_\rho$ **then**
6:         Sample $\mathbf{x}_{-\varepsilon}$ and $\mathbf{x}_\varepsilon$ using Eq. (11)
7:     **else**
8:         Sample $\mathbf{x}_{-\varepsilon}$ and $\mathbf{x}_\varepsilon$ using Eq. (12)
9:     **end if**
10:    Compute $\mathcal{L} = \min(L(\mathbf{x}_{-\varepsilon}), L(\mathbf{x}_\varepsilon))$
11:    **if** $\mathcal{L} < L(\mathbf{x}^{(k)})$ **then**
12:        Update $\mathbf{x}^{(k+1)}$ using Eq. (13)
13:    **else**
14:        Update $\mathbf{x}^{(k+1)} := \mathbf{x}_\gamma$, with γ given in Eq. (14)
15:        Update $\mathcal{L}$ using interpolation in Eq. (15)
16:    **end if**
17:    $k := k + 1$
18: **end while**
19: **return** $\mathbf{x}^{(k)}$

---

imizer of the parabola to $\mathbf{x}^{(k+1)}$. The geodesic (or standard) distance between this minimizer and $\mathbf{x}^{(k)}$ can be computed as

$$\gamma = \frac{\varepsilon}{2} \frac{L(\mathbf{x}_\varepsilon) - L(\mathbf{x}_{-\varepsilon})}{L(\mathbf{x}_\varepsilon) - 2\,L(\mathbf{x}^{(k)}) + L(\mathbf{x}_{-\varepsilon})}. \quad (14)$$

As a result, $\mathbf{x}^{(k+1)} = \mathbf{x}_\gamma$, where $\mathbf{x}_\gamma$ is defined similarly to $\mathbf{x}_\varepsilon$ in Eq. (12) when searching on $\mathcal{S}_\rho$ or Eq. (11) when searching within $\mathcal{B}_\rho$ with γ replaces ε. It is easy to see that the update is not zero when $L(\mathbf{x}_\varepsilon) \neq L(\mathbf{x}_{-\varepsilon})$. Moreover, we use the interpolated loss value

$$L_{\text{interp}} = L(\mathbf{x}^{(k)}) + \frac{1}{8} \frac{(L(\mathbf{x}_\varepsilon) - L(\mathbf{x}_{-\varepsilon}))^2}{L(\mathbf{x}_\varepsilon) - 2\,L(\mathbf{x}^{(k)} + L(\mathbf{x}_{-\varepsilon})}, \quad (15)$$

to approximate the current best loss value, instead of querying the loss function at $\mathbf{x}^{(k+1)}$. The present strategy continuously updates the iterates with small moves, when the random queries cannot find a new candidate. The effectiveness of this strategy relies on the interpolation accuracy. When generating adversarial examples in the frequency domain, the interpolation error is sufficiently small and able to lead the random search towards the loss descent direction (justified by the parabolic landscape of the adversarial loss).

5   Experimental Evaluation

5.1   Results of BABIES on MNIST, CIFAR-10 and ImageNet

We evaluate BABIES-DCT and compare with established algorithms from the literature: Bandits-TD ℓ_2 attack [19], SimBA-DCT [16] and ℓ_2-Square Attack [3] on the MNIST, CIFAR-10 and ImageNet datasets. We use the default hyperparameters suggested by the authors of the baseline methods. We use the following standard metrics to evaluate the attack performance: the mean number of queries of successful attacks (**Avg. QY**), the median number of query of successful attacks (**Med. QY**) and the success rate (**SR**). Additional evaluations with two other baselines, PPBA [20] and PRGF [12], are provided in the Appendix.

Setup. For MNIST and CIFAR tests, we attack 1,000 correctly labeled images randomly selected from their corresponding testing sets. Evaluation on ImageNet is performed on a set of 1,000 images from the ImageNetV2 [28]. In targeted attack, the target labels are uniformly sampled at random, and the same target labels are used for all methods. The search subspace of BABIES-DCT on ImageNet is set to the first 1/8-th of all frequencies, and includes additional 1/32-th of the next frequencies when all available frequencies are used up without success. Due to the low dimensionality of CIFAR-10 images, we initialize the random search on the first 5/8-th of all frequency, and add an additional 1/8-th

Table 1. The target classifiers and experiment parameters. The first numbers are for *untargeted* attack. Numbers in parentheses are for *targeted* attack. Additional results on sensitivity of BABIES's performance to hyperparameters are included in Appendix.

Classifiers	Dataset	Type	B	ρ	ε
Inception_v3 [32]	ImageNet	Standard	10000 (50000)	5 (12)	2 (3)
ResNet50 [17]	ImageNet	Standard	10000 (50000)	5 (12)	2 (3)
Inception_v3 [32]	CIFAR10	Standard	6144 (6144)	2.4 (4)	2 (2)
VGG13 [31]	CIFAR10	Standard	6144 (6144)	2.4 (4)	2 (2)
ResNet18 [29]	ImageNet	ℓ_2-robust ($\epsilon = 3$)	10000 (50000)	12 (32)	8 (8)
ResNet50 [29]	ImageNet	ℓ_2-robust ($\epsilon = 3$)	10000 (50000)	12 (32)	8 (8)
ResNet50 [13]	CIFAR10	ℓ_2-robust ($\epsilon = 1$)	6144 (6144)	2 (3)	0.5 (0.5)
SmallCNN [35]	MNIST	ℓ_2-robust ($\epsilon = 0.005$)	10000 (10000)	1 (2)	0.5 (0.5)

of the frequencies at a time, if necessary. We use our method and the other base-lines to attack eight pre-trained classifiers (four standard and four ℓ_2-robust). For each attack, we limit the number of queries (B) the attacker can make and the allowable ℓ_2 distortion (ρ). We use different values of ρ since our experiments span various types of datasets and classifiers. In particular, larger ρ is used if the attacks are more challenging (i.e., on ImageNet dataset, robust models and/or targeted attack). We make minimal tuning of the step size ε, just setting it to be a fraction of ρ. Details of the target classifiers and test parameters here are shown in Table 1. Additional results to show the performance of BABIES is not sensitive with ε are presented in the Appendix.

Results on the Standard Models (Tables 2 and 3). The main comparison results evaluated in the attacks on CIFAR-10 images are reported in Table 2. Here, the median queries of BABIES-DCT are significantly lower than those of other baselines in all of the tests, highlighting that for many images, our method can find an adversarial perturbation in the DCT domain with very few queries. We also achieve the best success rates in three out of four cases. On the aver-age query count, BABIES-DCT and Square-attack each lead in two tests. Both being random-search based method, BABIES-DCT samples from a pre-defined sets of DCT directions while Square-attack crafts random perturbations from a more flexible space. For low dimensional images like CIFAR-10, the set of DCT directions are limited, so eventually all directions will be chosen and recycled. The ability of generating more flexible random directions is an advantage for Square-attack in this case.

Table 3 shows the comparison results on ImageNet. Our method has a very strong performance on the targeted attacks, where it outperforms the others in all three metrics and requires much fewer number of queries (39% and 13% less than the next baseline for Inception_v3 and ResNet50 respectively). On untargeted attacks, the results are more comparable, where BABIES-DCT is slightly better than Square-attack in the success rate, and slightly worse in the number of queries of successful attacks. SimBA does not look particularly strong here, but it should be note that SimBA can find adversarial examples with very small distortions in $\mathcal{B}_\rho$, while other methods focus on searching on the hypersphere $\mathcal{S}_\rho$. As such, with the same maximum allowable distortion, SimBA always achieves lowest average distortion on successful attacks.

Table 2. Comparison on attacks against the **standard models** for **CIFAR-10**. BABIES-DCT leads in success rate in 3/4 tests and achieves significantly lower median queries than other baselines in 4/4 tests.

Attack	Inception v3 (untargeted)			Inception v3 (targeted)			VGG13 (untargeted)			VGG13 (targeted)		
	Avg. QY	Med. QY	SR	Avg. QY	Med. QY	SR	Avg. QY	Med. QY	SR	Avg. QY	Med. QY	SR
Bandits	409	46	94.5%	817	314	82.9%	199	46	99.6%	601	252	97.7%
Square-attack	170	41	97.5%	345	91	89.4%	96	28	**99.9%**	130	51	**99.3%**
SimBA-DCT	203	177	65.9%	603	486	46%	184	140	83.2%	492	356	86.9%
BABIES-DCT	329	**17**	**97.9%**	**239**	62	**97.1%**	94	**5**	99.2%	159	47	**99.3%**

Table 3. Comparison on attacks against the **standard models** for **ImageNet**. For targeted attacks, BABIES outperforms other baselines in all three metrics. For untargeted attacks, the performance of tested methods are more comparable.

	Inception v3 (untargeted)			Inception v3 (targeted)			ResNet50 (untargeted)			ResNet50 (targeted)		
Attack	Avg. QY	Med. QY	SR	Avg. QY	Med. QY	SR	Avg. QY	Med. QY	SR	Avg. QY	Med. QY	SR
Bandits	2200	1118	66.6%	21067	19416	77.9%	1238	672	96.6%	4166	3278	**100%**
Square-attack	**1543**	**777**	87.8%	15412	11600	91.3%	**1130**	**563**	97.3%	6189	4840	99.5%
SimBA-DCT	1897	1183	78%	16746	13530	82.5%	1673	1115	94.4%	8075	6126	94.6%
BABIES-DCT	1907	908	**87.9%**	**9429**	**6700**	**99.2%**	1276	742	**98%**	**3670**	**2923**	**100%**

Results on Defended Models (Tables 4 and 5). Here, none of the evaluated attacks can achieve success rates close to 100%, so we will evaluate them based on the success rate before other metrics, because with low success rate, a method can achieve a low number of queries. For MNIST and CIFAR-10 attacks (Table 4), BABIES-DCT has a significant lead in success rate in three out of four tests (14%–27% to the next baseline). The gap between our method and Bandits is close for untargeted SmallCNN attack, but then, our method posts a much lower average and median query counts. For ImageNet attacks (Table 5), BABIES-DCT leads by a large margin in untargeted ResNet18 (18%), targeted ResNet18 (29%) and untargeted ResNet50 (19%) attacks. Our method is close to Bandits in the targeted ResNet50, but again, it requires much fewer queries. We observe that BABIES shows more significant advantages in attacking defended models, which is consistent with the empirical result (in Fig. 3) that the loss landscape of defended models are closer to parabolas than that of the standard models.

Table 4. Comparison on attacks against the ℓ_2 **robust models** for **CIFAR-10** and **MNIST**. None of the attacks achieve success rates close to 100%, so we evaluate methods on success rate before other metrics. BABIES-DCT leads in success rate in 4/4 tests (and over 14% to the next baseline in 3/4 tests).

	ResNet50, eps=1 (untargeted)			ResNet50, eps=1 (targeted)			SmallCNN, eps=0.005 (untargeted)			SmallCNN, eps=0.005 (targeted)		
Attack	Avg. QY	Med. QY	SR	Avg. QY	Med. QY	SR	Avg. QY	Med. QY	SR	Avg. QY	Med. QY	SR
Bandits	2238	1804	45.1%	2992	2919	37.9%	3020	2453	19%	3608	2968	52.5%
Square-attack	1194	**302**	39%	2464	1978	29.9%	1919	**1044**	12.9%	**2310**	**1532**	41.1%
SimBA-DCT	1280	1232	33.1%	2085	1792	23.8%	**1892**	2012	8.9%	2440	2660	16.6%
BABIES-DCT	**1060**	824	**59.5%**	**1489**	**1420**	**63.3%**	1961	1464	**19.6%**	2560	1898	**67.4%**

Table 5. Comparison on attacks against the ℓ_2**-robust models** for **ImageNet**. Success rate is the most important metric. BABIES-DCT leads in success rate by over 18% to the next baseline in 3/4 tests. For targeted ResNet50, our method is close to Bandits in success rate, but it requires 50% less queries.

	ResNet18, eps=3 (untargeted)			ResNet18, eps=3 (targeted)			ResNet50, eps=3 (untargeted)			ResNet50, eps=3 (targeted)		
Attack	Avg. QY	Med. QY	SR	Avg. QY	Med. QY	SR	Avg. QY	Med. QY	SR	Avg. QY	Med. QY	SR
Bandits	2745	1660	54.3%	13728	12905	33.9%	3952	3558	43.6%	16171	13018	82.4%
Square-attack	**1027**	**209**	48.9%	11923	7707	46.5%	**1614**	**758**	33.4%	13025	9092	49.9%
SimBA-DCT	4563	3839	50.7%	18321	18843	42.3%	5554	5160	43.2%	19268	19469	21%
BABIES-DCT	2553	1594	**71.8%**	**8283**	**5700**	**85.8%**	3348	2898	**63.2%**	**8285**	**5684**	**83.8%**

Qualitative Results (Fig. 4). Since the distortion metric is only an approximation of the imperceptibility, we would like to compare how imperceptible the adversarial images are to the human eye. For that purpose, we selected four images from the targeted attack (on Inception_v3) experiment to explain our observations. The clean images and the distorted images are shown in Fig. 4. All adversarial images have approximately same ℓ_2 distortion norm $\|\delta\|_2 \simeq 12$. It is easy to see that different methods lead to different types of distortion. Even though Bandits is less efficient in our experiments, it generates the most imperceptible adversarial images with comparable ℓ_2 norms. The adversarial images from BABIES-DCT and SimBA-DCT (not shown here) exhibit noticeable wave-like distortions for some images, especially when the background color is light. Finally, Square-attack adds more noticeable sharp distortions. The distortion mass is distinctively concentrated in a set of small squares, coded by the design of searching space by this method.

5.2   Results on Attacking Google Cloud Vision

We perform attacks on the Google Cloud Vision API, which is a powerful image analysis tool capable to identify the dominant entities/objects in images. For an input image, the API provides a list of top concepts appearing in the image, together with their probabilities. We consider an untargeted attack that aims to remove the top 3 objects in the original images. We define the adversarial loss as the maximum of the probabilities of original top 3 concepts, similar to [16,20], and minimize this loss with BABIES, until an adversarial example is found. We allow maximum 2000 queries for each image and a maximum distortion $\rho = 12.0$ in ℓ_2 norm. Our attack on 50 images randomly selected from ImageNetV2 shows that BABIES achieves an 82% success rate with 205 average queries on successful attacks. In Fig. 5, we show some example images before and after the attack. We observe that the leading concepts in the original images, related to food, laundry, camel and insect, are completely removed in the adversarial images and replaced by

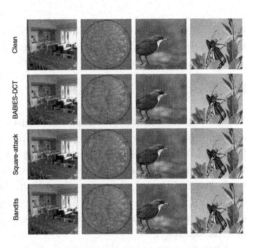

Fig. 4. Qualitative comparison of the imperceptibility of distortion. The distorted images are selected from the targeted attack (on Inception_v3) experiment and have approximately same distortion norm $\|\delta\|_2 \simeq 12$. Bandits generates perturbations with a grainy look and can blend with the background. The wave-like distortions from BABIES-DCT are noticeable for some images. Square attack generates in general more noticeable distortions compared with the other methods.

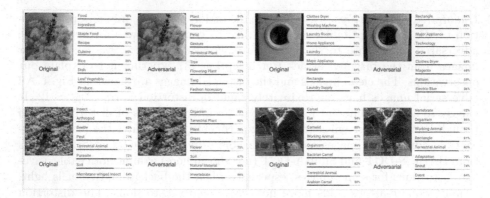

Fig. 5. Example images in our BABIES attack on the Google Cloud Vision API to remove top 3 labels. Labels related to the main objects of original images (clockwise from top left: food, laundry, camel, insect) are completely removed and replaced by less important or incorrect labels.

less important or incorrect labels. This test demonstrates that our method is highly effective against real world systems.

6   Discussion and Conclusion

We propose to exploit the parabolic landscape of the adversarial loss with respect to DCT perturbation to improve the query efficiency of random search methods for black-box adversarial attack. Using a simple quadratic interpolation strategy, we demonstrate that the loss smoothness can greatly improve query efficiency without additional query per iteration. Our algorithm solve a constraint optimization problem on ℓ_2 sphere. Thus we propose to use large query step for better exploration of the search space. Our evaluation shows a remarkable advantage of this strategy.

Our theoretical and empirical study on the landscape of the adversarial loss provides a new angle to investigate the vulnerability of an image classifier. From this perspective, the theoretical insight on the loss landscape may be even more valuable to the community than the BABIES algorithm. For example, an intriguing observation from theoretical study and our experiment is that the relative performance of BABIES-DCT (in comparison to other baselines) is strongest in attacking ℓ_2-robust models. One possible reason is that the loss landscapes of the defended models are closer to parabolas, which provides a favorable setting for our method. While defended classifiers have been studied extensively recently, ℓ_∞ models have got more attention and less is known about ℓ_2 models. Understanding the properties and possible weakness of ℓ_2 models is an interesting problem we plan to study next. Despite the superior performance, our method has several limitations. First, our method is designed for ℓ_2 attack, which may not outperform the state-of-the-art methods in ℓ_∞ attack. Second, since the perturbation is made in the Fourier domain, the perturbation is combination of cosine functions which is easier to be distinguished by naked eyes than pixel perturbations, even though the ℓ_2 norm satisfies the constraint.

There are several possible directions to pursue in the future research. One is to investigate the loss smoothness in other spaces, e.g., replacing DCT with wavelet transform. In fact, the idea of Square Attack makes Haar wavelet transform a good candidate to study. An advantage of using wavelet transform is that wavelet is only supported locally, which means perturbing a wavelet mode will result in a smaller distortion than perturbing a globally supported cosine basis. Another area for improvement is to perturb multiple DCT modes within each iteration for more efficient exploration. We leave these directions for future work.

Acknowledgments. This work was supported by the U.S. Department of Energy, Office of Science, Office of Advanced Scientific Computing Research, Applied Mathematics program; and by the Artificial Intelligence Initiative at the Oak Ridge National Laboratory (ORNL). ORNL is operated by UT-Battelle, LLC., for the U.S. DOE under Contract DE-AC05-00OR22725.

References

1. Al-Dujaili, A., O'Reilly, U.: Sign bits are all you need for black-box attacks. In: 8th International Conference on Learning Representations, ICLR 2020, Addis Ababa, Ethiopia, 26–30 April 2020. OpenReview.net (2020). https://openreview.net/forum?id=SygW0TEFwH
2. Alzantot, M., Sharma, Y., Chakraborty, S., Zhang, H., Hsieh, C.J., Srivastava, M.: Genattack: practical black-box attacks with gradient-free optimization (2019)
3. Andriushchenko, M., Croce, F., Flammarion, N., Hein, M.: Square attack: a query-efficient black-box adversarial attack via random search (2020)
4. Bhagoji, A.N., He, W., Li, B., Song, D.: Practical black-box attacks on deep neural networks using efficient query mechanisms. In: Proceedings of the European Conference on Computer Vision (ECCV), September 2018
5. Brendel, W., Rauber, J., Bethge, M.: Decision-based adversarial attacks: reliable attacks against black-box machine learning models. In: 6th International Conference on Learning Representations, ICLR 2018, Vancouver, BC, Canada, 30 April–3 2018 May, Conference Track Proceedings. OpenReview.net (2018). https://openreview.net/forum?id=SyZI0GWCZ
6. Brunner, T., Diehl, F., Truong-Le, M., Knoll, A.C.: Guessing smart: biased sampling for efficient black-box adversarial attacks. In: 2019 IEEE/CVF International Conference on Computer Vision, ICCV 2019, Seoul, Korea (South), 27 October–2 November 2019, pp. 4957–4965. IEEE (2019). https://doi.org/10.1109/ICCV.2019.00506
7. Carlini, N., Wagner, D.: Towards evaluating the robustness of neural networks. In: 2017 IEEE Symposium on Security and Privacy (SP), pp. 39–57 (2017)
8. Chen, J., Zhou, D., Yi, J., Gu, Q.: A frank-wolfe framework for efficient and effective adversarial attacks. In: The Thirty-Fourth AAAI Conference on Artificial Intelligence, AAAI 2020, The Thirty-Second Innovative Applications of Artificial

Intelligence Conference, IAAI 2020, The Tenth AAAI Symposium on Educational Advances in Artificial Intelligence, EAAI 2020, New York, NY, USA, 7–12 February 2020, pp. 3486–3494. AAAI Press (2020). http://aaai.org/ojs/index.php/AAAI/article/view/5753

9. Chen, P.Y., Zhang, H., Sharma, Y., Yi, J., Hsieh, C.J.: Zoo: zeroth order optimization based black-box attacks to deep neural networks without training substitute models. In: Proceedings of the 10th ACM Workshop on Artificial Intelligence and Security, AISec 2017, pp. 15–26. Association for Computing Machinery, New York (2017). https://doi.org/10.1145/3128572.3140448

10. Cheng, M., Le, T., Chen, P., Zhang, H., Yi, J., Hsieh, C.: Query-efficient hard-label black-box attack: an optimization-based approach. In: 7th International Conference on Learning Representations, ICLR 2019, New Orleans, LA, USA, 6–9 May 2019. OpenReview.net (2019). https://openreview.net/forum?id=rJlk6iRqKX

11. Dolatabadi, H.M., Erfani, S.M., Leckie, C.: Advflow: inconspicuous black-box adversarial attacks using normalizing flows. In: Larochelle, H., Ranzato, M., Hadsell, R., Balcan, M., Lin, H. (eds.) Advances in Neural Information Processing Systems 33: Annual Conference on Neural Information Processing Systems 2020, NeurIPS 2020, 6–12 December 2020, virtual (2020). https://proceedings.neurips.cc//paper/2020/hash/b6cf334c22c8f4ce8eb920bb7b512ed0-Abstract.html

12. Dong, Y., Cheng, S., Pang, T., Su, H., Zhu, J.: Query-efficient black-box adversarial attacks guided by a transfer-based prior. IEEE Trans. Pattern Anal. Mach. Intell. (2021). https://doi.org/10.1109/TPAMI.2021.3126733

13. Engstrom, L., Ilyas, A., Salman, H., Santurkar, S., Tsipras, D.: Robustness (python library) (2019). https://github.com/MadryLab/robustness

14. Goodfellow, I.J., Shlens, J., Szegedy, C.: Explaining and harnessing adversarial examples. CoRR abs/1412.6572 (2015)

15. Guo, C., Frank, J.S., Weinberger, K.Q.: Low frequency adversarial perturbation. In: Globerson, A., Silva, R. (eds.) Proceedings of the Thirty-Fifth Conference on Uncertainty in Artificial Intelligence, UAI 2019, Tel Aviv, Israel, 22–25 July 2019. Proceedings of Machine Learning Research, vol. 115, pp. 1127–1137. AUAI Press (2019). http://proceedings.mlr.press/v115/guo20a.html

16. Guo, C., Gardner, J.R., You, Y., Wilson, A.G., Weinberger, K.Q.: Simple black-box adversarial attacks. In: Chaudhuri, K., Salakhutdinov, R. (eds.) Proceedings of the 36th International Conference on Machine Learning, ICML 2019, 9–15 June 2019, Long Beach, California, USA. Proceedings of Machine Learning Research, vol. 97, pp. 2484–2493. PMLR (2019). http://proceedings.mlr.press/v97/guo19a.html

17. He, K., Zhang, X., Ren, S., Sun, J.: Deep residual learning for image recognition. In: 2016 IEEE Conference on Computer Vision and Pattern Recognition (CVPR), pp. 770–778 (2016)

18. Ilyas, A., Engstrom, L., Athalye, A., Lin, J.: Black-box adversarial attacks with limited queries and information. In: Dy, J., Krause, A. (eds.) Proceedings of the 35th International Conference on Machine Learning. Proceedings of Machine Learning Research, Stockholmsmässan, Stockholm Sweden, 10–15 July 2018, vol. 80, pp. 2137–2146. PMLR (2018). http://proceedings.mlr.press/v80/ilyas18a.html

19. Ilyas, A., Engstrom, L., Madry, A.: Prior convictions: black-box adversarial attacks with bandits and priors. In: 7th International Conference on Learning Representations, ICLR 2019, New Orleans, LA, USA, 6–9 May 2019. OpenReview.net (2019). https://openreview.net/forum?id=BkMiWhR5K7

20. Li, J., et al.: Projection and probability-driven black-box attack. In: Proceedings of the IEEE Conference on Computer Vision and Pattern Recognition (CVPR) (2020)
21. Li, Q., Guo, Y., Chen, H.: Practical no-box adversarial attacks against DNNs. In: Larochelle, H., Ranzato, M., Hadsell, R., Balcan, M., Lin, H. (eds.) Advances in Neural Information Processing Systems 33: Annual Conference on Neural Information Processing Systems 2020, NeurIPS 2020, 6–12 December 2020, virtual (2020). https://proceedings.neurips.cc/paper/2020/hash/96e07156db854ca7b00b5df21716b0c6-Abstract.html
22. Li, Y., Li, L., Wang, L., Zhang, T., Gong, B.: NATTACK: learning the distributions of adversarial examples for an improved black-box attack on deep neural networks. In: Chaudhuri, K., Salakhutdinov, R. (eds.) Proceedings of the 36th International Conference on Machine Learning, ICML 2019, 9–15 June 2019, Long Beach, California, USA. Proceedings of Machine Learning Research, vol. 97, pp. 3866–3876. PMLR (2019). http://proceedings.mlr.press/v97/li19g.html
23. Madry, A., Makelov, A., Schmidt, L., Tsipras, D., Vladu, A.: Towards deep learning models resistant to adversarial attacks. arXiv abs/1706.06083 (2018)
24. Moon, S., An, G., Song, H.O.: Parsimonious black-box adversarial attacks via efficient combinatorial optimization. In: Chaudhuri, K., Salakhutdinov, R. (eds.) Proceedings of the 36th International Conference on Machine Learning, ICML 2019, 9–15 June 2019, Long Beach, California, USA. Proceedings of Machine Learning Research, vol. 97, pp. 4636–4645. PMLR (2019). http://proceedings.mlr.press/v97/moon19a.html
25. Narodytska, N., Kasiviswanathan, S.: Simple black-box adversarial attacks on deep neural networks. In: 2017 IEEE Conference on Computer Vision and Pattern Recognition Workshops (CVPRW), pp. 1310–1318 (2017). https://doi.org/10.1109/CVPRW.2017.172
26. Papernot, N., McDaniel, P., Goodfellow, I.J.: Transferability in machine learning: from phenomena to black-box attacks using adversarial samples. arXiv abs/1605.07277 (2016)
27. Papernot, N., McDaniel, P., Goodfellow, I., Jha, S., Celik, Z.B., Swami, A.: Practical black-box attacks against machine learning. In: Proceedings of the 2017 ACM on Asia Conference on Computer and Communications Security, ASIA CCS 2017, pp. 506–519. Association for Computing Machinery, New York (2017). https://doi.org/10.1145/3052973.3053009
28. Recht, B., Roelofs, R., Schmidt, L., Shankar, V.: Do ImageNet classifiers generalize to ImageNet? In: Chaudhuri, K., Salakhutdinov, R. (eds.) Proceedings of the 36th International Conference on Machine Learning. Proceedings of Machine Learning Research, 09–15 June 2019, vol. 97, pp. 5389–5400. PMLR (2019)
29. Salman, H., Ilyas, A., Engstrom, L., Kapoor, A., Madry, A.: Do adversarially robust imagenet models transfer better? arXiv preprint arXiv:2007.08489 (2020)
30. Sharma, Y., Ding, G.W., Brubaker, M.: On the Effectiveness of Low Frequency Perturbations. arXiv e-prints arXiv:1903.00073, February 2019
31. Simonyan, K., Zisserman, A.: Very deep convolutional networks for large-scale image recognition. In: Bengio, Y., LeCun, Y. (eds.) 3rd International Conference on Learning Representations, ICLR 2015, San Diego, CA, USA, 7–9 May 2015, Conference Track Proceedings (2015). arxiv.org/abs/1409.1556
32. Szegedy, C., Vanhoucke, V., Ioffe, S., Shlens, J., Wojna, Z.: Rethinking the inception architecture for computer vision. In: 2016 IEEE Conference on Computer Vision and Pattern Recognition (CVPR), pp. 2818–2826 (2016)

33. Szegedy, C., et al.: Intriguing properties of neural networks. In: International Conference on Learning Representations (2014). arxiv.org/abs/1312.6199
34. Tu, C.C., et al.: Autozoom: autoencoder-based zeroth order optimization method for attacking black-box neural networks. In: AAAI (2019)
35. Zhang, H., Yu, Y., Jiao, J., Xing, E.P., Ghaoui, L.E., Jordan, M.I.: Theoretically principled trade-off between robustness and accuracy. In: International Conference on Machine Learning (2019)

Generative Domain Adaptation for Face Anti-Spoofing

Qianyu Zhou[1], Ke-Yue Zhang[2], Taiping Yao[2], Ran Yi[1],
Kekai Sheng[2], Shouhong Ding[2(✉)], and Lizhuang Ma[1(✉)]

[1] Shanghai Jiao Tong University, Shanghai, China
{zhouqianyu,ranyi}@sjtu.edu.cn, ma-lz@cs.sjtu.edu.cn
[2] Youtu Lab, Tencent, Shanghai, China
{zkyezhang,taipingyao,saulsheng,ericshding}@tencent.com

Abstract. Face anti-spoofing (FAS) approaches based on unsupervised domain adaption (UDA) have drawn growing attention due to promising performances for target scenarios. Most existing UDA FAS methods typically fit the trained models to the target domain via aligning the distribution of semantic high-level features. However, insufficient supervision of unlabeled target domains and neglect of low-level feature alignment degrade the performances of existing methods. To address these issues, we propose a novel perspective of UDA FAS that directly fits the target data to the models, *i.e.*, stylizes the target data to the source-domain style via image translation, and further feeds the stylized data into the well-trained source model for classification. The proposed Generative Domain Adaptation (GDA) framework combines two carefully designed consistency constraints: 1) Inter-domain neural statistic consistency guides the generator in narrowing the inter-domain gap. 2) Dual-level semantic consistency ensures the semantic quality of stylized images. Besides, we propose intra-domain spectrum mixup to further expand target data distributions to ensure generalization and reduce the intra-domain gap. Extensive experiments and visualizations demonstrate the effectiveness of our method against the state-of-the-art methods.

Keywords: Face anti-spoofing · Unsupervised domain adaptation

1 Introduction

Face recognition (FR) techniques [12,35,45,71,80,114] have been widely utilized in identity authentication products, *e.g.,* smartphones login, access control, *etc.*. Despite its gratifying progress in recent years, FR systems are vulnerable to face presentation attacks (PA), *e.g.,* printed photos, video replay, and *etc.*. To protect such FR systems from various face presentation attacks, face anti-spoofing (FAS) attracts great attention. Nowadays, based on hand-crafted

---

Q. Zhou and K.-Y. Zhang—Equal contributions.
Q. Zhou—Work done during an internship at Youtu Lab, Tencent.

ⓒ The Author(s), under exclusive license to Springer Nature Switzerland AG 2022
S. Avidan et al. (Eds.): ECCV 2022, LNCS 13665, pp. 335–356, 2022.
https://doi.org/10.1007/978-3-031-20065-6_20

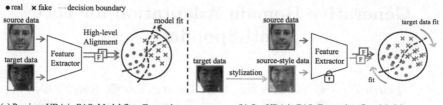

(a) Previous UDA in FAS: Model fit to Target data   (b) Our UDA in FAS: Target data fit to Model

Fig. 1. Conventional UDA FAS methods typically force the model fit to the target data via performing the high-level feature alignment across domains. However, insufficient supervisions and neglect of low-level feature alignment inevitably affect the discrimination ability of FAS models. Instead, we aim to directly fit the target data to the source-trained models in a reverse manner via both the high-level and low-level alignment. By generating source-style images and predicting with a well-trained model, we address these issues without changing models

features [2,16,37,55,88], and deeply-learned features [13,44,47,61,97,101,102], several methods achieve promising performance in intra-dataset scenarios. However, they all suffer from performance degradation when adapting to the target domains in real-world scenarios due to the domain gap across different domains.

To improve the generalization, FAS approaches based on domain generalization (DG) and unsupervised domain adaption (UDA) have been proposed on cross-domain scenarios. However, DG FAS approaches [9,31,48,49,68,69,111] only utilize the seen data in the training stage, which fail in utilizing the information of the target data, thus resulting in unsatisfactory performance on the target domain. Although UDA FAS methods [32,40,66,72,76,77,107] utilize both the labeled source domain and the unlabeled target domain to bridge the domain gap, most of them typically fit the models to the target domain via aligning the distribution of semantic high-level features, as shown in Fig. 1(a), without considering the specificity of FAS task. On the one hand, since the insufficient supervision of the target domain, fitting to it may inevitably affect the discrimination ability of the source model. On the other hand, as pointed out in [34], low-level features are especially vital to the FAS task. Thus, the above towards-target distribution alignment based on only high-level features may not be the most suitable way for UDA FAS.

To address the above issues, we propose a novel perspective of unsupervised domain adaptation (UDA) for face anti-spoofing (FAS). Different from existing methods that fit the models to the target data, we aim to directly fit the target data to the well-trained models, keeping the source-trained models unchanged, as shown in Fig. 1(b). To achieve such fitting, we reformulate the unsupervised domain adaptation (UDA) in FAS as a domain stylization problem to stylize the target data with the source-domain style, and the stylized data is further fed into the well-trained source model for classification. In this work, we propose Generative Domain Adaptation (GDA) framework combining two carefully designed consistency constraints. Specifically, we present inter-domain neural statistic consistency (NSC) to guide the generator toward producing the source-style images, which fully aligns the target feature statistics with the source ones in both high-levels and low-levels, and narrows the inter-domain gap efficiently. Besides, to maintain the semantic qualities and liveness information of the target data during the stylization procedure, we introduce a dual-level semantic consistency (DSC) on both image level and feature level. Moreover, intra-domain spectrum mixup (SpecMix) is presented to further expand the target data distribution to ensure that the generator could correctly translate the unseen target domain to the source-style domain. To the best of our knowledge, this is the first work that reveals the potential of image translation for UDA FAS.

Our main contributions can be summarized as follows:

- We propose a novel perspective of unsupervised domain adaptation for face anti-spoofing that directly fits the target data to the source model by stylizing the target data with the source-domain style via image translation.
- To ensure the stylization, we present a Generative Domain Adaptation framework combined with two carefully designed consistency constraints, inter-domain neural statistic consistency (NSC) and dual-level semantic consistency (DSC). And intra-domain spectrum mixup (SpecMix) is presented to further expand the target data distribution to ensure generalization.
- Extensive experiments and visualizations demonstrate the effectiveness of our proposed method against the state-of-the-art competitors.

2   Related Work

Face Anti-Spoofing. Face anti-spoofing (FAS) aims to detect a face image whether taken from a real person or various face presentation attacks [4,7,8,10]. Pioneer works utilize handcrafted features to tackle this problem, such as SIFT [62], LBP [2,16,55], and HOG [37,88]. Several methods utilize the information from different domains, such as HSV and YCrCb color spaces [2,3], temporal domains [1,70], and Fourier spectrum [43]. Recent approaches leverage CNN to model FAS with binary classification [13,44,61,100] or additional supervision, e.g., depth map [97], reflection map [101] and r-ppg signal [27,47]. Other methods adopt disentanglement [52,102] and custom operators [6,96,98] to improve the performance. Despite good outcomes in the intra-dataset setting, their performances still drop significantly on target domains due to large domain shifts.

Cross-Domain Face Anti-Spoofing. To improve the performances under the cross-domain settings, domain generalization (DG) [39,41,57,106] is introduced into FAS tasks. Nevertheless, DG FAS methods [9,31,48,49,68,69,111] aim to map the samples into a common feature space and lack the specific information of the unseen domains, inevitably resulting in unsatisfactory results. Considering the availability of the unlabeled target data in real-world applications, several works tackle the above issue based on unsupervised domain adaptation (UDA) methods. Recent studies of UDA FAS mainly rely on pseudo labeling [54,66], adversarial learning [32,40,76,77] or minimizing domain discrepancy [32,40] to narrow the domain shifts. However, they still suffer from insufficient supervision of the unlabeled target domains, which may cause the negative transfer to the source models. Besides, most works mainly focus on the alignment of high-level semantic features, overlooking the low-level features which are essential to the FAS tasks. In contrast, we aim to address these two issues for UDA FAS.

Unsupervised Domain Adaptation. Unsupervised domain adaptation (UDA) aims to bridge the domain shifts between the labeled source domain and unlabeled target domain. Recent methods focus on adversarial learning [17,56, 63,73], self-training [14,84,115,116], consistency regularization [11,108,109,112], prototypical alignment [33,85,103], feature disentanglement [5,82,110] and image translation [20,21,24–26,30,53,93,94,105]. Despite its gratifying progress, such "model-fitting-to data" paradigm is not practical for FAS task due to plenty of different domains in real-world scenarios. Besides, the discrimination ability of the source model may also be affected during re-training. In contrast, we propose a new yet practical approach that adapts the target data to the source model, keeping the source model unchanged. To the best of our knowledge, this is the first work that reveals the potential of image translation for UDA FAS.

3   Methodology

3.1   Overview

In UDA FAS, we have access to the labeled source domain, denoted as $D_s = \{(x_s, y_s) \mid x_s \subset \mathbb{R}^{H \times W \times 3}, y_s \in [0, 1]\}$, and the unlabeled target domain, denoted as $D_t = \{(x_t) \mid x_t \subset \mathbb{R}^{H \times W \times 3}\}$. Regarding that insufficient supervision and neglect of low-level feature alignment in previous UDA FAS approaches lead to inferior performances, we are motivated to perform both the high-level and low-level feature alignment and make the target data fit to the model in a reverse manner. Our training include two stages: the first phase using the source domains only for training the FAS models, including a feature extractor F, a classifier H, a depth estimator R; the second phase for domain adaptation. During the latter phase, only the image generator G is optimized, and other source models with an ImageNet pre-trained VGG module ϕ are fixed during the adaptation.

Figure 2 shows the overall GDA framework. We aim to stylize the unlabeled target domain to the source-style domain, making the unlabeled target data fit to the source models, so that the well-trained models do not need to be changed. To mitigate the intra-domain gap, input images are firstly diversified in continuous frequency space via intra-domain spectrum mixup (SpecMix) to produce augmented images. Then, the generator translates both the original and the diversified target images into the source-style images. To extract the source style information to guide the image translation, we match the generated statistics of the source-style images with those stored source statistics in the pre-trained

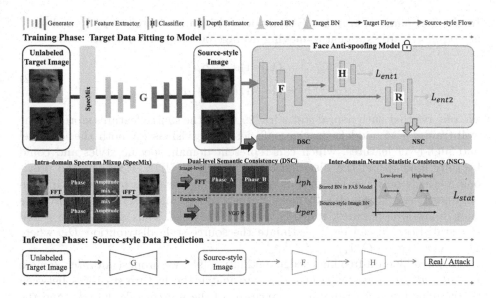

Fig. 2. Overview of Generative Domain Adaptation framework. The parameters of the source-trained models are fixed during adaptation. Given the unlabeled target data, we only optimize the parameters of the generator G. Firstly, we generate diversified target images via *intra-domain spectrum mixup* (SpecMix), thus enhancing the generalization abilities of the generator G in bridging the intra-domain gap. Then, *inter-domain neural statistic consistency* (NSC) fully matches generated feature statistics with the stored ones in high level and low levels, thus mitigating the inter-domain gap. Thus, the translated images can retain the source style. Furthermore, we introduce *dual-level semantic consistency* (DSC) to ensure content-preserving and prevent form semantic distortions

model via inter-domain neural statistic consistency (NSC), thus bridging the inter-domain gap. Finally, to preserve the target content and prevent semantic distortions during the generation, we propose a dual-level semantic consistency (DSC) on both the feature level and image level.

3.2   Generative Domain Adaptation

Inter-domain Neural Statistic Consistency. Batch normalization (BN) [29] normalizes each input feature within a mini-batch in a channel-wise manner so that the output has zero-mean and unit-variance. Let B and $\{z_i\}_{i=1}^{B}$ denote the mini-batch size and the input features to the batch normalization, respectively. The key to the BN layer is to compute the batch-wise statistics, *e.g.*, means μ and variances σ^2 of the features within the mini-batch:

$$\mu \leftarrow \frac{1}{B} \sum_{i=1}^{B} x_i, \ \sigma^2 \leftarrow \frac{1}{B} \sum_{i=1}^{B} (x_i - \mu)^2, \tag{1}$$

In the first phase of training FAS models, the source statistics $\bar{\mu}_s^{n+1}$ and $\bar{\sigma}_s^{n+1}$ at step $n+1$ are exponential moving average of that at step n with a ratio α:

$$\bar{\mu}_s^{n+1} = (1 - \alpha)\bar{\mu}_s^n + \alpha\mu_s^n$$
$$\left(\bar{\sigma}_s^{n+1}\right)^2 = (1 - \alpha)\left(\bar{\sigma}_s^n\right)^2 + \alpha\left(\sigma_s^n\right)^2 \tag{2}$$

We observe that such neural statistics [29,67] of the source features stored in the well-trained FAS models provide sufficient supervisions for both the low-level and high-level features, which can represent domain-specific styles and could be fully used to aid the distribution alignment in UDA. However, the previous methods only use the output features of high-level layers for distribution alignment, and are unable to make full use of rich and discriminative liveness cues in low-level features, which is vital to FAS tasks. Thus, given those stored BN statistics, we can easily estimate the source-style distribution $D_{\tilde{s}}$, where $D_{\tilde{s}} = \left\{(x_{\tilde{s}}) \mid x_{\tilde{s}} = G(x_t) \subset \mathbb{R}^{H \times W \times 3}\right\}$.

Inspired by data-free knowledge distillation [95], we propose an *inter-domain neural statistic consistency loss* $\mathcal{L}_{\text{stat}}$ to match the feature statistics between the running mean $\bar{\mu}_{\tilde{s}}$, running variances $\bar{\sigma}_{\tilde{s}}$ of the source-style data $D_{\tilde{s}}$ and the stored statistics $\bar{\mu}_s$, $\bar{\sigma}_s$ of source models M, thus bridging the inter-domain gap:

$$\mathcal{L}_{\text{stat}} = \frac{1}{L}\sum_{l=1}^{L}\left\{\left\|\bar{\mu}_{\tilde{s}}^l - \bar{\mu}_s{}^l\right\|_2 + \left\|\bar{\sigma}_{\tilde{s}}^l - \bar{\sigma}_s^l\right\|_2\right\} \tag{3}$$

where $l \in \{1, 2, ..., L\}$ denotes the layer l in the source-trained models, including the feature extractor F, classifier H, and depth estimator R. Guided by loss $\mathcal{L}_{\text{stat}}$, we could approximate the source-style domain that has the similar style as the source domain. Different from [95] that generates image contents from an input random noise, our NSC uses BN statistics alignment as one constraint to stylize the input images without changing contents.

Dual-Level Semantic Consistency. To preserve the semantic contents during the image translation, we propose a *dual-level semantic consistency* on both feature level and image level to constrain the contents.

On the feature level, given the generated source-style image $x_{\tilde{s}}$ and the original target image x_t as inputs, a perceptual loss $\mathcal{L}_{\text{per}}$ is imposed onto the latent features of the ImageNet pre-trained VGG module ϕ, thus narrowing the perceptual differences between them:

$$\mathcal{L}_{\text{per}}^{\phi}(x_{\tilde{s}}, x_s) = \frac{1}{CHW}\|\phi(x_{\tilde{s}}) - \phi(x_t)\|_2^2 \tag{4}$$

However, merely using this perceptual loss in the spatial space is not powerful enough to ensure semantic consistency. This is mainly because the latent features are deeply-encoded, and some important semantic cues may be lost. Many previous works [19,22,36,60,64,93,94] suggest that the Fourier transformations from one domain to another only affect the amplitude, but not the phase of their spectrum, where the phase component retains most of the contents in the original signals, while the amplitude component mainly contains styles. And inspired by [93], we consider explicitly penalizing the semantic inconsistency by ensuring the phase is retained before and after the image translation. For a single-channel image x, its Fourier transformation $\mathcal{F}(x)$ is formulated:

$$\mathcal{F}(x)(u,v) = \sum_{h=0}^{H-1} \sum_{w=0}^{W-1} x(h,w) e^{-j2\pi \left(\frac{h}{H}u + \frac{w}{W}v \right)} \tag{5}$$

As such, we enforce phase consistency between the original target image x_t and the source-style image $x_{\tilde{s}}$ by minimizing the following loss $\mathcal{L}_{ph}$:

$$\mathcal{L}_{ph}(x_{\tilde{s}}, x_t) = -\sum_j \frac{\langle \mathcal{F}(x_t)_j, \mathcal{F}(x_{\tilde{s}})_j \rangle}{\|\mathcal{F}(x_t)_j\|_2 \cdot \|\mathcal{F}(x_{\tilde{s}})_j\|_2} \tag{6}$$

where $\langle , \rangle$ is the dot-product, and $\| \cdot \|_2$ is the L_2 norm. Note that Eq. (6) is the negative cosine distance between the original phases and the generated phases. Therefore, by minimizing $\mathcal{L}_{ph}$, we can directly minimize their image-level differences on the Fourier spectrum and keep the phase consistency.

Intra-domain Spectrum Mixup. Given the unlabeled target data, we observe that the generator cannot perform well due to the lack of consideration of intra-domain domain shifts across different target subsets. If training only on the seen training subsets of the target domain and testing on the unseen testing subsets of the target domain, image qualities of the source-style domain could be less-desired. As such, we wish to a learn more robust generator G under varying environmental changes, *e.g.*, illumination, color.

Since previous findings [19,22,36,60,64,86,93,94] reveal that phase tends to preserve most contents in the Fourier spectrum of signals, while the amplitude mainly contains domain-specific styles, we propose to generate diversified images that retain contents but with new styles in the continuous frequency space. Through the FFT algorithm [59], we can efficiently compute the Fourier transformation $\mathcal{F}(x_t)$ and its inverse transformation $\mathcal{F}^{-1}(x_t)$ of the target image $x_t \in D_t$ via Eq. 5. The amplitude and phase components are formulated as:

$$\mathcal{A}(x_t)(u,v) = \left[R^2(x_t)(u,v) + I^2(x_t)(u,v) \right]^{1/2}$$
$$\mathcal{P}(x_t)(u,v) = \arctan \left[\frac{I(x_t)(u,v)}{R(x_t)(u,v)} \right], \tag{7}$$

where $R(x_t)$ and $I(x_t)$ denote the real and imaginary part of $\mathcal{F}(x_t)$, respectively. For RGB images, the Fourier transformation for each channel is computed independently to get the corresponding amplitude and phase components.

Inspired from [86,99], we introduce *intra-domain spectrum mixup* (SpecMix) by linearly interpolating between the amplitude spectrums of two arbitrary images x_t^k, $x_t^{k'}$ from the same unlabeled target domain D_t:

$$\hat{\mathcal{A}}(x_t^k) = (1 - \lambda)\mathcal{A}(x_t^k) + \lambda\mathcal{A}(x_t^{k'}), \tag{8}$$

where $\lambda \sim U(0, \eta)$, and the hyper-parameter η controls the strength of the augmentation. The mixed amplitude spectrum is then combined with the original phase spectrum to reconstruct a new Fourier representation:

$$\mathcal{F}(\hat{x}_t^k)(u, v) = \hat{\mathcal{A}}(x_t^k)(u, v) * e^{-j*\mathcal{P}(x_t^k)(u,v)}, \tag{9}$$

which is then fed to inverse Fourier transformation to generate the interpolated image: $\hat{x}_t^k = \mathcal{F}^{-1}[\mathcal{F}(\hat{x}_t^k)(u, v)]$.

This proposed *intra-domain spectrum mixup* is illustrated in Fig. 2. By conducting the aforementioned steps, we could generate unseen target samples with new style and the original content in continuous frequency space. Thus, by feeding forward those diversified images to the generator G, the generalization abilities across different subsets within the target domain could be further enhanced.

3.3 Overall Objective and Optimization

Entropy loss. Minimizing the Shannon entropy of the label probability distribution has been proved to be effective in normal UDA task [58,65,74,75,83]. In this paper, we compute entropy loss via the classifier and depth estimator, respectively. The total entropy loss are penelized with $\mathcal{L}_{ent} = \mathcal{L}_{ent1} + \mathcal{L}_{ent2}$.

$$\mathcal{L}_{ent1} = \sum_{c=1}^{C} -\langle p_c(x_{\tilde{s}}) \cdot \log(p_c(x_{\tilde{s}})) \rangle$$

$$\mathcal{L}_{ent2} = \sum_{c=1}^{C} \sum_{h=1}^{H} \sum_{w=1}^{W} -\langle r_c(x_{\tilde{s}})(h, w) \cdot \log(r_c(x_{\tilde{s}}(h, w))) \rangle \tag{10}$$

Total Loss. During the adaptation procedure, the parameters of the source model F, H R, and the VGG module ϕ are fixed, and we only optimize the parameters of the generator G. The total loss L_{total} is the weighted sum of the aforementioned loss functions:

$$\mathcal{L}_{total} = \mathcal{L}_{stat} + \mathcal{L}_{per} + \lambda_{ent}\mathcal{L}_{ent} + \lambda_{ph}\mathcal{L}_{ph}, \tag{11}$$

where λ_{ent}, λ_{ph}, are the weighting coefficients for the loss $\mathcal{L}_{ent}$, $\mathcal{L}_{ph}$ respectively.

4   Experiments

In this section, we first describe the experimental setup in Sect. 4.1, including the benchmark datasets and the implementation details. Then, in Sect. 4.2, we demonstrate the effectiveness of our proposed method compared to the state-of-the-art approaches and related works on multi-source scenarios and single-source scenarios. Next, in Sect. 4.3, we conduct ablation studies to investigate the role of each component in the method. Finally, we provide more visualization and analysis in Sect. 4.4 to reveal the insights of the proposed method.

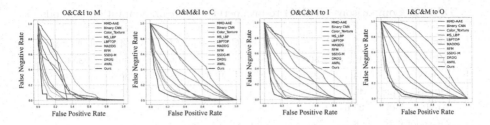

Fig. 3. ROC curves compared to the state-of-the-art FAS approaches

Table 1. Comparisons to the-state-of-art FAS methods on four testing domains

Methods	O&C&I to M		O&M&I to C		O&C&M to I		I&C&M to O	
	HTER(%)	AUC(%)	HTER(%)	AUC(%)	HTER(%)	AUC(%)	HTER(%)	AUC(%)
IDA [81]	66.6	27.8	55.1	39.0	28.3	78.2	54.2	44.6
LBPTOP [15]	36.9	70.8	42.6	61.5	49.5	49.5	53.1	44.0
MS_LBP [55]	29.7	78.5	54.2	44.9	50.3	51.6	50.2	49.3
ColorTexture [3]	28.0	78.4	30.5	76.8	40.4	62.7	63.5	32.7
Binary CNN [87]	29.2	82.8	34.8	71.9	34.4	65.8	29.6	77.5
Auxiliary (ALL) [51]	-	-	28.4	-	27.6	-	-	-
Auxiliary (Depth) [51]	22.7	85.8	33.5	73.1	29.1	71.6	30.1	77.6
MMD-AAE [42]	27.0	83.1	44.5	58.2	31.5	75.1	40.9	63.0
MADDG [68]	17.6	88.0	24.5	84.5	22.1	84.9	27.9	80.0
RFM [69]	13.8	93.9	20.2	88.1	17.3	90.4	16.4	91.1
SSDG-M [31]	16.7	90.5	23.1	85.5	18.2	94.6	25.2	81.8
DRDG [49]	12.4	95.8	19.1	88.8	15.6	91.8	15.6	91.8
ANRL [48]	10.8	96.8	17.9	89.3	16.0	91.0	15.7	91.9
SDA-FAS [78]	15.4	91.8	24.5	84.4	15.6	90.1	23.1	84.3
DIPE-FAS [15]	18.2	-	25.5	-	20.0	-	17.5	-
VLAD-VSA [79]	11.4	96.4	20.8	86.3	12.3	93.0	21.2	86.9
Ours	**9.2**	**98.0**	**12.2**	**93.0**	**10.0**	**96.0**	**14.4**	**92.6**

4.1   Experimental Setup

Datasets. We use four public datasets that are widely-used in FAS research to evaluate the effectiveness of our method: OULU-NPU [4] (denoted as O), CASIA-MFSD [104] (denoted as C), Idiap Replay-Attack [10] (denoted as I), and MSU-MFSD [81] (denoted as M). Strictly following the same protocols as previous UDA FAS methods [32,54,77–79], we use source domains to train the source model, the training set of the target domain for adaptation, and the testing set of the target domain for inference. Half Total Error Rate (HTER) and Area Under Curve (AUC) are used as the evaluation metrics [68].

Implementation Details. Our method is implemented via PyTorch on $24G$ NVIDIA 3090Ti GPU. We use the same backbone as existing works [48,49]. Note that we do not use any domain generalization techniques but just a binary classification loss and a depth loss during the first stage. We extract RGB channels of images, thus the input size is $256 \times 256 \times 3$. In the second stage, the

Table 2. Comparisons (HTER) to unsupervised domain adaptation methods

Method	C ⟶ I	C ⟶ M	I ⟶ C	I ⟶ M	M ⟶ C	M ⟶ I	Average
ADDA [73]	41.8	36.6	49.8	35.1	39.0	35.2	39.6
DRCN [18]	44.4	27.6	48.9	42.0	28.9	36.8	38.1
Dup-GAN [28]	42.4	33.4	46.5	36.2	27.1	35.4	36.8
Auxliary [50]	27.6	–	28.4	–	–	–	–
De-spoof [34]	28.5	–	41.1	–	–	–	–
STASN [92]	31.5	–	30.9	–	–	–	–
Yang et al. [89]	49.2	18.1	39.6	36.7	49.6	49.6	40.5
KSA [40]	39.2	14.3	**26.3**	33.2	**10.1**	33.3	26.1
ADA [76]	17.5	9.3	41.6	30.5	17.7	5.1	20.3
DIPE-FAS [54]	18.9	–	30.1	–	–	–	–
DR-UDA [77]	15.6	9.0	34.2	29.0	16.8	3.0	17.9
USDAN-Un [32]	16.0	9.2	30.2	25.8	13.3	3.4	16.3
Ours	**15.1**	**5.8**	29.7	**20.8**	12.2	**2.5**	**14.4**

Table 3. Comparison to the source-free domain adaptation methods

Methods	O&C&I to M		O&M&I to C		O&C&M to I		I&C&M to O	
	HTER(%)	AUC(%)	HTER(%)	AUC(%)	HTER(%)	AUC(%)	HTER(%)	AUC(%)
AdaBN [38]	20.5	88.0	34.5	72.0	27.7	80.3	28.2	80.8
TENT [75]	20.1	88.0	35.0	71.2	27.2	79.6	28.3	80.7
SDAN [23]	17.7	90.0	25.9	81.3	28.2	84.2	32.9	75.0
SHOT [46]	15.0	87.6	20.1	84.3	40.2	57.8	25.3	78.2
G-SFDA [90]	37.5	67.8	38.9	67.2	32.6	73.6	40.4	63.7
NRC [91]	15.0	87.4	47.8	52.4	22.1	82.3	26.6	78.8
DIPE-FAS [54]	18.2	-	25.5	-	20.0	-	17.5	-
SDA-FAS [78]	15.4	91.8	24.5	84.4	16.4	92.0	23.1	84.3
Ours	**9.2**	**98.0**	**12.2**	**93.0**	**10.0**	**96.0**	**14.4**	**92.6**

coefficients λ_{ph} and λ_{ent} are set to 0.01 and 0.01 respectively. The generator G [113] is trained with the Adam optimizer with a learning rate of 1e-4.

4.2   Comparisons to the State-of-the-Art Methods

To validate the generalization capability towards the target domain on the FAS task, we perform two experimental settings of UDA FAS, *i.e.,* multi-source domain adaptation and single-source domain adaptation, respectively.

Comparisons to FAS Methods in Multi-source Adaptation. As shown in Table 1 and Fig. 3, our method outperforms all the state-of-the-art FAS methods under four challenging benchmarks, which demonstrates the effectiveness of our method. Conventional FAS approaches [3,15,51,55,81,87] do not consider learning the domain-invariant representations across domains and show less-desired performances. Besides, almost all DG FAS methods [31,42,48,49,68,69] lack a

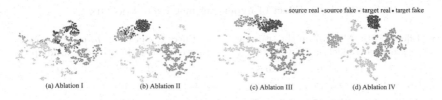

source real ▪source fake ▪ target real▪ target fake

(a) Ablation I   (b) Ablation II   (c) Ablation III   (d) Ablation IV

Fig. 4. The t-SNE visualization of features in different ablation studies

Table 4. Ablation of each component on four benchmarks

ID	Baseline	NSC	DSC	SpecMix	O&C&I to M		O&M&I to C		O&C&M to I		I&C&M to O	
					HTER	AUC	HTER	AUC	HTER	AUC	HTER	AUC
I	✓	-	-	-	29.2	77.8	32.7	76.4	19.4	85.8	27.1	80.9
II	✓	✓	-	-	20.0	89.0	28.7	79.7	17.3	88.4	21.1	84.9
III	✓	✓	✓	-	14.1	92.0	14.4	90.8	13.8	91.5	16.5	90.7
IV	✓	✓	✓	✓	**9.2**	**98.0**	**12.2**	**93.0**	**10.0**	**96.0**	**14.4**	**92.6**

clear target direction for generalization, resulting in unsatisfactory performance in the target domain. Our method outperforms all the DG approaches by significant improvements in both HTER and AUC. A few DA approaches [15,78,79] conduct the experiments under this multi-source setting, while they all directly fit the model to the target domain with insufficient supervision and neglect the low-level features for adaptation, leading to undesirable outcomes. In contrast, our method is superior to them by a large margin in four challenging benchmarks.

Comparisons to FAS Methods in Single-Source Adaptation. To make a fair comparison to the normal UDA approaches in the FAS task, we also conduct experiments in single-source scenarios, where source models are pre-trained on the single-source domain. From Table 2, it is obvious to find that our proposed approach shows superiority under four of the six adaptation settings and achieves the best average HTER results. In some hard adaptation tasks, e.g., I → C, and M → C, we can achieve the competitive results to the state-of-the-art methods. Interestingly, we find that some results in Table 2 are superior to results of Table 1. We guess the reason is that when training on multi-source domains, the style distribution is complicated, and it is hard to train a stable generator G, leading to inferior performances. Instead, training on only one source domain with simple style distribution is easier to obtain a better generator G.

Comparison to the Related SFDA Methods. Table 3 presents the comparison results with source-free domain adaptation (SFDA) approaches in four multi-source scenarios. As we can see, if we directly adapt the state-of-the-art SFDA approaches to the FAS task, the performances are less-desired. For example, some unsupervised/self-supervised techniques utilize pseudo labeling [54], neighborhood clustering [90,91], entropy minimization [46,75] and meta-learning [78] to reduce the domain gap between the source pre-trained model and the unlabeled

Table 5. Effect of hyper-parameter η of SpecMix

(a) Effect of SpecMix (η) on the training of our proposed model on O&C&I to M

η	0	0.1	0.2	0.3	0.4	0.5
HTER	14.1	9.2	10.0	10.0	10.0	10.0
AUC	92.0	98.0	97.9	97.8	97.3	97.2

(b) Effect of SpecMix (η) on the inference of a well-trained FAS model on Idiap (I)

η	0	0.1	0.2	0.3	0.4	0.5
HTER	0	0	0	0	0	0.4
AUC	100	100	100	100	100	99.9

target domain. The main reasons are two-fold. 1) Almost all of them do not fully utilize the source domain knowledge stored in the pre-trained model, which is not sufficient for feature alignment. 2) They largely neglect the intra-domain gap in the target domain itself, and do not consider learning a more robust domain-invariant representation under varying environmental changes within the target. In contrast, we address these two issues in an explicit manner, and show outstanding improvements on these challenging benchmarks.

4.3 Ablation Studies

In this section, we perform ablation experiments to investigate the effectiveness of each component, including inter-domain neural statistic consistency (NSC), intra-domain spectrum mixup (SpecMix), dual-level semantic consistency (DSC).

Effectiveness of Each Component. Table 4 shows the ablation studies of each component in four different settings. The baseline means directly feeding forward the target image to the source-trained FAS model for prediction, and the results are with 77.8%, 76.4%, 85.8%, 80.9% AUC, respectively on O&C&I to M, O&M&I to C, O&C&M to I, and I&C&M to O, setting. By adding NSC, we boost the AUC performances to 89.0%, 79.7%, 88.4%, and 84.9%, respectively. Moreover, by adding DSC, we effectively achieve 92.0%, 90.8%, 91.5%, and 90.7%, respectively. Finally, our proposed SpecMix effectively increases the performance to 98.0%, 93.0%, 96.0%, 92.6% on four benchmarks, respectively. These improvements reveal the effectiveness and the complementarities of individual components of our proposed approach.

The t-SNE Visualization of Features. To understand how GDA framework aligns the feature representations, we utilize t-SNE to visualize the feature distributions of both the source and target datasets. As shown in Fig. 4(a), we observe that the source data can be well discriminated by binary classification, however, the target data can not be well-classified between the real and fake faces without domain adaptation. From Fig. 4(b), by adding NSC, the classification boundary becomes more clear but there are still some samples misclassified near the decision boundary, the main reason is that it lacks the constraints on the image contents during the generation. As such, by further adding DSC in Fig. 4(c), the above issue is alleviated to some extent. By bridging both the inter-domain gap

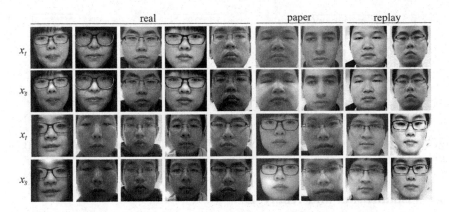

Fig. 5. Visualization of the target image x_t and the source-style image $x_{\tilde{s}}$

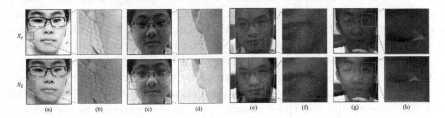

Fig. 6. Spoof details in the target images x_t and source-style images $x_{\tilde{s}}$

and intra-domain gap in Fig. 4(d), our approach manages to learn a better decision boundary between these two categories, and meanwhile, our target features between different domains become more compact to align.

Discussions on SpecMix. Regarding that SpecMix could generate new styles in continuous frequency space, it it natural to ask several questions: *Will SpecMix change the category during the adaptation? Will mixing amplitude information affect the face liveness?* We conduct several experiments to answer the questions. Note that we use a hyper-parameter η to control the strength of augmentation in our SpecMix. Higher η leads to a larger upper bound ratio to mix another image's amplitude from the same batch with that of the current image. (1). In Table 5(a), we investigate the effect of η on the training of our proposed GDA framework. During the adaptation, we find that if we set $\eta = 0$, which means the intra-domain gaps are neglected, the performance is not perfect. If ranging η from 0.1 to 0.5, the performance changes are very slight compared to the best one when setting $\eta = 0.1$, but still achieves the state-of-the-art results. (2). As shown in Table 5(b), we study the sensitivity of η during the inference of a well-trained FAS model on Idiap Replay-Attack dataset. If ranging η from 0.1 to 0.4, there are no performance changes, and when $\eta = 0.5$, the effect is still slight. From these two aspects, we set $\eta = 0.1$ in all experiments, and under such cases, we argue that mixing the amplitude will not affect the face liveness.

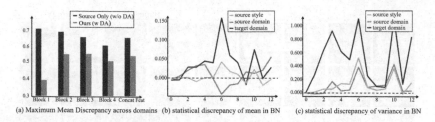

Fig. 7. Visualization of domain discrepancy (MMD and BN variance) of features (Color figure online)

4.4 Visualization and Analysis

Visualizations of Generated Images with Source Styles. To further explore whether the generator succeeds or not in stylizing the target images x_t to a generated images $x_{\bar{s}}$ that preserves the target content with the source style, we visualize the adapted knowledge in the setting of I&C&M to O. As shown in Fig. 5, with the help of our proposed NSC, no matter what kind of faces they are, real faces or fake faces, the style differences between the source domain and the target domain are successfully captured by the generator, which illustrates the effectiveness of our proposed NSC. Besides, as shown in Fig. 6, the semantic consistency, especially the spoof details, *e.g.,* moire patterns, paper reflection, are well-maintained between the original target images and the pseudo source images, which demonstrates the effectiveness of our proposed DSC.

Visualizations of Cross-Domain Discrepancy. As shown in Fig. 7(a), we measure the maximum mean discrepancy (MMD) across domains. Source Only denotes directly forwarding the testing image to the source model without any domain adaptation techniques. Compared to Source Only, our model effectively reduce the MMD in both the shallow blocks and deep blocks, especially in the shallow blocks, which confirms that our framework successfully translate the target images to the source-style images. In Fig. 7(b), we visualize the curve of mean discrepancy and variance discrepancy of each BN layer. As we can see, if directly feeding the target images to the source model in the test phase, the variation of the mean in BN between the source and the target (the red curve) is much larger than our method with domain adaptation methods (yellow curve). Our approach effectively prevents such feature misalignment. Besides, from Fig. 7(c), we observe that the variation of variance in BN by feeding the source image to the source model (blue curve) is similar to that with our GDA (yellow curve), which means that our BN statistics effectively align with the source ones.

5 Conclusion

In this work, we reformulate UDA FAS as a domain stylization problem, aiming to fit the target data onto the well-trained models without changing the models. We propose Generative Domain Adaptation (GDA) framework with several carefully designed components. Firstly, we present an inter-domain neural statistic consistency (NSC) to guide the generator generating the source-style domain. Then, we introduce a dual-level semantic consistency (DSC) to prevent the generation from semantic distortions. Finally, we design an intra-domain spectrum mixup (SpecMix) to reduce the intra-domain gaps. Extensive experiments with analysis demonstrate the effectiveness of our proposed approach.

Acknowledgment. This work is supported by National Key Research and Development Program of China (2019YFC1521104), National Natural Science Foundation of China (72192821, 61972157), Shanghai Municipal Science and Technology Major Project (2021SHZDZX0102), Shanghai Science and Technology Commission (21511101200, 22YF1420300), and Art major project of National Social Science Fund (I8ZD22).

References

1. Bao, W., Li, H., Li, N., Jiang, W.: A liveness detection method for face recognition based on optical flow field. In: International Conference on Image Analysis and Signal Processing, pp. 233–236. IEEE (2009)
2. Boulkenafet, Z., Komulainen, J., Hadid, A.: Face anti-spoofing based on color texture analysis. In: IEEE International Conference on Image Processing (ICIP), pp. 2636–2640. IEEE (2015)
3. Boulkenafet, Z., Komulainen, J., Hadid, A.: Face spoofing detection using colour texture analysis. IEEE Trans. Inf. Forensics Secur. (TIFS) **11**(8), 1818–1830 (2016)
4. Boulkenafet, Z., Komulainen, J., Li, L., Feng, X., Hadid, A.: Oulu-NPU: a mobile face presentation attack database with real-world variations. In: 12th IEEE International Conference on Automatic Face & Gesture Recognition (FG 2017), pp. 612–618. IEEE (2017)
5. Chang, W.L., Wang, H.P., Peng, W.H., Chiu, W.C.: All about structure: adapting structural information across domains for boosting semantic segmentation. In: Proceedings of the IEEE/CVF Conference on Computer Vision and Pattern Recognition (CVPR), pp. 1900–1909 (2019)
6. Chen, S., et al.: A dual-stream framework for 3D mask face presentation attack detection. In: Proceedings of the IEEE/CVF International Conference on Computer Vision (ICCV), pp. 834–841 (2021)
7. Chen, Z., Li, B., Wu, S., Xu, J., Ding, S., Zhang, W.: Shape matters: deformable patch attack. In: European Conference on Computer Vision (ECCV) (2022)
8. Chen, Z., Li, B., Xu, J., Wu, S., Ding, S., Zhang, W.: Towards practical certifiable patch defense with vision transformer. In: Proceedings of the IEEE/CVF Conference on Computer Vision and Pattern Recognition (CVPR), pp. 15148–15158 (2022)
9. Chen, Z., et al.: Generalizable representation learning for mixture domain face anti-spoofing. In: Proceedings of the AAAI Conference on Artificial Intelligence (AAAI), vol. 35, pp. 1132–1139 (2021)
10. Chingovska, I., Anjos, A., Marcel, S.: On the effectiveness of local binary patterns in face anti-spoofing. In: International Conference of Biometrics Special Interest Group, pp. 1–7. IEEE (2012)

11. Choi, J., Kim, T., Kim, C.: Self-ensembling with GAN-based data augmentation for domain adaptation in semantic segmentation. In: Proceedings of the IEEE/CVF International Conference on Computer Vision (ICCV), pp. 6830–6840 (2019)

12. Deng, J., Guo, J., Xue, N., Zafeiriou, S.: Arcface: additive angular margin loss for deep face recognition. In: Proceedings of the IEEE/CVF Conference on Computer Vision and Pattern Recognition (CVPR), pp. 4690–4699 (2019)

13. Feng, L., et al.: Integration of image quality and motion cues for face anti-spoofing: a neural network approach. J. Vis. Communi. Image Represent. (JVCIR) **38**, 451–460 (2016)

14. Feng, Z., et al.: DMT: dynamic mutual training for semi-supervised learning. Pattern Recognit. (PR) 108777 (2022)

15. Freitas Pereira, T., et al.: Face liveness detection using dynamic texture. EURASIP J. Image Video Process. **2014**(1), 1–15 (2014). https://doi.org/10.1186/1687-5281-2014-2

16. de Freitas Pereira, T., Anjos, A., De Martino, J.M., Marcel, S.: *LBP − TOP* based countermeasure against face spoofing attacks. In: Park, J.-I., Kim, J. (eds.) ACCV 2012. LNCS, vol. 7728, pp. 121–132. Springer, Heidelberg (2013). https://doi.org/10.1007/978-3-642-37410-4_11

17. Ganin, Y., Lempitsky, V.: Unsupervised domain adaptation by backpropagation. In: International Conference on Machine Learning (ICML), pp. 1180–1189. PMLR (2015)

18. Ghifary, M., Kleijn, W.B., Zhang, M., Balduzzi, D., Li, W.: Deep reconstruction-classification networks for unsupervised domain adaptation. In: Leibe, B., Matas, J., Sebe, N., Welling, M. (eds.) ECCV 2016. LNCS, vol. 9908, pp. 597–613. Springer, Cham (2016). https://doi.org/10.1007/978-3-319-46493-0_36

19. Grandvalet, Y., Bengio, Y.: Semi-supervised learning by entropy minimization. In: Proceedings of Advances in Neural Information Processing Systems (NeurIPS) (2005)

20. Gu, Q., et al.: PIT: position-invariant transform for cross-FoV domain adaptation. In: Proceedings of the IEEE/CVF International Conference on Computer Vision (ICCV), pp. 8761–8770 (2021)

21. Guo, S., et al.: Label-free regional consistency for image-to-image translation. In: IEEE International Conference on Multimedia and Expo (ICME), pp. 1–6. IEEE (2021)

22. Hansen, B.C., Hess, R.F.: Structural sparseness and spatial phase alignment in natural scenes. JOSA A **24**(7), 1873–1885 (2007)

23. He, Y., Carass, A., Zuo, L., Dewey, B.E., Prince, J.L.: Self domain adapted network. In: International Conference on Medical Image Computing and Computer-Assisted Intervention (MICCAI) (2020)

24. Hoffman, J., et al.: Cycada: cycle-consistent adversarial domain adaptation. In: International Conference on Machine Learning (ICML), pp. 1989–1998. PMLR (2018)

25. Hou, Y., Zheng, L.: Source free domain adaptation with image translation. arXiv preprint arXiv:2008.07514 (2020)

26. Hou, Y., Zheng, L.: Visualizing adapted knowledge in domain transfer. In: Proceedings of the IEEE/CVF Conference on Computer Vision and Pattern Recognition (CVPR), pp. 13824–13833 (2021)

27. Hu, C., et al.: An end-to-end efficient framework for remote physiological signal sensing. In: Proceedings of the IEEE/CVF International Conference on Computer Vision (ICCV), pp. 2378–2384 (2021)

28. Hu, L., Kan, M., Shan, S., Chen, X.: Duplex generative adversarial network for unsupervised domain adaptation. In: Proceedings of the IEEE Conference on Computer Vision and Pattern Recognition (CVPR), pp. 1498–1507 (2018)
29. Ioffe, S., Szegedy, C.: Batch normalization: accelerating deep network training by reducing internal covariate shift. In: International Conference on Machine Learning (ICML), pp. 448–456 (2015)
30. Isobe, T., et al.: Multi-target domain adaptation with collaborative consistency learning. In: Proceedings of the IEEE/CVF Conference on Computer Vision and Pattern Recognition (CVPR), pp. 8187–8196 (2021)
31. Jia, Y., Zhang, J., Shan, S., Chen, X.: Single-side domain generalization for face anti-spoofing. In: Proceedings of the IEEE Conference on Computer Vision and Pattern Recognition (CVPR) (2020)
32. Jia, Y., Zhang, J., Shan, S., Chen, X.: Unified unsupervised and semi-supervised domain adaptation network for cross-scenario face anti-spoofing. Pattern Recognit. (PR) **115**, 107888 (2021)
33. Jiang, Z., et al.: Prototypical contrast adaptation for domain adaptive segmentation. In: European Conference on Computer Vision (ECCV) (2022)
34. Jourabloo, A., Liu, Y., Liu, X.: Face de-spoofing: anti-spoofing via noise modeling. In: Proceedings of the European Conference on Computer Vision (ECCV), pp. 290–306 (2018)
35. Kemelmacher-Shlizerman, I., Seitz, S.M., Miller, D., Brossard, E.: The megaface benchmark: 1 million faces for recognition at scale. In: Proceedings of the IEEE Conference on Computer Vision and Pattern Recognition (CVPR), pp. 4873–4882 (2016)
36. Kermisch, D.: Image reconstruction from phase information only. JOSA **60**(1), 15–17 (1970)
37. Komulainen, J., Hadid, A., Pietikäinen, M.: Context based face anti-spoofing. In: 2013 IEEE Sixth International Conference on Biometrics: Theory, Applications and Systems (BTAS), pp. 1–8. IEEE (2013)
38. Li, Y., Wang, N., Shi, J., Hou, X., Liu, J.: Adaptive batch normalization for oractical domain adaptation. Pattern Recognit. (PR) **80**, 109–117 (2018)
39. Li, D., Yang, Y., Song, Y.Z., Hospedales, T.: Learning to generalize: meta-learning for domain generalization. In: Proceedings of the AAAI Conference on Artificial Intelligence (AAAI), vol. 32 (2018)
40. Li, H., Li, W., Cao, H., Wang, S., Huang, F., Kot, A.C.: Unsupervised domain adaptation for face anti-spoofing. IEEE Trans. Inf. Forensics Secur. (TIFS) **13**(7), 1794–1809 (2018)
41. Li, H., Pan, S.J., Wang, S., Kot, A.C.: Domain generalization with adversarial feature learning. In: Proceedings of the IEEE Conference on Computer Vision and Pattern Recognition (CVPR), pp. 5400–5409 (2018)
42. Li, H., Pan, S.J., Wang, S., Kot, A.C.: Domain generalization with adversarial feature learning. In: Proceedings of the IEEE Conference on Computer Vision and Pattern Recognition (CVPR), pp. 5400–5409 (2018)
43. Li, J., Wang, Y., Tan, T., Jain, A.K.: Live face detection based on the analysis of fourier spectra. In: Biometric Technology for Human Identification, vol. 5404, pp. 296–303. SPIE (2004)
44. Li, L., Feng, X., Boulkenafet, Z., Xia, Z., Li, M., Hadid, A.: An original face anti-spoofing approach using partial convolutional neural network. In: International Conference on Image Processing Theory, Tools and Applications (IPTA) (2016)

45. Li, S., Xu, J., Xu, X., Shen, P., Li, S., Hooi, B.: Spherical confidence learning for face recognition. In: Proceedings of the IEEE/CVF Conference on Computer Vision and Pattern Recognition (CVPR), pp. 15629–15637 (2021)

46. Liang, J., Hu, D., Feng, J.: Do we really need to access the source data? Source hypothesis transfer for unsupervised domain adaptation. In: International Conference on Machine Learning (ICML), pp. 6028–6039. PMLR (2020)

47. Lin, B., Li, X., Yu, Z., Zhao, G.: Face liveness detection by RPPG features and contextual patch-based CNN. In: International Conference on Biometric Engineering and Applications (ICBEA) (2019)

48. Liu, S., et al.: Adaptive normalized representation learning for generalizable face anti-spoofing, pp. 1469–1477 (2021)

49. Liu, S., et al.: Dual reweighting domain generalization for face presentation attack detection. In: International Joint Conference on Artificial Intelligence (IJCAI) (2021)

50. Liu, S., Lan, X., Yuen, P.C.: Remote photoplethysmography correspondence feature for 3D mask face presentation attack detection. In: Proceedings of the European Conference on Computer Vision (ECCV) (2018)

51. Liu, Y., Jourabloo, A., Liu, X.: Learning deep models for face anti-spoofing: binary or auxiliary supervision. In: Proceedings of the IEEE Conference on Computer Vision and Pattern Recognition (CVPR), pp. 389–398 (2018)

52. Liu, Y., Stehouwer, J., Liu, X.: On disentangling spoof trace for generic face anti-spoofing. In: Vedaldi, A., Bischof, H., Brox, T., Frahm, J.-M. (eds.) ECCV 2020. LNCS, vol. 12363, pp. 406–422. Springer, Cham (2020). https://doi.org/10.1007/978-3-030-58523-5_24

53. Liu, Y., Zhang, W., Wang, J.: Source-free domain adaptation for semantic segmentation. In: Proceedings of the IEEE/CVF Conference on Computer Vision and Pattern Recognition (CVPR), pp. 1215–1224 (2021)

54. Lv, L., et al.: Combining dynamic image and prediction ensemble for cross-domain face anti-spoofing. In: IEEE International Conference on Acoustics, Speech and Signal Processing (ICASSP), pp. 2550–2554 (2021)

55. Maatta, J., Hadid, A., Pietikainen, M.: Face spoofing detection from single images using micro-texture analysis. In: Proceedings of the IEEE International Joint Conference on Biometrics (IJCB) (2011)

56. Meng, R., et al.: Slimmable domain adaptation. In: Proceedings of the IEEE/CVF Conference on Computer Vision and Pattern Recognition (CVPR), pp. 7141–7150 (2022)

57. Meng, R., et al.: Attention diversification for domain generalization. In: European Conference on Computer Vision (ECCV) (2022)

58. Morerio, P., Cavazza, J., Murino, V.: Minimal-entropy correlation alignment for unsupervised deep domain adaptation. arXiv preprint arXiv:1711.10288 (2017)

59. Nussbaumer, H.J.: The fast fourier transform. In: Nussbaumer, H.J. (ed.) Fast Fourier Transform and Convolution Algorithms, pp. 80–111. Springer, Heidelberg (1981). https://doi.org/10.1007/978-3-662-00551-4_4

60. Oppenheim, A.V., Lim, J.S.: The importance of phase in signals. Proc. IEEE **69**(5), 529–541 (1981)

61. Patel, K., Han, H., Jain, A.K.: Cross-database face antispoofing with robust feature representation. In: You, Z., et al. (eds.) CCBR 2016. LNCS, vol. 9967, pp. 611–619. Springer, Cham (2016). https://doi.org/10.1007/978-3-319-46654-5_67

62. Patel, K., Han, H., Jain, A.K.: Secure face unlock: spoof detection on smartphones. IEEE Trans. Inf. Forensics Secur. (TIFS) **11**(10), 2268–2283 (2016)

63. Pei, Z., Cao, Z., Long, M., Wang, J.: Multi-adversarial domain adaptation. In: Thirty-Second AAAI Conference on Artificial Intelligence (AAAI) (2018)
64. Piotrowski, L.N., Campbell, F.W.: A demonstration of the visual importance and flexibility of spatial-frequency amplitude and phase. Perception 11(3), 337–346 (1982)
65. Prabhu, V., Khare, S., Kartik, D., Hoffman, J.: Sentry: selective entropy optimization via committee consistency for unsupervised domain adaptation. In: Proceedings of the IEEE/CVF International Conference on Computer Vision (ICCV), pp. 8558–8567 (2021)
66. Quan, R., Wu, Y., Yu, X., Yang, Y.: Progressive transfer learning for face anti-spoofing. IEEE Trans. Image Process. (TIP) 30, 3946–3955 (2021)
67. Santurkar, S., Tsipras, D., Ilyas, A., Madry, A.: How does batch normalization help optimization? In: Advances in Neural Information Processing Systems, vol. 31 (2018)
68. Shao, R., Lan, X., Li, J., Yuen, P.C.: Multi-adversarial discriminative deep domain generalization for face presentation attack detection. In: Proceedings of the IEEE Conference on Computer Vision and Pattern Recognition (CVPR) (2019)
69. Shao, R., Lan, X., Yuen, P.C.: Regularized fine-grained meta face anti-spoofing. In: Proceedings of the AAAI Conference on Artificial Intelligence (AAAI) (2020)
70. Siddiqui, T.A., et al.: Face anti-spoofing with multifeature videolet aggregation. In: 2016 23rd International Conference on Pattern Recognition (ICPR), pp. 1035–1040. IEEE (2016)
71. Taigman, Y., Yang, M., Ranzato, M., Wolf, L.: Deepface: closing the gap to human-level performance in face verification. In: Proceedings of the IEEE Conference on Computer Vision and Pattern Recognition (CVPR), pp. 1701–1708 (2014)
72. Tu, X., Zhang, H., Xie, M., Luo, Y., Zhang, Y., Ma, Z.: Deep transfer across domains for face antispoofing. J. Electron. Imaging 28(4), 043001 (2019)
73. Tzeng, E., Hoffman, J., Saenko, K., Darrell, T.: Adversarial discriminative domain adaptation. In: Proceedings of the IEEE Conference on Computer Vision and Pattern Recognition (CVPR), pp. 7167–7176 (2017)
74. Vu, T.H., Jain, H., Bucher, M., Cord, M., Pérez, P.: Advent: adversarial entropy minimization for domain adaptation in semantic segmentation. In: Proceedings of the IEEE/CVF Conference on Computer Vision and Pattern Recognition (CVPR), pp. 2517–2526 (2019)
75. Wang, D., Shelhamer, E., Liu, S., Olshausen, B., Darrell, T.: Fully test-time adaptation by entropy minimization. In: International Conference on Learning Representations (ICLR) (2021)
76. Wang, G., Han, H., Shan, S., Chen, X.: Improving cross-database face presentation attack detection via adversarial domain adaptation. In: Proceedings of the IEEE International Conference on Biometrics (ICB) (2019)
77. Wang, G., Han, H., Shan, S., Chen, X.: Unsupervised adversarial domain adaptation for cross-domain face presentation attack detection. IEEE Trans. Inf. Forensics Secur. (TIFS) 16, 56–69 (2021)
78. Wang, J., Zhang, J., Bian, Y., Cai, Y., Wang, C., Pu, S.: Self-domain adaptation for face anti-spoofing. In: Proceedings of the AAAI Conference on Artificial Intelligence (AAAI), vol. 35, pp. 2746–2754 (2021)
79. Wang, J., et al.: VLAD-VSA: cross-domain face presentation attack detection with vocabulary separation and adaptation. In: Proceedings of the 29th ACM International Conference on Multimedia (ACM MM), pp. 1497–1506 (2021)

80. Wang, J., Liu, Y., Hu, Y., Shi, H., Mei, T.: Facex-zoo: a pytorch toolbox for face recognition. In: Proceedings of the 29th ACM International Conference on Multimedia (ACM MM), pp. 3779–3782 (2021)

81. Wen, D., Han, H., Jain, A.K.: Face spoof detection with image distortion analysis. IEEE Trans. Inf. Forensics Secur. (TIFS) 10(4), 746–761 (2015)

82. Wu, A., Han, Y., Zhu, L., Yang, Y.: Instance-invariant domain adaptive object detection via progressive disentanglement. IEEE Trans. Pattern Anal. Mach. Intell. (TPAMI) (2021). https://doi.org/10.1109/TPAMI.2021.3060446

83. Wu, X., Zhang, S., Zhou, Q., Yang, Z., Zhao, C., Latecki, L.J.: Entropy minimization versus diversity maximization for domain adaptation. IEEE Trans. Neural Netw. Learn. Syst. (TNNLS) (2021)

84. Xu, H., et al.: Semi-supervised 3D object detection via adaptive pseudo-labeling. In: 2021 IEEE International Conference on Image Processing (ICIP), pp. 3183–3187. IEEE (2021)

85. Xu, M., Wang, H., Ni, B., Tian, Q., Zhang, W.: Cross-domain detection via graph-induced prototype alignment. In: Proceedings of the IEEE/CVF Conference on Computer Vision and Pattern Recognition (CVPR), pp. 12355–12364 (2020)

86. Xu, Q., Zhang, R., Zhang, Y., Wang, Y., Tian, Q.: A fourier-based framework for domain generalization. In: Proceedings of the IEEE/CVF Conference on Computer Vision and Pattern Recognition (CVPR), pp. 14383–14392 (2021)

87. Yang, J., Lei, Z., Li, S.Z.: Learn convolutional neural network for face anti-spoofing. arXiv preprint arXiv:1408.5601 (2014)

88. Yang, J., Lei, Z., Liao, S., Li, S.Z.: Face liveness detection with component dependent descriptor. In: 2013 International Conference on Biometrics (ICB), pp. 1–6. IEEE (2013)

89. Yang, J., Lei, Z., Yi, D., Li, S.Z.: Person-specific face antispoofing with subject domain adaptation. IEEE Trans. Inf. Forensics Secur. (TIFS) 10(4), 797–809 (2015)

90. Yang, S., Wang, Y., van de Weijer, J., Herranz, L., Jui, S.: Generalized source-free domain adaptation. In: Proceedings of the IEEE/CVF International Conference on Computer Vision (ICCV), pp. 8978–8987 (2021)

91. Yang, S., van de Weijer, J., Herranz, L., Jui, S., et al.: Exploiting the intrinsic neighborhood structure for source-free domain adaptation. In: Advances in Neural Information Processing Systems (NeurIPS), vol. 34, pp. 29393–29405 (2021)

92. Yang, X., et al.: Face anti-spoofing: model matters, so does data. In: Proceedings of the IEEE/CVF Conference on Computer Vision and Pattern Recognition (CVPR), pp. 3507–3516 (2019)

93. Yang, Y., Lao, D., Sundaramoorthi, G., Soatto, S.: Phase consistent ecological domain adaptation. In: Proceedings of the IEEE/CVF Conference on Computer Vision and Pattern Recognition (CVPR), pp. 9011–9020 (2020)

94. Yang, Y., Soatto, S.: FDA: fourier domain adaptation for semantic segmentation. In: Proceedings of the IEEE/CVF Conference on Computer Vision and Pattern Recognition (CVPR), pp. 4085–4095 (2020)

95. Yin, H., et al.: Dreaming to distill: data-free knowledge transfer via deepinversion. In: Proceedings of the IEEE/CVF Conference on Computer Vision and Pattern Recognition (CVPR), pp. 8715–8724 (2020)

96. Yu, Z., Li, X., Niu, X., Shi, J., Zhao, G.: Face anti-spoofing with human material perception. In: Vedaldi, A., Bischof, H., Brox, T., Frahm, J.-M. (eds.) ECCV 2020. LNCS, vol. 12352, pp. 557–575. Springer, Cham (2020). https://doi.org/10.1007/978-3-030-58571-6_33

97. Yu, Z., Li, X., Shi, J., Xia, Z., Zhao, G.: Revisiting pixel-wise supervision for face anti-spoofing. IEEE Trans. Biom. Behav. Identity Sci. (TBIOM) **3**(3), 285–295 (2021)
98. Yu, Z., et al.: Searching central difference convolutional networks for face anti-spoofing. In: Proceedings of the IEEE/CVF Conference on Computer Vision and Pattern Recognition (CVPR), pp. 5295–5305 (2020)
99. Zhang, H., Cisse, M., Dauphin, Y.N., Lopez-Paz, D.: mixup: beyond empirical risk minimization. arXiv preprint arXiv:1710.09412 (2017)
100. Zhang, J., et al.: Aurora guard: reliable face anti-spoofing via mobile lighting system. arXiv preprint arXiv:2102.00713 (2021)
101. Zhang, K.Y., et al.: Structure destruction and content combination for face anti-spoofing. In: 2021 IEEE International Joint Conference on Biometrics (IJCB), pp. 1–6. IEEE (2021)
102. Zhang, K.-Y., et al.: Face anti-spoofing via disentangled representation learning. In: Vedaldi, A., Bischof, H., Brox, T., Frahm, J.-M. (eds.) ECCV 2020. LNCS, vol. 12364, pp. 641–657. Springer, Cham (2020). https://doi.org/10.1007/978-3-030-58529-7_38
103. Zhang, P., Zhang, B., Zhang, T., Chen, D., Wang, Y., Wen, F.: Prototypical pseudo label denoising and target structure learning for domain adaptive semantic segmentation. In: Proceedings of the IEEE/CVF Conference on Computer Vision and Pattern Recognition (CVPR), pp. 12414–12424 (2021)
104. Zhang, Z., Yan, J., Liu, S., Lei, Z., Yi, D., Li, S.Z.: A face antispoofing database with diverse attacks. In: 2012 5th IAPR International Conference on Biometrics (ICB), pp. 26–31. IEEE (2012)
105. Zhao, Y., Zhong, Z., Luo, Z., Lee, G.H., Sebe, N.: Source-free open compound domain adaptation in semantic segmentation. IEEE Trans. Circuits Syst. Video Technol. (TCSVT) (2022)
106. Zhao, Y., et al.: Learning to generalize unseen domains via memory-based multi-source meta-learning for person re-identification. In: Proceedings of the IEEE/CVF Conference on Computer Vision and Pattern Recognition (CVPR), pp. 6277–6286 (2021)
107. Zhou, F., et al.: Face anti-spoofing based on multi-layer domain adaptation. In: 2019 IEEE International Conference on Multimedia & Expo Workshops (ICMEW), pp. 192–197. IEEE (2019)
108. Zhou, Q., et al.: Uncertainty-aware consistency regularization for cross-domain semantic segmentation. Comput. Vis. Image Underst. (CVIU) 103448 (2022)
109. Zhou, Q., et al.: Context-aware mixup for domain adaptive semantic segmentation. IEEE Trans. Circuits Syst. Video Technol., 1 (2022). https://doi.org/10.1109/TCSVT.2022.3206476
110. Zhou, Q., et al.: Self-adversarial disentangling for specific domain adaptation. arXiv preprint arXiv:2108.03553 (2021)
111. Zhou, Q., Zhang, K.Y., Yao, T., Yi, R., Ding, S., Ma, L.: Adaptive mixture of experts learning for generalizable face anti-spoofing. In: Proceedings of the 30th ACM International Conference on Multimedia (ACM MM) (2022)
112. Zhou, Q., Zhuang, C., Lu, X., Ma, L.: Domain adaptive semantic segmentation with regional contrastive consistency regularization. In: 2022 IEEE International Conference on Multimedia and Expo (ICME). IEEE (2022)
113. Zhu, J.Y., Park, T., Isola, P., Efros, A.A.: Unpaired image-to-image translation using cycle-consistent adversarial networks. In: Proceedings of the IEEE International Conference on Computer Vision (ICCV), pp. 2223–2232 (2017)

114. Zhu, W., Wang, C.Y., Tseng, K.L., Lai, S.H., Wang, B.: Local-adaptive face recognition via graph-based meta-clustering and regularized adaptation. In: Proceedings of the IEEE/CVF Conference on Computer Vision and Pattern Recognition (CVPR), pp. 20301–20310 (2022)
115. Zou, Y., Yu, Z., Kumar, B., Wang, J.: Unsupervised domain adaptation for semantic segmentation via class-balanced self-training. In: Proceedings of the European Conference on Computer Vision (ECCV), pp. 289–305 (2018)
116. Zou, Y., Yu, Z., Liu, X., Kumar, B., Wang, J.: Confidence regularized self-training. In: Proceedings of the IEEE/CVF International Conference on Computer Vision (ICCV), pp. 5982–5991 (2019)

MetaGait: Learning to Learn an Omni Sample Adaptive Representation for Gait Recognition

Huanzhang Dou[1], Pengyi Zhang[1], Wei Su[1], Yunlong Yu[2(✉)] [iD],
and Xi Li[1,3,4(✉)] [iD]

[1] College of Computer Science and Technology, Zhejiang University,
Hangzhou, China
{hzdou,pyzhang,weisuzju,xilizju}@zju.edu.cn
[2] College of Information Science and Electronic Engineering, Zhejiang University,
Hangzhou, China
yuyunlong@zju.edu.cn
[3] Shanghai Institute for Advanced Study, Zhejiang University, Hangzhou, China
[4] Shanghai AI Laboratory, Shanghai, China

Abstract. Gait recognition, which aims at identifying individuals by their walking patterns, has recently drawn increasing research attention. However, gait recognition still suffers from the conflicts between the limited binary visual clues of the silhouette and numerous covariates with diverse scales, which brings challenges to the model's adaptiveness. In this paper, we address this conflict by developing a novel MetaGait that learns to learn an omni sample adaptive representation. Towards this goal, MetaGait injects meta-knowledge, which could guide the model to perceive sample-specific properties, into the calibration network of the attention mechanism to improve the adaptiveness from the omni-scale, omni-dimension, and omni-process perspectives. Specifically, we leverage the meta-knowledge across the entire process, where Meta Triple Attention and Meta Temporal Pooling are presented respectively to adaptively capture omni-scale dependency from spatial/channel/temporal dimensions simultaneously and to adaptively aggregate temporal information through integrating the merits of three complementary temporal aggregation methods. Extensive experiments demonstrate the state-of-the-art performance of the proposed MetaGait. On CASIA-B, we achieve rank-1 accuracy of 98.7%, 96.0%, and 89.3% under three conditions, respectively. On OU-MVLP, we achieve rank-1 accuracy of 92.4%.

Keywords: Gait recognition · Attention mechanism · Sample adaptive · Learning to learn

Supplementary Information The online version contains supplementary material available at https://doi.org/10.1007/978-3-031-20065-6_21.

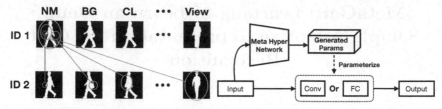

(a) Diverse scales of covariates.   (b) Meta-knowledge parameterization.

Fig. 1. Illustration of the conflicts and the meta-knowledge. **Left:** The conflicts between limited binary visual clues (colorless and textureless) and numerous covariates with diverse scales, such as bag and clothing, which poses a challenge to the model's adaptiveness. **Right:** Meta Hyper Network (MHN) learns to learn the meta-knowledge, which could guide the model to perceive sample-specific properties and adaptively parameterize the calibration network.

1 Introduction

As one of the most promising biometric patterns, gait could be recognized at a long distance without the explicit cooperation of humans, thus having wide applications ranging from security check [11], video retrieval [7], to identity identification [3,49]. Most existing approaches [20,43,44] address gait recognition with a two-step process [53]: feature extraction and temporal aggregation. Though significant advances have been achieved, gait recognition still suffers from the conflict between the *limited* binary visual clues (colorless and textureless) and *numerous covariates* with diverse scales of the silhouette shown in Fig. 1a, which poses a huge challenge to the model's adaptiveness.

Most existing methods tackle this conflict by utilizing the *adaptiveness* of the attention mechanism. For example, the attention mechanism for gait recognition on spatial [34], channel [20], temporal [10], or two of them [33] has been effectively explored. However, the existing attention mechanism still has some limitations, which may harm the adaptiveness. First, the calibration network [32] that performs feature rescaling in the attention mechanism, is static and limited in capturing dependency at a specific scale. Second, the attention mechanism is applied at most two dimensions while leaving one out. Third, only the feature extraction process is considered, while temporal aggregation is ignored.

To address these limitations, we propose a novel framework called MetaGait, to enhance the adaptiveness of the attention mechanism for gait recognition from three perspectives: *omni scale*, *omni dimension*, and *omni process*. The core idea of MetaGait is to leverage *meta-knowledge* [13,30,65], which could guide the model to perceive sample-specific properties, into the calibration network of attention mechanism. Specifically, the meta-knowledge is learned by a Meta Hyper Network (MHN) shown in Fig. 1b and MHN could parameterize the calibration network in a sample adaptive manner instead of being fixed.

Specifically, benefited from the meta-knowledge, we first present Meta Triple Attention (MTA) to adaptively capture the omni-scale dependency in the feature extraction process, leading to the ability to extract walking patterns from diverse scales. The calibration network of MTA is achieved by a weighted dynamic multi-branch structure with diverse receptive fields and parameterized by the meta-knowledge. Second, MTA is designed in homogeneous and applied on spatial/channel/temporal dimensions simultaneously. Third, apart from the feature extraction process, we present Meta Temporal Pooling (MTP) on temporal aggregation for adaptively integrating temporal information. MTP leverages the meta-knowledge to parameterize an attention-based weighting network, which could excavate the relation between three mainstream temporal aggregation methods with complementary properties (*i.e.,* Max/Average/GeM Pooling [44]). Therefore, MTP could adaptively aggregate their merits for comprehensive and discriminative representation.

Extensive experiments are conducted on two widely used datasets to evaluate the proposed MetaGait framework. The superior results demonstrate that MetaGait outperforms other state-of-the-art methods by a considerable margin, which verifies its effectiveness and adaptiveness.

The major contributions of this work are summarized as follows:

- We present MetaGait framework to address the conflict between limited binary visual clues and numerous covariates with diverse scales. The core idea is to introduce the meta-knowledge learned from Meta Hyper Network to enhance the calibration network's adaptiveness in the attention mechanism.
- We present Meta Triple Attention (MTA) for the feature extraction process, which aims at adaptively capturing the omni-scale dependency on spatial, channel, and temporal dimensions simultaneously.
- We present attention-based Meta Temporal Pooling (MTP), which could adaptively integrate the merits of three temporal aggregation methods with complementary properties in the temporal aggregation process.

2   Related Work

2.1   Gait Recognition

Model-Based Approaches. These methods [2,6,8,24,38,42] aim at modeling the structure of human body from pose information [9,56]. For example, Wang *et al.* [60] propose to use the angle change of body joints to model the walking pattern of different individuals. The advantage of these methods is that they are robust to the clothing and viewpoints conditions. Nevertheless, the model-based approaches suffer from expensive computational costs, accurate pose estimation results, missing ID-related shape information, and extra data collection devices.

Appearance-Based Approaches. These methods [4,17,23,25,39,40,50,52, 64] learn the features from the silhouette sequences without explicitly modeling the human body structure. For example, GaitSet [10] and GLN [31] deem each silhouette sequence as an unordered set for recognition. GaitPart [20] utilizes 1D convolutions to extract temporal information and aggregate it by a

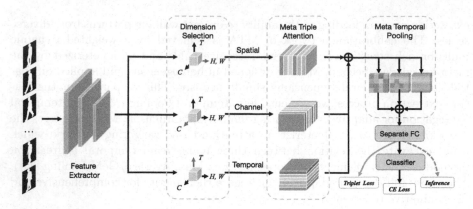

Fig. 2. Overview of MetaGait. Dimension selection refers to the transpose operation for Meta Triple Attention on the selected dimension. Meta Temporal Pooling adaptively aggregates the merits of three temporal aggregation methods with complementary properties. Separate FC is followed by [10,44].

summation or a concatenation. MT3D [43] and 3DLocal [36] propose to exploit 3D convolutions to extract spatial and temporal information at the same time. Appearance-based approaches become popular for their flexibility, conciseness, and effectiveness. The proposed MetaGait is in the scope of appearance-based gait recognition.

Attention Mechanism. Visual attention [27,32,59,62], which highlights the informative clues and suppresses the useless ones, has drawn research attention, and it has been applied to gait recognition successfully. GaitPart [20] performs short-range modeling by channel attention. Zhang *et al.* [66] introduce temporal attention to learn the attention score of each frame by LTSM [18]. Besides, there are methods [34,41] that apply spatial attention. In this paper, we propose to alleviate the conflict between limited visual clues and various covariates with diverse scales from the perspective of the attention mechanism's adaptiveness.

2.2 Dynamic Networks

Dynamic networks can adjust the structures/parameters in an input-dependent manner, leading to several advantages like efficiency, representation power, adaptiveness, and generalizability. Dynamic networks can be mainly divided into dynamic architectures [5,19,37,45,47,58,61] and dynamic parameters [12, 14,15,22,26,54,55,63]. SkipNet [61] and conv-AIG [58] are two representative approaches to enabling layer skipping to control the architecture. CondConv [63] utilizes the weighted sum of the candidate convolutions according to the input.

Further, Zhang *et al.* [65] point out that dynamic network can be seen as a form of meta-learning [1,16,21,30,65] in learning to learn fashion. In this paper, we leverage the dynamic network for the first time to inject meta-knowledge into the calibration network for improving the model's adaptiveness.

3   Method

In this section, we first present the overview of MetaGait in Fig. 2 and then elaborate on the meta-knowledge learned by Meta Hyper Network (MHN). Further, we introduce two modules that use meta-knowledge in two separate processes, *i.e.*, Meta Triple Attention for feature extraction and Meta Temporal Pooling for temporal aggregation. Finally, the details of the optimization are described.

3.1   Overview

The overview of MetaGait is shown in Fig. 2. First, the gait sequences are fed into the feature extractor, and the feature maps are transposed to perform Meta Triple Attention, which models the omni-scale representation on spatial/channel/temporal dimensions simultaneously. Then, Meta Temporal Pooling adaptively integrates the temporal information with three complementary temporal aggregation methods. Finally, the final objective is computed by the features from separated fully-connected layer [10, 44].

3.2   Meta Hyper Network

Considering the fact that most attention mechanism in gait recognition applies a static strategy to their calibration network [32], which may harm the model's adaptiveness, we propose Meta Hyper Network (MHN) to parameterize the calibration network of the attention mechanism adaptively. As shown in Fig. 1b, MHN learns information on data-specific properties of input gait silhouette sequences, *i.e.*, *meta-knowledge*, and generates the parameters of calibration network in a sample adaptive manner.

Given the input $X \in \mathbb{R}^{C \times T \times H \times W}$, let $F(\cdot)$ be a mapping network, the key to MHN is learning a mapping $\boldsymbol{F}_{meta}$ from $\mathbb{R}^C$ to $\mathbb{R}^N$ that is used to parameterize the calibration network $\boldsymbol{F}_{cali}$ with its parameters $\boldsymbol{W}_{cali}$, *i.e.*, fully connected layer ($N = C' \times C$) or convolution ($N = C' \times C \times k_h \times k_w \times k_t$). C, C', and k are the input channel, output channel, and kernel size, respectively. Therefore, the attention mechanism with the meta-knowledge can be formulated as:

$$\boldsymbol{f} = \boldsymbol{F}_{cali}(X) \otimes X, \quad s.t. \ \boldsymbol{W}_{cali} = \boldsymbol{F}_{meta}(X), \tag{1}$$

where $\otimes$ is element-wise multiplication. Specifically, MHN first utilizes Global Average Pooling (GAP) on spatial and temporal dimensions to computes the statics $m \in \mathbb{R}^{C \times 1 \times 1 \times 1}$ for MHN as:

$$m = GAP(X) = \frac{1}{H \times W \times T} \sum_{i=1}^{H} \sum_{j=1}^{W} \sum_{k=1}^{T} X(i, j, k). \tag{2}$$

Then, the meta-knowledge $\boldsymbol{W}_{meta} = \{\boldsymbol{W}_{meta_1} \in \mathbb{R}^{C \times C}, \boldsymbol{W}_{meta_2} \in \mathbb{R}^{N \times C}\}$ learned by MHN generates the sample adaptive parameters $\boldsymbol{W}_{cali}$ of the calibration network by a Multi-Layer Perceptron (MLP) with Leaky ReLU δ as:

$$\boldsymbol{W}_{cali} = \delta(\boldsymbol{W}_{meta_2} \delta(\boldsymbol{W}_{meta_1} m)). \tag{3}$$

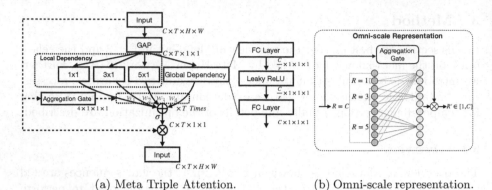

(a) Meta Triple Attention.   (b) Omni-scale representation.

Fig. 3. Illustration of Meta Triple Attention (MTA) and omni-scale representation. (a) MTA is composed of a multi-branch structure with diverse receptive fields weighted by the aggregation gate. (b) MTA achieves omni-scale representation via adaptively weighting the multi-branch structure by soft aggregation gate, leading to the outputs's receptive field $R' \in [1, C]$.

In this paper, the meta-knowledge is used to improve the adaptiveness of the attention mechanism on the modules as follows: the global/local calibration stream in Meta Triple Attention (MTA), the soft aggregation gate in MTA, and the weighting network of Meta Temporal Pooling described in Sect. 3.4.

3.3 Meta Triple Attention

Though previous attention methods in feature extraction achieve great success, they mainly suffer from two issues. First, they could only capture fixed-scale dependency while numerous covariates present diverse scales, which may harm the model's adaptiveness. For example, the covariates with small visual changes like bag carrying only require a small receptive field while a large one would bring noises. In contrast, the covariates with significant visual changes like viewpoints require a large receptive field while the small one cannot cover complete visual changes. Second, they only perform attention on two dimensions at most while leaving one dimension out, which is ineffective and insufficient.

To enhance the adaptiveness of the attention mechanism in the feature extraction process, we propose Meta Triple Attention (MTA), which injects the meta-knowledge into its feature rescaling and feature aggregation to capture omni-scale dependency and perform the omni-dimension attention mechanism sufficiently. Thus, MTA differs from the previous attention mechanism in two corresponding aspects: 1) MTA could cope with the numerous covariates at omni scale; 2) MTA performs homogeneous attention mechanism on spatial, channel, and temporal dimensions simultaneously rather than one or two of them. Note that we describe MTA in channel attention on each frame for simplicity while applied in all three dimensions in practice.

Specifically, we leverage the global and local dependency modeling in frame-level with the weighted multi-branch structure to achieve omni-scale representation. As shown in Fig. 3a, for the global channel dependency relation modeling in frame level, a GAP is first applied on the spatial to obtain each frame's statistics $s \in \mathbb{R}^{C \times 1 \times 1 \times 1}$. Then, to effectively capture dimension-wise non-linear global dependency f_{global} and evaluate the channel-wise importance, MTA utilizes an MLP activated by Leaky ReLu, which follows the bottleneck design [28,32] with a dimension reduction ratio r:

$$f_{global} = F_{global}(s) = W_{g_2} \delta(W_{g_1} s), \qquad (4)$$

where the parameters $W_g = \{W_{g_1} \in \mathbb{R}^{\frac{C}{r} \times C}, W_{g_2} \in \mathbb{R}^{C \times \frac{C}{r}}\}$ of global calibration stream F_{cali}^{global} is adaptively parameterized by MHN.

For local dependency modeling of the calibration network, we design a multi-branch convolutional structure with diverse receptive fields (*i.e.*, kernel size). Therefore, each local calibration stream could capture dependency at a specific scale. To learn omni-scale representation, we propose to aggregate the output f_{global} and f_{local} of global and local streams in a sample adaptive manner as Eq. (5) instead of being fixed, which is achieved by a soft aggregation gate G with meta-knowledge. Next, Sigmoid σ is applied to mapping the values of the attention vector into $[0, 1]$:

$$f_{mta} = \sigma(G(s)[L+1] * f_{global} + \sum_{l=1}^{L} G(s)[l] * f_{local}^l) \otimes X, \quad s.t. \ L \geq 1, \qquad (5)$$

where L denotes the number of the receptive field sizes in local stream of the calibration network. The output of the soft aggregation gate G is a vector with $\mathbb{R}^{L+1}$ to weight each stream according to the input. Specifically, G is implemented by GAP, an MLP mapping from $\mathbb{R}^{C \times 1 \times 1 \times 1}$ to $\mathbb{R}^{(L+1) \times 1 \times 1 \times 1}$, and Sigmoid in sequential. Therefore, the output's receptive field R' is adaptively ranging from 1 to global receptive field C, which could capture omni-scale dependency.

Besides, previous approaches design heterogeneous attention modules for each dimension to fit the dependency scale that each dimension needs to model. Benefited from the omni-scale dependency modeling, MTA can be efficiently performed on three different dimensions in homogeneous.

3.4 Meta Temporal Pooling

To achieve omni-process sample adaptive representation, the meta-knowledge is injected into the temporal aggregation apart from feature extraction. In the recent gait literature [10,20,44], Global Max Pooling (GMP), Global Average Pooling (GAP), and GeM Pooling [51] along the temporal dimension are the mainstream temporal aggregation methods, which represent the salient information, overall information, and an intermediate form between the former two methods, respectively. They can be formulated as:

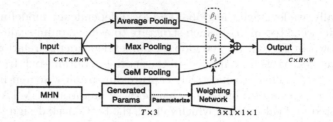

Fig. 4. The illustration of Meta Temporal Pooling (MTP), which aims at leveraging meta-knowledge from MHN to adaptively integrate the merits from three complementary temporal aggregation methods.

$$Max(\cdot) = Pool_{Max}^{T \times 1 \times 1}(\cdot), \tag{6a}$$

$$Mean(\cdot) = Pool_{Avg}^{T \times 1 \times 1}(\cdot), \tag{6b}$$

$$GeM(\cdot) = (Mean(\cdot)^p)^{\frac{1}{p}}, \tag{6c}$$

where p in GeM Pooling is a learnable parameter. Though these temporal aggregation methods have been validated their effectiveness individually, their relation is under-explored. We argue that different temporal aggregation methods have their own merits and complementarities to each other, which can be excavated to adaptively integrated temporal clues according to the properties of inputs. Specifically, GMP preserves the most salient information along the temporal dimension while ignoring the majority of information. By contrast, GAP includes the overall temporal information, but the salient information would be diluted out. Though GeM, an intermediate form, can obtain salient temporal information while preserving overall one, it is less robust than GAP and GMP due to the learning stability of unconstrained learnable parameter p.

To fully exploit their merits, we leverage the meta-knowledge learned by MHN to adaptively integrate the features produced by three temporal aggregation methods as shown in Fig. 4. In detail, we first compute the statics using GAP on spatial and channel dimensions, and we utilize MHN to generate the parameter ($N = 3T$), which is used to parameterize the weighting network, *i.e.*, an FC layer with $W_t \in \mathbb{R}^{3 \times T}$ followed by a Sigmoid. Therefore, the weights of different temporal aggregation methods $\beta \in \mathbb{R}^3$ can be obtained as:

$$\beta = \sigma(W_t(GAP(f_{mta}))). \tag{7}$$

Then, β adaptively weights the features of three complementary temporal aggregation methods and obtain omni sample adaptive representation f_{omni} as:

$$f_{omni} = \beta_1 Mean(f_{mta}) + \beta_2 Max(f_{mta}) + \beta_3 GeM(f_{mta}) \tag{8}$$

3.5 Optimization

Following the optimization strategy [31,33,44], we apply Triplet Loss [29] $\mathcal{L}_{tri}$ and Cross-Entropy loss $\mathcal{L}_{ce}$ on each horizontal feature independently to train our model as Eq. (9). The similarity metric is set to Euclidean distance.

$$\mathcal{L}_{total} = \mathcal{L}_{tri} + \mathcal{L}_{ce}. \tag{9}$$

4 Experiments

4.1 Datasets

CASIA-B [64]. It is composed of 124 IDs, each of which has 10 groups of sequences, *i.e.*, 6 normal walking (NM), 2 walking with a bag (BG), 2 walking in coats (CL). The views are uniformly distributed in $[0°, 180°]$. For evaluation, the protocol is adopted as [10], *i.e.*, small-scale training (ST), medium-scale training (MT), and large-scale training (LT). These three settings select the first 24/62/74 IDs as the training set and the rest 100/62/50 IDs as the test set, respectively. During the evaluation, the first four sequences of each ID under NM are deemed as the gallery, and the rest are used as the probe.

OU-MVLP [57]. It is the largest dataset consisting of 10,307 IDs. In OU-MVLP, there are 1 waling condition (NM) with 2 sequences and 14 views, which are uniformly distributed between $[0°, 90°]$ and $[180°, 270°]$. The training set and test set are composed of 5,153 IDs and 5,154 IDs, respectively. For evaluation, the first sequence of each ID is adopted as the gallery, and the rest is the probe.

4.2 Implementation Details

Hyper-Parameters. 1) The resolution of the silhouette is resized to 64×44 or 128×88 following [31,33,36]; 2) In a mini-batch, the number of the IDs and the sequences of each ID is set to (8, 8) for CASIA-B and (32, 8) for OU-MVLP; 3) Adam optimizer is used with a learning rate of $1e-4$; 4) We train our model for 100k iterations for CASIA-B and 250k for OU-MVLP, where the learning rate is reduced to $1e-5$ at 150k iterations; 5) The margin of Triplet loss is set to 0.2; 6) The reduction ratio r in this paper is all set to 2.

Training Details. 1) The feature extractor is following the global and local backbone in [44]; 2) The channels of the feature extractor in the three stages are set to (32, 64, 128) for CASIA-B and double for OU-MVLP. 3) The local stream of MTA is implemented with Conv1d and Conv2d for channel/temporal and spatial dimensions, respectively. The receptive fields of the local stream are set to {1, 3, 5}. Refer to supplementary materials for more details.

Table 1. Averaged rank-1 accuracy on CASIA-B, excluding identical views cases.

Gallery NM #1-4			$0°$–$180°$											Mean
Prob.	Res.	Method	$0°$	$18°$	$36°$	$54°$	$72°$	$90°$	$108°$	$126°$	$144°$	$162°$	$180°$	
NM	64×44	GaitSet	90.8	97.9	99.4	96.9	93.6	91.7	95.0	97.8	98.9	96.8	85.8	95.0
		GaitPart	94.1	98.6	99.3	98.5	94.0	92.3	95.9	98.4	99.2	97.8	90.4	96.2
		MT3D	95.7	98.2	99.0	97.5	95.1	93.9	96.1	98.6	99.2	98.2	92.0	96.7
		CSTL	97.2	99.0	99.2	98.1	96.2	95.5	**97.7**	98.7	99.2	98.9	96.5	97.8
		3DLocal	96.0	99.0	99.5	98.9	97.1	94.2	96.3	99.0	98.8	98.5	95.2	97.5
		GaitGL	96.0	98.3	99.0	97.9	96.9	95.4	97.0	98.9	99.3	98.8	94.0	97.4
		MetaGait	**97.3**	**99.2**	**99.5**	**99.1**	**97.2**	**95.5**	97.6	**99.1**	**99.3**	**99.1**	**96.7**	**98.1**
	128×88	GaitSet	91.4	98.5	98.8	97.2	94.8	92.9	95.4	97.9	98.8	96.5	89.1	95.6
		GLN	93.2	99.3	99.5	98.7	96.1	95.6	97.2	98.1	99.3	98.6	90.1	96.9
		CSTL	97.8	99.4	99.2	98.4	97.3	95.2	96.7	98.9	99.4	99.3	96.7	98.0
		3DLocal	97.8	99.4	99.7	99.3	97.5	96.0	98.3	99.1	99.9	99.2	94.6	98.3
		MetaGait	**98.1**	**99.4**	**99.8**	**99.4**	**97.6**	**96.7**	**98.5**	**99.3**	**99.9**	**99.6**	**97.0**	**98.7**
BG	64×44	GaitSet	83.8	91.2	91.8	88.8	83.3	81.0	84.1	90.0	92.2	94.4	79.0	87.2
		GaitPart	89.1	94.8	96.7	95.1	88.3	84.9	89.0	93.5	96.1	93.8	85.8	91.5
		MT3D	91.0	95.4	97.5	94.2	92.3	86.9	91.2	95.6	97.3	96.4	86.6	93.0
		CSTL	91.7	96.5	97.0	95.4	90.9	88.0	91.5	95.8	97.0	95.5	90.3	93.6
		3DLocal	92.9	95.9	**97.8**	96.2	93.0	87.8	92.7	96.3	97.9	98.0	88.5	94.3
		GaitGL	92.6	96.6	96.8	95.5	93.5	89.3	92.2	96.5	98.2	96.9	91.5	94.5
		MetaGait	**92.9**	**96.7**	97.1	**96.4**	**94.7**	**90.4**	**92.9**	**97.2**	**98.5**	**98.1**	**92.3**	**95.2**
	128×88	GaitSet	89.0	95.3	95.6	94.0	89.7	86.7	89.7	94.3	95.4	92.7	84.4	91.5
		GLN	91.1	97.7	97.8	95.2	92.5	91.2	92.4	96.0	97.5	95.0	88.1	94.0
		CSTL	95.0	96.8	97.9	96.0	94.0	90.5	92.5	96.8	97.9	**99.0**	**94.3**	95.4
		3DLocal	94.7	98.7	98.8	97.5	93.3	91.7	92.8	96.5	98.1	97.3	90.7	95.5
		MetaGait	**95.1**	**98.9**	**99.0**	**97.8**	**94.0**	**92.0**	**92.9**	**96.9**	**98.2**	98.4	93.5	**96.0**
CL	64×44	GaitSet	61.4	75.4	80.7	77.3	72.1	70.1	71.5	73.5	73.5	68.4	50.0	70.4
		GaitPart	70.7	85.5	86.9	83.3	77.1	72.5	76.9	82.2	83.8	80.2	66.5	78.7
		MT3D	76.0	87.6	89.8	85.0	81.2	75.7	81.0	84.5	85.4	82.2	68.1	81.5
		CSTL	78.1	89.4	91.6	86.6	82.1	79.9	81.8	86.3	88.7	86.6	75.3	84.2
		3DLocal	78.2	90.2	92.0	87.1	83.0	76.8	83.1	86.6	86.8	84.1	70.9	83.7
		GaitGL	76.6	90.0	90.3	87.1	84.5	79.0	84.1	87.0	87.3	84.4	69.5	83.6
		MetaGait	**80.0**	**91.8**	**93.0**	**87.8**	**86.5**	**82.9**	**85.2**	**90.0**	**90.8**	**89.3**	**78.4**	**86.9**
	128×88	GaitSet	66.3	79.4	84.5	80.7	74.6	73.2	74.1	80.3	79.7	72.3	62.9	75.3
		GLN	70.6	82.4	85.2	82.7	79.2	76.4	76.2	78.9	77.9	78.7	64.3	77.5
		CSTL	84.1	92.1	91.8	87.2	84.4	81.5	84.5	88.4	91.6	91.2	79.9	87.0
		3DLocal	78.5	88.9	91.0	89.2	83.7	80.5	83.2	84.3	87.9	87.1	74.7	84.5
		MetaGait	**87.8**	**94.6**	**93.5**	**90.3**	**87.1**	**84.3**	**86.1**	**89.7**	**93.9**	**93.4**	**81.7**	**89.3**

(a) NM   (b) BG   (c) CL   (d) Mean

Fig. 5. Comparison with state-of-the-art methods under ST/MT setting.

Table 2. Comparison with SOTA methods of rank-1 accuracy (%) and mAP (%).

Method	Pub.	Rank-1				mAP
		NM	BG	CL	Mean	
GaitSet [10]	AAAI19	95.0	87.2	70.4	84.2	86.2
GaitPart [20]	CVPR20	96.2	91.5	78.7	88.8	88.7
GLN [31]	ECCV20	96.9	94.0	77.5	89.5	89.2
MT3D [46]	ACM MM20	96.7	93.0	81.5	90.4	90.1
CSTL [35]	ICCV21	97.8	93.6	84.2	91.9	-
3DLocal [36]	ICCV21	97.5	94.3	83.7	91.8	-
GaitGL [44]	ICCV21	97.4	94.5	83.6	91.8	91.5
MetaGait	-	**98.1**	**95.2**	**86.9**	**93.4**	**93.2**

Table 3. Averaged rank-1 accuracy on OU-MVLP across different views excluding identical-view cases.

Method	Probe view														Mean
	0°	15°	30°	45°	60°	75°	90°	180°	195°	210°	225°	240°	255°	270°	
GEINet	11.4	29.1	41.5	45.5	39.5	41.8	38.9	14.9	33.1	43.2	45.6	39.4	40.5	36.3	35.8
GaitSet	79.5	87.9	89.9	90.2	88.1	88.7	87.8	81.7	86.7	89.0	89.3	87.2	87.8	86.2	87.1
GaitPart	82.6	88.9	90.8	91.0	89.7	89.9	89.5	85.2	88.1	90.0	90.1	89.0	89.1	88.2	88.7
GLN	83.8	90.0	91.0	91.2	90.3	90.0	89.4	85.3	89.1	90.5	90.6	89.6	89.3	88.5	89.2
CSTL	87.1	91.0	91.5	91.8	90.6	90.8	90.6	89.4	90.2	90.5	90.7	89.8	90.0	89.4	90.2
3DLocal	86.1	91.2	92.6	92.9	92.2	91.3	91.1	86.9	90.8	92.2	92.3	91.3	91.1	90.2	90.9
GaitGL	84.9	90.2	91.1	91.5	91.1	90.8	90.3	88.5	88.6	90.3	90.4	89.6	89.5	88.8	89.7
MetaGait (64 × 44)	88.2	92.3	93.0	93.5	93.1	92.7	92.6	89.3	91.2	92.0	92.6	92.3	91.9	91.1	91.9
MetaGait (128 × 88)	**88.5**	**92.6**	**93.4**	**93.7**	**93.8**	**93.0**	**93.3**	**90.1**	**91.7**	**92.4**	**93.3**	**92.9**	**92.6**	**91.6**	**92.4**

4.3   Comparison with State-of-the-Art Methods

Results on CASIA-B. To evaluate MetaGait on cross-view and large resolution scenarios, we conduct a comparison between MetaGait and latest SOTA as shown in Table 1, where MetaGait outperforms SOTA at most views and both two resolutions. Specifically, under NM/BG/CL conditions, MetaGait outperforms previous methods by **0.3%/0.4%**, **0.7%/0.5%**, and **2.7%/2.3%** at the resolution of $64 \times 44/128 \times 88$ **at least**. Further, MetaGait achieves rank-1 accuracies over **98%** and **96%** under NM and BG, respectively. More importantly, the considerable performance gain on the most challenging condition CL narrows the gap between the performance of NM and CL to less than **10%**, which verifies the robustness of MetaGait under the cross-walking-condition scenario.

Then, we evaluate MetaGait under the data-limited scenarios following the protocol in [10]. As the experimental results are shown in Fig. 5, MetaGait outperforms state-of-the-art methods with a significant margin, which further shows the efficiency and robustness of MetaGait under small data scenarios.

Further, to evaluate the comprehensive retrieval performance of MetaGait, we present the average rank-1/mAP performance in Table 2, where mAP is com-

Table 4. Ablation study on the effectiveness of each component of MetaGait, including Meta Triple Attention and Meta Temporal Aggregation.

Method	NM	BG	CL	Mean
Baseline	96.1	90.5	80.3	89.0
Baseline + MTA	97.5	94.2	85.4	92.3
Baseline + MTP	96.8	93.8	84.0	91.5
MetaGait	**98.1**	**95.2**	**86.9**	**93.4**

Table 5. Ablation study on the combination of receptive field of the local branch in omni-scale representation of Meta Triple Attention.

Local	NM	BG	CL	Mean
{1}	97.3	94.0	85.3	92.2
{1,3}	97.8	94.7	86.4	93.0
{1,3,5}	**98.1**	**95.2**	**86.9**	**93.4**
{1,3,5,7}	97.4	94.3	85.6	92.4
{1,3,5,7,9}	97.2	93.7	84.8	91.9

Table 6. Analysis of Meta Triple Attention, including the attention on three dimension, the calibration network, and the soft aggregation gate.

Attention			Calibration		Aggregation gate	NM	BG	CL	Mean
Spatial	Channel	Temporal	Static	Meta					
						96.8	93.8	84.0	91.5
✓			✓			97.4	94.0	84.5	92.0
	✓		✓			97.0	94.1	84.1	91.7
		✓	✓			96.8	94.0	84.7	91.8
✓	✓		✓			97.5	94.2	84.8	92.2
✓		✓	✓			97.6	94.3	85.0	92.3
	✓	✓	✓			97.1	94.1	84.9	92.0
✓	✓	✓	✓			97.7	94.5	85.2	92.5
✓	✓	✓	✓		✓	97.8	94.8	86.0	92.9
✓	✓	✓		✓		98.0	95.0	86.4	93.1
✓	✓	✓		✓	✓	**98.1**	**95.2**	**86.9**	**93.4**

puted by the reproduced methods. Specifically, MetaGait outperforms GaitSet by **9.2%/7%**, GaitPart by **4.6%/4.5%**, and GaitGL by **1.6%/1.7%**, which indicates the superior retrieval performance of MetaGait.

Results on OU-MVLP. To verify the effectiveness of MetaGait on the large dataset, we evaluate it on the largest public dataset OU-MVLP. As shown in Table 3, it can be seen that MetaGait outperforms other SOTA methods by considerable margins, which proves the generalizability of MetaGait.

4.4   Ablation Study

This section presents ablation studies to validate the effectiveness of MTA and MTP, including the quantitative and qualitative analysis.

Effectiveness of MTA and MTP. The individual impacts of the MTA and MTP module are presented in Table 4. The baseline model refers to the feature extractor in [44] with traditional temporal aggregation (Max Pooling) and

Table 7. The ablation study on Meta Temporal Aggregation.

Aggregation			Weight network		NM	BG	CL	Mean
Max	Mean	GeM	Static	Meta				
✓			–	–	97.5	94.2	85.4	92.3
	✓		–	–	96.3	93.4	84.0	91.2
		✓	–	–	97.3	94.3	85.6	92.4
✓	✓		✓		97.3	94.2	85.7	92.4
	✓	✓	✓		97.6	94.5	85.7	92.6
✓		✓	✓		97.7	94.5	85.9	92.7
✓	✓	✓	✓		97.9	94.7	86.2	92.9
✓	✓	✓		✓	**98.1**	**95.2**	**86.9**	**93.4**

(a) Baseline   (b) Ours

Fig. 6. The visualization of feature space using t-SNE [48].

a separate FC layer. From the results, several conclusions are summarized as:
1) Using MTA or MTP individually can obtain **3.3%** and **2.5%** performance
gain, respectively, which indicates the effectiveness of these modules. And Meta-
Gait improves the performance by **4.4%**; 2) Both MTA and MTP significantly
improve the performance under the most challenging condition (*i.e.*, CL) by
5.1% and **3.7%**. 3) The performance gain with MTP is mainly reflected in the
BG/CL condition, where temporal aggregation would be more crucial [33].

Receptive Field in Omni-scale Representation. In MTA, we use the re-
weighted combination of receptive fields in diverse scales to achieve omni-scale
representation. To explore the effects of the different combinations, we use the
convolutions with the kernel size of 1, 3, 5, 7, 9 in the local calibration network
of MTA as shown in Table 5. It can be seen that the performance is improved
with the increase of the receptive field scale until the combination of {1, 3, 5}.
In contrast, a larger receptive field decreases the performance, which may lie in
that larger and more diverse receptive fields could improve the ability of feature
representation, but the over-parameterized convolution is hard to optimize.

Analysis of MTA. To evaluate the effectiveness of MTA, we analyze it from
three aspects, *i.e.*, the attention design, the kind of the calibration network, and
the soft aggregation gate. From the results shown in Table 6, we could conclude:
1) MTA effectively improves the performance either using alone or in dimension
combination; 2) The calibration network and the soft aggregation gate, which

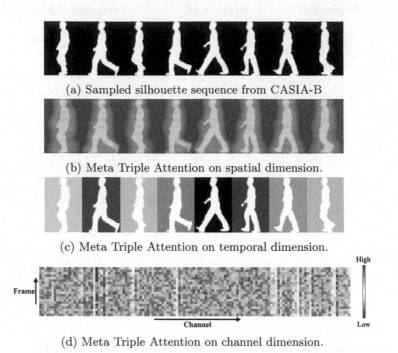

(a) Sampled silhouette sequence from CASIA-B

(b) Meta Triple Attention on spatial dimension.

(c) Meta Triple Attention on temporal dimension.

(d) Meta Triple Attention on channel dimension.

Fig. 7. The visualization of the attention maps of Meta Triple Attention. The transparency of the silhouette in (c) represents its attention value.

are parameterized by the meta-knowledge, clearly improve the rank-1 accuracy by **1.2%**. The above experimental results indicate that our MHN can effectively improve the model's adaptiveness.

Analysis of MTP. The results in Table 7 shows the impacts of different temporal aggregation methods and weighting network. It can be seen that: 1) Different temporal aggregation methods used together provide performance gain by **0.6%**. 2) Weighting network with meta-knowledge could effectively integrate the merits of three aggregation methods than the static one, which indicates that MTP could achieve more comprehensive and discriminative representation.

Visualization of Feature Space. To validate the effectiveness of MetaGait intuitively, we randomly choose 10 IDs from CASIA-B to visualize their feature distribution. As shown in Fig. 6, we find that MetaGait improves the intra-class compactness and inter-class separability than baseline.

Visualization of Attention Maps. To qualitatively analyze MTA, we visualize the attention map shown in Fig. 7. For spatial dimension, MTA effectively learns the shape-aware attention map to guide the learning process adaptively. For temporal dimension, MTA can adaptively highlight important frames and suppress irrelevant frames to model the temporal representation. For channel dimension, it can be observed that MTA can learn a sample adaptive representation. Further, we can observe that different samples have low attention weights in certain channels, which may be caused by the channel redundancy in common.

5 Conclusion

We propose a novel MetaGait framework to alleviate the conflicts between limited visual clues and various covariates with diverse scales. The key idea is to leverage meta-knowledge learned from Meta Hyper Network to improve the adaptiveness of attention mechanism. Specifically, Meta Triple Attention utilizes meta-knowledge to parameterize the calibration network and simultaneously conduct omni-scale attention on spatial/channel/temporal dimensions. Further, Meta Temporal Pooling excavates the relation between three complementary temporal aggregation methods and aggregates them in a sample adaptive manner. Finally, extensive experiments validate the effectiveness of MetaGait.

Acknowledgement. This work is supported in part by the National Natural Science Foundation of China under Grant U20A20222, National Key Research and Development Program of China under Grant 2020AAA0107400, Zhejiang Provincial Natural Science Foundation of China under Grant LR19F020004, NSFC (62002320, U19B2043) and the Key R&D Program of Zhejiang Province, China (2021C01119).

References

1. Antoniou, A., Edwards, H., Storkey, A.: How to train your MAML. arXiv preprint arXiv:1810.09502 (2018)
2. Ariyanto, G., Nixon, M.S.: Model-based 3D gait biometrics. In: International Joint Conference on Biometrics, pp. 1–7 (2011)
3. Balazia, M., Plataniotis, K.N.: Human gait recognition from motion capture data in signature poses. IET Biom. **6**, 129–137 (2017)
4. Bashir, K., Xiang, T., Gong, S.: Gait recognition using gait entropy image. In: IET International Conference on Imaging for Crime Detection and Prevention, pp. 1–6 (2009)
5. Bengio, E., Bacon, P.L., Pineau, J., Precup, D.: Conditional computation in neural networks for faster models. arXiv preprint arXiv:1511.06297 (2015)
6. Bodor, R., Drenner, A., Fehr, D., Masoud, O., Papanikolopoulos, N.: View-independent human motion classification using image-based reconstruction. Image Vis. Comput. **27**(8), 1194–1206 (2009)
7. Bouchrika, I.: A survey of using biometrics for smart visual surveillance: gait recognition. In: Karampelas, P., Bourlai, T. (eds.) Surveillance in Action, pp. 3–23. Springer, Cham (2018). https://doi.org/10.1007/978-3-319-68533-5_1
8. Boulgouris, N.V., Chi, Z.X.: Gait recognition based on human body components. In: IEEE International Conference on Image Processing, pp. 353–356 (2007)
9. Cao, Z., Simon, T., Wei, S.E., Sheikh, Y.: Realtime multi-person 2D pose estimation using part affinity fields. In: IEEE Conference on Computer Vision and Pattern Recognition, pp. 7291–7299 (2017)

10. Chao, H., He, Y., Zhang, J., Feng, J.: GaitSet: regarding gait as a set for cross-view gait recognition. In: AAAI (2019)
11. Chattopadhyay, P., Sural, S., Mukherjee, J.: Frontal gait recognition from incomplete sequences using RGB-D camera. IEEE Trans. Inf. Forensics Secur. **9**(11), 1843–1856 (2014)
12. Chen, Y., Dai, X., Liu, M., Chen, D., Yuan, L., Liu, Z.: Dynamic convolution: attention over convolution kernels. In: IEEE Conference on Computer Vision and Pattern Recognition, pp. 11030–11039 (2020)
13. Cheng, H.P., et al.: Swiftnet: using graph propagation as meta-knowledge to search highly representative neural architectures. arXiv preprint arXiv:1906.08305 (2019)
14. Dai, J., et al.: Deformable convolutional networks. In: IEEE Conference on Computer Vision and Pattern Recognition, pp. 764–773 (2017)
15. Denil, M., Shakibi, B., Dinh, L., Ranzato, M., De Freitas, N.: Predicting parameters in deep learning. In: Advances in Neural Information Processing Systems (2013)
16. Devos, A., Chatel, S., Grossglauser, M.: Reproducing meta-learning with differentiable closed-form solvers. In: International Conference on Learning Representations (2019)
17. Dou, H., et al.: Versatilegait: a large-scale synthetic gait dataset with fine-grainedattributes and complicated scenarios. arXiv preprint arXiv:2101.01394 (2021)
18. Du, Y., Wang, W., Wang, L.: Hierarchical recurrent neural network for skeleton based action recognition. In: IEEE Conference on Computer Vision and Pattern Recognition, pp. 1110–1118 (2015)
19. Eigen, D., Ranzato, M., Sutskever, I.: Learning factored representations in a deep mixture of experts. arXiv preprint arXiv:1312.4314 (2013)
20. Fan, C., et al.: Gaitpart: temporal part-based model for gait recognition. In: IEEE Conference on Computer Vision and Pattern Recognition (2020)
21. Finn, C., Rajeswaran, A., Kakade, S., Levine, S.: Online meta-learning. In: International Conference on Machine Learning, pp. 1920–1930 (2019)
22. Gao, H., Zhu, X., Lin, S., Dai, J.: Deformable kernels: adapting effective receptive fields for object deformation. In: International Conference on Learning Representations (2019)
23. Goffredo, M., Bouchrika, I., Carter, J.N., Nixon, M.S.: Self-calibrating view-invariant gait biometrics. IEEE Trans. Cybern. **40**(4), 997–1008 (2009)
24. Zhao, G., Liu, G., Li, H., Pietikainen, M.: 3D gait recognition using multiple cameras. In: International Conference on Automatic Face Gesture Recognition, pp. 529–534 (2006)
25. Han, J., Bhanu, B.: Individual recognition using gait energy image. IEEE Trans. Pattern Anal. Mach. Intell. **28**(2), 316–322 (2006)
26. Harley, A.W., Derpanis, K.G., Kokkinos, I.: Segmentation-aware convolutional networks using local attention masks. In: International Conference on Computer Vision, pp. 5038–5047 (2017)
27. He, B., Yang, X., Wu, Z., Chen, H., Lim, S.N., Shrivastava, A.: GTA: global temporal attention for video action understanding. arXiv preprint arXiv:2012.08510 (2020)
28. He, K., Zhang, X., Ren, S., Sun, J.: Deep residual learning for image recognition. In: IEEE Conference on Computer Vision and Pattern Recognition, pp. 770–778 (2016)
29. Hermans, A., Beyer, L., Leibe, B.: In defense of the triplet loss for person re-identification. arXiv preprint arXiv:1703.07737 (2017)

30. Hospedales, T., Antoniou, A., Micaelli, P., Storkey, A.: Meta-learning in neural networks: a survey. arXiv preprint arXiv:2004.05439 (2020)
31. Hou, S., Cao, C., Liu, X., Huang, Y.: Gait lateral network: learning discriminative and compact representations for gait recognition. In: Vedaldi, A., Bischof, H., Brox, T., Frahm, J.-M. (eds.) ECCV 2020. LNCS, vol. 12354, pp. 382–398. Springer, Cham (2020). https://doi.org/10.1007/978-3-030-58545-7_22
32. Hu, J., Shen, L., Sun, G.: Squeeze-and-excitation networks. In: IEEE Conference on Computer Vision and Pattern Recognition, pp. 7132–7141 (2018)
33. Huang, X., et al.: Context-sensitive temporal feature learning for gait recognition. In: International Conference on Computer Vision, pp. 12909–12918, October 2021
34. Huang, Y., Zhang, J., Zhao, H., Zhang, L.: Attention-based network for cross-view gait recognition. In: Advances in Neural Information Processing Systems, pp. 489–498 (2018)
35. Huang, Y., et al.: Curricularface: adaptive curriculum learning loss for deep face recognition. In: IEEE Conference on Computer Vision and Pattern Recognition (2020)
36. Huang, Z., et al.: 3D local convolutional neural networks for gait recognition. In: International Conference on Computer Vision, pp. 14920–14929, October 2021
37. Jacobs, R.A., Jordan, M.I., Nowlan, S.J., Hinton, G.E.: Adaptive mixtures of local experts. Neural Comput. 3(1), 79–87 (1991)
38. Kastaniotis, D., Theodorakopoulos, I., Fotopoulos, S.: Pose-based gait recognition with local gradient descriptors and hierarchically aggregated residuals. J. Electron. Imaging 25(6), 063019 (2016)
39. Kusakunniran, W., Wu, Q., Zhang, J., Li, H., Wang, L.: Recognizing gaits across views through correlated motion co-clustering. IEEE Trans. Image Process. 23(2), 696–709 (2014)
40. Kusakunniran, W., Wu, Q., Zhang, J., Ma, Y., Li, H.: A new view-invariant feature for cross-view gait recognition. IEEE Trans. Inf. Forensics Secur. 8(10), 1642–1653 (2013)
41. Li, S., Liu, W., Ma, H.: Attentive spatial-temporal summary networks for feature learning in irregular gait recognition. IEEE Trans. Multimedia 21(9), 2361–2375 (2019)
42. Liao, R., Yu, S., An, W., Huang, Y.: A model-based gait recognition method with body pose and human prior knowledge. Pattern Recog. 98, 107069 (2020)
43. Lin, B., Zhang, S., Bao, F.: Gait recognition with multiple-temporal-scale 3D convolutional neural network. In: ACM International Conference on Multimedia, pp. 3054–3062 (2020)
44. Lin, B., Zhang, S., Yu, X.: Gait recognition via effective global-local feature representation and local temporal aggregation. In: International Conference on Computer Vision, pp. 14648–14656, October 2021
45. Lin, J., Rao, Y., Lu, J., Zhou, J.: Runtime neural pruning. In: Advances in Neural Information Processing Systems (2017)
46. Lin, P., Sun, P., Cheng, G., Xie, S., Li, X., Shi, J.: Graph-guided architecture search for real-time semantic segmentation. In: IEEE Conference on Computer Vision and Pattern Recognition, June 2020
47. Ma, J., Zhao, Z., Yi, X., Chen, J., Hong, L., Chi, E.H.: Modeling task relationships in multi-task learning with multi-gate mixture-of-experts. In: SIGKDD, pp. 1930–1939 (2018)
48. Van der Maaten, L., Hinton, G.: Visualizing data using t-SNE. J. Mach. Learn. Res. 9(11) (2008)

49. Macoveciuc, I., Rando, C.J., Borrion, H.: Forensic gait analysis and recognition: standards of evidence admissibility. J. Forensic Sci. **64**(5), 1294–1303 (2019)
50. Makihara, Y., Sagawa, R., Mukaigawa, Y., Echigo, T., Yagi, Y.: Gait recognition using a view transformation model in the frequency domain. In: Leonardis, A., Bischof, H., Pinz, A. (eds.) ECCV 2006. LNCS, vol. 3953, pp. 151–163. Springer, Heidelberg (2006). https://doi.org/10.1007/11744078_12
51. Radenović, F., Tolias, G., Chum, O.: Fine-tuning CNN image retrieval with no human annotation. IEEE Trans. Pattern Anal. Mach. Intell. **41**(7), 1655–1668 (2018)
52. Samangooei, S., Nixon, M.S.: Performing content-based retrieval of humans using gait biometrics. Multimed. Tools Appl. **49**, 195–212 (2010)
53. Sepas-Moghaddam, A., Etemad, A.: Deep gait recognition: a survey. arXiv preprint arXiv:2102.09546 (2021)
54. Shan, S., Li, Y., Oliva, J.B.: Meta-neighborhoods. In: Advances in Neural Information Processing Systems, vol. 33, pp. 5047–5057 (2020)
55. Su, H., Jampani, V., Sun, D., Gallo, O., Learned-Miller, E., Kautz, J.: Pixel-adaptive convolutional neural networks. In: IEEE Conference on Computer Vision and Pattern Recognition, pp. 11166–11175 (2019)
56. Sun, K., Xiao, B., Liu, D., Wang, J.: Deep high-resolution representation learning for human pose estimation. In: IEEE Conference on Computer Vision and Pattern Recognition (2019)
57. Takemura, N., Makihara, Y., Muramatsu, D., Echigo, T., Yagi, Y.: Multi-view large population gait dataset and its performance evaluation for cross-view gait recognition. IPSJ Trans. Comput. Vis. Appl. **10**(1), 1–14 (2018). https://doi.org/10.1186/s41074-018-0039-6
58. Veit, A., Belongie, S.: Convolutional networks with adaptive inference graphs. In: European Conference on Computer Vision, pp. 3–18 (2018)
59. Wang, D., Zhang, S.: Unsupervised person re-identification via multi-label classification. In: IEEE Conference on Computer Vision and Pattern Recognition (2020)
60. Wang, L., Ning, H., Tan, T., Hu, W.: Fusion of static and dynamic body biometrics for gait recognition. IEEE TCSVT **14**(2), 149–158 (2004)
61. Wang, X., Yu, F., Dou, Z.Y., Darrell, T., Gonzalez, J.E.: Skipnet: learning dynamic routing in convolutional networks. In: European Conference on Computer Vision, pp. 409–424 (2018)
62. Woo, S., Park, J., Lee, J.Y., Kweon, I.S.: CBAM: convolutional block attention module. In: European Conference on Computer Vision, pp. 3–19 (2018)
63. Yang, B., Bender, G., Le, Q.V., Ngiam, J.: Condconv: conditionally parameterized convolutions for efficient inference. In: Advances in Neural Information Processing Systems (2019)
64. Yu, S., Tan, D., Tan, T.: A framework for evaluating the effect of view angle, clothing and carrying condition on gait recognition. In: International Conference on Pattern Recognition, pp. 441–444 (2006)
65. Zhang, F., Wah, B.W.: Supplementary meta-learning: towards a dynamic model for deep neural networks. In: International Conference on Computer Vision, pp. 4344–4353 (2017)
66. Zhang, Y., Huang, Y., Yu, S., Wang, L.: Cross-view gait recognition by discriminative feature learning. IEEE Trans. Image Process. **29**, 1001–1015 (2019)

GaitEdge: Beyond Plain End-to-End Gait Recognition for Better Practicality

Junhao Liang[1], Chao Fan[1], Saihui Hou[2,4], Chuanfu Shen[1,3],
Yongzhen Huang[2,4], and Shiqi Yu[1(✉)]

[1] Southern University of Science and Technology, Shenzhen, China
yusq@sustech.edu.cn
[2] School of Artificial Intelligence, Beijing Normal University, Beijing, China
[3] The University of Hong Kong, Hong Kong, China
[4] WATRIX.AI, Beijing, China

Abstract. Gait is one of the most promising biometrics to identify individuals at a long distance. Although most previous methods have focused on recognizing the silhouettes, several end-to-end methods that extract gait features directly from RGB images perform better. However, we demonstrate that these end-to-end methods may inevitably suffer from the gait-irrelevant noises, *i.e.* low-level texture and color information. Experimentally, we design the **cross-domain** evaluation to support this view. In this work, we propose a novel end-to-end framework named **GaitEdge** which can effectively block gait-irrelevant information and release end-to-end training potential. Specifically, GaitEdge synthesizes the output of the pedestrian segmentation network and then feeds it to the subsequent recognition network, where the synthetic silhouettes consist of trainable edges of bodies and fixed interiors to limit the information that the recognition network receives. Besides, **GaitAlign** for aligning silhouettes is embedded into the GaitEdge without losing differentiability. Experimental results on CASIA-B and our newly built TTG-200 indicate that GaitEdge significantly outperforms the previous methods and provides a more practical end-to-end paradigm. All the source code are available at https://github.com/ShiqiYu/OpenGait.

Keywords: Gait recognition · End-to-end · Gait alignment · Cross-domain

1 Introduction

In recent years, human identification by walking pattern, *i.e.* gait, has become an attractive research topic. Compared with other biometrics, *e.g.*, face, fingerprint and iris, human gait can be easily captured at a long distance without the cooperation of subjects, which means gait can be promising for crimes investigation and suspects tracing under real-world uncontrolled conditions. It is noticed that most

---

J. Liang and C. Fan—Equal contributions.

© The Author(s), under exclusive license to Springer Nature Switzerland AG 2022
S. Avidan et al. (Eds.): ECCV 2022, LNCS 13665, pp. 375–390, 2022.
https://doi.org/10.1007/978-3-031-20065-6_22

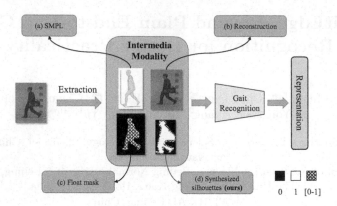

Fig. 1. Three typical end-to-end approaches: (a) model-based end-to-end [13,14], (b) Zhang's GaitNet [30], (c) Song's GaitNet [20] and (d) our **GaitEdge**. *Shaded areas* for the float-point numbers ranging from 0 to 1

of the studies treat gait recognition as a two-step approach, including extracting the intermediate modality, *e.g.*, silhouette mask or skeleton keypoints, from RGB images and putting them into the downstream gait recognition network. However, some researches [4,5,7,16] indicate that those multi-step pipelines usually give rise to the weakness in efficiency and effectiveness; increasing works tend to infer the final results directly in end-to-end [14,20,30].

To the best of our knowledge, there are three typical end-to-end gait recognition methods in the recent literature. As illustrated in Fig. 1(a), Li *et al.* [13,14] utilize a fashion human mesh recovery model [11] to reconstruct the three-dimensional human body and train the recognition network by taking the parameters of the skinned multi-person linear (SMPL) [17] model as inputs. Another typical approach proposed by Zhang *et al.* [30] introduces an autoencoder framework to disentangle the motion-relevant gait patterns and motion-irrelevant appearance features explicitly from the sequential RGB images, as shown in Fig. 1(b). In addition, Song *et al.* propose GaitNet [20], which integrates two tasks, *i.e.* pedestrian segmentation and gait recognition, as illustrated in Fig. 1(c). It extracts gait features straightly from the intermediate float mask instead of the classical binary silhouettes.

To achieve higher performance than those two-step methods, those end-to-end methods cannot ensure that the learned characteristics for human identification only consist of walking patterns. Since the intermediate modalities of previous end-to-end frameworks, *e.g.*, the SMPL reconstruction in [13,14], posture features disentanglement in [30], and pedestrian segmentation supervision in [20], are float-coding, they may introduce some background and texture information. Furthermore, while the previous methods all attempt to exclude gait-irrelevant features, they lack convincing experiments to validate.

To alleviate these issues, we notice that gait features are generally more robust to the variations of camera viewpoints, carrying and clothing than other gait-irrelevant noises, *i.e.* texture and color. If those uncorrelated texture and color features dominate in the extracted gait representations, the recognition performance will drop obviously when the model is directly exploited in unseen domains (new dataset) [8]. Hence, in this paper, we introduce the **cross-domain** evaluation to expose the side effects of texture and color. More importantly, we propose a concise yet compelling end-to-end framework named **GaitEdge** to deal with this challenging evaluation. As shown in Fig. 1(d), the intermediate modality of GaitEdge is a novel synthetic silhouette, while its edge is composed of the trainable float mask, and other regions are classical binary silhouettes. The design is inspired by two intuitive phenomena. First, the RGB-informed noises are mainly distributed in the non-edge regions, *e.g.*, the human body and background. Therefore, treating these regions as binary silhouettes can effectively prevent the leakage of gait-irrelevant noises. Second, the edge region plays a vital role in describing the shape of the human body. Hence, making the only edge region trainable can liberate the potential of the end-to-end training strategy. In addition, we observe that the size-normalized alignment [9] is necessary for the silhouette pre-processing to keep the body in aspect ratio. Unfortunately, this operation used to be offline and thus non-differentiable, which means it can not be directly applied to align the synthetic silhouette. To solve this problem, inspired by the RoIAlign [6], we propose **GaitAlign** module to complete the framework of GaitEdge, which can be regarded as a differentiable version of the alignment method proposed by [9].

In summary, the three major contributions are as follows:

- We point out that gait-irrelevant noises may be mixed into gait representations in end-to-end solutions, and introduce a cross-domain testing to verify the leakage of RGB-informed noises. Besides, due to the lack of a gait dataset to provide RGB videos, we collect the *Ten Thousand Gaits* (TTG-200) dataset which has a similar size to the popular CASIA-B [26] dataset.
- We propose GaitEdge, a concise yet compelling end-to-end gait recognition framework. Experiments on both CASIA-B and TTG-200 demonstrate that GaitEdge outperforms state-of-the-arts. GaitEdge can also effectively prevent irrelevant RGB-informed noises.
- We propose a differentiable size-normalization module, GaitAlign, for silhouette-based end-to-end gait recognition. GaitAlign makes the total solution is end-to-end and trainable.

2   Related Work

2.1   Gait Recognition

As a kind of biometrics, gait is defined by early research [23] as the walking pattern that a given person will perform in a fairly repeatable and characteristic way. On the other hand, another similar task, *i.e.* person re-identification (ReID) [31], aims to find a person presented in one camera in another place by another camera. Despite the similarity, they are still fundamentally different:

gait recognition focuses on walking patterns, while ReID uses clothing primarily for identification. Therefore, it is worth emphasizing that we can not let the gait recognition network acquire information other than gait patterns, such as RGB-informed texture and color.

At present, the mainstream visual-based gait recognition methods can be roughly divided into model-based and appearance-based. The former model-based approaches [2,14,15,22] usually extract the underlying structure of the human body first, e.g., 2D or 3D skeleton key-points, and then model the human walking patterns. In general, such methods can better mitigate the effects of clothing and more accurately describe the body's posture. Nonetheless, all of them are difficult to model the human body structure under the practical surveillance scene due to the low quality of the video.

Appearance-based gait recognition [4,5,7,16,24,28,29] is more popular than model-based gait recognition in the literature. A recent method, GaitSet [4], takes a sequence of silhouettes as input and makes great progress. Subsequently, Fan et al. [5] propose a focal convolutional layer to learn the part-level feature and utilize micro-motion capture module to model short-range temporal patterns. Besides, Lin et al. [16] propose a 3D CNN-based global and local feature extractor module to extract discriminative global and local representations from frames, which outperforms most other methods remarkably.

2.2   End-to-End Learning

End-to-end learning refers to integrating several separate gradient-based deep learning modules in a differentiable manner. This training paradigm has a natural advantage in that the system optimizes components for overall performance rather than optimizing human-selected intermediates [3].

Recently, some research topics have been benefited from the end-to-end learning paradigm. Amodei et al. [1] replace entire pipelines of hand-engineered components with neural networks to overcome the diverse variety of speech by end-to-end learning. Another notable work [3] is Nvidia's end-to-end training for autonomous driving systems. It only gives the system the human steering angle as the training signal. Still, the system can automatically learn the internal representation of the necessary processing steps, such as detecting lane lines.

As the end-to-end philosophy becomes increasingly popular, several studies [14,20,30] have applied it to gait recognition. Zhang et al. [30] propose an autoencoder to disentangle the appearance and gait information without the explicit appearance and gait label for supervision. Li et al. [13,14] use the newly developed 3D human mesh model [17] as an intermediate modality and make the silhouettes generated by the neural 3D mesh renderer [12] consistent with the silhouette segmented from RGB images. Because the 3D mesh model provides more helpful information than silhouettes, this approach achieves state-of-the-art results. However, using a 3D mesh model requires high resolution input RGB images which is not feasible in the real surveillance scenario. Different from the previous two, Song et al. [20] propose another type of end-to-end gait recognition framework. It is formed by directly connecting the pedestrian segmentation and gait recognition networks, which is supervised by a joint loss, *i.e.* segmentation loss and recognition loss. This approach looks more applicable, but it may make the gait-irrelevant noises leak into the recognition network due to the absence of explicit restrictions. Differently, our GaitEdge mainly poses and addresses two pivotal problems: cross-domain evaluation and silhouette misalignment.

3   Cross Domain Problem

From the previous perspective, we argue that although the existing end-to-end approaches [13,14,20,30] greatly improve the accuracy, it is natural to suspect that the introduction of RGB information is the cause of the improvement. To verify our conjecture, we introduce two gait recognition paradigms and compare them experimentally.

Firstly, one of the best-performing two-step gait recognition methods, *i.e.* **GaitGL** [16], is adopted as a baseline. In addition, a simple and straightforward end-to-end model named **GaitGL-E2E** that provides a fair comparison is introduced. As shown in Fig. 2(a) and (b), both methods use the same modules except that GaitGL-E2E replaces binary mask with float-coding silhouettes through a trainable segmentation network, *i.e.* U-Net [18]. Experimentally, we define the **single-domain** evaluation as training and testing on CASIA-B*[1] [26]. Correspondingly, the **cross-domain** evaluation is defined as training on another dataset, *i.e.* TTG-200, but testing the trained model on CASIA-B*. More implementation details will be elaborated in Sect. 5.

As shown in the single-domain part of Fig. 2(d), GaitGL-E2E easily outperforms GaitGL because it has more trainable parameters, and more information is contained in the float-point mask than the binary mask. However, it is inevitable to doubt that float-point numbers flowing into the recognition network bring in texture and color from RGB images, which makes the recognition network learn gait-irrelevant information and leads to the degradation of cross-domain performance. On the other hand, the cross-domain part of Fig. 2(d) shows that GaitGL-E2E does not achieve the same advantages as it does in single-domain and is even much lower than GaitGL (GaitGL: 40.34%, GaitGL-E2E: 27.18%) in the most challenging case, *i.e.* CL (walking with cloth change). This phenomenon indicates it is easier for end-to-end models to learn easily identifiable coarse-grained RGB information rather than fine-grained imperceptible gait patterns.

The above two experiments demonstrate that GaitGL-E2E does absorb RGB noises so that it is no longer reliable for gait recognition with practical cross-domain requirements. Therefore, we propose a novel framework GaitEdge composed of our carefully designed Gait Synthesis module and differentiable GaitAlign module, as shown in Fig. 2(c). The most significant difference between GaitEdge and GaitGL-E2E is that we control the transmission of RGB information through manual silhouettes synthesis.

---

[1] We reprocess CASIA-B and denote the newly processed one as CASIA-B*.

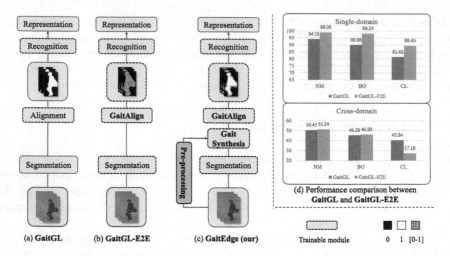

Fig. 2. (a), (b) and (c) are three different frameworks. (d) The rank-1 accuracy (%) on CASIA-B* excluding identical-view cases. *NM* for normal walking, *BG* for walking with bags, and *CL* for walking with cloth change

4 Our Framework

4.1 Gait Synthesis

We generally believe that the edge (the contour of the silhouette) contains the most discriminative information in silhouette images [25]. The interior of a silhouette can be regarded as low-frequency content with less information, whereas the information will be too compact to train the recognition network if we get rid of the interior. Therefore, the designed module, named **Gait Synthesis**, focuses on combining trainable edges with fixed interiors through mask operation. It only trains the edge part of the silhouette image, and the region other than edges are extracted from the frozen segmentation network. As shown in Fig. 3, to clarify how our framework works, we use yellow for the trainable module and illustrate the flow of gradient transfer, in which the dotted orange line represents the backward propagation, and the solid blue line represents the forward propagation. The masks of edge and interior are denoted as M_e and M_i. The output probability of the segmentation network is denoted as P. Then, the output of Gait Synthesis denoted M_s can be obtained by several element-wise operations:

$$M_s = M_e \times P + M_i \tag{1}$$

As shown in Eq. 1, we explicitly multiply P_s by M_e and then add it to M_i, which blocks most information, including the gait-relevant and gait-irrelevant. However, we can still fine-tune the edges of the silhouettes, making it automatically optimized for recognition.

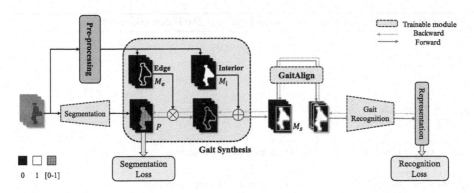

Fig. 3. Illustration of GaitEdge, $\oplus$ for *add element-wise*, $\otimes$ for *multiply element-wise*, and *shaded areas* for float-point numbers ranging from 0 to 1. More details about **Pre-processing** module can be found in Fig. 4.

Pre-processing. We design an untrainable pre-processing operation to get M_e and M_i, shown in Fig. 4. Specifically, we divide it to three steps. First, we segment the input RGB image with the trained segmentation model to obtain the silhouette M. Then, in the second step, we use the classic morphological algorithms to get the dilation and erosion silhouettes(M_i) with a 3×3 flat structuring element. Finally, we get M_e by element-wise exclusive or $\veebar$. Formally:

$$M_i = erode(M)$$
$$M_e = M_i \veebar dilate(M) \tag{2}$$

Overall, *Gait Synthesis* takes the most intuitive approach by limiting the adjustable region to retain the most valuable silhouette features while eliminate most of low-level RGB-informed noises. It is worth mentioning that, *Gait Synthesis* can be detachably integrated into previous silhouette-based end-to-end methods due to the simplicity of the design.

4.2 Gait Alignment Module

Alignment is very crucial for all silhouette-based gait recognition methods. Since the size-normalization of the silhouette was used for the first time on the OU-ISIR Gait Database [9], almost all silhouette-based methods pre-process the

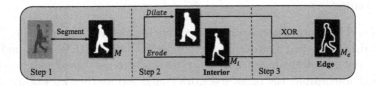

Fig. 4. The **Pre-processing** module in GaitEdge

Algorithm 1. Pseudocode of GaitAlign in a PyTorch-like style.

```
# s_in : silhouettes from segmentation output, (nx1xhxw)
# size : the target size, (H,W)
# r : aspect ratio of human body, (n)
# s_out : aligned silhouettes, (nx1xHxW)

# pad along the x axis so as not to exceed the boundary
s_in = ZeroPad2d((w // 2, w // 2), 0, 0)) # (nx1xhx2w)
binary_mask = round(s_in) # binary silhouette

# compute the coordinates and restore the aspect ratio r
left, top, right, bottom = bbox(binary_mask, r, size)

# get the new silhouettes by differentiable roi_align
s_out = roi_align(s_in, (left, top, right, bottom), size)
```

bbox: Get the four regularly locations of bounding box keeping aspect ratio. We hide this tedious engineering trick, and the source code will be released.
roi_align: Crop and resize the interested region without the loss of spatial alignment.

silhouette input via size-normalization, which removes the noise and benefits the recognition. However, the previous end-to-end approach, *i.e.* GaitNet [20], feeds the segmented silhouette into the recognition network directly, which hardly handles the situation mentioned above. Therefore, we propose a differentiable Gait Alignment Module called *GaitAlign* to make the body be the center of the image and fill the entire image vertically.

We first review the size-normalization [9] procedure because GaitAlign can be regarded as a differentiable version. In size-normalization, by figuring out the top, bottom, and horizontal center of the body, we can scale the body to the target height in aspect ratio and then pad the x-axis with zeros to reach the target width. In our case, pseudo-code in Algorithm 1 depicts the procedure of GaitAlign. We first need to pad the left and right sides with half the width of zeros, which ensures that crop operation will not exceed the boundary. According to the aspect ratio and the target size, then we compute the exact values of four regularly sampled locations. Finally, RoIAlign [6] is applied to the locations given by the previous step. As a result, we get the standard-size, image-filled silhouettes, and its aspect ratio remains the same (refer to the output of GaitAlign in Fig. 3). Another noteworthy point is that the GaitAlign module is still **differentiable**, making our end-to-end training feasible.

5   Experiment

5.1   Settings

Datasets. There are a few available datasets for gait recognition, *e.g.*, CASIA-B [26], OUMVLP [21], Outdoor-Gait [20], FVG [30], GREW [32], and so on. However, not all of them are useful for the end-to-end based gait recognition methods. For example, the proposed work cannot apply the two worldwide most enormous gait datasets, OUMVLP [21] and GREW [32], because neither provides

CASIA-B   TTG-200

Fig. 5. Examples of CASIA-B and TTG-200. The left (CASIA-B) consists of six views of one sequence. The right (TTG-200) consists of six subjects with different views

RGB videos. In short, our ideal gait dataset owns several vital attributes: RGB videos available, rich camera viewpoints, and multiple walking conditions.

CASIA-B [26] seems to be a good choice. Nevertheless, there still needs another similar dataset to fit our cross-domain settings. Consequently, we collect a private dataset named *Ten Thousand Gaits 200 (TTG-200)* and show its statistics in Table 1.

CASIA-B. There are 124 subjects walking indoor in CASIA-B. It is probably the most popular dataset that consists of 11 views ($[0°-180°]$) and three walking conditions, *i.e.* normal walking (NM#01-06), walking with bags (BG#01-02), and walking with cloth change (CL#01-02). We strictly follow previous studies, which group the first 74 subjects into the training set and others into the test set. Furthermore, for the test stage, the first 4 sequences (NM#01-04) are regarded as the gallery set, while the left 6 sequences are grouped into 3 probe subsets, *i.e.* NM#05-06, BG#01-02, CL#01-02. Besides, since the silhouettes of CASIA-B were obtained by the outdated background subtraction, there exists much noise caused by the background and clothes of subjects. Hence, we re-annotate the silhouettes of CASIA-B and denote it as *CASIA-B**. All our experiments are conducted on this newly annotated one.

TTG-200. This dataset contains 200 subjects walking in the wild, and each subject is required to walk under 6 various conditions, *i.e.* carrying, clothing, taking on the phone, and so on. For each walking process, the subject will be captured by 12 cameras located around the different viewpoints (unlabelled), which means each subject ideally owns $6 \times 12 = 72$ gait sequences. In the fol-

Table 1. The statistics of existing gait datasets and our collected TTG-200

Dataset	Subjects	Environment	Format	Variations	#Sequences
CASIA-B	124	Indoor	RGB	11 views, carrying, clothing	13,636
OUMVLP	10,307	Indoor	Silhouette	14 views	267,388
FVG	226	Outdoor	RGB	3 frontal views, walking speed, carrying, clothing, background	2,856
Outdoor-Gait	138	Outdoor	RGB	carrying, clothing	4,964
GREW	26,345	Outdoor	Silhouette	multiple camera	128,671
TTG-200 (our)	200	Outdoor	RGB	12 views, carrying, clothing, talking on the phone, background	14,198

lowing experiments, we take the first 120 subjects for training and the last 80 subjects for the test. In addition, the first sequence (#1) is regarded as gallery set, and the left 5 sequences (#2-6) are regarded as probe set.

As shown in Fig. 5, compared with CASIA-B, TTG-200 has three main differences: (1) The backgrounds of TTG-200 are more complex and diverse (collected in multiple different outdoor scenes); (2) The data of TTG-200 are mostly aerial view, while data of CASIA-B are mostly horizontal view; (3) TTG-200 has better image quality. Therefore, we can treat these two datasets as different domains.

Implementation Details

Data Pre-processing. We first employ ByteTrack [27] to detect and track pedestrians from the raw RGB videos for both CASIA-B [26] and TTG-200, and then conduct the human segmentation and silhouette alignment [9] to extract the gait sequences. The obtained silhouettes are resized to 64×44 and can be taken as the input of these two-stage gait recognition methods or be the ground-truth for the pedestrian segmentation network in these end-to-end based approaches.

Pedestrian Segmentation. We use the popular U-Net [18] as our segmentation network that is supervised by Binary Cross-Entropy [10] loss L_{seg}. We set the input size as $128 \times 128 \times 3$ and the channels of U-Net as {3, 16, 32, 64, 128, 64, 32, 16, 1} and train it via SGD [19] (batch size = 960, momentum = 0.9, initial learning rate = 0.1, weight decay = 5×10^{-4}). For each dataset, we train the network with learning rate scaled to $1/10$ two times for every 10000 iterations until convergence.

Gait Recognition. We use the latest GaitGL [16] as our recognition network and strictly follow the original paper's settings.

Joint Training Details. In this step, the training data sampler and batch size are similar to the gait recognition network. We jointly fine-tune the segmentation and recognition networks with the joint loss $L_{joint} = \lambda L_{seg} + L_{rec}$, where L_{rec} denotes the loss of recognition network. The λ represents the loss weight of segmentation network and is set to 10. Besides, to make the joint training process converge faster, we use the trained segmentation and recognition networks parameters to initialize the end-to-end model, and accordingly, their initial learning rate is set to 10^{-5} and 10^{-4}, respectively. Moreover, we fix the first half of the segmentation network, *i.e.* U-Net, to keep the segmentation result in human shape. We jointly train the end-to-end network for a total of 20,000 iterations and reduce the learning rate by $1/10$ at the 10,000th iteration.

5.2   Performance Comparison

To demonstrate the reliable cross-domain capability of GaitEdge, we conduct the single-domain and cross-domain evaluations on CASIA-B* and TTG-200, as shown in Table 2.

Table 2. The rank-1 accuracy (%) on CASIA-B* and TTG-200. The identical-view cases in CASIA-B* are excluded. The **bold** and **(bold)** numbers for the two highest accuracies of single-domain and that of cross-domain, respectively

Training set	Method		Test set				
			CASIA-B*				TTG-200
			NM	BG	CL	Mean	-
CASIA-B*	Two-step	GaitSet [4]	92.30	86.10	73.36	83.92	40.26
		GaitPart [5]	93.14	85.99	75.05	84.72	42.23
		GaitGL [16]	94.15	89.98	81.42	88.52	**(48.74)**
	End2end	GaitGL-E2E	99.06	98.24	89.45	**95.58**	37.18
		GaitEdge	97.94	96.06	86.36	**93.45**	**(49.12)**
TTG-200	Two-step	GaitSet [4]	41.32	35.15	21.59	32.69	77.62
		GaitPart [5]	45.21	38.75	25.92	36.62	80.24
		GaitGL [16]	50.47	45.29	40.34	**(45.37)**	80.46
	End2end	GaitGL-E2E	51.24	45.93	27.18	41.45	**90.37**
		GaitEdge	54.76	49.85	38.16	**(47.59)**	**88.66**

The diagonal of Table 2 shows the single-domain performance comparisons, where these methods are trained and evaluated in the identical dataset. On the opposite, the anti-diagonal shows the cross-domain performance comparisons, where these methods are trained and evaluated in the different datasets.

Single-Domain Evaluation. From the diagonal results in Table 2, we observe that the performance of traditional two-step gait recognition methods is far inferior to that of two end-to-end ones. For example, GaitGL-E2E exceeds Gait-Set [4] by 11.66% for CASIA-B* and 12.75% for TTG-200, respectively. On the other hand, the accuracy of our proposed GaitEdge is slightly lower than that of GaitGL-E2E, *i.e.* −2.13% for CASIA-B* and −1.71% for TTG-200. However, we argue that GaitGL-E2E owns the higher risk of overfitting in the gait-irrelevant noises since it directly takes the float mask generated by the segmentation network as the input of the recognition network. Hence, we further conduct the cross-domain evaluation to support this notion experimentally.

Cross-Domain Evaluation. If some irrelevant noises dominate the gait representations used for human identification, *i.e.* texture and color, the recognition accuracy would drop dramatically in the case of cross-domain settings since the extracted features impotently represent the relatively robust gait patterns. The anti-diagonal results in Table 2 show that all these methods have significant performance degradation compared to single-domain due to the significant difference between CASIA-B* and TTG-200. We notice that although GaitGL-E2E has the highest accuracy in single-domain, it achieves the poorest performance for crossing the domain from CASIA-B* to TTG-200. In contrast, our GaitEdge

Table 3. The rank-1 accuracy (%) on CASIA-B* across different views excluding the identical-view cases. For evaluation, the first 4 sequences (NM#01-04) are regarded as the gallery set, while the left 6 sequences are grouped into 3 probe subsets, *i.e.* NM#05-06, BG#01-02, CL#01-02. The original paper of Song GaitNet [20] does not mention the results of BG and CL

Probe	Method	Probe view											Mean
		0°	18°	36°	54°	72°	90°	108°	126°	144°	162°	180°	
NM	Song GaitNet [20]	75.6	91.3	91.2	92.9	92.5	91.0	91.8	93.8	92.9	94.1	81.9	89.9
	Zhang GaitNet [30]	93.1	92.6	90.8	92.4	87.6	95.1	94.2	95.8	92.6	90.4	90.2	92.3
	ModelGait [14]	96.9	97.1	98.5	98.4	**97.7**	98.2	97.6	97.6	98.0	98.4	**98.6**	97.9
	MvModelGait [13]	**97.5**	97.6	98.6	**98.8**	**97.7**	**98.9**	**98.9**	97.3	97.6	97.8	97.9	**98.1**
	GaitEdge	97.2	**99.1**	**99.2**	98.3	97.3	95.5	97.1	**99.4**	**99.3**	**98.5**	96.4	97.9
BG	Zhang GaitNet [30]	88.8	88.7	88.7	94.3	85.4	**92.7**	91.1	92.6	84.9	84.4	86.7	88.9
	ModelGait [14]	94.8	92.9	93.8	94.5	93.1	92.6	**94.0**	94.5	89.7	93.6	90.4	93.1
	MvModelGait [13]	93.9	92.5	92.9	94.1	93.4	93.4	95.0	94.7	92.9	93.1	92.1	93.4
	GaitEdge	**95.3**	**97.4**	**98.4**	**97.6**	**94.3**	90.6	93.1	**97.8**	**99.1**	**98.0**	**95.0**	**96.1**
CL	Zhang GaitNet [30]	50.1	60.7	72.4	72.1	74.6	78.4	70.3	68.2	53.5	44.1	40.8	62.3
	ModelGait [14]	78.2	81.0	82.1	82.8	80.3	76.9	75.5	77.4	72.3	73.5	74.2	77.6
	MvModelGait [13]	77.0	80.0	83.5	86.1	84.5	**84.9**	80.6	80.4	77.4	76.6	76.9	80.7
	GaitEdge	**84.3**	**92.8**	**94.3**	**92.2**	**84.6**	83.0	**83.0**	**87.5**	**87.4**	**85.9**	75.0	**86.4**

reaches the best performance than any other posted method in cross-domain evaluations, although it is about 2% lower than GaitGL-E2E in single domain.

Hence, this cross-domain evaluation not only indicates the robustness of Gait-Edge is far superior to that of GaitGL-E2E but also claims the GaitEdge is a practical and advanced framework for the end-to-end gait recognition task.

Comparison with Other End-to-End Methods. Last but not least, the proposed GaitEdge is compared to three previous end-to-end gait recognition methods across different views on CASIA-B*. Table 3 shows that GaitEdge reaches

Table 4. The ablation study for the size of structuring element. The larger size for the larger edge region. The **bold** and **(bold)** numbers for the highest accuracy of single-domain and that of cross-domain, respectively

Training set	Method	Structuring element	Test set				
			CASIA-B*				TTG-200
			NM	BG	CL	Mean	-
CASIA-B*	**GaitEdge**	3 × 3	97.94	96.06	86.36	93.45	49.12
		5 × 5	98.88	97.36	88.24	94.83	**(50.98)**
		7 × 7	98.97	97.90	88.36	95.08	49.15
		9 × 9	99.02	98.19	89.05	95.42	44.47
	GaitGL-E2E	-	99.06	98.24	89.45	**95.58**	37.18
TTG-200	**GaitEdge**	3 × 3	54.76	49.85	38.16	**(47.59)**	88.66
		5 × 5	49.21	45.22	33.71	42.71	89.62
		7 × 7	50.26	44.20	32.43	42.29	90.00
		9 × 9	48.84	41.72	27.66	39.41	**90.39**
	GaitGL-E2E	-	51.24	45.93	27.18	41.45	90.37

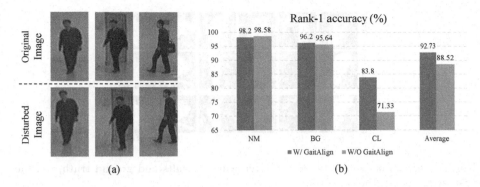

(a) (b)

Fig. 6. (a) The original images (top) *vs.* the disturbed images (bottom). We make random pixel offset to the disturbed images, including vertical and horizontal direction. (b) The ablation study for the *GaitAlign* module. The results are reported on CASIA-B* after disturbance

almost the highest accuracy on various walking conditions, especially for CL (+5.7% than MvModelGait), which reveals that GaitEdge is remarkably robust to color and texture (cloth change).

5.3 Ablation Study

Impact of Edge. Table 4 shows the impact of body edge size. We extract the edges by several sizes of structuring elements-the larger the structuring element, the larger the edge area. According to the results shown in Table 4, as the size of the structuring element increases, the performance of single-domain accordingly increases, but the performance of cross-domain almost decreases at the same time. This result claims that the area of the float mask occupying the intermediate synthetic silhouette is negatively associated with the cross-domain performance for GaitEdge. Therefore, we can argue that the reason why GaitGL-E2E fails in cross-domain evaluation is that it is equivalent to GaitEdge in the case of the infinite structural element. Furthermore, those non-edge regions of silhouette, *i.e.* human body and background, are unsuitable in float-coding for the end-to-end gait recognition framework.

Impact of GaitAlign. Notably, we observe that the result of pedestrian detection (upstream task) in natural scenes, is often much worse than that of the controlled environment, *i.e.* CASIA-B* and TTG-200. In order to simulate this complex situation, we first apply object detection on the videos of CASIA-B* and then perform random pixel offset along with vertical and horizontal coordinates with a probability of 0.5. As shown in Fig. 6 (a), the bottom images are disturbed, aiming to simulate the natural situation. Figure 6 (b) shows that alignment improves the average accuracy significantly. In addition, we also notice that the accuracy of normal walking (NM) drops a little, *i.e.* −0.38%. However, we believe this is because the accuracy of NM is approaching the upper limit.

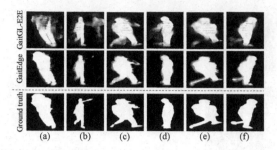

Fig. 7. The comparison between the intermediate results and ground truth, *i.e.* the first two rows *v.s.* the third row

5.4   Visualization

To better understand the performance degradation of GaitGL-E2E and the effectiveness of GaitEdge, we illustrate the intermediate results generated by GaitGL-E2E and GaitEdge respectively as well as the ground truth corresponding to the same frame, as shown in Fig. 7. Specifically, for GaitGL-E2E, the intermediate results in (a), (b), (c) and (d) capture more background and texture information, and some body parts are eliminated such as legs in (e) and (f). While for GaitEdge, the intermediate results are much more stable and reasonable making it more robust.

6   Conclusion

This paper presents a novel end-to-end gait recognition framework termed Gait-Edge that can solve the performance degradation in cross-domain situation. Specifically, we design a Gait Synthesis module to mask the fixed body with tunable edges obtained by morphological operation. Besides, a differentiable alignment module named GaitAlign is proposed to solve the body position jitter caused by the upstream pedestrian detection task. We also conduct extensive and comprehensive experiments on two datasets, including CASIA-B* and our newly built TTG-200. Experimental results show that GaitEdge significantly outperforms the previous methods, indicating that GaitEdge is a more practical end-to-end paradigm that can effectively block RGB noise. Moreover, this work exposes the cross-domain problem neglected by previous studies, which provides a new perspective for future research.

Acknowledgments. We would like to thank the helpful discussion with Dr. Chunshui Cao and Dr. Xu Liu. This work was supported in part by the National Natural Science Foundation of China under Grant 61976144, in part by the Stable Support Plan Program of Shenzhen Natural Science Fund under Grant 20200925155017002, in part by the National Key Research and Development Program of China under Grant 2020AAA0140002, and in part by the Shenzhen Technology Plan Program (Grant No. KQTD20170331093217368).

References

1. Amodei, D., et al.: Deep speech 2: end-to-end speech recognition in English and mandarin. In: International Conference on Machine Learning, pp. 173–182. PMLR (2016)
2. An, W., et al.: Performance evaluation of model-based gait on multi-view very large population database with pose sequences. IEEE Trans. Biometrics Behav. Identity Sci. **2**(4), 421–430 (2020)
3. Bojarski, M., et al.: End to end learning for self-driving cars. arXiv preprint arXiv:1604.07316 (2016)
4. Chao, H., He, Y., Zhang, J., Feng, J.: GaitSet: regarding gait as a set for cross-view gait recognition. In: Proceedings of the AAAI Conference on Artificial Intelligence, pp. 8126–8133 (2019)
5. Fan, C., et al.: GaitPart: temporal part-based model for gait recognition. In: Proceedings of the IEEE/CVF Conference on Computer Vision and Pattern Recognition, pp. 14225–14233 (2020)
6. He, K., Gkioxari, G., Dollár, P., Girshick, R.: Mask R-CNN. In: Proceedings of the IEEE International Conference on Computer Vision, pp. 2961–2969 (2017)
7. Hou, S., Cao, C., Liu, X., Huang, Y.: Gait lateral network: learning discriminative and compact representations for gait recognition. In: Vedaldi, A., Bischof, H., Brox, T., Frahm, J.-M. (eds.) ECCV 2020. LNCS, vol. 12354, pp. 382–398. Springer, Cham (2020). https://doi.org/10.1007/978-3-030-58545-7_22
8. Huang, H., et al.: EANet: enhancing alignment for cross-domain person re-identification. arXiv preprint arXiv:1812.11369 (2018)
9. Iwama, H., Okumura, M., Makihara, Y., Yagi, Y.: The OU-ISIR gait database comprising the large population dataset and performance evaluation of gait recognition. IEEE Trans. Inf. Forensics Secur. **7**(5), 1511–1521 (2012)
10. Jadon, S.: A survey of loss functions for semantic segmentation. In: 2020 IEEE Conference on Computational Intelligence in Bioinformatics and Computational Biology (CIBCB), pp. 1–7. IEEE (2020)
11. Kanazawa, A., Black, M.J., Jacobs, D.W., Malik, J.: End-to-end recovery of human shape and pose. In: Proceedings of the IEEE Conference on Computer Vision and Pattern Recognition, pp. 7122–7131 (2018)
12. Kato, H., Ushiku, Y., Harada, T.: Neural 3D mesh renderer. In: Proceedings of the IEEE Conference on Computer Vision and Pattern Recognition, pp. 3907–3916 (2018)
13. Li, X., Makihara, Y., Xu, C., Yagi, Y.: End-to-end model-based gait recognition using synchronized multi-view pose constraint. In: Proceedings of the IEEE/CVF International Conference on Computer Vision, pp. 4106–4115 (2021)
14. Li, X., Makihara, Y., Xu, C., Yagi, Y., Yu, S., Ren, M.: End-to-end model-based gait recognition. In: Ishikawa, H., Liu, C.-L., Pajdla, T., Shi, J. (eds.) ACCV 2020. LNCS, vol. 12624, pp. 3–20. Springer, Cham (2021). https://doi.org/10.1007/978-3-030-69535-4_1
15. Liao, R., Yu, S., An, W., Huang, Y.: A model-based gait recognition method with body pose and human prior knowledge. Pattern Recogn. **98**, 107069 (2020)
16. Lin, B., Zhang, S., Yu, X.: Gait recognition via effective global-local feature representation and local temporal aggregation. In: Proceedings of the IEEE/CVF International Conference on Computer Vision, pp. 14648–14656 (2021)
17. Loper, M., Mahmood, N., Romero, J., Pons-Moll, G., Black, M.J.: SMPL: a skinned multi-person linear model. ACM Trans. Graph. (TOG) **34**(6), 1–16 (2015)

18. Ronneberger, O., Fischer, P., Brox, T.: U-Net: convolutional networks for biomedical image segmentation. In: Navab, N., Hornegger, J., Wells, W.M., Frangi, A.F. (eds.) MICCAI 2015. LNCS, vol. 9351, pp. 234–241. Springer, Cham (2015). https://doi.org/10.1007/978-3-319-24574-4_28
19. Ruder, S.: An overview of gradient descent optimization algorithms. arXiv preprint arXiv:1609.04747 (2016)
20. Song, C., Huang, Y., Huang, Y., Jia, N., Wang, L.: GaitNet: an end-to-end network for gait based human identification. Pattern Recogn. **96**, 106988 (2019)
21. Takemura, N., Makihara, Y., Muramatsu, D., Echigo, T., Yagi, Y.: Multi-view large population gait dataset and its performance evaluation for cross-view gait recognition. IPSJ Trans. Comput. Vis. Appl. **10**(1), 1–14 (2018). https://doi.org/10.1186/s41074-018-0039-6
22. Teepe, T., Khan, A., Gilg, J., Herzog, F., Hörmann, S., Rigoll, G.: Gaitgraph: graph convolutional network for skeleton-based gait recognition. In: 2021 IEEE International Conference on Image Processing (ICIP), pp. 2314–2318. IEEE (2021)
23. Winter, D.A.: Biomechanics and motor control of human gait: normal, elderly and pathological (1991)
24. Wu, Z., Huang, Y., Wang, L., Wang, X., Tan, T.: A comprehensive study on cross-view gait based human identification with deep CNNs. IEEE Trans. Pattern Anal. Mach. Intell. **39**(2), 209–226 (2016)
25. Yu, S., Tan, D., Huang, K., Tan, T.: Reducing the effect of noise on human contour in gait recognition. In: Lee, S.-W., Li, S.Z. (eds.) ICB 2007. LNCS, vol. 4642, pp. 338–346. Springer, Heidelberg (2007). https://doi.org/10.1007/978-3-540-74549-5_36
26. Yu, S., Tan, D., Tan, T.: A framework for evaluating the effect of view angle, clothing and carrying condition on gait recognition. In: 18th International Conference on Pattern Recognition (ICPR 2006), vol. 4, pp. 441–444. IEEE (2006)
27. Zhang, Y., et al.: ByteTrack: multi-object tracking by associating every detection box. arXiv preprint arXiv:2110.06864 (2021)
28. Zhang, Y., Huang, Y., Yu, S., Wang, L.: Cross-view gait recognition by discriminative feature learning. IEEE Trans. Image Process. **29**, 1001–1015 (2019)
29. Zhang, Z., Tran, L., Liu, F., Liu, X.: On learning disentangled representations for gait recognition. IEEE Trans. Pattern Anal. Mach. Intell. (2020)
30. Zhang, Z., et al.: Gait recognition via disentangled representation learning. In: Proceedings of the IEEE/CVF Conference on Computer Vision and Pattern Recognition, pp. 4710–4719 (2019)
31. Zheng, L., Yang, Y., Hauptmann, A.G.: Person re-identification: past, present and future. arXiv preprint arXiv:1610.02984 (2016)
32. Zhu, Z., et al.: Gait recognition in the wild: a benchmark. In: Proceedings of the IEEE/CVF International Conference on Computer Vision, pp. 14789–14799 (2021)

UIA-ViT: Unsupervised Inconsistency-Aware Method Based on Vision Transformer for Face Forgery Detection

Wanyi Zhuang, Qi Chu$^{(\boxtimes)}$, Zhentao Tan, Qiankun Liu, Haojie Yuan, Changtao Miao, Zixiang Luo, and Nenghai Yu

CAS Key Laboratory of Electromagnetic Space Information, University of Science and Technology of China, Hefei, China
{wy970824,tzt,liuqk3,doubihj,miaoct,zxluo}@mail.ustc.edu.cn,
qchu@ustc.edu.cn, ynh@ustc.edu.cn

Abstract. Intra-frame inconsistency has been proved to be effective for the generalization of face forgery detection. However, learning to focus on these inconsistency requires extra pixel-level forged location annotations. Acquiring such annotations is non-trivial. Some existing methods generate large-scale synthesized data with location annotations, which is only composed of real images and cannot capture the properties of forgery regions. Others generate forgery location labels by subtracting paired real and fake images, yet such paired data is difficult to collected and the generated label is usually discontinuous. To overcome these limitations, we propose a novel Unsupervised Inconsistency-Aware method based on Vision Transformer, called UIA-ViT, which only makes use of video-level labels and can learn inconsistency-aware feature without pixel-level annotations. Due to the self-attention mechanism, the attention map among patch embeddings naturally represents the consistency relation, making the vision Transformer suitable for the consistency representation learning. Based on vision Transformer, we propose two key components: Unsupervised Patch Consistency Learning (UPCL) and Progressive Consistency Weighted Assemble (PCWA). UPCL is designed for learning the consistency-related representation with progressive optimized pseudo annotations. PCWA enhances the final classification embedding with previous patch embeddings optimized by UPCL to further improve the detection performance. Extensive experiments demonstrate the effectiveness of the proposed method.

Supplementary Information The online version contains supplementary material available at https://doi.org/10.1007/978-3-031-20065-6_23.

1   Introduction

Face forgery technologies [4,6,29] have been greatly promoted with the development of image generation and manipulation. The forged facial images can even deceive human beings, which may be abused for malicious purposes, leading to serious security and privacy concerns, e.g. fake news and evidence. Thus, it's of great significance to develop powerful techniques to detect fake faces.

Early face forgery detection methods [2,20,31] regard this task as a binary classification problem and achieve admirable performance in the intra-dataset detection with the help of deep neural networks. However, they fail easily when generalizing to other unseen forgery datasets where the identities, manipulation types, compression rate, *etc.* are quite different. To improve the generalization of detection, common forged artifacts or inconsistency produced by face manipulation techniques are explored by recent methods, such as eye blinking frequency [13], affine warping [14], image blending [12], temporal inconsistency [27,35], intra-frame inconsistency [1,34] and so on. Among them, intra-frame inconsistency has been proved to be able to effectively improve the generalization performance of the detection, since the common face forgery strategy (manipulation and blending) causes the inconsistency between the forged region and the original background. However, learning to focus on these inconsistency requires extra pixel-level forged location annotations. Acquiring such annotations is non-trivial. Generating the large-scale synthesized data (e.g. simulated stitched images [34]) with pixel-level forged location annotations seems to be an intuitive solution. Although it can produce accurate pixel-level location annotations, models can not capture the properties of forgery regions, since the generated data is only composed of real images. Other works [1,27] attempt to generate annotated forged location labels by subtracting forgery image with its corresponding real image. However, these paired images are usually unavailable, especially in the real-world scenes. Even though such paired data can be collected, the forgery region annotations tend to be discontinuous and inaccurate, which are sub-optimal for intra-frame consistency supervision. Therefore, we propose an unsupervised inconsistency-aware method that extracts intra-frame inconsistency cues without pixel-level forged location annotations.

The key of unsupervised inconsistency-aware learning is how to realize forgery location estimation. In this paper, we apply the widely used multivariate Gaussian estimation (MVG) [9,23] to represent the real/fake features and generate pseudo annotations through it. Based on this idea, we can force the model to focus on intra-inconsistency using pseudo annotations. In addition, different from the previous works [1,27] which specially design a module to obtain the consistency-related representation, we find that Vision Transformer [5] naturally provides the consistency representation from the attention map among patch embeddings, thanks to their self-attention mechanism. Therefore, we apply it to build the detection network and propose two key components: **UPCL** (Unsupervised Patch Consistency Learning) and **PCWA** (Progressive Consistency Weighted Assemble).

UPCL is a training strategy for learning the consistency-related representations through an unsupervised forgery location method. We approximately estimate forgery location maps by comparing the Mahalanobis distances between the MVGs of real/fake features and the patch embedding from the middle layer of Vision Transformer (ViT) [5]. During training, forgery location maps are progressively optimized. To model the consistency constraint, we use the Multi-head Attention Map existed in ViT itself as the representation and constrain them in multi-layers for better learning.

PCWA is a feature enhancement module and can take full advantage of the consistency representation through the proposed UPCL module. In details, we utilize the Attention Map between classification embedding and patch embeddings to progressively weighted average the patch embedding of final layer, and concatenate it with classification embedding before feed them into final MLP for forgery classification. The layers providing these Attention Maps are optimized by **UPCL** for further improvement.

The main contributions of this work are summarized as follows:

- We propose an unsupervised patch consistency learning strategy based on vision Transformer to make it possible for face forgery detection to focus on intra-frame inconsistency without pixel-level annotations. It greatly improves the generalization of detection without additional overhead.
- We take full advantage of feature representations under the proposed learning strategy to progressively combine global classification features and local patch features, by weighted averaging the latter using the Attention Map between classification embedding and patch embeddings.
- Extensive experiments demonstrate the superior generalization ability of proposed method and the effectiveness of unsupervised learning strategy.

2 Related Work

2.1 Face Forgery Detection

Early face manipulation methods usually produce obvious artifacts or inconsistencies on generated face images. Such flaws are important cues for early face forgery detection works. For example, Li *et al.* [13] observed that the eye blinking frequency of the forgery video is lower than the normal. Later methods extended it to check the inconsistency of 3D head poses to help forgery videos detection [32]. Similarly, Matern *et al.* [17] used hand-crafted visual features in eyes, noses, teeth to distinguish the fake faces.

Besides seeking for visual artifacts, frequency clues has also been introduced in forgery detection to improve detection accuracy, such as Two-branch [16], F3-Net [22], FDFL [11]. Meanwhile, attention mechanism proved to be effective in recent studies like Xception+Reg [3] and Multi-attention [19,33]. Although these methods have achieved perfect performance in the intra-dataset detection, they suffer big performance drop while generalizing to other unseen forgery datasets.

To overcome the difficulties on generalizing to unseen forgeries, works have been done to discover universal properties shared by different forgery methods.

Some works focused on inevitable procedures in forgery, such as affine warping (DSP-FWA [14]) and blending (Face X-ray [12]). While others observed that certain type of inconsistency exists in different kinds of forgery videos, such as temporal inconsistency (LipForensics [7], FTCN+TT [35]) and intra-frame inconsistency (Local-related [1], PCL+I2G [34], Dual [27]). However, in order to learn corresponding artifacts or inconsistency cues, Face X-ray [12] and PCL+I2G [34] try to generate the large-scale datasets with annotated forged location for their pixel-level supervised learning. The generation process is time consuming and cannot capture the properties of forgery regions. Local-related [1] and DCL [27] try to generate annotated forged location labels by subtracting forgery image with its corresponding real image. However, these paired images are usually unavailable, especially in the real-world scenes. Even though such paired data can be collected, the forgery region annotations tend to be discontinuous and inaccurate, which are sub-optimal for intra-frame consistency supervision. To tackle these issues, we introduce the unsupervised inconsistency-aware method to learn inconsistency cues for general face forgery detection.

2.2   Transformer

Transformers [30] are proposed for machine translation and have become the state of the art method in NLP tasks for their strong ability in modeling long-range context information. Vision Transformer (ViT) [5] adjusted Transformers for computer vision tasks, by modeling image as a sequences of image patches. Several works leveraging transformers to boost face forgery detection have been done: Miao *et al.* [18] extend transformer using bag-of-feature to learn local forgery features. Khan *et al.* [8] propose a video transformer to extract spatial features with the temporal information for detecting forgery. Zheng *et al.* [35] design a light-weight temporal transformer after their proposed fully temporal convolution network to explore the temporal coherence for general manipulated video detection. In this paper, we also extend transformer to dig the relationships among different regions and capture more local consistency information for general forgery image detection.

3   Method

In this section, we introduce the details of the proposed Vision Transformer based unsupervised inconsistency-aware face forgery detection. As shown in Fig. 1, given an image I, our network splits I into fixed-size patches, linearly embeds each of them, adds position embeddings and feeds the resulting sequence into the Transformer encoder. The patch embeddings $\mathcal{F}_P$ from layer K are accumulated for unsupervised approximate forgery location, and the estimated location maps are used for modeling consistency constraint. The Attention Map Υ_P and Υ_C are averaged from layer $N - n$ to layer N. Υ_P is used for patch consistency learning, and Υ_C is used as consistency weighted matrix in PCWA. In the end, PCWA outputs consistency-aware feature $F = \text{UIA}(I)$, and an MLP head is used to do the final prediction.

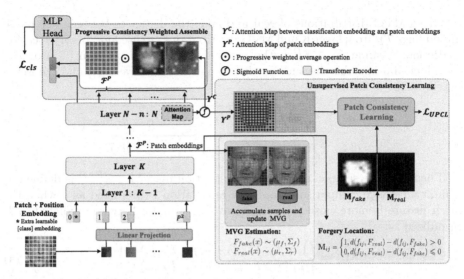

Fig. 1. An overview of the proposed UIA-ViT. The UPCL module uses the patch embeddings from layer K to make MVG estimation. The averaged Attention Map from layer $N - n$ to layer N is used for patch consistency learning in UPCL module and as consistency weighted matrix in PCWA module.

3.1 Unsupervised Patch Consistency Learning

Unsupervised Approximate Forgery Location. We apply the widely used multivariate Gaussian estimation (MVG) to represent the real/fake image patch features and generate pseudo annotations. To be concrete, we try to fit a MVG of original image patches and a MVG of forged image patches within **General Forgery Region (GFR)**. We define GFR as the general manipulated region among different forgery datasets, where the patch features can approximately represent the distribution of actual manipulated face region. Specifically, we designate the GFR as the center square region of the cropped faces.

Assume x_r represents the patch feature from layer K of real sample, and x_f represents the patch feature from layer K within GFR of fake sample. We model the probability density function (PDF) of x_r using the MVG, defined as:

$$F_{real}(x_r) = \frac{1}{\sqrt{(2\pi)^D |det \Sigma_r|}} e^{-\frac{1}{2}(x_r - \mu_r)^T \Sigma_r^{-1}(x_r - \mu_r)}, \tag{1}$$

where $\mu_r \in \mathbb{R}^D$ is the mean vector and $\Sigma_r \in \mathbb{R}^{D \times D}$ is the symmetric covariance matrix of the real distribution. Similarly, the PDF of x_f is defined as $F_{fake}(x_f)$ with mean vector μ_f and covariance matrix Σ_f.

During training, F_{real} and F_{fake} are updated by new (μ_r, Σ_r) and (μ_f, Σ_f), which are approximated with the sample mean and sample covariance from the observations $(x_r^1, x_r^2, ..., x_r^n \in \mathbb{R}^D)$ and $(x_f^1, x_f^2, ..., x_f^n \in \mathbb{R}^D)$. We accumulate the feature observations from every mini batch of training samples and experimentally update two MVG distributions every 0.5 training epochs.

Given MVG distributions of real and fake, the distances between the patch embeddings $\mathcal{F}_P$ from layer K and MVG distributions are used for forgery location prediction. Assume $f_{ij} \in \mathbb{R}^D$ is the particular feature in position (i, j) of $\mathcal{F}_P$. We adopt Mahalanobis distance for distance measure between f_{ij} and the MVG distributions, defined as

$$d(f_{ij}, F_{real}) = \sqrt{(f_{ij} - \mu_r)^T \Sigma_r^{-1}(f_{ij} - \mu_r)}, \tag{2}$$

$$d(f_{ij}, F_{fake}) = \sqrt{(f_{ij} - \mu_f)^T \Sigma_f^{-1}(f_{ij} - \mu_f)}. \tag{3}$$

Then, for fake samples, the predicted location map $\mathbf{M} \in \mathbb{R}^{P \times P}$ is defined as a binary distance comparison map. The annotation is predicted as 0 when the patch feature is more closed to F_{real} than F_{fake}, and otherwise predicted as 1, formalized as:

$$\mathbf{M}_{ij} = \begin{cases} 1, d(f_{ij}, F_{real}) - d(f_{ij}, F_{fake}) > 0 \\ 0, d(f_{ij}, F_{real}) - d(f_{ij}, F_{fake}) \leqslant 0 \end{cases}. \tag{4}$$

Note that location map $\mathbf{M}$ is fixes as the all-zero matrix for real samples. In particular, in order to guarantee that such patch embeddings from our network capture more local texture information rather than high-level semantic information, we perform several visualizations as shown in Fig. 5, and finally utilize the patch embeddings $\mathcal{F}_P$ from Block 6 of UIA-ViT network (i.e. $K = 6$) for approximately estimating forgery location map.

Patch Consistency Loss. In each transformer block of the standard Transformer Encoder, there is a Multi-head Attention layer that firstly calculate the compatibility between queries and keys from different input embeddings, called Attention Map. Unlike PCL+I2G [34] that specially computes the pair-wise similarity of their extracted feature, our ViT based method directly uses Attention Map from middle layers for self-consistency learning.

Define the mean Attention Map between different patch embeddings from $N - n$ to N Transformer layers as $\Upsilon^P \in \mathbb{R}^{P^2 \times P^2}$, where P^2 is the number of patch embeddings. $\Upsilon^P_{(i,j),(k,l)}$ represents the consistency between the embedding in position (i, j) and other patch embedding in position (k, l), and higher value means two positions have higher consistency. With the approximate forgery location map $\mathbf{M}$, we design the consistency loss to supervise the Attention Map, formalized as:

$$\mathbf{C}_{(i,j),(k,l)} = \begin{cases} c_1, if \ \mathbf{M}_{ij} = 0 \ and \ \mathbf{M}_{kl} = 0 \\ c_2, if \ \mathbf{M}_{ij} = 1 \ and \ \mathbf{M}_{kl} = 1 \\ c_3, \qquad else \end{cases}, \tag{5}$$

$$\mathcal{L}_{UPCL} = \frac{1}{P^2} \sum_{i,j,k,l} |\text{sigmoid}(\Upsilon^P_{(i,j),(k,l)}) - \mathbf{C}_{(i,j),(k,l)}|, \tag{6}$$

where c_1, c_2, c_3 are learnable parameters to avoid instability optimization when MVG estimation is biased in the early training. During training process, we initialize them as $(0.6, 0.6, 0.2)$, and also optimize c_1, c_2 to increase and optimize c_3 to decrease gradually. After convergence, c_1, c_2, c_3 eventually tend to $(0.8, 0.8, 0.0)$ in our experiments.

3.2 Progressive Consistency Weighted Assemble

In order to perform classification, we use the standard approach of adding an extra learnable classification token to the sequence. However, due to final classification embedding capturing more global semantic information rather than local texture, it is not sufficient to utilize the intra-frame inconsistency clues if merely feed the final classification embedding into MLP head. Therefore, we propose a novel module, named Progressive Consistency Weighted Assemble (PCWA), which progressively combines global features and local inconsistency-aware patch features for final binary classification.

Specifically, the patch embeddings of final layer are weighted average with $\Upsilon^C \in \mathbb{R}^{P \times P}$, which is defined as the mean Attention Map between classification embedding and other patch embeddings from $N - n$ to N Transformer layers. Denote classification embedding and patch embeddings of final layer as $\mathcal{F}^C \in \mathbb{R}^D$, $\mathcal{F}^P \in \mathbb{R}^{P^2 \times D}$. To avert instability optimization in the early training stage, we adopt variable weight w along with the current iterations. The scalar w is gradually decreased to zero controlled by the decreasing function with hyper-parameters ρ and θ. Then the weighted matrix $\mathbf{A}^P$ gradually transfers from averaged weighting (all-one matrix) to consistency weighting, formalized as:

$$w = \text{sigmoid}(-\rho(step - \theta)), step = \frac{current\_iters}{total\_iters} \in [0, 1], \tag{7}$$

$$\mathbf{A}^P = w * \mathbb{1} + (1 - w) * \text{sigmoid}(\Upsilon^C). \tag{8}$$

Ideally, the well optimized Υ^C can capture consistency information between the input global classification embedding and other local patch embeddings, and suggest which regions should be great considered by the classifier at the end of network. We adopt $\mathbf{A}^P$ as the weighted matrix and apply weighted average operation to patch embeddings $\mathcal{F}^P$. In the end, the average weighted feature $\mathcal{F}^{AP}$ is concatenated with $\mathcal{F}^C$ for final binary classification. The above procedure can be formulated as:

$$\mathcal{F}^{AP} = \mathbf{A}^P \odot \mathcal{F}^P = \frac{1}{P^2} \sum_{i,j}^{P} \mathbf{A}_{ij}^P * \mathcal{F}_{ij}^P, \tag{9}$$

$$\hat{\mathbf{y}} = \text{MLP}(concat\{\mathcal{F}^C, \mathcal{F}^{AP}\}), \tag{10}$$

where $\hat{\mathbf{y}}$ is the final predicted probability from MLP concatenated after the PCWA module.

3.3 Loss Functions

Assume $\mathbf{y}$ represents the binary labels indicating real or fake of input image. We use cross-entropy loss to supervise the final predicted probability $\hat{\mathbf{y}}$ to given binary labels 0/1, defined as:

$$\mathcal{L}_{cls} = -[\mathbf{y}\log\hat{\mathbf{y}} + (1-\mathbf{y})\log(1-\hat{\mathbf{y}})]. \tag{11}$$

The total loss functions of the proposed method are described as:

$$\mathcal{L}_{total} = \mathcal{L}_{cls} + \lambda_1\mathcal{L}_{UPCL} + \lambda_2(\frac{1}{|c1|} + \frac{1}{|c2|}) + \lambda_3|c3|, \tag{12}$$

where the final two losses are used for optimizing the learnable parameters c_1, c_2 to be increased and c_3 to be decreased along with the training process. λ_1, λ_2 and λ_3 are hyper-parameters used to balance the cross-entropy loss and consistency loss, meanwhile adjust the variations of consistency factors c_1, c_2 and c_3.

4   Experiment

4.1   Experimental Setting

Datasets. We conduct the experiments on four forgery datasets: 1) **FaceForensics++** [24] consists of 1,000 original videos and corresponding fake videos which are generated by four manipulation methods: DeepFakes [4], Face2Face [29], FaceSwap [6], NeuralTextures [28]. It provides forgery videos of three quality levels (raw, high, low quality). 2) **Celeb-DF** [15] is tempered by the Deep-Fake method and has a diversified distribution of scenarios. The author publishes two versions of their dataset, called Celeb-DF(v1) and Celeb-DF(v2). 3) **DeepFakeDetection (DFD)** [21] is produced by Google/Jigsaw, which contains 3,068 facial fake videos clips generated from 363 original videos. Forgery videos are tempered by the improved DeepFake method. 4) **Deepfake Detection Challenge** [25] (DFDC) preview dataset is generated by two kinds of synthesis methods on 1,131 original videos. Use the stand testset consisted 780 videos for our experiments.

Implement Details. Following [29], we employ the open source dlib algorithm to do face detection and landmark localization. All the detected faces are cropped around the center of the face, and then resized to 224 × 224. We adopt the ViT-Base architecture [5] as backbone where the input patch size is 16 × 16 and the number of encoder layer is set to 12. The designed GFR is assigned as 8 × 8 patches in the center region of cropped face. In the training process, the model is optimized only by cross-entropy loss in the first one epoch, and optimized by the total loss in the next epoch. Batch size is set to 96 and the Adam optimizer with the initial learning rate 3e-5 is adopted. The learning rate is reduced when the validation accuracy arrives at plateau. For the PCWA module, the hyper-parameters ρ, θ of variable weight w is set to 12, 0.7, respectively. In loss function Eq. (12), we experimentally set the weight λ_1, λ_2 and λ_3 to 0.06, 0.05, 0.5. These hyper-parameters are experimentally explored in supplementary materials. While testing, we set the *step* in Eq. (7) to 1.0 and use 110 frames per testing videos following FaceForensics++ [24].

Table 1. Cross-dataset experimental results. Our models are trained on Face-Forensics++ and tested on unseen datasets. We report the video-level AUC(%) on FaceForensics++(high quality) and frame level AUC(%) on other testing datasets

Methods	FF++.HQ	DFD	Celeb-DF-v2	Celeb-DF-v1	DFDC-P
Xception [24]	96.30	70.47	65.50	62.33	72.2
Capsule [20]	96.46	62.75	57.50	60.49	65.95
Multi-Attention [33]	99.29	75.53	67.44	54.01	66.28
FRLM [19]	99.50	68.17	70.58	76.52	69.81
Face X-ray [12]	87.40	85.60	74.20	80.58	70.0
LTW [26]	99.17	88.56	77.14	–	74.58
PCL+I2G [34]	99.11	–	81.80	–	–
Local-relation [1]	99.46	89.24	78.26	–	76.53
DCL [27]	99.30	91.66	82.30	–	**76.71**
UIA-ViT	99.33	**94.68**	**82.41**	**86.59**	75.80

Table 2. Cross manipulation experimental results. Test on each forgery method dataset (Deepfakes, Face2Face, FaceSwap, NeuralTexture) while training the model on the remaining three datasets

Methods	Training on the remaining three forgery dataset							
	Deepfakes		Face2Face		FaceSwap		NeuralTextures	
	ACC(%)	AUC(%)	ACC(%)	AUC(%)	ACC(%)	AUC(%)	ACC(%)	AUC(%)
Xception [24]	85.5	92.5	77.5	84.5	49.3	51.6	**70.9**	77.3
MLDG [10]	84.2	91.8	63.4	77.1	52.7	60.9	62.1	78.0
LTW [26]	85.6	92.7	65.6	80.2	**54.9**	64.0	65.3	77.3
DCL [27]	87.7	94.9	68.4	82.9	–	–	–	–
UIA-ViT	**90.4**	**96.7**	**86.4**	**94.2**	51.4	**70.7**	60.0	**82.8**

4.2 Quantitative Results

Cross Dataset Experiment. We first evaluate the detection performance on unseen datasets to demonstrate the generalization ability of our method in Table 1. We train the face forgery detectors on all the four types of fake data in FF++(HQ) and evaluate them on four unseen datasets, including DeepFakeDetection (DFD), Celeb-DF-v2, Celeb-DF-v1 and DFDC preview (DFDC-P). We report the cross-dataset AUC(%) in frame level of several state-of-art methods, each of which detects forgery using single frame rather than a video clip.

Table 1 shows that the proposed UIA-ViT outperforms other detection methods on several unseen datasets compared with recently general face forgery detection methods. Although our method adopts unsupervised forgery location method, it also superior to **PCL+I2G** [34] and **Local-relation** [1] on Celeb-DF, which both devote to extract intra-frame inconsistency cues with forgery location annotation. And we also slightly outperform the newly proposed **DCL** [27], which designs contrastive learning at different granularities to learn general-

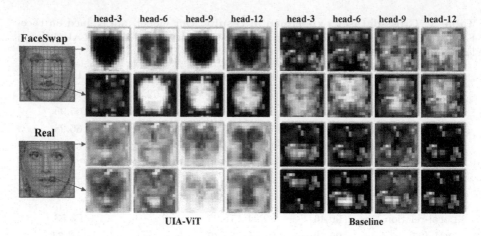

Fig. 2. Attention Maps of different queries in head-3/6/9/12 of the 11-th layer. Small squares denotes the query location.

ized feature representation for face forgery detection. Except DFDC-P, UIA-ViT achieves the best performance on unseen datasets. For example, UIA-ViT greatly outperforms other methods by 3.0+% on DFD, demonstrating the effectiveness of our method to improve the generalization ability for face forgery detection.

Cross Manipulation Experiment. To assess the generalization ability to unseen manipulations without perturbations such as variations in lighting and facial identities, we conduct the experiments on FaceForensics++ which is consisted of four types of manipulations and the same source videos. We utilize the fake videos created by four different forgery methods: DeepFakes, Face2Face, FaceSwap and NeuralTextures. We evaluate face forgery detectors with the leave-one-out strategy. Specifically, we test on each forgery method data using the model trained on the remaining three forgery methods in the high quality setting (FF++.HQ).

We compare the proposed method with other state of the art methods, and report the video-level ACC(%) and AUC(%). In the Table 2, there are four compared methods: **1) Xception** [24] is trained with official code by ourselves, **2) MLDG** [10] uses meta-learning for domain generalization, which is adapted to generalized face forgery detection in the work **LTW** [26]. **3) LTW** [26] also uses meta-learning strategy to learn domain-invariant model for unseen domain detection. This work reports the cross-manipulation results of LTW and MLDG. **4) DCL** [27] designs contrastive learning at different granularity to learn generalized feature representation. It reports their cross-manipulation results only on Deepfakes and Face2Face. The results in Table 2 show that the proposed method consistently achieves superior generalization performance compared to other frame-level methods, especially on Face2Face and FaceSwap with AUC(%) evaluation metrics. For example, out method achieves 9.7+% and 6.7+% higher AUC than other methods, demonstrating the state-of-the-art generalization ability of UIA-ViT to unseen forgeries.

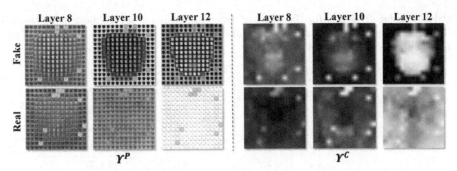

Fig. 3. Attention Map of layer 8/10/12 (averaged from multiple heads). The left Υ^P denotes the attention map between patch embeddings. The right Υ^C denotes the attention map between classification embedding and patch embeddings.

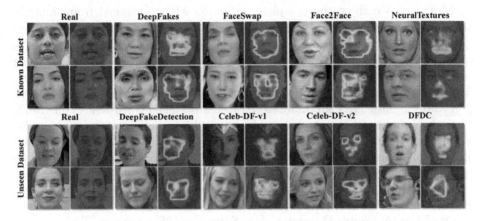

Fig. 4. Predicted Location Map of different datasets.

4.3 Visualization

To visually illustrate the consistency-aware embeddings learned by the proposed method, some attention maps of different queries from real or fake samples are shown in Fig. 2. We choose different query locations and show their attention map with keys of all patch embeddings. The dashed red rectangle in forgery sample represents the **GFR** location where the patch embeddings are used for MVG estimation. The query locations are indicated by green and red squares. From the visualizations, we conclude following observations: 1) patch embeddings among original background of the forged face are similar to each other, and so as those among forgery regions of the forged face. 2) patch embeddings between original background and forgery region is less similar. 3) the similarity between patch embeddings among different locations of real face are relatively equal. Such observations further illustrate the effectiveness of the proposed method to learn the consistency-related representations.

Table 3. Ablation Study for the effect of different components. All models are trained in FaceForensics++ and tested on the unseen forgery dataset Celeb-DF. The default components are expressed in bold

PCL	UPCL-hard	UPCL	CWA	PCWA	Celeb-DF-v1	Celeb-DF-v2
-	-	-	-	-	75.32	76.25
✓					77.88	79.85
		✓			78.54	78.55
			✓		82.96	80.86
			✓	✓	84.77	81.77
			✓	✓	**86.59**	**82.41**

Moreover, we show the complete Attention Map (averaged from multiple heads) from middle layers of our model in Fig. 3. $\Upsilon^P \in \mathbb{R}^{P^2 \times P^2}$ is the combination of P^2 small attention maps, each of which is of the size $P \times P$. $\Upsilon^C \in \mathbb{R}^{P \times P}$ is conducted by calculating the attention map between the classification embedding and the other patch embeddings. The visualizations show the similar observations described in the preceding paragraph. Meanwhile, it shows that Attention Maps in later layer are more closed to our designed consistency constraint. Though Υ^C has not been constrained by particular attention information, it also contains consistency cues between the input global classification embedding and other local patch embeddings, which indicates the importance regions should be great considered by the final classifier.

More **Predicted Location Map** of different datasets are further shown in Fig. 4. The UIA-ViT model is trained on FaceForensics++ consisted of four manipulation datasets, Deepfakes, FaceSwap, Face2Face, NeuralTextures and original videos (Real). We observe that our model can well concentrate on the manipulated regions, e.g. DF, F2F, FS replace the most areas of source faces with manipulated target faces, and NT manipulates the low-half faces, mainly on mouth and nose regions. We also show the predicted location maps of other unseen datasets, including DeepFakeDetection, Celeb-DF-v1, Celeb-DF-v2 and DFDC. They all use face swapping methods, which manipulate the identity of source faces and retain the original background. Their forgery regions should locate in center area of faces, like eyes, nose and mouth. When generalizing to these unseen datasets, we can find that most predicted forgery regions are consistent with the speculation.

4.4 Ablation Study

To explore the effectiveness of different components of the proposed UIA-ViT, we spilt each part separately for verification. Specifically, we develop the following experiment comparisons: 1) **baseline**: ViT-Base with the same training details. 2) **PCL**: Patch consistency learning which supervised by fixed GRF as general location map. 3) **UPCL-hard**: Unsupervised patch consistency learning module, but fix consistency factors $c_1 = 1, c_2 = 1$ and $c_3 = 0$. 4) **UPCL**:

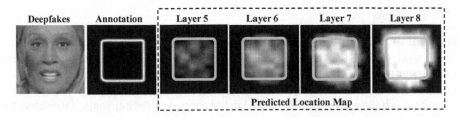

Fig. 5. Predicted Location Map of different layers.

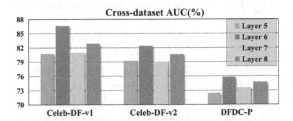

Fig. 6. Compare cross-dataset AUC of Layer 5–8.

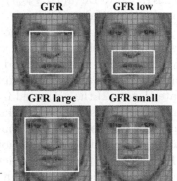

Fig. 7. Different GFR.

Table 4. Cross-dataset AUC of different GFR

AUC(%)	GFR low	GFR large	GFR small	GFR
Celeb-DF-v2	79.68	79.33	79.04	**82.41**
DFDC-P	74.61	73.78	73.13	**75.80**

Stand unsupervised patch consistency learning module. **5) CWA**: Consistency Weighted Assemble which fixes progressive weighted function as zero in Eq. (7). **6) PCWA**: Stand progressive consistency weighted assemble module.

The experimental results are shown in Table 3, and all models are trained on FaceForensics++ and tested on the unseen forgery dataset Celeb-DF. We draw the following conclusions: 1) Compared with **UPCL**, the model equipped with **PCL** and **UPCL-hard** are less generalized to Celeb-DF. Because MVG estimation in UPCL can help to amend the prior GFR and generate the predicted location map more closed to correct manipulated region. And soft consistency factors guarantee stable learning in early stage of training. 2) Both **CWA** and **PCWA** further improve the performance based on **UPCL**, demonstrating the importance of Attention Map Υ^C which indicates noteworthy regions for final classifier. Between them, **PCWA** performs better because of the progressive mechanism. 3) Comparing the results of **baseline**, **UPCL** and **UPCL+PCWA**, it demonstrates that both of proposed modules can improve the forgery detection performance. The model equipped with both components can obtain further improvements by 11% on Celeb-DF-v1 comparing to baseline, which demonstrates that the two components are complementary to each other.

4.5   Analysis

Determine Which Layer for MVG Estimation. In order to determine which layer is the best choice to conduct MVG estimation for forgery location prediction, we train the baseline ViT-Base model, and extract the patch embeddings from different middle layers for updating corresponding MVG distributions. Then, we visualize the predicted forgery location maps estimated by MVG distributions from 5-th, 6-th, 7-th and 8-th layers. Notice that different from the binary operation in Eq. (4), here predicted location map is computed as $M_{ij} = \text{ReLU}(d(f_{ij}, F_{real}) - d(f_{ij}, F_{fake}))$, where non-zero value indicates predicting as fake.

The visualizations are shown in Fig. 5. The annotation of forgery location is produced using the mask generation method mentioned in Face X-ray [12] which delimits the foreground manipulated region of forged image. We observe that: 1) the distances between real and fake MVG distributions are larger in the later layers; 2) the extracted features in the foreground and background are also more distinguishable in the later layers; 3) the predicted location map gradually expands to the whole image, because features in later layers capture more high-level semantic information rather than local texture information. Among them, we find that the predicted location map from 6-th layer is more closed to the annotation and apply it to conduct MVG estimation for forgery location prediction. We further make the quantitative analysis on this issue, as shown in Fig. 6. The experimental results show that utilizing the embeddings of 6-th layer to conduct unsupervised forgery location can achieve better generalization performance on several unseen datasets.

Determine Which GFR for MVG Estimation. We further explore the effect of different locations and sizes of General Forgery Region (GFR), and develop following experiments: **GFR low**, **GFR large**, **GFR small**, as shown in Fig. 7. GFR low is assigned as the low-half face, where nearly all pixels are manipulated in FaceForensics++ but eye region is missing. GFR large is assigned as the bigger region which contains most manipulated region and several mistake real pixels. Relatively, GFR small contains less manipulated region and less mistake real pixels. GFR is a trade-off proposal that locates in the center square region of faces, which covers most manipulated region of FaceForensics++. Comparing the performance of different locations and sizes of GFR in Table 4, we find that the standard GFR is superior than others. It further demonstrates that the features within GFR in FaceForensics++ can represent the distribution of actual manipulated face region and thus generalize well to other unseen datasets.

5   Conclusions

In this paper, we propose a novel face forgery detector named UIA-ViT, which is based on Vision Transformer and equipped with two key components UPCL and

PCWA. UPCL is a training strategy for learning the consistency-related representations through an unsupervised forgery location method. PCWA is a feature enhancement module and can take full advantage of the consistency representation. Visualizations show the great capabilities on learning consistency-related representations of our proposed method. Extensive experiments evidence effectiveness of our method for general face forgery detection.

Acknowledgements. This work is supported by the National Natural Science Foundation of China (No. 62002336, No. U20B2047) and Exploration Fund Project of University of Science and Technology of China under Grant YD3480002001.

References

1. Chen, S., Yao, T., Chen, Y., Ding, S., Li, J., Ji, R.: Local relation learning for face forgery detection. In: Proceedings of the AAAI Conference on Artificial Intelligence, pp. 1081–1088 (2021)
2. Chollet, F.: Xception: deep learning with depthwise separable convolutions. In: Proceedings of the IEEE/CVF Conference on Computer Vision and Pattern Recognition (CVPR) (2017)
3. Dang, H., Liu, F., Stehouwer, J., Liu, X., Jain, A.K.: On the detection of digital face manipulation. In: Proceedings of the IEEE/CVF Conference on Computer Vision and Pattern Recognition (CVPR) (2020)
4. DeepFakes (2019). www.github.com/deepfakes/faceswap
5. Dosovitskiy, A., et al.: An image is worth 16×16 words: transformers for image recognition at scale. I (2020)
6. FaceSwap (2019). www.github.com/MarekKowalski/FaceSwap
7. Haliassos, A., Vougioukas, K., Petridis, S., Pantic, M.: Lips don't lie: a generalisable and robust approach to face forgery detection. In: Proceedings of the IEEE/CVF Conference on Computer Vision and Pattern Recognition (CVPR), pp. 5039–5049 (2021)
8. Khan, S.A., Dai, H.: Video transformer for deepfake detection with incremental learning. In: Proceedings of the 29th ACM International Conference on Multimedia, pp. 1821–1828 (2021)
9. Li, C.L., Sohn, K., Yoon, J., Pfister, T.: CutPaste: self-supervised learning for anomaly detection and localization. In: Proceedings of the IEEE/CVF Conference on Computer Vision and Pattern Recognition (CVPR), pp. 9664–9674 (2021)
10. Li, D., Yang, Y., Song, Y.Z., Hospedales, T.M.: Learning to generalize: meta-learning for domain generalization. In: Thirty-Second AAAI Conference on Artificial Intelligence (2018)
11. Li, J., Xie, H., Li, J., Wang, Z., Zhang, Y.: Frequency-aware discriminative feature learning supervised by single-center loss for face forgery detection. In: Proceedings of the IEEE/CVF Conference on Computer Vision and Pattern Recognition (CVPR) (2021)
12. Li, L., et al.: Face X-ray for more general face forgery detection. In: Proceedings of the IEEE/CVF Conference on Computer Vision and Pattern Recognition (CVPR) (2020)
13. Li, Y., Chang, M.C., Lyu, S.: In ictu oculi: exposing AI created fake videos by detecting eye blinking. In: Workshop on Information Forensics and Security (WIFS) (2018)

14. Li, Y., Lyu, S.: Exposing deepfake videos by detecting face warping artifacts. arXiv preprint arXiv:1811.00656 (2018)
15. Li, Y., Yang, X., Sun, P., Qi, H., Lyu, S.: Celeb-DF: a large-scale challenging dataset for deepfake forensics. In: Proceedings of the IEEE/CVF Conference on Computer Vision and Pattern Recognition (CVPR) (2020)
16. Masi, I., Killekar, A., Mascarenhas, R.M., Gurudatt, S.P., AbdAlmageed, W.: Two-branch recurrent network for isolating deepfakes in videos. In: Vedaldi, A., Bischof, H., Brox, T., Frahm, J.-M. (eds.) ECCV 2020. LNCS, vol. 12352, pp. 667–684. Springer, Cham (2020). https://doi.org/10.1007/978-3-030-58571-6_39
17. Matern, F., Riess, C., Stamminger, M.: Exploiting visual artifacts to expose deep-fakes and face manipulations. In: Winter Applications of Computer Vision Workshops (WACVW) (2019)
18. Miao, C., Chu, Q., Li, W., Gong, T., Zhuang, W., Yu, N.: Towards generalizable and robust face manipulation detection via bag-of-feature. In: 2021 International Conference on Visual Communications and Image Processing (VCIP), pp. 1–5. IEEE (2021)
19. Miao, C., et al.: Learning forgery region-aware and ID-independent features for face manipulation detection. IEEE Trans. Biometrics Behav. Identity Sci. 4, 71–84 (2021)
20. Nguyen, H.H., Yamagishi, J., Echizen, I.: Capsule-forensics: using capsule networks to detect forged images and videos. In: IEEE International Conference on Acoustics, Speech and Signal Processing (ICASSP) (2019)
21. Nicholas, D., et al.: Deepfakes detection dataset by Google & Jigsaw (2019)
22. Qian, Y., Yin, G., Sheng, L., Chen, Z., Shao, J.: Thinking in frequency: face forgery detection by mining frequency-aware clues. In: Vedaldi, A., Bischof, H., Brox, T., Frahm, J.-M. (eds.) ECCV 2020. LNCS, vol. 12357, pp. 86–103. Springer, Cham (2020). https://doi.org/10.1007/978-3-030-58610-2_6
23. Rippel, O., Mertens, P., Merhof, D.: Modeling the distribution of normal data in pre-trained deep features for anomaly detection. In: 2020 25th International Conference on Pattern Recognition (ICPR), pp. 6726–6733. IEEE (2021)
24. Rossler, A., Cozzolino, D., Verdoliva, L., Riess, C., Thies, J., Nießner, M.: Face-Forensics++: learning to detect manipulated facial images. In: Proceedings of the IEEE/CVF International Conference on Computer Vision (2019)
25. Seferbekov, S.: (2020). https://github.com/selimsef/dfdc_deepfake_challenge
26. Sun, K., et al.: Domain general face forgery detection by learning to weight. In: Proceedings of the AAAI Conference on Artificial Intelligence, pp. 2638–2646 (2021)
27. Sun, K., Yao, T., Chen, S., Ding, S., Ji, R., et al.: Dual contrastive learning for general face forgery detection. In: Proceedings of the AAAI Conference on Artificial Intelligence (2021)
28. Thies, J., Zollhöfer, M., Nießner, M.: Deferred neural rendering: image synthesis using neural textures. ACM TOG 38, 1–12 (2019)
29. Thies, J., Zollhofer, M., Stamminger, M., Theobalt, C., Nießner, M.: Face2Face: real-time face capture and reenactment of RGB videos. In: CVPR (2016)
30. Vaswani, A., et al.: Attention is all you need. In: Advances in Neural Information Processing Systems, vol. 30 (2017)
31. Wang, S.Y., Wang, O., Zhang, R., Owens, A., Efros, A.A.: CNN-generated images are surprisingly easy to spot... for now. In: Proceedings of the IEEE/CVF Conference on Computer Vision and Pattern Recognition (CVPR), pp. 8695–8704 (2020)
32. Yang, X., Li, Y., Lyu, S.: Exposing deep fakes using inconsistent head poses. In: IEEE International Conference on Acoustics, Speech and Signal Processing (ICASSP) (2019)

33. Zhao, H., Zhou, W., Chen, D., Wei, T., Zhang, W., Yu, N.: Multi-attentional deepfake detection. In: Proceedings of the IEEE/CVF Conference on Computer Vision and Pattern Recognition (CVPR) (2021)
34. Zhao, T., Xu, X., Xu, M., Ding, H., Xiong, Y., Xia, W.: Learning self-consistency for deepfake detection. In: Proceedings of the IEEE/CVF International Conference on Computer Vision, pp. 15023–15033 (2021)
35. Zheng, Y., Bao, J., Chen, D., Zeng, M., Wen, F.: Exploring temporal coherence for more general video face forgery detection. In: Proceedings of the IEEE/CVF International Conference on Computer Vision, pp. 15044–15054 (2021)

Effective Presentation Attack Detection Driven by Face Related Task

Wentian Zhang[1,2,3], Haozhe Liu[1,2,3,4], Feng Liu[1,2,3($\boxtimes$)],
Raghavendra Ramachandra[5], and Christoph Busch[5]

[1] College of Computer Science and Software Engineering, Shenzhen University,
Shenzhen, China
[2] SZU Branch, Shenzhen Institute of Artificial Intelligence and Robotics for Society,
Shenzhen, China
[3] Guangdong Key Laboratory of Intelligent Information Processing,
Shenzhen University, Shenzhen 518060, China
feng.liu@szu.edu.cn
[4] King Abdullah University of Science and Technology, Thuwal, Saudi Arabia
[5] Norwegian Biometrics Laboratory (NBL), Norwegian University of Science
and Technology, 2818 Gjøvik, Norway

Abstract. The robustness and generalization ability of Presentation
Attack Detection (PAD) methods is critical to ensure the security of
Face Recognition Systems (FRSs). However, in a real scenario, Presentation Attacks (PAs) are various and it is hard to predict the Presentation Attack Instrument (PAI) species that will be used by the attacker.
Existing PAD methods are highly dependent on the limited training set
and cannot generalize well to unknown PAI species. Unlike this specific
PAD task, other face related tasks trained by huge amount of real faces
(e.g. face recognition and attribute editing) can be effectively adopted
into different application scenarios. Inspired by this, we propose to trade
position of PAD and face related work in a face system and apply the free
acquired prior knowledge from face related tasks to solve face PAD, so
as to improve the generalization ability in detecting PAs. The proposed
method, first introduces task specific features from other face related
task, then, we design a Cross-Modal Adapter using a Graph Attention
Network (GAT) to re-map such features to adapt to PAD task. Finally,
face PAD is achieved by using the hierarchical features from a CNN-based
PA detector and the re-mapped features. The experimental results show
that the proposed method can achieve significant improvements in the
complicated and hybrid datasets, when compared with the state-of-the-
art methods. In particular, when training on the datasets OULU-NPU,
CASIA-FASD, and Idiap Replay-Attack, we obtain HTER (Half Total

---

W. Zhang and H. Liu—Equal Contribution
This work was done when Haozhe Liu was a visiting student at NTNU, Norway, under
the supervision of R. Ramanchandra and C. Busch.

Supplementary Information The online version contains supplementary material
available at https://doi.org/10.1007/978-3-031-20065-6_24.

Error Rate) of 5.48% for the testing dataset MSU-MFSD, outperforming the baseline by 7.39%. The source code is available at https://github.com/WentianZhang-ML/FRT-PAD.

Keywords: Face · Presentation attack detection · Graph neural network

1   Introduction

Face Recognition Systems (FRSs) are widely deployed in authentication applications especially in access control and mobile phone unlocking in our daily life [17,35]. However, recent studies [15,26] demonstrate the existing face recognition systems are lacking robustness, since they are easily spoofed by presentation attacks (PAs), such as photographs, video replays, low-cost artificial masks [3] and facial make-up attacks [7]. Meanwhile, the face images can be easily obtained from social media, which seriously increases the risk of PAs. These issues raise wide concerns about the vulnerability of facial recognition technologies. Consequently, it is crucial to detect PAs to achieve robust and reliable FRS.

To tackle such challenge, many face PAD methods have been proposed, which can be divided into hardware and software based methods. Hardware based solutions [14,25] generally employ specific sensors to acquire presentations with different image modalities to detect PAs. Although, these methods provide strong robustness, their applicability is still limited because of unsatisfying performance to new application scenarios and cost limitations. Software based algorithms usually explore the distinctive features between bona fides (live faces) and PAs, such as hand-crafted features [1,8,24,33] and deep features [10,34]. Due to the advances of deep learning in recent years, deep feature based methods have been widely used in the community, since better performance can be achieved by adopting convolutional neural networks (CNNs) [12,16,32].

However, such learning-based method might not obtain ideal generalization to different unseen attacks, since they often needs comparable bona fide and PA samples for training. In the real scenario, PAs with different materials and instruments are hard to collect, the PAD mechanisms are limited by the unbalanced training data [18,20]. On the contrary, face related tasks (e.g. face, expression and attribute editing) possess strong generalization capability, since they are trained by millions of live faces cross genders, ages and ethnic groups from specific datasets. We argue that face PAD task should share some common patterns with other face related tasks, and the performance of PA detection might be boosted by the features adopted from such tasks.

As shown in Fig. 1(a), in traditional face systems, existing PAD mechanism like CNN-based PA detector, always plays a forward in face system and is independent with the following face related tasks. However, it is rarely discussed to contact PAD mechanism with face related tasks in the community. Since the face related tasks have already been trained, we consider that why not directly use these **free acquired** face-related features from face related tasks to serve for PAD. As shown in Fig. 1(b), different from traditional face systems, we attempt

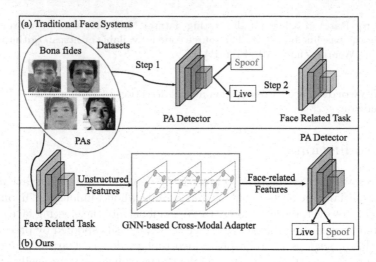

Fig. 1. The diagram of (a) traditional face systems with PA detector and (b) the proposed scheme. In the proposed method, face systems, including face, expression and attribute editing, are directly implemented. We then apply a GNN-based Cross-Modal Adapter to adapt their extracted features, which contain abundant generalization knowledge, to facilitate PAD.

to directly implement the trained face related tasks in face systems, and then utilize their extracted task specific features to make PAD mechanism generalize well in real scenarios.

In this paper, we propose a PAD method utilizing feature-level prior knowledge from face related task, denoted as **FRT-PAD** to solve the above mentioned problem. First, we trade the position of PAD mechanism and face related task in a face system. The task specific features, which contain abundant generalization knowledge, are directly obtained from face related tasks. By following a Graph Neural Network (GNN), a Cross-Modal Adapter is put forward to re-map and adapt the task specific features to PAD task. The generalization capability is finally improved by alleviating the problem resulting in limited PA samples for training. The main contributions of this work are concluded as follows,

- Existing PAD mechanism trained on the limited datasets are vulnerable to unseen PAs. To address this problem, we rethink the order of PAD mechanism and face related task in face system and directly introduce the free acquired features from face related tasks in PAD, which can improve generalization ability of PAD model.
- A Cross-Modal Adapter is designed to obtain face-related features, which can adapt task specific features into PAD space.
- The effectiveness and superiority of our method is evaluated on the public datasets. Particularly, when OULU-NPU [3], CASIA-FASD [38], and Idiap Replay-Attack [4] are adopted as training set and MSU-MFSD [33] is used as test set, the HTER (Half Total Error Rate) of the proposed method can outperform the baseline by 7.39%.

2   Related Works

As face related task is for the first time introduced in face PAD, the proposed face PAD scheme is different from existing PAD methods. Hence, our reviews mainly include face PAD methods and face related tasks.

2.1   Face Presentation Attack Detection

Existing face PAD methods can be categorized into hand-crafted and deep learning based methods. Hand-crafted methods employ the algorithms, e.g. LBP [8], IDA [33], SIFT [24], and SURF [1] to extract the features and then adopt traditional classifiers such as LDA and SVM to detect PAs. However, the hand-crafted features can be easily influenced by the variations of imaging quality and illumination. As a result, feature based methods generally can not generalize well to different application scenarios.

To address such challenges, deep learning models are then proposed for face PAD. Yang et al. [34] proposed to use CNNs to extract deep discriminative features for face PAD. Nguyen et al. [23] designed a multi-task learning model, which locates the most important regions of the input to detect PAs. Yu et al. [36] proposed a Central Difference Convolution (CDC) structure to capture intrinsic detailed patterns for face PAD and then used Neural Architecture Search (NAS) in CDC based network to achieve a better result. Besides applying only RGB images, auxiliary information of face, e.g. face depth, are considered to establish a more robust detector. Liu et al. [21] explored face depth as auxiliary information and estimated rPPG signal of RGB images through a CNN-RNN model for face PAD. George et al. [12] introduced a cross-modal loss function to supervise the multi-stream model, which extracted features from both RGB and depth channels. Liu et al. [19] proposed a self-supervised learning based method to search the better initialization for face PAD. Although such deep learning methods can achieve better PAD performance, their dependence on training data would inevitably leads a bias when accessible data is limited. In particular, numerous studies [11,28,30] have shown that, PA detectors trained on one dataset can not generalize to other datasets effectively.

To improve the generalization, researchers have further proposed one-class and domain generalization methods. A one-class multi-channel CNN model [11] was proposed to learn the discriminative representation for bona fides within a compact embedding space. Different from one-class methods, domain generalization based methods pay more attention to the disparities among the domains. Shao et al. [28] proposed a multi-adversarial deep domain generalization framework to learn a generalized feature space within the dual-force triplet-mining constraint. Since the learned feature space is discriminative and shared by multiple source domains, the generalization to new face PAs can be ensured effectively. Wang et al. [30] disentangled PAD informative features from subject-driven features and then designed a multi-domain learning based network to learn domain-independent features cross different domains for face PAD. Generally speaking, when training data is adequate for the aforementioned method, the detector can achieve very competitive performance. However, unlike other face related tasks,

Presentation Attacks (PAs) are hard to collect and the types/instruments of attacks are consistently increasing. Due to such open challenges, we propose a PAD mechanism based on face related task in a common face system to decrease the dependence of the PA detector on data scale. In particular, we obtain face-related features from face related tasks for a more robust representation with better generalization capability. Benefit from extensive samples collected in other tasks, face PA detector can achieve significant improvement within limited data.

2.2   Face Related Tasks

With the advances in deep learning, face related tasks including face recognition, face expression recognition, face attribute editing, etc., have become a very active field [5,6,31]. In this section, we briefly introduce some representative tasks adopted in this work due to the limited scope of the paper. For large-scale face recognition, Deng et al. [6] proposed an Additive Angular Margin Loss (Arc-Face), which has a clear geometric interpretation, to obtain highly discriminative features. ArcFace is a solid work evaluated on the various face recognition benchmarks, including image datasets with trillions of pairs and a large-scale video dataset. In the terms of facial expression recognition, Wang et al. [31] proposed a Self-Cure Network (SCN) to address uncertainties in facial expressions. By combining self-attention and relabelling mechanism, such method can prevent deep networks from over-fitting uncertain facial images. Choi1 et al. [5] proposed a scalable approach called StarGAN, to perform image-to-image translations for multiple domains and achieve facial attribute transfer. StarGAN can flexibly learn reliable features universally applicable to multiple domains of images with different facial attribute values, which is always set as a famous baseline in generative task. As the representative works for the corresponding tasks, the aforementioned solutions are conducted in this paper to investigate the relationship between PAD and face related tasks.

3   Proposed Method

In this paper, we propose a face-related-task based PAD mechanism (**FRT-PAD**) to improve the generalization capability of PAD model. As shown in Fig. 2, the proposed **FRT-PAD** method consists of two branches, including a CNN based PA detector and an auxiliary branch. The CNN based PA detector disentangles disparities between bona fides and PAs by directly extracting features from image space. The auxiliary branch aims to extract face-related features from a model trained by face related tasks. In such auxiliary branch, we firstly hierarchically obtain the task-specific features from multiple layers of the trained model. Then, we design a Cross-Modal Adapter based on GNN to adapt the features to PAD. The features from both branches are fused comprehensively for the final PAD. In the following sections, we will present the detailed discussion on the proposed method.

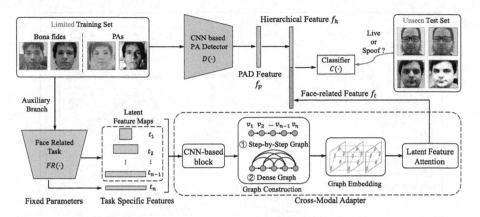

Fig. 2. The pipeline of our proposed PAD mechanism based on face related task in a common face system (**FRT-PAD**). In auxiliary branch, the task specific features t_i can be extracted by the parameter-fixed model $FR(\cdot)$, which has been trained from face related tasks. Then, a CNN-based block is used to transform t_i to graph vertexes. We construct a Graph Attention Network (GAT) to re-map t_i to fit PAD. By following latent feature attention, the face-related feature f_t is obtained, and finally fused with the main branch to achieve face PAD.

3.1   Task Specific Features from Face Related Tasks

As some face related tasks are trained from huge amount of faces, features extracted by such trained networks have better generalization capability. The hypothesis of this work is that face related tasks share some common patterns in face feature learning. For example, expression recognition requires the model to localize the action unit of the face, which also serves as a potential feature for PAD. Through transferring the knowledge contained in trained tasks, the dependence of PA detector on a large training data can be reduced. Hence features from face related tasks not only perform strong generalization in the trained task, but can also boost the performance of PA detector. Let x refers to a face in training set, and denote $FR(\cdot)$ as the network trained by face related tasks, e.g. face recognition, expression recognition and attribute editing. As shown in Fig. 2, $FR(\cdot)$ embeds x to a task specific feature $T = \{t_i | i \in [1, n]\}$, where t_i refers to the feature map extracted from the i-th layer. As a multi-level representation of x, the features from different layer represent different properties of the face. To prevent from the loss of information, the proposed method regards such non-structure feature map as the input of the auxiliary branch.

3.2   Cross-Modal Representation Using GAT

As $FR(\cdot)$ is trained by face related tasks, the extracted features t_i might contain information unrelated to the face PAD task. To alleviate the potential negative influence of the irrelevant information, we propose a Cross-Modal Adapter to re-map them for PAD. Considering that task specific features are non-structural,

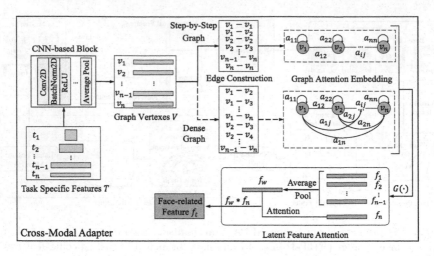

Fig. 3. The pipeline of Cross-Modal Adapter. To transform the task specific features $t_i \in T$ to graph vertexes, t_i are reconstructed to one-dimension vectors $v_i \in V$ using a CNN-based block. We design two different graphs, including Step-by-Step Graph and Dense Graph. In both graphs, attention mechanisms are used to specify the connection strength between different v_i. Through graph embedding $G(\cdot)$, v_i can be re-mapped to f_i. Then, the latent feature f_i is used to compute latent feature attention f_w by an average pool operation. The final face-related feature f_t is obtained by $f_w * f_n$.

a Graph Neural Network (GNN), denoted as $G(V, E)$, is employed to process T. $v_i \in V$ denotes vertex feature of graph. E is the edge matrix of graph to connect neighboring vertexes given by:

$$E = \begin{cases} e_{ij} = 1 \ v_i \rightarrow v_j \\ e_{ij} = 0 \ v_i \xrightarrow{\times} v_j \end{cases} \tag{1}$$

Given two graph vertexes v_i and v_j, $e_{ij} = 1$ presents an undirected edge existing between them. To construct neighboring v_i properly in E, the relationship among v_i is needed to be exploited. Since t_i is extracted by $FR(\cdot)$ step by step, T can perform as a sequence. Based on such observation, we propose two potential graph structures, including Step-by-Step Graph and Dense Graph, to investigate the reasonable utilization of T.

However, matrix E can only reflect the connection of each v_i. The importance of different v_i is unknown. Thus, we adopt an attention mechanism in GNN (i.e. GAT) embedding to find out the contribution of neighboring vertex to the central vertex. More important vertex features will obtain larger weights. Formally, the relative weights of the connected graph vertexes can be computed by:

$$A = E * (q_1 WV + (q_2 WV)^T) \tag{2}$$

where $Q = \{q_1, q_2\}$ is set as the shared attention parameter. A shared learnable weight matrix W is set to achieve graph convolutional operation, which can map each vertex v_i to a high-level feature. A stands for the attention matrix of graph vertexes V. Then, we use softmax to normalize $a_{ij} \in A$ by following the rule of connection:

$$A_s(i,j) = \frac{exp(a_{ij})}{\sum_{k \in [1,n]} exp(a_{ik}))} \tag{3}$$

Given two connected points v_i and v_j, $A_s(i,j)$ and $A_s(j,i)$ measures the connection strength coefficient of them. For one-layer attention, the vertex features with attention weights can be obtained:

$$V' = A_s W V \tag{4}$$

As shown in Fig. 3, task specific features t_i are firstly embedded into graph vertex features v_i by a CNN-based block. Then, for Step-by-Step Graph, two graph vertexes v_i and v_{i+1} are sequentially connected by a single edge. Different graph vertexes are fully connected in Dense Graph. Through the multi-layer graph embedding $G(V', E)$, the transformed features f_i are obtained. We regard latent features as the attention weights to strengthen the representation of f_n. Through an average pooling operation along with $f_i, i \in [1, n-1]$, the latent feature attention f_w can be computed. The final face-related feature f_t is represented by $f_w * f_n$.

3.3   Face-Related-Task Based Presentation Attack Detection

To adopt the re-mapped face-related feature in face PAD, the proposed method introduces a CNN based PA detector $D(\cdot)$ to learn the PAD feature f_p. Then,

---

Algorithm 1. Presentation Attack Detection Using FRT-PAD

Input:
  Training Set $\mathcal{X}_T$; CNN based PA detector $D(\cdot)$; Face recognition network $FR(\cdot)$;
  Classifier $C(\cdot)$; Graph embedding $G(\cdot)$;
Output:
  Trained $D(\cdot)$, $G(\cdot)$ and $C(\cdot)$;
1: Fixed parameters of Trained $FR(\cdot)$;
2: **for** x_j in $\mathcal{X}_T$ **do**
3:      Extract **PAD feature** f_p through $D(x_j)$;
4:      Derive task specific features $t_i \in T$ from $FR(x_j)$;
5:      Transform t_i to vector $v_i \in V$ as graph vertexes;
6:      Construct edge matrix E;
7:      Derive vertex features V' with attention weighs;
8:      Extract transformed features f_i through $G(V', E)$;
9:      Obtain attention weights f_w from $f_i, i \in [1, n-1]$;
10:     Calculate **face-related feature** f_t by $f_w * f_n$;
11:     Derive **hierarchical feature** f_h from f_p and f_t;
12:     Predict the PAD result by $C(f_h)$;
13:     Update $D(\cdot)$, $G(\cdot)$ and $C(\cdot)$by minimizing Eq. 5;
14: **end for**
15: Return $D(\cdot)$, $G(\cdot)$ and $C(\cdot)$;

---

a hierarchical feature f_h is derived by concatenating PAD feature f_p and face-related feature f_t. Through f_h, classifier $C(\cdot)$ can effectively distinguish bona fides with PAs. In the training process, $D(\cdot)$, $G(\cdot)$ and $C(\cdot)$ are trained by a cross entropy as follows:

$$\mathcal{L}_{x_j \in \mathcal{X}_T}(x_j, y_j') = -\frac{1}{N} \sum_{j=1}^{N} [y_j log(y_j') + (1 - y_j)log(1 - y_j')] \tag{5}$$

where $(x_j, y_j), j \in [1, N]$ are the paired samples from training set $\mathcal{X}_T$, and y_j' is the prediction result of $C(\cdot)$. For clarity, the proposed method is summarized in Algorithm 1.

4   Experimental Results and Analysis

In this section, we evaluate the performance of the proposed method by carrying experiments on the publicly-available datasets [3,4,33,38], First, the datasets and the corresponding implementation details are introduced. Then, we validate the effectiveness of the proposed method through analyzing the influences of each network component to PAD performance. Finally, to prove the superiority of our method, we compare the PAD performance of the proposed method with the state-of-the-art methods.

4.1   Datasets and Implementation Details

We use four public face anti-spoofing datasets, including OULU-NPU [3] (denoted as O), CASIA-FASD [38] (denoted as C), Idiap Replay-Attack [4] (denoted as I) and MSU-MFSD [33] (denoted as M) to evaluate the effectiveness of our method. Existing methods were evaluated on the protocol [16], denoted as Protocol-I. In this protocol, three of datasets are used as training set and the remaining one is used for test. However, in the reality, there are much more unseen PAs than the known ones in the training set. Using 3/4 datasets to train model is not strict to the real application scenario. Thus, we design a different cross-dataset protocol (Protocol-II) to evaluate the generalization ability of our method. In detail, we only use two datasets from [O, M, C, I] to train model and the remaining two datasets to test. Due to the number of samples varies greatly among each dataset, some data divisions will be unreasonable for model training. To make the number of training set and test set as close as possible, we only divide the datasets into two groups, i.e. [O, M] and [C, I]. To reduce the influence caused by the background, resolution, and illustration, MTCNN algorithm [37] is used for face detection and alignment. All the detected faces are resized to (256, 256). ResNet18 [13] is fine-tuned as the CNN based PA detector. Three network trained through the face related tasks are used to obtain task specific features. ResNet18 trained by face related task [6] and face expression recognition [31] is set as the feature extractor. For face attribute editing task, the trained discriminator of StarGAN [5] is set to extract task specific features.

In the graph embedding, a two-layer GAT with two-head attention mechanisms is adopted. In the training phase, the parameters of networks with face related tasks are fixed and the weight of task specific features are automatically determined. In terms of connection among vertexes, the attention mechanisms can specify the connection strength between them to show the most beneficial vertex. To evaluate the cross-modal adapter of our method, besides GAT, we adopt other deep learning methods, including ResNet18 [13] and transformer [29], as the competing methods.

In summary, we train PA detector, classifier and cross-modal adapter by Adam with 1e-4 learning rate and 5e-5 weight decay. Batch size for training is 32. To validate the superiority of our FRT-PAD method, the state-of-the-art PAD methods, including DeepPixBiS [10], SSDG-R [16], CDC [36], and IF-OM [19] are conducted in this paper. Following the work of [19], We use Half Total Error Rate (HTER), Area Under Curve (AUC) and Bona Fide Presentation Classification Error Rate (BPCER) when Attack Presentation Classification Error Rate ($APCER_{AP}$) is 1% to evaluate the performance of PAD. This paper adopts the public platform pytorch for all experiments using a work station with CPUs of 2.8GHz, RAM of 512GB and GPUs of NVIDIA Tesla V100.

4.2 Effectiveness Analysis of the Proposed Method

Face-Related Features. We perform the ablation study to quantify the influence of each component in our model for face PAD. First, to evaluate the effectiveness of face-related features, we test the performance of PAD with or without the face-related features. Table 1 shows the results carried on the cross-dataset protocol. The baseline is set as the ResNet18 model pretrained from ImageNet. We use three face related tasks, including face recognition, face expression recognition, and face attribute editing to extract task specific features. Then, by a step-by-step GAT, we can respectively obtain three different face-related features ($F.R.$, $F.E.$, $F.A.$). Compared with the baseline, all three face-related features can improve the PAD performance. Specifically, $F.A.$ feature adapted from face attribute editing task improves the HTER of baseline from 26.90% to 15.08%. This indicates that face-related features are useful to face PAD. As experiments are carried on the cross-dataset protocol, it also indicates that face-related features can improve generalization ability of face PAD.

Table 1. Performance of the proposed method with or without face-related features obtained from three different tasks.

	[O, M] to [C, I]			[C, I] to [O, M]		
	HTER(%)↓	AUC(%)↑	BPCER(%)↓	HTER(%)↓	AUC(%)↑	BPCER(%)↓
Baseline	25.65	79.14	95.93	28.14	79.05	81.34
Baseline w/$F.R.$	18.17	87.37	78.52	16.47	90.68	62.81
Baseline w/$F.E.$	17.93	85.97	90.90	16.62	91.78	55.66
Baseline w/$F.A.$	**16.98**	**90.66**	**58.32**	**13.18**	**94.36**	**43.70**

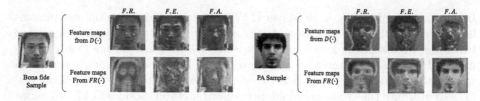

Fig. 4. The visualization on CASIA-FASD using Grad-CAM. The first row for each sample shows the discriminative regions obtained from CNN-based PA detector $D(\cdot)$ and the second row for each sample illustrate the region localization extracted from network of face related tasks $FR(\cdot)$.

To further verify the effectiveness of face-related features, we adopt Grad-CAM [27] to visualize the discriminative regions from feature maps in our proposed FRT-PAD model. We compare the visualization results with three face-related features. Cross-Modal Adapters are set as the Step-by-Step Graphs. As shown in Fig. 4, when using face-related features, the model can find discriminative features for both bona fide and PA samples. In the visualization region obtained form $FR(\cdot)$, the visualization shows that the hair, eyes, nose and mouth are important to distinguish live faces and spoofs. This further indicates the effectiveness of the face-related features. Typically, comparing with the visualization of $F.R.$ and $F.E.$ face-related features, $F.A.$ features can provide more effective region of face attributes.

Cross-Modal Adapter. For each task specific feature v_i, we further compare two other different deep learning models with GAT, i.e. CNN based model and transformer model, to justify the effectiveness of the Cross-Modal Adapter. In CNN based model, we use the same CNN-based block and latent feature attention in Fig. 3 to obtain the face-related feature. In transformer based model, each v_i is transformed to vector adopting CNN-based block in Fig. 3 and encoded with position encoding module in [29]. Then, we adopt six-layer transformer encoders with eight-head-attention to obtain the face-related feature. As CNN model and transformer model are sequential models, we only use the Step-by-Step Graph to ensure the fairness of the comparison. The PAD results in Table 2 show that the performance of the proposed method with different deep learning models in Cross-Modal Adapter and face-related features is better than the baseline.

Corresponding to Table 2, Fig. 5 presents the ROC (Receiver Operating Characteristic) curves of baseline and three face-related features when using different model in Cross-Modal Adapters. It can be seen that, for all face-related features, Cross-Modal Adapter using GAT model (with red lines in Fig. 5) achieves a higher performance than CNN model and transformer model. This indicates that GAT model is more suitable for the Cross-Model Adapter. In particular, face-related feature $F.A.$ re-mapped from GAT can obtain the best results in [C, I] to [O, M] protocol, and achieve an HTER of 13.18% and AUC of 94.36%.

Table 2. Performance of the proposed method using different models in cross-modal adapter for three face-related features.

Face-related features	Cross-modal adapters	[O, M] to [C, I]			[C, I] to [O, M]		
		HTER(%)↓	AUC(%)↑	BPCER(%)↓	HTER(%)↓	AUC(%)↑	BPCER(%)↓
×	×	25.65	79.14	95.93	28.14	79.05	81.34
F.R.	CNN	19.89	87.56	78.71	16.70	91.59	52.60
	Transformer	19.53	86.18	81.69	17.72	90.53	68.14
	GAT	18.17	87.37	78.52	16.47	90.68	62.81
F.E.	CNN	21.58	86.47	65.95	17.94	89.93	57.86
	Transformer	19.23	85.40	91.19	16.76	91.31	56.16
	GAT	17.93	85.97	90.90	16.62	91.78	55.66
F.A.	CNN	18.05	86.34	89.93	16.55	90.50	60.16
	Transformer	20.59	87.72	65.49	20.58	87.57	67.87
	GAT	**16.98**	**90.66**	**58.32**	**13.18**	**94.36**	**43.70**

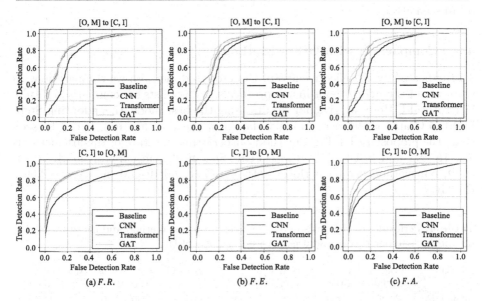

Fig. 5. ROC curves for the ablation study when using different models in Cross-Modal Adapter. The experiments are under the cross-dataset setting (Protocol-II) and adopting three different face-related features, which are (a) *F.R.*, (b) *F.E.* and (c) *F.A.*. Baseline (black line) in the figure represents the model without Cross-Modal Adapter.

These results can verify the contribution of Cross-Modal Adapter to improve the PAD performance and generalization.

Different Backbones. To further verify the effectiveness of face related task for PAD, we apply existing PAD methods, including CDC [36], DeepPixBiS [10] and SSDG-R [16] as backbones. We compare the PAD results when above PAD methods with or without face-related features (*F.A.*) from face related tasks on Protocol-II. As shown in Table 3, the proposed face-related features can improve

Table 3. Performance of other PAD backbones with or without face-related feature from FRT on protocol-II.

	[O, M] to [C, I]			[C, I] to [O, M]		
	HTER(%)↓	AUC(%)↑	BPCER(%)↓	HTER(%)↓	AUC(%)↑	BPCER(%)↓
CDC [36]	28.94	78.96	86.07	23.30	83.42	74.17
CDC w/FRT	**25.95**	**82.93**	**81.82**	**22.59**	**84.06**	**69.86**
DeepPixBiS [10]	22.93	79.13	100.0	22.45	85.70	75.63
DeepPixBiS w/FRT	**21.93**	**80.01**	100.0	**19.44**	**88.89**	**65.46**
SSDG-R [16]	20.92	88.07	90.28	22.57	85.61	84.05
SSDG-R w/FRT	**15.63**	**91.77**	**71.46**	**18.68**	**88.51**	**54.92**

performance of all three methods. It indicates that the proposed method can be adopted to existing PAD methods and improve their generalization capability on unseen attacks.

4.3 Comparison with Other Methods

To further verify the effectiveness of the proposed method, we compare it with the state-of-the-art methods in two protocols. Table 4 lists the comparison results in Protocol-I. Here, we give our results using the best model (i.e. adopting Step-by-Step Graph as the cross-modal Adapter of the *F.A.* feature). It can be seen that, the proposed FRT-PAD method outperforms the state-of-the-art methods e.g. IF-OM and SSDG-R by the HTER. Specifically, in experiment [I, C, M] to O, our method can outperform both SSDG-R and IF-OM by average 2.60% HTER.

Table 4. Performance comparison between the proposed method and the state-of-the-art methods under the cross-dataset setting. (protocol-I).

Method	[O, C, I] to M		[O, M, I] to C		[O, C, M] to I		[I, C, M] to O	
	HTER (%)↓	AUC(%)↑	HTER (%)↓	AUC(%)↑	HTER (%)↓	AUC(%)↑	HTER (%)↓	AUC(%)↑
MS-LBP [22]	29.76	78.50	54.28	44.98	50.30	51.64	50.29	49.31
Binary CNN [34]	29.25	82.87	34.88	71.94	34.47	65.88	29.61	77.54
IDA [33]	66.67	27.86	55.17	39.05	28.35	78.25	54.20	44.59
Color Texture [2]	28.09	78.47	30.58	76.89	40.40	62.78	63.59	32.71
LBP-TOP [9]	36.90	70.80	33.52	73.15	29.14	71.69	30.17	77.61
Auxiliary [21]	-	-	28.40	-	27.60	-	-	-
MADDG [28]	17.69	88.06	24.50	84.51	22.19	84.99	27.89	80.02
SSDG-R [16]	7.38	97.17	_10.44_	_95.94_	_11.71_	**96.59**	_15.61_	91.54
IF-OM [19]	_7.14_	_97.09_	15.33	91.41	14.03	94.30	16.68	_91.85_
Baseline	13.10	92.76	16.44	91.25	24.58	79.50	22.31	85.65
Ours: FRT-PAD	**5.71**	**97.21**	**10.33**	**96.73**	**11.37**	_94.79_	**13.55**	94.64

Moreover, in more challenge Protocol-II (two datasets as training set and other two datasets as test set), we can obtain good results with both adapters (Dense Graph and Step-by-Step Graph) using the *F.A.* feature. As shown in

Table 5. Performance comparison between the proposed method and the state-of-the-art methods under the cross-dataset setting. (protocol-II).

	[O, M] to [C, I]			[C, I] to [O, M]		
	HTER(%)↓	AUC(%)↑	BPCER(%)↓	HTER(%)↓	AUC(%)↑	BPCER(%)↓
CDC [36]	28.94	78.96	86.07	23.30	83.42	74.17
DeepPixBiS [10]	22.93	79.13	100.0	22.45	85.70	75.63
SSDG-R [16]	20.92	88.07	90.28	22.57	85.61	84.05
IF-OM [19]	18.96	89.48	69.52	18.60	89.76	69.70
Baseline	25.65	79.14	95.93	28.14	79.05	81.34
Ours: FRT-PAD w/Dense Graph	18.78	87.99	87.93	16.30	92.32	52.73
Ours: FRT-PAD w/Step-by-Step Graph	**16.98**	**90.66**	**58.32**	**13.18**	**94.36**	**43.70**

Table 5, the proposed method based on Step-by-Step Graph can outperform other methods by a large margin. Compared with CDC [36], our method can improve the HTER of PAD from 23.30% to 13.18% and AUC from 83.42% to 94.36%. These results indicate that the proposed method can generalize better than other PAD methods in both protocols, which further prove the superiority of our method.

5 Conclusion

Existing face presentation attack detection methods cannot generalize well to unseen PAs, due to the highly dependence on the limited datasets. In this paper, to improve generalization ability of face PAD, we proposed a face PAD mechanism using feature-level prior knowledge from face related task in a common face system. By designing a Cross-Modal Adapter, features from other face related tasks can re-map to more effective features for PAD. Experimental results have shown the effectiveness of the proposed method. Compared with the state-of-the-art methods in existing dataset partition (i.e. Protocol-I), we can improve HTER to 5.71%. Furthermore, when the dataset partition becomes more challenging (i.e. Protocol-II where more PAs are unseen to the model), our method largely improve the HTER to 13.18%, which demonstrates the strong generalization ability of our method to handle unpredictable PAs.

Acknowledgements. This work was supported in part by the National Natural Science Foundation of China (Grant 62076163 and Grant 91959108), and the Shenzhen Fundamental Research Fund (Grant JCYJ20190808163401646). Raghavendra Ramachandra is supported by SALT project funded by the Research Council of Norway.

References

1. Boulkenafet, Z., Komulainen, J., Hadid, A.: Face antispoofing using speeded-up robust features and fisher vector encoding. IEEE Signal Process. Lett. **24**(2), 141–145 (2016)

2. Boulkenafet, Z., Komulainen, J., Hadid, A.: Face spoofing detection using colour texture analysis. IEEE Trans. Inf. Forensics Secur. **11**(8), 1818–1830 (2016)
3. Boulkenafet, Z., Komulainen, J., Li, L., Feng, X., Hadid, A.: OULU-NPU: a mobile face presentation attack database with real-world variations. In: 2017 12th IEEE International Conference on Automatic Face & Gesture Recognition (FG 2017), pp. 612–618. IEEE (2017)
4. Chingovska, I., Anjos, A., Marcel, S.: On the effectiveness of local binary patterns in face anti-spoofing. In: 2012 BIOSIG-Proceedings of the International Conference of Biometrics Special Interest Group (BIOSIG), pp. 1–7. IEEE (2012)
5. Choi, Y., Choi, M., Kim, M., Ha, J.W., Kim, S., Choo, J.: StarGAN: unified generative adversarial networks for multi-domain image-to-image translation. In: Proceedings of the IEEE Conference on Computer Vision and Pattern Recognition, pp. 8789–8797 (2018)
6. Deng, J., Guo, J., Xue, N., Zafeiriou, S.: ArcFace: additive angular margin loss for deep face recognition. In: CVPR, pp. 4690–4699 (2019)
7. Drozdowski, P., Grobarek, S., Schurse, J., Rathgeb, C., Stockhardt, F., Busch, C.: Makeup presentation attack potential revisited: skills pay the bills. In: 2021 IEEE International Workshop on Biometrics and Forensics (IWBF), pp. 1–6. IEEE (2021)
8. de Freitas Pereira, T., Anjos, A., De Martino, J.M., Marcel, S.: Can face anti-spoofing countermeasures work in a real world scenario? In: 2013 International Conference on Biometrics (ICB), pp. 1–8. IEEE (2013)
9. Freitas Pereira, T., et al.: Face liveness detection using dynamic texture. EURASIP J. Image Video Process. **2014**(1), 1–15 (2014). https://doi.org/10.1186/1687-5281-2014-2
10. George, A., Marcel, S.: Deep pixel-wise binary supervision for face presentation attack detection. In: 2019 International Conference on Biometrics (ICB), pp. 1–8. IEEE (2019)
11. George, A., Marcel, S.: Learning one class representations for face presentation attack detection using multi-channel convolutional neural networks. IEEE Trans. Inf. Forensics Secur. **16**, 361–375 (2020)
12. George, A., Marcel, S.: Cross modal focal loss for RGBD face anti-spoofing. In: CVPR, pp. 7882–7891 (2021)
13. He, K., Zhang, X., Ren, S., Sun, J.: Deep residual learning for image recognition. In: CVPR, pp. 770–778 (2016)
14. Heusch, G., George, A., Geissbühler, D., Mostaani, Z., Marcel, S.: Deep models and shortwave infrared information to detect face presentation attacks. IEEE Trans. Biometrics Behavi. Identity Sci. **2**(4), 399–409 (2020)
15. Jia, S., Guo, G., Xu, Z.: A survey on 3D mask presentation attack detection and countermeasures. Pattern Recogn. **98**, 107032 (2020)
16. Jia, Y., Zhang, J., Shan, S., Chen, X.: Single-side domain generalization for face anti-spoofing. In: CVPR, pp. 8484–8493 (2020)
17. Karasugi, I.P.A., Williem: Face mask invariant end-to-end face recognition. In: Bartoli, A., Fusiello, A. (eds.) ECCV 2020. LNCS, vol. 12539, pp. 261–276. Springer, Cham (2020). https://doi.org/10.1007/978-3-030-68238-5_19
18. Liu, F., Liu, H., Zhang, W., Liu, G., Shen, L.: One-class fingerprint presentation attack detection using auto-encoder network. IEEE Trans. Image Process. **30**, 2394–2407 (2021)
19. Liu, H., Kong, Z., Ramachandra, R., Liu, F., Shen, L., Busch, C.: Taming self-supervised learning for presentation attack detection: in-image de-folding and out-of-image de-mixing. arXiv preprint arXiv:2109.04100 (2021)

20. Liu, H., Zhang, W., Liu, F., Wu, H., Shen, L.: Fingerprint presentation attack detector using global-local model. IEEE Trans. Cybern. (2021)
21. Liu, Y., Jourabloo, A., Liu, X.: Learning deep models for face anti-spoofing: binary or auxiliary supervision. In: CVPR, pp. 389–398 (2018)
22. Määttä, J., Hadid, A., Pietikäinen, M.: Face spoofing detection from single images using micro-texture analysis. In: 2011 International Joint Conference on Biometrics (IJCB), pp. 1–7. IEEE (2011)
23. Nguyen, S.M., Tran, L.D., Arai, M.: Attended-auxiliary supervision representation for face anti-spoofing. In: ACCV (2020)
24. Patel, K., Han, H., Jain, A.K.: Secure face unlock: spoof detection on smartphones. IEEE Trans. Inf. Forensics Secur. **11**(10), 2268–2283 (2016)
25. Raghavendra, R., Raja, K.B., Busch, C.: Presentation attack detection for face recognition using light field camera. TIP **24**(3), 1060–1075 (2015)
26. Ramachandra, R., Busch, C.: Presentation attack detection methods for face recognition systems: a comprehensive survey. ACM Comput. Surv. (CSUR) **50**(1), 1–37 (2017)
27. Selvaraju, R.R., Cogswell, M., Das, A., Vedantam, R., Parikh, D., Batra, D.: Grad-CAM: visual explanations from deep networks via gradient-based localization. In: ICCV, pp. 618–626 (2017)
28. Shao, R., Lan, X., Li, J., Yuen, P.C.: Multi-adversarial discriminative deep domain generalization for face presentation attack detection. In: CVPR, pp. 10023–10031 (2019)
29. Vaswani, A., et al.: Attention is all you need. In: Advances in Neural Information Processing Systems, pp. 5998–6008 (2017)
30. Wang, G., Han, H., Shan, S., Chen, X.: Cross-domain face presentation attack detection via multi-domain disentangled representation learning. In: CVPR, pp. 6678–6687 (2020)
31. Wang, K., Peng, X., Yang, J., Lu, S., Qiao, Y.: Suppressing uncertainties for large-scale facial expression recognition. In: CVPR, pp. 6897–6906 (2020)
32. Wang, Y., Song, X., Xu, T., Feng, Z., Wu, X.J.: From RGB to depth: domain transfer network for face anti-spoofing. IEEE Trans. Inf. Forensics Secur. **16**, 4280–4290 (2021)
33. Wen, D., Han, H., Jain, A.K.: Face spoof detection with image distortion analysis. IEEE Trans. Inf. Forensics Secur. **10**(4), 746–761 (2015)
34. Yang, J., Lei, Z., Li, S.Z.: Learn convolutional neural network for face anti-spoofing. arXiv preprint arXiv:1408.5601 (2014)
35. Yu, J., Hao, X., Xie, H., Yu, Y.: Fair face recognition using data balancing, enhancement and fusion. In: Bartoli, A., Fusiello, A. (eds.) ECCV 2020. LNCS, vol. 12540, pp. 492–505. Springer, Cham (2020). https://doi.org/10.1007/978-3-030-65414-6_34
36. Yu, Z., et al.: Searching central difference convolutional networks for face anti-spoofing. In: CVPR, pp. 5295–5305 (2020)
37. Zhang, K., Zhang, Z., Li, Z., Qiao, Y.: Joint face detection and alignment using multitask cascaded convolutional networks. IEEE Signal Process. Lett. **23**(10), 1499–1503 (2016)
38. Zhang, Z., Yan, J., Liu, S., Lei, Z., Yi, D., Li, S.Z.: A face antispoofing database with diverse attacks. In: 2012 5th IAPR International Conference on Biometrics (ICB), pp. 26–31. IEEE (2012)

PPT: Token-Pruned Pose Transformer for Monocular and Multi-view Human Pose Estimation

Haoyu Ma[1(✉)], Zhe Wang[1], Yifei Chen[2], Deying Kong[1], Liangjian Chen[3], Xingwei Liu[1], Xiangyi Yan[1], Hao Tang[3], and Xiaohui Xie[1]

[1] University of California, Irvine, Irvine, USA
{haoyum3,zwang15,deyingk,xingweil,xiangyy4,xhx}@uci.edu
[2] Tencent Inc., Shenzhen, China
dolphinchen@tencent.com
[3] Meta Reality Lab, Meta AI, Menlo Park, USA
{clj,haotang}@fb.com

Abstract. Recently, the vision transformer and its variants have played an increasingly important role in both monocular and multi-view human pose estimation. Considering image patches as tokens, transformers can model the global dependencies within the entire image or across images from other views. However, global attention is computationally expensive. As a consequence, it is difficult to scale up these transformer-based methods to high-resolution features and many views.

In this paper, we propose the token-Pruned Pose Transformer (PPT) for 2D human pose estimation, which can locate a rough human mask and performs self-attention only within selected tokens. Furthermore, we extend our PPT to multi-view human pose estimation. Built upon PPT, we propose a new cross-view fusion strategy, called human area fusion, which considers all human foreground pixels as corresponding candidates. Experimental results on COCO and MPII demonstrate that our PPT can match the accuracy of previous pose transformer methods while reducing the computation. Moreover, experiments on Human 3.6M and Ski-Pose demonstrate that our Multi-view PPT can efficiently fuse cues from multiple views and achieve new state-of-the-art results. Source code and trained model can be found at https://github.com/HowieMa/PPT.

Keywords: Vision transformer · Token pruning · Human pose estimation · Multi-view pose estimation

1 Introduction

Human pose estimation aims to localize anatomical keypoints from images. It serves as a foundation for many down-stream tasks such as AR/VR, action recognition [21,65], and medical diagnosis [11]. Over the past decades, deep convolutional neural networks (CNNs) play a dominant role in human pose estimation

S. Avidan et al. (Eds.): ECCV 2022, LNCS 13665, pp. 424–442, 2022.
https://doi.org/10.1007/978-3-031-20065-6_25

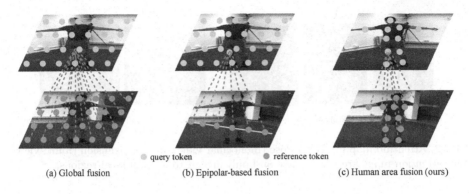

(a) Global fusion   (b) Epipolar-based fusion   (c) Human area fusion (ours)

Fig. 1. Different types of cross-view fusion. The first row is the current view, and the second row is the reference view.

tasks [40,50,53,59,61–63]. However, cases including occlusions and oblique viewing are still too difficult to be solved from a monocular image. To this end, some works apply a multi-camera setup [6,22,48,60] to boost the performance of 2D pose detection [19,43], since difficult cases in one view are potentially easier to be resolved in other views. Meanwhile, human body joints are highly correlated, constrained by strong kinetic and physical constraints [52]. However,since the reception fields of CNNs are limited, the long-range constraints among joints are often poorly captured [31].

Recently, the ViT [14] demonstrates that the transformers [55] can achieve impressive performance on many vision tasks [2,54]. Compared with CNN, the self-attention module of transformers can easily model the global dependencies among all visual elements. In the field of pose estimation, many tansformer-based works [31,33,37,67,74] suggest that the global attention is necessary. In single-view 2D human pose estimation, TransPose [67] and TokenPose [31] achieve new state-of-the-art performance and learn the relationship among keypoints with transformers. In multi-view human pose estimation, the TransFusion [36] uses the transformer to fuse cues from both current and reference views. Typically, these works flatten the feature maps into 1D token sequences, which are then fed into the transformer. In multi-view settings, tokens from all views are usually concatenated together to yield a long sequence. However, the dense global attention of transformers is computationally extensive. As a result, it is challenging to scale up these methods to high-resolution feature maps and many views. For example, the TransFusion [36] can only compute global attention between two views due to the large memory cost. Meanwhile, as empirically shown in Fig. 2, the attention map of keypoints is very sparse, which only focuses on the body or the joint area. This is because the constraints among human keypoints tend to be adjacent and symmetric [31]. This observation also suggests that the dense attention among all locations in the image is relatively extravagant.

In this paper, we propose a compromised and yet efficient alternative to the global attention in pose estimation, named token-Pruned Pose Transformer

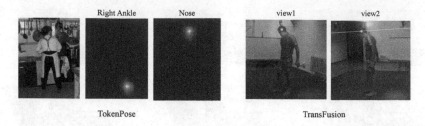

Fig. 2. Attention map for TokenPose (monocular view) and TransFusion (multi-view). The attention maps are very sparse and only attend to a small local regions.

(PPT). We calculate attention only within the human body area, rather than over the entire input image. Specifically, we select human body tokens and prune background tokens with the help of attention maps. As the human body only takes a small area of the entire image, the majority of input tokens can be pruned. We reveal that pruning these less informative tokens does not hurt the pose estimation accuracy, but can accelerate the entire networks. Interestingly, as a by-product, PPT can also predict a rough human mask without the guidance of ground truth mask annotations.

Moreover, we extend PPT to multi-view settings. As in Fig. 1, previous cross-view fusion methods consider all pixels in the reference view (global fusion) or pixels along the epipolar line (epipolar-based fusion) as candidates. The former is computationally extensive and inevitably introduces noise from the background, and the latter requires accurate calibration and lacks semantic information. Built upon PPT, we propose a new fusion strategy, called *human area fusion*, which considers human foreground pixels as corresponding candidates. Specifically, we firstly use PPT to locate the human body tokens on each view, and then perform the multi-view fusion among these selected tokens with transformers. Thus, our method is an efficient fusion strategy and can easily be extended to many views.

Our main contributions are summarized as follows:

1. We propose the token-Pruned Pose Transformer (PPT) for efficient 2D human pose estimation, which can locate the human body area and prune background tokens with the help of a Human Token Identification module.
2. We propose the strategy of "Human area fusion" for multi-view pose estimation. Built upon PPT, the multi-view PPT can efficiently fuse cues from human areas of multiple views.
3. Experimental results on COCO and MPII demonstrate that our PPT can maintain the pose estimation accuracy while significantly reduce the computational cost. Results on Human 3.6M and Ski-Pose show that human area fusion outperforms previous fusion methods on 2D and 3D metrics.

2   Related Work

2.1   Efficient Vision Transformers

Recently, the transformer [55] achieves great progresses on many computer vision tasks, such as classification [14,54], object detection [2,15,76], and semantic segmentation [58,66,68,75]. While being promising in accuracy, the vanilla ViT [14] is cumbersome and computationally intensive. Therefore, many algorithms have been proposed to improve the efficiency of vision transformers. Recent works demonstrate that some popular model compression methods such as network pruning [7,8,17,70], knowledge distillation [9,20,54], and quantization [46,51] can be applied to ViTs. Besides, other methods introduce CNN properties such as hierarchy and locality into the transformers to alleviate the burden of computing global attention [5,35]. On the other hand, some works accelerate the model by slimming the input tokens [3,29,32,38,44,45,71]. Specifically, the Token-to-tokens [71] aims to reduce the number of tokens by aggregating neighboring tokens into one token. The TokenLearner [45] mines important tokens by learnable attention weights conditioned on the input feature. The DynamicViT [44] prunes less informative tokens with an extra learned token selector. The EViT [32] reduces and reorganizes image tokens based on the classification token. However, all these models have only been designed for classification, where the final prediction only depends on the special classification token.

2.2   Human Pose Estimation

Monocular 2D Pose Estimation. In the past few years, many successful CNNs are proposed in 2D human pose estimation. They usually capture both low-level and high-level representations [12,13,40,50,62,63], or use the structural of skeletons to capture the spatial constraints among joints [10,24,26–28,42,52]. Recently, many works introduce transformers into pose estimation tasks [30,31,33,37,67,74]. Specifically, TransPose [67] utilizes transformers to explain dependencies of keypoint predictions. TokenPose [31] applies additional keypoint tokens to learn constraint relationships and appearance cues. Both works demonstrate the necessity of global attention in pose estimation.

Efficient 2D Pose Estimation. Some recent works also explore efficient architecture design for real-time pose estimation [39,41,47,57,69,72]. For example, EfficientPose [72] designs an efficient backbone with neural architecture search. Lite-HRNet [69] proposes the conditional channel weighting unit to replace the heavy shuffle blocks of HRNet. However, these works all focus on CNN-based networks, and none of them study transformer-based networks.

Multi-view Pose Estimation. 3D pose estimation from multiple views usually takes two steps: predicting 2D joints on each view separately with a 2D pose detector, and lifting 2D joints to 3D space via triangulation. Recently, many

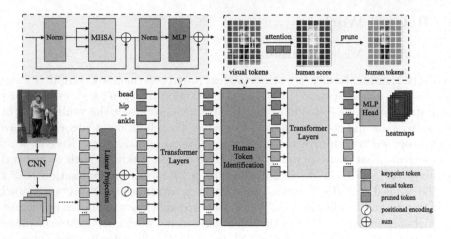

Fig. 3. Framework of the token-Pruned Pose Transformer (PPT). The visual tokens are obtained from the flattened CNN feature maps. The keypoint tokens are added to represent each joint and predict the keypoints heatmaps. The Human Token Identification (HTI) module is inserted inside the transformer layers to locate human visual tokens and prune background tokens. Thus the followed transformer layers are only performed on these selected tokens.

methods focus on enabling the 2D pose detector to fuse information from other views [19,36,43,64,73]. They can be categorized into two groups: 1) Epipolar-based fusion. The features of one pixel in one view is augmented by fusing features along the corresponding epipolar line of other views. Specifically, the AdaFuse [73] adds the largest response on the heatmap along the epipolar line. The epipolar transformer [19] applies the non-local module [56] on intermediate features to obtain the fusion weights. However, this fusion strategy requires precise camera calibration and discard information outside the epipolar lines. 2) Global fusion. The features of one pixel in one view are augmented by fusing features of all locations in other views. In detail, the Cross-view Fusion [43] learns a fixed attention matrix to fuse heatmaps in all other views. The TransFusion [36] applies the transformers to fuse features of the reference views and demonstrates that global attention is necessary. However, the computation complexity of global fusion is quadratic to the resolution of input images and number of views. Thus, both categories have their limitations. A fusion algorithm that can overcome these drawbacks and maintains their advantages is in need.

3   Methodology

3.1   Token-Pruned Pose Transformer

Overview. Figure 3 is an overview of our token-Pruned Pose Transformer. Following [31], the input RGB image **I** first go through a shallow CNN backbone

$\mathcal{B}(\cdot)$ to obtain the feature map $\mathbf{F} \in \mathbb{R}^{H \times W \times C}$. Then $\mathbf{F}$ is decomposed into flattened image patches $\mathbf{F}_p \in \mathbb{R}^{N_v \times (C \cdot P_h \cdot P_w)}$, where (P_h, P_w) is the resolution of each image patch, and $N_v = \frac{H}{P_h} \cdot \frac{W}{P_w}$ is the total number of patches [14]. Then a linear projection is applied to project $\mathbf{F}_p$ into $\mathbf{X}_p \in \mathbb{R}^{N_v \times D}$, where D is the dimension of hidden embeddings. The 2D positional encodings $\mathbf{E} \in \mathbb{R}^{N_v \times D}$ are added to make the transformer aware of position information [55], $i.e.$, $\mathbf{X}_v = \mathbf{X}_p + \mathbf{E}$, namely the visual token. Meanwhile, following TokenPose [31], we have J additional learnable keypoint tokens $\mathbf{X}_k \in \mathbb{R}^{J \times D}$ to represent J target keypoints. The input sequence to the transformer is $\mathbf{X}^0 = [\mathbf{X}_k, \mathbf{X}_v] \in \mathbb{R}^{N \times D}$, where $N = N_v + J$ and $[\dots]$ is the concatenation operation.

The transformer has L encoder layers in total. At the L_1^{th} layer, the Human Token Identification (HTI) module locates K most informative visual tokens where human body appears and prunes the remaining tokens. We denote $r = \frac{K}{N_v}(0 < r < 1)$ as the keep ratio. As a result, the length of the sequence is reduced to $N' = rN_v + J$ for the following transformer layers. The HTI is conducted e times at the $L_1^{th}, L_2^{th}, \dots, L_e^{th}$ layers. Thus, PPT can progressively reduce the length of visual tokens. Finally, the total number of tokens is $r^e N_v + J$. The prediction head projects the keypoint tokens in the last layer $\mathbf{X}_k^L \in \mathbb{R}^{J \times D}$ into the output heatmaps $\mathbf{H} \in \mathbb{R}^{J \times (H_h \cdot W_h)}$.

Transformer Encoder Layer. The encoder layer consists of the multi-headed self-attention (MHSA) and multi-layer perceptron (MLP). Operations in one encoder layer is shown in Fig. 3. The self-attention aims to match a query and a set of key-value pairs to an output [55]. Given the input $\mathbf{X}$, three linear projections are applied to transfer $\mathbf{X}$ into three matrices of equal size, namely the query $\mathbf{Q}$, the key $\mathbf{K}$, and the value $\mathbf{V}$. The self-attention (SA) operation is calculated by:

$$\text{SA}(\mathbf{X}) = \text{Softmax}(\frac{\mathbf{Q}\mathbf{K}^T}{\sqrt{D}})\mathbf{V}, \tag{1}$$

For MHSA, H self-attention modules are applied to $\mathbf{X}$ separately, and each of them produces an output sequence.

Human Token Identification (HTI). The TokenPose [31] conducts self-attention among all visual tokens, which is cumbersome and inefficient. From Eq. 1, we know that each keypoint token $\mathbf{X}_k^j$ interacts with all visual tokens $\mathbf{X}_v$ via the attention mechanism:

$$\text{Softmax}(\frac{\mathbf{q}_k^j \mathbf{K}_v^T}{\sqrt{D}})\mathbf{V}_v = \mathbf{a}^j \mathbf{V}_v, \tag{2}$$

where $\mathbf{q}_k^j$ denotes the query vector of $\mathbf{X}_k^j$, $\mathbf{K}_v$ and $\mathbf{V}_v$ are the keys and values of visual tokens $\mathbf{X}_v$. To this end, each keypoint token is a linear combination of all value vectors of visual tokens. The combination coefficients $\mathbf{a}^j \in \mathbb{R}^{N_v}$ are the attention values from the query vector for that keypoint token with respect to all visual tokens. To put it differently, the attention value determines how much

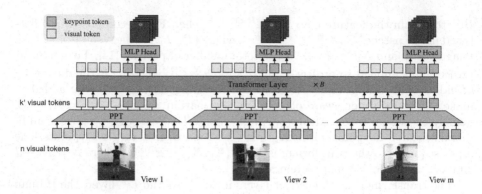

Fig. 4. Overall framework of the Multi-view PPT. A share-weight PPT is applied to extract a subset of visual tokens for each view. Then B transformer layers are applied to the concatenated tokens from each view to perform cross-view fusion. The output head takes keypoint tokens in each view to predict heatmaps.

information of each visual token is fused into the output. Thus, it is natural to assume that the attention value $\mathbf{a}^j$ indicates the importance of each visual token in the keypoint prediction [32]. Typically, a large attention value suggests that the target joint is inside or nearby the corresponded visual token.

With this assumption, we propose the Human Token Identification module to select informative visual tokens with the help of attention scores of keypoint tokens. However, each keypoint token usually only attends to a few visual tokens around the target keypoint. And some keypoint tokens (such as the eye and the nose) may attend to close-by or even the same visual tokens. Thus, it is difficult to treat the attention values of each keypoint separately. For simplicity, as all human keypoints make up a rough human body area, we use $\mathbf{a} = \sum_j \mathbf{a}^j$ as the criterion to select visual tokens, which is the summation of all joints' attention maps. In detail, we keep visual tokens with the K largest corresponding values in $\mathbf{a}$ as the human tokens, and prune the remaining tokens. As a result, only K visual tokens and J keypoint tokens are sent to the following layers.

3.2   Multi-view Pose Estimation with PPT

Human Area Fusion. We propose the concept of *Human area fusion* for cross-view fusion in multi-view pose estimation, which considers pixels where human appears as corresponding candidates. Suppose there are m cameras, and each view maintains n pixels (tokens) in its feature map. We summarize three typical types of cross-view fusion strategies in Fig. 1. 1) For global fusion, each pixel in each view calculates attention with respect to all n pixels in feature maps of other $m-1$ views. Thus the computational complexity is $\mathcal{O}(m^2n^2)$. 2) For epipolar-based fusion, each pixel in each view calculates attention with $k(k \ll n)$ pixels along the corresponded epipolar lines of other $m-1$ views. Thus the computational complexity is $\mathcal{O}(m^2nk)$. 3) For our human area fusion, we firstly select k' human foreground pixels in each view. Then we perform dense attention among these foreground tokens. As we also reduce the number of query pixels, the computational complexity is $\mathcal{O}(m^2 k'^2)$. Typically, $k < k' \ll n$. Thus, our method is an efficient way to perform cross-view fusion. Moreover, it also avoids the useless or even disturbing information from the background tokens and thus makes the model focus on the constraints within the human body.

Multi-view PPT. Naturally, we can apply an off-the-shelf segmentation network [18] to obtain human foreground pixels and then perform human area fusion. However, a large amount of densely annotated images are required to train a segmentation model. To this end, we utilize PPT to efficiently locate a rough human foreground area without any mask labels, and further propose the *multi-view PPT* for multi-view pose estimation. Specifically, we design our network in a two-stage paradigm, as shown in Fig. 4. Given the image $\mathbf{I}^m$ in each view, the share-weight PPT firstly produces selected human tokens $\tilde{\mathbf{X}}_v^m$ and keypoint tokens $\mathbf{X}_k^m$. Then we concatenate tokens from all views together and perform the dense attention among them with B transformer encoder layers. To help the network perceive the 3D space information, we also add the 3D positional encodings [36] on all selected visual tokens. Thus, each keypoint token can fuse visual information from all views. Moreover, it can learn correspondence constraints between keypoints both in the same view and among different views. Finally, a share-weight MLP head is placed on top of the keypoint token of each view to predicts keypoint heatmaps.

4   Experiments on Monocular Image

4.1   Settings

Datasets and Evaluation Metrics. We firstly evaluate PPT on monocular 2D human pose estimation benchmarks. COCO [34] contains $200K$ images in the wild and $250K$ human instances with 17 keypoints. Following top-down methods [31,50,63], we crop human instances with the ground truth bounding boxes for training and with the bounding boxes provided by SimpleBaseline [63] for inference. The evaluation is based on object keypoint similarity, which measures the distance between the detected keypoint and the corresponding ground truth. The standard average precision (AP) and recall (AR) scores are reported. MPII [1] contains about $25K$ images and $40K$ human instances with 16 keypoints. The evaluation is based on the head-normalized probability of correct keypoint (PCKh) score [1]. A keypoint is correct if it falls within a predefined threshold to the groundtruth location. We report the PCKh@0.5 score by convention.

Implementation Details. For fair comparison, we build our PPT based upon TokenPose-S, TokenPose-B, and TokenPose-L/D6 [31], namely PPT-S, PPT-B, and PPT-L/D6, respectively. For PPT-S and PPT-B, the number of encoder layers L is set to 12, the embedding size D is set to 192, the number of heads

H is set to 8. They take the shallow stem-net and the HRNet-W32 as the CNN backbone, respectively. Following [32,44], the HTI is performed $e = 3$ times and is inserted before the 4th, 7th, and 10th encoder layers. The PPT-L/D6 has $L = 12$ encoder layers and takes HRNet-W48 as the backbone. the HTI is inserted before the 2th, 4th, and 5th encoder layers. The number of visual tokens N_v is 256 for all networks, and the keep ratio r is set to 0.7 by default. Thus, only 88 visual tokens are left after three rounds pruning. We follow the same training recipes as [31]. In detail, all networks are optimized by Adam optimizer [25] with Mean Square Error (MSE) loss for 300 epochs. The learning rate is initialized with 0.001 and decays at the 200-th and the 260-th epoch with ratio 0.1. As locating human is difficult at early training stages, the keep ratio is gradually reduced from 1 to r with a cosine schedule during the early 100 epochs.

Table 1. Results on COCO validation dataset. The input size is 256×192. GFLOPs^T means the GFLOPs for the transformers only following equations from [29], as our method only focus on accelerating the transformers.

Method	#Params	GFLOPs	GFLOPs^T	AP	AP^{50}	AP^{75}	AP^M	AP^L	AR
SimpleBaseline-Res50 [63]	34M	8.9	-	70.4	88.6	78.3	67.1	77.2	76.3
SimpleBaseline-Res101 [63]	53M	12.4	-	71.4	89.3	79.3	68.1	78.1	77.1
SimpleBaseline-Res152 [63]	68.6M	15.7	-	72.0	89.3	79.8	68.7	78.9	77.8
HRNet-W32 [50]	28.5M	7.1	-	74.4	90.5	81.9	70.8	81.0	79.8
HRNet-W48 [50]	63.6M	14.6	-	75.1	90.6	82.2	71.5	81.8	80.4
Lite-HRNet-18 [69]	1.1M	0.20	-	64.8	86.7	73.0	62.1	70.5	71.2
Lite-HRNet-30 [69]	1.8M	0.31	-	67.2	88.0	75.0	64.3	73.1	73.3
EfficientPose-B [72]	3.3M	1.1	-	71.1	-	-	-	-	-
EfficientPose-C [72]	5.0M	1.6	-	71.3	-	-	-	-	-
TransPose-R-A4 [67]	6.0M	8.9	3.38	72.6	89.1	79.9	68.8	79.8	78.0
TransPose-H-S [67]	8.0M	10.2	4.88	74.2	89.6	80.8	70.6	81.0	79.5
TransPose-H-A6 [67]	17.5M	21.8	11.4	75.8	90.1	82.1	71.9	82.8	80.8
TokenPose-S [31]	6.6M	2.2	1.44	72.5	89.3	79.7	68.8	79.6	78.0
TokenPose-B [31]	13.5M	5.7	1.44	74.7	89.8	81.4	71.3	81.4	80.0
TokenPose-L/D6 [31]	20.8M	9.1	0.72	75.4	90.0	81.8	71.8	82.4	80.4
PPT-S (ours)	6.6M	1.6(−27%)	0.89(−38%)	72.2(−0.3)	89.0	79.7	68.6	79.3	77.8
PPT-B (ours)	13.5M	5.0(−12%)	0.89(−38%)	74.4(−0.3)	89.6	80.9	70.8	81.4	79.6
PPT-L/D6 (ours)	20.8M	8.7(−4%)	0.50(−31%)	75.2(−0.2)	89.8	81.7	71.7	82.1	80.4

Table 2. Results on the MPII validation set (PCKh@0.5). The input size is 256×256.

Method	#Params	GFLOPs	Head	Sho	Elb	Wri	Hip	Kne	Ank	Mean
SimpleBaseline-Res50 [63]	34M	12.0	96.4	95.3	89.0	83.2	88.4	84.0	79.6	88.5
SimpleBaseline-Res101 [63]	53M	16.5	96.9	95.9	89.5	84.4	88.4	84.5	80.7	89.1
SimpleBaseline-Res152 [63]	53M	21.0	97.0	95.9	90.0	85.0	89.2	85.3	81.3	89.6
HRNet-W32. [50]	28.5M	9.5	96.9	96.0	90.6	85.8	88.7	86.6	82.6	90.1
TokenPose-S [31]	7.7M	2.5	96.0	94.5	86.5	79.7	86.7	80.1	75.2	86.2
PPT-S	7.7M	1.9 (−24%)	96.6	94.9	87.6	81.3	87.1	82.4	76.7	87.3 (+1.1)
TokenPose-B [31]	14.4M	7.1	97.0	96.1	90.1	85.6	89.2	86.1	80.3	89.7
PPT-B	14.4M	6.2 (−13%)	97.0	95.7	90.1	85.7	89.4	85.8	81.2	89.8 (+0.1)

4.2 Results

The results are shown in Table 1 and Table 2 for COCO and MPII, respectively. Generally, the transformer-based methods [31,67] maintain less number of parameters. On COCO, compared with the TokenPose, PPT achieves significant acceleration while matching its accuracy. For example, PPT-S reduces 27% total inference FLOPs while only reducing 0.3 AP. Compared to SimpleBaseline-ResNet152 [63], PPT-S achieves equal performance but only requires 10% FLOPS. We can also observe consistent conclusion on PPT-B and PPT-L. Note that, for PPT-B and PPT-L, the CNN backbone takes a large portion of computation. Thus, the reduction of total FLOPs is relatively small. Meanwhile, compared with other efficient pose estimation networks [69,72], the AP of PPT-S is 72.2, which is much better than EfficientPose-C [72] with 71.3 AP at the same FLOPs level. More over, On MPII, our PPT-S can even improve on the PCKh of TokenPose-S by 1.1%. We believe that slimming the number of tokens can also make the attention focus on key elements [76]. Thus, our PPT is efficient yet powerful, and it is applicable to any TokenPose variants. All of these results suggest that pruning background tokens does not hurt the overall accuracy and calculating attention among human foreground tokens is sufficient for 2D human pose estimation.

4.3 Visualizations

We visualize the selected tokens from PPT-S in Fig. 5. We present the original images and the selected tokens at different layers. Remarkably, the human areas

Table 3. Results of PPT-S on COCO and MPII with different keep ratio r.

Method	Keep Ratio	# Visual Tokens	COCO			MPII		
			AP	AR	FLOPs	PCKh@0.5	PCKh@0.1	FLOPs
TokenPose-S	1.0	256 (100%)	72.5	78.0	2.23	86.2	32.2	2.53
PPT-S	0.8	131 (51%)	72.0 (−0.5)	77.6(−0.4)	1.75 (−22%)	86.9 (+0.7)	32.9 (+0.7)	2.06 (−19%)
PPT-S	0.7	88 (34%)	72.2 (−0.3)	77.8 (−0.2)	1.61 (−27%)	87.3 (+1.1)	34.1 (+1.9)	1.92 (−24%)
PPT-S	0.6	56 (22%)	71.8 (−0.7)	77.5 (−0.5)	1.52 (−32%)	86.7 (+0.5)	32.3 (+0.1)	1.82 (−28%)

are gradually refined as the network deepens. The final selected tokens can be considered as a rough human mask. Thus, our HTI can successfully locate human tokens as expected. Moreover, the HTI can handle quite a few complicated situations such as man-object interaction (Fig. 5(b)), oblique body pose (Fig. 5(c)), occlusion (Fig. 5(d)), and multiple persons (Fig. 5(e) 5(f)). Nevertheless, when only part of human body appears in the image (Fig. 5(g)5(h)), the quality of the located human mask could be imperfect. In these cases, we hypothesize that some keypoint tokens such as ankle and knee cannot locate the corresponding joints as they are invisible. Thus, they may just give equal attention score, which leads to inaccurate token selection.

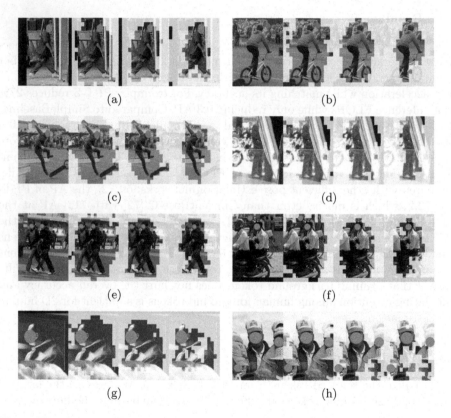

Fig. 5. Visualizations of the selected tokens at each HTI module on COCO. The masked regions represent the pruned tokens (We use blue circles to mask out face for privacy issue). For each image group, the first column is the original image, the 2nd, 3rd, and 4th columns are the selected tokens by HTI at the 4th, 7th, and 10th layers, respectively. (Color figure online)

Table 4. 2D pose estimation on Human3.6M. The metric is JDR on original image. All inputs are resized to 256×256. #V means the number of views used in cross-view fusion step. The FLOPs is the total computation for each view and cross-view fusion.

Method	#V	MACs	shlder	elb	wri	hip	knee	ankle	root	belly	neck	nose	head	Avg
ResNet50 [63]	1	51.7G	97.0	91.9	87.3	99.4	95.0	90.8	100.0	98.3	99.4	99.3	99.5	95.2
TransPose [67]	1	43.6G	96.0	92.9	88.4	99.0	95.0	91.8	100.0	97.5	99.0	99.4	99.6	95.3
TokenPose [31]	1	11.2G	96.0	91.3	85.8	99.4	95.2	91.5	100.0	98.1	99.1	99.1	99.1	94.9
Epipolar Transformer [19]	2	51.7G	97.0	93.1	91.8	99.1	96.5	91.9	100.0	99.3	99.8	99.8	99.3	96.3
TransFusion [36]	2	50.2G	97.2	96.6	93.7	99.0	96.8	91.7	100.0	96.5	98.9	99.3	99.5	96.7
Crossview Fusion [43]	4	55.1G	97.2	94.4	92.7	**99.8**	97.0	92.3	100.0	98.5	99.1	99.1	99.1	96.6
TokenPose+Transformers	4	11.5G	97.1	97.3	95.2	99.2	98.1	93.1	100.0	98.8	99.2	99.3	99.1	97.4
PPT	1	9.6G	96.0	91.8	86.5	99.2	95.6	92.2	100.0	98.4	99.3	99.5	99.4	95.3
Multi-view PPT	2	9.7G	97.1	95.5	91.9	99.4	96.4	92.1	100.0	99.0	99.2	99.3	99.0	96.6
Multi-view PPT	4	9.7G	97.6	**98.0**	96.4	99.7	98.4	93.8	100.0	99.0	**99.4**	**99.5**	**99.5**	**97.9**
Multi-view PPT + 3DPE	4	9.7G	**98.0**	**98.0**	96.4	99.7	**98.5**	**94.0**	100.0	**99.1**	99.2	99.4	99.3	**98.0**

Table 5. The MPJPE of each pose sequence on Human 3.6M.

Method	Dir	Disc	Eat	Greet	Phone	Pose	Purch	Sit	SitD	Smoke	Photo	Wait	WalkD	Walk	WalkT	Avg
Crossview Fusion [43]	24.0	28.8	25.6	24.5	28.3	24.4	26.9	30.7	34.4	29.0	32.6	25.1	24.3	30.8	24.9	27.8
Epipolar Trans. [19]	23.2	27.1	23.4	22.4	32.4	**21.4**	**22.6**	37.3	35.4	29.0	27.7	24.2	21.2	26.6	**22.3**	27.1
TransFusion [36]	24.4	**26.4**	23.4	**21.1**	25.2	23.2	24.7	33.8	**29.8**	26.4	26.8	24.2	23.2	26.1	23.3	25.8
Multi-PPT+3DPE	**21.8**	26.5	**21.0**	22.4	**23.7**	23.1	23.2	**27.9**	30.7	**24.6**	**26.7**	**23.3**	21.2	**25.3**	22.6	**24.4**

4.4 Ablation Studies

The keep ratio r controls the trade-off between the acceleration and the accuracy. Meanwhile, reducing tokens also introduces some regularization [76]. We take PPT-S and vary r from 0.6 to 0.8 on both COCO and MPII. The results are shown in Table 3. The reduction of AP is always less than 1%. When the r is relatively small, PPT can achieve considerable speedup but may not cover the entire human body. As a result, the accuracy of pose estimation is slightly dropped. To maintain the accuracy, we choose 0.7 as our default keep ratio.

5 Experiments on Multi-view Pose Estimation

5.1 Settings

Datasets and Evaluation Metrics. We evaluate multi-view PPT on two single-person datasets of multi-view 3D human pose estimation, i.e., Human 3.6M [4,22] and Ski-Pose [16,49][1]. Human 3.6M contains video frames captured by $M = 4$ indoor cameras. It includes many daily activities such as eating and

---

[1] Only authors from UCI downloaded and accessed these two datasets. Authors from Tencent and Meta don't have access to them.

Table 6. 2D and 3D pose estimation accuracy comparison on Ski-Pose.

Method	MACs	2D Pose/JDR (%) ↑	3D Pose/MPJPE (mm) ↓
Simple Baseline-Res50 [63]	77.6G	94.5	39.6
TokenPose [31]	16.8G	95.0	35.6
Epipolar Transformer [19]	77.6G	94.9	34.2
Multi-view PPT	**14.5G**	**96.3**	**34.1**

discussion. We follow the same train-test split as in [19,23,43], where subjects 1, 5, 6, 7, 8 are used for training, and 9, 11 are for testing. We also exclude some scenes of $S9$ from the evaluation as their 3D annotations are damaged [23]. Ski-Pose contains video frames captured by outdoor cameras. It is created to help analyze skiers's giant slalom. There are 8, 481 and 1, 716 frames in the training and testing sets, respectively. We use the Joint Detection Rate (JDR) on original images [43] to evaluate the 2D pose accuracy. JDR measures the percentage of successfully detected keypoints within a predefined distance of the ground truth location. The 3D pose is evaluated by Mean Per Joint Position Error (MPJPE) between the ground truth 3D pose in world coordinates and the estimated 3D pose.

Implementation Details. We build multi-view PPT upon PPT-S. The first 9 transformer layers are used to extract human tokens, and the last 3 transformer layers are used for cross-view fusion. Thus, no additional parameters are introduced. Following the settings in [19,36], we start from a PPT-S pre-trained on COCO and finetune it on multi-view human pose datasets, as it is difficult to train the transformer from scratch with examples in limited scenes. We apply Adam optimizer and train the model for 20 epochs with MSE loss. The learning rate starts with 0.001 and later on decays at 10-th and 15-th epoch with ratio 0.1. The keep ratio r is set to 0.7 through the entire training process. We resize input images to 256×256 and follow the same data augmentation in [36,43].

5.2   Results

The 2D results on Human 3.6 m is shown in Table 4. The MACs (multiply-add operations) consider both single-view forward MACs of all views and cross-view fusion MACs. Noticeably, our multi-view PPT outperforms all previous cross-view fusion methods on JDR. The JDR can be further improved with the 3D positional encodings (3DPE) [36] on visual tokens. Meanwhile, it can significantly reduce the computation of all 4 view fusion, *i.e.*, the MACs is reduced from 55.1G to 9.7G. When only fusing 2 views, multi-view PPT still achieves comparable accuracy with other two-view-fusion methods [19,36], Moreover, we add the baseline that adds transformers on top of TokenPose to perform cross-view fusion, which can be considered as multi-view PPT without token pruning. The JDR is 97.4% (−0.7% with respect to our multi-view PPT), which supports that our human area fusion is better than global attention in both accuracy

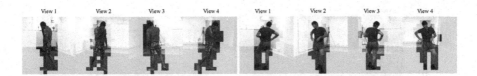

Fig. 6. Visualizations of the final located tokens on Human 3.6M validation set. For each group, each column is an image from one view. The masked regions represent the pruned tokens. We perform cross-view fusion among these selected tokens.

and efficiency. The MPJPE of estimated 3D pose is reported in Table 5. We can observe that multi-view PPT also achieves the best MPJPE on 3D pose, especially on sophisticated action sequences such as "Phone" and "Smoke", as the result of 3D pose is determined by the accuracy of 2D pose. Therefore, our "human area fusion" strategy is better than previous fusion strategies as it strikes a good balance between efficiency and accuracy. We can also observe consistent conclusion on Ski-Pose from Table 6. Nevertheless, it seems that the performance in this datatset tends to be saturated. The reason might be that there is limited number of training examples, thus the transformer is easy to overfit.

5.3 Visualizations

Human Tokens. Figure 6 presents the selected human tokens in all views. Similar to the conclusion on COCO, our PPT accurately locates all human areas and prunes background areas in all views. Moreover, the tokens used in the cross-view fusion step can be significantly reduced.

Qualitative Results. We present examples of predicted 2D heatmaps on the image in Fig. 7, and compare our methods with TransFusion [36]. It is observed that our method can solve heavy occlusion cases very well, while TransFusion cannot. For two-view-fusion method, occlusion cases in current view may still be occluded in the neighbor view. For example, the heatmap marked with red box is inaccurate in both view 2 and view 4. Thus, fusing this bad quality heatmap cannot improve the final prediction. However, our method can avoid this problem by fusing clues from all views.

Attentions. We present an example of the attention map between keypoint tokens in Fig. 8. Given keypoint tokens in one view, they pay attention to keypoints tokens in all views. For example, the left wrist in the first view (blue dot) is occluded, thus its corresponded keypoint token attends to the keypoint token in the second view, where the keypoint is visible. Therefore, the keypoint token in multi-view PPT can learn the dependencies among joints in different views.

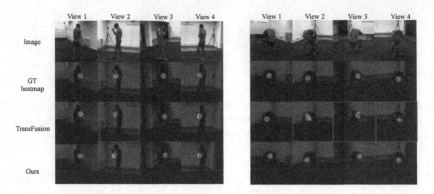

Fig. 7. Sample heatmaps of our approach.

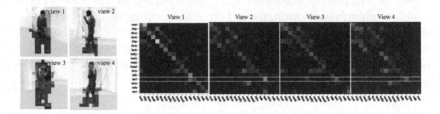

Fig. 8. Attention maps among keypoint tokens.

6   Conclusion

In this paper, we propose the PPT for 2D human pose estimation. Experiments on COCO and MPII show that the PPT achieves similar accuracy compared with previous transformer-based networks but reduces the computation significantly. We also empirically show that PPT can locate a rough human mask as expected. Furthermore, we propose the multi-view PPT to perform the cross-view fusion among human areas. We demonstrate that multi-view PPT efficiently fuses cues from many views and outperforms previous cross-view fusion methods on Human 3.6M and Ski-Pose.

References

1. Andriluka, M., Pishchulin, L., Gehler, P., Schiele, B.: 2D human pose estimation: new benchmark and state of the art analysis. In: CVPR (2014)
2. Carion, N., Massa, F., Synnaeve, G., Usunier, N., Kirillov, A., Zagoruyko, S.: End-to-end object detection with transformers. In: Vedaldi, A., Bischof, H., Brox, T., Frahm, J.-M. (eds.) ECCV 2020. LNCS, vol. 12346, pp. 213–229. Springer, Cham (2020). https://doi.org/10.1007/978-3-030-58452-8_13
3. Caron, M., et al.: Emerging properties in self-supervised vision transformers. In: ICCV (2021)

4. Ionescu, C., Li, F., Sminchisescu, C.: Latent structured models for human pose estimation. In: ICCV (2011)

5. Chen, C.F., Fan, Q., Panda, R.: CrossViT: cross-attention multi-scale vision transformer for image classification. In: ICCV (2021)

6. Chen, L., Lin, S.Y., Xie, Y., Lin, Y.Y., Xie, X.: MVHM: a large-scale multi-view hand mesh benchmark for accurate 3D hand pose estimation. In: WACV, pp. 836–845 (2021)

7. Chen, T., Cheng, Y., Gan, Z., Yuan, L., Zhang, L., Wang, Z.: Chasing sparsity in vision transformers: an end-to-end exploration. In: NeurIPS (2021)

8. Chen, T., Zhang, Z., Cheng, Y., Awadallah, A., Wang, Z.: The principle of diversity: training stronger vision transformers calls for reducing all levels of redundancy. In: CVPR (2022)

9. Chen, X., Cao, Q., Zhong, Y., Zhang, J., Gao, S., Tao, D.: DearKD: data-efficient early knowledge distillation for vision transformers. In: CVPR (2022)

10. Chen, Y., et al.: Nonparametric structure regularization machine for 2D hand pose estimation. In: WACV (2020)

11. Chen, Y., Ma, H., Wang, J., Wu, J., Wu, X., Xie, X.: PD-Net: quantitative motor function evaluation for Parkinson's disease via automated hand gesture analysis. In: KDD (2021)

12. Chen, Y., Wang, Z., Peng, Y., Zhang, Z., Yu, G., Sun, J.: Cascaded pyramid network for multi-person pose estimation. In: CVPR (2018)

13. Chu, X., Yang, W., Ouyang, W., Ma, C., Yuille, A.L., Wang, X.: Multi-context attention for human pose estimation. In: CVPR (2017)

14. Dosovitskiy, A., et al.: An image is worth 16×16 words: transformers for image recognition at scale. In: ICLR (2021)

15. Fang, Y., et al.: You only look at one sequence: rethinking transformer in vision through object detection. In: NeurIPS (2021)

16. Fasel, B., Spörri, J., Chardonnens, J., Kröll, J., Müller, E., Aminian, K.: Joint inertial sensor orientation drift reduction for highly dynamic movements. IEEE J. Biomed. Health Inform. **22**, 77–86 (2017)

17. Han, S., Mao, H., Dally, W.J.: Deep compression: compressing deep neural networks with pruning, trained quantization and Huffman coding. In: ICLR (2016)

18. He, K., Gkioxari, G., Dollár, P., Girshick, R.: Mask R-CNN. In: ICCV (2017)

19. He, Y., Yan, R., Fragkiadaki, K., Yu, S.I.: Epipolar transformers. In: CVPR (2020)

20. Hinton, G., Vinyals, O., Dean, J.: Distilling the knowledge in a neural network. arXiv preprint arXiv:1503.02531 (2015)

21. Huang, Z., Wan, C., Probst, T., Van Gool, L.: Deep learning on lie groups for skeleton-based action recognition. In: CVPR (2017)

22. Ionescu, C., Papava, D., Olaru, V., Sminchisescu, C.: Human3.6m: large scale datasets and predictive methods for 3D human sensing in natural environments. IEEE Trans. Pattern Anal. Mach. Intell. **36**, 1325–1339 (2014)

23. Iskakov, K., Burkov, E., Lempitsky, V., Malkov, Y.: Learnable triangulation of human pose. In: ICCV (2019)

24. Ke, L., Chang, M.-C., Qi, H., Lyu, S.: Multi-scale structure-aware network for human pose estimation. In: Ferrari, V., Hebert, M., Sminchisescu, C., Weiss, Y. (eds.) ECCV 2018. LNCS, vol. 11206, pp. 731–746. Springer, Cham (2018). https://doi.org/10.1007/978-3-030-01216-8_44

25. Kingma, D.P., Ba, J.: Adam: a method for stochastic optimization. In: ICLR (2015)

26. Kong, D., Chen, Y., Ma, H., Yan, X., Xie, X.: Adaptive graphical model network for 2D handpose estimation. In: BMVC (2019)

27. Kong, D., Ma, H., Chen, Y., Xie, X.: Rotation-invariant mixed graphical model network for 2D hand pose estimation. In: WACV (2020)
28. Kong, D., Ma, H., Xie, X.: SIA-GCN: a spatial information aware graph neural network with 2D convolutions for hand pose estimation. In: BMVC (2020)
29. Kong, Z., et al.: SpViT: enabling faster vision transformers via soft token pruning. arXiv preprint arXiv:2112.13890 (2021)
30. Li, K., Wang, S., Zhang, X., Xu, Y., Xu, W., Tu, Z.: Pose recognition with cascade transformers. In: CVPR (2021)
31. Li, Y., et al.: TokenPose: learning keypoint tokens for human pose estimation. In: ICCV (2021)
32. Liang, Y., Ge, C., Tong, Z., Song, Y., Wang, J., Xie, P.: EViT: expediting vision transformers via token reorganizations. In: ICLR (2022)
33. Lin, K., Wang, L., Liu, Z.: End-to-end human pose and mesh reconstruction with transformers. In: CVPR (2021)
34. Lin, T.-Y., et al.: Microsoft COCO: common objects in context. In: Fleet, D., Pajdla, T., Schiele, B., Tuytelaars, T. (eds.) ECCV 2014. LNCS, vol. 8693, pp. 740–755. Springer, Cham (2014). https://doi.org/10.1007/978-3-319-10602-1_48
35. Liu, Z., et al.: Swin transformer: hierarchical vision transformer using shifted windows. In: ICCV (2021)
36. Ma, H., et al.: Transfusion: cross-view fusion with transformer for 3D human pose estimation. In: BMVC (2021)
37. Mao, W., Ge, Y., Shen, C., Tian, Z., Wang, X., Wang, Z.: TFPose: direct human pose estimation with transformers. arXiv preprint arXiv:2103.15320 (2021)
38. Meng, L., et al.: AdaViT: adaptive vision transformers for efficient image recognition. In: CVPR (2022)
39. Neff, C., Sheth, A., Furgurson, S., Tabkhi, H.: EfficientHRNet: efficient scaling for lightweight high-resolution multi-person pose estimation. arXiv preprint arXiv:2007.08090 (2020)
40. Newell, A., Yang, K., Deng, J.: Stacked hourglass networks for human pose estimation. In: Leibe, B., Matas, J., Sebe, N., Welling, M. (eds.) ECCV 2016. LNCS, vol. 9912, pp. 483–499. Springer, Cham (2016). https://doi.org/10.1007/978-3-319-46484-8_29
41. Osokin, D.: Real-time 2D multi-person pose estimation on CPU: lightweight openpose. arXiv preprint arXiv:1811.12004 (2018)
42. Papandreou, G., Zhu, T., Chen, L.-C., Gidaris, S., Tompson, J., Murphy, K.: PersonLab: person pose estimation and instance segmentation with a bottom-up, part-based, geometric embedding model. In: Ferrari, V., Hebert, M., Sminchisescu, C., Weiss, Y. (eds.) ECCV 2018. LNCS, vol. 11218, pp. 282–299. Springer, Cham (2018). https://doi.org/10.1007/978-3-030-01264-9_17
43. Qiu, H., Wang, C., Wang, J., Wang, N., Zeng, W.: Cross view fusion for 3D human pose estimation. In: ICCV (2019)
44. Rao, Y., Zhao, W., Liu, B., Lu, J., Zhou, J., Hsieh, C.J.: DynamicViT: efficient vision transformers with dynamic token sparsification. In: NeurIPS (2021)
45. Ryoo, M., Piergiovanni, A., Arnab, A., Dehghani, M., Angelova, A.: TokenLearner: adaptive space-time tokenization for videos. In: NeurIPS (2021)
46. Shen, S., et al.: Q-BERT: hessian based ultra low precision quantization of BERT. In: AAAI (2020)
47. Shen, X., et al.: Towards fast and accurate multi-person pose estimation on mobile devices. arXiv preprint arXiv:2106.15304 (2021)
48. Simon, T., Joo, H., Matthews, I., Sheikh, Y.: Hand keypoint detection in single images using multiview bootstrapping. In: CVPR (2017)

49. Spörri, J.: Research dedicated to sports injury prevention-the 'sequence of prevention' on the example of alpine ski racing. Habilitation with Venia Docendi in Biomechanics (2016)
50. Sun, K., Xiao, B., Liu, D., Wang, J.: Deep high-resolution representation learning for human pose estimation. In: CVPR (2019)
51. Sun, M., et al.: VAQF: fully automatic software-hardware co-design framework for low-bit vision transformer. arXiv preprint arXiv:2201.06618 (2022)
52. Tompson, J.J., Jain, A., LeCun, Y., Bregler, C.: Joint training of a convolutional network and a graphical model for human pose estimation. In: NIPS (2014)
53. Toshev, A., Szegedy, C.: DeepPose: human pose estimation via deep neural networks. In: CVPR (2014)
54. Touvron, H., Cord, M., Douze, M., Massa, F., Sablayrolles, A., Jégou, H.: Training data-efficient image transformers & distillation through attention. In: ICML (2021)
55. Vaswani, A., et al.: Attention is all you need. In: NIPS (2017)
56. Wang, X., Girshick, R., Gupta, A., He, K.: Non-local neural networks. In: CVPR (2018)
57. Wang, Y., Li, M., Cai, H., Chen, W.M., Han, S.: Lite pose: efficient architecture design for 2D human pose estimation. In: CVPR (2022)
58. Wang, Y., et al.: End-to-end video instance segmentation with transformers. In: CVPR (2021)
59. Wang, Z., Yang, J., Fowlkes, C.: The best of both worlds: combining model-based and nonparametric approaches for 3D human body estimation. In: CVPR ABAW Workshop (2022)
60. Wang, Z., Chen, L., Rathore, S., Shin, D., Fowlkes, C.: Geometric pose affordance: 3D human pose with scene constraints. arXiv preprint arXiv:1905.07718 (2019)
61. Wang, Z., Shin, D., Fowlkes, C.C.: Predicting camera viewpoint improves cross-dataset generalization for 3D human pose estimation. In: Bartoli, A., Fusiello, A. (eds.) ECCV 2020. LNCS, vol. 12536, pp. 523–540. Springer, Cham (2020). https://doi.org/10.1007/978-3-030-66096-3_36
62. Wei, S.E., Ramakrishna, V., Kanade, T., Sheikh, Y.: Convolutional pose machines. In: CVPR (2016)
63. Xiao, B., Wu, H., Wei, Y.: Simple baselines for human pose estimation and tracking. In: Ferrari, V., Hebert, M., Sminchisescu, C., Weiss, Y. (eds.) ECCV 2018. LNCS, vol. 11210, pp. 472–487. Springer, Cham (2018). https://doi.org/10.1007/978-3-030-01231-1_29
64. Xie, R., Wang, C., Wang, Y.: MetaFuse: a pre-trained fusion model for human pose estimation. In: CVPR (2020)
65. Yan, S., Xiong, Y., Lin, D.: Spatial temporal graph convolutional networks for skeleton-based action recognition. In: AAAI (2018)
66. Yan, X., Tang, H., Sun, S., Ma, H., Kong, D., Xie, X.: AFTer-UNet: axial fusion transformer UNet for medical image segmentation. In: WACV (2022)
67. Yang, S., Quan, Z., Nie, M., Yang, W.: TransPose: keypoint localization via transformer. In: ICCV (2021)
68. You, C., et al.: Class-aware generative adversarial transformers for medical image segmentation. arXiv preprint arXiv:2201.10737 (2022)
69. Yu, C., et al.: Lite-HRNet: a lightweight high-resolution network. In: CVPR (2021)
70. Yu, S., et al.: Unified visual transformer compression. In: ICLR (2022)
71. Yuan, L., et al.: Tokens-to-token ViT: training vision transformers from scratch on imagenet. In: ICCV (2021)

72. Zhang, W., Fang, J., Wang, X., Liu, W.: EfficientPose: efficient human pose estimation with neural architecture search. Comput. Vis. Media **7**(3), 335–347 (2021). https://doi.org/10.1007/s41095-021-0214-z
73. Zhang, Z., Wang, C., Qiu, W., Qin, W., Zeng, W.: AdaFuse: adaptive multiview fusion for accurate human pose estimation in the wild. IJCV **129**, 703–718 (2021)
74. Zheng, C., Zhu, S., Mendieta, M., Yang, T., Chen, C., Ding, Z.: 3D human pose estimation with spatial and temporal transformers. In: ICCV (2021)
75. Zheng, S., et al.: Rethinking semantic segmentation from a sequence-to-sequence perspective with transformers. In: CVPR (2021)
76. Zhu, X., Su, W., Lu, L., Li, B., Wang, X., Dai, J.: Deformable DETR: deformable transformers for end-to-end object detection. In: ICLR (2021)

AvatarPoser: Articulated Full-Body Pose Tracking from Sparse Motion Sensing

Jiaxi Jiang[1] , Paul Streli[1] , Huajian Qiu[1] , Andreas Fender[1] ,
Larissa Laich[2] , Patrick Snape[2] , and Christian Holz[1](✉)

[1] Department of Computer Science, ETH Zurich, Zurich, Switzerland
christian.holz@inf.ethz.ch
[2] Reality Labs at Meta, Zurich, Switzerland
https://github.com/eth-siplab/AvatarPoser

Abstract. Today's Mixed Reality head-mounted displays track the user's head pose in world space as well as the user's hands for interaction in both Augmented Reality and Virtual Reality scenarios. While this is adequate to support user input, it unfortunately limits users' virtual representations to just their upper bodies. Current systems thus resort to floating avatars, whose limitation is particularly evident in collaborative settings. To estimate full-body poses from the sparse input sources, prior work has incorporated additional trackers and sensors at the pelvis or lower body, which increases setup complexity and limits practical application in mobile settings. In this paper, we present *AvatarPoser*, the first learning-based method that predicts full-body poses in world coordinates using only motion input from the user's head and hands. Our method builds on a Transformer encoder to extract deep features from the input signals and decouples global motion from the learned local joint orientations to guide pose estimation. To obtain accurate full-body motions that resemble motion capture animations, we refine the arm joints' positions using an optimization routine with inverse kinematics to match the original tracking input. In our evaluation, *AvatarPoser* achieved new state-of-the-art results in evaluations on large motion capture datasets (AMASS). At the same time, our method's inference speed supports real-time operation, providing a practical interface to support holistic avatar control and representation for Metaverse applications.

Keywords: 3D human pose estimation · Inverse kinematics · Augmented reality · Virtual reality

1 Introduction

Interaction in today's Mixed Reality (MR) environments is driven by the user's head pose and input from the hands. Cameras embedded in head-mounted displays (HMD) track the user's position inside the world and estimate articulated hand poses during interaction, which finds frequent application in Augmented Reality (AR) scenarios. Virtual Reality (VR) systems commonly equip the user with two hand-held controllers for spatial input to render haptic feedback. In

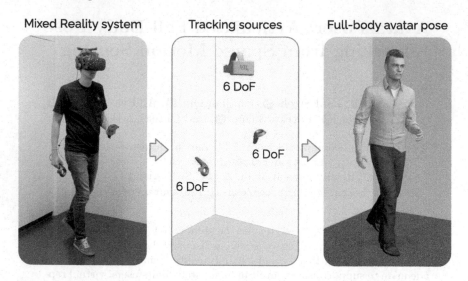

Fig. 1. We address the new problem of full-body avatar pose estimation from sparse tracking sources, which can significantly enhance embodiment, presence, and immersion in Mixed Reality. Our novel Transformer-based method *AvatarPoser* takes as input only the positions and orientations of one headset and two handheld controllers (or hands), and generates a full-body avatar pose over 22 joints. Our method reaches state-of-the-art pose accuracy, while providing a practical interface into the Metaverse.

both cases, even this sparse amount of tracking information suffices for interacting with a large variety of immersive first-person experiences (Fig. 1).

However, the lack of complete body tracking can break immersion and reduce the fidelity of the overall experience as soon as interactions exceed manual first-person tasks. This not just becomes evident as users see their own bodies during interaction in VR, but also in collaborative tasks in AR that necessarily limit the representation of other participants to their upper bodies, rendered to hover through space. Studies on avatar appearances have shown the importance of holistic avatar representations to achieve embodiment [49] and to establish presence in the virtual environment [19]. Applications such as telepresence or productivity meetings would greatly benefit from more holistic avatar representations that approach the fidelity of motion-capture animations.

This challenge will likely not be addressed by future hardware improvements, as MR systems increasingly optimize for mobile use outside controlled spaces that could accommodate comprehensive tracking. Therefore, we cannot expect future systems to expand much on the tracking information that is available today. While the headset's cameras may partially capture the user's feet in opportune moments with a wide field of view, head-mounted cameras are generally in a challenging location for capturing ego-centric poses [50].

Animating a complex full-body avatar based on the sparse input available on today's platforms is a vastly underdetermined problem. To estimate the complete set of joint positions from the limited tracking sources, previous work has constrained the extend of motion diversity [3] or used additional trackers on the user's body, such as a 6D pelvis tracker [53] or several body-worn inertial sensors [20]. Dittadi et al.'s recent method estimates full-body poses from only the head and hand poses with promising results [13]. However, since the method encodes all joints relative to the pelvis, it implicitly assumes knowledge of a fourth 3D input (i.e., the pelvis).

For practical application, existing methods for full-body avatar tracking come with three limitations: (1) Most general-purpose applications use Inverse Kinematics (IK) to estimate full-body poses. This often generates human motion that appears static and unnatural, especially for those joints that are far away from the known joint locations in the kinematic chain. (2) Despite the goal of using input from only the head and hands, existing deep learning-based methods implicitly assume knowledge of the pelvis pose. However, pelvis tracking may never be available in most portable MR systems, which increases the difficulty of full-body estimation. (3) Even with a tracked pelvis joint, animations from estimated lower-body joints sometimes contain jitter and sliding artifacts. These tend to arise from unintended movement of the pelvis tracker, which is attached to the abdomen and thus moves differently from the actual pelvis joint.

In this paper, we propose a novel Transformer-based method for full human pose estimation with only the sparse tracking information from the head and hand (or controller) poses as input. With *AvatarPoser*, we decouple the global motion from learned pose features and use it to guide our pose estimation. This provides robust results in the absence of other inputs, such as pelvis location or inertial trackers. To the best of our knowledge, our method is the first to recover the full-body motion from only the three inputs across a wide variety of motion classes. Because the predicted end effector poses of an avatar accumulate errors through the kinematic chain, we optimize our initial parameter estimations through inverse kinematics. This combination of our learning-based method with traditional model-based optimization strikes a good balance between full-body style realism and accurate hand control.

We demonstrate the effectiveness of *AvatarPoser* on the challenging AMASS dataset. Our proposed method achieves state-of-the-art accuracy on full-body avatar estimation from sparse inputs. For inference, our network reaches rates of up to 662 fps. In addition, we test our method on data we recorded with an HTC VIVE system and find good generalization of *AvatarPoser* to unseen user input. Taken together, our method provides a suitable solution for practical applications that operate based on the available tracking information on current MR headsets for application in both, Augmented Reality scenarios and Virtual Reality environments.

2   Related Work

Full-Body Pose Estimation from Sparse Inputs. Much prior work on full-body pose estimation from sparse inputs has used up to 6 body-worn inertial sensors [20,48,54,55]. Because these 6 IMUs are distributed over head, arms, pelvis and legs, motion capture becomes inflexible and unwieldly. CoolMoves [3] was first to use input from only the headset and hand-held controllers to estimate full-body poses. However, the proposed KNN-based method interpolates poses from a smaller dataset with only specific motion activities and it is unclear how well it scales to large datasets with diverse subjects and activities, also for inference. LoBSTr [53] used a GRU network to predict the lower-body pose from the past sequence of tracking signals of the head, hands, and pelvis, while it computes the upper-body pose to match the tracked end-effector transformations via an IK solver. The authors also highlight the difficulty of developing a system for estimations from 3 sources only, especially when distinguishing a wide range of human poses due to the large amount of ambiguity. More recently, Dittadi et al. proposed a VAE-based method to generate plausible and diverse body poses from sparse input [13]. However, their method implicitly uses knowledge of the pelvis as a fourth input location by encoding all joints relative to the pelvis, which leaves the highly ill-posed problem with only three inputs unsolved.

Vision Transformer. Transformers have achieved great success in their initial application in natural language processing [11,12,46]. The use of Transformer-based models has also significantly improved the performance on various computer vision tasks such as image classification [14,16,28], image restoration [26,52,56], object detection [8,44,62], and object tracking [33,43,59]. In the area of human pose estimation, METRO [27] was first to apply Transformer models to vertex-vertex and vertex-joint interactions for 3D human pose and mesh reconstruction from a single image. PoseFormer [60] and ST-Transformer [4] used Transformers to capture both body joint correlations and temporal dependencies. MHFormer [25] leveraged the spatio-temporal representations of multiple pose hypotheses to predict 3D human pose from monocular videos. In contrast to their offline setting where the complete time series of motions are available, our method focuses on the practical scenario where streaming data is processed by our Transformer in real-time without looking ahead.

Inverse Kinematics. Inverse kinematics (IK) is the process of calculating the variable joint parameters to produce a desired end-effector location. IK has been extensively studied in the past, with various applications in robotics [17,32,37, 40,51] and computer animation [2,18,36,42,58]. Because no analytical solution usually exists for an IK problem, the most common way to solve the problem is through numerical methods via iterative optimization, which is costly. To speed up computation, several heuristic methods have been proposed to approximate the solution [6,9,30,39]. Recently, learning-based IK solutions have attracted attention [5,7,10,15,38,47], because they can speed up inference. However, these methods are usually restricted to a scenario with a known data distribution and may not generalize well. To overcome this problem, recent works have combined IK with deep learning to make the prediction more robust and flexible [21,23, 24,41,53,57]. Our proposed method combines a deep neural network with IK optimization, where the IK component of our method refines the arm articulation to match the tracked hand positions from the original input (i.e., position of the hands or hand-held controllers).

3   Method

3.1   Problem Formulation

Although MR systems differ in the tracking technology they rely on, the global positions in Cartesian coordinates $\mathbf{p}^{1\times 3}$ and orientations in axis-angle representation $\mathbf{\Phi}^{1\times 3}$ of the headset and the hand-held controllers or hands are generally available. From these, *AvatarPoser* reconstructs the position of the articulated joints of the user's full body within the world $\mathbf{w}$. This mapping f is described through the following equation,

$$\mathbf{T}_{1:\tau}^{1:F} = f(\{\mathbf{p}^{\mathbf{w}}, \mathbf{\Phi}^{\mathbf{w}}\}_{1:\tau}^{1:S}), \tag{1}$$

where S corresponds to the number of joints tracked by the MR system, F is the number of joints of the full-body skeleton, τ matches the number of observed MR frames that are considered from the past, and $\mathbf{T} \in SE(3)$ is the body joint pose which is represented by $\mathbf{T} = \{\mathbf{p}, \mathbf{\Phi}\}$.

Specifically, we use the SMPL model [29] to represent and animate our human body pose. We use the first 22 joints defined in the kinematic tree of the SMPL human skeleton and ignore the pose of fingers similar to previous work [13].

3.2   Input and Output Representation

Since the 6D representation of rotations has proved effective for training neural networks due to its continuity [61], we convert the default axis-angle representation $\mathbf{\Phi}^{1\times 3}$ in the SMPL model to the rotation matrix $\mathbf{R}^{3\times 3}$ and discard the last row to get the 6D rotation representation $\theta^{1\times 6}$. During development, we observed that this 6D representation produces smooth and robust rotation predictions.

In addition to the accessible positions $\mathbf{p}^{1\times 3}$ and orientations $\mathbf{R}^{3\times 3}$ of the headset and hands, we also calculate the corresponding linear and angular velocities to obtain a signal of temporal smoothness. The linear velocity $\mathbf{v}$ is given by backward finite difference at each time step t:

$$\mathbf{v}_t = \mathbf{p}_t - \mathbf{p}_{t-1} \tag{2}$$

Similar, the angular velocity $\mathbf{\Omega}$ can be calculated by:

$$\mathbf{\Omega}_t = \mathbf{R}_{t-1}^{-1}\mathbf{R}_t \tag{3}$$

followed by also converting to its 6D representation $\omega^{1\times 6}$. As a result, the final input representation is a concatenated vector of position, linear velocity, rotation, and angular velocity from all given sparse inputs, which we write as:

$$\mathbf{X}_t^{1\times 18S} = [\{\mathbf{p}_t^1, \mathbf{v}_t^1, \theta_t^1, \omega_t^1\}^{1\times 18}, \ldots, \{\mathbf{p}_t^S, \mathbf{v}_t^S, \theta_t^S, \omega_t^S\}^{1\times 18}] \tag{4}$$

Therefore, when the number of sparse trackers S equals 3, the number of input features at each time step is 54.

The output of our rotation-based pose estimation network is the local rotation at each joint with respect to the parent joints θ_{local}. The rotation value at the pelvis, which is the root of the SMPL model, refers to the global orientation θ_{global}. As we use 22 joints to represent the full-body motion, the output dimension at each time step is 132.

3.3 Overall Framework for Avatar Full-Body Pose Estimation

Figure 2 illustrates the overall framework of our proposed method *AvatarPoser*. *AvatarPoser* is a time series network that takes as input the 6D signals from the sparse trackers over the previous $N - 1$ frames and the current N^{th} frame and predicts global orientation of the human body as well as the local rotations at each joint with respect to its parent joint. Specifically, *AvatarPoser* consists of four components: a Transformer Encoder, a Stabilizer, a Forward-Kinematics (FK) Module, and an Forward-Kinematics (IK) Module. We designed the network such that each component solves a specific task.

Transformer Encoder. Our method builds on a Transformer model to extract the useful information from time-series data, following its benefits in efficiency, scalability, and long-term modeling capabilities. We particularly leverage the Transformer's self-attention mechanism to distinctly capture global long-range dependencies in the data. Specifically, given the input signals, we apply a linear embedding to enrich the features to 256 dimensions. Next, our Transformer Encoder extracts deep pose features from previous time steps from the headset and hands, which are shared by the Stabilizer for global motion prediction, and a 2-layer multi-layer perceptron (MLP) for local pose estimation, respectively. We set the number of heads to 8 and the number of self-attention layers to 3.

Stabilizer. The Stabilizer is a 2-layer MLP that takes as input the 256-dimensional pose features from our Transformer Encoder. We set the number of nodes in the hidden layer to 256. The output of the network produces the estimated global orientation represented as the rotation of the pelvis; therefore, it is responsible for global motion navigation by decoupling global orientation from pose features and obtaining global translation from the head position through the body kinematic chain. Although it may be intuitive and possible to calculate the global orientation from a given head pose through the kinematic chain, the user's head rotation is often independent of the motions of other joints. As a result, the global orientation at the pelvis is sensitive to the rotation of the head. Considering the scenario where a user stands still and only rotates their head, it is likely that the global orientation may have a large error, which often results in a floating avatar.

Forward-Kinematics Module. The Forward-Kinematics (FK) Module calculates all joint positions given a human skeleton model and predicted local rotations as input. While rotation-based methods provide robust results without the need to reproject onto skeleton constraints to avoid bone stretching and invalid configurations, they are prone to error accumulating along the kinematic chain.

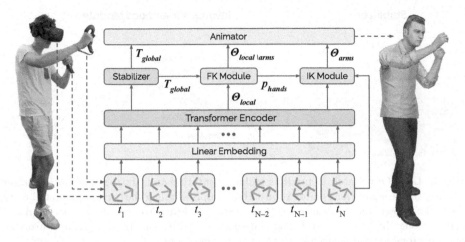

Fig. 2. The framework of our proposed *AvatarPoser* for Mixed Reality avatar full-pose estimation integrates four parts: a Transformer Encoder, a Stabilizer, a Forward-Kinematics Module, and an Inverse-Kinematics Module. The Transformer Encoder extracts deep pose features from previous time step signals from the headset and hands, which are split into global and local branches and correspond to global and local pose estimation, respectively. The Stabilizer is responsible for global motion navigation by decoupling global orientation from pose features and estimating global translation from the head position through the body's kinematic chain. The Forward-Kinematics Module calculates joint positions from a human skeleton model and a predicted body pose. The Inverse-Kinematics Module adjusts the estimated rotation angles of joints on the shoulder and elbow to reduce hand position errors.

Training the network without FK could only minimize the rotation angles, but would not consider the actually resulting joint positions during optimization.

Inverse-Kinematics Module. A main problem of rotation-based pose estimation is that the prediction of end-effectors may deviate from their actual location—even if the end effector served as a known input, such as in the case of hands. This is because for end-effectors, the error accumulates along the kinematic chain. Accurately estimating the position of end-effectors is particularly important in MR, however, because hands typically often used for providing input and even small errors in position can significantly disturb interaction with virtual interface elements. To account for this, we integrate a separate IK algorithm that adjusts the arm limb positions according to the known hand positions.

Our methods performs IK-based optimization based on the estimated parameters output by our neural network. This combines the individual benefits of both approaches as explored in prior work (e.g., [24,53]). Specifically, after our network produces an output, our IK Module adjusts the estimated rotation angles of joints on the shoulder and elbow to reduce the error of hand positions as shown in Fig. 3. We thereby fix the position of the shoulder and do not optimize

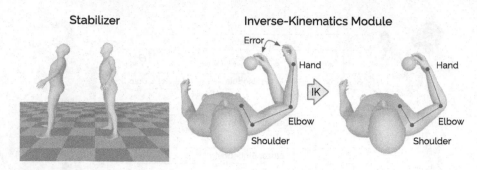

Fig. 3. Left: Our Stabilizer predicts global orientation and, thus, global motion (right avatar) that is significantly more robust than simply aligning the head of predicted body with the known input orientation (left avatar). **Right:** To account for accumulated errors along the joint hierarchy, we integrate an additional IK step to optimize the end-effectors' locations and match their target positions.

the other rotation angles, because we found the resulting overall body posture to appear more accurate than the output of the IK algorithm.

Given the initial rotation values $\theta_0 = \{\theta_0^{\text{shoulder}}, \theta_0^{\text{elbow}}\}$ estimated from our Transformer network, we calculate the positional error $\mathbf{E}$ of the hand according to the input signals and estimated hand position through the FK Module by

$$\mathbf{E}(\theta_i) = \left\| \mathbf{p}_{\text{gt}}^{\text{hand}} - \text{FK}(\theta_i)^{\text{hand}} \right\|_2^2 \tag{5}$$

Then the rotation value is updated by:

$$\theta_{i+1} = \theta_i + \eta \cdot f(\nabla \mathbf{E}(\theta_i)) \tag{6}$$

where η is the learning rate and $f(\cdot)$ is decided by the specific optimizer. To enable fast inference for real application, we stop the optimization after a fixed number of iterations.

There are several classical non-linear optimization algorithms that are suitable for optimizing inverse kinematics problems, such as Gauss-Newton method or the Levenberg-Marquardt method [34]. In our experiment, we leverage the Adam optimizer [22] due to its compatibility with Pytorch. We set the learning rate as 1×10^{-3}.

Loss Function. The final loss function is composed of an L1 local rotational loss, an L1 global orientation loss, and an L1 positional loss, denoted by:

$$\mathbf{L}_{total} = \lambda_{ori}\mathbf{L}_{ori} + \lambda_{rot}\mathbf{L}_{rot} + \lambda_{fk}\mathbf{L}_{fk} \tag{7}$$

We set the weights λ_{ori}, λ_{rot}, and λ_{fk} to 0.05, 1, and 1, respectively. For fast training, we do not include our IK Module into the training stage.

Table 1. Comparisons of MPJRE [°], MPJPE [cm], and MPJVE [cm/s] to State-of-the-Arts on AMASS dataset. For each metric, the best result is highlighted in **boldface**.

Methods	Four inputs			Three inputs		
	MPJRE	MPJPE	MPJVE	MPJRE	MPJPE	MPJVE
Final IK	12.39	9.54	36.73	16.77	18.09	59.24
CoolMoves	4.58	5.55	65.28	5.20	7.83	100.54
LoBSTr	8.09	5.56	30.12	10.69	9.02	44.97
VAE-HMD	3.12	3.51	28.23	4.11	6.83	37.99
AvatarPoser (Ours)	**2.59**	**2.61**	**22.16**	**3.21**	**4.18**	**29.40**

4 Experiments

4.1 Data Preparation and Network Training

We use the subsets CMU [1], BMLrub [45] and HDM05 [35] in AMASS [31] dataset for training and testing. The AMASS dataset is a large human motion database that unifies different existing optical marker-based MoCap datasets by converting them into realistic 3D human meshes represented by SMPL [29] model parameters. We split the three datasets into random training and test sets with 90% and 10% of the data, respectively. For use on VR devices, we unified the frame rate 60 Hz.

To optimize the parameters of *AvatarPoser*, we adopt the Adam solver [22] with batch size 256. We set the chunk size of input as 40 frames. The learning rate starts from 1×10^{-4} and decays by a factor of 0.5 every 2×10^4 iterations. We train our model with PyTorch on one NVIDIA GeForce GTX 3090 GPU. It takes about two hours to train *AvatarPoser*.

4.2 Evaluation Results

We use MPJRE (Mean Per Joint Rotation Error [°]), MPJPE (Mean Per Joint Position Error [cm]), and MPJVE (Mean Per Joint Velocity Error [cm/s]) as our evaluation metrics. We compare our proposed *AvatarPoser* with Final IK [2], CoolMoves [3], LoBSTr [53], and VAE-HMD [13], which are state-of-the-art methods working on the problems of avatar pose estimation from sparse inputs.

Since these state-of-the-art methods do not provide public source codes, we directly run Final IK in Unity [2] and reproduce other methods to the best of our knowledge. For a fair comparison, we train all the methods on the same training and testing data. It should be noted that the original CoolMoves is a position-based method, we adapt it to rotation-based method for a fair comparison with other methods. We make all the methods work with both three (headset, controllers) and four inputs (headset, controllers, pelvis tracker). When only three inputs are provided, for input representation we do not use the pose of pelvis as a reference frame, and for the output we calculate the global orientation and

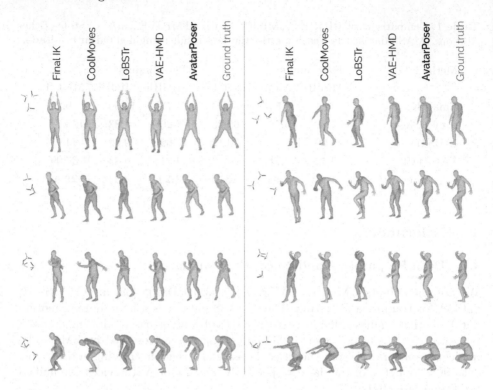

Fig. 4. Visual comparisons of different methods based on given sparse inputs for various motions. Avatars are color-coded to show errors in red. (Color figure online)

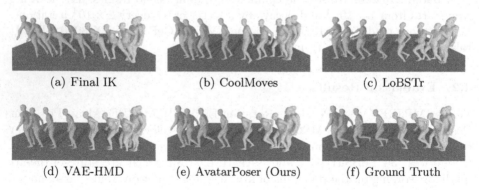

(a) Final IK   (b) CoolMoves   (c) LoBSTr

(d) VAE-HMD   (e) AvatarPoser (Ours)   (f) Ground Truth

Fig. 5. Visual results of our proposed method *AvatarPoser* compared to SOTA alternatives for a running motion. The change of color denotes different timestamp. (Color figure online)

translation of human body at pelvis through the kinematic chains from the given global pose of head (Figs. 4 and 5).

The numerical results for the considered metrics (MRJRE, MPJPE, and MPJVE) for both four and three inputs are reported in Table 1. It can be seen that our proposed *AvatarPoser* achieves the best results on all three metrics and outperforms all other methods. VAE-HMD achieves the second best performance on MPJPE, which is followed by CoolMoves (KNN). Final IK gives the worst result on MPJPE and MPJRE because it optimizes the pose of the end-effectors without considering the smoothness of other body joints. As a result, the performance of LoBSTr, which uses Final IK for upper body pose estimation, is also low. We believe this shows the value in data-driven methods to learn motion from existing mocap datasets. However, it does not mean that traditional optimization methods are not useful. In our ablation studies, we show how inverse kinematics when combined with deep learning can improve the accuracy of hand positions.

To further evaluate the generalization ability of our proposed method, we perform a 3-fold cross-dataset evaluation among different methods. To do so, we train on two subsets and test on the other subset in a round robin fashion. Table 2 shows the experimental results of different methods tested on CMU, BMLrub, and HDM05 datasets. We achieve the best results over almost all evaluation metrics in all three datasets. Although Final IK performs slightly better than *AvatarPoser* in terms of MPJVE in CMU, which can only means the motions are a little bit smoother. However, the rotation error MPJRE and the position error MPJPE of Final IK, which represent the accuracy of predictions, are much larger than our method.

Table 2. Results of cross-dataset evaluation between different methods. The input signals are from only three devices, i.e., one headset and two controllers. The best results for each dataset and each evaluation metrics are highlighted in **boldface**.

Dataset	Methods	MPJRE	MPJPE	MPJVE
CMU	Final IK	17.80	18.82	56.83
	CoolMoves	9.20	18.77	139.17
	LoBSTr	12.51	12.96	49.94
	VAE-HMD	6.53	13.04	51.69
	AvatarPoser (Ours)	**5.93**	**8.37**	**35.76**
BMLrub	Final IK	15.93	17.58	60.64
	CoolMoves	7.93	13.30	134.77
	LoBSTr	10.79	11.00	60.74
	VAE-HMD	5.34	9.69	51.80
	AvatarPoser (Ours)	**4.92**	**7.04**	**43.70**
HDM05	Final IK	18.64	18.43	62.39
	CoolMoves	9.47	17.90	140.61
	LoBSTr	13.17	11.94	48.26
	VAE-HMD	6.45	10.21	40.07
	AvatarPoser (Ours)	**6.39**	**8.05**	**30.85**

Table 3. Ablation studies. Best results are highlighted in **bold** for each metric.

Configurations	MPJRE	MPJPE-Full Body	MPJPE-Hand
Default	6.39	**8.05**	**1.86**
No Stabilizer	6.39	9.29	2.15
Predict Pelvis Position	6.42	8.82	2.11
No FK Module	**6.24**	8.41	2.04
No IK Module	6.41	8.07	3.17

4.3 Ablation Studies

We perform an ablation study on the different submodules of our method and provide results in Table 3. The experiments are conducted on the same test set as HDM05 in Table 2. We use MPJRE [°], MPJPE [cm] as our evaluation metrics in the ablation studies to show the need for each component. In addition to the position error across the full-body joints, we specifically calculate the mean error on hands to show how the IK module helps improve the hand positions.

No Stabilizer. We remove the Stabilizer module, which predicts the global orientation, and calculate the global orientation through the body kinematic chain directly from the given orientation of the head. Table 3 shows that the MPJPE drops without Stabilizer. This is because the rotation of the head is relatively independent to the rest of the body. Therefore, the global orientation is highly sensitive to random rotations of the head. Learning the global orientation from richer information via the network is a superior way to solve the problem.

Predict Pelvis Position. In our final model, we calculate the global translation of the human body, which is located at the pelvis, from the input head position through the kinematic chain. We also try directly regressing to the global translation within the network, but the result is worse than computing via the kinematic chain according to our evaluation results.

No FK Module. We also remove the FK Module, which means the network is only trained to minimize the rotation angles without considering the positions of joints after forward kinematics calculation. When we remove the FK module, the MPJPE increases and the MPJRE decreases. This is intuitive as we only optimize the joint rotations without the IK module. While rotation-based methods provide robust results without the need to reproject onto skeleton constraints to avoid bone stretching and invalid configurations, they are prone to error accumulation along the kinematic chain.

No IK Module. We remove IK Module and only provide the results directly predicted by our neural network. Removing the IK module has little effect on the average position error of full-body joints. However, the average position error of the hands increases by almost 41%.

4.4   Running Time Analysis

We evaluated the run-time inference performance of our network *AvatarPoser* and compared it to the inference of VAE-HMD [13], LoBSTr [53], CoolMoves [3] as shown in Fig. 6. Note that we did not include Final IK [2], because its integration into Unity makes accurate measurements difficult. To conduct our comparison, we modified LoBSTr to directly predict full-body motion via the GRU (denoted as LoBSTr-GRU) instead of combining Final IK and the GRU together. We measured the run time per frame (in milliseconds) on the evaluated test set on one NVIDIA 3090 GPU. For a fair comparison, we only calculated the network inference time of *AvatarPoser* here. Our *AvatarPoser* achieves a good trade-off between performance and inference speed.

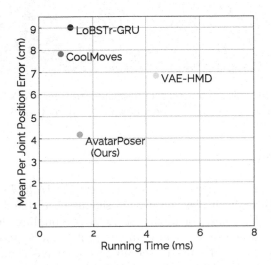

Fig. 6. Comparisons of network inference time across several methods. Due to the powerful and efficient Transformer encoder, our method achieves the smallest average position error while providing fast inference.

Our method also requires executing an IK algorithm after the network forward pass. Each iteration costs approximately 6 ms, so we set the number of iterations to 5 to keep a balance between inference speed and the accuracy of the final hand position. Note that the speed could be accelerated by adopting a more standard non-linear optimization.

4.5   Test on a Commercial VR System

To qualitatively assess the robustness of our method, we executed our algorithm on live recordings from an actual VR system. We used an HTC VIVE HMD as well as two controllers, each providing real-time input with six degrees of freedom (rotation and translation). Figure 7 shows a few examples of our method's output based on sparse inputs.

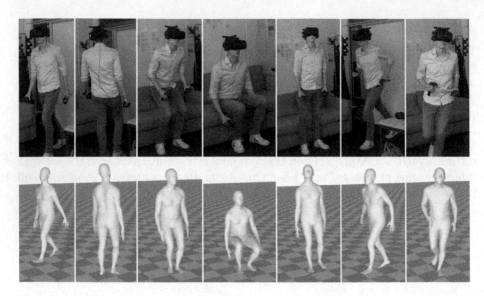

Fig. 7. We tested our method on recorded motion data from a VIVE Pro headset and two VIVE controllers. Columns show the user's pose (top) and our prediction (bottom).

5   Conclusions

We presented our novel Transformer-based method *AvatarPoser* to estimate realistic human poses from just the motion signals of a Mixed Reality headset and the user's hands or hand-held controllers. By decoupling the global motion information from learned pose features and using it to guide pose estimation, we achieve robust estimation results in the absence of pelvis signals. By combing learning-based methods with traditional model-based optimization, we keep a balance between full-body style realism and accurate hand control. Our extensive experiments on the AMASS dataset demonstrated that *AvatarPoser* surpasses the performance of state-of-the-art methods and, thus, provides a useful learning-based IK solution for practical VR/AR applications.

Acknowledgments. We thank Christian Knieling for his early explorations of learning-based methods for pose estimation with us at ETH Zürich. We thank Zhi Li, Xianghui Xie, and Dengxin Dai from Max Planck Institute for Informatics for their helpful discussions. We also thank Olga Sorkine-Hornung and Alexander Sorkine-Hornung for early discussions.

References

1. CMU MoCap Dataset (2004). http://mocap.cs.cmu.edu/
2. RootMotion Final IK (2018). https://assetstore.unity.com/packages/tools/animation/final-ik-14290

3. Ahuja, K., Ofek, E., Gonzalez-Franco, M., Holz, C., Wilson, A.D.: CoolMoves: user motion accentuation in virtual reality. Proc. ACM Interact. Mob. Wearable Ubiquit. Technol. **5**(2), 1–23 (2021)
4. Aksan, E., Kaufmann, M., Cao, P., Hilliges, O.: A spatio-temporal transformer for 3D human motion prediction. In: International Conference on 3D Vision (3DV) (2021)
5. Ames, B., Morgan, J.: IKFlow: generating diverse inverse kinematics solutions. IEEE Robot. Autom. Lett. **7**, 7177–7184 (2022)
6. Aristidou, A., Lasenby, J.: FABRIK: a fast, iterative solver for the inverse kinematics problem. Graph. Models **73**(5), 243–260 (2011)
7. Bócsi, B., Nguyen-Tuong, D., Csató, L., Schoelkopf, B., Peters, J.: Learning inverse kinematics with structured prediction. In: 2011 IEEE/RSJ International Conference on Intelligent Robots and Systems, pp. 698–703. IEEE (2011)
8. Carion, N., Massa, F., Synnaeve, G., Usunier, N., Kirillov, A., Zagoruyko, S.: End-to-end object detection with transformers. In: Vedaldi, A., Bischof, H., Brox, T., Frahm, J.-M. (eds.) ECCV 2020. LNCS, vol. 12346, pp. 213–229. Springer, Cham (2020). https://doi.org/10.1007/978-3-030-58452-8_13
9. Çavdar, T., Mohammad, M., Milani, R.A.: A new heuristic approach for inverse kinematics of robot arms. Adv. Sci. Lett. **19**(1), 329–333 (2013)
10. Csiszar, A., Eilers, J., Verl, A.: On solving the inverse kinematics problem using neural networks. In: 2017 24th International Conference on Mechatronics and Machine Vision in Practice (M2VIP), pp. 1–6. IEEE (2017)
11. Dai, Z., Yang, Z., Yang, Y., Carbonell, J.G., Le, Q., Salakhutdinov, R.: Transformer-XL: attentive language models beyond a fixed-length context. In: Proceedings of the 57th Annual Meeting of the Association for Computational Linguistics, pp. 2978–2988 (2019)
12. Devlin, J., Chang, M.W., Lee, K., Toutanova, K.: BERT: pre-training of deep bidirectional transformers for language understanding. In: Annual Conference of the North American Chapter of the Association for Computational Linguistics (2019)
13. Dittadi, A., Dziadzio, S., Cosker, D., Lundell, B., Cashman, T.J., Shotton, J.: Full-body motion from a single head-mounted device: generating SMPL poses from partial observations. In: Proceedings of the IEEE/CVF International Conference on Computer Vision, pp. 11687–11697 (2021)
14. Dosovitskiy, A., et al.: An image is worth 16 × 16 words: transformers for image recognition at scale. In: International Conference on Learning Representations (2021)
15. Duka, A.V.: Neural network based inverse kinematics solution for trajectory tracking of a robotic arm. Procedia Technol. **12**, 20–27 (2014)
16. Fan, H., et al.: Multiscale vision transformers. In: Proceedings of the IEEE/CVF International Conference on Computer Vision, pp. 6824–6835 (2021)
17. Goldenberg, A., Benhabib, B., Fenton, R.: A complete generalized solution to the inverse kinematics of robots. IEEE J. Robot. Autom. **1**(1), 14–20 (1985)
18. Grochow, K., Martin, S.L., Hertzmann, A., Popović, Z.: Style-based inverse kinematics. In: ACM SIGGRAPH 2004 Papers, pp. 522–531 (2004)
19. Heidicker, P., Langbehn, E., Steinicke, F.: Influence of avatar appearance on presence in social VR. In: 2017 IEEE Symposium on 3D User Interfaces (3DUI), pp. 233–234 (2017)
20. Huang, Y., Kaufmann, M., Aksan, E., Black, M.J., Hilliges, O., Pons-Moll, G.: Deep inertial poser: learning to reconstruct human pose from sparse inertial measure-

ments in real time. ACM Trans. Graph. (Proc. SIGGRAPH Asia) **37**, 185:1–185:15 (2018)

21. Kang, M., Cho, Y., Yoon, S.E.: RCIK: real-time collision-free inverse kinematics using a collision-cost prediction network. IEEE Robot. Autom. Lett. **7**(1), 610–617 (2021)

22. Kingma, D.P., Ba, J.: Adam: a method for stochastic optimization. In: International Conference on Learning Representations (2015)

23. Li, J., Xu, C., Chen, Z., Bian, S., Yang, L., Lu, C.: HybrIK: a hybrid analytical-neural inverse kinematics solution for 3D human pose and shape estimation. In: Proceedings of the IEEE/CVF Conference on Computer Vision and Pattern Recognition, pp. 3383–3393 (2021)

24. Li, S., et al.: A mobile robot hand-arm teleoperation system by vision and IMU. In: 2020 IEEE/RSJ International Conference on Intelligent Robots and Systems (IROS), pp. 10900–10906. IEEE (2020)

25. Li, W., Liu, H., Tang, H., Wang, P., Van Gool, L.: MHFormer: multi-hypothesis transformer for 3D human pose estimation. In: Proceedings of the IEEE/CVF Conference on Computer Vision and Pattern Recognition, pp. 13147–13156 (2022)

26. Liang, J., Cao, J., Sun, G., Zhang, K., Van Gool, L., Timofte, R.: SwinIR: image restoration using swin transformer. In: Proceedings of the IEEE/CVF International Conference on Computer Vision, pp. 1833–1844 (2021)

27. Lin, K., Wang, L., Liu, Z.: End-to-end human pose and mesh reconstruction with transformers. In: Proceedings of the IEEE/CVF Conference on Computer Vision and Pattern Recognition, pp. 1954–1963 (2021)

28. Liu, Z., et al.: Swin transformer: hierarchical vision transformer using shifted windows. In: Proceedings of the IEEE/CVF International Conference on Computer Vision, pp. 10012–10022 (2021)

29. Loper, M., Mahmood, N., Romero, J., Pons-Moll, G., Black, M.J.: SMPL: a skinned multi-person linear model. ACM Trans. Graph. (TOG) **34**(6), 1–16 (2015)

30. Luenberger, D.G., Ye, Y., et al.: Linear and Nonlinear Programming, vol. 2. Springer, Heidelberg (1984)

31. Mahmood, N., Ghorbani, N., Troje, N.F., Pons-Moll, G., Black, M.J.: AMASS: archive of motion capture as surface shapes. In: International Conference on Computer Vision, pp. 5442–5451 (2019)

32. Marić, F., Giamou, M., Hall, A.W., Khoubyarian, S., Petrović, I., Kelly, J.: Riemannian optimization for distance-geometric inverse kinematics. IEEE Trans. Rob. **38**(3), 1703–1722 (2021)

33. Meinhardt, T., Kirillov, A., Leal-Taixe, L., Feichtenhofer, C.: TrackFormer: multi-object tracking with transformers. In: Proceedings of the IEEE/CVF Conference on Computer Vision and Pattern Recognition, pp. 8844–8854 (2022)

34. Moré, J.J.: The Levenberg-Marquardt algorithm: implementation and theory. In: Watson, G.A. (ed.) Numerical Analysis. LNM, vol. 630, pp. 105–116. Springer, Heidelberg (1978). https://doi.org/10.1007/BFb0067700

35. Müller, M., Röder, T., Clausen, M., Eberhardt, B., Krüger, B., Weber, A.: Documentation mocap database hdm05. Technical report. CG-2007-2, Universität Bonn (2007)

36. Parger, M., Mueller, J.H., Schmalstieg, D., Steinberger, M.: Human upper-body inverse kinematics for increased embodiment in consumer-grade virtual reality. In: Proceedings of the 24th ACM Symposium on Virtual Reality Software and Technology, pp. 1–10 (2018)

37. Parker, J.K., Khoogar, A.R., Goldberg, D.E.: Inverse kinematics of redundant robots using genetic algorithms. In: 1989 IEEE International Conference on Robotics and Automation, pp. 271–272. IEEE Computer Society (1989)

38. Ren, H., Ben-Tzvi, P.: Learning inverse kinematics and dynamics of a robotic manipulator using generative adversarial networks. Robot. Auton. Syst. **124**, 103386 (2020)

39. Rokbani, N., Casals, A., Alimi, A.M.: IK-FA, a new heuristic inverse kinematics solver using firefly algorithm. In: Azar, A.T., Vaidyanathan, S. (eds.) Computational Intelligence Applications in Modeling and Control. SCI, vol. 575, pp. 369–395. Springer, Cham (2015). https://doi.org/10.1007/978-3-319-11017-2_15

40. Ruppel, P., Hendrich, N., Starke, S., Zhang, J.: Cost functions to specify full-body motion and multi-goal manipulation tasks. In: 2018 IEEE International Conference on Robotics and Automation (ICRA), pp. 3152–3159. IEEE (2018)

41. Starke, S., Zhang, H., Komura, T., Saito, J.: Neural state machine for character-scene interactions. ACM Trans. Graph. **38**(6), 209–1 (2019)

42. Sumner, R.W., Zwicker, M., Gotsman, C., Popović, J.: Mesh-based inverse kinematics. ACM Trans. Graph. (TOG) **24**(3), 488–495 (2005)

43. Sun, P., et al.: TransTrack: multiple object tracking with transformer. arXiv preprint arXiv:2012.15460 (2020)

44. Sun, Z., Cao, S., Yang, Y., Kitani, K.M.: Rethinking transformer-based set prediction for object detection. In: Proceedings of the IEEE/CVF International Conference on Computer Vision, pp. 3611–3620 (2021)

45. Troje, N.F.: Decomposing biological motion: a framework for analysis and synthesis of human gait patterns. J. Vis. **2**(5), 2 (2002)

46. Vaswani, A., et al.: Attention is all you need. In: Advances in Neural Information Processing Systems, vol. 30 (2017)

47. Villegas, R., Yang, J., Ceylan, D., Lee, H.: Neural kinematic networks for unsupervised motion retargetting. In: Proceedings of the IEEE Conference on Computer Vision and Pattern Recognition, pp. 8639–8648 (2018)

48. Von Marcard, T., Rosenhahn, B., Black, M.J., Pons-Moll, G.: Sparse inertial poser: automatic 3D human pose estimation from sparse IMUs. In: Computer Graphics Forum, vol. 36, pp. 349–360. Wiley Online Library (2017)

49. Waltemate, T., Gall, D., Roth, D., Botsch, M., Latoschik, M.E.: The impact of avatar personalization and immersion on virtual body ownership, presence, and emotional response. IEEE Trans. Visual Comput. Graph. **24**(4), 1643–1652 (2018)

50. Wang, J., Liu, L., Xu, W., Sarkar, K., Theobalt, C.: Estimating egocentric 3D human pose in global space. In: Proceedings of the IEEE/CVF International Conference on Computer Vision, pp. 11500–11509 (2021)

51. Wang, L.C., Chen, C.C.: A combined optimization method for solving the inverse kinematics problems of mechanical manipulators. IEEE Trans. Robot. Autom. **7**(4), 489–499 (1991)

52. Wang, Z., Cun, X., Bao, J., Zhou, W., Liu, J., Li, H.: Uformer: a general U-shaped transformer for image restoration. In: Proceedings of the IEEE/CVF Conference on Computer Vision and Pattern Recognition, pp. 17683–17693 (2022)

53. Yang, D., Kim, D., Lee, S.H.: LoBSTr: real-time lower-body pose prediction from sparse upper-body tracking signals. In: Computer Graphics Forum, vol. 40, pp. 265–275. Wiley Online Library (2021)

54. Yi, X., et al.: Physical inertial poser (PIP): physics-aware real-time human motion tracking from sparse inertial sensors. In: Proceedings of the IEEE/CVF Conference on Computer Vision and Pattern Recognition, pp. 13167–13178 (2022)

55. Yi, X., Zhou, Y., Xu, F.: Transpose: real-time 3D human translation and pose estimation with six inertial sensors. ACM Trans. Graph. (TOG) **40**(4), 1–13 (2021)
56. Zamir, S.W., Arora, A., Khan, S., Hayat, M., Khan, F.S., Yang, M.H.: Restormer: efficient transformer for high-resolution image restoration. In: Proceedings of the IEEE/CVF Conference on Computer Vision and Pattern Recognition, pp. 5728–5739 (2022)
57. Zhang, X., Bhatnagar, B.L., Guzov, V., Starke, S., Pons-Moll, G.: COUCH: towards controllable human-chair interactions. In: Avidan, S., et al. (eds.) ECCV 2022. LNCS, pp. 518–535. Springer, Cham (2022)
58. Zhao, J., Badler, N.I.: Inverse kinematics positioning using nonlinear programming for highly articulated figures. ACM Trans. Graph. (TOG) **13**(4), 313–336 (1994)
59. Zhao, Z., Wu, Z., Zhang, Y., Li, B., Jia, J.: Tracking objects as pixel-wise distributions. In: Proceedings of the European Conference on Computer Vision (ECCV) (2022)
60. Zheng, C., Zhu, S., Mendieta, M., Yang, T., Chen, C., Ding, Z.: 3D human pose estimation with spatial and temporal transformers. In: Proceedings of the IEEE International Conference on Computer Vision (ICCV) (2021)
61. Zhou, Y., Barnes, C., Lu, J., Yang, J., Li, H.: On the continuity of rotation representations in neural networks. In: Proceedings of the IEEE/CVF Conference on Computer Vision and Pattern Recognition, pp. 5745–5753 (2019)
62. Zhu, X., Su, W., Lu, L., Li, B., Wang, X., Dai, J.: Deformable DETR: deformable transformers for end-to-end object detection. In: International Conference on Learning Representations (2020)

P-STMO: Pre-trained Spatial Temporal Many-to-One Model for 3D Human Pose Estimation

Wenkang Shan[1], Zhenhua Liu[1,3], Xinfeng Zhang[2], Shanshe Wang[1,4], Siwei Ma[1,4(✉)], and Wen Gao[1,4]

[1] National Engineering Research Center of Visual Technology, Peking University, Beijing, China
{wkshan,liu-zh,sswang,swma,wgao}@pku.edu.cn
[2] University of Chinese Academy of Sciences, Beijing, China
xfzhang@ucas.ac.cn
[3] Huawei Noah's Ark Lab, Beijing, China
[4] Peng Cheng Laboratory, Shenzhen, China

Abstract. This paper introduces a novel Pre-trained Spatial Temporal Many-to-One (P-STMO) model for 2D-to-3D human pose estimation task. To reduce the difficulty of capturing spatial and temporal information, we divide this task into two stages: pre-training (Stage I) and fine-tuning (Stage II). In Stage I, a self-supervised pre-training sub-task, termed *masked pose modeling*, is proposed. The human joints in the input sequence are randomly masked in both spatial and temporal domains. A general form of denoising auto-encoder is exploited to recover the original 2D poses and the encoder is capable of capturing spatial and temporal dependencies in this way. In Stage II, the pre-trained encoder is loaded to STMO model and fine-tuned. The encoder is followed by a many-to-one frame aggregator to predict the 3D pose in the current frame. Especially, an MLP block is utilized as the spatial feature extractor in STMO, which yields better performance than other methods. In addition, a temporal downsampling strategy is proposed to diminish data redundancy. Extensive experiments on two benchmarks show that our method outperforms state-of-the-art methods with fewer parameters and less computational overhead. For example, our P-STMO model achieves 42.1 mm MPJPE on Human3.6 M dataset when using 2D poses from CPN as inputs. Meanwhile, it brings a 1.5–7.1× speedup to state-of-the-art methods. Code is available at https://github.com/paTRICK-swk/P-STMO.

Keywords: 3D human pose estimation · Transformer · Pre-training · Masked pose modeling

Supplementary Information The online version contains supplementary material available at https://doi.org/10.1007/978-3-031-20065-6_27.

1   Introduction

Monocular 3D human pose estimation in videos is a long-standing computer vision task with extensive applications, such as virtual reality, medical assistance, and self-driving. Two-step estimation methods [13,17,21,23,25] first detect 2D human keypoints, and then regress the 3D position of each joint. They use an off-the-shelf 2D keypoint detector (e.g., [8,30]) to obtain 2D poses and mainly focus on lifting 3D poses from these 2D keypoints. Despite considerable success achieved, this task remains an ill-posed problem due to depth ambiguity.

Existing works [6,9,26,27,32,49] rely on fully-connected (*fc*) layers, graph convolutions, or 1D convolutions to integrate information over spatial and temporal domains. Recently, some works [22,24,50] introduce Transformer [40] to 3D human pose estimation. The self-attention mechanism of Transformer is exploited to depict spatial dependencies between joints in each frame or temporal dependencies between frames in a sequence. However, there are two drawbacks to these methods: (1) They directly learn 2D-to-3D spatial and temporal correlations, which is a challenging task. This might make it difficult to optimize the model. (2) Previous works [12] show that Transformer requires more training data than convolutional neural networks.

For these two issues, self-supervised pre-training of Transformer, which has proven to be effective in natural language processing (NLP) and computer vision (CV), is a promising solution. Previous approaches [1,5,11,15] randomly mask a portion of input data and then recover the masked content. In this way, the model is enabled to represent the inherent characteristics within the data. Thus, we are motivated to exploit the self-supervised pre-training method for 3D human pose estimation.

In this paper, we propose a Pre-trained Spatial Temporal Many-to-One (P-STMO) model for 2D-to-3D human pose estimation. The whole process is split into two stages: pre-training (Stage I) and fine-tuning (Stage II). In Stage I, a self-supervised spatial temporal pre-training task, called *masked pose modeling* (MPM), is constructed. We randomly mask some frames[1] (temporally) as well as some 2D joints (spatially) in the remaining frames. The model in this stage, a general form of denoising auto-encoder [41], is intended to reconstruct the corrupted 2D poses. This gives the network a favorable initialization. In Stage II, the pre-trained encoder, combined with a many-to-one frame aggregator, is retrained to predict the 3D pose of the current (middle) frame by using a sequence of 2D poses as input. With this two-stage strategy, the encoder is supposed to capture 2D spatial temporal dependencies in Stage I and extract 3D spatial and temporal features in Stage II. Experimental results show that this strategy can reduce the optimization difficulty of STMO and improve the prediction performance.

The proposed STMO model consists of three modules: (*i*) spatial encoding module (SEM): capturing spatial information within a single frame, (*ii*) temporal encoding module (TEM): capturing temporal dependencies between different frames, (*iii*) many-to-one frame aggregator (MOFA): aggregating information from multiple frames to assist in the prediction of the current pose. These three

---

[1] If not specified, "frame" in the following text refers to the 2D pose in this frame.

modules play different roles and are organically linked to each other, which improves the overall performance. Herein, we propose to use an MLP block as the backbone network of SEM. Compared with fc [22] and Transformer [50], it achieves better performance while having moderate computational complexity. In addition, a temporal downsampling strategy (TDS) is introduced on the input side to reduce data redundancy while enlarging the temporal receptive field.

Our contributions can be summarized as follows:

- To the best of our knowledge, P-STMO is the first approach that introduces the pre-training technique to 3D human pose estimation. A pre-training task, namely MPM, is proposed in a self-supervised manner to better capture both spatial and temporal dependencies.
- The proposed STMO model simplifies the responsibility of each module and therefore significantly reduces the optimization difficulty. An MLP block is utilized as an effective spatial feature extractor for SEM. In addition, a temporal downsampling strategy is employed to mitigate the data redundancy problem for TEM.
- Compared with other approaches, our method achieves state-of-the-art performance on two benchmarks with fewer parameters and smaller computational budgets.

2   Related Work

2.1   3D Human Pose Estimation

Recently, there is a research trend that uses 2D keypoints to regress corresponding 3D joint positions. The advantage is that it is compatible with any existing 2D pose estimation method. Our approach falls under this category. Extensive works [13,27,29,31,38,42,44] have been carried out around an important issue in videos, which is how to exploit the information in spatial and temporal domains. Some works [13,27,38,48] only focus on 3D single-frame pose estimation and ignore temporal dependencies. Other recent approaches [3,16,43,44,50] explore the way of integrating spatio-temporal information. The following are the shortcomings of these methods. Approaches relying on recurrent neural network (RNN) [16,20] suffer from high computational complexity. Graph convolutional network (GCN)-based methods [17,43] perform graph convolutions on the spatial temporal graph, and predict all poses in the sequence. This diminishes the capability of the network to model the 3D pose in a particular frame. The Transformer-based method [50] predicts the 3D pose of the current (middle) frame by performing a weighted average at the last layer over the features of all frames in the sequence. It ignores the importance of the current pose and its near neighbors.

On the other hand, some works [6,26,32] focus on the process of many-to-one frame aggregation. Pavllo et al. [32] first propose a temporal convolutional network (TCN) that uses multiple frames to aid the modeling of one frame by progressively reducing the temporal dimension. Since then many methods [6,26,37,47] have been proposed based on TCN. However, these methods do not explicitly extract spatial and temporal features. Li et al. [22] alleviate this problem by using a vanilla Transformer to capture long-range temporal dependencies in the sequence. But they acquire spatial information by a single *fc* layer, which has insufficient representation capability.

In contrast, we propose a Spatial Temporal Many-to-One (STMO) model. The most important steps in 3D human pose estimation are represented as three modules in STMO: SEM, TEM, and MOFA. Our method clearly delineates the responsibility of each module and promotes the modeling of intrinsic properties.

2.2 Pre-training of Transformer

Transformer [40] has become the *de facto* backbone in NLP [2,10,11,34,35] and CV [4,7,12,14,39]. Transformer owes its widespread success to the pre-training technique [1,11,33,45,46]. In NLP, Devlin *et al.* [11] propose a *masked language modeling* (MLM) task, which triggers a wave of research on pre-training. They randomly mask some words and aim to predict these masked words based only on their context. Subsequent developments in CV have followed a similar trajectory to NLP. Some works [1,12,15] transfer self-supervised pre-trained models to image-based CV tasks, such as classification, object detection, semantic segmentation, etc. They replace the words to be reconstructed in MLM with pixels or discrete visual tokens. The pre-training task in CV is termed as *masked image modeling* (MIM).

Inspired by these works, we apply the pre-training technique to 3D human pose estimation and propose a *masked pose modeling* (MPM) task similarly. We randomly mask some joints in spatial and temporal domains and try to recover the original 2D poses. Note that METRO [24] also masks the input 2D poses, but the goal is to directly regress 3D joint positions rather than recovering the input. This approach is essentially a data augmentation method and therefore different from the proposed pre-training task.

3   Method

3.1   Overview

Figure 1 depicts an overview of the proposed P-STMO method, which divides the optimization process into two stages: pre-training and fine-tuning. Firstly, a part of STMO model is pre-trained by solving the *masked pose modeling* (MPM) task in a self-supervised manner. The goal of this stage is to recover the input sequence from the corrupted 2D poses. Secondly, STMO model is fine-tuned to predict the 3D pose in the current (middle) frame given a sequence of 2D poses obtained by an off-the-shelf 2D pose detector. For both stages, we take a sequence of 2D poses as input, denoted as

$$X = \{x_n\}_{n=-(N-1)/2}^{(N-1)/2}, \quad x_n = \{p_i\}_{i=1}^{J}, \tag{1}$$

where $p_i \in \mathbb{R}^2$ is the 2D position of ith joint. N, J are the number of frames and human joints in each frame, respectively. Usually, N is an odd number, which means that the current frame and $(N-1)/2$ frames to the left and right of it are used as inputs.

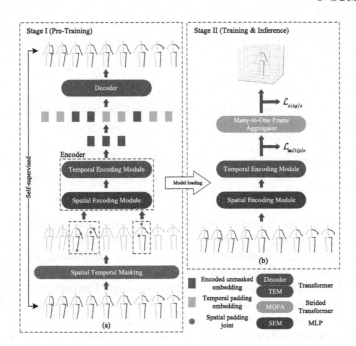

Fig. 1. (a) The pre-training procedure for STMO. The 2D pose sequence is randomly masked and fed to the encoder. The encoded unmasked embeddings as well as the temporal padding embeddings are sent to the decoder to reconstruct the original 2D poses in the input sequence. (b) Overview of our STMO model, which consists of SEM, TEM, and MOFA in series.

Stage I: As shown in Fig. 1a, a proportion of frames as well as some joints in the remaining frames are randomly masked. This spatially and temporally masked input is denoted as X^{ST}. The whole network architecture consists of a spatial temporal encoder (SEM+TEM) that maps the masked input X^{ST} to the latent space, and a decoder that recovers the original 2D poses X from latent representations. To predict the complete 2D poses, the model has to seek relevant unmasked joints for help. In this way, SEM and TEM are enabled to learn 2D spatial and temporal relationships. Since monocular motion contributes to depth estimation [36], acquiring 2D spatio-temporal relationships is beneficial for 3D human pose estimation.

Stage II: Figure 1b shows the proposed STMO model. The pre-trained encoder is loaded and fine-tuned in this stage to obtain knowledge about the 3D space. This encoder is followed by MOFA that aggregates multiple frames to estimate the 3D pose in the middle frame of the sequence, denoted as $Y = \{y_0\}, y_0 \in \mathbb{R}^{J \times 3}$.

3.2 Pre-training of STMO

The spatial and temporal dependencies of the pose sequence are mainly captured by SEM and TEM in our STMO model. To improve the overall estimation

Fig. 2. Illustration of three masking strategies. (a) Temporal masking. (b) Spatial masking. (c) Spatial temporal masking.

accuracy, we propose a self-supervised spatial temporal pre-training task, namely MPM. As shown in Fig. 2, we use three masking strategies to mask the input 2D poses, which are described in detail below.

Temporal Masking. A portion of input frames are randomly masked, which is called temporal masking. The masked frame is replaced with a *temporal padding embedding* e^{T} which is a shared learnable vector. Similar to [15], to improve the efficiency of the model, we only use the unmasked frames as inputs to the encoder, excluding the temporal padding embeddings. Instead, the decoder takes the temporal padding embeddings as well as the encoded unmasked embeddings as inputs and reconstructs the original 2D poses. In this way, the encoder models temporal dependencies between two unmasked frames that are not adjacent to each other in the original sequence, and then the decoder fills in the missing 2D poses between these two frames. We denote the indices of the masked frames as a set: $\mathcal{M}^{\mathrm{T}} \subseteq \{-\frac{N-1}{2}, -\frac{N-1}{2}+1, \ldots, \frac{N-1}{2}\}, |\mathcal{M}^{\mathrm{T}}| = q^{\mathrm{T}} \cdot N$, where $q^{\mathrm{T}} \in \mathbb{R}$ is the temporal masking ratio. We use a large temporal masking ratio (e.g., 90%), so this task cannot be solved easily by interpolation. The input X to the encoder (Eq. 1) is modified to

$$X^{\mathrm{T}} = \{x_n^{\mathrm{T}} : n \notin \mathcal{M}^{\mathrm{T}}\}_{n=-(N-1)/2}^{(N-1)/2}, \quad x_n^{\mathrm{T}} = \{p_i\}_{i=1}^{J}. \tag{2}$$

After that, the input to the decoder is denoted as

$$\{h_n : n \notin \mathcal{M}^{\mathrm{T}}\}_{n=-(N-1)/2}^{(N-1)/2} \bigcup \{e^{\mathrm{T}} : n \in \mathcal{M}^{\mathrm{T}}\}_{n=-(N-1)/2}^{(N-1)/2}, \tag{3}$$

where $h_n, e^{\mathrm{T}} \in \mathbb{R}^d$ are the encoded unmasked embedding and temporal padding embedding respectively. d is the dimension of the latent features. The output is $Y = \{y_n\}_{n=-(N-1)/2}^{(N-1)/2}$, where $y_n \in \mathbb{R}^{J \times 2}$ is the recovered 2D pose in frame n.

Spatial Masking. A fixed number of joints in each frame are randomly masked, which is called spatial masking. The masked joint is replaced with a *spatial padding joint* e^{S} that is a shared learnable vector. The spatial padding joints, together with other unmasked joints, are sent to the encoder. Since the pose sequence is not masked temporally, no temporal padding embedding is used at the decoder side. In such manner, the encoder models spatial dependencies between joints, and then the decoder is capable of recovering the contaminated joints. The indices of the masked joints in frame n are denoted as a set: $\mathcal{M}_n^{\mathrm{S}} \subseteq \{-\frac{N-1}{2}, -\frac{N-1}{2}+1, \ldots, \frac{N-1}{2}\}, |\mathcal{M}_n^{\mathrm{S}}| = m^{\mathrm{S}}$, where $m^{\mathrm{S}} \in \mathbb{N}$ is the number of masked joints. The spatial masking ratio is $q^S = m^S/J$. Although the number of masked joints is the same for each frame, the indices of the masked joints are various in different frames to increase the diversity. The input X to the encoder (Eq. 1) is modified to

$$X^S = \{x_n^S\}_{n=-(N-1)/2}^{(N-1)/2}, \quad x_n^S = \{p_i : i \notin \mathcal{M}_n^S\}_{i=1}^J \bigcup \{e^S : i \in \mathcal{M}_n^S\}_{i=1}^J, \quad (4)$$

where $e^S \in \mathbb{R}^2$ is the spatial padding joint.

Spatial Temporal Masking. To integrate the information on the spatio-temporal domain, we propose a spatial temporal masking strategy, which is a combination of the above two masking methods. Specifically, the temporal masking is implemented on the input pose sequence, followed by the spatial masking on the unmasked frames. This strategy is utilized in the proposed P-STMO model. The total spatial temporal masking ratio is calculated by $q^{ST} = q^T + (1 - q^T) \cdot q^S$. The input X to the encoder (Eq. 1) is modified to

$$X^{ST} = \{x_n^{ST} : n \notin \mathcal{M}^T\}_{n=-(N-1)/2}^{(N-1)/2}, \quad (5)$$

$$x_n^{ST} = \{p_i : i \notin \mathcal{M}_n^S\}_{i=1}^J \bigcup \{e^S : i \in \mathcal{M}_n^S\}_{i=1}^J. \quad (6)$$

3.3   Spatial Temporal Many-to-One (STMO) Model

In Stage II, the pre-trained encoder is loaded to the proposed STMO model and fine-tuned on 3D poses. The detailed architecture of STMO is provided in the supplementary material. The input sequence will go through SEM, TEM, and MOFA to obtain the final output. The role of each module is described in detail below.

Spatial Encoding Module (SEM). SEM aims to capture the characteristics of each frame in the spatial domain. Zheng *et al.* [50] propose to use a Transformer [40] as the backbone network of SEM to integrate information across all joints in a single frame. However, the self-attention operation brings a great computational overhead, which limits the scalability of the network in the case of using multiple frames as inputs. Therefore, we propose to use a simple MLP block as the backbone network to establish spatial relationships between joints. Compared to [50], this lightweight design allows the network to accommodate more frames with the same computational budget. Each 2D pose in the input sequence is independently sent to the MLP block whose weights are shared across all frames.

Temporal Encoding Module (TEM). As 2D keypoints are used as inputs to the network, the amount of data per frame is small. Thus, we can take advantage of the extra-long 2D input pose sequence (e.g., 243 frames). Since the objective of this module is to exploit temporal information from the changes of human posture within this sequence, it is inefficient to focus on the relationships between highly redundant frames in a local region. Therefore convolution operations, which introduce the inductive bias of *locality*, can be discarded. Instead, the self-attention mechanism is exploited, which allows the network to easily focus on correlations between frames that are far apart. We use a standard Transformer architecture as the backbone network of TEM. It is capable of capturing non-local self-attending associations. TEM takes a sequence of latent features from SEM as input and treats the features in each frame as an individual token. As the inputs are already embedded, the *token embedding* process in Transformer is skipped.

Previous works [6,32] show that the performance of 3D human pose estimation can be improved with more frames as inputs. However, there are two drawbacks when increasing the number of frames. (1) The computational complexity of Transformer is $O(N^2)$, which constrains the network from utilizing a larger scale of temporal information. (2) The input data is highly redundant. For example, the video frame rate of Human3.6M [19] is 50 fps, which means that there is only a slight change between adjacent frames. To alleviate these two problems, we propose to use a temporal downsampling strategy (TDS), which uniformly downsamples the input pose sequence. In this way, the network can accommodate a longer time span of information with the same number of input frames. In other words, the receptive field in the temporal domain can be expanded without increasing the number of parameters and computational complexity. Meanwhile, TDS removes highly similar neighboring frames, thus promoting data diversity. After TDS is applied, the input X is modified to $X^{\text{TDS}} = \{x_{n \cdot s}\}_{n=-(N-1)/2}^{(N-1)/2}$, where $s \in \mathbb{N}^+$ is the downsampling rate. The output Y remains unchanged. Some works [18,29,51] also downsample the data, but they reduce the size of the dataset. Since the scale of the dataset is preserved by TDS, the proposed strategy is more effective than these works.

Many-to-One Frame Aggregator (MOFA). TEM mainly concerns the understanding of the temporal dependencies in the overall sequence, while MOFA aims to aggregate information from multiple frames and extract the 3D pose of the current frame. Therefore, it is effective to leverage local information around the current pose, which allows convolution to shine in this module. Li *et al.* [22] propose a Strided Transformer Encoder (STE), which is a combination of Transformer and convolution. Specifically, STE replaces the MLP block in Transformer with strided 1D temporal convolutions proposed by TCN [32]. We use STE as the backbone network of MOFA. For the MLP block in vanilla Transformer, the *fc* layer is formulated as $l_{i,n}^{(k)} = \sum_{j=0}^{d_{k-1}} w_{i,j} * l_{j,n}^{(k-1)}$, where $l_{i,n}^{(k)}$ is the ith channel of nth token (frame) in k^{th} layer, $w_{i,j}$ is the weight shared across frames, and d_{k-1} is the number of channels in $(k-1)^{th}$ layer. In the case that 1D temporal convolution is used instead of the *fc* layer, the formulation is modified to $l_{i,n}^{(k)} = \sum_{j=0}^{d_{k-1}} \sum_{m=-(M-1)/2}^{(M-1)/2} w_{i,j,m} * l_{j,n+m}^{(k-1)}$, where M is the kernel size. It aggregates adjacent M frames in the sequence into a single frame. The stride is set to M so that there will be no overlap between any two convolution operations. The stacking of multiple layers of 1D temporal convolution eventually enables the mapping from N frames to one frame (current frame).

3.4   Loss Function

Stage I. The objective of the pre-training stage is to minimize the negative log-likelihood of the correct 2D pose $x_n = \{p_i\}_{i=1}^J$ in each frame given the corrupted input sequence:

$$\mathcal{L}_{pretrain} = \sum_{x \in \mathcal{D}} \mathbb{E}_n \left[\sum_{n=-(N-1)/2}^{(N-1)/2} - \log p\left(x_n \mid X^{ST}\right) \right], \qquad (7)$$

where $\mathcal{D}$ is the training corpus, and $p(\cdot \mid \cdot)$ is the conditional probability.

Stage II. The final estimated 3D pose of the middle frame in the sequence is obtained via a linear projection after MOFA. To optimize the network, we use L2 loss to minimize the errors between predictions and ground truths :

$$\mathcal{L}_{single} = \frac{1}{J} \sum_{i=1}^J \|y_i - \widetilde{y}_i\|_2, \qquad (8)$$

where y_i and $\widetilde{y}_i$ are the ground truth and estimated 3D positions of ith joint in the current pose respectively.

In addition, to better supervise the optimization, we append a multi-frame loss [22] after TEM. To be specific, a linear projection is added to obtain the 3D poses of all frames in the sequence. In this way, we force TEM to exploit the temporal relationships between frames to predict 3D poses in all frames. Since the output features of TEM are quite close to 3D poses after applying the multi-frame loss, the role of MOFA is to aggregate these 3D pose-related features of all frames into a single representation. The multi-frame loss is formulated as:

$$\mathcal{L}_{multiple} = \frac{1}{J \cdot N} \sum_{i=1}^J \sum_{n=-(N-1)/2}^{(N-1)/2} \|y_{i,n} - \widetilde{y}_{i,n}\|_2. \qquad (9)$$

The final loss function of the whole network is $\mathcal{L} = \mathcal{L}_{single} + \lambda \mathcal{L}_{multiple}$, where λ is the balance factor.

4   Experiments

4.1   Datasets and Evaluation Metrics

Human3.6M [19] is the most commonly used indoor dataset, which consists of 3.6 million frames captured by 50 Hz cameras. The dataset is divided into 15 daily activities (e.g., walking and sitting) performed by 11 subjects. Following [3, 32, 37], we use 5 subjects for training (S1, S5, S6, S7, S8), and 2 subjects for testing (S9, S11).

We report the mean per joint position error (MPJPE) and Procrustes MPJPE (P-MPJPE) for Human3.6M dataset. The former computes the Euclidean distance between the predicted joint positions and the ground truth positions. The latter is the MPJPE after the predicted results align to the ground truth via a rigid transformation.

MPI-INF-3DHP [28] is a more challenging dataset with both indoor and outdoor scenes. The training set comprises of 8 subjects, covering 8 activities. The test set covers 7 activities, containing three scenes: green screen, non-green screen, and outdoor. Following [6,50], we train the proposed method using all activities from 8 camera views in the training set and evaluate on valid frames in the test set.

We report MPJPE, percentage of correct keypoints (PCK) within 150 mm range, and area under curve (AUC) as the evaluation metrics for MPI-INF-3DHP dataset.

4.2   Comparison with State-of-the-Art Methods

Results on Human3.6M. We compare our P-STMO with existing state-of-the-art methods on Human3.6M dataset. Following [22,26,32,50], we use CPN [8] as the 2D keypoint detector, and then train our networks on the detected 2D pose sequence. As shown in Table 1, our method achieves promising results under MPJPE (42.8 mm) when using 243 frames as inputs. We also train our model using the same refining module as [3,22,43]. It achieves 42.1 mm under MPJPE, which surpasses all other methods. Our method yields better performance on hard poses (such as *Photo* and *SittingDown*) than the previous works. This demonstrates the robustness of our model in the case of depth ambiguity and severe self-occlusion. Additionally, we propose a smaller model P-STMO-*Small*. The only difference between P-STMO and P-STMO-S lies in the number of Transformer layers. For more details, please refer to the supplementary materials. Compared with P-STMO, P-STMO-S achieves 43.0 mm MPJPE with a smaller number of FLOPs and parameters.

Results on MPI-INF-3DHP. Table 2 reports the performance of state-of-the-art methods and the proposed method on MPI-INF-3DHP dataset. Following [17,43,50], we adopt the ground truth of 2D poses as inputs. Since the sequence length in this dataset is shorter than that in Human3.6M dataset, we set the number of input frames to 81. Our method achieves significant improvements in terms of AUC (9.1%) and MPJPE (24.2%). The PCK metric is at a competitive level compared to [17]. The results suggest that our method has a strong generalization ability.

Qualitative Results. We provide some qualitative results in Fig. 3. We compare the proposed method with Poseformer [50] on Human3.6M and MPI-INF-3DHP datasets. Our method achieves good qualitative performance in both indoor scenes and complex outdoor scenes.

Table 1. Results on Human3.6M in millimeter under MPJPE. 2D poses detected by CPN are used as inputs. N is the number of input frames. (*) - uses the refining module proposed in [3]. The best result is shown in bold, and the second-best result is underlined.

MPJPE (CPN)	Dir.	Disc.	Eat	Greet	Phone	Photo	Pose	Pur.	Sit	SitD.	Smoke	Wait	WalkD.	Walk	WalkT.	Avg
Pavllo et al. [32] CVPR'19 ($N = 243$)	45.2	46.7	43.3	45.6	48.1	55.1	44.6	44.3	57.3	65.8	47.1	44.0	49.0	32.8	33.9	46.8
Lin et al. [23] BMVC'19 ($N = 50$)	42.5	44.8	42.6	44.2	48.5	57.1	42.6	41.4	56.5	64.5	47.4	43.0	48.1	33.0	35.1	46.6
Xu et al. [44] CVPR'20 ($N = 9$)	**37.4**	43.5	42.7	42.7	46.6	59.7	41.3	45.1	**52.7**	60.2	45.8	43.1	47.7	33.7	37.1	45.6
Wang et al. [43] ECCV'20 ($N = 96$)	41.3	43.9	44.0	42.2	48.0	57.1	42.2	43.2	57.3	61.3	47.0	43.5	47.0	32.6	31.8	45.6
Liu et al. [26] CVPR'20 ($N = 243$)	41.8	44.8	41.1	44.9	47.4	54.1	43.4	42.2	56.2	63.6	45.3	43.5	45.3	31.3	32.2	45.1
Zeng et al. [47] ECCV'20 ($N = 243$)	46.6	47.1	43.9	41.6	45.8	_49.6_	46.5	40.0	53.4	61.1	46.1	42.6	43.1	31.5	32.6	44.8
Zeng et al. [48] ICCV'21 ($N = 9$)	–	–	–	–	–	–	–	–	–	–	–	–	–	–	–	45.7
Zheng et al. [50] ICCV'21 ($N = 81$)	41.5	44.8	39.8	42.5	46.5	51.6	42.1	42.0	_53.3_	60.7	45.5	43.3	46.1	31.8	32.2	44.3
Shan et al. [37] MM'21 ($N = 243$)	40.8	44.5	41.4	42.7	46.3	55.6	41.8	41.9	53.7	60.8	45.0	**41.5**	44.8	30.8	31.9	44.3
Chen et al. [6] TCSVT'21 ($N = 243$)	41.4	43.5	40.1	42.9	46.6	51.9	41.7	42.3	53.9	60.2	45.4	41.7	46.0	31.5	32.7	44.1
Hu et al. [17] MM'21 ($N = 96$)	_38.0_	43.3	_39.1_	**39.4**	45.8	53.6	41.4	41.4	55.5	61.9	44.6	41.9	44.5	31.6	_29.4_	43.4
Li et al. [22] TMM'22 ($N = 351$)(*)	39.9	43.4	40.0	40.9	46.4	50.6	42.1	_39.8_	55.8	61.6	44.9	43.3	44.9	29.9	30.3	43.6
P-STMO-S ($N = 81$)	41.7	44.5	41.0	42.9	46.0	51.3	42.8	41.3	54.9	61.8	45.1	42.8	43.8	30.8	30.7	44.1
P-STMO-S ($N = 243$)	40.0	_42.5_	**38.3**	41.5	45.8	50.8	41.6	40.0	54.2	_59.3_	_44.4_	41.9	43.6	30.3	30.1	43.0
P-STMO ($N = 243$)	38.9	42.7	40.4	41.1	_45.6_	49.7	_40.9_	39.9	55.5	59.4	44.9	42.2	_42.7_	_29.4_	_29.4_	_42.8_
P-STMO ($N = 243$)(*)	38.4	42.1	39.8	_40.2_	45.2	48.9	40.4	**38.3**	53.8	57.3	**43.9**	_41.6_	**42.2**	29.3	29.3	**42.1**

Table 2. Results on MPI-INF-3DHP under three evaluation metrics.

Method	PCK↑	AUC↑	MPJPE↓
Mehta et al. [28] 3DV'17 ($N = 1$)	75.7	39.3	117.6
Pavllo et al. [32] CVPR'19 ($N = 81$)	86.0	51.9	84.0
Lin et al. [23] BMVC'19 ($N = 25$)	83.6	51.4	79.8
Zeng et al. [47] ECCV'20 ($N = 1$)	77.6	43.8	–
Wang et al. [43] ECCV'20 ($N = 96$)	86.9	62.1	68.1
Zheng et al. [50] ICCV'21 ($N = 9$)	_88.6_	56.4	77.1
Chen et al. [6] TCSVT'21 ($N = 81$)	87.9	54.0	78.8
Hu et al. [17] MM'21 ($N = 96$)	**97.9**	_69.5_	_42.5_
P-STMO ($N = 81$)	**97.9**	**75.8**	**32.2**

4.3 Ablation Study

To verify the effectiveness of each component, we conduct ablation experiments on Human3.6M dataset using our P-STMO-S model. We utilize 2D keypoints from CPN as inputs. MPJPE is reported for analysis.

Impact of Each Component. As shown in Table 3, we validate the contributions of different modules in STMO model and the overall performance gain brought by the proposed MPM and TDS methods. A network consisting of only SEM achieves 51.0 mm under MPJPE. To evaluate the effect of TEM, we use a vanilla Transformer as the backbone and yield a result of 49.6 mm. After combining SEM and TEM, MPJPE drops to 46.0 mm. Finally, we end up with the proposed STMO model by assembling SEM, TEM as well as MOFA, and achieve 44.2 mm under MPJPE. Furthermore, MPM and TDS improve upon STMO by

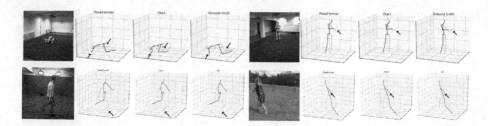

Fig. 3. Qualitative comparison between our P-STMO method and Poseformer [50] on Human3.6M and MPI-INF-3DHP datasets.

Table 3. The effectiveness of different components.

SEM	TEM	MOFA	MPM	TDS	Params (M)	FLOPs (M)	MPJPE↓
✓	✗	✗	✗	✗	1.1	536	51.0
✗	✓	✗	✗	✗	1.6	769	49.6
✓	✓	✗	✗	✗	2.2	1094	46.0
✓	✓	✓	✗	✗	6.2	1482	44.2
✓	✓	✓	✓	✗	6.2	1482	43.2
✓	✓	✓	✓	✓	6.2	1482	**43.0**

Table 4. Analysis on designs of SEM. L is the number of sub-blocks in MLP.

Backbone	N	Params(M)	FLOPs(M)	MPJPE↓
fc	243	1.6	769	49.6
Transformer	81	7.2	1218	48.8
MLP ($L = 1$)	243	2.3	1094	<u>46.0</u>
MLP ($L = 2$)	243	2.8	1350	**45.9**
MLP ($L = 3$)	243	3.3	1608	46.1

1.0 mm and 0.2 mm respectively. Previous works [26,32] observe decreasing returns when increasing the temporal receptive field, so a small gain (0.2 mm) from TDS is to be expected in the case of 243 input frames.

Analysis on Masking Ratio of Pre-training. Figure 4 shows the influence of the masking ratio of three masking strategies in the pre-training stage. As shown in Fig. 4a, the optimal ratio is $q^T = 90\%$ when only temporal masking is used. This ratio is higher than MAE [15] in CV and BERT [11] in NLP, whose masking ratios are 75% and 15%, respectively. This is because 2D pose sequences are more redundant than images and sentences. Since two adjacent poses are very similar, we need a high masking ratio to increase the difficulty of the task. We observe a negative correlation between the loss of Stage I and the error of Stage II. This implies that increasing the difficulty of the MPM task in Stage I does promote the fitting ability of the encoder, thus aiding the training of Stage II.

The way of spatial masking is different from that of temporal masking. In the case of temporal masking, the decoder perceives the indices of the masked frames through positional embeddings. In the case of spatial masking, only the latent features in each frame are visible to the decoder, so the indices of the masked joints cannot be inferred directly. For the above reasons, it is clear that the spatial masking task is more troublesome than the temporal masking task. Therefore, the optimal masking ratio of the former should be smaller than that of the latter. Figure 4b shows that the optimal number is $m^S = 7$ ($q^S = 41.1\%$) when only spatial masking is used. When the masking number is greater than 7,

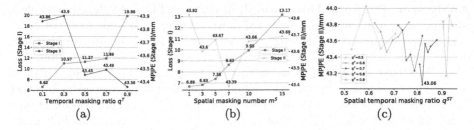

Fig. 4. Performance of three different masking strategies. (a) Temporal masking. (b) Spatial masking. (c) Spatial temporal masking.

Table 5. Analysis on temporal downsampling rate s. RF is the temporal receptive field.

Table 6. Analysis on computational complexity. Top table: taken from [50]. Bottom table: our implementation.

N	s	RF	Params(M)	FLOPs(M)	MPJPE↓
27	1	27	4.6	163	48.2
27	3	81	4.6	163	46.8
27	9	243	4.6	163	46.1
81	1	81	5.4	493	45.6
81	3	243	5.4	493	44.1
243	1	243	6.2	1482	43.2
243	2	486	6.2	1482	**43.0**

Method	Params(M)	FLOPs(M)	FPS	MPJPE↓
Pavllo *et al.* [32] CVPR'19 ($N = 243$)	16.9	33	863	46.8
Chen *et al.* [6] TCSVT'21 ($N = 243$)	58.1	116	264	44.1
Zheng *et al.* [50] ICCV'21 ($N = 81$)	9.5	1358	269	44.3
Chen *et al.* [6] TCSVT'21 ($N = 243$)	58.1	656	429	44.1
Zheng *et al.* [50] ICCV'21 ($N = 81$)	9.5	1624	1952	44.3
P-STMO-S ($N = 81$)	5.4	493	**7824**	44.1
P-STMO-S ($N = 243$)	6.2	1482	<u>3504</u>	<u>43.0</u>
P-STMO ($N = 243$)	6.7	1737	3040	**42.8**

continuing to increase the difficulty of the task will result in too much noise in the input data. Subsequently, the encoder is unable to obtain useful information.

We illustrate the effect of combining temporal masking and spatial masking in Fig. 4c. Since this hybrid masking strategy is more challenging, the spatial masking ratio and temporal masking ratio should be slightly reduced. The best performance is achieved when $q^{\mathrm{T}} = 80\%$ and $m^{\mathrm{S}} = 2$ ($q^{\mathrm{S}} = 11.7\%$). The optimal spatial temporal masking ratio is $q^{\mathrm{ST}} = 82.3\%$. The performance improvement of spatial temporal masking over spatial masking and temporal masking is 0.33 mm and 0.3 mm, respectively.

Analysis on Different Designs of SEM. To verify the superiority of using an MLP block as the backbone network of SEM, we evaluate different architecture designs in Table 4. The results show that MLP outperforms fc and Transformer by 3.7 mm and 2.9 mm respectively. The structure of a single fc layer is so simple that it does not have sufficient capability to represent spatial characteristics. Meanwhile, Transformer is too complex and thus difficult to optimize. Therefore, they are not as effective as an MLP block. MLP achieves better performance than the other two methods, while its parameters and FLOPs are in between. Additionally, we explore the influence of the number of sub-blocks L in MLP. The best performance is achieved when $L = 2$. We choose $L = 1$ in other experiments because it is less computationally intensive and achieves similar performance compared to the best one.

Analysis on Temporal Downsampling Rate of TDS. As shown in Table 5, we investigate the impact of temporal downsampling rate s for different numbers of input frames N. TDS brings up to 2.1 mm, 1.5 mm, 0.2 mm performance improvement in the case of $N = 27, 81, 243$ respectively. The results show that when N is fixed, increasing s can enlarge the temporal receptive field (RF) and reduce data redundancy, thus improving the prediction performance. In other words, when RF is fixed, TDS is an effective approach to reduce computational overhead without much performance sacrifice. Besides, the gain from TDS gradually decreases as N becomes larger. When $N = 27$ and $s = 3$, TDS improves the performance by 1.4 mm. However, when $N = 243$ and $s = 2$, TDS only brings 0.2 mm improvement. This can be explained by the fact that the farther the two frames are separated in the time domain, the less they are correlated. Therefore, the farther the added frames are from the middle frame, the less help it brings to the 3D pose estimation of the middle frame.

Computational Complexity. We report the number of parameters of our framework, the number of output frames per second (FPS), floating-point operations (FLOPs) per frame at inference time, and the performance. We conduct experiments on a single GeForce GTX 3080Ti GPU. For our method, we do not include the number of parameters and FLOPs of Stage I in the calculation results, because we only care about the speed of inference. Once the training is completed, the decoder in Stage I is discarded, which does not impose any burden on the inference process. As shown in Table 6, our 243-frame P-STMO-S has fewer parameters and FLOPs than 81-frame Poseformer. P-STMO outperforms PoseFormer and anatomy-aware model [6] by 1.5/1.3 mm while bringing a ~1.5/7.1× speedup. This reveals the effectiveness and efficiency of the proposed method. Note that we only calculate the time for the input data to pass through the model, which does not include data pre-processing time. Therefore, the FPS we report for Poseformer is larger than the result in the original paper.

5 Conclusion

In this paper, we present P-STMO, a Pre-trained Spatial Temporal Many-to-One model for 3D human pose estimation. A pre-training task, called MPM, is proposed to enhance the representation capability of SEM and TEM. For SEM, an MLP block is used as the backbone, which is more effective than Transformer and *fc*. For TEM, a temporal downsampling strategy is introduced to mitigate input data redundancy and increase the temporal receptive field. Comprehensive experiments on two datasets demonstrate that our method achieves superior performance over state-of-the-art methods with smaller computational budgets.

Acknowledgment. This work was supported in part by the National Natural Science Foundation of China under grantn (U21B2012, 62025101); in part by the National Postdoctoral Program for Innovative Talents under Grant BX2021009; and in part by the High Performance Computing Platform of Peking University, which are gratefully acknowledged.

References

1. Bao, H., Dong, L., Piao, S., Wei, F.: BEit: BERT pre-training of image transformers. In: International Conference on Learning Representations (2022)
2. Brown, T., et al.: Language models are few-shot learners. Adv. Neural. Inf. Process. Syst. **33**, 1877–1901 (2020)
3. Cai, Y., et al.: Exploiting spatial-temporal relationships for 3d pose estimation via graph convolutional networks. In: Proceedings of the IEEE/CVF International Conference on Computer Vision, pp. 2272–2281 (2019)
4. Carion, N., Massa, F., Synnaeve, G., Usunier, N., Kirillov, A., Zagoruyko, S.: End-to-end object detection with transformers. In: Vedaldi, A., Bischof, H., Brox, T., Frahm, J.-M. (eds.) ECCV 2020. LNCS, vol. 12346, pp. 213–229. Springer, Cham (2020). https://doi.org/10.1007/978-3-030-58452-8_13
5. Chen, M., et al.: Generative pretraining from pixels. In: International Conference on Machine Learning, pp. 1691–1703. PMLR (2020)
6. Chen, T., Fang, C., Shen, X., Zhu, Y., Chen, Z., Luo, J.: Anatomy-aware 3d human pose estimation with bone-based pose decomposition. IEEE Trans. Circ. Syst. Video Technol. **32**(1), 198–209 (2021)
7. Chen, X., Xie, S., He, K.: An empirical study of training self-supervised vision transformers. In: Proceedings of the IEEE/CVF International Conference on Computer Vision, pp. 9640–9649 (2021)
8. Chen, Y., Wang, Z., Peng, Y., Zhang, Z., Yu, G., Sun, J.: Cascaded pyramid network for multi-person pose estimation. In: Proceedings of the IEEE Conference on Computer Vision and Pattern Recognition, pp. 7103–7112 (2018)
9. Ci, H., Wang, C., Ma, X., Wang, Y.: Optimizing network structure for 3d human pose estimation. In: Proceedings of the IEEE/CVF International Conference on Computer Vision, pp. 2262–2271 (2019)
10. Conneau, A., Lample, G.: Cross-lingual language model pretraining. Adv. Neural. Inf. Process. Syst. **32**, 7059–7069 (2019)
11. Devlin, J., Chang, M.W., Lee, K., Toutanova, K.: Bert: Pre-training of deep bidirectional transformers for language understanding. arXiv preprint arXiv:1810.04805 (2018)
12. Dosovitskiy, A., et al.: An image is worth 16×16 words: transformers for image recognition at scale. In: International Conference on Learning Representations (2021)
13. Fang, H.S., Xu, Y., Wang, W., Liu, X., Zhu, S.C.: Learning pose grammar to encode human body configuration for 3d pose estimation. In: Proceedings of the AAAI Conference on Artificial Intelligence, vol. 32 (2018)
14. Han, K., et al.: A survey on vision transformer. In: IEEE Transactions on Pattern Analysis and Machine Intelligence, pp. 1–1 (2022)
15. He, K., Chen, X., Xie, S., Li, Y., Dollár, P., Girshick, R.: Masked autoencoders are scalable vision learners. In: Proceedings of the IEEE/CVF Conference on Computer Vision and Pattern Recognition, pp. 16000–16009 (2022)
16. Hossain, M.R.I., Little, J.J.: Exploiting temporal information for 3d human pose estimation. In: Proceedings of the European Conference on Computer Vision (ECCV), pp. 68–84 (2018)
17. Hu, W., Zhang, C., Zhan, F., Zhang, L., Wong, T.T.: Conditional directed graph convolution for 3d human pose estimation. In: Proceedings of the 29th ACM International Conference on Multimedia, pp. 602–611 (2021)

18. Ionescu, C., Carreira, J., Sminchisescu, C.: Iterated second-order label sensitive pooling for 3d human pose estimation. In: Proceedings of the IEEE Conference on Computer Vision and Pattern Recognition, pp. 1661–1668 (2014)
19. Ionescu, C., Papava, D., Olaru, V., Sminchisescu, C.: Human 3.6 m: large scale datasets and predictive methods for 3d human sensing in natural environments. IEEE Trans. Pattern Anal. Mach. Intell. **36**(7), 1325–1339 (2013)
20. Lee, K., Lee, I., Lee, S.: Propagating lstm: 3d pose estimation based on joint interdependency. In: Proceedings of the European Conference on Computer Vision (ECCV), pp. 119–135 (2018)
21. Li, C., Lee, G.H.: Generating multiple hypotheses for 3d human pose estimation with mixture density network. In: Proceedings of the IEEE/CVF Conference on Computer Vision and Pattern Recognition, pp. 9887–9895 (2019)
22. Li, W., Liu, H., Ding, R., Liu, M., Wang, P., Yang, W.: Exploiting temporal contexts with strided transformer for 3d human pose estimation. In: IEEE Transactions on Multimedia (2022)
23. Lin, J., Lee, G.H.: Trajectory space factorization for deep video-based 3d human pose estimation. In: Proceedings of the British Machine Vision Conference (BMVC) (2019)
24. Lin, K., Wang, L., Liu, Z.: End-to-end human pose and mesh reconstruction with transformers. In: Proceedings of the IEEE/CVF Conference on Computer Vision and Pattern Recognition, pp. 1954–1963 (2021)
25. Liu, K., Zou, Z., Tang, W.: Learning global pose features in graph convolutional networks for 3d human pose estimation. In: Proceedings of the Asian Conference on Computer Vision (2020)
26. Liu, R., Shen, J., Wang, H., Chen, C., Cheung, S.c., Asari, V.: Attention mechanism exploits temporal contexts: real-time 3d human pose reconstruction. In: Proceedings of the IEEE/CVF Conference on Computer Vision and Pattern Recognition, pp. 5064–5073 (2020)
27. Martinez, J., Hossain, R., Romero, J., Little, J.J.: A simple yet effective baseline for 3d human pose estimation. In: Proceedings of the IEEE International Conference on Computer Vision, pp. 2640–2649 (2017)
28. Mehta, D., et al.: Monocular 3d human pose estimation in the wild using improved cnn supervision. In: 2017 International Conference on 3D Vision (3DV), pp. 506–516. IEEE (2017)
29. Mehta, D., et al.: Vnect: real-time 3d human pose estimation with a single rgb camera. ACM Trans. Graph. (TOG) **36**(4), 1–14 (2017)
30. Newell, A., Yang, K., Deng, J.: Stacked hourglass networks for human pose estimation. In: Leibe, B., Matas, J., Sebe, N., Welling, M. (eds.) ECCV 2016. LNCS, vol. 9912, pp. 483–499. Springer, Cham (2016). https://doi.org/10.1007/978-3-319-46484-8_29
31. Pavlakos, G., Zhou, X., Daniilidis, K.: Ordinal depth supervision for 3d human pose estimation. In: Proceedings of the IEEE Conference on Computer Vision and Pattern Recognition, pp. 7307–7316 (2018)
32. Pavllo, D., Feichtenhofer, C., Grangier, D., Auli, M.: 3d human pose estimation in video with temporal convolutions and semi-supervised training. In: Proceedings of the IEEE/CVF Conference on Computer Vision and Pattern Recognition, pp. 7753–7762 (2019)
33. Peters, M.E., et al.: Deep contextualized word representations. In: Proceedings of the 2018 Conference of the North American Chapter of the Association for Computational Linguistics: Human Language Technologies, Volume 1 (Long Papers) (2018)

34. Qiu, X.P., Sun, T.X., Xu, Y.G., Shao, Y.F., Dai, N., Huang, X.J.: Pre-trained models for natural language processing: a survey. Sci. China Technol. Sci. **63**(10), 1872–1897 (2020). https://doi.org/10.1007/s11431-020-1647-3

35. Radford, A., Wu, J., Child, R., Luan, D., Amodei, D., Sutskever, I., et al.: Language models are unsupervised multitask learners. OpenAI blog **1**(8), 9 (2019)

36. Rogers, B., Graham, M.: Motion parallax as an independent cue for depth perception. Perception **8**(2), 125–134 (1979)

37. Shan, W., Lu, H., Wang, S., Zhang, X., Gao, W.: Improving robustness and accuracy via relative information encoding in 3d human pose estimation. In: Proceedings of the 29th ACM International Conference on Multimedia, pp. 3446–3454 (2021)

38. Sun, X., Shang, J., Liang, S., Wei, Y.: Compositional human pose regression. In: Proceedings of the IEEE International Conference on Computer Vision, pp. 2602–2611 (2017)

39. Touvron, H., Cord, M., Douze, M., Massa, F., Sablayrolles, A., Jégou, H.: Training data-efficient image transformers & distillation through attention. In: International Conference on Machine Learning, pp. 10347–10357. PMLR (2021)

40. Vaswani, A., et al.: Attention is all you need. In: Advances in Neural Information Processing Systems, pp. 5998–6008 (2017)

41. Vincent, P., Larochelle, H., Bengio, Y., Manzagol, P.A.: Extracting and composing robust features with denoising autoencoders. In: Proceedings of the 25th International Conference on Machine Learning, pp. 1096–1103 (2008)

42. Wang, C., Wang, Y., Lin, Z., Yuille, A.L., Gao, W.: Robust estimation of 3d human poses from a single image. In: Proceedings of the IEEE Conference on Computer Vision and Pattern Recognition, pp. 2361–2368 (2014)

43. Wang, J., Yan, S., Xiong, Y., Lin, D.: Motion guided 3D pose estimation from videos. In: Vedaldi, A., Bischof, H., Brox, T., Frahm, J.-M. (eds.) ECCV 2020. LNCS, vol. 12358, pp. 764–780. Springer, Cham (2020). https://doi.org/10.1007/978-3-030-58601-0_45

44. Xu, J., Yu, Z., Ni, B., Yang, J., Yang, X., Zhang, W.: Deep kinematics analysis for monocular 3d human pose estimation. In: Proceedings of the IEEE/CVF Conference on Computer Vision and Pattern Recognition, pp. 899–908 (2020)

45. Yan, Q., Zheng, J., Reding, S., Li, S., Doytchinov, I.: Crossloc: scalable aerial localization assisted by multimodal synthetic data. In: Proceedings of the IEEE/CVF Conference on Computer Vision and Pattern Recognition, pp. 17358–17368 (2022)

46. Yosinski, J., Clune, J., Bengio, Y., Lipson, H.: How transferable are features in deep neural networks? In: Advances in Neural Information Processing Systems 27 (2014)

47. Zeng, A., Sun, X., Huang, F., Liu, M., Xu, Q., Lin, S.: SRNet: improving generalization in 3D human pose estimation with a split-and-recombine approach. In: Vedaldi, A., Bischof, H., Brox, T., Frahm, J.-M. (eds.) ECCV 2020. LNCS, vol. 12359, pp. 507–523. Springer, Cham (2020). https://doi.org/10.1007/978-3-030-58568-6_30

48. Zeng, A., Sun, X., Yang, L., Zhao, N., Liu, M., Xu, Q.: Learning skeletal graph neural networks for hard 3d pose estimation. In: Proceedings of the IEEE/CVF International Conference on Computer Vision, pp. 11436–11445 (2021)

49. Zhao, L., Peng, X., Tian, Y., Kapadia, M., Metaxas, D.N.: Semantic graph convolutional networks for 3d human pose regression. In: Proceedings of the IEEE/CVF Conference on Computer Vision and Pattern Recognition, pp. 3425–3435 (2019)

50. Zheng, C., Zhu, S., Mendieta, M., Yang, T., Chen, C., Ding, Z.: 3d human pose estimation with spatial and temporal transformers. In: Proceedings of the IEEE/CVF International Conference on Computer Vision, pp. 11656–11665 (2021)
51. Zhou, X., Zhu, M., Leonardos, S., Derpanis, K.G., Daniilidis, K.: Sparseness meets deepness: 3d human pose estimation from monocular video. In: Proceedings of the IEEE Conference on Computer Vision and Pattern Recognition, pp. 4966–4975 (2016)

D&D: Learning Human Dynamics from Dynamic Camera

Jiefeng Li[1], Siyuan Bian[1], Chao Xu[2], Gang Liu[2], Gang Yu[2], and Cewu Lu[1(✉)]

[1] Shanghai Jiao Tong University, Shanghai, China
{ljf_likit,biansiyuan,lucewu}@sjtu.edu.cn
[2] Tencent, Shenzhen, China
{dasxu,sylvainliu,skicyyu}@tencent.com

Abstract. 3D human pose estimation from a monocular video has recently seen significant improvements. However, most state-of-the-art methods are kinematics-based, which are prone to physically implausible motions with pronounced artifacts. Current dynamics-based methods can predict physically plausible motion but are restricted to simple scenarios with static camera view. In this work, we present D&D (Learning Human **D**ynamics from **D**ynamic Camera), which leverages the laws of physics to reconstruct 3D human motion from the in-the-wild videos with a moving camera. D&D introduces *inertial force control (IFC)* to explain the 3D human motion in the non-inertial local frame by considering the inertial forces of the dynamic camera. To learn the ground contact with limited annotations, we develop *probabilistic contact torque (PCT)*, which is computed by differentiable sampling from contact probabilities and used to generate motions. The contact state can be weakly supervised by encouraging the model to generate correct motions. Furthermore, we propose an attentive PD controller that adjusts target pose states using temporal information to obtain smooth and accurate pose control. Our approach is entirely neural-based and runs without offline optimization or simulation in physics engines. Experiments on large-scale 3D human motion benchmarks demonstrate the effectiveness of D&D, where we exhibit superior performance against both state-of-the-art kinematics-based and dynamics-based methods. Code is available at https://github.com/Jeff-sjtu/DnD.

Keywords: 3D Human Pose Estimation · Physical Awareness · Human Motion Dynamics

---

Cewu Lu—The member of Qing Yuan Research Institute and MoE Key Lab of Artificial Intelligence, AI Institute, Shanghai Jiao Tong University, China and Shanghai Qi Zhi institute.

Supplementary Information The online version contains supplementary material available at https://doi.org/10.1007/978-3-031-20065-6_28.

1 Introduction

Recovering 3D human pose and shape from a monocular image is a challenging problem. It has a wide range of applications in activity recognition [20,21], character animation, and human-robot interaction. Despite the recent progress, estimating 3D structure from the 2D observation is still an ill-posed and challenging task due to the inherent ambiguity.

A number of works [6,13,14,23,50,62] turn to temporal input to incorporate body motion priors. Most state-of-the-art methods [12,14,15,19,33,50,56] are only based on kinematics modeling, i.e., body motion modeling with body part rotations and joint positions. Kinematics modeling directly captures the geometric information of the 3D human body, which is easy to learn by neural networks. However, methods that entirely rely on kinematics information are prone to physical artifacts, such as motion jitter, abnormal root actuation, and implausible body leaning.

Recent works [7,40,43,44,59] have started modeling human motion dynamics to improve the physical plausibility of the estimated motion. Dynamics modeling considers physical forces such as contact force and joint torque to control human motion. These physical properties can help analyze the body motion and understand human-scene interaction. Compared to widely adopted kinematics, dynamics gains less attention in 3D human pose estimation. The reason is that there are lots of limitations in current dynamics methods. For example, existing methods fail in daily scenes with dynamic camera movements (e.g., the 3DPW dataset [26]) since they require a static camera view, known ground plane and gravity vector for dynamics modeling. Besides, they are hard to deploy for real-time applications due to the need for highly-complex offline optimization or simulation with physics engines.

In this work, we propose a novel framework, D&D, a 3D human pose estimation approach with learned *Human **D**ynamics from **D**ynamic Camera*. Unlike previous methods that build the dynamics equation in the world frame, we re-devise the dynamics equations in the non-inertial camera frame. Specifically, when the camera is moving, we introduce inertial forces in the dynamics equation to relate physical forces to local pose accelerations. We develop dynamics networks that directly estimate physical properties (forces and contact states). Then we can use the physical properties to compute the pose accelerations and obtain final human motion based on the accelerations. To train the dynamics network with only a limited amount of contact annotations, we propose *probabilistic contact torque (PCT)* for differentiable contact torque estimation. Concretely, we use a neural network to predict contact probabilities and conduct differentiable sampling to draw contact states from the predicted probabilities. Then we use the sampled contact states to compute the torque of the ground reaction forces and control the human motion. In this way, the contact classifier can be weakly supervised by minimizing the difference between the generated human motion and the ground-truth motion. To further improve the smoothness of the estimated motion, we propose a novel control mechanism called *attentive PD controller*. The output of the conventional PD controller [44,44,59] is proportional to the distance of the current pose state from the target state, which is sensitive to the unstable and jittery target. Instead, our attentive PD controller allows accurate control by globally adjusting the target state and is robust to the jittery target.

We benchmark D&D on the 3DPW [26] dataset captured with moving cameras and the Human3.6M [9] dataset captured with static cameras. D&D is compared against both state-of-the-art kinematics-based and dynamics-based methods and obtains state-of-the-art performance.

The contributions of this paper can be summarized as follows:

- We present the idea of inertial force control (IFC) to perform dynamics modeling for 3D human pose estimation from a dynamic camera view.
- We propose probabilistic contact torque (PCT) that leverages large-scale motion datasets without contact annotations for weakly-supervised training.
- Our proposed attentive PD controller enables smooth and accurate character control against jittery target motion.
- Our approach outperforms previous state-of-the-art kinematics-based and dynamics-based methods. It is fully differentiable and runs without offline optimization or simulation in physics engines.

2   Related Work

Kinematics-Based 3D Human Pose Estimation. Numerous prior works estimate 3D human poses by locating the 3D joint positions [2,8,18,27,28,30, 32,34,35,37,41,46,47,51,54,61,63]. Although these methods obtain impressive performance, they cannot provide physiological and physical constraints of the human pose. Many works [5,12,15,16,19,33] adopt parametric statistical human body models [22,36,52] to improve physiological plausibility since they provide a well-defined human body structure. Optimization-based approaches [5,16,36,49] automatically fit the SMPL body model to 2D observations, e.g., 2D keypoints and silhouettes. Alternatively, learning-based approaches use a deep neural network to regress the pose and shape parameters directly [12,14,15,19,33]. Several works [11,15,16] combine the optimization-based and learning-based methods to produce pseudo supervision or conduct test-time optimization.

For better temporal consistency, recent works have started to exploit temporal context [4,6,13,14,29,31,39,48,50]. Kocabas et al. [14] propose an adversarial framework to leverage motion prior from large-scale motion datasets [25]. Sun et al. [48] model temporal information with a bilinear Transformer. Rempe et al. [39] propose a VAE model to learn motion prior and optimize ground contacts. All the aforementioned methods disregard human dynamics. Although they achieve high accuracy on pose metrics, e.g., Procrustes Aligned MPJPE, the resulting motions are often physically implausible with pronounced physical artifacts such as improper balance and inaccurate body leaning.

Dynamics-Based 3D Human Pose Estimation. To reduce physical artifacts, a number of works leverage the laws of physics to estimate human
motion [7,40,43,44,57,59]. Some of them are optimization-based approaches [7,
40,44]. They use trajectory optimization to obtain the physical forces that induce
human motion. Shimada et al. [44] consider a complete human motion dynamics
equation for optimization and obtain motion with fewer artifacts. Dabral et al. [7]
propose a joint 3D human-object optimization framework for human motion
capture and object trajectory estimation. Recent works [43,60] have started to
use regression-based methods to estimate human motion dynamics. Shimada
et al. [43] propose a fully-differentiable framework for 3D human motion capture with physics constraints. All previous approaches require a static camera,
restricting their applications in real-world scenarios.

On the other hand, deep reinforcement learning and motion imitation are
widely used for 3D human motion estimation [24,38,55,57,59]. These works
rely on physics engines to learn the control policies. Peng et al. [38] propose a
control policy that allows a simulated character to mimic realistic motion capture
data. Yuan et al. [59] present a joint kinematics-dynamics reinforcement learning
framework that learns motion policy to reconstruct 3D human motion. Luo et
al. [24] propose a dynamics-regulated training procedure for egocentric pose
estimation. The work of Yu et al. [55] is most related to us. They propose a policy
learning algorithm with a scene fitting process to reconstruct 3D human motion
from a dynamic camera. Training their RL model and the fitting process is time-
consuming. It takes $24 \sim 96$ hours to obtain the human motion of one video clip.
Unlike previous methods, our regression-based approach is fully differentiable
and does not rely on physics engines and offline fitting. It predicts accurate
and physically plausible 3D human motion for in-the-wild scenes with dynamic
camera movements.

3   Method

The overall framework of the proposed D&D (*Learning Human **D**ynamics from
Dynamic Camera*) is summarized in Fig. 1. The input to D&D is a video $\{I^t\}_{t=1}^T$
with T frames. Each frame I^t is fed into the kinematics backbone network to
estimate the initial human motion $\widehat{q}^t$ in the local camera frame. The dynamics
networks take as input the initial local motion $\{\widehat{q}^t\}_{t=1}^T$ and estimate physical
properties (forces and contact states). Then we apply the forward dynamics
modules to compute the pose and trajectory accelerations from the estimated
physical properties. Finally, we use accelerations to obtain 3D human motion
with physical constraints iteratively.

In this section, before introducing our solution, we first review the formulation of current dynamics-based methods in Sect. 3.1. In Sect. 3.2, we present
the formulation of *Inertial Force Control (IFC)* that introduces inertial forces
to explain the human motion in the dynamic camera view. Then we elaborate
on the pipeline of D&D: **i**) learning physical properties with neural networks
in Sect. 3.3, **ii**) analytically computing accelerations with forward dynamics in

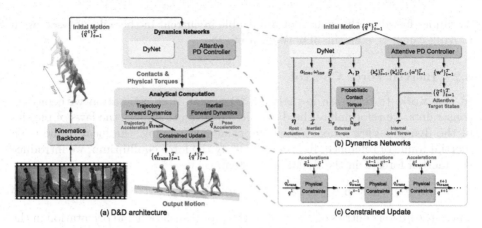

Fig. 1. Overview of the proposed framework. The video clip is fed into the kinematics backbone network to estimate the initial motion $\{\hat{q}^t\}_{t=1}^T$. The dynamics networks take as input the initial motion and estimate physical properties. Then we compute pose and trajectory accelerations analytically via forward dynamics. Finally, we utilize accelerations to obtain human motion with physical constraints.

Sect. 3.4, **iii**) obtaining final pose with the constrained update in Sect. 3.5. The objective function of training the entire framework is further detailed in Sect. 3.6.

3.1 Preliminaries

The kinematic state of the human body can be represented by a pose vector q. The pose vector is parameterized as Euler angles with root translation and orientation to build the dynamics formula, i.e., $q \in \mathbb{R}^{3N_j+6}$, where N_j denotes the total number of human body joints. In previous methods [43,44,58], the first six entries of q are set as the root translation and orientation in the *world frame*. All remaining $3N_j$ entries encode joint angles of the human body. The laws of physics are imposed by considering Newtonian rigid body dynamics as:

$$M(q)\ddot{q} - \tau = h_{\mathrm{grf}}(q, b, \lambda) - h_g(q, \dot{q}) - h_c(q, \dot{q}), \tag{1}$$

where $M \in \mathbb{R}^{(3N_j+6)\times(3N_j+6)}$ denotes the inertia matrix of the human body; $\dot{q} \in \mathbb{R}^{3N_j+6}$ and $\ddot{q} \in \mathbb{R}^{3N_j+6}$ denote the velocity and the acceleration of q, respectively; $h_{\mathrm{grf}} \in \mathbb{R}^{3N_j+6}$ denotes the resultant torque of the ground reaction forces; $b \in \mathbb{R}^{N_c}$ is the discrete contact states vector; $\lambda \in \mathbb{R}^{3N_c}$ is the linear contact forces; N_c denotes the number of joints to which the contact forces are applied; $h_g \in \mathbb{R}^{3N_j+6}$ is the gravity torque; $h_c \in \mathbb{R}^{3N_j+6}$ encompasses Coriolis and centripetal forces; $\tau \in \mathbb{R}^{3N_j+6}$ represents the internal joint torque of the human body, with the first six entries being the direct root actuation. In this formulation, the translation and orientation must be in the static world frame, which restricts the application of the model in real-world scenarios. Therefore, previous dynamics-based methods are not applicable in current in-the-wild datasets with moving cameras, e.g., the 3DPW dataset [26].

3.2 Inertial Force Control

In this work, to facilitate in-the-wild 3D human pose estimation with physics constraints, we reformulate the dynamics equation to impose the laws of physics in the dynamic-view video. When the camera is moving, the local frame is an inertial frame of reference. In order to satisfy the force equilibrium, we introduce the inertial force $\mathcal{I}$ in the dynamics system:

$$M(q)\ddot{q} - \boldsymbol{\tau} = h_{\text{grf}}(q, \mathbf{b}, \boldsymbol{\lambda}) - h_g(q, \dot{q}) - h_c(q, \dot{q}) + \mathcal{I}(q, \dot{q}, a_{\text{ine}}, \omega_{\text{ine}}), \qquad (2)$$

where the first six entries of q are set as the root translation and orientation in the *local camera frame*, and the inertial force $\mathcal{I}$ is determined by the current motion state (q and $\dot{q}$) and camera movement state (linear acceleration $a_{\text{ine}} \in \mathbb{R}^3$ and angular velocity $\omega_{\text{ine}} \in \mathbb{R}^3$). Specifically, the inertial force encompasses linear, centripetal, and Coriolis forces. It is calculated as follows:

$$\mathcal{I} = \sum_i^{N_j} \underbrace{m_i J_{v_i}^{\mathsf{T}} a_{\text{ine}}}_{\text{linear force}} + \underbrace{m_i J_{v_i}^{\mathsf{T}} \omega_{\text{ine}} \times (\omega_{\text{ine}} \times r_i)}_{\text{centripetal force}} + \underbrace{2 m_i J_{v_i}^{\mathsf{T}} (\omega_{\text{ine}} \times v_i)}_{\text{Coriolis force}}, \qquad (3)$$

where $J_{v_i} \in \mathbb{R}^{3 \times (3N_j + 6)}$ denotes the linear Jacobian matrix that describes how the linear velocity of the i-th joint changes with pose velocity $\dot{q}$, m_i denotes the mass of the i-th joint, r_i denotes the position of the i-th joint in the local frame, and v_i is the velocity of the i-th joint. J_{v_i}, r_i, and v_i can be analytically computed using the pose q and the velocity $\dot{q}$.

The inertial force control (IFC) establishes the relation between the physical properties and the pose acceleration in the local frame. The pose acceleration can be subsequently used to calculate the final motion. In this way, we can estimate physically plausible human motion from *forces* to *accelerations* to *poses*. The generated motion is smooth and natural. Besides, it provides extra physical information to understand human-scene interaction for high-level activity understanding tasks.

Discussion. The concept of *residual force* [58] is widely adopted in previous works [3,17,43,44,58] to explain the direct root actuation in the global static frame. Theoretically, we can adopt a residual term to explain the inertia in the local camera frame implicitly. However, we found explicit inertia modeling obtains better estimation results than implicit modeling with a residual term. Detailed comparisons are provided in Sect. 4.4.

3.3 Learning Physical Properties

In this subsection, we elaborate on the neural networks for physical properties estimation. We first use a kinematics backbone to extract the initial motion

$\{\widehat{q}^t\}_{t=1}^T$. The initial motion is then fed to a dynamics network (DyNet) with *probabilistic contact torque* for contact, external force, and inertial force estimation and the *attentive PD controller* for internal joint torque estimation.

Contact, External Force, and Inertial Force Estimation. The root motion of the human character is dependent on external forces and inertial forces. To explain root motion, we propose DyNet that directly regresses the related physical properties, including the ground reaction forces $\boldsymbol{\lambda} = (\lambda_1, \cdots, \lambda_{N_c})$, the gravity $\vec{g}$, the direct root actuation $\boldsymbol{\eta}$, the contact probabilities $\mathbf{p} = (p_1, p_2, \cdots, p_{N_c})$, the linear camera acceleration a_{ine}, and the angular camera velocity ω_{ine}. The detailed network structure of DyNet is provided in the supplementary material.

The inertial force $\mathcal{I}$ can be calculated following Eq. 3 with the estimated a_{ine} and ω_{ine}. The gravity torque h_g can be calculated as:

$$\mathrm{h}_g = -\sum_i^{N_j} m_i J_{v_i}^\mathsf{T} \vec{g}. \tag{4}$$

When considering gravity, bodyweight will affect human motion. In this paper, we let the shape parameters $\boldsymbol{\beta}$ control the body weight. We assume the standard weight is 75 kg when $\boldsymbol{\beta}_0 = \mathbf{0}$, and there is a linear correlation between the body weight and the bone length. We obtain the corresponding bodyweight based on the bone-length ratio of $\boldsymbol{\beta}$ to $\boldsymbol{\beta}_0$.

Probabilistic Contact Torque: For the resultant torque of the ground reaction forces, previous methods [43,44,58] compute it with the discrete contact states $\mathbf{b} = (b_1, b_2, \cdots, b_{N_c})$ of N_c joints:

$$\mathrm{h}_{\text{grf}}(q, \mathbf{b}, \boldsymbol{\lambda}) = \sum_j^{N_c} b_j J_{v_j}^\mathsf{T} \lambda_j, \tag{5}$$

where $b_j = 1$ for contact and $b_j = 0$ for non-contact. Note that the output probabilities $\mathbf{p}$ are continuous. We need to discretize p_j with a threshold of 0.5 to obtain b_j. However, the discretization process is not differentiable. Thus the supervision signals for the contact classifier only come from a limited amount of data with contact annotations.

To leverage the large-scale motion dataset without contact annotations, we propose *probabilistic contact torque (PCT)* for weakly-supervised learning. During training, PCT conducts differentiable sampling [10] to draw a sample $\widehat{\mathbf{b}}$ that follows the predicted contact probabilities $\mathbf{p}$ and computes the corresponding ground reaction torques:

$$\widehat{\mathrm{h}}_{\text{grf}}(q, \widehat{\mathbf{b}}, \boldsymbol{\lambda}) = \sum_j^{N_c} \widehat{b}_j J_{v_j}^\mathsf{T} \lambda_j = \sum_j^{N_c} \frac{p_j e^{g_{j1}}}{p_j e^{g_{j1}} + (1 - p_j) e^{g_{j2}}} J_{v_j}^\mathsf{T} \lambda_j, \tag{6}$$

where $g_{j1}, g_{j2} \sim \text{Gumbel}(0, 1)$ are i.i.d samples drawn from the Gumbel distribution. When conducting forward dynamics, we use the sampled torque $\widehat{\mathrm{h}}_{\text{grf}}(q, \widehat{\mathbf{b}}, \boldsymbol{\lambda})$

instead of the torque $h_{grf}(q, \mathbf{b}, \boldsymbol{\lambda})$ from the discrete contact states $\mathbf{b}$. To generate accurate motion, DyNet is encouraged to predict higher probabilities for the correct contact states so that PCT can sample the correct states as much as possible. Since PCT is differentiable, the supervision signals for the physical force and contact can be provided by minimizing the motion error. More details of differentiable sampling are provided in the supplementary material.

Internal Joint Torque Estimation. Another key process to generate human motions is internal joint torque estimation. PD controller is widely adopted for physics-based human motion control [43,44,59]. It controls the motion by outputting the joint torque $\boldsymbol{\tau}$ in proportion to the difference between the current state and the target state. However, the target pose states estimated by the kinematics backbone are noisy and contain physical artifacts. Previous works [43,59] adjust the gain parameters dynamically for smooth motion control. However, we find that this local adjustment is still challenging for the model and the output motion is still vulnerable to the jittery and incorrect input motion.

Attentive PD Controller: To address this problem, we propose the attentive PD controller, a method that allows global adjustment of the target pose states. The attentive PD controller is fed with initial motion $\{\widehat{q}^t\}_{t=1}^T$ and dynamically predicts the proportional parameters $\{\mathbf{k}_p^t\}_{t=1}^T$, derivative parameters $\{\mathbf{k}_d^t\}_{t=1}^T$, offset torques $\{\boldsymbol{\alpha}^t\}_{t=1}^T$, and attention weights $\{\mathbf{w}^t\}_{t=1}^T$. The attention weights $\mathbf{w}^t = (w^{t1}, w^{t2}, \cdots, w^{tT})$ denotes how the initial motion contributes to the target pose state at the time step t and $\sum_{j=1}^T w^{tj} = 1$. We first compute the attentive target pose state $\widetilde{q}^t$ as:

$$\widetilde{q}^t = \sum_{j=1}^T w^{tj} \widehat{q}^j, \tag{7}$$

where $\widehat{q}^j$ is the initial kinematic pose at the time step j. Then the internal joint torque $\boldsymbol{\tau}^t$ at the time step t can be computed following the PD controller rule with the compensation term h_c^t [53]:

$$\boldsymbol{\tau}^t = \mathbf{k}_p^t \circ (\widetilde{q}^{t+1} - q^t) - \mathbf{k}_d^t \circ \dot{q}^t + \boldsymbol{\alpha}^t + h_c^t, \tag{8}$$

where $\circ$ denotes Hadamard matrix product and h_c^t represents the sum of centripetal and Coriolis forces at the time step t. This attention mechanism allows the PD controller to leverage the temporal information to refine the target state and obtain a smooth motion. Details of the network structure are provided in the supplementary material.

3.4   Forward Dynamics

To compute the accelerations analytically from physical properties, we build two forward dynamics modules: *inertial forward dynamics* for the local pose acceleration and *trajectory forward dynamics* for the global trajectory acceleration.

Inertial Forward Dynamics. Prior works [43, 44, 59] adopt a proxy model to simulate human motion in physics engines or simplify the optimization process. In this work, to seamlessly cooperate with the kinematics-based backbone, we directly build the dynamics equation for the SMPL model [22]. The pose acceleration $\ddot{q}$ can be derived by rewriting Eq. 2 with PCT:

$$\ddot{q} = M^{-1}(q)(\tau + \widehat{h}_{\text{grf}} - h_g - h_c + \mathcal{I}). \tag{9}$$

To obtain $\ddot{q}$, we need to compute the inertia matrix M and other physical torques in each time step using the current pose q. The time superscript t is omitted for simplicity. M can be computed recursively along the SMPL kinematics tree. The derivation is provided in the supplementary material.

Trajectory Forward Dynamics. To train DyNet without ground-truth force annotations, we leverage a key observation: the gravity and ground reaction forces should explain the global root trajectory. We devise a trajectory forward dynamics module that controls the global root motion with external forces. It plays a central role in the success of weakly supervised learning.

Let q_{trans} denote the root translation in the *world frame*. The dynamics equation can be written as:

$$\ddot{q}_{\text{trans}} = \frac{1}{m_0} R_{\text{cam}}^{\mathsf{T}} (\boldsymbol{\eta} + \widehat{h}_{\text{grf}}^{\{0:3\}} - h_g^{\{0:3\}}), \tag{10}$$

where m_0 is the mass of the root joint, R_{cam} denotes the camera orientation computed from the estimated angular velocity $\omega_{\text{ine}} = (\omega_x, \omega_y, \omega_z)$, $\boldsymbol{\eta}$ denotes the direct root actuation, and $\widehat{h}_{\text{grf}}^{\{0:3\}}$ and $h_g^{\{0:3\}}$ denote the first three entries of $\widehat{h}_{\text{grf}}$ and h_g, respectively.

3.5   Constrained Update

After obtaining the pose and trajectory accelerations via forward dynamics modules, we can control the human motion and global trajectory by discrete simulation. Given the frame rate $1/\Delta t$ of the input video, we can obtain the kinematic 3D pose using the finite differences:

$$\dot{q}^{t+1} = \dot{q}^t + \Delta t\, \ddot{q}^t, \tag{11}$$

$$q^{t+1} = q^t + \Delta t\, \dot{q}^t. \tag{12}$$

Similarly, we can obtain the global root trajectory:

$$\dot{q}_{\text{trans}}^{t+1} = \dot{q}_{\text{trans}}^t + \Delta t\, \ddot{q}_{\text{trans}}^t, \tag{13}$$

$$q_{\text{trans}}^{t+1} = q_{\text{trans}}^t + \Delta t\, \dot{q}_{\text{trans}}^t. \tag{14}$$

In practice, since we predict the local and global motions simultaneously, we can impose contact constraints to prevent foot sliding. Therefore, instead of using

Eq. 12 and 14 to update q^{t+1} and q_{trans}^{t+1} directly, we first refine the velocities $\dot{q}^{t+1}$ and $\dot{q}_{\text{trans}}^{t+1}$ with contact constraints. For joints in contact with the ground at the time step t, we expect they have zero velocity in the world frame. The velocities of non-contact joints should stay close to the original velocities computed from the accelerations. We adopt the differentiable optimization layer following the formulation of Agrawal et al. [1]. This custom layer can obtain the solution to the optimization problem and supports backward propagation. However, the optimization problem with zero velocity constraints does not satisfy the DPP rules (Disciplined Parametrized Programming), which means that the custom layer cannot be directly applied. Here, we use soft velocity constraints to follow the DPP rules:

$$
\begin{aligned}
\dot{q}^*, \dot{q}_{\text{trans}}^* = \underset{\dot{q}^*, \dot{q}_{\text{trans}}^*}{\arg\min} \ \|\dot{q}^* - \dot{q}\| + \|\dot{q}_{\text{trans}}^* - \dot{q}_{\text{trans}}\|, \\
s.t. \quad \forall i \in \{i | p_i > 0.5\}, \ \|R_{\text{cam}}^{\mathsf{T}}(J_{v_i}\dot{q}^* - \dot{q}^{*\{0:3\}}) + \dot{q}_{\text{trans}}^*\| \le \epsilon,
\end{aligned}
\tag{15}
$$

where $\epsilon = 0.01$ and $\dot{q}^{*\{0:3\}}$ is the first three entries of $\dot{q}^*$. We omit the superscript t for simplicity. After solving Eq. 15, the estimated $\dot{q}^*$ and $\dot{q}_{\text{trans}}^*$ are used to compute the final physically-plausible 3D pose q and the global trajectory q_{trans}.

3.6 Network Training

The overall loss of D&D is defined as:

$$
\mathcal{L} = \mathcal{L}_{3\text{D}} + \mathcal{L}_{2\text{D}} + \mathcal{L}_{\text{con}} + \mathcal{L}_{\text{trans}} + \mathcal{L}_{\text{reg}}.
\tag{16}
$$

The 3D loss $\mathcal{L}_{3\text{D}}$ includes the joint error and the pose error:

$$
\mathcal{L}_{3\text{D}} = \|X - \check{X}\|_1 + \|q \ominus \check{q}\|_2^2,
\tag{17}
$$

where X denotes the 3D joints regressed from the SMPL model, "$\ominus$" denotes a difference computation after converting the Euler angle into a rotation matrix, and the symbol "$\check{\ }$" denotes the ground truth. The time superscript t is omitted for simplicity. The 2D loss $\mathcal{L}_{2\text{D}}$ calculates the 2D reprojection error:

$$
\mathcal{L}_{2\text{D}} = \|\Pi(X) - \Pi(\check{X})\|_1,
\tag{18}
$$

where Π denotes the projection function. The loss $\mathcal{L}_{\text{trans}}$ is added for the supervision of the root translation and provides weak supervision signals for external force and contact estimation:

$$
\mathcal{L}_{\text{trans}} = \|q_{\text{trans}} - \check{q}_{\text{trans}}\|_1.
\tag{19}
$$

The contact loss is added for the data with contact annotations:

$$
\mathcal{L}_{\text{con}} = \frac{1}{N_c} \sum_i^{N_c} \left[-\check{b}_i \log p_i - (1 - \check{b}_i) \log (1 - p_i) \right].
\tag{20}
$$

Table 1. Quantitative comparisons with state-of-the-art methods on the 3DPW dataset. Symbol "-" means results are not available, and "∗" means self-implementation.

Method	Dynamics	MPJPE ↓	PA-MPJPE ↓	PVE ↓	ACCEL ↓
HMR [12]	✗	130.0	81.3	–	37.4
SPIN [15]	✗	96.9	59.2	116.4	29.8
VIBE [14]	✗	82.9	51.9	99.1	23.4
TCMR [6]	✗	86.5	52.7	102.9	7.1
HybrIK∗ [19]	✗	76.2	45.1	89.1	22.8
MAED [50]	✗	79.1	45.7	92.6	17.6
Ours	✓	**73.7**	**42.7**	**88.6**	**7.0**

The regularization loss $\mathcal{L}_{\text{reg}}$ is defined as:

$$\mathcal{L}_{\text{reg}} = \|\boldsymbol{\eta}\|_2^2 + \frac{1}{N_c} \sum_i^{N_c} \left[- p_i \log p_i - (1 - p_i) \log (1 - p_i) \right], \qquad (21)$$

where the first term minimizes the direct root actuation, and the second term minimizes the entropy of the contact probability to encourage confident contact predictions.

4 Experiment

4.1 Datasets

We perform experiments on two large-scale human motion datasets. The first dataset is 3DPW [26]. 3DPW is a challenging outdoor benchmark for 3D human motion estimation. It contains 60 video sequences obtained from a hand-held moving camera. The second dataset we use is Human3.6M [9]. Human3.6M is an indoor benchmark for 3D human motion estimation. It includes 7 subjects, and the videos are captured at 50Hz. Following previous works [14,15,19,59], we use 5 subjects (S1, S5, S6, S7, S8) for training and 2 subjects (S9, S11) for evaluation. The videos are subsampled to 25Hz for both training and testing. We further use the AMASS dataset [25] to obtain annotations of foot contact and root translation for training.

4.2 Implementation Details

We adopt HybrIK [19] as the kinematics backbone to provide the initial motion. The original HybrIK network only predicts 2.5D keypoints and requires a separate RootNet [32] to obtain the final 3D pose in the camera frame. Here, for integrity and simplicity, we implement an extended version of HybrIK as our

Table 2. Quantitative comparisons with state-of-the-art methods on the Human3.6M dataset. Symbol "-" means results are not available, "∗" means self-implementation, and "†" means the method reports results on 17 joints.

Method	Dynamics	MPJPE ↓	PA-MPJPE ↓	PVE ↓	ACCEL ↓	FS ↓	GP ↓
VIBE [14]	✗	61.3	43.1	–	15.2	15.1	12.6
NeurGD [45]	✗	57.3	42.2	–	14.2	16.7	24.4
MAED† [50]	✗	56.3	38.7	–	–	–	–
HybrIK∗ [19]	✗	56.4	36.7	–	10.9	18.3	10.6
PhysCap [44]	✓	113.0	68.9	–	–	–	–
EgoPose [57]	✓	130.3	79.2	–	31.3	5.9	3.5
NeurPhys [43]	✓	76.5	–	–	–	–	–
SimPoE [59]	✓	56.7	41.6	–	6.7	**3.4**	1.6
Ours	✓	**52.5**	**35.5**	**72.9**	**6.1**	5.8	**1.5**

kinematics backbone that can directly predict the 3D pose in the camera frame by estimating the camera parameters. The network structures are detailed in the supplementary material. The learning rate is set to 5×10^{-5} at first and reduced by a factor of 10 at the 15th and 25th epochs. We use the Adam solver and train for 30 epochs with a mini-batch size of 32. Implementation is in PyTorch. During training on the Human3.6M dataset, we simulate a moving camera by cropping the input video with bounding boxes.

4.3   Comparison to state-of-the-Art methods

Results on Moving Camera. We first compare D&D against state-of-the-art methods on 3DPW, an in-the-wild dataset captured with the hand-held moving camera. Since previous dynamics-based methods are not applicable in the moving camera, prior arts on the 3DPW dataset are all kinematics-based. Mean per joint position error (MPJPE) and Procrustes-aligned mean per joint position error (PA-MPJPE) are reported to assess the 3D pose accuracy. The acceleration error (ACCEL) is reported to assess the motion smoothness. We also report Per Vertex Error (PVE) to evaluate the entire estimated body mesh.

Table 1 summarizes the quantitative results. We can observe that D&D outperforms the most accurate kinematics-based methods, HybrIK and MAED, by 2.5 and 5.4 mm on MPJPE, respectively. Besides, D&D improves the motion smoothness significantly by 69.3% and 60.2% relative improvement on ACCEL, respectively. It shows that D&D retains the benefits of the accurate pose in kinematics modeling and physically plausible motion in dynamics modeling.

Results on Static Camera. To compare D&D with previous dynamics-based methods, we evaluate D&D on the Human3.6M dataset. Following the previous method [59], we further report two physics-based metrics, foot sliding (FS) and ground penetration (GP), to measure the physical plausibility. To assess the effectiveness of IFC, we simulate a moving camera by cropping the input

Fig. 2. Qualitative comparisons on the 3DPW dataset. D&D estimates accurate poses with physically plausible foot contact and global movement.

Table 3. Ablation experiments on 3DPW and Human3.6M dataset.

	3DPW			Human3.6M		
	MPJPE ↓	PA-MPJPE ↓	ACCEL ↓	MPJPE ↓	PA-MPJPE ↓	ACCEL ↓
w/o IFC	76.0	45.2	10.0	53.8	36.4	6.7
w/o PCT	74.6	43.4	9.8	53.4	36.1	6.7
w/o Att PD Controller	73.8	42.8	8.0	52.5	35.7	6.3
D&D (Ours)	**73.7**	**42.7**	**7.0**	**52.5**	**35.5**	**6.1**

video with bounding boxes, i.e., the input to D&D is the video from a moving camera. Table 2 shows the quantitative comparison against kinematics-based and dynamics-based methods. D&D outperforms previous kinematics-based and dynamics-based methods in pose accuracy. For physics-based metrics (ACCEL, FS, and GP), D&D shows comparable performance to previous methods that require physics simulation engines.

We further follow GLAMR [56] to evaluate the global MPJPE (G-MPJPE) and global PVE (G-PVE) on the Human3.6M dataset with the simulated moving camera. The root translation is aligned with the GT at the first frame of the video sequence. D&D obtains 785.1mm G-MPJPE and 793.3mm G-PVE. More comparisons are reported in the supplementary material.

4.4   Ablation Study

Inertial Force *vs.* Residual Force. In this experiment, we compare the proposed inertial force control (IFC) with residual force control (RFC). To control the human motion with RFC in the local camera frame, we directly estimate the residual force instead of the linear acceleration and angular velocity. Quantitative results are reported in Table 3. It shows that explicit modeling of the inertial components can better explain the body movement than implicit modeling with residual force. IFC performs more accurate pose control and significantly reduces the motion jitters, showing a 30% relative improvement of ACCEL on 3DPW.

Effectiveness of PCT. To study the effectiveness of the probabilistic contact torque, we remove PCT in the baseline model. When training the baseline, the output contact probabilities are discretized to 0 or 1 with the threshold of 0.5 and we compute the discrete contact torque instead of the probabilistic contact torque. Quantitative results in Table 3 show that PCT is indispensable to have smooth and accurate 3D human motion.

Effectiveness of Attentive PD Controller. To further validate the effectiveness of the attentive mechanism, we report the results of the baseline model without the attentive PD controller. In this baseline, we adopt the meta-PD controller [43,59] that dynamically predicts the gain parameters based on the state of the character, which only allows local adjustment. Table 3 summarizes the quantitative results. The attentive PD controller contributes to a more smooth motion control as indicated by a smaller acceleration error.

4.5   Qualitative Results

In Fig. 3, we plot the contact forces estimated by D&D of the walking motion from the Human3.6M test set. Note that our approach does not require any ground-truth force annotations for training. The estimated forces fall into a reasonable force range for walking motions [42]. We also provide qualitative comparisons in Fig. 2. It shows that D&D can estimate physically plausible motions with accurate foot-ground contacts and no ground penetration.

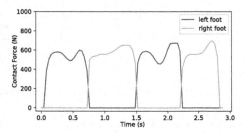

Fig. 3. Estimated contact forces of the walking sequences. The forces remain in a reasonable range for walking.

5   Conclusion

In this paper, we propose D&D, a physics-aware framework for 3D human motion capture with dynamic camera movements. To impose the laws of physics in the moving camera, we introduce inertial force control that explains the 3D human motion by taking the inertial forces into consideration. We further develop the probabilistic contact torque for weakly-supervised training and the attentive PD controller for smooth and accurate motion control. We demonstrate the effectiveness of our approach on standard 3D human pose datasets. D&D outperforms state-of-the-art kinematics-based and dynamics-based methods. Besides, it is entirely neural-based and runs without offline optimization or physics simulators. We hope D&D can serve as a solid baseline and provide a new perspective for dynamics modeling in 3D human motion capture.

Acknowledgments. This work was supported by the National Key R&D Program of China (No. 2021ZD0110700), Shanghai Municipal Science and Technology Major Project (2021SHZDZX0102), Shanghai Qi Zhi Institute, SHEITC (2018-RGZN-02046) and Tencent GY-Lab.

References

1. Agrawal, A., Amos, B., Barratt, S., Boyd, S., Diamond, S., Kolter, J.Z.: Differentiable convex optimization layers. In: NeurIPS (2019)
2. Akhter, I., Black, M.J.: Pose-conditioned joint angle limits for 3D human pose reconstruction. In: CVPR (2015)
3. Andrews, S., Huerta, I., Komura, T., Sigal, L., Mitchell, K.: Real-time physics-based motion capture with sparse sensors. In: CVMP (2016)
4. Arnab, A., Doersch, C., Zisserman, A.: Exploiting temporal context for 3D human pose estimation in the wild. In: CVPR (2019)
5. Bogo, F., Kanazawa, A., Lassner, C., Gehler, P., Romero, J., Black, M.J.: Keep It SMPL: automatic estimation of 3D human pose and shape from a single image. In: Leibe, B., Matas, J., Sebe, N., Welling, M. (eds.) ECCV 2016. LNCS, vol. 9909, pp. 561–578. Springer, Cham (2016). https://doi.org/10.1007/978-3-319-46454-1_34
6. Choi, H., Moon, G., Chang, J.Y., Lee, K.M.: Beyond static features for temporally consistent 3D human pose and shape from a video. In: CVPR (2021)
7. Dabral, R., Shimada, S., Jain, A., Theobalt, C., Golyanik, V.: Gravity-aware monocular 3D human-object reconstruction. In: ICCV (2021)
8. Fang, H., Xu, Y., Wang, W., Liu, X., Zhu, S.C.: Learning pose grammar to encode human body configuration for 3D pose estimation. In: AAAI (2017)
9. Ionescu, C., Papava, D., Olaru, V., Sminchisescu, C.: Human3. 6m: large scale datasets and predictive methods for 3D human sensing in natural environments. In: TPAMI (2013)
10. Jang, E., Gu, S., Poole, B.: Categorical reparameterization with Gumbel-Softmax. In: ICLR (2017)
11. Joo, H., Neverova, N., Vedaldi, A.: Exemplar fine-tuning for 3D human model fitting towards in-the-wild 3D human pose estimation. In: 3DV (2021)
12. Kanazawa, A., Black, M.J., Jacobs, D.W., Malik, J.: End-to-end recovery of human shape and pose. In: CVPR (2018)
13. Kanazawa, A., Zhang, J.Y., Felsen, P., Malik, J.: Learning 3D human dynamics from video. In: CVPR (2019)
14. Kocabas, M., Athanasiou, N., Black, M.J.: Vibe: video inference for human body pose and shape estimation. In: CVPR (2020)
15. Kolotouros, N., Pavlakos, G., Black, M.J., Daniilidis, K.: Learning to reconstruct 3D human pose and shape via model-fitting in the loop. In: ICCV (2019)
16. Lassner, C., Romero, J., Kiefel, M., Bogo, F., Black, M.J., Gehler, P.V.: Unite the people: closing the loop between 3D and 2D human representations. In: CVPR (2017)
17. Levine, S., Popović, J.: Physically plausible simulation for character animation. In: SIGGRAPH (2012)

18. Li, J., et al.: Localization with sampling-argmax. Adv. Neural. Inf. Process. Syst. **34**, 27236–27248 (2021)
19. Li, J., Xu, C., Chen, Z., Bian, S., Yang, L., Lu, C.: Hybrik: a hybrid analytical-neural inverse kinematics solution for 3D human pose and shape estimation. In: CVPR (2021)
20. Li, Y.L., et al.: Detailed 2D–3D joint representation for human-object interaction. In: Proceedings of the IEEE/CVF Conference on Computer Vision and Pattern Recognition, pp. 10166–10175 (2020)
21. Li, Y.L., et al.: Pastanet: toward human activity knowledge engine. In: Proceedings of the IEEE/CVF Conference on Computer Vision and Pattern Recognition, pp. 382–391 (2020)
22. Loper, M., Mahmood, N., Romero, J., Pons-Moll, G., Black, M.J.: SMPL: a skinned multi-person linear model. In: TOG (2015)
23. Luo, Z., Golestaneh, S.A., Kitani, K.M.: 3D human motion estimation via motion compression and refinement. In: ACCV (2020)
24. Luo, Z., Hachiuma, R., Yuan, Y., Kitani, K.: Dynamics-regulated kinematic policy for egocentric pose estimation. In: NeurIPS (2021)
25. Mahmood, N., Ghorbani, N., Troje, N.F., Pons-Moll, G., Black, M.J.: Amass: archive of motion capture as surface shapes. In: ICCV (2019)
26. von Marcard, T., Henschel, R., Black, M.J., Rosenhahn, B., Pons-Moll, G.: Recovering accurate 3D human pose in the wild using IMUS and a moving camera. In: ECCV (2018)
27. Martinez, J., Hossain, R., Romero, J., Little, J.J.: A simple yet effective baseline for 3D human pose estimation. In: ICCV (2017)
28. Mehta, D., et al.: Monocular 3D human pose estimation in the wild using improved CNN supervision. In: 3DV (2017)
29. Mehta, D., et al.: XNect: real-time multi-person 3D motion capture with a single RGB camera. TOG (2020)
30. Mehta, D., et al.: Single-shot multi-person 3D pose estimation from monocular RGB. In: 3DV (2018)
31. Mehta, D., et al.: Vnect: real-time 3D human pose estimation with a single RGB camera. TOG **36**(4), 1–14 (2017)
32. Moon, G., Chang, J.Y., Lee, K.M.: Camera distance-aware top-down approach for 3D multi-person pose estimation from a single RGB image. In: ICCV (2019)
33. Moon, G., Lee, K.M.: I2L-MeshNet: Image-to-lixel prediction network for accurate 3D human pose and mesh estimation from a single RGB image. In: Vedaldi, A., Bischof, H., Brox, T., Frahm, J.-M. (eds.) ECCV 2020. LNCS, vol. 12352, pp. 752–768. Springer, Cham (2020). https://doi.org/10.1007/978-3-030-58571-6_44
34. Moreno-Noguer, F.: 3D human pose estimation from a single image via distance matrix regression. In: CVPR (2017)
35. Park, S., Hwang, J., Kwak, N.: 3D human pose estimation using convolutional neural networks with 2D pose information. In: Hua, G., Jégou, H. (eds.) ECCV 2016. LNCS, vol. 9915, pp. 156–169. Springer, Cham (2016). https://doi.org/10.1007/978-3-319-49409-8_15
36. Pavlakos, G., et al.: Expressive body capture: 3D hands, face, and body from a single image. In: CVPR (2019)
37. Pavlakos, G., Zhou, X., Derpanis, K.G., Daniilidis, K.: Coarse-to-fine volumetric prediction for single-image 3D human pose. In: CVPR (2017)
38. Peng, X.B., Chang, M., Zhang, G., Abbeel, P., Levine, S.: MCP: learning composable hierarchical control with multiplicative compositional policies. arXiv preprint arXiv:1905.09808 (2019)

39. Rempe, D., Birdal, T., Hertzmann, A., Yang, J., Sridhar, S., Guibas, L.J.: Humor: 3D human motion model for robust pose estimation. In: ICCV (2021)
40. Rempe, D., Guibas, L.J., Hertzmann, A., Russell, B., Villegas, R., Yang, J.: Contact and human dynamics from monocular video. In: Vedaldi, A., Bischof, H., Brox, T., Frahm, J.-M. (eds.) ECCV 2020. LNCS, vol. 12350, pp. 71–87. Springer, Cham (2020). https://doi.org/10.1007/978-3-030-58558-7_5
41. Rogez, G., Weinzaepfel, P., Schmid, C.: LCR-net: localization-classification-regression for human pose. In: CVPR (2017)
42. Shahabpoor, E., Pavic, A.: Measurement of walking ground reactions in real-life environments: a systematic review of techniques and technologies. Sensors (2017)
43. Shimada, S., Golyanik, V., Xu, W., Pérez, P., Theobalt, C.: Neural monocular 3D human motion capture with physical awareness. TOG (2021)
44. Shimada, S., Golyanik, V., Xu, W., Theobalt, C.: Physcap: physically plausible monocular 3D motion capture in real time. TOG (2020)
45. Song, J., Chen, X., Hilliges, O.: Human body model fitting by learned gradient descent. In: Vedaldi, A., Bischof, H., Brox, T., Frahm, J.-M. (eds.) ECCV 2020. LNCS, vol. 12365, pp. 744–760. Springer, Cham (2020). https://doi.org/10.1007/978-3-030-58565-5_44
46. Sun, X., Shang, J., Liang, S., Wei, Y.: Compositional human pose regression. In: ICCV (2017)
47. Sun, X., Xiao, B., Wei, F., Liang, S., Wei, Y.: Integral human pose regression. In: Ferrari, V., Hebert, M., Sminchisescu, C., Weiss, Y. (eds.) ECCV 2018. LNCS, vol. 11210, pp. 536–553. Springer, Cham (2018). https://doi.org/10.1007/978-3-030-01231-1_33
48. Sun, Y., Ye, Y., Liu, W., Gao, W., Fu, Y., Mei, T.: Human mesh recovery from monocular images via a skeleton-disentangled representation. In: ICCV (2019)
49. Varol, G., Ceylan, D., Russell, B., Yang, J., Yumer, E., Laptev, I., Schmid, C.: BodyNet: volumetric inference of 3D human body shapes. In: Ferrari, V., Hebert, M., Sminchisescu, C., Weiss, Y. (eds.) ECCV 2018. LNCS, vol. 11211, pp. 20–38. Springer, Cham (2018). https://doi.org/10.1007/978-3-030-01234-2_2
50. Wan, Z., Li, Z., Tian, M., Liu, J., Yi, S., Li, H.: Encoder-decoder with multi-level attention for 3D human shape and pose estimation. In: ICCV (2021)
51. Wang, C., Li, J., Liu, W., Qian, C., Lu, C.: HMOR: hierarchical multi-person ordinal relations for monocular multi-person 3D pose estimation. In: Vedaldi, A., Bischof, H., Brox, T., Frahm, J.-M. (eds.) ECCV 2020. LNCS, vol. 12348, pp. 242–259. Springer, Cham (2020). https://doi.org/10.1007/978-3-030-58580-8_15
52. Xu, H., Bazavan, E.G., Zanfir, A., Freeman, W.T., Sukthankar, R., Sminchisescu, C.: Ghum & ghuml: generative 3D human shape and articulated pose models. In: CVPR (2020)
53. Yang, C., Huang, Q., Jiang, H., Peter, O.O., Han, J.: PD control with gravity compensation for hydraulic 6-DOF parallel manipulator. Mech. Mach. Theory **45**(4), 666–677 (2010)
54. Yasin, H., Iqbal, U., Kruger, B., Weber, A., Gall, J.: A dual-source approach for 3D pose estimation from a single image. In: CVPR (2016)
55. Yu, R., Park, H., Lee, J.: Human dynamics from monocular video with dynamic camera movements. TOG (2021)
56. Yuan, Y., Iqbal, U., Molchanov, P., Kitani, K., Kautz, J.: Glamr: global occlusion-aware human mesh recovery with dynamic cameras. In: CVPR (2022)
57. Yuan, Y., Kitani, K.: Ego-pose estimation and forecasting as real-time PD control. In: ICCV (2019)

58. Yuan, Y., Kitani, K.: Residual force control for agile human behavior imitation and extended motion synthesis. In: NeurIPS (2020)
59. Yuan, Y., Wei, S.E., Simon, T., Kitani, K., Saragih, J.: Simpoe: simulated character control for 3D human pose estimation. In: CVPR (2021)
60. Zell, P., Rosenhahn, B., Wandt, B.: Weakly-supervised learning of human dynamics. In: Vedaldi, A., Bischof, H., Brox, T., Frahm, J.-M. (eds.) ECCV 2020. LNCS, vol. 12371, pp. 68–84. Springer, Cham (2020). https://doi.org/10.1007/978-3-030-58574-7_5
61. Zeng, A., Sun, X., Huang, F., Liu, M., Xu, Q., Lin, S.: SRNet: improving generalization in 3D human pose estimation with a split-and-recombine approach. In: Vedaldi, A., Bischof, H., Brox, T., Frahm, J.-M. (eds.) ECCV 2020. LNCS, vol. 12359, pp. 507–523. Springer, Cham (2020). https://doi.org/10.1007/978-3-030-58568-6_30
62. Zeng, A., Yang, L., Ju, X., Li, J., Wang, J., Xu, Q.: Smoothnet: a plug-and-play network for refining human poses in videos. arXiv preprint arXiv:2112.13715 (2021)
63. Zhou, X., Huang, Q., Sun, X., Xue, X., Wei, Y.: Towards 3D human pose estimation in the wild: a weakly-supervised approach. In: ICCV (2017)

Explicit Occlusion Reasoning for Multi-person 3D Human Pose Estimation

Qihao Liu[1], Yi Zhang[1], Song Bai[2(✉)], and Alan Yuille[1]

[1] Johns Hopkins University, Baltimore, USA
[2] ByteDance, Singapore, Singapore
songbai.site@mail.com

Abstract. Occlusion poses a great threat to monocular multi-person 3D human pose estimation due to large variability in terms of the shape, appearance, and position of occluders. While existing methods try to handle occlusion with pose priors/constraints, data augmentation, or implicit reasoning, they still fail to generalize to unseen poses or occlusion cases and may make large mistakes when multiple people are present. Inspired by the remarkable ability of humans to infer occluded joints from visible cues, we develop a method to explicitly model this process that significantly improves bottom-up multi-person human pose estimation with or without occlusions. First, we split the task into two subtasks: visible keypoints detection and occluded keypoints reasoning, and propose a Deeply Supervised Encoder Distillation (DSED) network to solve the second one. To train our model, we propose a Skeleton-guided human Shape Fitting (SSF) approach to generate pseudo occlusion labels on the existing datasets, enabling explicit occlusion reasoning. Experiments show that explicitly learning from occlusions improves human pose estimation. In addition, exploiting feature-level information of visible joints allows us to reason about occluded joints more accurately. Our method outperforms both the state-of-the-art top-down and bottom-up methods on several benchmarks. The code is available for research purposes https://github.com/qihao067/HUPOR.

Keywords: Human pose estimation · 3D from a single image

1 Introduction

Monocular 3D multi-person human pose estimation (HPE) is a fundamental task in computer vision with wide applications in robotics, human activation recognition, human-computer interaction, *etc.*. Despite great advances brought by neural networks, it remains a very challenging task due to the depth ambiguity, high degrees of freedom in human poses, and frequent occlusion of various

---

Supplementary Information The online version contains supplementary material available at https://doi.org/10.1007/978-3-031-20065-6_29.

S. Avidan et al. (Eds.): ECCV 2022, LNCS 13665, pp. 497–517, 2022.
https://doi.org/10.1007/978-3-031-20065-6_29

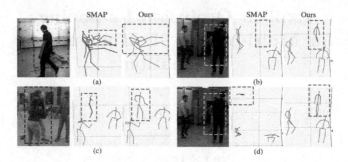

Fig. 1. Current methods may still fail in presence of heavy occlusion, and lead to (a) extra person, (b) missing person, (c) incomplete skeleton, and (d) wrong position estimate. We improve the robustness by enabling the network to infer occluded joints from visible cues explicitly. Red box is only used for visualization. (Color figure online)

forms. Among these challenges, we focus on occlusion which accounts for huge errors in state-of-the-art (SOTA) methods, *e.g.* SMAP [84], as shown in Fig. 1.

Some existing methods handle occlusion by imposing pose prior and kinematic constraints either explicitly [64] or implicitly [65]. These priors are learned from a limited training set thus may not generalize well. Others reason about occlusion implicitly through redundant pose encoding [46,47] or attention mechanism [17,30], where models need to identify occluded joints implicitly without any supervision during training and deal with unreliable intermediate representations with complex conflicts, making learning increasingly difficult. More importantly, most of these methods, even those designed for multi-person tasks, still solve the problem of occlusion from the perspective of single-person, thus requiring assembling pose first. However, the task of grouping human joints from incomplete keypoints detection is already error-prone. Thus these methods may make large mistakes when multiple people are present.

To alleviate the occlusion problem in multi-person scenarios, we revisit human's ability to reason about occluded joints. Given an image with occluded people (*e.g.* Fig. 1), humans can first precisely 'detect' visible joints and visible skeleton information. Then we can reasonably infer the occluded keypoints based on the detected information/cues, combined with local and global contexts, and our prior knowledge on human pose, shape, and motion. We argue that if we allow the network to fully and properly exploit the detected and restructured cues at the feature level, our method should also be able to reason about occluded joints more accurately, just like humans, without bells and whistles.

To achieve this, we follow the discussion above and split the commonly used single-step keypoint detection into two steps: visible keypoint detection and occluded keypoint reasoning. For the first part, any detection method that provides heatmaps of detected keypoints and skeleton information should work. We directly adopt the SOTA bottom-up method as our detection module. Then based on the intermediate results, we propose a reasoning module that efficiently learns structure information to explicitly infer occluded joints from visible ones. After that, we group both detected and inferred joints into individuals and refine the results. We name this model HUPOR (HUman Pose estimation via Occlusion Reasoning). We show that even using the same detection network and grouping policy, our method significantly improves the ability of 3D bottom-up methods to precisely predict visible keypoints and reasonably infer occluded joints. Furthermore, our method also benefits 2D human pose estimation, by using 2D keypoint detection methods as the detection module and slightly modifying the reasoning module of our method.

Although explicit occlusion reasoning is to some degree intuitive, not enough attention has been paid to it due to the lack of annotations and the poor performance of existing networks (*e.g.* hourglass [37,53]) in occlusion reasoning. We propose two methods to solve these problems separately:

First, explicit occlusion reasoning requires per-joint visibility label which is not available on most 3D human pose datasets. To this end, we first fit parametric shape models [41] to the image and then use projection relationships to determine whether the joint is visible. For human shape fitting, the SOTA 2D/3D pose-based methods [14] usually fail to predict accurate shape while the image-based methods [27,31] may get better shape but worse pose estimate and are very sensitive to noise. Therefore, we propose a Skeleton-guided human Shape Fitting (SSF) method that combines the advantage of these two lines of work. From the reconstructed mesh, pseudo occlusion labels are then generated. Unlike previous work [13] which only captures self-occlusion, our method finds self-occlusion, object occlusion, and occlusion by other people. We demonstrate that SSF is crucial to generate accurate occlusion labels for explicit occlusion reasoning, while previous methods are either inaccurate [13] or require manual labeling [83].

Another challenge is how to effectively reason about occlusions. We find that directly training an hourglass model to predict occluded joints from visible joints or images does not yield good results. This is due to the complexity that the network should identify useful information among all input features for reconstructing occluded joints. To solve this problem, we propose a stacked Deeply Supervised Encoder Distillation (DSED) network. DSED splits the reasoning task into two: reconstruct and imitate, with the help of two encoders. The first encoder acts as a teacher to select the most useful information for occluded joint reconstruction, and the second one learns to extract the same information from just visible cues. Compared with the vanilla hourglass model, DSED has a much stronger capability to reason about occluded joints. Compared with using pre-defined constraints, our method improves the performance by giving the network freedom to extract the information it finds the most useful, leading to better cues for occlusion reasoning. More importantly, occlusion reasoning in feature level before assembling pose makes our method more suitable for handling occlusion in multi-person scenarios than previous methods.

To evaluate the performance of our method, we perform experiments on the MuPoTS-3D [47], MuPoTS-synthOcc, 3DPW [43], 3DPW-OCC [43,83], CMU Panoptic [26], and Human3.6M [23] datasets. The results show that our method yields consistently higher accuracy than the SOTA methods for both occlusion and non-occlusion cases. Our bottom-up method surpasses the SOTA bottom-up methods by 6.0 PCK and SOTA top-down methods by 2.8 PCK on MuPoTS.

In addition, we apply our DSED-based reasoning module to two recent 2D HPE methods (*i.e.*PifPaf [32] and HigherHRNet [11]) and we also observe consistent improvements, ranging from 0.9 to 1.7 AP, on COCO [39] and CrowdPose [35].

In summary, our contributions are three folds:

- We advance the bottom-up pose estimation paradigm by exploiting its intermediate results for explicit occlusion reasoning, to which not enough attention has been paid before. We demonstrate its efficacy and potential in both 3D and 2D human pose estimation (HPE).
- We propose **DSED** network to infer occluded joints efficiently. It solves the reasoning tasks that hourglass fails. We demonstrate that it is superior in scalability and performance, and is crucial for explicit occlusion reasoning.
- Our 3D HPE method, denoted as **HUPOR**, enables more accurate visible keypoints detection and occluded keypoints reasoning, and significantly outperforms SOTA methods on several benchmarks for both occlusion and non-occlusion cases, while generalizing well to in-the-wild images.

2   Related Work

2D Multi-person Human Pose Estimation.   Current methods typically follow one of two paradigms:

Top-down methods [6, 10, 15, 16, 18, 20, 21, 29, 35, 50, 53, 55, 63, 67, 68, 73, 76, 82] split the task into two subtasks: (1) detecting bounding box for all people in the image, and (2) performing single person pose estimator for each detected region. These methods typically work better than bottom-up methods and are currently the best performers on datasets such as COCO [39] due to the single human assumption and the pose prior the assumption implies. However, these methods struggle in cases of occlusion [35] and interactions [29]. In addition, these two-step methods lack efficiency due to the need for separate human detectors and the repeat of pose estimation for each bounding box.

Bottom-up methods [5, 8, 11, 22, 25, 32, 34, 52, 54, 62, 87] start by first detecting identity-free keypoints over the entire image and then grouping joints into individuals. They are usually superior in speed but inferior in accuracy. To handle the grouping problems, recent work predicts offset fields [54,62] or part affinity fields [8,32], or uses associative embeddings [52] to get joint relationships. Different from the work that only uses PAFs to associate body parts, we also use them for occlusion reasoning since they encode useful context information.

3D Multi-person Human Pose Estimation.   In recent years a lot of work focuses on single-person 3D poses [1,9,28,44,45,48,51,59,60,69,79,86]. Only a few methods explore multi-person pose estimation:

Top-down methods [38,49,65,66,72] require off-the-shelf human detection, then anchor poses-based classification [65,66] or root-joint localization [49] is performed for better estimation. Recent work exploits the prior knowledge of human size [38] or ordinal relations among multiple people [72] to get more accurate depth estimation. However, these methods only focus on depth relations and discards many other useful cues. In addition, similar to the 2D top-down methods, they struggle in cases of occlusion and interactions and lack efficiency.

Although **bottom-up** methods [46,47,81,84] are inferior in accuracy, they have their inherent advantage in handling occlusion using joint relationships. Mehta *et al.* [47] propose occlusion-robust pose-map (ORPM) for full-body pose inference. It utilizes joint location redundancy to infer occluded joints, but can only be applied to extremity joints, and needs a predefined skeleton and an extra read-out process. Recently, Xnect [46] encodes joint's immediate local context in the kinematic tree to handle occlusion. However, this method can only use joint locations but fails to use link orientation and other cues. Zhen *et al.* [84] propose a depth-aware part association algorithm to add robustness to occlusion. However, it is only designed for associating body parts but cannot infer occluded joints. In addition, all these methods handle occlusion from the perspective of single-person and require grouping joints into individuals first, which leads to error-prone estimates in multi-person.

Occluded Pose. In addition to the bottom-up methods above [46–48,81], many methods have made good progress in occluded pose estimation. One common way to infer occlusion is to first reconstruct a full-body skeleton and then complete missing joints according to statistical and geometric models [3,46,64,65]. However, these methods only work for a single person but as mentioned, are less effective in multi-person scenarios, and depend on a library of known poses and structure that is easily biased to training data. Attention mechanism is introduced to enforce the model to focus on non-occluded areas and thus adding robustness to occlusion [17,30,85]. Temporal information [2,7,13,40,56,71,74,77] is another commonly used cue, but such methods require videos input. Using data augmentation [12,57,61,78] can also alleviate the problem but with minimal effects compared with other methods and does not fully capture the complexity of occlusions in real world [30]. Some recent methods regress multiple plausible poses [4,24,33,75] to handle heavy occlusion, in which almost no cue exists. For many occluded cases, human can infer occluded joints from pose prior or local and global context cues. Unlike previous work, we explore explicit modeling of occlusion reasoning. Recently, Zhang *et al.* [83] represent human meshes by UV maps and handle occluded parts reconstruction as image-inpainting problem. The requirement of accurate saliency maps limits the performance and generalization ability, and it is designed for single person scenarios.

3   HUPOR

The overall framework of our HUman Pose estimaion network via Occlusion Reasoning (HUPOR) is depicted in Fig. 2. It consists of three main stages: given an image $\mathcal{I} \in \mathbb{R}^{4h \times 4w}$, we first use a **visible keypoints detection** module to detect visible cues, then an **occluded keypoints reasoning** module is used to reasoning about the invisible information from the visible ones, and finally, all representations are combined to reconstruct 3D poses by the **grouping and refinement module**. Implementation details are provided in Sup. Mat.

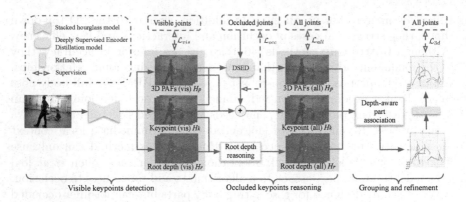

Fig. 2. Schematic view: HUPOR splits the two-step bottom-up methods into three separate tasks: visible keypoint detection, occluded keypoint reasoning, and grouping. In the detection module, a stacked hourglass model [37,53] is used to extract the intermediate results of all visible joints from the input image. In the reasoning module, DESD network is proposed to better infer occlusion joints from detected visible cues. Finally, all intermediate results are fed to the grouping module to reconstruct the human pose.

3.1   Visible Keypoints Detection

Following SMAP [84], we use a stacked hourglass [37] model to regress several intermediate representations, including 2D keypoint heatmaps, 3D part affinity fields (PAFs), and root depth maps. Let J be the number of joints being considered. Keypoint heatmaps $H_k \in \mathbb{R}^{h \times w \times J}$ indicate the probability location of each type of joint for all people in the image. 3D PAFs $H_p \in \mathbb{R}^{h \times w \times 3(J-1)}$ are extension of 2D PAFs [8]. 2D PAFs describe a set of 2D unit vectors pointing from the father node to the child node of the skeleton. For 3D tasks, the relative depth is added to the third dimension. Notice that the first two dimensions are defined in pixel and normalized while the relative depth is in mm without normalization. Root depth maps $H_r \in \mathbb{R}^{h \times w \times 7}$ represent the absolute root depth of all people in the images. Different from previous work [49,84] that directly estimates the pelvis depth, we estimate the depth of all the 7 torso joints, including shoulders, pelvis, neck, head, and hips. By doing so, it provides redundant information to infer pelvis depth under occlusion.

During training, we treat the occluded joints as noises and only provide supervision of visible joints. It makes our model more accurate when detecting visible keypoints and PAFs. This module is trained by minimizing $\mathcal{L}_{vis} = \lambda_k^{vis} \cdot \mathcal{L}_k^{vis} + \lambda_p^{vis} \cdot \mathcal{L}_p^{vis} + \lambda_r^{vis} \cdot \mathcal{L}_r^{vis}$, where

$$\mathcal{L}_k^{vis} = ||H_k - \hat{H}_k^{vis}||_2^2 \qquad \mathcal{L}_p^{vis} = ||H_p - \hat{H}_p^{vis}||_2^2 \tag{1}$$

$$\mathcal{L}_r^{vis} = \sum_{t=1}^{7} \sum_{i=1}^{N} ||H_{r,t}(u_i^t, v_i^t) - \hat{Z}_i^t||_1 \tag{2}$$

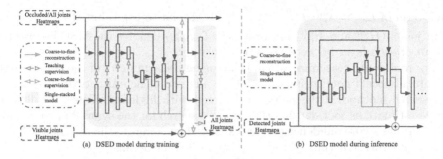

Fig. 3. Overview of DSED network: We only illustrate a single-stacked network here. We also use feature aggregation [37] but omit it for clear visualization.

where $\hat{H}_k^{vis}$ and $\hat{H}_p^{vis}$ denote ground-truth heatmaps of visible keypoints and visible PAFs, respectively. (u_i^t, v_i^t) is the detected position of the tth torso joint of the ith person, $H_{r,t}$ denotes the predicted depth map of torso joint t (*i.e.*, root depth map), and $\hat{Z}$ is the ground-truth normalized depth.

3.2 Occluded Keypoints Reasoning

The goal of this module is to infer occluded joints from visible joints. A straight-forward idea is to reuse the stacked hourglass model [37,53]. However, our experiments show that such a model cannot solve this problem. This indicates the difficulty of identifying useful information for occlusion reconstruction from all input information. Therefore, inspired by knowledge transfer [58], we propose DSED network to alleviate the difficulty of learning by splitting the task into two subtasks, reconstruct and imitate. This is done by adding an encoder to serve as a teacher to select the most useful information from occluded joints[2] and supervise the second encoder to extract the same information from just visible cues. This model is summarized in Fig. 3.

During training, the first encoder (blue) takes heatmaps of occluded joints as input, followed by a decoder to reconstruct these heatmaps, aiming to learn the best feature-level information needed for reconstruction. The second encoder (red) uses detected/visible joints as input and learns to extract the same information used for occlusion reconstruction, but only from visible cues. During inference, only the second encoder and the decoder are used. The reconstructed heatmaps of occluded joints and the detected heatmaps of visible joints are added together as the output of this module. Our experiments also show that using all joints as the input of the teacher can also improve performance, by enabling students to denoise and refine the detected joints while inferring occluded joints.

To train this model, we deeply supervise each layer of the encoders and the decoder and seek the parameters that minimize the loss function

$$\mathcal{L}_{reason} = \mathcal{L}_{all} + \omega_{extract} \cdot \mathcal{L}_{extract} \tag{3}$$

---

[2] In this section, joints represent both keypoints and 3D PAFs.

Each term of $\mathcal{L}_{all} = \lambda_k^{all} \cdot \mathcal{L}_k^{all} + \lambda_p^{all} \cdot \mathcal{L}_p^{all}$ is similar to Eq. 1, but the supervision of all joints ($\hat{H}_k^{all}$ and $\hat{H}_p^{all}$) are provided. $\mathcal{L}_{extract}$ denotes the MSE loss for the output of each layer between these two encoders.

For root depth reasoning, we find that using the symmetry of the human torso can already yield good results. Therefore, instead of neural networks, we use a tree search method: if the pelvis is detected with high confidence, we directly use its estimate as root depth, otherwise, we search for the symmetry torso joint pair that has high-confidence estimates, and then compute the root depth based on the skeleton structure. (Please see Sup. Mat. for details.)

Joint Training with Real and Synthetic Data. One problem of HPE is the lack of generalization ability. Meanwhile, 3D dataset generation and multi-person motion capture under strong occlusions are expensive and challenging, which worsen this problem. To better capture the complexity of occlusions and generalize to in-the-wild data, the reasoning module is designed to be trained without image input, thus is free from the domain gap between real data and synthetic. This enables us to build a synthetic dataset with a large range of pose and occlusion distribution and train our model on it. We design two training modes to train the reasoning module alternately: the first mode uses the output of the detection module as input while the second one uses artificially generated heatmaps of visible joints from the synthetic data as input. The former makes the occlusion reasoning more targeted at what the keypoint detection module can detect and the latter ensures the generalization ability of the reasoning module. Note that Gaussian distribution is used to model uncertainties when generating supervisions $\hat{H}_k$, but the output of the detection module cannot be a perfect Gaussian distribution. When training with the first mode, the reasoning module is more likely to prune the given heatmaps of detected joints instead of predicting occluded joints. Thus we provided extra supervision $\mathcal{L}_{occ} = \lambda_k^{occ} \cdot \mathcal{L}_k^{occ} + \lambda_p^{occ} \cdot \mathcal{L}_p^{occ}$ for occluded joints to avoid converging to this trivial solution. $\mathcal{L}_k^{occ}$ and $\mathcal{L}_p^{occ}$ are similar to $\mathcal{L}_k^{vis}$ and $\mathcal{L}_p^{vis}$ in Eq. 1, but only for occluded joints.

3.3 Grouping and Refinement

This module is not the main contribution of our method. For joint association, we directly use the depth-aware part association from SMAP [84] to get the connection relations, followed by a standard process to get the 3D pose from 2D joint location and relative depth. Finally a RefineNet is used to refine 3D root-relative pose. (Please refer to [84] for details.)

4   SSF for Occlusion Label Generation

To explicitly learn from occluded joints, we need the occlusion label for each joint. However, existing 3D human pose datasets have no occlusion labels. Recently, Cheng et al. [13] propose the "Cylinder Man Model", in which they model the human body as cylindrical segments with pre-defined diameters and then project

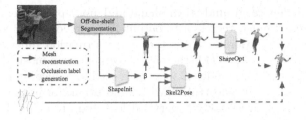

Fig. 4. Schematic view of human shape estimation and occlusion label generation. Test-time-optimization is used when generating occlusion labels.

the human model into 2D to determine the degree of occlusion for each joint. This model is simple enough, but using cylinders with fixed diameters causes a very rough representation of human shape and low accuracy. More importantly, It cannot handle occlusion caused by other people and objects. Using a more complex human body model like SMPL [41] is a straightforward extension. However, current methods cannot provide a sufficiently accurate estimate to generate occlusion labels. To solve the problem of human shape estimation from given poses and to enable the occlusion-label generation model to accurately detect occlusion of self, objects, and other people, we proposed Skeleton-guided human Shape Fitting (SSF). Note that SSF is not our major novelty, but an essential step to generate occlusion labels (Sect. 5.5) and requires extra effort.

The overall framework of this method is illustrated in Fig. 4. Given an image I and the 3D pose P of all people in the image as input, an off-the-shelf instance segmentation method is used to generate instance masks S_{ins} for objects and people in the image. Then for each person, we learn the shape parameters $\beta \in \mathbb{R}^{10}$ from the ShapeInit model. The shape parameters β are then used to obtain the canonical human mesh M_c with body part segmentation from the SMPL model. Next, a Skeleton2Pose model is utilized to predict the pose parameters $\theta \in \mathbb{R}^{24 \times 3}$ from M_c, β, and P. Due to the same function and similar input, we modify the Adaptive HybrIK [36] and use it as the Skeleton2Pose model here. After that, we use the shape β and the pose θ to calculate the SMPL body mesh $M_{init} = \mathcal{M}(\theta, \beta)$. Finally, mask S_{ins} and reconstructed mesh M_{init} are passed through the ShapeOpt model to obtain a more accurate mesh reconstruction M_{opt}. More details are provided in the Sup. Mat.

The overall loss function for training this model is given by:

$$\mathcal{L}_{HS} = \lambda_\beta \mathcal{L}_\beta + \lambda_\theta \mathcal{L}_\theta + \lambda_{pos} \mathcal{L}_{pose} + \lambda_{sil} \mathcal{L}_{silhouette} \tag{4}$$

where for the i-th person,

$$\mathcal{L}_\beta = ||\beta^i - \hat{\beta}^i||_2 \qquad \mathcal{L}_\theta = ||\theta^i - \hat{\theta}^i||_2 \tag{5}$$

$$\mathcal{L}_{pose} = ||W_{15}(\mathcal{M}(\theta^i, \beta^i)) - P^i||_2^2 \tag{6}$$

$$\mathcal{L}_{silhouette} = ||\Pi_c(\mathcal{M}(\theta^i, \beta^i)) - b^i(I)||_2^2 \tag{7}$$

where $\hat{\beta}$ and $\hat{\theta}$ denote ground-truth shape and pose parameters respectively. W_{15} is a pretrained linear regressor to output 15 joints locations consistent with the MPI15 keypoint ordering, Π_c is the image formation function of a weak-perspective camera c, and $b^i(I)$ is the binary segmentation mask of person i provided by the segmentation model. $\mathcal{L}_{silhouette}$ is used to reduce the error caused by the inaccurate pseudo-ground-truth SMPL annotations for in-the-wild datasets. $\mathcal{L}_{pose}$ and $\mathcal{L}_{silhouette}$ are weakly supervised loss and are also used to optimize the shape parameters when generating occlusion labels.

After getting the human part segmentation labels S_{part} of the reconstructed human mesh M_{opt} from the SMPL model, we can then generate the occlusion label $o_j \in \{0, 1, 2\}$ of joint j by checking the pixel label of (u_j, v_j) given by the instance segmentation masks S_{ins} and the human part segmentation labels S_{part}. $o_j = 0, 1, 2$ denote truncated, occluded, and visible, respectively.

5   Experiments

5.1   Dataset and Metrics

Dataset. For 3D human poes estimation (Sect. 5.2), we report results on MuPoTS-3D [47], CMU Panoptic [26], 3DPW [43], 3DPW-OCC [43,83], 3DOH [83] and Human3.6M [23] datasets. Inspired by PARE [30], we randomly generate synthetic occlusions on the image of MuPoTS-3D and name it MuPoTS-synthOcc. It is only used for evaluation. For experiments on MuPoTS-3D, MuPoTS-synthOcc, 3DPW, and 3DPW-OCC, we follow SMAP [84] and train our model on the MuCo-3DHP [47] dataset. In addition, for a fair comparison, we mix the data with COCO2017 [39] during training and 50% of data in each mini-batch is from it (same as [47,48,84]). For Panoptic, following [80,84], we choose cameras 16 and 30, and randomly select 9600 images from four activities (Haggling, Mafia, Ultimatum, Pizza) as test set, and 160k images from other sequences as training set. The synthetic dataset for training the DSED reasoning module is built based on AMASS [42]. Results on Human3.6M are reported in Sup. Mat.

For the broader study of the reasoning module and the DSED network (Sect. 5.4), we apply our reasoning module to two SOTA methods (PifPaf [32] and HigherHRNet [11]) and evaluate them on COCO [39] and CrowdPose [35]. For a fair comparison, we directly adopt the official implementation and use the same training data. Results on CrowdPose are reported in Sup. Mat.

Metrics. For pose estimation, we consider mean per joint position error (MPJPE) in mm and percentage of correct keypoints (PCK) in 3D. Following [84], a keypoint is declared correct if the Euclidean distance error is smaller than 150mm. We evaluate absolute pose accuracy (subscript abs), relative pose accuracy with root alignment (subscript rel), and relative pose accuracy of occluded joints (subscript occ). For human mesh reconstruction, we consider MPJPE, Procrustes-aligned mean per joint position error (PA-MPJPE), and per vertex error (PVE).

Table 1. Comparisons on MuPoTS-3D and MuPoTS-synthOCC. Results on MuPoTS-synthOcc are generated from the official pre-trained model and code if they are released. The PCK$_{occ}$ evaluates the same joints in both datasets to better analyze the occlusion reasoning ability under different levels of occlusion. Best in **bold**, second best underlined.

| | | MuPoTS-3D | | | | | MuPoTS-synthOCC | | | | |
| | | Matched people | | | All people | | Matched people | | | All people | |
		PCK$_{abs}$	PCK$_{rel}$	PCK$_{occ}$	PCK$_{abs}$	PCK$_{rel}$	PCK$_{abs}$	PCK$_{rel}$	PCK$_{occ}$	PCK$_{abs}$	PCK$_{rel}$
top down	Lcr-net++ [66]	–	74.0	–	–	–	–	–	–	–	–
	Moon et al. [49]	31.8	82.5	66.8	31.5	**81.8**	26.9	74.2	57.9	15.4	45.8
	HMOR [72]	**43.8**	82.0	–	–	–	–	–	–	–	–
	HDNet [38]	35.2	83.7	–	–	–	25.8	72.3	55.9	–	–
bottom up	ORPM [47]	–	69.8	–	–	–	–	–	–	–	–
	XNect [46]	–	75.8	57.8	–	–	–	69.2	56.2	–	–
	SMAP [84]	38.7	80.5	72.9	35.4	73.5	36.4	76.1	68.9	23.9	49.1
	Ours	38.9	84.3	74.1	35.8	76.9	36.3	80.1	71.0	24.3	52.6
	Ours (w/ synthetic)	39.3	**86.5**	74.9	**36.5**	79.4	**37.9**	**81.7**	**72.1**	**25.5**	**53.7**

Table 2. Comparisons on 3DPW, 3DPW-OCC, 3DOH, and Panoptic. Our method yields clear improvements among all datasets. MPJPE is used.

	3DPW	3DPW-OCC	3DOH
Moon et al. [49]	98.4	104.3	89.5
XNect [46]	118.5	124.7	–
SMAP [84]	101.5	105.2	90.6
Ours	95.8	96.9	–
Ours (w/ Synth)	**93.1**	**94.4**	**80.9**

	Haggling	Mafia	Ultim.	Pizza	Average
Moon et al. [49]	89.6	91.3	79.6	90.1	87.6
Zanfir et al. [81]	72.4	78.8	66.8	94.3	72.1
SMAP [84]	63.1	60.3	56.6	67.1	61.8
Ours	**54.7**	55.2	50.1	66.4	56.1
Ours (w/ Synth)	55.2	55.0	50.4	61.4	**55.0**

(a) 3DPW, 3DPW-OCC, and 3DOH   (b) CMU Panoptic

5.2 Benchmark Evaluation

MuPoTS-3D and MuPoTS-synthOCC. Table 1 compares our method with previous monocular HPE methods. In terms of the relative pose accuracy on which our work mainly focuses, our method significantly surpasses previous bottom-up methods in both visible and occluded joints estimate. Remarkably, even though we use a very similar detection module and the same grouping method, our method outperforms SMAP, which is also the previous SOTA bottom-up method, by 6 PCK$_{rel}$ and 5.6 PCK$_{rel}$ on matched people of MuPoTS-3D and MuPoTS-synthOCC, respectively. When considering all people, we still surpass previous art by 5.9 PCK$_{rel}$ and 4.6 PCK$_{rel}$ on these two datasets.

More importantly, although top-down methods have the inherent advantage on accuracy since they can use off-the-shelf human detection method and can simplify the problem to single-person pose estimation, our method still outperforms them by 2.8 PCK$_{rel}$ on MuPoTS-3D when considering matched people, and is comparable to them when considering all people. Meanwhile, depending on the number of people in the image, we are faster than the SOTA top-down methods during inference. Overall, the strong results and the relatively fast inference speed prove the effectiveness and efficiency of our method.

Table 3. Ablation studies on MuPoTS-3D dataset. Det, Reason, and Ref stand for detection, reasoning, and refinement module, respectively. Hg stands for hourglass model, NL for nonlocal blocks. Det of SMAP uses all joints during training and Det of ours uses visible joints only.

	PCK_{rel} ↑	$MPJPE_{rel}$ ↓	PCK_{occ} ↑	$MPJPE_{occ}$ ↓
Effect of each module of SMAP [84]				
SMAP Det	70.9	122.1	56.8	158.4
SMAP Det + Ref	80.5	103.3	72.9	122.8
Effect of each module				
Det	74.87	116.36	51.48	184.31
Det + Reason	79.28	104.33	61.24	145.94
Det + Reason + Ref	86.54	87.28	74.92	118.60
Training without occlusion label (OccL)				
Det (w/o OccL)	71.12	123.02	56.53	163.74
Det (w/o OccL) + Reason	74.76	112.77	58.70	118.61
Deeply Supervised Encoder Distillation				
Det + Reason (Hg)	75.58	113.35	55.30	154.76
Det + Reason (DSED)	79.28	104.33	61.24	145.94
Det + Reason (DSED + NL)	79.81	102.32	61.56	143.59

3DPW, 3DPW-OCC, and 3DOH. These dataset are designed for multi-person human shape reconstruction. It is unfair to compare the errors between the skeleton-based method with SMPL model-based method due to the different definitions of joints. Table 2 mainly focuses on skeleton-based methods. Results of baselines are generated from the official model. We use the same scripts to match the predicted person with ground-truth and compute the error based on MPI15 joint definition. Therefore, the relative values are more meaningful.

5.3 Ablation Study

Effect of Each Module. Compared with other bottom-up methods, we add the occlusion keypoint reasoning module. First, we validate the efficiency of this module and the continuous improvement of different modules. The results can be found in *Effect of each module* in Table 3. We achieve a continuous improvement in the accuracy of both visible and occluded joints with different modules. In addition, compared with SMAP that predicts all keypoints at the same time and then uses single-person refinement to complete the missing prediction, the idea of splitting the detection step into detection and reasoning already yields an improvement of 3.97 PCK_{rel} after detection module and 8.38 PCK_{rel} after reasoning module. Note that SMAP and our method use the same three-stacked hourglass architecture and output similar intermediate results.

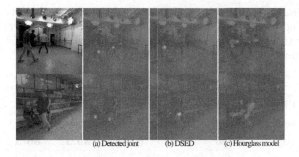

Fig. 5. Keypoint detection and reasoning. We visualize the right knee here. More results are provided in Sup. Mat. From left to right: input image, (a) detected keypoints, keypoints inferred by (b) DSED, and by (c) hourglass model.

Table 4. Broader study on 2D human pose. We show results in single-scale testing setting. Reason stands for reasoning module, Hg for hourglass model.

COCO val-dev	AP	AP^{50}	AP^{75}	AP^{M}	AP^{L}	AR	COCO test-dev	AP	AP^{50}	AP^{75}	AP^{M}	AP^{L}	AR
PifPaf [32]	67.4	–	–	–	–	–	PifPaf [32]	66.7	–	–	62.4	72.9	–
+ Reason (Hg)	67.5	86.5	73.6	62.0	75.8	70.9	+ Reason (Hg)	66.9	88.1	72.9	62.3	73.1	70.4
+ Reason (DSED)	69.1	87.0	75.3	64.7	76.9	75.5	+ Reason (DSED)	68.0	88.7	75.2	64.1	74.7	75.6
HrHRNet-W48 [11]	69.9	87.2	76.1	–	–	–	HrHRNet-W48 [11]	68.4	88.2	75.1	64.4	74.2	–
+ Reason (Hg)	68.2	86.7	75.9	64.3	76.6	72.1	+ Reason (Hg)	67.2	87.4	74.6	63.0	73.8	71.8
+ Reason (DSED)	70.8	87.9	77.0	66.0	78.3	76.6	+ Reason (DSED)	69.5	89.0	76.6	65.2	76.2	75.7
(a) COCO val-dev 2017							(b) COCO test-dev 2017						

Training with Occlusion Label. Next, we evaluate the effect of using occlusion labels. We can find that without using occlusion labels, the network will try to estimate both visible and occluded joints at the same time. It achieves a higher accuracy (56.53 PCK$_{occ}$ vs.51.48 PCK$_{occ}$) on occluded joint detection but gets a lower accuracy (71.12 PCK$_{rel}$ vs.74.87 PCK$_{rel}$) on all joints. Training the detection module with occluded joints can to some degree improve the ability of occluded joint detection, but increasing the training difficulty and adding noises by many unpredictable joints. When the reasoning module is used in this case, the accuracy is enhanced but still lower than the model trained with occlusion labels by 4.52 PCK$_{rel}$ due to the false-positive prediction and the noise on visible keypoint prediction that is hard to be fixed by the following reasoning module.

DSED Network. Compared with only using the detection model, both the hourglass-based reasoning model and DSED-based reasoning model yield improvement on occluded joints prediction. However, the DSED model achieves a much higher accuracy on occlusion reasoning by 5.94 PCK$_{occ}$. More importantly, the overall accuracy only improves 0.71 PCK$_{rel}$ when using the hourglass model but 4.41 PCK$_{rel}$ with the DSED model. This is mainly due to the false-positive estimates and noises given by the hourglass model (see Fig. 5). In addition, using non-local (NL) blocks can also yield an improvement of 0.53 PCK$_{rel}$ after carefully design, but it also increases the memory and time required for training. We do not add it to our final model but only show the results here.

Table 5. Evaluation of occluded joint detection. The left half compares the generated occlusion labels and the right half shows the model performance trained on these labels. For the left half, we randomly select 500 from 200k images in MuCo-3DHP and manually annotate them to get ground-truth labels.

	Precision	Recall	F1-score	PCK_{abs}	PCK_{rel}	PCK_{occ}
Cylinder [13]	0.653	0.401	0.497	–	–	–
HybrIK-based [36]	0.800	0.602	0.687	38.4	83.1	73.0
Ours (SSF-based)	0.885	0.805	0.843	**39.3**	**86.5**	**74.9**

5.4   Broader Study of the Reasoning Module and DSED Network

The previous section discusses the effect of the reasoning module and DSED network in 3D HPE, now we consider a more general task, *i.e.*, 2D human pose estimation. We delete the depth-related structure of the reasoning module and modify the DSED network, then apply them to PifPaf and HigherHRNet. We use the official implementation with small modifications on their network to make it compatible with our 2D reasoning module (see Sup. Mat. for details). The results are reported in Table 4. All methods are trained on 2017 COCO training set. We can see that even though the reasoning module is not designed for 2D tasks since the bone length is more accurate when computed in 3D, it still yields stable improvement (up to 1.7 AP) and achieves SOTA performances. We can also find that DSED is crucial for the reasoning module.

5.5   SSF and Occlusion Label Generation

Occlusion Label Generation. We compare our method with the Cylinder human model and the SMPL-based human mesh fitting method (*i.e.*, Adaptive HybrIK). We implement the Cylinder model and modify it to detect occlusion by other people. For comparison with HybrIK, we directly use the official model to fit the SMPL models and then use the same graphics pipeline in our SSF to generate the occlusion labels. Note that the ground-truth skeleton is provided for all methods. The results can be found in Table 5. Our method generates more accurate occlusion labels with much higher precision and recall. More importantly, the labels generated by previous methods reduce performance. SSF is essential to generate occlusion labels for explicit occlusion reasoning.

3D Human Mesh Reconstruction. We evaluate our SSF on the 3DPW dataset. We use the proposed HUPOR to generate 3D skeletons, and then use the estimated skeletons and the image as input to estimate SMPL parameters. For a fair comparison, we strictly follow HybrIK [36] to prepare the training data and use ResNet-34 [19] as backbone. The results are reported in Table 6. Compared with baselines, SSF can recover body mesh more accurately. Qualitative results on human shape estimation can be found in Sup. Mat.

Table 6. Evaluation of human mesh recovery on 3DPW dataset.

	MPJPE	PA-MPJPE	PVE
SPIN [31]	96.9	59.2	116.4
ROMP (ResNet-50) [70]	91.3	54.9	108.3
PARE (ResNet-50) [30]	84.3	51.2	101.2
Adaptive HybrIK (ResNet-34) [36]	<u>80.0</u>	**48.8**	<u>94.5</u>
Ours (w/o Synth, ResNet-34)	**79.1**	<u>49.3</u>	**92.3**

6   Conclusions

Although occlusion is a well-known problem in HPE, not enough attention has been paid to *learning from occlusion*. In this work, we show its value by incorporating our proposed 3D occlusion reasoning method in an existing framework, and present HUPOR. It solves the keypoint detection in a detect-and-reason pipeline, which is effective but being ignored. For occlusion reasoning, we propose a Deeply Supervised Encoder Distillation (DSED) network to effectively infer occluded joints from visible cues, and greatly improve current SOTA 3D and 2D methods. We also propose a Skeleton-guided human Shape Fitting (SSF) method for better human mesh reconstruction and occlusion label generation. Experiments show the effectiveness of our reasoning method in both 2D and 3D HPS. Meanwhile, we demonstrate that both the SSF and the DSED are crucial.

Acknowledgements. This work was supported by NIH R01 EY029700. We thank the anonymous reviewers for their efforts and valuable feedback to improve our work.

References

1. Akhter, I., Black, M.J.: Pose-conditioned joint angle limits for 3D human pose reconstruction. In: Proceedings of the IEEE Conference on Computer Vision and Pattern Recognition, pp. 1446–1455 (2015)
2. Artacho, B., Savakis, A.: Unipose: unified human pose estimation in single images and videos. In: Proceedings of the IEEE/CVF Conference on Computer Vision and Pattern Recognition, pp. 7035–7044 (2020)
3. de Bem, R., Arnab, A., Golodetz, S., Sapienza, M., Torr, P.: Deep fully-connected part-based models for human pose estimation. In: Asian Conference on Machine Learning, pp. 327–342. PMLR (2018)
4. Biggs, B., Ehrhadt, S., Joo, H., Graham, B., Vedaldi, A., Novotny, D.: 3D multi-bodies: fitting sets of plausible 3D human models to ambiguous image data. Adv. Neural. Inf. Process. Syst. **33**, 20496–20507 (2020)
5. Brasó, G., Kister, N., Leal-Taixé, L.: The center of attention: center-keypoint grouping via attention for multi-person pose estimation. In: Proceedings of the IEEE/CVF International Conference on Computer Vision, pp. 11853–11863 (2021)

6. Cai, Y., et al.: Learning delicate local representations for multi-person pose estimation. In: Vedaldi, A., Bischof, H., Brox, T., Frahm, J.-M. (eds.) ECCV 2020. LNCS, vol. 12348, pp. 455–472. Springer, Cham (2020). https://doi.org/10.1007/978-3-030-58580-8_27

7. Cai, Y., et al.: Exploiting spatial-temporal relationships for 3D pose estimation via graph convolutional networks. In: Proceedings of the IEEE/CVF International Conference on Computer Vision, pp. 2272–2281 (2019)

8. Cao, Z., Simon, T., Wei, S.E., Sheikh, Y.: Realtime multi-person 2D pose estimation using part affinity fields. In: Proceedings of the IEEE Conference on Computer Vision and Pattern Recognition, pp. 7291–7299 (2017)

9. Chen, C.H., Ramanan, D.: 3D human pose estimation= 2D pose estimation+ matching. In: Proceedings of the IEEE Conference on Computer Vision and Pattern Recognition, pp. 7035–7043 (2017)

10. Chen, Y., Wang, Z., Peng, Y., Zhang, Z., Yu, G., Sun, J.: Cascaded pyramid network for multi-person pose estimation. In: Proceedings of the IEEE Conference on Computer Vision and Pattern Recognition, pp. 7103–7112 (2018)

11. Cheng, B., Xiao, B., Wang, J., Shi, H., Huang, T.S., Zhang, L.: Higherhrnet: scale-aware representation learning for bottom-up human pose estimation. In: Proceedings of the IEEE/CVF Conference on Computer Vision and Pattern Recognition, pp. 5386–5395 (2020)

12. Cheng, Y., Yang, B., Wang, B., Tan, R.T.: 3D human pose estimation using spatio-temporal networks with explicit occlusion training. In: Proceedings of the AAAI Conference on Artificial Intelligence, vol. 34, pp. 10631–10638 (2020)

13. Cheng, Y., Yang, B., Wang, B., Yan, W., Tan, R.T.: Occlusion-aware networks for 3D human pose estimation in video. In: Proceedings of the IEEE/CVF International Conference on Computer Vision, pp. 723–732 (2019)

14. Choi, H., Moon, G., Lee, K.M.: Pose2Mesh: graph convolutional network for 3D human pose and mesh recovery from a 2D human pose. In: Vedaldi, A., Bischof, H., Brox, T., Frahm, J.-M. (eds.) ECCV 2020. LNCS, vol. 12352, pp. 769–787. Springer, Cham (2020). https://doi.org/10.1007/978-3-030-58571-6_45

15. Chu, X., Yang, W., Ouyang, W., Ma, C., Yuille, A.L., Wang, X.: Multi-context attention for human pose estimation. In: Proceedings of the IEEE Conference on Computer Vision and Pattern Recognition, pp. 1831–1840 (2017)

16. Fang, H.S., Xie, S., Tai, Y.W., Lu, C.: RMPE: regional multi-person pose estimation. In: Proceedings of the IEEE International Conference on Computer Vision, pp. 2334–2343 (2017)

17. Gu, R., Wang, G., Hwang, J.N.: Exploring severe occlusion: multi-person 3D pose estimation with gated convolution. In: 2020 25th International Conference on Pattern Recognition (ICPR), pp. 8243–8250. IEEE (2021)

18. He, K., Gkioxari, G., Dollár, P., Girshick, R.: Mask R-CNN. In: Proceedings of the IEEE International Conference on Computer Vision, pp. 2961–2969 (2017)

19. He, K., Zhang, X., Ren, S., Sun, J.: Deep residual learning for image recognition. In: Proceedings of the IEEE Conference on Computer Vision and Pattern Recognition, pp. 770–778 (2016)

20. Huang, J., Zhu, Z., Guo, F., Huang, G.: The devil is in the details: delving into unbiased data processing for human pose estimation. In: Proceedings of the IEEE/CVF Conference on Computer Vision and Pattern Recognition, pp. 5700–5709 (2020)

21. Huang, S., Gong, M., Tao, D.: A coarse-fine network for keypoint localization. In: Proceedings of the IEEE International Conference on Computer Vision, pp. 3028–3037 (2017)

22. Insafutdinov, E., Pishchulin, L., Andres, B., Andriluka, M., Schiele, B.: DeeperCut: a deeper, stronger, and faster multi-person pose estimation model. In: Leibe, B., Matas, J., Sebe, N., Welling, M. (eds.) ECCV 2016. LNCS, vol. 9910, pp. 34–50. Springer, Cham (2016). https://doi.org/10.1007/978-3-319-46466-4_3
23. Ionescu, C., Papava, D., Olaru, V., Sminchisescu, C.: Human3. 6m: large scale datasets and predictive methods for 3D human sensing in natural environments. IEEE Trans. Pattern Anal. Mach. Intell. **36**(7), 1325–1339 (2013)
24. Jahangiri, E., Yuille, A.L.: Generating multiple diverse hypotheses for human 3D pose consistent with 2D joint detections. In: Proceedings of the IEEE International Conference on Computer Vision Workshops, pp. 805–814 (2017)
25. Jin, S., et al.: Differentiable hierarchical graph grouping for multi-person pose estimation. In: Vedaldi, A., Bischof, H., Brox, T., Frahm, J.-M. (eds.) ECCV 2020. LNCS, vol. 12352, pp. 718–734. Springer, Cham (2020). https://doi.org/10.1007/978-3-030-58571-6_42
26. Joo, H., et al.: Panoptic studio: a massively multiview system for social motion capture. In: Proceedings of the IEEE International Conference on Computer Vision, pp. 3334–3342 (2015)
27. Joo, H., Neverova, N., Vedaldi, A.: Exemplar fine-tuning for 3D human model fitting towards in-the-wild 3D human pose estimation. arXiv preprint arXiv:2004.03686 (2020)
28. Kanazawa, A., Black, M.J., Jacobs, D.W., Malik, J.: End-to-end recovery of human shape and pose. In: Proceedings of the IEEE Conference on Computer Vision and Pattern Recognition, pp. 7122–7131 (2018)
29. Khirodkar, R., Chari, V., Agrawal, A., Tyagi, A.: Multi-hypothesis pose networks: rethinking top-down pose estimation. In: Proceedings of the IEEE International Conference on Computer Vision, pp. 3122–3131 (2021)
30. Kocabas, M., Huang, C.H.P., Hilliges, O., Black, M.J.: Pare: part attention regressor for 3D human body estimation. In: Proceedings of the IEEE International Conference on Computer Vision (2021)
31. Kolotouros, N., Pavlakos, G., Black, M.J., Daniilidis, K.: Learning to reconstruct 3D human pose and shape via model-fitting in the loop. In: Proceedings of the IEEE/CVF International Conference on Computer Vision, pp. 2252–2261 (2019)
32. Kreiss, S., Bertoni, L., Alahi, A.: Pifpaf: composite fields for human pose estimation. In: Proceedings of the IEEE/CVF Conference on Computer Vision and Pattern Recognition, pp. 11977–11986 (2019)
33. Li, C., Lee, G.H.: Generating multiple hypotheses for 3D human pose estimation with mixture density network. In: Proceedings of the IEEE/CVF Conference on Computer Vision and Pattern Recognition, pp. 9887–9895 (2019)
34. Li, J., Su, W., Wang, Z.: Simple pose: rethinking and improving a bottom-up approach for multi-person pose estimation. In: Proceedings of the AAAI Conference on Artificial Intelligence, vol. 34, pp. 11354–11361 (2020)
35. Li, J., Wang, C., Zhu, H., Mao, Y., Fang, H.S., Lu, C.: Crowdpose: efficient crowded scenes pose estimation and a new benchmark. In: Proceedings of the IEEE/CVF Conference on Computer Vision and Pattern Recognition, pp. 10863–10872 (2019)
36. Li, J., Xu, C., Chen, Z., Bian, S., Yang, L., Lu, C.: Hybrik: a hybrid analytical-neural inverse kinematics solution for 3D human pose and shape estimation. In: Proceedings of the IEEE/CVF Conference on Computer Vision and Pattern Recognition, pp. 3383–3393 (2021)
37. Li, W., et al.: Rethinking on multi-stage networks for human pose estimation. arXiv preprint arXiv:1901.00148 (2019)

38. Lin, J., Lee, G.H.: HDNet: human depth estimation for multi-person camera-space localization. In: Vedaldi, A., Bischof, H., Brox, T., Frahm, J.-M. (eds.) ECCV 2020. LNCS, vol. 12363, pp. 633–648. Springer, Cham (2020). https://doi.org/10.1007/978-3-030-58523-5_37

39. Lin, T.-Y., et al.: Microsoft COCO: common objects in context. In: Fleet, D., Pajdla, T., Schiele, B., Tuytelaars, T. (eds.) ECCV 2014. LNCS, vol. 8693, pp. 740–755. Springer, Cham (2014). https://doi.org/10.1007/978-3-319-10602-1_48

40. Liu, J., et al.: A graph attention spatio-temporal convolutional network for 3D human pose estimation in video. In: 2021 IEEE International Conference on Robotics and Automation (ICRA), pp. 3374–3380. IEEE (2021)

41. Loper, M., Mahmood, N., Romero, J., Pons-Moll, G., Black, M.J.: SMPL: a skinned multi-person linear model. ACM Trans. Graph. (Proc. SIGGRAPH Asia) 34(6), 2481–24816 (2015)

42. Mahmood, N., Ghorbani, N., Troje, N.F., Pons-Moll, G., Black, M.J.: Amass: archive of motion capture as surface shapes. In: Proceedings of the IEEE/CVF International Conference on Computer Vision, pp. 5442–5451 (2019)

43. von Marcard, T., Henschel, R., Black, M.J., Rosenhahn, B., Pons-Moll, G.: Recovering accurate 3D human pose in the wild using IMUS and a moving camera. In: Proceedings of the European Conference on Computer Vision (ECCV), pp. 601–617 (2018)

44. Martinez, J., Hossain, R., Romero, J., Little, J.J.: A simple yet effective baseline for 3D human pose estimation. In: Proceedings of the IEEE International Conference on Computer Vision, pp. 2640–2649 (2017)

45. Mehta, D., et al.: Monocular 3D human pose estimation in the wild using improved CNN supervision. In: 2017 International Conference on 3D Vision (3DV), pp. 506–516. IEEE (2017)

46. Mehta, D., et al.: XNect: real-time multi-person 3D human pose estimation with a single RGB camera. ACM Trans. Graph. (TOG) (2020)

47. Mehta, D., et al.: Single-shot multi-person 3D pose estimation from monocular RGB. In: 2018 International Conference on 3D Vision (3DV), pp. 120–130. IEEE (2018)

48. Mehta, D., et al.: Vnect: real-time 3D human pose estimation with a single RGB camera. ACM Trans. Graph. (TOG) 36(4), 1–14 (2017)

49. Moon, G., Chang, J.Y., Lee, K.M.: Camera distance-aware top-down approach for 3D multi-person pose estimation from a single RGB image. In: Proceedings of the IEEE/CVF International Conference on Computer Vision, pp. 10133–10142 (2019)

50. Moon, G., Chang, J.Y., Lee, K.M.: Posefix: model-agnostic general human pose refinement network. In: Proceedings of the IEEE/CVF Conference on Computer Vision and Pattern Recognition, pp. 7773–7781 (2019)

51. Moreno-Noguer, F.: 3D human pose estimation from a single image via distance matrix regression. In: Proceedings of the IEEE Conference on Computer Vision and Pattern Recognition, pp. 2823–2832 (2017)

52. Newell, A., Huang, Z., Deng, J.: Associative embedding: end-to-end learning for joint detection and grouping. arXiv preprint arXiv:1611.05424 (2016)

53. Newell, A., Yang, K., Deng, J.: Stacked hourglass networks for human pose estimation. In: Leibe, B., Matas, J., Sebe, N., Welling, M. (eds.) ECCV 2016. LNCS, vol. 9912, pp. 483–499. Springer, Cham (2016). https://doi.org/10.1007/978-3-319-46484-8_29

54. Papandreou, G., Zhu, T., Chen, L.C., Gidaris, S., Tompson, J., Murphy, K.: Personlab: person pose estimation and instance segmentation with a bottom-up, part-

based, geometric embedding model. In: Proceedings of the European Conference on Computer Vision (ECCV), pp. 269–286 (2018)

55. Papandreou, G., et al.: Towards accurate multi-person pose estimation in the wild. In: Proceedings of the IEEE Conference on Computer Vision and Pattern Recognition, pp. 4903–4911 (2017)

56. Parger, M., et al.: UNOC: Understanding occlusion for embodied presence in virtual reality. IEEE Trans. Vis. Comput. Graph. (2021)

57. Park, S., Park, J.: Localizing human keypoints beyond the bounding box. In: Proceedings of the IEEE/CVF International Conference on Computer Vision, pp. 1602–1611 (2021)

58. Passalis, N., Tefas, A.: Learning deep representations with probabilistic knowledge transfer. In: Proceedings of the European Conference on Computer Vision (ECCV), pp. 268–284 (2018)

59. Pavlakos, G., Zhou, X., Derpanis, K.G., Daniilidis, K.: Coarse-to-fine volumetric prediction for single-image 3D human pose. In: Proceedings of the IEEE Conference on Computer Vision and Pattern Recognition, pp. 7025–7034 (2017)

60. Pavllo, D., Feichtenhofer, C., Grangier, D., Auli, M.: 3D human pose estimation in video with temporal convolutions and semi-supervised training. In: Proceedings of the IEEE/CVF Conference on Computer Vision and Pattern Recognition, pp. 7753–7762 (2019)

61. Peng, X., Tang, Z., Yang, F., Feris, R.S., Metaxas, D.: Jointly optimize data augmentation and network training: adversarial data augmentation in human pose estimation. In: Proceedings of the IEEE Conference on Computer Vision and Pattern Recognition, pp. 2226–2234 (2018)

62. Pishchulin, L., et al.: Deepcut: joint subset partition and labeling for multi person pose estimation. In: Proceedings of the IEEE Conference on Computer Vision and Pattern Recognition, pp. 4929–4937 (2016)

63. Qiu, L., et al.: Peeking into occluded joints: a novel framework for crowd pose estimation. In: Vedaldi, A., Bischof, H., Brox, T., Frahm, J.-M. (eds.) ECCV 2020. LNCS, vol. 12364, pp. 488–504. Springer, Cham (2020). https://doi.org/10.1007/978-3-030-58529-7_29

64. Radwan, I., Dhall, A., Goecke, R.: Monocular image 3D human pose estimation under self-occlusion. In: Proceedings of the IEEE International Conference on Computer Vision, pp. 1888–1895 (2013)

65. Rogez, G., Weinzaepfel, P., Schmid, C.: LCR-net: localization-classification-regression for human pose. In: Proceedings of the IEEE Conference on Computer Vision and Pattern Recognition, pp. 3433–3441 (2017)

66. Rogez, G., Weinzaepfel, P., Schmid, C.: LCR-net++: multi-person 2D and 3D pose detection in natural images. IEEE Trans. Pattern Anal. Mach. Intell. **42**(5), 1146–1161 (2019)

67. Su, K., Yu, D., Xu, Z., Geng, X., Wang, C.: Multi-person pose estimation with enhanced channel-wise and spatial information. In: Proceedings of the IEEE/CVF Conference on Computer Vision and Pattern Recognition, pp. 5674–5682 (2019)

68. Sun, K., Xiao, B., Liu, D., Wang, J.: Deep high-resolution representation learning for human pose estimation. In: Proceedings of the IEEE/CVF Conference on Computer Vision and Pattern Recognition, pp. 5693–5703 (2019)

69. Sun, X., Shang, J., Liang, S., Wei, Y.: Compositional human pose regression. In: Proceedings of the IEEE International Conference on Computer Vision, pp. 2602–2611 (2017)

70. Sun, Y., Bao, Q., Liu, W., Fu, Y., Black, M.J., Mei, T.: Monocular, one-stage, regression of multiple 3D people. In: Proceedings of the IEEE/CVF International Conference on Computer Vision, pp. 11179–11188 (2021)
71. Véges, M., Lőrincz, A.: Temporal smoothing for 3D human pose estimation and localization for occluded people. In: Yang, H., et al. (eds.) ICONIP 2020. LNCS, vol. 12532, pp. 557–568. Springer, Cham (2020). https://doi.org/10.1007/978-3-030-63830-6_47
72. Wang, C., Li, J., Liu, W., Qian, C., Lu, C.: HMOR: hierarchical multi-person ordinal relations for monocular multi-person 3D pose estimation. In: Vedaldi, A., Bischof, H., Brox, T., Frahm, J.-M. (eds.) ECCV 2020. LNCS, vol. 12348, pp. 242–259. Springer, Cham (2020). https://doi.org/10.1007/978-3-030-58580-8_15
73. Wang, J., Long, X., Gao, Y., Ding, E., Wen, S.: Graph-PCNN: two stage human pose estimation with graph pose refinement. In: Vedaldi, A., Bischof, H., Brox, T., Frahm, J.-M. (eds.) ECCV 2020. LNCS, vol. 12356, pp. 492–508. Springer, Cham (2020). https://doi.org/10.1007/978-3-030-58621-8_29
74. Wang, J., Xu, E., Xue, K., Kidzinski, L.: 3D pose detection in videos: focusing on occlusion. arXiv preprint arXiv:2006.13517 (2020)
75. Wehrbein, T., Rudolph, M., Rosenhahn, B., Wandt, B.: Probabilistic monocular 3D human pose estimation with normalizing flows. In: Proceedings of the IEEE/CVF International Conference on Computer Vision, pp. 11199–11208 (2021)
76. Xiao, B., Wu, H., Wei, Y.: Simple baselines for human pose estimation and tracking. In: Proceedings of the European conference on computer vision (ECCV), pp. 466–481 (2018)
77. Xu, J., Yu, Z., Ni, B., Yang, J., Yang, X., Zhang, W.: Deep kinematics analysis for monocular 3D human pose estimation. In: Proceedings of the IEEE/CVF Conference on Computer Vision and Pattern Recognition, pp. 899–908 (2020)
78. Xu, Y., Wang, W., Liu, T., Liu, X., Xie, J., Zhu, S.C.: Monocular 3D pose estimation via pose grammar and data augmentation. IEEE Trans. Pattern Anal. Mach. Intell. (2021)
79. Yang, W., Ouyang, W., Wang, X., Ren, J., Li, H., Wang, X.: 3D human pose estimation in the wild by adversarial learning. In: Proceedings of the IEEE Conference on Computer Vision and Pattern Recognition, pp. 5255–5264 (2018)
80. Zanfir, A., Marinoiu, E., Sminchisescu, C.: Monocular 3D pose and shape estimation of multiple people in natural scenes-the importance of multiple scene constraints. In: Proceedings of the IEEE Conference on Computer Vision and Pattern Recognition, pp. 2148–2157 (2018)
81. Zanfir, A., Marinoiu, E., Zanfir, M., Popa, A.I., Sminchisescu, C.: Deep network for the integrated 3D sensing of multiple people in natural images. Adv. Neural. Inf. Process. Syst. **31**, 8410–8419 (2018)
82. Zhang, F., Zhu, X., Dai, H., Ye, M., Zhu, C.: Distribution-aware coordinate representation for human pose estimation. In: Proceedings of the IEEE/CVF conference on computer vision and pattern recognition, pp. 7093–7102 (2020)
83. Zhang, T., Huang, B., Wang, Y.: Object-occluded human shape and pose estimation from a single color image. In: Proceedings of the IEEE/CVF Conference on Computer Vision and Pattern Recognition, pp. 7376–7385 (2020)
84. Zhen, J., et al.: SMAP: single-shot multi-person absolute 3D pose estimation. In: Vedaldi, A., Bischof, H., Brox, T., Frahm, J.-M. (eds.) ECCV 2020. LNCS, vol. 12360, pp. 550–566. Springer, Cham (2020). https://doi.org/10.1007/978-3-030-58555-6_33

85. Zhou, L., Chen, Y., Gao, Y., Wang, J., Lu, H.: Occlusion-aware siamese network for human pose estimation. In: Vedaldi, A., Bischof, H., Brox, T., Frahm, J.-M. (eds.) ECCV 2020. LNCS, vol. 12365, pp. 396–412. Springer, Cham (2020). https://doi.org/10.1007/978-3-030-58565-5_24
86. Zhou, X., Huang, Q., Sun, X., Xue, X., Wei, Y.: Towards 3D human pose estimation in the wild: a weakly-supervised approach. In: Proceedings of the IEEE International Conference on Computer Vision, pp. 398–407 (2017)
87. Zhou, X., Wang, D., Krähenbühl, P.: Objects as points. arXiv preprint arXiv:1904.07850 (2019)

COUCH: Towards Controllable Human-Chair Interactions

Xiaohan Zhang[1,2]($\boxtimes$), Bharat Lal Bhatnagar[1,2], Sebastian Starke[3,4], Vladimir Guzov[1,2], and Gerard Pons-Moll[1,2]

[1] University of Tübingen, Tübingen, Germany
{xiaohan.zhang,bharat.bhatnagar,vladimir.guzov,
gerard.pons-moll}@uni-tuebingen.de
[2] Max Planck Institute for Informatics, Saarland Informatics Campus, Saarbrücken, Germany
[3] Electronic Arts, Redwood City, USA
sstarke@ea.com
[4] University of Edinburgh, Edinburgh, UK

Abstract. Humans interact with an object in many different ways by making contact at different locations, creating a highly complex motion space that can be difficult to learn, particularly when synthesizing such human interactions in a controllable manner. Existing works on synthesizing human scene interaction focus on the high-level control of action but do not consider the fine-grained control of motion. In this work, we study the problem of synthesizing scene interactions conditioned on different contact positions on the object. As a testbed to investigate this new problem, we focus on human-chair interaction as one of the most common actions which exhibit large variability in terms of contacts. We propose a novel synthesis framework COUCH that plans ahead the motion by predicting contact-aware control signals of the hands, which are then used to synthesize contact-conditioned interactions. Furthermore, we contribute a large human-chair interaction dataset with clean annotations, the COUCH Dataset. Our method shows significant quantitative and qualitative improvements over existing methods for human-object interactions. More importantly, our method enables control of the motion through user-specified or automatically predicted contacts.

1 Introduction

To synthesize realistic virtual humans which can achieve goals and act upon the environment, reasoning about the interactions and in turn contacts, is necessary. Reaching a goal, like sitting on a chair, is often preceded by intentional contact with the hand to support the body. In this work, we investigate a motion synthesis method which exploits predictable contact to achieve more control and diversity over the animations.

Supplementary Information The online version contains supplementary material available at https://doi.org/10.1007/978-3-031-20065-6_30.

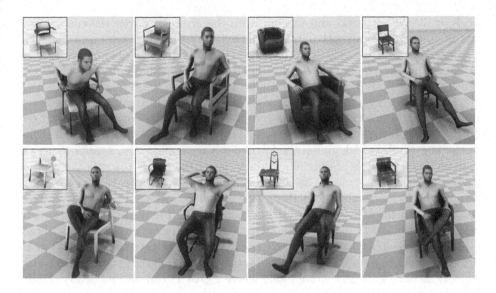

Fig. 1. We present COUCH. A dataset and model for synthesizing controllable, contact-driven human-chair interactions.

Although most applications in VR/AR [33,39], digital content creation and robotics require synthesizing motion *within the environment*, it is not considered in the majority of works in human motion synthesis [37,44,45,47]. Recent work does take the environment into account but is limited to synthesizing *static poses* [26,65]. Synthesizing dynamic human motion coherent with the environment is a substantially harder task [25,29,52–54] and recent works show promising results. However, these methods do not reason about intentional contacts with the environment, and can not be controlled with user provided contacts.

Thus, in this work, we investigate a new problem: synthesizing human motion conditioned on contact positions on the object to allow for controllable movement variations. As a testbed to investigate this new problem, we focus on human-chair interactions as one of the most common actions, which are of crucial importance for ergonomics, avatars in virtual reality or video game animation. Contact-driven motion synthesis is a more challenging learning problem compared to conditioning only on coarse object geometry [25,52]. First, the human needs to approach the chair differently depending on the contacts, regardless of the starting position, walking around it if necessary. Second, a chair can be approached and contacted in many different ways; we can directly sit without using our hands, or we can first support the body weight using the left/right or both hands with different parts of the chair, as illustrated in Fig. 1. Furthermore, different styled free-interactions can be modeled such as leaning back, stretching legs, using hands to support the head, and so on.

Contact-driven motion allows for providing more detailed instructions to the virtual human such as approaching to sit on the chair, while supporting the body with the left hand and placing it on the armrest. Given the contact and the goal, the full-body needs to coordinate at run-time to achieve a plausible sequence of pose transitions. Intuitively, this emulates our planning of motion as real humans: we plan in terms of goals and intermediate object contacts to reach; the full-body then moves to follow such desired trajectories.

To this end, we propose COUCH, a method for controllable contact-driven human-chair interactions, which is composed of two core components: 1) *ControlNet* is responsible for motion planning by predicting the future control signal of the body limbs which guides the future body movement. Our spatial-temporal control signal consists of dynamic trajectories of the hands towards the contact points and the local phase, an auxiliary continuous variable that encodes the temporal information of a limb during a particular movement (e.g. the left hand reaching an armrest). 2) *PoseNet* conditions on the predicted control signal to synthesize motion that follows the dynamic trajectories, ensuring the contact point is reached. At runtime, COUCH can operate in two modes. First, in an interactive mode where the user specifies the desired contact points on the target object. Second, in a generative mode where COUCH can automatically sample diverse intentional contacts on the object with a novel neural network called *ContactNet*. Training and evaluating COUCH calls for a dataset of rich and accurate human chair interactions. Existing interaction 3D datasets [52] are captured with Inertial Sensors, and hence do not capture the real body motion and the contacts with the real chair geometry – instead synthetic chairs are fit to the avatar as post-process in those works. Hence, to jointly capture real human-chair interactions with fine-grained contacts, we fit the SMPL model [42] and scanned chair models to data obtained from multiple Kinects and IMUs. The dataset (the COUCH dataset, Table 1) consists of 3 h (over 500 sequences) of motion capture (MoCap) on human-chair interactions. Moreover it features multiple subjects, accurately captured contacts with registered chairs, and annotation on the type of hand contact. Our experiments demonstrate that COUCH runs in real-time at 30 fps, COUCH generalizes across chairs of varied geometry, and different starting positions relative to the chair. Compared to SoTA models (trained on the same data) adapted to incorporate contacts, our method significantly outperforms them in terms of control by improving the average contact distance by 55%.

The contributions of our work can be summarized as follows:

- We propose COUCH, the first method for synthesizing controllable contact-based human-chair interactions. Given the same input control, COUCH can achieve diverse sitting motions. By specifying different control signals, the user enables control over the style of interaction with the object. Results show our method outperforms the state of the art both qualitatively and quantitatively.
- To train COUCH, we captured a large-scale MoCap dataset consisting of 3 h (over 500 sequences) of human interacting with chairs in different styles of sitting and free movements. The dataset features multiple subject, real chair geometry, accurately annotated hand contacts, and RGB-D images.

- To stimulate further research in controllable synthesis of human motion, we release the COUCH model and dataset [1].

2 Related Work

Scene Agnostic Human Motion Prediction. Synthesizing realistic human motion has drawn much attention from the computer vision and graphics communities. However, many methods do not take the scene into account. Existing methods on short ($\sim$1 s) [5,17,21,27,45,47,57,60,62] and long (>1 min) [19,31] term 3D human motion prediction aim to produce realistic-looking human motion (typically walking and its variants). There also exists work on conditional motion generation based on music [37]. These methods have two major limitations, i) except for work that use generative models [6,20,24,28,41], these methods are largely deterministic and cannot be used to generate diverse motions and ii) this body of work is unfortunately agnostic to scene geometry [36,44], which is critical to model human scene interactions. Our method on the other hand can generate *realistic motion and interactions*, taking into account the 3D scene.

Affordance and Static Scene Interactions. Although the focus of our work is to model human-scene interactions over time, we find the works predicting static affordances in a 3D scene [38] relevant. This branch of work aims at predicting and reconstructing static humans in a scene [26,59,61,64,65] that satisfies the scene constraints. More recently there have been attempts to model fine-grained interactions (contacts) between the hand and objects [10,16,35,55,56,66].

The aforementioned methods focus on predicting static humans/human poses that satisfy the scene constraints in case of affordances or grasping an object in case of hand-object interactions. But these methods cannot produce a full sequence of human motion and interaction with the scene. Ours is the first approach that can model fine-grained interactions (contacts) between an object in the scene and the human.

Dynamic Scene Interactions. Although various algorithms have been proposed for scene-agnostic motion prediction, affordance prediction as well as the synthesis of static human-scene interaction, capturing [22,23,46], let alone generating dynamic human-scene interactions is less explored. Recent advances include predicting human motion from scene images [11], and using a semantic graph and RNN to predict human and object movements [15]. More recently, Wang et al. [58] introduce a hierarchical framework that generates 'in-between' locations and poses on the scene and interpolates between the goal poses. However, it requires a carefully tuned post-optimization step over the full motion synthesis to solve the discontinuity of motion between sub-goals and to achieve robust foot contacts with the scene. Alternatively, Chao et al. [14] use a reinforcement learning based approach by training a meta controller to coordinate

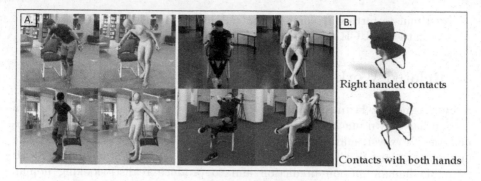

Fig. 2. (A) The COUCH dataset captures a diverse range of chair interaction with an emphasis on hand contacts. It consists of RGB-D images, corresponding MoCap in the SMPL [42] format, chair geometry and annotations on types of hand interaction. (B) COUCH dataset captures natural modes of interactions with a chair, as demonstrated by the heatmaps of contact clusters. Most common contacts while sitting, include right hand support or both hands.

sub-controllers to complete a sitting task. An important category of human-scene interaction involves performing locomotion on uneven terrains. The Phase-functioned Neural Network [30] first introduced the use of external phase variables to represent the state of the motion cycle. Zhang et al. [63] applies same concept for quadruped motion and further incorporates a gating network that segments the locomotion modes based on foot velocities. Both works show impressive results thanks to the mixture of experts [18] styled architectures.

The most relevant work to us, are the Neural State Machine (NSM) [52] and SAMP [25]. While NSM is a powerful method and models human-scene interactions such as sitting, carrying boxes and opening doors, it does not generate motion variations for the same task and object geometry. SAMP predicts diverse goal locations in the scene for the virtual human, which is then used to drive the motion generation. Our work takes inspiration from these works, but it is demonstrated qualitatively and quantitatively from our experiments that neither of the work enables control over the style of interaction (Sect. 5.2). Our work focus on controllable, fine-grained interactions given on contacts on the object. To the best of our knowledge, no previous work has tackled the problem of generating controllable human-chair interactions.

3   The COUCH Dataset

Large scale datasets of human motion such as AMASS [43] and H3.6m [32] have been instrumental to build models of human motion. Unfortunately, these datasets only contain sequences of 3D poses but no information about the 3D environment, making these datasets unsuitable for learning human interactions. On the other hand, datasets containing human-object interactions are either

Table 1. Comparison with existing motion capture datasets for human chair interactions. The COUCH dataset features registered real chairs models, multiple subject, and RGB-D data. The types of hand contact are also annotated.

Features	NSM [52]	SAMP [25]	Ours
Real Objects	✗	✓	✓
Multiple Subjects	✗	✗	✓
Contact Types	✗	✗	✓
RGB-D	✗	✗	✓

restricted to just grasping [10,56], contain only static human poses [26] without any motion, or have little variation in motion [52].

We present a multi-subject dataset of human chair interactions (see Fig. 2). Our dataset consists of 6 different subjects interacting with chairs with over 500 motion sequences. We collect our dataset using 17 wearable Inertial Measurement Units (XSens) [4], from which we obtain high-quality pose sequences in SMPL [42] format using Unity [34]. The total capture length is 3 h.

Motion capture with marker-based capture systems is restrictive to capturing human-object interactions because markers often get occluded during the interactions leading to inaccurate tracking. IMU-based systems are prevalent for large-scale motion capture, however, the error from its calibration can lower the accuracy of the motion. We propose to combine IMUs with Kinect-based capture system as an efficient trade-off between scalability and accuracy. Our capture system is lightweight and can be generalized to capture many human scene interactions. We use the SMPL registration method similar to [7–9,50] to obtain SMPL fits for our data. The dataset is captured in four different indoor scenes. The average fitting error for the SMPL human model, and the chair scans to the point clouds from the Kinects are 3.12 cm and 1.70 cm, respectively (in Chamfer distance). More details about data capture can be found in supp. mat.

Diversity on Starting Points and Styles. We capture people approaching the chairs from different starting points surrounding the chairs. Each subject then performs different styles of interactions with the chairs during sitting. This includes, one hand touching the arm of the chair, both hands touching the armrests of the chair, one hand touching the sitting plane of the chair before sitting down, and no hand contacts. It also includes free interactions such as crossing legs or leaning forward and backward on the chairs. To ensure the naturalness of motion, each subject is only provided with high-level instruction before capturing each sequence and was asked to perform their styles freely. Annotations of the direction of the starting points relative to the chair as well as the type of hand contact are included in the dataset.

Objects. Our dataset contains three different chair models that vary in terms of their shapes, as well as a sofa. The objects are 3D scanned [2,3] before registering into the Kinect captured point clouds. To generalize the synthesized motion to unseen objects, we perform data augmentation as in [52].

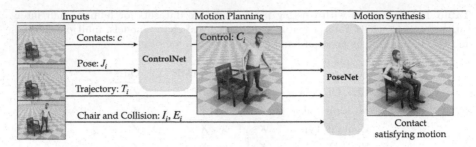

Fig. 3. Given user specified or model generated contacts, our method which consists of the ControlNet and the PoseNet, auto-regressively synthesizes contact satisfying motion.

Contacts. Studying contact-conditioned interaction calls for accurate contacts to be annotated in the dataset. Since we capture both the body motion and the object pose, it is possible to capture contacts between the body and the object. We detect the contacts of five key joints of the virtual human skeleton, which are the pelvis, hands, and feet. We then augment our data by randomly switching or scaling the object at each frame. The data augmentation is performed on 30 instances from ShapeNet [13] over categories of straight chairs, chairs with arms, and sofas. At every frame, we project the contacts detected from the ground truth data to the new object, and apply full-body inverse kinematics to recompute the pose such that the contacts are consistent, keeping the original context of the motion.

4   Method

We address the problem of synthesizing 3D human motion that is natural and satisfies environmental geometry constraints and user-defined contacts with the chair. COUCH allows fine-grained control over how the human interacts with the chair. At run-time, our model operates in two modes. First, a generative mode where COUCH can automatically sample diverse intentional contacts on the object with our proposed generative model. Second, an interactive mode where the user specifies the desired contact points on the target object.

As illustrated in Fig. 3, the input to our method is the current character pose, the target chair geometry as well the target contacts for the hands that need to be met. Our method takes these inputs and predicts the future poses that satisfy the desired contacts auto-regressively.

4.1   Key Insights

While prior work generates human motion based on a single specified goal location [25,30,52], our model is driven by a set of user-specified or predicted body contacts on the object. This significantly more challenging task allows fine-grained control. Our model is motivated by the way humans execute complex interactions e.g., to sit on the chair, we first prepare a mental model (planning) of how we will sit (place a hand on the arm-rest and sit, place a hand on the sitting plane and sit or just sit without using the hands etc.) and then we move our bodies accordingly. Hence, we propose two neural networks *ControlNet* $f^{\mathrm{CN}}(\cdot)$, and *PoseNet* $f^{\mathrm{PN}}(\cdot)$, for *motion planning* and *motion prediction* respectively.

Furthermore, we observe that it is only useful to perform detailed hand motion planning only when we are close to the chair right before sitting. Thus, we decompose the motion synthesis into *approaching* and *sitting*. The *approaching* motion can be generated directly with *PoseNet*, but both networks *ControlNet* and *PoseNet*, are required for generating the *sitting* motion that satisfies the given contacts.

4.2   Motion Planning with ControlNet

ControlNet is the core of our method and plays an important role in motion planning, that is predicting the future control signals of the key joints which are used to guide the body motions. At a high level, the contact-aware control signal contains the local phases and the future locations of the key joints (in our case, the two hands). The local phase is an auxiliary variable that encodes the temporal alignment of motion for each of the hands and prepares for a future contact to be made. When the virtual human is ready to make contact with the chair, and at the beginning of the hand movement, the local phase is equal to 0, and it gradually reaches the value 1 as the hand comes closer to the contact. The hand trajectory, on the other hand, encodes the spatial relationship between the hand joint and the given contact location.

More formally, we define our spatial-temporal control signal at frame $i+1$ to be $\mathbf{C}_{i+1}^{+} = \{\mathbf{h}_{i+1}^{+}, \phi_{i+1}^{+}\}$, where $\mathbf{h}_{i+1}^{+} \in \mathbb{R}^{2 \times 3 \times \mathcal{T}^{+}}$ represents the future position of the two hand joints relative to their corresponding desired contact point $c \in \mathbb{R}^{2 \times 3}$, and their local phases are represented by $\phi_{i}^{+} \in \mathbb{R}^{2 \times \mathcal{T}^{+}}$. We predict the control signal for $\mathcal{T}^{+} = 7$ time stamps sampled uniformly between $[0, 1]$ second window centered at frame $i + 1$.

We use an LSTM based $f^{\mathrm{CN}}(\cdot)$ to predict the control signal,

$$\mathbf{C}_{i+1}^{+} = f^{\mathrm{CN}}(\tilde{\mathbf{h}}_i, \phi_i), \tag{1}$$

where $\tilde{\mathbf{h}}_i \in \mathbb{R}^{2 \times 3 \times \mathcal{T}^{+}}$ denote $\mathcal{T}^{+}$ points interpolated uniformly on the straight line from the current hand locations to their desired contact locations c. Intuitively, these interpolated positions encourages the ControlNet to predict future hand trajectories that always reach the given contacts. $\phi_i \in \mathbb{R}^{2 \times \mathcal{T}}$ denotes the local phases of the hands over $\mathcal{T} = 13$ frames sampled uniformly between the $[-1, 1]$ second window centered at frame i.

The ControlNet is trained to minimize the following MSE loss on the future hand trajectories and the local phase, which is formulated as follows:

$$L_{\mathrm{control}} = \lambda_1 \|\mathbf{h}_{i+1}^{+} - \hat{\mathbf{h}}_{i+1}^{+}\|_2^2 + \lambda_2 \|\phi_{i+1}^{+} - \hat{\phi}_{i+1}^{+}\|_2^2 + \lambda_3 L_{\mathrm{reg}}. \tag{2}$$

Here, $\mathbf{h}_{i+1}^+, \phi_{i+1}^+$ are the network predicted future trajectories and local phases. $\hat{\mathbf{h}}_{i+1}^+, \hat{\phi}_{i+1}^+$ are the corresponding GT. We also introduce an additional regularization term $L_{\text{reg}} = \|\mathbf{h}_{i+1}^+ - \tilde{\mathbf{h}}_i\|_2$. Please see supplementary for implementation details regarding the network architectures and training.

4.3   Motion Synthesis with PoseNet

ControlNet generates important signals that guide the motion of the person such that user-defined contacts are satisfied. To this end, we train PoseNet $f^{\text{PN}}(\cdot)$, that takes as input the control signals predicted by the ControlNet along with the 3D scene and motion in the past and predicts full body motion.

$$\mathbf{J}_{i+1}, \mathbf{T}_{i+1}^+, \mathbf{G}_{i+1}^+, \mathbf{\Phi}_{i+1}, \tilde{\boldsymbol{j}}_{i+1}^p, \tilde{\mathbf{T}}_{i+1}, \boldsymbol{b}_{i+1} = f^{\text{PN}}(\mathbf{C}_i^+, \mathbf{J}_i, \mathbf{T}_i, \mathbf{G}_i, \mathbf{I}_i, \mathbf{E}_i, \mathbf{\Phi}_i), \quad (3)$$

where $\mathbf{C}_i^+$ is the control signal generated by the *ControlNet*. We represent the current state of motion for the human model: $\mathbf{J}_i = (\boldsymbol{j}_i^p, \boldsymbol{j}_i^v, \boldsymbol{j}_i^r)$ contains root relative position $\boldsymbol{j}_i^p \in R^{j\times3}$, rotation $\boldsymbol{j}_i^v \in R^{j\times6}$ and velocity $\boldsymbol{j}_i^r \in R^{j\times3}$ of each joint at frame i. We use $j = 22$ joints for our human model. $\mathbf{T}_i = (\boldsymbol{t}_i^p, \boldsymbol{t}_i^d, \boldsymbol{t}_i^a)$ contains the root positions $\boldsymbol{t}_i^p \in R^{\mathcal{T}\times3}$ and rotation $\boldsymbol{t}_i^d \in R^{\mathcal{T}\times6}$ for $\tau = 13$ frames sampled uniformly between the [-1, 1] second window centered at frame i. $\boldsymbol{t}_i^a \in R^{\mathcal{T}\times3}$ are the soft labels which describe current action over ours three action classes, namely, idle, walk, and sit. Inspired by Starke et al., [52], we also use intermediate goals $\mathbf{G}_i = (\boldsymbol{g}_i^p, \boldsymbol{g}_i^d, \boldsymbol{g}_i^a)$, where $\boldsymbol{g}_i^p \in R^{\mathcal{T}\times3}$, $\boldsymbol{g}_i^d \in R^{\mathcal{T}\times6}$ are the goal positions and orientations at frame i. $\boldsymbol{g}_i^a \in R^{\mathcal{T}\times3}$ are the one-hot labels describing the intended goal action.

To accurately capture the spatial relation between the person and the chair, we voxelize the chair into an $8 \times 8 \times 8$ grid and store at each voxel its occupancy ($\mathbb{R}$) and the relative vector between the root joint of the person and the voxel ($\mathbb{R}^3$). This allows us to reason about the distance between the person and different parts of the chair. We flatten this grid to obtain our chair encoding $\mathbf{I}_i \in \mathbb{R}^{2048}$ at time-step i.

In order to explicitly reason about the collisions of the person with the chair, we voxelize the region around the person into a cylindrical ego-centric grid and store the occupancies corresponding to the chair (if it is inside the grid). We flatten the occupancy feature to obtain $\mathbf{E}_i \in \mathbb{R}^{1408}$. It is important to note that although $\mathbf{I}_i$ and $\mathbf{E}_i$ are scene encodings, they serve different purposes. $\mathbf{I}_i$ is chair-centric and entails information about how far is the person from the chair and the geometry of the chair, while $\mathbf{E}_i$ is ego-centric and detects collisions in the surrounding of the human model. In addition, we also introduce an auxiliary variable $\mathbf{\Phi} \in [0, 1]$ as in [30,47], which encodes the global phase of the motion. When approaching the goal, the represents the timing within a walking cycle, for sitting the phase equals 0 when the person is still standing and reaches 1 when the person has sat.

The components of the output of the network differs from the input to a small extend by additionally predicting $\tilde{\boldsymbol{j}}_{i+1}^p$ are the joint positions relative to future root 1 s ahead. To ensure the human model can reach the chair, we introduce the goal-relative root trajectory $\tilde{\mathbf{T}}_{i+1} = \{\tilde{t}^p_{i+1}, \tilde{t}^d_{i+1}\}$ which include the root positions and forward directions relative to the chair of frame $i + 1$. The rest of the components remain consistent with the input include the the the future pose $\mathbf{J}_{i+1}$, future root trajectory $\mathbf{T}^+_{i+1}$, the future intermediate goals $\mathbf{G}^+_{i+1}$, and the future global phase $\mathbf{\Phi}_{i+1}$. The PoseNet $f^{\mathrm{PN}}(\cdot)$ adopts a mixture-of-experts [25, 30,52,53] and is trained to minimize the standard MSE loss.

4.4   Contact Generation with ContactNet

From the user's perspective, it is useful to automatically generate plausible contact points on any given chairs. To this reason, we propose *ContactNet*. The network adopts a conditional variational auto-encoder [51] architecture (cVAE) which encodes the chair geometry $\mathbf{I}$ introduced in Sect. 4.3 and the contact positions $\mathbf{c} \in R^{2\times3}$ to a latent vector $\mathbf{z}$. The decoder of the network then reconstructs the hand contacts $\hat{\mathbf{c}} \in R^{2\times3}$. Note, the position of each voxel in the scene representation $\mathbf{I}$ in this case is computed relative to the center of the chair instead of the character's root. During training, the network is trained to minimize the following loss,

$$L_{\mathrm{contact}} = \|\hat{\mathbf{c}} - \mathbf{c}\|^2_2 + \beta KL(q(\mathbf{z}|\mathbf{c},\mathbf{I})\|p(\mathbf{z})), \tag{4}$$

where KL denotes the Kullback-Leibler divergence. During inference, given the scene representation $\mathbf{I}$ of a novel chair, we sample the latent vector $\mathbf{z}$ from the uniform Gaussian distribution $\mathbf{N}(0, I)$, and use the decoder to generate plausible hand contacts $\mathbf{c} \in \mathbb{R}^{2\times3}$.

4.5   Decomposition of *Approaching* and *Sitting* Motion

Detailed hand motion planning is only required when the human model is close enough to the chair right before sitting as sitting requires synthesizing more precise full-body motion, especially for the hands, such that the person makes the desired contacts and sits on the chair. For this reason, we decompose our synthesis into approaching and sitting by only activating the ControlNet during the sitting. When the ControlNet is deactivated the control signal or when a "no contact" signal is present the control signal for the corresponding hand is zeroed.

5   Evaluation

Studying contact-conditioned interaction with chairs requires accurately labelled contacts and a diverse range of styled interactions. The COUCH dataset is captured to meet such needs. We evaluate our contact constrained motion synthesis method on the COUCH dataset qualitatively and quantitatively. Our method is the first approach that allows the user to explicitly define how the person should contact the chair and we generate natural and diverse motions satisfying these contacts. As such we evaluate our method on three axis, (i) accuracy in reaching the contacts, (ii) diversity and (iii) naturalness of the synthesized motion. For qualitative results, we highly encourage the readers to see our supplementary video. It can be seen that our method can generate diverse and natural motions while reaching the user-specified contacts. We quantitatively evaluate the accuracy of contacts and motion diversity on a total of 120 testing sequences on six subject-specific models trained on corresponding subsets of our COUCH dataset. Note that we evaluate raw synthesized motion without post-processing.

5.1 Baselines

To our best knowledge, the most related work to ours are the Neural State Machine (NSM) [52] and the SAMP [25] since they both synthesize human-scene interactions. However, neither of the methods allows the use of fine-grained control over how the interaction should take place. We adapt these baselines for our task by additionally conditioning on the contact positions and refer to these new baselines as NSM+Control and SAMP+Control. Quantitative results are reported for both the original baselines and their adapted version. For each of the methods, we train subject-specific models with the corresponding subset of our COUCH dataset using the code provided by the authors. Our experiments, detailed below, show that naively providing contacts as input to existing motion synthesis approaches does not ensure that the generated motion satisfies the contacts. Our method, on the other hand, does not suffer from this limitation.

5.2 Evaluation on Control

In order to evaluate how well our synthesized motion meets the given contacts, we report the *average contact error (ACE)* as the mean squared error between the predicted hand contact and the corresponding given contact. We use the closest position of the predicted hand motion to the given contact as our hand contact. Since ACE might be susceptible to outliers and inspired by the literature on object detection [12,40,48,49], we also report *average contact precision* (AP@k), where we consider a contact as correctly predicted if it is closer than k cm.

We compare our method with NSM+Control and SAMP+Control in Table 2. It can be observed that COUCH outperforms prior methods by a significant margin. Prior methods are trained to condition on the contact positions, however it is shown (Fig. 4) that they over-fit to the training contacts and cannot reason correctly about the given contacts during auto-regresssion. As a result the constraints are often not met. This highlights the importance of motion planning in form of trajectory predictors in order to reach the desired contacts. Our ControlNet provides valuable information on how to synthesize motion such that the given contacts are satisfied. Our motion prediction network PoseNet uses these control signals to generate contact constrained motions.

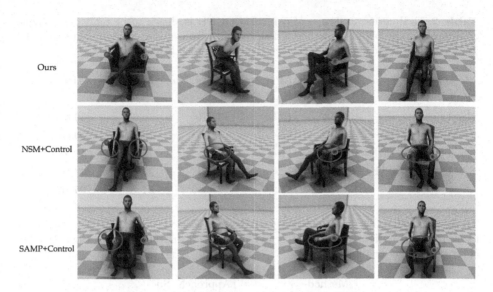

Fig. 4. We demonstrate qualitatively and quantitatively (Table 2) that motion generated by our approach satisfies the contacts much better than the baselines, NSM+Control [52] and SAMP+Control [25].

5.3   Evaluation on Motion Diversity

Diversity is an essential element for our motion synthesis, since a chair can be approached and interacted with in different ways. To quantify diversity, we evaluate using the Average Pairwise Distance (APD) [25,62,65] on the synthesized pose features of the virtual human $\mathbf{J}_i = (\boldsymbol{j}_i^p, \boldsymbol{j}_i^v, \boldsymbol{j}_i^r)$. defined as:

$$APD = \frac{1}{N(N-1)} \sum_{i=1}^{N} \sum_{j \neq i}^{N} D(\mathbf{J}_i', \mathbf{J}_j'), \tag{5}$$

where N is the total number of frames in all the testing sequences. Note that for evaluation, the virtual human is initialized at different starting points and is instructed to approach and sit on randomly selected chairs with randomly sampled contact points from the dataset, and motion is synthesized for 16 s for each sequence. We compare the diversity of synthesized motion in Table 3 and it can be seen that using explicit contacts allows our method to generate more varied motion.

5.4   Contact Prediction on Novel Shapes

Apart from user-specified contacts, we can additionally generate the contacts on the surface of a given chair using our proposed ContactNet. This allows us to generate fully automatic and diverse motions for sitting. To measure the diversity of the generated contacts from ContactNet, we compute the Average Pairwise

Table 2. Evaluation on degree of control. COUCH is shown to be more controllable compared to the baseline methods. The distance from given contact points and the joint position are measured. The success rate of control is also reported.

Method	Distance to Contact$^\downarrow$	AP@ 3 cm$^\uparrow$	AP@ 5 cm$^\uparrow$	AP@ 7 cm$^\uparrow$	AP@ 9 cm$^\uparrow$
NSM [52]	10.69	15.52	38.20	46.05	56.61
SAMP [25]	11.96	6.54	14.57	20.94	50.83
NSM+Control [52]	10.52	17.46	35.7	48.4	57.93
SAMP+Control [25]	12.09	7.20	15.2	23.2	48.80
Ours	**4.73**	**47.97**	**78.86**	**87.8**	**91.87**

Table 3. Evaluation on the diversity of the synthesized motion. APD is measured for segmented motion of approaching and sitting. Our approach attains the best score compared to the baselines.

Method	Approach	Sit
NSM [52]	5.15	5.76
SAMP [25]	5.34	5.81
NSM+Control [52]	5.07	5.80
SAMP+Control [25]	5.21	5.88
Ours	**5.55**	**6.02**
Ground Truth	5.69	6.30

Fig. 5. *ContactNet* enables sampling of diverse contact positions across various chair shapes. These contacts can be used by our ControlNet and PoseNet to generate fully automatic and diverse motions.

Distance (APD) among the generated hand contact positions c_j with unseen chair shapes. A total number of 200 unseen chairs are chosen, and for each chair 10 contact positions are predicted for both hands.

$$APD = \frac{1}{2LN(N-1)} \sum_{k=1}^{2} \sum_{l=1}^{L} \sum_{i=1}^{N} \sum_{j \neq i}^{N} \|X_i' - X_j'\|_2^2 \qquad (6)$$

$L = 200$ is the number of objects and $N = 10$ is the number of contacts generated per object. The APD on contact positions is **11.82** cm which is comparable to the ground truth dataset which has an APD of **14.07** cm. As shown qualitatively in Fig. 5, we can generate diverse and plausible contact positions on chairs, which can generalize to unseen shapes. The average minimal distance between predicted and ground truth contacts is **4.31** cm. This low value indicates our generated samples are plausible are well-aligned with the ground truth contacts.

6   Conclusion

We propose COUCH, the first method for synthesizing controllable contact-driven human-chair interactions. Given initial conditions and the contacts on the chair, our model plans the trajectory of the hands, which drives the full body motion to satisfy contacts. In addition to the model, we introduce the COUCH dataset for human chair interactions which includes a wide variety of sitting motions that approach and contact the chairs in different ways. It consists of 3 h of motion capture with 6 subjects interacting with registered 3D chair models, captured in high quality with IMUs and Kinects. Experiments demonstrate that our method consistently outperforms the SoTA by improving the average contact accuracy by ∼55% to better satisfy contact constraints. In addition to better control, it can be seen in the supplementary video that our approach generates more natural motion compared to the baseline methods. In the future, we want to extend our dataset to new activities and train a multi-activity contact-driven model. In the supplementary, we discuss further future directions in this new problem of fine-grained controlled motion synthesis. Our dataset and code will be released to foster further work in this new research direction [1].

Acknowledgement. This work was supported by the German Federal Ministry of Education and Research (BMBF): Tübingen AI Center, FKZ: 01IS18039A. This work is funded by the Deutsche Forschungsgemeinschaft (DFG, German Research Foundation) - 409792180 (Emmy Noether Programme, project: Real Virtual Humans). Gerard Pons-Moll is a member of the Machine Learning Cluster of Excellence, funded by the Deutsche Forschungsgemeinschaft (DFG, German Research Foundation) under Germany's Excellence Strategy - EXC number 2064/1 - Project number 390727645. We would like to thank Xianghui Xie for assisting the data processing, and we are grateful for all the participants involved in the data capture.

References

1. http://virtualhumans.mpi-inf.mpg.de/couch/
2. https://www.treedys.com/

3. Agisoft metashape. https://www.agisoft.com/
4. Xsens MVN: full 6DOF human motion tracking using miniature inertial sensors. https://www.xsens.com/. Accessed 30 Sep 2010
5. Aksan, E., Kaufmann, M., Hilliges, O.: Structured prediction helps 3D human motion modelling. In: Proceedings of the IEEE/CVF International Conference on Computer Vision (ICCV) (2019)
6. Aliakbarian, S., Saleh, F.S., Salzmann, M., Petersson, L., Gould, S.: A stochastic conditioning scheme for diverse human motion prediction. In: Proceedings of the IEEE/CVF Conference on Computer Vision and Pattern Recognition (CVPR) (2020)
7. Alldieck, T., Magnor, M., Bhatnagar, B.L., Theobalt, C., Pons-Moll, G.: Learning to reconstruct people in clothing from a single RGB camera. In: IEEE Conference on Computer Vision and Pattern Recognition (CVPR) (2019)
8. Bhatnagar, B.L., Sminchisescu, C., Theobalt, C., Pons-Moll, G.: Combining implicit function learning and parametric models for 3D human reconstruction. In: Vedaldi, A., Bischof, H., Brox, T., Frahm, J.-M. (eds.) ECCV 2020. LNCS, vol. 12347, pp. 311–329. Springer, Cham (2020). https://doi.org/10.1007/978-3-030-58536-5_19
9. Bhatnagar, B.L., Xie, X., Petrov, I.A., Sminchisescu, C., Theobalt, C., Pons-Moll, G.: Behave: dataset and method for tracking human object interactions. In: Proceedings of the IEEE/CVF Conference on Computer Vision and Pattern Recognition (2022)
10. Brahmbhatt, S., Ham, C., Kemp, C.C., Hays, J.: ContactDB: analyzing and predicting grasp contact via thermal imaging, cVPR (2019)
11. Cao, Z., Gao, H., Mangalam, K., Cai, Q.-Z., Vo, M., Malik, J.: Long-term human motion prediction with scene context. In: Vedaldi, A., Bischof, H., Brox, T., Frahm, J.-M. (eds.) ECCV 2020. LNCS, vol. 12346, pp. 387–404. Springer, Cham (2020). https://doi.org/10.1007/978-3-030-58452-8_23
12. Carion, N., Massa, F., Synnaeve, G., Usunier, N., Kirillov, A., Zagoruyko, S.: End-to-end object detection with transformers. In: Vedaldi, A., Bischof, H., Brox, T., Frahm, J.-M. (eds.) ECCV 2020. LNCS, vol. 12346, pp. 213–229. Springer, Cham (2020). https://doi.org/10.1007/978-3-030-58452-8_13
13. Chang, A.X., et al.: Shapenet: an information-rich 3D model repository. CoRR abs/1512.03012 (2015)
14. Chao, Y., Yang, J., Chen, W., Deng, J.: Learning to sit: synthesizing human-chair interactions via hierarchical control. CoRR abs/1908.07423 (2019)
15. Corona, E., Pumarola, A., Alenyà, G., Moreno-Noguer, F.: Context-aware human motion prediction. CoRR abs/1904.03419 (2019)
16. Corona, E., Pumarola, A., Alenya, G., Moreno-Noguer, F., Rogez, G.: Ganhand: predicting human grasp affordances in multi-object scenes. In: Proceedings of the IEEE/CVF Conference on Computer Vision and Pattern Recognition (CVPR) (2020)
17. Cui, Q., Sun, H., Yang, F.: Learning dynamic relationships for 3D human motion prediction. In: Proceedings of the IEEE/CVF Conference on Computer Vision and Pattern Recognition (CVPR) (2020)
18. Eigen, D., Ranzato, M., Sutskever, I.: Learning factored representations in a deep mixture of experts. In: Bengio, Y., LeCun, Y. (eds.) 2nd International Conference on Learning Representations, ICLR 2014, Banff, AB, Canada, 14–16 April 2014, Workshop Track Proceedings (2014)
19. Ghosh, P., Song, J., Aksan, E., Hilliges, O.: Learning human motion models for long-term predictions. In: s International Conference on 3D Vision 3DV (2017)

20. Gui, L.-Y., Wang, Y.-X., Liang, X., Moura, J.M.F.: Adversarial geometry-aware human motion prediction. In: Ferrari, V., Hebert, M., Sminchisescu, C., Weiss, Y. (eds.) ECCV 2018. LNCS, vol. 11208, pp. 823–842. Springer, Cham (2018). https://doi.org/10.1007/978-3-030-01225-0_48
21. Gui, L.-Y., Wang, Y.-X., Ramanan, D., Moura, J.M.F.: Few-shot human motion prediction via meta-learning. In: Ferrari, V., Hebert, M., Sminchisescu, C., Weiss, Y. (eds.) ECCV 2018. LNCS, vol. 11212, pp. 441–459. Springer, Cham (2018). https://doi.org/10.1007/978-3-030-01237-3_27
22. Guzov, V., Mir, A., Sattler, T., Pons-Moll, G.: Human poseitioning system (HPS): 3D human pose estimation and self-localization in large scenes from body-mounted sensors. In: IEEE Conference on Computer Vision and Pattern Recognition (CVPR). IEEE (2021)
23. Guzov, V., Sattler, T., Pons-Moll, G.: Visually plausible human-object interaction capture from wearable sensors. arXiv (2022)
24. Habibie, I., Holden, D., Schwarz, J., Yearsley, J., Komura, T.: A recurrent variational autoencoder for human motion synthesis. In: Proceedings of the British Machine Vision Conference (BMVC), pp. 119.1-119.12. BMVA Press (2017)
25. Hassan, M., et al.: Stochastic scene-aware motion prediction. In: Proceedings of the International Conference on Computer Vision 2021 (2021)
26. Hassan, M., Choutas, V., Tzionas, D., Black, M.J.: Resolving 3D human pose ambiguities with 3D scene constraints. In: International Conference on Computer Vision, pp. 2282–2292 (2019)
27. Henter, G.E., Alexanderson, S., Beskow, J.: Moglow: probabilistic and controllable motion synthesis using normalising flows. ACM Trans. Graph. **39**(6), 236:1-236:14 (2020)
28. Hernandez, A., Gall, J., Moreno-Noguer, F.: Human motion prediction via spatio-temporal inpainting. In: Proceedings of the IEEE/CVF International Conference on Computer Vision (ICCV) (2019)
29. Holden, D., Kanoun, O., Perepichka, M., Popa, T.: Learned motion matching. ACM Trans. Graph. **39**(4), 53 (2020)
30. Holden, D., Komura, T., Saito, J.: Phase-functioned neural networks for character control. ACM Trans. Graph. **36**(4), 42:1-42:13 (2017)
31. Holden, D., Saito, J., Komura, T.: A deep learning framework for character motion synthesis and editing. ACM Trans. Graph. **35**(4), 1–11 (2016)
32. Ionescu, C., Papava, D., Olaru, V., Sminchisescu, C.: Human3.6m: large scale datasets and predictive methods for 3D human sensing in natural environments. IEEE Trans. Pattern Anal. Mach. Intell. **36**(7), 1325–1339 (2014)
33. Jiang, J., Streli, P., Fender, A., Qiu, H., Laich, L., Snape, P., Holz, C.: Avatarposer: Articulated full-body pose tracking from sparse motion sensing. In: European Conference on Computer Vision (ECCV) (2022)
34. Juliani, A., et al.: Unity: a general platform for intelligent agents. CoRR abs/1809.02627 (2018)
35. Karunratanakul, K., Yang, J., Zhang, Y., Black, M., Muandet, K., Tang, S.: Grasping field: learning implicit representations for human grasps. In: International Conference on 3D Vision (3DV) (2020)
36. Li, M., Chen, S., Zhao, Y., Zhang, Y., Wang, Y., Tian, Q.: dynamic multiscale graph neural networks for 3D skeleton based human motion prediction. In: Proceedings of the IEEE/CVF Conference on Computer Vision and Pattern Recognition (CVPR) (2020)
37. Li, R., Yang, S., Ross, D.A., Kanazawa, A.: Ai choreographer: music conditioned 3D dance generation with aist++ (2021)

38. Li, X., Liu, S., Kim, K., Wang, X., Yang, M.H., Kautz, J.: Putting humans in a scene: learning affordance in 3D indoor environments. In: Proceedings of the IEEE/CVF Conference on Computer Vision and Pattern Recognition (CVPR) (2019)

39. Liao, Z., Yang, J., Saito, J., Pons-Moll, G., Zhou, Y.: Skeleton-free pose transfer for stylized 3D characters. In: European Conference on Computer Vision (ECCV). Springer (2022)

40. Lin, T.Y., Dollár, P., Girshick, R.B., He, K., Hariharan, B., Belongie, S.J.: Feature pyramid networks for object detection. In: CVPR. IEEE Computer Society (2017)

41. Ling, H.Y., Zinno, F., Cheng, G., van de Panne, M.: Character controllers using motion vaes. ACM Trans. Graph. **39**(4) (2020)

42. Loper, M., Mahmood, N., Romero, J., Pons-Moll, G., Black, M.J.: SMPL: a skinned multi-person linear model. ACM Trans. Graph. (Proc. SIGGRAPH Asia) **34**(6), 2481–24816 (2015)

43. Mahmood, N., Ghorbani, N., Troje, N.F., Pons-Moll, G., Black, M.J.: AMASS: archive of motion capture as surface shapes. In: 2019 IEEE/CVF International Conference on Computer Vision, ICCV 2019, Seoul, Korea (South), 27 October – 2 November, 2019

44. Mao, W., Liu, M., Salzmann, M., Li, H.: Learning trajectory dependencies for human motion prediction. In: Proceedings of the IEEE/CVF International Conference on Computer Vision (ICCV) (2019)

45. Martinez, J., Black, M.J., Romero, J.: On human motion prediction using recurrent neural networks. In: 2017 IEEE Conference on Computer Vision and Pattern Recognition, CVPR 2017, Honolulu, HI, USA, 21–26 July 2017

46. Nie, Y., Dai, A., Han, X., Nießner, M.: Pose2room: understanding 3D scenes from human activities. In: Proceedings of the European Conference on Computer Vision (ECCV) (2022)

47. Pavllo, D., Grangier, D., Auli, M.: Quaternet: a quaternion-based recurrent model for human motion. In: British Machine Vision Conference (BMVC) (2018)

48. Ren, S., He, K., Girshick, R., Sun, J.: Faster R-CNN: towards real-time object detection with region proposal networks. In: Cortes, C., Lawrence, N., Lee, D., Sugiyama, M., Garnett, R. (eds.) Advances in Neural Information Processing Systems, vol. 28 (2015)

49. Ren, S., He, K., Girshick, R.B., Sun, J.: Faster R-CNN: towards real-time object detection with region proposal networks. CoRR abs/1506.01497 (2015)

50. Rong, Y., Shiratori, T., Joo, H.: Frankmocap: a monocular 3D whole-body pose estimation system via regression and integration. In: IEEE International Conference on Computer Vision Workshops (2021)

51. Sohn, K., Lee, H., Yan, X.: Learning structured output representation using deep conditional generative models. In: Cortes, C., Lawrence, N.D., Lee, D.D., Sugiyama, M., Garnett, R. (eds.) Advances in Neural Information Processing Systems 28: Annual Conference on Neural Information Processing Systems 2015, 7–12 December 2015, pp. 3483–3491, Montreal, Quebec, Canada (2015)

52. Starke, S., Zhang, H., Komura, T., Saito, J.: Neural state machine for character-scene interactions. ACM Trans. Graph. **38**(6), 209:1-209:14 (2019)

53. Starke, S., Zhao, Y., Komura, T., Zaman, K.A.: Local motion phases for learning multi-contact character movements. ACM Trans. Graph. **9**(4), 1–54 (2020)

54. Starke, S., Zhao, Y., Zinno, F., Komura, T.: Neural animation layering for synthesizing martial arts movements. ACM Trans. Graph. **40**(4), 1–16 (2021)

55. Taheri, O., Choutas, V., Black, M.J., Tzionas, D.: GOAL: generating 4D whole-body motion for hand-object grasping. In: Conference on Computer Vision and Pattern Recognition (CVPR) (2022)
56. Taheri, O., Ghorbani, N., Black, M.J., Tzionas, D.: GRAB: a dataset of whole-body human grasping of objects. In: Vedaldi, A., Bischof, H., Brox, T., Frahm, J.-M. (eds.) ECCV 2020. LNCS, vol. 12349, pp. 581–600. Springer, Cham (2020). https://doi.org/10.1007/978-3-030-58548-8_34
57. Wang, H., Feng, J.: VRED: A position-velocity recurrent encoder-decoder for human motion prediction. CoRR abs/1906.06514 (2019)
58. Wang, J., Xu, H., Xu, J., Liu, S., Wang, X.: Synthesizing long-term 3D human motion and interaction in 3D scenes. In: IEEE Conference on Computer Vision and Pattern Recognition, CVPR 2021, virtual, 19–25 June 2021, pp. 9401–9411. Computer Vision Foundation / IEEE (2021)
59. Xie, X., Bhatnagar, B.L., Pons-Moll, G.: Chore: contact, human and object reconstruction from a single RGB image. In: European Conference on Computer Vision (ECCV). Springer (2022)
60. Xu, J., Xu, H., Ni, B., Yang, X., Wang, X., Darrell, T.: Hierarchical style-based networks for motion synthesis. In: Vedaldi, A., Bischof, H., Brox, T., Frahm, J. (eds.) Computer Vision - ECCV 2020–16th European Conference, Glasgow, UK, 23–28 August 2020, Proceedings, Part XI
61. Yi, H., et al.: Human-aware object placement for visual environment reconstruction. In: Computer Vision and Pattern Recognition (CVPR) (2022)
62. Yuan, Y., Kitani, K.: DLow: diversifying latent flows for diverse human motion prediction. In: Vedaldi, A., Bischof, H., Brox, T., Frahm, J.-M. (eds.) ECCV 2020. LNCS, vol. 12354, pp. 346–364. Springer, Cham (2020). https://doi.org/10.1007/978-3-030-58545-7_20
63. Zhang, H., Starke, S., Komura, T., Saito, J.: Mode-adaptive neural networks for quadruped motion control. ACM Trans. Graph. **37**(4), 145:1-145:11 (2018)
64. Zhang, S., Zhang, Y., Ma, Q., Black, M.J., Tang, S.: PLACE: proximity learning of articulation and contact in 3D environments. In: International Conference on 3D Vision (3DV) (2020)
65. Zhang, Y., Hassan, M., Neumann, H., Black, M.J., Tang, S.: Generating 3D people in scenes without people. In: Proceedings of the IEEE/CVF Conference on Computer Vision and Pattern Recognition (CVPR) (2020)
66. Zhou, K., Bhatnagar, B.L., Lenssen, J.E., Pons-Moll, G.: Toch: spatio-temporal object correspondence to hand for motion refinement. In: European Conference on Computer Vision (ECCV). Springer (2022)

Identity-Aware Hand Mesh Estimation and Personalization from RGB Images

Deying Kong[1]([✉]), Linguang Zhang[2], Liangjian Chen[2], Haoyu Ma[1],
Xiangyi Yan[1], Shanlin Sun[1], Xingwei Liu[1], Kun Han[1], and Xiaohui Xie[1]

[1] University of California-Irvine, Irvine, CA 92697, USA
{deyingk,haoyum3,xiangyy4,shanlins,xingweil,khan7,xhx}@uci.edu
[2] Reality Labs at Meta, Irvine, USA
{linguang,clj}@fb.com

Abstract. Reconstructing 3D hand meshes from monocular RGB images has attracted increasing amount of attention due to its enormous potential applications in the field of AR/VR. Most state-of-the-art methods attempt to tackle this task in an anonymous manner. Specifically, the identity of the subject is ignored even though it is practically available in real applications where the user is unchanged in a continuous recording session. In this paper, we propose an *identity-aware* hand mesh estimation model, which can incorporate the identity information represented by the intrinsic shape parameters of the subject. We demonstrate the importance of the identity information by comparing the proposed *identity-aware* model to a baseline which treats subject anonymously. Furthermore, to handle the use case where the test subject is *unseen*, we propose a novel personalization pipeline to calibrate the intrinsic shape parameters using only a few unlabeled RGB images of the subject. Experiments on two large scale public datasets validate the state-of-the-art performance of our proposed method.

Keywords: Pose estimation · Hand pose · Personalization · MANO · Mesh

1 Introduction

Hand pose estimation has been one of the most popular computer vision problems because of its critical role in many applications, including hand gesture recognition, virtual and augmented reality, sign language translation and human-computer interaction [3]. With recent advances in deep learning techniques [17,33,40] and development of large hand pose datasets [39,51,54,56], 2D hand pose estimation has been extensively investigated and deployed in real-time applications with compelling results [6,19,39]. However, 3D hand pose estimation still remains a challenging problem due to the diversity of hand shapes, occlusion and depth ambiguity when monocular RGB image is used.

Supplementary Information The online version contains supplementary material available at https://doi.org/10.1007/978-3-031-20065-6_31.

Current state-of-the-art methods for 3D hand reconstruction from RGB images either try to directly regress 3D vertices of the hand mesh [9,11,22,24,25], or utilize the parametric MANO model [38] by regressing the low-dimensional parameters [2,4,16,50,52]. While these methods could generalize reasonably across different subjects, nearly all of them estimate the 3D hand pose in an anonymous manner. The identity information of the subject, which is practically available in real applications, is typically ignored in these methods. In many real-world use cases, such as virtual and augmented reality, the device is often personal and the user is typically identifiable.

We ask the question, can 3D hand reconstruction from RGB images be further improved with the help of identity information? If so, how should we calibrate the personalized hand model for *unseen* subjects during the test phase, using only RGB images? In depth image based hand tracking systems, the hand model personalization has been well studied and its benefits on improving hand tracking performance has been demonstrated [42,43]. However, using only RGB images to perform personalization is underexplored.

To close this gap and answer the above question, we investigate the problem of hand model personalization from RGB images and design a simple yet effective network to incorporate the identity information. Specifically, we propose an *identity-aware* hand mesh estimation model, which can take in the personalized hand model along with the input RGB image. Motivated by MANO [38], we choose to use MANO shape parameters to represent the hand model. To enable a fair comparison, we then construct a strong baseline by adapting our proposed identity-aware network slightly. Instead of being given the groundtruth hand shape parameters, the baseline regresses the shape parameters directly from the input image via a multi-layer perceptron. We show through experiments that with ground truth shape parameters, more accurate 3D hand reconstruction can be obtained. Lastly, we propose a novel personalization method which can calibrate the hand model for *unseen* subjects, using only unannotated RGB images. The calibrated hand model can then be utilized in our identity-aware network. Our main contributions are summarized as follows:

- Our work is the first to systematically investigate the problem of hand mesh personalization from RGB images and demonstrate its benefits to hand mesh and keypoints reconstruction.
- For unknown subjects that are *not seen* in training, we develop a novel hand model personalization method that is capable of calibrating the hand model using a few unannotated images of the same subject.
- We demonstrate that our method outperforms existing methods on two large-scale public datasets, showing the benefit of utilizing the identity information, which is an underexplored topic in the field.
- We design a simple but competitive baseline that features the same optimization augmented inference step and further validate the effectiveness of leveraging the identity information.

2   Related Work

There are many research works on human/hand pose estimation [24,25,28–30, 46–48], including well-developed 2D hand pose estimation algorithms [6,10,19–21,39,45] and fast developing 3D hand pose estimation algorithms [1,5,12,41, 55]. In this section, we will mainly discuss literature on 3D hand mesh reconstruction.

Model-Based Methods. The popular model-based method usually rely on the MANO model [38], developed from the SMPL human model [27]. As a parameterized model, the MANO model factorizes the hand mesh into shape and pose parameters, by utilizing principal component analysis. Massive literature has tried to predict the MANO parameters in order to reconstruct the hand mesh. Boukhayma *et al.* [4] regressed the MANO shape and pose parameters from 2D keypoint heatmaps. This was the first end-to-end deep learning based method that can predict both 3D hand shape and pose from RGB images in the wild. Zhang *et al* [52] proposed to use an iterative regression module to regress the MANO parameters in a coarse-to-fine manner. Baek *et al* [2] also exploited iterative refinement. In addition to that, a differentiable renderer was also deployed, which can be supervised by 2D segmentation masks and 3D skeletons. Hasson *et al* [16] exploited the MANO model to solve the task of reconstructing hands and objects during manipulation. Yang *et al* [50] proposed a multi-stage bisected network, which can regress the MANO params using 3D heatmaps and depth map.

Model-Free Methods. In [30], Moon *et al* designed I2L-MeshNet, an image-to-lixel prediction network. Many other works are based on graph convolutional network, directly regressing the vertex locations. In [11], Ge *et al* proposed a graph neural network based method to reconstruct a full 3D mesh of hand surface. In [23], Lim *et al* proposed an efficient graph convolution, SpiralConv, to process mesh data in the spatial domain. Leveraging spiral mesh convolutions, Kulon *et al* [22] devised a simple and effective network architecture for monocular 3D hand pose estimation consisting of an image encoder followed by a mesh decoder. Most recently, Chen *et al* [9] exploited the similar architecture, with more advanced designs. They divide the camera-space mesh recovery into two sub-tasks, i.e., root-relative mesh recovery and root recovery. To estimate the root-relative mesh, the authors proposed a novel aggregation method to collect effective 2D cues from the image, and then are decoded by a spiral graph convolutional decoder to regress the vertex coordinates. Apart from graph neural network, Transformer [44] has also been introduced into the field of computer vison, solving different tasks [7,26,49]. Several methods [14,24,25,34] have been proposed for hand pose and mesh reconstruction.

Hand Model Personalization. Tan *et al* [42] and Tkach *et al* [43] studied hand model personalization in the scenario where multiple *depth* images are available, and successfully demonstrated its importance in hand tracking. Hampali *et al* [13] used the same method to generate annotations when creating a new dataset. However, hand model personlization from RGB images has been underexplored. Qian *et al* [37] focused on hand *texture* personalization from RGB images. While hand model (mesh) personalization is also performed, the effectiveness of mesh personalization is not validated by quantitative results. There is also no investigation on whether the personalized mesh model can be used to improve hand pose estimation. Moon *et al* [31] proposed to personalize each subject using a randomly generated Gaussian vector. The subject ID vectors were generated prior to training and experiments were performed where all subjects in the test set were already seen in the training set. The trained model is only applicable to known subjects and there exists no principle way to handle unseen subjects during the testing phase. MEgATrack [15] is a multi-view monochrome egocentric hand tracking system that calibrates the hand model for unseen users, but the calibration is limited to a single hand scaling factor.

To our best knowledge, our work is the *first* to systematically investigate the hand model personalization from RGB images and its benefits to 3D hand pose estimation and mesh reconstruction.

3   Method

We first review the MANO hand model which is used extensively in this work, and then propose our identity-aware hand mesh estimation method that takes as input the identity information represented by the hand MANO shape parameters along with the input image. Next, by a slight modification of our method, we propose the baseline which would be compared with. Lastly, to address the practical use case where the hand model is not provided for the test subject, we propose a novel personalization pipeline that estimates the hand model for an *unseen* subject using only a few unannotated images.

3.1   MANO Model

MANO [38] is a popular parameterized hand model extended from the 3D human model SMPL [27]. The MANO model factorizes the hand mesh into two groups of parameters: the shape parameters and the pose parameters. The shape parameters control the intrinsic shape of the hand, e.g., size of the hand, thickness of the fingers, length of the bones, etc. The pose parameters represent the hand pose, i.e., how the hand joints are transformed, which subsequently deforms the hand mesh. Mathematically, the model is defined as below:

$$\mathcal{M}(\beta, \theta) = W(T_P(\beta, \theta), J(\beta), \theta, \mathcal{W}) \tag{1}$$

where a skinning function W is applied to an articulated mesh with shape T_P, joint locations J, pose parameter θ, shape parameter β, and blend weights $\mathcal{W}$ [38].

3.2   Identity-Aware Hand Mesh Estimation

Existing methods assume that the subject in every image frame is anonymous, even though the input is recorded in a continuous session. To fully leverage

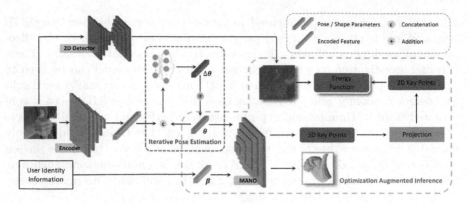

Fig. 1. Overview of our proposed identity-aware hand mesh estimation model. The model mainly contains three parts, i.e., the iterative pose regressor, the 2D detector and the optimization module. Note that in our proposed model, along with the RGB image, we also feed the user's identity information, i.e. the ground truth or calibrated MANO shape parameters of the user.

the fact that the subject is often fixed within each recording session in real applications, we propose a new hand mesh estimation pipeline. In addition to the input image, we also feed the user's identity information into the network.

There are various ways to represent the identity of a subject. The most straightforward method is to label each subject with a unique identifier, such as a high-dimensional random vector [31]. However, identity information that does not have physical meaning can be hard for the model to utilize. More importantly, models trained with this type of identity information usually only generalize to *known* subjects included in the training set. In this work, we are interested in an identity representation that allows generalizing to *unseen* subjects.

Inspired by MANO model [38], we utilize the MANO shape parameters as the identity information for a specific subject. As shown in Fig. 1, our proposed identity-aware hand mesh estimator takes in directly the ground truth or calibrated MANO shape parameters, enabling the network to be subject-aware. The main parts of our proposed model is explained as follows.

MANO Pose Parameter Regressor. Motivated by [52], the pose parameter θ is obtained by using an iterative pose regressor. We include the global rotation in θ, and use the 6D rotation representation [53] to represent the rotation of each joint. With 15 hand joints and the global rotation, θ is a vector in $\mathbb{R}^{96}$. Let $\mathcal{F} \in \mathbb{R}^N$ denote the image feature after the encoder and $\theta^{(i)}$ denote the estimated pose after i iterations. Initially, we set $\theta^{(0)}$ as the rotation 6D representation of identity matrices. Then, the pose is predicted iteratively as follows

$$\Delta\theta^{(i)} = MLP_\theta\left(\text{cat}(\mathcal{F}, \theta^{(i-1)})\right) \tag{2}$$

$$\theta^{(i)} = \Delta\theta^{(i)} \oplus \theta^{(i-1)}, \tag{3}$$

where $\oplus$ means adding the new rotation increment onto the predicted rotation from the previous iteration. The operator $\oplus$ is implemented by transforming both $\Delta\theta^{(i)}$ and $\theta^{(i-1)}$ from rotation 6D representations to rotation matrices, then multiplying them, and finally converting the result back to rotation 6D representation. We adopt three iterations in the experiments.

Optimization Augmented Inference. During inference time, we can further improve the estimated hand mesh by enforcing the consistency between the 3D pose and the 2D pose predictions. The 2D predictions are obtained via a stacked hourglass-style neural network [33].

Let $\mathbf{x}^d \in \mathbb{R}^{21\times2}$ denote the 2D keypoints predictions, $f_{\mathrm{MANO}}(\cdot)$ represent the mapping function from (β, θ) to 3D keypoints positions, $\mathcal{P}(\cdot)$ denote the projection operator from 3D space to image space, and $\mathbf{r} \in \mathbb{R}^3$ denote the root-position of the hand. We aim to optimize the following energy function

$$\mathcal{E}(\theta, \mathbf{r}, \beta) = \left\| \mathbf{x}^d - \mathcal{P}(f_{\mathrm{MANO}}(\beta, \theta) + \mathbf{r}) \right\|_2. \tag{4}$$

We adopt a two-stage optimization procedure. In the first stage, we optimize $\mathbf{r}$ only. In the second stage, we optimize θ and $\mathbf{r}$ jointly. Note that the MANO parameters are not optimized from scratch. The prediction from the MANO parameter regressor is used as the initial guess.

3.3 Baseline Method

To further validate that the accuracy improvement of hand mesh reconstruction is a result of leveraging the identity information, we construct a baseline by slightly modifying our identity-aware model. Instead of feeding ground truth/calibrated shape parameters into the model, we use an extra MLP to regress the shape parameters from the input image. For a fair comparison, all the other modules from our identity-aware model are kept the same in this baseline model. Formally, let $\mathcal{F} \in \mathbb{R}^N$ denote the image feature produced by the encoder. The MANO shape parameter $\beta \in \mathbb{R}^{10}$ is directly regressed by a multilayer perceptron from $\mathcal{F}$ as

$$\beta = MLP_\beta(\mathcal{F}). \tag{5}$$

3.4 Personalization Pipeline

In most practical applications, the test subject is usually *unknown* and there is no corresponding hand model (shape parameters) available for the proposed identity-aware hand mesh estimation pipeline. To handle this practical issue, we propose a novel hand model personalization method, which could calibrate the hand model from a few *unannotated* RGB images.

Confidence Predictor. Our personalization pipeline takes in multiple images of a same subject and perform a joint attention-based optimization to get the personalized shape parameter. Naively, the images can be treated equally and contribute the same weight during the optimization. However, images usually differ from each other in terms of quality, view angles, occlusions and so on. Thus,

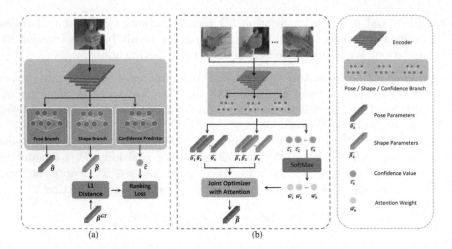

Fig. 2. Proposed personalization pipeline with attention mechanism. Images used for personalization capture the same subject who is never seen during training.

the images should be attended with different importance. To achieve this goal, we propose a light weight confidence predictor on top of the baseline network, as shown in Fig. 2(a). The confidence predictor takes as input the feature extracted by the ResNet50 encoder and outputs a scalar via one fully connected layer. The predicted confidence value indicates the quality of the predicted shape parameter from the input image. Note that our confidence predictor is only trained on the training split. Subjects in the test split are different from the training split and are **not seen** during the training phase.

Joint Optimization with Attention. Figure 2(b) illustrates the whole process during the personalization phase. Denote the collection of K unannotated images from the same user as $\mathcal{I} = \{I_1, I_2, \cdots, I_K\}$. The images are fed into the baseline model equipped with confidence predictor, which outputs $\{c_i, \hat{\beta}_i, \hat{\theta}_i\}$ for each image I_i, where $c_i \in \mathbb{R}$ is the confidence value, $\hat{\beta}_i, \hat{\theta}_i$ are the predicted MANO shape and pose parameters. The confidence values $\{c_i\}_{i=1}^{K}$ then go through a SoftMax layer, which generates the attention weights $\{w_i\}_{i=1}^{K}$ as following

$$w_i = \frac{e^{c_i/T}}{\sum_{k=1}^{K} e^{c_k/T}}, \tag{6}$$

where T is the temperature parameter. Afterwards, $\{w_i, \hat{\beta}_i, \hat{\theta}_i\}_{i=1}^{K}$ are sent into the attention based optimization module, where the following optimization is solved

$$\min_{\tilde{\beta}} \sum_{k=1}^{K} w_k \cdot \|\mathcal{M}(\tilde{\beta}, \hat{\theta}_k) - \mathcal{M}(\hat{\beta}_k, \hat{\theta}_k)\|_F, \tag{7}$$

where $\mathcal{M}(\cdot)$ is the MANO model. Note that, now all the K images from the same subject share same shape parameter $\tilde{\beta}$. After the personalization process, $\tilde{\beta}$ would be used as the identity information for the subject.

3.5   Loss Functions

The Baseline. To train the baseline, we apply loss terms on the predicted 3D hand mesh, following [9], and also on the predicted MANO shape and pose parameters.

a) Loss functions on hand mesh. Denote the vertices and faces of the hand mesh as $\mathcal{V}$ and Ω. We impose $L1$ loss on the predicted hand mesh, and also deploy edge length loss and normal loss, following [9]. The loss functions on the mesh can be expressed as

$$L_{\text{mesh}} = \sum_{i=1}^{N} \|\hat{\mathcal{V}}_i - \mathcal{V}_i\|_1$$

$$L_{\text{norm}} = \sum_{\omega \in \Omega} \sum_{(i,j) \subset \omega} \left| \frac{\hat{\mathcal{V}}_i - \hat{\mathcal{V}}_j}{\|\hat{\mathcal{V}}_i - \hat{\mathcal{V}}_j\|_2} \cdot \mathbf{n}_\omega \right| \tag{8}$$

$$L_{\text{edge}} = \sum_{\omega \in \Omega} \sum_{(i,j) \subset \omega} \left| \|\hat{\mathcal{V}}_i - \hat{\mathcal{V}}_j\|_2 - \|\mathcal{V}_i - \mathcal{V}_j\|_2 \right|,$$

where the $\mathbf{n}_\omega$ is the unit normal vector of face $\omega \in \Omega$.

b) Loss function on MANO parameters. We use $L_{\text{pose}} = \|\hat{\theta} - \theta\|_1$ and $L_{\text{shape}} = \|\hat{\beta} - \beta\|_1$, where θ and β are ground truth MANO pose and shape parameters. The $\hat{\theta}$ is the predicted pose parameter from the last iteration of the iterative pose regressor.

c) Loss function on 2D heatmap. A binary cross entropy function is imposed on 2D heatmaps of hand keypoints as in $L_{\text{pose2D}} = \text{BCE}(\hat{U}, U)$, where $\hat{U}$ and U are the predicted and ground truth 2D heatmaps of each keypoint, respectively. The groud-truth heatmap U is generated with a Gaussian distribution.

The 2D detector is trained by using L_{pose2D}. The other parts are trained under the following loss function

$$L_{\text{total}} = L_{\text{mesh}} + 0.1 \cdot L_{\text{norm}} + L_{\text{edge}} + L_{\text{pose}} + L_{\text{shape}}. \tag{9}$$

Our Identity-Aware Model. Since for our identity-aware model, the subject identity information (the MANO shape parameter) is provided, either ground truth or calibrated, the loss function is given by Eq. (10) with the shape loss removed,

$$L'_{\text{total}} = L_{\text{mesh}} + 0.1 \cdot L_{\text{norm}} + L_{\text{edge}} + L_{\text{pose}}. \tag{10}$$

Confidence Predictor. We use margin ranking loss for training of the confidence predictor. Given N_b images in the batch, the baseline model equipped with confidence predictor would output confidence values $\{c_i\}_{i=1}^{N_b}$ and MANO shape parameter predictions $\{\hat{\beta}_i\}_{i=1}^{N_b}$. With ground truth shape parameters $\{\beta_i\}_{i=1}^{N_b}$, the difference l_i between the predicted and ground truth shape parameters can be calculated as $l_i = |\beta_i - \hat{\beta}_i|_1$. We generate $N_b \times (N_b - 1)/2$ pairs of $\{(c_i, l_i), (c_j, l_j)\}$, and calculate ranking loss on each pair [36]. The total loss is the sum of ranking losses from all pairs.

4   Experiments

4.1   Experimental Setups

Datasets. We conduct experiments on two large-scale public hand pose datasets, i.e., HUMBI [51] and DexYCB [8]. There are two major reasons why these two datasets are chosen. First, they both have a diverse collection of subjects, which allows us to split the datasets into different subject groups for training and evaluating our identity-aware pipeline. More importantly, they annotate the shape parameters of the same subject in a consistent way. Each hand image in the dataset is associated with a subject ID and all the hands from the same subject share the same MANO shape annotation. Note that our method cannot be directly evaluated on other popular benchmarks such as FreiHAND [56] or InterHand [32] because they either do not associate images with subject IDs or guarantee consistent shape parameters for the same subject.

HUMBI is a large multiview image dastaset of human body expressions with natural clothing. For each hand image, the 3D mesh annotation is provided, along with the fitted MANO parameters. The shape parameters are fitted across all instances of the same subject. This means that the same shape parameters are *shared* among all the hand meshes from the same subject. In our experiments, we use all the right hand images from the released dataset. We split the dataset into training (90%) and test (10%), by subjects. The split results into 269 subjects (474,472 images) in the training set and 30 subjects (50,894 images) in the test set. Note that none of the subjects in the test set appear in the training set.

DexYCB is a large dataset capturing hand grasping of objects. The dataset consists of 582K RGB-D frames over 1,000 sequences of 10 subjects from 8 views. It also provides MANO parameters for each hand image. Same as the HUMBI dataset, the hand shape parameters for each subject are calibrated and fixed throughout each subject's sequences. While object pose estimation is beyond the scope of this work, extra occlusions introduced by the objects makes the DexYCB dataset more challenging for hand mesh estimation. In our experiments, similar to the set up for the HUMBI dataset, we use the provided split in [8] which splits the dataset by subjects. In this set up, there are 7, 1, 2 subjects in the training, validation and test set, respectively.

Metrics for 3D Hand Estimation. Following the protocol used by existing methods, we use the following two metrics, both in millimeter.

a) *Mean Per Joint Position Error* (MPJPE) measures the Euclidean distance between the root-relative prediction and ground truth 3D hand keypoints.
b) *Mean Per Vertex Position Error* (MPVPE) measures the Euclidean distance between the root-relative prediction and groud-truth 3D hand mesh.

Metrics for Hand Shape Calibration. We propose three metrics to evaluate the performance of the calibrated hand shape.

a) MSE_{mano} measures the mean square error between the estimated MANO shape parameters and the ground truth values.
b) *W-error* measures the mean hand width error between the calibrated hands and the ground truth hands at the flat pose, which is defined as the distance between the metacarpophalangeal joints of index finger and ring finger.
b) *L-error* measures the mean hand length error between the calibrated hands and the ground truth hands at the flat pose, which is defined as the distance between the wrist joint and the tip of middle finger as the hand length.

Implementation Details. We implement our model in PyTorch [35] and deploy ResNet50 [17] as our encoder. Input images are resized to 224×224 before being fed into the network. We use the Adam optimizer [18] and a batch size of 32 to train all the models except for the confidence predictor. For a fair comparison, both the baseline model and our proposed identity-aware model are trained using the same learning rate schedule. On the HUMBI dataset, both models are trained for 15 epochs, with an initial learning rate of 1e−4 which is dropped by a factor of 10 at the 10-th epoch. On the DexYCB dataset, models are also trained for 15 epochs, with the same initial learning rate, while the learning rate is dropped at the 5-th and 10-th epochs. With the baseline model trained and frozen, the lightweight confidence predictor is trained with a batch size of 128, with the intuition that larger batch size allows more image pairs to train the ranking loss. The temperature parameter is set to 0.33 in Eq. (6). During all the training, input images are augmented with random color jitter and normalization. In the inference stage, we use the Adam optimizer in PyTorch to optimize Eq. (4). Specifically, 200 and 60 iterations are performed with learning rate of 1e−2 and 1e−3 in the first and second optimization stages, respectively. On one Titan RTX graphics card, it takes 8 min to process all test images (50 k) in HUMBI dataset, and 7.5 min for those (48 k) in DexYCB dataset. We emphasize again that all our experiments are conducted in the scenarios where there is **no overlap** between the subjects in the test set and the training set.

4.2 Quantitative Evaluation

3D Hand Estimation. We evaluate the benefit of our pipeline under two settings, i.e., with and without the optimization module during inference time. As shown in Table 1, our proposed pipeline improves the baseline consistently across different datasets. With calibrated hand model, our proposed method can achieve close performance to that with ground truth hand model, which validates

Table 1. Numerical results on DexYCB and HUMBI datasets.

Method	DexYCB		HUMBI	
	MPJPE ↓	MPVPE ↓	MPJPE ↓	MPVPE ↓
CMR-PG [9]	20.34	19.88	11.64	11.37
Without optimization at inference time				
Baseline	21.58	20.95	12.13	11.82
Ours, GT shape	18.83	18.27	11.41	11.11
Ours, Calibrated	18.97	18.42	11.51	11.21
With optimization at inference time				
Baseline	18.03	17.92	10.75	10.60
Ours, GT shape	16.60	16.29	10.17	9.94
Ours, Calibrated	**16.81**	**16.55**	**10.31**	**10.28**

Table 2. Comparison with existing methods on Dex-YCB.

Methods	MPJPE↓	MPVPE ↓
Boukhayma et al. [4]	27.94	27.28
Spurr et al [41] + ResNet50	22.71	–
Spurr et al [41] + HRNet32	22.26	–
Boukhayma et al. [4] [†]	21.20	21.56
CMR-PG [9]	20.34	19.88
Metro [24]	19.05	17.71

Table 3. Performance of hand model calibration.

Metrics	HUMBI	DexYCB
MSE_{mano}	0.07	0.04
W-error (mm)	0.88	1.02
L-error (mm)	1.71	1.20

the effectiveness of our personalization pipeline. Furthermore, our method also achieves the state-of-the-art performance, as shown by Table 1 and Table 2. To ensure fair comparison, same data augmentation are applied to all the methods, i.e., random color jitter and normalization. All the models are trained for 15 epochs including ours, with the exception of Metro [24] which is trained for 70 epochs, as transformers are much harder to converge. The superscript [†] in Table 2 means adding our optimization module on top of the original method. It shows that our optimization module can be generalized to other model-based methods efficiently. We emphasize that, *none* of the existing methods produces consistent shape estimation across images originating from the same subject. In contrast, our method guarantees shape consistency with zero hand shape variation.

Hand Shape Calibration. Table 3 reports the performance of our personalization pipeline, which achieves less than 2 mm in terms of hand width and hand length errors, by calibrating on 20 unannotated images.

Our proposed method inherently guarantees the hand shape consistency among different images from the same subject. Figure 3 demonstrates this advantage of our method over the baseline model. As shown in Fig. 3, for a specific subject, the baseline model outputs hand meshes with big variations in terms

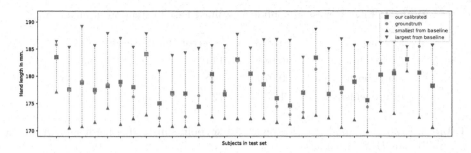

Fig. 3. Hand shape consistency comparison between our proposed method and the baseline. The x-axis corresponds to different subjects in the test dataset, while the y-axis corresponds to the length of the hand of each subject.

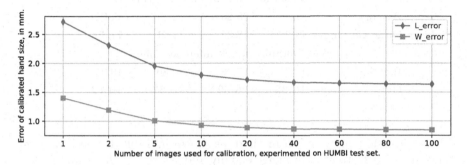

Fig. 4. Impact of the number of images used in calibration.

of hand length, up to 20 mm. This is because the baseline model is subject-agnostic and predicts hand shape parameters based on a single input image. Even if the input images are from the same user, the baseline model could predict hand meshes with big variations in size. In contrast, our proposed method outputs consistent hand shape inherently, with *zero* hand shape variation across images from the same user. Also shown in Fig. 3, the hand size calibrated by our proposed method stays close to the ground truth hand size in most cases.

4.3 Ablation Study

Number of Images Used for Personalization. Figure 4 shows hand size errors (in mm) when different number of images are utilized during calibration. With $K = 20$ images, the hand model can already be well calibrated with length error less than 2 mm and width error less than 1 mm. In all the other experiments, we use $K = 20$ images for hand model calibration.

Attention During Calibration. During the calibration, different weights are imposed across the input images according to their confidence values, as formulated in Eq. (7). We compare the calibration performance of our attention-based

Table 4. Effectiveness of confidence-valued based attention mechanism.

Metrics	MSE_{mano}	W-error (mm)	L-error (mm)
No attention	0.084	1.00	1.93
Ours, with attention	0.070	0.88	1.71
Improvement	16%	12%	11%

Table 5. Evaluating models trained with 3D keypoints instead of mesh supervision on DexYCB and HUMBI datasets.

Method	DexYCB		HUMBI	
	MPJPE↓	MPVPE ↓	MPJPE ↓	MPVPE ↓
Without optimization at inference time				
Baseline	21.85	20.26	12.34	12.02
Ours, GT shape	18.92	18.35	11.61	11.30
With optimization at inference time				
Baseline	17.71	17.58	10.80	10.95
Ours, GT shape	**16.63**	**16.32**	**10.37**	**10.12**

method with the non-attention method, as shown in Table 4. Specifically, non-attention means to treat each image equally and set $w_i = 1/K$ in Eq. (7) for all images. As shown by Table 4, our attention-based calibration can improve the performance by a noticeable margin comparing to the naive calibration.

Optimization Augmented Inference from Scratch. In this experiment, we remove the MANO parameter regressor from the model in Fig. 1. Without being initialized by the MANO parameter regressor, the initial pose is set to the neutral pose prior to optimization. This pure optimization procedure results in an MJPJE > 50 mm on both DexYCB and HUMBI datasets. This validates the necessity of the MANO parameter regressor, which can give good initial values of MANO parameters for later optimization.

Training Model with 3D Keypoints Instead of 3D Mesh Supervision. In Table 5, we report the performance of the baseline and our proposed identity-aware model when trained with 3D keypoints supervision, instead of 3D mesh. Under this setting, our identity-aware method still improves the accuracy.

Qualitative Results. The qualitative results of our personalization method and the identity-aware hand mesh estimator are shown in Fig. 5. On the left side, it can be seen that the calibrated hand mesh is very close to the ground truth hand mesh. On the right side, qualitative results of our identity-aware model are demonstrated. When generating the third row, we align the predicted mesh with ground truth root position before projecting the mesh back to the image space. As seen from Fig. 5, our model can robustly recover the hand mesh under moderate occlusion and can handle a wide range of hand poses.

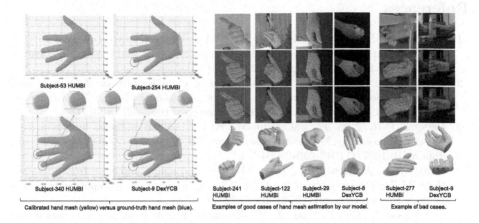

Fig. 5. Qualitative results. a) Left: calibrated hand model versus ground truth hand model. b) Right: visualization of our identity-aware hand mesh estimator. From top row to bottom row are the input RGB images, the projected ground truth meshes, the projected predicted meshes, and the predicted meshes viewed from two different angles.

Limitations. The guarantee of consistent hand shape primarily comes from explicitly incorporating a 3D hand model i.e., the MANO in our pipeline. A future direction is to explore model free approaches to enforce shape consistency at inference time. We also observe that images with severe occlusions and blurs may affect the quality of shape calibration. We currently mitigate this issue by predicting confidence values, which helps lower the importance of these suboptimal images greatly. A better approach might be to detect and remove these images prior to the calibration step.

5   Conclusion

In this paper, we propose an *identity-aware* hand mesh estimation pipeline for 3D hand mesh recovery from monocular images. Different from existing methods which estimate the hand mesh anonymously, our method leverages the fact that the user is usually unchanged in real applications and identity information of the subject can be utilized for 3D hand mesh recovery. More specifically, our model not only takes as input the RGB image, but also the identity information represented by the intrinsic shape parameters of the subject. We also design a novel personalization pipeline, through which the intrinsic shape parameters of an *unknown* subject can be calibrated from a few RGB images. With the personalization pipeline, our model can operate in scenarios where ground truth hand shape parameters of subjects are not provided, which are common in real world AR/VR applications. We experimented on two large-scale public datasets, HUMBI and DexYCB, demonstrating the state-of-the-art performance of our proposed method.

References

1. Athitsos, V., Sclaroff, S.: Estimating 3d hand pose from a cluttered image. In: 2003 IEEE Computer Society Conference on Computer Vision and Pattern Recognition 2003. Proceedings, vol. 2, pp. II-432. IEEE (2003)
2. Baek, S., Kim, K.I., Kim, T.K.: Pushing the envelope for rgb-based dense 3d hand pose estimation via neural rendering. In: Proceedings of the IEEE/CVF Conference on Computer Vision and Pattern Recognition, pp. 1067–1076 (2019)
3. Beddiar, D.R., Nini, B., Sabokrou, M., Hadid, A.: Vision-based human activity recognition: a survey. Multimedia Tools Appl. **79**(41), 30509–30555 (2020). https://doi.org/10.1007/s11042-020-09004-3
4. Boukhayma, A., Bem, R.d., Torr, P.H.: 3d hand shape and pose from images in the wild. In: Proceedings of the IEEE/CVF Conference on Computer Vision and Pattern Recognition, pp. 10843–10852 (2019)
5. Cai, Y., Ge, L., Cai, J., Yuan, J.: Weakly-supervised 3d hand pose estimation from monocular rgb images. In: Proceedings of the European Conference on Computer Vision (ECCV), pp. 666–682 (2018)
6. Cao, Z., Hidalgo, G., Simon, T., Wei, S.E., Sheikh, Y.: Openpose: realtime multi-person 2d pose estimation using part affinity fields. IEEE Trans. Pattern Anal. Mach. Intell. **43**(1), 172–186 (2019)
7. Carion, N., Massa, F., Synnaeve, G., Usunier, N., Kirillov, A., Zagoruyko, S.: End-to-end object detection with transformers. In: Vedaldi, A., Bischof, H., Brox, T., Frahm, J.-M. (eds.) ECCV 2020. LNCS, vol. 12346, pp. 213–229. Springer, Cham (2020). https://doi.org/10.1007/978-3-030-58452-8_13
8. Chao, Y.W., et al.: Dexycb: a benchmark for capturing hand grasping of objects. In: Proceedings of the IEEE/CVF Conference on Computer Vision and Pattern Recognition, pp. 9044–9053 (2021)
9. Chen, X., et al.: Camera-space hand mesh recovery via semantic aggregation and adaptive 2d–1d registration. In: Proceedings of the IEEE/CVF Conference on Computer Vision and Pattern Recognition, pp. 13274–13283 (2021)
10. Chen, Y., et al.: Nonparametric structure regularization machine for 2d hand pose estimation. In: Proceedings of the IEEE/CVF Winter Conference on Applications of Computer Vision, pp. 381–390 (2020)
11. Ge, L., et al.: 3d hand shape and pose estimation from a single rgb image. In: Proceedings of the IEEE/CVF Conference on Computer Vision and Pattern Recognition, pp. 10833–10842 (2019)
12. Ge, L., Ren, Z., Yuan, J.: Point-to-point regression pointnet for 3d hand pose estimation. In: Proceedings of the European Conference on Computer Vision (ECCV) (2018)
13. Hampali, S., Rad, M., Oberweger, M., Lepetit, V.: Honnotate: a method for 3d annotation of hand and object poses. In: Proceedings of the IEEE/CVF Conference on Computer Vision and Pattern Recognition, pp. 3196–3206 (2020)
14. Hampali, S., Sarkar, S.D., Rad, M., Lepetit, V.: Keypoint transformer: solving joint identification in challenging hands and object interactions for accurate 3d pose estimation. In: Proceedings of the IEEE/CVF Conference on Computer Vision and Pattern Recognition, pp. 11090–11100 (2022)
15. Han, S., Liu, B., Cabezas, R., Twigg, C.D., Zhang, P., Petkau, J., Yu, T.H., Tai, C.J., Akbay, M., Wang, Z., et al.: Megatrack: monochrome egocentric articulated hand-tracking for virtual reality. ACM Trans. Graph. (TOG) **39**(4), 1–87 (2020)

16. Hasson, Y., et al.: Learning joint reconstruction of hands and manipulated objects. In: Proceedings of the IEEE/CVF Conference on Computer Vision and Pattern Recognition, pp. 11807–11816 (2019)
17. He, K., Zhang, X., Ren, S., Sun, J.: Deep residual learning for image recognition. In: Proceedings of the IEEE Conference on Computer Vision and Pattern Recognition, pp. 770–778 (2016)
18. Kingma, D.P., Ba, J.: Adam: a method for stochastic optimization. arXiv preprint arXiv:1412.6980 (2014)
19. Kong, D., Chen, Y., Ma, H., Yan, X., Xie, X.: Adaptive graphical model network for 2d handpose estimation. arXiv preprint arXiv:1909.08205 (2019)
20. Kong, D., Ma, H., Chen, Y., Xie, X.: Rotation-invariant mixed graphical model network for 2d hand pose estimation. In: Proceedings of the IEEE/CVF Winter Conference on Applications of Computer Vision, pp. 1546–1555 (2020)
21. Kong, D., Ma, H., Xie, X.: Sia-gcn: a spatial information aware graph neural network with 2d convolutions for hand pose estimation. arXiv preprint arXiv:2009.12473 (2020)
22. Kulon, D., Guler, R.A., Kokkinos, I., Bronstein, M.M., Zafeiriou, S.: Weakly-supervised mesh-convolutional hand reconstruction in the wild. In: Proceedings of the IEEE/CVF Conference on Computer Vision and Pattern Recognition, pp. 4990–5000 (2020)
23. Lim, I., Dielen, A., Campen, M., Kobbelt, L.: A simple approach to intrinsic correspondence learning on unstructured 3d meshes. In: Proceedings of the European Conference on Computer Vision (ECCV) Workshops (2018)
24. Lin, K., Wang, L., Liu, Z.: End-to-end human pose and mesh reconstruction with transformers. In: Proceedings of the IEEE/CVF Conference on Computer Vision and Pattern Recognition, pp. 1954–1963 (2021)
25. Lin, K., Wang, L., Liu, Z.: Mesh graphormer. In: Proceedings of the IEEE/CVF International Conference on Computer Vision, pp. 12939–12948 (2021)
26. Liu, Z., et al.: Swin transformer: hierarchical vision transformer using shifted windows. In: Proceedings of the IEEE/CVF International Conference on Computer Vision, pp. 10012–10022 (2021)
27. Loper, M., Mahmood, N., Romero, J., Pons-Moll, G., Black, M.J.: Smpl: a skinned multi-person linear model. ACM Trans. Graph. (TOG) **34**(6), 1–16 (2015)
28. Ma, H., et al.: Transfusion: cross-view fusion with transformer for 3d human pose estimation. arXiv preprint arXiv:2110.09554 (2021)
29. Moon, G., Chang, J.Y., Lee, K.M.: V2v-posenet: voxel-to-voxel prediction network for accurate 3d hand and human pose estimation from a single depth map. In: Proceedings of the IEEE Conference on Computer Vision and Pattern Recognition, pp. 5079–5088 (2018)
30. Moon, G., Lee, K.M.: I2L-MeshNet: image-to-lixel prediction network for accurate 3D human pose and mesh estimation from a single RGB image. In: Vedaldi, A., Bischof, H., Brox, T., Frahm, J.-M. (eds.) ECCV 2020. LNCS, vol. 12352, pp. 752–768. Springer, Cham (2020). https://doi.org/10.1007/978-3-030-58571-6_44
31. Moon, G., Shiratori, T., Lee, K.M.: DeepHandMesh: a weakly-supervised deep encoder-decoder framework for high-fidelity hand mesh modeling. In: Vedaldi, A., Bischof, H., Brox, T., Frahm, J.-M. (eds.) ECCV 2020. LNCS, vol. 12347, pp. 440–455. Springer, Cham (2020). https://doi.org/10.1007/978-3-030-58536-5_26
32. Moon, G., Yu, S.-I., Wen, H., Shiratori, T., Lee, K.M.: InterHand2.6M: a dataset and baseline for 3D interacting hand pose estimation from a single RGB image. In: Vedaldi, A., Bischof, H., Brox, T., Frahm, J.-M. (eds.) ECCV 2020. LNCS, vol.

12365, pp. 548–564. Springer, Cham (2020). https://doi.org/10.1007/978-3-030-58565-5_33

33. Newell, A., Yang, K., Deng, J.: Stacked hourglass networks for human pose estimation. In: Leibe, B., Matas, J., Sebe, N., Welling, M. (eds.) ECCV 2016. LNCS, vol. 9912, pp. 483–499. Springer, Cham (2016). https://doi.org/10.1007/978-3-319-46484-8_29

34. Park, J., Oh, Y., Moon, G., Choi, H., Lee, K.M.: Handoccnet: Occlusion-robust 3d hand mesh estimation network. In: Proceedings of the IEEE/CVF Conference on Computer Vision and Pattern Recognition, pp. 1496–1505 (2022)

35. Paszke, A., et al.: Pytorch: an imperative style, high-performance deep learning library. Adv. Neural. Inf. Process. Syst. **32**, 8026–8037 (2019)

36. Pytorch: Pytorch margin ranking loss (2022). https://pytorch.org/docs/stable/generated/torch.nn.MarginRankingLoss.html

37. Qian, N., Wang, J., Mueller, F., Bernard, F., Golyanik, V., Theobalt, C.: HTML: a parametric hand texture model for 3D hand reconstruction and personalization. In: Vedaldi, A., Bischof, H., Brox, T., Frahm, J.-M. (eds.) ECCV 2020. LNCS, vol. 12356, pp. 54–71. Springer, Cham (2020). https://doi.org/10.1007/978-3-030-58621-8_4

38. Romero, J., Tzionas, D., Black, M.J.: Embodied hands: modeling and capturing hands and bodies together. ACM Trans. Graph. (ToG) **36**(6), 1–17 (2017)

39. Simon, T., Joo, H., Matthews, I., Sheikh, Y.: Hand keypoint detection in single images using multiview bootstrapping. In: Proceedings of the IEEE conference on Computer Vision and Pattern Recognition, pp. 1145–1153 (2017)

40. Simonyan, K., Zisserman, A.: Very deep convolutional networks for large-scale image recognition. arXiv preprint arXiv:1409.1556 (2014)

41. Spurr, A., Iqbal, U., Molchanov, P., Hilliges, O., Kautz, J.: Weakly supervised 3D hand pose estimation via biomechanical constraints. In: Vedaldi, A., Bischof, H., Brox, T., Frahm, J.-M. (eds.) ECCV 2020. LNCS, vol. 12362, pp. 211–228. Springer, Cham (2020). https://doi.org/10.1007/978-3-030-58520-4_13

42. Tan, D.J., et al.: Fits like a glove: rapid and reliable hand shape personalization. In: Proceedings of the IEEE Conference on Computer Vision and Pattern Recognition, pp. 5610–5619 (2016)

43. Tkach, A., Tagliasacchi, A., Remelli, E., Pauly, M., Fitzgibbon, A.: Online generative model personalization for hand tracking. ACM Trans. Graph. (ToG) **36**(6), 1–11 (2017)

44. Vaswani, A., et al.: Attention is all you need. In: Advances in Neural Information Processing Systems 30 (2017)

45. Wang, Y., Peng, C., Liu, Y.: Mask-pose cascaded cnn for 2d hand pose estimation from single color image. IEEE Trans. Circuits Syst. Video Technol. **29**(11), 3258–3268 (2018)

46. Wang, Z., Chen, L., Rathore, S., Shin, D., Fowlkes, C.: Geometric pose affordance: 3d human pose with scene constraints. In: Arxiv 1905.07718 (2019)

47. Wang, Z., Shin, D., Fowlkes, C.C.: Predicting camera viewpoint improves cross-dataset generalization for 3D human pose estimation. In: Bartoli, A., Fusiello, A. (eds.) ECCV 2020. LNCS, vol. 12536, pp. 523–540. Springer, Cham (2020). https://doi.org/10.1007/978-3-030-66096-3_36

48. Wang, Z., Yang, J., Fowlkes, C.: The best of both worlds: combining model-based and nonparametric approaches for 3d human body estimation. In: CVPR ABAW Workshop (2022)

49. Yan, X., Tang, H., Sun, S., Ma, H., Kong, D., Xie, X.: After-unet: axial fusion transformer unet for medical image segmentation. In: Proceedings of the IEEE/CVF Winter Conference on Applications of Computer Vision, pp. 3971–3981 (2022)

50. Yang, L., Li, J., Xu, W., Diao, Y., Lu, C.: Bihand: recovering hand mesh with multi-stage bisected hourglass networks. arXiv preprint arXiv:2008.05079 (2020)

51. Yu, Z., et al.: Humbi: a large multiview dataset of human body expressions. In: Proceedings of the IEEE/CVF Conference on Computer Vision and Pattern Recognition, pp. 2990–3000 (2020)

52. Zhang, X., Li, Q., Mo, H., Zhang, W., Zheng, W.: End-to-end hand mesh recovery from a monocular rgb image. In: Proceedings of the IEEE/CVF International Conference on Computer Vision, pp. 2354–2364 (2019)

53. Zhou, Y., Barnes, C., Lu, J., Yang, J., Li, H.: On the continuity of rotation representations in neural networks. In: Proceedings of the IEEE/CVF Conference on Computer Vision and Pattern Recognition, pp. 5745–5753 (2019)

54. Zimmermann, C., Brox, T.: Learning to estimate 3d hand pose from single rgb images. Technical report, arXiv:1705.01389 (2017). https://lmb.informatik.uni-freiburg.de/projects/hand3d/, https://arxiv.org/abs/1705.01389

55. Zimmermann, C., Brox, T.: Learning to estimate 3d hand pose from single rgb images. In: Proceedings of the IEEE International Conference on Computer Vision, pp. 4903–4911 (2017)

56. Zimmermann, C., Ceylan, D., Yang, J., Russell, B., Argus, M., Brox, T.: Freihand: a dataset for markerless capture of hand pose and shape from single rgb images. In: Proceedings of the IEEE/CVF International Conference on Computer Vision, pp. 813–822 (2019)

C3P: Cross-Domain Pose Prior Propagation for Weakly Supervised 3D Human Pose Estimation

Cunlin Wu[1], Yang Xiao[1(✉)], Boshen Zhang[2], Mingyang Zhang[1], Zhiguo Cao[1], and Joey Tianyi Zhou[3]

[1] Key Laboratory of Image Processing and Intelligent Control, Ministry of Education, School of AIA, Huazhong University of Science and Technology, Wuhan, China
{cunlin_wu, Yang_Xiao, izmy, zgcao}@hust.edu.cn
[2] YouTu Lab, Tencent, Shanghai, China
boshenzhang@tencent.com
[3] A*STAR Centre for Frontier AI Reasearch (CFAR), Singapore, Singapore
zhouty@ihpc.a-star.edu.sg

Abstract. This paper first proposes and solves weakly supervised 3D human pose estimation (HPE) problem in point cloud, via propagating the pose prior within unlabelled RGB-point cloud sequence to 3D domain. Our approach termed C3P does not require any labor-consuming 3D keypoint annotation for training. To this end, we propose to transfer 2D HPE annotation information within the existing large-scale RGB datasets (e.g., MS COCO) to 3D task, using unlabelled RGB-point cloud sequence easy to acquire for linking 2D and 3D domains. The self-supervised 3D HPE clues within point cloud sequence are also exploited, concerning spatial-temporal constraints on human body symmetry, skeleton length and joints' motion. And, a refined point set network structure for weakly supervised 3D HPE is proposed in encoder-decoder manner. The experiments on CMU Panoptic and ITOP datasets demonstrate that, our method can achieve the comparable results to the 3D fully supervised state-of-the-art counterparts. When large-scale unlabelled data (e.g., NTU RGB+D 60) is used, our approach can even outperform them under the more challenging cross-setup test setting. The source code is released at https://github.com/wucunlin/C3P for research use only.

Keywords: 3D human pose estimation · Weak supervision · RGB-point cloud sequence · Spatial-temporal constraints

Supplementary Information The online version contains supplementary material available at https://doi.org/10.1007/978-3-031-20065-6_32.

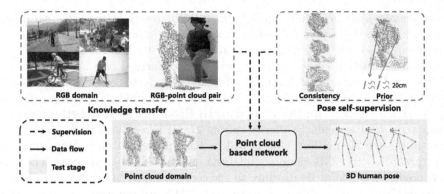

Fig. 1. The main research idea of our weakly supervised 3D human pose estimation approach in point cloud. RGB-point cloud pairs bridge 2D and 3D domain. 3D priors of human pose in point cloud sequences are also utilized as self-supervision signals. For test, we only need point cloud as input, and output 3D human pose in world coordinate.

1   Introduction

3D human pose estimation (HPE) in depth data (e.g., depth map or point cloud) is of wide-range applications towards human action recognition [1,22,23], human-robot interaction [38], virtual [29], etc. With the introduction of deep learning technologies (e.g., CNN [12,36] or PointNet [30,31]), 3D HPE's performance has been enhanced remarkably in fully supervised learning manner. However, deep network's data-hungry property leads to the high demand on 3D pose annotation both on quality and quantity, which is essentially labor and time consuming. Nevertheless, the existing annotated 3D HPE datasets are generally of relative small size. For example, ITOP [11] only involves 50K samples from 20 subjects in laboratory setting. While, as the 2D RGB counterpart MS COCO [21] contains over 200K samples from 250K subjects under in the wild conditions. Accordingly, the existing RGB-based 2D HPE approaches [4,5,28,42,43] are generally of stronger generality. Thus, we raise the question that *whether the rich 2D annotation information within RGB domain can be transferred to depth domain for facilitating 3D HPE*, which has not been well concerned before.

Due to the emergency of low-cost RGB-D cameras (e.g., MS Kinect [24,25]), 3D human pose's unlabelled RGB-D pair sequence can be easily acquired to link 2D and 3D domains. It also involves rich human pose prior information. Particularly, for RGB stream 2D human pose can be acquired with the existing well-established 2D HPE approaches [43] pre-trained on large-scale RGB datasets (e.g., MS COCO [21]). Within depth stream, the physical 3D constraints on human body symmetry, skeleton length and joints' motion are maintained. Although the supervision priors above, to our knowledge, there is still no work that concerns applying unlabelled RGB-D pair sequence to address 3D HPE.

To fill this gap, a novel weakly supervised 3D HPE approach termed C3P for depth data is proposed by us, based on unlabelled RGB-D sequence. It *conducts cross-domain pose prior propagation from RGB to depth in weakly supervised manner, with self-supervised learning in depth domain jointly.* Human pose annotation supervision is only from the third-party 2D RGB datasets. To alleviate projection distortion [18], depth map will be transformed into point cloud.

For weakly supervised learning, the key idea is to build correspondence between 2D and 3D HPE results in 3D space. Compared with the existing 2D supervision manner [7] for RGB-based 3D HPE, our method can better reveal 3D characteristics. Particularly after acquiring 2D HPE result on RGB stream with state-of-the-art 2D method [43], it will be back projected into 3D space in ray form according to RGB camera's intrinsic and extrinsic parameters. Then, for each predicted 3D joint its distance to the corresponding 2D oriented projection ray is minimized to establish accurate 3D to 2D correspondence as supervision.

To leverage performance, self-supervised learning in 3D domain is jointly executed. The supervision information derives from the intrinsic natural constraints on human body symmetry, skeleton length limitation and joint's temporal motion continuity thanks to cloud sequence's spatial-temporal characteristics.

Technically, the encoder-decoder based point set network (i.e., P2P [9]) for 3D hand pose estimation is used as our backbone network. Since under weakly-supervised setting joint's ground-truth 3D heatmap cannot be acquired for P2P's training, we propose to refine it with an additional per point aggregation module with integral regression design [37]. Accordingly, 3D heatmap is no longer required. Overall, our main research idea is shown in Fig. 1.

The experiments on CMU Panoptic [16,17] and ITOP [11] datasets verify the effectiveness of our proposition. It is impressive that, when large-scale unlabelled data is introduced our weakly supervised approach can even outperform the fully supervised counterparts under the challenging cross-setup test setting.

The main contributions of this paper include:

- We first propose the research problem of weakly supervised 3D human pose estimation in point cloud without requiring 3D annotation;
- C3P: a novel weakly supervised 3D human pose estimation approach that relies on unlabelled RGB-point cloud sequence.

2   Related Work

In this section, we mainly introduce the depth image and point cloud based HPE methods. Since the proposed C3P is a weakly-supervised method, we also introduce other related weakly supervised HPE works.

Depth Image and Point Cloud Based HPE Methods. Non-deep learning approaches [13,34,45] plays an important role in early research on depth image based human pose estimation. These methods rely on hand-crafted features and subsequent processing by regression or classification to obtain results on human posture. However, due to the limited discriminative power of these features, their performance is usually not as high as that of deep learning methods. Recently, numerous deep learning based HPE methods [27,44,46,48,52] were proposed

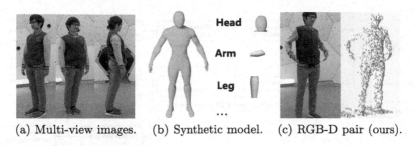

(a) Multi-view images.   (b) Synthetic model.   (c) RGB-D pair (ours).

Fig. 2. Illustration of the essential characteristics of different weakly-supervised 3D human pose estimation methods.

due to the fitting ability of neural networks. V2V-PoseNet [27] converts depth image to Voxel, and uses 3D CNN to predict the coordinate of human joints, however, the 3D CNN is time-consuming. A2J [44] proposes an anchor based 2D CNN method which predicts in-plain offset estimation branch, depth estimation branch and anchor proposal branch, and uses the element-wise multiplication to get final results. A2J does not fully consider the intrinsic 3D information in depth data, and the data augmentation strategies such as normalization, scale scaling will destroy the original 3D structure. Ge et al. [8,9] propose a series of point cloud based 3D hand pose estimation methods. Ying et al. [46] propose an RGB-D based 3D HPE method, which extracts the joint point heatmap based on the RGB image, and then regresses the joint point offset and distance on the point cloud to obtain the final prediction results. Compared to Ying's method [46], our method only requires point clouds during testing. Note that the methods mentioned above are based on fully supervised training paradigm with labeled 3D data. However, collecting the annotated 3D dataset is labor and time consuming, leading to the fact that existing annotated 3D HPE datasets in depth form are generally of relative small size [11].

Weakly Supervised HPE Methods. The difficulty of data collection for 3D HPE leads researchers to use unlabeled data for facilitating model training. Here, the mainstream weakly supervised methods (i.e., multi-view and synthetic model based) are introduced as shown in Fig. 2. Most multi-view methods [15,19,26,32] need images from three or more views and the complex calibration using intrinsic and extrinsic camera parameters among these views. Thus, accumulated errors are often faced. Towards this problem, some works only use two views [32] or try to predict camera parameters by deep network [40], which reduces the dependence of multi-view data. However compared with single-view data, collecting multi-view images is essentially difficult, which hinders the practical application. Another research avenue resorts to generating more training samples with synthetic software [35] or rendering predicted keypoints to depth or RGB images with pre-defined human skeleton model [2,3,20,39]. Supervisory signals of synthetic data or rendered images facilitate training procedure of 3D pose estimator. However, these methods suffer from the domain shift problem between syn-

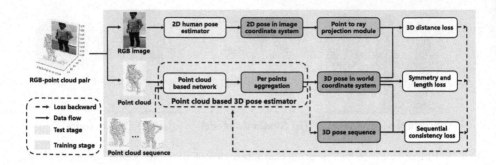

Fig. 3. The main technical pipeline of the proposed C3P approach.

thetic (or rendered) and real data. Human pose prior is also important for HPE. Some works use 2D annotation and limb proportions of human bodies [49,51]. These methods often suffer from incomplete 3D information in RGB domain [51]. The prior information cannot be fully utilized, resulting in the need on fully annotated samples [49,51]. In our work, unannotated RGB-point cloud pairs is used to link 2D and 3D domains. The 2D keypoints are obtained via pre-trained RGB pose estimator, which provides weak supervisory signals for 3D HPE. To the best of our knowledge, there is still no work that concerns applying unlabelled RGB-D pair sequence to address 3D HPE problem.

3   Method

Here, C3P will be illustrated in details. It takes point cloud $P = \{p_i\}_{i=1}^{N}$ as input, and yields body joints' position $J = \{j_k\}_{k=1}^{K}$, where N is the number of points as input, K indicates the number of body joints, and $j_k \in R^3$ is the coordinate of body joints in real world distance w.r.t. camera. Each input point is of form $p_i \in R^{3+D}$, where the first 3 dimensions denote the coordinate in world coordinate system and $D = 3$ is the surface normal of points as in P2P [9].

C3P's main technical pipeline is shown in Fig. 3. In training stage, the input is RGB-point cloud sequence. Two point cloud networks (P2P [9] and PT [50]) are used as backbone to extract high level semantic features of raw points. Offset between each point and joint location is predicted. Under weakly-supervised setting, joint's ground-truth 3D heatmap cannot be obtained for training P2P or PT. Thus we propose to refine it with additional per point aggregation module with integral regression design [37], which integrally ensembles all points' prediction to obtain 3D joint location. In C3P, RGB based 2D pose estimator plays the role of providing weak supervision for training 3D pose estimator. A state-of-the-art 2D HPE method [43] pre-trained on MS COCO is adopted in C3P to predict accurate 2D joint location. Then, it will be back projected into 3D space in ray form according to RGB camera's intrinsic and extrinsic parameters. For each predicted 3D joint, its distance to the corresponding 2D oriented

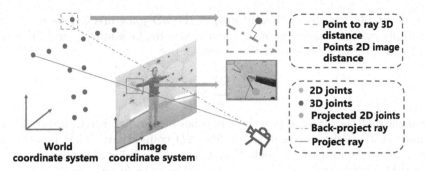

Fig. 4. Different supervision signals from RGB data. The solid line and sky blue box indicate that 3D keypoints are projected onto the image plane to calculate the planar pixel error. The dashed line and orange box indicate that the 2D keypoints are back-projected as 3D rays and the point-to-line distance error is calculated in 3D space. (Color figure online)

projection ray is minimized to establish accurate 3D to 2D correspondence as the supervision signal. Additionally, self-supervised learning in 3D domain is jointly proposed to leverage performance, including constraints on human body symmetry, skeleton length limitation and joint's temporal motion continuity.

In test stage, RGB image is no longer required. The weakly supervised P2P or PT will take point cloud as input and yield 3D joint position in world coordinate. Next, we will illustrate the weakly-supervised training part within C3P.

3.1 Weak Supervision Signal from RGB Image

As aforementioned, a 2D pose estimator [43] pre-trained on COCO dataset is used to get the RGB image based prediction results $C = \{c_k\}_{k=1}^{K}$, where K is the number of body joints, and $c_k \in R^2$ is the k-th joint on image plane. The point cloud based 3D pose estimator's output is $J = \{j_k\}_{k=1}^{K}$, and $j_k \in R^3$ is the k-th joint coordinate in world coordinate. Now the problem is how to use 2D joint prediction $C \in R^{2*K}$ to supervise the 3D output $J \in R^{3*K}$.

First, J is transformed into camera coordinate system using RGB camera's intrinsic and extrinsic parameters. We use $\hat{J} = \{\hat{j}_k\}_{k=1}^{K}$ to represent the 3D points in RGB camera coordinate system, and $\hat{C} = \{\hat{c}_k\}_{k=1}^{K}$ is the 2D projection results of $\hat{J}$. For one point $j_k = (x_k, y_k, z_k)^T$, $\hat{j}_k = (\hat{x}_k, \hat{y}_k, \hat{z}_k)^T$ and the projection result $\hat{c}_k = (\hat{u}_k, \hat{v}_k)^T$ is formulated as:

$$\begin{bmatrix} \hat{x}_k & \hat{y}_k & \hat{z}_k \end{bmatrix}^T = R_{p-r} \begin{bmatrix} x_k & y_k & z_k \end{bmatrix}^T + T_{p-r}, \tag{1}$$

$$\begin{bmatrix} \hat{u}_k & \hat{v}_k & 1 \end{bmatrix}^T = \frac{1}{\hat{z}_k} K_{rgb} \begin{bmatrix} \hat{x}_k & \hat{y}_k & \hat{z}_k \end{bmatrix}^T, \tag{2}$$

where R_{p-r} and T_{p-r} are the rotation and translation matrix from point cloud to RGB camera coordinate system, K_{rgb} is RGB camera's intrinsic parameter.

One simple idea is to directly project the 3D joint predictions to 2D RGB image plane, distance between the projected joint locations $\hat{c}_k$ and 2D pose c_k can be utilized to formulate the loss function as:

$$\mathcal{L}_{rgb} = \sum_{k=1}^{K} \|c_k - \hat{c}_k\|_2.$$
(3)

We argue that the above approach [7] may not be optimal. First, the optimization process of 3D estimator is different from 2D counterpart. That is, computing loss in 2D space inevitably yields discrepancy for training 3D network. Secondly for weakly-supervised task, in the initial stage of training network's prediction results are indeed inaccurate. The projection process will result in huge loss in 2D plane when z is small, which leads to unstable training. And the unit of $\mathcal{L}_{rgb}$ is pixel, which may cause difficulty in 3D model tuning.

Accordingly, we propose to back-project the pre-computed keypoints c_k on image plane to ray forms in 3D space, and then calculate the distance between predicted 3D points and back-projected 3D rays as in Fig. 4. The proposed back-projection method can yield more stable 3D training supervision signal.

Technically, the distance between j_k and the ray back-projected by c_k needs to be calculated. And, the point cloud and RGB camera coordinate system need to stay consistent. $\hat{j}_k$ is used to calculate divergence. $\mathcal{D}_{p-ray,k}$ is applied to denote distance between $\hat{j}_k = (\hat{x}_k, \hat{y}_k, \hat{z}_k)$ and the ray back-projected by $c_k = (u_k, v_k)$:

$$\mathcal{D}_{p-ray,k} = \frac{\left\| K_{rgb}^{-1}\hat{z}_k \left[u_k \; v_k \; 1\right]^T - \hat{j}_k \right\|_2}{\left\| K_{rgb}^{-1} \left[u_k \; v_k \; 1\right]^T \right\|_2}.$$
(4)

The weakly supervised signal from 2D keypoints is formulated as:

$$\mathcal{L}_{2d} = \sum_{k=1}^{K} \frac{\mathcal{D}_{p-ray,k}}{\mu},$$
(5)

where we set the hyper parameter $\mu = \left\|\hat{j}_k\right\|_2$ to prevent the network from converging to trivial solution (i.e., zero vector).

3.2   Self Supervision Signal from Point Cloud

To further exploit the intrinsic prior information of human pose in depth cloud, we propose to build self-training supervision signals with the constraints on human body symmetry, bone length and joint's temporal motion continuity.

Bone length is an important prior knowledge of human bodies, especially in point cloud based method. We can acquire the real world scale, and estimate the absolute coordinates under world coordinate. This prior naturally provides useful information to regularize the output of 3D joint prediction as:

$$\mathcal{L}_{len} = \sum_{n=1}^{N} \left\| B_n - \bar{B}_n \right\|_2^2,$$
(6)

where N is the number of pre-defined bones; B_n is the n-th bone length, $\bar{B}_n$ is the mean length of the n-th bone across the dataset. With $\mathcal{L}_{len}$, the predicted 3D human poses are limited to a reasonable scale.

Human body symmetry is also an important prior. Being different from most existing RGB based methods that adopt 2.5D pose representation [14] (i.e., 2D image coordinates and depth related to root joint), C3P is under world coordinates. This makes the human symmetry prior easy to incorporate into our proposition. Generally, the left bone (B_n) has almost equal length with the corresponding right counterpart (B_n^{cor}) as:

$$\mathcal{L}_{sym} = \sum_{n=1}^{N} \left\| \frac{B_n}{B_n^{cor}} - 1 \right\|. \tag{7}$$

It is worthy noting that, we do not use the form of loss like $\|B_n - B_n^{cor}\|$ since it may cause the final bone length approach to 0.

Motion consistency of joints in point cloud sequence is also a useful supervision signal. Intuitively, the movement of human joints in a temporal sequence is generally a continuous process. Requiring the 3D joints prediction to be continuous in the adjacent frames can well avoid jittering of ambiguous joints. In C3P, we concern the keypoints are moving at a constant speed:

$$\mathcal{L}_{con1} = \sum_{k=1}^{K} \sum_{i=2}^{I-1} \left\| j_k^i - \frac{j_k^{i-1} + j_k^{i+1}}{2} \right\|, \tag{8}$$

where I is number of video frames; j_k^i is location of k-th keypoint in i-th frame. In addition, the length of bones of the same person are constant in video:

$$\mathcal{L}_{con2} = \sum_{n=1}^{N} \left\| \frac{B_n}{\bar{B}_n^v} - 1 \right\|, \tag{9}$$

where $\bar{B}_n^v$ is the mean bone length in video for n-th bone.

The overall consistency loss is formulated as:

$$\mathcal{L}_{con} = \mathcal{L}_{con1} + \lambda_0 \mathcal{L}_{con2}, \tag{10}$$

where λ_0 is weight factor to balance two loss terms.

3.3 Per Points Aggregation

The network used by us for point cloud based 3D human pose estimation is P2P [9] and PT [50]. The two networks are designed for 3D hand pose estimation and point cloud semantic segmentation, which directly takes the 3D point cloud as input and yields dense prediction of each point. While our network output the per point heatmap and unit vector field to joint on the point cloud (similar to P2P [9]). The original P2P [9] uses the ground-truth heatmap to supervise the training procedure. However in weakly-supervised setting, there is no available annotation to generate 3D ground-truth heatmap and unit vector.

Towards this problem, we propose to use a points aggregation module to regress final predictions. During C3P's forward process, we select the results of the nearest points within a certain range to acquire the final joint prediction via weighted regression. The heatmap and unit vector field predictions of selected points integrally contribute to the final joint locations in ensemble manner [37]. This facilitates the training of 3D encoder-decoder based network without the need of ground-truth heatmap annotations.

In the predicted heatmap, the value of heatmap reflects the distance between current point and keypoint to be predicted, and the unit vector fields specify the direction. Small value in heatmaps means long distance. If the distance is above the threshold, this point will be abandoned when calculating the final result. The unit vector field specifies the direction between current point and target keypoint. Then, the result predicted by current point can be calculated.

The settings in our network enforces the final prediction results are surrounded by a set of points in point cloud. It is useful for our C3P method. Compared with the direct regression network [8], the dense prediction and per points aggregation module can guarantee the output of network at a relatively reasonable initial value, especially in the initial phase of training. This makes the weakly supervised training phase more stable.

3.4   Learning Procedure of C3P

In the C3P's training stage, RGB-point cloud pairs are used as input. The 2D RGB human pose estimator is a frozen model that provides human pose in 2D space as weak supervision signal. The parameters in 3D depth-based network are updated with the 2D supervision and 3D self-supervision signals as well:

$$\mathcal{L} = \lambda_1 \mathcal{L}_{2d} + \lambda_2 \mathcal{L}_{len} + \lambda_3 \mathcal{L}_{sym} + \lambda_4 \mathcal{L}_{con} \tag{11}$$

where $\mathcal{L}_{2d}$, $\mathcal{L}_{len}$, $\mathcal{L}_{sym}$, $\mathcal{L}_{con}$ are defined by Eq. (5)–(10). We set $\lambda_1 = 10$, $\lambda_2 = 1$, $\lambda_3 = 0.002$, $\lambda_4 = 0.1$ to balance each loss term.

In test phase, RGB images are no longer required. Given the raw 3D point cloud input, the trained 3D human pose estimator can yield 3D joint locations directly. This essentially expands the application scenarios of C3P.

4   Experiment

4.1   Datasets and Evaluation Metrics

CMU Panoptic Dataset [16,17] contains 480 VGA videos, 31 HD videos and 10 Kinect videos, including depth and RGB images in indoor scene. Calibration and synchronous data are also provided. The 3D human pose annotation for VGA and HD videos are provided at the same time. We use 3D human pose in HD videos, the calibration clue, and synchronous data to get 3D human pose labels

Table 1. Performance comparison on CMU Panoptic Dataset [16,17]. C3P (P2P) and C3P (PT) indicate C3P with the different backbone networks (i.e., P2P [9] and PT [50]). The unit of test error is cm.

	Nose	Eyes	Ears	Shoulders	Elbows	Wrists	Hips	Knees	Ankles	mAP	Error
Fully-supervised methods											
HandPoint [8]	79.8	78.9	79.6	80.6	5.3	0.2	89.6	84.5	75.1	62.8	12.0
P2P [9]	98.1	98.1	98.2	96.9	95.0	89.8	94.5	94.1	93.7	95.2	4.1
PT [50]	**99.6**	**99.3**	**99.2**	**98.8**	**97.0**	**92.0**	**96.8**	**95.0**	**95.7**	**96.9**	**3.3**
Weakly-supervised methods											
C3P (P2P)	96.3	95.8	95.0	93.9	91.4	81.5	90.9	78.4	85.2	89.4	6.1
C3P (PT)	**99.1**	**98.6**	**95.9**	**95.4**	**94.4**	**85.4**	**93.1**	**91.1**	**94.0**	**93.8**	**5.3**

for Kinect. Since we only focus on point cloud based 3D human pose estimation for single person, experiments are carried on the "range of motion" class Kinect data with 9 available video sequences. The 6th and 9th videos ("171204_pose6, 171206_pose3") are used for testing, and the remaining 7 videos are for training. The evaluation metrics is the **mean average precision (mAP)** with 10-cm rule [11]. The average 3D distance error [9] is also used as evaluation metric.

ITOP Dataset [11] is a widely used benchmark dataset in depth image based and point cloud based 3D human pose estimation. It contains 40K training and 10K testing depth images and point clouds data for each front-view and top-view track. This dataset contains 20 actors and 15 human body parts are labeled with 3D coordinates relative to the depth camera. In our experiment, we use the front-view data to evaluate the effectiveness of the method. The evaluation metrics is the **mean average precision (mAP)** with 10-cm rule [11].

NTU RGB+D Dataset [33] is a large-scale RGB-D action recognition dataset. It contains over 40 subjects and 60 actions. The actions can cover most daily behavior. There are 17 different scenes in it. The size and diversity are much larger than current human pose dataset. This dataset also contains 3D skeleton joint position labeled by Kinect V2 SDK. But the annotation accuracy is not satisfactory. Nevertheless, the weakly-supervised setting in C3P can well leverage this large-scale RGB-D dataset. We conduct the cross-dataset test to demonstrate that, C3P trained on large-scale unannotated dataset can even better adapt to scene variation than the fully-supervised counterparts.

4.2 Implementation Details

C3P is implemented using PyTorch. The input point number is set to 2048, and point cloud normalization operations is the same as P2P [9]. Adam is used as optimizer. The learning rate is set to 0.0001 in all cases. C3P is trained for 140 epoch. The learning rate decay by 0.1 at 90-th and 110-th epoch.

4.3   Comparison with Fully-Supervised Method

Here, C3P is compared with the state-of-the-art fully-supervised depth-based 3D HPE methods. The network structure and experimental setup are the same for the different datasets.

Results on CMU Panoptic Dataset. C3P is compared with the fully-supervised 3D HPE methods (i.e., HandPoint [8], P2P [9], and PT [50]). Two different point cloud based networks (i.e., P2P [9] and PT [50]) are used to validate C3P's generality. Experimental results are listed in Table 1. We can see that:

- C3P achieves comparable results to fully-supervised counterparts. Without labeled data, its result is only inferior about 3% in mAP and 2 cm in mean error;
- C3P can be applied to the different point cloud networks [9,50]. This indicates that the proposed weakly-supervised 3D HPE manner is not sensitive to the choice of backbone network;
- Although performance drop for joints (e.g., hand and feet) of fine appearance pattern, C3P's performance is still high (93.8 at mAP and 5.3 mm at error).

Table 2. Performance comparison on ITOP Dataset [11]. C3P (P2P) and C3P (PT) indicate C3P with the different backbone networks (i.e., P2P [9] and PT [50]).

	Head	Neck	Shoulders	Elbows	Hands	Torso	Hips	Knees	Feet	Mean
Fully-supervised methods										
RF [34]	63.8	86.4	83.3	73.2	51.3	65.0	50.8	65.7	61.3	65.8
RTW [47]	97.8	95.8	94.1	77.9	70.5	93.8	90.3	68.8	68.4	80.5
IEF [6]	96.2	85.2	77.2	45.4	30.9	84.7	83.5	81.8	80.9	71.0
VI [11]	98.1	97.5	96.5	73.3	68.7	85.6	72.0	69.0	60.8	77.4
CMB [41]	97.7	98.5	75.9	62.7	**84.4**	96.0	87.9	84.4	83.8	83.3
REN-9*6*6 [10]	**98.7**	**99.4**	96.1	74.7	55.2	**98.7**	91.8	89.0	81.1	84.9
V2V* [27]	98.3	99.1	**99.2**	**80.4**	67.3	**98.7**	**93.2**	**91.8**	**87.6**	**88.7**
A2J [44]	98.5	99.2	96.2	78.9	68.4	98.5	90.9	90.8	86.9	88.0
P2P [9]	97.6	98.6	95.5	78.0	63.9	97.8	88.9	90.6	85.1	86.5
PT [50]	97.7	98.6	96.0	78.6	64.1	98.5	90.1	90.8	86.5	87.2
Weakly-supervised method										
C3P (P2P)	97.0	**97.4**	**91.4**	75.6	63.1	**96.4**	**85.2**	**88.7**	**84.2**	**84.5**
C3P (PT)	**97.3**	97.0	91.3	**76.3**	**66.5**	94.9	81.7	87.8	83.4	84.3

Results on ITOP Dataset. ITOP Dataset only contains depth images. Accordingly, we use the 2D annotation on depth image to replace the "supervision signal from RGB image" in C3P. State-of-art fully-supervised methods [6,10,11,27,34,41,44,47] are compared to verify C2P's effectiveness. The performance comparison results are listed in Table 2. It can be observed that:

- C3P can achieve comparable results to fully-supervised methods. With the same 3D network, C3P's performance drop is slight (about 2–3% at mAP) .
- The results indicate that C3P can still work well when RGB images are missing. That is 2D annotation can also be used to train C3P.

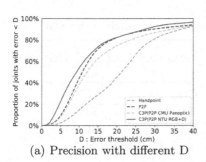
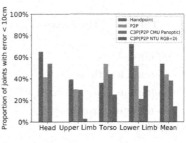

(a) Precision with different D   (b) Joints' mean precision

Fig. 5. Results on cross view test setting. C3P (P2P CMU Panoptic) and C3P (P2P NTU RGB+D) indicate C3P models with P2P [9] and are trained on CMU panoptic [16,17] and NTU RGB+D [33] respectively.

Cross View Test. To compare the generalization capacity of different 3D HPE methods, we conduct a cross view test on CMU Panoptic dataset. The HPE methods are trained on one view and tested on another. To enhance generalization ability of deep learning model, previous efforts often resort to complex data augmentation strategies [9,44]. However, C3P can use massive unannotated RGB-D data (e.g., NTU RGB+D [33] dataset) to achieve this goal. Specifically, we train C3P on NTU RGB+D dataset, and test it on CMU Panoptic dataset with cross view setting. The performance comparison among the different approaches is shown in Fig. 5. We can summarize that:

- In this challenging test case, performance of all 3D HPE methods drops remarkably. However compared to the fully-supervised counterpart (i.e., P2P), C3P can consistently acquire better performance when large-scale unannotated dataset (i.e., NTU RGB+D) is used to enhance generality;
- The results above reveal that C3P can benefit from large-scale unannotated RGB-D data easy to collect, which is preferred by practical applications. C3P's performance tends to be further facilitated when more unannotated data is used.

4.4   Ablation Study

Weak Supervision Signal. To verify the effectiveness of the proposed weak supervision information via 2D-to-3D ray projection against existing 3D-to-2D

Table 3. Performance comparison between different weak supervision methods (i.e., our 2D-to-3D ray projection manner vs. 3D-to-2D projection way) on ITOP dataset.

	mAP									
	Head	Neck	Shoulders	Elbows	Hands	Torso	Hips	Knees	Feet	Mean
3D-to-2D manner	95.9	95.0	90.0	67.8	48.6	91.7	80.5	85.6	76.5	78.7
2D-to-3D manner (ours)	**97.0**	**97.4**	**91.4**	**75.6**	**63.1**	**96.4**	**85.2**	**88.7**	**84.2**	**84.5**

Table 4. Effectiveness of self supervision signals within C3P.

Component	Mean error (cm)	mAP (@10 cm)
w/o bone length $\mathcal{L}_{len}$	6.9	86.6
w/o human body symmetry $\mathcal{L}_{sym}$	6.6	87.5
w/o motion consistency $\mathcal{L}_{con}$	7.4	85.5
C3P (ours)	**6.1**	**89.4**

projection way, they are compared on ITOP dataset. 2D ground-truth human pose annotation is used to resist the effect of 2D HPE. The results are listed in Table 3. It can be observed that:

- The proposed 2D-to-3D ray projection is superior to existing 3D-to-2D counterpart. This is mainly due to the fact that, our method can better measure the distance between the predicted and target joints in world coordinate system;
- For joints (e.g., feet and hands) of high freedom degrees, the 3D-to-2D ray projection supervision outperforms the 3D-to-2D projection strategy by large margins (i.e., +7.7% on feet and +14.5% on hands) at mAP.

Self Supervision Signal. In our method, three self supervision signals (i.e., bone length, human body symmetry and temporal consistency constrains of human pose) are proposed. To validate their effectiveness, we conduct ablation test on CMU Panoptic dataset by removing them item by item respectively. The results are listed in Table 4. It can be observed that:

- All the three self supervision signals are essential for leveraging performance. Among them, the temporal consistency constraint contributes the most towards the final result (i.e., 1.3cm at mean error and +3.9% at mAP).

Impact of 2D Human Pose Estimator. 2D human pose estimator plays the important role for generating C3P's weak supervision signals. Hence the effectiveness of 2D pose estimator can affect C3P's training phase remarkably. To investigate the impact of 2D human pose estimator, we compare it with the ground-truth 2D annotation on CMU Panoptic dataset. The results are listed in Table 5. It can be observed that:

- The impact of 2D pose estimator is remarkable to C3P. More accurate 2D pose estimation result leads to better 3D HPE;

Table 5. Impact of 2D human pose estimator on CMU Panoptic dataset. C3P* indicates C3P model trained with 2D ground-truth pose. The unit of error is cm.

	Nose	Eyes	Ears	Shoulders	Elbows	Wrists	Hips	Knees	Ankles	mAP	error
C3P* (P2P)	98.1	98.2	97.6	95.8	93.4	82.8	94.5	82.3	91.4	92.4	4.7
C3P* (PT)	**99.2**	**98.9**	**98.4**	**97.1**	**96.2**	**89.5**	**96.0**	**94.8**	**95.3**	**96.0**	**3.7**
C3P (P2P)	96.3	95.8	95.0	93.9	91.4	81.5	90.9	78.4	85.2	89.4	6.1
C3P (PT)	**99.1**	**98.6**	**95.9**	**95.4**	**94.4**	**85.4**	**93.1**	**91.1**	**94.0**	**93.8**	**5.3**

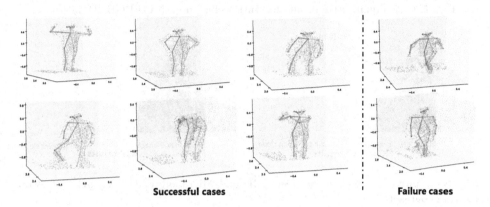

Successful cases   **Failure cases**

Fig. 6. C3P's qualitative results on CMU Panoptic dataset.

- The performance gain brought by more accurate 2D keypoint locations is consistent across all human joints. This reveals that, improving the quality of weak supervision signals (i.e., 2D pose estimation) is critical to C3P.

4.5   Qualitative Results

Some C3P's qualitative results on CMU Panoptic Dataset and NTU RGB+D Dataset are shown in Fig. 6. Generally, C3P works well towards variational human poses. The failure cases are mainly due to serious self-occlusion and missing points in point cloud. While, we also find that C3P is still of some anti-occlusion capacity as shown in Fig. 7, which may be due to the introduction of self supervision signals on temporal consistence and bone length. C3P is also compared with Kinect V2 SDK in Fig. 8. Under human-object interaction condition, C3P even outperforms Kinect V2. This indeed verifies C3P's application potentiality.

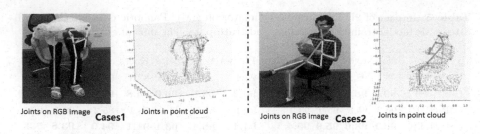

Fig. 7. C3P's qualitative results for anti-occlusion on NTU RGB+D dataset.

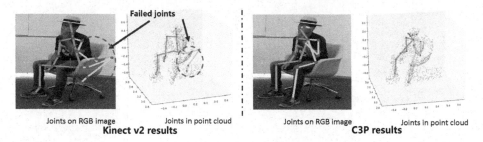

Fig. 8. Intuitive comparison between C3P and MicroSoft Kinect V2 SDK on NTU RGB+D dataset.

5   Conclusions

In this paper, C3P is proposed as a novel weakly supervised 3D HPE method towards point cloud. Its training phases does not require any 3D human pose annotation. Instead, we propose to propagate the 3D pose prior within the unlabelled RGB-point cloud sequence to 3D domain. The supervision signals derive from the well-established 2D pose estimator and the physical constrains of 3D human body. Extensive experiments demonstrate that C3P can achieve comparable or even better performance than the fully supervised counterparts. How to enhance C3P's anti-occlusion capacity is what we mainly concern in future.

Acknowledgements. This work is jointly supported by the National Natural Science Foundation of China (Grant No. 61502187 and 61876211). Joey Tianyi Zhou is supported by SERC Central Research Fund (Use-inspired Basic Research), Programmatic Grant No. A18A1b0045 from the Singapore government's Research, and Innovation and Enterprise 2020 plan (Advanced Manufacturing and Engineering domain).

References

1. Caetano, C., Sena, J., Brémond, F., Dos Santos, J.A., Schwartz, W.R.: SkeleMotion: a new representation of skeleton joint sequences based on motion information for 3D action recognition. In: Proceedings of IEEE International Conference on Advanced Video and Signal Based Surveillance (AVSS), pp. 1–8 (2019)

2. Cai, Y., Ge, L., Cai, J., Thalmann, N.M., Yuan, J.: 3D hand pose estimation using synthetic data and weakly labeled RGB images. IEEE Trans. Pattern Anal. Mach. Intell. **43**(11), 3739–3753 (2020)
3. Cai, Y., Ge, L., Cai, J., Yuan, J.: Weakly-supervised 3D hand pose estimation from monocular RGB images. In: Proceedings of the European Conference on Computer Vision (ECCV), pp. 666–682 (2018)
4. Cao, Z., Hidalgo Martinez, G., Simon, T., Wei, S., Sheikh, Y.A.: Realtime multi-person 2D pose estimation using part affinity fields. In: IEEE Transactions on Pattern Analysis and Machine Intelligence (2019)
5. Cao, Z., Simon, T., Wei, S.E., Sheikh, Y.: Realtime multi-person 2D pose estimation using part affinity fields. In: Proceedings of the IEEE Conference on Computer Vision and Pattern Recognition (CVPR) (2017)
6. Carreira, J., Agrawal, P., Fragkiadaki, K., Malik, J.: Human pose estimation with iterative error feedback. In: Proceedings of the IEEE Conference on Computer Vision and Pattern Recognition (CVPR), pp. 4733–4742 (2016)
7. Chen, X., Lin, K.Y., Liu, W., Qian, C., Lin, L.: Weakly-supervised discovery of geometry-aware representation for 3D human pose estimation. In: Proceedings of the IEEE Conference on Computer Vision and Pattern Recognition(CVPR), pp. 10895–10904 (2019)
8. Ge, L., Cai, Y., Weng, J., Yuan, J.: Hand pointnet: 3D hand pose estimation using point sets. In: Proceedings of the IEEE Conference on Computer Vision and Pattern Recognition (CVPR), pp. 8417–8426 (2018)
9. Ge, L., Ren, Z., Yuan, J.: Point-to-point regression pointnet for 3D hand pose estimation. In: Proceedings of the European Conference on Computer Vision (ECCV), pp. 475–491 (2018)
10. Guo, H., Wang, G., Chen, X., Zhang, C.: Towards good practices for deep 3D hand pose estimation. arXiv preprint arXiv:1707.07248 (2017)
11. Haque, A., Peng, B., Luo, Z., Alahi, A., Yeung, S., Fei-Fei, L.: Towards viewpoint invariant 3D human pose estimation. In: Proceedings of the European Conference on Computer Vision (ECCV), pp. 160–177 (2016)
12. He, K., Zhang, X., Ren, S., Sun, J.: Deep residual learning for image recognition. In: Proceedings of the IEEE Conference on Computer Vision and Pattern Recognition (CVPR), pp. 770–778 (2016)
13. He, L., Wang, G., Liao, Q., Xue, J.H.: Depth-images-based pose estimation using regression forests and graphical models. Neurocomputing **164**, 210–219 (2015)
14. Iqbal, U., Molchanov, P., Gall, T.B.J., Kautz, J.: Hand pose estimation via latent 2.5D heatmap regression. In: Proceedings of the European Conference on Computer Vision (ECCV) (2018)
15. Iqbal, U., Molchanov, P., Kautz, J.: Weakly-supervised 3D human pose learning via multi-view images in the wild. In: Proceedings of the IEEE Conference on Computer Vision and Pattern Recognition (CVPR), pp. 5243–5252 (2020)
16. Joo, H., et al.: Panoptic studio: a massively multiview system for social motion capture. In: Proceedings of the IEEE International Conference on Computer Vision (ICCV) (2015)
17. Joo, H., et al.: Panoptic studio: a massively multiview system for social interaction capture. IEEE Trans. Pattern Anal. Mach. Intell. (2017)
18. Kim, W.S., Ortega, A., Lai, P., Tian, D., Gomila, C.: Depth map distortion analysis for view rendering and depth coding. In: Proceedings of the IEEE International Conference on Image Processing (ICIP), pp. 721–724 (2009)
19. Kocabas, M., Karagoz, S., Akbas, E.: Self-supervised learning of 3D human pose using multi-view geometry. In: Proceedings of the IEEE Conference on Computer Vision and Pattern Recognition (CVPR), pp. 1077–1086 (2019)

20. Kundu, J.N., Seth, S., Jampani, V., Rakesh, M., Babu, R.V., Chakraborty, A.: Self-supervised 3D human pose estimation via part guided novel image synthesis. In: Proceedings of the IEEE Conference on Computer Vision and Pattern Recognition (CVPR), pp. 6152–6162 (2020)

21. Lin, T.-Y., et al.: Microsoft COCO: common objects in context. In: Fleet, D., Pajdla, T., Schiele, B., Tuytelaars, T. (eds.) ECCV 2014. LNCS, vol. 8693, pp. 740–755. Springer, Cham (2014). https://doi.org/10.1007/978-3-319-10602-1_48

22. Liu, J., Wang, G., Duan, L.Y., Abdiyeva, K., Kot, A.C.: Skeleton-based human action recognition with global context-aware attention LSTM networks. IEEE Trans. Image Process. **27**(4), 1586–1599 (2017)

23. Liu, J., Wang, G., Hu, P., Duan, L.Y., Kot, A.C.: Global context-aware attention LSTM networks for 3D action recognition. In: Proceedings of the IEEE Conference on Computer Vision and Pattern Recognition (CVPR), pp. 1647–1656 (2017)

24. Microsoft: Kinect for windows. https://developer.microsoft.com/en-us/windows/kinect/. Accessed 6 Feb 2022

25. Microsoft: Kinect for x-box 360. https://www.xbox.com/en-US/kinect. Accessed 6 Feb 2022

26. Mitra, R., Gundavarapu, N.B., Sharma, A., Jain, A.: Multiview-consistent semi-supervised learning for 3D human pose estimation. In: Proceedings of the IEEE Conference on Computer Vision and Pattern Recognition (CVPR), pp. 6907–6916 (2020)

27. Moon, G., Chang, J.Y., Lee, K.M.: V2V-PoseNet: voxel-to-voxel prediction network for accurate 3D hand and human pose estimation from a single depth map. In: Proceedings of the IEEE Conference on Computer Vision and Pattern Recognition (CVPR), pp. 5079–5088 (2018)

28. Newell, A., Yang, K., Deng, J.: Stacked hourglass networks for human pose estimation. In: Leibe, B., Matas, J., Sebe, N., Welling, M. (eds.) ECCV 2016. LNCS, vol. 9912, pp. 483–499. Springer, Cham (2016). https://doi.org/10.1007/978-3-319-46484-8_29

29. Obdržálek, Š., Kurillo, G., Han, J., Abresch, T., Bajcsy, R.: Real-time human pose detection and tracking for tele-rehabilitation in virtual reality. In: Medicine Meets Virtual Reality 19, pp. 320–324. IOS Press (2012)

30. Qi, C.R., Su, H., Mo, K., Guibas, L.J.: PointNet: deep learning on point sets for 3D classification and segmentation. In: Proceedings of the IEEE Conference on Computer Vision and Pattern Recognition, pp. 652–660 (2017)

31. Qi, C.R., Yi, L., Su, H., Guibas, L.J.: PointNet++: deep hierarchical feature learning on point sets in a metric space. Adv. Neural Inf. Process. Syst. **30** (2017)

32. Remelli, E., Han, S., Honari, S., Fua, P., Wang, R.: Lightweight multi-view 3D pose estimation through camera-disentangled representation. In: Proceedings of the IEEE Conference on Computer Vision and Pattern Recognition (CVPR), pp. 6040–6049 (2020)

33. Shahroudy, A., Liu, J., Ng, T.T., Wang, G.: NTU RGB+D: a large scale dataset for 3D human activity analysis. In: Proceedings of the IEEE Conference on Computer Vision and Pattern Recognition (CVPR), pp. 1010–1019 (2016)

34. Shotton, J., et al.: Real-time human pose recognition in parts from single depth images. In: Proceedings of the IEEE Conference on Computer Vision and Pattern Recognition (CVPR), pp. 1297–1304 (2011)

35. Shrivastava, A., Pfister, T., Tuzel, O., Susskind, J., Wang, W., Webb, R.: Learning from simulated and unsupervised images through adversarial training. In: Proceedings of the IEEE Conference on Computer Vision and Pattern Recognition (CVPR), pp. 2107–2116 (2017)

36. Simonyan, K., Zisserman, A.: Very deep convolutional networks for large-scale image recognition. arXiv preprint arXiv:1409.1556 (2014)
37. Sun, X., Xiao, B., Wei, F., Liang, S., Wei, Y.: Integral human pose regression. In: Proceedings of the European Conference on Computer Vision (ECCV), pp. 529–545 (2018)
38. Svenstrup, M., Tranberg, S., Andersen, H.J., Bak, T.: Pose estimation and adaptive robot behaviour for human-robot interaction. In: Proceedings of the IEEE International Conference on Robotics and Automation (ICRA), pp. 3571–3576 (2009)
39. Wan, C., Probst, T., Gool, L.V., Yao, A.: Self-supervised 3D hand pose estimation through training by fitting. In: Proceedings of the IEEE Conference on Computer Vision and Pattern Recognition (CVPR), pp. 10853–10862 (2019)
40. Wandt, B., Rosenhahn, B.: RepNet: weakly supervised training of an adversarial reprojection network for 3D human pose estimation. In: Proceedings of the IEEE Conference on Computer Vision and Pattern Recognition (CVPR), pp. 7782–7791 (2019)
41. Wang, K., Lin, L., Ren, C., Zhang, W., Sun, W.: Convolutional memory blocks for depth data representation learning. In: Proceedings of International Joint Conference on Artificial Intelligence (IJCAI), pp. 2790–2797 (2018)
42. Wei, S.E., Ramakrishna, V., Kanade, T., Sheikh, Y.: Convolutional pose machines. In: Proceedings of the IEEE Conference on Computer Vision and Pattern Recognition (CVPR) (2016)
43. Xiao, B., Wu, H., Wei, Y.: Simple baselines for human pose estimation and tracking. In: Proceedings of the European Conference on Computer Vision (ECCV) (2018)
44. Xiong, F., et al.: A2J: anchor-to-joint regression network for 3D articulated pose estimation from a single depth image. In: Proceedings of the IEEE International Conference on Computer Vision (ICCV), pp. 793–802 (2019)
45. Ye, M., Wang, X., Yang, R., Ren, L., Pollefeys, M.: Accurate 3D pose estimation from a single depth image. In: Proceedings of the IEEE Conference on Computer Vision and Pattern Recognition (CVPR), pp. 731–738 (2011)
46. Ying, J., Zhao, X.: RGB-D fusion for point-cloud-based 3D human pose estimation. In: Proceedings of IEEE International Conference on Image Processing (ICIP), pp. 3108–3112 (2021)
47. Yub Jung, H., Lee, S., Seok Heo, Y., Dong Yun, I.: Random tree walk toward instantaneous 3D human pose estimation. In: Proceedings of the IEEE Conference on Computer Vision and Pattern Recognition (CVPR), pp. 2467–2474 (2015)
48. Zhang, B., et al.: 3D human pose estimation with cross-modality training and multi-scale local refinement. Appl. Soft Comput. **122**, 108950 (2022)
49. Zhang, Z., Hu, L., Deng, X., Xia, S.: Weakly supervised adversarial learning for 3D human pose estimation from point clouds. IEEE Trans. Visual Comput. Graphics **26**(5), 1851–1859 (2020)
50. Zhao, H., Jiang, L., Jia, J., Torr, P.H., Koltun, V.: Point transformer. In: Proceedings of the IEEE International Conference on Computer Vision (ICCV), pp. 16259–16268 (2021)
51. Zhou, X., Huang, Q., Sun, X., Xue, X., Wei, Y.: Towards 3D human pose estimation in the wild: a weakly-supervised approach. In: Proceedings of the IEEE International Conference on Computer Vision (ICCV), pp. 398–407 (2017)
52. Zhou, Y., Dong, H., El Saddik, A.: Learning to estimate 3D human pose from point cloud. IEEE Sens. J. **20**(20), 12334–12342 (2020)

Pose-NDF: Modeling Human Pose Manifolds with Neural Distance Fields

Garvita Tiwari[1,2(✉)], Dimitrije Antić[1], Jan Eric Lenssen[2],
Nikolaos Sarafianos[3], Tony Tung[3], and Gerard Pons-Moll[1,2]

[1] University of Tübingen, Tübingen, Germany
{garvita.tiwari,dimirije.antic,gerard.pons-moll}@uni-tuebingen.de
[2] Max Planck Institute for Informatics, Saarland Informatics Campus, Saarbrücken,
Germany
jlenssen@mpi-inf.mpg.de
[3] Meta Reality Labs Research, Sausalito, USA
{nsarafianos,tony.tung}@fb.com

Abstract. We present Pose-NDF, a continuous model for plausible
human poses based on neural distance fields (NDFs). Pose or motion priors are important for generating realistic new poses and for reconstructing accurate poses from noisy or partial observations. Pose-NDF learns
a manifold of plausible poses as the zero level set of a neural implicit
function, extending the idea of modeling implicit surfaces in 3D to the
high-dimensional domain $SO(3)^K$, where a human pose is defined by
a single data point, represented by K quaternions. The resulting high-
dimensional implicit function can be differentiated with respect to the
input poses and thus can be used to project arbitrary poses onto the
manifold by using gradient descent on the set of 3-dimensional hyper-
spheres. In contrast to previous VAE-based human pose priors, which
transform the pose space into a Gaussian distribution, we model the
actual pose manifold, preserving the distances between poses. We demonstrate that Pose-NDF outperforms existing state-of-the-art methods as
a prior in various downstream tasks, ranging from denoising real-world
human mocap data, pose recovery from occluded data to 3D pose reconstruction from images. Furthermore, we show that it can be used to
generate more diverse poses by random sampling and projection than
VAE-based methods. We will release our code and pre-trained model for
further research at https://virtualhumans.mpi-inf.mpg.de/posendf/.

1 Introduction

Realistic and accurate human motion capture and generation is essential for
understanding human behavior and human interaction in the scene [9,23,41,
67,68]. Human motion capturing systems, like marker-based systems [34,37],
IMU-based methods [23,41], or reconstruction from RGB/RGB-D data [22,29,
55,70], often suffer from artifacts like skating, self-intersections and jitters and

---

Supplementary Information The online version contains supplementary material
available at https://doi.org/10.1007/978-3-031-20065-6_33.

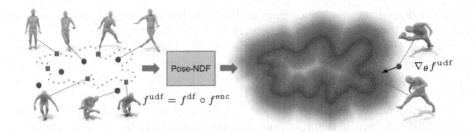

Fig. 1. We present Pose-NDF, a neural unsigned distance field in $SO(3)^K$, which learns the manifold of plausible poses as zero level set. We learn the distance field representation from samples of plausible (■) and unrealistic (●) poses (**left**). We encode the input pose (given as a set of quaternions) using a structural MLP f^{enc} and predict the distance from the joint representation using an MLP f^{df}. The gradient $\nabla_\theta f^{\mathrm{udf}}$ and distance value $f^{\mathrm{udf}}(\theta)$ are used to project implausible poses onto the manifold (**right**). (Color figure online)

produce non-realistic human poses, especially in the presence of noisy data and occlusion. To make the results applicable in fields like 3D scene understanding, human motion generation, or AR/VR applications, it is often required to apply exhaustive manual or automatic cleaning procedures.

In recent years, learned data priors to post-process such non-realistic human poses has become increasingly popular. Prior human pose models mainly focus on learning a joint distribution of individual joints in pose space [10] or recently in a latent space, using VAEs [49,52,66]. They have demonstrated to greatly improve the plausibility of poses after model fitting. However, VAE-based methods, such as VPoser [49] or HuMoR [52] make a Gaussian assumption on the space of possible poses, which leads to several limitations: **1)** They have the *tendency of producing more likely poses* that lie near the mean of the computed Gaussian. Those poses however, might not be the correct ones. **2)** Distances between individual human poses are *not preserved* in the VAE latent space. Hence, taking small steps towards the Gaussian mean might result in large steps in pose space. **3)** VAEs have been shown to *fold* a manifold into a Gaussian distribution [39], exposing *dead regions* without any data points in the outer parts of the distribution. Thus, they produce non-plausible samples that are far from the input when traversed in outer regions, as we demonstrate in our experiments.

To alleviate these issues, we present Pose-NDF, a human pose prior that models the full manifold of plausible poses in high-dimensional pose space. We represent the manifold as a surface, where plausible poses lie on the manifold, hence having a zero distance, and non-plausible poses lie outside of it, having a non-zero distance from the surface. We propose to learn this manifold using a high-dimensional neural field, analogously to representing 3D shapes using neural distance fields [13,48]. This formulation preserves distances between poses and allows to traverse the pose space along the negative gradient of the distance function, which points to the direction of maximum distance decrease. Using gradient descent in pose space from an initial potentially non-plausible pose, we always find the closest point on the manifold of plausible poses.

An overview of our method is given in Fig. 1. We formulate the problem of learning the pose manifold as a surface completion task in n-dimensional space. In order to learn a pose manifold, there are two key challenges: **a)** the input space is high-dimensional, and **b)** the input space is not Euclidean, as it is for 3-dimensional implicit surfaces [13,48]. Instead, the pose space is given as $SO(3)^K$, in which a single pose can be represented by K elements of the rotation group $SO(3)$, describing the orientations of joints in a human body model. To represent group elements, we opted for a quaternion representation, as they are continuous, have an easy-to-compute distance, and are subject to an efficient gradient descent algorithm. We map a given pose to a distance by applying a hierarchical implicit neural function, which encodes the pose based on the kinematic structure of the human body. We train our model using the AMASS dataset [38], where each sample from the dataset is treated as a point on the manifold. The learned neural field representation can be used to project any pose onto the manifold, similar to [13]. We leverage this property and use Pose-NDF for diverse pose generation, pose interpolation, as a pose prior for 3D pose estimation from images [10,49], and motion denoising [23,52], improving on state-of-the-art methods in all areas. In summary our contributions are:

- A novel high-dimensional neural field representation in $SO(3)^K$, Pose-NDF, which represents the manifold of plausible human poses.
- Pose-NDF improves the state of the art in human body fitting from images by acting as a pose prior. It outperforms other human pose priors, such as VPoser [49] and the human motion prior HuMoR [52] on motion denoising.
- Our method is as fast or faster than current state-of-the-art methods, is fully differentiable and the distance from the manifold can be leveraged for finding the optimal step size during optimization.
- Pose-NDF generates more diverse samples than previous methods with Gaussian assumptions, which are biased towards generating more likely poses.

2   Related Work

Our method is a *human pose prior* build as *neural field* in high-dimensional space. Thus, we review related work in both of these areas.

Pose and Motion Priors. Human pose and motion priors are crucial for preserving the realism of models estimated from captured data [23,38,40] and to estimate human pose from images [10,14,33,49,65] and videos [32,59]. Further, they can be powerful tools for data generation. Initial work along this direction mainly focused on learning constraints for joint limits in Euler angles [17] or swing and twist representations [1,6,56], to avoid twists and bends beyond certain limits. A next iteration of methods fits a Gaussian Mixture Model (GMM) to a pose dataset and uses the GMM-based prior for downstream tasks like image-based 3D pose estimation [10,54] or registration of 3D scans [4,8,60]. Additionally, simple statistical models, such as PCA, have been proposed [47,57,62]. With the rise of deep learning and GANs [20], adversarial training has been used to bring predicted poses close to real poses [19,31] and for motion prediction [7]. However these are task specific models, HMR [31] models $p(\boldsymbol{\theta}|I)$ and requires an image I. HP-GAN [7] models $p(\boldsymbol{\theta}_t|\boldsymbol{\theta}_{t-1})$ and requires pose parameters $\boldsymbol{\theta}_{t-1}$ for previous frame/time. Therefore they cannot be used as a prior for other tasks.

More recent work uses VAEs to learn pose priors [49], which can be used for generating pose samples, as prior in pose estimation, or 3d human reconstruction from images or sparse/occluded data. Some works [50,52,66] propose VAE-based human motion models. HuMoR [52] proposes to learn a distribution of possible pose transitions in motion sequences using a conditional VAE. ACTOR [50] learns an action conditioned VAE-Transformer prior. Further work designs pose representations along the hierarchy of human skeletons [2] and uses it for character animation [5]. Concurrent work [16] learns a human pose prior using GANs and highlights the shortcomings of Gaussian assumption based models like VPoser [49]. A VPoser decoder is used as generator (mapping $z \rightarrow \theta$) and an HMR [31]-like discriminator is used to train the model. As described in Sect. 1, our approach follows a different paradigm than the VAE and GAN-based methods, as we directly model the manifold of plausible poses in high-dimensional space, which leads to a distance-preserving representation.

Before the rise of deep learning, modeling partial pose spaces as implicit functions was common, e.g. as fields on a single shoulder joint quaternion [26] or an elbow joint quaternion, conditioned on the shoulder joint [25]. However, those ignore the real part of the quaternion, leading to ambiguities in representation, are not differentiable, and are limited to 2 joints in the human body model. In contrast, our method uses a fully differentiable neural network, which learns an implicit surface in higher dimension, taking all human joints and all four components of each quaternion into account.

Neural Fields. Neural fields [13,42,48] for surface modeling have received increasing interest over the recent years. They have been used to model fields in 2D or 3D, representing images or partial differentiable equations [21,58], signed or unsigned distances from static 3D shapes [13,24,27,48], pose-conditioned distance field [43,53,61], radiance fields [44,51] and more recently for human-object [9,63] and hand-object [69] interactions. For a more detailed overview of neural fields please refer to [64]. Neural fields have recently been brought to higher dimensions to model surfaces in Euclidean spaces [45]. In this work, we apply the concept to the high-dimensional, non-Euclidean space of $SO(3)^K$, modeling the unsigned distance to manifolds of plausible human body poses in pose space.

3 Method

In this section, we describe our method Pose-NDF, a model for manifolds of plausible human poses based on high-dimensional neural fields. We assume that the realistic and plausible human poses lie on a manifold embedded in pose space $SO(3)^K$, with K being the number of joints in the human body. Given a neural network $f : SO(3)^K \mapsto \mathbb{R}^+$, which maps a pose, $\boldsymbol{\theta} \in SO(3)^K$ to a non-negative scalar, we represent the manifold of plausible poses as the zero level set:

$$\mathcal{S} = \{\boldsymbol{\theta} \in SO(3)^K \mid f(\boldsymbol{\theta}) = 0\}, \tag{1}$$

such that the value of f represents the unsigned distance to the manifold, similar to neural fields-based 3D shape learning [12,13,21,48]. Without loss of generality, we use the SMPL body model [36,49], resulting in poses $\boldsymbol{\theta}$ with $K = 21$ joints.

3.1 Quaternions as Representation of SO(3)

A human pose is represented by 3D rotations of individual joints in the human skeleton. The 3-dimensional rotation group $SO(3)$ has several common vector space representations that are used to describe group elements in practice. Frequently used examples are rotation matrices, axis-angle representations or unit quaternions [28]. Pose-NDF requires the representation to have specific properties: a) we aim to model a *manifold*, continuously embedded in pose space. Thus, the chosen representation should be continuous in parameter space, which prohibits axis-angle representations; b) the representation should enable efficient computation of the geodesic distance between two elements; c) our algorithm requires *efficient gradient descent* in pose space. As described in Sect. 3.4, quaternions are subject to such a gradient descent algorithm that makes use of the efficient reprojection to $SO(3)$ by vector normalization. In contrast, rotation matrices would require more expensive orthogonalization. Therefore, we chose unit quaternions as the best-suited $SO(3)$ representation of joints, as they fulfill all three properties. We will use $\boldsymbol{\theta} = \{\boldsymbol{\theta}_1, ..., \boldsymbol{\theta}_K\}$ to denote the quaternions for all K joints of a pose. Each quaternion represents the rotation of a joint with respect to its parent node. Since quaternions lie on S^3 (embedded in 4-dimensional space) the full pose $\boldsymbol{\theta}$ can be easily used as input for a neural network $f : \mathbb{R}^{4K} \to \mathbb{R}^+$. We define the distance $d : (S^3)^K \times (S^3)^K \to \mathbb{R}^+$ between two poses $\boldsymbol{\theta} = \{\boldsymbol{\theta}_1, ..., \boldsymbol{\theta}_K\}$ and $\hat{\boldsymbol{\theta}} = \{\hat{\boldsymbol{\theta}}_1, ..., \hat{\boldsymbol{\theta}}_K\}$ as:

$$d(\boldsymbol{\theta}, \hat{\boldsymbol{\theta}}) = \sqrt{\sum_{i=1}^{K} \frac{w_i}{2}(\arccos |\boldsymbol{\theta}_i^\top \cdot \hat{\boldsymbol{\theta}}_i|)^2}, \tag{2}$$

where the individual elements of summation are a metric on $SO(3)$ [28] and w_i is the weight associated with each joint based on their position in the kinematic structure of the SMPL body model (i.e. early joints in the chain have higher weights). It should be noted that the double cover property of unit quaternions, that is, the quaternions $\mathbf{q}$ and $-\mathbf{q}$ represent the same $SO(3)$ element, does not lead to additional challenges. We simply train the network to be point symmetric by applying sign flip augmentation on input quaternions.

3.2 Hierarchical Implicit Neural Function

We represent the human pose with quaternions in local coordinate frames of the parent joint, using the kinematic structure of the SMPL body model. We treat the joints in local coordinate frame, so that continuous manipulation of a single joint corresponds to realistic motion. However, this might result in unrealistic combination of rotation of joints. The plausibility of individual joints depends on the ancestor rotations and thus needs to be conditioned on them. In order to incorporate this dependency, we use a hierarchical network f^{enc}, which encodes the human pose based on the model structure [2,19,43], before predicting the distance based on the joint representation.

Formally, for a given pose $\boldsymbol{\theta} = \{\boldsymbol{\theta}_1, ..., \boldsymbol{\theta}_K\}$, where $\boldsymbol{\theta}_k$ is the pose for joint k, and a function $\tau(k)$, mapping the index of each joint to its parent joints index, we encode each pose using an MLP as:

$$f_1^{\text{enc}} : (\boldsymbol{\theta}_1) \mapsto \mathbf{v}_1 \quad f_k^{\text{enc}} : (\boldsymbol{\theta}_k, \mathbf{v}_{\tau(k)}) \mapsto \mathbf{v}_k, \quad k \in \{2 \ldots K\} \tag{3}$$

which takes the quaternion pose and encoded feature $\mathbf{v}_{\tau(k)} \in \mathbb{R}^l$ of its parent joint as input and generates $\mathbf{v}_k \in \mathbb{R}^l$, where l is the dimension of feature. We then concatenate the encoded feature for every joint to get a combined pose embedding $\mathbf{p} = [\mathbf{v}_1 || \ldots || \mathbf{v}_K]$. This embedding is processed by an MLP $f^{\text{df}} : \mathbb{R}^{l \cdot K} \to \mathbb{R}^+$, which predicts the unsigned distance for the given pose representation $\mathbf{p}$. Collectively the complete model $f^{\text{udf}}(\boldsymbol{\theta}) = (f^{\text{df}} \circ f^{\text{enc}})(\boldsymbol{\theta})$, is termed as Pose-NDF, where $f^{\text{udf}} : SO(3)^K \mapsto \mathbb{R}^+$.

3.3   Loss Functions

We train the hierarchically structured neural field f^{udf} to predict the geodesic distance to the plausible pose manifold for a given pose. The training data is given as a set $\mathcal{D} = \{(\boldsymbol{\theta}_i, d_i)\}_{1 \leq i \leq N}$, containing pairs of poses $\boldsymbol{\theta}_i$ and distances d_i (Eq. 2). We train the network with the standard distance loss $\mathcal{L}_{\text{UDF}}$, and an Eikonal regularizer $\mathcal{L}_{\text{eikonal}}$, which encourages a unit-norm gradient for the distance field outside of the manifold [15,21]:

$$\mathcal{L}_{\text{UDF}} = \sum_{(\boldsymbol{\theta}, d) \in \mathcal{D}} \|f^{\text{udf}}(\boldsymbol{\theta}) - d_{\boldsymbol{\theta}}\|_2 \quad \mathcal{L}_{\text{eikonal}} = \sum_{(\boldsymbol{\theta}, d) \in \mathcal{D}, \, d \neq 0} (\|\nabla_{\boldsymbol{\theta}} f^{\text{udf}}(\boldsymbol{\theta})\| - 1)^2, \tag{4}$$

More details about training data, network architecture is provided in the supplementary material.

3.4   Projection Algorithm

Given a trained model f^{udf}, it can be applied to project an arbitrary pose $\boldsymbol{\theta}$ to the manifold of plausible poses. We use the predicted distance $f^{\text{udf}}(\boldsymbol{\theta})$ and gradient information $\nabla_{\boldsymbol{\theta}} f^{\text{udf}}(\boldsymbol{\theta})$ to project a query pose to the manifold surface $\mathcal{S}$, as was previously done in unsigned distances functions for 3D shapes [13]. In our case, given $SO(3)$ poses, this amounts to finding:

$$\hat{\boldsymbol{\theta}} = \arg\min_{\boldsymbol{\theta} \in SO(3)^K} d(\boldsymbol{\theta}, \mathcal{S}), \tag{5}$$

where $d(\boldsymbol{\theta}, \mathcal{S})$ is the distance (Eq. 2) of $\boldsymbol{\theta}$ to the closest point in $\mathcal{S}$. We find $\hat{\boldsymbol{\theta}}$ by applying gradient descent on the 3-sphere, using gradient information $\nabla_{\boldsymbol{\theta}} f(\boldsymbol{\theta})$ and distances $f(\boldsymbol{\theta})$, obtained from the implicit neural function f. One step is given as:

$$\boldsymbol{\theta}^i = \boldsymbol{\theta}^{i-1} - \alpha f(\boldsymbol{\theta}^{i-1}) \nabla_{\boldsymbol{\theta}} f(\boldsymbol{\theta}^{i-1}), \tag{6}$$

followed by a re-projection to the sphere (i.e. vector normalization) after several iterations. This algorithm is guaranteed to converge to local minima on the sphere, which in our case, assuming a correctly learned distance function, is the nearest point on the pose manifold.

4   Experiments and Results

In this section we evaluate Pose-NDF and show the different use cases of our pose model, which include the ability to serve as a *prior in denoising motion sequences or recovery* from partial observations (Sect. 4.2), *prior for recovering plausible poses* from images (Sect. 4.3) using an optimization-based method, *pose generation* (Sect. 4.4) and *pose interpolation* (Sect. 4.5). We demonstrate that the Pose-NDF method *outperforms the state-of-the-art VAE-based human pose prior methods*. We also show the *advantages* of our distance field formulation over VAEs or Gaussian assumption models (Sect. 4.6). Before turning to the results, we explain training and implementation details of Pose-NDF in Sect. 4.1.

4.1   Experimental Setup

We use the AMASS dataset [38] for training. As mentioned in Sect. 3.3, we train the network with supervision on predicted distance values, and hence we create a dataset of pose and distance pairs $(\boldsymbol{\theta}, d_{\boldsymbol{\theta}})$. Since the training samples from AMASS lie on the desired manifold, $d_{\boldsymbol{\theta}} = 0$ is assigned to all poses in the dataset. We then randomly generate negative samples with distance $d_{\boldsymbol{\theta}} > 0$ by adding noise to AMASS poses. Please find details of data preparation in supplementary. We train our model in a **multi-stage** regime by varying the type of training samples used. We start our training with manifold poses $\boldsymbol{\theta}_m$ and non-manifold poses $\boldsymbol{\theta}_{nm}$ with a large distance to the desired manifold. Then we increase the number of non-manifold poses $\boldsymbol{\theta}_{nm}$ with a small distance in each training batch. This training scheme helps to initially learn a smooth surface and to iteratively introduce the fine details over the course of training. Our **network architecture** consists of one 2-layer MLP f^{enc} with an output feature size of $l = 6$ for each joint, similar to [43]. Thus, the pose encoding network generates a feature vector $\mathbf{p} \in \mathbb{R}^{126}$. We implement the distance field network f^{df} as a 5-layer MLP. For training, we use the softplus activation in the hidden layer and train the network end-to-end using the loss functions described in Eq. (4).

Table 1. Motion denoising: We compare the per-vertex error (in *cm*) on mocap data from HPS (**left**) and AMASS (**middle**) and on artificially created noisy AMASS data (**right**). In all cases, Pose-NDF based motion denoising results in the least error. We also observe that in case of mocap data (HPS, AMASS), motion denoising using Pose-NDF results in very small error (small change from input), which is the desired behavior as these mocap poses are already realistic and hence close to our learned manifold. On the other hand, HuMoR changes the input pose significantly.

Data # frames	HPS [23]			AMASS [38]			Noisy AMASS		
	60	120	240	60	120	240	60	120	240
Method									
VPoser [49]	4.91	4.16	3.81	1.52	1.55	1.47	8.96	9.13	9.15
HuMoR [52]	9.69	8.73	10.86	3.21	3.62	3.67	11.04	17.14	30.31
Pose-NDF	**2.32**	**2.14**	**2.11**	**0.59**	**0.55**	**0.54**	**7.96**	**8.31**	**8.46**

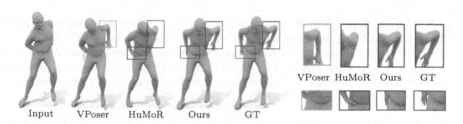

Fig. 2. Motion denoising: We observe that Pose-NDF based motion denoising makes the pose realistic and solves small intersection issues, while VPoser and HuMoR still result in unrealistic poses.

4.2 Denoising Mocap Data

Human motion capture has been done using diverse setups ranging from RGB, RGB-D to IMU based capture systems. The data captured from these sources often produce artifacts like jitters, unnaturally rigid joints or weird bends at some joints, or positions with only partial observations. Prior work [52] improves the quality of captured motion sequences by using an optimization-based method, with the goal of recovering the captured data and preserving the realism of human poses. A robust and expressive human pose prior is key to preserve the realism of optimized poses, along with preserving the original data. Following HuMoR [52], we demonstrate the effectiveness of our pose manifold for: 1) motion denoising and 2) fitting to partial data.

We follow the same experimental setup as [52], but only deal with human poses and thus, remove the terms corresponding to human-scene contact and translation of root joint. In total, we find the pose parameters $\hat{\theta}^t$ at frame t as:

$$\hat{\theta}^t = \arg \min_{\theta} \lambda_v \mathcal{L}_v + \lambda_\theta \mathcal{L}_\theta + \lambda_t \mathcal{L}_t, \tag{7}$$

HuMoR

GT

Ours

Time

Fig. 3. Motion denoising: We compare the results on motion denoising using Pose-NDF and HuMoR [52] as priors with GT data and visualize every 10th frame of a sequence. We observe that for HuMoR (**top**) the correction in input pose accumulates over time and makes the output pose significantly different from the GT (**middle**). Pose-NDF remains close to observations while correcting unrealistic poses (**bottom**).

where $\mathcal{L}_v$ makes sure that the optimized pose is close to the observation and the temporal smoothness term $\mathcal{L}_t$ enforces temporal consistency:

$$\mathcal{L}_v = ||\mathcal{J}(\boldsymbol{\beta}_0, \hat{\boldsymbol{\theta}}^t) - \mathcal{J}_{\text{obs}}||_2^2 \quad \mathcal{L}_t = ||M(\boldsymbol{\beta}_0, \hat{\boldsymbol{\theta}}^t) - M(\boldsymbol{\beta}_0, \boldsymbol{\theta}^{t-1})||_2^2. \quad (8)$$

Here, $\mathcal{J}(\boldsymbol{\beta}, \boldsymbol{\theta})$ represent vertices (mocap markers) and $M(\boldsymbol{\beta}, \boldsymbol{\theta})$ represents SMPL mesh vertices for a given pose ($\boldsymbol{\theta}$) and shape ($\boldsymbol{\beta}$) parameters of SMPL [36]. Finally, we use Pose-NDF as a pose prior term in the optimization by minimizing the distance of the current pose from our learned manifold, $\mathcal{L}_\theta = f^{\text{udf}}(\boldsymbol{\theta})$. We leverage the distance $f^{\text{udf}}(\boldsymbol{\theta})$ to get the optimal step size during optimization.

We evaluate on two different settings: 1) clean mocap datasets and 2) a noisy mocap dataset. For clean mocap datasets, we use HPS [23] and the test split of AMASS [38,49]. For the noisy mocap dataset, we create random noisy sequences by adding Gaussian noise to AMASS test sequences and call it "Noisy AMASS". The average noise introduced in "Noisy AMASS" is 9.3 *cm*. We use a list of SMPL mesh vertices $\mathcal{J}$ as observation during optimization. We created the data with a fixed shape and do not optimize for shape parameters $\boldsymbol{\beta}$. Instead of adding noise to joint locations, we add noise directly to the rotation of each joint. This is done for all methods to ensure a fair comparison. For HuMoR [52], we use the *TestOpt* optimization from the original work. VPoser does not have motion experiments, which is why we combine the latent space optimization from the original work with our optimization given in Eq. (7) to ensure that we compare against the best possible result. Specifically, we first encode the rotation matrix representation of noisy input pose $\boldsymbol{\theta}^t$ using the VPoser encoder as

Table 2. Motion estimation from partial 3D observations: We compare per-vertex error (in cm). It can be seen that for leg and arm/hand occlusions, Pose-NDF reconstructs the pose better than VPoser and HuMoR. For occluded shoulders, HuMoR takes the lead. We observe that results of Pose-NDF depend on the initialization of the occluded joint, as it is expected from manifold projection.

Data # frames	Occ. Leg			Occ. Arm+hand			Occ. Shoulder +Upper Arm		
	60	120	240	60	120	240	60	120	240
Method									
VPoser [49]	2.53	2.57	2.54	8.51	8.52	8.59	9.98	9.49	9.48
HuMoR [52]	5.60	6.19	9.09	7.83	8.44	10.25	**4.75**	**5.11**	**4.95**
Pose-NDF	**2.49**	**2.51**	**2.47**	**7.81**	**8.13**	**7.98**	7.63	7.89	6.76

$z^t = f_{\text{v\_enc}}(\boldsymbol{\theta}^t)$, then add random noise ($\hat{\epsilon}$) in the latent space and reconstruct the pose by $\tilde{\boldsymbol{\theta}}^t = f_{\text{v\_dec}}(z^t + \hat{\epsilon})$. Following [66], we observe that the temporal term in latent space yields better results than the temporal term in input pose/vertices, which we used in the VPoser experiment. The prior and temporal term for VPoser-based denoising are given as:

$$\mathcal{L}_\theta^{\text{VPoser}} = ||\hat{\epsilon}||_2 \qquad \mathcal{L}_t^{\text{VPoser}} = ||z^{t-1} - \hat{z}^t||_2. \qquad (9)$$

Results. We compare motion denoising between HuMoR [52] (*TestOpt*), Eq. (7) with VPoser prior [49], and Eq. (7) with Pose-NDF prior in Table 1. Pose-NDF achieves the lowest error in all settings. For mocap datasets like AMASS and HPS the motion is realistic, but can have small artifacts and jitter. Thus, an ideal motion/pose prior should not change the overall pose of these examples, but only fix these local artifacts. We observe that, numerically, VPoser and Pose-NDF-based optimization do not change the input pose significantly. However HuMoR changes the pose and this change increases with an increasing number of frames. This is because HuMoR is a motion-based prior (conditioned on the previous pose) and, hence, over time the correction in pose accumulates and makes the output pose significantly different from the input.

For the "Noisy AMASS" data, Pose-NDF-based optimization outperforms prior work. We visualise the denoising results in Fig. 2, and observe that the Pose-NDF-based method produces realistic and close to GT results. We further compare results of a sequence with HuMoR in Fig. 3. HuMoR results in large deviations from the input/GT, due to accumulation of correction over time.

Fitting to Partial Data. We use the test set of AMASS and randomly create occluded poses (e.g. missing arm or legs or shoulder joint) and quantitatively compare with HuMoR [52] and VPoser [49] in Table 2. We use Eq. (7) for VPoser and Pose-NDF-based optimization. We only optimize for the occluded joints and for our model, we initialize the occluded joint pose randomly (close to 0). For HuMoR, we use the *TestOpt* provided in their paper. We evaluate on three differ-ent type of occlusions: 1) occluded left leg, 2) occluded left arm and 3) occluded

LSP dataset [30]   High resolution LSP dataset [30]

COCO dataset [35]   3DPW dataset [40]

Fig. 4. 3D pose and shape estimation from in-the-wild images using Pose-NDF-based optimization method.

Table 3. 3D pose and shape estimation from images using Pose-NDF, GAN-S [16] and VPoser [49] as pose prior terms in optimization-based method (**left**). We also use proposed prior and optimization pipeline to further improve the results of the SoTA 3D pose and shape estimation network, ExPose [14] (**right**).

Method	Optimization			ExPose	ExPose + Optimization			
	VPoser [49]	GAN-S [16]	Pose-NDF	-	+No prior	+ VPoser [49]	+ GAN-S [16]	+Pose-NDF
Per-vertex error (*mm*)	60.34	59.18	57.39	54.76	99.78	67.23	54.09	53.81

right shoulder and upper arm. For the occluded leg case, VPoser and our prior-based method perform better. We believe this is because the majority of the poses in both AMASS training and test are upright with nearly straight legs and hence VPoser is biased towards these poses. For our method, it highly depends on initialization. Since we have used an initialization close to rest position, our optimization method generates smaller error for occluded legs but higher errors for occluded arms and shoulders, as they usually are more far away from the rest pose. For HuMoR, the motion generated is realistic and plausible, but in some cases results in large deviation from ground truth, because the correction in input pose accumulates over the time.

4.3   3D Pose Estimation from Images

We now show that Pose-NDF can also be used as a prior in optimization-based 3D pose estimation from images [49]. We use the objective function proposed in SMPLify-X [49], see Eq. (10). Since we are working with a SMPL body only (without hands or faces), we remove the respective loss and prior terms. Thus, we find the desired pose $\hat{\theta}$ and shape $\hat{\beta}$ as:

$$\hat{\beta}, \hat{\theta} = \arg\min_{\beta,\theta} \mathcal{L}_J + \lambda_\theta \mathcal{L}_\theta + \lambda_\beta \mathcal{L}_\beta + \lambda_\alpha \mathcal{L}_\alpha, \tag{10}$$

with data term $\mathcal{L}_J$, bending term $\mathcal{L}_\alpha$, shape regularizer $\mathcal{L}_\beta$, and prior term $\mathcal{L}_\theta$. The data term and the bending term are given as:

$$\mathcal{L}_J = \sum_{i \in \text{joints}} \gamma_i w_i \rho(\Pi_K(R_\theta(J(\beta))) - J_{\text{est,i}}) \quad \mathcal{L}_\alpha = \sum_{i \in (\text{elbow,knees})} \exp(\theta_i), \tag{11}$$

where $J_{est,i}$ are 2D pose keypoints estimated by a SoTA 2D-pose estimation method [11], R_θ transforms the joints along the kinematic tree according to the pose θ, Π_K represents a 3D to 2D projection with intrinsic camera parameters and ρ represents a robust Geman-McClure error [18]. Further, the bending term $\mathcal{L}_\alpha$ penalizes large bending near the elbow and knee joints, and the shape regularizer is given as $\mathcal{L}_\beta = ||\beta||^2$ [49]. For VPoser, the prior term is given as $\mathcal{L}_\theta = ||z||_2^2$, where z is the 32-dimensional latent vector of the VAE. In our model, we use $\mathcal{L}_\theta = f^{udf}(\theta)$ and minimize the distance of the pose from our learned manifold using our projection algorithm. We leverage the distance information provided by our model in optimization by setting $\lambda_\theta = wf^{udf}(\theta)$, where w has a fixed value. This ensures that if the pose is getting close to the manifold (i.e. $f^{udf}(\theta)$ is very small), the prior term is down-weighted, which results in faster convergence.

Results. We use the EHF dataset [49] for quantitative evaluation and compare our work with the state-of-the-art priors VPoser [49] and GAN-S [16]. A Pose-NDF prior term slightly improves on the VPoser and GAN-S based optimization (Table 3). We observe that the neural network based model ExPose [14] outperforms all optimization-based results. However, we show that such methods can benefit from an optimization-based refinement step. We refine the ExPose output using Eq (10) with Pose-NDF as prior and compare this refinement with no-prior and other priors (Table 3). With no prior, the optimization objective only minimizes the joint projection loss, resulting in unrealistic poses. In contrast, GAN and Pose-NDF improve the result (qualitatively and quantitatively), generating realistic poses, while Pose-NDF outperforms the GAN prior. Finally, in Fig. 4 we show qualitative results of optimization-based 3D pose estimation on in-the-wild images from 3DPW [40], LSP [30] and MS-COCO [35] datasets.

4.4 Pose Generation

We evaluate our model on the task of pose generation. Due to our distance field formulation, we can generate diverse poses by sampling a random point from $SO(3)^K$ and projecting it onto the manifold (Sect. 3.4). We compare the results of our model with sampling from the state-of-the-art pose prior VPoser [49], GMM [10,46] and GAN-S [16] in Fig. 5. We use Average Pairwise Distance (APD) [3], to quantify the diversity of generated poses. APD is defined as mean joint distance between all pairs of samples. We randomly sample 500 poses for each GMM, VPoser, GAN-S and Pose-NDF, which results in APD values of **48.24**, **23.13**, **27.52**, **32.31** (in cm), respectively. We see that numerically, the GMM produces very large variance, but also results in unrealistic poses, as seen in Fig. 5 (top-left). Pose-NDF generates more diverse poses than VPoser while producing only plausible poses. We also calculate the percentage of self-intersecting faces in generated poses, to evaluate one aspect of realism in poses. Pose-NDF generates poses with less self-intersecting faces (**0.89%**), as compared to the GAN-S (**1.43%**) and VPoser (**2.10%**).

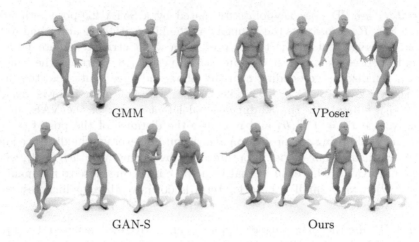

GMM   VPoser

GAN-S   Ours

Fig. 5. Pose generation: GMM generates wrong and unrealistic poses, whereas VPoser, GAN-S and Pose-NDF generate much more realistic poses. We notice from APD, that variance of poses generated by Pose-NDF (32.31 cm) is larger than VPoser (23.13 cm) and GAN-S (27.52 cm).

4.5   Pose Interpolation

Pose-NDF learns a manifold of plausible human poses, so it can be used to interpolate between two distinct poses by traversing the manifold. Specifically, for any given pose, we first project start (θ_0) and end pose (θ_T) on our manifold using Eq (6), to get θ_0' and θ_T'. We then move along the direction of θ_T' from θ_0' with step size τ using Eq (12). The interpolated pose (θ_t) is again projected on the manifold to get a realistic pose (θ_t'). In the subsequent interpolation steps, we move from θ_t' to θ_T', where θ_t' is updated after each step.

$$\theta_t = \theta_{t-1}' + \tau(\theta_T' - \theta_{t-1}') \tag{12}$$

Results: We compare the results of Pose-NDF with those from VPoser [49] and GAN-S [16] interpolation. For VPoser [49], we project the start and end pose into the latent space and perform linear interpolation using the latent vectors. For GAN-S [16], we use the spherical interpolation in latent space, as suggested in the work. We qualitatively evaluate the interpolation quality by calculating mean per-vertex distance between consecutive frames. Smaller value means smooth interpolation. We observe that Pose-NDF-based interpolation has a mean per-vertex distance of 2.72 ± 2.16, GAN-S has 2.71 ± 2.45 and VPoser has 2.53 ± 4.62, which shows that Pose-NDF and GAN-S based interpolation is smooth and the distance in input space is not entirely preserved in case of VAEs. We compare VPoser based interpolation with Pose-NDF in Fig. 6) and observe large jumps in VPoser interpolation. This behaviour is not observed in GAN-S and Pose-NDF based interpolation. Since the VAE learns a compact latent representation of poses, the distance between two input poses is not preserved in the latent space.

Fig. 6. Pose interpolation: We observe that VPoser-based interpolation (**top**) is less smooth than Pose-NDF-based pose interpolation (**bottom**).

4.6 Pose-NDF vs. Gaussian Assumption Models

Prior work [49,52] uses VAE-based models as pose/motion prior, which follow a Gaussian assumption in the latent space. This has three major limitations, as mentioned in Sect. 1. Conversely, Pose-NDF learns the manifold directly in the pose-space without such assumptions and, hence, overcomes these limitations.

We report the cumulative error based on deviation from the mean pose. We evaluate on AMASS Noisy (60 and 120 frames) and report cumulative error for samples with $\sigma, 2\sigma, 3\sigma$ for both Pose-NDF and VPoser motion denoising. We obtain per-vertex error of **8.18, 8.20, 8.21** *cm* for Pose-NDF and **8.35, 9.11, 9.13** *cm* for VPoser, and **10.08, 11.38, 16.86** *cm* for HuMoR which reflects that VPoser and HuMoR perform well for poses close to the mean but the error increases for samples deviating from mean pose. Since the Gaussian distribution is unbounded, it produces *dead regions*, without any data points in these parts of distribution. Hence sampling in these regions might result in completely unrealistic poses for GMM and VPoser (Fig. 5). Lastly, since we learn the manifold in pose space, the distance between individual poses is preserved and leads to smoother interpolation compared to VPoser (see Sect. 4.5).

5 Conclusion

We introduced a novel human pose prior model represented by a scalar neural distance field that describes a manifold of plausible poses as zero level set in $SO(3)^K$. The method extends the idea of classic 3D shape representation using neural fields to higher the dimensions of human poses and maps quaternion-based poses to an unsigned distance value, representing the distance to the pose manifold. The resulting network can be used to project arbitrary poses to the pose manifold, opening applications in several areas. We comprehensively evaluate the performance of our model in diverse pose sampling, pose estimation from images, and motion denoising. We show that our model is able to generate poses with much more diversity than prior VAE-based works and improves state-of-the-art results in reconstruction from images and motion estimation.

Acknowledgements. Special thanks to the RVH team and reviewers, their feedback helped improve the manuscript and Andrey Davydov, for providing the code for GAN-based pose prior. This work is funded by the Deutsche Forschungsgemeinschaft (DFG, German Research Foundation) - 409792180 (Emmy Noether Programme, project: Real Virtual Humans), German Federal Ministry of Education and Research (BMBF): Tübingen AI Center, FKZ: 01IS18039A and a Facebook research award. Gerard Pons-Moll is a member of the Machine Learning Cluster of Excellence, EXC number 2064/1 - Project number 390727645.

References

1. Akhter, I., Black, M.J.: Pose-conditioned joint angle limits for 3D human pose reconstruction. In: CVPR (2015)
2. Aksan, E., Kaufmann, M., Hilliges, O.: Structured prediction helps 3D human motion modelling. In: ICCV (2019)
3. Aliakbarian, S., Sadat Saleh, F., Salzmann, M., Petersson, L., Gould, S.: A stochastic conditioning scheme for diverse human motion prediction. In: CVPR (2020)
4. Alldieck, T., Magnor, M., Bhatnagar, B.L., Theobalt, C., Pons-Moll, G.: Learning to reconstruct people in clothing from a single RGB camera. In: CVPR (2019)
5. Andreou, N., Lazarou, A., Aristidou, A., Chrysanthou, Y.: A hierarchy-aware pose representation for deep character animation (2021)
6. Baerlocher, P., Boulic, R.: Parametrization and range of motion of the ball-and-socket joint. In: Proceedings of the IFIP TC5/WG5.10 DEFORM'2000 Workshop and AVATARS'2000 Workshop on Deformable Avatars (2000)
7. Barsoum, E., Kender, J., Liu, Z.: HP-GAN: probabilistic 3D human motion prediction via GAN. In: CVPR Workshops (2018)
8. Bhatnagar, B.L., Tiwari, G., Theobalt, C., Pons-Moll, G.: Multi-garment net: learning to dress 3D people from images. In: ICCV (2019)
9. Bhatnagar, B.L., Xie, X., Petrov, I., Sminchisescu, C., Theobalt, C., Pons-Moll, G.: BEHAVE: dataset and method for tracking human object interactions. In: CVPR (2022)
10. Bogo, F., Kanazawa, A., Lassner, C., Gehler, P., Romero, J., Black, M.J.: Keep it SMPL: automatic estimation of 3D human pose and shape from a single image. In: Leibe, B., Matas, J., Sebe, N., Welling, M. (eds.) ECCV 2016. LNCS, vol. 9909, pp. 561–578. Springer, Cham (2016). https://doi.org/10.1007/978-3-319-46454-1_34
11. Cao, Z., Hidalgo Martinez, G., Simon, T., Wei, S., Sheikh, Y.A.: OpenPose: real-time multi-person 2D pose estimation using part affinity fields. IEEE Trans. Pattern Anal. Mach. Intell. (2019)
12. Chabra, R., et al.: Deep local shapes: learning local SDF priors for detailed 3D reconstruction. In: Vedaldi, A., Bischof, H., Brox, T., Frahm, J.-M. (eds.) ECCV 2020. LNCS, vol. 12374, pp. 608–625. Springer, Cham (2020). https://doi.org/10.1007/978-3-030-58526-6_36

13. Chibane, J., Mir, A., Pons-Moll, G.: Neural unsigned distance fields for implicit function learning. In: NeurIPS (2020)
14. Choutas, V., Pavlakos, G., Bolkart, T., Tzionas, D., Black, M.J.: Monocular expressive body regression through body-driven attention. In: Vedaldi, A., Bischof, H., Brox, T., Frahm, J.-M. (eds.) ECCV 2020. LNCS, vol. 12355, pp. 20–40. Springer, Cham (2020). https://doi.org/10.1007/978-3-030-58607-2_2
15. Crandall, M.G., Lions, P.L.: Viscosity solutions of Hamilton-Jacobi equations. Trans. Am. Math. Soc. **277**(1), 1–42 (1983)
16. Davydov, A., Remizova, A., Constantin, V., Honari, S., Salzmann, M., Fua, P.: Adversarial parametric pose prior. In: CVPR (2022)
17. Engell-Nørregård, M., Niebe, S., Erleben, K.: A joint-constraint model for human joints using signed distance-fields. Multibody Syst. Dyn. **28**, 69–81 (2012)
18. Geman, S., McClure, D.E.. In: Statistical methods for tomographic image reconstruction (1987)
19. Georgakis, G., Li, R., Karanam, S., Chen, T., Košecká, J., Wu, Z.: Hierarchical kinematic human mesh recovery. In: Vedaldi, A., Bischof, H., Brox, T., Frahm, J.-M. (eds.) ECCV 2020. LNCS, vol. 12362, pp. 768–784. Springer, Cham (2020). https://doi.org/10.1007/978-3-030-58520-4_45
20. Goodfellow, I., et al.: Generative adversarial nets. In: NeurIPS (2014)
21. Gropp, A., Yariv, L., Haim, N., Atzmon, M., Lipman, Y.: Implicit geometric regularization for learning shapes. In: Proceedings of Machine Learning and Systems (2020)
22. Guo, C., et al.: Action2Motion: conditioned generation of 3D human motions. In: ACMMM (2020)
23. Guzov, V., Mir, A., Sattler, T., Pons-Moll, G.: Human POSEitioning System (HPS): 3D human pose estimation and self-localization in large scenes from body-mounted sensors. In: CVPR (2021)
24. He, T., Xu, Y., Saito, S., Soatto, S., Tung, T.: Arch++: animation-ready clothed human reconstruction revisited. In: Proceedings of the IEEE/CVF International Conference on Computer Vision (2021)
25. Herda, L., Urtasun, R., Fua, P.: Hierarchical implicit surface joint limits for human body tracking. In: ECCV (2004)
26. Herda, L., Urtasun, R., Hanson, A.: Automatic determination of shoulder joint limits using quaternion field boundaries. In: FG (2002)
27. Huang, Z., Xu, Y., Lassner, C., Li, H., Tung, T.: Arch: animatable reconstruction of clothed humans. In: Proceedings of the IEEE/CVF Conference on Computer Vision and Pattern Recognition, pp. 3093–3102 (2020)
28. Huynh, D.Q.: Metrics for 3D rotations: comparison and analysis. J. Math. Imaging Vis. **35**(2), 155–164 (2009)
29. Ji, Y., Xu, F., Yang, Y., Shen, F., Shen, H.T., Zheng, W.S.: A large-scale RGB-D database for arbitrary-view human action recognition. In: ACM International Conference on Multimedia (ACMMM) (2018)
30. Johnson, S., Everingham, M.: Clustered pose and nonlinear appearance models for human pose estimation. In: BMVC (2010)
31. Kanazawa, A., Black, M.J., Jacobs, D.W., Malik, J.: End-to-end recovery of human shape and pose. In: CVPR (2018)
32. Kocabas, M., Athanasiou, N., Black, M.J.: Vibe: video inference for human body pose and shape estimation. In: CVPR (2020)
33. Kolotouros, N., Pavlakos, G., Black, M.J., Daniilidis, K.: Learning to reconstruct 3D human pose and shape via model-fitting in the loop. In: ICCV (2019)

34. Krebs, F., Meixner, A., Patzer, I., Asfour, T.: The kit bimanual manipulation dataset. In: IEEE/RAS International Conference on Humanoid Robots (Humanoids) (2021)
35. Lin, T.-Y., et al.: Microsoft COCO: common objects in context. In: Fleet, D., Pajdla, T., Schiele, B., Tuytelaars, T. (eds.) ECCV 2014. LNCS, vol. 8693, pp. 740–755. Springer, Cham (2014). https://doi.org/10.1007/978-3-319-10602-1_48
36. Loper, M., Mahmood, N., Romero, J., Pons-Moll, G., Black, M.J.: SMPL: a skinned multi-person linear model. ACM Trans. Graph. (Proc. SIGGRAPH Asia) **34**(6), 248:1–248:16 (2015)
37. Loper, M.M., Mahmood, N., Black, M.J.: MoSh: motion and shape capture from sparse markers. ACM Trans. Graph. (Proc. SIGGRAPH Asia) (2014)
38. Mahmood, N., Ghorbani, N., Troje, N.F., Pons-Moll, G., Black, M.J.: AMASS: archive of motion capture as surface shapes. In: ICCV (2019)
39. Makhzani, A., Shlens, J., Jaitly, N., Goodfellow, I.: Adversarial autoencoders. In: ICLR (2016)
40. von Marcard, T., Henschel, R., Black, M., Rosenhahn, B., Pons-Moll, G.: Recovering accurate 3D human pose in the wild using IMUs and a moving camera. In: ECCV (2018)
41. von Marcard, T., Henschel, R., Black, M.J., Rosenhahn, B., Pons-Moll, G.: Recovering accurate 3D human pose in the wild using IMUs and a moving camera. In: ECCV (2018)
42. Mescheder, L., Oechsle, M., Niemeyer, M., Nowozin, S., Geiger, A.: Occupancy networks: learning 3D reconstruction in function space. In: CVPR (2019)
43. Mihajlovic, M., Zhang, Y., Black, M.J., Tang, S.: LEAP: learning articulated occupancy of people. In: CVPR (2021)
44. Mildenhall, B., Srinivasan, P.P., Tancik, M., Barron, J.T., Ramamoorthi, R., Ng, R.: NeRF: representing scenes as neural radiance fields for view synthesis. In: ECCV (2020)
45. Novello, T., da Silva, V., Lopes, H., Schardong, G., Schirmer, L., Velho, L.: Neural implicit surfaces in higher dimension (2022)
46. Omran, M., Lassner, C., Pons-Moll, G., Gehler, P., Schiele, B.: Neural body fitting: unifying deep learning and model based human pose and shape estimation. In: 3DV (2018)
47. Ormoneit, D., Sidenbladh, H., Black, M., Hastie, T.: Learning and tracking cyclic human motion. In: Advances in Neural Information Processing Systems, vol. 13 (2000)
48. Park, J.J., Florence, P., Straub, J., Newcombe, R., Lovegrove, S.: DeepSDF: learning continuous signed distance functions for shape representation. In: CVPR (2019)
49. Pavlakos, G., et al.: Expressive body capture: 3D hands, face, and body from a single image. In: CVPR (2019)
50. Petrovich, M., Black, M.J., Varol, G.: Action-conditioned 3D human motion synthesis with transformer VAE. In: ICCV (2021)
51. Pumarola, A., Corona, E., Pons-Moll, G., Moreno-Noguer, F.: D-NeRF: neural radiance fields for dynamic scenes. In: CVPR (2020)
52. Rempe, D., Birdal, T., Hertzmann, A., Yang, J., Sridhar, S., Guibas, L.J.: HuMoR: 3D human motion model for robust pose estimation. In: ICCV (2021)
53. Saito, S., Yang, J., Ma, Q., Black, M.J.: SCANimate: weakly supervised learning of skinned clothed avatar networks. In: CVPR (2021)
54. Sarafianos, N., Boteanu, B., Ionescu, B., Kakadiaris, I.A.: 3D human pose estimation: a review of the literature and analysis of covariates. Comput. Vis. Image Underst. **152**, 1–20 (2016)

55. Shahroudy, A., Liu, J., Ng, T.T., Wang, G.: NTU RGB+D: a large scale dataset for 3D human activity analysis. In: CVPR (2016)

56. Shao, W., Ng-Thow-Hing, V.: A general joint component framework for realistic articulation in human characters. In: Proceedings of the 2003 Symposium on Interactive 3D Graphics, pp. 11–18 (2003)

57. Sidenbladh, H., Black, M.J., Fleet, D.J.: Stochastic tracking of 3D human figures using 2D image motion. In: Vernon, D. (ed.) ECCV 2000. LNCS, vol. 1843, pp. 702–718. Springer, Heidelberg (2000). https://doi.org/10.1007/3-540-45053-X_45

58. Sitzmann, V., Martel, J.N., Bergman, A.W., Lindell, D.B., Wetzstein, G.: Implicit neural representations with periodic activation functions. In: NeurIPS (2020)

59. Stoll, C., Gall, J., de Aguiar, E., Thrun, S., Theobalt, C.: Video-based reconstruction of animatable human characters. In: ACM SIGGRAPH Asia (2010)

60. Tiwari, G., Bhatnagar, B.L., Tung, T., Pons-Moll, G.: SIZER: a dataset and model for parsing 3D clothing and learning size sensitive 3D clothing. In: Vedaldi, A., Bischof, H., Brox, T., Frahm, J.-M. (eds.) ECCV 2020. LNCS, vol. 12348, pp. 1–18. Springer, Cham (2020). https://doi.org/10.1007/978-3-030-58580-8_1

61. Tiwari, G., Sarafianos, N., Tung, T., Pons-Moll, G.: Neural-GIF: neural generalized implicit functions for animating people in clothing. In: ICCV (2021)

62. Urtasun, R., Fleet, D., Fua, P.: 3D people tracking with Gaussian process dynamical models. In: CVPR (2006)

63. Xie, X., Bhatnagar, B.L., Pons-Moll, G.: CHORE: contact, human and object reconstruction from a single RGB image. In: European Conference on Computer Vision (ECCV). Springer, Cham (2022)

64. Xie, Y., et al.: Neural fields in visual computing and beyond. Comput. Graph. Forum (2022)

65. Xu, Y., Zhu, S.C., Tung, T.: Denserac: joint 3D pose and shape estimation by dense render and compare. In: International Conference on Computer Vision (2019)

66. Zhang, S., Zhang, H., Bogo, F., Pollefeys, M., Tang, S.: Learning motion priors for 4D human body capture in 3D scenes. In: ICCV (2021)

67. Zhang, S., Zhang, Y., Ma, Q., Black, M.J., Tang, S.: PLACE: proximity learning of articulation and contact in 3D environments. In: 3DV (2020)

68. Zhang, Y., Hassan, M., Neumann, H., Black, M.J., Tang, S.: Generating 3D people in scenes without people. In: CVPR (2020)

69. Zhou, K., Bhatnagar, B.L., Lenssen, J.E., Pons-Moll, G.: TOCH: spatio-temporal object correspondence to hand for motion refinement. In: European Conference on Computer Vision (ECCV). Springer, Cham (2022)

70. Zou, S., et al.: 3D human shape reconstruction from a polarization image. In: Vedaldi, A., Bischof, H., Brox, T., Frahm, J.-M. (eds.) ECCV 2020. LNCS, vol. 12359, pp. 351–368. Springer, Cham (2020). https://doi.org/10.1007/978-3-030-58568-6_21

CLIFF: Carrying Location Information in Full Frames into Human Pose and Shape Estimation

Zhihao Li, Jianzhuang Liu, Zhensong Zhang, Songcen Xu,
and Youliang Yan[✉]

Huawei Noah's Ark Lab, Shenzhen, China
{zhihao.li,liu.jianzhuang,zhangzhensong,
xusongcen,yanyouliang}@huawei.com

Abstract. Top-down methods dominate the field of 3D human pose and shape estimation, because they are decoupled from human detection and allow researchers to focus on the core problem. However, cropping, their first step, discards the location information from the very beginning, which makes themselves unable to accurately predict the global rotation in the original camera coordinate system. To address this problem, we propose to Carry Location Information in Full Frames (CLIFF) into this task. Specifically, we feed more holistic features to CLIFF by concatenating the cropped-image feature with its bounding box information. We calculate the 2D reprojection loss with a broader view of the full frame, taking a projection process similar to that of the person projected in the image. Fed and supervised by global-location-aware information, CLIFF directly predicts the global rotation along with more accurate articulated poses. Besides, we propose a pseudo-ground-truth annotator based on CLIFF, which provides high-quality 3D annotations for in-the-wild 2D datasets and offers crucial full supervision for regression-based methods. Extensive experiments on popular benchmarks show that CLIFF outperforms prior arts by a significant margin, and reaches the first place on the AGORA leaderboard (the SMPL-Algorithms track). The code and data are available at https://github.com/huawei-noah/noah-research/tree/master/CLIFF.

Keywords: 3D human pose · Human body reconstruction · 2D to 3D · Global rotation · Projection · Global location · Pseudo annotation

1 Introduction

Given a single RGB image, 3D human pose and shape estimation aims to reconstruct human body meshes with the help of statistic models [3,29,37,52]. It is a fundamentally under-constrained problem due to the depth ambiguity. This

Supplementary Information The online version contains supplementary material available at https://doi.org/10.1007/978-3-031-20065-6_34.

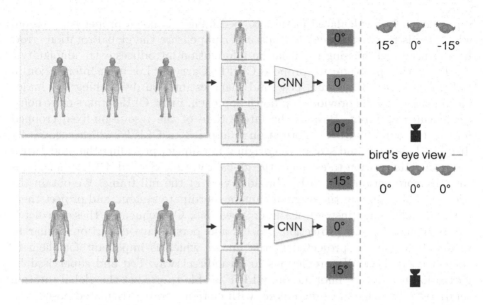

Fig. 1. In the upper part, the cropped images look similar and thus get close predictions from a CNN model. However, two of the three predictions are wrong (marked in red). Actually, they have clearly different global rotations relative to the original camera, which can be seen from the bird's eye view. In the lower part, the three global rotations are the same, but again two estimations are wrong. We only show the yaw angles of the global rotations here for simplicity. (Color figure online)

problem attracts a lot of research because of its key role in many applications such as AR/VR, telepresence, and action analysis.

With the popular parametric human model SMPL [29], regression-based methods [15,20,35] learn to predict the SMPL parameters from image features in a data-driven way, and obtain the meshes from these predictions through a linear function. Like most tasks in computer vision, there are two approaches to do this: top-down [15,19,20,22] and bottom-up [47,54]. The former first detects humans, then crops the regions of interest, and processes each cropped image independently. The latter takes a full image as input and gives the results for all individuals at once. The top-down approach dominates this field currently, because it is decoupled from human detection, and has high recall and precision performances thanks to the mature detection technique [5,41,42].

However, cropping, the first step in the top-down approach discards location information from the very beginning, which is essential in estimating the global rotation in the original camera coordinate system with respect to the full image. Take Fig. 1 as an example, where the original images come from a perspective camera with a common diagonal Field-of-View 55°. After cropping, the input images to the CNN model look similar, and thus get close predictions without surprise (see the upper part of Fig. 1). In fact, the three persons have clearly different global rotations, which can be inferred from the full image. The same problem exists for other 2D evidences such as 2D keypoints. As a result, the 2D reprojection loss calculated in the cropped images is not a proper supervision, which tends to twist articulated poses to compensate the global rotation error. In another word, missing the location information introduces extra ambiguity.

To fix this problem, we propose CLIFF: Carrying Location Information in Full Frames into 3D human pose and shape estimation, by making two major modifications to the previous top-down approach. First, CLIFF takes more holistic features as input. Besides the latent code of the resolution-fixed cropped image, the bounding box information is also fed to CLIFF, which encodes its discarded location and size in the original full image, providing the model with adequate information to estimate the global rotation. Second, CLIFF calculates the 2D reprojection loss with a broader view of the full frame. We obtain the predicted 3D joints in the original camera coordinate system, and project them onto the full image instead of the cropped one. Consequently, these predicted 2D keypoints have a projection process and perspective distortion similar to those of the person projected in the image, which is important for them to correctly supervise 3D predictions in an indirect way. Fed and supervised by global-location-aware information, CLIFF is able to predict the global rotation relative to the original camera along with more accurate articulated poses.

On the other hand, the regression-based methods need full supervision for SMPL parameters to boost their performances [22]. However, it costs a lot of time and effort to obtain these 3D annotations, using multi-view motion capture systems [13,32] or a set of IMU devices [31,48]. Moreover, the lack of diversity in actors and scenes limits the generalization abilities of these data-driven models. On the contrary, 2D keypoints are straightforward and inexpensive to annotate for a wide variety of in-the-wild images with diverse persons and backgrounds [2,27]. Hence, some CNN-based pseudo-ground-truth (pseudo-GT) annotators [14,22,34] are introduced to lift these 2D keypoints up to 3D poses for full supervision. Since these annotators are based on previous top-down models that are agnostic to the person location in the full frame, they produce inaccurate annotations, especially for the global rotation.

We propose a novel annotator based on CLIFF with a global perspective of the full frame, which produces high-quality annotations of human model parameters. Specifically, we first pretrain the CLIFF annotator on several datasets with available 3D ground truth, and then test it on the target dataset to predict SMPL parameters. Using these predictions as regularization and ground-truth 2D keypoints as weak supervision, we finetune the pretrained model on the target dataset, and finally test on it to infer SMPL parameters as pseudo-GT. With the implicit prior of the pretrained weights and the explicit prior of the SMPL parameter predictions, the CLIFF annotator alleviates the inherent depth ambiguity to recover feasible 3D annotations from monocular images.

Our contributions are summarized as follows:

– We reveal that the global rotations cannot be accurately inferred when only using cropped images, which is ignored by previous methods, and propose CLIFF to deal with this problem by feeding and supervising the model with global-location-aware information.

- Based on CLIFF, we propose a pseudo-GT annotator with strong priors to generate high-quality 3D annotations for in-the-wild images, which are demonstrated to be very helpful in performance boost.
- We conduct extensive experiments on popular benchmarks and show that CLIFF outperforms prior arts by significant margins on several evaluation metrics (e.g., 5.7 mm MPJPE and 6.5 mm PVE on 3DPW), and reaches the first place on the AGORA leaderboard (the SMPL-Algorithms track) way ahead of other methods.

2   Related Work

3D Human Pose Estimation. 3D human pose is usually represented as a skeleton of 3D joints [45,51,53], or a mesh of triangle vertices [7,15,19,25,26,33]. These vertex locations are inferred directly by model-free methods [7,25,26,33], or obtained indirectly from parametric model (e.g., SMPL [29]) predictions of model-based methods [15,19,22]. Optimization-based methods [4] are first proposed to iteratively fit the SMPL model to 2D evidences, while regression-based ones [15] make the predictions in a straightforward way that may support real time applications. Both top-down [20,22,24,26] and bottom-up [47] approaches can do the job. Because our method is a top-down framework to regress the SMPL parameters, we only review the most relevant work, and refer the reader to [28] for a more comprehensive survey.

Input and Supervision. Previous top-down methods take as input the cropped image [15] or/and 2D keypoints in the cropped region [7], perhaps with additional camera parameters [21]. They generally project the predicted 3D joints onto the cropped image to compute the reprojection loss for supervision. Since the location information is lost in the cropped image, it is difficult for them to estimate an accurate global rotation. To solve this problem, Kissos et al. [18] use the prediction with respect to the cropped image as initialization, and then use SMPLify [4] to refine the results for better pixel alignment. Since SMPLify computes the reprojection loss in the full image, they obtain a better global rotation in the end. However, as an optimization approach, SMPLify is very slow and may also harm the articulated pose estimation, as shown in EFT [14] and NeuralAnnot [34]. PCL [53] warps the cropped image to remove the perspective distortion, and corrects the global rotation via a post-processing, but the articulated poses cannot be corrected. Unlike these methods, CLIFF exploits the location information in both input and supervision, to predict more accurate global rotation and articulated poses simultaneously, without any post-processing.

Pseudo-GT Annotators. It is well known that training with in-the-wild images can bring significant benefits to the generalization performances of regression-based models. However, it is hard to obtain the corresponding 3D ground truth, so pseudo-GT annotators are proposed. Optimization-based annotators [4] throw the images away, and fit the human model to 2D keypoints by minimizing the reprojection loss. CNN-based annotators [10,14,22,23,34] are recently introduced to get better results, taking the cropped images as input. They all need priors to deal with the depth ambiguity. An extra model such as GMM [4], GAN [8,15] or VAE [19,40] is trained on a large motion capture dataset AMASS [30] to be an implicit prior. Other methods search for plausible SMPL parameters that may be close to the ground truth to be an explicit prior [10,36]. We propose a novel annotator based on CLIFF, which takes more than the cropped image as input and calculates the 2D supervision in the full image, and use the SMPL parameter predictions by the pretrained CLIFF annotator as an effective explicit prior, without an extra model and human actors mimicking the predefined poses [21,36].

3   Approach

In this section, we first briefly review the commonly-used parametric model SMPL and the baseline method HMR, then propose our model CLIFF, and finally present a novel pseudo-GT annotator for in-the-wild images.

3.1   SMPL Model

As a parametric human body model, SMPL [29] provides a differentiable function, which takes dozens of parameters $\Theta = \{\theta, \beta\}$ as input, and returns a posed 3D mesh of 6890 vertices V, where $\theta \in \mathbb{R}^{24 \times 3}$ and $\beta \in \mathbb{R}^{10}$ are the pose and shape parameters, respectively. The pose parameters θ consist of the global rotation of the root joint (pelvis) with respect to some coordinate system (e.g., the camera coordinate system in our work), and 23 local rotations of other articulated joints relative to their parents along the kinematic tree. The k joints of interest $J_{3D} \in \mathbb{R}^{k \times 3}$ can be obtained by the linear combination of the mesh vertices, $J_{3D} = MV$, where M is a pretrained sparse matrix for these k joints.

3.2   HMR Model

HMR [15] is a simple and widely-used top-down method for 3D human pose and shape estimation. Its architecture is shown in Fig. 2(a). A square cropped image is resized to 224×224 and passed through a convolutional encoder. Then an iterative MLP regressor predicts the SMPL parameters $\Theta = \{\theta, \beta\}$ and weak-perspective projection parameters $P_{weak} = \{s, t_x, t_y\}$ for a virtual camera M_{crop} with respect to the cropped image (see Fig. 3), where s is the scale parameter, and t_x and t_y are the root translations relative to M_{crop} along the X and Y axes, respectively. With a predefined large focal length $f_{HMR} = 5000$, P_{weak} can be transformed to perspective projection parameters $P_{persp} = \{f_{HMR}, \mathbf{t}^{crop}\}$, where $\mathbf{t}^{crop} = [t_X^{crop}, t_Y^{crop}, t_Z^{crop}]$ denotes the root translations relative to M_{crop} along the X, Y, and Z axes respectively:

$$t_X^{crop} = t_x, \; t_Y^{crop} = t_y, \; t_Z^{crop} = \frac{2 \cdot f_{HMR}}{r \cdot s}, \tag{1}$$

where $r = 224$ denotes the side resolution of the resized square crop.

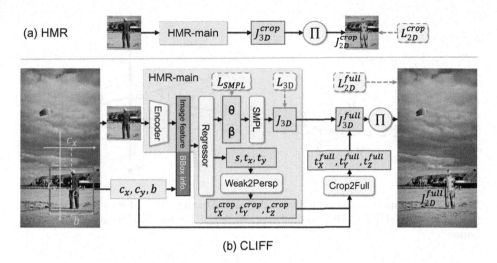

Fig. 2. (a) HMR architecture where the detail of its main part "HMR-main" is shown in the gray box in (b). (b) CLIFF architecture that takes HMR as its backbone and has two modifications: 1) CLIFF takes as input not only the cropped image but also the bounding box information. 2) CLIFF projects the predicted 3D joints onto the original full image plane to compute the 2D reprojection loss, while HMR does this in the cropped image. (Color figure online)

The loss of HMR is defined as:

$$L^{HMR} = \lambda_{SMPL}L_{SMPL} + \lambda_{3D}L_{3D} + \lambda_{2D}L_{2D}^{crop}, \qquad (2)$$

and its terms are calculated by:

$$L_{SMPL} = \left\| \Theta - \hat{\Theta} \right\|, L_{3D} = \left\| J_{3D} - \hat{J}_{3D} \right\|, L_{2D}^{crop} = \left\| J_{2D}^{crop} - \hat{J}_{2D}^{crop} \right\|, \qquad (3)$$

where $\hat{\Theta}$, $\hat{J}_{3D}$, and $\hat{J}_{2D}^{crop}$ are the ground truth, and the predicted 2D keypoints in the cropped image are obtained by the perspective projection Π:

$$J_{2D}^{crop} = \Pi J_{3D}^{crop} = \Pi(J_{3D} + \mathbf{1}t^{crop}), \qquad (4)$$

where $\mathbf{1} \in \mathbb{R}^{k \times 1}$ is an all-ones matrix.

3.3   CLIFF Model

As described above, previous top-down methods take only the cropped image as input, and calculate the reprojection loss in the cropped image, which may lead to inaccurate predictions, as emphasized in Sect. 1. To address this problem, we take HMR as the baseline and propose to make two modifications to build CLIFF, as shown in Fig. 2(b).

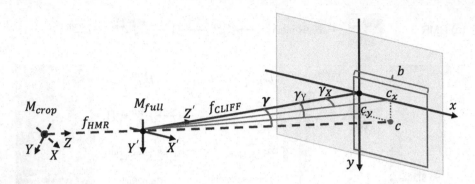

Fig. 3. The geometric relation between the virtual camera M_{crop} for the cropped image (the red rectangle) and the original camera M_{full} for the full image. (Color figure online)

First, CLIFF takes more holistic features as input. Besides the encoded image feature, the additional bounding box information I_{bbox} of the cropped region is also fed to the regressor,

$$I_{bbox} = [\frac{c_x}{f_{CLIFF}}, \frac{c_y}{f_{CLIFF}}, \frac{b}{f_{CLIFF}}], \tag{5}$$

where (c_x, c_y) is its location relative to the full image center, b its original size, and f_{CLIFF} the focal length of the original camera M_{full} used in CLIFF (see Fig. 3). Besides the effect of normalization, taking f_{CLIFF} as the denominator gives geometric meaning to the first two terms in I_{bbox}:

$$\tan \gamma_X = \frac{c_x}{f_{CLIFF}},$$
$$\tan \gamma_Y = \frac{c_y}{f_{CLIFF}}, \tag{6}$$

where $\gamma = [\gamma_X, \gamma_Y, 0]$ is the transformation angle from M_{crop} to the original camera M_{full} coordinate system with respect to the full image, as shown in Fig. 3. Therefore, fed with I_{bbox} as part of the input, the regressor can make the transformation implicitly to predict the global rotation relative to M_{full}, which also bring benefits to the articulated pose estimation. As for the focal length, we use the ground truth if it is known; otherwise we approximately estimate its value as $f_{CLIFF} = \sqrt{w^2 + h^2}$, where w and h are the width and height of the full image respectively, corresponding to a diagonal Field-of-View of $55°$ for M_{full}, following the previous work [18].

Second, CLIFF calculates the reprojection loss in the full image instead of the cropped one. The root translation is transformed from M_{crop} to M_{full}:

$$t_X^{full} = t_X^{crop} + \frac{2 \cdot c_x}{b \cdot s},$$
$$t_Y^{full} = t_Y^{crop} + \frac{2 \cdot c_y}{b \cdot s}, \tag{7}$$
$$t_Z^{full} = t_Z^{crop} \cdot \frac{f_{CLIFF}}{f_{HMR}} \cdot \frac{r}{b},$$

where $\mathbf{t}^{full} = [t_X^{full}, t_Y^{full}, t_Z^{full}]$ denotes the root translations relative to M_{full} along the X', Y', and Z' axes, respectively. The derivation can be found in our supplementary materials. Then we project the predicted 3D joints onto the full image plane:

$$J_{2D}^{full} = \Pi J_{3D}^{full} = \Pi(J_{3D} + \mathbf{1}\mathbf{t}^{full}), \tag{8}$$

to compute the 2D reprojection loss:

$$L_{2D}^{full} = \left\| J_{2D}^{full} - \hat{J}_{2D}^{full} \right\|, \tag{9}$$

where the ground truth $\hat{J}_{2D}^{full}$ is also relative to the full image center. Finally, the total loss of CLIFF is calculated by:

$$L^{CLIFF} = \lambda_{SMPL} L_{SMPL} + \lambda_{3D} L_{3D} + \lambda_{2D} L_{2D}^{full}. \tag{10}$$

The predicted 2D keypoints J_{2D}^{full} share a similar projection process and perspective distortion with the person in the image, especially when the focal length f_{CLIFF} is close to its ground truth. Thus, the corresponding loss L_{2D}^{full} can correctly supervise CLIFF to make more accurate prediction of 3D human poses, especially the global rotation, which is demonstrated in our experiments.

3.4   CLIFF Annotator

Full supervision from 3D ground truth (particularly the SMPL parameters) is crucial for regression-based methods to improve their performances on 3D human pose and shape estimation [22]. However, these annotations are scarce for in-the-wild datasets, since they require specialized devices and cost a lot of time and labor [13,31]. Recently, CNN-based pseudo-GT annotators [14,22,34] are proposed to address this problem. However, their base models are agnostic to the person locations in full frames, and thus they produce inaccurate annotations, especially for the global rotations, as mentioned in Sect. 1.

Hence, we propose an annotator based on CLIFF, which is fed and supervised with global-location-aware information, and thus produces better global rotation and articulated pose annotations simultaneously. As shown in Fig. 4, there are four steps in our pipeline to annotate an in-the-wild dataset with only 2D keypoint ground truth.

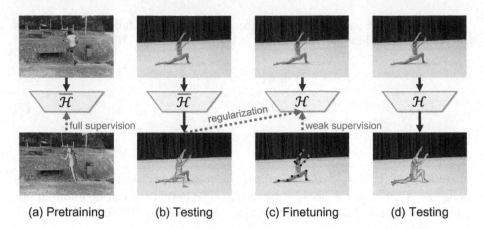

(a) Pretraining   (b) Testing   (c) Finetuning   (d) Testing

Fig. 4. Our pipeline to generate 3D annotations for a 2D dataset. (a) Pretrain CLIFF model $\bar{\mathcal{H}}$ with full supervision on available datasets. (b) Then test $\bar{\mathcal{H}}$ on the target dataset to predict SMPL parameters $\bar{\Theta}$. (c) Finetune $\bar{\mathcal{H}}$ with 2D keypoints as weak supervision and $\bar{\Theta}$ as regularization, obtaining the updated model $\mathcal{H}$. (d) Finally, test $\mathcal{H}$ on the target dataset to infer SMPL parameters as pseudo-GT.

1. We pretrain the CLIFF annotator $\bar{\mathcal{H}}$ on several datasets with ground-truth SMPL parameters, including 3D datasets and 2D datasets with pseudo-GT generated by EFT [14]. The pretrained weights serve as an implicit prior from these various datasets for the following optimization in Step 3.
2. Test the pretrained model $\bar{\mathcal{H}}$ on the target dataset to predict SMPL parameters $\bar{\Theta}$. Although these predictions may not be accurate, they can be an explicit prior to guide the optimization, and cost little without the need for crowd-sourced participants to mimick some predefined poses [21,36].
3. Finetune the pretrained model $\bar{\mathcal{H}}$ on the target dataset, using ground-truth 2D keypoints as weak supervision and $\bar{\Theta}$ as regularization, to get the updated annotator $\mathcal{H}$. Due to the depth ambiguity, these 2D keypoints are insufficient to supervise the optimization to recover their 3D ground truth. Thus, the priors are very important because they can prevent $\mathcal{H}$ from overfitting to these 2D keypoints and from offering implausible solutions.
4. Test $\mathcal{H}$ on the target dataset to get SMPL parameter predictions Θ as the final pseudo-GT. In our experiment, the reconstructed 3D meshes from these pseudo-GT are pixel-aligned to their 2D evidences, and also perceptually realistic which can be confirmed from novel views.

Compared with other annotators whose priors come from extra models [4, 40] trained on another large motion capture dataset AMASS [30], the CLIFF annotator contains strong priors that are efficient to obtain with no need for an extra model and AMASS. More importantly, based on CLIFF, the annotator produces much better pseudo-GT which is very helpful to boost the training performance as shown in the experiments.

3.5   Implementation Details

We train CLIFF for 244K steps with batch size 256, using the Adam optimizer [17]. The learning rate is set to $1 \times e^{-4}$ and reduced by a factor of 10 in the middle. The image encoder is pretrained on ImageNet [9]. The cropped images are resized to 224×224, preserving the aspect ratio. Data augmentation includes random rotations and scaling, horizontal flipping, synthetic occlusion [44], and random cropping [14,43]. To annotate an in-the-wild dataset, we train the CLIFF annotator for 30 epochs with learning rate $5 \times e^{-5}$ but no data augmentation. We use MindSpore [1] and PyTorch [38] for the implementation.

4   Experiments and Results

Datasets. Following previous work, we train CLIFF on a mixture of 3D datasets (Human3.6M [13] and MPI-INF-3DHP [32]), and 2D datasets (COCO [27] and MPII [2]) with pseudo-GT provided by the CLIFF annotator. The evaluation is performed on three datasets: 1) 3DPW [31], an in-the-wild dataset with 3D annotations from IMU devices; 2) Human3.6M, an indoor dataset providing 3D ground truth from optical markers with a multi-view setup; 3) AGORA [39], a synthetic dataset with highly accurate 3D ground truth. We use the 3DPW and AGORA training data when conducting experiments on them respectively.

Evaluation Metrics. The three standard metrics in our experiments are briefly described below. They all measure the Euclidean distances (in millimeter (mm)) of 3D points between the predictions and ground truth.

> **MPJPE** (Mean Per Joint Position Error) first aligns the predicted and ground-truth 3D joints at the pelvis, and then calculates their distances, which comprehensively evaluates the predicted poses and shapes, including the global rotations.
> **PA-MPJPE** (Procrustes-Aligned Mean Per Joint Position Error, or reconstruction error) performs Procrustes alignment before computing MPJPE, which mainly measures the articulated poses, eliminating the discrepancies in scale and global rotation.
> **PVE** (Per Vertex Error, or MVE used in the AGORA evaluation) does the same alignment as MPJPE at first, but calculates the distances of vertices on the human mesh surfaces.

4.1   Comparisons with State-of-the-Art Methods

Quantitative Results. We compare CLIFF with prior arts, including video-based methods [6,16,19,50] that exploit temporal information, and frame-based ones [7,22,24,26] that process each frame independently. They could be model-based [15,20] or model-free [25,33], and most of them are top-down methods, except for one bottom-up [47]. As shown in Table 1, CLIFF outperforms them

Table 1. Performance comparison between CLIFF and state-of-the-art methods on 3DPW, Human3.6M and AGORA.

Method		3DPW			Human3.6M		AGORA	
		MPJPE ↓	PA-MPJPE ↓	PVE ↓	MPJPE ↓	PA-MPJPE ↓	MPJPE ↓	MVE ↓
Video	HMMR [16]	116.5	72.6	-	-	56.9	-	-
	TCMR [6]	86.5	52.7	102.9	-	-	-	-
	VIBE [19]	82.7	51.9	99.1	65.6	41.1	-	-
	MAED [50]	79.1	45.7	92.6	56.4	38.7	-	-
Model-free	I2L-MeshNet [33]	93.2	58.6	110.1	-	-	-	-
	Pose2Mesh [7]	89.5	56.3	105.3	64.9	46.3	-	-
	HybrIK [24]	80.0	48.8	94.5	54.4	34.5	-	-
	METRO [25]	77.1	47.9	88.2	54.0	36.7	-	-
	Graphormer [26]	74.7	45.6	87.7	51.2	34.5	-	-
Model-based	HMR [15]	130.0	81.3	-	-	56.8	180.5	173.6
	SPIN [22]	96.9	59.2	116.4	-	41.1	153.4	148.9
	SPEC [21]	96.5	53.2	118.5	-	-	112.3	106.5
	HMR-EFT [14]	85.1	52.2	98.7	63.2	43.8	165.4	159.0
	PARE [20]	79.1	46.4	94.2	-	-	146.2	140.9
	ROMP [47]	76.7	47.3	93.4	-	-	116.6	113.8
	CLIFF (Res-50)	72.0	45.7	85.3	50.5	35.1	91.7	86.3
	CLIFF (HR-W48)	**69.0**	**43.0**	**81.2**	**47.1**	**32.7**	**81.0**	**76.0**

Table 2. Ablation study of CLIFF on Human3.6M.

Method	MPJPE ↓	PA-MPJPE ↓
CLIFF w/o CI & CS	85.2	54.5
CLIFF w/o CI	84.0	52.4
CLIFF	**81.4**	**52.1**

Table 3. Direct comparison among pseudo-GT annotators on 3DPW.

Annotator	MPJPE ↓	PA-MPJPE ↓	PVE ↓
ProHMR [23]	-	52.4	-
BOA [11]	77.2	49.5	-
EFT [14]	-	49.3	-
DynaBOA [10]	65.5	40.4	82.0
Pose2Mesh [7]	65.1	34.6	-
CLIFF (Ours)	**52.8**	**32.8**	**61.5**

by significant margins in all metrics on these three evaluation datasets. With the same image encoder backbone (ResNet-50 [12]) and similar computation cost, CLIFF beats its baseline HMR-EFT, reducing the errors by more than 13mm on MPJPE and PVE. In the case of similar PA-MPJPE to other methods, CLIFF still has lower MPJPE and PVE, since it has a better global rotation estimation. With HRNet-W48 [46], CLIFF has better performance and distinct advantages over previous state-of-the-art, including METRO [25] and Mesh Graphormer [26] which have similar image encoder backbones (HRNet-W64) and transformer-based architectures [49]. CLIFF reaches *the first place* on the AGORA leaderboard (the SMPL-Algorithms track) way ahead of other methods (whose results are from the leaderboard).

Qualitative Results. As shown in Fig. 5, we compare CLIFF with PARE [20] on the 3DPW testing data, which is one of the best cropped-image-based methods. We render the reconstructed meshes using the original camera with ground-

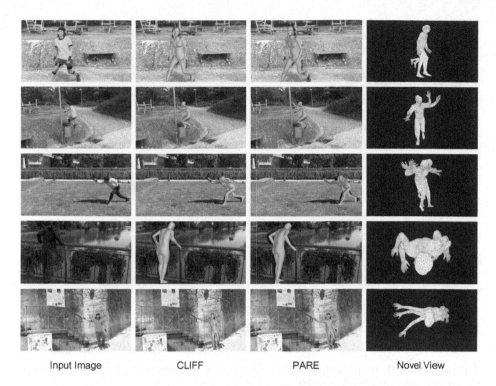

Input Image   CLIFF   PARE   Novel View

Fig. 5. Qualitative comparison on 3DPW. From left to right: input images, CLIFF predictions, PARE predictions, and their visualizations from novel views (green for the ground truth, blue for CLIFF, and red for PARE). (Color figure online)

truth intrinsic parameters. Even though accurate articulated poses can also be obtained by PARE, we can see clear pixel-misalignment of its results overlaid on the images, suffering from its inferior global rotation estimation. From the novel viewpoints, we can see that the predicted meshes by CLIFF overlay with the ground truth better than those by PARE, thanks to its more accurate global rotation estimation.

4.2   Ablation Study

We take HMR as the baseline and make two modifications to build CLIFF: additional input of the bounding box information (CI, denoting the CLIFF Input), and the 2D reprojection loss calculated in the full frame for supervision (CS, denoting the CLIFF Supervision). As shown in Table 2, we conduct an ablation study on Human3.6M, since it has accurate 3D ground truth. Without CI providing enough information, MPJPE increases significantly, indicating a worse global rotation estimation. It causes larger errors when we also drop CS that can guide CLIFF to better predictions. This study validates our intuition that global-location-aware information helps the model predict the global rotation and obtain more accurate articulated poses.

Input Image   Front View   Side View   Input Image   Front View   Side View

Fig. 6. Qualitative results of the CLIFF annotator on the MPII dataset. From left to right: input images, the front view and side view of the pseudo-GT.

Table 4. Indirect comparison among pseudo-GT annotators by training on COCO and then evaluating on 3DPW and Human3.6M.

Annotator	3DPW			Human3.6M	
	MPJPE ↓	PVE ↓	PA-MPJPE ↓	MPJPE ↓	PA-MPJPE ↓
SPIN [22]	101.2	119.2	65.2	115.0	66.9
EFT [14]	98.8	115.8	62.0	110.9	60.7
CLIFF (Ours)	**85.4**	**100.5**	**53.6**	**96.1**	**54.8**

4.3 Annotator Comparisons

Direct Comparison. In Table 3, we directly compare different pseudo-GT annotators on 3DPW, for it is an in-the-wild dataset with ground-truth SMPL parameters. The CLIFF annotator outperforms other methods in all metrics. Even with similar PA-MPJPE to Pose2Mesh [7], CLIFF reduces MPJPE by 12.3 mm, and PVE by 20.5 mm. Compared to EFT [14] that finetunes a pre-trained model on each example, the CLIFF annotator is trained in a mini-batch manner, which helps it maintain the implicit prior all the way. With the additional explicit prior, there is no need for our annotator to choose a generic stopping criterion carefully. It only takes about 30 min for the CLIFF annotator to annotate the whole 35,515 images with 4 T V100 GPUs (the finetuning and final testing steps described in Sect. 3.4).

Indirect Comparison. We train CLIFF on the COCO dataset with pseudo-GT from different annotators, and show their results on 3DPW and Human3.6M. The training lasts for 110K steps without learning rate decay. As shown in Table 4, the CLIFF annotator has much better performance than SPIN [22] and EFT [14] (more than 13mm margins on MPJPE and PVE). It demonstrates that the CLIFF annotator can generate high-quality pseudo-GT for in-the-wild images with only 2D annotations, which helps to improve performances significantly.

Qualitative Results. In Fig. 6, we show pseudo-GT samples generated by the CLIFF annotator. With good 2D keypoint annotations, the reconstructed meshes are pixel-aligned to the image evidence. From the side view, we can see that they are also perceptually realistic without obvious artifacts, thanks to the strong priors in the CLIFF annotator.

5   Discussion

In Sect. 3, we show how to build CLIFF based on HMR by making two modifications. We believe that the idea can also be applied to many other methods. First, it can benefit regression-based top-down methods that work on the cropped-region features (e.g., image, keypoint, edge, and silhouette). As for bottom-up methods that treat all the subjects without distinction of their different locations, we can take another form to encode the location information, for example, a location map which consists of a normalized coordinate for each pixel. Going beyond 3D human pose estimation, we can apply the idea to other 3D tasks that involve object global rotations (e.g., 3D object detection and 6-DoF object pose estimation). Even when there are perfect 3D annotations and thus no need for the 2D reprojection loss calculated in the full image, it is still important to take the global-location-aware information as input.

6   Conclusion

Although translation invariance is a key factor for CNN models to succeed in computer vision, we argue that the global location information in full frames matters in 3D human pose and shape estimation, and the global rotations cannot be accurately inferred when only using cropped images. To address this problem, we propose CLIFF by feeding and supervising the model with global-location-aware information. CLIFF takes not only the cropped image but also its bounding box information as input. It calculates the 2D reprojection loss in the full image instead of the cropped one, projecting the predicted 3D joints in a way similar to that of the person projected in the image. Moreover, based on CLIFF, we propose a novel pseudo-GT annotator for in-the-wild 2D datasets, which generates high-quality 3D annotations to help regression-based models boost their performances. Extensive experiments on popular benchmarks show that CLIFF outperforms state-of-the-art methods by a significant margin and reaches the first place on the AGORA leaderboard (the SMPL-Algorithms track).

References

1. Mindspore. https://www.mindspore.cn
2. Andriluka, M., Pishchulin, L., Gehler, P., Schiele, B.: 2D human pose estimation: new benchmark and state of the art analysis. In: CVPR (2014)
3. Anguelov, D., Srinivasan, P., Koller, D., Thrun, S., Rodgers, J., Davis, J.: Scape: shape completion and animation of people. In: SIGGRAPH (2005)
4. Bogo, F., Kanazawa, A., Lassner, C., Gehler, P., Romero, J., Black, M.J.: Keep It SMPL: automatic estimation of 3D human pose and shape from a single image. In: Leibe, B., Matas, J., Sebe, N., Welling, M. (eds.) ECCV 2016. LNCS, vol. 9909, pp. 561–578. Springer, Cham (2016). https://doi.org/10.1007/978-3-319-46454-1_34
5. Chen, K., et al.: Hybrid task cascade for instance segmentation. In: CVPR (2019)
6. Choi, H., Moon, G., Chang, J.Y., Lee, K.M.: Beyond static features for temporally consistent 3D human pose and shape from a video. In: CVPR (2021)
7. Choi, H., Moon, G., Lee, K.M.: Pose2Mesh: graph convolutional network for 3D human pose and mesh recovery from a 2D human pose. In: Vedaldi, A., Bischof, H., Brox, T., Frahm, J.-M. (eds.) ECCV 2020. LNCS, vol. 12352, pp. 769–787. Springer, Cham (2020). https://doi.org/10.1007/978-3-030-58571-6_45
8. Davydov, A., Remizova, A., Constantin, V., Honari, S., Salzmann, M., Fua, P.: Adversarial parametric pose prior. arXiv:2112.04203 (2021)
9. Deng, J., Dong, W., Socher, R., Li, L.J., Li, K., Fei-Fei, L.: Imagenet: a large-scale hierarchical image database. In: CVPR (2009)
10. Guan, S., Xu, J., He, M.Z., Wang, Y., Ni, B., Yang, X.: Out-of-domain human mesh reconstruction via dynamic bilevel online adaptation. arXiv:2111.04017 (2021)
11. Guan, S., Xu, J., Wang, Y., Ni, B., Yang, X.: Bilevel online adaptation for out-of-domain human mesh reconstruction. In: CVPR (2021)
12. He, K., Zhang, X., Ren, S., Sun, J.: Identity mappings in deep residual networks. In: Leibe, B., Matas, J., Sebe, N., Welling, M. (eds.) ECCV 2016. LNCS, vol. 9908, pp. 630–645. Springer, Cham (2016). https://doi.org/10.1007/978-3-319-46493-0_38
13. Ionescu, C., Papava, D., Olaru, V., Sminchisescu, C.: Human3.6m: large scale datasets and predictive methods for 3D human sensing in natural environments. PAMI **36**(7), 1325–1339 (2013)
14. Joo, H., Neverova, N., Vedaldi, A.: Exemplar fine-tuning for 3D human model fitting towards in-the-wild 3D human pose estimation. In: 3DV (2021)
15. Kanazawa, A., Black, M.J., Jacobs, D.W., Malik, J.: End-to-end recovery of human shape and pose. In: CVPR (2018)
16. Kanazawa, A., Zhang, J.Y., Felsen, P., Malik, J.: Learning 3D human dynamics from video. In: CVPR (2019)
17. Kingma, D.P., Ba, J.: Adam: a method for stochastic optimization. In: ICLR (2015)
18. Kissos, I., Fritz, L., Goldman, M., Meir, O., Oks, E., Kliger, M.: Beyond weak perspective for monocular 3D human pose estimation. In: Bartoli, A., Fusiello, A. (eds.) ECCV 2020. LNCS, vol. 12536, pp. 541–554. Springer, Cham (2020). https://doi.org/10.1007/978-3-030-66096-3_37
19. Kocabas, M., Athanasiou, N., Black, M.J.: Vibe: video inference for human body pose and shape estimation. In: CVPR (2020)
20. Kocabas, M., Huang, C.H.P., Hilliges, O., Black, M.J.: Pare: part attention regressor for 3D human body estimation. In: ICCV (2021)
21. Kocabas, M., Huang, C.H.P., Tesch, J., Müller, L., Hilliges, O., Black, M.J.: SPEC: seeing people in the wild with an estimated camera. In: ICCV (2021)

22. Kolotouros, N., Pavlakos, G., Black, M.J., Daniilidis, K.: Learning to reconstruct 3D human pose and shape via model-fitting in the loop. In: ICCV (2019)

23. Kolotouros, N., Pavlakos, G., Jayaraman, D., Daniilidis, K.: Probabilistic modeling for human mesh recovery. In: ICCV (2021)

24. Li, J., Xu, C., Chen, Z., Bian, S., Yang, L., Lu, C.: Hybrik: a hybrid analytical-neural inverse kinematics solution for 3D human pose and shape estimation. In: CVPR (2021)

25. Lin, K., Wang, L., Liu, Z.: End-to-end human pose and mesh reconstruction with transformers. In: CVPR (2021)

26. Lin, K., Wang, L., Liu, Z.: Mesh graphormer. In: ICCV (2021)

27. Lin, T.-Y., et al.: Microsoft COCO: common objects in context. In: Fleet, D., Pajdla, T., Schiele, B., Tuytelaars, T. (eds.) ECCV 2014. LNCS, vol. 8693, pp. 740–755. Springer, Cham (2014). https://doi.org/10.1007/978-3-319-10602-1_48

28. Liu, W., Bao, Q., Sun, Y., Mei, T.: Recent advances in monocular 2D and 3D human pose estimation: a deep learning perspective. arXiv:2104.11536 (2021)

29. Loper, M., Mahmood, N., Romero, J., Pons-Moll, G., Black, M.J.: SMPL: a skinned multi-person linear model. TOG **34**(6), 1–16 (2015)

30. Mahmood, N., Ghorbani, N., Troje, N.F., Pons-Moll, G., Black, M.J.: AMASS: archive of motion capture as surface shapes. In: ICCV (2019)

31. von Marcard, T., Henschel, R., Black, M.J., Rosenhahn, B., Pons-Moll, G.: Recovering accurate 3D human pose in the wild using IMUs and a moving camera. In: ECCV (2018)

32. Mehta, D., et al.: Monocular 3D human pose estimation in the wild using improved CNN supervision. In: 3DV (2017)

33. Moon, G., Lee, K.M.: I2L-MeshNet: image-to-lixel prediction network for accurate 3D human pose and mesh estimation from a single RGB image. In: Vedaldi, A., Bischof, H., Brox, T., Frahm, J.-M. (eds.) ECCV 2020. LNCS, vol. 12352, pp. 752–768. Springer, Cham (2020). https://doi.org/10.1007/978-3-030-58571-6_44

34. Moon, G., Lee, K.M.: Neuralannot: neural annotator for in-the-wild expressive 3D human pose and mesh training sets. arXiv:2011.11232 (2020)

35. Moon, G., Lee, K.M.: Pose2pose: 3D positional pose-guided 3D rotational pose prediction for expressive 3D human pose and mesh estimation. arXiv:2011.11534 (2020)

36. Muller, L., Osman, A.A., Tang, S., Huang, C.H.P., Black, M.J.: On self-contact and human pose. In: CVPR (2021)

37. Osman, A.A.A., Bolkart, T., Black, M.J.: STAR: sparse trained articulated human body regressor. In: Vedaldi, A., Bischof, H., Brox, T., Frahm, J.-M. (eds.) ECCV 2020. LNCS, vol. 12351, pp. 598–613. Springer, Cham (2020). https://doi.org/10.1007/978-3-030-58539-6_36

38. Paszke, A., et al.: Pytorch: an imperative style, high-performance deep learning library. In: NeurIPS (2019)

39. Patel, P., Huang, C.H.P., Tesch, J., Hoffmann, D.T., Tripathi, S., Black, M.J.: Agora: avatars in geography optimized for regression analysis. In: CVPR (2021)

40. Pavlakos, G., et al.: Expressive body capture: 3D hands, face, and body from a single image. In: CVPR (2019)

41. Redmon, J., Farhadi, A.: Yolov3: an incremental improvement. arXiv:1804.02767 (2018)

42. Ren, S., He, K., Girshick, R., Sun, J.: Faster R-CNN: towards real-time object detection with region proposal networks. In: Advances in Neural Information Processing Systems (2015)

43. Rockwell, C., Fouhey, D.F.: Full-body awareness from partial observations. In: Vedaldi, A., Bischof, H., Brox, T., Frahm, J.-M. (eds.) ECCV 2020. LNCS, vol. 12362, pp. 522–539. Springer, Cham (2020). https://doi.org/10.1007/978-3-030-58520-4_31

44. Sárándi, I., Linder, T., Arras, K.O., Leibe, B.: How robust is 3D human pose estimation to occlusion? arXiv:1808.09316 (2018)

45. Sharma, S., Varigonda, P.T., Bindal, P., Sharma, A., Jain, A.: Monocular 3D human pose estimation by generation and ordinal ranking. In: ICCV (2019)

46. Sun, K., Xiao, B., Liu, D., Wang, J.: Deep high-resolution representation learning for human pose estimation. In: CVPR (2019)

47. Sun, Y., Bao, Q., Liu, W., Fu, Y., Black, M.J., Mei, T.: Monocular, one-stage, regression of multiple 3D people. In: ICCV (2021)

48. Trumble, M., Gilbert, A., Malleson, C., Hilton, A., Collomosse, J.: Total capture: 3D human pose estimation fusing video and inertial sensors. In: BMVC (2017)

49. Vaswani, A., et al.: Attention is all you need. In: Advances in Neural Information Processing Systems (2017)

50. Wan, Z., Li, Z., Tian, M., Liu, J., Yi, S., Li, H.: Encoder-decoder with multi-level attention for 3D human shape and pose estimation. In: ICCV (2021)

51. Wehrbein, T., Rudolph, M., Rosenhahn, B., Wandt, B.: Probabilistic monocular 3D human pose estimation with normalizing flows. In: ICCV (2021)

52. Xu, H., Bazavan, E.G., Zanfir, A., Freeman, W.T., Sukthankar, R., Sminchisescu, C.: GHUM & GHUML: generative 3D human shape and articulated pose models. In: CVPR (2020)

53. Yu, F., Salzmann, M., Fua, P., Rhodin, H.: PCLS: geometry-aware neural reconstruction of 3D pose with perspective crop layers. In: CVPR (2021)

54. Zhang, J., Yu, D., Liew, J.H., Nie, X., Feng, J.: Body meshes as points. In: CVPR (2021)

DeciWatch: A Simple Baseline for 10× Efficient 2D and 3D Pose Estimation

Ailing Zeng[1], Xuan Ju[1], Lei Yang[2], Ruiyuan Gao[1], Xizhou Zhu[2], Bo Dai[3],
and Qiang Xu[1(✉)]

[1] The Chinese University of Hong Kong, Hong Kong, China
{alzeng,rygao,qxu}@cse.cuhk.edu.hk
[2] Sensetime Group Limited, Hong Kong, China
{yanglei,zhuwalter}@sensetime.com
[3] Shanghai AI Laboratory, Shanghai, China
doubledaibo@gmail.com

Abstract. This paper proposes a simple baseline framework for video-based 2D/3D human pose estimation that can achieve 10× efficiency improvement over existing works without any performance degradation, named *DeciWatch*. Unlike current solutions that estimate each frame in a video, *DeciWatch* introduces a simple yet effective *sample-denoise-recover* framework that only watches sparsely sampled frames, taking advantage of the continuity of human motions and the lightweight pose representation. Specifically, *DeciWatch* uniformly samples less than 10% video frames for detailed estimation, denoises the estimated 2D/3D poses with an efficient Transformer architecture, and then accurately recovers the rest of the frames using another Transformer-based network. Comprehensive experimental results on three video-based human pose estimation, body mesh recovery tasks and efficient labeling in videos with four datasets validate the efficiency and effectiveness of *DeciWatch*. Code is available at https://github.com/cure-lab/DeciWatch.

Keywords: Human Pose Estimation · Video Analysis · Efficiency

1 Introduction

2D/3D human pose estimation [7,36,63] has numerous applications, such as surveillance, virtual reality, and autonomous driving. Various high-performance image-based pose estimators [25,29,30,40,48,51] are proposed in the literature, but they are associated with substantial computational costs.

There are two main approaches to improving the efficiency of human pose estimators so that they can be deployed on resource-scarce edge devices (e.g., smart cameras). A straightforward way to improve the efficiency is designing

Supplementary Information The online version contains supplementary material available at https://doi.org/10.1007/978-3-031-20065-6_35.

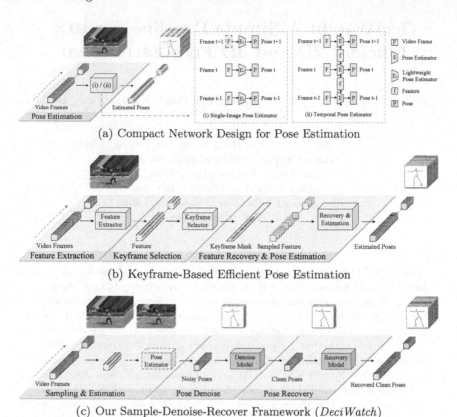

(a) Compact Network Design for Pose Estimation

(b) Keyframe-Based Efficient Pose Estimation

(c) Our Sample-Denoise-Recover Framework (*DeciWatch*)

Fig. 1. The workflows of three types of efficient pose estimation frameworks. (a) is compact model designs. The (green) pose estimation module has two design strategies: (i) shows single-frame efficient methods [3,4,6,18,21,35,42,60–62] that use lightweight models to reduce the costs of each frame; (ii) presents some temporal efficient strategies [9,41] that utilize feature similarities among consecutive frames via RNNs to decrease feature extraction cost. (b) is the keyframe-based efficient framework [10,59]. They first select about 30%–40% keyframes in a video by watching all frames, then recover the whole sequence based on features of selected keyframes. (c) is the proposed efficient *sample-denoise-recover* framework *DeciWatch* with 5%–10% frames watched. (Color figure online)

more compact models, such as numerous light-weighted image-level pose estimators [3,4,6,18,21,35,42,54,60–62] (see Fig. 1(a)(i)) and video-level pose estimators [9,41] (see Fig. 1(a)(ii)) introduced in previous literature. However, when estimating on a video, such approaches inevitably lead to a sub-optimal solution for efficiency improvement due to the frame-by-frame estimation scheme. In contrast, a promising but rarely explored direction is leveraging the semantic redundancy among frames of videos, where we can feed only keyframes to heavy and high-performance modules and recover or estimate the rest of the frames with light-weighted modules [10,59] (see Fig. 1(b)). While the computational efficiency of these works is improved due to the use of keyframes, they still need to conduct costly feature extraction on each frame for keyframe selection, making it hard to further reduce their computational complexity.

To achieve highly efficient 2D/3D pose estimation *without the need of watching every frame in a video*, we propose a novel framework based on the continuity of human motions, which conducts pose estimation only on sparsely sampled video frames. Since these detected poses ineluctably contain various noises, they will affect the effectiveness of the recovery. Subsequently, poses of those sampled frames should be denoised before recovered, where we formulate the three-step *sample-denoise-recover* framework. By doing so, the problem in the *recover* stage is similar to the long-standing motion completion task in the computer graphics literature [2,8,24,28,31,46]. However, there are two main differences: (i). our objective is to achieve highly efficient pose estimation, and hence we could only afford lightweight models for pose recovery on frames that are not processed by pose estimators; (ii). most existing motion completion works assume ground-truth poses on the given keyframes. In contrast, the visible frames in our task could have untrustworthy poses with challenging occlusion or rarely seen actions.

This work proposes a simple yet effective baseline framework (see Fig. 1(c)) that watches sparsely sampled frames for highly efficient 2D and 3D video-based human pose estimation. We empirically show that we could maintain and even improve the pose estimation accuracy, with less than 10% frames calculated with the costly pose estimator. We name the proposed framework *DeciWatch*, and the contributions of this work include:

- To the best of our knowledge, this is the first work that considers sparsely sampled frames in video-based pose estimation tasks. *DeciWatch* is compatible with any given single-frame pose estimator, achieving 10× efficiency improvement without any performance degradation. Moreover, the pose sequence obtained by *DeciWatch* is much smoother than existing solutions as it naturally models the continuity of human motions.
- We propose a novel sample-denoise-recover pipeline in *DeciWatch*. Specifically, we uniformly sample less than 10% of video frames for estimation, denoise the estimated 2D/3D poses with an efficient Transformer architecture named *DenoiseNet*, and then accurately recover the poses for the rest of the frames using another Transformer network called *RecoverNet*. Thanks to the lightweight pose representation, the two subnets in our design are much smaller than the costly pose estimator.
- We verify the efficiency and effectiveness of *DeciWatch* on three human pose estimation, body recovery tasks, and efficient labeling in videos with four widely-used datasets and five popular single-frame pose estimators as backbones. We also conduct extensive ablation studies and point out future research directions to further enhance video-based tasks' efficiency.

2   Related Work

2.1   Efficient Human Pose Estimation

Efficient attempts at human pose estimation can be divided into image-based and video-based. Image-based efficient pose estimators [3,4,6,21,35,42,54,60–62] mainly focus on employing well-designed network structures [3,4,42,54,56, 60,62], knowledge distillation [18,21,35], or low-resolution features [6,33,61] to reduce model capacity and decrease spatial redundancies, where they may suffer from accuracy reduction, especially in the cases of complex and rare poses. Moreover, when dealing with videos, these methods reveal their limitations for having to estimate poses frame-by-frame. Their outputs also suffer from unavoidable jitters because they lack the capability of using temporal information.

To cope with video inputs, other attempts exploit temporal co-dependency among consecutive frames to decrease unnecessary calculations. However, only a few video-based efficient estimation methods [9,10,41,59] are proposed in the literature, and they mainly target on 2D pose estimation. In particular, DKD [41] introduces a lightweight distillator to online distill the pose knowledge via leveraging temporal cues from the previous frame. In addition to using local information of adjacent frames, KFP [59] designs a keyframe proposal network that selects informative keyframes after estimating the whole sequence, and then applies a learned dictionary to recover the entire pose sequence. Lastly, MAPN [10] exploits the readily available motion and residual information stored in the compressed streams to dramatically boost the efficiency, and all the residual frames will be calculated by a dynamic gate.

These proposed methods reduce computation costs by employing adaptive operations on different frames, *i.e.*, complex operations on indispensable frames and simple ones on the rest. Despite obtaining efficiency improvement, they still fail to push the efficiency to a higher level since they ignore the fact that it is not necessary to watch each frame. What's more, relying on image features as intermediate representation is heavy for calculation.

2.2   Motion Completion

Motion completion is widely explored in the area of computer graphics, generally including motion capture data completion [1,12,20,24,31,32,44,46,50] and motion in-filling [2,8,11,14,14,15,17,28,55], which has great significance in the film, animation, and game applications. To be specific, points or sequences missing often occur in motion capture due to technical limitations and occlusions of markers. Accordingly, existing approaches include traditional methods (e.g. linear, Cubic Spline, Lagrange, and Newton's polynomial interpolation, low-rank matrix completion) [12,20,32,44] and learning-based methods (e.g., Recurrent Neural Networks (RNNs)) [24,31]. Motion in-filling aims to complete the absent poses with specific keyframe constraints. RNNs [11,14,14,15,52] and convolutional models [28,53] are commonly used in motion in-filling. Recently, Generative adversarial learning [17,27] and autoencoder [2,28] are also introduced for realistic and naturalistic output. Some recent works [8,19] also introduce self-attention models to infill the invisible frames.

Although both general motion completion and our target are to recover the full pose sequence, there are two main differences. On the one hand, the objective of motion completion is to generate diverse or realistic motions under certain assumptions, e.g., a recurring or repeated motion like walking. They may fail when motions are aperiodic and complex. In contrast, our goal is to achieve high efficiency in video-based pose estimation, where the benchmarks are usually from real-life videos. On the other hand, motion completion assumes having ground-truth poses as inputs rather than estimated poses. Current designs may not be able to handle unreliable and noisy poses generated from deep models.

3   Method

3.1   Problem Definition and Overview

Given an input video $\mathcal{I} = \{\mathbf{I}^t\}_{t=1}^T$ of length T, a pose estimation framework computes the corresponding sequence of poses $\hat{\mathcal{P}} = \{\hat{\mathbf{P}}^t\}_{t=1}^T$, aiming to minimize the distance between the estimated poses $\hat{\mathcal{P}}$ and the ground-truth poses $\mathcal{P}$. $\hat{\mathbf{P}}^t$ could be any human pose representation, including 2D keypoint position, 3D keypoint position, and 6D rotation matrix.

The main target of this work is to set a baseline for efficient video-based pose estimation without compromising accuracy. As shown in Fig. 1(c), we devise a three-step *sample-denoise-recover* flow to process video-based pose estimation efficiently and effectively. As adjacent frames usually contain redundant information and human motion is continuous, *DeciWatch* first samples a small percentage of frames (e.g., 10%) $\mathbf{I}^{sampled}$ and applies existing pose estimators [25,29,30,39,51] thereon to obtain the corresponding poses. However, recovering the full pose sequence from sparsely observed poses is challenging, especially when the poses are estimated by networks and often contain noise. Relying on a few poses to recover the entire sequence, the quality of sampled poses is the key. To tackle the challenge, we introduce two subnets, *DenoiseNet* and *RecoverNet*. Specifically, *DenoiseNet* refines sparse poses from pose estimator. Then *RecoverNet* performs motion recovery based on the refined sparse poses to recover the whole pose sequence, with the intuition that humans can perceive complete motion information through a small number of keyframes. With this new mechanism, the computation cost can be reduced significantly by watching only a small number of frames, which replaces high-cost image feature extraction and pose estimation with a low-cost pose recovery.

3.2   Getting Sampled Poses

Different from the previous keyframe-based efficient frameworks [10,59] using each frame's feature to select keyframes, we use a uniform sampling that watches one frame in every N frame to select sparse frames $\mathbf{I}^{sampled}$ as a baseline strategy.

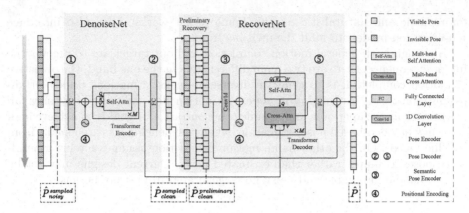

Fig. 2. Illustration of the *denoise and recovery* subnets. First, we denoise the sparsely sampled poses $\hat{\mathbf{P}}_{noisy}^{sampled}$ into a clean poses $\hat{\mathbf{P}}_{clean}^{sampled}$ by a transformer-based *DenoiseNet* to handle the dynamically various noises. Then, after a preliminary pose recovery, we embed the sequence into temporal semantic pose tokens and put them into another transformer-based *RecoverNet* that can leverage spatio-temporal correlations to recover realistic and natural poses.

Due to the redundancy in consecutive frames and continuity of human poses, a uniform sampling strategy under a certain ratio is capable of keeping enough information for recovery. Then we can estimate $\mathbf{I}^{sampled}$ by any existing pose estimators, such as SimplePose [51] for 2D poses, FCN [39] for 3D poses, and PARE [29] for 3D body mesh recovery, to get sparse poses $\hat{\mathbf{P}}_{noisy}^{sampled} \in \mathbb{R}^{\frac{T}{N} \times (K \cdot D)}$. K is the number of keypoints, and D is the dimensions for each keypoint. Notably, we experimentally show that uniform sampling can surpass complex keyframe selection methods from both efficiency and accuracy in Sect. 4.2.

3.3 Denoising the Sampled Poses

Motion completion often resorts to ground-truth sparse poses for infilling the whole sequence. However, in our scenario, the sampled poses are obtained by single-frame pose estimators, inevitably leading to noisy, sparse poses. Consequently, the quality of sparse poses is crucial for motion recovery. Before recovering the full motion, we develop a denoising network to refine the sampled poses $\hat{\mathbf{P}}_{noisy}^{sampled}$ to clean poses $\hat{\mathbf{P}}_{clean}^{sampled}$. Due to the temporal sparseness and noisy jitters, the key designs of *DenoiseNet* lie in two aspects: (i) A *dynamic* model for handling diverse possible pose noises; (ii) *Global* temporal receptive fields to capture useful Spatio-temporal information while suppressing distracting noises. Based on these two considerations, local operations, like convolutional or recurrent networks, are not well suited. Intuitively, Transformer-based models [49] are capable of capturing the global correlations among discrete tokens, so we use Transformer-based encoder modules to relieve noises from the sparse poses. The denoise process can be formulated as:

$$\hat{\mathbf{F}}_{clean}^{sampled} = \mathbf{TransformerEncoder}\left(\hat{\mathbf{P}}_{noisy}^{sampled}\mathbf{W}_{DE} + \mathbf{E}_{pos}\right) \tag{1}$$

As demonstrated in the left block of Fig. 2, after being encoded through a linear projection matrix $\mathbf{W}_{DE} \in \mathbb{R}^{(K \cdot D) \times C}$, summed with a positional embedding $\mathbf{E}_{pos} \in \mathbb{R}^{\frac{T}{N} \times C}$, and then processed by the **TransformerEncoder** composed of M Multi-head Self-Attention blocks as in [49], input noisy poses $\hat{\mathbf{P}}_{noisy}^{sampled}$ are embedded into a clean feature $\hat{\mathbf{F}}_{clean}^{sampled} \in \mathbb{R}^{\frac{T}{N} \times C}$, where C is the embedding dimension. Dropout, Layer Normalization, and Feedforward layers are the same as the original Transformer. Lastly, we use another linear projection matrix $\mathbf{W}_{DD} \in \mathbb{R}^{C \times (K \cdot D)}$ to obtain refined sparse poses.

$$\hat{\mathbf{P}}_{clean}^{sampled} = \hat{\mathbf{F}}_{clean}^{sampled} \mathbf{W}_{DD} \tag{2}$$

The learnable parameters in *DenoiseNet* are trained by minizing $\hat{\mathbf{P}}_{clean}^{sampled}$ with sampled ground-truth poses $\mathbf{P}^{sampled}$.

3.4   Recovering the Sampled Poses

After getting the sparse clean poses $\hat{\mathbf{P}}_{clean}^{sampled} \in \mathbb{R}^{\frac{T}{N} \times (K \cdot D)}$, we use another Spatio-temporal subnet, *RecoverNet*, to recover the absent poses. In order to learn the consistent temporal correlations, a simple temporal upsampling (e.g., a linear transformation $\mathbf{W}_{PR} \in \mathbb{R}^{T \times \frac{T}{N}}$) is applied to perform preliminary sequence recovery to get $\hat{\mathbf{P}}_{clean}^{preliminary} \in \mathbb{R}^{T \times (K \cdot D)}$.

$$\hat{\mathbf{P}}_{clean}^{preliminary} = \mathbf{W}_{PR} \hat{\mathbf{P}}_{clean}^{sampled} \tag{3}$$

To make the recovery more realistic and accurate, we adopt another transformer-based network for detailed poses recovery. Unlike the previous pose transformers [64], we bring temporal semantics into pose encoding to encode the neighboring D frames' poses into pose tokens via a temporal 1D convolutional layer. The main architecture of *RecoverNet* is also the same as Transformer, which employs M multi-head self-attention blocks.

$$\hat{\mathbf{P}} = \textbf{TransformerDecoder} \left(Conv1d \left(\hat{\mathbf{P}}_{clean}^{preliminary} \right) + \mathbf{E}_{pos}, \hat{\mathbf{F}}_{clean}^{sampled} \right) \mathbf{W}_{RD}, \tag{4}$$

where the pose decoder is $\mathbf{W}_{RD} \in \mathbb{R}^{C \times (K \cdot D)}$. As illustrated in the second block marked as *RecoverNet* in Fig. 2, we draw key information in the Cross-Attention block by leveraging denoised features $\hat{\mathbf{F}}_{clean}^{sampled}$.

Efficiency Calculation. The computational costs of *DeciWatch* is from three parts: (i) using existing backbones to estimate the sampled poses $\hat{\mathbf{P}}_{noisy}^{sampled}$, (ii) using *DenoiseNet* to get clean sampled poses $\hat{\mathbf{P}}_{clean}^{sampled}$, and (iii) using *RecoverNet* to recover the clean sampled poses to the complete pose sequence $\hat{\mathbf{P}}^t$. To summarize, FLOPs of *DeciWatch* is:

$$FLOPs = \frac{1}{T}(T/N * f(E) + T * (f(D) + f(R))), \tag{5}$$

where $f(\cdot)$ calculates the model's per frame FLOPs. $f(E)$, $f(D)$ and $f(R)$ represent per frame FLOPs of pose estimators, *DenoiseNet* and *RecoverNet*, respectively. Using poses instead of image features as representation makes two subnets computational efficient. Notably, $(f(D) + f(R)) \ll f(E)$ (more than $10^4 \times$. Details can be find in Tables 1 and 2). Since *DeciWatch* samples very few frames in step 1, the mean FLOPs can be reduced to $1/N$ compared with those watch-every-frame methods, resulting in a $10 \times$ speedup overalls.

3.5   Loss Function

We follow recent 3D pose estimation methods [43,57] to apply a simple L1 regression loss to minimize the errors between $\mathbf{P}^t$ and $\hat{\mathbf{P}}^t$ for 2D or 3D pose estimation. Particularly, to learn the noisy patterns from sampled estimated poses, we further add an L1 loss between sparse estimated poses $\hat{\mathbf{P}}_{clean}^{sampled}$ and the corresponding ground-truth poses $\mathbf{P}^{sampled}$. Therefore, the objective function is defined as follows.

$$\mathcal{L} = \lambda(\frac{1}{T}\sum_{t=1}^{T}|\hat{\mathbf{P}}^t - \mathbf{P}^t|) + \frac{1}{(T/N)}\sum_{n=1}^{T/N}|\hat{\mathbf{P}}_{clean}^{sampled(n)} - \mathbf{P}^{sampled(n)}|, \qquad (6)$$

where λ is a scalar to balance the losses between *RecoverNet* and *DenoiseNet*. We set $\lambda = 5$ by default.

4   Experiments

4.1   Experimental Settings

Datasets. We verify our baseline framework on three tasks[1] . For 2D pose estimation, we follow existing video-based efficient methods [10,59] using dataset Sub-JHMDB [23]. For 3D pose estimation, we choose the most commonly used dataset Human3.6M [22]. For 3D body recovery, we evaluate on an in-the-wild dataset 3DPW [38] and a dance dataset AIST++ [34] with fast-moving and diverse actions.

Evaluation Metrics. For 2D pose estimation, we follow previous works [10,41, 59] adopting the Percentage of the Correct Keypoints (*PCK*), where the matching threshold is set as 20% of the bounding box size under pixel level. For 3D pose estimation and body recovery, following [26,29,30,39,58], we report Mean Per Joint Position Error (*MPJPE*) and the mean Acceleration error (*Accel*) to respectively measure the localization precision and smoothness. Besides, we report efficiency metrics mean FLOPs (G) per frame, the number of parameters and the inference time tested on a single TITAN Xp GPU.

---

[1] Due to the limit of pages, we present *data description, comprehensive results of different sampling ratios, the effect of hyper-parameters, generalization ability, qualitative results, and failure cases analyses* in the supplementary material.

Implementation Details. To facilitate the training and testing in steps 2 and 3, we first prepare the detected poses on both training and test sets offline. The uniform sampling ratio is set to 10% by default, which means watching one frame in every $N = 10$ frames in videos. To deal with different input video lengths, we input non-overlapping sliced windows with fixed window sizes. It is important to make sure the first and last frames are visible, so the input and output window sizes are both $(N * Q + 1)$, where Q is the average number of visible frames in a window. We set $Q = 1$ for 2D poses due to the short video length of the 2D dataset and $Q = 10$ for others. We change embedding dimension C and video length T to adapt different datasets and estimators, which influence FLOPs slightly. For *DenoiseNet*, we apply $M = 5$ transformer blocks with embedding dimension $C = 128$ by default. For *RecoverNet*, we use the same settings as *DenoiseNet*. The temporal kernel size of the semantic pose encoder is 5. For more details, please refer to the supplementary material. All experiments can be conducted on a single TITAN Xp GPU.

4.2 Comparison with Efficient Video-Based Methods

Existing efficient video-based pose estimation methods [10,41,59] only validate on 2D poses. In this section, we compare the accuracy and the efficiency of *DeciWatch* with SOTAs. We follow their experiment settings for fair comparisons and use the same pose estimator SimplePose [51].

Table 1. Comparison on Sub-JHMDB [23] dataset with existing video-based efficient methods [10,41,59] for 2D pose estimation. R stands for ResNet backbone [16]. *Ratio* represents the sampling ratio. The pose estimator of *DeciWatch* is the single-frame model SimplePose (R50) [51]. Best results are in bold.

Sub-JHMDB dataset - 2D Pose Estimation										
Methods	Head	Sho.	Elb.	Wri.	Hip	Knee	Ank.	Avg. ↑	FLOPs(G) ↓	*Ratio*
Luo *et al.* [37]	98.2	96.5	89.6	86.0	98.7	95.6	90.0	93.6	70.98	100%
DKD (R50) [41]	98.3	96.6	90.4	87.1	99.1	96.0	92.9	94.0	8.65	100%
KFP (R50) [59]	95.1	96.4	95.3	91.3	96.3	95.6	92.6	94.7	10.69[a]	44.5%
KFP (R18) [59]	94.7	96.3	95.2	90.2	96.4	95.5	93.2	94.5	7.19[a]	40.8%
MAPN (R18) [10]	98.2	97.4	91.7	85.2	99.2	96.7	92.2	94.7	2.70	35.2%
SimplePose [51]	97.5	97.8	91.1	86.0	99.6	96.8	92.6	94.4	11.96	100%
DeciWatch	99.8	99.5	**99.7**	**99.7**	**98.7**	99.4	96.5	98.8	1.196 + 0.0005[b]	10.0%
DeciWatch	**99.9**	**99.8**	99.6	**99.7**	98.6	**99.6**	**96.6**	**98.9**	0.997 + 0.0005[b]	8.3%
DeciWatch	98.4	98.3	98.2	98.7	97.5	98.3	95.2	97.5	**0.598 + 0.0005[b]**	5.0%

[a] The results are recalculated according to *Ratio* and their tested FLOPs for SimplePose (i.e., 11.96 G).
[b] Tested with ptflops v0.5.2 [47].

As shown in Table 1, our approach shows significantly increased accuracy with the highest efficiency, achieving more than 20× improvement in the computation cost on the Sub-JHMDB dataset. Compared to the SOTA method [10], we surpass them by 4.3% and 4.4% on average *PCK* (Avg.) with 55.7% and 77.9% reduction in FLOPs. Our improvement mainly comes from elbows (Elb.) (from 91.7% to 99.6%) and ankles (Ank.) (from 92.2% to 96.6%) under a 8.3% ratio. These outer joints usually move faster than inner joints (e.g., Hips), which may cause motion blur and make estimators hard to detect precisely. However, previous efficient video-based pose estimation methods did not consider a denoising or refinement strategy. *DeciWatch* uses *DenoiseNet* to reduce noises. Then, *RecoverNet* interpolates the sparse poses using the assumption of continuity of motion without watching blurry frames, showing the superiority of *DeciWatch*.

To further verify the effectiveness of the denoise scheme in *DeciWatch*, we input the full sequence of outputs from SimplePose, which means the *Ratio* is 100%, and the result of *PCK* is 99.3. The additional improvement in accuracy shows that *DeciWatch* can also be used as an effective denoise/refinement model to further calibrate the output positions. Based on the above observations, using a lightweight *DeciWatch* in a regression manner to further refine heatmap-based 2D pose estimation methods can be a promising refinement strategy. For efficiency, the total number of parameters in *DenoiseNet* and *RecoverNet* is 0.60M and the inference time is about 0.58 ms/frame.

Besides, we argue that PCK@0.05 with lower thresholds will be better to reflect the effectiveness of the methods since the commonly used metric PCK@0.2 appears saturated. We report PCK@0.05 and PCK@0.1 of *DeciWatch* in Supp.

4.3 Boosting Single-Frame Methods

The Used Single-Frame Pose Estimators: We compare *DeciWatch* with the following single-frame pose estimators [25, 29, 30, 39] that watch each frame when estimating a video. We first introduce these methods as follows.
– FCN [39] is one of the most important 2D-to-3D methods with multiple fully connected layers along the spatial dimension.
– SPIN [30] is one of the most commonly used methods, which combines SMPL optimization in the training process.
– EFT [25] is trained on augmented data compared with SPIN [30] to get better performance and generalization ability.
– PARE [29] proposes a part-guided attention mechanism to handle partial occlusion scenes, achieving the state-of-the-art on many benchmarks.

The Comparisons: We demonstrate the comparison results in Table 2 at sampling ratios of 10% ($N = 10$) and 6.7% ($N = 15$). To be specific, when the sampling ratio is 10%, *DeciWatch* can reduce *MPJPE* by about 2% to 3% for most estimators and reduce *Accel* by about 73% to 92%, indicating *DeciWatch* achieves higher precision and smoothness with about 10% FLOPs. Moreover, with 6.7% watched frames, *DeciWatch* still has the capability to recover the complete pose sequence with competitive results. For the AIST++ dataset, we surprisingly find that training on sparse poses and recovering them can significantly improve output qualities by 33.8% and 23.6% with a sampling ratio of

Table 2. Comparing *DeciWatch* **with existing single-image 3D pose esti-mators on Human3.6M** [22], **3DPW** [38], **and AIST++** [34] **datasets.** Pose estimators used in *DeciWatch* keep the same as the corresponding methods.

Methods	MPJPE ↓	Accel ↓	FLOPs(G)↓	Ratio
Human3.6M [22] - 3D Pose Estimation				
FCN [39]	54.6	19.2	6.21	100.0%
DeciWatch	**52.8**$\downarrow_{1.8(3.3\%)}$	**1.5**$\downarrow_{17.7(92.2\%)}$	0.621+0.0007	**10.0%**
DeciWatch	53.5$\downarrow_{1.1(2.0\%)}$	**1.4**$\downarrow_{17.8(92.7\%)}$	0.414+0.0007	**6.7%**
3DPW [38] - 3D body recovery				
SPIN [30]	96.9	34.7	4.13	100.0%
DeciWatch	**93.3**$\downarrow_{3.6(3.7\%)}$	**7.1**$\downarrow_{27.6(79.5\%)}$	0.413+0.0004	**10.0%**
DeciWatch	96.7$\downarrow_{0.2(0.2\%)}$	**6.9**$\downarrow_{27.8(80.1\%)}$	0.275+0.0004	**6.7%**
EFT [25]	90.3	32.8	4.13	**100.0%**
DeciWatch	**89.0**$\downarrow_{1.3(1.4\%)}$	**6.8**$\downarrow_{26.0(79.3\%)}$	0.413+0.0004	**10.0%**
DeciWatch	92.3$\uparrow_{2.0(2.2\%)}$	**6.6**$\downarrow_{26.2(79.9\%)}$	0.275+0.0004	**6.7%**
PARE [29]	78.9	25.7	15.51	100.0%
DeciWatch	**77.2**$\downarrow_{1.7(2.2\%)}$	**6.9**$\downarrow_{18.8(73.2\%)}$	1.551+0.0004	**10.0%**
DeciWatch	80.7$\uparrow_{1.8(2.2\%)}$	**6.7**$\downarrow_{18.6(73.9\%)}$	1.034+0.0004	**6.7%**
AIST++ [34] - 3D Body Recovery				
SPIN [30]	107.7	33.8	4.13	100.0%
DeciWatch	**71.3**$\downarrow_{36.4(33.8\%)}$	**5.7**$\downarrow_{28.1(83.1\%)}$	0.413+0.0007	**10.0%**
DeciWatch	82.3$\downarrow_{25.4(23.6\%)}$	**5.5**$\downarrow_{28.3(83.7\%)}$	0.275+0.0007	**6.7%**

All estimation results are re-implemented or tested by us for fair comparisons

10% and 6.7% respectively. This indicates that our method is capable of datasets with fast movements and difficult actions, such as Hip-hop or Ballet dances.

In general, we attribute the high efficiency of *DeciWatch* to the use of lightweight and temporal continuous poses representation rather than the heavy features used by previous works [10,41,59]. Meanwhile, the superior effectiveness, especially for motion smoothness, comes from its ability to capture spatio-temporal dynamic relations in the denoising and recovery process and the well-designed sample-denoise-recover steps. Additionally, the inference speeds in step 2 and 3 are about 0.1ms/frame, significantly faster than image feature extraction.

4.4   Comparison with Motion Completion Techniques

The third step of *DeciWatch* is similar to motion completion/interpolation as introduced in Sect. 2.2. To assess existing interpolation methods quantitatively, we compare our model with four traditional methods and one of the latest learning-based interpolation methods [2] based on Conditional Variational Auto-Encoder(CVAE). The original experiments in the CAVE-based model are based

Table 3. Comparison of *MPJPE* with existing motion completion methods on Human3.6M dataset [22] for 3D pose estimation. Noted that [2] is originally trained and tested on ground-truth 3D poses (noted by ⋆) with random sampling (CVAE [2]-R.), we retrain their model with detected 3D poses to keep the same uniform sampling as us (CVAE [2]-U.). We use FCN [39] as the single-frame estimator to generate the sparse detected results, and its *MPJPE* is 54.6mm.

Ratio	Nearest	Linear	Quadratic	Cubic-Spline	CVAE-R.⋆	CVAE-R.	CVAE-U	DeciWatch
20%	54.4	54.4	<u>54.3</u>	54.5	87.4	114.1	119.4	**52.8**$\downarrow_{1.8(3.2\%)}$
10%	54.7	<u>54.3</u>	55.2	54.4	99.1	119.2	121.5	**52.8**$\downarrow_{1.8(3.2\%)}$
5%	57.6	57.5	<u>57.2</u>	57.3	134.9	140.5	123.1	**54.4**$\downarrow_{0.2(0.3\%)}$

All estimation results are re-implemented or tested by us for fair comparisons

Table 4. Comparison of *MPJPE* with traditional interpolation methods on AIST++ dataset [34]. We use 3D pose estimator SPIN [30] as the single-frame estimator, and its *MPJPE* is 107.7 mm.

Ratio	Nearest	Linear	Quadratic	Cubic-Spline	DeciWatch
20%	106.7	<u>104.6</u>	105.8	106.8	**67.6**$\downarrow_{39.7(37.0\%)}$
10%	108.3	<u>106.3</u>	108.2	108.9	**71.3**$\downarrow_{36.0(33.6\%)}$
5%	123.2	120.7	<u>119.9</u>	121.2	**90.8**$\downarrow_{16.5(15.4\%)}$

on the ground-truth of the Human3.6M dataset [22] (marked as CVAE [2]-R.⋆). We compare two additional settings on the same dataset: (i). CVAE [2]-R. inputs estimated 3D poses rather than ground-truth 3D poses and uses Random sampling; (ii). CVAE [2]-U. inputs estimated 3D poses and use Uniform sampling, which is the same setting as *DeciWatch*. For a fair comparison, we adjusted the sampling ratio of training and testing to be consistent as 20%, 10%, and 5%.

In Table 3, *DeciWatch* outperforms all methods. Specifically, we find that the results of the CVAE-based model are even twice as bad as the traditional methods at all ratios, especially with estimated poses inputs and uniform sampling. This is because CVAE-based methods try to encode a long sequence of motion into an embedding and then recover them, which is practically difficult to embed well and recover precisely for a specific video. Instead, our method and the traditional interpolation strategies directly utilize the continuity of human poses as a priori, making the interpolation process easier.

Owing to the relatively low *MPJPE* and the slow motions in the Human3.6M dataset, *DeciWatch* only have limited improvement over traditional methods. We evaluate on a more challenging dance dataset AIST++ [34] in Table 4. A tremendous lift is revealed to over 30% under a 10% ratio. The improvement of *DeciWatch* is from: *DeciWatch* can learn to minimize errors with data-driven training, especially poses with high errors, while traditional methods have no such prior knowledge to decrease the errors from both visible and invisible poses.

4.5   Ablation Study

As a baseline framework, we do not emphasize the novelty of network design but provide some possible designs in each step for further research. We have explored the impact of different pose estimators in Tables 1 and 2 in previous sections. This section will explore how designs in steps 2 and 3 influence the results. All experiments use the same input window length at 101 and a 10% sampling ratio by default. We keep the same setting in both training and testing.

Impact of Sampling Ratio and Input Window Size. Due to space limitation, we discuss this part *in Supp..* We summarize the key observations as follows :(i). With the increase in sampling ratio, the *MPJPEs* first drop before rising, and they are at the lowest when the sampling ratio is about 20%. *Accels* will decrease constantly. These observations give us a new perspective that in pose estimation, *it is not essential to watch all frames for achieving a better and smoother performance.* (ii). Besides, the *MPJPE* of *DeciWatch* surpasses the original baseline even when the sampling ratio is about 8%. (iii). Lastly, *DeciWatch* is robust to different window sizes from 11 to 201 frames.

Impact of Sampling Strategies. Although we use uniform sampling one frame for every N frame, there are other sampling strategies that can be adopted without watching each frame, such as (i). uniform sampling 2 or 3 frames for every N frames, which contains velocity and acceleration information (named as *U.-2* and *U.-3*); (ii). random sampling (*R.*); (iii). combining uniform sampling with random sampling (*U.-R.*). From Table 5, *U.-2* and *U.-3* get the worse

Table 5. Comparison of *MPJPE* with different sampling strategies on 3DPW dataset with EFT [25] pose estimator (*MPJPE* is 90.3 mm). *U.-2* and *U.-3* are uniform sampling 2 or 3 frames for every *N* frames. *U.-R.* conducts both uniform sampling and random sampling. *R.* is random sampling.

Ratio	U.(Ours)	U.-2	U.-3	U.-R.	R.
20%	**87.2**	89.3	91.5	94.2	97.1
10%	**89.0**	96.3	103.4	101.3	104.4

results compared to *U.(Ours)* because intervals between visible frames become longer, and the information in two or three adjacent frames is too similar to be helpful for the recovery. Moreover, random sampling shows is capable of recovery since a long invisible period may appear, which is hard for model learning. Combining uniform sampling (half of the frames) to avoid long invisible periods can slightly decrease the error in random sampling. In summary, uniform sampling one frame for every N frame (*U.(Ours)*) surpasses all other sampling strategies under the same model.

Impact of Denoise and Recovery Subnets. In Table 6, we comprehensively verify the effectiveness of *DenoiseNet* and *RecoverNet* at 10% sampling ratio on three datasets. When we remove any part of the two subnets, the results deteriorate to various degrees. Removing *RecoverNet* means we only use a preliminary recovery via a temporal linear layer, which leads to unsatisfying results as discussed in Sect. 4.4. In fact, *RecoverNet* is very important for the whole framework since it is supervised by the entire sequence's ground-truth, especially for the fast-moving dance dataset AIST++ [34]. *DenoiseNet* can remove

Table 6. Exploring impacts of the two *DenoiseNet* and *RecoverNet* subnets with 10% sampling ratio on three dataset and the corresponding backbones. *Ori.* means the original estimator (watching all frames) with 100% sampling ratio. No *RecoverNet* is preliminarily recovered via a temporal linear layer.

Dataset w/Backbone	Ori. (100%)	No *DenoiseNet*	No *RecoverNet*	*DeciWatch*
Human3.6M w/FCN [39]	54.6	54.5	54.7	**52.8**
3DPW w/PARE [29]	78.9	79.8	81.0	**77.2**
AIST++ w/SPIN [25]	107.7	91.5	95.3	**71.3**

noises in advance while giving a better initial pose sequence to *RecoverNet*, which can reduce the burden in the recovery stage. In summary, the two subnets are both essential and effectively improve the final performance.

4.6 An Application: Efficient Pose Labeling in Videos

A large amount of labeled data leads to the success of deep models. However, labeling each frame in videos is labor-intensive and high cost. It is also hard to guarantee continuity among adjacent frames, especially for 3D annotations. Due to the efficiency and smoothness of the pose sequences recovered by *DeciWatch*, reducing the need for dense labeling could be a potential application. We verify the effectiveness of this application on the Human3.6M and AIST++ dataset by directly inputting the sparse ground-truth 3D positions into the *RecoverNet* of *DeciWatch*. Due to limited pages, please see Supp. for details.

5 Conclusion and Future Work

This work proposes a sample-denoise-recover flow as a simple baseline framework for highly efficient video-based 2D/3D pose estimation. Thanks to the lightweight representation and continuity characteristics of human poses, this method can watch one frame in every 10 frame and achieve nearly 10× improvement in efficiency while maintaining competitive performance, as validated in the comprehensive experiments across various video-based human pose estimation and body mesh recovery tasks. There are many opportunities to further improve the proposed baseline solution:

Adaptive Sampling and Dynamic Recovery. In *DeciWatch*, we use a simple uniform sampling strategy for all the joints. In practice, the movements of different joints under different actions vary greatly. Consequently, an adaptive sampling strategy has the potential to further boost the efficiency of video-based pose estimators. For instance, combining multi-modality information (e.g., WIFI, sensors) to relieve visual computation can be interesting. Correspondingly, how to design a dynamic recovery network that can handle non-uniformly sampled poses is an interesting yet challenging problem to explore.

High-Performance Pose Estimator Design. While this work emphasizes the efficiency of pose estimators, our results show that watching fewer frames with our framework could achieve better per-frame precision compared with watching each frame. This is in line with the recent findings on multi-view pose estimation methods [5,13,45], showing better results without calculating every possible view simultaneously. We attribute the above phenomena to the same intrinsic principle that it is likely to achieve better results by discarding some untrustworthy estimation results. Therefore, designing such a strategy to achieve the best pose estimation performance is an interesting problem to explore.

Acknowledgement. This work is supported in part by Shenzhen-Hong Kong-Macau Science and Technology Program (Category C) of Shenzhen Science Technology and Innovation Commission under Grant No. SGDX2020110309500101, and Shanghai AI Laboratory.

References

1. Burke, M., Lasenby, J.: Estimating missing marker positions using low dimensional kalman smoothing. J. Biomech. **49**(9), 1854–1858 (2016)
2. Cai, Y., et al.: A unified 3d human motion synthesis model via conditional variational auto-encoder. In: Proceedings of the IEEE/CVF International Conference on Computer Vision, pp. 11645–11655 (2021)
3. Cao, Z., Hidalgo, G., Simon, T., Wei, S.E., Sheikh, Y.: Openpose: realtime multi-person 2d pose estimation using part affinity fields. IEEE Trans. Pattern Anal. Mach. Intell. **43**(1), 172–186 (2019)
4. Choi, S., Choi, S., Kim, C.: Mobilehumanpose: toward real-time 3d human pose estimation in mobile devices. In: Proceedings of the IEEE/CVF Conference on Computer Vision and Pattern Recognition, pp. 2328–2338 (2021)
5. Chu, H., et al.: Part-aware measurement for robust multi-view multi-human 3d pose estimation and tracking. In: Proceedings of the IEEE/CVF Conference on Computer Vision and Pattern Recognition (CVPR) Workshops, pp. 1472–1481 (2021)
6. Dai, H., Shi, H., Liu, W., Wang, L., Liu, Y., Mei, T.: Fasterpose: a faster simple baseline for human pose estimation. arXiv preprint arXiv:2107.03215 (2021)
7. Desmarais, Y., Mottet, D., Slangen, P., Montesinos, P.: A review of 3d human pose estimation algorithms for markerless motion capture. Comput. Vis. Image Underst. **212**, 103275 (2021)
8. Duan, Y., et al.: Single-shot motion completion with transformer. arXiv preprint arXiv:2103.00776 (2021)
9. Fan, Z., Liu, J., Wang, Y.: Adaptive computationally efficient network for monocular 3D hand pose estimation. In: Vedaldi, A., Bischof, H., Brox, T., Frahm, J.-M. (eds.) ECCV 2020. LNCS, vol. 12349, pp. 127–144. Springer, Cham (2020). https://doi.org/10.1007/978-3-030-58548-8_8
10. Fan, Z., Liu, J., Wang, Y.: Motion adaptive pose estimation from compressed videos. In: Proceedings of the IEEE/CVF International Conference on Computer Vision, pp. 11719–11728 (2021)
11. Fragkiadaki, K., Levine, S., Felsen, P., Malik, J.: Recurrent network models for human dynamics. In: Proceedings of the IEEE International Conference on Computer Vision, pp. 4346–4354 (2015)

12. Gløersen, Ø., Federolf, P.: Predicting missing marker trajectories in human motion data using marker intercorrelations. PLoS One, **11**(3), e0152616 (2016)
13. Gundavarapu, N.B., Srivastava, D., Mitra, R., Sharma, A., Jain, A.: Structured aleatoric uncertainty in human pose estimation. In: CVPR Workshops, vol. 2, p. 2 (2019)
14. Harvey, F.G., Pal, C.: Recurrent transition networks for character locomotion. In: SIGGRAPH Asia 2018 Technical Briefs, pp. 1–4 (2018)
15. Harvey, F.G., Yurick, M., Nowrouzezahrai, D., Pal, C.: Robust motion inbetweening. ACM Trans. Graph. (TOG) **39**(4), 60–1 (2020)
16. He, K., Zhang, X., Ren, S., Sun, J.: Deep residual learning for image recognition. In: Proceedings of the IEEE Conference on Computer Vision and Pattern Recognition, pp. 770–778 (2016)
17. Hernandez, A., Gall, J., Moreno-Noguer, F.: Human motion prediction via spatio-temporal inpainting. In: Proceedings of the IEEE/CVF International Conference on Computer Vision, pp. 7134–7143 (2019)
18. Hinton, G., Vinyals, O., Dean, J.: Distilling the knowledge in a neural network. arXiv preprint arXiv:1503.02531 (2015)
19. Ho, H.I., Chen, X., Song, J., Hilliges, O.: Render in-between: Motion guided video synthesis for action interpolation. arXiv preprint arXiv:2111.01029 (2021)
20. Howarth, S.J., Callaghan, J.P.: Quantitative assessment of the accuracy for three interpolation techniques in kinematic analysis of human movement. Comput. Meth. Biomech. Biomed. Eng. **13**(6), 847–855 (2010)
21. Hwang, D.H., Kim, S., Monet, N., Koike, H., Bae, S.: Lightweight 3d human pose estimation network training using teacher-student learning. In: Proceedings of the IEEE/CVF Winter Conference on Applications of Computer Vision, pp. 479–488 (2020)
22. Ionescu, C., Papava, D., Olaru, V., Sminchisescu, C.: Human3.6 m: large scale datasets and predictive methods for 3d human sensing in natural environments. IEEE Trans. Pattern Anal. Mach. Intell. **36**(7), 1325–1339 (2013)
23. Jhuang, H., Gall, J., Zuffi, S., Schmid, C., Black, M.J.: Towards understanding action recognition. In: Proceedings of the IEEE International Conference on Computer Vision, pp. 3192–3199 (2013)
24. Ji, L., Liu, R., Zhou, D., Zhang, Q., Wei, X.: Missing data recovery for human mocap data based on a-lstm and ls constraint. In: 2020 IEEE 5th International Conference on Signal and Image Processing (ICSIP), pp. 729–734. IEEE (2020)
25. Joo, H., Neverova, N., Vedaldi, A.: Exemplar fine-tuning for 3d human model fitting towards in-the-wild 3d human pose estimation. In: 2021 International Conference on 3D Vision (3DV), pp. 42–52. IEEE (2021)
26. Kanazawa, A., Black, M.J., Jacobs, D.W., Malik, J.: End-to-end recovery of human shape and pose. In: Proceedings of the IEEE Conference on Computer Vision and Pattern Recognition, pp. 7122–7131 (2018)
27. Karras, T., Laine, S., Aila, T.: A style-based generator architecture for generative adversarial networks. In: Proceedings of the IEEE/CVF Conference on Computer Vision and Pattern Recognition, pp. 4401–4410 (2019)
28. Kaufmann, M., Aksan, E., Song, J., Pece, F., Ziegler, R., Hilliges, O.: Convolutional autoencoders for human motion infilling. In: 2020 International Conference on 3D Vision (3DV), pp. 918–927. IEEE (2020)
29. Kocabas, M., Huang, C.H.P., Hilliges, O., Black, M.J.: Pare: part attention regressor for 3d human body estimation. In: Proceedings of the IEEE/CVF International Conference on Computer Vision, pp. 11127–11137 (2021)

30. Kolotouros, N., Pavlakos, G., Black, M.J., Daniilidis, K.: Learning to reconstruct 3d human pose and shape via model-fitting in the loop. In: Proceedings of the IEEE/CVF International Conference on Computer Vision, pp. 2252–2261 (2019)
31. Kucherenko, T., Beskow, J., Kjellström, H.: A neural network approach to missing marker reconstruction in human motion capture. arXiv preprint arXiv:1803.02665 (2018)
32. Lai, R.Y., Yuen, P.C., Lee, K.K.: Motion capture data completion and denoising by singular value thresholding. In: Eurographics (Short Papers), pp. 45–48 (2011)
33. Li, J., et al.: Human pose regression with residual log-likelihood estimation. In: ICCV (2021)
34. Li, R., Yang, S., Ross, D.A., Kanazawa, A.: Ai choreographer: music conditioned 3d dance generation with aist++. In: Proceedings of the IEEE/CVF International Conference on Computer Vision (ICCV), pp. 13401–13412 (2021)
35. Li, Z., Ye, J., Song, M., Huang, Y., Pan, Z.: Online knowledge distillation for efficient pose estimation. In: Proceedings of the IEEE/CVF International Conference on Computer Vision, pp. 11740–11750 (2021)
36. Liu, W., Bao, Q., Sun, Y., Mei, T.: Recent advances in monocular 2d and 3d human pose estimation: A deep learning perspective. arXiv preprint arXiv:2104.11536 (2021)
37. Luo, Y., et al.: Lstm pose machines. In: Proceedings of the IEEE Conference on Computer Vision and Pattern Recognition, pp. 5207–5215 (2018)
38. von Marcard, T., Henschel, R., Black, M.J., Rosenhahn, B., Pons-Moll, G.: Recovering accurate 3d human pose in the wild using imus and a moving camera. In: Proceedings of the European Conference on Computer Vision (ECCV), pp. 601–617 (2018)
39. Martinez, J., Hossain, R., Romero, J., Little, J.J.: A simple yet effective baseline for 3d human pose estimation. In: Proceedings of the IEEE International Conference on Computer Vision, pp. 2640–2649 (2017)
40. Newell, A., Yang, K., Deng, J.: Stacked hourglass networks for human pose estimation. In: Leibe, B., Matas, J., Sebe, N., Welling, M. (eds.) ECCV 2016. LNCS, vol. 9912, pp. 483–499. Springer, Cham (2016). https://doi.org/10.1007/978-3-319-46484-8_29
41. Nie, X., Li, Y., Luo, L., Zhang, N., Feng, J.: Dynamic kernel distillation for efficient pose estimation in videos. In: Proceedings of the IEEE/CVF International Conference on Computer Vision, pp. 6942–6950 (2019)
42. Osokin, D.: Real-time 2d multi-person pose estimation on cpu: lightweight openpose. arXiv preprint arXiv:1811.12004 (2018)
43. Pavllo, D., Feichtenhofer, C., Grangier, D., Auli, M.: 3d human pose estimation in video with temporal convolutions and semi-supervised training. In: Proceedings of the IEEE Conference on Computer Vision and Pattern Recognition, pp. 7753–7762 (2019)
44. Reda, H.E.A., Benaoumeur, I., Kamel, B., Zoubir, A.F.: Mocap systems and hand movement reconstruction using cubic spline. In: 2018 5th International Conference on Control, Decision and Information Technologies (CoDIT), pp. 1–5. IEEE (2018)
45. Shuai, H., Wu, L., Liu, Q.: Adaptively multi-view and temporal fusing transformer for 3d human pose estimation. arXiv preprint arXiv:2110.05092 (2021)
46. Skurowski, P., Pawlyta, M.: Gap reconstruction in optical motion capture sequences using neural networks. Sensors 21(18), 6115 (2021)
47. Sovrasov, V.: Flops counter for convolutional networks in pytorch framework (2022). https://github.com/sovrasov/flops-counter.pytorch, original-date: 2018-08-17T09:54:59Z

48. Sun, K., Xiao, B., Liu, D., Wang, J.: Deep high-resolution representation learning for human pose estimation. In: Proceedings of the IEEE/CVF Conference on Computer Vision and Pattern Recognition, pp. 5693–5703 (2019)
49. Vaswani, A., et al.: Attention is all you need. In: Advances in Neural Information Processing Systems 30 (2017)
50. Wu, Q., Boulanger, P.: Real-time estimation of missing markers for reconstruction of human motion. In: 2011 XIII Symposium on Virtual Reality, pp. 161–168. IEEE (2011)
51. Xiao, B., Wu, H., Wei, Y.: Simple baselines for human pose estimation and tracking. In: Proceedings of the European Conference on Computer Vision (ECCV), pp. 466–481 (2018)
52. Xu, J., et al.: Exploring versatile prior for human motion via motion frequency guidance. In: 2021 International Conference on 3D Vision (3DV), pp. 606–616. IEEE (2021)
53. Yan, S., Li, Z., Xiong, Y., Yan, H., Lin, D.: Convolutional sequence generation for skeleton-based action synthesis. In: Proceedings of the IEEE/CVF International Conference on Computer Vision, pp. 4394–4402 (2019)
54. Yu, C., et al.: Lite-hrnet: a lightweight high-resolution network. In: Proceedings of the IEEE/CVF Conference on Computer Vision and Pattern Recognition, pp. 10440–10450 (2021)
55. Yuan, Y., Iqbal, U., Molchanov, P., Kitani, K., Kautz, J.: Glamr: global occlusion-aware human mesh recovery with dynamic cameras. arXiv preprint arXiv:2112.01524 (2021)
56. Zeng, A., Sun, X., Huang, F., Liu, M., Xu, Q., Lin, S.: SRNet: improving generalization in 3D human pose estimation with a split-and-recombine approach. In: Vedaldi, A., Bischof, H., Brox, T., Frahm, J.-M. (eds.) ECCV 2020. LNCS, vol. 12359, pp. 507–523. Springer, Cham (2020). https://doi.org/10.1007/978-3-030-58568-6_30
57. Zeng, A., Sun, X., Yang, L., Zhao, N., Liu, M., Xu, Q.: Learning skeletal graph neural networks for hard 3d pose estimation. In: Proceedings of the IEEE International Conference on Computer Vision (2021)
58. Zeng, A., Yang, L., Ju, X., Li, J., Wang, J., Xu, Q.: Smoothnet: a plug-and-play network for refining human poses in videos. arXiv preprint arXiv:2112.13715 (2021)
59. Zhang, Y., Wang, Y., Camps, O., Sznaier, M.: Key frame proposal network for efficient pose estimation in videos. In: Vedaldi, A., Bischof, H., Brox, T., Frahm, J.-M. (eds.) ECCV 2020. LNCS, vol. 12362, pp. 609–625. Springer, Cham (2020). https://doi.org/10.1007/978-3-030-58520-4_36
60. Zhang, Z., Tang, J., Wu, G.: Simple and lightweight human pose estimation. arXiv preprint arXiv:1911.10346 (2019)
61. Zhao, L., Wang, N., Gong, C., Yang, J., Gao, X.: Estimating human pose efficiently by parallel pyramid networks. IEEE Trans. Image Process. 30, 6785–6800 (2021)
62. Zheng, C., Mendieta, M., Wang, P., Lu, A., Chen, C.: A lightweight graph transformer network for human mesh reconstruction from 2d human pose. arXiv preprint arXiv:2111.12696 (2021)
63. Zheng, C., et al.: Deep learning-based human pose estimation: a survey. arXiv preprint arXiv:2012.13392 (2020)
64. Zheng, C., Zhu, S., Mendieta, M., Yang, T., Chen, C., Ding, Z.: 3d human pose estimation with spatial and temporal transformers. In: Proceedings of the IEEE/CVF International Conference on Computer Vision, pp. 11656–11665 (2021)

SmoothNet: A Plug-and-Play Network for Refining Human Poses in Videos

Ailing Zeng[1], Lei Yang[2], Xuan Ju[1], Jiefeng Li[3], Jianyi Wang[4], and Qiang Xu[1(✉)]

[1] The Chinese University of Hong Kong, Shatin, Hong Kong
{alzeng,qxu}@cse.cuhk.edu.hk, juxuan27@link.cuhk.edu.hk
[2] Sensetime Group Ltd., Shatin, Hong Kong
yanglei@sensetime.com
[3] Shanghai Jiao Tong University, Shanghai, China
ljf_likit@sjtu.edu.cn
[4] Nanyang Technological University, Singapore, Singapore
JIANYI001@e.ntu.edu.sg

Abstract. When analyzing human motion videos, the output jitters from existing pose estimators are highly-unbalanced with varied estimation errors across frames. Most frames in a video are relatively easy to estimate and only suffer from slight jitters. In contrast, for rarely seen or occluded actions, the estimated positions of multiple joints largely deviate from the ground truth values for a consecutive sequence of frames, rendering significant jitters on them.

To tackle this problem, we propose to attach a dedicated *temporal-only* refinement network to existing pose estimators for jitter mitigation, named SMOOTHNET. Unlike existing learning-based solutions that employ spatio-temporal models to co-optimize per-frame precision and temporal smoothness at all the joints, SMOOTHNET models the natural smoothness characteristics in body movements by learning the long-range temporal relations of every joint without considering the noisy correlations among joints. With a simple yet effective motion-aware fully-connected network, SMOOTHNET improves the temporal smoothness of existing pose estimators significantly and enhances the estimation accuracy of those challenging frames as a side-effect. Moreover, as a temporal-only model, a unique advantage of SMOOTHNET is its strong transferability across various types of estimators, modalities, and datasets. Comprehensive experiments on *five datasets* with *eleven popular backbone networks* across *2D and 3D pose estimation and body recovery tasks* demonstrate the efficacy of the proposed solution. Code is available at https://github.com/cure-lab/SmoothNet.

Keywords: Human pose estimation · Jitter · Temporal models

Supplementary Information The online version contains supplementary material available at https://doi.org/10.1007/978-3-031-20065-6_36.

S. Avidan et al. (Eds.): ECCV 2022, LNCS 13665, pp. 625–642, 2022.
https://doi.org/10.1007/978-3-031-20065-6_36

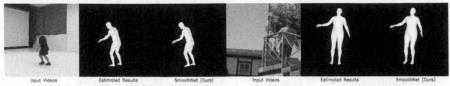

(a) Rare Pose Refinement   (b) Occluded Pose Refinement

Fig. 1. State-of-the-art human pose/shape estimators (e.g., VIBE [21]) suffer from severe jitters on videos containing rarely seen or occluded poses, resulting in untrustworthy perceptions. We propose a novel plug-and-play temporal refinement network, SMOOTHNET, significantly alleviating this problem. *See supplementary material for an animated version of the figure.*

1 Introduction

Human pose estimation has broad applications such as motion analysis and human-computer interaction. While significant advancements have been achieved with novel deep learning techniques (e.g., [5,18,22,34,38,47]), the estimation errors for rarely seen or occluded poses are still relatively high.

When applying existing image-based pose estimators for video analysis, significant jitters occur on those challenging frames with large estimation errors as L1/L2 loss optimization is directionless. Moreover, they often last for a consecutive sequence of frames, causing untrustworthy perceptions (see *Estimated Results* in Fig. 1). Various video-based pose estimators are proposed in the literature to mitigate this problem. Some use an end-to-end network that takes jitter errors into consideration [6,19,21,35,45], while the rest smooth the estimation results with spatial-temporal refinement models [20,27,43] or low-pass filters [4,8,11,13,17,36,41,46]. These solutions, however, do not consider the highly-unbalanced nature of the jitters in the estimated poses, resulting in unsatisfactory performance.

On the one hand, existing learning-based solutions (including end-to-end and refinement networks) employ Spatio-temporal models to co-optimize per-frame precision and temporal smoothness at all the joints. This is a highly challenging task as jittering frames typically persist for a while, and they are associated with untrustworthy local temporal features and noisy correlation among the estimated joints. On the other hand, applying low-pass filters on each estimated joint with a long filtering window could reduce jitters to an arbitrarily small value. Nevertheless, such fixed temporal filters usually lead to considerable precision loss (e.g., over-smoothing) without prior knowledge about the distribution of human motions.

Motivated by the above, this work proposes to attach a dedicated *temporal-only* refinement network to existing 2D/3D pose estimators for jitter mitigation, named SMOOTHNET. Without considering the noisy correlations (especially on jittering frames) among estimated joint positions, SMOOTHNET models the nat-

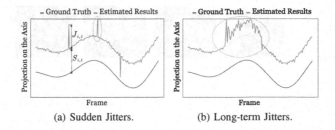

Fig. 2. Two kinds of jitters are caused by pose estimation errors. The horizontal coordinate represents frames, and the vertical coordinate shows joint position values. Output errors are composed of jitter errors J and biased errors S.

ural smoothness characteristics in body movements in a data-driven manner. The main contributions of this paper include:

- We investigate the highly-unbalanced nature of the jitter problem with existing pose estimators and empirically show that significant jitters usually occur on a consecutive sequence of challenging frames with poor image quality, occlusion, or rarely seen poses.
- To the best of our knowledge, this is the first data-driven temporal-only refinement solution for human motion jitter mitigation. Specifically, we design simple yet effective fully-connected networks with a long receptive field to learn the temporal relations of every joint for smoothing, and we show it outperforms other temporal models such as temporal convolutional networks (TCNs) and vanilla Transformers.
- As a temporal-only model, SmoothNet is a plug-and-play network with strong transferability across various types of estimators and datasets.

SMOOTHNET is conceptually simple yet empirically powerful. We conduct extensive experiments to validate its effectiveness and generalization capability on *five datasets*, *eleven backbone networks*, and *three modalities* (2D/3D position and 6D rotation matrix [54]). Our results show that SMOOTHNET improves the temporal smoothness of existing pose estimators significantly and enhances the estimation accuracy of the challenging frames as a side-effect, especially for those video clips with severe pose estimation errors and long-term jitters.

2 Preliminaries and Problem Definition

2.1 Human Pose Estimation

For video-based human pose estimation, L frames of a video $\mathbf{X}$ are inputs to the pose estimator f, and it outputs the estimated poses $\hat{\mathbf{Y}} \in \mathbb{R}^{L \times C}$, where $C = N \times D$. N is the number of keypoints associated with datasets, and D denotes the dimensions of each keypoint (2D [5,24,34,38] or 3D [29,35,47,48,50]). The above process can be simply formulated as $\hat{\mathbf{Y}} = f(\mathbf{X})$. The estimator is trained in a supervised manner with the labeled ground truth $\mathbf{Y} \in \mathbb{R}^{L \times C}$.

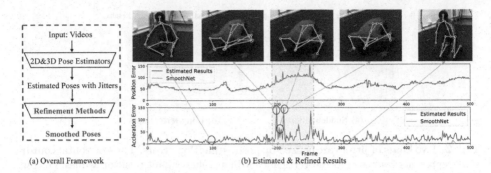

(a) Overall Framework   (b) Estimated & Refined Results

Fig. 3. SMOOTHNET is a plug-and-play temporal-only refinement network for jitter mitigation. (a) shows the refinement flow. (b) demonstrates the estimated results of a state-of-the-art estimator RLE [24] and how SMOOTHNET can improve the precision (upper curve) and smoothness (lower curve).

Key Evaluation Metrics. To evaluate the per-frame precision, the metric is the mean per joint position error (*MPJPE*). To measure the smoothness or jitter errors, the metric is the mean per joint acceleration error (*Accel*).

2.2 The Jitter Problem from Pose Estimators

An ideal pose estimator that outputs accurate joint positions would not suffer from jitters. In other words, the jitter problem is caused by pose estimation errors, which can be divided into two parts: the *jitter error* **J** between adjacent frames and the *biased error* **S** between the ground truth and smoothed poses. In Fig. 2, we differentiate sudden jitters and long-term jitters based on the duration of jitters. Moreover, according to the degree of jitters, existing jitters can be split into small jitters caused by inevitably inaccurate and inconsistent annotations in the training dataset (e.g., [1,26]) and large jitters caused by poor image quality, rare poses, or heavy occlusion.

State-of-the-art end-to-end estimators such as [21,24] can output relatively accurate estimation results and small jitters for most frames (see Fig. 3(b)). However, they tend to output large position errors when the video segments with rare/complex actions and these clips also suffer from significant jitters (e.g., from 200 to 250 frames in Fig. 3(b)).

The jitter problem in human pose estimation is hence highly unbalanced. Generally speaking, sudden jitters are easy to remove with low-pass filters [3, 36,46]. However, handling long-term jitters **J** is quite challenging because they usually entangle with ambiguous biased errors **S**.

3   Related Work and Motivation

3.1   Spatio-Temporal Models for Smoothing

Existing learning-based jitter mitigation solutions can be categorized into two types: end-to-end solutions and refinement networks after pose estimators. For the former category, various types of temporal models (e.g., gated recurrent units (GRUs) [6,21,27,53], temporal convolutional networks (TCNs) [35,47], and Transformers [44,51]) are used for temporal feature extraction. Other end-to-end solutions employ regularizers or loss functions to constrain the temporal consistency across successive frames [19,31,33,39,43,49]. Recent pose refinement works [15,20,43] take smoothness into consideration with spatial-temporal modeling. Specifically, Jiang *et al.* [15] designed a transformer-based network to smooth 3D poses in sign language recognition. Kim *et al.* [20] propose a non-local attention mechanism with convolutions represented by *quaternions*. Considering occlusions on multi-person scenes, Vege *et al.* [43] conduct energy optimization with visibility scores to adaptively filter the keypoint trajectories.

Without considering the highly-unbalanced nature of the jitter problem in pose estimation, the above solutions still cannot yield a smooth sequence of poses. There are mainly two reasons for such unsatisfactory performance. On the one hand, multiple joint positions largely deviate from the ground-truth for consecutive frames with long-term jitters, and the extracted spatial/temporal features themselves are untrustworthy, rendering less effective smoothing results. On the other hand, co-optimizing the jitter error $\mathbf{J}$ and the biased error $\mathbf{S}$ is challenging, and we name it the *spatio-temporal optimization bottleneck*.

We conduct comprehensive experiments on the popular 3D skeleton-based methods [29,35] and SMPL-based approaches [21,22] under single-frame, multi-frame, and smoothness loss settings. Due to space limitations, we put the results in the supplementary materials and summarize our key findings here: (i). compared to single-frame models, spatial-temporal models have better performance. However, the reduction in jitter errors $\mathbf{J}$ are still unsatisfactory (e.g., *Accels* are reduced from 33 mm to 27 mm [21]); (ii). further adding an acceleration loss between consecutive frames or enhancing temporal modeling in the decoder design can benefit *Accels* but harm MPJPEs (increase biased errors $\mathbf{S}$), due to the optimization bottleneck between per-frame precision and smoothness.

With the above, a temporal-only pose smoothing solution is more promising for jitter mitigation. Moreover, without using vastly different spatial information, such solutions have the potential to generalize across different datasets and motion modalities.

3.2   Low-Pass Filters for Smoothing

Low-pass filters are general smoothing solutions, and they are used for pose refinement in the literature. For example, moving averages [12] that calculate the mean values over a specified period of time can be used to smooth sudden jitters. Savitzky-Golay filter [36] uses a local polynomial least-squares function to fit the sequence within a given window size. Gaussian filter [46] modifies the input signal by convolution with a Gaussian function to obtain the minimum possible group delay. Recently, a One-Euro filter was proposed in [4] for real-time jitter mitigation with an adaptive cutoff frequency.

As a general temporal-only solution, low-pass filters can be applied to various pose refinement tasks without training. However, it inevitably faces the trade-off between jitters and lags, resulting in significant errors under long-term jitters. Motivated by the limitations of existing works, we propose a novel data-driven temporal-only refinement solution for 2D/3D human pose estimation tasks, as detailed in the following section.

4   Method

Instead of fusing spatial and temporal features for pose refinement, we explore long-range temporal receptive fields to capture robust temporal relations for mitigating large and long-term jitters. Specifically, the proposed SMOOTHNET g learns from the noisy estimated poses $\hat{\mathbf{Y}} \in \mathbb{R}^{L \times C}$ generated by any pose estimators f.

The refinement function can be simply formulated as $\hat{\mathbf{G}} = g(\hat{\mathbf{Y}})$, where $\hat{\mathbf{G}} \in \mathbb{R}^{L \times C}$ is the smoothed poses.

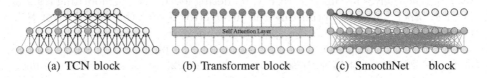

| (a) TCN block | (b) Transformer block | (c) SmoothNet   block |

Fig. 4. Temporal relation extraction with (a) TCN, (b) Transformer, and (c) FCN. The input circles mean T frames information in one spatial dimension.

4.1   Basic SmoothNet

Consider a fixed-length long sequence of the estimated joint positions, our objective is to capture temporal relations for smoothing. There are three popular temporal architectures that support long receptive fields without error accumulation, as illustrated in Fig. 4. Temporal convolutional networks (TCNs) [2] conduct local convolutions (e.g., kernel size is 3) at each layer and employ dilation operations with multiple layers to enlarge the receptive field. In contrast, Transformers [42] or fully-connected networks (FCNs) have global receptive fields at every layer, which can better tolerate long-term jitters than local convolutions in TCNs. While Transformers have become the *de facto* sequence-to-sequence models in many application scenarios [9,37,51,52], we argue it is less applicable to our problem when compared to FCNs. In a Transformer model, the critical issue is to extract the semantic correlations between any two elements in a long

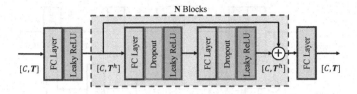

Fig. 5. A simple yet effective SMOOTHNET design.

sequence (e.g., words in texts or 2D patches in images) with self-attention mechanisms. However, for pose refinement, we are more interested in modeling the continuity of motions on each joint (instead of point-wise correlations), which spans a continuous sequence of poses.

Consequently, in this work, we propose to use FCNs as the backbone of our SMOOTHNET design, which is position-aware and easy to train with abundant pose data from human motion videos. Additionally, according to the superposition of movements [10], a movement can be decomposed as several movements performed independently. Based on this principle, each axis i in channel C can be processed independently.

The proposed network is shown in Fig. 5, where we construct multiple FC layers with N residual connected blocks along the temporal axis. The computation of each layer can be formulated as follows.

$$\hat{Y}_{i,t}^{l+1} = \sigma(\sum_{t=1}^{T} w_t^l * \hat{Y}_{i,t}^l + b^l), \tag{1}$$

where w_t^l and b^l are learnable weights and bias at the t_{th} frame and they are shared among different i_{th} axis, respectively. σ is the non-linear activation function (LeakyReLU is chosen by default). To process $\hat{Y}$ with SMOOTHNET, we adopt a sliding-window scheme similar to filters [23,36,46], where we first extract a chunk with size T, yield refined results thereon, and then move to the next chunk with a step size s ($s \leq T$), preventing a loss of the last few frames.

4.2 Motion-Aware SmoothNet

Our goal is to capture jitter patterns and reduce jitter errors **J**, which mainly present as acceleration errors. It is straightforward to model acceleration explicitly in addition to position. Accordingly, we further inject the movement function into our network, *i.e.*, velocity and acceleration. Given the prior with physical meaning, it is beneficial to leverage first-order and second-order motion information, making the learning process converge better and faster than the Basic SMOOTHNET. Specifically, given the input $\hat{Y}$, we first compute the velocity and acceleration (subtract by two consecutive frames) for each axis i, according to the Eq. 2.

$$\hat{V}_{i,t} = \hat{Y}_{i,t} - \hat{Y}_{i,t-1}, \quad \hat{A}_{i,t} = \hat{V}_{i,t} - \hat{V}_{i,t-1}. \tag{2}$$

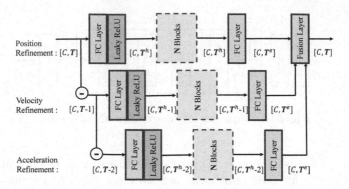

Fig. 6. The motion-aware SMOOTHNET design. It explicitly models the velocity and acceleration with adjacent frames to achieve better pose refinement.

As shown in Fig. 6, the top branch is the baseline stream to refine noisy positions $\hat{\mathbf{Y}}$. The other two branches input the corresponding noisy velocity $\hat{\mathbf{V}}$ and acceleration $\hat{\mathbf{A}}$. To capture the long-term temporal cue, we also employ Eq. 1 to refine the velocity and acceleration. All branches consist of the same FC layers and blocks. Then, we concatenate the top embedding of three branches to aggregate information from different order of motions and perform a linear fusion layer to obtain the final refined poses $\hat{\mathbf{G}}$. Similar to the basic scheme in Sect. 4.1, this motion-aware scheme also works in a sliding-window manner to process the whole input sequence.

4.3 Loss Function

SMOOTHNET aims to minimize both position errors and acceleration errors during training, and these objective functions are defined as follows.

$$L_{pose} = \frac{1}{T \times C} \sum_{t=0}^{T} \sum_{i=0}^{C} |\hat{G}_{i,t} - Y_{i,t}|, \tag{3}$$

$$L_{acc} = \frac{1}{(T-2) \times C} \sum_{t=0}^{T} \sum_{i=0}^{C} |\hat{G}''_{i,t} - A_{i,t}|, \tag{4}$$

where $\hat{G}''_{i,t}$ is the computed acceleration from predicted pose $\hat{G}_{i,t}$ and $A_{i,t}$ is the ground-truth acceleration. We simply add L_{pose} and L_{acc} as our final target.

5   Experiment

We validate the effectiveness of the proposed SMOOTHNET and show quantitative results in the following sections. Due to space limitations, we leave more analysis, discussions, and demos to the *supplementary material*. For more experimental details, please refer to the code.

5.1   Experimental Settings

Backbones. We validate the generalization ability on both smoothness and precision of the proposed SMOOTHNET covering three related tasks and several corresponding backbone models. For 2D pose estimation, we use Hourglass [34], CPN [5], HRNet [38] and RLE [24]; for 3D pose estimation, we implement FCN [29], RLE [24], TPoseNet [43] and VPose [35]; in terms of body recovery, we test on SPIN [22], EFT [16], VIBE [21] and TCMR [6].

Training Sets. To prepare training data, we first save the outputs of existing methods, including estimated 2D positions, 3D positions, or SMPL parameters. Then, we take these outputs as the inputs of SMOOTHNET and use the corresponding ground-truth data as the supervision to train our model. In particular, we use the outputs of FCN on Human3.6M, SPIN on 3DPW [28], and VIBE on AIST++ [25] to train SMOOTHNET.

Testing Sets. We validate SMOOTHNET on five dataset: Human3.6M [14], 3DPW [28], MPI-INF-3DHP [30], AIST++ [25,40] and MuPoTS-3D [32] datasets.

Evaluation Metrics. To measure the jitter errors, we follow the related works [6,19,21] to adopt *Accel*. This is measured in $mm/frame^2$ for 3D poses and $pixel/frame^2$ for 2D poses. To evaluate the precision for each frame, besides *MPJPE*, the *Procrustes Analysis MPJPE (PA-MPJPE)* is another commonly used metric, where it removes effects on the inherent scale, rotation, and translation issues. For the 3D pose, the unit is mm. For the 2D pose, we simply use *pixel* in an image to validate the accurate localization precision.

Implementation Details. The basic SMOOTHNET is an eight-layer model including the first layer, three cascaded blocks (N = 3), and the last layer as a decoder. The motion-aware SMOOTHNET contains three parallel branches with the first layer, one cascaded block, and the last layer for each branch. The input window size T is 32 and the moving step size s is 1. In addition, we use the sliding window average algorithm [23] based on smoothed results to avoid frame drop and reduce spikes. The parameters of SMOOTHNET is 0.33M, and the average inference time is less than 1.3k fps on a CPU and 46.8k on an A100-SXM4-40GB GPU.

5.2   Comparison with Existing Solutions

Comparison with Filters. We compare SMOOTHNET against three commonly used filters on the AIST++ dataset with pose estimator VIBE [21]. Experimental results are shown in Table 1. As can be observed, SMOOTHNET achieves the best performance, and it reduces *Accel* by 86.88% and *MPJPE* by 8.82% compared to the original pose estimation results. Since we can easily trade off smoothness and lag in filter designs, there could be a large set of solutions with different *Accel* and *MPJPE* values. In this table, we present two possible solutions with

Table 1. Comparison SmoothNet with widely-used filters on AIST++ [25]. The upper table with filters shows their lowest *MPJPEs*, and the lower table is when their *Accels* are comparable to ours. * means the inference speed is tested on a GPU.

	Method	Accel	MPJPE	PA-MPJPE	Test FPS
	VIBE [21]	31.64	106.90	72.84	-
Human Mesh Recovery	w/ One-Euro [4]	10.82	108.55	74.67	2.31k
	w/ Savitzky-Golay [36]	5.84	105.80	72.15	31.22k
	w/ Gaussian1d [46]	4.95	103.42	71.11	37.45k
	w/ One-Euro [4]	4.67	135.71	103.22	2.43k
	w/ Savitzky-Golay [36]	4.36	118.25	85.39	30.19k
	w/ Gaussian1d [46]	4.47	105.71	71.49	38.21k
	w/ Ours	**4.15**	**97.47**	**69.67**	1.30k/**46.82k***

the greedy search: one with comparable *Accel* with SMOOTHNET and the other with the minimum *MPJPE*.

As a data-driven approach, SMOOTHNET effectively learns the motion distribution of the complex movements in the dataset, resulting in much better *MPJPEs* values, especially when *Accel* is comparable. Among the three filters, the one-Euro filter shows inferior performance, and we attribute it to the real-time frame-by-frame jitter mitigation strategy used in it. Additionally, as SMOOTHNET can benefit from GPU acceleration, it yields a much faster inference speed than filters (marked by *).

We further plot the *MPJPE* and *Accel* distribution of the original pose output from VIBE, VIBE with a Gaussian filter, and VIBE with SMOOTHNET in Fig. 7. As can be observed, 98.7% of VIBE's original *Accel* output falls above 4 $mm/frame^2$. With Gaussian filter and SMOOTHNET, this percentage decreases to 56.5% and 41.6%, respectively. As for MPJPEs, 5.78% of VIBE's outputs

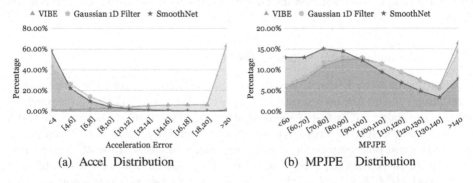

(a) Accel Distribution   (b) MPJPE Distribution

Fig. 7. Comparison of smoothness and precision distributions on AIST++.

are smaller than 60 mm and 16.43% estimated poses are larger than 140 mm. Gaussian filter increase the former proportion to 6.31% and decrease the latter proportion to 14.27%, improving precision slightly by removing some *small* jitters and *sudden* jitters. In contrast, SMOOTHNET can increase the former percentage to 13.01% and decrease the latter percentage to 7.82% (a relative 45.2% reduction). We attribute the much higher performance of our solution to the fact that SMOOTHNET can relieve large and long-term jitters effectively, thanks to its data-driven modeling of the smoothness characteristics in body movements.

5.3   Refinement Results for Existing Methods

As a plug-and-play network, SMOOTHNET can be combined with any existing pose estimators. Here, we show the results on both skeleton-based methods and SMPL-based methods.

Table 2. Results of SmoothNet attached to 2D and 3D pose estimators on Human3.6M dataset. * is spatio-temporal backbones.

	Method	Accel	MPJPE	PA-MPJPE	MPJPE-1%	Accel-1%
2D Pose Estimation	Hourglass [34]	1.54	9.42	7.64	55.81	2.71
	Hourglass w/ours	**0.15**	**9.25**	**7.57**	**55.50**	**0.23**
	CPN [5]	2.91	6.67	5.18	51.86	4.17
	CPN w/ours	**0.14**	**6.45**	**4.96**	**51.65**	**0.22**
	HRNet [38]	1.01	4.59	4.19	18.16	3.55
	HRNet w/ours	**0.13**	**4.54**	**4.13**	**16.98**	**0.26**
	RLE [24]	0.90	5.14	4.82	16.67	2.28
	RLE w/ours	**0.13**	**5.21**	**4.78**	**16.16**	**0.19**
3D Pose Estimation	FCN [29]	19.17	54.55	42.20	161.00	40.03
	FCN w/ours	**1.03**	**52.72**	**40.92**	**151.08**$\downarrow_{6.2\%}$	**1.52**$\downarrow_{96.2\%}$
	RLE [24]	7.75	48.87	38.63	139.04	16.54
	RLE w/ours	**0.90**	**48.27**	**38.13**	**136.70**$\downarrow_{1.7\%}$	**1.01**$\downarrow_{93.9\%}$
	VPose [35] (T = 27)*	3.53	50.13	39.13	153.87	7.95
	VPose (T = 27)* w/ours	**0.88**	**50.04**	**39.04**	**153.29**$\downarrow_{3.8\%}$	**0.94**$\downarrow_{88.2\%}$
	VPose (T = 81)*	3.06	48.97	38.27	149.97	6.52
	VPose (T = 81)* w/ours	**0.87**	**48.89**	**38.21**	**149.57**$\downarrow_{0.3\%}$	**0.85**$\downarrow_{87.0\%}$
	VPose (T = 243)*	2.82	48.11	37.71	150.25	6.01
	VPose (T = 243)* w/ours	**0.87**	**48.05**	**37.66**	**149.88**$\downarrow_{0.2\%}$	**0.83**$\downarrow_{86.2\%}$

All estimation results are re-implemented or tested by us for fair comparisons

2D and 3D Pose Estimation. In Table 2, we compare the results of skeleton-based methods on the Human3.6M dataset. The *Accel* of all the backbones followed by our pose refinement method is significantly reduced, and *MPJPE* is also reduced to some extent. Specifically, *Accel* and *MPJPE* are reduced to a greater extent for the single-frame networks. Also, we observe that the refined *Accel* is similar with different backbones, indicating that SMOOTHNET can effectively remove different kinds of jitters in pose estimation. Since SMOOTHNET is only trained with FCN-Human3.6M, the improvements on FCN [29] is larger than other backbones with 94.6%, 3.4% and 3.0% reduction in *Accel*, *MPJPE* and *PA-MPJPE*, respectively. To explore the impact on significant biased errors and long-term jitters, we further calculate the largest 1% of *MPJPE* (*MPJPE-1%*) and their corresponding *Accel* (*Accel-1%*) as the worst 1% estimated poses for each backbone. On average, the estimated *Accel* on these poses are decreased by about 90%. In particular, we could achieve an 6.2% improvement on the trained backbone FCN with *MPJPE* reduced from 161.00 mm to 151.08 mm. This is because significant position errors are usually accompanied by long-term and large jitters, and SMOOTHNETcan reduce them as a side-effect during smoothing. Moreover, the above results across backbones also validate the generalization capability of SMOOTHNET.

Human Mesh Recovery. In Table 3, we give results of SMPL-based methods for body recovery on 3DPW [28], MPI-INF-3DHP [30], and Human3.6M dataset [14]. SMOOTHNET is trained with the pose outputs from SPIN [22]. We test its performance across multiple backbone networks.

Table 3. Results of SmoothNet attached to human mesh recovery models on 3DPW [28], MPI-INF-3DHP [30], and Human3.6M [14] dataset. * is spatio-temporal backbones.

Method	3DPW			MPI-INF-3DHP			Human3.6M		
	Accel	*MPJPE*	*PA-MPJPE*	*Accel*	*MPJPE*	*PA-MPJPE*	*Accel*	*MPJPE*	*PA-MPJPE*
SPIN [22]	30.8	87.6	53.3	28.5	100.2	61.4	18.6	68.5	46.5
SPIN w/ours	**5.5**	**86.7**	**52.7**	**6.5**	**92.9**	**60.2**	**2.8**	**67.5**	**46.3**
VIBE* [21]	23.2	83.0	52.0	22.3	91.9	58.9	15.8	78.1	53.7
VIBE* w/ours	**6.0**	**81.5**	**51.7**	**6.5**	**87.6**	**58.8**	**2.9**	**77.2**	**53.4**
TCMR* [6]	6.8	**86.5**	**52.7**	8.0	92.6	58.2	3.8	**73.6**	52.0
TCMR w/MEVA* [27]	6.2	88.7	55.0	-	-	-	3.1	77.2	55.4
TCMR* w/ours	**6.0**	**86.5**	53.0	**6.5**	88.9	58.9	**2.8**	73.9	52.1

All estimation results are re-implemented or tested by us for fair comparisons

Overall, our method has a consistent improvement in smoothness and precision. Specifically, SMOOTHNET can reduce *Accel* on SPIN and VIBE by a large margin. Compared to the original estimated poses from SPIN, our method improves by about 82.1% and 1.0% on *Accel* and *MPJPE*, respectively. For the TCMR backbone, since it has used some smoothing strategies in its models, their original *Accel* is relatively small. However, the first and last few frames could not be smoothed out with their method. Our model can relieve such jitters and further enhance its performance. Moreover, we add the post-processing slerp filter to minimize Euclidean distance on quaternion from MEVA [27] on top of TCMR backbone. The filter can improve *Accel*, but causes over-smoothness, leading to higher position errors.

5.4   Ablation Study

Comparisons on Temporal Models. To further validate the capability of the proposed FCN-based temporal model SMOOTHNET, we compare it with (i). traditional Gaussian1d filter; (ii). temporal convolutional networks [2] with a small kernel size (here is 3) in each layer, with 6, 8, 10 layers to obtain 27, 81, and 243 final receptive fields, respectively; (iii). self-attention-based Transformer (Trans.); (iv). TCN (81)× with overlapped sliding window scheme to enhance the output quality. Same as the Sect. 5.2, we use inputs from VIBE-AIST++.

Results are shown in Table 4, which indicates (i). the performance of TCN improves with increased receptive fields; (ii). the *Accel* of TCNs are worse than that of the filter [46], implying local aggregation of noisy poses with the shared kernels cannot handle large and long-term jitters well; (iii) the *MPJPE* of TCNs and Transformers are lower than that of the filter, indicating learning-based methods can further reduce biased errors S with learning the noisy pose prior; (iv) Transformer achieves a good balance between *Accel* and *MPJPE* with the global receptive field at each layer, but not as good as SMOOTHNET. We attribute it to the unnecessary self-attention operations for the pose refinement task, which

Table 4. Comparison results with different temporal models on VIBE-AIST++. × is to use overlapped sliding-window scheme, which is used in SMOOTH-NET by default. Ours⋆ is the same model with a non-overlapping sliding window.

Method	Gaussian1d	TCN(27)	TCN(81)	TCN(81)×	TCN(243)	Trans.×	Ours⋆	Ours×
Accel	4.95	14.46	11.84	8.71	10.07	6.15	<u>5.45</u>	**4.15**
MPJPE	103.42	103.53	101.17	99.54	99.76	99.30	<u>98.34</u>	**97.47**
PA-MPJPE	71.11	72.99	72.30	71.80	71.92	71.89	<u>71.02</u>	**69.67**

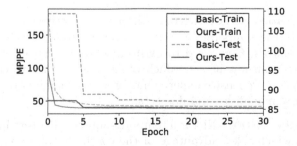

Fig. 8. Impact of model designs from the training and testing precision curves.

is no guarantee to model the smoothness pattern well. Lastly, our method show superiority in all metrics even without overlapped sliding window scheme. Note that the sliding window scheme can relieve the spikes at the junction of two sliding windows, especially when MPJPE is huge.

Comparison Between the Two Proposed Models. To capture the long-range temporal relations from noisy estimated pose sequences, we first propose a simple model with the residual fully connected network on temporal dimension, named *basic* SMOOTHNET. To further improve performance, we design a motion-aware temporal network as the SMOOTHNET in Sect. 4.2. Figure 8 illustrates the training and testing precision curves of these two models on 3DPW. We can observe that (i) *basic* model tends to somewhat overfit; (ii) SMOOTHNET fits better and obtain slightly lower position errors. In comprehensive studies, we summarize the motion-aware SMOOTHNET can fit better than the basic one, while the basic one can obtain impressive results with its simple design.

Impact of Window Size. The window size W will largely impact of smoothness from previous sliding-window-based methods [6,20,21,36]. We demonstrate the effects on different window sizes from 2 to 256 frames in Table 5. As the window size becomes longer, the *Accel* decreases consistently, but the *MPJPE* and *PA-MPJPE* initially decrease, then begin to increase slightly, indicating that when the size exceeds 64 frames, the results of the three metrics tend to be saturated. Therefore, 64 frames can be suitable to balance the smoothness and precision.

Table 5. Impact of window size W on VIBE-AIST++ [25].

W	VIBE	2	8	16	32	64	128	256
Accel	31.63	17.89	5.76	4.54	4.15	4.07	4.04	**4.03**
MPJPE	106.90	102.57	99.98	98.62	97.47	97.06	**93.20**	94.89
PA-MPJPE	72.84	71.48	70.51	69.85	**69.67**	69.89	70.57	71.52

6   Conclusion

In this work, we propose SMOOTHNET, a simple yet effective pose refinement network to improve the temporal smoothness and per-frame precision of existing pose/body estimators. Compared to existing solutions, SMOOTHNET can deal with long-term significant jitters, which often occur with rare/complex poses, as verified with comprehensive experiments on a large number of backbone networks, commonly modalities and datasets.

Broader Impact: SMOOTHNET is a temporal-only model targeting at removing various jitters, which takes advantage of the continuity of human motion, and generalizes well across backbones, modalities, and even datasets. Accordingly, this idea could be applied to other related tasks, such as whole-body estimation, pose tracking, and multi-object tracking, to further improve their smoothness and precision. Moreover, SMOOTHNET could potentially provide a smoothness prior over human motion, which is complementary to pose prior VPoser [7] and motion prior MPoser [21].

Limitation and Future Work: SMOOTHNET is a sliding-window-based model, which limits its use in real-time systems since we can not aggregate future poses to refine the historical poses. A real-time and accurate refinement model will be beneficial for online applications. We leave them for future work.

Acknowledgement. This work is supported in part by Shenzhen-Hong Kong-Macau Science and Technology Program (Category C) of Shenzhen Science Technology and Innovation Commission under Grant No. SGDX20201103095000101.

References

1. Andriluka, M., Pishchulin, L., Gehler, P., Schiele, B.: 2D human pose estimation: new benchmark and state of the art analysis. In: Proceedings of the IEEE Conference on computer Vision and Pattern Recognition, pp. 3686–3693 (2014)
2. Bai, S., Kolter, J.Z., Koltun, V.: An empirical evaluation of generic convolutional and recurrent networks for sequence modeling. arXiv arXiv:abs/1803.01271 (2018)
3. Brownrigg, D.R.: The weighted median filter. Commun. ACM **27**(8), 807–818 (1984)
4. Casiez, G., Roussel, N., Vogel, D.: 1€ filter: a simple speed-based low-pass filter for noisy input in interactive systems. In: Proceedings of the SIGCHI Conference on Human Factors in Computing Systems, pp. 2527–2530 (2012)
5. Chen, Y., Wang, Z., Peng, Y., Zhang, Z., Yu, G., Sun, J.: Cascaded pyramid network for multi-person pose estimation. In: Proceedings of the IEEE Conference on Computer Vision and Pattern Recognition, pp. 7103–7112 (2018)
6. Choi, H., Moon, G., Chang, J.Y., Lee, K.M.: Beyond static features for temporally consistent 3D human pose and shape from a video. In: Proceedings of the IEEE/CVF Conference on Computer Vision and Pattern Recognition, pp. 1964–1973 (2021)
7. Choutas, V., Pavlakos, G., Bolkart, T., Tzionas, D., Black, M.J.: Monocular expressive body regression through body-driven attention. In: Vedaldi, A., Bischof, H., Brox, T., Frahm, J.-M. (eds.) ECCV 2020. LNCS, vol. 12355, pp. 20–40. Springer, Cham (2020). https://doi.org/10.1007/978-3-030-58607-2_2
8. Coskun, H., Achilles, F., DiPietro, R.S., Navab, N., Tombari, F.: Long short-term memory kalman filters: recurrent neural estimators for pose regularization. 2017 IEEE International Conference on Computer Vision (ICCV), pp. 5525–5533 (2017)
9. Dosovitskiy, A., et al.: An image is worth 16x16 words: transformers for image recognition at scale. arXiv preprint arXiv:2010.11929 (2020)
10. Fischman, M.G.: Programming time as a function of number of movement parts and changes in movement direction. J. Mot. Behav. **16**(4), 405–423 (1984)
11. Gauss, J.F., Brandin, C., Heberle, A., Löwe, W.: Smoothing skeleton avatar visualizations using signal processing technology. SN Comput. Sci. **2**(6), 1–17 (2021)
12. Hunter, J.S.: The exponentially weighted moving average. J. Qual. Technol. **18**(4), 203–210 (1986)

13. Hyndman, R.J.: Moving averages (2011)
14. Ionescu, C., Papava, D., Olaru, V., Sminchisescu, C.: Human3.6m: large scale datasets and predictive methods for 3D human sensing in natural environments. IEEE Trans. Pattern Anal. Mach. Intell. **36**(7), 1325–1339 (2013)
15. Jiang, T., Camgoz, N.C., Bowden, R.: Skeletor: skeletal transformers for robust body-pose estimation. In: Proceedings of the IEEE/CVF Conference on Computer Vision and Pattern Recognition, pp. 3394–3402 (2021)
16. Joo, H., Neverova, N., Vedaldi, A.: Exemplar fine-tuning for 3d human model fitting towards in-the-wild 3D human pose estimation. In: 2021 International Conference on 3D Vision (3DV), pp. 42–52. IEEE (2021)
17. Kalman, R.E.: A new approach to linear filtering and prediction problems (1960)
18. Kanazawa, A., Black, M.J., Jacobs, D.W., Malik, J.: End-to-end recovery of human shape and pose. In: Proceedings of the IEEE Conference on Computer Vision and Pattern Recognition, pp. 7122–7131 (2018)
19. Kanazawa, A., Zhang, J.Y., Felsen, P., Malik, J.: Learning 3D human dynamics from video. In: Proceedings of the IEEE/CVF Conference on Computer Vision and Pattern Recognition, pp. 5614–5623 (2019)
20. Kim, D.Y., Chang, J.Y.: Attention-based 3D human pose sequence refinement network. Sensors **21**(13), 4572 (2021)
21. Kocabas, M., Athanasiou, N., Black, M.J.: Vibe: video inference for human body pose and shape estimation. In: Proceedings of the IEEE/CVF Conference on Computer Vision and Pattern Recognition, pp. 5253–5263 (2020)
22. Kolotouros, N., Pavlakos, G., Black, M.J., Daniilidis, K.: Learning to reconstruct 3D human pose and shape via model-fitting in the loop. In: Proceedings of the IEEE/CVF International Conference on Computer Vision, pp. 2252–2261 (2019)
23. Lee, C.H., Lin, C.R., Chen, M.S.: Sliding-window filtering: an efficient algorithm for incremental mining. In: Proceedings of the Tenth International Conference on Information and Knowledge Management, pp. 263–270 (2001)
24. Li, J., Bian, S., Zeng, A., Wang, C., Pang, B., Liu, W., Lu, C.: Human pose regression with residual log-likelihood estimation. In: ICCV (2021)
25. Li, R., Yang, S., Ross, D.A., Kanazawa, A.: AI choreographer: music conditioned 3D dance generation with AIST++. In: Proceedings of the IEEE/CVF International Conference on Computer Vision (ICCV), pp. 13401–13412, October 2021
26. Lin, T.-Y., et al.: Microsoft COCO: common objects in context. In: Fleet, D., Pajdla, T., Schiele, B., Tuytelaars, T. (eds.) ECCV 2014. LNCS, vol. 8693, pp. 740–755. Springer, Cham (2014). https://doi.org/10.1007/978-3-319-10602-1_48
27. Luo, Z., Golestaneh, S.A., Kitani, K.M.: 3D human motion estimation via motion compression and refinement. In: Proceedings of the Asian Conference on Computer Vision (2020)
28. von Marcard, T., Henschel, R., Black, M.J., Rosenhahn, B., Pons-Moll, G.: Recovering accurate 3D human pose in the wild using IMUs and a moving camera. In: Proceedings of the European Conference on Computer Vision (ECCV), pp. 601–617 (2018)
29. Martinez, J., Hossain, R., Romero, J., Little, J.J.: A simple yet effective baseline for 3D human pose estimation. In: Proceedings of the IEEE International Conference on Computer Vision, pp. 2640–2649 (2017)
30. Mehta, D., et al.: Monocular 3D human pose estimation in the wild using improved CNN supervision. In: 2017 International Conference on 3D Vision (3DV), pp. 506–516. IEEE (2017)
31. Mehta, D., et al.: XNect: real-time multi-person 3D motion capture with a single RGB camera. ACM Trans. Graph. (TOG) **39**(4), 82-1 (2020)

32. Mehta, D., et al.: Single-shot multi-person 3D pose estimation from monocular RGB. In: 2018 International Conference on 3D Vision (3DV), pp. 120–130 (2018)

33. Mehta, D., et al.: VNect: real-time 3D human pose estimation with a single RGB camera. ACM Trans. Graph. (TOG) **36**(4), 1–14 (2017)

34. Newell, A., Yang, K., Deng, J.: Stacked hourglass networks for human pose estimation. In: Leibe, B., Matas, J., Sebe, N., Welling, M. (eds.) ECCV 2016. LNCS, vol. 9912, pp. 483–499. Springer, Cham (2016). https://doi.org/10.1007/978-3-319-46484-8_29

35. Pavllo, D., Feichtenhofer, C., Grangier, D., Auli, M.: 3D human pose estimation in video with temporal convolutions and semi-supervised training. In: Proceedings of the IEEE Conference on Computer Vision and Pattern Recognition, pp. 7753–7762 (2019)

36. Press, W.H., Teukolsky, S.A.: Savitzky-Golay smoothing filters. Comput. Phys. **4**(6), 669–672 (1990)

37. So, D., Le, Q., Liang, C.: The evolved transformer. In: International Conference on Machine Learning, pp. 5877–5886. PMLR (2019)

38. Sun, K., Xiao, B., Liu, D., Wang, J.: Deep high-resolution representation learning for human pose estimation. In: Proceedings of the IEEE/CVF Conference on Computer Vision and Pattern Recognition, pp. 5693–5703 (2019)

39. Tripathi, S., Ranade, S., Tyagi, A., Agrawal, A.: Posenet3d: learning temporally consistent 3D human pose via knowledge distillation. In: 2020 International Conference on 3D Vision (3DV), pp. 311–321. IEEE (2020)

40. Tsuchida, S., Fukayama, S., Hamasaki, M., Goto, M.: AIST dance video database: multi-genre, multi-dancer, and multi-camera database for dance information processing. In: ISMIR, pp. 501–510 (2019)

41. Van Loan, C.: Computational frameworks for the fast Fourier transform. SIAM (1992)

42. Vaswani, A., et al.: Attention is all you need. In: Advances in Neural Information Processing Systems, vol. 30 (2017)

43. Véges, M., Lőrincz, A.: Temporal smoothing for 3D human pose estimation and localization for occluded people. In: Yang, H., Pasupa, K., Leung, A.C.-S., Kwok, J.T., Chan, J.H., King, I. (eds.) ICONIP 2020. LNCS, vol. 12532, pp. 557–568. Springer, Cham (2020). https://doi.org/10.1007/978-3-030-63830-6_47

44. Wan, Z., Li, Z., Tian, M., Liu, J., Yi, S., Li, H.: Encoder-decoder with multi-level attention for 3D human shape and pose estimation. In: Proceedings of the IEEE/CVF International Conference on Computer Vision, pp. 13033–13042 (2021)

45. Wang, J., Yan, S., Xiong, Y., Lin, D.: Motion guided 3D pose estimation from videos. arXiv abs/2004.13985 (2020)

46. Young, I.T., Van Vliet, L.J.: Recursive implementation of the gaussian filter. Signal Process. **44**(2), 139–151 (1995)

47. Zeng, A., Sun, X., Huang, F., Liu, M., Xu, Q., Lin, S.: SRNet: improving generalization in 3D human pose estimation with a split-and-recombine approach. In: Vedaldi, A., Bischof, H., Brox, T., Frahm, J.-M. (eds.) ECCV 2020. LNCS, vol. 12359, pp. 507–523. Springer, Cham (2020). https://doi.org/10.1007/978-3-030-58568-6_30

48. Zeng, A., Sun, X., Yang, L., Zhao, N., Liu, M., Xu, Q.: Learning skeletal graph neural networks for hard 3D pose estimation. In: Proceedings of the IEEE International Conference on Computer Vision (2021)

49. Zhang, S., Zhang, Y., Bogo, F., Pollefeys, M., Tang, S.: Learning motion priors for 4D human body capture in 3D scenes. In: Proceedings of the IEEE/CVF International Conference on Computer Vision, pp. 11343–11353 (2021)

50. Zhao, L., Peng, X., Tian, Y., Kapadia, M., Metaxas, D.N.: Semantic graph convolutional networks for 3D human pose regression. In: Proceedings of the IEEE Conference on Computer Vision and Pattern Recognition, pp. 3425–3435 (2019)
51. Zheng, C., Zhu, S., Mendieta, M., Yang, T., Chen, C., Ding, Z.: 3D human pose estimation with spatial and temporal transformers. arXiv preprint arXiv:2103.10455 (2021)
52. Zhou, H., et al.: Informer: beyond efficient transformer for long sequence time-series forecasting. In: Proceedings of AAAI (2021)
53. Zhou, K., Bhatnagar, B.L., Lenssen, J.E., Pons-Moll, G.: TOCH: spatio-temporal object correspondence to hand for motion refinement. arXiv, May 2022
54. Zhou, Y., Barnes, C., Lu, J., Yang, J., Li, H.: On the continuity of rotation representations in neural networks. In: 2019 IEEE/CVF Conference on Computer Vision and Pattern Recognition (CVPR), pp. 5738–5746 (2019)

PoseTrans: A Simple yet Effective Pose Transformation Augmentation for Human Pose Estimation

Wentao Jiang[1,2]ⓘ, Sheng Jin[2,3]ⓘ, Wentao Liu[2,4]ⓘ, Chen Qian[2]ⓘ,
Ping Luo[3]ⓘ, and Si Liu[1,5]([✉])

[1] Institute of Artificial Intelligence, Beihang University, Beijing, China
{jiangwentao,liusi}@buaa.edu.cn
[2] SenseTime Research and Tetras.AI, Pak Shek Kok, Hong Kong
js20@connect.hku.hk,{liuwentao,qianchen}@sensetime.com
[3] The University of Hong Kong, Pok Fu Lam, Hong Kong
pluo@cs.hku.hk
[4] Shanghai AI Laboratory, Shanghai, China
[5] State Key Lab. of VR Technology and Systems, SCSE, Beihang University, Beijing, China

Abstract. Human pose estimation aims to accurately estimate a wide variety of human poses. However, existing datasets often follow a long-tailed distribution that unusual poses only occupy a small portion, which further leads to the lack of diversity of rare poses. These issues result in the inferior generalization ability of current pose estimators. In this paper, we present a simple yet effective data augmentation method, termed Pose Transformation (PoseTrans), to alleviate the aforementioned problems. Specifically, we propose Pose Transformation Module (PTM) to create new training samples that have diverse poses and adopt a pose discriminator to ensure the plausibility of the augmented poses. Besides, we propose Pose Clustering Module (PCM) to measure the pose rarity and select the "rarest" poses to help balance the long-tailed distribution. Extensive experiments on three benchmark datasets demonstrate the effectiveness of our method, especially on rare poses. Also, our method is efficient and simple to implement, which can be easily integrated into the training pipeline of existing pose estimation models.

Keywords: Pose estimation · Data augmentation

1 Introduction

Human Pose Estimation (HPE) is the task of localizing human body keypoints (also referred to as joints) from an image. It serves as a fundamental technique for numerous applications, including action recognition, pedestrian tracking, and virtual/augmented reality. Recently, deep convolutional neural networks

Supplementary Information The online version contains supplementary material available at https://doi.org/10.1007/978-3-031-20065-6_37.

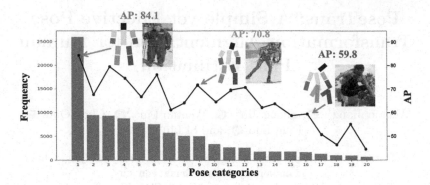

Fig. 1. We cluster the poses in the MS-COCO dataset into 20 categories and evaluate the AP with a pre-trained HRNet model [43]. The top-1 category has more than 25000 samples and high precision, while nearly half of the categories have less than 2000 samples and relatively low precision.

(DCNN) [34,35,41] have achieved drastic improvements on standard benchmark datasets. To fully exploit the power of DCNN, a large number of training data is indispensable for obtaining satisfactory performance in human pose estimation.

However, existing human pose estimation datasets do not uniformly represent all possible human poses in real life. We take MS-COCO dataset [31] as an example to analyze the distribution of the human poses, as shown in Fig. 1. We normalize the poses and cluster them into 20 categories. We observe that it follows a long-tailed distribution, with a few common pose categories (*e.g* standing and walking) occupying a large portion of the dataset and unusual posture types (*e.g* squatting and jumping) possessing a smaller portion. We also find that although current state-of-the-art data-driven methods achieve good performance on common poses, however, they still suffer performance degradation on some unusual poses, since the long-tailed categories have neither enough training samples nor enough diversity.

Due to the high cost of collecting and annotating examples with rare poses, a feasible way to tackle this problem is data augmentation. Previous methods augment the human pose mainly by global image-level transformations [12,35, 37,42,45] (*e.g* scaling and rotating) or local object-level transformations [5,18, 37] (*e.g* copy-paste and occluding). Since these methods fail to increase the diversity of poses and alleviate the long-tailed distribution, they contribute little to recognizing diverse rare poses.

In this paper, we propose a simple yet effective data augmentation approach, termed Pose Transformation (PoseTrans), to tackle the aforementioned challenges. PoseTrans consists of a Pose Transformation Module (PTM) with a pose discriminator, and a Pose Clustering Module (PCM). During training, PTM applies affine transformations to the original pose of the training sample and generates a pool of diverse new poses. The pre-trained pose discriminator is adopted to evaluate the plausibility of generated samples and then filter out unnatural samples. PCM is based on the Gaussian Mixture Model (GMM), which normalizes and clusters the human poses in the dataset. The rare types of poses are represented by the Gaussian components that have small weights. PCM evaluates the components' density for each candidate pose and selects the "rarest" one (*i.e* which has the minimal weighted sum of components' density) as the final augmented training sample. By transforming the existing poses, Pose-Trans helps generate diverse, plausible poses by PTM and alleviate the long-tail distribution problem by PCM. We also design a metric that focuses on rare poses called balanced AP/AR and observe more performance gain on this metric. Our method is simple to implement and can be easily integrated into the training pipeline of existing pose estimation models.

We summarize our contributions as follows:

- We present a simple yet effective data augmentation method, termed Pose-Trans. To tackle the problem of limited diversity of unusual human poses, we propose a novel Pose Transformation Module (PTM) with a pose discriminator to generate new training samples with diverse and plausible poses.
- We propose Pose Clustering Module (PCM) to measure the pose rarity and select rare poses for data augmentation, which helps to balance the long-tailed distribution of the training set.
- Extensive experiments on various pose estimation datasets show that Pose-Trans consistently improves the performance of various state-of-the-art pose estimators, especially on rare poses.

2   Related Works

2.1   2D Human Pose Estimation

In recent years, 2D human pose estimation has shown remarkable performance advancement. DeepPose [41] first applied deep neural networks to human pose estimation by directly regressing the 2D coordinates of key points from the input image. Since then, deep learning-based methods started to dominate this area. Recent multi-person human pose estimation approaches can be divided into bottom-up and top-down approaches. Bottom-up approaches [7,13,23–25, 28,34,36] first detect all the key points of every person in images and then group them into individuals. Top-down methods [11,21,40,45] first detect the bounding boxes and then predict the human body key points in each box.

Recent works mainly focus on designing powerful network architectures to improve the performance of pose estimation [11,26,35,40,45,46,48]. However, current state-of-the-art models often suffer performance drops on rare poses due to the long-tailed distribution problem in human pose data. In this work, we focus on tackling this important but ignored problem. Standing on the shoulder of the well-designed network structure, we propose a novel data augmentation method to generate diverse rare poses.

2.2 Data Augmentation

Data augmentation has been widely utilized to improve the model generalization ability. For image classification, popular augmentation methods include information dropping [9,16,52], multi-image information mixing [47,50] and automatic augmentation [15]. For human pose estimation, data augmentation mainly focus on global image-level transformations [12,35,37,42,45] (*e.g* scaling, rotating, and flipping) and local object-level transformations [5,37] (*e.g* copy-paste, occluding). These common data augmentation schemes enhance the global translational invariance and robustness in occlusion cases but struggle to improve the immunity to rare poses. Recently, some augmentation methods [18,19] propose to perform jitting on instances to increase the generalization of the model, but they do not change either the instance itself or the distribution of instances. Different from the existing data augmentation strategies, we propose a novel, simple and effective PoseTrans augmentation scheme that directly generates diverse rare poses.

2.3 Long-Tailed Distribution

In visual recognition, there exists a challenging problem of long-tailed training set distributions, where a small portion of classes have massive training samples while classes in the distribution tail have few samples [51]. Over-sampling [8] and re-weighting [17] are two popular methods to tackle the problem. The over-sampling method raises the frequency level of the minor classes by repeating the data samples during training. The re-weighting method assigns higher loss weights to these minor classes and thus increases their importance. However, such approaches do not increase the diversity of the data and tend to suffer from over-fitting which leads to a performance drop. Other approaches also include metric learning that enforces inter-class margins [22] and meta-learning that learns to regress many-shot model parameters from few-shot model parameters [44], but they are only designed for visual recognition. In human pose estimation, we encounter a similar problem. For many human pose estimation datasets [3, 29,31], *e.g* the MS-COCO dataset [31], the distribution of human poses is highly biased, which does not uniformly represent human poses in real life. These dataset biases lead to poor generalization and degraded detection accuracy of these "long-tailed" poses. To address the aforementioned issue, we propose a simple yet effective PoseTrans approach to create the needed diverse poses.

3 Method

3.1 Overview

To increase the diversity of poses and alleviate the long-tailed distribution problem, we propose the Pose Transformation (PoseTrans) to generate new training samples with diverse poses, as shown in Fig. 2. PoseTrans consists of a Pose Transformation Module (PTM) with a pose discriminator D and a Pose Clustering Module (PCM). Given a training sample $(\boldsymbol{x}, \boldsymbol{y})$ consisting of a single

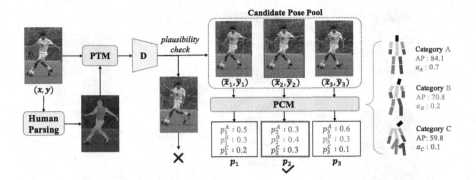

Fig. 2. Overview of PoseTrans. Given a single human image x and its keypoint annotations y, we first segment the human into different parts through human parsing. PTM applies affine transformations on the limbs of the human to construct new poses. A pretrained pose discriminator is used for the plausibility check. The plausible poses form a candidate pose pool $\{(\tilde{x}_t, \tilde{y}_t)\}$, where $t \in \{1, 2, 3\}$ as an example. For pose $\tilde{y}_t$, PCM predicts w_t, which is the probability of belonging to each category (3 categories as an example). PCM selects the rarest one with the minimal weighted sum of components' density as a new training sample, *i.e* $w_2^A \alpha_A + w_2^B \alpha_B + w_2^C \alpha_C$.

human image x and its keypoint annotation y, PTM aims to create a new training sample $(\tilde{x}, \tilde{y})$ by applying affine transformations on the limbs of the human, where $x, \tilde{x} \in \mathbb{R}^{H \times W \times 3}$, $y, \tilde{y} \in \mathbb{R}^{J \times 2}$. H, W and J indicate the height, width and the number of keypoints respectively. To ensure plausibility, we leverage the pose discriminator D to filter out implausible samples. PoseTrans applies PTM repeatedly until a candidate pose pool with T plausible generated poses is formed. PCM clusters human poses into N categories and evaluates the probability of belonging to each cluster for generated poses to select the rarest one among the pool as a new training sample. After each training epoch, we re-fit the PCM using the original training set and all the selected augmented samples.

3.2 Pose Transformation Module (PTM) and Pose Discriminator

By clustering the human poses in the existing dataset, it can be observed that many clusters only have a few examples. The lack of training examples of rare poses further leads to the lack of diversity of rare poses, which results in the inferior performance of current data-driven methods on these types of poses. To tackle this issue, we devise the Pose Transformation Module (PTM) and a pose discriminator to create plausible new poses based on the existing training samples. The detail of PTM is shown in Fig. 3.

Modeling the Body Part Movement. The body kinematic skeleton is constructed by a pose graph, where the human body is partitioned into several parts, *i.e* the head, the torso, the left/right arm, and the left/right leg. In this work, we mainly focus on the angular movement of the arms and legs. Angular movements (flexion and extension) take place at the shoulder, hip, elbow, knee, and

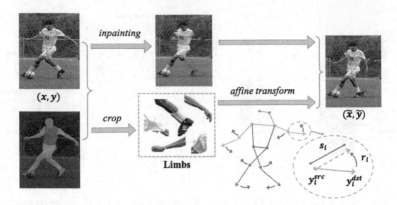

Fig. 3. By leveraging the human parsing results, we first erase the limbs from x and then transform each limb separately with a given probability $p = 0.5$. Limbs that do not appear or are obscured will not be transformed. The zoom-in view in the bottom right corner indicates the affine transformation with scale s_i and rotation r_i applied on the i-th limb (lower arm).

wrist. Flexion decreases the angle between the bones (bending of the joint), while extension increases the angle and straightens the joint. These body part movements in the image plane can be modeled by applying the affine transformation to a rigid body part segment. In our implementation, the affine transformation is composed of rotation and scaling.

We define the limb as a single rigid body part connecting natural adjacent joints y^{src} and y^{dst}, where $y^{src}, y^{dst} \in \mathbb{R}^2$ are the coordinates of the source and destination joint respectively. We define $K = 8$ limbs for each instance, including the lower arm, the upper arm, the lower leg, and the upper leg of both sides.

Pose Transformation. With human parsing results obtained through Dense-Pose [1] model, PTM first erases the original limbs in x by an efficient inpainting method [4]. After that, each limb is transformed by its affine transformation matrix separately. To increase the diversity, each limb has a probability of $p = 0.5$ to decide whether to transform or not. The transformed limbs and the inpainted image are composed to form the new augmented image $\tilde{x}$. And the pose annotations are also transformed accordingly to get $\tilde{y}$.

Specifically, the angular movement of the i-th limb can be modeled by the following affine transformation matrix

$$H_i = \begin{bmatrix} s_i \cos r_i & -s_i \sin r_i & (1 - \cos r_i)c_i^x + c_i^y \sin r_i \\ s_i \sin r_i & s_i \cos r_i & (1 - \cos r_i)c_i^y - c_i^x \sin r_i \\ 0 & 0 & 1 \end{bmatrix}, \tag{1}$$

where $s_i \in \mathbb{R}^+$ and $r_i \in \mathbb{R}$ denote the scale and rotation of the i-th limb, $y_i^{src} = \{c_i^x, c_i^y\}$ is the coordinates of the rotation center of the i-th limb. For the lower arm, the upper arm, the lower leg, and the upper leg, the rotation centers are the elbow, the shoulder, the knee, and the hip respectively. To ensure the diversity of augmented poses, the scale s_i and rotation r_i parameters in $\boldsymbol{H}_i$ are randomly sampled from a normal distribution in the neighboring space of identity transformation $(1, 0)$. The scale and rotation parameters are also restricted to a certain range in our implementation to ensure that the majority of the randomly generated poses are plausible. Note that, limbs that do not appear in the image or are obscured will not be transformed.

According to the kinematic skeleton hierarchy, the movement of the upper arm/leg will affect that of its lower part. Suppose the j-th limb is the lower arm/leg and the k-th limb is its corresponding upper part. Considering the combined effect, the total movement of the j-th limb can be modeled by matrix multiplication, $i.e$ $\boldsymbol{H}_k\boldsymbol{H}_j$.

Pose Discriminator for the Plausibility Check. Purely generating poses randomly may result in implausible poses that violate the biomechanical structure of the human body. Some other augmentation methods [10,30] rely on pre-defined rules for ensuring plausibility, which however limits the diversity of generated poses. Inspired by [20], we design a pose discriminator D that suits our task to avoid implausible poses that have unnatural joint angles or unreasonable positions in the scene. For the augmented sample $(\tilde{\boldsymbol{x}}_t, \tilde{\boldsymbol{y}}_t)$, the discriminator D is trained to predict the plausibility $e_t = D(\tilde{\boldsymbol{x}}_t, \tilde{\boldsymbol{y}}_t)$. We adopt the LS-GAN loss [33] to train the discriminator before training the pose estimatior:

$$\mathcal{L}_D = \mathbb{E}\left[(D(\boldsymbol{x}, \boldsymbol{y}) - 1)^2\right] + \mathbb{E}\left[D(\tilde{\boldsymbol{x}}, \tilde{\boldsymbol{y}})^2\right]. \tag{2}$$

With the pre-trained discriminator D, PoseTrans efficiently filter out the augmented sample whose plausibility is less than a pre-defined threshold $E \in [0, 1]$, and fill the candidate pose pool with samples that are plausible and diverse.

3.3   Pose Clustering Module (PCM)

After gaining the ability to create new human poses by PTM, we propose the Pose Clustering Module (PCM) to measure the pose rarity and select the needed poses for data augmentation.

Fitting the PCM. Our PCM is built upon the Gaussian Mixture Model (GMM) with N Gaussian components. As a soft clustering method, it predicts the probability of belonging to a certain category. Before pose clustering, human poses in the training set are first normalized. We crop every human instance on the image and re-scale the cropped image into the same height and width (256×256). The corresponding keypoint coordinates are also normalized at the same time. We fit the PCM using the normalized human poses in the training set. After fitting, given the pose $\boldsymbol{y}$, we model $P(\boldsymbol{y})$ as:

$$P(\boldsymbol{y}) = \sum_{n=1}^{N} \alpha_n \mathcal{N}\left(\boldsymbol{y}; \mu_n, \sigma_n\right), \tag{3}$$

where α_n is the weight of the n-th Gaussian component, $\mathcal{N}\left(\boldsymbol{y}; \mu_n, \sigma_n\right)$ denotes the n-th Gaussian distribution with mean μ_n and covariance σ_n.

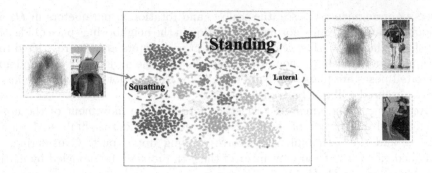

Fig. 4. The visualization of the clustering results using PCM by t-SNE. Different colored points indicate different clusters. Representative images and mean skeletons for the clusters of standing, squatting, and lateral poses are also visualized.

By predicting the probability of belonging to each Gaussian component, the human pose is classified as the component with the maximum probability. We visualize the probability vectors of every example using t-SNE [32], as shown in Fig. 4. With PCM, we cluster the human poses into N categories, where Gaussian components that have small weights (*i.e* few examples,) indicate the categories of rare poses. We observe the long-tailed problem that frontal standing accounts for a significant portion while squatting and lateral postures account for small percentages.

Pose Selection from the Candidate Pose Pool. PoseTrans repeats PTM to build a candidate pose pool $\{(\tilde{x}_t, \tilde{y}_t)\}$ with T samples for the training sample (x, y), where $t \in \{1, 2, ..., T\}$. PoseTrans select the rarest one $(\tilde{x}_{t^*}, \tilde{y}_{t^*})$ among the candidate pose pool by:

$$t^* = \underset{t}{\operatorname{argmin}} \left(\sum_{n=1}^{N} \alpha_n w_t^n \right), \tag{4}$$

where $w_t = \{w_t^1, w_t^2, ..., w_t^N\}$ is the predicted probability of $\tilde{y}_t$ belonging to N Gaussian components by the fitted PCM. We consider the transformed sample $(\tilde{x}_{t^*}, \tilde{y}_{t^*})$ with the minimal weighted sum of components' density as the rarest and select it as a new training sample.

4   Experiments

4.1   Datasets and Evaluation

Datasets. To verify the effectiveness of our proposed data augmentation approach, we conduct extensive experiments on popular datasets. **(1)** MS-COCO [31] pose estimation dataset. Our models are trained on the train set only and evaluated on the val set and the test-dev set. DensePose [1] provides a small portion of human parsing annotations for the MS-COCO dataset. To verify the performance on rare poses, both the traditional evaluation metrics (*i.e* AP/AR) and newly designed metrics (balanced AP/AR) are used for evaluation. The base learning rate of 1e-3, and decay the learning rate to 1e-4 and 1e-5 at the 170-th and 200-th epochs respectively. **(2)** PoseTrack'18 [2] dataset. Following common settings [14], we pre-train the model on the MS-COCO dataset and fine-tune it on the PoseTrack'18 dataset for 20 epochs. The basic learning rate is 1e-4 and drops to 1e-5 at 10 epochs then 1e-6 at 15 epochs. We test the model on the PoseTrack'18 validation set using the ground truth bounding boxes, and evaluate the AP on the whole body and also on different parts of the human. Due to the limited space, the results of some experiments are placed in the supplementary material.

Evaluation Metrics. We follow [31] to use Average Precision (AP) and Average Recall (AR) for evaluation on MS-COCO [31]. They are based on object keypoint similarity (OKS), which measures the distance between predicted keypoints and ground-truth keypoints normalized by the scale of the object. AP_{50} (AP at OKS = 0.5), AP_{75} (AP at OKS = 0.75), AP^M for medium objects, and AP^L for large objects are reported.

Balanced AP/AR. Since existing datasets mostly suffer the long-tailed distribution problem, simply calculating the AP/AR tends to ignore the minor pose categories. To solve this problem, we design the balanced AP/AR, which we term AP_{BAL}, AR_{BAL}. We first classify the ground-truth poses into categories based on the fitted PCM. Then we calculate the standard AP/AR separately for each category and calculate the average precision/recall among *categories* instead of *samples*. Therefore, AP_{BAL} and AR_{BAL} assign the same weights to all pose categories, which is helpful to analyze the "unbiased" performance.

4.2   Implementation Details

PoseTrans can be integrated into the training pipeline of any existing pose estimators together with other common data augmentation strategies. Except for the small portion of images that have human parsing annotations, we leverage DensePose [1] model for human parsing which segments humans into 14 semantic parts. In PCM, we have $N = 20$ and cluster the poses into 20 categories. We implement PoseTrans with scaling ($s \in [0.75, 1.25]$), rotating ($r \in [-35°, 35°]$), and apply it with the probability $p = 0.5$ for every limb in the training examples. We filter out the implausible samples whose plausibility is less than $E = 0.7$ and repeat PTM until the candidate pose pool has $T = 5$ augmented samples.

For *bottom-up* methods, PoseTrans is applied on every instance in the image separately. The experimental settings are the same as [13]. We apply image-level random scaling ($[-25\%, 25\%]$), random rotation ($[-30°, 30°]$), random translation ($[-40px, 40px]$) and random flipping. The models are trained for 300 epochs using the Adam optimizer [27]. The base learning rate is 1e-3, and it decreases to 1e-4 and 1e-5 at the 200-th and 260-th epochs respectively. For *top-down* approaches, the experimental settings are the same as [40]. We use the detected bounding boxes provided by Xiao *et al* [45]. The detection boxes are first extended to a fixed aspect ratio (*i.e* height:width = 4:3) and then

Table 1. Improvements on MS-COCO `val` set and `test-dev` set. PoseTrans consistently boosts the performance of the state of the arts.

Method	Input size	MS-COCO val						MS-COCO test-dev					
		AP	AP^{50}	AP^{75}	AP^M	AP^L	AR	AP	AP^{50}	AP^{75}	AP^M	AP^L	AR
Bottom-up methods w/o multi-scale test													
AE [34] + HRNet-W32 [40]	512 × 512	64.4	86.3	72.0	57.1	75.6	71.0	64.1	86.3	70.4	57.4	73.9	70.4
+ PoseTrans (Ours)	512 × 512	**66.2**	**86.4**	**72.1**	**59.3**	**76.5**	**71.6**	**65.4**	**87.6**	**72.1**	**58.8**	**74.7**	**71.0**
HigherHRNet-W32 [13]	512 × 512	67.1	86.2	73.0	61.5	76.1	72.3	66.4	87.5	72.8	61.2	74.2	71.4
+ PoseTrans (Ours)	512 × 512	**68.4**	**87.1**	**74.8**	**62.7**	**77.1**	**72.9**	**67.4**	**88.3**	**73.9**	**62.1**	**75.1**	**72.2**
Bottom-up methods with multi-scale test [×2, ×1, ×0.5]													
AE [34] + HRNet-W32 [40]	512 × 512	68.5	87.1	75.1	64.0	76.8	73.9	68.1	88.3	75.1	63.8	74.9	72.9
+ PoseTrans (Ours)	512 × 512	**70.5**	**87.8**	**76.7**	**65.1**	**78.1**	**75.2**	**69.4**	**88.8**	**76.3**	**64.4**	**76.2**	**74.2**
HigherHRNet-W32 [13]	512 × 512	69.9	87.1	76.0	65.3	77.0	74.7	68.8	88.8	75.7	64.4	75.0	73.5
+ PoseTrans (Ours)	512 × 512	**71.2**	**88.2**	**77.2**	**66.5**	**78.0**	**75.3**	**69.9**	**89.3**	**77.0**	**65.2**	**76.2**	**74.3**
Top-down methods													
SBL-ResNet-50 [45]	256 × 192	70.4	88.6	78.3	67.1	75.9	76.3	70.2	90.9	78.3	67.1	75.9	75.8
+ PoseTrans (Ours)	256 × 192	**72.3**	**89.9**	**80.0**	**68.3**	**79.2**	**77.8**	**71.5**	**91.8**	**80.0**	**68.1**	**77.3**	**77.0**
SBL-ResNet-101 [45]	256 × 192	71.4	89.3	79.3	68.1	78.1	77.1	71.1	91.5	79.6	67.7	76.8	76.6
+ PoseTrans (Ours)	256 × 192	**72.7**	**90.0**	**80.7**	**69.5**	**78.8**	**78.3**	**71.8**	**91.6**	**80.3**	**68.3**	**77.5**	**77.3**
HRNet-W32 [40]	256 × 192	74.4	90.5	81.9	70.8	81.0	79.8	73.5	92.2	82.0	70.4	79.0	79.0
+ PoseTrans (Ours)	256 × 192	**75.5**	**91.0**	**82.9**	**71.8**	**82.2**	**80.7**	**74.2**	**92.4**	**82.5**	**70.8**	**79.6**	**79.4**
HRNet-W32 [40] + Dark [49]	256 × 192	75.6	90.5	82.1	71.8	82.8	80.8	74.6	92.4	82.9	71.2	80.3	79.9
+ PoseTrans (Ours)	256 × 192	**76.0**	**90.8**	**83.0**	**72.1**	**83.2**	**81.1**	**75.0**	**92.5**	**82.9**	**71.5**	**80.6**	**80.1**
HRNet-W32 [40]	384 × 288	75.8	90.6	82.7	71.9	82.8	80.1	74.9	92.5	82.8	71.3	80.9	80.1
+ PoseTrans (Ours)	384 × 288	**76.5**	**90.9**	**83.3**	**72.5**	**83.3**	**81.5**	**75.4**	**92.5**	**83.0**	**71.6**	**81.1**	**80.4**
HRNet-W48 [40]	384 × 288	76.3	90.8	82.9	72.3	83.4	81.2	75.5	92.5	83.3	71.9	81.5	80.5
+ PoseTrans (Ours)	384 × 288	**76.8**	**91.0**	**83.1**	**72.7**	**83.7**	**81.6**	**75.7**	**92.6**	**83.4**	**72.0**	**81.7**	**80.6**

enlarged by a factor of 1.25 to include some context. We apply random scaling ($[-35\%, 35\%]$), random rotation ($[-45°, 45°]$), random flipping, and half-body crops. The models are trained on 16 GPUs for 210 epochs. We use Adam optimizer [27] for training. All networks are pre-trained on the ImageNet dataset [39].

4.3 Improvement of State-of-the-Art Methods by PoseTrans

Improvement of AP/AR. Table 1 reports the performance improvement of AP and AR on the MS-COCO `val` and MS-COCO `test-dev` set, where PoseTrans is applied to recent state-of-the-art pose estimators, *i.e* SBL [45], HRNet [40], and HigherHRNet [13]. Table 2 show the performance improvement on the PoseTrack dataset. PoseTrans consistently boosts the performance of both top-down and bottom-up approaches in various datasets.

Improvement of AP_{BAL} and AR_{BAL}. The results of AP_{BAL} and AR_{BAL} are reported in Table 3a. To calculate the new metrics, we use the bounding boxes and keypoint annotations to determine the category of predicted poses. Thanks to the design of PCM and PTM, PoseTrans increases the diversity of rare poses and balances the distribution, which enables PoseTrans to bring more improvements on the newly proposed AP_{BAL}/AR_{BAL} than traditional AP/AR.

4.4 Comparisons with Other Data Augmentation Techniques

In Table 3b, we compare PoseTrans with other data augmentation techniques, including non-learning [6,9,16] and learning/strategy-based methods [18,42].

Table 2. Improvements on PoseTrack2018 validation set.

Method	Input size	Head	Sho.	Elb.	Wri.	Hip	Knee	Ank.	Total AP
SBL-ResNet-50 [45]	256 × 192	86.5	87.5	82.3	75.6	79.9	78.6	74.0	81.0
+ PoseTrans (Ours)	256 × 192	**87.8**	**89.3**	**84.7**	**77.7**	**82.3**	**81.6**	**75.4**	**83.0**
HRNet-W32 [40]	256 × 192	87.4	88.6	84.3	78.5	79.7	81.8	78.8	83.0
+ PoseTrans (Ours)	256 × 192	**88.6**	**90.0**	**86.2**	**80.3**	**83.1**	**84.9**	**79.8**	**84.9**
HRNet-W32 [40]	384 × 288	88.5	89.5	86.0	80.4	81.6	83.4	78.9	84.3
+ PoseTrans (Ours)	384 × 288	**88.9**	**90.3**	**87.4**	**81.8**	**83.5**	**85.5**	**80.6**	**85.7**

Table 3. (a) Improvements of Balanced AP/AR on MS-COCO `val` set. **(b)** Comparisons of data augmentation techniques on MS-COCO `val` set. HRNet-W32 with an input size of 256 × 192 is adopted as the baseline. Results marked with '*' are reported by [38] using CascadeRCNN bounding boxes.

Method	Input size	MS-COCO val			
		AP	AR	AP$_{BAL}$	AR$_{BAL}$
SBL-ResNet50 [45]	256 × 192	70.4	76.3	60.6	66.3
+ PoseTrans (Ours)	256 × 192	**72.3**	**77.8**	**63.8**	**69.6**
HRNet-W32 [40]	256 × 192	74.4	79.8	65.4	72.3
+ PoseTrans (Ours)	256 × 192	**75.5**	**80.7**	**67.9**	**73.8**
HRNet-W32 [49]	384 × 288	75.8	80.1	67.7	73.8
+ PoseTrans (Ours)	384 × 288	**76.5**	**81.5**	**68.9**	**74.2**

(a)

Method	AP	AP^{50}	AP^{75}	AR
Baseline [40]	74.4	90.5	81.9	79.8
+ Cutout* [16]	74.5	90.5	81.7	78.8
+ GridMask [9]	74.7	90.6	82.0	80.1
+ Photometric Distortion [6]	74.6	90.3	81.9	80.0
+ AdvMix [42]	74.7	-	-	-
+ InstaBoost [18]	74.7	90.5	82.0	80.1
+ ASDA [5]	75.2	**91.0**	82.4	80.4
+ PoseTrans (Ours)	**75.5**	**91.0**	**82.9**	**80.7**

(b)

For non-learning methods, Cutout [16] randomly selects a rectangle region around the keypoint and fills in random values. GridMask [9] evenly replaces multiple rectangle regions in an image with all zeros. For Photometric Distortion, we follow [6] to adjust the brightness, contrast, hue, saturation, and noise of an image. These general data techniques are proven to be effective for image classification. However, they do not bring significant improvements for human pose estimation. Similar conclusions have also been reached by previous works [38]. This is probably because such techniques introduce undesirable artifacts and do not increase the diversity of human poses.

For learning/strategy-based methods, AdvMix [42] applies adversarial training to learn to mix up augmented samples generated by GridMask [9] and AutoAugment [15]. InstaBoost [18] is a recently proposed data augmentation technique which is originally designed for instance segmentation. It conducts crop-paste augmentation guided by the appearance consistency heatmaps. However, the improvements of AdvMix and InstaBoost are only marginal. ASDA [5] also employs human parsing and augments images by pasting the segmented body parts. PoseTrans outperforms all these approaches, which validates the importance of increasing the diversity of the human body poses.

Kindly note that PoseTrans is also complementary to other techniques. Effectively combining these techniques may further improve the final performance. As shown in the third row from the bottom in Table 1, combining PoseTrans with DarkPose [49] can further gain improvements.

4.5   Ablation Studies

Effect of PTM. Without using the PTM, we perform the over-sampling [8] and re-weighting [17] strategies, which are two popular methods to tackle the long-tailed problem. The over-sampling method raises the frequency level of the minor categories by duplicating the long-tailed data samples during model training. The re-weighting method assigns higher loss weights to rare samples and thus increases their importance. Based on the clustering results of PCM, we implement these methods as baselines, as shown in Table 4a. By increasing the importance of long-tailed training samples, both the over-sampling marginally improve the AP_{BAL}. However, such approaches do not increase the diversity of the data, which leads to slight performance drops on AP and AR. With the design of PTM, our proposed PoseTrans creates diverse long-tailed samples, which significantly outperforms the baseline methods.

Effect of PCM. Without PCM, PoseTrans randomly samples a transformed pose obtained from PTM as the training sample, instead of picking the "rarest" pose in the candidate pose pool. Note that, "w/o PCM" is equivalent to the case of $T = 1$ in PoseTrans. The studies of w/o PCM and the number of T in PCM are shown in Table 4b. By providing simple disturbance to training data, w/o PCM increases the generalization of the model, which leads to some performance improvements. While with the aid of PCM, our full model learns to alleviate the long-tailed distribution problem of the training set by selecting transformed poses, which brings greater performance gains, especially on AP_{BAL}/AR_{BAL}. Also, a larger candidate pose pool (*i.e* greater T) leads to better performance. However, T greater than 5 will not bring more performance boost.

Effect of Pose Discriminator. Without the pose discriminator (D), some implausible poses will lead to performance degradation as shown in Table 5a. Since the scale s and rotation r parameters are sampled from a normal distribution and are restricted to $[0.75, 1.25]$ and $[-35°, 35°]$ in the implementation, a majority of the randomly generated poses are plausible. In this situation, the PTM without the pose discriminator can still benefit the model.

Comparison with the Adversarial Learning Variant. Inspired by recent works [5,37,42] on adversarial data augmentation, we also build an adversarial training variant of PoseTrans, which we refer to as PoseTrans-Adv. PoseTrans-Adv has an additional generator that predicts the rotation r and scale s for a given single human image x. During training, the generator is asked to confuse the pose estimation model by maximizing the loss of the pose estimator. However, we observe that the generator will soon learn to choose the maximum rotation and scale for every training sample, which actually decreases the diversity of the training set. This leads to performance degradation in all the evaluation metrics as shown in the first row of Table 5b.

Comparison with PoseTrans-Par on the MS-COCO Dataset. As mentioned above, DensePose [1] provides a small portion of human parsing annotations for the MS-COCO dataset. Here, we compare with the PoseTrans-Par

Table 4. (a) Ablation studies of PTM. The over-sampling and re-weighting methods are based on the clustering results of PCM. **(b)** Ablation studies of PCM. HRNet-W32 with the input size of 256 × 192 is adopted for experiments.

Method	AP	AR	AP$_{BAL}$	AR$_{BAL}$
Baseline	74.4	79.8	65.4	72.3
Over-sampling [8]	74.3	79.7	66.0	72.3
Re-weighting [17]	74.2	79.6	65.8	72.2
PoseTrans (Ours)	**75.5**	**80.7**	**67.9**	**73.8**

(a)

Method	AP	AR	AP$_{BAL}$	AR$_{BAL}$
Baseline [40]	74.4	79.8	65.4	72.3
w/o PCM	74.9	80.1	66.1	72.6
PoseTrans ($T = 3$)	75.2	80.3	67.2	72.9
PoseTrans ($T = 5$)	**75.5**	**80.7**	**67.9**	**73.8**

(b)

Table 5. (a) Ablation studies of Discriminator (D). **(b)** Comparison with the variants of PoseTrans.

Method	AP	AR	AP$_{BAL}$	AR$_{BAL}$
PoseTrans w/o D	75.0	80.1	66.5	72.8
PoseTrans	**75.5**	**80.7**	**67.9**	**73.8**

(a)

Method	AP	AR	AP$_{BAL}$	AR$_{BAL}$
PoseTrans-Adv	72.7	78.4	65.2	71.5
PoseTrans-Par	75.3	80.4	67.3	73.3
PoseTrans	**75.5**	**80.7**	**67.9**	**73.8**

(b)

variant that replaces the human annotations with the pseudo-labels obtained from the parsing model. As shown in the second row of Table 5b, without human annotations, the performance of PoseTrans-Par is comparable with PoseTrans.

4.6   Analysis

Visualizations of the Augmented Samples. In Fig. 5, we visualize the original image and the augmented sample by PoseTrans. It can be observed that our proposed method generates diverse and plausible body postures that facilitate the model training and improve its generalization ability.

Visualizations of Pose Estimation Results. In Fig. 6, we visualize pose estimation results obtained by HRNet [40]. We observe that vanilla HRNet is easily confused by infrequent and difficult poses, *e.g* upside-down postures and serious occlusions. By generating training samples with diverse rare poses, our PoseTrans improves the performance in these challenging cases.

Limitations. Our limitations mainly lie in the artifacts produced by the inpainting method and the accuracy of the human parsing model. We choose a simple non-data-driven inpainting method in pose transformation for efficiency. An advanced inpainting and parsing model with higher resolution inputs may bring more improvements in pose estimation.

Fig. 5. Visualizations of PoseTrans augmented samples. We observe that our proposed method generates more diverse body postures which facilitates the model training and improves its generalization ability.

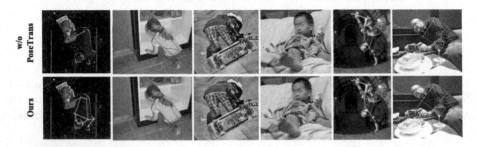

Fig. 6. Qualitative comparisons of vanilla HRNet [40] (upper row) and HRNet trained with PoseTrans (bottom row). PoseTrans improves the human pose estimation results, especially for rare poses.

5   Conclusions

In this paper, we study the performance degradation caused by unbalanced data distribution on human pose estimation. To tackle this issue, we propose Pose-Trans with PTM, PCM, and a pose discriminator to create diverse and plausible training samples that have infrequent poses. Comprehensive experiments on public benchmarks demonstrate the effectiveness of our method, especially on rare poses. Our implementation of PoseTrans is simple and efficient, which can be easily integrated into the training pipeline of existing pose estimators. We hope our work will draw the community's attention to the long-tail problem in human pose estimation and provide inspiration on how to tackle it for other tasks.

Acknowledgement. This work is supported in part by the National Natural Science Foundation of China under Grant 62122010 and Grant 61876177, in part by the Fundamental Research Funds for the Central Universities, and in part by the Key Research and Development Program of Zhejiang Province under Grant 2022C01082. Ping Luo is supported by the General Research Fund of HK No. 27208720, No. 17212120, and No. 17200622.

References

1. Alp Güler, R., Neverova, N., Kokkinos, I.: DensePose: dense human pose estimation in the wild. In: Proceedings of the IEEE Conference on Computer Vision and Pattern Recognition, pp. 7297–7306 (2018)
2. Andriluka, M., et al.: PoseTrack: a benchmark for human pose estimation and tracking. In: Proceedings of the IEEE Conference on Computer Vision and Pattern Recognition, pp. 5167–5176 (2018)
3. Andriluka, M., Pishchulin, L., Gehler, P., Schiele, B.: 2D human pose estimation: new benchmark and state of the art analysis. In: Proceedings of the IEEE Conference on Computer Vision and Pattern Recognition, pp. 3686–3693 (2014)
4. Bertalmio, M., Bertozzi, A.L., Sapiro, G.: Navier-stokes, fluid dynamics, and image and video inpainting. In: Proceedings of the 2001 IEEE Computer Society Conference on Computer Vision and Pattern Recognition, vol. 1, p. I. IEEE (2001)
5. Bin, Y., et al.: Adversarial semantic data augmentation for human pose estimation. In: Vedaldi, A., Bischof, H., Brox, T., Frahm, J.-M. (eds.) ECCV 2020. LNCS, vol. 12364, pp. 606–622. Springer, Cham (2020). https://doi.org/10.1007/978-3-030-58529-7_36
6. Bochkovskiy, A., Wang, C.Y., Liao, H.Y.M.: YOLOv4: optimal speed and accuracy of object detection. arXiv preprint arXiv:2004.10934 (2020)
7. Cao, Z., Simon, T., Wei, S.E., Sheikh, Y.: Realtime multi-person 2D pose estimation using part affinity fields. In: Proceedings of the IEEE Conference on Computer Vision and Pattern Recognition, pp. 7291–7299 (2017)
8. Chawla, N.V., Bowyer, K.W., Hall, L.O., Kegelmeyer, W.P.: SMOTE: synthetic minority over-sampling technique. J. Artif. Intell. Res. **16**, 321–357 (2002)
9. Chen, P., Liu, S., Zhao, H., Jia, J.: GridMask data augmentation. arXiv preprint arXiv:2001.04086 (2020)
10. Chen, W., et al.: Synthesizing training images for boosting human 3D pose estimation. In: 2016 Fourth International Conference on 3D Vision (3DV), pp. 479–488. IEEE (2016)
11. Chen, Y., Wang, Z., Peng, Y., Zhang, Z., Yu, G., Sun, J.: Cascaded pyramid network for multi-person pose estimation. In: Proceedings of the IEEE Conference on Computer Vision and Pattern Recognition, pp. 7103–7112 (2018)
12. Chen, Y., Shen, C., Wei, X.S., Liu, L., Yang, J.: Adversarial PoseNet: a structure-aware convolutional network for human pose estimation. In: Proceedings of the IEEE International Conference on Computer Vision, pp. 1212–1221 (2017)
13. Cheng, B., Xiao, B., Wang, J., Shi, H., Huang, T.S., Zhang, L.: HigherHRNet: scale-aware representation learning for bottom-up human pose estimation. In: Proceedings of the IEEE/CVF Conference on Computer Vision and Pattern Recognition, pp. 5386–5395 (2020)
14. MMP Contributors: OpenMMLab pose estimation toolbox and benchmark (2020). https://github.com/open-mmlab/mmpose
15. Cubuk, E.D., Zoph, B., Mane, D., Vasudevan, V., Le, Q.V.: AutoAugment: learning augmentation policies from data. arXiv preprint arXiv:1805.09501 (2018)
16. DeVries, T., Taylor, G.W.: Improved regularization of convolutional neural networks with cutout. arXiv preprint arXiv:1708.04552 (2017)
17. Elkan, C.: The foundations of cost-sensitive learning. In: International Joint Conference on Artificial Intelligence, vol. 17, pp. 973–978. Lawrence Erlbaum Associates Ltd. (2001)

18. Fang, H.S., Sun, J., Wang, R., Gou, M., Li, Y.L., Lu, C.: InstaBoost: boosting instance segmentation via probability map guided copy-pasting. In: Proceedings of the IEEE/CVF International Conference on Computer Vision, pp. 682–691 (2019)

19. Fang, H.S., Xie, Y., Shao, D., Li, Y.L., Lu, C.: DecAug: augmenting HOI detection via decomposition. In: Proceedings of the AAAI Conference on Artificial Intelligence, pp. 1300–1308 (2021)

20. Gong, K., Zhang, J., Feng, J.: PoseAug: a differentiable pose augmentation framework for 3D human pose estimation. In: Proceedings of the IEEE/CVF Conference on Computer Vision and Pattern Recognition, pp. 8575–8584 (2021)

21. He, K., Gkioxari, G., Dollár, P., Girshick, R.: Mask R-CNN. arXiv preprint arXiv:1703.06870 (2017)

22. Huang, C., Li, Y., Loy, C.C., Tang, X.: Learning deep representation for imbalanced classification. In: Proceedings of the IEEE Conference on Computer Vision and Pattern Recognition, pp. 5375–5384 (2016)

23. Insafutdinov, E., Pishchulin, L., Andres, B., Andriluka, M., Schiele, B.: DeeperCut: a deeper, stronger, and faster multi-person pose estimation model. In: Leibe, B., Matas, J., Sebe, N., Welling, M. (eds.) ECCV 2016. LNCS, vol. 9910, pp. 34–50. Springer, Cham (2016). https://doi.org/10.1007/978-3-319-46466-4_3

24. Jin, S., Liu, W., Ouyang, W., Qian, C.: Multi-person articulated tracking with spatial and temporal embeddings. In: Proceedings of the IEEE/CVF Conference on Computer Vision and Pattern Recognition, pp. 5664–5673 (2019)

25. Jin, S., et al.: Differentiable hierarchical graph grouping for multi-person pose estimation. In: Vedaldi, A., Bischof, H., Brox, T., Frahm, J.-M. (eds.) ECCV 2020. LNCS, vol. 12352, pp. 718–734. Springer, Cham (2020). https://doi.org/10.1007/978-3-030-58571-6_42

26. Jin, S., et al.: Whole-body human pose estimation in the wild. In: Vedaldi, A., Bischof, H., Brox, T., Frahm, J.-M. (eds.) ECCV 2020. LNCS, vol. 12354, pp. 196–214. Springer, Cham (2020). https://doi.org/10.1007/978-3-030-58545-7_12

27. Kingma, D.P., Ba, J.: Adam: a method for stochastic optimization. arXiv preprint arXiv:1412.6980 (2014)

28. Kreiss, S., Bertoni, L., Alahi, A.: PifPaf: composite fields for human pose estimation. In: Proceedings of the IEEE/CVF Conference on Computer Vision and Pattern Recognition, pp. 11977–11986 (2019)

29. Li, J., Wang, C., Zhu, H., Mao, Y., Fang, H.S., Lu, C.: CrowdPose: efficient crowded scenes pose estimation and a new benchmark. In: Proceedings of the IEEE/CVF Conference on Computer Vision and Pattern Recognition, pp. 10863–10872 (2019)

30. Li, S., Ke, L., Pratama, K., Tai, Y.W., Tang, C.K., Cheng, K.T.: Cascaded deep monocular 3D human pose estimation with evolutionary training data. In: Proceedings of the IEEE/CVF Conference on Computer Vision and Pattern Recognition, pp. 6173–6183 (2020)

31. Lin, T.-Y., et al.: Microsoft COCO: common objects in context. In: Fleet, D., Pajdla, T., Schiele, B., Tuytelaars, T. (eds.) ECCV 2014. LNCS, vol. 8693, pp. 740–755. Springer, Cham (2014). https://doi.org/10.1007/978-3-319-10602-1_48

32. Van der Maaten, L., Hinton, G.: Visualizing data using t-SNE. J. Mach. Learn. Res. 9(11), 2579–2605 (2008)

33. Mao, X., Li, Q., Xie, H., Lau, R.Y., Wang, Z., Paul Smolley, S.: Least squares generative adversarial networks. In: Proceedings of the IEEE International Conference on Computer Vision, pp. 2794–2802 (2017)

34. Newell, A., Huang, Z., Deng, J.: Associative embedding: end-to-end learning for joint detection and grouping. Adv. Neural Inform. Process. Syst. 30 (2017)

35. Newell, A., Yang, K., Deng, J.: Stacked hourglass networks for human pose esti-
    mation. In: Leibe, B., Matas, J., Sebe, N., Welling, M. (eds.) ECCV 2016. LNCS,
    vol. 9912, pp. 483–499. Springer, Cham (2016). https://doi.org/10.1007/978-3-319-
    46484-8_29

36. Papandreou, G., Zhu, T., Chen, L.C., Gidaris, S., Tompson, J., Murphy, K.: Per-
    sonLab: person pose estimation and instance segmentation with a bottom-up, part-
    based, geometric embedding model. arXiv preprint arXiv:1803.08225 (2018)

37. Peng, X., Tang, Z., Yang, F., Feris, R.S., Metaxas, D.: Jointly optimize data aug-
    mentation and network training: adversarial data augmentation in human pose
    estimation. In: Proceedings of the IEEE Conference on Computer Vision and Pat-
    tern Recognition, pp. 2226–2234 (2018)

38. Pytel, R., Kayhan, O.S., van Gemert, J.C.: Tilting at windmills: data augmentation
    for deep pose estimation does not help with occlusions. In: 2020 25th International
    Conference on Pattern Recognition (ICPR), pp. 10568–10575 (2021)

39. Russakovsky, O., et al.: ImageNet large scale visual recognition challenge. Int. J.
    Comput. Vis. **115**(3), 211–252 (2015). https://doi.org/10.1007/s11263-015-0816-y

40. Sun, K., Xiao, B., Liu, D., Wang, J.: Deep high-resolution representation learning
    for human pose estimation. arXiv preprint arXiv:1902.09212 (2019)

41. Toshev, A., Szegedy, C.: DeepPose: human pose estimation via deep neural net-
    works. In: Proceedings of the IEEE Conference on Computer Vision and Pattern
    Recognition, pp. 1653–1660 (2014)

42. Wang, J., Jin, S., Liu, W., Liu, W., Qian, C., Luo, P.: When human pose estimation
    meets robustness: adversarial algorithms and benchmarks. In: Proceedings of the
    IEEE/CVF Conference on Computer Vision and Pattern Recognition, pp. 11855–
    11864 (2021)

43. Wang, J., et al.: Deep high-resolution representation learning for visual recognition.
    IEEE Trans. Pattern Anal. Mach. Intell. **43**(10), 3349–3364 (2020)

44. Wang, Y.X., Ramanan, D., Hebert, M.: Learning to model the tail. Adv. Neural
    Inform. Process. Syst. **30**, 7032–7042 (2017)

45. Xiao, B., Wu, H., Wei, Y.: Simple baselines for human pose estimation and tracking.
    In: Proceedings of the European Conference on Computer Vision (ECCV), pp.
    466–481 (2018)

46. Xu, L., et al.: ViPNAS: efficient video pose estimation via neural architecture
    search. In: Proceedings of the IEEE/CVF Conference on Computer Vision and
    Pattern Recognition, pp. 16072–16081 (2021)

47. Yun, S., Han, D., Oh, S.J., Chun, S., Choe, J., Yoo, Y.: CutMix: regularization
    strategy to train strong classifiers with localizable features. In: Proceedings of the
    IEEE/CVF International Conference on Computer Vision, pp. 6023–6032 (2019)

48. Zeng, W., et al.: Not all tokens are equal: human-centric visual analysis via token
    clustering transformer. In: Proceedings of the IEEE/CVF Conference on Computer
    Vision and Pattern Recognition, pp. 11101–11111 (2022)

49. Zhang, F., Zhu, X., Dai, H., Ye, M., Zhu, C.: Distribution-aware coordinate repre-
    sentation for human pose estimation. In: Proceedings of the IEEE/CVF Conference
    on Computer Vision and Pattern Recognition, pp. 7093–7102 (2020)

50. Zhang, H., Cisse, M., Dauphin, Y.N., Lopez-Paz, D.: mixup: beyond empirical risk
    minimization. arXiv preprint arXiv:1710.09412 (2017)

51. Zhang, Y., Kang, B., Hooi, B., Yan, S., Feng, J.: Deep long-tailed learning: a survey.
    arXiv preprint arXiv:2110.04596 (2021)

52. Zhong, Z., Zheng, L., Kang, G., Li, S., Yang, Y.: Random erasing data augmenta-
    tion. Proc. AAAI Conf. Artif. Intell. **34**, 13001–13008 (2020)

Multi-Person 3D Pose and Shape Estimation via Inverse Kinematics and Refinement

Junuk Cha[1], Muhammad Saqlain[1,2], GeonU Kim[1], Mingyu Shin[1,3], and Seungryul Baek[1(✉)]

[1] UNIST, Ulsan, South Korea
srbaek@unist.ac.kr
[2] eSmart Systems, Halden, Norway
[3] Yeongnam University, Gyeongsan-si, South Korea

Abstract. Estimating 3D poses and shapes in the form of meshes from monocular RGB images is challenging. Obviously, it is more difficult than estimating 3D poses only in the form of skeletons or heatmaps. When interacting persons are involved, the 3D mesh reconstruction becomes more challenging due to the ambiguity introduced by person-to-person occlusions. To tackle the challenges, we propose a coarse-to-fine pipeline that benefits from 1) inverse kinematics from the occlusion-robust 3D skeleton estimation and 2) Transformer-based relation-aware refinement techniques. In our pipeline, we first obtain occlusion-robust 3D skeletons for multiple persons from an RGB image. Then, we apply inverse kinematics to convert the estimated skeletons to deformable 3D mesh parameters. Finally, we apply the Transformer-based mesh refinement that refines the obtained mesh parameters considering intra- and inter-person relations of 3D meshes. Via extensive experiments, we demonstrate the effectiveness of our method, outperforming state-of-the-arts on 3DPW, MuPoTS and AGORA datasets.

Keywords: Multi-person · 3D mesh reconstruction · Transformer

1 Introduction

Recovering 3D human body meshes for a single person or multi-person from a monocular RGB image has made great progress in recent years [3,10,12,17, 23,27,28,30–33,38,39,62,65,69,71,73]. The technique is essential to understand

---

M. Saqlain—This research was conducted when Dr. Saqlain was the post-doctoral researcher at UNIST
G. Kim and M. Shin—Were undergraduate interns at UNIST.

Supplementary Information The online version contains supplementary material available at https://doi.org/10.1007/978-3-031-20065-6_38.

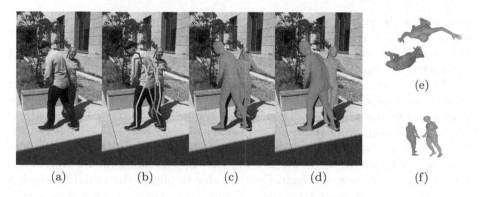

(a)   (b)   (c)   (d)   (f)

Fig. 1. Example outputs from our pipeline: (a) input RGB image, (b) initial skeleton estimation results obtained from the input image, (c) initial meshes obtained from the inverse kinematics process, (d) refined meshes obtained from the refinement Transformer, (e, f) top- and side-views for the refined meshes.

people's behaviors, intentions and person-to-person interactions. It has a wide range of real-world applications such as human motion imitation [41], virtual try on [48], motion capture [46], action recognition [5,58,67], etc.

Recently, deep convolutional neural network-based mesh reconstruction methods [6,10,12,17,23,27,28,30–33,38,39,62,65,69,71,73] have shown the practical performance on in-the-wild scenes [21,25,44,45]. Most of the existing 3D human body pose and shape estimation approaches [6,10,17,27,28,30–33,38,39,69] achieved promising results for single-person cases. Generally, firstly they crop the area with a person in an input image using bounding-box and then extract features for each detected person, which are further used for 3D human mesh regression.

Some of the recent studies [26–28,30–33,36,39,65,71] reconstruct each person 3D mesh individually for multi-person 3D mesh reconstruction using the same bounding-boxes detector [4,18,56]. Multiple persons can create severe person-to-person or person-to-environmental occlusions, erroneous monocular depth and diverse human body appearance which results in performance ambiguity in crowded scenes, while in these methods, proper modules that tackle the interacting persons have not been established yet. A few recent methods [23,73] applied direct regression for multiple persons which do not require individual person detection. Sun et al. [62] used body center heatmaps as the target representation to identify mesh parameter map. However, without applying the human detection, the human pose estimation result is frequently affected by unimportant pixels and it frequently fails to capture scale variations, which result in the inferior performance.

In parallel, there have been efforts to reduce the ambiguity of estimating 3D meshes from an RGB image. However in the aspect of the pose recovery, 3D body mesh recovery methods [27,30,31,33] still fall behind the 3D skeleton or heatmap estimation methods [8,9,22,61]. One drawback of 3D skeleton estimation method is that it cannot reconstruct the full 3D body mesh. Recently, Li et al. [36]

proposed an inverse kinematics method for single-person mesh reconstruction to recover 3D meshes from 3D skeletons. This approach is promising since it is able to deliver good poses obtained from 3D skeleton estimator to the 3D mesh reconstruction pipeline.

To tackle the multi-person 3D body mesh reconstruction task, we propose a coarse-to-fine pipeline that first estimates 3D skeletons, reconstruct 3D meshes from 3D skeletons via inverse kinematics and refine the initial 3D mesh parameters via relation-aware refinement. Inspired by [60], our 3D skeleton estimator involves metric-scale heatmaps and is trained by both relative and absolute positional 3D poses to be robust to occlusions. By extending the IK process [36] towards the multi-person scenario, we are able to obtain the initial 3D meshes for multiple persons from 3D skeletons; while the accuracy is limited especially for interacting person cases. To compensate for the limitation, we propose the relation-aware Transformer to refine the initial mesh parameters considering intra- and inter-person 3D mesh relationships. The Fig. 1 shows example outputs for intermediate steps. To summarize, our contributions are as follows:

- We propose a coarse-to-fine multi-person 3D body mesh reconstruction pipeline that first estimates 3D skeletons and then delivers it toward 3D meshes via inverse kinematics. To make our pipeline robust to interacting persons, we borrowed the occlusion-robust techniques for 3D skeleton estimation.
- To further boost the performance, we propose the Transformer-based architecture for relation-aware mesh refinement to refine the initial mesh parameters considering intra- and inter-person relationships.
- Extensive comparisons are conducted involving three challenging multi-person 3D body pose benchmarks (i.e. 3DPW, MuPoTS and AGORA) and we have demonstrated the state-of-the-art performance on each benchmark. Via ablation studies, we prove that each component works in the meaningful way.

2   Related Works

Single-Person 3D Mesh Regression. There is a long history of methods for predicting 3D human body meshes from monocular RGB images or video frames [16]. Recently, there has been quick advancement in this field thanks to SMPL [42] which provides a low dimensional parameterization of the 3D human body mesh. Here we focus on a 3D body mesh regressing by adopting a parametric model like SMPL from a monocular RGB image. Bogo et al. [3] represented an optimization-based method called SMPLify by fitting SMPL on the detected 2D body joints iteratively. However, this optimization-based approach is comparatively time-consuming and struggle with the higher inference time per input frame.

Some recent studies [34,51,54] use deep neural networks for SMPL parameters regression from images in a two-stage manner, which have been effective and can generate more accurate mesh reconstruction outputs in the presence of large-scale 3D datasets. They first determine intermediate renderings such as silhouettes and 2D keypoints from input images and then map them to the SMPL parameters. Impressive results have been achieved for in-the-wild images by applying diverse weak supervision signals such as semantic segmentation [69], texture consistency [53], efficient temporal features [30,64,66], 2D pose [11,27,35], motion dynamics [28], etc.

More recently, Li et al. [36] proposed a 3D human body pose and shape estimation method by collaborating the 3D keypoints and body meshes. Authors introduced an inverse kinematics process to find the relative rotations using twist-and-swing decomposition which estimates targeted body joint locations.

Multi-Person 3D Skeleton Regression. There have been variety of methods [13,47,49,57] that tackle the 3D body pose estimation for multi-person: Zanfir et al. [57] proposed LCR-Net that consists of localization, classification, and regression modules. The localization module detects multi-persons from a single image. The classification module classifies the detected human into several anchor-poses. Finally, the regression module refines the anchor-poses. Mehta et al. [47] proposed a single-shot method for multi-person 3D pose estimation from a single image. In addition, they introduced the MuCo-3DHP dataset which has multi-person interactions and occlusions images. Moon et al. [49] proposed top-down method for 3D multi-person pose estimation from a monocular RGB image. This method consists of human detection, absolute 3D human root localization, and root-relative 3D single-person pose estimation modules. Dong et al. [13] used the multi-view images for estimating the multi-person 3D pose. They proposed a coarse-to-fine method lifting the 2D joints to the 3D joints. They obtained the 2D joints candidates from [4]. The initial 3D joints are triangulated from 2D joints candidates of different camera views of the same image. In addition, the initial 3D joints are updated using the prior information using the SMPL [42] model.

Recent multi-person 3D pose regression works [7,55,60,72] tackled a variety of issues such as developing attention-based mechanism dedicated to the 3D pose estimation problem which considers 3D-to-2D projection process [72], combining the top-down and bottom-up networks [7], developing the tracking-based for multi-person [55] and so on. Sárándi et al. [60] recently proposed a metric-scale 3D pose estimation method that is robust to truncations. It is able to reason about the out-of-image joints well. Also, this method is robust to occlusion and bounding-box noise.

Multi-Person 3D Mesh Regression. There have been few works [12, 23,62,63,70,73] that concern the multi-person 3D body mesh regression: The approaches could be categorized into two: bottom-up and top-down methods.

Bottom-up methods [23,62,63,73] perform multi-person detection and 3D mesh reconstruction simultaneously. Zhang et al. [73] proposed a Body Mesh as Point (BMP) using a multi-scale 2D center map grid-level representation, which locates selective persons at the grid cell's center. Sun et al. [62] proposed a ROMP, which creates parameter maps (i.e. body center heatmap, camera map and mesh parameter map) for 2D human body detection, body positioning and 3D body mesh parameter regression, respectively. Jiang et al. [23] represented a coherent reconstruction of multiple humans (CRMH) model, which utilizes the Faster R-CNN based RoI-aligned feature of all persons to estimate SMPL parameters. They further defined the position relevance between multiple persons through a depth ordering-aware loss and an interpenetration. Sun et al. [63] further introduced Bird's-Eye-View (BEV) representation for reasoning the multi-person body centers and depth simultaneously and combining them to estimate 3D body positions.

Top-down methods [12,70] first detect each individual person in the frame using bounding-boxes and then estimate the 3D mesh parameters of each detected person. They are basically similar to the single-person 3D mesh reconstruction pipeline; however different in that they provide dedicated modules or loss functions for the multi-person scenario. For example, Zanfir et al. [70] proposed a 3D mesh reconstruction method to firstly infer 3D skeletons of each person and group estimated skeletons to infer the final 3D meshes for multi-person. Choi et al. [12] proposed a method for combining early-stage image features and estimated 2D pose heatmaps which are robust to occlusions, to reconstruct 3D meshes for multiple persons.

Bottom-up methods are frequently affected by unimportant image pixels and suffer from scale variations. They further fail to detect small persons since the person detection is not powerful enough compared to that of top-down methods. On the contrary, in top-down methods, proper modules that tackle the interacting persons have not been established yet. In this paper, we take the top-down approach to secure the robustness and propose to use the Transformer architecture to consider the interacting scenario.

3   Method

Our aim is to reconstruct 3D meshes $\{\mathbf{M}^i\}_{i=1}^M$ of the multiple persons in an RGB image $\mathbf{I}$, where M denotes the number of persons in $\mathbf{I}$. To achieve this goal, we propose the coarse-to-fine reconstruction pipeline as in Fig. 2 that 1) first estimates the 3D skeletons $\{\mathbf{P}^i\}_{i=1}^M$, 2) obtains the deformable 3D mesh parameters from 3D skeletons via the inverse kinematics (IK) process and 3) refines the initial 3D meshes $\{\mathbf{M}^i\}_{i=1}^M$ using the Transformer architecture that considers intra-person and inter-person relationships. In the remainder of this section, we will elaborate each step in detail.

SMPL Body Model. For the 3D mesh representation, we use the SMPL deformable 3D mesh model [42] for its compact representation. Variations of the SMPL model [42] are controlled by pose $\boldsymbol{\theta} \in \mathbb{R}^{24 \times 6}$ and shape parameters $\boldsymbol{\beta} \in \mathbb{R}^{1 \times 10}$. The pose and shape parameters contain 3D rotational information of 24 human body joints in 6D representation and the top-10 principal component analysis coefficients of the 3D shape space, respectively. Using the differentiable mapping between SMPL parameters (i.e. $\boldsymbol{\theta}$ and $\boldsymbol{\beta}$) and the 3D body mesh $\mathbf{M} = \{\mathbf{v}, \mathbf{f}\}$ defined in [42], we can differentiably obtain the 3D body mesh $\mathbf{M}$ from $\boldsymbol{\theta}$ and $\boldsymbol{\beta}$, where $\mathbf{v} \in \mathbb{R}^{6,890 \times 3}$, $\mathbf{f} \in \mathbb{R}^{13,776 \times 3}$ denote vertices having 6,890 vertices, 13,776 triangular faces that are defined by 3 vertices.

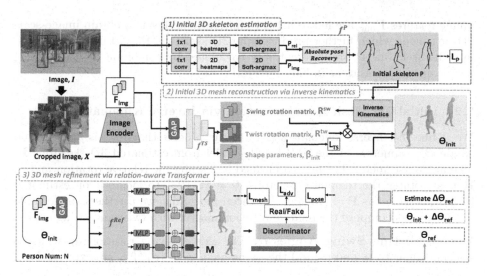

Fig. 2. The schematic diagram of our framework: We first detect persons from an image **I** and crop it to **X** and the image encoder extracts image features $\mathbf{F}_{\mathrm{img}}$ from **X**. Then, initial 3D skeletons **P** are estimated via the initial 3D skeleton estimator f^P and SMPL parameters Θ_{init} are reconstructed via the inverse kinematic process, involving the twist angle and shape estimator f^{TS} (GAP denotes global average pooling layer). Finally, we refine the initial SMPL parameters by inputting the image features $\mathbf{F}_{\mathrm{img}}$ and Θ_{init} to the relation-aware refiner f^{Ref} to produce the refined mesh parameters Θ_{ref}. The final 3D mesh **M** is obtained from the refined SMPL parameters Θ_{ref}. The blue boxes denote involved loss functions (L_{P}, L_{TS}, L_{mesh}, L_{adv} and L_{pose}).

3.1   Initial 3D Skeleton Estimation

We take the top-down approach for 3D skeleton estimation that first detect bounding boxes of the humans and estimate 3D skeletons within each bounding box. Following [43,50,59,60], we constituted the person detector using the YOLOv4 [2] to obtain the cropped image $\mathbf{X} \in \mathbb{R}^{256 \times 256 \times 3}$ from an image **I**. In order to develop the initial 3D skeleton estimation network $f^P : \mathbf{X} \to \mathbf{P} \in \mathbb{R}^{K \times 3}$ aiming to use it for the inverse kinematics (IK) process, it is necessary to align the output dimension K with the SMPL model [42]: We are required to set K as 24 to align it with the SMPL model which uses 24-dimensional pose parameters. The reason behind this is that the IK process we use (see Sect. 3.2) requires to calculate the SMPL pose parameters θ by comparing the 3D skeletons to the SMPL template skeletons having 24 joints.

To further obtain occlusion-robust 3D skeletons, we follow the architecture and loss functions of the recent 3D skeletal estimation approach [60] which utilizes the metric-scale heatmaps for 3D skeleton estimation and use both absolute-scale 3D skeletons and image aligned skeletons as the supervision. Within f^P, we applied ResNet [19] as a feature extractor that predicts image features $\mathbf{F}_{\mathrm{img}} \in \mathbb{R}^{8 \times 8 \times 2,048}$. They are fed to a 1×1 convolutional layer to extract 3D heatmaps that can produce the root-relative 3D skeletons $\mathbf{P}_{\mathrm{rel}}$. In parallel, the image features $\mathbf{F}_{\text{img}}$ are fed to a 1×1 convolutional layer to obtain image-scale 2D heatmaps which further produces the 2D skeletons $\mathbf{P}_{\text{img}}$. Finally, the absolute 3D skeletons $\mathbf{P}$ are differentiably calculated by combining $\mathbf{P}_{\text{img}}$ and $\mathbf{P}_{\text{rel}}$ with camera intrinsics as in [60].

3.2   Initial 3D Mesh Reconstruction via Inverse Kinematics

We define the inverse kinematics (IK) as the process that reveals angle θ and shape β parameters of the SMPL [42] model from estimated 3D skeletons $\mathbf{P}$. The angle parameter θ could be obtained by finding the relative rotation matrix $\mathbf{R}$ that rotates the template skeletons $\mathbf{T} = \{\mathbf{t}_k\}_{k=1}^{K}$ to locate it on estimated initial 3D skeletons $\mathbf{P} = \{\mathbf{p}_k\}_{k=1}^{K}$. To reconstruct this, we use the same formula as [36] that decompose the relative rotation matrix with twist and swing angles.

Reconstructing Swing Angles α. The axis of swing rotation $\mathbf{n}_k$ which is perpendicular to $\mathbf{t}_k$ and $\mathbf{p}_k$ and the swing angle $\alpha = \{\alpha_k\}_{k=1}^{K}$ are expressed as:

$$\mathbf{n}_k = \frac{\mathbf{t}_k \times \mathbf{p}_k}{\|\mathbf{t}_k \times \mathbf{p}_k\|}, \quad \cos \alpha_k = \frac{\mathbf{t}_k \cdot \mathbf{p}_k}{\|\mathbf{t}_k\|\|\mathbf{p}_k\|}, \quad \sin \alpha_k = \frac{\mathbf{t}_k \times \mathbf{p}_k}{\|\mathbf{t}_k\|\|\mathbf{p}_k\|} \tag{1}$$

By the Rodrigues formula, swing rotation matrix $\mathbf{R}_k^{\text{sw}}$ can be derived from the axis $\mathbf{n}_k$ and the angle α_k as follows:

$$\mathbf{R}_k^{\text{sw}} = \mathbf{I} + \sin \alpha_k [\mathbf{n}_k]_\times + (1 - \cos \alpha_k)[\mathbf{n}_k]_\times^2 \tag{2}$$

where $\mathbf{I}$ is 3×3 identity matrix and $[\mathbf{n}_k]_\times$ is the skew-symmetric matrix of $\mathbf{n}_k$.

Reconstructing Twist Angles ϕ and Shape Parameter β. While swing angles α could be obtained from $\mathbf{t}_k$ and $\mathbf{p}_k$ using Eq. 1; it is hard to find closed-form equations for twist angles ϕ. Furthermore, estimating shape parameter β is non-trivial. To bypass the challenges, similarly to [36], we involve the network called as twist angle and shape estimator $f^{\text{TS}} : \mathbf{F}_{\text{img}} \to [\phi, \beta_{\text{init}}]$ that estimates twist angle $\phi = \{\phi_k\}_{k=1}^{K}$ and shape parameter β_{init} from image features $\mathbf{F}_{\text{img}}$. To resolve the discontinuity issue, it directly estimates cosine value c_{ϕ_k} and sine value s_{ϕ_k} of twist angle instead of estimating ϕ_k. The axis of twist rotation is $\mathbf{t}_k$ and thus, twist rotation matrix $\mathbf{R}_k^{\text{tw}}$ can be derived by the axis $\mathbf{t}_k$ and the angle ϕ as follows:

$$\mathbf{R}_k^{\text{tw}} = \mathbf{I} + \frac{\sin \phi_k}{\|\mathbf{t}_k\|}[\mathbf{t}_k]_\times + \frac{(1 - \cos \phi_k)}{\|\mathbf{t}_k\|^2}[\mathbf{t}_k]_\times^2, \tag{3}$$

where $[\mathbf{t}_k]_\times$ is the skew-symmetric matrix of $\mathbf{t}_k$.

Finally, the relative rotation matrix $\mathbf{R}$ can be determined as follows:

$$\mathbf{R} = \mathbf{R}^{\text{sw}}\mathbf{R}^{\text{tw}}. \tag{4}$$

After obtaining the rotation matrix $\mathbf{R}$, we convert it to 6D rotation representation and obtain the pose parameters θ_{init}. We initialize the camera parameter $\mathbf{C}_{\text{init}}$ as $[0.9, 0, 0]$ and use the constant values during the inverse kinematics step.

3.3 3D Mesh Refinement via Relation-Aware Transformer

The relation-aware refiner $f^{\text{Ref}} : [\mathbf{F}_{\text{img}}, \boldsymbol{\Theta}_{\text{init}}] \rightarrow \boldsymbol{\Theta}_{\text{ref}}$ is proposed to refine the initial SMPL parameters based on the vision Transformer architecture [14]. Its input is the concatenation of image features $\mathbf{F}_{\text{img}}$ and SMPL parameters $\boldsymbol{\Theta}_{\text{init}} = [\boldsymbol{\theta}_{\text{init}}; \boldsymbol{\beta}_{\text{init}}; \mathbf{C}_{\text{init}}]$ which are obtained from the IK process. We use $N \times K$ as the sequence length of the Transformer where N is the maximum number of people for the input and K is the number of joints for one person. By rearranging and concatenating image features $\mathbf{F}_{\text{img}}$ with $\boldsymbol{\Theta}_{\text{init}}$, we generate the $(N \times K) \times 2,067$ array as the input to the Transformer (see supplemental for details). We obtain the $\Delta\boldsymbol{\Theta}_{\text{ref}}$ from the Transformer and the final SMPL parameter is obtained as follows:

$$\boldsymbol{\Theta}_{\text{ref}} = \boldsymbol{\Theta}_{\text{init}} + \Delta\boldsymbol{\Theta}_{\text{ref}}. \tag{5}$$

From the refined parameter $\boldsymbol{\Theta}_{\text{ref}} = [\boldsymbol{\theta}_{\text{ref}}; \boldsymbol{\beta}_{\text{ref}}; \mathbf{C}_{\text{ref}}]$, 3D meshes $\mathbf{M}$ are obtained, and corresponding 3D skeletons $\mathbf{P}_{\text{ref}}$ are further obtained by applying the mesh-to-joint regressor [42] to mesh vertices.

When constituting the Transformer, we use the masking input patch as METRO [38]: randomly 0 to 30% of input patches are masked and this makes the Transformer learn non-local interactions. We select not to use the positional embedding while using the masking scheme from results in Table 4.

Sampling Interacting Persons. The number of persons M varies depending on the image $\mathbf{I}$; while the relation-aware refiner f^{Ref} requires to fix N which is the maximum number of persons in the input. We set N as 3 according to the ablation study shown in Table 4. For images having less than N persons ($M < N$), we apply Transformer once by simply zero-padding unoccupied inputs, while for images having more than N persons ($M > N$), we need to apply Transformers multiple times by sampling the interacting persons. The sampling scheme during training and testing stages are proposed as follows: At training, we randomly sample multiple data consisting of N persons so that Transformer can see various combinations as epochs go. At testing, we run f^{Ref} exactly M times, getting results once for each person. At each run, we set each person as the target to refine, inputting $N - 1$ closest persons as contexts.

3.4 Training Method

We use PyTorch to implement our pipeline. A single NVIDIA TITAN GPU is used for each experiment with a batch size of 64. The Adam optimizer [29] is used for the optimization with a learning rate of 5×10^{-5} for relation-aware Transformer and 1×10^{-4} for all other networks, respectively. We decrease the learning rate exponentially by a factor of 0.9 per each epoch. Total 100 epochs are executed for completely training our network.

To train the proposed initial 3D skeleton estimation network f^{P}, twist angle and shape estimation network f^{TS} and relation-aware refiner f^{Ref}, we used the loss L defined as follows:

$$L(f^{\text{P}}, f^{\text{TS}}, f^{\text{Ref}}) = L_{\text{P}}(f^{\text{P}}) + L_{\text{TS}}(f^{\text{TS}}) + L_{\text{Ref}}(f^{\text{Ref}}). \tag{6}$$

Each loss term is detailed in the remainder of this subsection.

Skeleton Loss $L_{\mathbf{P}}$. We use multiple $L1$ losses using 2D and 3D skeletons in absolute and relative coordinate spaces to train the initial skeleton estimation network f^P using the loss $L_{\mathbf{P}}$ as follows:

$$L_{\mathbf{P}}(f^P) = \|\mathbf{P} - \hat{\mathbf{P}}_{\text{abs}}^{3D}\|_1 + \|\mathbf{P}_{\text{rel}} - \hat{\mathbf{P}}_{\text{rel}}^{3D}\|_1$$
$$+ \|\mathbf{P}_{\text{img}} - \hat{\mathbf{P}}^{2D}\|_1 + \|\Pi(\mathbf{P}_{\text{rel}}) - \hat{\mathbf{P}}^{2D}\|_1 \qquad (7)$$

where $\hat{\mathbf{P}}_{\text{abs}}^{3D}$, $\hat{\mathbf{P}}_{\text{rel}}^{3D}$ and $\hat{\mathbf{P}}^{2D}$ are ground-truth absolute 3D skeletons, relative 3D skeletons and 2D skeletons, respectively. Π is an orthographic projection.

Twist Angle and Shape Loss $L_{\mathbf{TS}}$. We use the loss L_{TS} to train the twist angle and shape estimator f^{TS} as follows:

$$L_{\text{TS}}(f^{\text{TS}}) = L_{\text{angle}}(f^{\text{TS}}) + L_{\text{shape}}(f^{\text{TS}}) \qquad (8)$$

where

$$L_{\text{angle}}(f^{\text{TS}}) = \frac{1}{K}\sum_{k=1}^{K}\|(c_{\phi_k}, s_{\phi_k}) - (\cos\hat{\phi}_k, \sin\hat{\phi}_k)\|_2, \qquad (9)$$

$$L_{\text{shape}}(f^{\text{TS}}) = \|\boldsymbol{\beta}_{\text{init}} - \hat{\boldsymbol{\beta}}\|_2, \qquad (10)$$

$\hat{\phi}_k$ denotes the ground-truth twist angle and $\hat{\boldsymbol{\beta}}$ denotes the ground-truth SMPL shape parameters.

Refinement Loss $L_{\mathbf{Ref}}$. We use the loss L_{Ref} combining several losses to train our relation-aware refinement network f^{Ref} and additional discriminators $D = \{D_\theta, D_\beta\}$ as follows:

$$L_{\text{Ref}}(f^{\text{Ref}}, D) = L_{\text{mesh}}(f^{\text{Ref}}) + L_{\text{pose}}(f^{\text{Ref}}) + L_{\text{adv}}(f^{\text{Ref}}) + L_{\text{adv}}(D) \qquad (11)$$

where

$$L_{\text{mesh}}(f^{\text{Ref}}) = \|\boldsymbol{\theta}_{\text{ref}} - \hat{\boldsymbol{\theta}}\|_2 + \|\boldsymbol{\beta}_{\text{ref}} - \hat{\boldsymbol{\beta}}\|_2 \qquad (12)$$

enforces the estimated pose $\boldsymbol{\theta}_{\text{ref}}$ and shape $\boldsymbol{\beta}_{\text{ref}}$ parameters close to the ground-truth pose $\hat{\boldsymbol{\theta}}$ and shape $\hat{\boldsymbol{\beta}}$ parameters of the meshes,

$$L_{\text{pose}}(f^{\text{Ref}}) = \|\mathbf{P}_{\text{ref}} - \hat{\mathbf{P}}_{\text{rel}}^{3D}\|_2^2 + \|\Pi(\mathbf{P}_{\text{ref}}) - \hat{\mathbf{P}}^{2D}\|_2^2 \qquad (13)$$

enforces estimated 3D skeletons $\mathbf{P}_{\text{ref}}$ and its orthographic projection $\Pi(\mathbf{P}_{\text{ref}})$ close to ground-truth 3D and 2D skeletons ($\hat{\mathbf{P}}_{\text{rel}}^{3D}$, $\hat{\mathbf{P}}^{2D}$), respectively,

$$L_{\text{adv}}(D) = \|D_\theta(\boldsymbol{\theta}_{\text{ref}}) - 0\|_2 + \|D_\theta(\boldsymbol{\theta}_{\text{real}}) - 1\|_2$$
$$+ \|D_\beta(\boldsymbol{\beta}_{\text{ref}}) - 0\|_2 + \|D_\beta(\boldsymbol{\beta}_{\text{real}}) - 1\|_2 \qquad (14)$$

trains discriminators D_θ, D_β to classify real SMPL parameter $\boldsymbol{\theta}_{\text{real}}$ and $\boldsymbol{\beta}_{\text{real}}$ as real (i.e. 1) and estimated SMPL parameter $\boldsymbol{\theta}_{\text{ref}}$ and $\boldsymbol{\beta}_{\text{ref}}$ as fake (i.e. 0) and

$$L_{\text{adv}}(f^{\text{Ref}}) = \|D_\theta(\boldsymbol{\theta}_{\text{ref}}) - 1\|_2 + \|D_\beta(\boldsymbol{\beta}_{\text{ref}}) - 1\|_2 \qquad (15)$$

enforces the estimated $\boldsymbol{\theta}_{\text{ref}}$ and $\boldsymbol{\beta}_{\text{ref}}$ become realistic to deceive two discriminators D_θ and D_β to say that it is the real sample (i.e. 1).

Table 1. SOTA comparisons on 3DPW.

Method	MPJPE(↓)	PA-MPJPE(↓)	PVE(↓)
HMR [27]	130.0	76.7	-
temporal HMR [28]	116.5	72.6	139.3
BMP [73]	104.1	63.8	119.3
SPIN [33]	96.6	59.2	116.4
VIBE [30]	93.5	56.5	116.4
ROMP(Resnet-50) [62]	89.3	53.5	105.6
ROMP(HRNet-32) [62]	85.5	53.3	103.1
PARE(Resnet-50) [31]	82.9	52.3	99.7
PARE(HRNet-50) [31]	82.0	50.9	97.9
3DCrowdNet [12]	82.8	52.2	100.2
HybrIK [36]	80.0	48.8	94.5
METRO [38]	77.1	47.9	88.2
MeshLeTemp [65]	74.8	46.8	86.5
Mesh Graphormer [39]	74.7	45.6	87.7
Ours	66.0	39.0	76.3

Table 2. SOTA Comparisons on AGORA.

Method	All		Matched	
	NMVE(↓)	NMJE(↓)	MVE(↓)	MPJPE(↓)
ROMP [62]	227.3	236.6	161.4	168.0
HMR [27]	217.0	226.0	173.6	180.5
SPIN [33]	216.3	223.1	168.7	175.1
PyMAF [71]	200.2	207.4	168.2	174.2
EFT [26]	196.3	203.6	159.0	165.4
HybrIK [36]	-	188.5	-	156.1
PARE [31]	167.7	174.0	140.9	146.2
SPEC [32]	126.8	133.7	106.5	112.3
Ours	104.5	110.4	86.7	91.6

Table 3. 3DPCK relevant on MuPoTS-3D dataset for all sequences. The above table shows accuracy only for all groundtruths. The below table shows accuracy only for matched groundtruths.

Method-3DPCK(↑)	S1	S2	S3	S4	S5	S6	S7	S8	S9	S10	S11	S12	S13	S14	S15	S16	S17	S18	S19	S20	Avg
Accuracy for all groundtruths																					
Jiang et al. [23]	-	-	-	-	-	-	-	-	-	-	-	-	-	-	-	-	-	-	-	-	69.1
ROMP [62]	89.8	73.1	67.2	68.4	78.9	41.0	68.7	68.2	70.1	85.4	69.2	63.2	66.5	60.9	78.1	77.4	75.1	80.7	74.0	61.1	71.9
SPEC [32]	87.2	69.4	69.0	71.5	78.5	63.8	69.1	66.2	71.5	85.7	69.2	63.2	66.5	60.9	78.1	77.4	75.1	80.7	74.0	61.1	71.9
BMP [73]	-	-	-	-	-	-	-	-	-	-	-	-	-	-	-	-	-	-	-	-	73.8
PARE [31]	87.7	65.4	66.4	67.7	81.9	62.5	64.9	69.9	73.8	88.5	80.1	79.2	74.5	62.9	81.6	84.5	89.6	83.7	73.7	66.5	75.3
Moon et al. [49]	94.4	77.5	79.0	81.9	85.3	72.8	81.9	75.7	90.2	90.4	79.2	79.9	75.1	72.7	81.1	89.9	89.6	81.8	81.7	76.2	81.8
Metrabs [60]	94.0	82.6	88.4	86.5	87.3	76.2	85.9	66.9	85.8	92.9	81.8	89.9	77.6	68.5	85.6	92.3	89.3	85.1	78.2	71.6	83.3
Cheng et al. [7]	93.4	91.3	84.7	83.3	89.1	85.2	95.4	92.1	89.5	93.1	85.4	85.7	89.9	90.1	88.8	93.7	92.2	87.9	89.7	91.9	89.6
Ours	97.3	84.7	91.1	89.9	92.9	89.8	92.2	87.1	89.1	94.0	88.6	92.9	84.6	80.4	94.3	96.7	98.8	91.5	86.1	76.7	89.9
Accuracy only for matched groundtruths.																					
Jiang et al. [23]	-	-	-	-	-	-	-	-	-	-	-	-	-	-	-	-	-	-	-	-	72.2
ROMP [62]	92.1	81.9	69.8	69.1	85.9	43.2	69.3	70.7	70.1	85.4	69.2	63.2	68.0	63.6	78.1	77.6	75.4	80.7	74.5	72.9	74.0
SPEC [32]	88.1	78.5	69.6	71.6	81.0	63.8	69.1	77.4	71.5	85.7	69.2	63.2	68.0	63.6	78.1	77.6	75.4	80.7	74.5	72.9	74.0
BMP [73]	-	-	-	-	-	-	-	-	-	-	-	-	-	-	-	-	-	-	-	-	75.3
PARE [31]	88.8	77.1	66.7	67.7	83.2	62.5	64.9	77.9	73.8	88.5	80.1	79.2	76.4	65.8	81.6	85.4	89.6	83.7	74.2	82.5	77.5
Moon et al. [49]	94.4	78.6	79.0	82.1	86.6	72.8	81.9	75.8	90.2	90.4	79.4	79.9	75.3	81.0	81.0	90.7	89.6	83.1	81.7	77.3	82.5
Metrabs [60]	94.0	86.5	89.0	87.1	91.1	77.4	90.2	75.7	85.8	92.9	86.0	90.7	83.8	82.0	85.6	94.3	89.8	89.6	86.5	91.7	87.5
Cheng et al. [7]	-	-	-	-	-	-	-	-	-	-	-	-	-	-	-	-	-	-	-	-	89.6
Ours	97.6	94.1	90.7	89.6	95.2	88.7	94.2	88.4	89.2	93.7	89.1	93.2	86.6	90.5	94.4	97.4	98.5	91.9	86.1	84.8	91.7

4 Experiments

Setup. We involved multiple datasets to train our model. We used Human3.6M [21], MPI-INF-3DHP [45], LPS [24], MSCOCO [40], MPII [1] datasets as the training data, which are the same setting as Kanazawa et al. [27]. Additionally, MuCo-3DHP [47], CMU-Panoptic [25], SAIL-VOS [20], SURREAL [68], AIST++ [37] are used to calculate the $L_P(f^P)$. For evaluation, we used 3DPW [44], MuPoTs [47], and AGORA [52]: The 3DPW dataset is an outdoor 3D human pose benchmark involving real sequences. It contains diverse subjects, various backgrounds and occlusion scenario. The MuPoTS dataset contains both real indoor and outdoor sequences having multiple persons occluding each other. AGORA is the synthetic benchmark having multi-person within it. Image contains many persons with various clothes, ages and ethnicities.

Table 4. Ablation study of the effectiveness of IK, refiner, positional embedding, masking input patch and comparison between the different number of Transformer's input persons on 3DPW.

Method	MPJPE($\downarrow$)	PA-MPJPE($\downarrow$)	MVE($\downarrow$)	Method	MPJPE($\downarrow$)	PA-MPJPE($\downarrow$)	MVE($\downarrow$)
Ours w/o IK, w/o Ref	71.8	42.5	–	Ours (N=1)	66.9	39.4	77.0
Ours w/o Ref	67.3	39.3	77.5	Ours (N=2)	66.7	39.3	76.7
Ours w/ positional embedding	68.3	39.4	78.3	Ours (N=3)	**66.0**	**39.0**	**76.3**
Ours w/o masking input patch	67.1	39.0	76.6	Ours (N=4)	66.6	39.4	77.2

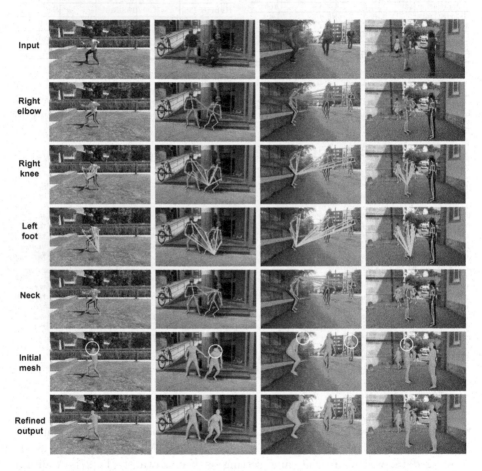

Fig. 3. Attention visualization: (Row 1) input image, (Row 2–5) part-based attentions obtained within an intra-person in the column 1, those among two persons in the column 2 and those among three persons in the column 3–4, (Row 6) initial mesh obtained from inverse kinematics, (Row 7) refined mesh after mesh refinement module. We visualize the self-attentions between a specified joint and all other joints, where brighter color and thicker line indicate stronger attentions.

Measures. For 3DPW dataset, we measure the accuracy of ours with widely used evaluation metrics to compare with others: MPJPE, PA-MPJPE and MVE: The MPJPE is the mean per joint position error which is calculated based on the Euclidean distance between ground-truth and estimated joint positions. For this, pelvis joint is aligned by moving the estimated pelvis joint to the ground-truth pelvis joint. The PA-MPJPE is Procrustes Aligned MPJPE which is calculated similarly to MPJPE; however it is measured after rigidly aligning the estimated joints to ground-truth joints via Procrustes Analysis [15]. The MVE is the mean vertex error which is calculated as the Euclidean distance between ground-truth and estimated mesh vertices. For MuPoTS dataset, we measure the performance of our methods using 3DPCK. The 3DPCK is the 3D percentage of correct keypoints. It counts the keypoints as correct when the Euclidean distance between the estimated joint position and its ground-truth is within a threshold. We used 150mm as the threshold following [49]. For AGORA dataset, we measure the performance of our methods on AGORA using MPJPE, MVE, NMJE and NMVE. The MPJPE and MVE are measured on matched detections. The NMJE and NMVE are normalized MPJPE and MVE by F1 score to punish misses and false alarms in the detection.

Baselines. In our experiments, we have involved several state-of-the-art 3D body mesh reconstruction [26–28,30–33,36,38,39,65,71] pipelines for single persons to compare with ours: HMR [27] and SPIN [33] are the pioneering works that first tried to infer SMPL pose and shape parameters using the CNN network for a single person. Temporal HMR [28] and VIBE [30] developed to further utilize the temporal information from a video. METRO [38] used transformer architecture for non-parametric mesh reconstruction. Mesh Graphormer [39] combines self-attention and graph convolution network for mesh reconstruction. Mesh-LeTemp [65] proposed the learnable template which reflects not only vertex-vertex interactions but also the human pose and body shape. PyMAF [71] uses a pyramidal mesh alignment feedback loop to refine the mesh based on the mesh-image alignment mechanism. EFT [26] trains HMR architecture with a large-scale dataset having pseudo ground-truths. SPEC [32] estimates the perspective camera to accurately infer the 3D mesh coordinates. PARE [31] learns the body-part-guided attention masks to be robust to occlusions. HybrIK [36] estimates SMPL pose and shape parameters from estimated 3D skeletons via inverse kinematics. The single-person mesh reconstruction methods take the top-down approach using bounding boxes obtained from YOLOv4 [2] for AGORA dataset, and using those obtained from ground-truth 3D skeletons for MuPoTS and 3DPW datasets, respectively.

Several multi-person frameworks are also involved for the comparisons [12, 23,62,73]: Jiang et al. [23], ROMP [62] and BMP [73] are bottom-up methods that estimate the multi-person SMPL pose and shape parameters at once and simultaneously localizes multi-person instances and predicts 3D body meshes in a single stage, respectively. Jiang et al. [23] proposed inter-penetration loss to avoid collision and depth ordering loss for the rendering. 3DCrowdNet [12] is a top-down method that proposed to concatenate image features and 2D pose heatmaps to exploit the 2D pose-guided features for better accuracy. We also involved 3D skeleton estimation approaches [7,49,60]: Moon et al. [49]'s work that estimates the absolute root position and root-relative 3D skeletons focusing on camera distance. Cheng et al. [7]'s work that integrates top-down method and bottom-up methods for estimating better 3D skeletons. Metrabs [60] that is robust to truncation/occlusion variations thanks to the metric-scale heatmap representation.

Results. We compared ours to state-of-the-art algorithms on three challenging datasets (i.e. 3DPW, MuPoTS and AGORA). The results are summarized in Tables 1, 2 and 3: From Tables 1 and 2, we could observe that ours obtained the superior performance compared to previous mesh reconstruction works. We obtained even better performance than works exploiting temporal information [28,30] and several multi-person 3D mesh reconstruction methods [12,23,62,73]. Also, in Table 1, we also compared ours to HybrIK [36] that applied the inverse kinematics process on the pre-estimated 3D skeleton results. We outperforms it by successfully extending it towards the multi-person scenario. As shown in Table 3, we have achieved the state-of-the-art accuracy on MuPoTS. Note that the 3D skeleton estimation methods [7,49,60] are also included in the comparison and they produced superior performance than 3D mesh estimation approaches [31,32,62,73]. However, our method outperforms them by delivering good pose accuracy from the initial 3D skeleton estimator, while reconstructing both poses and shapes in the form of 3D meshes.

Figure 3 shows the visualization for the attention learned in the relation-aware refinement network f^{Ref}. It learns the attentions for intra-person parts as in the column 1 and learns the inter-person attentions among at most $N = 3$ persons as in columns 2 through 4. From the visualization, we could see that the refinement network f^{Ref} refines the initial meshes (in the 6th row) a lot towards refined meshes (in the 7th row). Figure 4 shows the qualitative comparisons to competitive state-of-the-arts [31,32,62]. Ours faithfully reconstructs 3D human bodies with diverse artifacts while others frequently fails to capture the details.

Ablation Study. We conduct an ablation study for several design choices. The Table 4 shows the ablation results on 3DPW dataset: 'Ours w.o IK, w/o Ref', 'Ours w/o Ref', 'Ours w/ positional embedding', 'Ours w/o masking input patch' denote our results obtained without inverse kinematics process and refinement module which are 3D skeletons, our results without the refinement module, our results with positional embedding and our results without masking input patches, respectively. From the results, we can see that inverse kinematics and relation-aware refinements consistently increase the accuracy of our pipeline. Furthermore, we decided not to use positional embedding while using the masking input patch scheme. 'Ours (N = 1)' through 'Ours (N = 4)' denote experiments conducted by varying the maximum number of persons (i.e. N) of the Transformer input. We observe that $N = 3$ works best.

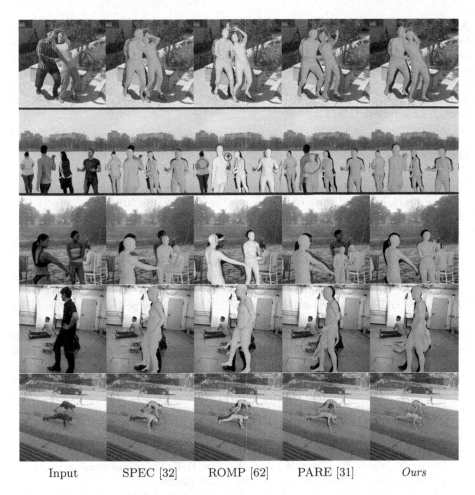

| Input | SPEC [32] | ROMP [62] | PARE [31] | *Ours* |

Fig. 4. Qualitative comparisons on 3DPW (Row 1), AGORA (Rows 2–3) and MuPoTS (Rows 4–5) datasets. Red circles highlight wrongly estimated parts.

5 Conclusion

In this paper, we proposed a coarse-to-fine pipeline for the multi-person 3D mesh reconstruction task, which first estimates occlusion-robust 3D skeletons, then reconstructs initial 3D meshes via the inverse kinematic process and finally refines them based on the relation-aware refiner considering intra- and inter-person relationships. By extensive experiments, we find that our idea of delivering the accurate occlusion-robust 3D poses to 3D meshes, and refining initial mesh parameters of interacting persons indeed works: Our pipeline consistently outperforms multiple 3D skeleton-based, 3D mesh-based baselines and each component proposed works meaningfully for the intended scenario.

Acknowledgements. This work was supported by IITP grants (No. 2021-0-01778 Development of human image synthesis and discrimination technology below the perceptual threshold; No. 2020-0-01336 Artificial intelligence graduate school program(UNIST); No. 2021-0-02068 Artificial intelligence innovation hub; No. 2022-0-00264 Comprehensive video understanding and generation with knowledge-based deep logic neural network) and the NRF grant (No. 2022R1F1A1074828), all funded by the Korean government (MSIT).

References

1. Andriluka, M., Pishchulin, L., Gehler, P., Schiele, B.: 2D human pose estimation: new benchmark and state of the art analysis. In: CVPR (2014)
2. Bochkovskiy, A., Wang, C.Y., Liao, H.Y.M.: Yolov4: optimal speed and accuracy of object detection. arXiv:2004.10934 (2020)
3. Bogo, F., Kanazawa, A., Lassner, C., Gehler, P., Romero, J., Black, M.J.: Keep It SMPL: automatic estimation of 3D human pose and shape from a single image. In: Leibe, B., Matas, J., Sebe, N., Welling, M. (eds.) ECCV 2016. LNCS, vol. 9909, pp. 561–578. Springer, Cham (2016). https://doi.org/10.1007/978-3-319-46454-1_34
4. Cao, Z., Hidalgo, G., Simon, T., Wei, S.E., Sheikh, Y.: Openpose: realtime multi-person 2D pose estimation using part affinity fields. TPAMI (2019)
5. Cha, J., Saqlain, M., Kim, D., Lee, S., Lee, S., Baek, S.: Learning 3D skeletal representation from transformer for action recognition. IEEE Access **10**, 67541-67550 (2022)
6. Cha, J., et al.: Towards single 2D image-level self-supervision for 3D human pose and shape estimation. Appl. Sci. **11**(20), 9724(2021)
7. Cheng, Y., Wang, B., Yang, B., Tan, R.T.: Monocular 3D multi-person pose estimation by integrating top-down and bottom-up networks. In: CVPR (2021)
8. Cheng, Y., Yang, B., Wang, B., Tan, R.T.: 3D human pose estimation using spatio-temporal networks with explicit occlusion training. In: AAAI (2020)
9. Cheng, Y., Yang, B., Wang, B., Yan, W., Tan, R.T.: Occlusion-aware networks for 3D human pose estimation in video. In: ICCV (2019)
10. Choi, H., Moon, G., Chang, J.Y., Lee, K.M.: Beyond static features for temporally consistent 3D human pose and shape from a video. In: CVPR (2021)
11. Choi, H., Moon, G., Lee, K.M.: Pose2Mesh: graph convolutional network for 3D human pose and mesh recovery from a 2D human pose. In: Vedaldi, A., Bischof, H., Brox, T., Frahm, J.-M. (eds.) ECCV 2020. LNCS, vol. 12352, pp. 769–787. Springer, Cham (2020). https://doi.org/10.1007/978-3-030-58571-6_45
12. Choi, H., Moon, G., Park, J., Lee, K.M.: 3Dcrowdnet: 2D human pose-guided3d crowd human pose and shape estimation in the wild. arXiv:2104.07300 (2021)
13. Dong, Z., Song, J., Chen, X., Guo, C., Hilliges, O.: Shape-aware multi-person pose estimation from multi-view images. In: ICCV (2021)
14. Dosovitskiy, A., et al.: An image is worth 16x16 words: transformers for image recognition at scale. ICLR (2021)
15. Gower, J.C.: Generalized procrustes analysis. Psychometrika **40**(1), 33–51 (1975)
16. Guan, P., Weiss, A., Balan, A.O., Black, M.J.: Estimating human shape and pose from a single image. In: ICCV (2009)
17. Guler, R.A., Kokkinos, I.: Holopose: Holistic 3D human reconstruction in-the-wild. In: CVPR (2019)
18. He, K., Gkioxari, G., Dollár, P., Girshick, R.: Mask R-CNN. In: ICCV (2017)

19. He, K., Zhang, X., Ren, S., Sun, J.: Identity mappings in deep residual networks. In: Leibe, B., Matas, J., Sebe, N., Welling, M. (eds.) ECCV 2016. LNCS, vol. 9908, pp. 630–645. Springer, Cham (2016). https://doi.org/10.1007/978-3-319-46493-0_38
20. Hu, Y.T., Chen, H.S., Hui, K., Huang, J.B., Schwing, A.G.: SAIL-VOS: semantic amodal instance level video object segmentation-a synthetic dataset and baselines. In: CVPR (2019)
21. Ionescu, C., Papava, D., Olaru, V., Sminchisescu, C.: Human3.6m: large scale datasets and predictive methods for 3D human sensing in natural environments. TPAMI **36**(7), 1325–1339 (2013)
22. Iskakov, K., Burkov, E., Lempitsky, V., Malkov, Y.: Learnable triangulation of human pose. In: ICCV (2019)
23. Jiang, W., Kolotouros, N., Pavlakos, G., Zhou, X., Daniilidis, K.: Coherent reconstruction of multiple humans from a single image. In: CVPR (2020)
24. Johnson, S., Everingham, M.: Clustered pose and nonlinear appearance models for human pose estimation. In: BMVC (2010)
25. Joo, H., et al.: Panoptic studio: a massively multiview system for social motion capture. In: ICCV (2015)
26. Joo, H., Neverova, N., Vedaldi, A.: Exemplar fine-tuning for 3D human model fitting towards in-the-wild 3D human pose estimation. In: 3DV (2021)
27. Kanazawa, A., Black, M.J., Jacobs, D.W., Malik, J.: End-to-end recovery of human shape and pose. In: CVPR (2018)
28. Kanazawa, A., Zhang, J.Y., Felsen, P., Malik, J.: Learning 3D human dynamics from video. In: CVPR (2019)
29. Kingma, D.P., Ba, J.: Adam: a method for stochastic optimization. ICLR (2015)
30. Kocabas, M., Athanasiou, N., Black, M.J.: Vibe: video inference for human body pose and shape estimation. In: CVPR (2020)
31. Kocabas, M., Huang, C.H.P., Hilliges, O., Black, M.J.: PARE: part attention regressor for 3d human body estimation. In: ICCV (2021)
32. Kocabas, M., Huang, C.H.P., Tesch, J., Müller, L., Hilliges, O., Black, M.J.: SPEC: seeing people in the wild with an estimated camera. In: ICCV (2021)
33. Kolotouros, N., Pavlakos, G., Black, M.J., Daniilidis, K.: Learning to reconstruct 3D human pose and shape via model-fitting in the loop. In: ICCV (2019)
34. Kolotouros, N., Pavlakos, G., Daniilidis, K.: Convolutional mesh regression for single-image human shape reconstruction. In: CVPR (2019)
35. Kundu, J.N., Rakesh, M., Jampani, V., Venkatesh, R.M., Venkatesh Babu, R.: Appearance consensus driven self-supervised human mesh recovery. In: Vedaldi, A., Bischof, H., Brox, T., Frahm, J.-M. (eds.) ECCV 2020. LNCS, vol. 12346, pp. 794–812. Springer, Cham (2020). https://doi.org/10.1007/978-3-030-58452-8_46
36. Li, J., Xu, C., Chen, Z., Bian, S., Yang, L., Lu, C.: HybrIk: a hybrid analytical-neural inverse kinematics solution for 3D human pose and shape estimation. In: CVPR (2021)
37. Li, R., Yang, S., Ross, D.A., Kanazawa, A.: Learn to dance with AIST++: music conditioned 3D dance generation. arXiv:2101.08779 (2021)
38. Lin, K., Wang, L., Liu, Z.: End-to-end human pose and mesh reconstruction with transformers. In: CVPR (2021)
39. Lin, K., Wang, L., Liu, Z.: Mesh graphormer. In: ICCV (2021)
40. Lin, T.-Y.: Microsoft COCO: common objects in context. In: Fleet, D., Pajdla, T., Schiele, B., Tuytelaars, T. (eds.) ECCV 2014. LNCS, vol. 8693, pp. 740–755. Springer, Cham (2014). https://doi.org/10.1007/978-3-319-10602-1_48

41. Liu, W., Piao, Z., Min, J., Luo, W., Ma, L., Gao, S.: Liquid warping GAN: a unified framework for human motion imitation, appearance transfer and novel view synthesis. In: ICCV (2019)
42. Loper, M., Mahmood, N., Romero, J., Pons-Moll, G., Black, M.J.: SMPL: a skinned multi-person linear model. TOG **34**(6), 1–16 (2015)
43. Ludl, D., Gulde, T., Curio, C.: Enhancing data-driven algorithms for human pose estimation and action recognition through simulation. IEEE Trans. Intell. Transp. Syst. **21**(9), 3990–3999 (2020)
44. von Marcard, T., Henschel, R., Black, M.J., Rosenhahn, B., Pons-Moll, G.: Recovering accurate 3D human pose in the wild using IMUs and a moving camera. In: ECCV (2018)
45. Mehta, D., et al.: Monocular 3D human pose estimation in the wild using improved CNN supervision. In: 3DV (2017)
46. Mehta, D., et al.: XNect: real-time multi-person 3D motion capture with a single RGB camera. TOG **39**(4), 1–82 (2020)
47. Mehta, D., et al.: Single-shot multi-person 3D pose estimation from monocular RGB. In: 3DV (2018)
48. Mir, A., Alldieck, T., Pons-Moll, G.: Learning to transfer texture from clothing images to 3D humans. In: CVPR (2020)
49. Moon, G., Chang, J.Y., Lee, K.M.: Camera distance-aware top-down approach for 3D multi-person pose estimation from a single RGB image. In: ICCV (2019)
50. Ning, G., Pei, J., Huang, H.: Lighttrack: a generic framework for online top-down human pose tracking. In: CVPR workshop (2020)
51. Omran, M., Lassner, C., Pons-Moll, G., Gehler, P., Schiele, B.: Neural body fitting: unifying deep learning and model based human pose and shape estimation. In: 3DV (2018)
52. Patel, P., Huang, C.H.P., Tesch, J., Hoffmann, D.T., Tripathi, S., Black, M.J.: AGORA: avatars in geography optimized for regression analysis. In: CVPR (2021)
53. Pavlakos, G., Kolotouros, N., Daniilidis, K.: TexturePose: supervising human mesh estimation with texture consistency. In: ICCV (2019)
54. Pavlakos, G., Zhu, L., Zhou, X., Daniilidis, K.: Learning to estimate 3D human pose and shape from a single color image. In: CVPR (2018)
55. Reddy, N.D., Guigues, L., Pishchulin, L., Eledath, J., Narasimhan, S.G.: Tesse-Track: end-to-end learnable multi-person articulated 3D pose tracking. In: CVPR (2021)
56. Redmon, J., Divvala, S., Girshick, R., Farhadi, A.: You only look once: unified, real-time object detection. In: CVPR (2016)
57. Rogez, G., Weinzaepfel, P., Schmid, C.: LCR-NET: localization-classification-regression for human pose. In: CVPR (2017)
58. Saqlain, M., Kim, D., Cha, J., Lee, C., Lee, S., Baek, S.: 3DMesh-GAR: 3D human body mesh-based method for group activity recognition. Sensors **22**(4), 1464(2022)
59. Sárándi, I., Linder, T., Arras, K.O., Leibe, B.: Synthetic occlusion augmentation with volumetric heatmaps for the 2018 ECCV posetrack challenge on 3D human pose estimation. arXiv:1809.04987 (2018)
60. Sárándi, I., Linder, T., Arras, K.O., Leibe, B.: Metrabs: metric-scale truncation-robust heatmaps for absolute 3D human pose estimation. IEEE Trans. Biometrics Behav. Identity Sci. **3**(1), 16–30 (2020)
61. Sun, X., Xiao, B., Wei, F., Liang, S., Wei, Y.: Integral human pose regression. In: ECCV (2018)
62. Sun, Y., Bao, Q., Liu, W., Fu, Y., Black, M.J., Mei, T.: Monocular, one-stage, regression of multiple 3D people. In: ICCV (2021)

63. Sun, Y., Liu, W., Bao, Q., Fu, Y., Mei, T., Black, M.J.: Putting people in their place: monocular regression of 3D people in depth. arXiv:2112.08274 (2021)
64. Sun, Y., Ye, Y., Liu, W., Gao, W., Fu, Y., Mei, T.: Human mesh recovery from monocular images via a skeleton-disentangled representation. In: ICCV (2019)
65. Tran, T.Q., Than, C.C., Nguyen, H.T.: MeshLeTemp: leveraging the learnable vertex-vertex relationship to generalize human pose and mesh reconstruction for in-the-wild scenes. arXiv:2202.07228 (2022)
66. Tung, H.Y.F., Tung, H.W., Yumer, E., Fragkiadaki, K.: Self-supervised learning of motion capture. In: NeurIPS (2017)
67. Varol, G., Laptev, I., Schmid, C., Zisserman, A.: Synthetic humans for action recognition from unseen viewpoints. Int. J. Comput. Vis. **129**(7), 2264–2287 (2021). https://doi.org/10.1007/s11263-021-01467-7
68. Varol, G., et al.: Learning from synthetic humans. In: CVPR (2017)
69. Xu, Y., Zhu, S.C., Tung, T.: DenseRaC: joint 3D pose and shape estimation by dense render-and-compare. In: ICCV (2019)
70. Zanfir, A., Marinoiu, E., Zanfir, M., Popa, A.I., Sminchisescu, C.: Deep network for the integrated 3D sensing of multiple people in natural images. In: NeurIPS (2018)
71. Zhang, H., et al.: PyMAF: 3D human pose and shape regression with pyramidal mesh alignment feedback loop. In: ICCV (2021)
72. Zhang, J., Cai, Y., Yan, S., Feng, J., et al.: Direct multi-view multi-person 3D pose estimation. In: NeurIPS (2021)
73. Zhang, J., Yu, D., Liew, J.H., Nie, X., Feng, J.: Body meshes as points. In: CVPR (2021)

Overlooked Poses Actually Make Sense: Distilling Privileged Knowledge for Human Motion Prediction

Xiaoning Sun[1], Qiongjie Cui[1], Huaijiang Sun[1(✉)], Bin Li[2], Weiqing Li[1], and Jianfeng Lu[1]

[1] Nanjing University of Science and Technology, Nanjing, China
{sunxiaoning,cuiqiongjie,sunhuaijiang,li_weiqing,lujf}@njust.edu.cn
[2] Tianjin AiForward Science and Technology Co., Ltd., Tianjin, China
libin@aiforward.com

Abstract. Previous works on human motion prediction follow the pattern of building a mapping relation between the sequence observed and the one to be predicted. However, due to the inherent complexity of multivariate time series data, it still remains a challenge to find the extrapolation relation between motion sequences. In this paper, we present a new prediction pattern, which introduces previously overlooked human poses, to implement the prediction task from the view of interpolation. These poses exist *after* the predicted sequence, and form the privileged sequence. To be specific, we first propose an InTerPolation learning Network (ITP-Network) that encodes both the observed sequence and the privileged sequence to interpolate the in-between predicted sequence, wherein the embedded Privileged-sequence-Encoder (Priv-Encoder) learns the privileged knowledge (PK) simultaneously. Then, we propose a Final Prediction Network (FP-Network) for which the privileged sequence is not observable, but is equipped with a novel PK-Simulator that distills PK learned from the previous network. This simulator takes as input the observed sequence, but approximates the behavior of Priv-Encoder, enabling FP-Network to imitate the interpolation process. Extensive experimental results demonstrate that our prediction pattern achieves state-of-the-art performance on benchmarked H3.6M, CMU-Mocap and 3DPW datasets in both short-term and long-term predictions.

Keywords: Human motion prediction · Privileged knowledge

1 Introduction

Human motion prediction, aimed at forecasting future poses according to the historical motion sequence, has been widely applied in the field of autonomous driving [38], human-machine interaction [21] and action detection [13]. To make the best of human body structure information, recent methods employ graph

S. Avidan et al. (Eds.): ECCV 2022, LNCS 13665, pp. 678–694, 2022.
https://doi.org/10.1007/978-3-031-20065-6_39

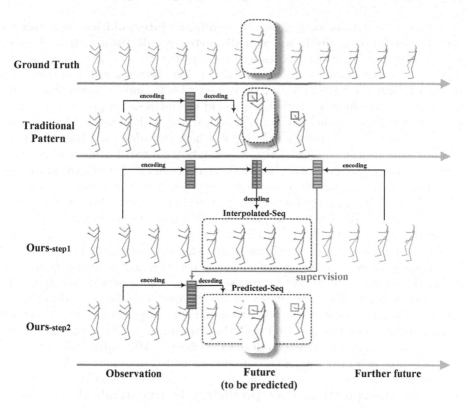

Fig. 1. Comparison between the traditional human motion prediction pattern and ours. Previous works predict future motions on historical ones by direct extrapolation, which may bring about outcomes opposite to targets (see red boxes in the figure). However, our pattern a) introduces poses from further future to learn a PK representation by interpolating the in-between poses during the first step, and b) extrapolates (i.e. predicts) the sequence given historical poses only, but with PK to be distilled that offers supervision on the process of encoding and decoding during the second step. (Color figure online)

convolutional networks (GCNs) [7,8,34,43] to model spatial dependencies or topological relations of body joints.

Classical sequential networks such as Recurrent Neural Networks (RNNs) [5,12,19] and Long Short-Term Memory (LSTM) [6,11,35] have been used to tackle certain sequence prediction frame-by-frame, yet suffer from error accumulation and convergence to the static mean pose [14,22]. Temporal Convolutional Networks (TCNs) [2,50] and the Discrete Cosine Transform (DCT) [31,32,34] method have also proved their ability to encode temporal information, and to be coordinated with GCNs to better predict human motions in terms of both spatial and temporal domain [7,31,32,34]. All the methods mentioned above follow the same prediction pattern, which is building a mapping relation between the sequence observed and the one to be predicted. However, it still remains tough to directly extrapolate a multivariate time series based on the historical sequence, and unexpected results or unreasonable poses may arise.

Inspired by the fact that, generally, **sequence interpolation is easier to operate and often yields an overall better result than extrapolation**, we introduce the overlooked poses which exist after the predicted sequence, in the hope of constructing a prediction pattern that **shares similar spirit with interpolation**. As these poses are only observable for interpolation and should not appear in the final prediction, we regard the information provided by them as privileged information. The concept of learning with privileged information is first presented by Vapnik *et al.* [46] in which the additional information of training samples can be used during training but discarded while testing. As is shown in the top half part of our prediction pattern in Fig. 1, when the privileged sequence is introduced, the poses to be predicted finally are first interpolated as we hope. With this preliminary step done, another problem that arises is how to let the prediction step acquire the privileged information, since the raw privileged sequence would not exist then.

Recently, it has been proved that knowledge distillation is able to transfer knowledge between different models, and has been applied to diverse fields such as image dehazing [17], object detection [48], and online action detection [53]. This advancement enlightens us to tackle the question above by designing a novel prediction network (see the bottom half of our pattern in Fig. 1), which distills privileged knowledge (PK) from the aforementioned interpolation period. The distillation process exactly reflects the effect of PK supervision, enabling the model to be armed with a certain amount of PK gradually without taking the privileged sequence as input. In this way, this model is able to **keep the merits of interpolation**, while **predicting in the standard manner of extrapolation** finally.

In this paper, we name the two steps of networks proposed above as InTer-Polation learning Network (ITP-Network) and Final Prediction Network (FP-Network), respectively. As our networks are created on the basis of GCN structure, the entire model is named as PK-GCN (see Fig. 2). This model embodies a new pattern of human motion prediction, instead of the traditional one that directly finds an extrapolation relation between the observed sequence and the one to be predicted. Specifically, the Privileged-sequence-Encoder (Priv-Encoder) in ITP learns a PK representation of the privileged sequence during interpolation, then the novel PK-Simulator embedded in FP implements the PK distillation process by approximating the PK representation, with only the observed sequence as input. Meanwhile, a PK simulation loss function is presented to measure this approximation.

The idea of introducing future information to provide additional supervision has been practiced in prediction-related tasks, such as using predicted future frames to assist online action detection [49], or encapsulating future information in observation representations with Jaccard similarity measures [10] for action anticipation, among which the information obtained from *future* are still limited to the traditional observed-predicted research window. However, 3D human motion data is more elaborated with abundant yet subtle spatio-temporal information, and focusing on this two-section research window is not enough. Compared with existing works, our novelty lies in that we extend it to the observed-

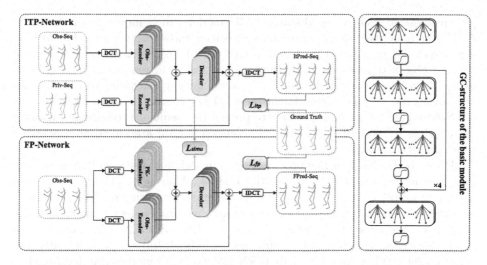

Fig. 2. The backbone of our PK-GCN. ITP is composed of an Observed-sequence-Encoder (Obs-Encoder), a Privileged-sequence-Encoder (Priv-Encoder) and a decoder to interpolate the in-between sequence. FP is composed of an Obs-Encoder, a PK-Simulator and a decoder. These basic modules share the same architecture of graph convolutional layers (GC-Layers) and residual structures shown in the right sub-figure. During the interpolation period, a PK representation is learned by Priv-Encoder, so that the PK-Simulator is able to distill PK by approximating this representation (we measure their similarity by PK simulation loss L_{simu}). Therefore, FP could take as input only the observed sequence but predict motions with PK assisted.

predicted-privileged window, in the seek of additional yet tailored information to provide supervision. To the best of our knowledge, this is the first work to involve poses existing after the predicted sequence to learn PK for human motion prediction.

In summary, our contributions are as follows: (i) ITP-Network: introducing the privileged sequence to learn PK during interpolation period; (ii) FP-Network: with the novel PK-Simulator distilling PK, to predict in the extrapolation manner while keeping the merits of interpolation; (iii) Entire model of PK-GCN: SOTA performance on benchmarked H3.6M, CMU-Mocap and 3DPW datasets.

2 Related Work

2.1 Human Motion Prediction

Since human motion data is composed of a time series of human poses, many works on human motion prediction rely on sequential networks such as RNNs [5,12,19], LSTM [11,35,44] or GRU [9,35,40] to extract temporal information, and has achieved success. Notably, there occurs a problem that the first predicted frame is discontinuous with the last observed frame, so Martinez *et al.*

[35] propose a residual single-layer GRU model which moves from the usual LSTM architectures [25] and predicts velocities rather than poses. Meanwhile, a zero-velocity baseline is proposed in this work to prove that the repetition of the last observed pose even outperform prediction performances in [11,19]. However, the crucial defect of RNNs, error accumulation, may lead to failure cases of convergence to unexpected mean poses. Other classical architectures such as CNN-based [22,26] make it possible to predict in a sequence-to-sequence manner rather than frame-by-frame, while GAN-based [14,15] are aimed at generating more realistic motions.

Recently, GCNs gain huge popularity to model spatial dependencies on predict human motions [7,8,24,28,30,31,34,43,54]. Mao *et al.* [34] first introduce a generic graph instead of the previous skeletal kinematic tree [3], with DCT encoding the short-term history in frequency domain. To depict the topological relations of body joints, Cui *et al.* [7] present a dynamic GCN, which learns both the natural connectivity of joint pairs and the implicit links of geometrically separated joints. Different multi-scale GNN [23]/GCN [8] models are developed to further explore the features of human motions. Sofianos *et al.* [43] realizes crosstalk over space and time within one graph and factorizes it into separable matrices for better understanding on both features. Meanwhile, stochastic motion prediction [1,29,32,33,52] gradually draw attention, which generate diverse yet plausible motion sequences given only one observed.

All the models mentioned above follow the traditional prediction pattern, limiting their research window within the observed-predicted sequence. Differently, our work goes further by adding a privileged window containing overlooked poses, so that a PK representation can be learned and distilled through our two-step model, to serve as a supplement of supervision information to assist prediction tasks.

2.2 Knowledge Distillation

Early knowledge distillation is utilized for deep model compression [16], wherein the knowledge from the larger teacher network helps the smaller student network to learn better [36]. The teacher provides the soft target for the student to imitate the output logits and intermediate features [4,42,45,51]. Subsequently, it has been proved that knowledge distillation is able to transfer knowledge between different models, and has its applications in image classification [41, 45], action detection [53], semantic segmentation [27], trajectory prediction [37] and stochastic motion prediction [29]. However, the teachers in these models provides additional information about training samples either with no privileged information involved, or with it involved but irrelevant to distill knowledge from future further away. In addition, our design of distillation process ensures that a) PK would be distilled into FP as much as possible, and b) only the observed sequence would be taken as input. We embed the PK-Simulator in FP to be fed with the observed sequence but approximate the PK representation learned by Priv-Encoder, and present a PK simulation loss L_{simu} (also denoted as PKSL) to measure this approximation.

3   Proposed Method

We present a new formulation for human motion prediction. Different from existing works, our notation involves three research windows (i.e. the observed-predicted-privileged sequence), with N poses $\mathbf{X}_{1:N} = [\mathbf{x}_1, \mathbf{x}_2, \ldots, \mathbf{x}_N]$ given, T poses $\mathbf{X}_{N+1:N+T}$ to predict, and particularly another P poses after the predicted sequence $\mathbf{X}_{N+T+1:N+T+P}$ as the privileged sequence, where $\mathbf{x}_i \in \mathbb{R}^K$, with K parameters depicting each pose based on joint coordinates or angles. The entire architecture of PK-GCN is shown in Fig. 2. To be specific, ITP-Network encodes both the observed sequence and the privileged sequence to interpolate the predicted sequence, during which PK is learned and to be distilled to the next step, enabling FP-Network to predict in the standard manner of extrapolation finally, but with PK assisted.

3.1   Spatio-Temporal Encoding

To encode both the spatial and temporal information of human motions, we employ the remarkable encoding method from [34]. We treat each human skeleton as a fully-connected graph of K nodes, and use an adjacency matrix $A \in \mathbb{R}^{K \times K}$ to depict its edges. Formally, we define $H^{(l)} \in \mathbb{R}^{K \times F^{(l)}}$ to be fed into the lth layer of GCN (i.e. the lth GC-Layer), $W^{(l)} \in \mathbb{R}^{F^{(l)} \times F^{(l+1)}}$ as weight matrix, and output (also the input of next GC-Layer) as:

$$H^{(l+1)} = \sigma(A^{(l)} H^{(l)} W^{(l)}), \tag{1}$$

where $\sigma(\cdot)$ is an activation function. Particularly, a DCT-based representation is employed to extract temporal information, which transforms the observed sequence into its DCT coefficients $H^{(1)} \in \mathbb{R}^{K \times C}$ before being input into our network, with C the DCT coefficient number. The output is $H^{(last)} \in \mathbb{R}^{K \times C}$, and should also be transformed into its sequence form by IDCT.

3.2   Network Structure

The InTerPolation Learning Network (ITP-Network), based on residual GCN architecture, is composed of two encoders to encode the observed sequence (Obs-Encoder) and the privileged sequence (Priv-Encoder), and one decoder to interpolate the in-between sequence (see the top half of Fig. 2). In each of the encoders/decoder, we employ 4 residual blocks and 2 separate GC-Layers with one at the beginning and one at the end (see the right part of Fig. 2). Each residual block is composed of 2 GC-Layers, and the activation function is set to $tanh(\cdot)$. The outputs of the Obs-Encoder and the Priv-Encoder are integrated by element-wise addition.

It should be emphasized that PK *only* serves as a supplement of supervision information, and it is unreasonable to hold this advantage as an excuse to diminish the original predictability of Obs-Encoder in FP. Additionally, overly complicated PK is not conducive to distill. Therefore, in this PK preparation step, we intend to reduce the relative weight of Priv-Encoder. However, this variation will lead to degradation on the interpolation performance, so we alternatively set the weight ratio of the outermost residual connection to 0.7:0.3, sum of which is 1 in line with the residual weight in FP.

Since the input of both encoders and the output of the decoder are all DCT coefficients of the corresponding sequences, motivated by zero-velocity baseline [35] and inspired by the padding operation in [34], we propose a new data preprocessing method which replicates the last pose of the observed sequence, $\mathbf{x}_N$, $T + P$ times (represented as $\mathbf{ObsX}_{1:N+T+P}$), and the first pose of the privileged sequence, $\mathbf{x}_{N+T+1}$, $N + T$ times (represented as $\mathbf{PrivX}_{1:N+T+P}$), to form residual vectors in frequency domain as the input $H_{\text{obs}}^{(1)}$, $H_{\text{priv}}^{(1)}$. After epochs of training to find the interpolation relation $\mathcal{I}$:

$$H_{\text{itp}}^{(last)} = \mathcal{I}(H_{\text{obs}}^{(1)}, H_{\text{priv}}^{(1)}), \tag{2}$$

where the interpolation result $H_{\text{itp}}^{(last)}$ is close to the ground truth, the Priv-Encoder could obtain its most accurate representation of PK, which is aimed to be distilled to the final prediction period.

The Final Prediction Network (FP-Network) consists of an Obs-Encoder to encode the observed sequence, a novel PK-Simulator to approximate the representation obtained from Priv-Encoder, and a decoder to extrapolate the predicted sequence. We construct each module the same as in ITP with residual blocks and GC-Layers. We pad the observed sequence to the length of $N+T+P$ the same as in ITP, and operate DCT transformation to form the input $H_{\text{obs}}^{(1)}$ to be fed into the network, in the seek of a predictive function $\mathcal{P}$:

$$H_{\text{fp}}^{(last)} = \mathcal{P}(H_{\text{obs}}^{(1)}), \tag{3}$$

with distilled PK assisted. Since the privileged sequence does not exist at this moment, the embedded PK-Simulator should undertake the assistant role by distilling PK but without direct use of raw privileged data. A PK simulation loss is introduced in this step, to measure the discrepancy between the output of PK-Simulator and Priv-Encoder (i.e. how well does PK-Simulator imitate the PK representation learned by Priv-Encoder), and notably, the PK representation learned by Priv-Encoder has been well-trained previously and should remain fixed. Moreover, the distillation process is not damage-free. The PK-Simulator is doomed not to obtain entire PK from ITP, but is still capable of reflecting PK to some extent.

3.3   Training

Human poses are depicted mainly based on their 3D coordinates (i.e. 3D positions) or angles of body joints. In this section, we follow [8,31,34,43] to employ Mean Per Joint Position Error (MPJPE) for position-based representation, and Mean Angle Error (MAE) [34,35,43] for angle-based representation.

Loss for ITP-Network. The MPJPE interpolation loss is expressed as:

$$L_{\text{itp(mp)}} = \frac{1}{(N+T+P)J} \sum_{n=1}^{N+T+P} \sum_{j=1}^{J} \|\hat{\mathbf{m}}_{j,n} - \mathbf{m}_{j,n}\|_2 , \tag{4}$$

where $\hat{\mathbf{m}}_{j,n} \in \mathbb{R}^3$ is the interpolated jth joint position of the pose $\mathbf{x}_n$, and $\mathbf{m}_{j,n}$ is the corresponding ground truth one. Note that the length of the interpolated sequence should be consistent with the padded observed/privileged sequences (i.e. $N+T+P$), and is denoted as $\textbf{ItPredX}_{1:N+T+P}$. This design is inspired by [34], which calculates the sum of l_2 over the entire sequence sample, and we extend it to the longer observed-predicted-privileged window to fit our privileged design. Meanwhile, the minimization on $L_{\text{itp(mp)}}$ ensures that the optimal PK representation is obtained by Priv-Encoder, denoted as $\mathbf{E}_m$.

Similarly, the MAE interpolation loss is expressed as:

$$L_{\text{itp(ma)}} = \frac{1}{(N+T+P)K} \sum_{n=1}^{N+T+P} \sum_{k=1}^{K} \|\hat{\mathbf{a}}_{k,n} - \mathbf{a}_{k,n}\|_1 , \tag{5}$$

where $\hat{\mathbf{a}}_{k,n}$ is the interpolated kth angle of the pose $\mathbf{x}_n$, and $\mathbf{a}_{k,n}$ is the corresponding ground truth one. We minimize $L_{\text{itp(ma)}}$ to gain the optimal output of the Priv-Encoder represented as $\mathbf{E}_a$.

Loss for FP-Network. As FP is aimed at imitating the interpolation process, then the input form should maintain the length of $N+T+P$ in previous step, and the predicted sequence is also the same, denoted as $\textbf{FPredX}_{1:N+T+P}$. But notably, we only take into account the loss of $N+T$ poses because the following P ones are not our prediction target, and the corresponding ground truth (i.e. the privileged sequence) is not observable for this step. To measure the discrepancy between the predicted sequence and its ground truth, we present MPJPE prediction loss

$$L_{\text{fp(mp)}} = \frac{1}{(N+T)J} \sum_{n=1}^{N+T} \sum_{j=1}^{J} \|\hat{\mathbf{m}}_{j,n} - \mathbf{m}_{j,n}\|_2 \tag{6}$$

for position-based joint representation and MAE prediction loss

$$L_{\text{fp(ma)}} = \frac{1}{(N+T)K} \sum_{n=1}^{N+T} \sum_{k=1}^{K} \|\hat{\mathbf{a}}_{k,n} - \mathbf{a}_{k,n}\|_1 \tag{7}$$

for angle-based one. Meanwhile, we denote the output of the PK-Simulator as $\mathbf{S}_m$ for MPJPE and $\mathbf{S}_a$ for MAE, which approximate $\mathbf{E}_m$ and $\mathbf{E}_a$ respectively to implement distillation process. The PK simulation loss L_{simu} (i.e. PKSL) we introduce to measure this approximation is formulated as:

$$L_{\text{simu(mp)}} = \|\mathbf{S}_m - \mathbf{E}_m\|_F \quad \text{or} \quad L_{\text{simu(ma)}} = \|\mathbf{S}_a - \mathbf{E}_a\|_F . \tag{8}$$

Therefore, the MPJPE/MAE total loss are:

$$L_{\text{total(mp)}} = L_{\text{fp(mp)}} + \lambda L_{\text{simu(mp)}} \quad \text{or} \quad L_{\text{total(ma)}} = L_{\text{fp(ma)}} + \lambda L_{\text{simu(ma)}}, \quad (9)$$

where λ is the relative weight of the final prediction error and the simulation error, and is set to 0.6.

4   Experiments

To evaluate our proposed model, we conduct experiments on benchmarked motion capture datasets, including Human3.6M (H3.6M), CMU-Mocap, and 3DPW datasets. In this section, we first introduce these datasets, the evaluation metrics, and the baselines which we compare with, and then present our results.

4.1   Datasets and Evaluation Metrics

Human3.6M. (H3.6M) [18], depicting seven actors which perform 15 actions (walking, eating, smoking, discussing, etc.), is the most widely used dataset for human motion processing tasks. Each human pose is represented by 32 joints to form a skeleton. In line with previous methods [14,22,34,35], we set the global rotation and translation to zero and down-sample the sequences to 25 frames per second. We train our model on Subject 1 (S1), S6, S7, S8, S9 and test on S5 the same as [14,22,34,35].

CMU-Mocap. Based on [22], eight actions are selected for experiments after removing sequences with multiple actors, insufficient poses, or actions with repetitions. The other pre-processing operations are the same as on H3.6M.

3DPW. The 3D Pose in the Wild dataset [47] consists of 60 sequences about both indoor and outdoor actions captured by a moving camera at 30 fps. We follow the setting in [34] to evaluate the effectiveness of our models on challenging activities.

Evaluation Metrics. We employ Mean Per Joint Position Error (MPJPE) [18] in millimeter [8,34,43] to measure the position discrepancy between the interpolated/predicted joint and the corresponding ground truth, and Mean Angle Error (MAE) [34,35,43] to measure the angle one. As is stated in [34] that MAE may fail due to ambiguous representation, we focus mainly on MPJPE results.

4.2   Baselines

Recent methods are involved to evaluate the effectiveness of our model, denoted as Res.sup. [35], Traj-GCN [34], MSR-GCN [8] and STS-GCN [43]. Specifically, Traj-GCN [34] is the first work that introduces an unconstrained graph convolutional network on human motion prediction. MSR-GCN [8] presents a GCN with

Table 1. Comparisons of short-term MPJPE error on H3.6M dataset. The best result is highlighted in bold.

Millisecond (ms)	Walking				Eating				Smoking				Discussion				Directions			
	80	160	320	400	80	160	320	400	80	160	320	400	80	160	320	400	80	160	320	400
Res. sup [35]	29.4	50.8	76.0	81.5	16.8	30.6	56.9	68.7	23.0	42.6	70.1	82.7	32.9	61.2	90.9	96.2	35.4	57.3	76.3	87.7
Traj-GCN [34]	12.3	23.0	39.8	46.1	8.4	**16.9**	33.2	40.7	8.0	16.2	31.9	38.9	12.5	27.4	58.5	71.7	9.0	19.9	43.4	**53.7**
MSR-GCN [8]	12.2	22.7	38.6	45.2	8.4	17.1	**33.0**	40.4	8.0	16.3	31.3	38.2	12.0	26.8	57.1	69.7	8.6	**19.7**	**43.3**	53.8
STS-GCN [43]	16.7	27.1	43.4	51.0	11.7	18.9	35.2	43.3	12.3	19.8	35.6	42.3	15.3	28.1	58.5	71.9	12.8	23.7	51.1	63.2
PK-GCN	**8.9**	**15.9**	**28.0**	**31.6**	**8.1**	17.7	33.6	41.8	**7.4**	**14.3**	**24.4**	**29.2**	**10.3**	**22.9**	**42.0**	**47.2**	**8.6**	23.7	46.5	56.2

Millisecond (ms)	Greeting				Phoning				Posing				Purchases				Sitting			
	80	160	320	400	80	160	320	400	80	160	320	400	80	160	320	400	80	160	320	400
Res. sup [35]	34.5	63.4	124.6	142.5	38.0	69.3	115.0	126.7	36.1	69.1	130.5	157.1	36.3	60.3	86.5	95.9	42.6	81.4	134.7	151.8
Traj-GCN [34]	18.7	38.7	77.7	93.4	10.2	21.0	42.5	52.3	13.7	29.9	66.6	84.1	15.6	32.8	65.7	79.3	10.6	**21.9**	**46.3**	57.9
MSR-GCN [8]	16.5	37.0	77.3	93.4	**10.1**	20.7	41.5	51.3	12.8	29.4	67.0	85.0	14.8	32.4	66.1	79.6	10.5	22.0	**46.3**	57.8
STS-GCN [43]	18.7	34.9	71.6	86.4	13.7	22.4	43.6	53.8	16.4	30.4	67.6	84.7	19.1	35.8	70.2	83.1	10.6	24.6	47.8	57.9
PK-GCN	**13.3**	**27.2**	**67.3**	**83.1**	11.4	**20.2**	**37.7**	**43.2**	**9.1**	**23.6**	**65.8**	**81.2**	**15.2**	**31.4**	**57.9**	68.0	**10.1**	24.6	47.8	**57.3**

Millisecond (ms)	Sittingdown				Takingphoto				Waiting				Walkingdog				Walkingtogether			
	80	160	320	400	80	160	320	400	80	160	320	400	80	160	320	400	80	160	320	400
Res. sup [35]	47.3	86.0	145.8	168.9	26.1	47.6	81.4	94.7	30.6	57.8	106.2	121.5	64.2	102.1	141.1	164.4	26.8	50.1	80.2	92.2
Traj-GCN [34]	16.1	31.1	61.5	75.5	9.9	20.9	45.0	56.6	11.4	24.0	50.1	61.5	23.4	46.2	83.5	96.0	10.5	21.0	38.5	45.2
MSR-GCN [8]	16.1	31.6	62.5	76.8	9.9	21.0	44.6	56.3	10.7	23.1	**48.3**	**59.2**	**20.7**	42.9	**80.4**	**93.3**	10.6	20.9	37.4	**43.9**
STS-GCN [43]	22.1	37.2	66.5	79.4	14.5	23.4	47.8	59.4	14.5	24.8	50.4	62.0	26.5	46.1	83.6	97.3	14.3	23.9	41.3	49.1
PK-GCN	**11.5**	**27.5**	**56.8**	**67.3**	**7.6**	**16.1**	**39.7**	**51.3**	**9.5**	**23.0**	55.9	63.6	21.3	**42.4**	83.7	95.1	**9.4**	**19.3**	**36.3**	44.8

Table 2. Comparisons of long-term MPJPE error on some actions in H3.6M dataset. The best result is highlighted in bold.

Millisecond (ms)	Walking		Eating		Smoking		Discussion		Directions		Greeting	
	560	1000	560	1000	560	1000	560	1000	560	1000	560	1000
Res. sup [35]	81.7	100.7	79.9	100.2	94.8	137.4	121.3	161.7	110.1	152.5	156.1	166.5
Traj-GCN [34]	54.1	59.8	53.4	77.8	50.7	72.6	91.6	121.5	**71.0**	101.8	115.4	148.8
MSR-GCN [8]	52.7	63.0	**52.5**	77.1	49.5	71.6	88.6	117.6	71.2	**100.6**	116.3	147.2
STS-GCN [43]	58.0	70.2	57.4	82.6	55.5	76.1	91.1	118.9	79.9	109.6	106.3	136.1
PK-GCN	**42.5**	**47.0**	57.9	**69.7**	**33.3**	**60.2**	**75.8**	112.0	74.7	101.9	**90.1**	**108.8**

multi-scale residual structure which abstracts human poses on different levels. STS-GCN [43] realizes cross-talk of space and time within only one graph, and is able to factorize the graph into separable space and time matrices for better understanding of both features. We follow them to predict 10 (i.e. short-term) or 25 (i.e. long-term) poses with the observed 10 poses. It should be added that errors in [8, 34, 35] are shown by per frame, while the one in [43] is shown by averaging on all previous frames. To keep in line with Traj-GCN and MSR-GCN, we re-demonstrate the error in [43] as the same protocol in [8, 34, 35].

4.3 Implement Details

We implement our model using PyTorch [39] on an NVIDIA 2080TI GPU. The optimizer is ADAM [20], and the learning rate is set to 0.0005 with a 0.96 decay every two epochs. Each GC-Layer has a dropout rate of 0.5, with the learnable weight matrix $\mathbf{W}$ of size 256×256. The batch size is set to 16. The ITP-Network and the FP-Network are trained separately. We first train the former one for 50

Table 3. Comparisons of average MPJPE error (left) and MAE error (right) on H3.6M dataset. The best result is highlighted in bold.

Millisecond (ms)	Average-MPJPE						Average-MAE					
	80	160	320	400	560	1000	80	160	320	400	560	1000
Res. sup [35]	34.7	62.0	101.1	115.5	135.8	167.3	0.36	0.67	1.02	1.15	–	–
Traj-GCN [34]	12.7	26.1	52.3	63.5	81.6	114.3	0.32	0.55	0.91	1.04	1.27	1.66
MSR-GCN [8]	12.1	25.6	51.6	62.9	81.1	114.2	–	–	–	–	–	–
STS-GCN [43]	16.3	28.1	54.4	65.8	85.1	117.0	0.31	0.57	0.91	1.03	1.22	1.61
PK-GCN	**10.8**	**23.3**	**48.2**	**57.4**	**76.1**	**106.4**	**0.29**	**0.54**	**0.85**	**0.96**	**1.15**	**1.57**

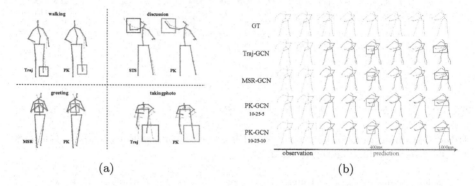

(a)   (b)

Fig. 3. (a) Visualized comparisons between three baselines [8,34,43] and PK-GCN on actions *walking, discussion, greeting, takingphoto* in H3.6M at the 1000 ms testpoint (i.e. 25th frame). Performances marked in green boxes are better than in red. The dashed lines denote ground truth. (b) Visualized comparisons of short-term and long-term predictions on a motion sequence *Washwindow* in CMU-Mocap. We show the ground truth, Traj-GCN [34], MSR-GCN [8], ours with 5 privileged poses of PK, and ours with 10 privileged poses of PK. The prediction deviations on left wrist are marked with red/green boxes. Our results are much closer to the ground truth.

epochs, then fix it and train the latter for another 50 epochs. The size of our model is 2.8M for both stages.

4.4 Results

Following the baselines [8,34,43], we evaluate our prediction performance by showing the results of 400 ms short-term and 1000 ms long-term predictions on H3.6M, CMU-Mocap, and 3DPW with 10-pose sequence observed. The length of the privileged sequence offered to PK-GCN is also set to 10.

H3.6M. Table 1 and Table 2 show quantitative comparisons for MPJPE error between short/long-term prediction and the ground truth. We find that error obtained by PK-GCN is smaller than other baselines in most cases. Particularly, activities with larger ranges of motions, such as *discussion* and *takingphoto*, achieve more improvements than the others, in that the distilled PK restricts the overall moving trend/orientation of an activity from the future further away.

Table 4. Comparisons of average MPJPE error of short/long-term prediction on CMU-Mocap (left) and 3DPW (right) datasets. The best results are highlighted in bold.

Millisecond (ms)	CMU-Average						3DPW-Average				
	80	160	320	400	560	1000	200	400	600	800	1000
Res. sup [35]	24.0	43.0	74.5	87.2	105.5	136.3	113.9	173.1	191.9	201.1	210.7
Traj-GCN [34]	11.5	20.4	37.8	46.8	55.8	86.2	35.6	67.8	90.6	106.9	117.8
MSR-GCN [8]	**8.1**	18.7	34.2	42.9	53.7	83.0	-	-	-	-	-
PK-GCN	9.4	**17.1**	**32.8**	**40.3**	**52.2**	**79.3**	**34.8**	**66.2**	**88.1**	**104.3**	**114.2**

Taking a sequence from *greeting* as an example, when the person makes a bow with hands folded in front, the prediction trajectory of hands is forced to move from the chest to down with PK foretelling that the hands will be at down in the end. On the other hand, the failure of *eating* and *sitting* confirms our assumption that activities with relatively motionless status are less likely to benefit much from our model, as the information in observations is sufficient to generate a nearly static sequence.

We further present the average MPJPE and MAE errors in Table 3, wherein the omitted cells indicate no data source available. Meanwhile, visualization of prediction at 1000 ms testpoint on four actions in H3.6M is given in Fig. 3 (a).

CMU-Mocap and 3DPW. Similar experiments are conducted on CMU-Mocap and 3DPW datasets, and the MPJPE errors of which are shown in Table 4. Apparently, our PK-GCN achieves state-of-the-art performance on CMU-Mocap among the baselines. In Fig. 3 (b), qualitative visualization results of *Washwindow* are demonstrated with the ground truth. The prediction results of Traj-GCN [34], MSR-GCN [8], our PK-GCN with 5 privileged poses of PK, and ours with 10 privileged poses of PK, are from the top to the bottom. These comparisons show that our model performs better than that of the baselines. It should be emphasized that the first and second numbers behind our model indicate the length of the observed sequence and the predicted sequence, while the third number n means that we train our ITP-Network by introducing n privileged poses to learn PK, and distill it to assist the final prediction. Errors in Table 1, 2, 3, 4 are all obtained with PK of 10 poses.

In addition, the improvement achieved on 3DPW proves that PK is effective when faced with more complex data, but notably, it should be guaranteed that poses in one sample should be consistent. Two irrelevant actions in one sequence sample (such as *arguing* to *dancing*) is not suitable for PK distillation.

4.5   Ablation Study

In this section, we conduct more experiments on three parts for deeper analysis on our PK-GCN. Following the previous notation, any numbers of the form a-b-c indicate predicting b poses on a historical poses, with c poses of PK introduced.

Interpolation Results. During the training of ITP, the loss between the interpolated sequence and the corresponding ground truth is minimized. In Fig. 4 (a),

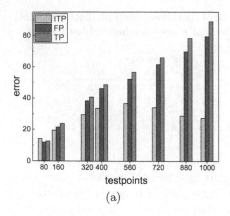 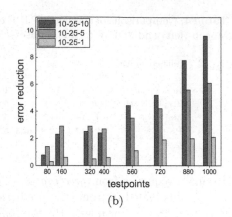

(a)   (b)

Fig. 4. (a) The average MPJPE 10-25-10 interpolated error from ITP, final predicted error from FP, and error obtained under traditional prediction pattern (TP) on CMU-Mocap. (b) Comparison of the advancement achieved with different lengths of PK on CMU-Mocap.

among the eight testpoints within the range of 1000 ms, the interpolation error show the performance of first increasing then decreasing, which is consistent with the variation trend of general interpolation problems, and the final prediction error appears a continuous increasing trend as expected.

A phenomenon easily neglected has emerged, that the interpolation process yields higher error than extrapolation at the beginning testpoint (i.e. 80 ms), which seemingly contradicts our previous statement that interpolation often yields better results than extrapolation. In fact, human motions are of highly smoothness with little difference between adjacent frames, and therefore the beginning predicted poses are quite close to observations. In other words, 10 poses of observation is sufficient to predict the following few frames directly. However, when the Priv-Encoder is involved in ITP to form an interpolation structure, the Obs-Encoder is compelled to sacrifice part of its original predictive property, to collaborate with Priv-Encoder for an *overall* (especially long-term) better prediction performance and thereby a relatively accurate representation of PK. Concerning FP-Network, where we reduce the weight of PKSL, it is acceptable even if the PK simulation is not *that* accurate, as PK just serves as an assistance in the extrapolation process, which leads to a continuous error-increase trend as standard extrapolation does, but lower than that without PK assisted. We regard the traditional prediction pattern that has no PK involved as TP, and the discrepancy between FP and TP is due to the distilled PK taking effects.

Privileged Sequences with Different Lengths. We further set the length of the privileged sequence to 10, 5, 1 and 0, to evaluate how different lengths of privileged poses influence the final prediction performance. When the privileged length is down to 0, the two-step structure vanishes and is equivalent to

Table 5. Comparisons of MPJPE error of 10-25-10 prediction on baselines with/without PSL and our PK-GCN on CMU-Mocap.

Millisecond (ms)		Average					
		80	160	320	400	560	1000
Traj-GCN [34]	w/o PSL	13.9	24.8	43.3	52.7	55.8	86.2
	1*PSL/0.6*PSL	14.3/14.2	26.0/25.3	44.6/43.9	54.2/53.7	57.6/56.6	88.4/87.2
MSR-GCN [8]	w/o PSL	**10.5**	23.1	39.7	48.8	53.7	83.0
	1*PSL/0.6*PSL	11.2/10.6	24.0/23.6	41.6/39.3	49.5/48.8	55.5/54.3	85.6/85.0
PK-GCN		11.8	**21.5**	**38.3**	**46.2**	**52.2**	**79.3**

predicting directly without PK (i.e. TP). In Fig. 4 (b), we plot the advancement of PK-GCN trained with PK obtained from different lengths of privileged sequences on CMU-Mocap. From the figure, once PK is introduced, the final prediction performance is improved even when there only exists 1 privileged pose of PK. The higher error reduction of 10-25-5 than 10-25-10 at early testpoints indicates that too much PK may become a burden for short-term prediction.

Baselines with PK. In order to a) explore the impact of introducing PK on baselines under the traditional prediction pattern, and b) dispel the uncertainty whether our progress is *only* due to PK while irrelevant to our two-step structure, we re-train Traj-GCN [34] and MSR-GCN [8] by also predicting poses in the privileged window and adding a loss (i.e. Privileged Sequence Loss, PSL) on them. Table 5 shows errors of baselines with/without PSL for 10–25-10 prediction. We further involve a reduction of PSL weight to 0.6, in line with the weight λ of PKSL in PK-GCN.

From the table, baselines with PSL yield even higher errors than without PSL, where the gap in-between exactly reflects the superiority of our two-step design. For baselines, when introducing PSL, the minimization of the total loss transforms the original 25-pose prediction into a 35-pose one. Since extrapolation becomes much harder when the prediction goes far, the last 10 poses, not belonging to the prediction object, waste big proportion of model resource and therefore lead to a worse performance of the previous 25 poses. Although an alleviation on PSL weight provides limited improvement, the direct use of PSL still harms the 25-pose prediction. However, our two-step spirit allows PK-GCN to remove these wastes during the training of FP-Network, focusing mainly on the prediction of 25 poses as we need.

5 Conclusion

In this paper, we introduce the overlooked poses existing after the predicted sequence to provide PK for human motion prediction from the view of interpolation. We extend the research window to the observed-predicted-privileged sequence, and propose a two-step model PK-GCN, wherein the ITP-Network learns a PK representation while interpolating the middle sequence, and the FP-Network predicts with the distilled PK assisted. Moreover, a novel PK-Simulator embedded in FP approximates the PK representation to implement the distillation process, enabling FP to imitate the behavior of ITP, and thereby keep the merits of interpolation during the final prediction. Our model outperforms the state-of-the-art methods on three benchmarked datasets, especially those activities with large ranges of motions.

Acknowledgements. This work was supported in part by the National Natural Science Foundation of China (NO. 62176125, 61772272).

References

1. Aliakbarian, S., Saleh, F.S., Salzmann, M., Petersson, L., Gould, S.: A stochastic conditioning scheme for diverse human motion prediction. In: CVPR, pp. 5223–5232 (2020)
2. Bai, S., Kolter, J.Z., Koltun, V.: An empirical evaluation of generic convolutional and recurrent networks for sequence modeling. arXiv preprint arXiv:1803.01271 (2018)
3. Butepage, J., Black, M.J., Kragic, D., Kjellstrom, H.: Deep representation learning for human motion prediction and classification. In: CVPR, pp. 6158–6166 (2017)
4. Cho, J.H., Hariharan, B.: On the efficacy of knowledge distillation. In: ICCV, pp. 4794–4802 (2019)
5. Corona, E., Pumarola, A., Alenyà, G., Moreno-Noguer, F.: Context-aware human motion prediction. In: CVPR, pp. 6992–7001 (2020)
6. Cui, Q., Sun, H., Li, Y., Kong, Y.: A deep bi-directional attention network for human motion recovery. In: IJCAI, pp. 701–707 (2019)
7. Cui, Q., Sun, H., Yang, F.: Learning dynamic relationships for 3D human motion prediction. In: CVPR, pp. 6519–6527 (2020)
8. Dang, L., Nie, Y., Long, C., Zhang, Q., Li, G.: MSR-GCN: multi-scale residual graph convolution networks for human motion prediction. In: ICCV, pp. 11467–11476 (2021)
9. Dong, M., Xu, C.: Skeleton-based human motion prediction with privileged supervision. IEEE Trans. Neural Netw. Learn. Syst. (2022)
10. Fernando, B., Herath, S.: Anticipating human actions by correlating past with the future with Jaccard similarity measures. In: CVPR, pp. 13224–13233 (2021)
11. Fragkiadaki, K., Levine, S., Felsen, P., Malik, J.: Recurrent network models for human dynamics. In: ICCV, pp. 4346–4354 (2015)
12. Gopalakrishnan, A., Mali, A., Kifer, D., Giles, L., Ororbia, A.G.: A neural temporal model for human motion prediction. In: CVPR, pp. 12116–12125 (2019)
13. Gu, C., et al.: Ava: a video dataset of spatio-temporally localized atomic visual actions. In: CVPR, pp. 6047–6056 (2018)
14. Gui, L.Y., Wang, Y.X., Liang, X., Moura, J.M.: Adversarial geometry-aware human motion prediction. In: ECCV, pp. 786–803 (2018)
15. Hernandez, A., Gall, J., Moreno-Noguer, F.: Human motion prediction via spatio-temporal inpainting. In: ICCV, pp. 7134–7143 (2019)
16. Hinton, G., Vinyals, O., Dean, J.: Distilling the knowledge in a neural network. arXiv preprint arXiv:1503.02531 (2015)
17. Hong, M., Xie, Y., Li, C., Qu, Y.: Distilling image dehazing with heterogeneous task imitation. In: CVPR, pp. 3462–3471 (2020)

18. Ionescu, C., Papava, D., Olaru, V., Sminchisescu, C.: Human3.6m: large scale datasets and predictive methods for 3D human sensing in natural environments. IEEE Trans. Pattern Anal. Mach. Intell. **36**(7), 1325–1339 (2013)
19. Jain, A., Zamir, A.R., Savarese, S., Saxena, A.: Structural-RNN: deep learning on spatio-temporal graphs. In: CVPR, pp. 5308–5317 (2016)
20. Kingma, D.P., Ba, J.: Adam: a method for stochastic optimization. arXiv preprint arXiv:1412.6980 (2014)
21. Koppula, H.S., Saxena, A.: Anticipating human activities for reactive robotic response. In: IROS, p. 2071 (2013)
22. Li, C., Zhang, Z., Lee, W.S., Lee, G.H.: Convolutional sequence to sequence model for human dynamics. In: CVPR, pp. 5226–5234 (2018)
23. Li, M., Chen, S., Zhao, Y., Zhang, Y., Wang, Y., Tian, Q.: Dynamic multiscale graph neural networks for 3D skeleton based human motion prediction. In: CVPR, pp. 214–223 (2020)
24. Liang, M., et al.: Learning lane graph representations for motion forecasting. In: Vedaldi, A., Bischof, H., Brox, T., Frahm, J.-M. (eds.) ECCV 2020. LNCS, vol. 12347, pp. 541–556. Springer, Cham (2020). https://doi.org/10.1007/978-3-030-58536-5_32
25. Liu, J., Shahroudy, A., Xu, D., Wang, G.: Spatio-temporal LSTM with trust gates for 3D human action recognition. In: Leibe, B., Matas, J., Sebe, N., Welling, M. (eds.) ECCV 2016. LNCS, vol. 9907, pp. 816–833. Springer, Cham (2016). https://doi.org/10.1007/978-3-319-46487-9_50
26. Liu, X., Yin, J., Liu, J., Ding, P., Liu, J., Liu, H.: Trajectorycnn: a new spatio-temporal feature learning network for human motion prediction. IEEE Trans. Circuits Syst. Video Technol. **31**(6), 2133–2146 (2020)
27. Liu, Y., Chen, K., Liu, C., Qin, Z., Luo, Z., Wang, J.: Structured knowledge distillation for semantic segmentation. In: CVPR, pp. 2604–2613 (2019)
28. Liu, Z., et al.: Motion prediction using trajectory cues. In: ICCV, pp. 13299–13308 (2021)
29. Ma, H., Li, J., Hosseini, R., Tomizuka, M., Choi, C.: Multi-objective diverse human motion prediction with knowledge distillation. In: CVPR, pp. 8161–8171 (2022)
30. Ma, T., Nie, Y., Long, C., Zhang, Q., Li, G.: Progressively generating better initial guesses towards next stages for high-quality human motion prediction. In: CVPR, pp. 6437–6446 (2022)
31. Mao, W., Liu, M., Salzmann, M.: History repeats itself: human motion prediction via motion attention. In: Vedaldi, A., Bischof, H., Brox, T., Frahm, J.-M. (eds.) ECCV 2020. LNCS, vol. 12359, pp. 474–489. Springer, Cham (2020). https://doi.org/10.1007/978-3-030-58568-6_28
32. Mao, W., Liu, M., Salzmann, M.: Generating smooth pose sequences for diverse human motion prediction. In: ICCV, pp. 13309–13318 (2021)
33. Mao, W., Liu, M., Salzmann, M.: Weakly-supervised action transition learning for stochastic human motion prediction. In: CVPR, pp. 8151–8160 (2022)
34. Mao, W., Liu, M., Salzmann, M., Li, H.: Learning trajectory dependencies for human motion prediction. In: ICCV, pp. 9489–9497 (2019)
35. Martinez, J., Black, M.J., Romero, J.: On human motion prediction using recurrent neural networks. In: CVPR, pp. 2891–2900 (2017)
36. Mishra, A., Marr, D.: Apprentice: using knowledge distillation techniques to improve low-precision network accuracy. arXiv preprint arXiv:1711.05852 (2017)
37. Monti, A., Porrello, A., Calderara, S., Coscia, P., Ballan, L., Cucchiara, R.: How many observations are enough? knowledge distillation for trajectory forecasting. In: CVPR, pp. 6553–6562 (2022)

38. Paden, B., Čáp, M., Yong, S.Z., Yershov, D., Frazzoli, E.: A survey of motion planning and control techniques for self-driving urban vehicles. IEEE Trans. Intell. Veh. **1**(1), 33–55 (2016)
39. Paszke, A., et al.: Automatic differentiation in pytorch (2017)
40. Pavllo, D., Feichtenhofer, C., Auli, M., Grangier, D.: Modeling human motion with quaternion-based neural networks. Int. J. Comput. Vis. **128**(4), 855–872 (2020)
41. Romero, A., Ballas, N., Kahou, S.E., Chassang, A., Gatta, C., Bengio, Y.: Fitnets: hints for thin deep nets. arXiv preprint arXiv:1412.6550 (2014)
42. Shen, Z., He, Z., Xue, X.: Meal: multi-model ensemble via adversarial learning. In: AAAI, pp. 4886–4893 (2019)
43. Sofianos, T., Sampieri, A., Franco, L., Galasso, F.: Space-time-separable graph convolutional network for pose forecasting. In: ICCV, pp. 11209–11218 (2021)
44. Sun, J., Lin, Z., Han, X., Hu, J.F., Xu, J., Zheng, W.S.: Action-guided 3D human motion prediction. NeurIPS **34**, 30169–30180 (2021)
45. Tung, F., Mori, G.: Similarity-preserving knowledge distillation. In: ICCV, pp. 1365–1374 (2019)
46. Vapnik, V., Vashist, A.: A new learning paradigm: learning using privileged information. Neural Netw. **22**(5–6), 544–557 (2009)
47. Von Marcard, T., Henschel, R., Black, M.J., Rosenhahn, B., Pons-Moll, G.: Recovering accurate 3D human pose in the wild using IMUs and a moving camera. In: ECCV, pp. 601–617 (2018)
48. Wang, T., Yuan, L., Zhang, X., Feng, J.: Distilling object detectors with fine-grained feature imitation. In: CVPR, pp. 4933–4942 (2019)
49. Xu, M., Gao, M., Chen, Y.T., Davis, L.S., Crandall, D.J.: Temporal recurrent networks for online action detection. In: CVPR, pp. 5532–5541 (2019)
50. Yan, S., Xiong, Y., Lin, D.: Spatial temporal graph convolutional networks for skeleton-based action recognition. In: AAAI (2018)
51. Yang, C., Xie, L., Su, C., Yuille, A.L.: Snapshot distillation: teacher-student optimization in one generation. In: CVPR, pp. 2859–2868 (2019)
52. Yuan, Y., Kitani, K.: DLow: diversifying latent flows for diverse human motion prediction. In: Vedaldi, A., Bischof, H., Brox, T., Frahm, J.-M. (eds.) ECCV 2020. LNCS, vol. 12354, pp. 346–364. Springer, Cham (2020). https://doi.org/10.1007/978-3-030-58545-7_20
53. Zhao, P., Xie, L., Zhang, Y., Wang, Y., Tian, Q.: Privileged knowledge distillation for online action detection. arXiv preprint arXiv:2011.09158 (2020)
54. Zhong, C., Hu, L., Zhang, Z., Ye, Y., Xia, S.: Spatio-temporal gating-adjacency GCN for human motion prediction. In: CVPR, pp. 6447–6456 (2022)

Structural Triangulation: A Closed-Form Solution to Constrained 3D Human Pose Estimation

Zhuo Chen⬤, Xu Zhao(✉)⬤, and Xiaoyue Wan⬤

Department of Automation, Shanghai Jiao Tong University, Shanghai, China
{chzh9311, zhaoxu, sherrywaan}@sjtu.edu.cn

Abstract. We propose *Structural Triangulation*, a closed-form solution for optimal 3D human pose considering multi-view 2D pose estimations, calibrated camera parameters, and bone lengths. To start with, we focus on embedding structural constraints of human body in the process of 2D-to-3D inference using triangulation. Assume bone lengths are known in prior, then the inference process is formulated as a constrained optimization problem. By proper approximation, the closed-form solution to this problem is achieved. Further, we generalize our method with *Step Constraint Algorithm* to help converge when large error occurs in 2D estimations. In experiment, public datasets (Human3.6M and Total Capture) and synthesized data are used for evaluation. Our method achieves state-of-the-art results on Human3.6M Dataset when bone lengths are known and competitive results when they are not. The generality and efficiency of our method are also demonstrated.

Keywords: Multi-view 3D human pose estimation · Constrained optimization · Triangulation

1 Introduction

3D Human Pose Estimation (3D HPE) is a fundamental yet difficult problem in computer vision. From the perspective of sensor utilization, this problem could be divided into two categories, namely, monocular [9,17,18,26,27,33,36] and multi-view [2,6,10,16,20,25] based, both obtaining increasing attention in recent years. Different from monocular 3D HPE, multi-view systems can acquire depth information theoretically from multiple measurement instead of merely

---

This work has been funded in part by the NSFC grants 62176156 and the Science and Technology Commission of Shanghai Municipality under Grant 20DZ2220400. The code is available at https://github.com/chzh9311/structural-triangulation.

Supplementary Information The online version contains supplementary material available at https://doi.org/10.1007/978-3-031-20065-6_40.

S. Avidan et al. (Eds.): ECCV 2022, LNCS 13665, pp. 695–711, 2022.
https://doi.org/10.1007/978-3-031-20065-6_40

training data, which is an inherent advantage. In this paper, we try to improve multi-view 3D HPE via a novel pathway.

Triangulation is a basic and common module in 3D HPE, which estimates the 3D joint positions by leveraging their 2D counterparts measured in multiple images to 3D space [13]. The module is usually used in a two-stage procedure: first estimating 2D poses in multi-view images, then applying triangulation to obtain 3D human pose [16,19,32]. Remarkable progress has been achieved under this pipeline. However, conventional triangulation methods are designed for individual points, and the associations between points are not specially considered. But human body possesses an innate structure, containing relations between joints, which can provide strong priors for 3D HPE. To overcome this shortcoming, some methods, like 3DPSM [4,23] and post-process methods [10,18] are proposed, and exceed previous methods in precision so the effectiveness of using human priors is demonstrated. But some aspects are still out of focus of these works. 3DPSM is usually time-consuming due to the large search space; post-process methods have limited effects, where priors are not naturally and thoroughly applied.

Ideally, we expect to build a grace and simple expression for the optimal 3D pose considering 2D poses, camera settings, and human priors. Thus, 2D-to-3D inference can be more efficient and accurate, while keeping the simplicity of linear triangulation. We start from a simple idea of embedding structural information in triangulation. The problem is formulated as a process to minimize weighted square re-projection error. Using predefined bone lengths, a constrained optimization problem is constructed. The solution to this problem is made closed-form by proper approximations and linearizations. It directly produces the optimal pose of a certain tree structure with predefined edge lengths. We call this novel triangulation method as *Structural Triangulation* (ST).

To make aforementioned approximations feasible, some conditions should be satisfied, but they may not always hold in practice, causing ST to diverge. So we propose the *Step Constraint Algorithm* (SCA) to promote its adaptivity. The algorithm split the optimization problem into small steps. and the optimal pose gets updated when stepping from one point to the next, meanwhile, the preconditions are satisfied at each step.

We conduct comprehensive experimental evaluation to the proposed method. First, we use the 2D backbone provided in [16] to capture 2D pose, and then the 3D pose is estimated using our method. Two public datasets, Human3.6M [15] and Total Capture [29], are used. We achieve state-of-the-art result with precise bone lengths, and promising result with bone lengths estimated from T-pose. Next, we generate multi-view 2D estimations by shifting ground truth re-projection randomly, and the test result shows that our method can work well regardless of the choice of 2D backbones. Finally, the efficiency of our method is validated by comparing the run time with previous methods.

In sum, the contributions of this work are in the following three aspects.

1. We construct a novel constrained 3D HPE problem and derive a closed-form solution called Structural Triangulation. For the first time, structural priors (bone lengths) are embedded in triangulation in a simple analytical form.
2. We design the Step Constraint Algorithm, which helps ST converge when 2D pose estimations are not precise enough.
3. We evaluate our method on Human3.6M Dataset, Total Capture Dataset, and synthesized data. The precision and efficiency of our method are validated by comparing with other state-of-the-art methods.

2   Related Work

Recently, many works are proposed to solve the problem pf Multi-view 3D HPE. We roughly classify them as geometry and optimization based methods.

Geometry-Based Methods. Epipolar geometry is the theory basis of triangulation. A two-stage framework is commonly used in multi-view 3D HPE [16,20,25]. In the first stage, 2D poses are estimated from the given views separately. Secondly, 3D pose is inferred from 2D poses by triangulation methods. This framework is straightforward, practical, and proved effective. Recent works make difference mainly in 2D estimations or 3D volume introduction. The triangulation itself, however, remain conventional as concluded in [13].

Under the framework of epipolar geometry, feature fusion is another concern in recent [6,24,25,32,35]. The method generally connects 2D backbones of different views to fuse information from all views before outputting 2D heatmaps. The effectiveness of this kind of methods in promoting both 2D and 3D estimations is validated. Further, [25] provides a light-weighted version, and [32] contributes in generalizing it.

Recently, in some works, information loss in the process of 2D pose estimation, is significantly concerned. So the 2D estimation step is eliminated and 3D pose is obtained directly from multi-view images, like fusing heatmaps directly in volumes [16] and 3D pose regression [30]. Although having the benefit of precision improvement, the computational cost is also increased.

Optimization-Based Methods. Early works of multi-view 3D HPE start from optimizing human pose given 2D features [12]. Although the development of deep learning offers a better solution for feature extraction, optimization is still active in recent works. Such methods generally solve the problem by designing an objective function that fuses all known information.

The most common and effective method under this pipeline, is 3D Pictorial Structure Model (3DPSM). The original PSM was first proposed in [11] to match certain structures on images. After PSM achieved promising performance in 2D pose estimation [34], 3DPSM was developed to deal with 3D HPE [2,4]. It succeeds in optimizing posterior probability given observations and human priors. But global optimization is generally implemented by grid sampling and therefore is time-consuming. To balance time and precision, recurrent PSM is proposed in [24] so a faster convergence is realized.

Besides 3DPSM, there are other ways to solve such a problem. In [10], SMPL model [3] is used to fit 3D pose by optimization so that pose and shape are reconstructed simultaneously. Shape models can eliminate some unfeasible poses. However, the increase in pose precision is quite limited because of redundant shape parameters. In [5], Maximum A Posteriori (MAP) is integrated with trust region method [8] to optimize 3D pose, but it suffers from initialization.

In conclusion, to achieve better precision, the current models become increasingly complicated with less efficiency. Moreover, current triangulation methods generally treat joints independently, yet the significance of human priors has been well proved. So in this work, we propose to produce optimal 3D pose based on a closed-form solution by utilizing human priors in a novel way.

3   Method

The whole framework of the proposed method is shown in Fig. 1. In this section, we focus on describing the process of formulation, while the detailed inductions can be found in Sec. 1 in Supplementary.

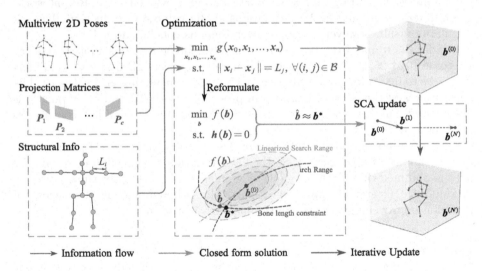

Fig. 1. The framework of our method. With the 2D poses and camera projection matrices, we formulate a quadratic objective function based on re-projection error, which produces the initial solution $b^{(0)}$. And bone lengths are used as constraints to relate joints. Then the unknowns are converted from joint positions to bone vectors and the problem is reformulated. In the lower middle figure, brown line is the analytical search range given by KKT condition, we linearize it so that a closed-form solution $\hat{b}$ is derived, which is close to the analytical one b^*. It is further used in SCA to update from $b^{(0)}$ to the final solution $b^{(N)}$. (Color figure online)

3.1   Problem Formulation

Given multiple images taken by several calibrated cameras, we are going to estimate the 3D human pose in scene, where only the case of a single person is considered. Suppose the 2D poses in each view, along with the lengths of body bones, could be available, obtained from other existing methods.

First of all, we model the overall human body as a tree structure with joints as nodes and bones as edges, where in total $n + 1$ joints indexed by $i = 0, 1, \ldots, n$ are considered, and 0 represents the root joint (usually hip). Bones are represented in form of (i, j), where i is the parent of j. Mark the bone set as $\mathcal{B}$.

Now we can organize the known and unknown variables. The projection matrices P_k of all cameras indexed from 1 to c, the bone length L_j of each bone (i, j), the 2D location $\hat{x}_{i,k}$ of joint i on image from camera k, and the corresponding weight $w_{i,k}$ (usually the belief given by 2D backbones) are known. The 3D coordinates of human joints, denoted by $x_0, x_1, \ldots, x_n$, are unknowns and need to be determined. Then our goal is to minimize the total weighted square re-projection error with predefined values of all the bone lengths, i.e.:

$$\min_{x_0, x_1, \ldots, x_n} \sum_{i=0}^{n} \sum_{k=1}^{c} w_{i,k} \left\| H^{-1} \left(P_k H(x_i) \right) - \hat{x}_{i,k} \right\|^2, \tag{1}$$

$$\text{s.t.} \quad \|x_i - x_j\| = L_j, \forall (i, j) \in \mathcal{B}. \tag{2}$$

where H maps a inhomogeneous coordinate to equivalent homogeneous one. Note that H^{-1} is the inverse process of H, not the function inverse:

$$y \xrightarrow{H} \begin{bmatrix} y \\ 1 \end{bmatrix}; \quad \begin{bmatrix} y \\ w \end{bmatrix} \xrightarrow{H^{-1}} \frac{y}{w} (w \neq 0). \tag{3}$$

3.2   Closed-Form Solution

Reformulation of the Objective Function. First, we analyze the objective function Eq. (1). Split the projection matrix by $P_k = [P_k^{u\top}, p_k]^\top$ where $P_k^u \in \mathbb{R}^{2 \times 4}, p_k \in \mathbb{R}^4$. Then the objective function in Eq. (1) equals to

$$g(x) = \sum_{i=0}^{n} \sum_{k=1}^{c} w'_{i,k} \left\| P_k^u H(x_i) - \hat{x}_{i,k} \left(p_k^\top H(x_i) \right) \right\|^2. \tag{4}$$

where $x = [x_0^\top, x_1^\top, \ldots, x_n^\top]^\top$ represents the full human pose, and the weight becomes $w'_{i,k} = w_{i,k} / \left(p_k^\top H(x_i) \right)^2$. We can ignore the term $p_k^\top H(x_i)$ and directly treat $w'_{i,k}$ as the new weight. Thus $g(x)$ becomes a quadratic function, whose minimization is trivial. Actually, if all weights are set the same, minimizing $g(x)$ will produce exactly the same result as linear-LS triangulation [13].

To better describe the constraints on bones in Eq. (2), we represent human pose with bones. Define a *bone vector* as a vector that points from proximal to distal joint of the bone. Use b_i to represent the bone vector with distal joint i $(i = 1, 2, \ldots, n$, no b_0 because joint 0 is the root). Like x, we concatenate all bone vectors to a single column vector $b = [b_1^\top, b_2^\top, \ldots, b_n^\top]^\top$. Since b implies no global position, $\tilde{b} = [x_0^\top, b^\top]$ is a comprehensive representation of human pose.

As is indicated in Kinematic Chain Space (KCS) [31], the conversion between joint positions and bone vectors is a linear process, and can be accomplished by matrix multiplication. Here, the matrix is defined as $\mathcal{G} = \{\mathcal{G}_{ij}\}$, where

$$\mathcal{G}_{ij} = \begin{cases} I_3, & \text{if } i = j \text{ or joint } j - 1 \text{ is the parent of } i - 1; \\ -I_3, & \text{if joint } j - 1 \text{ is the child of } i - 1; \\ 0, & \text{otherwise.} \end{cases} \tag{5}$$

Note that no bone vector can be linearly represented by the others, so all row vectors of $\mathcal{G}$ are linearly independent and $\mathcal{G}$ is non-singular. Then we have

$$\tilde{b} = \mathcal{G}x; \quad x = \mathcal{G}^{-1}\tilde{b}. \tag{6}$$

The conversion by Eq. (6) is not thorough because in $\tilde{b}$, x_0 is the root joint coordinate, not a bone vector. The constraints set no direct limit on x_0, so we can fix b and solve x_0 from an unconstrained quadratic optimization problem, which has a trivial solution. The optimal x_0 is obtained via the following equation:

$$x_0 = Qb + p \tag{7}$$

where $Q \in \mathbb{R}^{3 \times 3n}, p \in \mathbb{R}^3$ are known constants, whose expressions are provided in Sec. 1.1 Supplementary. We illustrate the full converting process from joint coordinates to bone vectors, as well as the inverse process, in Fig. 2.

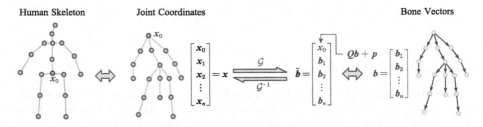

Fig. 2. The conversion between joint coordinates and bone vectors. From left to right, the human skeleton is represented by joint positions x, which is further converted to $\tilde{b}$ by Eq. (6). Then the root joint coordinate x_0 is expressed by bone vectors and the conversion to b is done. The process is fully invertible.

With Eq. (7), Eq. (4) can be formulated as a quadratic function of b. To help description, we mark the line as $l_{i,k}$, which connects the optic center of camera k and the 2D estimation of joint i on the image plane. Then we derive a property of the formulation of Eq. (4) and leave its proof in Sec. 1.2 in Supplementary.

Property 1. The optimization problem in Eq. (1) and (2) is formulated as

$$\min_{b} \quad f(b) = \frac{1}{2}b^{\top}Ab - \beta^{\top}b + d \tag{8}$$

$$\text{s.t.} \quad h_i(b_i) = \|b_i\|^2 = L_i^2, \ i = 1, 2, \ldots, n. \tag{9}$$

where $A \in \mathbb{R}^{3n \times 3n}$ is a symmetric positive semi-definite constant matrix, $\beta \in \mathbb{R}^{3n}$ and $d \in \mathbb{R}$ are constants. A is singular if and only if $\exists i = 0, 1, \ldots, n$, there holds $\forall k_1, k_2 = 1, 2, \ldots, c, l_{i,k_1} /\!/ l_{i,k_2}$.

Actually when A is singular, excluding the factor of 2D estimation errors, all camera optic centers have to be approximately collinear with one of the joints. If we set up the cameras properly, such conditions can be easily avoided.

Approximation and Linearization. In Eq. (8), $f(b)$ is a convex function, but due to non-affine constraint in Eq. (9), the optimization problem is non-convex. Generally, we need to consider the necessary condition, i.e., Karush-Kuhn-Tucker (KKT) condition. The condition produces a nonlinear equation group, but we show that it is solvable under proper approximations.

Define three vectors: $h(b) = [h_1(b_1), h_2(b_2), \ldots, h_n(b_n)]^{\top}$ represents the function that calculates square bone length vector given b, $L = [L_1^2, L_2^2, \ldots, L_n^2]^{\top}$ is the target square bone length vector, and $\lambda = [\lambda_1, \lambda_2, \ldots, \lambda_n]^{\top}$ is the multiplier vector. Then the Lagrange multiplier is written as:

$$l(b, \lambda) = f(b) + \lambda^{\top}(h(b) - L). \tag{10}$$

The KKT condition gives us an equation group purely about λ.

$$h\left((A + 2\Lambda)^{-1}\beta\right) = L, \tag{11}$$

where $\Lambda = \text{diag}\{\lambda\} \otimes I_3$ and "$\otimes$" is the Kronecker product. The unknown λ is inside a matrix inverse, which is highly non-linear. But we can make linear approximations about $(A + 2\Lambda)^{-1}$ under certain assumptions. To support this, we introduce the following lemma (proof see Sec. 1.3 in Supplementary):

Lemma 1. *Suppose $A, B \in \mathbb{R}^{n \times n}$ and A is non-singular. $\|\cdot\|$ is the spectral norm of a matrix. If $\|A^{-1}B\| < 1$, then $A - B$ is non-singular and the following inequality holds:*

$$\left\|(A - B)^{-1} - (A^{-1} + A^{-1}BA^{-1})\right\| \leq \frac{\|A^{-1}B\|^2 \|A^{-1}\|}{1 - \|A^{-1}B\|}. \tag{12}$$

By substituting -2Λ for B in Lemma 1, we directly conclude that

$$(A + 2\Lambda)^{-1} \approx A^{-1} - 2A^{-1}\Lambda A^{-1}. \tag{13}$$

Equation (13) provides a linear approximation for matrix inverse. After replacing $(A + 2\Lambda)^{-1}$ in Eq. (11), there is still a second-order term of λ. We can abandon it with respect to $\|2A^{-1}\Lambda\| \ll 1$ so that Eq. (11) becomes totally linear. Define some notations. $L^{(i)} = \left[\|b_1^{(i)}\|^2, \|b_2^{(i)}\|^2, \cdots, \|b_n^{(i)}\|^2 \right]^\top$, $b^{(0)} = A^{-1}\beta$ is the minimizer of $f(b)$ with no constraint, which is later referred to as the *initial solution*, and $D_n^{(3 \times 1)} \in \mathbb{R}^{3n \times n}$ represents a block diagonal matrix whose diagon is filled by n 3-dimensional all-1 column vectors. Then the expression of λ is

$$\lambda = \frac{1}{4} \left(D_n^{(3\times1)\top} \mathrm{diag}\{b^{(0)}\} A^{-1} \mathrm{diag}\{b^{(0)}\} D_n^{(3\times1)} \right)^{-1} (L^{(0)} - L). \tag{14}$$

The bone vector estimation is given by

$$\hat{b} = b^{(0)} - 2A^{-1}\Lambda b^{(0)}, \tag{15}$$

With Eq. (15), we can derive root joint coordinate from $\hat{b}$ by Eq. (7), and then applying Eq. (6) reversely will produce the optimal pose. This is the theory of Structural Triangulation. The process is illustrated more clearly in Fig. 3a.

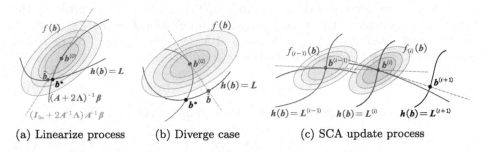

(a) Linearize process   (b) Diverge case   (c) SCA update process

Fig. 3. Illustrations of solution finding process. Groups of ellipses represent the level sets of objective functions. In (a) and (b), blue curve is the bone length constraint, brown line is the range of $(A + \Lambda)^{-1}\beta$ as λ varies, and orange virtual line is the linearized range by Eq. (13). b^* is the analytical solution while $\hat{b}$ is the approximated one. They are usually close, as (a) shows, but sometimes not, like (b). For diverge cases, SCA will be helpful. Figure (c) shows the update process, where we mark variables at adjacent stages with different colors. From step $i - 1$ to i, the solution is updated to $b^{(i)}$ in the way shown in (a) and a new quadratic objective function is formed with $b^{(i)}$ as the minimizer. Then we target for the bone lengths constraint, i.e., $h(b) = L^{(i+1)}$ and repeat the process. (Color figure online)

3.3 SCA: Step Constraint Algorithm

The above analysis is under the assumption of $\|2A^{-1}\Lambda\| \ll 1$, but sometimes it fails to hold. Structural Triangulation may be regarded as a process to correct a pose so that the squared bone length vector changes from $L^{(0)}$ to the target

---

Algorithm 1: Structural Triangulation + Step Constraint Algorithm

---

Input : $A, \beta, L, N, \alpha_0, \alpha_1, \ldots, \alpha_N$

Output: b

1 $T^{(0)} \longleftarrow A^{-1}$;

2 $b^{(0)} \longleftarrow T^{(0)}\beta$;

3 **for** $i \leftarrow 1$ **to** N **do**

4     $L_{real}^{(i-1)} \longleftarrow h(b^{(i-1)})$; // when i=1, initialize L0.

5     $L^{(i)} \longleftarrow \left(\alpha_i L_{real}^{(i-1)} + (\alpha_{i-1} - \alpha_i)L\right)/\alpha_{i-1}$;

6     $\lambda \longleftarrow \left(D_n^{(3\times1)\top}\mathrm{diag}\{b^{(i-1)}\}T^{(0)}\mathrm{diag}\{b^{(i-1)}\}D_n^{(3\times1)}\right)^{-1}(L_{real}^{(i-1)} - L^{(i)})/4$;

7     $\Lambda \longleftarrow \mathrm{diag}\{\lambda\} \otimes I_3$;

8     $T^{(i)} \longleftarrow (I_n - 2T^{(i-1)}\Lambda)T^{(i-1)}$;

9     $b^{(i)} \longleftarrow T^{(i)}\beta$;

10 **end**

11 $b \longleftarrow b^{(N)}$;

L. In Eq. (14), it is obvious that if the initial bone lengths are far from target, which is possible when 2D estimations are not precise enough, then $\|\lambda\|$ can be large and the assumption may be contradicted. Consequently, the result may diverge (as shown in Fig. 3b).

However, this case is still in reach with some modifications. We can interpolate some points between $L^{(0)}$ and L and use ST to correct pose from one point to the next. Adjacent points are near so the assumption is confirmed to hold each time. This is the basic idea of *Step Constraint Algorithm*.

First we need to determine a *step number* N and $N-1$ step points between $L^{(0)}$ and L, which are marked as $L^{(1)}, L^{(2)}, \ldots, L^{(N-1)}$. Let $L^{(N)} = L$. A way to generate them is by constructing a decreasing series $\{\alpha_i\}_{i=0}^N$ ($\alpha_0 = 1, \alpha_N = 0$), and calculate by linear interpolating, where the series serve as the proportions, i.e., $L^{(i)} = \alpha_i L^{(0)} + (1-\alpha_i)L$. However, in iteration from $i-1$ to i, $h(b^{(i)})$ does not exactly equal to the predefined splitting point $L^{(i)}$ due to approximations. So a better way is to determine these splitting points in-the-run. In other words, we first calculate the real square bone length vector $L_{real}^{(i-1)} = h(b^{(i-1)})$, then find $L^{(i)}$ by $(L^{(i)} - L)/\alpha_i = (L^{(i-1)} - L)/\alpha_{i-1}$.

$$L^{(i)} = \frac{\alpha_i}{\alpha_{i-1}}L_{real}^{(i-1)} + \frac{\alpha_{i-1} - \alpha_i}{\alpha_{i-1}}L \tag{16}$$

In our experiment, we use the in-the-run method and determine $\{\alpha_i\}_{i=0}^N$ simply by $\alpha_i = (N-i)/N$. In experiment, if not specified, then N is set to 3.

The pseudo-code of ST + SCA is shown in Algorithm 1. Besides $b^{(i)}$ and $L^{(i)}$, $T^{(i)}$ represents another important variable to update - the approximation of $(A + 2\Lambda)^{-1}$. The update is done in line 8 of Algorithm 1, by the linear expression provided in Eq. (13). Figure 3c illustrates the whole process.

4   Experiments

4.1   Experimental Settings

Datasets and Metrics. In the experiments, we use two public datasets: Human3.6M [15] and Total Capture [29] datasets.

In Human3.6M Dataset, the images are acquired by 4 cameras at 50 Hz and the dataset contains more than 3.6 million images, which are organized by different subjects. By convention, S1, S5, S6, S7, and S8 are used for training, while S9 and S11 are used for testing. Note that Human3.6M provides pose labels in 32-joint form, and we follow the common criterion to use the 17-joint subset.

In Total Capture Dataset, 8 cameras are used to capture images, where we use cameras 1, 3, 5, and 7. The data are also organized by subjects. The test set contains "Walking-2"(W2), "Freestyle-3"(FS3), and "Acting-3" (A3) of all 5 subjects. Note that the original labels are arranged in 21-joint form, with which "Nose" joint in previous 17-joint model fails to make correspondence. So we use a 16-joint subset (details see Sec. 2 in Supplementary) for ST, where "RightArm" and "Neck", "LeftArm" and "Neck" are not directly connected in the original skeletal model and the lengths may vary in a limited range.

For metrics, we use Mean Per Joint Position Error (MPJPE) to measure joint precision, along with some new metrics on bone lengths. Two types of MPJPEs are used: (1) absolute MPJPE (MPJPE-ab) calculate the position errors directly without alignment; (2) relative MPJPE (MPJPE-re), usually known as Protocol #1 [22], measures position errors after aligning the pelvis. Since labels of some subsets in S9 is shifted, we follow [16] to present MPJPE-ab after eliminating these bad samples. Additionally, we introduce some metrics on bones: (1) Mean Per Bone Length Error (MPBLE) measures the average over all bone length errors, the same as MPLLE in [21]. (2) Mean Bone Length Standard deviation (MBLS) equals the square root of average variance over all bone lengths. (3) Percentage of Inlier Bones (PIB) is the rate of bones with reasonable lengths, to be exact, 0.8~1.2 times the true bone lengths.

The Choice of 2D Estimation Model. Because 2D HPE is not involved in our work, a proper 2D backbone is needed to test our method on public datasets. We choose the algebraic triangulation model by Iskakov et al. [16] because it is a precise and simple framework. The model, which serves as our *baseline*, consists of a 2D backbone and a SVD triangulation module. It also provides beliefs for cameras which we use as weights in Eq. (4). In our experiment, the model is pretrained on MPII [1] and fine-tuned on Human3.6M dataset. We keep the 2D backbone and replace the triangulation module with our method.

Virtual Test Settings. We aim to prove that our method outperforms conventional triangulation methods once the bone lengths are known, regardless of camera settings and 2D backbones. So we synthesize 2D estimations randomly by modeling the 2D estimations as "ground truth re-projection + Gaussian noise".

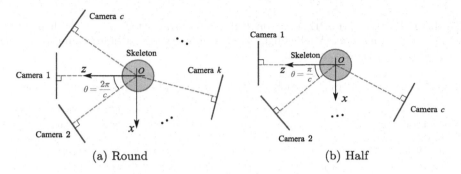

(a) Round (b) Half

Fig. 4. Two patterns to set up virtual cameras, where c is the camera number and θ is the angle interval between adjacent camera optic axes. O is the global coordinate origin, which all skeleton root joints are aligned to. All image planes are orthogonal to the principal optic axes, while these axes all point to O and distribute uniformly in predefined angle range, i.e., 2π in (a) and π in (b). The axis of camera 1 is right on z axis.

After generating c virtual cameras with projection matrices $P_1, P_2, \ldots, P_c$, we can re-project 3D pose and get the ground truth 2D poses. Concatenate these coordinates as a column vector $x_{2d} \in \mathbb{R}^{2(n+1)}$. Then generate a noise vector $\epsilon \in \mathbb{R}^{2(n+1)}$, each of whose element obeys Gaussian distribution $N(0, \sigma)$. Finally the generated 2D estimations are calculated by $\hat{x}_{2d} = x_{2d} + \epsilon$.

In our experiment, all cameras share the same intrinsics, along with two types of camera extrinsic settings: round and half (Fig. 4). We use ground truth labels from sampled test set of Human3.6M Dataset - totally 2181 frames - as our base 3D pose to confirm feasibility and variety.

4.2 Experiments on Public Datasets

Quantitative Results and Analysis. The test result of two datasets are reported in Table 1, 2, and 3.

The acquisition of bone lengths is simple in public datasets since we can use the ground truth of one frame to calculate. In practice, it is also available by mature human measurement techniques. However, we need to consider the errors in bone length measurements. We therefore provide a simple estimation by averaging all symmetric bone lengths in linear triangulation results of T-pose frames. We mark experiments using such bone lengths with "*".

Table 1 and 2 show the experiment result on Human3.6M dataset. Besides linear triangulation, we also implement an iterative optimization algorithm - Lagrangian algorithm [7] - to solve the problem described by Eq. (8) and (9) to serve as a baseline (details see Sec. 3.1 in Supplementary). As is shown, our method exceeds the previous state-of-the-art method (Volumetric Triangulation [16]) by 4.9% in MPJPE-re. Absolute MPJPE error is also reduced by 0.15 mm. We can also observe that SCA helps lower MPJPE-re by 0.87 mm and MPJPE-

Table 1. Relative MPJPE (mm) on Human3.6M Dataset compared with previous state-of-the-art methods. We highlight tests in our method in light gray, and "*" means estimated bone lengths are used.

Method	Dire.	Disc.	Eat	Greet	Phone	Photo	Pose	Purch.
Tome et al. [28]	43.3	49.6	42.0	48.8	51.1	64.3	40.3	43.3
Yihui and Rui et al.[14]	28.9	32.5	26.6	28.1	28.3	29.3	28.0	36.8
Remelli et al. [25]	27.3	32.1	25.0	26.5	29.3	35.4	28.8	31.6
Qiu et al. [24]	23.98	26.71	23.19	24.30	24.77	22.82	24.12	28.62
AT by Iskakov et al. [16]	20.42	22.83	19.98	19.48	21.73	20.69	19.11	22.39
VT by Iskakov et al. [16]	18.06	19.63	19.45	18.36	19.95	19.36	17.79	20.68
Lagrangian algorithm [7]	19.33	20.85	18.68	18.49	21.77	20.05	17.97	20.89
Ours*	18.67	21.27	17.95	18.90	21.00	19.18	18.48	22.07
Ours (w/o SCA)	17.56	20.03	16.22	17.86	20.49	19.06	17.38	22.08
Ours	**17.37**	**19.70**	**15.56**	**17.46**	**19.61**	**18.82**	**16.95**	**20.24**

Method	Sit	SitD	Smoke	Wait	Walk	WalkD	WalkT	Avg.
Tome et al. [28]	66.0	95.2	50.2	52.2	51.1	43.9	45.3	52.8
Yihui and Rui et al. [14]	42.0	30.5	35.6	30.0	29.3	30.0	30.5	31.2
Remelli et al. [25]	36.4	31.7	31.2	29.9	26.9	33.7	30.4	30.2
Qiu et al. [24]	32.12	26.87	30.98	25.56	25.02	28.07	24.37	26.21
AT by Iskakov et al. [16]	26.10	31.80	22.85	20.94	20.13	23.50	21.12	22.33
VT by Iskakov et al. [16]	23.27	29.43	20.58	19.38	18.66	21.15	19.12	20.35
Lagrangian algorithm [7]	24.99	29.18	21.89	19.94	19.37	22.05	20.28	21.18
Ours*	23.34	28.17	20.73	20.27	20.25	21.87	20.19	20.86
Ours (w/o SCA)	24.07	29.87	20.44	19.83	17.96	20.97	18.91	20.22
Ours	**21.92**	**26.71**	**19.25**	**18.90**	**17.88**	**20.64**	**18.69**	**19.35**

Table 2. Average absolute MPJPE (mm) on Human3.6M Dataset.

Method	MPJPE-ab
Baseline	19.26
Vol. [16]	17.93
Ours*	18.90
Ours (w/o SCA)	17.98
Ours	**17.78**

Table 3. Relative MPJPE (mm) on Total Capture Dataset. The bone lengths used in tests of the last line are the average over all ground truth labels instead of one frame.

Method	W2	FS3	A3	Average
Baseline	**69.0**	65.8	56.0	63.3
Ours*	73.0	70.2	58.4	66.9
Ours	69.2	**60.2**	**50.2**	**59.6**

ab by 0.20 mm. Our method outperforms the iterative baseline, and reaches satisfying accuracy when imprecise bone lengths are used.

We also study how the step number N in SCA affects precision. Relatie MPJPE generally decreases with N and gets 19.33 mm at $N = 9$. However, when $N \geq 10$ the estimations in some frames will diverge, causing an abnormal error increase. So a relatively small number is recommended, like 3 in our tests.

In experiments on Total Capture Dataset, we focus on whether our method works in case some connection lengths are not actually fixed. We report the result in Table 3. Though our method does not correct 3D pose successfully when bone length estimations are imprecise, a 3.7 mm decrease in MPJPE-re error is obtained when bone lengths are known.

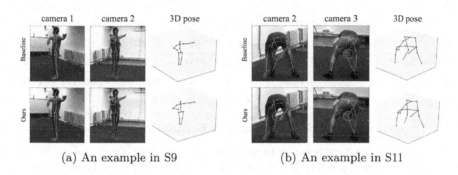

(a) An example in S9   (b) An example in S11

Fig. 5. Examples on how Structural Triangulation corrects human pose. The upper row is the result by SVD triangulation while the lower is by ours. Only 2 representative views are selected from the 4 views for illustration. The circled point in (a) gets 61.7% reduction in relative joint position error, while in (b) the reduction is 24.3%.

Qualitative Analysis. To describe how our method corrects poses, we take two examples from test subjects in Human3.6M dataset and mark the remarkably improved points with circles in Fig. 5. The initial pose possesses shorter right arms in Fig. 5a and longer right leg in Fig. 5b. We can see how the pose is corrected while pursuing the correct bone lengths.

Ablation Study. In this section, our major concern is the improvement on bone lengths of our method, and the affect of whether precise bone lengths are given. The metrics on bones proposed in Sect. 4.1 are used. We report the result in Table 4. The use of ground truth bone lengths is treated as a component to help analyze the effect of imprecise bone length input.

In the first two rows, it is clear that merely ST is enough to decrease MPBLE by over 35% in S9 and S11 even with estimated bone lengths. It implies the increase in bone length precision, yet we still need to study MBLS and PIB to conclude the reason. Actually, smaller MBLS means stabler bone lengths in estimation, and larger PIB indicates larger proportion of reasonable poses.

Compared to baseline, ST has the effect to stabilize bone lengths, and SCA makes the effect even stronger. In the last two rows, small MBLS and 100% PIB indicate that the bone lengths are nearly invariant, which proves that our method constrains the bone lengths in a strict way.

Table 4. Effects of whether SCA is involved ("SCA") or whether ground truth bone lengths are used ("GT"). The unit for MPBLE and MBLS is mm. PIB is presented in percentage (%). Down arrows mean the smaller the better while up arrows mean the contrary. "*" means estimated bone lengths are used.

Method	SCA	GT	S9			S11		
			MPBLE ↓	MBLS ↓	PIB ↑	MPBLE ↓	MBLS ↓	PIB ↑
Baseline	–	–	12.2	15.9	97.4	7.62	9.88	97.5
ST*	×	×	7.93	0.350	99.9	5.48	0.156	**100**
ST	×	✓	1.31	4.35	99.8	0.531	1.19	**100**
ST + SCA*	✓	×	7.93	**0.122**	**100**	5.48	0.0243	**100**
ST + SCA	✓	✓	**0.129**	0.151	**100**	**0.0555**	**0.0178**	**100**

4.3   Experiments on Synthesized 2D Estimations

We conduct experiments on data generated in the way proposed in Sect. 4.1, where noise standard deviation σ varies from 2 px to 20 px, and camera number c varies from 2 to 10 and all combinations are considered. Some representative results are plotted in Fig. 6 and the full results are available in Sec. 3.4 in Supplementary.

Clearly, our method shows better precision than SVD triangulation. In Fig. 6, we observe boundary effect in the promotion of ST, but ST has certain positive effect in all experiment settings. We also calculate the proportion of frames when ST outperforms the baseline under all combinations of σ and c which is always more than 82% and nearly 100% when there are more than 2 cameras. In conclusion, the generality of our method is validated.

4.4   Running Time

Now we would like to validate the computational efficiency. We conduct experiments to compare our method with Volumetric Triangulation Model [16], RPSM [24], and SVD Triangulation method. Since [16] does not generate 2D estimations but require algobraic model to generate a rough estimation, the time is how much the whole end-to-end process takes. We run different methods on the same computer with a 16-core 2.10 GHz Intel E5-2620 v4 CPU, an Nvidia Titan Xp GPU, 32 GB RAM. The experiment results are reported in Table 5.

As shown in Table 5, our method is much faster than RPSM and Volumetric Triangulation. Additionally, more steps in SCA is not costing much time. Though it takes more time than basic SVD triangulation, compared to time cost in 2D backbones (about 400 ms) in our test, the increase is not obvious.

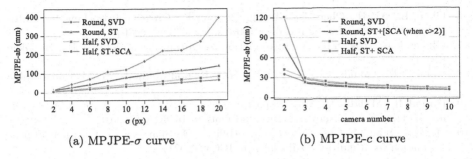

(a) MPJPE-σ curve   (b) MPJPE-c curve

Fig. 6. Curves on how absolute MPJPE varies with the change of noise standard deviation σ and camera number c. In (a) we set $c = 2$, while in (b) we set $\sigma = 10$ px. When there are only 2 cameras in round camera setting, they are right on the opposite directions to each other, which causes singularity in SCA. So in such experiments we eliminate SCA step and apply pure ST.

Table 5. Per frame inference time of different methods. The numbers of steps is the values of N used in SCA.

Method	SVD	RPSM [24]	Vol. [16]	Ours (3 steps)	Ours (9 steps)
Inference time (ms)	1.95	1.82×10^3	305.4	6.63	8.96

5   Conclusions

In this paper we formulate the problem of 2D-to-3D inference in multi-view 3D HPE as a constrained optimization problem, and propose a novel closed-form solution, i.e., Structural Triangulation. To further generalize our method, we design SCA to make it compatible with the situation when large error occurs in 2D estimations. Experiments on open datasets and synthesized data prove our method is effective, generally applicable, and efficient.

References

1. Andriluka, M., Pishchulin, L., Gehler, P., Schiele, B.: 2D human pose estimation: new benchmark and state of the art analysis. In: CVPR (2014)
2. Belagiannis, V., Amin, S., Andriluka, M., Schiele, B., Navab, N., Ilic, S.: 3D pictorial structures for multiple human pose estimation. In: CVPR (2014)
3. Bogo, F., et al.: Keep it SMPL: automatic estimation of 3D human pose and shape from a single image. In: Leibe, B., Matas, J., Sebe, N., Welling, M. (eds.) ECCV 2016. LNCS, vol. 9909, pp. 561–578. Springer, Cham (2016). https://doi.org/10.1007/978-3-319-46454-1_34
4. Burenius, M., Sullivan, J., Carlsson, S.: 3D pictorial structures for multiple view articulated pose estimation. In: CVPR (2013)
5. Chen, H., Guo, P., Li, P., Lee, G.H., Chirikjian, G.: Multi-person 3D pose estimation in crowded scenes based on multi-view geometry. In: Vedaldi, A., Bischof, H., Brox, T., Frahm, J.-M. (eds.) ECCV 2020. LNCS, vol. 12348, pp. 541–557. Springer, Cham (2020). https://doi.org/10.1007/978-3-030-58580-8_32

6. Chen, L., Ai, H., Chen, R., Zhuang, Z., Liu, S.: Cross-view tracking for multi-human 3D pose estimation at over 100 fps. In: CVPR (2020)
7. Chong, E.K., Zak, S.H.: An Introduction to Optimization. John Wiley, Hoboken (2004)
8. Conn, A.R., Gould, N.I., Toint, P.L.: Trust Region Methods. SIAM, Philadelphia (2000)
9. Dabral, R., Mundhada, A., Kusupati, U., Afaque, S., Sharma, A., Jain, A.: Learning 3D human pose from structure and motion. In: ECCV (2018)
10. Dong, Z., Song, J., Chen, X., Guo, C., Hilliges, O.: Shape-aware multi-person pose estimation from multi-view images. In: ICCV (2021)
11. Fischler, M., Elschlager, R.: The representation and matching of pictorial structures. IEEE Trans. Comput. C- **22**(1), 67–92 (1973). https://doi.org/10.1109/T-C.1973.223602
12. Gall, J., Stoll, C., de Aguiar, E., Theobalt, C., Rosenhahn, B., Seidel, H.P.: Motion capture using joint skeleton tracking and surface estimation. In: CVPR (2009)
13. Hartley, R.I., Sturm, P.: Triangulation. CVIU **68**(2), 146–157 (1997). https://doi.org/10.1006/cviu.1997.0547, http://www.sciencedirect.com/science/article/pii/S1077314297905476
14. He, Y., Yan, R., Fragkiadaki, K., Yu, S.I.: Epipolar transformers. In: CVPR (2020)
15. Ionescu, C., Papava, D., Olaru, V., Sminchisescu, C.: Human3.6m: large scale datasets and predictive methods for 3D human sensing in natural environments. TPAMI **36**(7), 1325–1339 (2014). https://doi.org/10.1109/TPAMI.2013.248
16. Iskakov, K., Burkov, E., Lempitsky, V., Malkov, Y.: Learnable triangulation of human pose. In: ICCV (2019)
17. Kolotouros, N., Pavlakos, G., Black, M.J., Daniilidis, K.: Learning to reconstruct 3d human pose and shape via model-fitting in the loop. In: ICCV (2019)
18. Li, J., Xu, C., Chen, Z., Bian, S., Yang, L., Lu, C.: Hybrik: a hybrid analytical-neural inverse kinematics solution for 3D human pose and shape estimation. In: CVPR (2021)
19. Li, X., Fan, Z., Liu, Y., Li, Y., Dai, Q.: 3D pose detection of closely interactive humans using multi-view cameras. Sensors **19**(12), 2831 (2019). https://doi.org/10.3390/s19122831, https://www.mdpi.com/1424-8220/19/12/2831
20. Lin, J., Lee, G.H.: Multi-view multi-person 3D pose estimation with plane sweep stereo. In: CVPR (2021)
21. Ma, X., Su, J., Wang, C., Ci, H., Wang, Y.: Context modeling in 3D human pose estimation: a unified perspective. In: CVPR (2021)
22. Martinez, J., Hossain, R., Romero, J., Little, J.J.: A simple yet effective baseline for 3D human pose estimation. In: ICCV (2017)
23. Pavlakos, G., Zhou, X., Derpanis, K.G., Daniilidis, K.: Harvesting multiple views for marker-less 3D human pose annotations. In: CVPR (2017)
24. Qiu, H., Wang, C., Wang, J., Wang, N., Zeng, W.: Cross view fusion for 3D human pose estimation. In: ICCV (2019)
25. Remelli, E., Han, S., Honari, S., Fua, P., Wang, R.: Lightweight multi-view 3D pose estimation through camera-disentangled representation. In: CVPR (2020)
26. Rhodin, H., et al.: Learning monocular 3D human pose estimation from multi-view images. In: CVPR (2018)
27. Sharma, S., Varigonda, P.T., Bindal, P., Sharma, A., Jain, A.: Monocular 3D human pose estimation by generation and ordinal ranking. In: ICCV (2019)
28. Tome, D., Toso, M., Agapito, L., Russell, C.: Rethinking pose in 3D: multi-stage refinement and recovery for markerless motion capture. In: 3DV (2018)

29. Trumble, M., Gilbert, A., Malleson, C., Hilton, A., Collomosse, J.: Total capture: 3d human pose estimation fusing video and inertial sensors. In: BMCV (2017)

30. Tu, H., Wang, C., Zeng, W.: VoxelPose: towards multi-camera 3D human pose estimation in wild environment. In: Vedaldi, A., Bischof, H., Brox, T., Frahm, J.-M. (eds.) ECCV 2020. LNCS, vol. 12346, pp. 197–212. Springer, Cham (2020). https://doi.org/10.1007/978-3-030-58452-8_12

31. Wandt, B., Ackermann, H., Rosenhahn, B.: A kinematic chain space for monocular motion capture. In: ECCV Workshops (2018)

32. Xie, R., Wang, C., Wang, Y.: Metafuse: a pre-trained fusion model for human pose estimation. In: CVPR (2020)

33. Xu, J., Yu, Z., Ni, B., Yang, J., Yang, X., Zhang, W.: Deep kinematics analysis for monocular 3D human pose estimation. In: CVPR (2020)

34. Yang, Y., Ramanan, D.: Articulated pose estimation with flexible mixtures-of-parts. In: CVPR (2011)

35. Yao, Y., Jafarian, Y., Park, H.S.: Monet: Multiview semi-supervised keypoint detection via epipolar divergence. In: ICCV (2019)

36. Zeng, A., Sun, X., Yang, L., Zhao, N., Liu, M., Xu, Q.: Learning skeletal graph neural networks for hard 3D pose estimation. In: ICCV (2021)

Audio-Driven Stylized Gesture Generation with Flow-Based Model

Sheng Ye[1], Yu-Hui Wen[1(✉)], Yanan Sun[1], Ying He[2], Ziyang Zhang[3], Yaoyuan Wang[3], Weihua He[4], and Yong-Jin Liu[1(✉)]

[1] CS Department BNRist, Tsinghua University, Beijing, China
{ye-c18,wenyh1616,sunyn20,liuyongjin}@tsinghua.edu.cn
[2] School of Computer Science and Engineering, Nanyang Technological University, Singapore, Singapore
yhe@ntu.edu.sg
[3] Advanced Computing and Storage Lab, Huawei Technologies Co Ltd., Shenzhen, China
{zhangziyang11, wangyaoyuan1}@huawei.com
[4] Department of Precision Instrument, Tsinghua University, Beijing, China
hwh20@tsinghua.edu.cn

Abstract. Generating stylized audio-driven gestures for robots and virtual avatars has attracted increasing considerations recently. Existing methods require style labels (e.g. speaker identities), or complex preprocessing of data to obtain the style control parameters. In this paper, we propose a new end-to-end flow-based model, which can generate audio-driven gestures of arbitrary styles with neither preprocessing nor style labels. To achieve this goal, we introduce a global encoder and a gesture perceptual loss into the classic generative flow model to capture both global and local information. We conduct extensive experiments on two benchmark datasets: the TED Dataset and the Trinity Dataset. Both quantitative and qualitative evaluations show that the proposed model outperforms state-of-the-art models.

Keywords: Stylized gesture · Flow-based model · Global encoder

1 Introduction

When people speak, they often make arm and hand movements that accompany what they say. These movements, called co-speech gestures, are important in human communication, as they contain rich non-verbal information [8,39]. Existing studies have shown that co-speech gestures can help listeners concentrate and better understand the meaning conveyed in oral messages [7,39]. Therefore, when developing virtual avatars or interactive robots, it is highly desired to generate natural co-speech gestures accompanying their messages, which can improve communication and enhance vividness and realism.

Supplementary Information The online version contains supplementary material available at https://doi.org/10.1007/978-3-031-20065-6_41.

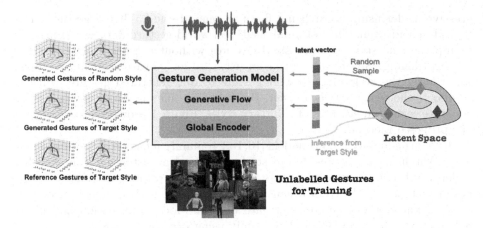

Fig. 1. Overview of our proposed stylized audio-driven gesture generation method. We jointly train a generative flow model with a global encoder using unlabelled gesture data. In the synthesis stage, we can manipulate the gesture style given an extra gesture sequence as the target style.

Yet, the problem of audio-driven co-speech gesture synthesis is challenging and intrinsically ill-posed due to the one-to-many relationship between audios and gestures, i.e., the same audio input may correspond to multiple reasonable gestures. Most of the early approaches are rule-based [9,25,26,40], which require complicated mapping rules from audio to motion. These approaches not only need a great deal of efforts in designing rules, but also are often too fragile to work for complicated application scenarios. In recent years, data-driven approaches [16,27,43] have demonstrated their potential in gesture generation. These methods utilize CNN or RNN based models, which are trained in an end-to-end manner. Since conventional deterministic networks that they use [16,27,43] tend to learn one-to-one mapping functions, the generated results often become the average of all potential target gestures and thereby lack diversity.

Furthermore, different people have different styles of co-speech gestures. Previous studies attempt to control the styles of generated gestures. Yoon et al. [42] and Ahuja et al. [2] directly use the speaker's identity as style label and embed it into a latent style space during training. However, it is often difficult to obtain such labelled data in the real-world application scenarios. Alexanderson et al. [5] provide more fine-grained style control, such as movement speed and hand position, but the price is a tedious preprocessing of motion data for obtaining control parameters.

Due to the multi-modal nature of co-speech gestures, we prefer stochastic over deterministic model. Flow-based generative models [10,18,24] can generate different plausible results for a single input by randomly sampling the latent distribution, which is much desired for the gesture synthesis task. Therefore in this paper, building upon MoGlow [18], we propose a probabilistic and autoregressive model using normalizing flows to generate audio-driven gestures. Due to widespread availability of unlabelled, real-world gesture data, we propose to manipulate the style of synthesized gestures without the need for style labels during training. Specifically, given an extra target gesture sequence as input, we transfer the style of the target gesture to our generated gesture, which is similar to the task of style transfer. By assigning different target styles, we can generate co-speech gestures of arbitrary styles. Figure 1 provides an overview of our proposed method.

Existing generative flow models [10,18,24] mainly focus on capturing dependency within local features. In our study, we also draw attention from AutoEncoder which can effectively capture the global feature. In particular, our proposed method jointly train a generative flow model with a global encoder in an AutoEncoder manner to aggregate both the local information and global information. Moreover, we find that only using ordinary L_1 or L_2 loss cannot effectively measure the difference between the real motion and the generated motion well. Inspired by the success of perceptual losses [22] used in image style transfer tasks, we design a new gesture perceptual loss to help the joint training process and improve the generation quality. We observe that our model can synthesize a large variety of natural and human-like gestures that match the audio input well. We evaluate our proposed model on two benchmark datasets: TED Dataset [43] and Trinity Dataset [12,29]. Results show that our approach surpasses other state-of-the-art methods in both datasets.

2   Related Work

2.1   Audio-Driven Gesture Synthesis

Early methods for generating co-speech gestures are typically rule-based [9,25, 26] before flourishing development of deep learning methods. Wagner et al. [40] provide a detailed survey of these rule-based methods, which require a great deal of human efforts to design mapping rules. To alleviate human efforts, some data-driven methods are proposed to learn the mapping between prosody features and motions. Specifically, Hidden Markov Models (HMMs) have been used to generate prosody-driven motion sequences [30,31].

In recent years, VAEs [23] and GANs [15] achieve a great success on image generation problems. These neural network models are also used to predict gesture sequences. Ginosar et al. [14] propose an encoder-decoder structure and train the network with both regression and adversarial losses. Li et al. [32] introduce a conditional VAE model to solve this co-speech gesture generation task.

Classic deep learning models (e.g. CNN or RNN) are deterministic and often suffer from the mean problem when applying to regression problems such as gesture synthesis. Although adversarial learning can reduce this problem to some extent, GAN has its limitations, including intractable log-likelihood and unstable training processes. Henter et al. [18] propose a probabilistic network to model the conditional probability distribution of gesture data, which can not only describe the one-to-many mapping elegantly but also increase the diversity of generated results. However, each flow step of their model only supports linear operations, restricting its expressiveness. Qian et al. [37] complement the audio input with a learnable vector, which reduces ambiguity and turns the one-to-many mapping between the input audio and generated gesture into a one-to-one mapping.

2.2   Style Transfer of Motion

Image style transfer, which extracts and transfers the artistic style of one image to another, has been well studied. Gatys et al. [13] first introduce a neural style transfer algorithm. Johnson et al. [22] train a feed-forward network to solve the optimization problem in real time. Huang et al. [21] propose an AdaIN layer to transfer arbitrary styles.

These image-oriented methods are further extended to motion style transfer. Holden et al. [20] introduce a framework that enables motion edition and style transfer. Du et al. [11] propose to use a conditional VAE to learn motion styles, which improve the efficiency of previous approaches. Aberman et al. [1] train their network with unpaired motion data using the AdaIN mechanism and can disentangle motion content and style automatically. Wen et al. [41] propose an unsupervised motion style transfer method using a generative flow model.

Similarly, in gesture synthesis, it is also desired to edit and/or transfer the style of the generated gestures. Though there are previous works on synthesizing such stylized gestures [14,30,35], these methods are only able to learn individual styles. To overcome the challenges, Yoon et al. [42] use speaker identity as an additional input and project it into a style embedding space. By sampling through this space, they can manipulate the gesture styles. Bhattacharya et al. [6] further improve their work [42] by adding an Affective Encoder to learn affective features from the seed poses. Ahuja et al. [2] introduce a supervised learning method that can perform gesture style preservation and style transfer tasks. Another study [5] provides high-level controls over gesturing styles, such as movement speed and spatial extent. But the motion data needs to be preprocessed first to extract control parameters. In contrast, our model is trained on unlabelled gesture data, and can transfer arbitrary styles without any preprocessing procedure, thereby is more suitable for practical applications.

3   Approach

3.1   Preliminaries on Generative Flow Model

Generative flows, which belongs to generative models, provide advantages such as tractable log-likelihood and efficient inference. Given a set of data $X = \{x_1, x_2, \ldots, x_n\}$, that subject to an unknown distribution, generative flows aim to model the probability distribution $p_\theta(X)$ of X by minimizing the negative log-likelihood:

$$NLL(X) = \frac{1}{n} \sum_{i=1}^{n} -\ln p_\theta(x_i) \tag{1}$$

Unlike VAEs or GANs, generative flows are capable of optimizing this negative log-likelihood exactly. The main idea is to find an invertible and differentiable function g that transforms a simple, fixed distribution Z to a new, complicated distribution X. As the function g is invertible, generative flows can perform efficient sampling as well as efficient inference: $x = g(z), z = g^{-1}(x)$, where x is a data sample and z is a latent variable corresponding to x.

The mapping function g can be extremely complex. To increase expressiveness, flow models compose plenty of simple nonlinear transformations $\{g_i\}_{i=1}^{L}$ together to construct the final function: $g = g_1 \circ g_2 \circ ... \circ g_L$. The transformation between two distributions can be described as follows

$$z = h_L \xrightarrow{g_L} h_{L-1} \xrightarrow{g_{L-1}} ... \xrightarrow{g_2} h_1 \xrightarrow{g_1} h_0 = x \tag{2}$$

$$z = g^{-1}(x) = g_L^{-1}(g_{L-1}^{-1}(...g_1^{-1}(x))) \tag{3}$$

$$x = g(z) = g_1(g_2(...g_L(z))). \tag{4}$$

The stacked sequence of inverse transformations $\{g_i^{-1}\}_{i=1}^{L}$ is called normalizing flow. By applying the change-of-variables formula, we can derive the exact log-likelihood of one data sample x as:

$$\ln p_\theta(x) = \ln p_\phi(z) + \sum_{i=1}^{L} \ln \left| \det \left(\frac{\partial h_i}{\partial h_{i-1}} \right) \right|, \tag{5}$$

where $p_\phi(z)$ is the tractable, fixed probability distribution (typically Gaussian distribution or Student's t distribution) and $\det \left(\frac{\partial h_i}{\partial h_{i-1}} \right)$ is the determinant of the Jacobian matrix of g_i^{-1}. Calculating the determinant of a dense matrix is computationally expensive. Thus, in usual cases, flow transformations are carefully designed to make the Jacobian matrix diagonal or triangular.

3.2 Generative Flow with Global Encoder

Our proposed model can be regarded as an autoregressive sequence-to-sequence model. When generating the t-th frame of a gesture sequence x, our model is conditioned on τ frames of previous poses $x_{t-\tau:t-1}$ and $\tau + 1$ frames of audio control signals $a_{t-\tau:t}$. Specifically, all the condition information are fed into every affine coupling layer in the network. Thus, the gesture synthesis procedure can be developed as:

$$p(x|a) = p(x_{1:\tau}|a_{1:\tau}) \prod_{t=\tau+1}^{T} p(x_t|x_{t-\tau:t-1}, a_{t-\tau:t}) \tag{6}$$

Previous studies [19,33,34] find that flow-based models have the problem of local dependency, meaning that each flow transformation mainly focuses on capturing dependency within local features. To address this issue, we design

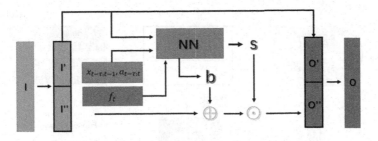

Fig. 2. Architecture of the affine coupling layer. We first split the input feature I into two parts, then keep the first part I' unchanged and transform the other I'' into O''. Finally, we concatenate O'' with O' to get the output. $\oplus$ denotes the element-wise sum and $\odot$ is the Hadamard product.

an additional global encoder, which is shared by every flow transformation, to provide the global information required by the flow model. The detailed structure of our global encoder can be found in Sect. 3.4. At each time step, this encoder embeds the previous pose histories and audio control signals separately and then integrates them to obtain the final global feature f_t. The global feature is then concatenated with original autoregressive poses as well as audio signals and fed into neural networks to produce the bias and scaling parameters $[b_t, s_t]$ used in affine coupling layers (shown in Fig. 2). Mathematically, at time step t, we denote the input feature and output feature of the affine coupling layer as I_t and O_t. The input is first split into two equal parts $[I'_t, I''_t]$. We keep half of the input unchanged, then shift and scale the other half of the input based on parameters extracted by the neural network of the affine coupling layer. The coupling operation can be defined as:

$$[O'_t, O''_t] = [I'_t, (I''_t + b_t) \odot s_t] \tag{7}$$

$$[b_t, s_t] = NN(I'_t; x_{t-\tau:t-1}; a_{t-\tau:t}; f_t) \tag{8}$$

where $\odot$ is the Hadamard product. Note that the inverse operation can also be easily obtained

$$[I'_t, I''_t] = \left[O'_t, s_t^{-1}O''_t - b_t\right]. \tag{9}$$

As Fig. 3 shows, we propose to jointly train the global encoder with the generative flow in an end-to-end manner. Specifically, we use the invertible flow model as our decoder and train our model like an AutoEncoder. The complete training process can be described as follows. Firstly, we transform the training gesture data into the latent vector conditioned on control signals and global features through the forward normalizing flow. In the meantime, we minimize the NLL loss derived in Sect. 3.1. Then, we sample from the latent, fixed distribution randomly to get the new latent vector and transform it into the synthesized gesture pose conditioned on the same global features and controls through the backward

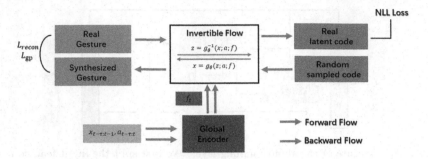

Fig. 3. Overview of our proposed training framework. Through the pass of the forward flow and backward flow, we can jointly train the global encoder with the generative flow to complement each other in an end-to-end manner.

normalizing flow. We simultaneously minimize the reconstruction loss L_{recon}, which measures the L_1 distance between the real motion and the synthesized motion. Through the pass of the forward flow, we train the flow model to take full advantage of global features. Through the pass of the backward flow, we train the global encoder to capture meaningful features. See the supplementary material for the detailed structure of the invertible flow.

3.3 Gesture Peceptual Loss

Our reconstruction loss L_{recon} computes the difference between the generated gesture and the ground-truth gesture. However, the low-level L_1 loss is insufficient to measure the difference well. Inspired by the image perceptual losses [22], we further propose a new gesture perceptual loss to train our model. To the best of our knowledge, there is no pre-trained inception network for gesture data (like VGG-Nets [38] for images). Therefore, we train our own feature extraction net using the training set. Our feature extractor has a convolutional encoder-decoder structure. Denote by x the real gesture motion, $\hat{x}$ the synthesized gesture motion, and ω the 4-th layer of our feature extractor encoder. As ω is a convolutional layer, $\omega(x)$ and $\omega(\hat{x})$ are feature maps of dimension $C \times H \times W$. Thus, we can describe our proposed loss as:

$$L_{gp}(\hat{x}, x) = \frac{1}{C \times H \times W} \|\omega(\hat{x}) - \omega(x)\|_1. \tag{10}$$

Note that this loss encourages synthesized motion and real motion to have similar feature representations. Our ablation study further demonstrates that this loss facilitates the joint training process of our model and improves the quality of generated results. Finally, we train our model with the combined loss:

$$L = NLL + \lambda_1 L_{recon} + \lambda_2 L_{gp}, \tag{11}$$

where λ_1 and λ_2 are the pre-defined weights. In our experiments, we empirically set $\lambda_1 = 1.0$ and $\lambda_2 = 0.1$.

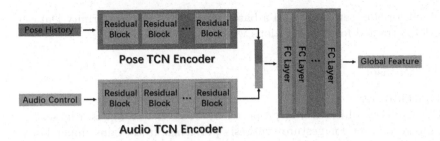

Fig. 4. Structure of proposed global encoder. Autoregressive pose histories and audio control signals are encoded as low-dimensional vectors by two TCN encoders, respectively. The two vectors are then concatenated together and passed through a series of fully connected layers to get the final global feature.

3.4 Network Structure

Our neural network builds upon the MoGlow [5] network. Specifically, we keep the structure of Actnorm layers and invertible 1×1 convolutions. As for affine coupling layers, we replace LSTMs with GRUs. We observe that in this task, GRU can generate results comparable to LSTM, but is more concise and computationally efficient, and has a faster convergence rate due to the fewer parameters. Besides, the previous MoGlow model with LSTM has a limitation in that the generated results rely more heavily on autoregressive histories than audio control signals. A possible reason for this is the overly complex gating mechanism of LSTM, which makes the network retain too much redundant information from previous states. Our proposed model with GRU can alleviate this problem to some extent. We also adapt the zero initialization technique proposed by Kingma et al. [24], making each affine coupling layer performs the identity function at the initial state.

Our global encoder (shown in Fig. 4) consists of a series of fully connected layers and two TCN (Temporal Convolution Network) encoders stacked by many residual building blocks. Each building block is initialized by Kaiming Normal [17] and includes four basic operations: a 1D convolution, a batch normalization, a residual operation, and a ReLU activation. Empirically, we assume that this architecture is designed to extract the global features of gestures and audio sequences and the correlations between them. Furthermore, the global encoder can be trained efficiently as it is based on temporal convolutions.

4 Experiments

We implement our network using PyTorch. Our model is optimized using Adam on an NVIDIA A100 GPU. We choose the Student's t distribution as the fixed latent distribution as it provides a more robust training process [4]. We conduct our experiments on two benchmark datasets (described in detail in Sect. 4.1), namely, TED Dataset and Trinity Dataset. For the TED Dataset, our model is trained for 80k iterations with a batch size of 200. For the Trinity Dataset, our model is trained for 30k iterations with a batch size of 100.

4.1 Datasets

TED Dataset
TED Dataset, which is first proposed by Yoon et al. [43], is a large, English-language dataset for gesture synthesis problems. It contains upper body pose sequences, audio waveforms, transcribed speech texts, and speaker identities. Pose data is extracted from 1,714 videos of TED lectures and converted to 3D data by using a pose estimator [36]. We resample the pose data at 15 fps and slice each training sample into 42 frames. We use the initial 12 frames as autoregressive pose histories and, following Yoon et al. [42], train our model to generate the remaining 30 frames. The dataset is partitioned into a training set (200,038 samples), a test set (26,245 samples), and a validation set (26,903 samples). We use the training set to train our model, the test set for quantitative and qualitative evaluation, and the validation set for tuning our network.

Trinity Dataset
Trinity Dataset (GENEA Challenge 2020 [29]) proposed by Ferstl et al. [12] is a dataset containing speaking gestures and corresponding audio signals. Unlike TED Dataset, this dataset only consists of a single speaker and is collected using a professional motion capture system, which results in better data quality. Moreover, this dataset contains full-body motion, including the speaker changing the standing posture or taking a few steps back and forth. Following Alexanderson et al. [5], we downsample the motion data at 20 fps and slice each training sample into 120 frames. The total duration of valid data is about 242 min and *Recording_008* session is held out for validation and evaluation. We take 5 frames as historic poses and 20 frames as audio lookahead. We also augment the data by mirroring the gesture motion with the speech unchanged.

4.2 Evaluation

Quantitative Evaluation
We compare our model with several state-of-the-art models on two datasets using different metrics. On the TED Dataset, we compare with six representative methods: attentional Seq2Seq (Seq2Seq) [43], Speech2Gesture (S2G) [14], Joint Embedding Model (JEM) [3], MoGlow [5], Gestures from Trimodal Context (GTC) [42], and Speech2AffectiveGestures (S2AG) [6]. On the Trinity Dataset, we compare with two methods: Gesticulator [28] and MoGlow [5]. We use Fréchet Gesture Distance (FGD), Percent of Correct Keypoints (PCK), Diversity (Div), BeatAlign Score (BA), and Multi-modality Score (MM) for evaluation. Please refer to our supplementary material for detailed descriptions of these metrics.

For Seq2Seq, S2G, JEM, we directly use some metric values as documented in [42]. For GTC, S2AG, and Gesticulator, we utilize the pre-trained models

Table 1. Comparison of our method with previous methods on two benchmark datasets. Bold indicates the best.

Dataset	Method	FGD	PCK	Div	BA ($\sigma = 5$)	MM
TED	Seq2Seq [43]	18.15	0.809	40.08	0.319	–
	S2G [14]	19.25	0.877	44.46	0.620	–
	JEM [3]	22.08	**0.880**	44.61	0.508	–
	MoGlow [5]	5.15	0.842	50.63	0.617	22.56
	GTC [42]	4.40	0.850	48.70	0.618	–
	S2AG [6]	7.22	0.861	47.25	0.619	–
	Ours	**3.30**	0.850	**52.00**	**0.622**	**22.63**
Trinity	Gesticulator [28]	9.95	0.701	3.50	0.844	–
	MoGlow [5]	7.61	0.726	3.81	0.852	**2.12**
	Ours	**6.76**	**0.730**	**4.34**	**0.875**	1.60

provided by the authors. We train MoGlow from scratch following the same configuration as in [5].

Table 1 summarizes the comparison results. On the TED Dataset, our method achieves the best performance for almost all the metrics except PCK, indicating that our generated gestures are high quality. Specifically, for FGD metric, we achieve improvements of 25.0% and 54.3% over GTC and S2AG, which both need trimodal contexts. Note that JEM, S2G, and S2AG are better than our model in the PCK metric. A possible reason is that our model generates plausible gestures from a probabilistic model, while the other methods tend to generate averaged motion which lacks diversity. On the Trinity Dataset, our model also surpasses two other state-of-the-art models. Although MoGlow achieves better MM scores than ours, we emphasize that higher MM is only preferred when the generated gestures are realistic and natural, because invalid and jitter motion can also result in high MM scores.

Qualitative Evaluation

Figure 5 shows the qualitative results of our method on the TED Dataset. The synthesized poses are plotted as stick figures. We also demonstrate the full-body generation results of the Trinity Dataset in Fig. 6. For better visualization, we retarget the motion sequences to several 3D characters using Blender. Note that the generated gestures are diverse and human-like, and match the input audio well.

User Study

To further evaluate the quality of our results based on human perception, we conducted a user study with 12 participants. Specifically, we asked the participants to watch six groups of videos, where each group contained three gesture sequences synthesized by GTC [42], S2AG [6], and our method, respectively.

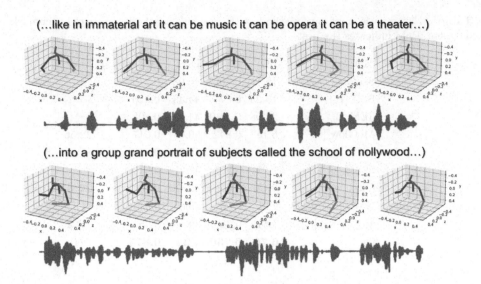

Fig. 5. Qualitative results (visualized as 3D stick figures) of our method on the TED Dataset. We also show the corresponding audio waveforms and texts.

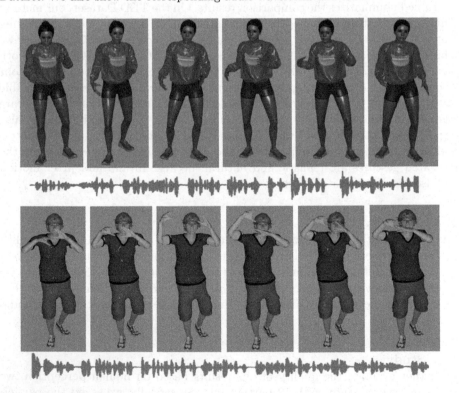

Fig. 6. Full-body generated poses and corresponding audio waveform of the Trinity Dataset. We retarget the pose sequences to 3D characters using Blender.

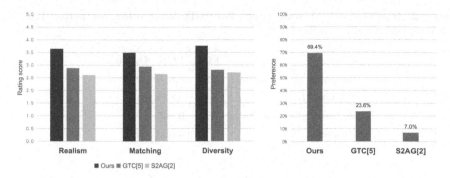

Fig. 7. User study results of comparing our method with two state-of-the-art methods on TED Dataset, i.e., GTC [42], and S2AG [6]. The left figure shows human rating scores on three aspects: Realism, Matching Degree, and Diversity. The right figure shows human preference over results generated by different method.

They were asked to rate each gesture sequence in terms of Realism, Matching Degree, and Diversity. Moreover, the participants were required to choose one gesture sequence in each group that they liked the most.

Figure 7 shows the user study results. The left histogram demonstrates that our proposed method outperforms the other two state-of-the-art methods. The right histogram shows that the majority of participants (almost 70%) preferred our synthesized gestures, again confirming that our results are more visually appealing than the others. See also the supplementary material and demo video for more results.

4.3   Ablation Study

We conduct an ablation study on TED Dataset to understand each part of our model in detail. Specifically, we remove two components of the proposed model separately: the global encoder and the gesture perceptual loss, and measure FGD, PCK, and Div metrics. Table 2 shows the results of our ablation study.

By removing both global encoder and gesture perceptual loss, our model are degenerate and become MoGlow, except that the LSTMs are replaced with GRUs. We take this as our baseline. Without L_{gp} or global encoder, the FGD and Div scores get worse, implying that the results are less natural and lack diversity. Note that our proposed gesture perceptual loss is used to facilitate the joint training process of the flow model and the global encoder. Therefore, adding L_{gp} without the global encoder makes little sense and results in a slightly worse performance than the baseline (Table 2, third row). As our proposed global encoder and gesture perceptual loss are mainly used to enhance the global features of gestures, thus, the improvement of our model under the FGD metric is more significant than PCK and Div metrics. The ablation study confirms that both the global encoder and the gesture perceptual loss have positive effects on co-speech gesture generation.

Table 2. Results of our ablation study. For FGD, lower values are better. For PCK and Div, higher values are better.

Config	FGD	PCK	Div (mm)
Proposed (no ablation)	3.30	0.850	52
Without L_{gp}	4.62	0.845	51
Without global encoder	6.26	0.848	50
Baseline	6.10	0.850	49

4.4 Latent Space Visualization

The GAN-based models usually lack latent representation of the data samples. In contrast, normalizing flows can directly transform a gesture to its corresponding latent code through the pass of the forward flow. By projecting these latent codes onto a 2D space using t-SNE and coloring each sample according to its style label (speaker's identity), we can visualize the distribution of the latent space of gestures. We observe that the models trained on the full TED Dataset tend to extract general features and thereby cannot distinguish different samples well in the latent space. Therefore, we train our model on a subset (with only 15 speakers) of the TED Dataset and visualize the results in Fig. 8 left.

Table 3. Comparison of the clustering results of our method and MoGlow on a subset (15 speakers) of the TED Dataset. Higher CHI and SCoeff values indicate better performance.

Method	CHI	SCoeff
MoGlow [5]	908.47	0.443
Ours	**1149.34**	**0.517**

We observe that latent codes are clustered into different groups, and samples from the same speaker tend to be in adjacent spaces. It means that although our model does not need labels and is trained in an unsupervised manner, it can still learn the styles of gestures and can encode gestures with similar styles into nearby locations in the latent space. Moreover, compared to MoGlow, we find that latent codes inferred by our model are clustered more reasonably and the gap between different categories is more significant. Mathematically, we compute the Calinski-Harabaz Index (CHI) and the Silhouette Coefficient (SCoeff) to measure the clustering result. Table 3 shows that our model can learn the distribution of gesture styles better.

4.5 Manipulating Gesture Styles

Section 4.4 has demonstrated that the latent codes contain high-level properties of gesture styles. Thus, by manipulating the latent codes during inference time,

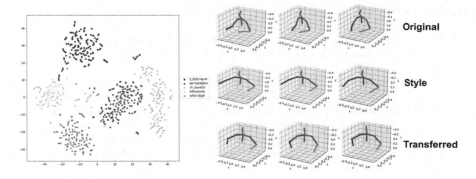

Fig. 8. Visualization of the latent space (left) and a typical example of gesture style transfer (right). We project the latent codes to $\mathbb{R}^2$ and color them based on their labels. Gestures are transferred to a drastic and exaggerated style.

we can control the style of synthesized gestures. Specifically, when generating the stylized gesture, we replace the randomly sampled latent code with the specific latent code inferred from the target style gesture sequence. Therefore, we can generate audio-driven gestures with a specific style.

Figure 8 (right) shows such an example. The original poses are gentle and restrained with slight arm movement (first row). However, we want to generate passionate and drastic motions (second row). The transferred results (third row) show exaggerated gestures with widely open arms. Furthermore, the rhythm of the transferred gestures is consistent with the original movements.

5   Conclusions

In this paper, we propose an end-to-end flow-based model to synthesize stylized audio-driven gestures in an unsupervised manner. Our model is novel in that it utilizes a global encoder to capture both the local and global features by jointly training the encoder and the generative flow. We also design a gesture perceptual loss to facilitate the joint training procedure and improve the quality of the generated results. Both quantitative and qualitative evaluations on two benchmark datasets show that the proposed approach outperforms state-of-the-art methods. Moreover, the flow-based model allows us to explore the latent space to transfer the styles of target gestures to our generated gestures.

Acknowledgments. This work was supported by the Natural Science Foundation of China (No.61725204), Tsinghua University Initiative Scientific Research Program, China Postdoctoral Science Foundation (No.2021M701891).

References

1. Aberman, K., Weng, Y., Lischinski, D., Cohen-Or, D., Chen, B.: Unpaired motion style transfer from video to animation. ACM Trans. Graph. (TOG) **39**(4), 64–1 (2020)
2. Ahuja, C., Lee, D.W., Nakano, Y.I., Morency, L.-P.: Style transfer for co-speech gesture animation: a multi-speaker conditional-mixture approach. In: Vedaldi, A., Bischof, H., Brox, T., Frahm, J.-M. (eds.) ECCV 2020. LNCS, vol. 12363, pp. 248–265. Springer, Cham (2020). https://doi.org/10.1007/978-3-030-58523-5_15
3. Ahuja, C., Morency, L.P.: Language2pose: Natural language grounded pose forecasting. In: 2019 International Conference on 3D Vision (3DV), pp. 719–728 IEEE (2019)
4. Alexanderson, S., Henter, G.E.: Robust model training and generalisation with studentising flows. In: ICML Workshop on Invertible Neural Networks, Normalizing Flows, and Explicit Likelihood Models (INNF+ 2020). vol. 2, pp. 25–1 (2020)
5. Alexanderson, S., Henter, G.E., Kucherenko, T., Beskow, J.: Style-controllable speech-driven gesture synthesis using normalising flows. In: Computer Graphics Forum, vol. 39, pp. 487–496. Wiley Online Library (2020)
6. Bhattacharya, U., Childs, E., Rewkowski, N., Manocha, D.: Speech2affectivegestures: synthesizing co-speech gestures with generative adversarial affective expression learning. In: Proceedings of the 29th ACM International Conference on Multimedia, pp. 2027–2036 (2021)
7. Bremner, P., Pipe, A.G., Melhuish, C., Fraser, M., Subramanian, S.: The effects of robot-performed co-verbal gesture on listener behaviour. In: 2011 11th IEEE-RAS International Conference on Humanoid Robots, pp. 458–465. IEEE (2011)
8. Cassell, J., McNeill, D., McCullough, K.E.: Speech-gesture mismatches: evidence for one underlying representation of linguistic and nonlinguistic information. Pragmatics Cogn. **7**(1), 1–34 (1999)
9. Cassell, J., et al.: Animated conversation: rule-based generation of facial expression, gesture & spoken intonation for multiple conversational agents. In: Proceedings of the 21st Annual Conference On Computer Graphics And Interactive Techniques, pp. 413–420 (1994)
10. Dinh, L., Sohl-Dickstein, J., Bengio, S.: Density estimation using real NVP. In: International Conference on Learning Representations (2017)
11. Du, H., Herrmann, E., Sprenger, J., Cheema, N., Hosseini, S., Fischer, K., Slusallek, P.: Stylistic locomotion modeling with conditional variational autoencoder. In: Eurographics (Short Papers), pp. 9–12 (2019)
12. Ferstl, Y., McDonnell, R.: Investigating the use of recurrent motion modelling for speech gesture generation. In: Proceedings of the 18th International Conference on Intelligent Virtual Agents, pp. 93–98 (2018)
13. Gatys, L.A., Ecker, A.S., Bethge, M.: Image style transfer using convolutional neural networks. In: Proceedings of the IEEE Conference on Computer Vision and Pattern Recognition, pp. 2414–2423 (2016)
14. Ginosar, S., Bar, A., Kohavi, G., Chan, C., Owens, A., Malik, J.: Learning individual styles of conversational gesture. In: Proceedings of the IEEE/CVF Conference on Computer Vision and Pattern Recognition, pp. 3497–3506 (2019)
15. Goodfellow, I., et al.: Generative adversarial nets. In: Advances in Neural Information Processing Systems, vol. 27 (2014)
16. Hasegawa, D., Kaneko, N., Shirakawa, S., Sakuta, H., Sumi, K.: Evaluation of speech-to-gesture generation using bi-directional LSTM network. In: Proceedings of the 18th International Conference on Intelligent Virtual Agents, pp. 79–86 (2018)

17. He, K., Zhang, X., Ren, S., Sun, J.: Delving deep into rectifiers: surpassing human-level performance on ImageNet classification. In: Proceedings of the IEEE International Conference on Computer Vision, pp. 1026–1034 (2015)
18. Henter, G.E., Alexanderson, S., Beskow, J.: MoGlow: probabilistic and controllable motion synthesis using normalising flows. ACM Trans. Graph. (TOG) **39**(6), 1–14 (2020)
19. Ho, J., Chen, X., Srinivas, A., Duan, Y., Abbeel, P.: Flow++: improving flow-based generative models with variational dequantization and architecture design. In: International Conference on Machine Learning, pp. 2722–2730. PMLR (2019)
20. Holden, D., Saito, J., Komura, T.: A deep learning framework for character motion synthesis and editing. ACM Transa. Graph. (TOG) **35**(4), 1–11 (2016)
21. Huang, X., Belongie, S.: Arbitrary style transfer in real-time with adaptive instance normalization. In: Proceedings of the IEEE International Conference on Computer Vision, pp. 1501–1510 (2017)
22. Johnson, J., Alahi, A., Fei-Fei, L.: Perceptual losses for real-time style transfer and super-resolution. In: Leibe, B., Matas, J., Sebe, N., Welling, M. (eds.) ECCV 2016. LNCS, vol. 9906, pp. 694–711. Springer, Cham (2016). https://doi.org/10.1007/978-3-319-46475-6_43
23. Kingma, D.P., Welling, M.: Auto-encoding variational bayes. In: International Conference on Learning Representations (2014)
24. Kingma, D.P., Dhariwal, P.: Glow: generative flow with invertible 1x1 convolutions. In: Advances in Neural Information Processing Systems, vol. 31 (2018)
25. Kipp, M.: Gesture Generation by Imitation: From Human Behavior to Computer Character Animation. Universal-Publishers, Irvine (2005)
26. Kopp, S., et al.: Towards a common framework for multimodal generation: the behavior markup language. In: Gratch, J., Young, M., Aylett, R., Ballin, D., Olivier, P. (eds.) IVA 2006. LNCS (LNAI), vol. 4133, pp. 205–217. Springer, Heidelberg (2006). https://doi.org/10.1007/11821830_17
27. Kucherenko, T., Hasegawa, D., Henter, G.E., Kaneko, N., Kjellström, H.: Analyzing input and output representations for speech-driven gesture generation. In: Proceedings of the 19th ACM International Conference on Intelligent Virtual Agents, pp. 97–104 (2019)
28. Kucherenko, T., et al.: Gesticulator: a framework for semantically-aware speech-driven gesture generation. In: Proceedings of the 2020 International Conference on Multimodal Interaction, pp. 242–250 (2020)
29. Kucherenko, T., Jonell, P., Yoon, Y., Wolfert, P., Henter, G.E.: A large, crowd-sourced evaluation of gesture generation systems on common data: the GENEA challenge 2020. In: 26th International Conference on Intelligent User Interfaces, pp. 11–21 (2021)
30. Levine, S., Krähenbühl, P., Thrun, S., Koltun, V.: Gesture controllers. In: ACM SIGGRAPH 2010 papers, pp. 1–11. Association for Computing Machinery, New York, NY, United States (2010)
31. Levine, S., Theobalt, C., Koltun, V.: Real-time prosody-driven synthesis of body language. In: ACM SIGGRAPH Asia 2009 papers, pp. 1–10. Association for Computing Machinery, New York, NY, United States (2009)
32. Li, J., et al.: Audio2gestures: generating diverse gestures from speech audio with conditional variational autoencoders. In: Proceedings of the IEEE/CVF International Conference on Computer Vision, pp. 11293–11302 (2021)
33. Ma, X., Kong, X., Zhang, S., Hovy, E.: MaCow: masked convolutional generative flow. In: Advances in Neural Information Processing Systems, vol. 32 (2019)

34. Ma, X., Kong, X., Zhang, S., Hovy, E.H.: Decoupling global and local representations via invertible generative flows. In: International Conference on Learning Representations (2020)
35. Neff, M., Kipp, M., Albrecht, I., Seidel, H.P.: Gesture modeling and animation based on a probabilistic re-creation of speaker style. ACM Trans. Graph. (TOG) **27**(1), 1–24 (2008)
36. Pavllo, D., Feichtenhofer, C., Grangier, D., Auli, M.: 3D human pose estimation in video with temporal convolutions and semi-supervised training. In: Proceedings of the IEEE/CVF Conference on Computer Vision and Pattern Recognition, pp. 7753–7762 (2019)
37. Qian, S., Tu, Z., Zhi, Y., Liu, W., Gao, S.: Speech drives templates: co-speech gesture synthesis with learned templates. In: Proceedings of the IEEE/CVF International Conference on Computer Vision, pp. 11077–11086 (2021)
38. Simonyan, K., Zisserman, A.: Very deep convolutional networks for large-scale image recognition. In: International Conference on Learning Representations (2015)
39. Studdert-Kennedy, M.: Hand and mind: what gestures reveal about thought. Lang. Speech **37**(2), 203–209 (1994)
40. Wagner, P., Malisz, Z., Kopp, S.: Gesture and speech in interaction: an overview. Speech Commun. **57**, 209–232 (2014)
41. Wen, Y.H., Yang, Z., Fu, H., Gao, L., Sun, Y., Liu, Y.J.: Autoregressive stylized motion synthesis with generative flow. In: Proceedings of the IEEE/CVF Conference on Computer Vision and Pattern Recognition, pp. 13612–13621 (2021)
42. Yoon, Y., et al.: Speech gesture generation from the trimodal context of text, audio, and speaker identity. ACM Trans. Graph. (TOG) **39**(6), 1–16 (2020)
43. Yoon, Y., Ko, W.R., Jang, M., Lee, J., Kim, J., Lee, G.: Robots learn social skills: End-to-end learning of co-speech gesture generation for humanoid robots. In: 2019 International Conference on Robotics and Automation (ICRA), pp. 4303–4309. IEEE (2019)

Self-Constrained Inference Optimization on Structural Groups for Human Pose Estimation

Zhehan Kan, Shuoshuo Chen, Zeng Li, and Zhihai He$^{(\boxtimes)}$

Southern University of Science and Technology, Shenzhen, China
{kanzh2021,chenss2021}@mail.sustech.edu.cn
{liz9,hezh}@sustech.edu.cn

Abstract. We observe that human poses exhibit strong group-wise structural correlation and spatial coupling between keypoints due to the biological constraints of different body parts. This group-wise structural correlation can be explored to improve the accuracy and robustness of human pose estimation. In this work, we develop a self-constrained prediction-verification network to characterize and learn the structural correlation between keypoints during training. During the inference stage, the feedback information from the verification network allows us to perform further optimization of pose prediction, which significantly improves the performance of human pose estimation. Specifically, we partition the keypoints into groups according to the biological structure of human body. Within each group, the keypoints are further partitioned into two subsets, high-accuracy proximal keypoints and low-accuracy distal keypoints. We develop a self-constrained prediction-verification network to perform forward and backward predictions between these keypoint subsets. One fundamental challenge in pose estimation, as well as in generic prediction tasks, is that there is no mechanism for us to verify if the obtained pose estimation or prediction results are accurate or not, since the ground truth is not available. Once successfully learned, the verification network serves as an accuracy verification module for the forward pose prediction. During the inference stage, it can be used to guide the local optimization of the pose estimation results of low-accuracy keypoints with the self-constrained loss on high-accuracy keypoints as the objective function. Our extensive experimental results on benchmark MS COCO and CrowdPose datasets demonstrate that the proposed method can significantly improve the pose estimation results.

Keywords: Human pose estimation · Self-constrained · Structural inference · Prediction optimization

Supplementary Information The online version contains supplementary material available at https://doi.org/10.1007/978-3-031-20065-6_42.

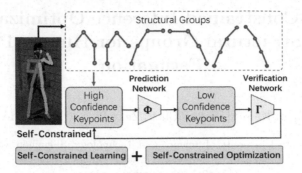

Fig. 1. Illustration of the proposed idea of self-constrained inference optimization of structural groups for human pose estimation.

1 Introduction

Human pose estimation aims to correctly detect and localize keypoints, i.e., human body joints or parts, for all persons in an input image. It is one of the fundamental computer vision tasks which plays an important role in a variety of downstream applications, such as motion capture [5,24], activity recognition [1,31], and person tracking [30,35]. Recently, remarkable process has been made in human pose estimation based on deep neural network methods [2,3,10,23,25,27]. For regular scenes, deep learning-based methods have already achieved remarkably accurate estimation of body keypoints and there is little space for further performance improvement [11,29,37]. However, for complex scenes with person-person occlusions, large variations of appearance, and cluttered backgrounds, pose estimation remains very challenging [11,32]. We notice that, in complex scenes, the performance of pose estimation on different keypoints exhibits large variations. For example, for those visible keypoints with little interference from other persons or background, their estimation results are fairly accurate and reliable. However, for some keypoints, for example the distal keypoints at tip locations of body parts, it is very challenging to achieve accurate pose estimation. The low accuracy of these challenging keypoints degrades the overall pose estimation performance. Therefore, the main challenge in pose estimation is how to improve the estimation accuracy of these challenging keypoints.

As summarized in Fig. 1, this work is motivated by the following two important observations: (1) human poses, although exhibiting large variations due to the free styles and flexible movements of human, are however restricted by the biological structure of the body. The whole body consists of multiple parts, such as the upper limbs and lower limbs. Each body part corresponds to a subgroup of keypoints. We observe that the keypoint correlation across different body parts remains low since different body parts, such as the left and right arms, can move with totally different styles and towards different directions. However, within the same body part or within the same structural group, keypoints are more

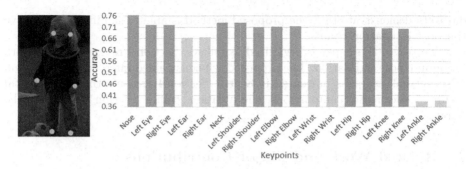

Fig. 2. Keypoints at the tip locations of body parts suffer from low accuracy scores obtained from the heatmap during pose estimation.

spatially constrained by each other. This implies that keypoints can be potentially predictable from each other by exploring this unique structural correlation. Motivated by this observation, in this work, we propose to partition the body parts into a set of structural groups and perform group-wise structure learning and keypoint prediction refinement.

(2) We have also observed that, within each group of keypoints, distal keypoints at tip locations of the body parts, such as ankle and wrist keypoints, often suffer from lower estimation accuracy. This is because they have much larger freedom of motion and are more easily to be occluded by other objects. Figure 2 shows the average prediction accuracy (computed based on the distance between the predicted keypoint position and its ground-truth with normalization.) of all keypoints with yellow dots and bars representing the locations and estimation accuracy for distal keypoints, for example, wrist or ankle keypoints. We can see that the average estimation accuracy of distal keypoints are much lower than the rest.

Motivated by the above two observations, we propose to partition the body keypoints into 6 structural groups according to their biological parts, and each structural group is further partitioned into two subsets: *distal keypoints* and *proximal keypoints* (the rest keypoints). We develop a self-constrained prediction-verification network to learn the structural correlation between these two subsets within each structural group. Specifically, we learn two tightly coupled networks, the prediction network Φ which performs the forward prediction of distal keypoints from proximal keypoints, and the verification network Γ which performs backward prediction of the proximal keypoints from distal keypoints. This prediction-verification network aims to characterize the structural correlation between keypoints within each structural group. They are jointly learned using a self-constraint loss. Once successfully learned, the verification network Γ is then used as a performance assessment module to optimize the prediction of low-accuracy distal keypoints based on local search and refinement within each structural group. Our extensive experimental results on benchmark MS COCO datasets demonstrate that the proposed method is able to significantly improve the pose estimation results.

The rest of the paper is organized as follows. Section 2 reviews related work on human pose estimation. The proposed self-constrained inference optimization of structural groups is presented in Sect. 3. Section 4 presents the experimental results, performance comparisons, and ablation studies. Section 5 concludes the paper.

2   Related Work and Major Contributions

In this section, we review related works on heatmap-based pose estimation, multi-person pose estimation, pose refinement and error correction, and reciprocal learning. We then summarize the major contributions of this work.

(1) **Heatmap-based pose estimation.** In this paper, we use heatmap-based pose estimation. The probability for a pixel to be the keypoint can be measured by its response in the heatmap. Recently, heatmap-based approaches have achieved the state-of-the-art performance in pose estimation [4,27,32,34]. The coordinates of keypoints are obtained by decoding the heatmaps [25]. [4] predicted scale-aware high-resolution heatmaps using multi-resolution aggregation during inference. [34] processed graph-structured features across multi-scale human skeletal representations and proposed a learning approach for multi-level feature learning and heatmap estimation.

(2) **Multi-person pose estimation.** Multi-person pose estimation requires detecting keypoints of all persons in an image [6]. It is very challenging due to overlapping between body parts from neighboring persons. Top-down methods and bottom-up methods have been developed in the literature to address this issue. (a) **Top-down** approaches [10,21,25,28] first detect all persons in the image and then estimates keypoints of each person. The performance of this method depends on the reliability of object detection which generates the bounding box for each person. When the number of persons is large, accurate detection of each person becomes very challenging, especially in highly occluded and cluttered scenes [23]. (b) **Bottom-up** approaches [2,8,20] directly detect keypoints of all persons and then group keypoints for each person. These methods usually run faster than the top-down methods in multi-person pose estimation since they do not require person detection. [8] activated the pixels in the keypoint regions and learned disentangled representations for each keypoint to improve the regression result. [20] developed a scale-adaptive heatmap regression method to handle large variations of body sizes.

(3) **Pose refinement and error correction.** A number of methods have been developed in the literature to refine the estimation of body keypoints [13,21,29]. [7] proposed a pose refinement network which takes the image and the predicted keypoint locations as input and learns to directly predict refined keypoint locations. [13] designed two networks where the correction network guides the refinement to correct the joint locations before generating the final pose estimation. [21] introduced a model-agnostic pose refinement method using

statistics of error distributions as prior information to generate synthetic poses for training. [29] introduced a localization sub-net to extract different visual features and a graph pose refinement module to explore the relationship between points sampled from the heatmap regression network.

(4) **Cycle consistency and reciprocal learning.** This work is related to cycle consistency and reciprocal learning. [39] translated an image from the source domain into the target domain by introducing a cycle consistence constraint so that the distribution of images from translated domain is indistinguishable from the distribution of target domain. [26] developed a pair of jointly-learned networks to predict human trajectory forward and backward. [33] developed a reciprocal cross-task architecture for image segmentation, which improves the learning efficiency and generation accuracy by exploiting the commonalities and differences across tasks. [18] developed a Temporal Reciprocal Learning (TRL) approach to fully explore the discriminative information from the disentangled features. [38] designed a support-query mutual guidance architecture for few-shot object detection.

(5) **Major contributions of this work.** Compared to the above related work, the major contributions of this work are: (a) we propose to partition the body keypoints into structural groups and explore the structural correlation within each group to improve the pose estimation results. Within each structural group, we propose to partition the keypoints into high-accuracy and low-accuracy ones. We develop a prediction-verification network to characterize structural correlation between them based on a self-constraint loss. (b) We introduce a self-constrained optimization method which uses the learned verification network as a performance assessment module to optimize the pose estimation of low-accuracy keypoints during the inference stage. (c) Our extensive experimental results have demonstrated that our proposed method is able to significantly improve the performance of pose estimation and outperforms the existing methods by large margins.

Compared to existing methods on cycle consistency and reciprocal learning, our method has the following unique novelty. First, it addresses an important problem in prediction: how do we know if the prediction is accurate or not since we do not have the ground-truth. It establishes a self-matching constraint on high-accuracy keypoints and uses the successfully learned verification network to verify if the refined predictions of low-accuracy keypoints are accurate or not. Unlike existing prediction methods which can only perform forward inference, our method is able to perform further optimization of the prediction results during the inference stage, which can significantly improve the prediction accuracy and the generalization capability of the proposed method.

3   Method

In this section, we present our self-constrained inference optimization (SCIO) of structural groups for human pose estimation.

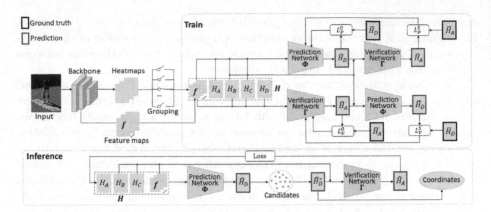

Fig. 3. The overall framework of our proposed network. For an input image, heatmaps of all keypoints predicted by the backbone are partitioned into 6 structural groups. During training stage, each group **H** is divided into two subsets: proximal keypoints and distal keypoints. A prediction-verification network with self-constraints is developed to characterize the structural correlation between these two subsets. During testing, the learned verification network is used to refine the prediction results of the low-accuracy distal keypoints.

3.1 Problem Formulation

Human pose estimation, as a keypoint detection task, aims to detect the locations of body keypoints from the input image. Specifically, let I be the image of size $W \times H \times 3$. Our task is to locate K keypoints $X = \{X_1, X_2, ..., X_K\}$ from I precisely. Heatmap-based methods transform this problem to estimate K heatmaps $\{H_1, H_2, ..., H_K\}$ of size $W' \times H'$. Given a heatmap, the keypoint location can be determined using different grouping or peak finding methods [21,25]. For example, the pixel with the highest heatmap value can be designated as the location of the corresponding keypoint. Meanwhile, given a keypoint at location (p_x, p_y), the corresponding heatmap can be generated using the Gaussian kernel

$$C(x, y) = \frac{1}{2\pi\sigma^2} e^{-[(x-p_x)^2 + (y-p_y)^2]/2\sigma^2}. \tag{1}$$

In this work, the ground-truth heatmaps are denoted by $\bar{H}_1, \bar{H}_2, ..., \bar{H}_K$.

3.2 Self-constrained Inference Optimization on Structural Groups

Figure 3 shows the overall framework of our proposed SCIO method for pose estimation. We first partition the detected human body keypoints into 6 structural groups, which correspond to different body parts, including lower and upper limbs, as well as two groups for the head part, as illustrated in Fig. 4. Each group contains four keypoints. We observe that these structural groups of four keypoints are the basic units for human pose and body motion. They are constrained by the biological structure of the human body. There are significant freedom and variations between structural groups. For example, the left arm and the right arm could move and pose in totally different ways. In the meantime, within each group, the set of keypoints are constraining each other with strong structural correlation between them.

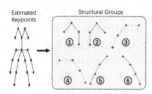

Fig. 4. Partition of the body keypoints into 6 structural groups corresponding to different body parts. Each group has 4 keypoints.

As discussed in Sect. 1, we further partition each of these 6 structural groups into proximal keypoints and distal keypoints. The proximal keypoints are near the body torso while the distal keypoints are at the end or tip locations of the corresponding body part. Figure 2 shows that the distal keypoints are having much lower estimation accuracy scores than those proximal keypoints during pose estimation. In this work, we denote these 4 keypoints within each group by

$$\mathbf{G} = \{X_A, X_B, X_C \mid X_D\}, \tag{2}$$

where X_D is the distal keypoint and the rest three $\{X_A, X_B, X_C\}$ are the proximal keypoints near the torso. The corresponding heatmap are denoted by $\mathbf{H} = \{H_A, H_B, H_C \mid H_D\}$. To characterize the structural correlation within each structural group $\mathbf{H}$, we propose to develop a self-constrained prediction-verification network. As illustrated in Fig. 3, the prediction network $\mathbf{\Phi}$ predicts the heatmap of the distal keypoint H_D from the proximal keypoints $\{H_A, H_B, H_C\}$ with feature map $\mathbf{f}$ as the visual context:

$$\hat{H}_D = \mathbf{\Phi}(H_A, H_B, H_C; \mathbf{f}). \tag{3}$$

We observe that the feature map $\mathbf{f}$ provides important visual context for keypoint estimation. The verification network $\mathbf{\Gamma}$ shares the same structure as the prediction network. It performs the backward prediction of keypoint H_A from the rest three:

$$\hat{H}_A = \mathbf{\Gamma}(H_B, H_C, H_D; \mathbf{f}). \tag{4}$$

Coupling the prediction and verification network together by passing the prediction output $\hat{H}_D$ of the prediction network into the verification network as input, we have the following prediction loop

$$\hat{H}_A = \mathbf{\Gamma}(H_B, H_C, \hat{H}_D; \mathbf{f}) \tag{5}$$
$$= \mathbf{\Gamma}(H_B, H_C, \mathbf{\Phi}(H_A, H_B, H_C; \mathbf{f}); \mathbf{f}). \tag{6}$$

This leads to the following self-constraint loss

$$\mathcal{L}_A^s = ||\bar{H}_A - \hat{H}_A||_2. \tag{7}$$

This prediction-verification network with a forward-backward prediction loop learns the internal structural correlation between the proximal keypoints and the distal keypoint. The learning process is guided by the self-constraint loss. If the internal structural correlation is successfully learned, then the self-constraint loss $\mathcal{L}_A^s$ generated by the forward and backward prediction loop should be small. This step is referred to as *self-constrained learning*.

Once successfully learned, the verification network Γ can be used to verify if the prediction $\hat{X}_D$ is accurate or not. In this case, the self-constraint loss is used as an objective function to optimize the prediction $\hat{X}_D$ based on local search, which can be formulated as

$$\hat{X}_D^* = \arg\min_{\hat{X}_D} ||H_A - \hat{H}_A||_2, \tag{8}$$

$$= \arg\min_{\hat{X}_D} ||H_A - \Gamma(H_B, H_C, \mathbb{H}(\hat{X}_D); \mathbf{f})||_2,$$

where $\mathbb{H}(\hat{X}_D)$ represents the heatmap generated from keypoint $\hat{X}_D$ using the Gaussian kernel. This provides an effective mechanism for us to iteratively refine the prediction result based on the specific statistics of the test sample. This adaptive prediction and optimization is not available in traditional network prediction which is purely forward without any feedback or adaptation. This feedback-based adaptive prediction will result in better generalization capability on the test sample. This step is referred to as *self-constrained optimization*. In the following sections, we present more details about the proposed self-constrained learning (SCL) and self-constrained optimization (SCO) methods.

3.3   Self-constrained Learning of Structural Groups

In this section, we explain the self-constrained learning in more details. As illustrated in Fig. 3, the input to the prediction and verification networks, namely, $\{H_A, H_B, H_C\}$ and $\{H_B, H_C, H_D\}$, are all heatmaps generated by the baseline pose estimation network. In this work, we use the HRNet [27] as our baseline, on top of which our proposed SCIO method is implemented. We observe that the visual context surrounding the keypoint location provides important visual cues for refining the locations of the keypoints. For example, the correct location of the knee keypoint should be at the center of the knee image region. Motivated by this, we also pass the feature map $\mathbf{f}$ generated by the backbone network to the prediction and verification network as inputs.

In our proposed scheme of self-constrained learning, the prediction and verification networks are jointly trained. Specifically, as illustrated in Fig. 3, the top branch shows the training process of the prediction network. Its input includes heatmaps $\{H_A, H_B, H_C\}$ and the visual feature map $\mathbf{f}$. The output of the prediction network is the predicted heatmap for keypoint X_D, denoted by $\hat{H}_D$. During the training stage, this prediction is compared to its ground-truth $\bar{H}_D$ and form the prediction loss $\mathcal{L}_P^O$ which is given by

$$\mathcal{L}_P^O = ||\hat{H}_D - \bar{H}_D||_2. \tag{9}$$

The predicted heatmap $\hat{H}_D$, combined with the heatmaps H_B and H_C and the visual feature map $\mathbf{f}$, is passed to the verification network Γ as input. The output of Γ will be the predicted heatmap for keypoint X_A, denoted by $\hat{H}_A$. We then compare it with the ground-truth heatmap $\bar{H}_A$ and define the following self-constraint loss for the prediction network

$$\mathcal{L}_P^S = ||\hat{H}_A - \bar{H}_A||_2. \tag{10}$$

These two losses are combined as $\mathcal{L}_P = \mathcal{L}_P^O + \mathcal{L}_P^S$ to train the prediction network Φ.

Similarly, for the verification network, the inputs are heatmaps $\{H_B, H_C, H_D\}$ and visual feature map $\mathbf{f}$. It predicts the heatmap $\hat{H}_A$ for keypoint X_A. It is then, combined with $\{H_B, H_C\}$ and $\mathbf{f}$ to form the input to the prediction network Φ which predicts the heatmap $\hat{H}_D$. Therefore, the overall loss function for the verification network is given by

$$\mathcal{L}_V = ||\hat{H}_A - \bar{H}_A||_2 + ||\hat{H}_D - \bar{H}_D||_2. \tag{11}$$

The prediction and verification network are jointly trained in an iterative manner. Specifically, during the training epochs for the prediction network, the verification network is fixed and used to compute the self-constraint loss for the prediction network. Similarly, during the training epochs for the verification network, the prediction network is fixed and used to compute the self-constraint loss for the verification network.

3.4   Self-constrained Inference Optimization of Low-Accuracy Keypoints

As discussed in Sect. 1, one of the major challenges in pose estimation is to improve the accuracy of hard keypoints, for example, those distal keypoints. In existing approaches for network prediction, the inference process is purely forward. The knowledge learned from the training set is directly applied to the test set. There is no effective mechanism to verify if the prediction result is accurate or not since the ground-truth is not available. This forward inference process often suffers from generalization problems since there is no feedback process to adjust the prediction results based on the actual test samples.

The proposed self-constrained inference optimization aims to address the above issue. The verification network Γ, once successfully learned, can be used as a feedback module to evaluate the accuracy of the prediction result. This is achieved by mapping the prediction result $\hat{H}_D$ for the low-accuracy keypoint back to the high-accuracy keypoint $\hat{H}_A$. Using the self-constraint loss as an objective function, we can perform local search or refinement of the prediction result $\hat{X}_D$ to minimize the objective function, as formulated in (8). Here, the basic idea is that: if the prediction $\hat{X}_D$ becomes accurate during local search, then, using it as the input, the verification network should be able to accurately predict the high-accuracy keypoint $\hat{H}_A$, which implies that the self-constraint loss $||H_A - \hat{H}_A||_2$ on the high-accuracy keypoint X_A should be small.

Motivated by this, we propose to perform local search and refinement of the low-accuracy keypoint. Specifically, we add a small perturbation Δ_D onto the predicted result $\hat{X}_D$ and search its small neighborhood to minimize the self-constraint loss:

$$\hat{X}_D^* = \arg\min_{\tilde{H}_D} ||H_A - \mathbf{\Gamma}(H_B, H_C, \tilde{H}_D; \mathbf{f})||_2$$

$$\tilde{H}_D = \mathbb{H}(\hat{X}_D + \Delta_D), \quad ||\Delta_D||_2 \leq \delta. \tag{12}$$

Here, δ controls the search range and direction of the keypoint, and the direction will be dynamically adjusted with the loss. $\mathbb{H}(\hat{X}_D + \Delta_D)$ represents the heatmap generated from the keypoint location $\hat{X}_D + \Delta_D$ using the Gaussian kernel. In the Supplemental Material section, we provide further discussion on the extra computational complexity of the proposed SCIO method.

4 Experiments

In this section, we present experimental results, performance comparisons with state-of-the-art methods, and ablation studies to demonstrate the performance of our SCIO method.

4.1 Datasets

The comparison and ablation experiments are performed on MS COCO dataset [17] and CrowdPose [15] dataset, both of which contain very challenging scenes for pose estimation.

MS COCO Dataset: The COCO dataset contains challenging images with multi-person poses of various body scales and occlusion patterns in unconstrained environments. It contains 64K images and 270K persons labeled with 17 keypoints. We train our models on train2017 with 57K images including 150K persons and conduct ablation studies on val2017. We test our models on test-dev for performance comparisons with the state-of-the-art methods. In evaluation, we use the metric of Object Keypoint Similarity (OKS) score to evaluate the performance.

CrowdPose Dataset: The CrowdPose dataset contains 20K images and 80K persons labeled with 14 keypoints. Note that, for this dataset, we partition the keypoints into 4 groups, instead of 6 groups as in the COCO dataset. CrowdPose has more crowded scenes. For training, we use the train set which has 10K images and 35.4K persons. For evaluation, we use the validation set which has 2K images and 8K persons, and the test set which has 8K images and 29K persons.

4.2 Implementation Details

For fair comparisons, we use HRNet and ResNet as our backbone and follow the same training configuration as [32] and [27] for ResNet and HRNet, respectively. For the prediction and verification networks, we choose the FCN network [19]. The networks are trained with the Adam optimizer. We choose a batch size of 36 and an initial learning rate of 0.001. The whole model is trained for 210 epochs. During the search process of inference, we used perturbations with different step size and chose the best step size of 1.5. The number of search steps is set to be 50. More details are provided in the Supplemental Material.

4.3 Evaluation Metrics and Methods

Following existing papers [27], we use the standard Object Keypoint Similarity (OKS) metric which is defined as:

$$OKS = \frac{\sum_i e^{-d_i^2/2s^2k_i^2} \cdot \delta(v_i > 0)}{\sum_i \delta(v_i > 0)}. \tag{13}$$

Here d_i is the Euclidean distance between the detected keypoint and the corresponding ground truth, v_i is the visibility flag of the ground truth, s is the object scale, and k_i is a per-keypoint constant that controls falloff. $\delta(*)$ means if * holds, $\delta(*)$ equals to 1, otherwise, $\delta(*)$ equals to 0. We report standard average precision and recall scores: AP^{50}, AP^{75}, AP, AP^M, AP^L, AR, AP^{easy}, AP^{med}, AP^{hard} at various OKS [8,27].

Table 1. Comparison with the state-of-the-arts methods on COCO test-dev.

Method	Backbone	Size	AP	AP^{50}	AP^{75}	AP^M	AP^L	AR
G-RMI [23]	R101	353 × 257	64.9	85.5	71.3	62.3	70.0	69.7
AE [22]	-	512 × 512	65.5	86.8	72.3	60.6	72.6	70.2
Integral Pose [28]	R101	256 × 256	67.8	88.2	74.8	63.9	74.0	-
RMPE [6]	PyraNet	320 × 256	72.3	89.2	79.1	68.0	78.6	-
CFN [12]	-	-	72.6	86.1	69.7	**78.3**	64.1	-
CPN(ensemble) [3]	ResNet-Incep	384 × 288	73.0	91.7	80.9	69.5	78.1	79.0
CSM+SCARB [25]	R152	384 × 288	74.3	91.8	81.9	70.7	80.2	80.5
CSANet [36]	R152	384 × 288	74.5	91.7	82.1	71.2	80.2	80.7
HRNet [27]	HR48	384 × 288	75.5	92.5	83.3	71.9	81.5	80.5
MSPN [16]	MSPN	384 × 288	76.1	93.4	83.8	72.3	81.5	_81.6_
DARK [37]	HR48	384 × 288	76.2	92.5	83.6	72.5	82.4	81.1
UDP [11]	HR48	384 × 288	76.5	_92.7_	84.0	73.0	82.4	_81.6_
PoseFix [21]	HR48+R152	384 × 288	76.7	92.6	84.1	73.1	82.6	81.5
Graph-PCNN [29]	HR48	384 × 288	_76.8_	92.6	_84.3_	73.3	_82.7_	_81.6_
SCIO (Ours)	HR48	384 × 288	**79.2**	**93.9**	**85.8**	_75.1_	84.2	81.6
Performance Gain			**+2.4**	**+0.5**	**+1.5**	**-3.2**	**+1.5**	**+0.0**

Table 2. Comparison with the state-of-the-arts methods on CrowdPose test-dev.

Method	Backbone	AP	AP^{med}
Mask-RCNN [10]	ResNet101	60.3	-
OccNet [9]	ResNet50	65.5	66.6
JC-SPPE [15]	ResNet101	66	66.3
HigherHRNet [4]	HR48	67.6	-
MIPNet [14]	HR48	70.0	71.1
SCIO (Ours)	HR48	**71.5**	**72.2**
Performance Gain		**+1.5**	**+1.1**

Table 3. Comparison with state-of-the-art of three backbones on COCO test-dev.

Method	Backbone	Size	AP	AP^{50}	AP^{75}	AP^M	AP^L	AR
SimpleBaseline [32]	R152	384 × 288	73.7	91.9	81.1	70.3	80.0	79.0
SimpleBaseline +**SCIO** (Ours)	R152	384 × 288	**77.9**	**93.1**	**83.3**	**74.2**	**82.3**	**80.9**
Performance Gain			**+4.2**	**+1.2**	**+2.2**	**+3.9**	**+2.3**	**+1.9**
HRNet [27]	HR32	384 × 288	74.9	92.5	82.8	71.3	80.9	80.1
HRNet+**SCIO** (Ours)	HR32	384 × 288	**78.6**	**93.5**	**85.6**	**74.5**	**82.9**	**81.5**
Performance Gain			**+3.7**	**+1.0**	**+1.8**	**+3.2**	**+2.0**	**+1.4**
HRNet [27]	HR48	384 × 288	75.5	92.5	83.3	71.9	81.5	80.5
HRNet+**SCIO** (Ours)	HR48	384 × 288	**79.2**	**93.9**	**85.8**	**75.1**	**84.2**	**81.6**
Performance Gain			**+3.7**	**+1.4**	**+2.5**	**+3.2**	**+2.7**	**+1.1**

4.4 Comparison to State of the Art

We compare our SCIO method with other top-performing methods on the COCO test-dev and CrowdPose datasets. Table 1 shows the performance comparisons with state-of-the-art methods on the MS COCO dataset. It should be noted that the best performance is reported here for each method. We can see that our SCIO method outperforms the current best by a large margin, up to 2.5%, which is quite significant. Table 2 shows the results on challenging CrowdPose. In the literature, there are only few methods have reported results on this challenging dataset. Compared to the current best method MIPNet [14], our SCIO method has improved the pose estimation accuracy by up to 1.5%, which is quite significantly.

In Table 3, we compare our SCIO with state-of-the-art methods using different backbone networks, including R152, HR32, and HR48 backbone networks. We can see that our SCIO method consistently outperforms existing methods.

4.5 Ablation Studies

To systematically evaluate our method and study the contribution of each algorithm component, we use the HRNet-W48 backbone to perform a number of

Table 4. Ablations study on COCO val2017.

	AP	AP^{50}	AP^{75}	AR
Baseline	76.3	90.8	82.9	81.2
Baseline + SCL	78.3	92.9	84.9	81.3
Baseline + SCL + SCO	**79.5**	**93.7**	**86.0**	**81.6**

Table 5. Ablations study of distal keypoints accuracy on COCO val2017.

	Left Ear	Right Ear	Left Wrist	Right Wrist	Left Ankle	Right Ankle
HRNet	0.6637	0.6652	0.5476	0.5511	0.3843	0.3871
HRNet + SCIO(Ours)	**0.7987**	**0.7949**	**0.7124**	**0.7147**	**0.5526**	**0.5484**
Performance Gain	**+0.1350**	**+0.1297**	**+0.1648**	**+0.1636**	**+0.1683**	**+0.1613**

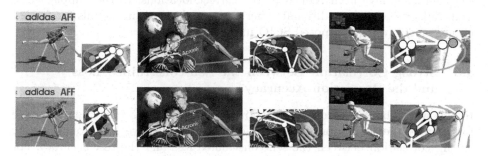

Fig. 5. Three examples of refinement of predicted keypoints. The top row is the original estimation. The bottom row is the refined version.

ablation experiments on the COCO val2017 dataset. Our algorithm has two major new components, the Self-Constrained Learning (SCL) and the Self-Constrained optimization (SCO). In the first row of Table 4, we report the baseline (HRNet-W48) results. The second row shows the results with the SCL. The third row shows results with the SCL and SCO of the prediction results. We can clearly see that each algorithm component is contributing significantly to the overall performance. In Table 5, We also use normalization and sigmoid functions to evaluate the loss of distal keypoints, and the results show that the accuracy of each keypoint from HRNet has been greatly improved after using SCIO.

Figure 5 shows three examples of how the estimation keypoints have been refined by the self-constrained inference optimization method. The top row shows the original estimation of the keypoints. The bottom row shows the refined estimation of the keypoints. Besides each result image, we show the enlarged image of those keypoints whose estimation errors are large in the original method. However, using our self-constrained optimization method, these errors have been successfully corrected. Figure 6(a) shows how the self-constraint loss decreases and the corresponding accuracy improves during the search process. We can

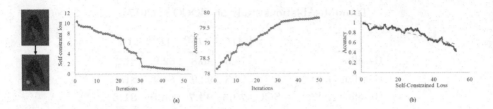

Fig. 6. (a) shows the decreasing of the self-constraint loss and the corresponding improving of the accuracy during local search and refinement of the predicted keypoint. (b) shows the correlation between the self-constrained loss and the test accuracy.

see that the loss drops quickly with accuracy increasing at the same time and the keypoints have been refined to the correct locations. In the Supplemental Materials, we provide additional experiments and algorithm details for further understanding of the proposed SCIO method.

4.6 Strong Correlation Between the Self-constrained Loss and the Prediction Accuracy

In this work, the proposed self-constrained loss provides an important guidance for refining the prediction results. In our experiments, we have found a very strong correlation between the self-constrained loss and the test accuracy. For example, the following Fig. 6(b) shows their strong correlation with a correlation coefficient of -0.85 over 1000 test samples. Thus, this self-constrained loss can be used to guide the search and refinement of the prediction results based on feedback from the test samples, resulting in better generalization capability.

5   Conclusion

In this work, we observed that human poses exhibit strong structural correlation within keypoint groups, which can be explored to improve the accuracy and robustness of their estimation. We developed a self-constrained prediction-verification network to learn this coherent spatial structure and to perform local refinement of the pose estimation results during the inference stage. We partition each keypoint group into two subsets, proximal keypoints and distal keypoints, and develop a self-constrained prediction-verification network to perform forward and backward predictions between them. This prediction-verification network design is able to capture the local structural correlation between keypoints. Once successfully learned, we used the verification network as a feedback module to guide the local optimization of pose estimation results for low-accuracy keypoints with the self-constraint loss on high-accuracy keypoints as the objective function. Our extensive experimental results on benchmark MS COCO datasets demonstrated that the proposed SCIO method is able to significantly improve the pose estimation results.

Acknowledgments. Zeng Li's research is partially supported by NSFC (No. 12031005 and No. 12101292).

References

1. Bagautdinov, T.M., Alahi, A., Fleuret, F., Fua, P., Savarese, S.: Social scene understanding: end-to-end multi-person action localization and collective activity recognition. In: CVPR, pp. 3425–3434 (2017)
2. Cao, Z., Simon, T., Wei, S., Sheikh, Y.: Realtime multi-person 2D pose estimation using part affinity fields. In: CVPR, pp. 1302–1310 (2017)
3. Chen, Y., Wang, Z., Peng, Y., Zhang, Z., Yu, G., Sun, J.: Cascaded pyramid network for multi-person pose estimation. In: CVPR, pp. 7103–7112 (2018)
4. Cheng, B., Xiao, B., Wang, J., Shi, H., Huang, T.S., Zhang, L.: HigherHRNet: scale-aware representation learning for bottom-up human pose estimation. In: CVPR, pp. 5385–5394 (2020)
5. Elhayek, A., et al.: Efficient convnet-based marker-less motion capture in general scenes with a low number of cameras. In: CVPR, pp. 3810–3818 (2015)
6. Fang, H.S., Xie, S., Tai, Y.W., Lu, C.: RMPE: regional multi-person pose estimation. In: ICCV, pp. 2353–2362 (2017)
7. Fieraru, M., Khoreva, A., Pishchulin, L., Schiele, B.: Learning to refine human pose estimation. In: 2018 IEEE/CVF Conference on Computer Vision and Pattern Recognition Workshops (CVPRW), pp. 318–31809 (2018)
8. Geng, Z., Sun, K., Xiao, B., Zhang, Z., Wang, J.: Bottom-up human pose estimation via disentangled keypoint regression. In: CVPR, pp. 14676–14686 (2021)
9. Golda, T., Kalb, T., Schumann, A., Beyerer, J.: Human pose estimation for real-world crowded scenarios. In: AVSS, pp. 1–8 (2019)
10. He, K., Gkioxari, G., Dollar, P., Girshick, R.: Mask R-CNN. In: ICCV, pp. 2980–2988 (2017)
11. Huang, J., Zhu, Z., Guo, F., Huang, G.: The devil is in the details: delving into unbiased data processing for human pose estimation. In: CVPR, pp. 5699–5708 (2020)
12. Huang, S., Gong, M., Tao, D.: A coarse-fine network for keypoint localization. In: ICCV, pp. 3047–3056 (2017)
13. Kamel, A., Sheng, B., Li, P., Kim, J., Feng, D.D.: Hybrid refinement-correction heatmaps for human pose estimation. IEEE Trans. Multimed. **23**, 1330–1342 (2021)
14. Khirodkar, R., Chari, V., Agrawal, A., Tyagi, A.: Multi-instance pose networks: rethinking top-down pose estimation. In: Proceedings of the IEEE/CVF International Conference on Computer Vision (ICCV), pp. 3122–3131 (2021)
15. Li, J., Wang, C., Zhu, H., Mao, Y., Fang, H., Lu, C.: CrowdPose: efficient crowded scenes pose estimation and a new benchmark. In: CVPR, pp. 10863–10872 (2019)
16. Li, W., et al.: Rethinking on multi-stage networks for human pose estimation. CoRR abs/1901.00148 (2019)
17. Lin, T.-Y., et al.: Microsoft COCO: common objects in context. In: Fleet, D., Pajdla, T., Schiele, B., Tuytelaars, T. (eds.) ECCV 2014. LNCS, vol. 8693, pp. 740–755. Springer, Cham (2014). https://doi.org/10.1007/978-3-319-10602-1_48
18. Liu, X., Zhang, P., Yu, C., Lu, H., Yang, X.: Watching you: global-guided reciprocal learning for video-based person re-identification. In: Proceedings of the IEEE/CVF Conference on Computer Vision and Pattern Recognition, pp. 13334–13343 (2021)

744   Z. Kan et al.

19. Long, J., Shelhamer, E., Darrell, T.: Fully convolutional networks for semantic segmentation. In: Proceedings of the IEEE Conference on Computer Vision and Pattern Recognition, pp. 3431–3440 (2015)
20. Luo, Z., Wang, Z., Huang, Y., Wang, L., Tan, T., Zhou, E.: Rethinking the heatmap regression for bottom-up human pose estimation. In: CVPR, pp. 13264–13273 (2021)
21. Moon, G., Chang, J.Y., Lee, K.M.: PoseFix: model-agnostic general human pose refinement network. In: CVPR, pp. 7773–7781 (2019)
22. Newell, A., Huang, Z., Deng, J.: Associative embedding: end-to-end learning for joint detection and grouping. In: NeurIPS, pp. 2277–2287 (2017)
23. Papandreou, G., et al.: Towards accurate multi-person pose estimation in the wild. In: CVPR, pp. 3711–3719 (2017)
24. Rhodin, H., Constantin, V., Katircioglu, I., Salzmann, M., Fua, P.: Neural scene decomposition for multi-person motion capture. In: CVPR, pp. 7703–7713 (2019)
25. Su, K., Yu, D., Xu, Z., Geng, X., Wang, C.: Multi-person pose estimation with enhanced channel-wise and spatial information. In: CVPR, pp. 5674–5682. Computer Vision Foundation/IEEE (2019)
26. Sun, H., Zhao, Z., He, Z.: Reciprocal learning networks for human trajectory prediction. In: CVPR, pp. 7414–7423 (2020)
27. Sun, K., Xiao, B., Liu, D., Wang, J.: Deep high-resolution representation learning for human pose estimation. In: CVPR, pp. 5693–5703 (2019)
28. Sun, X., Xiao, B., Wei, F., Liang, S., Wei, Y.: Integral human pose regression. In: Ferrari, V., Hebert, M., Sminchisescu, C., Weiss, Y. (eds.) ECCV 2018. LNCS, vol. 11210, pp. 536–553. Springer, Cham (2018). https://doi.org/10.1007/978-3-030-01231-1_33
29. Wang, J., Long, X., Gao, Y., Ding, E., Wen, S.: Graph-PCNN: two stage human pose estimation with graph pose refinement. In: Vedaldi, A., Bischof, H., Brox, T., Frahm, J.-M. (eds.) ECCV 2020. LNCS, vol. 12356, pp. 492–508. Springer, Cham (2020). https://doi.org/10.1007/978-3-030-58621-8_29
30. Wang, M., Tighe, J., Modolo, D.: Combining detection and tracking for human pose estimation in videos. In: CVPR, pp. 11085–11093 (2020)
31. Wu, J., Wang, L., Wang, L., Guo, J., Wu, G.: Learning actor relation graphs for group activity recognition. In: CVPR, pp. 9964–9974 (2019)
32. Xiao, B., Wu, H., Wei, Y.: Simple baselines for human pose estimation and tracking. In: Ferrari, V., Hebert, M., Sminchisescu, C., Weiss, Y. (eds.) ECCV 2018. LNCS, vol. 11210, pp. 472–487. Springer, Cham (2018). https://doi.org/10.1007/978-3-030-01231-1_29
33. Xu, C., Howey, J., Ohorodnyk, P., Roth, M., Zhang, H., Li, S.: Segmentation and quantification of infarction without contrast agents via spatiotemporal generative adversarial learning. Med. Image Anal. **59**, 101568 (2020)
34. Xu, T., Takano, W.: Graph stacked hourglass networks for 3D human pose estimation. In: CVPR, pp. 16105–16114 (2021)
35. Yang, Y., Ren, Z., Li, H., Zhou, C., Wang, X., Hua, G.: Learning dynamics via graph neural networks for human pose estimation and tracking. In: CVPR, pp. 8074–8084 (2021)
36. Yu, D., Su, K., Geng, X., Wang, C.: A context-and-spatial aware network for multi-person pose estimation. CoRR abs/1905.05355 (2019)
37. Zhang, F., Zhu, X., Dai, H., Ye, M., Zhu, C.: Distribution-aware coordinate representation for human pose estimation. In: CVPR, pp. 7091–7100 (2020)

38. Zhang, L., Zhou, S., Guan, J., Zhang, J.: Accurate few-shot object detection with support-query mutual guidance and hybrid loss. In: Proceedings of the IEEE/CVF Conference on Computer Vision and Pattern Recognition, pp. 14424–14432 (2021)
39. Zhu, J.Y., Park, T., Isola, P., Efros, A.A.: Unpaired image-to-image translation using cycle-consistent adversarial networks. In: ICCV, pp. 2242–2251 (2017)

Author Index

Printed in the United States
by Baker & Taylor Publisher Services